Basic College Mathematics

MT 055 Pre-Algebra

Second Custom Edition for Jefferson Community and Technical College

Elayn Martin-Gay

Taken from:
Basic College Mathematics, Third Edition
by Elayn Martin-Gay

Custom Publishing

New York Boston San Francisco
London Toronto Sydney Tokyo Singapore Madrid
Mexico City Munich Paris Cape Town Hong Kong Montreal

Cover Art: Courtesy of Jefferson Community and Technical College.

Taken from:

Basic College Mathematics, Third Edition
by Elayn Martin-Gay
Copyright © 2006, 2003, 1999 by Pearson Education, Inc.
Published by Prentice Hall
Upper Saddle River, New Jersey 07458

Printed in the United States of America

10 9 8 7 6 5 4 3 2 1

2009361008

JM/LD

Pearson
Custom Publishing
is a division of

www.pearsonhighered.com

ISBN 10: 0-558-31535-6
ISBN 13: 978-0-558-31535-1

Jefferson Community & Technical College

MT055 Pre-Algebra

Supplemental Material

Table of Contents

Acknowledgements

The Developmental Mathematics Department extends much deserved thanks and sincere appreciation to the following faculty and college administration members for their contribution toward creation of this customized Pre-algebra book for the Jefferson Community and Technical College and the University of Louisville Pathways Program's students:

Mrs. Shari Bennett

Mrs. Lisa Brosky

Mrs. Venita Dobson

Dr. Dennis Guagliardo

Mrs. Linda Hook

Mrs. Monica Jones

Mr. Dan Kesterson

Mr. Paul Klein

Mrs. Karen Klingenfus

Mrs. Caroline Martinson

Mr. Bob Olsen

Dr. Frank Pecchioni

Mrs. Donna Riedel

Hamid Attarzadeh
Associate Professor, Mathematics
Developmental Mathematics Department Head
Jefferson Community and Technical College Downtown
(502) 213 – 5038
Hamid.attarzadeh@kctcs.edu

MT055 Pre- Algebra
Important Information

Class Information	Instructor Information
Section	Name
Class Number	Office Location
Meeting Days	Phone Number
Meeting Time	Email Address
Classroom Location	Office Hours

The Natural Sciences/Mathematics Division office is located in HFD 1111. The phone number for the Division office is 213-5012 or 213-5013.

This course is part of the Developmental Mathematics Department. Please contact Developmental Mathematics Department Head Hamid Attarzadeh at 213-5038 for further information.

Natural Sciences/Mathematics Learning Lab is Located in HFD 505. Call 213-5086 for hours of operation.

Natural Sciences/Mathematics Computer Lab is Located in HFD 1110. Call 213-5083 for hours of operation.

Natural Sciences/Mathematics Computer Classroom is Located in HFD 607A. Call 213-5012 or 213-5013 for hours of operation.

Steps for Registering as a new student with MyMathLab®

1) Go to www.coursecompass.com.
2) Click on REGISTER button for Students.
3) Make sure that the button for Get access to a new course is selected and click Next.
4) Enter the course ID provided by your teacher and click FIND THE COURSE button.
5) Select Access Code.
6) Enter your code in the space below (using tab to move between the fields) and Click on NEXT.
7) Create a login name and a password that you will use in the future.
8) Retype the password and record them for future use with MyMathLab®.
9) Put in the School's zip code, which is 40202.
10) Select United States as the country.
11) Select Your College (Jefferson Community College).
12) Select a security question and enter your answer, then select NEXT.
13) Enter first name, last name, email address.
13) Click NEXT button.
14) If your information is complete you will now be on the confirmation screen.
15) Click on the button to LOGIN with MyMathLab®.
16) You will be returned to the main login screen.
17) Enter the login name and password you just created to enter MyMathLab®.
18) Click on your course.
19) Click on your Homework, Quizzes, or Tests.
20) Click on your questions.
21) Submit or save after you finish all the questions.
22) If you have problem with your login, call 1-800-677-6337.

Organization of 3-Ring Binder

Some of your instructors may require that you organize your work in a 3-ring binder. You will use this to keep important materials that you will receive in class. **Much of your success in college is based on your ability to organize information so that you can use it easily.**

Please buy dividers with tabs and organize your 3-ring binder. Your instructor may give you specific titles for the dividers in your notebook. If you are not directed to use specific titles, you might want to organize your binder as follows:

1st Divider Tab - Syllabus, etc.

Remember your syllabus is an important document that you may need to reference regarding class requirements and policies regarding attendance, exams, and grading. Other important papers might include the class calendar, assignment sheet and/or grade sheet to record quiz and exam grades.

2nd Divider Tab   Current Book and Class Notes

Before you attend class you should always read the section that will be covered and take notes. Write down important vocabulary words and definitions. Write down examples of problems that will be covered in class. When you attend class you will be prepared to listen and add to your notes any notes from the class lecture or discussion. It is a good idea to review notes and reorganize any that are unclear. Use a highlighter to mark vocabulary or examples that your instructor emphasizes in class.

3rd Divider Tab   Documentation of Homework

Homework may be from your math textbook or MyMathLab. Label each section and number each problem. If you are doing homework from the textbook be sure to check your answers in the back of the textbook. This will help you prepare for quizzes and exams.

4th Divider Tab   Returned Quizzes and Exams

These will help you study for the comprehensive final exam.

5th Divider Tab...Handouts and Study Aids

You will receive many important handouts from your instructor during the semester. Now when you need one of those important papers in class, you will not have to turn your backpack upside down to find it!

Better Math Study Techniques

Good study strategies are the foundation of being a successful student in mathematics courses. The following are study habits that are specifically geared for use in your math class. If you make it a priority to do them, soon they will become a part of your life.

Before Class

- Review your previous class notes.
- Be sure you have worked all assigned problems from the previous class. Write down all questions exactly where you ran into trouble.
- Go to the math lab or seek help from other resources if you are having trouble.
- Read over the material that will be covered in the next class lecture. Don't worry if you don't understand. This will give you a general idea of what the lecture will cover and help you formulate possible questions for class.
- Bring a pencil, textbook, notebook, and a calculator ready to class.

During Class

- Attend class regularly.
- Be on time to class.
- Participate in class. Ask questions and answer questions posed by the teacher.
- Take good notes. Make sure your notes can be read and understood weeks later.
- Sit near the front of class
- Don't space out during lecture. Try to stay focused at all times during class.
- Don't compare your progress in class with that of your class mates. Everyone's mathematical background is different.

Studying for a test

- Don't cram. Make a study schedule. Work on math everyday.
- Review your notes, homework, and the textbook sections that will be covered on the test. If you missed a class, get the notes from a classmate or the teacher.
- Make a list of all concepts, formulas, and rules that will be covered on the test.

- Get help if you need assistance with the material or if you have test anxiety.
- Make a sample test.
- Review and relax the night before the test. Get a good night's sleep.

The Test
- Arrive early
- Ignore what other students have to say right before the test. Often they are confused and anxiously searching for solutions at the last minute.
- Bring pencils, paper, and a calculator to class.
- Write down all memorized formulas on your test paper before you begin working the test.
- Read all directions. If you don't understand the directions, ask the teacher for clarification.
- Look over the test and do what you know first.
- Show all your steps in a neat and orderly fashion.
- Check your work. Careless errors can make you lose points.
- Keep track of the time. If you get stuck, move on. Come back to that problem later. Do not spend 20 minutes on a problem that will give you few or no points.
- Try all problems. You may be able to get partial credit by just writing the formula or for setting up the problem.
- Watch out for math anxiety. Don't fool yourself into thinking you won't do well on the test before you have given your best effort.

The Returned Test
- Don't throw the test away.
- Read all the teacher comments and suggestions.
- Correct your test. Write the corrections on a separate piece of paper.
- Go see your teacher if you have questions about your grade or if you don't understand a problem.
- See if your mistakes have a common pattern.
- Use the returned test as a review for the final exam.

Effectively Using Your Resources

Tutors should be coaches, not crutches. They should not be expected to completely do the problem for you. Tutors are there to encourage you, give you hints, and sometimes show you how to do the problems. They are there to help you discover how to learn math for yourself. To effectively use your resources, you should remember the following:

1. Don't get behind. Get help before a test is near or you fail a test.

2. Read your textbook and notes on the material that is confusing you and try to do some problems before you ask for help.

3. If you get stuck on a problem, do not erase your work. The tutor or teacher can look at your steps and see where you are going wrong.

4. Ask questions. Don't pretend to understand.

5. Do not become dependent on a tutor or your teacher constantly giving you hints or working problems for you. You are the one that has to take the test.

6. Tell your teacher or tutor how you feel about math and your math history. This can help them relate to your situation.

Check Yourself

Many students say that Math is difficult for them or that they are not "good" in Math. The reality may be that they are not putting the effort into the subject or using the support services available. Here is a list of behaviors that are necessary to succeed in Math at the college level.

Check the boxes that apply to you.

- ❑ I go to all classes.
- ❑ I know what's on the syllabus and have marked it in my day-planner
- ❑ I take notes in class.
- ❑ I read the textbook before class (and after if necessary.)
- ❑ I do the practice problems.
- ❑ I get help from the instructor – office hours or e-mail
- ❑ I use the study guide.
- ❑ I use the publisher's computer program.
- ❑ I go to the NS/Math Learning Lab – HFD 505.
- ❑ I belong to a Study group.
- ❑ I talk to other students.
- ❑ I have a private tutor.
- ❑ I get help from math oriented family or friends.

What can you add to your math study plan that can make you more successful?

_____

_____

_____

_____

_____

_____

_____

_____

_____

_____

JCTC's Mathematics Courses

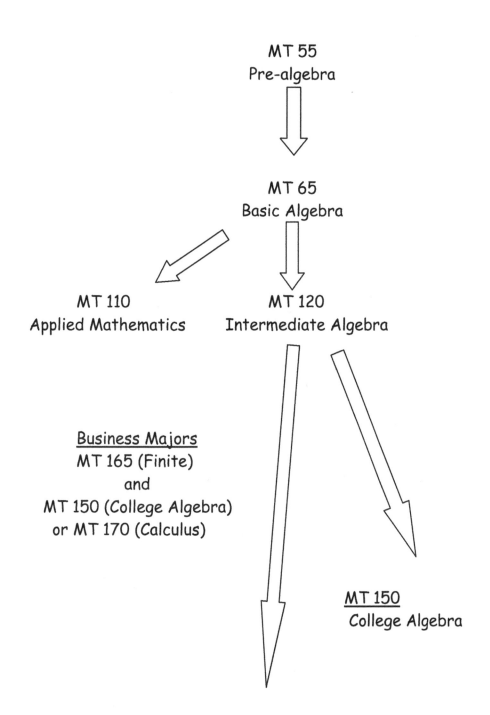

MT 55
Pre-algebra

MT 65
Basic Algebra

MT 110
Applied Mathematics

MT 120
Intermediate Algebra

Business Majors
MT 165 (Finite)
and
MT 150 (College Algebra)
or MT 170 (Calculus)

MT 150
College Algebra

If you don't need a particular Math
MT 145
(Contemporary College Mathematics)

To the Student: Reading Math Textbooks

A Brain-Based/Conceptual Learning Approach to Reading and Learning Math

Learning arithmetic is a partnership between the instructor and the student. Textbooks are limited in how much clarification they can offer. Learning math can be thought of as involving the constant interaction between the mind of the instructor, the learner (the reader), the text, and the context. Gone are the days when learning math meant that the instructor has the math knowledge, the student was an empty vessel to fill up, and the process of learning was the instructor only wrote and explained the problem on the board, and the student copied the problem. It doesn't work. Today the modern math instructor's focus is on helping the learner learn how to think with math, which involves learning how to read math textbooks. Both the instructor and math student have to take responsibility for ensuring that the student is understanding, actively organizing what they are learning (developing conceptual frameworks), connecting new knowledge to prior knowledge, and elaborating.

Taking Control of Learning Math

A goal of both the instructor and student is enabling the student to take control of learning math, that is, to not only learn math, but to learn how to learn by learning thinking strategies that increase understanding of math concepts and procedures, and increase the probability of being able to use the math learned in new situations. It is therefore essential that math instructors teach and math students learn how to learn math by reading math textbooks. The goal is not only learning math, but learning how to become self-regulated math learners.

Brain-Based Learning

Learning / Constructing Meaning

The brain learns naturally when whatever you are trying to learn (math) gets connected to related knowledge your brain already knows (prior knowledge). The more the learner already knows about what is being read, the easier it is to construct meaning (comprehend what is being read). When the reader has little prior knowledge, the harder it is to learn. When the brain learns something new, it is because the brain was able to make a connection with what the reader already knows and the new information.

What the Learner Should Know about Arithmetic

Arithmetic is about counting. We count to find out "How many?"

Arithmetic as Language

Arithmetic is a language and has a vocabulary, that is it has symbols that represent counting (ex. numbers - 0, 1, 2, 3 or words - zero, one, two, three). These symbols represent "How many." I have two birds, one sparrow and one robin. A sparrow and a robin are birds. Notice that birds is the language we use to lump those animals that have the characteristics shared by both sparrow and robins.

Research in cognitive science has shown that people remember better, longer, and in more detail if they understand, actively organize what they are learning, connect new knowledge to prior knowledge, and elaborate. - *Moschkovich*

If we look on page 7 in this book (go ahead, take a look), we find in bold print **"digits"** followed by 1, 2, 3, 4, 5, 6, 7, 8, 9. The numbers 1 through 9 have been lumped together and labeled "digits." If we read further, we see in bold print "whole numbers." We know to look for the meaning of **"whole numbers"** and we find 0, 1, 2, 3, 4, 5, 6, 7, 8, 9…. The numbers zero through 9 and continuing on indefinitely are a group of numbers lumped together and labeled "Whole Numbers." Remember the brain learns by tying new information to old information the reader already knows – this causes new dendrites to grown on older dendrites of brain cells (neurons) that are information the reader already knows. (See Figure 1)

Let's assume that you do not know the meaning of digits or whole numbers. The brain needs to find related information it already knows about the new words "digits and whole numbers" in order to learn. Fortunately almost all readers will know the numbers 0, 1, 2, 3, 4, 5, 6, 7, 8, 9… To truly make the concept of whole numbers meaningful, the brain needs to find concrete examples of whole numbers as it did when we counted the number of birds I have – 2 birds.

Concepts: New Math Words and Their levels

Concepts are mental categories for objects, events, or ideas that have a common set of features. Concepts allow us to classify objects and

events by giving them a label (words, new terminology). This is done by concept formation (concept learning) in which the reader has developed the reading ability by which they can respond to the common features of categories of objects or events and can organize the information.

Example

Concept: bird

Shared Common Features: birds are warm-blooded, egg-laying, vertebrates, characterized by feathers and forelimbs modified as wings

Examples of Birds: robin, sparrow, hawk, woodpecker, owl, ostrich, etc.

For example:

New Word - whole numbers

Numbers New Word Represents - 0, 1, **2**, 3, 4...

Concrete Example – counting two birds

It has been argued that many mathematics curricula emphasize ...not so much a form of thinking as a substitute for thinking. The process of calculation or computation only involves the deployment of a set routine with no room for ingenuity or flair, no place for guess work or surprise, no chance for discovery, no need for the human being, in fact.
The argument here is not that students should never learn to compute, but that they should also learn other things about mathematics, especially the fact that it is possible for them to make sense of mathematics and to think mathematically. - Bransford

Math Words as Concepts for Counting: Many arithmetic words are labels for concepts (ex. whole numbers), which share common features (in this case, numbers starting with zero and going on indefinitely (0, 1, 2, 3...) that can be used for counting whole things, (ex. counting the 6 birds in the apple tree).

When the reader comes across a new math word, they should immediately ask themselves (1) if the new word is referring to *numbers* that can be used to count something and (2) what are *examples* of those somethings it could be counting. **Strategy:** (1) reader encounters

new word, (2) reader looks for representative numbers, the reader looks for concrete example(s). Why?

Mathematics is the study of the *relationships* involved in reality. Reality (concrete examples) is the two birds that you want to count. You count them with numbers (whole numbers) that have been lumped together and given a name (birds). This is how concepts are formed. This is what the brain needs to construct meaning (connecting new information to the learner's prior knowledge).

For example:

New Word - whole numbers

Numbers New Word Represents - 0, 1, **2**, 3, 4...

Concrete Example – counting two birds

Math Words as Actions: Not all new words are numbers. For example, the new word may be telling you what action you can take with numbers, such as addition, subtraction, multiplication, or division. These new words may be represented by symbols (+, -, *, /). Words that tell you what to do with more than one number to count them may be lumped together and given a label, such as "operations", which refers to addition, subtraction, multiplication, or division.

How the Brain Learns Naturally

Growing Dendrites: Dendrites are fiber-like structures that grow on each brain cell as new information is learned. Learn something new and new dendrites grow; therefore learning is the growing of new dendrites and new dendrites mean new learning has occurred.

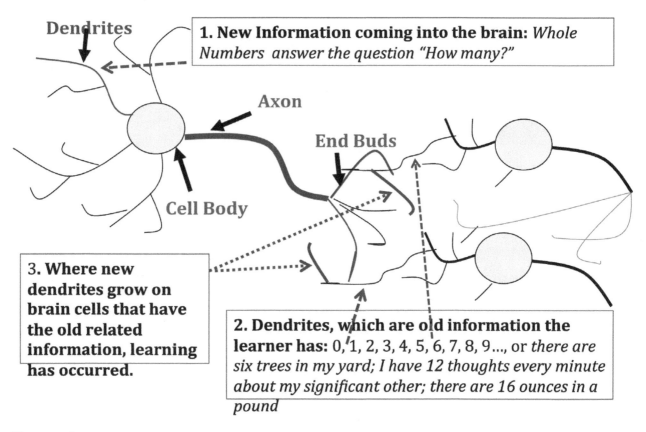

Dendrites

1. New Information coming into the brain: *Whole Numbers answer the question "How many?"*

Axon

End Buds

Cell Body

3. Where new dendrites grow on brain cells that have the old related information, learning has occurred.

2. Dendrites, which are old information the learner has: 0, 1, 2, 3, 4, 5, 6, 7, 8, 9..., or *there are six trees in my yard; I have 12 thoughts every minute about my significant other; there are 16 ounces in a pound*

Figure 1

Figure 1: (1)Beginning in the upper left hand corner, new information (*whole numbers answer the question "How many?"*) enters through the Dendrites of neurons; it then travels to the Cell Body and on down the Axon as an electrical signal to the End Buds. (2) The End Buds look for related or associated information the reader already knows (*there are six trees in my yard*); that information is called prior knowledge and is stored as dendrites on other neurons. (3) When the end buds find related prior knowledge, new dendrites grow off the older related dendrites of prior knowledge. The new dendrites are new learning.

Constructing Meaning in Math: The brain does not store math language or steps for solving problems easily, rather the brain stores meaning. Remember this: new information becomes "meaningful" only when what the reader is reading is interconnected with what the reader already knows (the reader knows reality (concrete examples or math concepts it learned earlier). To learn new math concepts, it is always important to constantly always make a connection with a concrete example,

even when doing practice exercises. Memorized steps for working a problem (computing) or definitions are easily forgotten by the brain because memorizing without "meaning" does not enable the reader to make interconnections in the brain between the new information being learned and what the reader already knows. Most of the reading strategies you will learn deliberately focus on helping the learner make a connection between what they are reading and what they already know – that is, construct meaning.

Learning How to Learn So One Can Remember Over Time

Learning: Comprehending or constructing meaning is not enough when learning math and will be forgotten if it is not used or reinforced. There are many thinking strategies that reinforce or strengthen new dendrites of learning.

Communication should include multiple modes (talking, listening, writing, drawing, etc., because making connections among multiple ways of representing mathematical concepts is central to developing conceptual understanding. - Moschkovich

The Brain Connection: *Forgetting* - When a reader reads new information in textbooks, they forget on average 50% within the first twenty-four hours. The reader forgets 80% within the first two weeks if they do not do something with the information to strengthen their memory. A bigger problem for many struggling math students is depending only on learning math by watching the instructor work a problem on the board and copying the worked problem as notes and not reading the math textbook or really learning the language of the math problem so that one can thinking and reason with the problem.

Pruning Dendrites: Information that is not used is forgotten. The new dendrites that grow when learning occurs are absorbed by the brain (pruned) if the reader does not do something to strengthen the new dendrites at the point of learning and within the first twenty-four hours.

Practice is Essential, But Elaborating While Learning and Practicing is the Key: Using Elaborations: *Elaborations* are mental strategies the reader can use to increase the likelihood that new information will get connected in the brain to what the reader already knows. For example, research clearly shows us that once the reader identifies and read about what is important

to learn using text clues such as headings, words in bold print or italics, summaries, etc. that if we make sure we can explain what is important to learn in our own words, we increase memory by four times. This is called *reciting* and it helps not only in the construction of meaning by tapping the reader's prior knowledge, but also by strengthening the newly formed dendrites of learning in the brain.

Creating Conceptual Frameworks

Conceptual Framework: Increasing the likelihood that the reader will be able to think and reason with what they read

A key finding in the learning and transfer literature is that organizing information into a conceptual framework allows for greater "transfer"; that is, it allows the student to apply what was learned in new situations and to learn related information more quickly. – Bransford

Learning: The point of reading and learning from textbooks is not to accumulate a lot of information, but rather to be able to use the information to think and reason with the information. This involves critical thinking – can the reader use the information to make decisions or solve problems? Perhaps the most important skill a reader can develop to make what they learn useful is the ability to organize information into conceptual frameworks which moves information from pieces of isolated information to knowledge. It is organized information (knowledge) that increases the likelihood of information becoming useful.

The Brain Connection: The brain is made up of 100 billion brain cells each cell capable of making 10,000 connections. These connections represent learning and, as more and more information is interconnected by related meaning, the more neural networks with which to learn.

Neural Networks of Dendrites: Consider what you know about food. Your brain has organized all the information you know into neural networks of interrelated information. You know thousands of pieces of information about where food comes from, where to find it, if the food is animal of plant, if it is nutritious and why, and on and on it goes. Therefore, you can easily make decisions or solve problems about food. The more

S–17

you know (knowledge – organized information) the easier it is to use it.

Chapter 1: Whole Numbers – how to start thinking conceptually about basic operations on *whole numbers*

Look on page 1 of your text, which introduces "whole numbers."

"Whole numbers are the building blocks of mathematics. The whole numbers answer the question "How Many?"

Mile Wide/Inch Deep

NCTM Standards

The process, standards are based on the belief that mathematics must be approached as a unified whole. Its concepts, procedures, and intellectual processes are so interrelated that, in a significant sense, its "Whole is greater than the sum of its parts."

The Chapter covers the basic operations on whole numbers. Knowledge of these operations provides a good foundation on which to build further mathematical skills."

What the Textbook Tell Us and What it Does Not Tell Us

From what we have just read, we know that whole numbers answer the question "How many?" We also know that the chapter will cover the basic operations on whole numbers. What the text does not tell us is what operations are. We can search the whole book and never find an explanation of "operations." Yes, it will tell us what the "order of operations" are, but not what operations are. We will find plenty of examples of operations on whole numbers in the chapter, but the text will never tell us that the "operations" are addition, subtraction, multiplication and division. If we do not already know what "operations" are, we are not likely to comprehend what we just read. Remember, if the brain does not find a way to connect new information to prior knowledge, construction of meaning is not constructed – learning does not occur. As readers, we must become very sensitive to whether we understand or not. This sensitivity is key to using thinking strategies for making what we read useful.

Overview (a cognitive strategy): Using Text Clues to Begin Forming a Mathematical Conceptual Framework

Text Clues are clues about the organization of the chapter and clues about what is important to learn in the chapter such as table of contents, objectives, title, headings, new terminology, examples, and summary.

Keep in mind that as readers, we want to make sense of mathematics and to learn to think mathematically, not just learn to perform computations. In order to do so we must learn to build mathematical concepts – What is the concept we want to develop in chapter 1? Here is the problem for us as readers. We have virtually no text clues to help us identify the concept we will want to learn, which is essential if we want to develop a mathematical conceptual framework. With no meaningful text clues, the reader is forced to learn the contents of chapter 1 as isolated pieces of information.

Table of Contents and Chapter Text Clues: The reader will want to find as quickly as possible the main arithmetic concept they will be developing into a conceptual framework within the chapter. Let's look at the table of contents for chapter 1.

The main concept is not whole numbers as table of contents and the chapter title suggests; rather the main concept is "**the basic operations on whole numbers",** which is made up of many other concepts – for example, whole numbers, place value, adding whole numbers (total, sum, addend, addition, properties), and the other operations with their special language, etc.

Table of Contents

The Whole Numbers (the reader is left to discover that the main concept of the chapter is "the basic operations on whole numbers", which increases the likelihood that the reader will learn the operations in isolation, rather than building conceptual understanding)

Where Are We Heading?

We are going to learn how to incorporate cognitive strategies when reading and learning which are in line with how the brain learns naturally and in line with developing conceptual understanding so that we can think with, reason with and use the math we learn. The following are the main cognitive strategies with which we will be working.

Cognitive Strategies

{Overview} – Getting an overview of the chapter or reading selection before reading in order to identify the concepts and procedures to be learned, to identify the organization of the text, and to begin identifying what the reader already knows.

{Question/Read} – Always ask questions, especially when encountering while reading headings, new math vocabulary, steps in procedures. Then read to find the answer to your question(s)

{Find Example(s)} – Find examples of numbers and concrete examples of those numbers representing the concept being learned.

> **For example:**
>
> **New Word** - whole numbers
>
> **Examples of Numbers Representing New Word** - 0, 1, **2**, 3, 4…
>
> **Concrete Example** – counting two birds

{Visualize} – Arithmetic is about counting something. Always create a mental image of something that is being counted – see it in your mind's eye.

{Describe and Explain} – It is essential that the learner can describe the visualization (imagery) they created of the concept in words, and that they can explain their imagery in their own words.

{Mind Mapping} – Mind mapping is a visual/graphic way of taking notes that reflects the reader's understanding of the information, their organization of the information, their connections with prior knowledge.

Mind Mapping for a Concept

1. The main concept in the reading selection should be in the center of the map (ex. **Proper Fractions, Improper Fractions, and Mixed Numbers)**
2. Each main branch off the map center should have printed on it new terminology (ex. **Proper fraction**)
3. Off each main branch should be examples of numbers representing new word (ex. **!**)
4. Also off each branch should be a drawing of a concrete example representing the new terminology (ex. **Draw three slices of pizza cut from a whole pizza that has been cut into four equal slices**)

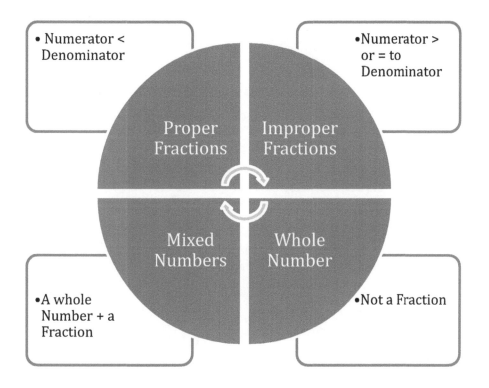

Mind Mapping for a Procedure

1. The name of the procedure in the reading selection should be in the center of the map (ex. **Writing Mixed Numbers as Improper Fraction)**

2. Each main branch off the map center should have printed on it a step in the procedure being learned. (ex. **Multiply the denominator of the fraction by the whole number.** HINT: use abbreviations**)**

3. Off each main branch should be examples of numbers representing the step being learned. (ex. **For 1 1/3 , write 3 x 1 = 2)**

4. Also off the main branch should be a drawing of a concrete example representing the step being learned. (ex. **Draw 3 cookies being cut in half**.)

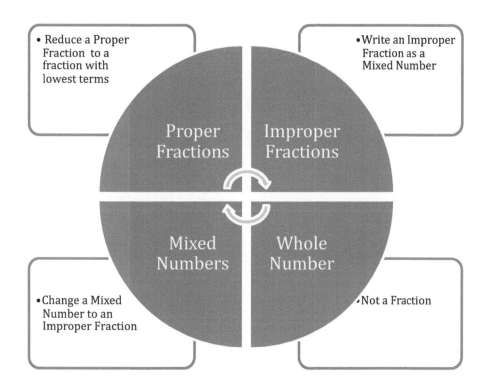

Double Entry Organizer

FROM THE TEXT CONCEPTS/FACTS/INFORMATION	FROM THE READER QUESTIONS/IDEAS/OPINIONS

Reprinted by permission of the Collaborative for Teaching and Learning.

Activity 1
The Whole Numbers

Multiplication Table

Complete the multiplication table. Use it to practice your multiplication facts.

×	0	1	2	3	4	5	6	7	8	9	10	11	12
0													
1													
2													
3													
4													
5													
6													
7													
8													
9													
10													
11													
12													

Timed Integer Addition

Time yourself on this set of questions. Do these without the aid of a calculator. You should be able t answer all of the questions in about 2 minutes. You want to practice until you don't even have t think about the answers. Remember to add when signs are alike and subtract when signs are not the same. There are three timed additions in this supplement.

Timed Integer Addition 1

$-5 + (-4) =$	$-9 + 6 =$	$7 + (-8) =$	$-1 + 5 =$	$5 + (-8) =$
$4 + (-9) =$	$-7 + 5 =$	$2 + (-1) =$	$8 + 6 =$	$-6 + (-5) =$
$7 + (-1) =$	$9 + (-7) =$	$8 + 1 =$	$-6 + 8 =$	$-1 + (-6) =$
$-4 + (-6) =$	$-5 + (-3) =$	$3 + (-1) =$	$-1 + 0 =$	$-9 + (-4) =$
$-8 + 9 =$	$8 + (-7) =$	$-7 + (-8) =$	$-4 + (-7) =$	$5 + (-8) =$
$-7 + (-1) =$	$-8 + 8 =$	$-3 + (-4) =$	$2 + (-1) =$	$8 + 5 =$
$-8 + 1 =$	$-4 + (-7) =$	$-8 + (-4) =$	$7 + (-9) =$	$-5 + (-9) =$
$6 + (-5) =$	$-4 + 1 =$	$-5 + (-2) =$	$-9 + (-7) =$	$8 + (-6) =$
$8 + 9 =$	$-7 + (-8) =$	$8 + (-5) =$	$9 + (-6) =$	$5 + (-7) =$
$-7 + 2 =$	$-8 + (-9) =$	$-8 + (-8) =$	$9 + (-3) =$	$-6 + (-5) =$

Timed Integer Addition 2

$-4 + (-8) =$	$-8 + 4 =$	$0 + (-6) =$	$-7 + 3 =$	$4 + (-6) =$
$3 + (-7) =$	$-4 + 3 =$	$1 + (-9) =$	$7 + 4 =$	$-3 + (-8) =$
$6 + (-9) =$	$8 + (-7) =$	$7 + 9 =$	$-3 + 6 =$	$-9 + (-3) =$
$-1 + (-4) =$	$-2 + (-1) =$	$2 + (-9) =$	$-9 + 9 =$	$-6 + (-2) =$
$-5 + 7 =$	$9 + (-7) =$	$-6 + (-8) =$	$-3 + (-7) =$	$8 + (-8) =$
$-4 + (-9) =$	$-9 + 6 =$	$-2 + (-2) =$	$1 + (-9) =$	$9 + 3 =$
$-9 + 8 =$	$-1 + (-5) =$	$-5 + (-2) =$	$6 + (-7) =$	$-2 + (-7) =$
$5 + (-3) =$	$-1 + 9 =$	$-2 + (-9) =$	$-6 + (-5) =$	$9 + (-6) =$
$8 + 7 =$	$-4 + (-6) =$	$9 + (-3) =$	$8 + (-4) =$	$4 + (-5) =$
$-4 + 0 =$	$-5 + (-7) =$	$-7 + (-6) =$	$9 + (-2) =$	$-3 + (-3) =$

Timed Integer Addition 3

$-3 + (-9) =$	$-7 + 3 =$	$9 + (-7) =$	$-8 + 2 =$	$3 + (-7) =$
$2 + (-8) =$	$-5 + 2 =$	$0 + (-8) =$	$6 + 3 =$	$-4 + (-9) =$
$5 + (-8) =$	$7 + (-8) =$	$6 + 8 =$	$-4 + 7 =$	$-9 + (-5) =$
$-2 + (-5) =$	$-3 + (-2) =$	$1 + (-8) =$	$-9 + 7 =$	$-7 + (-3) =$
$-6 + 8 =$	$8 + (-8) =$	$-7 + (-9) =$	$-4 + (-8) =$	$5 + (-9) =$
$-4 + (-9) =$	$-8 + 5 =$	$-1 + (-3) =$	$0 + (-7) =$	$8 + 2 =$
$-9 + 8 =$	$-2 + (-6) =$	$-6 + (-3) =$	$5 + (-8) =$	$-3 + (-8) =$
$4 + (-4) =$	$-2 + 8 =$	$-7 + (-9) =$	$-7 + (-6) =$	$8 + (-7) =$
$6 + 6 =$	$-5 + (-7) =$	$8 + (-4) =$	$7 + (-5) =$	$3 + (-6) =$
$-5 + (-1) =$	$-6 + (-8) =$	$-6 + (-7) =$	$9 + (-4) =$	$-4 + (-4) =$

Timed Integer Subtraction

Time yourself on this set of questions. Do these without the aid of a calculator. You should be able to answer all of the questions in about 2 minutes. You want to practice until you don't even have t think about the answers. Remember to add the opposite of the second number.

$-5 - 7 =$	$9 - 11 =$	$-12 - 12 =$	$9 - 0 =$	$7 - (-4) =$
$-15 - 7 =$	$19 - 7 =$	$12 - 8 =$	$8 - 8 =$	$-11 - 7 =$
$-52 - 17 =$	$-25 - (-17) =$	$13 - 17 =$	$-18 - 0 =$	$14 - 12 =$
$-13 - (-2) =$	$23 - 4 =$	$8 - 7 =$	$-8 - 2 =$	$-16 - 1 =$
$-4 - 2 =$	$-4 - 4 =$	$-8 - (-8) =$	$-13 - (-4) =$	$-9 - 27 =$
$21 - 11 =$	$41 - 1 =$	$-17 - 17 =$	$11 - 23 =$	$-19 - 6 =$
$17 - 17 =$	$26 - 8 =$	$25 - 5 =$	$6 - 8 =$	$-14 - 7 =$
$-6 - 6 =$	$-8 - 12 =$	$-20 - 7 =$	$-1 - 3 =$	$-8 - 23 =$
$-2 - 7 =$	$8 - 19 =$	$-25 - 25 =$	$-4 - 3 =$	$-1 - 16 =$

Timed Integer Multiplication

Time yourself on this set of questions. Do these without the aid of a calculator. You should be able t answer all of the questions in about 2 minutes. You want to practice until you don't even have t think about the answers. Remember that the product is a positive when signs are alike and a negative number when signs are not the same. There are three timed multiplications in this supplement.

Timed Integer Multiplication 1

$-5 \# (-8) =$	$-9 \# 6 =$	$9 \times (\#8) =$	$-0 \# 5 =$	$5 \times (\#8) =$
$4 \times (\#9) =$	$-7 \# 5 =$	$2 \times (\#1) =$	$8 \times 6 =$	$-6 \# (-0) =$
$7 \times (\#1) =$	$9 \times (\#9) =$	$8 \times 1 =$	$-6 \# 8 =$	$-1 \# (-6) =$
$-4 \# (-6) =$	$-5 \# (-3) =$	$3 \times (\#1) =$	$-1 \# 0 =$	$-9 \# (-4) =$
$-8 \# 9 =$	$0 \times (\#9) =$	$-9 \# (-8) =$	$-6 \# (-9) =$	$7 \times (\#8) =$
$-7 \# (-1) =$	$-0 \# 8 =$	$-3 \# (-5) =$	$2 \times (\#9) =$	$8 \times 5 =$
$-8 \# 2 =$	$-4 \# (-7) =$	$-8 \# (-4) =$	$7 \times (\#9) =$	$-5 \# (-9) =$
$6 \times (\#5) =$	$-3 \# 9 =$	$-5 \# (-1) =$	$-9 \# (-7) =$	$0 \times (\#8) =$
$8 \times 9 =$	$-7 \# (-8) =$	$0 \times (\#5) =$	$9 \times (\#6) =$	$5 \times (\#7) =$
$-7 \# 2 =$	$-8 \# (-9) =$	$-8 \# (-8) =$	$1 \times (\#5) =$	$-6 \# (-5) =$

Timed Integer Multiplication 2

$-4 \# (-8) =$	$-8 \# 4 =$	$0 \times (\#6) =$	$-7 \# 3 =$	$4 \times (\#6) =$
$3 \times (\#7) =$	$-4 \# 3 =$	$1 \times (\#9) =$	$7 \times 4 =$	$-3 \# (-8) =$
$6 \times (\#9) =$	$8 \times (\#7) =$	$7 \times 9 =$	$-3 \# 6 =$	$-9 \# (-3) =$
$-1 \# (-4) =$	$-2 \# (-1) =$	$2 \times (\#9) =$	$-9 \# 9 =$	$-6 \# (-2) =$
$-5 \# 7 =$	$9 \times (\#7) =$	$-6 \# (-8) =$	$-3 \# (-7) =$	$8 \times (\#8) =$
$-4 \# (-9) =$	$-9 \# 6 =$	$-2 \# (-2) =$	$1 \times (\#9) =$	$9 \times 3 =$
$-9 \# 8 =$	$-1 \# (-5) =$	$-5 \# (-2) =$	$6 \times (\#7) =$	$-2 \# (-7) =$
$5 \times (\#3) =$	$-1 \# 9 =$	$-2 \# (-9) =$	$-6 \# (-5) =$	$9 \times (\#6) =$
$8 \times 7 =$	$-4 \# (-6) =$	$9 \times (\#3) =$	$8 \times (\#4) =$	$4 \times (\#5) =$
$-4 \# 0 =$	$-5 \# (-7) =$	$-7 \# (-6) =$	$9 \times (\#2) =$	$-3 \# (-3) =$

$-3 \# (-9) =$	$-7 \# 3 =$	$9 \times (\#7) =$	$-8 \# 2 =$	$3 \times (\#7) =$
$2 \times (\#8) =$	$-5 \# 2 =$	$0 \times (\#8) =$	$6 \times 3 =$	$-4 \# (-9) =$
$5 \times (\#8) =$	$7 \times (\#8) =$	$6 \times 8 =$	$-4 \# 7 =$	$-9 \# (-5) =$
$-2 \# (-5) =$	$-3 \# (-2) =$	$1 \times (\#8) =$	$-9 \# 7 =$	$-7 \# (-3) =$
$-6 \# 8 =$	$8 \times (\#8) =$	$-7 \# (-9) =$	$-4 \# (-8) =$	$5 \times (\#9) =$
$-4 \# (-9) =$	$-8 \# 5 =$	$-1 \# (-3) =$	$0 \times (\#7) =$	$8 \times 2 =$
$-9 \# 8 =$	$-2 \# (-6) =$	$-6 \# (-3) =$	$5 \times (\#8) =$	$-3 \# (-8) =$
$4 \times (\#4) =$	$-2 \# 8 =$	$-7 \# (-9) =$	$-7 \# (-6) =$	$8 \times (\#7) =$
$6 \times 6 =$	$-5 \# (-7) =$	$8 \times (\#4) =$	$7 \times (\#5) =$	$3 \times (\#6) =$
$-5 \# (-1) =$	$-6 \# (-8) =$	$-6 \# (-7) =$	$9 \times (\#4) =$	$-4 \# (-4) =$

No Calculator Part.

1.   A rectangle measures 5 m by 4 m. Find the perimeter and area.

   a) $P = 9\,m;\ A = 20\,m^2$ b) $P = 20\,m;\ A = 9\,m^2$ c) $P = 18\ m;\ A = 20\ m^2$

   d) $P = 20\ m;\ A = 9\ m^2$ e) $P = 18\ m^2;\ A = 20\ m$

2.   What property is illustrated by the equation $7 \cdot (5 \cdot 4) = (7 \cdot 5) \cdot 4$?

   a) Multiplicative Identity
   b) Associative property of multiplication
   c) Reciprocal property of multiplication
   d) Commutative property of multiplication
   e) Distributive property of multiplication over addition

3.   Write in decimal notation: eighty and three tenths.

   a) 80.003   b) 8.03   c) 8.3   d) 80.03   e) 80.3

4.   Write $\dfrac{74}{4}$ as a mixed number with the fraction in lowest terms.

   a) $18\dfrac{1}{2}$ b) $\dfrac{37}{2}$ c) $\dfrac{35}{2}$ d) $17\dfrac{1}{2}$ e) None of these

5.   Find the product of 0.8 and 0.6.

   a) 4.8   b) 0.048   c) 0.0048   d) 0.48   e) 48

6.   Find the prime factorization for 50.

   a) $25 \cdot 2$ b) $5 \cdot 10$ c) $2 \cdot 5^2$ d) $2^2 \cdot 5$ e) 25^2

7.   Using the tests for divisibility, list all the numbers in {2, 3, 5} that divide into 5205 evenly.

   a) {3,5}   b) {3}   c) {5}   d) {2,3,5}   e) {2,5}

8. Find the LCM of 18, 27, and 60.

 a) 270 b) 360 c) 720 d) 1080 e) 540

9. Find the difference between 40.8 and 19.06.

 a) – 21.74 b) 777.65 c) 21.74 d) 59.86 e) 2.14

10. Find the average of $\frac{1}{4}$ and $\frac{1}{2}$.

 a) $\frac{3}{4}$ b) $\frac{2}{6}$ c) $\frac{2}{3}$ d) $\frac{1}{8}$ e) $\frac{3}{8}$

11. Write 0.238 in words.

 a) Two hundred and thirty-eight ten thousandths
 b) Two hundred and thirty-eight thousandths
 c) Two hundred thirty-eight
 d) Two hundred thirty-eight thousandths
 e) Two hundred thirty-eight thousands

12. Find the difference between $\frac{3}{4}$ and $\frac{2}{3}$

 a) $-\frac{1}{12}$ b) $\frac{1}{1}$ c) $\frac{-1}{-1}$ d) $\frac{1}{2}$ e) $\frac{1}{12}$

13. Find the product of $\frac{3}{5}$ and $\frac{5}{9}$

 a) $\frac{25}{27}$ b) $\frac{1}{3}$ c) $\frac{52}{45}$ d) $\frac{27}{25}$ e) $\frac{8}{14}$

14. Find the value of $3 - 6 \cdot 2 + 8 \div 2$.

 a) – 2 b) 10 c) 19 d) – 5 e) 1

15. Find the quotient of 0.027 and 0.03.

   a) 0.9   b) 0.09   c) 9   d) 90   e) 0.009

16. 20% is equivalent to:

   a) 0.02 or $\dfrac{1}{50}$ b) 0.2 or $\dfrac{1}{5}$ c) 0.02 or $\dfrac{1}{5}$ d) 0.2 or $\dfrac{1}{4}$ e) 0.02 or $\dfrac{1}{4}$

17. Find the value of $2(6-3)+7(5-12)$.

   a) 13   b) -43 c) 32   d) 55   e) 5

18. 0.8 is equivalent to:

   a) 0.8% or $\dfrac{4}{50}$ b) 80% or $\dfrac{4}{5}$ c) 8% or $\dfrac{4}{5}$ d) 8% or $\dfrac{4}{50}$

   e) 0.08% or $\dfrac{4}{50}$

19. Find the sum of $\dfrac{3}{5}$, $\dfrac{1}{2}$, and $\dfrac{3}{10}$.

   a) $\dfrac{9}{10}$ b) $1\dfrac{2}{5}$ c) $\dfrac{7}{17}$ d) $\dfrac{7}{10}$ e) $\dfrac{14}{30}$

20. According to the distributive law:

   a) $3\cdot(2\cdot 5)=(3\cdot 2)\cdot 5$
   b) $3+(2+5)=3+2+3+5$
   c) $3+(2+5)=(3+2)+5$
   d) $3+(2+5)=(2+5)+3$
   e) $3(2+5)=3\cdot 2+3\cdot 5$

21. Write $6\dfrac{3}{8}$ as an improper fraction.

   a) $\dfrac{63}{8}$ b) 6.38   c) $\dfrac{51}{8}$ d) 63.8   e) $3\dfrac{3}{4}$

22. $\frac{2}{3}$ is equivalent to:

   a) 320% or 3.2   b) $66\frac{2}{3}$% or 0.67   c) 230% or 2.3

   d) 150% or 1.5   e) $33\frac{1}{3}$% or 0.3

23. Find the average of 0.1, 0.08, 0.12, and 0.06.

   a) 0.36   b) 0.27   c) 0.9   d) 0.675   e) 0.09

24. Find the quotient of $\frac{14}{15}$ and $\frac{6}{35}$.

   a) $\frac{49}{9}$ b) $\frac{4}{25}$ c) $\frac{25}{4}$ d) $\frac{20}{50}$ e) $\frac{9}{49}$

25. Find the sum of 3.02, 10.4, and 0.015.

   a) 0.013425   b) 0.421   c) 13.57   d) 13.435   e) 4.21

Answers

1.	C
2.	B
3.	E
4.	A
5.	D
6.	C
7.	A
8.	E
9.	C
10.	E
11.	D
12.	E
13.	B
14.	D
15.	A
16.	B
17.	B
18.	B
19.	B
20.	E
21.	C
22.	B
23.	E
24.	A
25.	D

You may use a Calculator.

26.   Find the value of: $5 - [-2(8-2)^2 + 7] + 3(6-9)$.

       a) 61   b) -9 c) -184 d) 166 e) -13

27.   Find the quotient of 3.62 and 0.64; round to the nearest tenth.

       a) 5.7   b) 4.3   c) 0.2 d) 2.0 e) -3.0

28.   Find the value of: $\dfrac{3}{8} \cdot \dfrac{2}{5} + \dfrac{3}{4} \div \dfrac{5}{8} - 2\dfrac{1}{2}$

       a) $-1\dfrac{3}{20}$ b) $-1\dfrac{3}{50}$ c) $-1\dfrac{141}{160}$ d) $-\dfrac{3}{20}$ e) $1\dfrac{3}{20}$

29.   Sara earns a 7% commission on every refrigerator he sells. How much did she
       earn in commission on the sale of a refrigerator for $1250?

       a) $895.00   b) $17.86   c) $87.50   d) $178.58   e) $875.00

30.   David figured he saved $7.50 by buying a basketball at a 30% discount. What did
       the basketball cost him?

       a) $17.50   b) $25.00   c) $37.50   d) $9.75   e) 25.285

31.   What is $3\dfrac{1}{2}$ more than the product of $2\dfrac{1}{3}$ and $3\dfrac{1}{4}$?

       a) $11\dfrac{5}{11}$ b) $9\dfrac{1}{12}$ c) $4\dfrac{17}{78}$ d) $18\dfrac{23}{24}$ e) $11\dfrac{1}{12}$

32.   Find the value of: $16.8 - 2.7(8.2 - 6.75) + 12.4$

       a) 27.75   b) 0.31   c) -20.595 d) 16303   e) 25.285

33. Find the average of $\frac{7}{8}, \frac{3}{16}$, and $\frac{5}{6}$.

   a) $\frac{59}{96}$ b) $\frac{91}{144}$ c) $\frac{37}{48}$ d) $\frac{73}{128}$ e) $1\frac{43}{48}$

34. 84 is 16% of what number?

   a) 5.25   b) 1344   c) 134.4   d) 525   e) 13.44

35. 16 is what percent of 200?

   a) 0.08%   b) 0.8%   c) 12.5%   d) 8% e) 0.385%

36. 3.6 is how much more than $1\frac{3}{4}$?

   a) −5.35   b) 6.3   c) 1.85   d) 5.35   e) −1.85

37. Find the perimeter of a rectangle whose length is 8.33 cm and whose width is 4.8 cm.

   a) 17.93 cm^2 b) 13.13 cm   c) 26.26 cm   d) 25.26 cm   e) 39.984 cm^2

38. A board is $14\frac{5}{8}$ feet long. If a piece $8\frac{3}{10}$ feet long is cut from the board, what is the length of the remaining piece?

   a) $6\frac{1}{4}$ ft   b) $6\frac{2}{3}$ ft   c) $6\frac{5}{8}$ ft   d) $6\frac{3}{20}$ ft   e) $6\frac{13}{40}$ ft

39. The price of salami is $1.25 per quarter-pound. How many pounds can you buy with $8.75?

   a) 1.25 lbs.   b) 1.5 lbs.   c) 1.75 lbs.   d) 2.5 lbs.   e) 7 lbs.

40. Jim walked $\frac{3}{8}$ mile to the grocery, $\frac{5}{6}$ mile from there to the post office, and $\frac{1}{3}$ mile back home. How far did he walk?

   a) $\frac{3}{8}$ mile   b)   mile   c)   mile   d) $\frac{37}{24}$ mile   e) None of these

41. Mary's test scores were 86, 92, 78, and 84. Find Mary's average grade.

a) 340   b) 277   c) 85   d) 84   e) 86

42. If you can drive your car 540 miles on $26\frac{2}{3}$ gallons of gasoline, how many miles can you drive on one gallon?

a) 22 miles   b) $20\frac{1}{4}$ miles   c) $18\frac{2}{3}$ miles   d) $23\frac{1}{3}$ miles

e) $513\frac{1}{3}$ miles

43. John had $\frac{2}{3}$ gallon of milk in the refrigerator; he used $\frac{3}{8}$ of it. How much did he use?

a) $\frac{7}{24}$ gallon   b) $\frac{1}{4}$ gallon   c) $\frac{9}{16}$ gallon   d) $\frac{1}{5}$ gallon   e) $\frac{5}{11}$ gallon

44. Convert 336 yards to feet.

a) 1008 ft   b) 112 ft   c) 28 ft   d) 56 ft   e) 132.28 ft

45. If Amy drove 7.2 hours at an average speed of 44.8 miles per hour, how far did she drive?

a) 380.16 miles   b) 322.56 miles   c) 260.71 miles   d) 422.22 miles
e) 52 miles

46. If sales tax is 7.5%, what is the total price of a $500 television?

a) $875.00   b) $575.00   c) $525.50   d) $605.25   e) $537.50

47. Jasmine had $327.18 in her checking account. She wrote checks for $83.75, $29, and $37.50. The monthly fee for the account is $7. What did Jasmine have in her account at the end of the month?

a) $176.93   b) $171.57   c) $171.64   d) $183.93   e) $169.93

48. In three fill-ups, Terri bought 17.35, 16.2, and 18.036 gallons of gas. How much gas did she buy in these fill-ups?

a) 17.195 gallons   b) 51.586 gallons   c) 19.933 gallons
d) 39.562 gallons   e) 79.09 gallons

49. If the product of 8 and -5 is added to the quotient of -8 and -2, what is the sum?

a) – 44   b) 56 c) – 36   d) – 1   e) – 30

50. The graph compares American teenagers' weight to their ideal weights. Approximately how many teens are more than 5 pounds overweight?

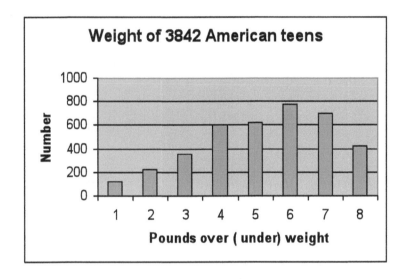

a) 60 teens   b) 2500 teens c) 1900 teens d) 1200 teens e) 70 teens

Answers:

26.	A
27.	A
28.	A
29.	C
30.	A
31.	E
32.	E
33.	B
34.	D
35.	D
36.	C
37.	C
38.	E
39.	C
40.	D
41.	C
42.	B
43.	B
44.	A
45.	B
46.	E
47.	E
48.	B
49.	C
50.	C

Pre-Algebra

Extra Practice Problems - No Calculator Part.

1. Find the value of $6[2(4-5)+7]$.

   a) 54   b) 19   c) 30   d) -5 e) 50

2. If we divide 30 by $\dfrac{1}{2}$ and add 10 to the result, we will have:

   a) 25   b) 15   c) 70   d) 45   e) 40

3. Andrea read $\dfrac{1}{3}$ of her book, which has 69 pages. How many pages left for her to read?

   a) 23   b) 46   c) 207   d) 21   e) 13

4. Using one or more of these conversions to answer the question below.

   1 kilometer = 1000 meters
   10 decimeters = 1 meter
   100 centimeters = 1 meter
   1000 millimeters = 1 meter

   Convert 285 cm to m.

   a) 28.5 m   b) 2.85 m   c) 285 m   d) 0.285 m   e) 0.0285 m

5. 40% of what number is 20?

   a) 80   b) 60   c) 50   d) 8   e) 800

Answers

1.	C
2.	C
3.	B
4.	B
5.	C

Pre-Algebra

<u>**Extra Practice Problems - You may use calculator.**</u>

1. Normal body temperature is **98.6°** Fahrenheit. What is normal body temperature on Celsius scale?

    a) 209.48°   b) 22.78°   c) 235.08°
    d) Celsius temperature is not normal.   e) 37°

2. Find the difference between $18\frac{1}{12}$ and $14\frac{2}{3}$.

    a) $4\frac{5}{12}$ b) $3\frac{7}{12}$ c) $4\frac{7}{12}$ d) $3\frac{5}{12}$ e) $4\frac{-7}{12}$

3. $\frac{2}{3}$ of a number is 16. Find the number.

    a) 24   b) 10.67   c) 48   d) 32   e) 50

4. The total number of cans in a soft drink machine is 300. If 78 soft drinks have been sold, find the percent of soft drink cans that have been left in the machine.

    a) 26%   b) 78%   c) 74%   d) 222%   e) None of these

5. Find the total amount due on a loan of $5,500 for 9 years at 12.5% simple interest.

    a) $74,250   b) $11,687.50   c) $61,875   d) $618,750   e) $6,187.50

6. Using one or more of these conversions to answer the question below.

    1 kilometer = 1000 meters   1 inch = 2.54 cm
    10 decimeters = 1 meter
    100 centimeters = 1 meter
    1000 millimeters = 1 meter

    Convert 0.95 km to centimeters.

    a) 95,000 cm b) 950 cm   c) 9500 cm d) 0.00095 cm   e) 0.0095 cm

7. Find the sale price of an item originally priced at $540 and on sale at 30% off.

    a) $358   b) $402   c) $372   d) $386   e) $378

8. A chain link fence sells for $ 1.50 an inch. What would be the cost of 12 meters of fence?

   a) $45.72   b) $16,764   c) $526   d) $708.66   e) $186

9. 78 inches is equal to how many meters?

   a) 1.98 meters   b) 198.12 meters   c) 19.812 meters
   d) 30.71 meters   e) None of these

10. Multiply $\dfrac{5}{9} \cdot \dfrac{2}{25} \cdot \dfrac{-3}{10}$ and reduce to lowest terms.

   a) $-\dfrac{1}{3}$ b) $-\dfrac{1}{30}$ c) $-\dfrac{1}{6}$ d) $-\dfrac{1}{75}$ e) $-\dfrac{30}{2250}$

Answers

1.	E
2.	D
3.	A
4.	C
5.	B
6.	A
7.	E
8.	D
9.	A
10.	D

Dear Faculty,

Below is the new Advising Recommendation form for the current students. Students need to have one before his or her advising appointment.

Advising Recommendation

Student's Name: _____

Student's ID#: _____

Is currently taking:
- MT 055
- MT065
- MT120

And should enroll in:
- MT055
- MT065
- MT120 or MT110 or MT105*
- MT150 or MT145 or MT 151*

Faculty Signature: _____

Note to students: give this recommendation to your advisor during early advising/advanced registration (EA/AR). However, you must still complete this course. Your final grade in this course may require you to go through drop/add next semester.

* Choice of course depends on the requirements for your major.

You may re-take the Compass test, if you wish. If the test places you in a higher class, you may enroll in that class. Take a copy of Compass score with you when you register.

To my mother, Barbara M. Miller,
and her husband, Leo Miller, and to the memory of
my father, Robert J. Martin

Contents

1 The Whole Numbers   1

2 Multiplying and Dividing Fractions   111

3 Adding and Subtracting Fractions   178

4 Decimals   249

5 Ratio and Proportion   320

6 Percent   369

7 Measurement 441

9 Statistics and Probability 591

10 Signed Numbers 641

Tools to Help Students Succeed

Your textbook includes a number of features designed to help you succeed in this math course—as well as the next math course you take. These features include:

Feature	Benefit	Page
Well-crafted Exercise Sets: We learn math by doing math	The exercise sets in your text offer an ample number of exercises carefully ordered so you can master basic mathematical skills and concepts while developing all-important problem solving skills. Exercise sets include Mixed Practice exercises to help you master multiple key concepts, as well as Mental Math, Writing, Applications, Concept Check, Concept Extension, and Review exercises.	151–56
Solutions-to-Selected Exercises: Built-in solutions at the back of the text	If you need to review problems you find difficult, this built-in solutions manual at the back of the text provides the step-by-step solutions to every other odd-numbered exercise in the exercise sets.	A23
Study Skills Builders: Maximize your chances for success	Study Skills Builders reinforce the material in *Section 1.1—Tips for Success in Mathematics*. Study Skills Builders are a great resource for study ideas and self-assessment to maximize your opportunity for success in this course. Take your new study skills with you to help you succeed in your next math course.	156
The Bigger Picture: Succeed in this math course and the next one you take	The Bigger Picture focuses on the key concept of this course—operations (addition, subtraction, multiplication, division)—and asks you to keep an ongoing outline so you can recognize and perform operations on different types of numbers. A strong foundation in operations on different sets of numbers will help you succeed in this basic math course, as well as the next math course you take.	165
Examples: Step-by-step instruction for you	Examples in the text provide you with clear, concise step-by-step instructions to help you learn. Annotations in the examples provide additional instruction.	195
Helpful Hints: Help where you'll need it most	Helpful Hints provide tips and advice at exact locations where students need it most. Strategically placed where you might have the most difficulty, Helpful Hints will help you work through common trouble spots.	136
Practice Problems: Immediate reinforcement	Practice Problems offer immediate reinforcement after every example. Try each Practice Problem after studying the corresponding example to make sure you have a good working knowledge of the concept.	195
Integrated Review: Mid-chapter progress check	To ensure that you understand the key concepts covered in the first sections of the chapter, work the exercises in the Integrated Review before you continue with the rest of the chapter.	144
Vocabulary Check: Key terms and vocabulary	Make sure you understand key terms and vocabulary in each chapter with the Vocabulary Check.	166
Chapter Highlights: Study smart	Chapter Highlights outline the key concepts of the chapter along with examples to help you focus your studying efforts as you prepare for your test.	166–68
Chapter Test: Take a practice test	In preparation for your classroom test, take this practice test to make sure you understand the key topics in the chapter. Be sure to use the **Chapter Test Prep Video CD** included with this text to see the author present a fully worked-out solution to each exercise in the Chapter Test.	173

Martin-Gay's CD VIDEO RESOURCES Help Students Succeed

Martin-Gay's **Chapter Test Prep Video CD (available with this text)**

- Provides students with help during their most "teachable moment"—while they are studying for a test.
- Text author Elayn Martin-Gay presents step-by-step solutions to the exact exercises found in each Chapter Test in the book.
- Easy video navigation allows students to instantly access the worked-out solutions to the exercises they want to review.
- A close-captioned option for the hearing impaired is provided.

Martin-Gay's **CD Lecture Series (with Tips for Success in Mathematics)**

- Text author Elayn Martin-Gay presents the key concepts from every section of the text in 10–15 minute mini-lectures.
- Students can easily review a section or a specific topic before a homework assignment, quiz, or test.
- Includes fully worked-out solutions to exercises marked with a CD Video icon () in each section.
- Includes *Section 1.1, Tips for Success in Mathematics.*
- A close-captioned option for the hearing impaired is provided.
- Ask your bookstore for information about Martin-Gay's, *Basic College Mathematics,* Third Edition, CD Lecture Series, or visit www.prenhall.com.

Additional Resources to Help You Succeed

Student Study Pack

A single, easy-to-use package–available bundled with your textbook or by itself–for purchase through your bookstore. This package contains the following resources to help you succeed:

Student Solutions Manual
- Contains worked-out solutions to odd-numbered exercises from each section exercise set, Practice Problems, Mental Math exercises, and all exercises found in the Chapter Review and Chapter Tests.

Prentice Hall Math Tutor Center
- Staffed by qualified math instructors who provide students with tutoring on examples and odd-numbered exercises from the textbook. Tutoring is available via toll-free telephone, toll-free fax, email, or the Internet.

Martin-Gay's CD Lecture Series
- Text author Elayn Martin-Gay presents the key concepts from every section of the text with 10–15 minute mini-lectures. Students can easily review a section or a specific topic before a homework assignment, quiz, or test.
- Includes fully worked-out solutions to exercises marked with a CD Video icon () in each section. Also includes *Section 1.1, Tips for Success in Mathematics.*

Online Homework and Tutorial Resources

MyMathLab *MyMathLab*

MyMathLab is a series of text specific, easily customizable, online courses for Prentice Hall textbooks in mathematics and statistics. MyMathLab is powered by Course Compass™—Pearson Education's online teaching and learning environment—and by MathXL®—our online homework, tutorial, and assessment system. MyMathLab gives instructors the tools they need to deliver all or a portion of their course online, whether students are in a lab setting or working from home. MyMathLab provides a rich and flexible set of course materials, featuring free-response exercises that are algorithmically generated for unlimited practice and mastery. Students can also use online tools, such as video lectures, animations, and a multimedia textbook, to independently improve their understanding and performance. MyMathLab is available to qualified adopters. For more information, visit our Web site at www.mymathlab.com or contact your Prentice Hall sales representative. (MyMathLab must be set up and assigned by your instructor.)

MathXL® www.mathxl.com *MathXL* MathXL®

MathXL is a powerful online homework, tutorial, and assessment system that accompanies the text. With MathXL, instructors can create, edit, and assign online homework and tests using algorithmically generated exercises correlated to your textbook. All student work is tracked in MathXL's online gradebook. Students can take chapter tests in MathXL and receive personalized study plans based on their test results. The study plan diagnoses weaknesses and links students directly to tutorial exercises for the objectives they need to study and retest. Students can also access supplemental animations and video clips directly from selected exercises. MathXL is available to qualified adopters. For more information, visit our Web site at www.mathxl.com, or contact your Prentice Hall sales representative for a product demonstration. (MathXL must be set up and assigned by your instructor.)

Preface

Basic College Mathematics, **Third Edition** was written to provide a solid foundation in the basics of college mathematics, including the topics of whole numbers, fractions, decimals, ratio, and proportion, percent, and measurement as well as introductions to geometry, statistics and probability, and algebra topics. Specific care was taken to make sure students have the most up-to-date relevant text preparation for their next mathematics course or for nonmathematical courses that require an understanding of basic mathematical concepts. I have tried to achieve this by writing a user-friendly text that is keyed to objectives and contains many worked-out examples. As suggested by AMATYC and the NCTM Standards (plus Addenda), real-life and real-data applications, data interpretation, conceptual understanding, problem solving, writing, cooperative learning, appropriate use of technology, mental mathematics, number sense, estimation, critical thinking, and geometric concepts are emphasized and integrated throughout the book.

The many factors that contributed to the success of the previous editions have been retained. In preparing the Third Edition, I considered comments and suggestions of colleagues, students, and many users of the prior edition throughout the country.

What's New in the Third Edition?

Enhanced Exercise Sets

- **NEW!** Three forms of mixed sections of exercises have been added to the Third Edition.
  - **Mixed Practice** exercises combining objectives within a section
  - **Mixed Practice** exercises combining previous sections
  - **Mixed Review** exercises included at the end of the Chapter Review

  These exercises require students to determine the problem type and strategy needed in order to solve it. In doing so, students need to think about key concepts to proceed with a correct method of solving—just as they would need to do on a test.

- **NEW! Concept Check exercises** have been added to the section exercise sets. These exercises are related to the Concept Check(s) found within the section. They help students measure their understanding of key concepts by focusing on common trouble areas. These exercises may ask students to identify a common error, and/or provide an explanation.

- **NEW! Concept Extensions** (formerly Combining Concepts) have been revised. These exercises extend the concepts and require students to combine several skills or concepts to solve the exercises in this section.

Increased Emphasis on Study Skills and Student Success

- **NEW! Study Skills Builders** (formerly Study Skill Reminders) Found at the end of many exercise sets, Study Skills Builders allow instructors to assign exercises that will help students improve their study skills and take responsibility for their part of the learning process. Study Skills Builders reinforce the material found in Section 1.1, "Tips for Success in Mathematics" and serve as an excellent tool for self-assessment.

- **NEW! The Bigger Picture** is a recurring feature that focuses on the key concepts of the course—operations, sets of numbers, and solving equations—and helps students develop an outline to recognize and perform operations on different sets of numbers or to solve different types of equations. By working the exercises and developing this outline throughout the text, students can begin to transition from thinking "section by section" to thinking about how the mathematics in this course is part of the "bigger picture" of mathematics in general. A completed outline is provided in Appendix B so students have a model for their work.

- **NEW! Chapter Test Prep Video CD** provides students with help during their most "teachable moment"—while they are studying for a test. Included with every copy of the student edition of the text, this video CD provides fully worked-out solutions by the author to every exercise from each Chapter Test in the text. The easy video navigation allows students to instantly access the solutions to the exercises they want to review. The problems are solved by the author in the same manner as in the text.

- **NEW! Chapter Test files in TestGen** provide algorithms specific to each exercise from each Chapter Test in the text. Allows for easy replication of Chapter Tests with consistent, algorithmically generated problem types for additional assignments or assessment purposes.

Content Changes in the Third Edition

- Increased attention to writing equivalent fractions by multiplying by a form of 1 (for example $\frac{2}{2}$), or "removing" a form of 1. For example, see **Sections 2.3, 3.3, and 4.6.**

- Increased emphasis on estimation, for example, when performing operations on mixed numbers and decimals. **See Sections 2.4 and 4.3.**

- More examples and exercises on concepts of geometry, for example, the difference between perimeter, area, and volume. **See Section 3.6.**

- New and updated applications throughout this text. For example, **see Sections 1.6 and 4.1.**

- All exercise sets have been reviewed and updated to ensure that even- and odd-numbered exercises are paired.

Key Pedagogical Features

The following key features have been retained and/or updated for the Third Edition of the text:

Problem Solving Process   This is formally introduced in Chapter 1 with a four-step process that is integrated throughout the text. The four steps are **Understand, Translate, Solve,** and **Interpret.** The repeated use of these steps in a variety of examples shows their wide applicability. Reinforcing the steps can increase students' comfort level and confidence in tackling problems.

Exercise Sets Revised and Updated   The exercise sets have been carefully examined and extensively revised. Special focus was placed on making sure that even- and odd-numbered exercises are paired.

Examples   Detailed step-by-step examples were added, deleted, replaced, or updated as needed. Many of these reflect real life. Additional instructional support is provided in the annotated examples.

Practice Problems   Throughout the text, each worked-out example has a parallel Practice Problem. These invite students to be actively involved in the learning process. Students should try each Practice Problem after finishing the corresponding example. Learning by doing will help students grasp ideas before moving on to other concepts. Answers to the Practice Problems are provided at the bottom of each page.

Helpful Hints   Helpful Hints contain practical advice on applying mathematical concepts. Strategically placed where students are most likely to need immediate reinforcement, Helpful Hints help students avoid common trouble areas and mistakes.

Concept Checks   This feature allows students to gauge their grasp of an idea as it is being presented in the text. Concept Checks stress conceptual understanding at the point-of-use and help suppress misconceived notions before they start. Answers appear at the bottom of the page. Exercises related to Concept Checks are now included in the exercise sets.

Selected Solutions   Solutions to every-other odd exercise are included in the back of the text. This built-in solutions manual allows students to check their work.

Integrated Reviews   A unique, mid-chapter exercise set that helps students assimilate new skills and concepts that they have learned separately over several sections. These reviews provide yet another opportunity for students to work with "mixed" exercises as they master the topics.

Vocabulary Check   Provides an opportunity for students to become more familiar with the use of mathematical terms as they strengthen their verbal skills. These appear at the end of each chapter before the Chapter Highlights.

Chapter Highlights   Found at the end of every chapter, these contain key definitions and concepts with examples to help students understand and retain what they have learned and help them organize their notes and study for tests.

Chapter Review   The end of every chapter contains a comprehensive review of topics introduced in the chapter. The Chapter Review offers exercises keyed to every section in the chapter, as well as Mixed Review **(NEW!)** exercises that are not keyed to sections.

Chapter Test and Chapter Test Prep Video CD   The Chapter Test is structured to include those problems that involve common student errors. The **Chapter Test Prep Video CD** gives students instant author access to a step-by-step video solution of each exercise in the Chapter Test.

Cumulative Review   Follows every chapter in the text (except Chapter 1). Each odd-numbered exercise contained in the Cumulative Review is an earlier worked example in the text that is referenced in the back of the book along with the answer.

Mental Math   Found at the beginning of an exercise set, these mental warm-ups reinforce concepts found in the accompanying section and increase student's confidence before they tackle an exercise set.

Writing Exercises ✎   These exercises occur in almost every exercise set and require students to provide a written response to explain concepts or justify their thinking.

Applications   Real-world and real-data applications have been thoroughly updated and many new applications are included. These exercises occur in almost every exercise set and show the relevance of mathematics and help students gradually, and continuously develop their problem solving skills.

Review Exercises (formerly Review and Preview exercises)   These exercises occur in each exercise set (except in Chapter 1) and are keyed to earlier sections. They review concepts learned earlier in the text that will be needed in the next section or chapter.

Exercise Set Resource Icons at the opening of each exercise set remind students of the resources available for extra practice and support:

CD/Video for Review

MyMathLab

MathXL®

PH Math/Tutor Center

Student Solutions Manual

See Student Resource descriptions pages xviii–xix for details on the individual resources available.

Exercise Icons These icons facilitate the assignment of specialized exercises and let students know what resources can support them.

- CD Video icon: exercise worked on Martin-Gay's CD Lecture Series.
- △ Triangle icon: identifies exercises involving geometric concepts.
- Pencil icon: indicates a written response is needed.
- Calculator icon: optional exercises intended to be solved using a scientific or graphing calculator.

Group Activities Found at the end of each chapter, these activities are for individual or group completion, and are usually hands-on or data-based activities that extend the concepts found in the chapter allowing students to make decisions and interpretations and to think and write about algebra.

Optional: Calculator Exploration Boxes and Calculator Exercises The optional Calculator Explorations provide key strokes and exercises at appropriate points to provide an opportunity for students to become familiar with these tools. Section exercises that are best completed by using a calculator are identified by ▦ for ease of assignment.

A Word about Textbook Design and Student Success

The design of developmental mathematics textbooks has become increasingly important. As students and instructors have told Prentice Hall in focus groups and market research surveys, these textbooks cannot look "cluttered" or "busy." A "busy" design can distract a student from what is most important in the text. It can also heighten math anxiety.

As a result of the conversations and meetings we have had with students and instructors, we concluded the design of this text should be understated and focused on the most important pedagogical elements. Students and instructors helped us to identify the primary elements that are central to student success. These primary elements include:

- Exercise Sets

- Examples and Practice Problems

- Helpful Hints

- Rules, Property, and Definition boxes

As you will notice in this text, these primary features are the most prominent elements in the design. We have made every attempt to make sure these elements are the features the eye is drawn to. The remaining features, the secondary elements in the design, blend into the "fabric" or "grain" of the overall design. These secondary elements complement the primary elements without becoming distractions.

Prentice Hall's thanks goes to all of the students and instructors (as noted by the author in Acknowledgments) who helped us develop the design of this text. At every step in the design process, their feedback proved valuable in helping us to make the right decisions. Thanks to your input, we're confident the design of this text will be both practical and engaging as it serves its educational and learning purposes.

Sincerely,

Paul Murphy

Executive Editor
Developmental Mathematics
Prentice Hall

Instructor and Student Resources

The following resources are available to help instructors and students use this text more effectively.

Instructor Resources

Annotated Instructor's Edition (0-13-194310-3)

- Answers to all exercises printed on the same text page
- Teaching Tips throughout the text placed at key points
- Includes Vocabulary Check at the beginning of relevant sections
- General tips and suggestions for classroom or group activities

Instructor Solutions Manual (0-13-188115-9)

- Solutions to the even-numbered exercises
- Solutions to every Mental Math exercise
- Solutions to every Practice Problem
- Solutions to every exercise in the Integrated Reviews, Chapter Reviews, Chapter Tests, and Cumulative Reviews

Instructor's Resource Manual with Tests (0-13-188113-2)

- **NEW!** Includes Mini-Lectures for every section from the text
- Group Activities
- Free Response Test Forms, Multiple Choice Test Forms, Cumulative Tests, and Additional Exercises
- Answers to all items

TestGen (0-13-188110-8)

- Enables instructors to build, edit, print, and administer tests
- Features a computerized bank of questions developed to cover all text objectives
- Available on dual-platform Windows/Macintosh CD-Rom

Instructor Adjunct Resource Kit (0-13-188109-4)

The Martin-Gay Instructor/Adjunct Resource Kit (IARK) contains tools and resources to help adjuncts and instructors succeed in the classroom. The IARK includes:

- Instructor-to-Instructor CD Videos that offer tips, suggestions, and strategies for engaging students and presenting key topics
- PDF files of the Instructor Solutions Manual and the Instructor's Resource Manual
- TestGen

MyMathLab Instructor Version (0-13-147898-2)
MyMathLab www.mymathlab.com

MyMathLab is a series of text specific, easily customizable, online courses for Prentice Hall textbooks in mathematics and statistics. MyMathLab is powered by Course Compass™—Pearson Education's online teaching and learning environment—and by MathXL®—our online homework, tutorial, and assessment system. MyMathLab gives instructors the tools they need to deliver all or a portion of their course online, whether students are in a lab setting or working from home. MyMathLab provides a rich and flexible set of course materials, featuring free-response exercises that are algorithmically generated for unlimited practice and mastery. Students can also use online tools, such as video lectures, animations, and a multimedia textbook, to independently improve their understanding and performance. Instructors can use

MyMathLab's homework and test managers to select and assign online exercises correlated directly to the text, and they can import TestGen tests into MyMathLab for added flexibility. MyMathLab's online gradebook—designed specifically for mathematics and statistics—automatically tracks students' homework and test results and gives the instructor control over how to calculate final grades. Instructors can also add offline (paper-and-pencil) grades to the gradebook. MyMathLab is available to qualified adopters. For more information, visit our website at www.mymathlab.com or contact your Prentice Hall sales representative.

MathXL Instructor Version (0-13-147895-8)
MathXL® www.mathxl.com

MathXL is a powerful online homework, tutorial, and assessment system that accompanies the text. With MathXL, instructors can create, edit, and assign online homework and tests using algorithmically generated exercises correlated to your textbook. All student work is tracked in MathXL's online gradebook. Students can take chapter tests in MathXL and receive personalized study plans based on their test results. The study plan diagnoses weaknesses and links students directly to tutorial exercises for the objectives they need to study and retest. Students can also access supplemental animations and video clips directly from selected exercises. MathXL is available to qualified adopters. For more information, visit our Web site at www.mathxl.com, or contact your Prentice Hall sales representative for a product demonstration.

Interact Math® Tutorial Web site www.interactmath.com

Get practice and tutorial help online! This interactive tutorial Web site provides algorithmically generated practice exercises that correlate directly to the exercises in your textbook. You can retry an exercise as many times as you like with new values each time for unlimited practice and mastery. Every exercise is accompanied by an interactive guided solution that gives you helpful feedback if you enter an incorrect answer, and you can also view a worked-out sample problem that steps you through an exercise similar to the one you're working on.

Student Resources

Student Solutions Manual (0-13-188107-8)

- Solutions to the odd-numbered section exercises
- Solutions to the Practice Problems
- Solutions to every Mental Math exercise
- Solutions to every exercise found in the Chapter Reviews and Chapter Tests

Martin-Gay's CD Lecture Series (0-13-188102-7)

- Perfect for review of a section or a specific topic, these mini-lectures by Elayn Martin-Gay cover the key concepts from each section of the text in approximately 10–15 minutes
- Includes fully worked-out solutions to exercises in each section marked with a 🌐
- Includes coverage of Section 1.1, "Tips for Success Mathematics"
- Closed-captioned for the hearing impaired

Prentice Hall Math Tutor Center (0-13-064604-0)

- Staffed by qualified math instructors who provide students with tutoring on examples and odd-numbered exercises from the textbook
- Tutoring is available via toll-free telephone, toll-free fax, e-mail, or the Internet
- Whiteboard technology allows tutors and students to see problems worked while they "talk" in real time over the Internet during tutoring sessions

Basic College Mathematics, Third Edition *Student Study Pack (0-13-196302-3)*

The Student Study Pack includes:

- Martin-Gay's CD Lecture Series
- Student Solutions Manual
- Prentice Hall Math Tutor Center access code

Chapter Test Prep Video CD—Standalone (0-13-188108-6)

- Includes fully worked-out solutions to every problem from each Chapter Test in the text.

MathXL Tutorials on CD—Standalone (0-13-186833-0)

- Provides algorithmically generated practice exercises that correlate to exercises at the end of sections.
- Every exercise is accompanied by an example and a guided solution, selected exercises include a video clip.
- The software recognizes student errors and provides feedback. It can also generate printed summaries of students progress.

Interact Math® Tutorial Web Site www.interactmath.com

Get practice and tutorial help online! This interactive tutorial Web site provides algorithmically generated practice exercises that correlate directly to the exercises in your textbook. You can retry an exercise as many times as you like with new values each time for unlimited practice and mastery. Every exercise is accompanied by an interactive guided solution that gives you helpful feedback if you enter an incorrect answer, and you can also view a worked-out sample problem that steps you through an exercise similar to the one you're working on.

Acknowledgments

There are many people who helped me develop this text, and I will attempt to thank some of them here. Cindy Trimble was *invaluable* for contributing to the overall accuracy of the text. Chris Callac, Laura Wheel, and Lori Mancuso were *invaluable* for their many suggestions and contributions during the development and writing of this Third Edition. Ingrid Mount provided guidance throughout the production process.

A special thanks to my editor, Paul Murphy, for all of his assistance, support, and contributions to this project. A very special thank you goes to my project manager, Mary Beckwith, for being there 24/7/365, as my students say. Last, my thanks to the staff at Prentice Hall for all their support: Linda Behrens, Alan Fischer, Patty Burns, Tom Benfatti, Paul Belfanti, Maureen Eide, Suzanne Behnke, Kate Valentine, Patrice Jones, Chris Hoag, Paul Corey, and Tim Bozik.

I would like to thank the following reviewers for their input and suggestions:

Anita Aikman, *Collin County Community College*

Sheila Anderson, *Housatonic Community College*

Adrianne Arata, *College of the Siskyous*

Cedric Atkins, *Mott Community College*

Laurel Berry, *Bryant & Stratton College*

Connie Buller, *Metropolitan Community College*

Lisa Feintech, *Cabrillo College*

Chris Ford, *Shasta College*

Cindy Fowler, *Central Piedmont Communty College*

Pam Gerszewski, *College of the Albemarle*

Doug Harley, *Del Mar College*

Sonya Johnson, *Central Piedmont Community College*

Deborah Jones, *High Tech College*

Nancy Lange, *Inver Hills Community College*

Paul Laverty, *Wachusett Commmunity College*

Donna Martin, *Florida Community College–Jacksonville*

Robbin Miller, *Erie Community College*

Kris Mundunuri, *Long Beach City College*

Gary Piercy, *Moraine Valley Community College*

Marilyn Platt, *Gaston Community College*

Carolyn Poos, *Southwestern Illinois Community College*

Johnny Reaves, *Central Piedmont Community College*

Mary Lee Seitz, *Erie Community College*

Rhonda Watts, *College of the Albemarle*

I would also like to thank the following dedicated group of instructors who participated in our focus groups, Martin-Gay Summits, and our design review for this edition of the text. Their feedback and insights have helped to strengthen this edition of the text. These instructors include:

Cedric Atkins, *Mott Community College*

Laurel Berry, *Bryant & Stratton*

Bob Brown, *Community College of Baltimore County–Essex*

Lisa Brown, *Community College of Baltimore County–Essex*

Gail Burkett, *Palm Beach Community College*

Cheryl Cantwell, *Seminole Community College*

Jackie Cohen, *Augusta State College*

Janice Ervin, *Central Piedmont Community College*

Pauline Hall, *Iowa State College*

Sonya Johnson, *Central Piedmont Community College*

Irene Jones, *Fullerton College*

Nancy Lange, *Inver Hills Community College*

Jean McArthur, *Joliet Junior College*

Marica Molle, *Metropolitan Community College*

Linda Padilla, *Joliet Junior College*

Carole Shapero, *Oakton Community College*

Jennifer Strehler, *Oakton Community College*

Tanomo Taguchi, *Fullerton College*

Leigh Ann Wheeler, *Greenville Technical Community College*

Valerie Wright, *Central Piedmont Community College*

A special thank you to those students who participated in our design review: Katherine Browne, Mike Bulfin, Nancy Canipe, Ashley Carpenter, Jeff Chojnachi, Roxanne Davis, Mike Dieter, Amy Dombrowski, Kay Herring, Todd Jaycox, Kaleena Levan, Matt Montgomery, Tony Plese, Abigail Polkinghorn, Harley Price, Eli Robinson, Avery Rosen, Robyn Schott, Cynthia Thomas, and Sherry Ward.

Additional Acknowledgments

As usual, I would like to thank my husband, Clayton, for his constant encouragement. I would also like to thank my children, Eric and Bryan, for providing most of the cooking and humor in our household. I would also like to thank my extended family for their help and wonderful sense of humor. Their contributions are too numerous to list. They are Rod and Karen Pasch; Peter, Michael, Christopher, Matthew, and Jessica Callac; Stuart and Earline Martin; Josh, Mandy, Bailey, Ethan, and Avery Barnes; Mark, Sabrina, and Madison Martin; Leo and Barbara Miller; and Jewett Gay.

Elayn Martin-Gay

About the Author

Elayn Martin-Gay has taught mathematics at the University of New Orleans for more than 25 years. Her numerous teaching awards include the local University Alumni Association's Award for Excellence in Teaching, and Outstanding Developmental Educator at University of New Orleans, presented by the Louisiana Association of Developmental Educators.

Prior to writing textbooks, Elayn Martin-Gay developed an acclaimed series of lecture videos to support developmental mathematics students in their quest for success. These highly successful videos originally served as the foundation material for her texts. Today, the videos are specific to each book in the Martin-Gay series. The author has also created Chapter Test Prep Videos to help students during their most "teachable moment"—as they prepare for a test, along with Instructor-to-Instructor videos that provide teaching tips, hints, and suggestions for each developmental mathematics course, including basic mathematics, prealgebra, beginning algebra, and intermediate algebra.

Elayn is the author of 10 published textbooks as well as multimedia interactive mathematics, all specializing in developmental mathematics courses. She has participated as an author across the broadest range of educational materials: textbooks, videos, tutorial software, and Interactive Math courseware. All of these components are designed to work together. This offers an opportunity of various combinations for an integrated teaching and learning package offering great consistency for the student.

Applications Index

1

The Whole Numbers

Whole numbers are the basic building blocks of mathematics. The whole numbers answer the question "How many?"

This chapter covers basic operations on whole numbers. Knowledge of these operations provides a good foundation on which to build further mathematical skills.

Yosemite National Park was established on October 1, 1890, and it is a favorite tourist destination in the Sierra Nevada Mountains in central California. Its nearly 750,000 acres are home to many of nature's most beautiful sites, including rock formations, giant sequoias, and waterfalls. In Exercise 65, Section 1.3, on page 25, we will see how whole numbers can be used to measure the height of Yosemite Falls, the highest waterfall in the United States.

Highest U.S. Waterfalls

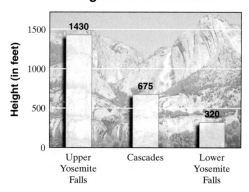

1

1.1 TIPS FOR SUCCESS IN MATHEMATICS

Before reading this section, remember that your instructor is your best source of information. Please see your instructor for any additional help or information.

Objective **A** Getting Ready for This Course

Now that you have decided to take this course, remember that a *positive attitude* will make all the difference in the world. Your belief that you can succeed is just as important as your commitment to this course. Make sure that you are ready for this course by having the time and positive attitude that it takes to succeed.

Next, make sure that you have scheduled your math course at a time that will give you the best chance for success. For example, if you are also working, you may want to check with your employer to make sure that your work hours will not conflict with your course schedule.

On the day of your first class period, double-check your schedule and allow yourself extra time to arrive on time in case of traffic problems or difficulty locating your classroom. Make sure that you bring at least your textbook, paper, and a writing instrument. Are you required to have a lab manual, graph paper, calculator, or some other supply besides this text? If so, also bring this material with you.

Objective **B** General Tips for Success

Below are some general tips that will increase your chance for success in a mathematics class. Many of these tips will also help you in other courses you may be taking.

Exchange names and phone numbers or e-mail addresses with at least one other person in class. This contact person can be a great help if you miss an assignment or want to discuss math concepts or exercises that you find difficult.

Choose to attend all class periods. If possible, sit near the front of the classroom. This way, you will see and hear the presentation better. It may also be easier for you to participate in classroom activities.

Do your homework. You've probably heard the phrase "practice makes perfect" in relation to music and sports. It also applies to mathematics. You will find that the more time you spend solving mathematics exercises, the easier the process becomes. Be sure to schedule enough time to complete your assignments before the next class period.

Check your work. Review the steps you made while working a problem. Learn to check your answers in the original problems. You may also compare your answers with the answers to selected exercises section in the back of the book. If you have made a mistake, try to figure out what went wrong. Then correct your mistake. If you can't find what went wrong, don't erase your work or throw it away. Bring your work to your instructor, a tutor in a math lab, or a classmate. It is easier for someone to find where you had trouble if they look at your original work.

Learn from your mistakes. Everyone, even your instructor, makes mistakes. Use your errors to learn and to become a better math student. The key is finding and understanding your errors. Was your mistake a careless one, or did you make it because you can't read your own math writing? If so, try to work more slowly or write more neatly and make a conscious effort to carefully check your work. Did you make a mistake because you don't understand a concept? If so, take the time to review the concept or ask questions to better understand it.

Know how to get help if you need it. It's all right to ask for help. In fact, it's a good idea to ask for help whenever there is something that you don't understand. Make sure you know when your instructor has office hours and how to find his or her office. Find out whether math tutoring services are available on your campus. Check on the hours, location, and requirements of the tutoring service. Know whether software is available and how to access this resource.

Organize your class materials, including homework assignments, graded quizzes and tests, and notes from your class or lab. All of these items will make valuable references throughout your course and when studying for upcoming tests and the final exam. Make sure that you can locate these materials when you need them.

Read your textbook before class. Reading a mathematics textbook is unlike reading a novel or a newspaper. Your pace will be much slower. It is helpful to have paper and a pencil with you when you read. Try to work out examples on your own as you encounter them in your text. You should also write down any questions that you want to ask in class. When you read a mathematics textbook, sometimes some of the information in a section will be unclear. But after you hear a lecture or watch a videotape on that section, you will understand it much more easily than if you had not read your text beforehand.

Don't be afraid to ask questions. You are not the only person in class with questions. Other students are normally grateful that someone has spoken up.

Hand in assignments on time. This way you can be sure that you will not lose points for being late. Show every step of a problem and be neat and organized. Also be sure that you understand which problems are assigned for homework. If allowed, you can always double-check the assignment with another student in your class.

Objective C Using This Text

There are many helpful resources that are available to you in this text. It is important that you become familiar with and use these resources. They should increase your chances for success in this course.

- *Practice Problems.* Each example in every section has a parallel Practice Problem. As you read a section, try each Practice Problem after you've finished the corresponding example. This "learn-by-doing" approach will help you grasp ideas before you move on to other concepts.

- *Chapter Test Prep Video CD.* This book contains a CD. This CD contains all of the Chapter Test exercises worked out by the author. This supplement is very helpful before a classroom chapter test.

- *Lecture Video CDs.* Exercises marked with a ⊚ are fully worked out by the author on video CDs. Check with your instructor for the availability of these video CDs.

- *Symbols at the beginning of an exercise set.* If you need help with a particular section, the symbols listed at the beginning of each exercise set will remind you of the numerous supplements available.

- *Objectives.* The main section of exercises in each exercise set is referenced by an objective, such as **A** or **B**, and also an example(s). There is also often a section of exercises entitled "Mixed Practice," which is referenced by two or more objectives or sections. These are mixed exercises written to prepare you for your next exam. Use all of this referencing if you have trouble completing an assignment from the exercise set.

- *Icons (Symbols).* Make sure that you understand the meaning of the icons that are beside many exercises. ⊚ tells you that the corresponding exercise may be viewed on the video segment that corresponds to that section. ✎ tells you that this exercise is a writing exercise in which you should answer in complete sentences. △ icon tells you that the exercise involves geometry.

- *Integrated Reviews.* Found in the middle of each chapter, these reviews offer you a chance to practice — in one place — the many concepts that you have learned separately over several sections.

- *End of Chapter Opportunities.* There are many opportunities at the end of each chapter to help you understand the concepts of the chapter.

  Chapter Highlights contain chapter summaries and examples.

  Chapter Reviews contain review problems. The first part is organized section by section and the second part contains a set of mixed exercises.

  Chapter Tests are sample tests to help you prepare for an exam. The Chapter Test Prep Video CD, found in this text, contains all the Chapter Test exercises worked by the author.

  Cumulative Reviews are reviews consisting of material from the beginning of the book to the end of that particular chapter.

- *Study Skills Builder.* This feature is found at the end of many exercise sets. In order to increase your chance of success in this course, please read and answer the questions in the Study Skills Builder.

- *The Bigger Picture.* This feature contains the directions for building an outline to be used throughout the course. The purpose of this outline is to help you make the transition from thinking "section by section" to thinking about how the mathematics in this course is part of a bigger picture.

See the preface at the beginning of this text for a more thorough explanation of the features of this text.

Objective D Getting Help

If you have trouble completing assignments or understanding the mathematics, get help as soon as you need it! This tip is presented as an objective on its own because it is so important. In mathematics, usually the material presented in one section builds on your understanding of the previous section. This means that if you don't understand the concepts covered during a class period, there is a good chance that you will not understand the concepts covered during the next class period. If this happens to you, get help as soon as you can.

Where can you get help? Many suggestions have been made in this section on where to get help, and now it is up to you to do it. Try your instructor, a tutoring center, or a math lab, or you may want to form a study group with fellow classmates. If you do decide to see your instructor or go to a tutoring center, make sure that you have a neat notebook and are ready with your questions.

Objective E Preparing for and Taking an Exam

Make sure that you allow yourself plenty of time to prepare for a test. If you think that you are a little "math anxious," it may be that you are not preparing for a test in a way that will ensure success. The way that you prepare for a test in mathematics is important. To prepare for a test:

1. Review your previous homework assignments.
2. Review any notes from class and section-level quizzes you have taken. (If this is a final exam, also review chapter tests you have taken.)
3. Review concepts and definitions by reading the Highlights at the end of each chapter.
4. Practice working out exercises by completing the Chapter Review found at the end of each chapter. (If this is a final exam, go through a Cumulative Review. There is one found at the end of each chapter except Chapter 1. Choose the review found at the end of the latest chapter that you have covered in your course.) *Don't stop here!*
5. It is important that you place yourself in conditions similar to test conditions to find out how you will perform. In other words, as soon as you feel that you know the material, get a few blank sheets of paper and take a sample test. There is a Chapter Test available at the end of each chapter, or you can work selected

problems from the Chapter Review. Your instructor may also provide you with a review sheet. During this sample test, do not use your notes or your textbook. Then check your sample test. If you are not satisfied with the results, study the areas that you are weak in and try again.

6. On the day of the test, allow yourself plenty of time to arrive at where you will be taking your exam.

When taking your test:

1. Read the directions on the test carefully.
2. Read each problem carefully as you take the test. Make sure that you answer the question asked.
3. Watch your time and pace yourself so that you can attempt each problem on your test.
4. If you have time, check your work and answers.
5. Do not turn your test in early. If you have extra time, spend it double-checking your work.

Objective 🇫 Managing Your Time

As a college student, you know the demands that classes, homework, work, and family place on your time. Some days you probably wonder how you'll ever get everything done. One key to managing your time is developing a schedule. Here are some hints for making a schedule:

1. Make a list of all of your weekly commitments for the term. Include classes, work, regular meetings, extracurricular activities, etc. You may also find it helpful to list such things as laundry, regular workouts, grocery shopping, etc.
2. Next, estimate the time needed for each item on the list. Also make a note of how often you will need to do each item. Don't forget to include time estimates for the reading, studying, and homework you do outside of your classes. You may want to ask your instructor for help estimating the time needed.
3. In the exercise set that follows, you are asked to block out a typical week on the schedule grid given. Start with items with fixed time slots like classes and work.
4. Next, include the items on your list with flexible time slots. Think carefully about how best to schedule items such as study time.
5. Don't fill up every time slot on the schedule. Remember that you need to allow time for eating, sleeping, and relaxing! You should also allow a little extra time in case some items take longer than planned.
6. If you find that your weekly schedule is too full for you to handle, you may need to make some changes in your workload, classload, or in other areas of your life. You may want to talk to your advisor, manager or supervisor at work, or someone in your college's academic counseling center for help with such decisions.

1. What is your instructor's name?

2. What are your instructor's office location and office hours?

3. What is the best way to contact your instructor?

4. Do you have the name and contact information of at least one other student in class?

5. Will your instructor allow you to use a calculator in this class?

6. Is tutorial software available to you? If so, what type and where?

7. Is there a tutoring service available on campus? If so, what are its hours? What services are available?

8. Have you attempted this course before? If so, write down ways that you might improve your chances of success during this second attempt.

9. List some steps that you can take if you begin having trouble understanding the material or completing an assignment.

10. How many hours of studying does your instructor advise for each hour of instruction?

11. What does the ✎ icon in this text mean?

12. What does the ⊙ icon in this text mean?

13. What does the △ icon in this text mean?

14. Search the minor columns in your text. What are Practice Problems?

15. When might be the best time to work a Practice Problem?

16. Where are the answers to Practice Problems?

17. What answers are contained in this text and where are they?

18. What solutions are contained in this text and where are they?

19. What and where are Integrated Reviews?

20. What video CD is contained in this book, where is it, and what material is on it?

21. Chapter Highlights are found at the end of each chapter. Find the Chapter 1 Highlights and explain how you might use it and how it might be helpful.

22. Chapter Reviews are found at the end of each chapter. Find the Chapter 1 Review and explain how you might use it and how it might be useful.

23. Chapter Tests are found at the end of each chapter. Find the Chapter 1 Test and explain how you might use it and how it might be helpful when preparing for an exam on Chapter 1. Include how the Chapter Test Prep Video in this book may help.

24. Read or reread objective **F** and fill out the schedule grid below.

	Monday	Tuesday	Wednesday	Thursday	Friday	Saturday	Sunday
7:00 a.m.							
8:00 a.m.							
9:00 a.m.							
10:00 a.m.							
11:00 a.m.							
12:00 a.m.							
1:00 p.m.							
2:00 p.m.							
3:00 p.m.							
4:00 p.m.							
5:00 p.m.							
6:00 p.m.							
7:00 p.m.							
8:00 p.m.							
9:00 p.m.							

1.2 PLACE VALUE AND NAMES FOR NUMBERS

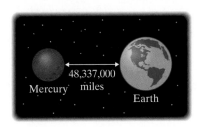
The **digits** 0, 1, 2, 3, 4, 5, 6, 7, 8, and 9 can be used to write numbers. For example, the **whole numbers** are

0, 1, 2, 3, 4, 5, 6, 7, 8, 9, 10, 11, . . .

The three dots (. . .) after the 11 mean that this list continues indefinitely. That is, there is no largest whole number. The smallest whole number is 0.

Objective A Finding the Place Value of a Digit in a Whole Number

The position of each digit in a number determines its **place value.** For example, the distance (in miles) between the planet Mercury and the planet Earth can be represented by the whole number 48,337,000.

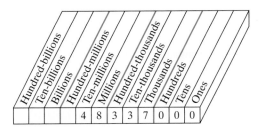

Below is a place-value chart for this whole number.

The two 3s in 48,337,000 represent different amounts because of their different placements. The place value of the 3 on the left is hundred-thousands. The place value of the 3 on the right is ten-thousands.

EXAMPLES Find the place value of the digit 4 in each whole number.

1. 48,761
↑
ten-thousands

2. 249
↑
tens

3. 524,007,656
↑
millions

 Work Practice Problems 1–3

Objective B Writing a Whole Number in Words and in Standard Form

A whole number such as 1,083,664,500 is written in **standard form.** Notice that commas separate the digits into groups of three, starting from the right. Each group of three digits is called a **period.** The names of the first four periods are shown in blue.

PRACTICE PROBLEMS 1–3

Find the place value of the digit 7 in each whole number.
1. 72,589,620
2. 67,890
3. 50,722

Answers
1. ten-millions, **2.** thousands,
3. hundreds

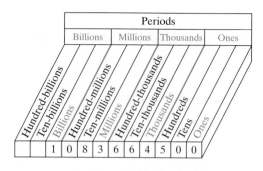

Periods			
Billions	Millions	Thousands	Ones

Hundred-billions / Ten-billions / Billions / Hundred-millions / Ten-millions / Millions / Hundred-thousands / Ten-thousands / Thousands / Hundreds / Tens / Ones

| | 1 | 0 | 8 | 3 | 6 | 6 | 4 | 5 | 0 | 0 |

Writing a Whole Number in Words

To write a whole number in words, write the number in each period followed by the name of the period. (The ones period is usually not written.) This same procedure can be used to read a whole number.

For example, we write 1,083,664,500 as

one **billion,**

eighty-three **million,**

six hundred sixty-four **thousand,**

five **hundred**

> **Helpful Hint** Notice the commas after the name of each period.

> **Helpful Hint** The name of the ones period is not used when reading and writing whole numbers. For example,
>
> 9,265
>
> is read as
>
> "nine **thousand,** two **hundred** sixty-five."

PRACTICE PROBLEMS 4–6

Write each number in words.
4. 67
5. 395
6. 12,804

EXAMPLES Write each number in words.

4. 85   eighty-five
5. 126   one hundred twenty-six
6. 27,034   twenty-seven thousand, thirty-four

▣ **Work Practice Problems 4–6**

> **Helpful Hint** The word "and" is *not* used when reading and writing whole numbers. It is used when reading and writing mixed numbers and some decimal values, as shown later in this text.

PRACTICE PROBLEM 7

Write 321,670,200 in words.

EXAMPLE 7 Write 106,052,447 in words.

Solution: 106,052,447 is written as

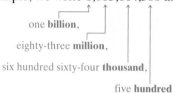

one hundred six **million,** fifty-two **thousand,** four **hundred** forty-seven

▣ **Work Practice Problem 7**

Answers

4. sixty-seven, **5.** three hundred ninety-five, **6.** twelve thousand, eight hundred four, **7.** three hundred twenty-one million, six hundred seventy thousand, two hundred

✔ **Concept Check Answer**

false

✔**Concept Check** True or false? When writing a check for $2600, the word name we write for the dollar amount of the check is "two thousand sixty." Explain your answer.

Writing a Whole Number in Standard Form

To write a whole number in standard form, write the number in each period, followed by a comma.

EXAMPLES Write each number in standard form.

8. sixty-one   61

9. eight hundred five   805

10. two million, five hundred sixty-four thousand, three hundred fifty

2,564,350

11. nine thousand, three hundred eighty-six

9,386   or   9386

Work Practice Problems 8–11

Helpful Hint
A comma may or may not be inserted in a four-digit number. For example, both

9,386   and   9386

are acceptable ways of writing nine thousand, three hundred eighty-six.

PRACTICE PROBLEMS 8–11

Write each number in standard form.

8. twenty-nine

9. seven hundred ten

10. twenty-six thousand, seventy-one

11. six thousand, five hundred seven

Objective C Writing a Whole Number in Expanded Form

The place value of a digit can be used to write a number in expanded form. The **expanded form** of a number shows each digit of the number with its place value. For example, 5672 is written in expanded form as

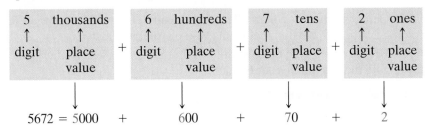

$$5672 = 5000 + 600 + 70 + 2$$

EXAMPLE 12 Write 706,449 in expanded form.

Solution: $700{,}000 + 6000 + 400 + 40 + 9$

Work Practice Problem 12

PRACTICE PROBLEM 12

Write 1,047,608 in expanded form.

Objective D Reading Tables

Now that we know about place value and names for whole numbers, we introduce one way that whole number data may be presented. **Tables** are often used to organize and display facts that involve numbers. The following table shows the countries that won the most medals during the 2004 Olympic summer games. (Although the medals are truly won by athletes from the various countries, for simplicity we will state that countries have won the medals.)

Answers

8. 29, **9.** 710, **10.** 26,071, **11.** 6507,
12. $1{,}000{,}000 + 40{,}000 + 7000 + 600 + 8$

Most Medals—2004 Olympic Summer Games

Country	Gold	Silver	Bronze	Total	Country	Gold	Silver	Bronze	Total
United States	35	39	27	101	Italy	10	11	11	32
Russia	27	27	38	92	Great Britain	9	9	12	30
China	32	17	14	63	South Korea	9	12	9	30
Australia	17	16	16	49	Cuba	9	7	11	27
Germany	14	16	18	48	Ukraine	9	5	9	23
Japan	16	9	12	37	Netherlands	4	9	9	22
France	11	9	13	33	(*Source:* ESPN.com)				

For example, by reading from left to right along the row marked "U.S." we find that the United States won 35 gold, 39 silver, and 27 bronze medals during the 2004 Summer Games.

PRACTICE PROBLEM 13

Use the Summer Games table to answer the following questions:

a. How many bronze medals did Australia win during the Summer Games of the 2004 Olympics?

b. Which countries shown won more than 30 gold medals?

EXAMPLE 13 Use the Summer Games table to answer each question.

a. How many total medals did China win during the 2004 Summer Games of the Olympics?

b. Which country shown won fewer gold medals than Great Britain?

Solution:

a. Find "China" in the left column. Then read from left to right until the "Total" column is reached. We find that China won 63 total medals.

b. Great Britain won 9 gold medals while Netherlands won 4, so Netherlands won fewer gold medals than Great Britain.

🔲 **Work Practice Problem 13**

Answers

13. a. 16,   **b.** United States and China

1.2 EXERCISE SET

Objective Ⓐ *Determine the place value of the digit 5 in each whole number. See Examples 1 through 3.*

1. 352

2. 905

3. 5890

4. 6527

5. 62,500,000

6. 79,050,000

7. 5,070,099

8. 51,682,700

Objective Ⓑ *Write each whole number in words. See Examples 4 through 7.*

9. 542

10. 316

11. 7896

12. 5445

13. 26,990

14. 42,009

15. 1,620,000

16. 3,204,000

17. 53,520,170

18. 47,033,107

Write each number in the sentence in words. See Examples 4 through 7.

19. At this writing, the population of Bermuda is 64,482. (*Source:* 2004 *World Almanac*)

20. Each Home Depot store in the United States and Canada stocks at least 40,000 different kinds of building materials, home improvement supplies, and lawn and garden products. (*Source:* The Home Depot, Inc.)

21. The world's tallest building, the Taipei 101 building in Taiwan is 1679 feet tall. (*Source:* Council on Tall Buildings and Urban Habitat)

22. In a recent year, there were 3895 patients in the United States waiting for a heart transplant. (*Source:* United Network for Organ Sharing)

23. Each day, UPS delivers 13,600,000 packages and documents worldwide. (*Source:* United Parcel Service of America, Inc.)

24. Liz Harold has the number 16,820,409 showing on her calculator display.

25. The highest point in Idaho is at Granite Peak, at an elevation of 12,662 feet. (*Source:* U.S. Geological Survey)

26. The highest point in New Mexico is Wheeler Peak, at an elevation of 13,161 feet. (*Source:* U.S. Geological Survey)

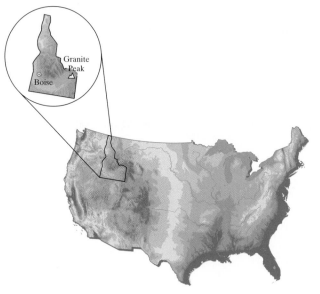

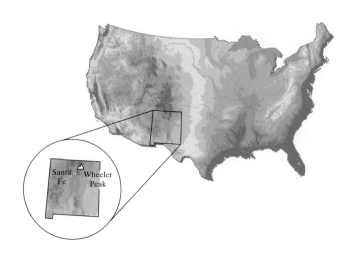

27. The Goodyear blimp *Eagle* holds 202,700 cubic feet of helium. (*Source:* The Goodyear Tire & Rubber Company)

28. In a recent year, zinc mines in the United States mined 799,000 metric tons of zinc. (*Source:* U.S. Dept. of Interior)

Write each whole number in standard form. See Examples 8 through 11.

29. Six thousand, five hundred eighty-seven

30. Three thousand, three hundred seventy-nine

31. Twenty-nine thousand, nine hundred

32. Forty-two thousand, six

33. Sixteen million, five hundred four thousand, nineteen

34. Ten million, thirty-seven thousand, sixteen

35. Three million, fourteen

36. Seven million, twelve

Write the whole number in each sentence in standard form. See Examples 8 through 11.

37. The International Space station orbits above Earth at an altitude of two hundred twenty miles. (*Source:* NASA)

38. The average distance between the surfaces of the Earth and the Moon is about two hundred thirty-four thousand miles.

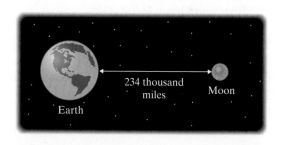

39. The price for a 2005 Porsche Carrera GT is four hundred forty thousand, two hundred seventy-six dollars. (*Source:* Porsche Cars North America)

40. You might know that the zip code for Beverly Hills, California, is 90210, but did you know that one of its area codes is three hundred ten?

41. The Disney/Pixar film *Finding Nemo* set the world record for opening weekend income when it took in seventy million, two hundred fifty-one thousand, seven hundred ten dollars during the weekend of May 30, 2003. (*Source: Guinness Book,* 2005)

42. In 2004, there were one hundred eight million, four hundred thousand U.S. households that owned at least one television set. (*Source:* Nielsen Media Research)

43. The world's tallest self-supporting structure is the CN Tower in Toronto, Canada. It is one thousand, eight hundred fifteen feet tall. (*Source: The World Almanac,* 2005)

44. As of 2004, there were one thousand, eight hundred twenty-four species classified as either threatened or endangered in the United States. (*Source:* U.S. Fish & Wildlife Service)

45. Hank Aaron holds the career record for home runs in Major League baseball since 1974, with a total of seven hundred fifty-five home runs. (*Source:* Major League Baseball)

46. Barry Bonds is approaching Hank Aaron's career record for home runs in Major League baseball (see Exercise 45). Barry has seven hundred three home runs through 2004.

Objective **C** *Write each whole number in expanded form. See Example 12.*

47. 406

48. 789

49. 5290

50. 6040

51. 62,407

52. 20,215

53. 30,680

54. 99,032

55. 39,680,000

56. 47,703,029

Objectives **B** **C** **D** **Mixed Practice** *The table shows the six tallest mountains in New England and their elevations. Use this table to answer Exercises 57 through 62. See Example 13.*

Mountain (State)	Elevation (in feet)
Boott Spur (NH)	5492
Mt. Adams (NH)	5774
Mt. Clay (NH)	5532
Mt. Jefferson (NH)	5712
Mt. Sam Adams (NH)	5584
Mt. Washington (NH)	6288
Source: U.S. Geological Survey	

Elevation in feet

57. Write the elevation of Mt. Clay in standard form and then in words.

58. Write the elevation of Mt. Washington in standard form and then in words.

59. Write the height of Boott Spur in expanded form.

60. Write the height of Mt. Jefferson in expanded form.

61. Which mountain is the tallest in New England?

62. Which mountain is the second tallest in New England?

The table shows the top ten popular breeds of dogs in 2003 according to the American Kennel Club. Use this table to answer Exercises 63 through 68. See Example 13.

Top Ten American Kennel Club Registrations in 2003			
Breed	Number of Registered Dogs	Average Dog Maximum Height (in inches)	Average Dog Maximum Weight (in pounds)
Beagle	45,033	15	30
Boxer	34,136	25	70
Chihuahua	24,930	9	6
Dachshund	39,473	9	25
German shepherd dog	43,950	26	95
Golden retriever	52,530	24	80
Labrador retriever	144,934	25	75
Poodle (standard, miniature, and toy)	32,176	standard: 26	standard: 70
Shih Tzu	26,935	11	16
Yorkshire terrier	38,256	9	7

(*Source:* American Kennel Club)

63. Which breed has more dogs registered, Chihuahua or Golden retriever?

64. Which breed has fewer dogs registered, Beagle or Yorkshire terrier?

65. Which breed has the most American Kennel Club registrations? Write the number of registrations for this breed in words.

66. Which of the listed breeds has the fewest registrations? Write the number of registered dogs for this breed in words.

67. What is the maximum weight of an average-size Dachshund?

68. What is the maximum height of an average-size Yorkshire terrier?

Concept Extensions

69. Write the largest four-digit number that can be made from the digits 3, 6, 7, and 2 if each digit must be used once.

____ ____ ____ ____

70. Write the largest five-digit number that can be made using the digits 4, 5, and 3 if each digit must be used at least once.

____ ____, ____ ____ ____

Check to see whether each number written in standard form matches the number written in words. If not, correct the number in words. See the Concept Check in this section.

71.

	60–8124/7233 1000613331	1401
	DATE _____
PAY TO THE ORDER OF _____	$ *105.00*
One Hundred Fifty and ⁰⁰⁄₁₀₀ ——————— DOLLARS
FIRST STATE BANK OF FARTHINGTON FARTHINGTON, IL 64422
MEMO _____
⑆621497260⑆ 1000613331⑈ 1401

72.

	60–8124/7233 1000613331	1402
	DATE _____
PAY TO THE ORDER OF _____	$ *7030.00*
Seven Thousand Thirty and ⁰⁰⁄₁₀₀ ——————— DOLLARS
FIRST STATE BANK OF FARTHINGTON FARTHINGTON, IL 64422
MEMO _____
⑆621497260⑆ 1000613331⑈ 1402

73. If a number is given in words, describe the process used to write this number in standard form.

74. If a number is written in standard form, describe the process used to write this number in expanded form.

75. The Pro-Football Hall of Fame was established on September 7, 1963, in this town. Use the information and the diagram to the right to find the name of the town.

- Alliance is east of Massillon.
- Dover is between Canton and New Philadelphia.
- Massillon is not next to Alliance.
- Canton is north of Dover.

Pro-Football
Hall of Fame

OHIO

76. The world's fastest super computer is Japan's Earth Simulator, which is programmed to simulate weather patterns and other massive systems. It can perform thirty-five trillion calculations in a second. Look up "trillion" in a dictionary and use the definition to write this number in standard form. (*Source:* 2005 *World Almanac*)

Objectives

A Add Whole Numbers.

B Find the Perimeter of a Polygon.

C Solve Problems by Adding Whole Numbers.

1.3 ADDING WHOLE NUMBERS AND PERIMETER

Objective A Adding Whole Numbers

The iPod is a hard drive–based portable audio player. As of 2004, it is the most popular digital music player in the United States.

Suppose that a small computer store received a shipment of two iPods one day and an additional four iPods the next day. The **total** shipment in the two days can be found by adding 2 and 4.

$$2 \text{ iPods } + 4 \text{ iPods } = 6 \text{ iPods}$$

The **sum** (or total) is 6 iPods. Each of the numbers 2 and 4 is called an **addend,** and the process of finding the sum is called **addition.**

$$
\underset{\text{addend}}{2} \quad + \quad \underset{\text{addend}}{4} \quad = \quad \underset{\text{sum}}{6}
$$

To add whole numbers, we add the digits in the ones place, then the tens place, then the hundreds place, and so on. For example, let's add $2236 + 160$.

$$
\begin{array}{r}
2236 \\
+160 \\
\hline
2396
\end{array}
$$

Line up numbers vertically so that the place values correspond. Then add digits in corresponding place values, starting with the ones place.

— sum of ones
— sum of tens
— sum of hundreds
— sum of thousands

PRACTICE PROBLEM 1

Add: $7235 + 542$

EXAMPLE 1 Add: $23 + 136$

Solution:
$$
\begin{array}{r}
23 \\
+136 \\
\hline
159
\end{array}
$$

Work Practice Problem 1

When the sum of digits in corresponding place values is more than 9, **carrying** is necessary. For example, to add $365 + 89$, add the ones-place digits first.

Carrying
$$
\begin{array}{r}
\overset{1}{3}65 \\
+\ 89 \\
\hline
4
\end{array}
$$
5 ones + 9 ones = **14 ones** or **1 ten** + **4 ones**
Write the 4 ones in the ones place and carry the 1 ten to the tens place.

Next, add the tens-place digits.

$$
\begin{array}{r}
\overset{1\ 1}{3}65 \\
+\ 89 \\
\hline
54
\end{array}
$$
1 ten + 6 tens + 8 tens = **15 tens** or **1 hundred** + **5 tens**
Write the 5 tens in the tens place and carry the 1 hundred to the hundreds place.

Next, add the hundreds-place digits.

$$
\begin{array}{r}
\overset{1\ 1}{3}65 \\
+\ 89 \\
\hline
454
\end{array}
$$
1 hundred + 3 hundreds = 4 hundreds
Write the 4 hundreds in the hundreds place.

Answer

1. 7777

EXAMPLE 2 Add: $34,285 + 149,761$

Solution:

$$
\begin{array}{r}
\overset{1\,1\ \ 1}{34{,}285} \\
+\ 149{,}761 \\
\hline
184{,}046
\end{array}
$$

■ Work Practice Problem 2

PRACTICE PROBLEM 2
Add: $27,364 + 92,977$

✔Concept Check   What is wrong with the following computation?

$$
\begin{array}{r}
394 \\
+\ 283 \\
\hline
577
\end{array}
$$

Before we continue adding whole numbers, let's review some properties of addition that you may have already discovered. The first property that we will review is the **addition property of 0.** This property reminds us that the sum of 0 and any number is that same number.

Addition Property of 0

The sum of 0 and any number is that number. For example,

$$7 + 0 = 7$$
$$0 + 7 = 7$$

Next, notice that we can add any two whole numbers in any order and the sum is the same. For example,

$$4 + 5 = 9 \quad \text{and} \quad 5 + 4 = 9$$

We call this special property of addition the **commutative property of addition.**

Commutative Property of Addition

Changing the **order** of two addends does not change their sum. For example,

$$2 + 3 = 5 \quad \text{and} \quad 3 + 2 = 5$$

Another property that can help us when adding numbers is the **associative property of addition.** This property states that when adding numbers, the grouping of the numbers can be changed without changing the sum. We use parentheses to group numbers. They indicate which numbers to add first. For example, let's use two different groupings to find the sum of $2 + 1 + 5$.

$$(2 + 1) + 5 = 3 + 5 = 8$$

Also,

$$2 + (1 + 5) = 2 + 6 = 8$$

Both groupings give a sum of 8.

Answer
2. 120,341

✔ Concept Check Answer
forgot to carry 1 hundred to the hundreds place

Associative Property of Addition

Changing the **grouping** of addends does not change their sum. For example,

$$3 + (5 + 7) = 3 + 12 = 15 \quad \text{and} \quad (3 + 5) + 7 = 8 + 7 = 15$$

The commutative and associative properties tell us that we can add whole numbers using any order and grouping that we want.

When adding several numbers, it is often helpful to look for two or three numbers whose sum is 10, 20, and so on. Why? Adding multiples of 10 such as 10 and 20 is easier.

PRACTICE PROBLEM 3

Add: $11 + 7 + 8 + 9 + 13$

EXAMPLE 3 Add: $13 + 2 + 7 + 8 + 9$

Solution: $13 + 2 + 7 + 8 + 9 = 39$

$$20 + 10 + 9$$

$$39$$

■ **Work Practice Problem 3**

Feel free to use the process of Example 3 anytime when adding.

PRACTICE PROBLEM 4

Add: $19 + 5042 + 638 + 526$

EXAMPLE 4 Add: $1647 + 246 + 32 + 85$

Solution:

```
  1 2 2
  1647
   246
    32
+   85
  2010
```

■ **Work Practice Problem 4**

Objective B Finding the Perimeter of a Polygon

In geometry addition is used to find the perimeter of a polygon. A **polygon** can be described as a flat figure formed by line segments connected at their ends. (For more review, see Appendix A3.) Geometric figures such as triangles, squares, and rectangles are called polygons.

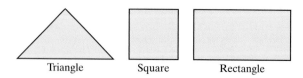

Triangle   Square   Rectangle

The **perimeter** of a polygon is the *distance around* the polygon. This means that the perimeter of a polygon is the sum of the lengths of its sides.

Answers
3. 48, **4.** 6225

 Find the perimeter of the polygon shown.

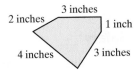

Solution: To find the perimeter (distance around), we add the lengths of the sides.

2 in. + 3 in. + 1 in. + 3 in. + 4 in. = 13 in.

The perimeter is 13 inches.

▢ **Work Practice Problem 5**

To make the addition appear simpler, we will often not include units with the addends. If you do this, make sure units are included in the final answer.

⚠ **EXAMPLE 6** **Calculating the Perimeter of a Building**

The largest commercial building in the world under one roof is the flower auction building of the cooperative VBA in Aalsmeer, Netherlands. The floor plan is a rectangle that measures 776 meters by 639 meters. Find the perimeter of this building. (A meter is a unit of length in the metric system.) (*Source: The Handy Science Answer Book,* Visible Ink Press)

Solution: Recall that opposite sides of a rectangle have the same length. To find the perimeter of this building, we add the lengths of the sides. The sum of the lengths of its sides is

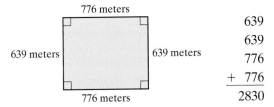

$$\begin{array}{r} 639 \\ 639 \\ 776 \\ +\ 776 \\ \hline 2830 \end{array}$$

The perimeter of the building is 2830 meters.

▢ **Work Practice Problem 6**

Objective ⓒ **Solving Problems by Adding**

Often, real-life problems occur that can be solved by writing an addition statement. The first step in solving any word problem is to *understand* the problem by reading it carefully. Descriptions of problems solved through addition *may* include any of these key words or phrases:

Key Words or Phrases	Example	Symbols
added to	5 added to 7	7 + 5
plus	0 plus 78	0 + 78
increased by	12 increased by 6	12 + 6
more than	11 more than 25	25 + 11
total	the total of 8 and 1	8 + 1
sum	the sum of 4 and 133	4 + 133

To solve a word problem that involves addition, we first use the facts given to write an addition statement. Then we write the corresponding solution of the real-life

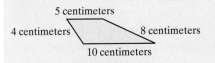

problem. It is sometimes helpful to write the statement in words (brief phrases) and then translate to numbers.

PRACTICE PROBLEM 7

Texas produces 90 million pounds of pecans per year. Georgia is the world's top pecan producer and produces 15 million pounds more pecans than Texas. How much does Georgia produce? (*Source: Absolute Trivia.com*)

Texas   Georgia

EXAMPLE 7 Finding a Salary

The governor's salary in the state of Alabama was recently increased by $1706. If the old salary was $94,655, find the new salary. (*Source: The World Almanac and Book of Facts,* 2003 and 2005)

Montgomery

Solution: The key phrase here is "increased by," which suggests that we add. To find the new salary, we add the increase, $1706, to the old salary.

In Words		Translate to Numbers
old salary	→	94,655
+ increase	→	+ 1 706
new salary	→	96,361

The Alabama governor's salary is now $96,361.

🖱 **Work Practice Problem 7**

Graphs can be used to visualize data. The graph shown next is called a **bar graph.** For this bar graph, the height of each bar is labeled above the bar. To check this height, follow the top of each bar to the vertical line to the left. For example, the second bar is labeled 15. Follow the top of that bar to the left until the vertical line is reached, halfway between 10 and 20, or 15.

PRACTICE PROBLEM 8

Use the graph in Example 8 to answer the following:

a. Which rating had the least number of Best Picture nominees?

b. Find the total number of Best Picture nominees that were rated PG, PG-13, or R.

EXAMPLE 8 Reading a Bar Graph

The graph below shows the ratings of Best Picture nominees since PG-13 was introduced in 1984. In this graph, each bar represents a different rating, and the height of each bar represents the number of Best Picture nominees for that rating.

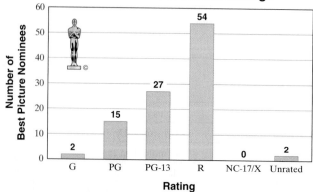

Best Picture Nominee Ratings

Source: Academy of Motion Picture Arts and Sciences; Internet Movie Database

a. Which rating did most Best Picture nominees have?

b. Find the total number of Best Picture nominees that were rated G, PG, or PG-13.

Answers

7. 105 million lb,

8. a. NC-17/X,   b. 96

Solution:

a. The rating for most Best Picture nominees is the one corresponding to the highest bar, which is an R rating.

b. The key word here is "total." To find the total number of Best Picture nominees that were rated G, PG, or PG-13, we add.

In Words		Translate to Numbers
G-rated nominees	$\rightarrow$	2
PG-rated nominees	$\rightarrow$	15
PG-13–rated nominees	$\rightarrow$	+ 27
Total		44

The number of Best Picture nominees rated G, PG, or PG-13 is 44.

Work Practice Problem 8

CALCULATOR EXPLORATIONS Adding Numbers

To add numbers on a calculator, find the keys marked $+$ and $=$ or $\boxed{\text{ENTER}}$.

For example, to add 5 and 7 on a calculator, press the keys $\boxed{5}$ $\boxed{+}$ $\boxed{7}$ $\boxed{=}$ or $\boxed{\text{ENTER}}$.

The display will read $\boxed{\quad 12}$.
Thus, $5 + 7 = 12$.

To add 687, 981, and 49 on a calculator, press the keys $\boxed{687}$ $\boxed{+}$ $\boxed{981}$ $\boxed{+}$ $\boxed{49}$ $\boxed{=}$ or $\boxed{\text{ENTER}}$.
The display will read $\boxed{\quad 1717}$.

Thus, $687 + 981 + 49 = 1717$. (Although entering 687, for example, requires pressing more than one key, here numbers are grouped together for easier reading.)

Use a calculator to add.

1. $89 + 45$

2. $76 + 97$

3. $285 + 55$

4. $8773 + 652$

5.
$$
\begin{array}{r}
985 \\
1210 \\
562 \\
+ \quad 77 \\
\end{array}
$$

6.
$$
\begin{array}{r}
465 \\
9888 \\
620 \\
+ 1550 \\
\end{array}
$$

Mental Math

Find each sum.

1. $9 + 7$ **2.** $20 + 30$ **3.** $5000 + 4000$ **4.** $4300 + 26$ **5.** $1620 + 0$ **6.** $6 + 126 + 4$

1.3 EXERCISE SET

FOR EXTRA HELP

Student Solutions Manual PH Math/Tutor Center CD/Video for Review MathXL MyMathLab

Objective **A** *Add. See Examples 1 through 4.*

1.
$$\begin{array}{r} 14 \\ +22 \end{array}$$

2.
$$\begin{array}{r} 27 \\ +31 \end{array}$$

3.
$$\begin{array}{r} 62 \\ +230 \end{array}$$

4.
$$\begin{array}{r} 37 \\ +542 \end{array}$$

5.
$$\begin{array}{r} 12 \\ 13 \\ +24 \end{array}$$

6.
$$\begin{array}{r} 23 \\ 45 \\ +30 \end{array}$$

7.
$$\begin{array}{r} 5267 \\ +\ 132 \end{array}$$

8.
$$\begin{array}{r} 236 \\ +6243 \end{array}$$

9. $53 + 64$

10. $41 + 74$

11. $22 + 490$ **12.** $35 + 470$ **13.** $22,781 + 186,297$ **14.** $17,427 + 821,059$

15.
$$\begin{array}{r} 8 \\ 9 \\ 2 \\ 5 \\ +1 \end{array}$$

16.
$$\begin{array}{r} 3 \\ 5 \\ 8 \\ 5 \\ +7 \end{array}$$

17.
$$\begin{array}{r} 6 \\ 21 \\ 14 \\ 9 \\ +12 \end{array}$$

18.
$$\begin{array}{r} 12 \\ 4 \\ 8 \\ 26 \\ +10 \end{array}$$

19.
$$\begin{array}{r} 81 \\ 17 \\ 23 \\ 79 \\ +12 \end{array}$$

20.
$$\begin{array}{r} 64 \\ 28 \\ 56 \\ 25 \\ +32 \end{array}$$

21. $62 + 18 + 14$

22. $23 + 49 + 18$

23. $40 + 800 + 70$ **24.** $30 + 900 + 20$ **25.** $7542 + 49 + 682$

26. $1624 + 32 + 976$ **27.** $24 + 9006 + 489 + 2407$ **28.** $16 + 1056 + 748 + 7770$

22

29.   627
           628
        + 629

30.   427
           383
        + 229

31.   6820
           4271
        + 5626

32.   6789
           4321
        + 5555

33.   507
           593
        +   10

34.   864
            33
        + 356

35.   4200
           2107
        + 2692

36.   5000
           1400
        + 3021

37.   49
              628
            5 762
        + 29,462

38.   26
              582
            4 763
        + 62,511

39.   121,742
            57,279
            26,586
        + 426,782

40.   504,218
           321,920
            38,507
        + 594,687

Objective **B** *Find the perimeter of each figure. See Examples 5 and 6.*

△ **41.**
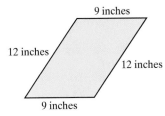
9 inches
12 inches
12 inches
9 inches

△ **42.**
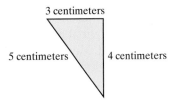
3 kilometers   3 kilometers
5 kilometers   5 kilometers

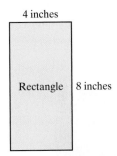 **43.**
△
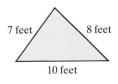
7 feet   8 feet
10 feet

△ **44.**
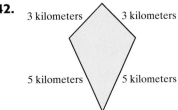
3 centimeters
5 centimeters   4 centimeters

△ **45.**
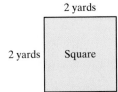
4 inches
Rectangle   8 inches

△ **46.**
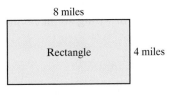
8 miles
Rectangle   4 miles

△ **47.**
2 yards
2 yards   Square

△ **48.**
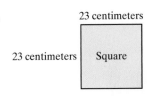
23 centimeters
23 centimeters   Square

△ **49.**
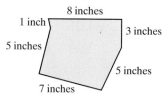

△ **50.**
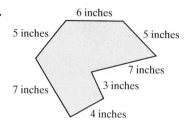

Objectives Ⓐ Ⓑ Ⓒ **Mixed Practice** *Solve. See Examples 1 through 8.*

51. Find the sum of 297 and 1796.

52. Find the sum of 802 and 6487.

53. Find the total of 76, 39, 8, 17, and 126.

54. Find the total of 89, 45, 2, 19, and 341.

55. What is 452 increased by 92?

56. What is 712 increased by 38?

57. What is 2686 plus 686 plus 80?

58. What is 3565 plus 565 plus 70?

59. The highest point in South Carolina is Sassafras Mountain at 3560 feet above sea level. The highest point in North Carolina is Mt. Mitchell, whose peak is 3124 feet increased by the height of Sassafras Mountain. Find the height of Mt. Mitchell. (*Source:* U.S. Geological Survey)

60. The distance from Kansas City, Kansas, to Hays, Kansas, is 285 miles. Colby, Kansas, is 98 miles farther from Kansas City than Hays. Find the total distance from Kansas City to Colby.

△ **61.** Leo Callier is installing an invisible fence in his backyard. How many feet of wiring are needed to enclose the yard below?

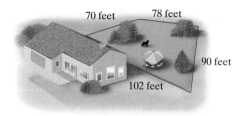

△ **62.** A homeowner is considering installing gutters around her home. Find the perimeter of her rectangular home.

63. In 2003, Harley-Davidson sold 228,400 of its motorcycles domestically. In addition, 62,747 Harley-Davidson motorcycles were sold internationally. What was the total number of Harley-Davidson motorcycles sold in 2003? (*Source: Harley-Davidson, Inc.*)

64. Dan Marino holds the NFL career record for most passes completed. He completed 2305 passes from the beginning of his NFL career in 1983 through 1989. He completed another 2662 passes from 1990 through 1999, his last season before retiring from professional football. How many total passes did he complete during his NFL career? (*Source: National Football League*)

65. The highest waterfall in the United States is Yosemite Falls in Yosemite National Park in California. Yosemite Falls is made up of three sections, as shown in the graph. What is the total height of Yosemite Falls? (*Source: U.S. Department of the Interior*)

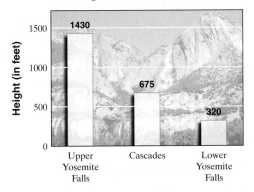

Highest U.S. Waterfalls

66. Jordan White, a nurse at Mercy Hospital, is recording fluid intake on a patient's medical chart. During his shift, the patient had the following types and amounts of intake measured in cubic centimeters (cc). What amount should Jordan record as the total fluid intake for this patient?

Oral	Intravenous	Blood
240	500	500
100	200	
355		

67. The State of Alaska has 1795 miles of urban highways and 11,460 miles of rural highways. Find the total highway mileage in Alaska. (*Source: U.S. Federal Highway Administration*)

68. The state of Hawaii has 1851 miles of urban highways and 2291 miles of rural highways. Find the total highway mileage in Hawaii. (*Source: U.S. Federal Highway Administration*)

69. The largest permanent Monopoly board is made of granite and located in San Jose, California. Find the perimeter of the square playing board.

31 ft

31 ft

70. The smallest commercially available jigsaw puzzle is a 1000-piece puzzle manufactured in Spain. Find the perimeter of this rectangular-shaped puzzle.

12 in.

18 in.

71. The two top-selling automobiles in the United States are the Honda Accord, with sales of 397,750 and the Toyota Camry with sales of 369,562 in 2003. What is the total amount of Accords and Camrys sold in 2003? (*Source:* J. D. Power and Associates)

72. In the country of New Zealand, there are 40,748,693 more sheep than there are people. If the human population of New Zealand is 3,951,307, what is the sheep population? (*Source:* Food and Agricultural Organization of the United States)

73. In 2004, there were 5670 Blockbuster video rental stores located in the United States and 3197 located outside the United States. How many Blockbuster rental stores were located worldwide? (*Source:* Blockbuster Inc.)

74. Wilma Rudolph, who won three gold medals in track and field events in the 1960 Summer Olympics, was born in 1940. Marion Jones, who also won three gold medals in track and field events but in the 2000 Summer Olympics, was born 35 years later. In what year was Marion Jones born?

The table shows the number of Target stores in ten states. Use this table to answer Exercises 75 through 80.

The Top States for Target Stores in 2003	
State	**Number of Stores**
Arizona	36
California	184
Florida	78
Georgia	38
Illinois	62
New York	37
Michigan	51
Minnesota	65
Ohio	44
Texas	104
(*Source:* Target Corporation)	

75. Which state has the most Target stores?

76. Which of the states listed in the table has the fewest number of Target stores?

77. What is the total number of Target stores located in the three states with the most Target stores?

78. How many Target stores are located in the ten states listed in the table?

79. Which pair of neighboring states have more Target stores combined, Florida and Georgia or Michigan and Ohio?

80. Target operates stores in 47 states. There are 526 Target stores located in the states not listed in the table. How many Target stores are in the United States?

Concept Extensions

81. In your own words, explain the commutative property of addition.

82. In your own words, explain the associative property of addition.

83. Give any three whole numbers whose sum is 100.

84. Give any four whole numbers whose sum is 25.

85. Find the perimeter of the figure.

8 ft

3 ft

4 ft

?

5 ft

?

86. Add: 78,962 + 129,968,350 + 36,462,880

87. Add: 56,468,980 + 1,236,785 + 986,768,000

Check each addition below. If it is incorrect, find the correct answer. See the Concept Check in this section.

88.	**89.**	**90.**	**91.**
566	773	14	19
932	659	173	214
+ 871	+ 481	86	49
2369	1913	+ 257	+ 651
		520	923

STUDY SKILLS BUILDER

Learning New Terms?

Many of the terms used in this text may be new to you. It will be helpful to make a list of new mathematical terms and symbols as you encounter them and to review them frequently. Placing these new terms (including page references) on 3 × 5 index cards might help you later when you're preparing for a quiz.

Answer the following.

1. Name one way you might place a word and its definition on a 3 × 5 card.

2. How do new terms stand out in this text so that they can be found?

1.4 SUBTRACTING WHOLE NUMBERS

Objective **A** Subtracting Whole Numbers

If you have $5 and someone gives you $3, you have a total of $8, since $5 + 3 = 8$. Similarly, if you have $8 and then someone borrows $3, you have $5 left. **Subtraction** is finding the **difference** of two numbers.

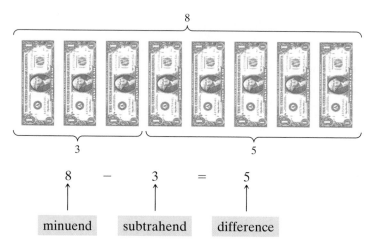

$$8 - 3 = 5$$

minuend   subtrahend   difference

Notice that addition and subtraction are very closely related. In fact, subtraction is defined in terms of addition.

$$8 - 3 = 5 \text{ because } 5 + 3 = 8$$

This means that subtraction can be *checked* by addition, and we say that addition and subtraction are reverse operations.

PRACTICE PROBLEM 1

Subtract. Check each answer by adding.

a. $14 - 9$

b. $20 - 8$

c. $9 - 9$

d. $4 - 0$

EXAMPLE 1 Subtract. Check each answer by adding.

a. $12 - 9$ **b.** $11 - 6$ **c.** $5 - 5$ **d.** $7 - 0$

Solution:

a. $12 - 9 = 3$ because $3 + 9 = 12$
b. $11 - 6 = 5$ because $5 + 6 = 11$
c. $5 - 5 = 0$ because $0 + 5 = 5$
d. $7 - 0 = 7$ because $7 + 0 = 7$

Work Practice Problem 1

Look again at Examples 1(c) and 1(d).

1(c) $5 - 5 = 0$

same number   difference is 0

1(d) $7 - 0 = 7$

a number minus 0   difference is the same number

Answers

1. a. 5, **b.** 12, **c.** 0, **d.** 4

These two examples illustrate the subtraction properties of 0.

Subtraction Properties of 0

The difference of any number and that same number is 0. For example,

$$11 - 11 = 0$$

The difference of any number and 0 is that same number. For example,

$$45 - 0 = 45$$

To subtract whole numbers we subtract the digits in the ones place, then the tens place, then the hundreds place, and so on. When subtraction involves numbers of two or more digits, it is more convenient to subtract vertically. For example, to subtract $893 - 52$,

$$
\begin{array}{r}
893 \quad \longleftarrow \text{minuend} \\
-52 \quad \longleftarrow \text{subtrahend} \\
\hline
841 \quad \longleftarrow \text{difference}
\end{array}
$$

Line up the numbers vertically so that the minuend is on top and the place values correspond. Subtract in corresponding places, starting with the ones place.

$$
\begin{array}{l}
3 - 2 \\
9 - 5 \\
8 - 0
\end{array}
$$

To check, add.

$$
\begin{array}{r}
\text{difference} \quad \text{or} \quad 841 \\
+ \text{subtrahend} \quad \quad\quad + 52 \\
\hline
\text{minuend} \quad\quad\quad 893 \quad \longleftarrow
\end{array}
$$

Since this is the original minuend, the problem checks.

EXAMPLE 2 Subtract: $7826 - 505$. Check by adding.

Solution:

$$
\begin{array}{r}
7826 \\
-505 \\
\hline
7321
\end{array}
\qquad
\textbf{Check:}
\begin{array}{r}
7321 \\
+505 \\
\hline
7826
\end{array}
$$

🔲 **Work Practice Problem 2**

Objective B **Subtracting with Borrowing**

When subtracting vertically, if a digit in the second number (subtrahend) is larger than the corresponding digit in the first number (minuend), **borrowing** is necessary. For example, consider

$$
\begin{array}{r}
8|1 \\
-6|3
\end{array}
$$

Since the 3 in the ones place of 63 is larger than the 1 in the ones place of 81, borrowing is necessary. We borrow 1 ten from the tens place and add it to the ones place.

Borrowing

$$
\begin{array}{c}
8 - 1 = 7 \longrightarrow \quad 7 \;\; 11 \leftarrow 1 \text{ ten } + 1 \text{ one} = 11 \text{ ones} \\
\text{tens} \quad \text{ten} \quad \text{tens} \quad\quad \cancel{8}\,\cancel{1} \\
\quad\quad\quad\quad\quad\quad -6\;3
\end{array}
$$

Answers
2. a. 4436, **b.** 351

Now we subtract the ones-place digits and then the tens-place digits.

$$
\begin{array}{r}
\overset{7\ 11}{\cancel{8}\cancel{1}} \\
-6\,3 \\
\hline
1\,8 \leftarrow 11 - 3 = 8 \\
\;\; 7 - 6 = 1
\end{array}
$$

Check:

$$
\begin{array}{r}
18 \\
+63 \\
\hline
81 \quad \text{The original minuend}
\end{array}
$$

PRACTICE PROBLEM 3

Subtract. Check by adding.

a.   227
     − 175

b.   1136
     − 914

c.   8627
     − 4119

EXAMPLE 3   Subtract: 543 − 29. Check by adding.

Solution:
$$
\begin{array}{r}
\overset{3\ 13}{5\cancel{4}\cancel{3}} \\
-2\,9 \\
\hline
5\,1\,4
\end{array}
$$

Check:
$$
\begin{array}{r}
514 \\
+29 \\
\hline
543
\end{array}
$$

■ **Work Practice Problem 3**

Sometimes we may have to borrow from more than one place. For example, to subtract 7631 − 152, we first borrow from the tens place.

$$
\begin{array}{r}
76\overset{2\ 11}{\cancel{3}\cancel{1}} \\
-\ 1\,5\,2 \\
\hline
9 \leftarrow 11 - 2 = 9
\end{array}
$$

In the tens place, 5 is greater than 2, so we borrow again. This time we borrow from the hundreds place.

6 hundreds − **1 hundred** = 5 hundreds

$$
\begin{array}{r}
\overset{5\ \overset{12}{\cancel{2}}\ 11}{7\cancel{6}\cancel{3}\cancel{1}} \\
-\ 1\,5\,2 \\
\hline
7\,4\,7\,9
\end{array}
$$

1 hundred + 2 tens
or
10 tens + 2 tens = 12 tens

Check:

$$
\begin{array}{r}
7479 \\
+\ 152 \\
\hline
7631 \quad \text{The original minuend}
\end{array}
$$

PRACTICE PROBLEM 4

Subtract. Check by adding.

a.   400
     − 164

b.   200
     − 45

c.   1000
     − 762

EXAMPLE 4   Subtract: 900 − 174. Check by adding.

Solution: In the ones place, 4 is larger than 0, so we borrow from the tens place. But the tens place of 900 is 0, so to borrow from the tens place we must first borrow from the hundreds place.

$$
\begin{array}{r}
\overset{8\ \ 10}{\cancel{9}\ \cancel{0}\ 0} \\
-1\,7\,4
\end{array}
$$

Answers
3. a. 52, b. 222, c. 4508,
4. a. 236, b. 155, c. 238

Now borrow from the tens place.

$$
\begin{array}{r}
\overset{\scriptstyle 9}{}\\
\overset{8}{\cancel{9}}\ \overset{\cancel{10}}{\cancel{0}}\ \overset{10}{\cancel{0}}\\
-\ 1\ 7\ 4\\
\hline
7\ 2\ 6
\end{array}
$$

Check:

$$
\begin{array}{r}
726\\
+\ 174\\
\hline
900
\end{array}
$$

◪ **Work Practice Problem 4**

Objective ⓒ Solving Problems by Subtracting

Descriptions of real-life problems that suggest solving by subtraction include these key words or phrases:

Key Words or Phrases	Examples	Symbols
subtract	subtract 5 from 8	8 − 5
difference	the difference of 10 and 2	10 − 2
less	17 less 3	17 − 3
less than	2 less than 20	20 − 2
take away	14 take away 9	14 − 9
decreased by	7 decreased by 5	7 − 5
subtracted from	9 subtracted from 12	12 − 9

✔**Concept Check** In each of the following problems, identify which number is the minuend and which number is the subtrahend.

a. What is the result when 9 is subtracted from 20?
b. What is the difference of 15 and 8?
c. Find a number that is 15 fewer than 23.

EXAMPLE 5 Finding the Radius of a Planet

The radius of Venus is 6052 kilometers. The radius of Mercury is 3612 kilometers less than the radius of Venus. Find the radius of Mercury. (*Source:* National Space Science Data Center)

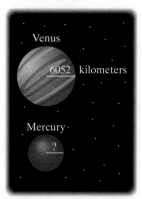

PRACTICE PROBLEM 5

The radius of Earth is 6378 kilometers. The radius of Mars is 2981 kilometers less than the radius of Earth. What is the radius of Mars? (*Source:* National Space Science Data Center)

Answer
5. 3397 km

✔ **Concept Check Answers**
a. minuend: 20; subtrahend: 9,
b. minuend: 15; subtrahend: 8,
c. minuend: 23; subtrahend: 15

Continued on next page

Solution: In Words   **Translate to Numbers**

$$
\begin{array}{rcr}
\text{radius of Venus} & \longrightarrow & 6052 \\
-\,3612 & \longrightarrow & -\,3612 \\
\hline
\text{radius of Mercury} & \longrightarrow & 2440
\end{array}
$$

The radius of Mercury is 2440 kilometers.

🔲 **Work Practice Problem 5**

PRACTICE PROBLEM 6

During a sale, the price of a new suit is decreased by $47. If the original price was $92, find the sale price of the suit.

EXAMPLE 6 Calculating Miles per Gallon

A subcompact car gets 42 miles per gallon of gas. A full-size car gets 17 miles per gallon of gas. Find the difference between the subcompact car miles per gallon and the full-size car miles per gallon.

Solution: In Words   **Translate to Numbers**

$$
\begin{array}{rcr}
\text{subcompact miles per gallon} & \longrightarrow & \overset{3\;\;12}{\cancel{4}\,\cancel{2}} \\
-\quad\text{full-size miles per gallon} & \longrightarrow & -\,1\,7 \\
\hline
\text{difference in miles per gallon} & & 2\,5
\end{array}
$$

The difference in the subcompact car miles per gallon and the full-size car miles per gallon is 25 miles per gallon.

🔲 **Work Practice Problem 6**

Helpful Hint

Since subtraction and addition are reverse operations, don't forget that a subtraction problem can be checked by adding.

📇 CALCULATOR EXPLORATIONS   Subtracting Numbers

To subtract numbers on a calculator, find the keys marked $\boxed{-}$ and $\boxed{=}$ or $\boxed{\text{ENTER}}$.

For example, to find $83 - 49$ on a calculator, press the keys $\boxed{83}\;\boxed{-}\;\boxed{49}\;\boxed{=}$ or $\boxed{\text{ENTER}}$.

The display will read $\boxed{34}$. Thus, $83 - 49 = 34$.

Use a calculator to subtract.

1. $865 - 95$ **2.** $76 - 27$

3. $147 - 38$ **4.** $366 - 87$

5. $9625 - 647$ **6.** $10,711 - 8925$

Answer

6. $45

Mental Math

Find each difference. See Example 1.

1. $9 - 2$ **2.** $6 - 6$ **3.** $5 - 0$ **4.** $44 - 22$ **5.** $93 - 93$

6. $700 - 400$ **7.** $700 - 300$ **8.** $700 - 700$ **9.** $600 - 100$ **10.** $600 - 0$

1.4 EXERCISE SET

FOR EXTRA HELP

Student Solutions Manual   PH Math/Tutor Center   CD/Video for Review   MathXL® MathXL   MyMathLab MyMathLab

Objective A *Subtract. Check by adding. See Examples 1 and 2.*

1. $\begin{array}{r} 67 \\ -23 \\ \hline \end{array}$ **2.** $\begin{array}{r} 72 \\ -41 \\ \hline \end{array}$ **3.** $\begin{array}{r} 389 \\ -124 \\ \hline \end{array}$ **4.** $\begin{array}{r} 572 \\ -321 \\ \hline \end{array}$

5. $\begin{array}{r} 167 \\ -32 \\ \hline \end{array}$ **6.** $\begin{array}{r} 286 \\ -45 \\ \hline \end{array}$ **7.** $2677 - 423$ **8.** $5766 - 324$

9. $6998 - 1453$ **10.** $4912 - 2610$ **11.** $\begin{array}{r} 749 \\ -149 \\ \hline \end{array}$ **12.** $\begin{array}{r} 257 \\ -257 \\ \hline \end{array}$

Objectives A B Mixed Practice *Subtract. Check by adding. See Examples 1 through 4.*

   13. $\begin{array}{r} 62 \\ -37 \\ \hline \end{array}$ **14.** $\begin{array}{r} 55 \\ -29 \\ \hline \end{array}$ **15.** $\begin{array}{r} 70 \\ -25 \\ \hline \end{array}$ **16.** $\begin{array}{r} 80 \\ -37 \\ \hline \end{array}$ **17.** $\begin{array}{r} 938 \\ -792 \\ \hline \end{array}$ **18.** $\begin{array}{r} 436 \\ -275 \\ \hline \end{array}$

19. $\begin{array}{r} 922 \\ -634 \\ \hline \end{array}$ **20.** $\begin{array}{r} 674 \\ -299 \\ \hline \end{array}$ **21.** $\begin{array}{r} 600 \\ -432 \\ \hline \end{array}$ **22.** $\begin{array}{r} 300 \\ -149 \\ \hline \end{array}$ **23.** $\begin{array}{r} 142 \\ -36 \\ \hline \end{array}$ **24.** $\begin{array}{r} 773 \\ -29 \\ \hline \end{array}$

25. $\begin{array}{r} 923 \\ -476 \\ \hline \end{array}$ **26.** $\begin{array}{r} 813 \\ -227 \\ \hline \end{array}$ **27.** $\begin{array}{r} 6283 \\ -560 \\ \hline \end{array}$ **28.** $\begin{array}{r} 5349 \\ -720 \\ \hline \end{array}$ **29.** $\begin{array}{r} 533 \\ -29 \\ \hline \end{array}$ **30.** $\begin{array}{r} 724 \\ -16 \\ \hline \end{array}$

31. $\begin{array}{r} 200 \\ -111 \\ \hline \end{array}$ **32.** $\begin{array}{r} 300 \\ -211 \\ \hline \end{array}$ **33.** $\begin{array}{r} 1983 \\ -1904 \\ \hline \end{array}$ **34.** $\begin{array}{r} 1983 \\ -1914 \\ \hline \end{array}$ **35.** $\begin{array}{r} 56{,}422 \\ -16{,}508 \\ \hline \end{array}$ **36.** $\begin{array}{r} 76{,}652 \\ -29{,}498 \\ \hline \end{array}$

37. 50,000 − 17,289

38. 40,000 − 23,582

39. 7020 − 1979

40. 6050 − 1878

41. 51,111 − 19,898

42. 62,222 − 39,898

Objective **C** *Solve. See Examples 5 and 6.*

43. Subtract 5 from 9.

44. Subtract 9 from 21.

45. Find the difference of 41 and 21.

46. Find the difference of 16 and 5.

47. Subtract 56 from 63.

48. Subtract 41 from 59.

49. Find 108 less 36.

50. Find 25 less 12.

51. Find 12 subtracted from 100.

52. Find 86 subtracted from 90.

53. Dyllis King is reading a 503-page book. If she has just finished reading page 239, how many more pages must she read to finish the book?

54. When Lou and Judy Zawislak began a trip, the odometer read 55,492. When the trip was over, the odometer read 59,320. How many miles did they drive on their trip?

55. In 1997, the hole in the Earth's ozone layer over Antartica was about 21 million square kilometers in size. In 2001, the hole had grown to 25 million square kilometers. By how much has the hole grown from 1997 to 2001? (*Source:* U.S. Environmental Protection Agency EPA)

56. Bamboo can grow to 98 feet while Pacific giant kelp (a type of seaweed) can grow to 197 feet. How much taller is the kelp than the bamboo?

Bamboo

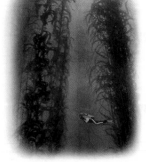

Kelp

57. The peak of Mt. McKinley in Alaska is 20,320 feet above sea level. The peak of Long's Peak in Colorado is 14,255 feet above sea level. How much higher is the peak of Mt. McKinley than Long's Peak? (*Source:* U.S. Geological Survey)

Mt. McKinley, Alaska   Long's Peak, Colorado

58. On one day in May the temperature in Paddin, Indiana, dropped 27 degrees from 2 p.m. to 4 p.m. If the temperature at 2 p.m. was 73° Fahrenheit, what was the temperature at 4 p.m.?

59. During the 2003–2004 regular season, Kevin Garnett of the Minnesota Timberwolves led the NBA in total points scored with 1987. The Sacramento Kings' Predrag Stojakovic placed second for total points scored with 1964. How many more points did Garnett score than Stojakovic during the 2003–2004 regular season? (*Source:* National Basketball Association)

60. In 2002, Americans bought 243,199 Ford Focus cars. In 2003, 13,846 fewer Focuses were sold in the United States. How many Focuses were sold in the United States in 2003? (*Source:* Ford Motor Company)

61. Buhler Gomez has a total of $538 in his checking account. If he writes a check for his electric bill of $129, how much money will be left in his account?

62. Pat Salanki's blood cholesterol level is 243. The doctor tells him it should be decreased to 185. How much of a decrease is this?

63. The distance from Kansas City to Denver is 645 miles. Hays, Kansas, lies on the road between the two and is 287 miles from Kansas City. What is the distance between Hays and Denver?

64. Alan Little is trading his car in on a new car. The new car costs $ 15,425. His car is worth $7998. How much more money does he need to buy the new car?

65. A new VCR with remote control costs $525. Prunella Pasch has $914 in her savings account. How much will she have left in her savings account after she buys the VCR?

66. A stereo that regularly sells for $547 is discounted by $99 in a sale. What is the sale price?

67. The population of Florida grew from 12,937,926 in 1990 to 15,982,378 in 2000. What was Florida's population increase over this time period? (*Source:* U.S. Census Bureau)

68. The population of El Paso, Texas, was 515,342 in 1990 and 563,662 in 2000. By how much did the population of El Paso grow from 1990 to 2000? (*Source:* U.S. Census Bureau)

El Paso

69. In 2000, there were 29,393 cocker spaniels registered with the American Kennel Club. In 2003, there were 10,357 fewer cocker spaniels registered. How many cocker spaniels were registered with the AKC in 2003? (*Source:* American Kennel Club)

70. In the United States, there were 41,589 tornadoes from 1950 through 2000. In all, 13,205 of these tornadoes occurred from 1990 through 2000. How many tornadoes occurred during the period prior to 1990? (*Source:* Storm Prediction Center, National Weather Service)

71. Until recently, the world's largest permanent maze was located in Ruurlo, Netherlands. This maze of beech hedges covers 94,080 square feet. A new hedge maze using hibiscus bushes at the Dole Plantation in Wahiawa, Hawaii, covers 100,000 square feet. How much larger is the Dole Plantation maze than the Ruurlo maze? (*Source: The Guinness Book of Records*)

72. There were only 27 California condors in the entire world in 1987. By 2004, the number of California condors had increased to 221. How much of an increase was this? (*Source:* California Department of Fish and Game)

The bar graph shows the top five U.S. airports according to number of passengers arriving and departing in 2003. Use this graph to answer Exercises 73 through 76.

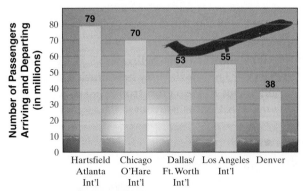

Source: Airports Council International

73. Which airport is the busiest?

74. Which airports have fewer than 60 million passengers per year?

75. How many more passengers per year does the Chicago O'Hare International Airport have than the Denver Airport?

76. How many more passengers per year does the Hartsfield Atlanta International Airport have than the Dallas/Ft. Worth International Airport?

The table shows the top ten leading advertisers in the United States in 2003 and the amount of money each spent in that year on advertising. Use this table to answer Exercises 77 through 80.

Advertiser	Amount Spent on Advertising in 2003 (in millions of dollars)
DaimlerChrysler AG	2318
General Motors Corp.	3430
Pfizer	2839
Ford Motor Co.	2234
Johnson & Johnson	1996
Sony Corp.	1815
Walt Disney Co.	2129
Toyota Motor Corp.	1683
Time Warner	3097
Procter & Gamble Co.	3323
Source: Television Bureau of Advertising, Inc.	

77. Which companies spent more than $3000 million on advertising?

78. Which companies shown spent fewer than $2000 million on advertising?

79. How much more money did General Motors Corp. spend on advertising than DaimlerChrysler AG?

80. How much more money did Pfizer spend on advertising than Toyota Motor Corp.?

Mixed Practice (Sections 1.3 and 1.4) *Add or subtract as indicated.*

81. 986
+ 48

82. 986
− 48

83. $76 - 67$

84. $80 + 93 + 17 + 9 + 2$

85. 9000
− 482

86. 10,000
− 1786

87. 10,962
4851
+ 7063

88. 12,468
3211
+ 1988

Concept Extensions

For each exercise, identify which number is the minuend and which number is the subtrahend. See the Concept Check in this section.

89. 48
− 1

90. 2863
− 1904

91. Subtract 7 from 70.

92. Find 86 decreased by 25.

Solve.

93. Jo Keen and Trudy Waterbury were candidates for student government president. Who won the election if the votes were cast as follows? By how many votes did the winner win?

Class	Candidate	
	Jo	Trudy
Freshman	276	295
Sophomore	362	122
Junior	201	312
Senior	179	18

94. Two students submitted advertising budgets for a student government fund-raiser.

	Student A	Student B
Radio ads	$600	$300
Newspaper ads	$200	$400
Posters	$150	$240
Handbills	$120	$170

If $1200 is available for advertising, how much excess would each budget have?

Identify each answer as correct or incorrect. Use addition to check. If the answer is incorrect, then write the correct answer.

95. 741
      − 56
      ‾‾‾‾
      675

96. 478
      − 89
      ‾‾‾‾
      389

97. 1029
      − 888
      ‾‾‾‾
      141

98. 7615
      − 547
      ‾‾‾‾
      7168

Fill in the missing digits in each problem.

99.   526_
       − 2_85
       ‾‾‾‾‾
        28_4

100.   10,_4_
        − 8_5_4
        ‾‾‾‾‾‾
         _710

101. Is there a commutative property of subtraction? In other words, does order matter when subtracting? Why or why not?

102. Explain why the phrase "Subtract 7 from 10" translates to "10 − 7."

103. The local college library is having a Million Pages of Reading promotion. The freshmen have read a total of 289,462 pages; the sophomores have read a total of 369,477 pages; the juniors have read a total of 218,287 pages; and the seniors have read a total of 121,685 pages. Have they reached a goal of one million pages? If not, how many more pages need to be read?

1.5 ROUNDING AND ESTIMATING

Objectives

A Round Whole Numbers.

B Use Rounding to Estimate Sums and Differences.

C Solve Problems by Estimating.

Objective **A** Rounding Whole Numbers

Rounding a whole number means approximating it. A rounded whole number is often easier to use, understand, and remember than the precise whole number. For example, instead of trying to remember the Iowa state population as 2,851,792, it is much easier to remember it rounded to the nearest million: 3 million people.

To understand rounding, let's first understand how we can visualize whole numbers by points on a line. The line below is called a **number line.** This number line has equally spaced marks for each whole number. The arrow to the right simply means that there is no largest whole number.

To **graph** a whole number, we darken the point representing the location of the whole number. For example, the number 4 is graphed below.

On the number line, the whole number 36 is closer to 40 than 30, so 36 rounded to the nearest ten is 40.

The whole number 52 rounded to the nearest ten is 50 because 52 is closer to 50 than to 60.

In trying to round 25 to the nearest ten, we see that 25 is halfway between 20 and 30. It is not closer to either number. In such a case, we round to the larger ten, that is, to 30.

To round a whole number without using a number line, follow these steps:

Rounding Whole Numbers to a Given Place Value

Step 1: Locate the digit to the right of the given place value.

Step 2: If this digit is 5 or greater, add 1 to the digit in the given place value and replace each digit to its right by 0.

Step 3: If this digit is less than 5, replace it and each digit to its right by 0.

PRACTICE PROBLEM 1

Round to the nearest ten.

a. 46

b. 731

c. 125

 EXAMPLE 1 Round 568 to the nearest ten.

Solution: 5 6⑧ The digit to the right of the tens place is the ones place, which is circled.

↑
tens place

5 6⑧ Since the circled digit is 5 or greater, add 1 to the 6 in the tens place and replace the digit to the right by 0.

↑ ↘
Add 1. Replace with 0.

We find that 568 rounded to the nearest ten is 570.

■ **Work Practice Problem 1**

PRACTICE PROBLEM 2

Round to the nearest thousand.

a. 56,702

b. 7444

c. 291,500

EXAMPLE 2 Round 278,362 to the nearest thousand.

Solution:

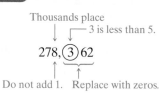

Thousands place
↓ ┌─ 3 is less than 5.
278,③62
↑   ↑
Do not add 1. Replace with zeros.

The number 278,362 rounded to the nearest thousand is 278,000.

■ **Work Practice Problem 2**

PRACTICE PROBLEM 3

Round to the nearest hundred.

a. 2777

b. 38,152

c. 762,955

EXAMPLE 3 Round 248,982 to the nearest hundred.

Solution:

Hundreds place
↓ ┌─ 8 is greater than or equal to 5.
248,9⑧2
↑
Add 1. $9 + 1 = 10$, so replace the digit 9 by 0 and carry 1 to the place value to the left.

$8+1$ 0
2 4 8, 9̸ 8 2
↑   ↑
Add 1.   Replace with zeros.

The number 248,982 rounded to the nearest hundred is 249,000.

■ **Work Practice Problem 3**

✔ **Concept Check** Round each of the following numbers to the nearest *hundred*. Explain your reasoning.

a. 79   b. 33

Answers

1. a. 50, b. 730, c. 130,
2. a. 57,000, b. 7000, c. 292,000,
3. a. 2800, b. 38,200, c. 763,000

✔ **Concept Check Answers**

a. 100, b. 0

Objective B Estimating Sums and Differences

By rounding addends, we can estimate sums. An estimated sum is appropriate when an exact sum is not necessary. To estimate the sum shown, round each number to the nearest hundred and then add.

```
 768   rounds to     800
1952   rounds to    2000
 225   rounds to     200
+ 149  rounds to    + 100
                    3100
```

The estimated sum is 3100, which is close to the exact sum of 3094.

EXAMPLE 4

Round each number to the nearest hundred to find an estimated sum.

```
 294
 625
1071
+ 349
```

Solution:

```
 294   rounds to     300
 625   rounds to     600
1071   rounds to    1100
+ 349  rounds to    + 300
                    2300
```

The estimated sum is 2300. (The exact sum is 2339.)

⬛ Work Practice Problem 4

EXAMPLE 5

Round each number to the nearest hundred to find an estimated difference.

```
 4725
-2879
```

Solution:

```
 4725  rounds to    4700
-2879  rounds to  - 2900
                    1800
```

The estimated difference is 1800. (The exact difference is 1846.)

⬛ Work Practice Problem 5

Objective C Solving Problems by Estimating

Making estimates is often the quickest way to solve real-life problems when solutions do not need to be exact.

PRACTICE PROBLEM 4

Round each number to the nearest ten to find an estimated sum.

```
 79
 35
 42
 21
+98
```

PRACTICE PROBLEM 5

Round each number to the nearest thousand to find an estimated difference.

```
 4725
-2879
```

Answers
4. 280, **5.** 2000

PRACTICE PROBLEM 6

Tasha Kilbey is trying to estimate how far it is from Grove, Kansas, to Hays, Kansas. Round each given distance on the map to the nearest ten to estimate the total distance.

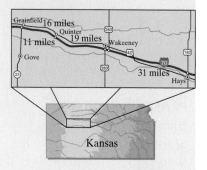

EXAMPLE 6 **Estimating Distances**

Jose Guillermo is trying to estimate quickly the distance from Temple, Texas, to Brenham, Texas. Round each distance given on the map to the nearest ten to estimate the total distance.

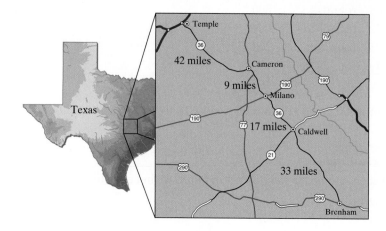

Solution:

Distance		Estimation
42	rounds to	40
9	rounds to	10
17	rounds to	20
+33	rounds to	+ 30
		100

It is approximately 100 miles from Temple to Brenham. (The exact distance is 101 miles.)

🔲 **Work Practice Problem 6**

PRACTICE PROBLEM 7

In a recent year, there were 120,624 reported cases of chicken pox, 22,866 reported cases of tuberculosis, and 45,970 reported cases of salmonellosis in the United States. Round each number to the nearest ten-thousand to estimate the total number of cases reported for these diseases. (*Source:* Centers for Disease Control and Prevention)

EXAMPLE 7 **Estimating Data**

In three recent years the numbers of reported cases of mumps in the United States were 906, 1537, and 1692. Round each number to the nearest hundred to estimate the total number of cases reported over this period. (*Source:* Centers for Disease Control and Prevention)

Solution:

Number of Cases		Estimation
906	rounds to	900
1537	rounds to	1500
+ 1692	rounds to	+ 1700
		4100

The approximate number of cases reported over this period was 4100.

🔲 **Work Practice Problem 7**

Answers

6. 80 mi, **7.** 190,000

1.5 EXERCISE SET

Objective A *Round each whole number to the given place. See Examples 1 through 3.*

1. 632 to the nearest ten

2. 273 to the nearest ten

3. 635 to the nearest ten

4. 275 to the nearest ten

5. 1792 to the nearest hundred

6. 9394 to the nearest hundred

7. 395 to the nearest ten

8. 898 to the nearest ten

9. 51,096 to the nearest thousand

10. 82,198 to the nearest thousand

11. 42,682 to the nearest thousand

12. 42,682 to the nearest ten-thousand

13. 248,695 to the nearest hundred

14. 179,406 to the nearest hundred

15. 36,499 to the nearest thousand

16. 96,501 to the nearest thousand

17. 99,995 to the nearest ten

18. 39,994 to the nearest ten

19. 59,725,642 to the nearest ten-million

20. 39,523,698 to the nearest million

Complete the table by estimating the given number to the given place value.

		Tens	Hundreds	Thousands
21.	5281			
22.	7619			
23.	9444			
24.	7777			
25.	14,876			
26.	85,049			

Round each number to the indicated place.

27. The number of active duty U.S. Air Force personnel in 2004 was 379,884. Round this number to the nearest thousand. (*Source:* U.S. Department of Defense)

28. The number of passengers handled in 2004 by the Hartsfield Atlanta International Airport was 79,086,792. Round this number to the nearest hundred-thousand. (*Source:* Airports Council International)

29. It takes 10,759 days for Saturn to make a complete orbit around the Sun. Round this number to the nearest hundred. (*Source:* National Space Science Data Center)

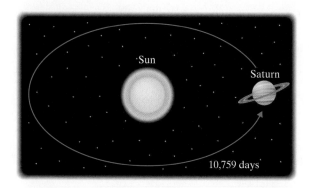

30. Kareem Abdul-Jabbar holds the NBA record for points scored, a total of 38,387 over his NBA career. Round this number to the nearest thousand. (*Source:* National Basketball Association)

31. The most valuable brand in the world in 2003 was Coca-Cola, with an estimated brand value of $70,450,000,000. Round this to the nearest billion. (*Source: Interbrand/Business Week*)

32. According to the 2000 U.S. Census, the population of the United States was 281,421,906. Round this population figure to the nearest million. (*Source:* U.S. Census Bureau)

33. The average salary for a Major League baseball player during the 2004 season was $2,486,609. Round this average salary to the nearest hundred-thousand. (*Source:* Major League Baseball Players Association)

34. In 2004, the Procter & Gamble Company had $51,407,000,000 in sales. Round this sales figure to the nearest billion. (*Source:* The Procter & Gamble Company)

35. The United States currently has 158,722,000 cellular mobile phone users (about 54% of population) while Austria has 7,094,500 users (about 88% of population). Round each of the user numbers to the nearest million. (*Note:* We will study percents in a later chapter.) (*Source:* Siemens AG, International Telecom Statistics, 2003)

36. In 2003, U.S. farms produced 144,649,000 bushels of oats. Round the oat production figure to the nearest ten-million. (*Source:* U.S. Department of Agriculture)

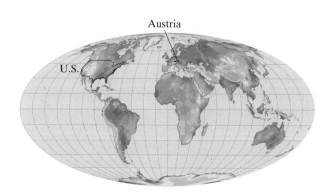

Objective **B** *Estimate the sum or difference by rounding each number to the nearest ten. See Examples 4 and 5.*

37.	**38.**	**39.**	**40.**
29	62	649	555
35	72	− 272	− 235
42	15		
+ 16	+ 19		

Estimate the sum or difference by rounding each number to the nearest hundred. See Examples 4 and 5.

41. 1812
         1776
       + 1945

42. 2010
         2001
       + 1984

43. 1774
       − 1492

44. 1989
       − 1870

45. 2995
         1649
       + 3940

46. 799
         1655
       + 271

Two of the given calculator answers below are incorrect. Find them by estimating each sum.

47. 362 + 419   781

48. 522 + 785   1307

49. 432 + 679 + 198   1139

50. 229 + 443 + 606   1278

51. 7806 + 5150   12,956

52. 5233 + 4988   9011

> **Helpful Hint**
> Estimation is useful to check for incorrect answers when using a calculator. For example, pressing a key too hard may result in a double digit, while pressing a key too softly may result in the digit not appearing in the display.

Objective **C** *Solve each problem by estimating. See Examples 6 and 7.*

53. Campo Appliance Store advertises three refrigerators on sale at $799, $1299, and $999. Round each cost to the nearest hundred to estimate the total cost.

54. Jared Nuss scored 89, 92, 100, 67, 75, and 89 on his biology tests. Round each score to the nearest ten to estimate his total score.

55. Round each distance given on the map to the nearest ten miles to estimate the total distance from Stockton to LaCrosse.

56. The Gonzales family took a trip and traveled 458, 489, 377, 243, 69, and 702 miles on six consecutive days. Round each distance to the nearest hundred to estimate the distance they traveled.

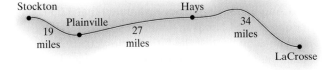

Stockton
Plainville   Hays
19 miles   27 miles   34 miles
                           LaCrosse

57. The peak of Mt. McKinley, in Alaska, is 20,320 feet above sea level. The top of Mt. Rainier, in Washington, is 14,410 feet above sea level. Round each height to the nearest thousand to estimate the difference in elevation of these two peaks. (*Source:* U.S. Geological Survey)

58. A student is pricing new car stereo systems. One system sells for $1895 and another system sells for $1524. Round each price to the nearest hundred dollars to estimate the difference in price of these systems.

59. In 2003 the population of Chicago was 2,896,121, and the population of Philadelphia was 1,479,339. Round each population to the nearest hundred-thousand to estimate how much larger Chicago was than Philadelphia. (*Source:* U.S. Census Bureau, 2003 census)

60. The distance from Kansas City to Boston is 1429 miles and from Kansas City to Chicago, 530 miles. Round each distance to the nearest hundred to estimate how much farther Boston is from Kansas City than Chicago is.

61. In the 1964 presidential election, Lyndon Johnson received 41,126,233 votes and Barry Goldwater received 27,174,898 votes. Round each number of votes to the nearest million to estimate the number of votes by which Johnson won the election.

62. Enrollment figures at Normal State University showed an increase from 49,713 credit hours in 2003 to 51,746 credit hours in 2004. Round each number to the nearest thousand to estimate the increase.

63. Head Start is a national program that provides developmental and social services for America's low-income preschool children ages three to five. Enrollment figures in Head Start programs showed an increase from 857,664 children in 2000 to 909,608 children in 2003. Round each number of children to the nearest thousand to estimate this increase. (*Source:* Head Start Bureau)

64. In 2002, General Motors produced 244,356 Saturn cars. Similarly, in 2003 only 183,448 Saturns were produced. Round each number of cars to the nearest thousand to estimate the decrease in Saturn production from 2002 to 2003. (*Source:* General Motors Corporation)

Mixed Practice (*Sections 1.2 and 1.5*) *The following table (from Section 1.4) shows a few of the top leading advertisers in the United States for 2003 and the amount of money spent in that year on advertising. Complete this table. The first line is completed for you.*

	Advertiser	Amount Spent on Advertising in 2003 (in millions of dollars)	Amount Written in Standard Form	Standard Form Rounded to Nearest Hundred-Million	Standard Form Rounded to Nearest Billion
	DaimlerChrysler AG	2318	$2,318,000,000	$2,300,000,000	$2,000,000,000
65.	General Motors Corp.	3430			
66.	Pfizer	2839			
67.	Ford Motor Co.	2234			
68.	Johnson & Johnson	1996			
	(*Source:* Television Bureau of Advertising, Inc.)				

Concept Extensions

69. Find one number that when rounded to the nearest hundred is 4600.

70. Find one number that when rounded to the nearest ten is 4600.

71. A number rounded to the nearest hundred is 8600.
  a. Determine the smallest possible number.
  b. Determine the largest possible number.

72. On August 23, 1989, it was estimated that 1,500,000 people joined hands in a human chain stretching 370 miles to protest the fiftieth anniversary of the pact that allowed what was then the Soviet Union to annex the Baltic nations in 1939. If the estimate of the number of people is to the nearest hundred-thousand, determine the largest possible number of people in the chain.

73. In your own words, explain how to round a number to the nearest thousand.

74. Estimate the perimeter of the triangle by first rounding the length of each side to the nearest hundred.

5950 miles, 7693 miles, 8203 miles

75. Estimate the perimeter of the rectangle by first rounding the length of each side to the nearest ten.

54 meters

Rectangle   17 meters

1.6 MULTIPLYING WHOLE NUMBERS AND AREA

Objectives

A Use the Properties of Multiplication.

B Multiply Whole Numbers.

C Multiply by Whole Numbers Ending in Zero(s).

D Find the Area of a Rectangle.

E Solve Problems by Multiplying Whole Numbers.

Multiplication Shown as Repeated Addition Suppose that we wish to count the number of laptops provided in a computer class. The laptops are arranged in 5 rows, and each row has 6 laptops.

6 laptops in each row

1

2

3

Adding 5 sixes gives the total number of laptops:
6 + 6 + 6 + 6 + 6 = 30 laptops. When each addend is the same, we refer to this as **repeated addition.**

Multiplication is repeated addition but with different notation.

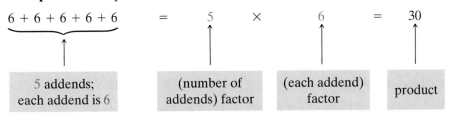

6 + 6 + 6 + 6 + 6	=	5	×	6	=	30

5 addends; each addend is 6	(number of addends) factor	(each addend) factor	product

The × is called a **multiplication sign.** The numbers 5 and 6 are called **factors.** The number 30 is called the **product.** The notation 5 × 6 is read as "five times six." The symbols · and ( ) can also be used to indicate multiplication.

$$5 \times 6 = 30, \quad 5 \cdot 6 = 30, \quad (5)(6) = 30, \quad \text{and} \quad 5(6) = 30$$

✔ Concept Check

a. Rewrite 4 + 4 + 4 + 4 + 4 + 4 + 4 using multiplication.

b. Rewrite 3 × 16 as repeated addition. Is there more than one way to do this? If so, show all ways.

Objective A Using the Properties of Multiplication

As with addition, we memorize products of one-digit whole numbers and then use certain properties of multiplication to multiply larger numbers. (If necessary, review the multiplication of one-digit numbers in Appendix A2.) Notice in the appendix that when any number is multiplied by 0, the result is always 0. This is called the **multiplication property of 0.**

✔ **Concept Check Answers**

a. 7 × 4 = 28,

b. 16 + 16 + 16 = 48; yes,
3 + 3 + 3 + 3 + 3 + 3 + 3 +
3 + 3 + 3 + 3 + 3 + 3 + 3 + 3 + 3 = 48

Multiplication Property of 0

The product of 0 and any number is 0. For example,

$$5 \cdot 0 = 0 \quad \text{and} \quad 0 \cdot 8 = 0$$

Also notice in the appendix that when any number is multiplied by 1, the result is always the original number. We call this result the **multiplication property of 1.**

Multiplication Property of 1

The product of 1 and any number is that same number. For example,

$$1 \cdot 9 = 9 \quad \text{and} \quad 6 \cdot 1 = 6$$

PRACTICE PROBLEM 1

Multiply.
a. 3×0
b. $4(1)$
c. $(0)(34)$
d. $1 \cdot 76$

EXAMPLE 1 Multiply.

a. 6×1 b. $0(8)$ c. $1 \cdot 45$ d. $(75)(0)$

Solution:

a. $6 \times 1 = 6$ b. $0(8) = 0$
c. $1 \cdot 45 = 45$ d. $(75)(0) = 0$

■ Work Practice Problem 1

Like addition, multiplication is commutative and associative. Notice that when multiplying two numbers, the order of these numbers can be changed without changing the product. For example,

$$3 \cdot 5 = 15 \quad \text{and} \quad 5 \cdot 3 = 15$$

This property is the **commutative property of multiplication.**

Commutative Property of Multiplication

Changing the **order** of two factors does not change their product. For example,

$$9 \cdot 2 = 18 \quad \text{and} \quad 2 \cdot 9 = 18$$

Another property that can help us when multiplying is the **associative property of multiplication.** This property states that when multiplying numbers, the grouping of the numbers can be changed without changing the product. For example,

$$(2 \cdot 3) \cdot 4 = 6 \cdot 4 = 24$$

Also,

$$2 \cdot (3 \cdot 4) = 2 \cdot 12 = 24$$

Both groupings give a product of 24.

Answers
1. a. 0, b. 4, c. 0, d. 76

Associative Property of Multiplication

Changing the **grouping** of factors does not change their product. From above, we know that for example,

$$(2 \cdot 3) \cdot 4 = 2 \cdot (3 \cdot 4)$$

With these properties, along with the **distributive property,** we can find the product of any whole numbers. The distributive property says that multiplication **distributes** over addition. For example, notice that $3(2 + 5)$ simplifies to the same number as $3 \cdot 2 + 3 \cdot 5$.

$$3(2 + 5) = 3(7) = 21$$

$$3 \cdot 2 + 3 \cdot 5 = 6 + 15 = 21$$

Since $3(2 + 5)$ and $3 \cdot 2 + 3 \cdot 5$ both simplify to 21, then

$$3(2 + 5) = 3 \cdot 2 + 3 \cdot 5$$

Notice in $3(2 + 5) = 3 \cdot 2 + 3 \cdot 5$ that each number inside the parentheses is multiplied by 3.

Distributive Property

Multiplication distributes over addition. For example,

$$2(3 + 4) = 2 \cdot 3 + 2 \cdot 4$$

EXAMPLE 2 Rewrite each using the distributive property.

a. $3(4 + 5)$ **b.** $10(6 + 8)$ **c.** $2(7 + 3)$

Solution: Using the distributive property, we have

a. $3(4 + 5) = 3 \cdot 4 + 3 \cdot 5$
b. $10(6 + 8) = 10 \cdot 6 + 10 \cdot 8$
c. $2(7 + 3) = 2 \cdot 7 + 2 \cdot 3$

■ **Work Practice Problem 2**

Objective B Multiplying Whole Numbers

Let's use the distributive property to multiply $7(48)$. To do so, we begin by writing the expanded form of 48 (see Section 1.2) and then applying the distributive property.

$$7(48) = 7(40 + 8) \quad \text{Write 48 in expanded form.}$$
$$= 7 \cdot 40 + 7 \cdot 8 \quad \text{Apply the distributive property.}$$
$$= 280 + 56 \quad \text{Multiply.}$$
$$= 336 \quad \text{Add.}$$

PRACTICE PROBLEM 2

Rewrite each using the distributive property.

a. $5(2 + 3)$
b. $9(8 + 7)$
c. $3(6 + 1)$

Answers

2. a. $5(2 + 3) = 5 \cdot 2 + 5 \cdot 3,$
   b. $9(8 + 7) = 9 \cdot 8 + 9 \cdot 7,$
   c. $3(6 + 1) = 3 \cdot 6 + 3 \cdot 1$

This is how we multiply whole numbers. When multiplying whole numbers, we will use the following notation.

$$\overset{5}{4}8$$
$$\times 7$$
$$\overline{336} \leftarrow 7\cdot8 = 56$$

Write 6 in the ones place and carry 5 to the tens place.

$7\cdot4 = 28$ and $28 + 5 = 33$

PRACTICE PROBLEM 3
Multiply.
a. $\begin{array}{r}36\\ \times\ 4\end{array}$ b. $\begin{array}{r}132\\ \times\ 9\end{array}$

EXAMPLE 3 Multiply:

a. $\begin{array}{r}25\\ \times\ 8\end{array}$ b. $\begin{array}{r}246\\ \times\ 5\end{array}$

Solution:

a. $\begin{array}{r}\overset{4}{2}5\\ \times\ 8\\ \hline 200\end{array}$ b. $\begin{array}{r}\overset{23}{2}46\\ \times\ 5\\ \hline 1230\end{array}$

◻ **Work Practice Problem 3**

To multiply larger whole numbers, use the following similar notation. Multiply 89×52.

Step 1
$\begin{array}{r}\overset{1}{8}9\\ \times\ 52\\ \hline 178\end{array} \leftarrow$ Multiply 89×2.

Step 2
$\begin{array}{r}\overset{4}{8}9\\ \times\ 52\\ \hline 178\\ 4450\end{array} \leftarrow$ Multiply 89×50.

Step 3
$\begin{array}{r}89\\ \times\ 52\\ \hline 178\\ 4450\\ \hline 4628\end{array}$ Add.

The numbers 178 and 4450 are called **partial products.** The sum of the partial products, 4628, is the product of 89 and 52.

PRACTICE PROBLEM 4
Multiply.
a. $\begin{array}{r}594\\ \times\ 72\end{array}$ b. $\begin{array}{r}306\\ \times\ 81\end{array}$

EXAMPLE 4 Multiply: 236×86

Solution:
$\begin{array}{r}236\\ \times\ 86\\ \hline 1\,416\\ 18\,880\\ \hline 20{,}296\end{array}$ $\leftarrow 6(236)$
$\leftarrow 80(236)$
Add.

◻ **Work Practice Problem 4**

PRACTICE PROBLEM 5
Multiply.
a. $\begin{array}{r}726\\ \times142\end{array}$ b. $\begin{array}{r}288\\ \times\ 4\end{array}$

EXAMPLE 5 Multiply: 631×125

Solution:
$\begin{array}{r}631\\ \times\ 125\\ \hline 3\,155\\ 12\,620\\ 63\,100\\ \hline 78{,}875\end{array}$ $\leftarrow 5(631)$
$\leftarrow 20(631)$
$\leftarrow 100(631)$
Add.

◻ **Work Practice Problem 5**

Answers
3. a. 144, b. 1188,
4. a. 42,768, b. 24,786,
5. a. 103,092, b. 1152

SECTION 1.6 | MULTIPLYING WHOLE NUMBERS AND AREA

✔ **Concept Check** Find and explain the error in the following multiplication problem.

$$
\begin{array}{r}
102 \\
\times\ 33 \\
\hline
306 \\
306 \\
\hline
612
\end{array}
$$

Objective C Multiplying by Whole Numbers Ending in Zero(s)

Interesting patterns occur when we multiply by a number that ends in zeros. To see these patterns, let's multiply a number, say 34, by 10, then 100, then 1000.

1 zero
$34 \cdot 10 = 340$ 1 zero attached to 34.

2 zeros
$34 \cdot 100 = 3400$ 2 zeros attached to 34.

3 zeros
$34 \cdot 1000 = 34,000$ 3 zeros attached to 34.

These patterns help us develop a shortcut for multiplying by whole numbers ending in zeros.

To multiply by 10, 100, 1000 and so on,
   Form the product by attaching the number of zeros in that number to the other factor.
   For example, $41 \cdot 100 = 4100$.
                    2 zeros

EXAMPLES Multiply.

6. $176 \cdot 1000 = 176,000$ Attach 3 zeros.

7. $2041 \cdot 100 = 204,100$ Attach 2 zeros.

■ **Work Practice Problems 6–7**

We can use a similar format to multiply by any whole number ending in zeros. For example, since

$$15 \cdot 500 = 15 \cdot 5 \cdot 100,$$

we find the product by multiplying 15 and 5, then attaching two zeros to the product.

$$
\begin{array}{r}
\overset{2}{15} \\
\times\ 5 \\
\hline
75
\end{array}
\qquad 15 \cdot 500 = 7500
$$

Multiply.
6. $75 \cdot 100$
7. $808 \cdot 1000$

Answers
6. 7500, **7.** 808,000

✔ **Concept Check Answer**

$$
\begin{array}{r}
102 \\
\times\ 33 \\
\hline
306 \\
3060 \\
\hline
3366
\end{array}
$$

PRACTICE PROBLEMS 8–9

Multiply.

8. $35 \cdot 3000$

9. $600 \cdot 600$

EXAMPLES Multiply.

8. $25 \cdot 9000 = 225,000$ $\overset{4}{25}$ Attach 3 zeros.
$$\underline{\times 9}$$
$$225$$

9. $20 \cdot 7000 = 140,000$ Attach 4 zeros.
$$2 \cdot 7$$

◾ **Work Practice Problems 8–9**

Objective D Finding the Area of a Rectangle

A special application of multiplication is finding the area of a region. Area measures the amount of surface of a region. For example, we measure a plot of land or the living space of a home by area. The figures show two examples of units of area measure. (A centimeter is a unit of length in the metric system.)

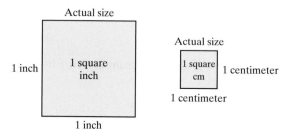

To measure the area of a geometric figure such as the rectangle shown, count the number of square units that cover the region.

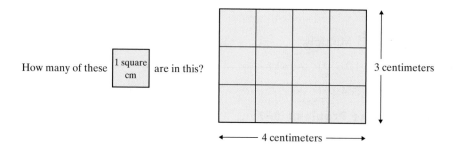

This rectangular region contains 12 square units, each 1 square centimeter. Thus, the area is 12 square centimeters. This total number of squares can be found by counting or by multiplying **4 · 3**(length · width).

Area of a rectangle $=$ length · width
$$= (4 \text{ centimeters})(3 \text{ centimeters})$$
$$= 12 \text{ square centimeters}$$

In this section, we find the areas of rectangles only. In later sections, we find the areas of other geometric regions.

Answers

8. 105,000,   **9.** 360,000

EXAMPLE 10 Finding the Area of a State

The state of Colorado is in the shape of a rectangle whose length is 380 miles and whose width is 280 miles. Find its area.

Solution:

The area of a rectangle is the product of its length and its width.

Area = length · width
     = (380 miles)(280 miles)
     = 106,400 square miles

The area of Colorado is 106,400 square miles.

■ Work Practice Problem 10

PRACTICE PROBLEM 10

The state of Wyoming is in the shape of a rectangle whose length is 360 miles and whose width is 280 miles. Find its area.

Objective E Solving Problems by Multiplying

There are several words or phrases that indicate the operation of multiplication. Some of these are as follows:

Key Words or Phrases	Example	Symbols
multiply	multiply 5 by 7	$5 \cdot 7$
product	the product of 3 and 2	$3 \cdot 2$
times	10 times 13	$10 \cdot 13$

Many key words or phrases describing real-life problems that suggest addition might be better solved by multiplication instead. For example, to find the **total** cost of 8 shirts, each selling for $27, we can either add 27 + 27 + 27 + 27 + 27 + 27 + 27 + 27, or we can multiply 8(27).

EXAMPLE 11 Finding DVD Space

A digital video disc (DVD) can hold about 4800 megabytes (MB) of information. How many megabytes can 12 DVDs hold?

Solution:

Twelve DVDs will hold 12 × 4800 megabytes.

In Words   **Translate to Numbers**

megabytes per disk →   4800
+   DVDs →   × 12
                              9600
                            48000
total megabytes   57,600

Twelve DVDs will hold 57,600 megabytes.

■ Work Practice Problem 11

PRACTICE PROBLEM 11

A particular computer printer can print 15 pages per minute in color. How many pages can it print in 45 minutes?

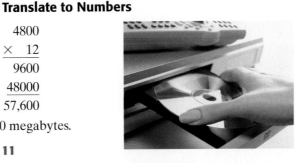

Answers

10. 100,800 sq mi,   **11.** 675 pages

PRACTICE PROBLEM 12

Softball T-shirts come in two styles: plain at $6 each and striped at $7 each. The team orders 4 plain shirts and 5 striped shirts. Find the total cost of the order.

EXAMPLE 12 **Budgeting Money**

Earline Martin agrees to take her children and their cousins to the San Antonio Zoo. The ticket price for each child is $4 and for each adult, $6. If 8 children and 1 adult plan to go, how much money is needed for admission?

Solution: If the price of one child's ticket is $4, the price for 8 children is $8 \cdot 4 = \$32$. The price of one adult ticket is $6, so the total cost is

In Words		Translate to Numbers
price of 8 children	→	32
+ price of 1 adult	→	+ 6
total cost		38

The total cost is $38.

⬛ **Work Practice Problem 12**

PRACTICE PROBLEM 13

If an average page in a book contains 171 words, estimate, rounding each number to the nearest hundred, the total number of words contained on 395 pages.

EXAMPLE 13 **Estimating Word Count**

The average page of a book contains 259 words. Estimate, rounding each number to the nearest hundred, the total number of words contained on 212 pages.

Solution: The exact number of words is 259×212. Estimate this product by rounding each factor to the nearest hundred.

$$259 \quad \text{rounds to} \quad 300$$
$$\times 212 \quad \text{rounds to} \quad \times 200, \qquad 300 \times 200 = 60,000$$
$$3 \cdot 2 = 6$$

There are approximately 60,000 words contained on 212 pages.

⬛ **Work Practice Problem 13**

🖩 **CALCULATOR EXPLORATIONS** Multiplying Numbers

To multiply numbers on a calculator, find the keys marked × and = or ENTER . For example, to find $31 \cdot 66$ on a calculator, press the keys 31   ×   66   = or ENTER . The display will read 2046 . Thus, $31 \cdot 66 = 2046$.

Use a calculator to multiply.

1. 72×48
2. 81×92
3. $163 \cdot 94$
4. $285 \cdot 144$
5. $983(277)$
6. $1562(843)$

Answers
12. $59, **13.** 80,000 words

Mental Math

Objective A *Multiply. See Example 1.*

1. $1 \cdot 24$ **2.** $55 \cdot 1$ **3.** $0 \cdot 19$ **4.** $27 \cdot 0$

5. $8 \cdot 0 \cdot 9$ **6.** $7 \cdot 6 \cdot 0$ **7.** $87 \cdot 1$ **8.** $1 \cdot 41$

1.6 EXERCISE SET

FOR EXTRA HELP

Student Solutions Manual   PH Math/Tutor Center   CD/Video for Review   MathXL®   MyMathLab

Objective A *Use the distributive property to rewrite each expression. See Example 2.*

1. $4(3 + 9)$ **2.** $5(8 + 2)$ **3.** $2(4 + 6)$ **4.** $6(1 + 4)$ **5.** $10(11 + 7)$ **6.** $12(12 + 3)$

Objective B *Multiply. See Example 3.*

7. $\begin{array}{r} 42 \\ \times\ 6 \\ \hline \end{array}$ **8.** $\begin{array}{r} 79 \\ \times\ 3 \\ \hline \end{array}$ **9.** $\begin{array}{r} 624 \\ \times\ 3 \\ \hline \end{array}$ **10.** $\begin{array}{r} 638 \\ \times\ 5 \\ \hline \end{array}$

11. 277×6 **12.** 882×2 **13.** 1062×5 **14.** 9021×3

Multiply. See Examples 4 and 5.

15. $\begin{array}{r} 98 \\ \times 14 \\ \hline \end{array}$ **16.** $\begin{array}{r} 91 \\ \times 72 \\ \hline \end{array}$ **17.** $\begin{array}{r} 231 \\ \times\ 47 \\ \hline \end{array}$ **18.** $\begin{array}{r} 526 \\ \times\ 23 \\ \hline \end{array}$ **19.** $\begin{array}{r} 809 \\ \times\ 14 \\ \hline \end{array}$ **20.** $\begin{array}{r} 307 \\ \times\ 16 \\ \hline \end{array}$

21. $(620)(40)$ **22.** $(720)(80)$ **23.** $(998)(12)(0)$ **24.** $(593)(47)(0)$ **25.** $(590)(1)(10)$

26. $(240)(1)(20)$ **27.** 1234×48 **28.** 1357×79 **29.** 609×234 **30.** 505×127

31. $\begin{array}{r} 5621 \\ \times\ 324 \\ \hline \end{array}$ **32.** $\begin{array}{r} 1234 \\ \times\ 567 \\ \hline \end{array}$ **33.** $\begin{array}{r} 1941 \\ \times 2035 \\ \hline \end{array}$ **34.** $\begin{array}{r} 1876 \\ \times 1407 \\ \hline \end{array}$ **35.** $\begin{array}{r} 589 \\ \times 110 \\ \hline \end{array}$ **36.** $\begin{array}{r} 426 \\ \times 110 \\ \hline \end{array}$

Objective **C** *Multiply. See Examples 6 through 9.*

37. 8×100 **38.** 6×100 **39.** 11×1000 **40.** 26×1000 **41.** $7406 \cdot 10$ **42.** $9054 \cdot 10$

43. $6 \cdot 4000$ **44.** $3 \cdot 9000$ **45.** $50 \cdot 900$ **46.** $70 \cdot 300$ **47.** $41 \cdot 80,000$ **48.** $27 \cdot 50,000$

Objectives **D** **E** **Mixed Practice** *Estimate the products by rounding each factor to the nearest hundred. See Example 13.*

49. 576×354 **50.** 982×650 **51.** 604×451 **52.** 111×999

Without actually calculating, mentally round, multiply, and choose the best estimate.

53. $38 \times 42 =$
  a. 16
  b. 160
  c. 1600
  d. 16,000

54. 2872×12
  a. 2872
  b. 28,720
  c. 287,200
  d. 2,872,000

55. $612 \times 29 =$
  a. 180
  b. 1800
  c. 18,000
  d. 180,000

56. 706×409
  a. 280
  b. 2800
  c. 28,000
  d. 280,000

Find the area of each rectangle. See Example 10.

57.

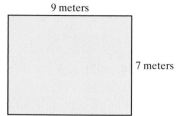

9 meters

7 meters

58. 4 inches

12 inches

59. 13 feet

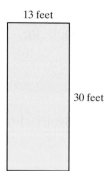

30 feet

60. 25 centimeters

20 centimeters

Solve. See Examples 10 through 13.

61. Multiply 70 by 11.   **62.** Multiply 80 by 12.   **63.** Find the product of 9 and 600.

64. Find the product of 4 and 400.   **65.** Find 2 times 2240.   **66.** Find 3 times 3310.

67. One tablespoon of olive oil contains 125 calories. How many calories are in 3 tablespoons of olive oil? (*Source: Home and Garden Bulletin No. 72*, U.S. Department of Agriculture).

68. One ounce of hulled sunflower seeds contains 14 grams of fat. How many grams of fat are in 6 ounces of hulled sunflower seeds? (*Source: Home and Garden Bulletin No. 72*, U.S. Department of Agriculture).

69. The textbook for a course in Civil War history costs $54. There are 35 students in the class. Find the total cost of the history books for the class.

70. The seats in the mathematics lecture hall are arranged in 12 rows with 34 seats in each row. Find how many seats are in this room.

71. A case of canned peas has *two layers* of cans. In each layer are 8 rows with 12 cans in each row.
   a. How many cans are in 1 layer?
   b. How many cans are in a case?

72. An apartment building has *three floors*. Each floor has five rows of apartments with four apartments in each row.
   a. How many apartments are on 1 floor?
   b. How many apartments are in the building?

△ **73.** A plot of land measures 90 feet by 110 feet. Find its area.

△ **74.** A house measures 45 feet by 60 feet. Find the floor area of the house.

△ **75.** The largest hotel lobby can be found at the Hyatt Regency in San Francisco, CA. It is in the shape of a rectangle that measures 350 feet by 160 feet. Find its area.

△ **76.** Recall from an earlier section that the largest commercial building in the world under one roof is the flower auction building of the cooperative VBA in Aalsmeer, Netherlands. The floor plan is a rectangle that measures 776 meters by 639 meters. Find the area of this building. (A meter is a unit of length in the metric system.) (*Source: The Handy Science Answer Book*, Visible Ink Press)

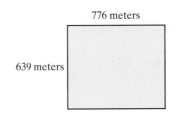

77. A pixel is a rectangular dot on a graphing calculator screen. If a graphing calculator screen contains 62 pixels in a row and 94 pixels in a column, find the total number of pixels on a screen.

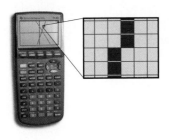

78. A compact disc (CD) can hold 700 megabytes (MB) of information. How many MBs can 17 discs hold?

79. A line of print on a computer contains 60 characters (letters, spaces, punctuation marks). Find how many characters there are in 25 lines.

80. An average cow eats 3 pounds of grain per day. Find how much grain a cow eats in a year. (Assume 365 days in 1 year.)

81. One ounce of Planters® Dry Roasted Peanuts has 160 calories. How many calories are in 8 ounces? (*Source:* RJR Nabisco, Inc.)

82. One ounce of Planters® Dry Roasted Peanuts has 13 grams of fat. How many grams of fat are in 8 ounces? (*Source:* RJR Nabisco, Inc.)

83. The diameter of the planet Saturn is 9 times as great as the diameter of Earth. The diameter of Earth is 7927 miles. Find the diameter of Saturn.

84. The planet Uranus orbits the Sun every 84 Earth years. Find how many Earth days two orbits take. (Assume 365 days in 1 year.)

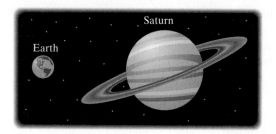

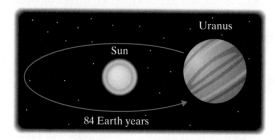

85. The Thespian club at a local community college is ordering T-shirts. T-shirts size S, M, or L cost $10 each and T-shirts size XL or XXL cost $12 each. Use the table below to find the total cost. (The first row is filled in for you.)

T-Shirt Size	Number of Shirts Ordered	Cost per Shirt	Cost per Size Ordered
S	3	$10	$30
M	5		
L	10		
XL	2		
XXL	2		

Total Cost ___

86. A field trip to the planetarium is planned by the student teacher of a third-grade class. For parent supervisors, the cost is $10 per person. For the third grade students, the cost is $8 per person. For the teacher and student teacher, the cost is $5 per person. Use the table below to find the total cost. (The first row is filled in for you.)

Person	Number of Persons	Cost per Person	Cost per Category
Teacher/ student teacher	2	$5	$10
Third graders	25		
Parents	5		

Total Cost ___

87. Hershey's main chocolate factory in Hershey, Pennsylvania, uses 700,000 quarts of milk each day. How many quarts of milk would be used during the month of March, assuming that chocolate is made at the factory every day of the month? (*Source:* Hershey Foods Corp.)

88. Among older Americans (age 65 years and older), there are about 4 times as many widows as widowers. There were 1,974,000 widowers in 2002. How many widows were there in 2002? (*Sources:* Administration on Aging, U.S. Census Bureau)

Mixed Practice (*Sections 1.3, 1.4, 1.6*) *Perform each indicated operation.*

89. 126
    + 8

90. 126
    − 8

91. 126
    × 8

92. 47 + 26 + 10 + 231 + 50

93. Find the sum of 18 and 6.

94. Find the product of 18 and 6.

95. Find the difference of 18 and 6.

96. Find the total of 18 and 6.

Concept Extensions

Solve. See the first Concept Check in this section.

97. Rewrite $3 + 3 + 3 + 3 + 3$ using multiplication.

98. Rewrite $11 + 11 + 11 + 11 + 11 + 11$ using multiplication.

99. a. Rewrite $4 \cdot 7$ as repeated addition.
   b. Explain why there is more than one way to do this?

100. a. Rewrite $2 \cdot 5$ as repeated addition.
   b. Explain why there is more than one way to do this.

Find and explain the error in each multiplication problem. See the second Concept Check in this section.

101.
$$
\begin{array}{r}
203 \\
\times\ \ 14 \\
\hline
812 \\
203\ \ \\
\hline
1015
\end{array}
$$

102.
$$
\begin{array}{r}
31 \\
\times\ 50 \\
\hline
155
\end{array}
$$

Fill in the missing digits in each problem.

103.
$$
\begin{array}{r}
4\_ \\
\times\ \ 3\_ \\
\hline
\cdot\ 126 \\
3780\ \ \\
\hline
3906
\end{array}
$$

104.
$$
\begin{array}{r}
\_7 \\
\times\ 6\_ \\
\hline
171 \\
3420\ \ \\
\hline
3591
\end{array}
$$

105. Explain how to multiply two 2-digit numbers using partial products.

106. During the NBA's 2003–2004 season, Kevin Garnett of the Minnesota Timberwolves scored 11 three-point field goals, 793 two-point field goals, and 368 free throws (worth one point each). How many points did Garnett score during the 2003–2004 season? (*Source:* National Basketball Association)

107. A window washer in New York City is bidding for a contract to wash the windows of a 23-story building. To write a bid, the number of windows in the building is needed. If there are 7 windows in each row of windows on 2 sides of the building and 4 windows per row on the other 2 sides of the building, find the total number of windows.

1.7 DIVIDING WHOLE NUMBERS

Suppose three people pooled their money and bought a raffle ticket at a local fundraiser. Their ticket was the winner and they won a $60 cash prize. They then divided the prize into three equal parts so that each person received $20.

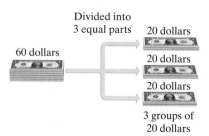

Objective **A** Dividing Whole Numbers

The process of separating a quantity into equal parts is called **division.** The division above can be symbolized by several notations.

quotient
$$3\overline{)60} \leftarrow \text{dividend}$$
↑
divisor

dividend
$$\frac{60}{3} = 20 \leftarrow \text{quotient}$$
↑
divisor

quotient
$$60 \div 3 = 20$$
↑ ↑
dividend divisor

dividend quotient
$$60/3 = 20$$
↑
divisor

(In the notation $\frac{60}{3}$, the bar separating 60 and 3 is called a **fraction bar.**) Just as subtraction is the reverse of addition, division is the reverse of multiplication. This means that division can be checked by multiplication.

$$3\overline{)60}^{\,20} \quad \text{because} \quad 20 \cdot 3 = 60$$

| Quotient | · | Divisor | = | Dividend |

Since multiplication and division are related in this way, you can use the multiplication table in Appendix A.2 to review quotients of one-digit divisors if necessary.

EXAMPLE 1 Find each quotient. Check by multiplying.

a. $42 \div 7$ **b.** $\dfrac{81}{9}$ **c.** $4\overline{)24}$

Solution:

a. $42 \div 7 = 6$ because $6 \cdot 7 = 42$

b. $\dfrac{81}{9} = 9$ because $9 \cdot 9 = 81$

c. $4\overset{6}{\overline{)24}}$ because $6 \cdot 4 = 24$

▣ **Work Practice Problem 1**

EXAMPLE 2 Find each quotient. Check by multiplying.

a. $1\overline{)8}$ **b.** $11 \div 1$ **c.** $\dfrac{9}{9}$ **d.** $7 \div 7$ **e.** $\dfrac{10}{1}$ **f.** $6\overline{)6}$

Solution:

a. $1\overset{8}{\overline{)8}}$ because $8 \cdot 1 = 8$

b. $11 \div 1 = 11$ because $11 \cdot 1 = 11$

c. $\dfrac{9}{9} = 1$ because $1 \cdot 9 = 9$

d. $7 \div 7 = 1$ because $1 \cdot 7 = 7$

e. $\dfrac{10}{1} = 10$ because $10 \cdot 1 = 10$

f. $6\overset{1}{\overline{)6}}$ because $1 \cdot 6 = 6$

▣ **Work Practice Problem 2**

Example 2 illustrates the important properties of division described next:

Division Properties of 1

The quotient of any number and that same number is 1. For example,

$$8 \div 8 = 1 \qquad \frac{7}{7} = 1 \qquad 4\overset{1}{\overline{)4}}$$

The quotient of any number and 1 is that same number. For example,

$$9 \div 1 = 9 \qquad \frac{6}{1} = 6 \qquad 1\overset{3}{\overline{)3}} \qquad \frac{0}{1} = 0$$

EXAMPLE 3 Find each quotient. Check by multiplying.

a. $9\overline{)0}$ **b.** $0 \div 12$ **c.** $\dfrac{0}{5}$ **d.** $\dfrac{3}{0}$

Solution:

a. $9\overset{0}{\overline{)0}}$ because $0 \cdot 9 = 0$ **b.** $0 \div 12 = 0$ because $0 \cdot 12 = 0$

c. $\dfrac{0}{5} = 0$ because $0 \cdot 5 = 0$

Continued on next page

Continued on next page

PRACTICE PROBLEM 1

Find each quotient. Check by multiplying.

a. $8\overline{)48}$

b. $35 \div 5$

c. $\dfrac{49}{7}$

PRACTICE PROBLEM 2

Find each quotient. Check by multiplying.

a. $\dfrac{8}{8}$ **b.** $3 \div 1$

c. $1\overline{)12}$ **d.** $2 \div 1$

e. $\dfrac{5}{1}$ **f.** $11 \div 11$

PRACTICE PROBLEM 3

Find each quotient. Check by multiplying.

a. $\dfrac{0}{7}$ **b.** $5\overline{)0}$

c. $9 \div 0$ **d.** $0 \div 6$

Answers

1. a. 6, **b.** 7, **c.** 7, **2. a.** 1, **b.** 3,
c. 12, **d.** 2, **e.** 5, **f.** 1,
3. a. 0, **b.** 0, **c.** undefined, **d.** 0

d. If $\dfrac{3}{0}$ = a **number,** then the **number** times 0 = 3. Recall from Section 1.6 that any number multiplied by 0 is 0 and not 3. We say, then, that $\dfrac{3}{0}$ is **undefined.**

■ **Work Practice Problem 3**

Example 3 illustrates important division properties of 0.

Division Properties of 0

The quotient of 0 and any number (except 0) is 0. For example,

$$0 \div 9 = 0 \quad \frac{0}{5} = 0 \quad 14\overline{)0}$$

The quotient of any number and 0 is not a number. We say that

$$\frac{3}{0}, \quad 0\overline{)3}, \quad \text{and} \quad 3 \div 0$$

are **undefined.**

Objective B Performing Long Division

When dividends are larger, the quotient can be found by a process called **long division.** For example, let's divide 2541 by 3.

$$3\overline{)2541}$$

We can't divide 3 into 2, so we try dividing 3 into the first two digits.

$$3\overline{)2541}^{\,8}$$ 25 ÷ 3 = 8 with 1 left, so our best estimate is 8. We place 8 over the 5 in 25.

Next, multiply 8 and 3 and subtract this product from 25. Make sure that this difference is less than the divisor.

$$\begin{array}{r} 8 \\ 3\overline{)2541} \\ -24 \\ \hline 1 \end{array}$$ 8(3) = 24; 25 − 24 = 1, and 1 is less than the divisor 3.

Bring down the next digit and go through the process again.

$$\begin{array}{r} 84 \\ 3\overline{)2541} \\ -24\downarrow \\ \hline 14 \\ -12 \\ \hline 2 \end{array}$$ 14 ÷ 3 = 4 with 2 left; 4(3) = 12; 14 − 12 = 2

Once more, bring down the next digit and go through the process.

$$\begin{array}{r} 847 \\ 3\overline{)2541} \\ -24 \\ \hline 14 \\ -12\downarrow \\ \hline 21 \\ -21 \\ \hline 0 \end{array}$$ 21 ÷ 3 = 7; 7(3) = 21; 21 − 21 = 0

The quotient is 847. To check, see that 847 × 3 = 2541.

EXAMPLE 4 Divide: 3705 ÷ 5. Check by multiplying.

Solution:

$$
\begin{array}{r}
7 \\
5\overline{)3705} \\
-35\downarrow \\
\hline
20
\end{array}
$$

37 ÷ 5 = 7 with 2 left. Place this estimate, 7, over the 7 in 37.

7(5) = 35

37 − 35 = 2, and 2 is less than the divisor 5.

└── Bring down the 0.

$$
\begin{array}{r}
74 \\
5\overline{)3705} \\
-35 \\
\hline
20 \\
-20\downarrow \\
\hline
05
\end{array}
$$

20 ÷ 5 = 4

4(5) = 20

20 − 20 = 0, and 0 is less than the divisor 5.

└── Bring down the 5.

$$
\begin{array}{r}
741 \\
5\overline{)3705} \\
-35 \\
\hline
20 \\
-20\downarrow \\
\hline
5 \\
-5 \\
\hline
0
\end{array}
$$

5 ÷ 5 = 1

1(5) = 5

5 − 5 = 0

Check:

$$
\begin{array}{r}
741 \\
\times \quad 5 \\
\hline
3705
\end{array}
$$

🔲 **Work Practice Problem 4**

> **Helpful Hint**
>
> Since division and multiplication are reverse operations, don't forget that a division problem can be checked by multiplying.

EXAMPLE 5 Divide and check: 1872 ÷ 9

Solution:

$$
\begin{array}{r}
208 \\
9\overline{)1872} \\
-18\downarrow\downarrow \\
\hline
07 \\
-0\downarrow \\
\hline
72 \\
-72 \\
\hline
0
\end{array}
$$

2(9) − 18

18 − 18 = 0; bring down the 7.

0(9) = 0

7 − 0 = 7; bring down the 2.

8(9) = 72

72 − 72 = 0

Check: 208 · 9 = 1872

🔲 **Work Practice Problem 5**

PRACTICE PROBLEM 4

Divide. Check by multiplying.

a. 5382 ÷ 6

b. 2212 ÷ 4

c. 753 ÷ 3

PRACTICE PROBLEM 5

Divide and check.

a. $3\overline{)2115}$

b. $7\overline{)28{,}700}$

Answers

4. a. 897,   **b.** 553,   **c.** 251,

5. a. 705,   **b.** 4100

Naturally, quotients don't always "come out even." Making 4 rows out of 26 chairs, for example, isn't possible if each row is supposed to have exactly the same number of chairs. Each of 4 rows can have 6 chairs, but 2 chairs are still left over.

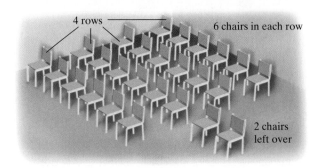

4 rows — 6 chairs in each row
2 chairs left over

We signify "leftovers" or **remainders** in this way:

$$4\overline{)26} \quad 6 \text{ R } 2$$

The **whole number part of the quotient** is 6; the **remainder part of the quotient** is 2. Checking by multiplying,

whole number part	·	divisor	+	remainder part	=	dividend
6	·	4	+	2		
		24	+	2	=	26

PRACTICE PROBLEM 6

Divide and check.

a. $5\overline{)949}$

b. $6\overline{)4399}$

EXAMPLE 6 Divide and check: $2557 \div 7$

Solution:

$$
\begin{array}{r}
365 \text{ R } 2 \\
7\overline{)2557} \\
-21 \\
\hline
45 \\
-42 \\
\hline
37 \\
-35 \\
\hline
2
\end{array}
$$

$3(7) = 21$
$25 - 21 = 4$; bring down the 5.
$6(7) = 42$
$45 - 42 = 3$; bring down the 7.
$5(7) = 35$
$37 - 35 = 2$; the remainder is 2.

Check: $365 \cdot 7 + 2 = 2557$

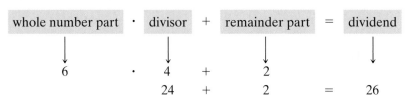

whole number part	·	divisor	+	remainder part	=	dividend

■ **Work Practice Problem 6**

Answers
6. a. 189 R 4, **b.** 733 R 1

EXAMPLE 7 Divide and check: 56,717 ÷ 8

Solution:

```
      7089  R 5
   8)56717
    −56↓||
      07|         7(8) = 56
     −0↓|         Subtract and bring down the 7.
      71|         0(8) = 0
     −64↓         Subtract and bring down the 1.
      77          8(8) = 64
     −72          Subtract and bring down the 7.
       5          9(8) = 72
                  Subtract. The remainder is 5.
```

Check:

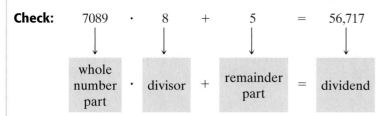

$$7089 \cdot 8 + 5 = 56{,}717$$

whole number part · divisor + remainder part = dividend

■ Work Practice Problem 7

When the divisor has more than one digit, the same pattern applies. For example, let's find 1358 ÷ 23.

```
      5        135 ÷ 23 = 5 with 20 left over. Our estimate is 5.
  23)1358
   −115↓      5(23) = 115
     208       135 − 115 = 20. Bring down the 8.
```

Now we continue estimating.

```
      59  R 1   208 ÷ 23 = 9 with 1 left over.
  23)1358
   −115
     208
    −207       9(23) = 207
       1       208 − 207 = 1. The remainder is 1.
```

To check, see that 59 · 23 + 1 = 1358.

EXAMPLE 8 Divide: 6819 ÷ 17

Solution:

```
      401  R 2
  17)6819
   −68↓|
     01|        4(17) = 68
    −0↓|        Subtract and bring down the 1.
     19         0(17) = 0
    −17         Subtract and bring down the 9.
      2         1(17) = 17
                Subtract. The reminder is 2.
```

To check, see that 401 · 17 + 2 = 6819.

■ Work Practice Problem 8

Answers

7. a. 8168 R 1,   **b.** 3204 R 2,
8. 302 R 2

PRACTICE PROBLEM 9

Divide: 16,589 ÷ 247

EXAMPLE 9 Divide: 51,600 ÷ 403

Solution:

$$
\begin{array}{r}
128 \quad \text{R } 16 \\
403\overline{)51600} \\
-403\downarrow \\
\hline
1130 \\
-806\downarrow \\
\hline
3240 \\
-3224 \\
\hline
16
\end{array}
$$

1(403) = 403

Subtract and bring down the 0.

2(403) = 806

Subtract and bring down the 0.

8(403) = 3224

Subtract. The remainder is 16.

To check, see that 128 · 403 + 16 = 51,600.

◾ **Work Practice Problem 9**

Division Shown as Repeated Subtraction To further understand division, recall from Section 1.6 that addition and multiplication are related in the following manner:

$$\underbrace{3 + 3 + 3 + 3}_{\text{4 addends; each addend is 3}} = 4 \times 3 = 12$$

In other words, multiplication is repeated addition. Likewise, division is repeated subtraction.

For example, let's find

35 ÷ 8

by repeated subtraction. Keep track of the number of times 8 is subtracted from 35. We are through when we can subtract no more because the difference is less than 8.

35 ÷ 8: Repeated Subtraction

$$
\begin{array}{r}
35 \\
-8
\end{array}\Big\}\text{ 1 time}
$$

$$
\begin{array}{r}
27 \\
-8
\end{array}\Big\}\text{ 2 times}
$$

$$
\begin{array}{r}
19 \\
-8
\end{array}\Big\}\text{ 3 times}
$$

$$
\begin{array}{r}
11 \\
-8
\end{array}\Big\}\text{ 4 times}
$$

$$3 \longleftarrow \text{ Remainder}$$

(We cannot subtract 8 again.)

35 ÷ 8: Illustration

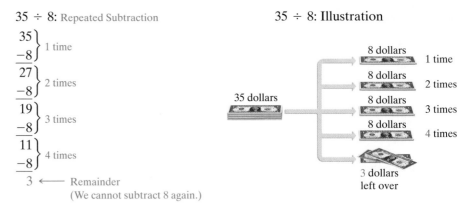

Thus, 35 ÷ 8 = 4 R 3.

To check, perform the same multiplication as usual, but finish by adding in the remainder.

whole number part of quotient	·	divisor	+	remainder	=	dividend
4	·	8	+	3	=	35

Objective C Solving Problems by Dividing

Below are some key words and phrases that may indicate the operation of division:

Key Words or Phrases	Examples	Symbols
divide	divide 10 by 5	$10 \div 5$ or $\frac{10}{5}$
quotient	the quotient of 64 and 4	$64 \div 4$ or $\frac{64}{4}$
divided by	9 divided by 3	$9 \div 3$ or $\frac{9}{3}$
divided or shared equally among	$100 divided equally among five people	$100 \div 5$ or $\frac{100}{5}$

✔ Concept Check Which of the following is the correct way to represent "the quotient of 20 and 5"? Or are both correct? Explain your answer.

a. $5 \div 20$
b. $20 \div 5$

EXAMPLE 10 Finding Shared Earnings

Zachary, Tyler, and Stephanie McMillan share a paper route to earn money for college expenses. The total in their fund after expenses was $2895. How much is each person's equal share?

Solution:

In words: Each person's share = total money ÷ number of persons

Translate: Each person's share = 2895 ÷ 3

Then
$$\begin{array}{r} 965 \\ 3\overline{)2895} \\ -27 \\ \hline 19 \\ -18 \\ \hline 15 \\ -15 \\ \hline 0 \end{array}$$

Each person's share is $965.

■ Work Practice Problem 10

PRACTICE PROBLEM 10

Marina, Manual, and Min bought 120 high-density computer diskettes to share equally. How many diskettes did each person get?

Answer
10. 40 diskettes

✔ Concept Check Answers
a. incorrect, b. correct

Peanut butter and cheese cracker sandwiches come in 6 sandwiches to a package. How many full packages are formed with 195 sandwiches?

EXAMPLE 11 Calculating Shipping Needs

How many boxes are needed to ship 56 pairs of Nikes to a shoe store in Texarkana if 9 pairs of shoes will fit in each shipping box?

Solution:

In words:	number of boxes	=	total pairs of shoes	÷	how many pairs in a box
	↓		↓		↓
Translate:	number or boxes	=	56	÷	9

$$\begin{array}{r} 6 \;\; R\,2 \\ 9\overline{)56} \\ -54 \\ \hline 2 \end{array}$$

There are 6 full boxes with 2 pairs of shoes left over, so 7 boxes will be needed.

🔲 **Work Practice Problem 11**

Calculators can be packed 24 to a box. If 497 calculators are to be packed but only full boxes are shipped, how many full boxes will be shipped? How many calculators are left over and not shipped?

EXAMPLE 12 Dividing Holiday Favors Among Students

Mary Schultz has 48 kindergarten students. She buys 260 stickers as Thanksgiving Day favors for her students. How many stickers will each person receive? How many stickers will be left over?

Solution:

In words:	Number of stickers for each person	=	number of stickers	÷	number of students
	↓		↓		↓
Translate:	Number of stickers for each person	=	260	÷	48

$$\begin{array}{r} 5 \;\; R\,20 \\ 48\overline{)260} \\ -240 \\ \hline 20 \end{array}$$

Each student will receive 5 stickers. The stickers cannot be divided equally among her students since there is a nonzero remainder. There will be 20 stickers left over.

🔲 **Work Practice Problem 12**

Objective D Finding Averages

A special application of division (and addition) is finding the average of a list of numbers. The **average** of a list of numbers is the sum of the numbers divided by the *number* of numbers.

$$\text{average} = \frac{\text{sum of numbers}}{\textit{number} \text{ of numbers}}$$

EXAMPLE 13 **Averaging Scores**

Liam Reilly's scores in his mathematics class so far are 93, 86, 71, and 82. Find his average score.

Solution: To find his average score, we find the sum of his scores and divide by 4, the number of scores.

$$\begin{array}{r} 93 \\ 86 \\ 71 \\ +82 \\ \hline 332 \text{ sum} \end{array}$$

$$\text{average} = \frac{332}{4} = 83$$

$$\begin{array}{r} 83 \\ 4\overline{)332} \\ -32 \\ \hline 12 \\ -12 \\ \hline 0 \end{array}$$

His average score is 83.

Work Practice Problem 13

PRACTICE PROBLEM 13

To compute a safe time to wait for reactions to occur after allergy shots are administered, a lab technician is given a list of elapsed times between administered shots and reactions. Find the average of the times 5 minutes, 7 minutes, 20 minutes, 6 minutes, 9 minutes, 3 minutes, and 48 minutes.

Answer

13. 14 min

■ CALCULATOR EXPLORATIONS Dividing Numbers

To divide numbers on a calculator, find the keys marked ÷ and = or ENTER . For example, to find 435 ÷ 5 on a calculator, press the keys 435 ÷ 5 = or ENTER . The display will read 87 . Thus, 435 ÷ 5 = 87.

Use a calculator to divide.

1. 848 ÷ 16

2. 564 ÷ 12

3. $95\overline{)5890}$

4. $27\overline{)1053}$

5. $\dfrac{32,886}{126}$

6. $\dfrac{143,088}{264}$

7. 0 ÷ 315

8. 315 ÷ 0

Mental Math

Objective **A** *Find each quotient. See Examples 1 through 3.*

1. 40 ÷ 8

2. 72 ÷ 9

3. 45 ÷ 5

4. 24 ÷ 3

5. 0 ÷ 5

6. 0 ÷ 8

7. 9 ÷ 1

8. 12 ÷ 1

9. $\dfrac{16}{16}$

10. $\dfrac{49}{49}$

11. $\dfrac{25}{5}$

12. $\dfrac{45}{9}$

13. 6 ÷ 0

14. $\dfrac{12}{0}$

15. 7 ÷ 1

16. 6 ÷ 6

17. 0 ÷ 4

18. 7 ÷ 0

19. 16 ÷ 2

20. 18 ÷ 3

Objective **A** **B** **Mixed Practice** *Divide and then check by multiplying. See Examples 1 through 5.*

1. $3\overline{)78}$ **2.** $5\overline{)85}$ **3.** $6\overline{)222}$ **4.** $8\overline{)640}$ **5.** $3\overline{)1014}$ **6.** $4\overline{)2104}$

7. $\dfrac{20}{0}$ **8.** $\dfrac{0}{20}$ **9.** $48 \div 6$ **10.** $56 \div 8$ **11.** $125 \div 5$ **12.** $121 \div 11$

Divide and then check by multiplying. See Examples 6 and 7.

13. $9\overline{)589}$ **14.** $7\overline{)426}$ **15.** $5\overline{)1129}$ **16.** $3\overline{)1240}$

17. $186 \div 5$ **18.** $167 \div 3$ **19.** $2125 \div 8$ **20.** $3333 \div 4$

Divide and then check by multiplying. See Examples 8 and 9.

21. $23\overline{)1127}$ **22.** $42\overline{)2016}$ ⊙ **23.** $55\overline{)715}$ **24.** $23\overline{)736}$ **25.** $97\overline{)9449}$

26. $1938 \div 44$ **27.** $3718 \div 18$ **28.** $7224 \div 12$ **29.** $6578 \div 13$ **30.** $5670 \div 14$

⊙ **31.** $9299 \div 46$ **32.** $2539 \div 64$ **33.** $\dfrac{10,620}{236}$ **34.** $\dfrac{5781}{123}$ **35.** $\dfrac{10,194}{103}$

36. $\dfrac{23,048}{240}$ **37.** $20,619 \div 102$ **38.** $40,853 \div 203$ **39.** $244,989 \div 423$ **40.** $164,592 \div 543$

Divide. See Examples 1 through 9.

41. $7\overline{)133}$ **42.** $9\overline{)153}$ **43.** $3\overline{)1540}$ **44.** $5\overline{)3017}$

45. $30\overline{)62,486}$ **46.** $50\overline{)85,747}$ **47.** $139\overline{)699,170}$ **48.** $213\overline{)866,910}$

Objective **C** *Solve. See Examples 10 through 12.*

49. Find the quotient of 85 and 4.

50. Find the quotient of 90 and 7.

51. Find 100 divided by 35.

52. Find 121 divided by 29.

53. Find the quotient of 62 and 3.

54. Find the quotient of 78 and 5.

55. Kathy Gomez teaches Spanish lessons for $85 per student for a 5-week session. From one group of students, she collects $4930. Find how many students are in the group.

56. Martin Thieme teaches American Sign Language classes for $55 per student for a 7-week session. He collects $1430 from the group of students. Find how many students are in the group.

57. Twenty-one people pooled their money and bought lottery tickets. One ticket won a prize of $5,292,000. Find how many dollars each person received.

58. The gravity of Jupiter is 318 times as strong as the gravity of Earth, so objects on Jupiter weigh 318 times as much as they weigh on Earth. If a person would weigh 52,470 pounds on Jupiter, find how much the person weighs on Earth.

59. A truck hauls wheat to a storage granary. It carries a total of 5810 bushels of wheat in 14 trips. How much does the truck haul each trip if each trip it hauls the same amount?

60. An 18-hole golf course is 5580 yards long. If the distance to each hole is the same, find the distance between holes.

61. The white stripes dividing the lanes on a highway are 25 feet long, and the spaces between them are 25 feet long. Let's call a "lane divider" a stripe followed by a space. Find how many whole "lane dividers" there are in 1 mile of highway. (A mile is 5280 feet.)

62. There is a bridge over highway I-35 every three miles. The first bridge is at the beginning of a 265-mile stretch of highway. Find how many bridges there are over 265 miles of I-35.

63. Wendy Holladay has a piece of rope 185 feet long that she wants to cut into pieces for an experiment in her second-grade class. Each piece of rope is to be 8 feet long. Determine whether she has enough rope for her 22-student class. Determine the amount extra or the amount short.

64. Jesse White is in the requisitions department of Central Electric Lighting Company. Light poles along a highway are placed 492 feet apart. The first light pole is at the beginning of a 1-mile strip. Find how many poles he should order for the 1-mile strip of highway. (A mile is 5280 feet.)

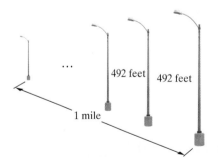

65. Priest Holmes of the Kansas City Chiefs led the NFL in touchdowns during the 2003 football season, scoring a total of 162 points from touchdowns. If a touchdown is worth 6 points, how many touchdowns did Priest make during 2003? (*Source:* National Football League)

66. Broad Peak in Pakistan is the twelfth-tallest mountain in the world. Its elevation is 26,400 feet. A mile is 5280 feet. How many miles tall is Broad Peak? (*Source:* National Geographic Society)

67. Find how many yards are in 1 mile. (A mile is 5280 feet; a yard is 3 feet.)

68. Find how many whole feet are in 1 rod. (A mile is 5280 feet; 1 mile is 320 rods.)

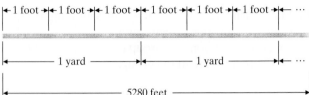

Objective **D** *Find the average of each list of numbers. See Example 13.*

69. 14, 22, 45, 18, 30, 27

70. 37, 26, 15, 29, 51, 22

71. 204, 968, 552, 268

72. 121, 200, 185, 176, 163

73. 86, 79, 81, 69, 80

74. 92, 96, 90, 85, 92, 79

The normal monthly temperature in degrees Fahrenheit for Minneapolis, Minnesota, is given in the graph. Use this graph to answer Exercises 75 and 76. (Source: National Climatic Data Center)

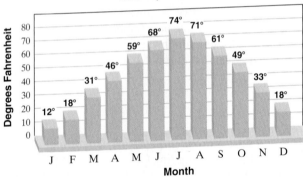

75. Find the average temperature for December, January, and February.

76. Find the average temperature for the entire year.

Mixed Practice (*Sections 1.3, 1.4, 1.6, 1.7*) *Perform each indicated operation. Watch the operation symbol.*

77. 78 + 236 + 42 + 8506

78. 23 + 407 + 92 + 7011

79.
$$\begin{array}{r} 635 \\ \times\ 46 \\ \hline \end{array}$$

80.
$$\begin{array}{r} 712 \\ \times\ 54 \\ \hline \end{array}$$

81.
$$\begin{array}{r} 635 \\ -\ 46 \\ \hline \end{array}$$

82.
$$\begin{array}{r} 712 \\ -\ 54 \\ \hline \end{array}$$

83. $\dfrac{86}{0}$

84. $\dfrac{0}{80}$

85. $211 \div 28$

86. $304 \div 31$

Concept Extensions

Match each word phrase to the correct translation. (Not all letter choices will be used.) See the Concept Check in this section.

87. The quotient of 35 and 7

a. $100 \div 10$

88. The quotient of 100 and 10

b. $10 \div 100$

89. 100 divided by 10

c. $7 \div 35$

90. 35 divided by 7

d. $35 \div 7$

The following table shows the top five leading U.S. advertisers in 2003 and the amount of money spent in that year on advertising. Use this table to answer Exercises 91 and 92.

Company	2003 Advertising Expenditures
General Motors Corp.	$3,430,000,000
DaimlerChrysler AG	$2,318,000,000
Procter & Gamble Co.	$3,323,000,000
Pfizer	$2,839,000,000
Time Warner Inc.	$3,097,000,000
(*Source:* Crain Communications)	

91. Find the average amount of money spent on ads for the year by the top two companies.

92. Find the average amount of money spent on ads by DaimlerChrysler AG, Procter & Gamble Co., Pfizer, and Time Warner Inc.

In Example 13 in this section, we found that the average of 93, 86, 71, and 82 is 83. Use this information to answer Exercises 93 and 94.

93. If the number 71 is removed from the list of numbers, does the average increase or decrease? Explain why.

94. If the number 93 is removed from the list of numbers, does the average increase or decrease? Explain why.

95. Without computing it, tell whether the average of 126, 135, 198, 113 is 86. Explain why it is or why it is not.

96. If the area of a rectangle is 30 square feet and its width is 3 feet, what is its length?

97. Write down any two numbers whose quotient is 15.

98. Find 26 ÷ 5 using the process of repeated subtraction.

THE BIGGER PICTURE   Operations on Sets of Numbers

This is a special feature that we begin in this section. Among other concepts introduced later in the text, it is very important for you to be able to perform operations on different sets of numbers. To help you remember these operations, we begin an outline below and continually expand this outline throughout this text. Although suggestions are given, this outline should be in your own words. Once you complete the new portion of your outline, try the exercises below. Remember: Study your outline often as you proceed through this text.

I. Some Operations on Sets of Numbers

   A. Whole Numbers

      1. Add or Subtract:

$$\begin{array}{r} 14 \\ +39 \\ \hline 53 \end{array} \qquad \begin{array}{r} 300 \\ -27 \\ \hline 273 \end{array}$$

2. Multiply or Divide:

$$\begin{array}{r} 238 \\ \times\ 47 \\ \hline 1666 \\ 9520 \\ \hline 11186 \end{array} \qquad \begin{array}{r} 127\ \text{R}\ 2 \\ 7\overline{)891} \\ -7 \\ \hline 19 \\ -14 \\ \hline 51 \\ -49 \\ \hline 2 \end{array}$$

Perform indicated operations.

1. 73 + 45

2. 73 − 45

3. 73 × 45

4. 2592 ÷ 29

5. 0 · 28

6. 0 ÷ 11

7. 19 · 1

8. 36 ÷ 0

9. 64 ÷ 1

10. 2000 − 156

Operations on Whole Numbers

Perform each indicated operation.

1. 23
46
$+79$

2. 7006
$- 451$

3. 36
$\times 45$

4. $8\overline{)4496}$

5. $1 \cdot 79$

6. $\dfrac{36}{0}$

7. $9 \div 1$

8. $9 \div 9$

9. $0 \cdot 13$

10. $7 \cdot 0 \cdot 8$

11. $0 \div 2$

12. $12 \div 4$

13. $4219 - 1786$

14. $1861 + 7965$

15. $5\overline{)1068}$

16. 1259
$\times\ \ 63$

17. $3 \cdot 9$

18. $45 \div 5$

19. 207
$-\ 69$

20. 207
$+\ 69$

21. $7\overline{)7695}$

22. $9\overline{)1000}$

23. $32\overline{)21{,}222}$

24. $65\overline{)70{,}000}$

25. $4000 - 2976$

26. $10{,}000 - 101$

27. 303
$\times 101$

28. $(475)(100)$

29. Find the total of 57 and 8.

30. Find the product of 57 and 8.

31. Find the quotient of 57 and 8.

32. Find the difference of 57 and 8.

33. Subtract 14 from 100.

34. Find the difference of 43 and 21.

Complete the table by rounding the given number to the given place value.

		Tens	Hundreds	Thousands
35.	8625			
36.	1553			
37.	10,901			
38.	432,198			

Find the perimeter and area of each figure.

△ **39.**

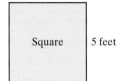

Square — 5 feet

△ **40.**

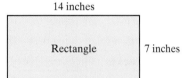

14 inches

Rectangle — 7 inches

Find the perimeter of each figure.

△ **41.**

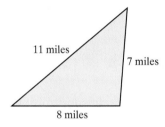

11 miles, 7 miles, 8 miles

△ **42.**

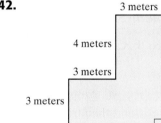

3 meters, 4 meters, 3 meters, 3 meters

Find the average of each list of numbers.

43. 19, 15, 25, 37, 24

44. 108, 131, 98, 159

45. The Mackinac Bridge is a suspension bridge that connects the lower and upper peninsulas of Michigan across the Straits of Mackinac. Its total length is 26,372 feet. The Lake Pontchartrain Bridge is a twin concrete trestle bridge in Slidell, Louisiana. Its total length is 28,547 feet. Which bridge is longer and by how much? (*Sources:* Mackinac Bridge Authority and Federal Highway Administration, Bridge Division)

Slidell, LA

Straits of Mackinac, MI

46. In North America, the average toy expenditure per child is $328 per year. On average, how much is spent on toys for a child by the time he or she reaches age 18? (*Source:* The NPD Group Worldwide)

31. _____

32. _____

33. _____

34. _____

39. _____

40. _____

41. _____

42. _____

43. _____

44. _____

45. _____

46. _____

Objectives

A Solve Problems by Adding, Subtracting, Multiplying, or Dividing Whole Numbers.

B Solve Problems That Require More Than One Operation.

1.8 AN INTRODUCTION TO PROBLEM SOLVING

Objective **A** Solving Problems Involving Addition, Subtraction, Multiplication, or Division

In this section, we decide which operation to perform in order to solve a problem. Don't forget the key words and phrases that help indicate which operation to use. Some of these are listed below and were introduced earlier in the chapter. Also included are several words and phrases that translate to the symbol "=".

Addition (+)	Subtraction (−)	Multiplication (·)	Division (÷)	Equality (=)
sum	difference	product	quotient	equals
plus	minus	times	divide	is equal to
added to	subtract	multiply	shared equally	is/was
more than	less than	multiply by	among	yields
increased by	decreased by	of	divided by	
total	less	double/triple	divided into	

The following problem-solving steps may be helpful to you:

Problem-Solving Steps

1. UNDERSTAND the problem. Some ways of doing this are to read and reread the problem, construct a drawing and look for key words to identify an operation.
2. TRANSLATE the problem. That is, write the problem in short form using words, and then translate to numbers and symbols.
3. SOLVE the problem. It is helpful to estimate the solution by rounding. Then carry out the indicated operation from step 2.
4. INTERPRET the results. *Check* the proposed solution in the stated problem and *state* your conclusions. Write your results with the correct units attached.

EXAMPLE 1 Calculating the Length of a River

The Hudson River in New York State is 306 miles long. The Snake River in the northwestern United States is 732 miles longer than the Hudson River. How long is the Snake River? (*Source:* U.S. Department of the Interior)

Solution:

1. UNDERSTAND. Read and reread the problem, and then draw a picture. Notice that we are told that Snake River is 732 miles longer than the Hudson River. The phrase "longer than" means that we add.

PRACTICE PROBLEM 1

The Bank of America Building is the second-tallest building in San Francisco, California, at 779 feet. The tallest building in San Francisco is the Transamerica Pyramid, which is 74 feet taller than the Bank of America Building. How tall is the Transamerica Pyramid? (*Source: The World Almanac, 2005*)

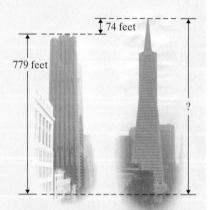

Bank of America   Transamerica Pyramid

Answer
1. 853 ft

2. TRANSLATE.

In words: | Snake River | is | 732 miles | longer than | the Hudson River |

↓   ↓   ↓   ↓   ↓

Translate: Snake River   =   732   +   306

3. SOLVE: Let's see if our answer is reasonable by also estimating. We will estimate each addend to the nearest hundred.

732	rounds to	700
+306	rounds to	300
1038	exact	1000	estimate

4. INTERPRET. *Check* your work. The answer is reasonable since 1038 is close to our estimated answer of 1000. *State* your conclusion: The Snake River is 1038 miles long.

◼ **Work Practice Problem 1**

EXAMPLE 2 **Filling a Shipping Order**

How many cases can be filled with 9900 cans of jalapeños if each case holds 48 cans? How many cans will be left over? Will there be enough cases to fill an order for 200 cases?

Solution:

1. UNDERSTAND. Read and reread the problem. Draw a picture to help visualize the situation.

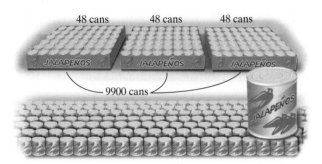

Since each case holds 48 cans, we want to know how many 48s there are in 9900. We find this by dividing.

2. TRANSLATE.

In words: | Number of cases | is | 9900 | divided by | 48 |

↓   ↓   ↓   ↓   ↓

Translate: Number of cases   =   9900   ÷   48

3. SOLVE: Let's estimate a reasonable solution before we actually divide. Since 9900 rounded to the nearest thousand is 10,000 and 48 rounded to the nearest ten is 50, $10{,}000 \div 50 = 200$. Now find the exact quotient.

$$
\begin{array}{r}
206 \text{ R } 12 \\
48\overline{)9900} \\
-96 \\
\hline
300 \\
-288 \\
\hline
12
\end{array}
$$

Continued on next page

PRACTICE PROBLEM 2

Four friends bought a lottery ticket and won $65,000. If each person is to receive the same amount of money, how much does each person receive?

Answer

2. $16,250

4. INTERPRET. *Check* your work. The answer is reasonable since 206 R 12 is close to our estimate of 200. *State* your conclusion: 206 cases will be filled, with 12 cans left over. There will be enough cases to fill an order for 200 cases.

▣ **Work Practice Problem 2**

PRACTICE PROBLEM 3

The director of the learning lab also needs to include in the budget a line for 425 blank CDs at a cost of $4 each. What is this total cost for the blank CDs?

EXAMPLE 3 Calculating Budget Costs

The director of a learning lab at a local community college is working on next year's budget. Thirty-three new DVD players are needed at a cost of $187 each. What is the total cost of these DVD players?

Solution:

1. UNDERSTAND. Read and reread the problem, and then draw a diagram.

33 DVD Players

$187 $187   ... $187

From the phrase "total cost," we might decide to solve this problem by adding. This would work, but repeated addition, or multiplication, would save time.

2. TRANSLATE.

In words:	Total cost	is	number of DVD players	times	cost of a DVD player
	↓	↓	↓	↓	↓
Translate:	Total cost	=	33	×	$187

3. SOLVE: Once again, let's estimate a reasonable solution.

$$
\begin{array}{rl}
187 & \text{rounds to} \quad 200 \\
\times\ 33 & \text{rounds to} \quad \times\ 30 \\
\hline
561 & \qquad\qquad 6000 \ \text{estimate} \\
5610 & \\
\hline
6171 & \text{exact}
\end{array}
$$

4. INTERPRET. *Check* your work. *State* your conclusion: The total cost of the video players is $6171.

▣ **Work Practice Problem 3**

PRACTICE PROBLEM 4

In 2002, the average salary of a public school teacher in North Dakota was $32,300. For the same year, the average salary for a public school teacher in South Dakota was $1000 less than this. What was the average public school teacher's salary in South Dakota? (*Source:* National Education Association)

EXAMPLE 4 Calculating a Public School Teacher's Salary

In 2002, the average salary of a public school teacher in California was $54,300. For the same year, the average salary for a public school teacher in Louisiana was $18,000 less than this. What was the average public school teacher's salary in Louisiana? (*Source:* National Education Association)

Solution:

1. UNDERSTAND. Read and reread the problem. Notice that we are told that the Louisiana salary is $18,000 less than the California salary. The phrase "less than" indicates subtraction.

Answers

3. $1700,   4. $31,300

2. TRANSLATE. Remember that order matters when subtracting, so be careful when translating.

In words: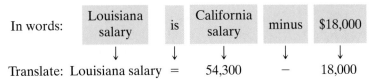

Translate: Louisiana salary = 54,300 − 18,000

3. SOLVE: This time, instead of estimating, let's check by adding

$$\begin{array}{r} 54{,}300 \\ -18{,}000 \\ \hline 36{,}300 \end{array}$$

Check:

$$\begin{array}{r} \overset{1}{36{,}300} \\ +18{,}000 \\ \hline 54{,}300 \end{array}$$

4. INTERPRET. *Check* your work. The check is above. *State* your conclusion: The average Louisiana teacher's salary in 2002 was $36,300.

■ **Work Practice Problem 4**

Objective B Solving Problems That Require More Than One Operation

We must sometimes use more than one operation to solve a problem.

EXAMPLE 5 Planting a New Garden

A gardener bought enough plants to fill a rectangular garden with length 30 feet and width 20 feet. Because of shading problems from a nearby tree, the gardener changed the width of the garden to 15 feet. If the area is to remain the same, what is the new length of the garden?

Solution:

1. UNDERSTAND. Read and reread the problem. Then draw a picture to help visualize the problem.

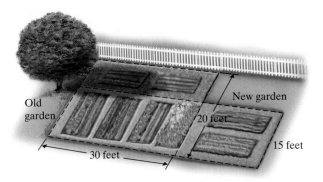

2. TRANSLATE. Since the area of the new garden is to be the same as the area of the old garden, let's find the area of the old garden. Recall that

Area = length × width = 30 feet × 20 feet = 600 square feet

Continued on next page

PRACTICE PROBLEM 5

A gardener is trying to decide how much fertilizer to buy for his yard. He knows that his lot is in the shape of a rectangle that measures 90 feet by 120 feet. He also knows that the floor of his house is in the shape of a rectangle that measures 45 feet by 65 feet. How much area of the lot is not covered by the house?

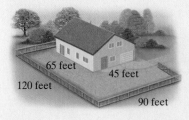

Answer

5. 7875 sq ft

Thus, the area of the new garden is to be 600 square feet. Also, we need to see how many 15s there are in 600. This means division. In other words,

In words: | New length | = | Area of garden | ÷ | New width |

Translate: New length = 600 ÷ 15

Since the area of the new garden is to be 600 square feet also, we need to see how many 15s there are in 600. This means division.

3. SOLVE.

$$
\begin{array}{r}
40 \\
15{\overline{\smash{\big)}\,600}} \\
\underline{-60} \\
00
\end{array}
$$

4. INTERPRET. *Check* your work. *State* your conclusion: The length of the new garden is 40 feet.

▣ **Work Practice Problem 5**

Objective A *Solve. See Examples 1 through 4.*

1. 41 increased by 8 is what number?

2. What is the product of 12 and 9?

3. What is the quotient of 1185 and 5?

4. 78 decreased by 12 is what number?

5. What is the total of 35 and 7?

6. What is the difference of 48 and 8?

7. 60 times 10 is what number?

8. 60 divided by 10 is what number?

9. A vacant lot in the shape of a rectangle measures 120 feet by 80 feet.
   a. What is the perimeter of the lot?
   b. What is the area of the lot?

10. A parking lot in the shape of a rectangle measures 100 feet by 150 feet.
   a. What is the perimeter of the lot?
   b. What is the area of the parking lot?

80 feet

120 feet

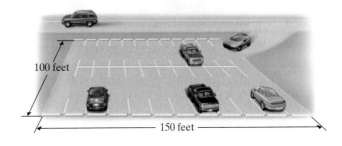

100 feet

150 feet

11. The Henrick family bought a house for $85,700 and later sold the house for $101,200. How much money did they make by selling the house?

12. Three people dream of equally sharing a $147 million lottery. How much would each person receive if they have the winning ticket?

13. There are 24 hours in a day. How many hours are in a week?

14. There are 60 minutes in an hour. How many minutes are in a day?

15. The country with the most higher education establishments is India, with 8407 of these establishments. In second place is the United States, with 2649 fewer higher education establishments. Find how many of these establishments there are in the United States.

16. The Goodyear Tire & Rubber Company maintains a fleet of five blimps. The *Spirit of Goodyear* can hold 202,700 cubic feet of helium. Its smaller sister, the *Spirit of Europe*, can hold 132,700 fewer cubic feet of helium than *Spirit of Goodyear*. How much helium can *Spirit of Europe* hold? (*Source:* Goodyear Tire & Rubber Company)

17. Yellowstone National Park in Wyoming was the first national park in the United States. It was created in 1872. One of the more recent additions to the National Park System is Governors Island National Monument in New York. It was established in 2001. How much older is Yellowstone than Governors Island? (*Source:* National Park Service)

18. Razor scooters were introduced in 2000. Radio Flyer Wagons were first introduced 83 years earlier. In what year were Radio Flyer Wagons introduced? (*Source:* Toy Industry Association, Inc.)

19. Since their introduction, the number of LEGO building bricks that have been sold is equivalent to the world's current population of approximately 6 billion people owning 52 LEGO bricks each. About how many LEGO bricks have been sold since their introduction? (*Source:* LEGO Company)

20. In 2003, the average weekly pay for a production worker in the United States was $517 per week. At that rate, how much would a production worker have earned working a 52-week year? (*Source:* U.S. Bureau of Labor Statistics)

21. The three most common city names in the United States are Fairview, Midway, and Riverside. There are 287 towns named Fairview, 252 named Midway, and 180 named Riverside. Find the total number of towns named Fairview, Midway, and Riverside.

22. In the game of Monopoly, a player must own all properties in a color group before building houses. The yellow color-group properties are Atlantic Avenue, Ventnor Avenue, and Marvin Gardens. These cost $260, $260, and $280, respectively, when purchased from the bank. What total amount must a player pay to the bank before houses can be built on the yellow properties? (*Source:* Hasbro, Inc.)

23. In 2003, the average weekly pay for a Financial Records Processing Supervisor in the United States was $840. If such a supervisor works 40 hours in one week, what is his or her hourly pay? (*Source:* U.S. Bureau of Labor Statistics)

24. In 2003, the average weekly pay for a computer programmer in the United States was $1160. If a computer programmer works 40 hours in one week, what is his or her hourly pay? (*Source:* U.S. Bureau of Labor Statistics)

25. Three ounces of canned tuna in oil has 165 calories. How many calories does 1 ounce have? (*Source: Home and Garden Bulletin No. 72,* U.S. Department of Agriculture)

26. A whole cheesecake has 3360 calories. If the cheesecake is cut into 12 equal pieces, how many calories will each piece have? (*Source: Home and Garden Bulletin No. 72,* U.S. Department of Agriculture)

27. The estimated 2003 U.S. population is 290,800,000 people. Between Memorial Day and Labor Day, 7 billion hot dogs are consumed. Approximately how many hot dogs are consumed per person between Memorial and Labor Days? Divide, but do not give remainder portion of quotient. (*Source:* U.S. Census Bureau, National Hot Dog and Sausage Council)

28. Diana Taurasi of the WNBA's Phoenix Mercury scored an average of 17 points per basketball game during the 2004 regular season. She played a total of 34 games during the season. What was the total number of points she scored during 2004? (*Source:* Women's National Basketball Association)

29. The May Department Stores Company operates Lord & Taylor, Foley's, Filene's, Kaufmann's, and other department stores around the country. It also operates 73 Robinsons-May and Meier & Frank stores in California, Oregon, Nevada, and Arizona. In 2003, Robinsons-May and Meier & Frank had sales of $2,446,000,050. What is the average amount of sales made by each of the 73 stores? (*Source:* The May Department Stores Company)

30. In 2003, the United States Postal Service delivered approximately 859,000,000 pieces of Priority Mail. The total weight of all items sent Priority Mail that year was approximately 1,718,000,000 pounds. What was the average weight of an item sent Priority Mail during 2003? (*Source:* United States Postal Service)

31. The enrollment of all students in elementary and secondary schools in the United States in 2008 is projected to be 54,268,000. Of these students, 16,234,000 are expected to be enrolled in secondary schools. How many students are expected to be enrolled in elementary schools in 2008? (*Source:* National Center for Education Statistics)

32. Kroger now operates convenience stores, food/grocery type stores, and department stores. In 2003, Kroger operated a total of 3774 stores. Of this total, 802 were convenience stores and 2532 were food/grocery type stores. How many department stores did Kroger operate in 2003? (*Source:* The Kroger Company)

33. The length of the southern boundary of the conterminous United States is 1933 miles. The length of the northern boundary of the conterminous United States is 2054 miles longer than this. What is the length of the northern boundary? (*Source:* U.S. Geological Survey)

34. In humans, 14 muscles are required to smile. It takes 29 more muscles to frown. How many muscles does it take to frown?

2054 miles longer

1933 miles

35. Marcel Rockett receives a paycheck every four weeks. Find how many paychecks he receives in a year. (A year has 52 weeks.)

36. A loan of $6240 is to be paid in 48 equal payments. How much is each payment?

Objective **B** *Solve. See Example 5.*

37. Find the total cost of 3 sweaters at $38 each and 5 shirts at $25 each.

38. Find the total cost of 10 computers at $2100 each and 7 boxes of diskettes at $12 each.

39. A college student has $950 in an account. She spends $205 from the account on books and then deposits $300 in the account. How much money is now in the account?

40. The temperature outside was 57°F (degrees Fahrenheit). During the next few hours, it decreased by 18 degrees and then increased by 23 degrees. Find the new temperature.

The table shows the menu from Corky's, a concession stand at the county fair. Use this menu to answer Exercises 41 and 42.

41. A hungry college student is debating between the following two orders:
  a. a hamburger, an order of onion rings, a candy bar, and a soda.
  b. a hot dog, an apple, an order of french fries, and a soda.
  Which order will be cheaper? By how much?

Corky's Concession Stand Menu	
Item	**Price**
Hot dog	$3
Hamburger	$4
Soda	$1
Onion rings	$3
French fries	$2
Apple	$1
Candy bar	$2

42. A family of four is debating between the following two orders:
  a. 6 hot dogs, 4 orders of onion rings, and 4 sodas.
  b. 4 hamburgers, 4 orders of french fries, 2 apples, and 4 sodas.
  Will the family save any money by ordering (b) instead of (a)? If so, how much?

Objectives **A** **B** **Mixed Practice** *Use the bar graph to answer Exercises 43 through 50.*

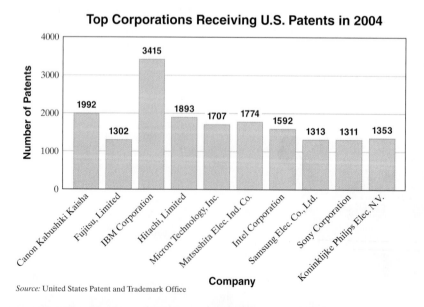

Top Corporations Receiving U.S. Patents in 2004

Number of Patents

Canon Kabushiki Kaisha: 1992
Fujitsu, Limited: 1302
IBM Corporation: 3415
Hitachi, Limited: 1893
Micron Technology, Inc.: 1707
Matsushita Elec. Ind. Co.: 1774
Intel Corporation: 1592
Samsung Elec. Co., Ltd.: 1313
Sony Corporation: 1311
Koninklijke Philips Elec. N.V.: 1353

Company

Source: United States Patent and Trademark Office

43. Which company listed received the most patents in 2004?

44. Which company listed received the fewest patents in 2004?

45. How many more patents did the company with the most patents receive than the company with the fewest patents?

46. How many more patents did Samsung receive than Sony?

47. How many more patents did Canon receive than Hitachi?

48. Which company received more patents, Matsushita or Fujitsu? How many more patents did it receive?

Find the average number of patents for the companies listed. Do not show remainders. Give whole number answers only.

49. The three companies with the greatest number of patents.

50. The four companies with the least number of patents shown.

Solve.

51. The learning lab at a local university is receiving new equipment. Twenty-two computers are purchased for $615 each and three printers for $408 each. Find the total cost for this equipment.

52. The washateria near the local community college is receiving new equipment. Thirty-six washers are purchased for $585 each and ten dryers are purchased for $388 each. Find the total cost for this equipment.

53. The American Heart Association recommends consuming no more than 2400 milligrams of salt per day. (This is about the amount in 1 teaspoon of salt.) How many milligrams of sodium is this in a week?

54. This semester a particular student pays $1750 for room and board, $709 for a meal ticket plan, and $2168 for tuition. What is her total bill?

△ **55.** The Meish's yard is in the shape of a rectangle and measures 50 feet by 75 feet. In their yard, they have a rectangular swimming pool that measures 15 feet by 25 feet.
   a. Find the area of the entire yard.
   b. Find the area of the swimming pool.
   c. Find the area of the yard that is not part of the swimming pool.

56. The community is planning to construct a rectangular-shaped playground within the local park. The park is in the shape of a square and measures 100 yards on each side. The playground is to measure 15 yards by 25 yards.
   a. Find the area of the entire park.
   b. Find the area of the playground.
   c. Find the area of the park that is not part of the playground.

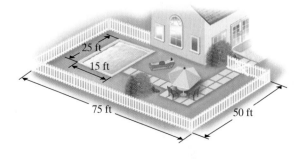

Concept Extensions

57. In 2003, the United States Postal Service issued approximately 202,500,000 money orders worth approximately $48,551,700,000. Round the value of the money orders issued to the nearest hundred-million to estimate the average value of each money order. (*Source:* United States Postal Service)

58. In 2003, there were about 2000 Hilton Hotels world-wide with a total of 348,483 guestrooms. Round the number of guestrooms to the nearest thousand to estimate the average number of guestrooms per hotel. (*Source:* Hilton Hotels Corporation)

59. Write an application of your own that uses the term "bank account" and the numbers 1036 and 524.

 STUDY SKILLS BUILDER

Are You Familiar with Your Textbook Supplements?

There are many student supplements available for additional study. Below, I have listed some of these. See the preface of this text or your instructor for further information.

Chapter Test Prep Video CD. This material is found in the back pocket of your textbook and is fully explained there. The CD contains videos clips solutions to the Chapter Test exercises in this text and are excellent help when studying for chapter tests.

Lecture Video CDs. These video segments are keyed to each section of the text. The material is presented by me, Elayn Martin-Gay, and I have placed a video icon by the exercises in the text that I have worked on the video.

The Student Solutions Manual. This contains worked out solutions to odd-numbered exercises as well as every exercise in the Integrated Reviews, Chapter Reviews, Chapter Tests, and Cumulative Reviews.

Prentice Hall Tutor Center. Mathematics questions may be phoned, faxed, or emailed to this center.

MyMathLab, MathXL, and Interact Math. These are computer and Internet tutorials. This supplement may already be available to you somewhere on campus, for example at your local learning resource lab. Take a moment and find the name and location of any such lab on campus.

As usual, your instructor is your best source of information.

Let's see how you are doing with textbook supplements:

1. Name one way the Chapter Test Prep Video can help you prepare for a chapter test.

2. List any textbook supplements that you have found useful.

3. Have you located and visited a learning resource lab located on your campus?

4. List the textbook supplements that are currently housed in your campus' learning resource lab.

1.9 EXPONENTS, SQUARE ROOTS, AND ORDER OF OPERATIONS

Objectives

A Write Repeated Factors Using Exponential Notation.

B Evaluate Expressions Containing Exponents.

C Evaluate the Square Root of a Perfect Square.

D Use the Order of Operations.

E Find the Area of a Square.

Objective **A** Using Exponential Notation

In the product $2 \cdot 2 \cdot 2 \cdot 2 \cdot 2$, notice that 2 is a factor several times. When this happens, we can use a shorthand notation, called an **exponent,** to write the repeated multiplication.

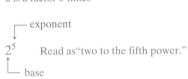

$\underbrace{2 \cdot 2 \cdot 2 \cdot 2 \cdot 2}_{\text{2 is a factor 5 times}}$ can be written as

2^5 Read as "two to the fifth power."

(exponent, base)

This is called **exponential notation.** The **exponent,** 5, indicates how many times the **base,** 2, is a factor.

The table below shows examples of reading exponential notation in words.

Expression	In Words
5^2	"five to the second power" or "five squared."
5^3	"five to the third power" or "five cubed."
5^4	"five to the fourth power."

Usually, an exponent of 1 is not written, so when no exponent appears, we assume that the exponent is 1. For example, $2 = 2^1$ and $7 = 7^1$.

EXAMPLES Write using exponential notation.

1. $4 \cdot 4 \cdot 4 = 4^3$
2. $7 \cdot 7 = 7^2$
3. $5 \cdot 5 \cdot 5 \cdot 5 = 5^4$
4. $6 \cdot 6 \cdot 6 \cdot 8 \cdot 8 \cdot 8 \cdot 8 \cdot 8 = 6^3 \cdot 8^5$

Work Practice Problems 1–4

Objective **B** Evaluating Exponential Expressions

To **evaluate** an exponential expression, we write the expression as a product and then find the value of the product.

EXAMPLES Evaluate.

5. $8^2 = 8 \cdot 8 = 64$
6. $9^1 = 9$
7. $2^5 = 2 \cdot 2 \cdot 2 \cdot 2 \cdot 2 = 32$
8. $5 \cdot 6^2 = 5 \cdot 6 \cdot 6 = 180$

Work Practice Problems 5–8

PRACTICE PROBLEMS 1–4

Write using exponential notation.
1. $2 \cdot 2 \cdot 2$
2. $3 \cdot 3$
3. $10 \cdot 10 \cdot 10 \cdot 10 \cdot 10 \cdot 10$
4. $5 \cdot 5 \cdot 4 \cdot 4 \cdot 4$

PRACTICE PROBLEMS 5–8

Evaluate.
5. 2^3 6. 5^2
7. 10^1 8. $4 \cdot 5^2$

Answers
1. 2^3, 2. 3^2, 3. 10^6, 4. $5^2 \cdot 4^3$,
5. 8, 6. 25, 7. 10, 8. 100

Example 8 illustrates an important property: An exponent applies only to its base. The exponent 2, in $5 \cdot 6^2$, applies only to its base, 6.

> **Helpful Hint**
> An exponent applies only to its base. For example, $4 \cdot 2^3$ means $4 \cdot 2 \cdot 2 \cdot 2$.

> **Helpful Hint**
> Don't forget that 2^4, for example, is *not* $2 \cdot 4$. The expression 2^4 means repeated multiplication of the same factor.
> $$2^4 = 2 \cdot 2 \cdot 2 \cdot 2 = 16, \quad \text{whereas } 2 \cdot 4 = 8$$

✔ **Concept Check** Which of the following statements is correct?

a. 3^6 is the same as $6 \cdot 6 \cdot 6$.
b. "Eight to the fourth power" is the same as 8^4.
c. "Ten squared" is the same as 10^3.
d. 11^2 is the same as $11 \cdot 2$.

Objective C Evaluating Square Roots

A **square root** of a number is one of two identical factors of the number. For example,

$7 \cdot 7 = 49$, so a square root of 49 is 7.

We use this symbol $\sqrt{}$ (called a radical sign) for finding square roots. Since
$7 \cdot 7 = 49$, then $\sqrt{49} = 7$.

PRACTICE PROBLEMS 9–11

Find each square root.

9. $\sqrt{100}$
10. $\sqrt{4}$
11. $\sqrt{1}$

EXAMPLES Find each square root.

9. $\sqrt{25} = 5$ because $5 \cdot 5 = 25$
10. $\sqrt{81} = 9$ because $9 \cdot 9 = 81$
11. $\sqrt{0} = 0$ because $0 \cdot 0 = 0$

▢ **Work Practice Problems 9–11**

> **Helpful Hint**
> Make sure you understand the difference between squaring a number and finding the square root of a number.
> $$9^2 = 9 \cdot 9 = 81 \quad \sqrt{9} = 3 \text{ because } 3 \cdot 3 = 9$$

Answers
9. 10, **10.** 2, **11.** 1

✔ **Concept Check Answer**
b

Not every square root simplifies to a whole number. We will study this more in a later chapter. In this section, we will find square roots of perfect squares only.

A **perfect square** is the product of a whole number multiplied by itself. It may be helpful to study the perfect squares below.

Perfect Squares

$0 = 0 \cdot 0$	$9 = 3 \cdot 3$	$36 = 6 \cdot 6$	$81 = 9 \cdot 9$	$144 = 12 \cdot 12$	$225 = 15 \cdot 15$
$1 = 1 \cdot 1$	$16 = 4 \cdot 4$	$49 = 7 \cdot 7$	$100 = 10 \cdot 10$	$169 = 13 \cdot 13$	$256 = 16 \cdot 16$
$4 = 2 \cdot 2$	$25 = 5 \cdot 5$	$64 = 8 \cdot 8$	$121 = 11 \cdot 11$	$196 = 14 \cdot 14$	$289 = 17 \cdot 17$

Objective D Using the Order of Operations

Suppose that you are in charge of taking inventory at a local bookstore. An employee has given you the number of a certain book in stock as the expression

$$3 + 2 \cdot 10$$

To calculate the value of this expression, do you add first or multiply first? If you add first, the answer is 50. If you multiply first, the answer is 23.

Mathematical symbols wouldn't be very useful if two values were possible for one expression. Thus, mathematicians have agreed that, given a choice, we multiply first.

$$3 + 2 \cdot 10 = 3 + 20 \quad \text{Multiply.}$$
$$= 23 \qquad \text{Add.}$$

This agreement is one of several **order of operations** agreements.

Order of Operations

1. Perform all operations within parentheses ( ), brackets [ ], or other grouping symbols such as fraction bars or square roots.
2. Evaluate any expressions with exponents.
3. Multiply or divide in order from left to right.
4. Add or subtract in order from left to right.

Below we practice using order of operations to simplify expressions.

EXAMPLE 12 Simplify: $2 \cdot 4 - 3 \div 3$

Solution: There are no parentheses and no exponents, so we start by multiplying and dividing, from left to right.

$$2 \cdot 4 - 3 \div 3 = 8 - 3 \div 3 \quad \text{Multiply.}$$
$$= 8 - 1 \qquad \text{Divide.}$$
$$= 7 \qquad \text{Subtract.}$$

■ **Work Practice Problem 12**

PRACTICE PROBLEM 12

Simplify: $8 \cdot 2 - 16 \div 4$

Answer

12. 12

PRACTICE PROBLEM 13

Simplify: $36 \div 3 \cdot 2^2$

EXAMPLE 13 Simplify: $4^2 \div 2 \cdot 4$

Solution: We start by evaluating 4^2.

$4^2 \div 2 \cdot 4 = 16 \div 2 \cdot 4$ Write 4^2 as 16.

Next we multiply or divide *in order* from left to right. Since division appears before multiplication from left to right, we divide first, then multiply.

$16 \div 2 \cdot 4 = 8 \cdot 4$ Divide.

$\quad\quad\quad\quad = 32$ Multiply.

■ **Work Practice Problem 13**

PRACTICE PROBLEM 14

Simplify: $(9 - 8)^3 + 3 \cdot 2^4$

EXAMPLE 14 Simplify: $(8 - 6)^2 + 2^3 \cdot 3$

Solution: $(8 - 6)^2 + 2^3 \cdot 3 = 2^2 + 2^3 \cdot 3$ Simplify inside parentheses.

$\quad\quad\quad = 4 + 8 \cdot 3$ Write 2^2 as 4 and 2^3 as 8.

$\quad\quad\quad = 4 + 24$ Multiply.

$\quad\quad\quad = 28$ Add.

■ **Work Practice Problem 14**

PRACTICE PROBLEM 15

Simplify:
$24 \div [20 - (3 \cdot 4)] + 2^3 - 5$

EXAMPLE 15 Simplify: $4^3 + [3^2 - (10 \div 2)] - 7 \cdot 3$

Solution: Here we begin with the innermost set of parentheses.

$4^3 + [3^2 - (10 \div 2)] - 7 \cdot 3 = 4^3 + [3^2 - 5] - 7 \cdot 3$ Simplify inside parentheses.

$\quad\quad\quad = 4^3 + [9 - 5] - 7 \cdot 3$ Write 3^3 as 9.

$\quad\quad\quad = 4^3 + 4 - 7 \cdot 3$ Simplify inside brackets.

$\quad\quad\quad = 64 + 4 - 7 \cdot 3$ Write 4^3 as 64.

$\quad\quad\quad = 64 + 4 - 21$ Multiply.

$\quad\quad\quad = 47$ Add and subtract from left to right.

■ **Work Practice Problem 15**

PRACTICE PROBLEM 16

Simplify: $\dfrac{49 + 4 \cdot 3 - 5^2}{3(1 + 1)}$

EXAMPLE 16 Simplify: $\dfrac{7 - 2 \cdot 3 + 3^2}{5(2 - 1)}$

Solution: Here, the fraction bar is like a grouping symbol. We simplify above and below the fraction bar separately.

$\dfrac{7 - 2 \cdot 3 + 3^2}{5(2 - 1)} = \dfrac{7 - 2 \cdot 3 + 9}{5(1)}$ Evaluate 3^2 and $(2 - 1)$.

$\quad\quad\quad = \dfrac{7 - 6 + 9}{5}$ Multiply $2 \cdot 3$ in the numerator and add 4 and 1 in the denominator.

$\quad\quad\quad = \dfrac{10}{5}$ Add and subtract from left to right.

$\quad\quad\quad = 2$ Divide.

■ **Work Practice Problem 16**

Answers

13. 48, **14.** 49, **15.** 6, **16.** 6

EXAMPLE 17 Simplify: $64 \div \sqrt{64} \cdot 2 + 4$

Solution: $64 \div \sqrt{64} \cdot 2 + 4 = \underline{64 \div 8} \cdot 2 + 4$ Find the square root.

$= \underline{8 \cdot 2} + 4$ Divide.

$= 16 + 4$ Multiply.

$= 20$ Add.

■ **Work Practice Problem 17**

PRACTICE PROBLEM 17

Simplify: $81 \div \sqrt{81} \cdot 5 + 7$

Objective E **Finding the Area of a Square**

Since a square is a special rectangle, we can find its area by finding the product of its length and its width.

Area of a rectangle = length · width

By recalling that each side of a square has the same measurement, we can use the following procedure to find its area:

Area of a square = length · width
= side · side
= (side)^2

Square | Side
Side

EXAMPLE 18 Find the area of a square whose side measures 5 inches.

Solution: Area of a square = (side)^2
= (5 inches)^2
= 25 square inches

5 inches

The area of the square is 25 square inches.

■ **Work Practice Problem 18**

PRACTICE PROBLEM 18

Find the area of a square whose side measures 11 centimeters.

Answers
17. 52, **18.** 121 sq cm

🖩 CALCULATOR EXPLORATIONS

Exponents

To evaluate an exponent such as 4^7 on a calculator, find the keys marked $\boxed{y^x}$ or $\boxed{\wedge}$ and $\boxed{=}$ or $\boxed{\text{ENTER}}$. To evaluate 4^7, press the keys $\boxed{4}$ $\boxed{y^x}$ (or $\boxed{\wedge}$) $\boxed{7}$ $\boxed{=}$ or $\boxed{\text{ENTER}}$. The display will read $\boxed{\qquad 16384}$. Thus, $4^7 = 16,384$.

Use a calculator to evaluate.

1. 3^6 **2.** 5^6 **3.** 4^5
4. 7^6 **5.** 2^{11} **6.** 6^8

Order of Operations

To see whether your calculator has the order of operations built in, evaluate $5 + 2 \cdot 3$ by pressing the keys $\boxed{5}$ $\boxed{+}$ $\boxed{2}$ $\boxed{\times}$ $\boxed{3}$ $\boxed{=}$ or $\boxed{\text{ENTER}}$. If the display reads $\boxed{11}$, your calculator does have the order of operations

built in. This means that most of the time you can key in a problem exactly as it is written and the calculator will perform operations in the proper order. When evaluating an expression containing parentheses, key in the parentheses. (If an expression contains brackets, key in parentheses.) For example, to evaluate $2[25 - (8 + 4)] - 11$, press the keys $\boxed{2}$ $\boxed{\times}$ $\boxed{(}$ $\boxed{25}$ $\boxed{-}$ $\boxed{(}$ $\boxed{8}$ $\boxed{+}$ $\boxed{4}$ $\boxed{)}$ $\boxed{)}$ $\boxed{-}$ $\boxed{11}$ $\boxed{=}$ or $\boxed{\text{ENTER}}$.

The display will read $\boxed{\quad 15}$.

Use a calculator to evaluate.

7. $7^4 + 5^3$
8. $12^4 - 8^4$
9. $63 \cdot 75 - 43 \cdot 10$
10. $8 \cdot 22 + 7 \cdot 16$
11. $4(15 \div 3 + 2) - 10 \cdot 2$
12. $155 - 2(17 + 3) + 185$

1.9 EXERCISE SET

Objective **A** *Write using exponential notation. See Examples 1 through 4.*

1. $3 \cdot 3 \cdot 3 \cdot 3$

2. $5 \cdot 5 \cdot 5$

3. $7 \cdot 7 \cdot 7 \cdot 7 \cdot 7 \cdot 7 \cdot 7 \cdot 7$

4. $6 \cdot 6 \cdot 6 \cdot 6 \cdot 6$

 5. $12 \cdot 12 \cdot 12$

6. $10 \cdot 10$

 7. $6 \cdot 6 \cdot 5 \cdot 5 \cdot 5$

8. $4 \cdot 4 \cdot 4 \cdot 3 \cdot 3$

9. $9 \cdot 9 \cdot 9 \cdot 8$

10. $7 \cdot 7 \cdot 7 \cdot 4$

11. $3 \cdot 2 \cdot 2 \cdot 2 \cdot 2 \cdot 2$

12. $4 \cdot 6 \cdot 6 \cdot 6 \cdot 6$

13. $3 \cdot 2 \cdot 2 \cdot 5 \cdot 5 \cdot 5$

14. $6 \cdot 6 \cdot 2 \cdot 9 \cdot 9 \cdot 9 \cdot 9$

Objective **B** *Evaluate. See Examples 5 through 8.*

15. 7^2

16. 6^2

 17. 5^3

18. 6^3

19. 2^6

20. 2^7

21. 1^{10}

22. 1^{12}

23. 7^1

24. 8^1

25. 3^5

26. 5^4

27. 2^8

28. 3^3

29. 4^3

30. 4^4

31. 9^2

32. 12^2

33. 9^3

34. 8^3

35. 10^2

36. 10^3

37. 20^1

38. 14^1

39. 3^6

40. 4^5

41. $3 \cdot 2^4$

42. $5 \cdot 3^2$

43. $2 \cdot 3^3$

44. $2 \cdot 7^2$

Objective C *Find each square root. See Examples 9 through 11.*

45. $\sqrt{9}$

46. $\sqrt{36}$

47. $\sqrt{64}$

48. $\sqrt{121}$

49. $\sqrt{144}$

50. $\sqrt{0}$

51. $\sqrt{16}$

52. $\sqrt{169}$

Objective D *Simplify. See Examples 12 through 16. (This section does not contain square roots.)*

53. $15 + 3 \cdot 2$

54. $24 + 6 \cdot 3$

55. $28 \div 7 \cdot 2 + 3$

56. $100 \div 10 \cdot 5 + 4$

57. $28 \div 4 - 3$

58. $42 \div 7 - 6$

59. $14 + \dfrac{24}{8}$

60. $32 + \dfrac{8}{2}$

61. $6 \cdot 5 + 8 \cdot 2$

62. $3 \cdot 4 + 9 \cdot 1$

63. $\dfrac{6 + 8 \div 2}{1^7}$

64. $\dfrac{6 + 9 \div 3}{3^2}$

65. $(3 + 5^2) \div 2 \cdot 3^2$

66. $(13 + 6^2) \div 7 \cdot 4^2$

67. $6^2 \cdot (10 - 8) + 2^3 + 5^2$

68. $5^3 \div (10 + 15) + 9^2 + 3^3$

69. $\dfrac{18 + 6}{2^4 - 2^2}$

70. $\dfrac{15 + 17}{5^2 - 3^2}$

71. $(2 + 5) \cdot (8 - 3)$

72. $(9 - 7) \cdot (12 + 18)$

73. $\dfrac{7(9 - 6) + 3}{3^2 - 3}$

74. $\dfrac{5(12 - 7) - 4}{5^2 - 18}$

75. $5 \div 0 + 24$

76. $18 - 7 \div 0$

77. $2^3 \cdot 4 - (10 \div 5)$

78. $2^4 \cdot 3 - (100 \div 10)$

79. $3^4 - [35 - (12 - 6)]$

80. $[40 - (8 - 2)] - 2^5$

81. $(7 \cdot 5) + [9 \div (3 \div 3)]$

82. $(18 \div 6) + [(3 + 5) \cdot 2]$

83. $8 \cdot [2^2 + (6 - 1) \cdot 2] - 50 \cdot 2$

84. $35 \div [3^2 + (9 - 7) - 2^2] + 10 \cdot 3$

85. $\dfrac{9^2 + 2^2 - 1^2}{8 \div 2 \cdot 3 \cdot 1 \div 3}$

86. $\dfrac{5^2 - 2^3 + 1^4}{10 \div 5 \cdot 4 \cdot 1 \div 4}$

Simplify. See Examples 12 through 17. (This section does contain square roots.)

87. $6 \cdot \sqrt{9} + 3 \cdot \sqrt{4}$

88. $3 \cdot \sqrt{25} + 2 \cdot \sqrt{81}$

89. $4 \cdot \sqrt{49} - 0 \div \sqrt{100}$

90. $7 \cdot \sqrt{36} - 0 \div \sqrt{64}$

91. $\dfrac{\sqrt{4} + 4^2}{5(20 - 16) - 3^2 - 5}$

92. $\dfrac{\sqrt{9} + 9^2}{3(10 - 6) - 2^2 - 1}$

93. $\sqrt{81} \div \sqrt{9} + 4^2 \cdot 2 - 10$

94. $\sqrt{100} \div \sqrt{4} + 3^3 \cdot 2 - 20$

95. $[\sqrt{225} \div (11 - 6) + 2^2] + (\sqrt{25} - \sqrt{1})^2$

96. $[\sqrt{169} \div (20 - 7) + 2^5] - (\sqrt{4} + \sqrt{9})^2$

97. $7^2 - \{18 - [40 \div (4 \cdot 2) + \sqrt{4}] + 5^2\}$

98. $29 - \{5 + 3[8 \cdot (10 - \sqrt{64})] - 50\}$

Objective **E** *Find the area of each square. See Example 18.*

△ **99.**

20 miles

△ **100.**

4 meters

△ **101.**

8 centimeters

△ **102.**

31 feet

Concept Extensions

Answer the following true or false. See the Concept Check in this section.

103. "Five to the sixth power" is the same as 6^5.

104. "Seven cubed" is the same as 7^3.

105. 2^5 is the same as $5 \cdot 5$.

106. 4^9 is the same as $4 \cdot 9$.

Insert grouping symbols (parentheses) so that each given expression evaluates to the given number.

107. $2 + 3 \cdot 6 - 2$; evaluate to 28

108. $2 + 3 \cdot 6 - 2$; evaluate to 20

109. $24 \div 3 \cdot 2 + 2 \cdot 5$; evaluate to 14

110. $24 \div 3 \cdot 2 + 2 \cdot 5$; evaluate to 15

△ **111.** A building contractor is bidding on a contract to install gutters on seven homes in a retirement community, all in the shape shown. To estimate the cost of materials, she needs to know the total perimeter of all seven homes. Find the total perimeter.

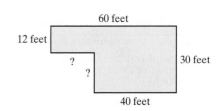

Simplify.

▦ **112.** $25^3 \cdot (45 - 7 \cdot 5) \cdot 5$

▦ **113.** $(7 + 2^4)^5 - (3^5 - 2^4)^2$

114. Explain why $2 \cdot 3^2$ is not the same as $(2 \cdot 3)^2$.

115. Write an expression that simplifies to 5. Use multiplication, division, addition, subtraction, and at least one set of parentheses.

THE BIGGER PICTURE   Operations on Sets of Numbers

Continue your outline started in Section 1.7. Suggestions are once again written to help you complete this part of your outline.

I. **Some Operations on Sets of Numbers**

   A. **Whole Numbers**

      1. **Add or Subtract** (Sections 1.3, 1.4)

      2. **Multiply or Divide** (Sections 1.6, 1.7)

      3. **Exponent:** $3^4 = \overbrace{3 \cdot 3 \cdot 3 \cdot 3}^{4 \text{ factors of } 3} = 81$

      4. **Square Root:** $\sqrt{25} = 5$ *because* $5 \cdot 5 = 25$

      5. **Order of Operations:**

$$24 \div 3 \cdot 2 - (2 + 8)$$
$$= 24 \div 3 \cdot 2 - (10) \quad \text{Parentheses.}$$
$$= 8 \cdot 2 - 10 \qquad\quad \text{Multiply or divide from left to right.}$$
$$= 16 - 10 \qquad\quad\; \text{Multiply or divide from left to right.}$$
$$= 6 \qquad\qquad\qquad \text{Add or subtract from left to right.}$$

Perform the indicated operations.

1. 4^3
2. $2^3 \cdot 6^1$
3. $\sqrt{81}$
4. $\sqrt{9} \cdot \sqrt{25}$
5. $2 + 5(10 - 6)$
6. $20 \div 2 \cdot 5$
7. $867 - 179$
8. $\quad 72$
    $\underline{\times\, 30}$
9. $626 \div 58$
10. $3[(7 - 3)^2 - (25 - 22)^2] + \sqrt{36}$

STUDY SKILLS BUILDER

What to Do the Day of an Exam?

Your first exam may be soon. On the day of an exam, don't forget to try the following:

- Allow yourself plenty of time to arrive.
- Read the directions on the test carefully.
- Read each problem carefully as you take your test. Make sure that you answer the question asked.
- Watch your time and pace yourself so that you may attempt each problem on your test.
- Check your work and answers.
- ***Do not turn your test in early.*** If you have extra time, spend it double-checking your work.

Good luck!

Answer the following questions based on your most recent mathematics exam, whenever that was.

1. How soon before class did you arrive?
2. Did you read the directions on the test carefully?
3. Did you make sure you answered the question asked for each problem on the exam?
4. Were you able to attempt each problem on your exam?
5. If your answer to question 4 is no, list reasons why.
6. Did you have extra time on your exam?
7. If your answer to question 6 is yes, describe how you spent that extra time.

CHAPTER 1   Group Activity

Modeling Subtraction of Whole Numbers

A mathematical concept can be represented or modeled in many different ways. For instance, subtraction can be represented by the following symbolic model:

$$11 - 4$$

The following verbal models can also represent subtraction of these same quantities:

"Four subtracted from eleven" or
"Eleven take away four"

Physical models can also represent mathematical concepts. In these models, a number is represented by that many objects. For example, the number 5 can be represented by five pennies, squares, paper clips, tiles, or bottle caps.

A physical representation of the number 5

Take-Away Model for Subtraction: 11 − 4

- Start with 11 objects.
- Take 4 objects away.
- How many objects remain?

Comparison Model for Subtraction: 11 − 4

- Start with a set of 11 of one type of object and a set of 4 of another type of object.

- Make as many pairs that include one object of each type as possible.

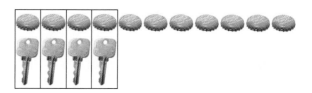

- How many more objects left are in the larger set?

Missing Addend Model for Subtraction: 11 − 4

- Start with 4 objects.
- Continue adding objects until a total of 11 is reached.
- How many more objects were needed to give a total of 11?

Group Activity

Use an appropriate physical model for subtraction to solve each of the following problems. Explain your reasoning for choosing each model.

1. Sneha has assembled 12 computer components so far this shift. If his quota is 20 components, how many more components must he assemble to reach his quota?

2. Yuko has 14 daffodil bulbs to plant in her yard. She planted 5 bulbs in the front yard. How many bulbs does she have left for planting in the backyard?

3. Todd is 19 years old and his sister Tanya is 13 years old. How much older is Todd than Tanya?

Chapter 1 Vocabulary Check

Fill in each blank with one of the words or phrases listed below.

difference	area	square root	addend	divisor	minuend
place value	factor	quotient	subtrahend	exponent	digits
sum	whole numbers	perimeter	dividend	product	

1. The _____ are 0, 1, 2, 3, . . .
2. The _____ of a polygon is its distance around or the sum of the lengths of its sides.
3. The position of each digit in a number determines its _____.
4. An _____ is a shorthand notation for repeated multiplication of the same factor.
5. To find the _____ of a rectangle, multiply length times width.
6. A _____ of a number is one of two identical factors of the number.
7. The _____ used to write numbers are 0, 1, 2, 3, 4, 5, 6, 7, 8, and 9.

Use the facts below for Exercises 8 through 17.

$$2 \cdot 3 = 6 \qquad 4 + 17 = 21 \qquad 20 - 9 = 11 \qquad 5)\overline{35}^{\,7}$$

8. The 21 above is called the _____.
9. The 5 above is called the _____.
10. The 35 above is called the _____.
11. The 7 above is called the _____.
12. The 3 above is called a _____.
13. The 6 above is called the _____.
14. The 20 above is called the _____.
15. The 9 above is called the _____.
16. The 11 above is called the _____.
17. The 4 above is called an _____.

Helpful Hint

Are you preparing for your test? Don't forget to take the Chapter 1 Test on page 109. Then check your answers at the back of the text and use the Chapter Test Prep Video CD to see the fully worked-out solutions to any of the exercises you want to review.

1 Chapter Highlights

DEFINITIONS AND CONCEPTS	EXAMPLES
Section 1.2 Place Value and Names for Numbers	
The **whole numbers** are 0, 1, 2, 3, 4, 5, . . . The position of each digit in a number determines its **place value.** A place-value chart is shown next with the names of the periods given.	0, 14, 968, 5,268,619

Periods

Billions	Millions	Thousands	Ones

Hundred-billions, Ten-billions, Billions, Hundred-millions, Ten-millions, Millions, Hundred-thousands, Ten-thousands, Thousands, Hundreds, Tens, Ones

DEFINITIONS AND CONCEPTS	EXAMPLES

Section 1.2 Place Value and Names for Numbers (*continued*)

To write a whole number in words, write the number in each period followed by the name of the period. (The name of the ones period is not included.)

9,078,651,002 is written as nine billion, seventy-eight million, six hundred fifty-one thousand, two.

To write a whole number in standard form, write the number in each period, followed by a comma.

Four million, seven hundred six thousand, twenty-eight is written as 4,706,028.

Section 1.3 Adding Whole Numbers and Perimeter

To add whole numbers, add the digits in the ones place, then the tens place, then the hundreds place, and so on, carrying when necessary.

Find the sum:

$$
\begin{array}{r}
\overset{2\ 1\ 1}{2689} \leftarrow \text{addend} \\
1735 \leftarrow \text{addend} \\
+\ \ 662 \leftarrow \text{addend} \\
\hline
5086 \leftarrow \text{sum}
\end{array}
$$

The **perimeter** of a polygon is its distance around or the sum of the lengths of its sides.

Find the perimeter of the polygon shown.

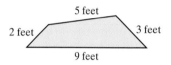

The perimeter is 5 feet + 3 feet + 9 feet + 2 feet = 19 feet.

Section 1.4 Subtracting Whole Numbers

To subtract whole numbers, subtract the digits in the ones place, then the tens place, then the hundreds place, and so on, borrowing when necessary.

Subtract:

$$
\begin{array}{r}
\overset{8\ 15}{79\cancel{5}4} \leftarrow \text{minuend} \\
-5673 \leftarrow \text{subtrahend} \\
\hline
2281 \leftarrow \text{difference}
\end{array}
$$

Section 1.5 Rounding and Estimating

ROUNDING WHOLE NUMBERS TO A GIVEN PLACE VALUE

Step 1. Locate the digit to the right of the given place value.

Step 2. If this digit is 5 or greater, add 1 to the digit in the given place value and replace each digit to its right with 0.

Step 3. If this digit is less than 5, replace it and each digit to its right with 0.

Round 15,721 to the nearest thousand.

15,⑦21   Since the circled digit is 5 or greater, add 1 to the given place value and replace digits to its right with zeros.
Add 1 ↑ Replace with zeros.

15,721 rounded to the nearest thousand is 16,000.

Section 1.6 Multiplying Whole Numbers and Area

To multiply 73 and 58, for example, multiply 73 and 8, then 73 and 50. The sum of these partial products is the product of 73 and 58. Use the notation to the right.

$$
\begin{array}{r}
73 \leftarrow \text{factor} \\
\times\ 58 \leftarrow \text{factor} \\
\hline
584 \leftarrow 73 \times 8 \\
3650 \leftarrow 73 \times 50 \\
\hline
4234 \leftarrow \text{product}
\end{array}
$$

continued

DEFINITIONS AND CONCEPTS	EXAMPLES
Section 1.6 Multiplying Whole Numbers and Area (*continued*)	

| To find the **area** of a rectangle, multiply length times width. | Find the area of the rectangle shown. 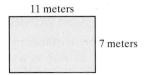 |

$$\text{area of rectangle} = \text{length} \cdot \text{width}$$
$$= (11 \text{ meters})(7 \text{ meters})$$
$$= 77 \text{ square meters}$$

| To multiply by 10, 100, 1000, and so on, form the product by attaching the number of 0s in that number to the other factor. | $39 \cdot 1000 = 39{,}000$
 └ Attach 3 zeros.

 $200 \cdot 4000 = 800{,}000$ Attach 5 zeros.
 ↑
 $2 \cdot 4$ |

Section 1.7   Dividing Whole Numbers

DIVISION PROPERTIES OF 0

The quotient of 0 and any number (except 0) is 0.

The quotient of any number and 0 is not a number. We say that this quotient is undefined.

$$\frac{0}{5} = 0$$

$$\frac{7}{0} \text{ is undefined}$$

To divide larger whole numbers, use the process called **long division** as shown to the right.

$$
\begin{array}{r}
507 \quad \text{R } 2 \leftarrow \text{quotient}\\
\text{divisor} \rightarrow 14\overline{)7100} \longleftarrow \text{dividend}\\
-70\downarrow|\\
\overline{10}|\\
-0\downarrow\\
\overline{100}\\
-98\\
\overline{2}
\end{array}
$$

$5(14) = 70$
Subtract and bring down the 0.
$0(14) = 0$
Subtract and bring down the 0.
$7(14) = 98$
Subtract. The remainder is 2.

To check, see that $507 \cdot 14 + 2 = 7100$.

The **average** of a list of numbers is

$$\text{average} = \frac{\text{sum of numbers}}{\text{number of numbers}}$$

Find the average of 23, 35, and 38.

$$\text{average} = \frac{23 + 35 + 38}{3} = \frac{96}{3} = 32$$

Section 1.8   An Introduction to Problem Solving

PROBLEM-SOLVING STEPS

1. UNDERSTAND the problem.

Suppose that 225 tickets are sold for each performance of a play. How many tickets are sold for 5 performances?

1. UNDERSTAND. Read and reread the problem. Since we want the number of tickets for 5 performances, we multiply.

DEFINITIONS AND CONCEPTS	**EXAMPLES**

| **Section 1.8   An Introduction to Problem Solving (*continued*)** ||

2. TRANSLATE the problem.

2. TRANSLATE.

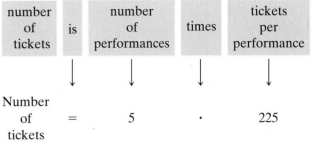

	number of tickets	is	number of performances	times	tickets per performance

$$\text{Number of tickets} = 5 \cdot 225$$

3. SOLVE the problem.

3. SOLVE: See if the answer is reasonable by also estimating.

$$\begin{array}{r} {\scriptstyle 1\,2} \\ 225 \\ \times\quad 5 \\ \hline 1125 \end{array} \text{ exact} \qquad \begin{array}{r} 200 \\ \times\quad 5 \\ \hline 1000 \end{array} \text{ estimate}$$

225 rounds to 200

4. INTERPRET the results.

4. INTERPRET. **Check** your work. The product is reasonable since 1125 is close to our estimated answer of 1000, and **state** your conclusion: There are 1125 tickets sold for 5 performances.

| **Section 1.9   Exponents, Square Roots, and Order of Operations** ||

An **exponent** is a shorthand notation for repeated multiplication of the same factor.

$$\overset{\text{exponent}}{3^{4}} = \underset{\text{4 factors of 3}}{\underbrace{3 \cdot 3 \cdot 3 \cdot 3}} = 81$$
base

A **square root** of a number is one of two identical factors of the number.

$$\sqrt{36} = 6 \quad \text{because} \quad 6 \cdot 6 = 36$$
$$\sqrt{121} = 11 \quad \text{because} \quad 11 \cdot 11 = 121$$
$$\sqrt{0} = 0 \quad \text{because} \quad 0 \cdot 0 = 0$$

ORDER OF OPERATIONS

1. Perform all operations within parentheses ( ), brackets [ ], or other grouping symbols such as square roots or fraction bars.

2. Evaluate any expressions with exponents.

3. Multiply or divide in order from left to right.

4. Add or subtract in order from left to right.

Simplify: $\dfrac{5 + 3^2}{2(7 - 6)}$

Simplify above and below the fraction bar separately.

$$\frac{5 + 3^2}{2(7 - 6)} = \frac{5 + 9}{2(1)} \quad \substack{\text{Evaluate } 3^2 \text{ above the fraction bar.} \\ \text{Subtract: } 7 - 6 \text{ below the fraction bar.}}$$
$$= \frac{14}{2} \quad \substack{\text{Add.} \\ \text{Multiply.}}$$
$$= 7 \quad \text{Divide.}$$

The **area of a square** is $(\text{side})^2$.

Find the area of a square with side length 9 inches.

$$\begin{aligned} \text{Area of the square} &= (\text{side})^2 \\ &= (9 \text{ inches})^2 \\ &= 81 \text{ square inches} \end{aligned}$$

(1.2) *Determine the place value of the digit 4 in each whole number.*

1. 5480

2. 46,200,120

Write each whole number in words.

3. 5480

4. 46,200,120

Write each whole number in expanded form.

5. 6279

6. 403,225,000

Write each whole number in standard form.

7. Fifty-nine thousand, eight hundred

8. Six billion, three hundred four million

The following table shows the populations of the ten largest cities in the United States. Use this table to answer Exercises 9 and 10 and other exercises throughout this review.

Rank	City	2000	1990	1980
1	New York, NY	8,008,278	7,322,564	7,071,639
2	Los Angeles, CA	3,694,820	3,485,398	2,968,528
3	Chicago, IL	2,896,016	2,783,726	3,005,072
4	Houston, TX	1,953,631	1,630,553	1,595,138
5	Philadelphia, PA	1,517,550	1,585,577	1,688,210
6	Phoenix, AZ	1,321,045	983,403	789,704
7	San Diego, CA	1,223,400	1,110,549	875,538
8	Dallas, TX	1,188,580	1,006,877	904,599
9	San Antonio, TX	1,144,646	935,933	785,940
10	Detroit, MI	951,270	1,027,974	1,203,368
(*Source:* U.S. Census Bureau)				

9. Find the population of Houston, Texas, in 1990.

10. Find the population of Los Angeles, California, in 1980.

11. Which city had the smallest population in 1990?

12. Which city had the largest population in 1990?

(1.3) *Add.*

13. $17 + 46$ **14.** $28 + 39$ **15.** $25 + 8 + 15$ **16.** $27 + 9 + 41$ **17.** $932 + 24$

18. $819 + 21$ **19.** $567 + 7383$ **20.** $463 + 6787$ **21.** $91 + 3623 + 497$ **22.** $82 + 1647 + 238$

Solve.

23. Find the sum of 86, 331, and 909.

24. Find the sum of 49, 529, and 308.

25. What is 26,481 increased by 865?

26. What is 38,556 increased by 744?

27. The distance from Chicago to New York City is 714 miles. The distance from New York City to New Delhi, India, is 7318 miles. Find the total distance from Chicago to New Delhi if traveling by air through New York City.

28. Susan Summerline earned salaries of $62,589, $65,340, and $69,770 during the years 2002, 2003, and 2004, respectively. Find her total earnings during those three years.

Find the perimeter of each figure.

△ **29.**
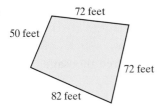
72 feet
50 feet
72 feet
82 feet

△ **30.**

11 kilometers   20 kilometers
35 kilometers

(1.4) *Subtract and then check.*

31. $93 - 79$ **32.** $61 - 27$ **33.** $462 - 397$ **34.** $583 - 279$ **35.** $4000 - 86$ **36.** $8000 - 92$

Solve.

37. Subtract 7965 from 25,862.

38. Subtract 4349 from 39,007.

Use the city population table for Exercises 39 and 40.

39. Find the increase in population for Phoenix, Arizona, from 1980 to 2000.

40. Find the decrease in population for Detroit, Michigan, from 1990 to 2000.

41. Bob Roma is proofreading the Yellow Pages for his county. If he has finished 315 pages of the total 712 pages, how many pages does he have left to proofread?

42. Shelly Winters bought a new car listed at $28,425. She received a discount of $1599 and a factory rebate of $1200. Find how much she paid for the car.

The following bar graph shows the monthly savings account balance for a freshman attending a local community college. Use this graph to answer Exercises 43 through 46.

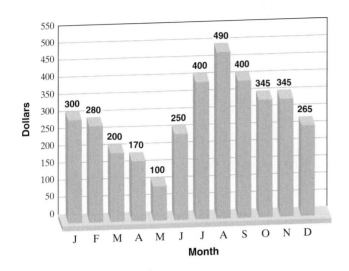

43. During what month was the balance the least?

44. During what month was the balance the greatest?

45. By how much did his balance decrease from February to April?

46. By how much did his balance increase from June to August?

(1.5) *Round to the given place.*

47. 93 to the nearest ten

48. 45 to the nearest ten

49. 467 to the nearest ten

50. 493 to the nearest hundred

51. 4832 to the nearest hundred

52. 57,534 to the nearest thousand

53. 49,683,712 to the nearest million

54. 768,542 to the nearest hundred-thousand

55. In 2003, there were 73,365,880 households in the United States subscribing to cable television services. Round this number to the nearest million. (*Source:* Nielsen Media Research-NTI)

56. In 2003, the total number of employees working for U.S. airlines was 570,868. Round this number to the nearest thousand. (*Source:* The Air Transport Association of America, Inc.)

Estimate the sum or difference by rounding each number to the nearest hundred.

57. $4892 + 647 + 1876$

58. $5925 - 1787$

59. A group of students took a week-long driving trip and traveled 628, 290, 172, 58, 508, 445, and 383 miles on seven consecutive days. Round each distance to the nearest hundred to estimate the distance they traveled.

60. According to the city population table, the 2000 population of Los Angeles was 3,694,820, and for Dallas it was 1,188,580. Round each number to the nearest hundred-thousand and estimate how much larger Los Angeles is than Dallas.

(1.6) *Multiply.*

61. 273
  $\times\ 7$

62. 349
  $\times\ 4$

63. 47
  $\times 30$

64. 69
  $\times 42$

65. 20(8)(5)

66. 25(9)(4)

67.   48
      × 77

68.   77
      × 22

69. 49 · 49 · 0

70. 62 · 88 · 0

71.   586
      × 29

72.   242
      × 37

73.   642
      × 177

74.   347
      × 129

75.   1026
      × 401

76.   2107
      × 302

77. 375 · 1000

78. 108 · 1000

79. 30 · 400

80. 50 · 700

81. 1700 · 3000

82. 1900 · 4000

Solve.

83. Find the product of 5 and 230.

84. Find the product of 6 and 820.

85. Multiply 9 and 12.

86. Multiply 8 and 14.

87. One ounce of Swiss cheese contains 8 grams of fat. How many grams of fat are in 3 ounces of Swiss cheese? (*Source: Home and Garden Bulletin No. 72*, U.S. Department of Agriculture)

88. There were 5283 students enrolled at Weskan State University in the fall semester. Each paid $927 in tuition. Find the total tuition collected.

Find the area of each rectangle.

△ **89.**
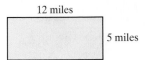
12 miles

5 miles

△ **90.**   20 centimeters
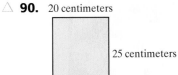
25 centimeters

(1.7) *Divide and then check.*

91. $\dfrac{18}{6}$

92. $\dfrac{36}{9}$

93. 42 ÷ 7

94. 35 ÷ 5

95. 27 ÷ 5

96. 18 ÷ 4

97. 16 ÷ 0

98. 0 ÷ 8

99. 9 ÷ 9

100. 10 ÷ 1

101. $918 \div 0$ **102.** $0 \div 668$ **103.** $5\overline{)167}$ **104.** $8\overline{)159}$ **105.** $26\overline{)626}$

106. $19\overline{)680}$ **107.** $47\overline{)23,792}$ **108.** $53\overline{)48,111}$ **109.** $207\overline{)578,291}$ **110.** $306\overline{)615,732}$

Solve.

111. Find the quotient of 92 and 5.

112. Find the quotient of 86 and 4.

113. One foot is 12 inches. Find how many feet there are in 5496 inches.

114. One mile is 1760 yards. Find how many miles there are in 22,880 yards.

115. Find the average of the numbers 76, 49, 32, and 47.

116. Find the average of the numbers 23, 85, 62, and 66.

(1.8) *Solve.*

117. A box can hold 24 cans of corn. How many boxes can be filled with 648 cans of corn?

118. If a ticket to a movie costs $6, how much do 32 tickets cost?

119. Aspirin was 100 years old in 1997 and was the first U.S. drug made in tablet form. Today, people take 11 billion tablets a year for heart disease prevention and 4 billion tablets a year for headaches. How many more tablets are taken a year for heart disease prevention? (*Source:* Bayer Market Research)

120. The cost to banks when a person uses an ATM (Automatic Teller Machine) is 27¢. The cost to banks when a person deposits a check with a teller is 48¢ more. How much is this cost?

121. A golf pro orders shirts for the company sponsoring a local charity golfing event. Shirts size large cost $32 while shirts size extra-large cost $38. If 15 large shirts and 11 extra-large shirts are ordered, find the cost.

122. Two rectangular pieces of land are purchased: one that measures 65 feet by 110 feet and one that measures 80 feet by 200 feet. Find the total area of land purchased. (*Hint:* Find the area of each rectangle, then add.)

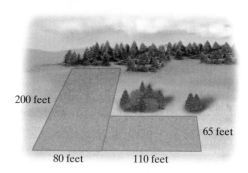

(1.9) *Simplify.*

123. 7^2

124. 5^3

125. $5 \cdot 3^2$

126. $4 \cdot 10^2$

127. $18 \div 3 + 7$

128. $12 - 8 \div 4$

129. $\dfrac{5(6^2 - 3)}{3^2 + 2}$

130. $\dfrac{7(16 - 8)}{2^3}$

131. $48 \div 8 \cdot 2$

132. $27 \div 9 \cdot 3$

133. $2 + 3[1^5 + (20 - 17) \cdot 3] + 5 \cdot 2$

134. $21 - [2^4 - (7 - 5) - 10] + 8 \cdot 2$

Simplify. These exercises contain roots.

135. $\sqrt{81}$

136. $\sqrt{4}$

137. $\sqrt{1}$

138. $\sqrt{0}$

139. $4 \cdot \sqrt{25} - 2 \cdot 7$

140. $8 \cdot \sqrt{49} - 3 \cdot 9$

141. $\left(\sqrt{36} - \sqrt{16}\right)^3 \cdot [10^2 \div (3 + 17)]$

142. $\left(\sqrt{49} - \sqrt{25}\right)^3 \cdot [9^2 \div (2 + 7)]$

143. $\dfrac{5 \cdot 7 - 3 \cdot \sqrt{25}}{2\left(\sqrt{121} - 3^2\right)}$

144. $\dfrac{4 \cdot 8 - 1 \cdot \sqrt{121}}{3\left(\sqrt{81} - 2^3\right)}$

Find the area of each square.

△ **145.** A square with side length of 7 meters.

△ **146.**

3 inches

Mixed Review

Perform the indicated operations.

147. $375 - 68$

148. $729 - 47$

149. 723×3

150. 629×4

151. $264 + 39 + 598$

152. $593 + 52 + 766$

153. $13\overline{)5962}$

154. $18\overline{)4267}$

155. 1968×36

156. 5324×18

157. $2000 - 356$

158. $9000 - 519$

Round to the given place.

159. 736 to the nearest ten

160. 258,371 to the nearest thousand

161. 1999 to the nearest hundred

162. 44,499 to the nearest ten thousand

Write each whole number in words.

163. 36,911

164. 154,863

Write each whole number in standard form.

165. Seventy thousand, nine hundred forty-three

166. Forty-three thousand, four hundred one

Simplify.

167. 4^3

168. 5^3

169. $\sqrt{144}$

170. $\sqrt{100}$

171. $24 \div 4 \cdot 2$

172. $\sqrt{256} - 3 \cdot 5$

173. $\dfrac{8(7-4)-10}{4^2-3^2}$

174. $\dfrac{\left(15+\sqrt{9}\right)\cdot(8-5)}{2^3+1}$

Solve.

175. 36 divided by 9 is what number?

176. What is the product of 2 and 12?

177. 16 increased by 8 is what number?

178. 7 subtracted from 21 is what number?

The following table shows the top-grossing movies for 2003 and 2004. Use this table to answer Exercises 179 and 180.

Movie (2003)	Gross	Movie (2004)	Gross
The Lord of the Rings: The Return of the King	$377,019,000	Shrek 2	$436,471,000
Finding Nemo	$339,714,000	Spider-Man 2	$373,378,000
Pirates of the Caribbean: The Curse of the Black Pearl	$305,389,000	The Passion of the Christ	$370,275,000
The Matrix Reloaded	$281,492,000	Harry Potter and the Prisoner of Azkaban	$249,359,000
Bruce Almighty	$242,590,000	The Incredibles	$242,426,000
(*Source:* Internet Movie Database)			

179. How much more did the top grossing film in 2004 make than the top-grossing film in 2003?

180. Find the total gross of the animated films *Finding Nemo* and *The Incredibles*.

181. A manufacturer of drinking glasses ships his delicate stock in special boxes that can hold 32 glasses. If 1714 glasses are manufactured, how many full boxes are filled? Are there any glasses left over?

182. A teacher orders 2 small white boards for $27 each and 8 boxes of dry erase pens for $4 each. What is her total bill before taxes?

1 CHAPTER TEST

 Use the Chapter Test Prep Video CD to see the fully worked-out solutions to any of the exercises you want to review.

Simplify.

1. Write 82,426 in words.

2. Write "four hundred two thousand, five hundred fifty" in standard form.

3. $59 + 82$

4. $600 - 487$

5. $\begin{array}{r} 496 \\ \times\ \ 30 \\ \hline \end{array}$

6. $52{,}896 \div 69$

7. $2^3 \cdot 5^2$

8. $\sqrt{4} \cdot \sqrt{25}$

9. $0 \div 49$

10. $62 \div 0$

11. $(2^4 - 5) \cdot 3$

12. $16 + 9 \div 3 \cdot 4 - 7$

13. $\dfrac{64 \div 8 \cdot 2}{\left(\sqrt{9} - \sqrt{4}\right)^2 + 1}$

14. $2[(6 - 4)^2 + (22 - 19)^2] + 10$

15. $5698 \cdot 1000$

16. $8000 \cdot 1400$

17. Round 52,369 to the nearest thousand.

Estimate each sum or difference by rounding each number to the nearest hundred.

18. $6289 + 5403 + 1957$

19. $4267 - 2738$

Answers

1. _____

2. _____

3. _____

4. _____

5. _____

6. _____

7. _____

8. _____

9. _____

10. _____

11. _____

12. _____

13. _____

14. _____

15. _____

16. _____

17. _____

18. _____

19. _____

20. _____

21. _____

22. _____

23. _____

24. _____

25. _____

26. _____

27. _____

28. _____

29. _____

Solve.

20. Subtract 15 from 107.

21. Find the sum of 15 and 107.

22. Find the product of 15 and 107.

23. Find the quotient of 107 and 15.

24. Twenty-nine cans of Sherwin-Williams paint cost $493. How much was each can?

25. Jo McElory is looking at two new refrigerators for her apartment. One costs $599 and the other costs $725. How much more expensive is the higher-priced one?

26. One tablespoon of white granulated sugar contains 45 calories. How many calories are in 8 tablespoons of white granulated sugar? (_Source: Home and Garden Bulletin No. 72, U.S. Department of Agriculture_)

27. A small business owner recently ordered 16 digital cameras that cost $430 each and 5 printers that cost $205 each. Find the total cost for these items.

Find the perimeter and the area of each figure.

△ **28.**

Square   5 centimeters

△ **29.**

20 yards

Rectangle   10 yards

2

Multiplying and Dividing Fractions

Fractions are numbers, and like whole numbers, they can be added, subtracted, multiplied, and divided. Fractions are very useful and appear frequently in everyday language, in common phrases like "half an hour," "quarter of a pound," and "third of a cup." This chapter introduces the concept of fractions, presents some basic vocabulary, and demonstrates how to multiply and divide fractions.

Sales of digital cameras are increasing as prices decrease and quality and ease of use increase.

In Section 2.4, Exercise 89, we calculate the face area of the currently smallest digital camera.

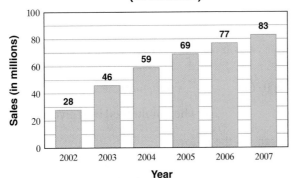

World-wide Sales of Digital Cameras (in millions)

Source: IDC; '05, '06, '07 are projected

A Identify the Numerator
and the Denominator of
a Fraction and Review
Division Properties for
0 and 1.

B Write a Fraction to
Represent the Shaded
Part of a Figure.

C Identify Proper Fractions,
Improper Fractions, and
Mixed Numbers.

D Write Mixed Numbers as
Improper Fractions.

E Write Improper Fractions
as Mixed Numbers or
Whole Numbers.

2.1 INTRODUCTION TO FRACTIONS AND MIXED NUMBERS

Objective **A** Identifying Numerators and Denominators and Reviewing Division Properties for 0 and 1

Whole numbers are used to count whole things or units, such as cars, horses, dollars, and people. To refer to a part of a whole, fractions can be used. Here are some examples of **fractions.** Study these examples for a moment.

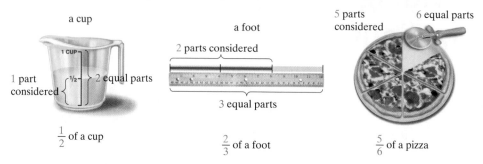

a cup

1 part considered $\left\{ \frac{1}{2} \right\}$ 2 equal parts

$\frac{1}{2}$ of a cup

a foot

2 parts considered

3 equal parts

$\frac{2}{3}$ of a foot

5 parts considered   6 equal parts

$\frac{5}{6}$ of a pizza

In a fraction, the top number is called the **numerator** and the bottom number is called the **denominator.** The bar between the numbers is called the **fraction bar.**

Names	Fraction	Meaning
numerator ⟶ denominator ⟶	$\frac{5}{6}$	⟵ number of parts being considered ⟵ number of equal parts in the whole

EXAMPLES Identify the numerator and the denominator of each fraction.

1. $\frac{3}{7}$ ← numerator
   ← denominator

2. $\frac{13}{5}$ ← numerator
   ← denominator

Helpful Hint Notice the fraction $\frac{11}{1} = 11$, or also $11 = \frac{11}{1}$.

■ **Work Practice Problems 1–2**

Before we continue further, don't forget from Section 1.7 that the fraction bar indicates division. Let's review some division properties for 1 and 0.

$\frac{9}{9} = 1$ because $1 \cdot 9 = 9$ $\frac{11}{1} = 11$ because $11 \cdot 1 = 11$

$\frac{0}{6} = 0$ because $0 \cdot 6 = 0$ $\frac{6}{0}$ *is undefined* because there is no number that when multiplied by 0 gives 6.

In general, we can say the following.

Let n be any whole number except 0.

$\frac{n}{n} = 1$ $\frac{0}{n} = 0$

$\frac{n}{1} = n$ $\frac{n}{0}$ is undefined.

EXAMPLES Simplify.

3. $\dfrac{5}{5} = 1$ **4.** $\dfrac{0}{7} = 0$ **5.** $\dfrac{10}{1} = 10$ **6.** $\dfrac{3}{0}$ is undefined

▣ **Work Practice Problems 3–6**

Objective B Writing Fractions to Represent Shaded Areas of Figures

One way to become familiar with the concept of fractions is to visualize fractions with shaded figures. We can then write a fraction to represent the shaded area of the figure.

EXAMPLES Write a fraction to represent the shaded part of each figure.

7. In this figure, 2 of the 5 equal parts are shaded. Thus, the fraction is $\dfrac{2}{5}$.

$\dfrac{2}{5}$ ← number of parts shaded
← number of equal parts

8. In this figure, 3 of the 10 rectangles are shaded. Thus, the fraction is $\dfrac{3}{10}$.

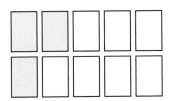

$\dfrac{3}{10}$ ← number of parts shaded
← number of equal parts

▣ **Work Practice Problems 7–8**

EXAMPLES Write a fraction to represent the shaded part of the diagram.

9.

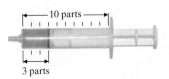

The fraction is $\dfrac{3}{10}$.

10.

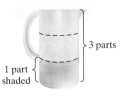

The fraction is $\dfrac{1}{3}$.

▣ **Work Practice Problems 9–10**

PRACTICE PROBLEMS 3–6

Simplify.

3. $\dfrac{0}{2}$ **4.** $\dfrac{8}{8}$

5. $\dfrac{4}{0}$ **6.** $\dfrac{20}{1}$

PRACTICE PROBLEMS 7–8

Write a fraction to represent the shaded part of each figure.

7.

8. ◯ ◯ ◯
◯ ◯ ◯

PRACTICE PROBLEMS 9–10

Write a fraction to represent the part of the whole shown.

9. Just consider this part of the syringe

10.

Answers

3. 0, **4.** 1, **5.** undefined, **6.** 20,

7. $\dfrac{3}{8}$, **8.** $\dfrac{1}{6}$, **9.** $\dfrac{7}{10}$, **10.** $\dfrac{9}{16}$

PRACTICE PROBLEMS 11–12

Draw and shade a part of a figure to represent each fraction.

11. $\frac{2}{3}$ of a figure

12. $\frac{7}{11}$ of a figure

EXAMPLES Draw a figure and then shade a part of it to represent each fraction.

11. $\frac{5}{6}$ of a figure

We will use a geometric figure such as a rectangle. Since the denominator is 6, we divide it into 6 equal parts. Then we shade 5 of the equal parts.

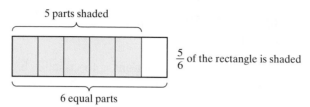

5 parts shaded

$\frac{5}{6}$ of the rectangle is shaded

6 equal parts

12. $\frac{3}{8}$ of a figure

If you'd like, our figure can consist of 8 triangles of the same size. We will shade 3 of the triangles.

3 triangles shaded

$\frac{3}{8}$ of the diagram is shaded

8 triangles

🔲 **Work Practice Problems 11–12**

✔**Concept Check** If  represents $\frac{6}{7}$ of a whole diagram, sketch the whole diagram.

PRACTICE PROBLEM 13

Of the nine planets in our solar system, seven are farther from the Sun than Venus is. What fraction of the planets are farther from the Sun than Venus is?

EXAMPLE 13 **Writing Fractions from Real-Life Data**

Of the nine planets in our solar system, two are closer to the Sun than Earth is. What fraction of the planets are closer to the Sun than Earth is?

Solution: The fraction of planets closer to the Sun than Earth is:

$\frac{2}{9}$ ← number of planets closer
    ← number of planets in our solar system

Thus, $\frac{2}{9}$ of the planets in our solar system are closer to the Sun than the Earth is.

🔲 **Work Practice Problem 13**

Answers

11. answers may vary; for example,

12. answers may vary; for example,

13. $\frac{7}{9}$

✔ **Concept Check Answer**

Objective C Identifying Proper Fractions, Improper Fractions, and Mixed Numbers

A **proper fraction** is a fraction whose numerator is less than its denominator. Proper fractions are less than 1. For example, the shaded portion of the triangle's area is represented by $\frac{2}{3}$.

$\frac{2}{3}$

An **improper fraction** is a fraction whose numerator is greater than or equal to its denominator. Improper fractions are greater than or equal to 1. The shaded part of the group of circles' area below is $\frac{9}{4}$.

The shaded part of the rectangle's area is $\frac{6}{6}$. (Recall from earlier that $\frac{6}{6}$ simplifies to 1 and notice that 1 whole figure or rectangle is shaded below.)

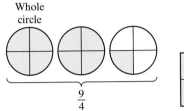

Whole circle

$\frac{9}{4}$

$\frac{6}{6}$

A **mixed number** contains a whole number and a fraction. Mixed numbers are greater than 1. Earlier, we wrote the shaded part of the group of circles below as the improper fraction $\frac{9}{4}$. Now let's write the shaded part as a mixed number. The shaded part of the group of circles' area is $2\frac{1}{4}$. (Read "two and one-fourth.")

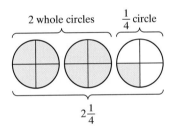

2 whole circles $\frac{1}{4}$ circle

$2\frac{1}{4}$

EXAMPLE 14 Identify each number as a proper fraction, improper fraction, or mixed number.

a. $\frac{6}{7}$ is a proper fraction

b. $\frac{13}{12}$ is an improper fraction

c. $\frac{2}{2}$ is an improper fraction

d. $\frac{99}{101}$ is a proper fraction

e. $1\frac{7}{8}$ is a mixed number

f. $\frac{93}{74}$ is an improper fraction

■ **Work Practice Problem 14**

> **Helpful Hint**
> The mixed number $2\frac{1}{4}$ represents $2 + \frac{1}{4}$.

PRACTICE PROBLEM 14

Identify each number as a proper fraction, improper fraction, or mixed number.

a. $\frac{5}{8}$ **b.** $\frac{7}{7}$

c. $\frac{14}{13}$ **d.** $\frac{13}{14}$

e. $5\frac{1}{4}$ **f.** $\frac{100}{49}$

Answers

14. a. proper fraction, **b.** improper fraction, **c.** improper fraction, **d.** proper fraction, **e.** mixed number, **f.** improper fraction

PRACTICE PROBLEMS 15-16

Represent the shaded part of each figure group as both an improper fraction and a mixed number.

15.

16.

EXAMPLES Represent the shaded part of each figure group's area as both an improper fraction and a mixed number.

15.

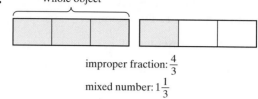

Whole object

improper fraction: $\frac{4}{3}$

mixed number: $1\frac{1}{3}$

16.

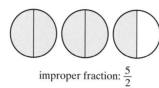

improper fraction: $\frac{5}{2}$

mixed number: $2\frac{1}{2}$

🔲 **Work Practice Problems 15-16**

✔**Concept Check** If you were to estimate $2\frac{1}{8}$ by a whole number, would you choose 2 or 3? Why?

Objective D Writing Mixed Numbers as Improper Fractions

Notice from Examples 15 and 16 that mixed numbers and improper fractions were both used to represent the shaded area of the figure groups. For example,

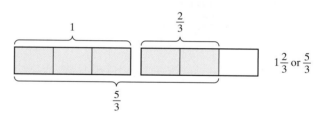

$1\frac{2}{3}$ or $\frac{5}{3}$

The following steps may be used to write a mixed number as an improper fraction:

Writing a Mixed Number as an Improper Fraction

To write a mixed number as an improper fraction:

Step 1: Multiply the denominator of the fraction by the whole number.

Step 2: Add the numerator of the fraction to the product from Step 1.

Step 3: Write the sum from Step 2 as the numerator of the improper fraction over the original denominator.

For example,

$$1\frac{2}{3} = \frac{\overbrace{3 \cdot 1}^{\text{Step 1}} + \overbrace{2}^{\text{Step 2}}}{3} = \frac{3 + 2}{3} = \frac{5}{3}$$

Step 3

EXAMPLE 17 Write each as an improper fraction.

a. $4\frac{2}{9} = \frac{9 \cdot 4 + 2}{9} = \frac{36 + 2}{9} = \frac{38}{9}$

b. $1\frac{8}{11} = \frac{11 \cdot 1 + 8}{11} = \frac{11 + 8}{11} = \frac{19}{11}$

▣ **Work Practice Problem 17**

PRACTICE PROBLEM 17

Write each as an improper fraction.

a. $2\frac{5}{7}$ b. $5\frac{1}{3}$

c. $9\frac{3}{10}$ d. $1\frac{1}{5}$

Objective **E** **Writing Improper Fractions as Mixed Numbers or Whole Numbers**

Just as there are times when an improper fraction is preferred, sometimes a mixed or a whole number better suits a situation. To write improper fractions as mixed or whole numbers, we use division. Recall once again from Section 1.7 that the fraction bar means division. This means that the fraction

$\frac{5}{3}$ $\begin{array}{l}\text{numerator}\\\text{denominator}\end{array}$ means $3\overline{)5}$
$\qquad\qquad\qquad\quad\uparrow\ \ \uparrow$
$\qquad\qquad\qquad\ \ \ \text{numerator}$
$\qquad\qquad\qquad \text{denominator}$

Writing an Improper Fraction as a Mixed Number or a Whole Number

To write an improper fraction as a mixed number or a whole number:

Step 1: Divide the denominator into the numerator.

Step 2: The whole number part of the mixed number is the quotient. The fraction part of the mixed number is the remainder over the original denominator.

$$\text{quotient}\,\frac{\text{remainder}}{\text{original denominator}}$$

For example,

$\qquad\quad$ Step 1
$\qquad\qquad\ \overset{\frown}{1}$
$\frac{5}{3}:\ 3\overline{)5}$
$\qquad\quad \underline{3}$
$\qquad\quad\ 2$

$\qquad\quad$ Step 2
$\frac{5}{3} = 1\frac{\overset{\frown}{2}}{3}\ \leftarrow \text{remainder}$
$\qquad\ \ \uparrow\ \ \ \leftarrow \text{original denominator}$
$\qquad \text{quotient}$

EXAMPLE 18 Write each as a mixed number or a whole number.

a. $\frac{30}{7}$ b. $\frac{16}{15}$ c. $\frac{84}{6}$

Solution:

a. $\frac{30}{7}:\ 7\overline{)30}$ $\qquad\frac{30}{7} = 4\frac{2}{7}$
$\qquad\quad\ \ \underline{28}$
$\qquad\qquad\ 2$

Continued on next page

PRACTICE PROBLEM 18

Write each as a mixed number or a whole number.

a. $\frac{8}{5}$ b. $\frac{17}{6}$ c. $\frac{48}{4}$

d. $\frac{75}{13}$ e. $\frac{51}{7}$ f. $\frac{21}{20}$

Answers

17. a. $\frac{19}{7}$, b. $\frac{16}{3}$, c. $\frac{93}{10}$, d. $\frac{6}{5}$,

18. a. $1\frac{3}{5}$, b. $2\frac{5}{6}$, c. 12,

d. $5\frac{10}{13}$, e. $7\frac{2}{7}$, f. $1\frac{1}{20}$

b. $\dfrac{16}{15}$ $15\overline{\smash{)}16}$ $\dfrac{1}{}$ $\dfrac{16}{15} = 1\dfrac{1}{15}$

$\dfrac{15}{1}$

c. $\dfrac{84}{6}$ $6\overline{\smash{)}84}$ $\dfrac{14}{}$ $\dfrac{84}{6} = 14$ Since the remainder is 0, the result is the whole number 14.

$\dfrac{6}{24}$

$\dfrac{24}{0}$

🔲 **Work Practice Problem 18**

Helpful Hint

When the remainder is 0, the improper fraction is a whole number. For example, $\dfrac{92}{4} = 23$.

$4\overline{\smash{)}92}$ $\dfrac{23}{}$

$\dfrac{8}{12}$

$\dfrac{12}{0}$

Mental Math

Objective A Mixed Practice *Identify the numerator and the denominator of each fraction and identify each fraction as proper or improper. See Examples 1, 2, and 14.*

1. $\dfrac{1}{2}$

2. $\dfrac{1}{4}$

3. $\dfrac{10}{3}$

4. $\dfrac{53}{21}$

5. $\dfrac{15}{15}$

6. $\dfrac{26}{26}$

Objective A *Simplify. See Examples 3 through 6.*

1. $\dfrac{21}{21}$ **2.** $\dfrac{14}{14}$ **3.** $\dfrac{5}{0}$ **4.** $\dfrac{1}{0}$ **5.** $\dfrac{13}{1}$ **6.** $\dfrac{14}{1}$

7. $\dfrac{0}{20}$ **8.** $\dfrac{0}{17}$ **9.** $\dfrac{10}{0}$ **10.** $\dfrac{0}{18}$ **11.** $\dfrac{16}{1}$ **12.** $\dfrac{18}{18}$

Objective B *Write a fraction to represent the shaded part of each. See Examples 7 through 10.*

13.

14.

15.
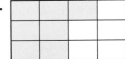

16.

17.

18.

19.

20.

21.

22.

23.

1 mile

24.

Draw and shade a part of a diagram to represent each fraction. See Examples 11 and 12.

25. $\frac{1}{5}$ of a diagram

26. $\frac{1}{16}$ of a diagram

27. $\frac{7}{8}$ of a diagram

28. $\frac{3}{5}$ of a diagram

29. $\frac{6}{7}$ of a diagram

30. $\frac{7}{9}$ of a diagram

31. $\frac{4}{4}$ of a diagram

32. $\frac{6}{6}$ of a diagram

Write each fraction. See Example 13.

33. Of the 131 students at a small private school, 42 are freshmen. What fraction of the students are freshmen?

34. Of the 78 executives at a private accounting firm, 61 are women. What fraction of the executives are women?

35. Use Exercise 33 to answer a and b.
   a. How many students are *not* freshmen?
   b. What fraction of the students are *not* freshmen?

36. Use Exercise 34 to answer a and b.
   a. How many of the executives are men?
   b. What fraction of the executives are men?

37. As of 2005, the United States has had 43 different presidents. A total of eight U.S. presidents were born in the state of Virginia, more than any other state. What fraction of U.S. presidents were born in Virginia? (*Source: 2005 World Almanac and Book of Facts*)

38. Of the nine planets in our solar system, four have days that are longer than the 24-hour Earth day. What fraction of the planets have longer days than Earth has? (*Source:* National Space Science Data Center)

Eight U.S. Presidents

39. The hard drive in Aaron Hawn's Computer can hold 70 gigabytes of information. He has currently used 27 gigabytes. What fraction of his hard drive has he used?

40. There are 12 inches in a foot. What fractional part of a foot does 5 inches represent?

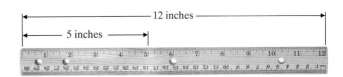

41. There are 31 days in the month of March. What fraction of the month does 11 days represent?

42. There are 60 minutes in an hour. What fraction of an hour does 37 minutes represent?

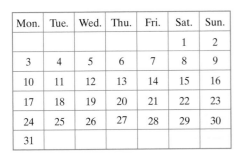

Mon.	Tue.	Wed.	Thu.	Fri.	Sat.	Sun.
					1	2
3	4	5	6	7	8	9
10	11	12	13	14	15	16
17	18	19	20	21	22	23
24	25	26	27	28	29	30
31						

43. In a basic college mathematics class containing 31 students, there are 18 freshmen, 10 sophomores, and 3 juniors. What fraction of the class is sophomores?

44. In a family with 11 children, there are 4 boys and 7 girls. What fraction of the children is girls?

45. Thirty-three states in the United States contain federal Indian reservations.
  a. What fraction of the states contain Indian reservations?
  b. How many states do not contain Indian reservations?
  c. What fraction of the states do not contain Indian reservations? (*Source:* Tiller Research, Inc., Albuquerque, NM)

46. Consumer fireworks are legal in 40 states in the United States.
  a. In what fraction of the states are consumer fireworks legal?
  b. In how many states are consumer fireworks illegal?
  c. In what fraction of the states are consumer fireworks illegal? (*Source:* United States Fireworks Safety Council)

47. A bag contains 50 red or blue marbles. If 21 marbles are blue,
  a. What *fraction* of the marbles are blue?
  b. How many marbles are red?
  c. What *fraction* of the marbles are red?

48. An art dealer is taking inventory. His shop contains a total of 37 pieces, which are all sculptures, watercolor paintings, or oil paintings. If there are 15 watercolor paintings and 17 oil paintings, answer each question.
  a. What fraction of the inventory is watercolor paintings?
  b. What fraction of the inventory is oil paintings?
  c. How many sculptures are there?
  d. What fraction of the inventory is sculptures?

Objective C *Write the shaded area in each figure group as (a) an improper fraction and (b) a mixed number. See Examples 15 and 16.*

49.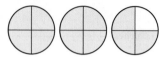

50.

51.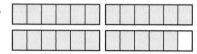

52.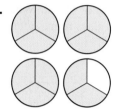

53.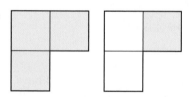

54.

55.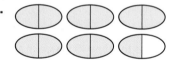

56.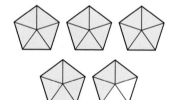

Objective D *Write each mixed number as an improper fraction. See Example 17.*

57. $2\frac{1}{3}$ **58.** $6\frac{3}{4}$ **59.** $3\frac{3}{5}$ **60.** $2\frac{5}{9}$ **61.** $6\frac{5}{8}$ **62.** $7\frac{3}{8}$

63. $2\frac{11}{15}$ **64.** $1\frac{13}{17}$ **65.** $11\frac{6}{7}$ **66.** $12\frac{2}{5}$ **67.** $6\frac{6}{13}$ **68.** $8\frac{9}{10}$

69. $4\dfrac{13}{24}$ **70.** $5\dfrac{17}{25}$ **71.** $17\dfrac{7}{12}$ **72.** $12\dfrac{7}{15}$ ◉ **73.** $9\dfrac{7}{20}$ **74.** $10\dfrac{14}{27}$

75. $2\dfrac{51}{107}$ **76.** $3\dfrac{27}{125}$ **77.** $166\dfrac{2}{3}$ **78.** $114\dfrac{2}{7}$

Objective **E** *Write each improper fraction as a mixed number or a whole number. See Example 18.*

◉ **79.** $\dfrac{17}{5}$ **80.** $\dfrac{13}{7}$ ◉ **81.** $\dfrac{37}{8}$ **82.** $\dfrac{64}{9}$ **83.** $\dfrac{47}{15}$ **84.** $\dfrac{65}{12}$

85. $\dfrac{46}{21}$ **86.** $\dfrac{67}{17}$ **87.** $\dfrac{198}{6}$ **88.** $\dfrac{112}{7}$ **89.** $\dfrac{225}{15}$ **90.** $\dfrac{196}{14}$

91. $\dfrac{200}{3}$ **92.** $\dfrac{300}{7}$ **93.** $\dfrac{247}{23}$ **94.** $\dfrac{437}{53}$ **95.** $\dfrac{319}{18}$ **96.** $\dfrac{404}{21}$

97. $\dfrac{182}{175}$ **98.** $\dfrac{149}{143}$ **99.** $\dfrac{737}{112}$ **100.** $\dfrac{901}{123}$

Review

Simplify. See Section 1.9.

101. 3^2 **102.** 4^3 **103.** 5^3 **104.** 3^4

Write each using exponents.

105. $7 \cdot 7 \cdot 7 \cdot 7 \cdot 7$ **106.** $5 \cdot 5 \cdot 5 \cdot 5$ **107.** $2 \cdot 2 \cdot 2 \cdot 3$ **108.** $4 \cdot 4 \cdot 10 \cdot 10 \cdot 10$

Concept Extensions

Write each fraction.

109. In your own words, explain how to write an improper fraction as a mixed number.

110. In your own words, explain how to write a mixed number as an improper fraction.

Identify the larger fraction for each pair.

111. $\frac{1}{2}$ or $\frac{2}{3}$ (*Hint:* Represent each fraction by the shaded part of equivalent figures. Then compare the shaded areas.)

112. $\frac{7}{4}$ or $\frac{3}{5}$ (*Hint:* Identify each as a proper fraction or an improper fraction.)

Solve. See the Concept Check in this section.

113. If  represents $\frac{4}{9}$ of a whole diagram, sketch the whole diagram.

114. If △ △ represents $\frac{1}{3}$ of a whole diagram, sketch the whole diagram.

115. The Wendy's Corporation owns restaurants with five different names, as shown on the bar graph. What fraction of restaurants owned by Wendy's corporation are named "Wendy's" restaurants? (*Source:* The Wendy's Corporation)

116. The Public Broadcasting Service (PBS) provides programming to the noncommercial public TV stations of the United States. The table shows a breakdown of the public television licensees by type. Each licensee operates one or more PBS member TV stations. What fraction of the public television licensees are universities or colleges? (*Source:* The Public Broadcast Service)

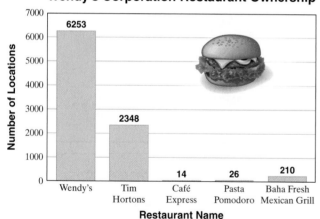

Wendy's Corporation Restaurant Ownership

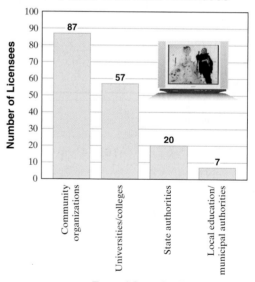

Public Television Licensees

117. Habitat for Humanity is a nonprofit organization that helps provide affordable housing to families in need. Habitat for Humanity does its work of building and renovating houses through 1651 local affiliates in the United States and 634 international affiliates. What fraction of the total Habitat for Humanity affiliates are located in the United States? (*Hint:* First find the total number of affiliates.) (*Source:* Habitat for Humanity International)

118. The United States Marine Corps (USMC) has five principal training centers in California, three in North Carolina, two in South Carolina, one in Arizona, one in Hawaii, and one in Virginia. What fraction of the total USMC principal training centers are located in California? (*Source:* U.S. Department of Defense)

 STUDY SKILLS BUILDER

Have You Decided to Complete This Course Successfully?

Ask yourself if one of your current goals is to complete this course successfully.

If it is not a goal of yours, ask yourself why? One common reason is fear of failure. Amazingly enough, fear of failure alone can be strong enough to keep many of us from doing our best in any endeavor.

Another common reason is that you simply haven't taken the time to make successfully completing this course one of your goals. How do you do this? Start by writing this goal in your mathematics notebook. Then list steps you will take to ensure success. A great first step is to read or reread Section 1.1 and make a commitment to try the suggestions in that section.

Good luck, and don't forget that a positive attitude will make a big difference.

Let's see how you are doing.

1. Have you decided to make "successfully completing this course" a goal of yours? If no, please list reasons why this has not happened. Study your list and talk to your instructor about this.

2. If your answer to question 1 is yes, take a moment and list in your notebook further specific goals that will help you achieve this major goal of successfully completing this course. (For example, "My goal this semester is not to miss any of my mathematics classes.")

3. Rate your commitment to this course with a number between 1 and 5. Use the diagram below to help.

High Commitment		Average Commitment		Not committed at all
5	4	3	2	1

4. If you have rated your personal commitment level (from the exercise above) as a 1, 2, or 3, list the reasons why this is so. Then determine whether it is possible to increase your commitment level to a 4 or 5.

2.2 FACTORS AND PRIME FACTORIZATION

To perform many operations with fractions, it is necessary to be able to factor a number. In this section, only the **natural numbers**—1, 2, 3, 4, 5, and so on—will be considered.

✔ **Concept Check** How are the natural numbers and the whole numbers alike? How are they different?

Objective **A** Finding Factors of Numbers

Recall that when numbers are multiplied to form a product, each number is called a factor. Since $5 \cdot 9 = 45$, both 5 and 9 are **factors** of 45, and $5 \cdot 9$ is called a **factorization** of 45.

The two-number factorizations of 45 are

$1 \cdot 45 \quad 3 \cdot 15 \quad 5 \cdot 9$

Thus, we say that the factors of 45 are $1, 3, 5, 9, 15,$ and 45.

Helpful Hint

From our definition of factor above, notice that a **factor** of a number divides the number evenly (with a remainder of 0). For example,

$$\frac{45}{1)\overline{45}} \quad \frac{15}{3)\overline{45}} \quad \frac{9}{5)\overline{45}} \quad \frac{5}{9)\overline{45}} \quad \frac{3}{15)\overline{45}} \quad \frac{1}{45)\overline{45}}$$

PRACTICE PROBLEM 1

Find all the factors of each number.

a. 15 **b.** 7 **c.** 24

EXAMPLE 1 Find all the factors of 20.

Solution: First we write all the two-number factorizations of 20.

$1 \cdot 20 = 20$
$2 \cdot 10 = 20$
$4 \cdot 5 = 20$

The factors of 20 are $1, 2, 4, 5, 10,$ and 20.

☐ **Work Practice Problem 1**

Objective **B** Identifying Prime and Composite Numbers

Of all the ways to factor a number, one special way is called the **prime factorization.** To help us write prime factorizations, we first review prime and composite numbers.

Prime Numbers

A **prime number** is a natural number that has exactly two different factors, 1 and itself.

The first several prime numbers are

$2, 3, 5, 7, 11, 13, 17$

It would be helpful to memorize these.

If a natural number other than 1 is not a prime number, it is called a **composite number.**

Answers

1. a. $1, 3, 5, 15,$ **b.** $1, 7,$
c. $1, 2, 3, 4, 6, 8, 12, 24$

✔ **Concept Check Answer**

answers may vary

Composite Numbers

A **composite number** is any natural number, other than 1, that is not prime.

> **Helpful Hint**
> The natural number 1 is neither prime nor composite.

EXAMPLE 2 Determine whether each number is prime or composite. Explain your answers.

3,   9,   11,   17,   26

Solution: The number 3 is prime. Its only factors are 1 and 3 (itself).
The number 9 is composite. It has more than two factors: 1, 3, and 9.
The number 11 is prime. Its only factors are 1 and 11.
The number 17 is prime. Its only factors are 1 and 17.
The number 26 is composite. Its factors are 1, 2, 13, and 26.

Work Practice Problem 2

Objective C Finding Prime Factorizations

Now we are ready to find **prime factorizations** of numbers.

Prime Factorization

The **prime factorization** of a number is the factorization in which all the factors are prime numbers.

For example, the prime factorization of 12 is $2 \cdot 2 \cdot 3$ because

$12 = 2 \cdot 2 \cdot 3$ and each number is a prime number.

There is only one prime factorization for any given number. In other words, the prime factorization of a number is unique.

> **Helpful Hint**
> Don't forget that multiplication is commutative, so $2 \cdot 2 \cdot 3$ can also be written as $2 \cdot 3 \cdot 2$ or $3 \cdot 2 \cdot 2$ or $2^2 \cdot 3$. Any one of these can be called *the prime factorization of* 12.

EXAMPLE 3 Find the prime factorization of 45.

Solution: The first prime number, 2, does not divide 45 evenly (with a remainder of 0). The second prime number, 3, does, so we divide 45 by 3.

$$\begin{array}{r} 15 \\ 3\overline{)45} \end{array}$$

Because 15 is not prime and 3 also divides 15 evenly, we divide by 3 again.

$$\begin{array}{r} 5 \\ 3\overline{)15} \\ 3\overline{)45} \end{array}$$

Continued on next page

PRACTICE PROBLEM 2

Determine whether each number is prime or composite. Explain your answers.

21, 13, 18, 29, 39

PRACTICE PROBLEM 3

Find the prime factorization of 28.

Answers

2. 13, 29 are prime. 21, 18, and 39 are composite.   **3.** $2^2 \cdot 7$

The quotient, 5, is a prime number, so we are finished. The prime factorization of 45 is

$$45 = 3 \cdot 3 \cdot 5 \quad \text{or} \quad 45 = 3^2 \cdot 5,$$

using exponents.

▣ Work Practice Problem 3

There are a few quick **divisibility tests** to determine whether a number is divisible by the primes 2, 3, or 5. (A number is divisible by 2, for example, if 2 divides it evenly.)

Divisibility Tests

A whole number is divisible by:

- **2** if the last digit is 0, 2, 4, 6, or 8.

  13↓2 is divisible by 2 since the last digit is a 2.

- **3** if the sum of the digits is divisible by 3.

  144 is divisible by 3 since $1 + 4 + 4 = 9$ is divisible by 3.

- **5** if the last digit is 0 or 5.

  111↓5 is divisible by 5 since the last digit is a 5.

Helpful Hint

Here are a few other divisibility tests you may find interesting. A whole number is divisible by:

- **4** if its last two digits are divisible by 4.

  1712 is divisible by 4.

- **6** if it's divisible by 2 and 3.

  9858 is divisible by 6.

- **9** if the sum of its digits is divisible by 9.

  5238 is divisible by 9 since $5 + 2 + 3 + 8 = 18$ is divisible by 9.

For the next few examples, we will begin the division process with the smallest prime number factor of the given number. Remember that since multiplication is commutative, this is not necessary. As long as the divisor is a prime number factor, this process works.

PRACTICE PROBLEM 4

Find the prime factorization of 120.

EXAMPLE 4 Find the prime factorization of 180.

Solution: We divide 180 by 2 and continue dividing until the quotient is no longer divisible by 2. We then divide by the next largest prime number, 3, until the quotient is no longer divisible by 3. We continue this process until the quotient is a prime number.

$$
\begin{array}{r}
5 \\
3\overline{)\ 15} \\
3\overline{)\ 45} \\
2\overline{)\ 90} \\
2\overline{)180}
\end{array}
$$

Answer

4. $2^3 \cdot 3 \cdot 5$

Thus, the prime factorization of 180 is

$$180 = 2 \cdot 2 \cdot 3 \cdot 3 \cdot 5 \quad \text{or} \quad 180 = 2^2 \cdot 3^2 \cdot 5,$$

using exponents.

🔲 **Work Practice Problem 4**

EXAMPLE 5 Find the prime factorization of 945.

Solution: This number is not divisible by 2 but is divisible by 3. We will begin by dividing 945 by 3.

$$
\begin{array}{r}
7 \\
5\overline{)35} \\
3\overline{)105} \\
3\overline{)315} \\
3\overline{)945}
\end{array}
$$

Thus, the prime factorization of 945 is

$$945 = 3 \cdot 3 \cdot 3 \cdot 5 \cdot 7 \quad \text{or} \quad 945 = 3^3 \cdot 5 \cdot 7$$

🔲 **Work Practice Problem 5**

Another way to find the prime factorization is to use a factor tree, as shown in the next example.

EXAMPLE 6 Use a factor tree to find the prime factorization of 18.

Solution: We begin by writing 18 as a product of two natural numbers greater than 1, say $2 \cdot 9$.

$$
\begin{array}{c}
18 \\
\diagup\diagdown \\
2 \cdot 9
\end{array}
$$

The number 2 is prime, but 9 is not. So we write 9 as $3 \cdot 3$.

$$
\begin{array}{c}
18 \\
\diagup\diagdown \\
2 \cdot 9 \\
\downarrow \quad \diagup\diagdown \\
2 \cdot 3 \cdot 3
\end{array}
$$

Each factor is now prime, so the prime factorization is

$$18 = 2 \cdot 3 \cdot 3 \quad \text{or} \quad 18 = 2 \cdot 3^2,$$

using exponents.

🔲 **Work Practice Problem 6**

In this text, we will write the factorization of a number from the smallest factor to the largest factor.

PRACTICE PROBLEM 5

Find the prime factorization of 756.

PRACTICE PROBLEM 6

Use a factor tree to find the prime factorization of 70.

Answers

5. $2^2 \cdot 3^3 \cdot 7$, **6.** $2 \cdot 5 \cdot 7$

PRACTICE PROBLEM 7

Use a factor tree to find the prime factorization of each number.

a. 30   **b.** 56   **c.** 72

 EXAMPLE 7 Use a factor tree to find the prime factorization of 24.

Solution:
$$24$$
$$4 \cdot 6$$
$$2 \cdot 2 \cdot 2 \cdot 3$$

The prime factorization of 24 is

$$24 = 2 \cdot 2 \cdot 2 \cdot 3 \quad \text{or} \quad 2^3 \cdot 3,$$

using exponents.

◻ **Work Practice Problem 7**

✔ **Concept Check** True or false? Two different numbers can have exactly the same prime factorization. Explain your answer.

Helpful Hint

When using a factor tree, we arrive at the same prime factorization of a number no matter what original factors we use. For example, let's factor 24 again from Example 7.

Still, $24 = 2^3 \cdot 3$.

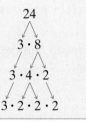
$$24$$
$$3 \cdot 8$$
$$3 \cdot 4 \cdot 2$$
$$3 \cdot 2 \cdot 2 \cdot 2$$

PRACTICE PROBLEM 8

Use a factor tree to find the prime factorization of 117.

EXAMPLE 8 Use a factor tree to find the prime factorization of 175.

Solution: We begin by writing 175 as a product of two numbers greater than 1, say $7 \cdot 25$.

$$175$$
$$7 \cdot 25$$
$$7 \cdot 5 \cdot 5$$

The prime factorization of 175 is

$$175 = 5 \cdot 5 \cdot 7 \quad \text{or} \quad 175 = 5^2 \cdot 7$$

◻ **Work Practice Problem 8**

Answers

7. a. $2 \cdot 3 \cdot 5$,   **b.** $2^3 \cdot 7$,   **c.** $2^3 \cdot 3^2$

8. $3^2 \cdot 13$

✔ **Concept Check Answer**

false; answers may vary

Objective A *List all the factors of each number. See Example 1.*

1. 8   **2.** 6   **3.** 25   **4.** 30   **5.** 4   **6.** 9

7. 18   **8.** 48   **9.** 29   **10.** 37   **11.** 80   **12.** 100

13. 12   **14.** 28   **15.** 34   **16.** 26

Objective B *Identify each number as prime or composite. See Example 2.*

17. 7   **18.** 5   **19.** 4   **20.** 10   **21.** 23   **22.** 13

23. 49   **24.** 45   **25.** 67   **26.** 89   **27.** 39   **28.** 21

29. 31   **30.** 27   **31.** 63   **32.** 51   **33.** 119   **34.** 147

Objective C *Find the prime factorization of each number. Write any repeated factors using exponents. See Examples 3 through 8.*

35. 32   **36.** 80   **37.** 15   **38.** 21   **39.** 40   **40.** 63

41. 36   **42.** 64   **43.** 39   **44.** 56   **45.** 60   **46.** 84

47. 110   **48.** 130   **49.** 85   **50.** 93   **51.** 128   **52.** 81

53. 154   **54.** 198   **55.** 300   **56.** 360   **57.** 240   **58.** 836

59. 828   **60.** 504   **61.** 882   **62.** 405   **63.** 637   **64.** 539

Objectives B C **Mixed Practice** *Find the prime factorization of each composite number. Write prime if the number is prime.*

65. 33   **66.** 48   **67.** 98   **68.** 54   **69.** 67   **70.** 59

71. 459   **72.** 208   **73.** 97   **74.** 103   **75.** 700   **76.** 1000

Review

Round each whole number to the indicated place value. See Section 1.5.

77. 4267 hundreds   **78.** 7,658,240 ten-thousands   **79.** 4,286,340 tens

80. 19,764 thousands   **81.** 10,292,876 millions

With all the recent low-carbohydrate diets, the number of new no- and low-carb ice cream products has greatly increased. Use this bar graph to answer the questions below. See Section 2.1.

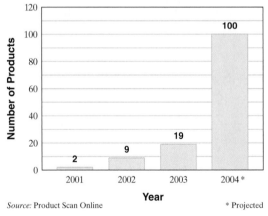

New No-Carb and Low-Carb Ice Cream Product

Number of Products vs. Year

2001: 2
2002: 9
2003: 19
2004*: 100

Source: Product Scan Online   * Projected

82. Find the total number of new products for the years shown.

83. What fraction of new products were introduced in 2003?

84. What fraction of new products were introduced in 2002?

Concept Extensions

Find the prime factorization of each number.

85. 34,020

86. 131,625

 87. In your own words, define a prime number.

88. The number 2 is a prime number. All other even natural numbers are composite numbers. Explain why.

89. Why are we interested in the prime factorization of nonzero whole numbers only?

90. Two students have different prime factorizations for the same number. Is this possible? Explain.

STUDY SKILLS BUILDER

Organizing a Notebook

It's never too late to get organized. If you need ideas about organizing a notebook for your mathematics course, try some of these:

- Use a spiral or ring binder notebook with pockets and use it for mathematics only.
- Start each page by writing the book's section number you are working on at the top.
- When your instructor is lecturing, take notes. *Always* include any examples your instructor works for you.
- Place your worked-out homework exercises in your notebook immediately after the lecture notes from that section. This way, a section's worth of material is together.
- Homework exercises: Attempt all assigned homework. For odd-numbered exercises, you are not through until you check your answers against the back of the book. Correct any exercises with incorrect answers. You may want to place a "?" by any homework exercises or notes that you need to ask questions about. Also, consider placing a "!" by any notes or exercises you feel are important.

- Place graded quizzes in the pockets of your notebook. If you are using a binder, you can place your quizzes in a special section of your binder.

Let's check your notebook organization by answering the following questions.

1. Do you have a spiral or ring binder notebook for your mathematics course only?

2. Have you ever had to flip through several sheets of notes and work in your mathematics notebook to determine what section's work you are in?

3. Are you now writing the textbook's section number at the top of each notebook page?

4. Have you ever lost or had trouble finding a graded quiz or test?

5. Are you now placing all your graded work in a dedicated place in your notebook?

6. Are you attempting all of your homework and placing all of your work in your notebook?

7. Are you checking and correcting your homework in your notebook? If not, why not?

8. Are you writing in your notebook the examples your instructor works for you in class?

2.3 SIMPLEST FORM OF A FRACTION

Objective **A** Writing Fractions in Simplest Form

Fractions that represent the same portion of a whole are called **equivalent fractions.**

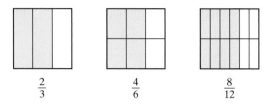

$$\frac{2}{3} \qquad \frac{4}{6} \qquad \frac{8}{12}$$

For example, $\frac{2}{3}, \frac{4}{6}$, and $\frac{8}{12}$ all represent the same shaded portion of the rectangle's area, so they are equivalent fractions.

$$\frac{2}{3} = \frac{4}{6} = \frac{8}{12}$$

A special form of a fraction is called **simplest form.**

Simplest Form of a Fraction

A fraction is written in **simplest form** or **lowest terms** when the numerator and the denominator have no common factors other than 1.

For example, the fraction $\frac{2}{3}$ is in simplest form because 2 and 3 have no common factor other than 1. The fraction $\frac{4}{6}$ is *not* in simplest form because 4 and 6 both have a factor of 2. That is, 2 is a common factor of 4 and 6. The process of writing a fraction in simplest form is called **simplifying** the fraction.

To simplify $\frac{4}{6}$ and write it as $\frac{2}{3}$, let's first study a few properties. Recall from Section 2.1 that any nonzero whole number n divided by itself is 1.

Any nonzero number n divided by itself is 1.

$$\frac{5}{5} = 1, \ \frac{17}{17} = 1, \ \frac{24}{24} = 1, \text{ or, in general, } \frac{n}{n} = 1$$

Also, in general, if $\frac{a}{b}$ and $\frac{c}{d}$ are fractions (with b and d not 0), the following is true.

$$\frac{a \cdot c}{b \cdot d} = \frac{a}{b} \cdot \frac{c}{d}*$$

These properties allow us to do the following:

$$\frac{4}{6} = \frac{2 \cdot 2}{2 \cdot 3} = \frac{2}{2} \cdot \frac{2}{3} = 1 \cdot \frac{2}{3} = \frac{2}{3}$$
$\quad \qquad \qquad \qquad \underset{\uparrow}{\llcorner \text{This is 1}}$

When 1 is multiplied by a number, the result is the same number.

*Note: We will study this concept further in the next section.

EXAMPLE 1 Write in simplest form: $\dfrac{12}{20}$

Solution: Notice that 12 and 20 have a common factor of 4.

$$\frac{12}{20} = \frac{4\cdot 3}{4\cdot 5} = \frac{4}{4}\cdot\frac{3}{5} = 1\cdot\frac{3}{5} = \frac{3}{5}$$

Since 3 and 5 have no common factors (other than 1), $\dfrac{3}{5}$ is in simplest form.

▪ **Work Practice Problem 1**

If you have trouble finding common factors, write the prime factorization of the numerator and the denominator.

EXAMPLE 2 Write in simplest form: $\dfrac{42}{66}$

Solution: Let's write the prime factorizations of 42 and 66.

$$\frac{42}{66} = \frac{2\cdot 3\cdot 7}{2\cdot 3\cdot 11} = \frac{2}{2}\cdot\frac{3}{3}\cdot\frac{7}{11} = 1\cdot 1\cdot\frac{7}{11} = \frac{7}{11}$$

▪ **Work Practice Problem 2**

In the example above, you may have saved time by noticing that 42 and 66 have a common factor of 6.

$$\frac{42}{66} = \frac{6\cdot 7}{6\cdot 11} = \frac{6}{6}\cdot\frac{7}{11} = 1\cdot\frac{7}{11} = \frac{7}{11}$$

Helpful Hint Writing the prime factorizations of the numerator and the denominator is helpful in finding any common factors.

EXAMPLE 3 Write in simplest form: $\dfrac{10}{27}$

Solution:

$$\frac{10}{27} = \frac{2\cdot 5}{3\cdot 3\cdot 3} \quad \text{Prime factorizations of 10 and 27.}$$

Since 10 and 27 have no common factors, $\dfrac{10}{27}$ is already in simplest form.

▪ **Work Practice Problem 3**

EXAMPLE 4 Write in simplest form: $\dfrac{30}{108}$

Solution:

$$\frac{30}{108} = \frac{2\cdot 3\cdot 5}{2\cdot 2\cdot 3\cdot 3\cdot 3} = \frac{2}{2}\cdot\frac{3}{3}\cdot\frac{5}{2\cdot 3\cdot 3} = 1\cdot 1\cdot\frac{5}{18} = \frac{5}{18}$$

▪ **Work Practice Problem 4**

We can use a shortcut procedure with common factors when simplifying.

$$\frac{4}{6} = \frac{\overset{1}{\cancel{2}}\cdot 2}{\underset{1}{\cancel{2}}\cdot 3} = \frac{1\cdot 2}{1\cdot 3} = \frac{2}{3} \quad \text{Divide out the common factor of 2 in the numerator and denominator.}$$

PRACTICE PROBLEM 1
Write in simplest form: $\dfrac{30}{45}$

PRACTICE PROBLEM 2
Write in simplest form: $\dfrac{39}{51}$

PRACTICE PROBLEM 3
Write in simplest form: $\dfrac{9}{50}$

PRACTICE PROBLEM 4
Write in simplest form: $\dfrac{49}{112}$

Answers
1. $\dfrac{2}{3}$, **2.** $\dfrac{13}{17}$, **3.** $\dfrac{9}{50}$, **4.** $\dfrac{7}{16}$

This procedure is possible because dividing out a common factor in the numerator and denominator is the same as removing a factor of 1 in the product.

Writing a Fraction in Simplest Form

To write a fraction in simplest form, write the prime factorization of the numerator and the denominator and then divide both by all common factors.

PRACTICE PROBLEM 5

Write in simplest form: $\dfrac{64}{20}$

EXAMPLE 5 Write in simplest form: $\dfrac{72}{26}$

Solution:

$$\frac{72}{26} = \frac{\overset{1}{\cancel{2}} \cdot 2 \cdot 2 \cdot 3 \cdot 3}{\underset{1}{\cancel{2}} \cdot 13} = \frac{1 \cdot 2 \cdot 2 \cdot 3 \cdot 3}{1 \cdot 13} = \frac{36}{13},$$

which can also be written as

$$2\frac{10}{13}$$

◻ **Work Practice Problem 5**

✔ **Concept Check** Which is the correct way to simplify the fraction $\dfrac{15}{25}$? Or are both correct? Explain.

a. $\dfrac{15}{25} = \dfrac{3 \cdot \overset{1}{\cancel{5}}}{5 \cdot \underset{1}{\cancel{5}}} = \dfrac{3}{5}$ **b.** $\dfrac{1\overset{1}{\cancel{5}}}{2\underset{1}{\cancel{5}}} = \dfrac{11}{21}$

PRACTICE PROBLEM 6

Write in simplest form: $\dfrac{8}{56}$

EXAMPLE 6 Write in simplest form: $\dfrac{6}{60}$

Solution:

$$\frac{6}{60} = \frac{\overset{1}{\cancel{2}} \cdot \overset{1}{\cancel{3}}}{\underset{1}{\cancel{2}} \cdot 2 \cdot \underset{1}{\cancel{3}} \cdot 5} = \frac{1 \cdot 1}{1 \cdot 2 \cdot 1 \cdot 5} = \frac{1}{10}$$

◻ **Work Practice Problem 6**

Helpful Hint

Be careful when all factors of the numerator or denominator are divided out. In Example 6, the numerator was $1 \cdot 1 = 1$, so the final result was $\dfrac{1}{10}$.

In the fraction of Example 6, $\dfrac{6}{60}$, you may have immediately noticed that the largest common factor of 6 and 60 is 6. If so, you may simply divide out that common factor.

$$\frac{6}{60} = \frac{\overset{1}{\cancel{6}}}{\underset{1}{\cancel{6}} \cdot 10} = \frac{1}{1 \cdot 10} = \frac{1}{10} \qquad \text{Divide out the common factor of 6.}$$

Answers

5. $\dfrac{16}{5}$ or $3\dfrac{1}{5}$, 6. $\dfrac{1}{7}$

✔ **Concept Check Answers**

a. correct, **b.** incorrect

Notice that the result, $\dfrac{1}{10}$, is in simplest form. If it were not, we would repeat the same procedure until the result was in simplest form.

EXAMPLE 7 Write in simplest form: $\dfrac{45}{75}$

Solution: You may write the prime factorizations of 45 and 75 or you may notice that these two numbers have a common factor of 15.

$$\frac{45}{75} = \frac{3 \cdot \overset{1}{\cancel{15}}}{5 \cdot \underset{1}{\cancel{15}}} = \frac{3 \cdot 1}{5 \cdot 1} = \frac{3}{5}$$

The numerator and denominator of $\dfrac{3}{5}$ have no common factors other than 1, so $\dfrac{3}{5}$ is in simplest form.

🔲 **Work Practice Problem 7**

PRACTICE PROBLEM 7

Write in simplest form: $\dfrac{42}{48}$

Objective B Determining Whether Two Fractions Are Equivalent

Recall that two fractions are equivalent if they represent the same part of a whole. One way to determine whether two fractions are equivalent is to see whether they simplify to the same fraction.

EXAMPLE 8 Determine whether $\dfrac{16}{40}$ and $\dfrac{10}{25}$ are equivalent.

Solution: Simplify each fraction.

$$\frac{16}{40} = \frac{\overset{1}{\cancel{8}} \cdot 2}{\underset{1}{\cancel{8}} \cdot 5} = \frac{1 \cdot 2}{1 \cdot 5} = \frac{2}{5}$$

$$\frac{10}{25} = \frac{2 \cdot \overset{1}{\cancel{5}}}{5 \cdot \underset{1}{\cancel{5}}} = \frac{2 \cdot 1}{5 \cdot 1} = \frac{2}{5}$$

Since these fractions are the same, $\dfrac{16}{40} = \dfrac{10}{25}$.

🔲 **Work Practice Problem 8**

PRACTICE PROBLEM 8

Determine whether $\dfrac{7}{9}$ and $\dfrac{21}{27}$ are equivalent.

There is a shortcut method you may use to check or test whether two fractions are equivalent. In the example above, we learned that the fractions are equivalent, or

$$\frac{16}{40} = \frac{10}{25}$$

In this example above, we call $25 \cdot 16$ and $40 \cdot 10$ **cross products** because they are the products one obtains by multiplying across.

Cross Products

$$25 \cdot 16 \qquad \qquad 40 \cdot 10$$

$$\frac{16}{40} = \frac{10}{25}$$

Notice that these cross products are equal

$$25 \cdot 16 = 400, \quad 40 \cdot 10 = 400$$

Answers

7. $\dfrac{7}{8}$, **8.** equivalent

In general, this is true for equivalent fractions.

Equality of Fractions

$$8 \cdot 6 \qquad\qquad \frac{6}{24} \stackrel{?}{=} \frac{2}{8} \qquad\qquad 24 \cdot 2$$

Since the cross products ($8 \cdot 6 = 48$ and $24 \cdot 2 = 48$) are equal, the fractions are equal.

Note: If the cross products are not equal, the fractions are not equal.

PRACTICE PROBLEM 9

Determine whether $\dfrac{4}{13}$ and $\dfrac{5}{18}$ are equivalent.

EXAMPLE 9 Determine whether $\dfrac{8}{11}$ and $\dfrac{19}{26}$ are equivalent.

Solution: Let's check cross products.

$$26 \cdot 8 = 208 \qquad \frac{8}{11} \stackrel{?}{=} \frac{19}{26} \qquad 11 \cdot 19 = 209$$

Since $208 \neq 209$, then $\dfrac{8}{11} \neq \dfrac{19}{26}$.

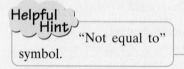

Helpful Hint "Not equal to" symbol.

◾ **Work Practice Problem 9**

Objective **C** ### Solving Problems by Writing Fractions in Simplest Form

Many real-life problems can be solved by writing fractions. To make the answers clearer, these fractions should be written in simplest form.

PRACTICE PROBLEM 10

Eighty pigs were used in a recent study of olestra, a calorie-free fat substitute. A group of 12 of these pigs were fed a diet high in fat. What fraction of the pigs were fed the high-fat diet in this study? Write your answer in simplest form. (*Source:* from a study conducted by the Procter & Gamble Company)

EXAMPLE 10 Calculating the Fraction of Memorials in Washington, D.C.

There are 28 national memorials in the United States. Seven of these are located in Washington, D.C. What fraction of the national memorials in the United States can be found in Washington, D.C.? Write the fraction in simplest form.
(*Source:* National Park Service)

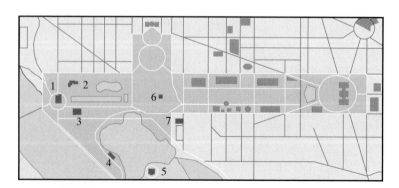

Solution: First we determine the fraction of national memorials located in Washington, D.C.

$\dfrac{7}{28}$ ← number of national memorials in Washington, D.C.
← total number of national memorials in U.S.

Next we simplify the fraction.

$$\frac{7}{28} = \frac{\overset{1}{\cancel{7}}}{\underset{1}{\cancel{7}} \cdot 4} = \frac{1}{1 \cdot 4} = \frac{1}{4}$$

Thus, $\dfrac{1}{4}$ of the United States' national memorials are in Washington, D.C.

🔲 **Work Practice Problem 10**

🖩 CALCULATOR EXPLORATIONS Simplifying Fractions

Scientific Calculator

Many calculators have a fraction key, such as $\boxed{a \, b/c}$, that allows you to simplify a fraction on the calculator. For example, to simplify $\dfrac{324}{612}$, enter

$\boxed{3}\ \boxed{2}\ \boxed{4}\ \boxed{a\,b/c}\ \boxed{6}\ \boxed{1}\ \boxed{2}\ \boxed{=}$

The display will read

$\boxed{\quad 9 \mid 17 \quad}$

which represents $\dfrac{9}{17}$, the original fraction simplified.

Helpful Hint

The Calculator Explorations boxes in this chapter provide only an introduction to fraction keys on calculators. Any time you use a calculator, there are both advantages and limitations to its use. Never rely solely on your calculator. It is very important that you understand how to perform all operations on fractions by hand in order to progress through later topics. For further information, talk to your instructor.

Use your calculator to simplify each fraction.

1. $\dfrac{128}{224}$ 2. $\dfrac{231}{396}$ 3. $\dfrac{340}{459}$ 4. $\dfrac{999}{1350}$

5. $\dfrac{810}{432}$ 6. $\dfrac{315}{225}$ 7. $\dfrac{243}{54}$ 8. $\dfrac{689}{455}$

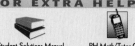

Objective Ⓐ *Write each fraction in simplest form. See Examples 1 through 7.*

1. $\dfrac{3}{12}$ **2.** $\dfrac{5}{30}$ **3.** $\dfrac{4}{42}$ **4.** $\dfrac{9}{48}$ 💿 **5.** $\dfrac{14}{16}$

6. $\dfrac{22}{34}$ **7.** $\dfrac{20}{30}$ **8.** $\dfrac{70}{80}$ **9.** $\dfrac{35}{50}$ **10.** $\dfrac{25}{55}$

11. $\dfrac{63}{81}$ **12.** $\dfrac{21}{49}$ 💿 **13.** $\dfrac{24}{40}$ **14.** $\dfrac{36}{54}$ **15.** $\dfrac{27}{64}$

16. $\dfrac{32}{63}$ **17.** $\dfrac{25}{40}$ **18.** $\dfrac{36}{42}$ **19.** $\dfrac{40}{64}$ **20.** $\dfrac{28}{60}$

21. $\dfrac{56}{68}$ **22.** $\dfrac{39}{42}$ **23.** $\dfrac{36}{24}$ **24.** $\dfrac{60}{36}$ **25.** $\dfrac{90}{120}$

26. $\dfrac{60}{150}$ 💿 **27.** $\dfrac{70}{196}$ **28.** $\dfrac{98}{126}$ **29.** $\dfrac{66}{308}$ **30.** $\dfrac{65}{234}$

31. $\dfrac{55}{85}$ **32.** $\dfrac{78}{90}$ **33.** $\dfrac{75}{350}$ **34.** $\dfrac{72}{420}$ **35.** $\dfrac{189}{216}$

36. $\dfrac{144}{162}$ **37.** $\dfrac{288}{480}$ **38.** $\dfrac{135}{585}$ **39.** $\dfrac{224}{16}$ **40.** $\dfrac{270}{15}$

Objective Ⓑ *Determine whether each pair of fractions is equivalent. See Examples 8 and 9.*

41. $\dfrac{3}{6}$ and $\dfrac{4}{8}$ **42.** $\dfrac{3}{9}$ and $\dfrac{2}{6}$ 💿 **43.** $\dfrac{7}{11}$ and $\dfrac{5}{8}$ **44.** $\dfrac{2}{5}$ and $\dfrac{4}{11}$

45. $\dfrac{10}{15}$ and $\dfrac{6}{9}$ **46.** $\dfrac{4}{10}$ and $\dfrac{6}{15}$ 💿 **47.** $\dfrac{3}{9}$ and $\dfrac{6}{18}$ **48.** $\dfrac{2}{8}$ and $\dfrac{7}{28}$

49. $\dfrac{10}{13}$ and $\dfrac{12}{15}$ **50.** $\dfrac{16}{20}$ and $\dfrac{9}{12}$ **51.** $\dfrac{8}{18}$ and $\dfrac{12}{24}$ **52.** $\dfrac{6}{21}$ and $\dfrac{14}{35}$

Objective **C** *Solve. Write each fraction in simplest form. See Example 10.*

53. A work shift for an employee at McDonald's consists of 8 hours. What fraction of the employee's work shift is represented by 2 hours?

54. Two thousand baseball caps were sold one year at the U.S. Open Golf Tournament. What fractional part of this total does 200 caps represent?

55. There are 5280 feet in a mile. What fraction of a mile is represented by 2640 feet?

56. There are 100 centimeters in 1 meter. What fraction of a meter is 20 centimeters?

57. Fifteen states in the United States have Ritz-Carlton hotels. (*Source:* Ritz-Carlton Hotel Company, LLC)

   a. What fraction of states can claim at least one Ritz-Carlton hotel?

   b. How many states do not have a Ritz-Carlton hotel?

   c. Write the fraction of states without a Ritz-Carlton hotel.

58. There were 74 national monuments in the United States. Ten of these monuments are located in New Mexico. (*Source:* National Park Service)

   a. What fraction of the national monuments in the United States can be found in New Mexico?

   b. How many of the national monuments in the United States are found outside New Mexico

   c. Write the fraction of national monuments found in states other than New Mexico.

59. The outer wall of the Pentagon is 24 inches wide. Ten inches is concrete, 8 inches is brick, and 6 inches is limestone. What fraction of the wall is concrete? (*Source: USA Today*, 1/28/2000)

60. There are 35 students in a biology class. If 10 students made an A on the first test, what fraction of the students made an A?

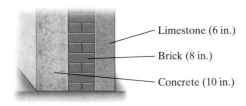

   Limestone (6 in.)

   Brick (8 in.)

   Concrete (10 in.)

61. As Internet usage grows in the United States, more and more state governments are placing services online. Twenty-eight states have Web sites that allow residents to pay their state income tax online.

   a. How many states do not have this type of Web site?

   b. What fraction of states do not have this type of Web site? (*Source:* Center for Digital Government)

62. Chris Callac just bought a brand new 2005 Toyota Camry for $22,000. His old car was traded in for $10,000.

   a. How much of his purchase price was not covered by his trade-in?

   b. What fraction of the purchase price was not covered by the trade-in?

Review

Multiply. See Section 1.6.

63.   91
      × 4

64.   73
      × 8

65.   387
      × 6

66.   562
      × 9

67.   72
      × 35

68.   238
      × 26

Concept Extensions

69. In your own words, define equivalent fractions.

70. Given a fraction, say $\frac{3}{8}$, how many fractions are there that are equivalent to it? Explain your answer.

Write each fraction in simplest form.

71. $\dfrac{3975}{6625}$

72. $\dfrac{9506}{12{,}222}$

There are generally considered to be eight basic blood types. The table shows the number of people with the various blood types in a typical group of 100 blood donors. Use the table to answer Exercises 73 through 77. Write each answer in simplest form.

Distribution of Blood Types in Blood Donors	
Blood Type	**Number of People**
O Rh-positive	37
O Rh-negative	7
A Rh-positive	36
A Rh-negative	6
B Rh-positive	9
B Rh-negative	1
AB Rh-positive	3
AB Rh-negative	1
(*Source:* American Red Cross Biomedical Services)	

73. What fraction of blood donors have blood type A Rh-positive?

74. What fraction of blood donors have an O blood type?

75. What fraction of blood donors have an AB blood type?

76. What fraction of blood donors have a B blood type?

77. What fraction of blood donors have the negative Rh-factor?

The following graph is called a circle graph or pie chart. Each sector (shaped like a piece of pie) shows the fraction of entering college freshmen who expect to major in each discipline shown. The whole circle represents the entire class of college freshmen. Use this graph to answer Exercises 78 through 81.

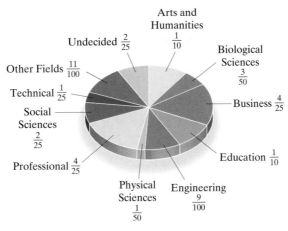

Arts and Humanities $\frac{1}{10}$

Undecided $\frac{2}{25}$

Other Fields $\frac{11}{100}$

Technical $\frac{1}{25}$

Social Sciences $\frac{2}{25}$

Professional $\frac{4}{25}$

Physical Sciences $\frac{1}{50}$

Engineering $\frac{9}{100}$

Education $\frac{1}{10}$

Business $\frac{4}{25}$

Biological Sciences $\frac{3}{50}$

Source: Higher Education Research Institute

78. What fraction of entering college freshmen plan to major in education?

79. What fraction of entering college freshmen plan to major in social sciences?

80. Why is the Professional sector the same size as the Business sector?

81. Why is the Physical Sciences sector smaller than the Biological Sciences sector?

Summary on Fractions, Mixed Numbers, and Factors

Answers

1. _____

2. _____

3. _____

4. _____

5. _____

6. _____

7. _____

8. _____

9. _____

10. _____

11. _____

12. _____

13. _____

14. _____

15. _____

16. _____

17. _____

18. _____

19. _____

20. _____

Use a fraction to represent the shaded area of each figure. If the fraction is improper, also write the fraction as a mixed number.

1.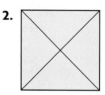

2.

Solve.

3. In a survey, 73 people out of 85 get fewer than 8 hours of sleep each night. What fraction of people in the survey get fewer than 8 hours of sleep?

4. Sketch a diagram to represent $\frac{9}{13}$.

Simplify.

5. $\frac{11}{11}$

6. $\frac{17}{1}$

7. $\frac{0}{3}$

8. $\frac{7}{0}$

Write each mixed number as an improper fraction.

9. $3\frac{1}{8}$

10. $5\frac{3}{5}$

11. $9\frac{6}{7}$

12. $20\frac{1}{7}$

Write each improper fraction as a mixed number or a whole number.

13. $\frac{20}{7}$

14. $\frac{55}{11}$

15. $\frac{39}{8}$

16. $\frac{98}{11}$

List the factors of each number.

17. 35

18. 40

Determine whether each number is prime or composite.

19. 72

20. 13

Write the prime factorization of each composite number. Write prime if the number is prime. Write any repeated factors using exponents.

21. 65   **22.** 70   **23.** 96   **24.** 132

25. 252   **26.** 31   **27.** 315   **28.** 441

29. 286   **30.** 41

Write each fraction in simplest form.

31. $\frac{2}{14}$ **32.** $\frac{24}{20}$ **33.** $\frac{18}{38}$ **34.** $\frac{42}{110}$

35. $\frac{56}{60}$ **36.** $\frac{72}{80}$ **37.** $\frac{54}{135}$ **38.** $\frac{90}{240}$

39. $\frac{165}{210}$ **40.** $\frac{245}{385}$

Determine whether each pair of fractions is equivalent.

41. $\frac{7}{8}$ and $\frac{9}{10}$ **42.** $\frac{10}{12}$ and $\frac{15}{18}$

43. Of the 50 states, 2 states are not adjacent to any other states.
   a. What fraction of the states are not adjacent to other states?
   b. How many states are adjacent to other states.
   c. What fraction of the states are adjacent to other states?

44. In a recent year, 460 films were released and rated. Of these, 275 were rated PG-13. (*Source:* Motion Picture Association)
   a. What fraction were rated PG-13?
   b. How many films were rated other than PG-13?
   c. What fraction of films were rated other than PG-13?

21. ____ 22. ____ 23. ____ 24. ____ 25. ____ 26. ____ 27. ____ 28. ____ 29. ____ 30. ____ 31. ____ 32. ____ 33. ____ 34. ____ 35. ____ 36. ____ 37. ____ 38. ____ 39. ____ 40. ____ 41. ____ 42. ____ 43. a. ____ b. ____ c. ____ 44. a. ____ b. ____ c. ____

2.4 MULTIPLYING FRACTIONS

Objective **A** Multiplying Fractions

Let's use a diagram to discover how fractions are multiplied. For example, to multiply $\frac{1}{2}$ and $\frac{3}{4}$, we find $\frac{1}{2}$ of $\frac{3}{4}$. To do this, we begin with a diagram showing $\frac{3}{4}$ of a rectangle's area shaded.

$\frac{3}{4}$ of the rectangle's area is shaded.

To find $\frac{1}{2}$ of $\frac{3}{4}$, we heavily shade $\frac{1}{2}$ of the part that is already shaded.

By counting smaller rectangles, we see that $\frac{3}{8}$ of the larger rectangle is now heavily shaded, so that

$$\frac{1}{2} \text{ of } \frac{3}{4} \text{ is } \frac{3}{8}, \text{ or } \frac{1}{2} \cdot \frac{3}{4} = \frac{3}{8} \quad \text{Notice that } \frac{1}{2} \cdot \frac{3}{4} = \frac{1 \cdot 3}{2 \cdot 4} = \frac{3}{8}.$$

Multiplying Fractions

To multiply two fractions, multiply the numerators and multiply the denominators.

If a, b, c, and d represent positive whole numbers, we have

$$\frac{a}{b} \cdot \frac{c}{d} = \frac{a \cdot c}{b \cdot d}$$

PRACTICE PROBLEMS 1–2

Multiply.

1. $\frac{3}{8} \cdot \frac{5}{7}$ **2.** $\frac{1}{3} \cdot \frac{1}{6}$

 **EXAMPLES** Multiply.

1. $\frac{2}{3} \cdot \frac{5}{11} = \frac{2 \cdot 5}{3 \cdot 11} = \frac{10}{33}$

This fraction is in simplest form since 10 and 33 have no common factors other than 1.

2. $\frac{1}{4} \cdot \frac{1}{2} = \frac{1 \cdot 1}{4 \cdot 2} = \frac{1}{8}$

◾ Work Practice Problems 1–2

Answers

1. $\frac{15}{56}$, **2.** $\frac{1}{18}$

EXAMPLE 3 Multiply and simplify: $\dfrac{6}{7} \cdot \dfrac{14}{27}$

Solution:

$$\frac{6}{7} \cdot \frac{14}{27} = \frac{6 \cdot 14}{7 \cdot 27}$$

We can simplify by finding the prime factorizations and using our shortcut procedure of dividing out common factors in the numerator and denominator.

$$\frac{6 \cdot 14}{7 \cdot 27} = \frac{2 \cdot \overset{1}{\cancel{3}} \cdot 2 \cdot \overset{1}{\cancel{7}}}{\underset{1}{\cancel{7}} \cdot \underset{1}{\cancel{3}} \cdot 3 \cdot 3} = \frac{2 \cdot 2}{3 \cdot 3} = \frac{4}{9}$$

■ **Work Practice Problem 3**

Helpful Hint
Remember that the shortcut procedure above is the same as removing factors of 1 in the product.

$$\frac{6 \cdot 14}{7 \cdot 27} = \frac{2 \cdot 3 \cdot 2 \cdot 7}{7 \cdot 3 \cdot 3 \cdot 3} = \frac{7}{7} \cdot \frac{3}{3} \cdot \frac{2 \cdot 2}{3 \cdot 3} = 1 \cdot 1 \cdot \frac{4}{9} = \frac{4}{9}$$

Helpful Hint
In simplifying a product, don't forget that it may be possible to identify common factors without actually writing the prime factorization. For example,

$$\frac{10}{11} \cdot \frac{1}{20} = \frac{10 \cdot 1}{11 \cdot 20} = \frac{\overset{1}{\cancel{10}} \cdot 1}{11 \cdot \underset{1}{\cancel{10}} \cdot 2} = \frac{1}{11 \cdot 2} = \frac{1}{22}$$

EXAMPLE 4 Multiply and simplify: $\dfrac{23}{32} \cdot \dfrac{4}{7}$

Solution: Notice that 4 and 32 have a common factor of 4.

$$\frac{23}{32} \cdot \frac{4}{7} = \frac{23 \cdot 4}{32 \cdot 7} = \frac{23 \cdot \overset{1}{\cancel{4}}}{\underset{1}{\cancel{4}} \cdot 8 \cdot 7} = \frac{23}{8 \cdot 7} = \frac{23}{56}$$

■ **Work Practice Problem 4**

After multiplying two fractions, always check to see whether the product can be simplified.

EXAMPLES Multiply.

5. $\dfrac{3}{4} \cdot \dfrac{8}{5} = \dfrac{3 \cdot 8}{4 \cdot 5} = \dfrac{3 \cdot \overset{1}{\cancel{4}} \cdot 2}{\underset{1}{\cancel{4}} \cdot 5} = \dfrac{6}{5}$

6. $\dfrac{6}{13} \cdot \dfrac{26}{30} = \dfrac{6 \cdot 26}{13 \cdot 30} = \dfrac{\overset{1}{\cancel{6}} \cdot \overset{1}{\cancel{13}} \cdot 2}{\underset{1}{\cancel{13}} \cdot \underset{1}{\cancel{6}} \cdot 5} = \dfrac{2}{5}$

7. $\dfrac{1}{3} \cdot \dfrac{2}{5} \cdot \dfrac{9}{16} = \dfrac{1 \cdot 2 \cdot 9}{3 \cdot 5 \cdot 16} = \dfrac{1 \cdot \overset{1}{\cancel{2}} \cdot \overset{1}{\cancel{3}} \cdot 3}{\underset{1}{\cancel{3}} \cdot 5 \cdot \underset{1}{\cancel{2}} \cdot 8} = \dfrac{3}{40}$

■ **Work Practice Problems 5–7**

Objective B Multiplying Fractions and Mixed Numbers or Whole Numbers

When multiplying a fraction and a mixed or a whole number, remember that mixed and whole numbers can be written as fractions.

Multiplying Fractions and Mixed Numbers or Whole Numbers

To multiply with mixed numbers or whole numbers, first write any mixed or whole numbers as fractions and then multiply as usual.

PRACTICE PROBLEM 8

Multiply and simplify: $2\dfrac{1}{2} \cdot \dfrac{8}{15}$

EXAMPLE 8 Multiply: $3\dfrac{1}{3} \cdot \dfrac{7}{8}$

Solution: The mixed number $3\dfrac{1}{3}$ can be written as the fraction $\dfrac{10}{3}$. Then,

$$3\frac{1}{3}\cdot\frac{7}{8}=\frac{10}{3}\cdot\frac{7}{8}=\frac{\overset{1}{\cancel{2}}\cdot 5\cdot 7}{3\cdot\underset{1}{\cancel{2}}\cdot 4}=\frac{35}{12}\quad\text{or}\quad 2\frac{11}{12}$$

☐ **Work Practice Problem 8**

Don't forget that a whole number can be written as a fraction by writing the whole number over 1. For example,

$$20 = \frac{20}{1} \qquad \text{and} \qquad 7 = \frac{7}{1}$$

PRACTICE PROBLEM 9

Multiply.

9. $\dfrac{2}{3} \cdot 18$

EXAMPLE 9 Multiply.

$$\frac{3}{4}\cdot 20=\frac{3}{4}\cdot\frac{20}{1}=\frac{3\cdot 20}{4\cdot 1}=\frac{3\cdot\overset{1}{\cancel{4}}\cdot 5}{\underset{1}{\cancel{4}}\cdot 1}=\frac{15}{1}\quad\text{or}\quad 15$$

☐ **Work Practice Problem 9**

When both numbers to be multiplied are mixed or whole numbers, it is a good idea to estimate the product to see if your answer is reasonable. To do this, we first practice rounding mixed numbers to the nearest whole. If the fraction part of the mixed number is $\dfrac{1}{2}$ or greater, we round the whole number part up. If the fraction part of the mixed number is less than $\dfrac{1}{2}$, then we do not round the whole number part up. Study the table below for examples.

Mixed Number		Rounding
$5\dfrac{1}{4}$	$\dfrac{1}{4}$ is less than $\dfrac{1}{2}$ $\dfrac{1}{4}$ ⬚⬚ ⬚⬚ $\dfrac{1}{2}$	Thus, $5\dfrac{1}{4}$ rounds to 5.
$3\dfrac{9}{16}$	← 9 is greater than 8 → Half of 16 is 8.	Thus, $3\dfrac{7}{16}$ rounds to 4.
$1\dfrac{3}{7}$	← 3 is less than $3\dfrac{1}{2}$. → Half of 7 is $3\dfrac{1}{2}$.	Thus, $1\dfrac{3}{7}$ rounds to 1.

Copyright 2006 Pearson Education, Inc.

Answers

8. $\dfrac{4}{3}$ or $1\dfrac{1}{3}$, **9.** 12

EXAMPLES Multiply. Check by estimating.

10. $1\frac{2}{3} \cdot 2\frac{1}{4} = \frac{5}{3} \cdot \frac{9}{4} = \frac{5 \cdot 9}{3 \cdot 4} = \frac{5 \cdot \overset{1}{\cancel{3}} \cdot 3}{\underset{1}{\cancel{3}} \cdot 4} = \frac{15}{4}$ or $3\frac{3}{4}$ Exact

Let's check by estimating.

$1\frac{2}{3}$ rounds to 2, $2\frac{1}{4}$ rounds to 2, and $2 \cdot 2 = 4$ Estimate

The estimate is close to the exact value, so our answer is reasonable.

11. $7 \cdot 2\frac{11}{14} = \frac{7}{1} \cdot \frac{39}{14} = \frac{7 \cdot 39}{1 \cdot 14} = \frac{\overset{1}{\cancel{7}} \cdot 39}{1 \cdot 2 \cdot \underset{1}{\cancel{7}}} = \frac{39}{2}$ or $19\frac{1}{2}$ Exact

To estimate,

$2\frac{11}{14}$ rounds to 3 and $7 \cdot 3 = 21$. Estimate

The estimate is close to the exact value, so our answer is reasonable.

Work Practice Problems 10–11

Recall from Section 1.6 that 0 multiplied by any number is 0. This is true of fractions and mixed numbers also.

EXAMPLES Multiply.

12. $0 \cdot \frac{3}{5} = 0$

13. $2\frac{3}{8} \cdot 0 = 0$

Work Practice Problems 12–13

✔ Concept Check

Find the error.

$2\frac{1}{4} \cdot \frac{1}{2} = 2\frac{1 \cdot 1}{4 \cdot 2} = 2\frac{1}{8}$

Objective **C** Solving Problems by Multiplying Fractions

To solve real-life problems that involve multiplying fractions, we use our four problem-solving steps from Chapter 1. In Example 14, a new key word that implies multiplication is used. That key word is "**of.**"

Helpful Hint

"of" usually translates to multiplication.

PRACTICE PROBLEMS 10–11

Multiply.

10. $3\frac{1}{5} \cdot 2\frac{3}{4}$ **11.** $5 \cdot 3\frac{11}{15}$

PRACTICE PROBLEMS 12–13

Multiply.

12. $\frac{9}{11} \cdot 0$ **13.** $0 \cdot 4\frac{1}{8}$

Answers

10. $\frac{44}{5}$ or $8\frac{4}{5}$, **11.** $\frac{56}{3}$ or $18\frac{2}{3}$, **12.** 0,

13. 0

✔ Concept Check Answer

forgot to change mixed number to fraction

PRACTICE PROBLEM 14

About $\frac{1}{3}$ of all plant and animal species in the United States are at risk of becoming extinct. There are 20,439 known species of plants and animals in the United States. How many species are at risk of extinction? (*Source:* The Nature Conservancy)

EXAMPLE 14 **Finding the Number of Roller Coasters in an Amusement Park**

Cedar Point is an amusement park located in Sandusky, Ohio. Its collection of 68 rides is the largest in the world. Of the rides, $\frac{7}{34}$ are roller coasters. How many roller coasters are in Cedar Point's collection of rides? (*Source:* Cedar Fair, L.P.)

Solution:

1. UNDERSTAND the problem. To do so, read and reread the problem. We are told that $\frac{7}{34}$ of Cedar Point's rides are roller coasters. The word "of" here means multiplication.

2. TRANSLATE.

In words:	Number of roller coasters	is	$\frac{7}{34}$	of	total rides at Cedar Point
	↓	↓	↓	↓	↓
Translate:	Number of roller coasters	=	$\frac{7}{34}$	·	68

3. SOLVE: Before we solve, let's estimate a reasonable answer. The fraction $\frac{7}{34}$ is less than $\frac{1}{2}$ (draw a diagram, if needed), and $\frac{1}{2}$ of 68 rides is 34 rides, so the number of roller coasters should be less than 34.

$$\frac{7}{34} \cdot 68 = \frac{7}{34} \cdot \frac{68}{1} = \frac{7 \cdot 68}{34 \cdot 1} = \frac{7 \cdot \overset{1}{34} \cdot 2}{\underset{1}{34} \cdot 1} = \frac{14}{1} \text{ or } 14$$

4. INTERPRET. *Check* your work. From our estimate, our answer is reasonable. *State* your conclusion: The number of roller coasters at Cedar Point is 14.

🔲 **Work Practice Problem 14**

Helpful Hint

To help visualize a fractional part of a whole number, look at the diagram below.

$\frac{1}{5}$ of 60 = ?

$\frac{1}{5}$ of 60 is 12.

Answer
14. 6813 species

Mental Math

Round each mixed number to the nearest whole number.

1. $7\frac{7}{8}$

2. $11\frac{3}{4}$

3. $6\frac{1}{5}$

4. $4\frac{1}{9}$

5. $8\frac{5}{22}$

6. $9\frac{7}{24}$

7. $19\frac{11}{20}$

8. $18\frac{12}{22}$

2.4 EXERCISE SET

FOR EXTRA HELP

Student Solutions Manual   PH Math/Tutor Center   CD/Video for Review   Math XL MathXL®   MyMathLab MyMathLab

Objective A *Multiply. Write each answer in simplest form. See Examples 1 through 7 and 12.*

1. $\frac{1}{3} \cdot \frac{2}{5}$

2. $\frac{2}{3} \cdot \frac{4}{7}$

3. $\frac{6}{5} \cdot \frac{1}{7}$

4. $\frac{7}{3} \cdot \frac{1}{4}$

5. $\frac{3}{10} \cdot \frac{3}{8}$

6. $\frac{2}{5} \cdot \frac{7}{11}$

7. $\frac{2}{7} \cdot \frac{5}{8}$

8. $\frac{7}{8} \cdot \frac{2}{3}$

9. $\frac{16}{5} \cdot \frac{3}{4}$

10. $\frac{8}{3} \cdot \frac{5}{12}$

11. $\frac{5}{28} \cdot \frac{2}{25}$

12. $\frac{4}{35} \cdot \frac{5}{24}$

13. $0 \cdot \frac{8}{9}$

14. $\frac{11}{12} \cdot 0$

15. $\frac{1}{10} \cdot \frac{1}{11}$

16. $\frac{1}{9} \cdot \frac{1}{13}$

17. $\frac{18}{20} \cdot \frac{36}{99}$

18. $\frac{5}{32} \cdot \frac{64}{100}$

19. $\frac{3}{8} \cdot \frac{9}{10}$

20. $\frac{4}{5} \cdot \frac{8}{25}$

21. $\frac{11}{20} \cdot \frac{1}{7} \cdot \frac{5}{22}$

22. $\frac{27}{32} \cdot \frac{10}{13} \cdot \frac{16}{30}$

23. $\frac{1}{3} \cdot \frac{2}{7} \cdot \frac{1}{5}$

24. $\frac{3}{5} \cdot \frac{1}{2} \cdot \frac{3}{7}$

25. $\frac{9}{20} \cdot 0 \cdot \frac{4}{19}$

26. $\frac{8}{11} \cdot \frac{4}{7} \cdot 0$

27. $\frac{3}{14} \cdot \frac{6}{25} \cdot \frac{5}{27} \cdot \frac{7}{6}$

28. $\frac{7}{8} \cdot \frac{9}{20} \cdot \frac{12}{22} \cdot \frac{11}{14}$

Objective B *Multiply. Write each answer in simplest form. For those exercises marked, find both an exact product and an estimated product. See Examples 8 through 11 and 13.*

29. $12 \cdot \frac{1}{4}$

30. $\frac{2}{3} \cdot 6$

31. $\frac{5}{8} \cdot 4$

32. $10 \cdot \frac{7}{8}$

33. $1\frac{1}{4} \cdot \frac{4}{25}$

34. $\dfrac{3}{22} \cdot 3\dfrac{2}{3}$　　　　**35.** $\dfrac{2}{5} \cdot 4\dfrac{1}{6}$　　　　**36.** $2\dfrac{1}{9} \cdot \dfrac{6}{7}$　　　　**37.** $\dfrac{2}{3} \cdot 1$　　　　**38.** $1 \cdot \dfrac{5}{9}$

39. $2\dfrac{1}{5} \cdot 3\dfrac{1}{2}$　　　　**40.** $2\dfrac{1}{4} \cdot 7\dfrac{1}{8}$　　　　**41.** $3\dfrac{4}{5} \cdot 6\dfrac{2}{7}$　　　　**42.** $5\dfrac{5}{6} \cdot 7\dfrac{3}{5}$　　　　**43.** $5 \cdot 2\dfrac{1}{2}$

　　Exact:　　　　　　　Exact:　　　　　　　Exact:　　　　　　　Exact:

　　Estimate:　　　　　Estimate:　　　　　Estimate:　　　　　Estimate:

44. $6 \cdot 3\dfrac{1}{3}$　　　　**45.** $1\dfrac{1}{5} \cdot 12\dfrac{1}{2}$　　　　**46.** $1\dfrac{1}{6} \cdot 7\dfrac{1}{5}$　　　　**47.** $\dfrac{3}{4} \cdot 16 \cdot \dfrac{1}{2}$　　　　**48.** $\dfrac{7}{8} \cdot 24 \cdot \dfrac{1}{3}$

49. $\dfrac{3}{10} \cdot 15 \cdot 2\dfrac{1}{2}$　　　　**50.** $\dfrac{11}{20} \cdot 12 \cdot 3\dfrac{1}{3}$　　　　**51.** $3\dfrac{1}{2} \cdot 1\dfrac{3}{4} \cdot 2\dfrac{2}{3}$　　　　**52.** $4\dfrac{1}{2} \cdot 2\dfrac{1}{9} \cdot 1\dfrac{1}{5}$

Objectives Ⓐ Ⓑ **Mixed Practice** *Multiply and simplify. See Examples 1 through 13.*

53. $\dfrac{1}{4} \cdot \dfrac{2}{15}$　　　　**54.** $\dfrac{3}{8} \cdot \dfrac{5}{12}$　　　　**55.** $\dfrac{19}{37} \cdot 0$　　　　**56.** $0 \cdot \dfrac{3}{31}$　　　　**57.** $2\dfrac{4}{5} \cdot 1\dfrac{1}{7}$

58. $3\dfrac{1}{5} \cdot 2\dfrac{11}{32}$　　　　**59.** $\dfrac{3}{2} \cdot \dfrac{7}{3}$　　　　**60.** $\dfrac{15}{2} \cdot \dfrac{3}{5}$　　　　**61.** $\dfrac{6}{15} \cdot \dfrac{5}{16}$　　　　**62.** $\dfrac{9}{20} \cdot \dfrac{10}{90}$

63. $\dfrac{7}{72} \cdot \dfrac{9}{49}$　　　　**64.** $\dfrac{3}{80} \cdot \dfrac{2}{27}$　　　　**65.** $20 \cdot \dfrac{11}{12}$　　　　**66.** $30 \cdot \dfrac{8}{9}$　　　　**67.** $9\dfrac{5}{7} \cdot 8\dfrac{1}{5} \cdot 0$

68. $4\dfrac{11}{13} \cdot 0 \cdot 12\dfrac{1}{13}$　　　　**69.** $12\dfrac{4}{5} \cdot 6\dfrac{7}{8} \cdot \dfrac{26}{77}$　　　　**70.** $14\dfrac{2}{5} \cdot 8\dfrac{1}{3} \cdot \dfrac{11}{16}$

Objective Ⓒ *Solve. Write each answer in simplest form. For Exercises 71 through 74, recall that "of" translates to multiplication. See Example 14.*

71. Find $\dfrac{1}{4}$ of 200.　　　　**72.** Find $\dfrac{1}{5}$ of 200.　　　　**73.** Find $\dfrac{5}{6}$ of 24.　　　　**74.** Find $\dfrac{5}{8}$ of 24.

75. Each turn of a screw sinks it $\frac{3}{16}$ of an inch deeper into a piece of wood. Find how deep the screw is after 8 turns.

$\frac{3}{16}$ inch

76. A veterinarian's dipping vat holds 36 gallons of liquid. She normally fills it $\frac{5}{6}$ full of a medicated flea dip solution. Find how many gallons of solution are normally in the vat.

36 gallons
$\frac{5}{6}$ full

77. The Oregon National Historic Trail is 2,170 miles long. It begins in Independence, Missouri, and ends in Oregon City, Oregon. Manfred Coulon has hiked $\frac{2}{5}$ of the trail before. How many miles has he hiked? (*Source:* National Park Service)

Oregon City

Independence

78. Movie theater owners received a total of $7660 million in movie admission tickets, about $\frac{7}{10}$ of this amount was for R-rated movies. Find the amount of money received from R-rated movies. (*Source:* Motion Picture Association of America)

79. An estimate for the measure of an adult's wrist is $\frac{1}{4}$ of the waist size. If Jorge has a 34-inch waist, estimate the size of his wrist.

80. An estimate for an adult's waist measurement is found by multiplying the neck size (in inches) by 2. Jock's neck measures $\frac{36}{2}$ inches. Estimate his waist measurement.

△ **81.** The radius of a circle is one-half of its diameter as shown. If the diameter of a circle is $\frac{3}{8}$ of an inch, what is its radius?

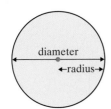

diameter
←radius→

82. The plans for a deck call for $\frac{2}{5}$ of a 4-foot post to be underground. Find the length of the post that is to be buried.

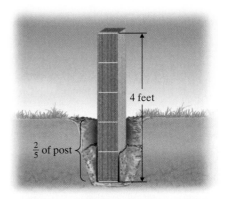

4 feet

$\frac{2}{5}$ of post

83. A patient was told that no more than $\frac{1}{5}$ of his calories should come from fat. If his diet consists of 3000 calories a day, how many of these calories can come from fat?

84. A recipe calls for $\frac{1}{3}$ of a cup of flour. How much flour should be used if only $\frac{1}{2}$ of the recipe is being made?

85. A special on a cruise to the Bahamas is advertised to be $\frac{2}{3}$ of the regular price. If the regular price is $2757, what is the sale price?

86. The Gonzales recently sold their house for $102,000, but $\frac{3}{50}$ of this amount goes to the real estate companies that helped them sell their house. How much money do the Gonzales pay to the real estate companies?

87. A sidewalk is built 6 bricks wide by laying each brick side by side. How many inches wide is the sidewalk if each brick measures $3\frac{1}{4}$ inches wide?

88. The nutrition label on a can of crushed pineapple shows 9 grams of carbohydrates for each cup of pineapple. How many grams of carbohydrates are in a $2\frac{1}{2}$-cup can?

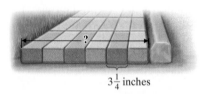

$3\frac{1}{4}$ inches

89. At this writing, the smallest digital camera is the SPYZ camera from a Japanese company called Che-ez! The face of the camera measures $2\frac{9}{25}$ inches by $1\frac{13}{25}$ inches and is slightly bigger than a Zippo lighter. Find the area of the face of this camera. (Area = length · width)

90. As part of his research, famous tornado expert Dr. T. Fujita studied approximately 31,050 tornadoes that occurred in the United States between 1916 and 1985. He found that roughly $\frac{7}{10}$ of these tornadoes occurred during April, May, June, and July. How many of these tornadoes occurred during these four months? (*Source: U.S. Tornadoes Part 1*, T. Fujita, University of Chicago)

$1\frac{13}{25}$ in.

$2\frac{9}{25}$ in.

Find the area of each rectangle. Recall that area = length · width.

△ **91.**

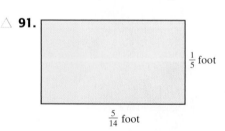

$\frac{1}{5}$ foot

$\frac{5}{14}$ foot

△ **92.** $\frac{1}{2}$ mile

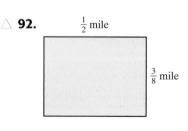

$\frac{3}{8}$ mile

△ **93.**

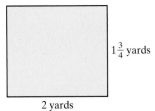

$1\frac{3}{4}$ yards

2 yards

△ **94.**

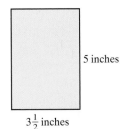

5 inches

$3\frac{1}{2}$ inches

*The following graph is called a **circle graph** or **pie chart**. Each sector (shaped like a piece of pie) shows the fractional part of a car's total mileage that falls into a particular category. The whole circle represents a car's total mileage.*

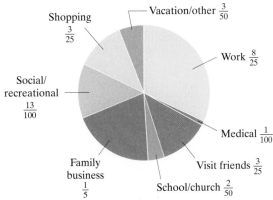

Vacation/other $\frac{3}{50}$

Shopping $\frac{3}{25}$

Work $\frac{8}{25}$

Social/ recreational $\frac{13}{100}$

Medical $\frac{1}{100}$

Family business $\frac{1}{5}$

Visit friends $\frac{3}{25}$

School/church $\frac{2}{50}$

Source: The American Automobile Manufacturers Association and The National Automobile Dealers Association

In one year, a family drove 12,000 miles in the family car. Use the circle graph to determine how many of these miles might be expected to fall in the categories shown in Exercises 95 through 98.

95. Work

96. Shopping

97. Family business

98. Medical

Review

Divide. See Section 1.7.

99. $8\overline{)1648}$

100. $7\overline{)3920}$

101. $23\overline{)1300}$

102. $31\overline{)2500}$

Concept Extensions

103. In your own words, explain how to multiply
  a. fractions
  b. mixed numbers

104. In your own words, explain how to round a mixed number to the nearest whole number.

Solve. See the Concept Check in this section.

105. A student asked you to check his work below. Is it correct? If not, where is the error?

$$3\frac{2}{3} \cdot 1\frac{1}{7} = 3\frac{2}{21}$$

Choose the best estimate for each product.

106. $3\frac{1}{5} \cdot 4\frac{5}{8}$

   a. 7
   b. 15
   c. 8
   d. $12\frac{1}{8}$

107. $\frac{11}{12} \cdot 4\frac{1}{16}$

   a. 16
   b. 1
   c. 4
   d. 8

108. $9 \cdot \frac{10}{11}$

   a. 9
   b. 90
   c. 99
   d. 0

109. $7\frac{1}{4} \cdot 4\frac{1}{5}$

   a. 40
   b. $\frac{7}{5}$
   c. 35
   d. 28

110. If $\frac{3}{4}$ of 36 students on a first bus are girls and $\frac{2}{3}$ of the 30 students on a second bus are *boys,* how many students on the two buses are girls.

111. According to the 2000 census, in that year there were 34,800,000 Americans age 65 or older. About $\frac{11}{20}$ of these older Americans had annual incomes *under* $15,000. How many older Americans had incomes greater than or equal to $15,000? (*Source:* U.S. Census Bureau)

112. In 2004, there were approximately 10,600 commercial radio stations broadcasting in the United States. Of these stations, $\frac{32}{265}$ were news/talk stations. How many radio stations were news/talk stations in 2004? (*Source:* Corporation for Public Broadcasting)

 STUDY SKILLS BUILDER

How Are Your Homework Assignments Going?

It is very important in mathematics to keep up with homework. Why? Many concepts build on each other. Often your understanding of a day's concepts depends on an understanding of the previous day's material.

Remember that completing your homework assignment involves a lot more than attempting a few of the problems assigned.

To complete a homework assignment, remember these four things:

- Attempt all of it.
- Check it.
- Correct it.
- If needed, ask questions about it.

Take a moment and review your completed homework assignments. Answer the questions below based on this review.

1. Approximate the fraction of your homework you have attempted.

2. Approximate the fraction of your homework you have checked (if possible).

3. If you are able to check your homework, have you corrected it when errors have been found?

4. When working homework, if you do not understand a concept, what do you do?

2.5 DIVIDING FRACTIONS

Objectives

A Find the Reciprocal of a Fraction.

B Divide Fractions.

C Divide Fractions and Mixed Numbers or Whole Numbers.

D Solve Problems by Dividing Fractions.

Objective A Finding Reciprocals of Fractions

Before we can divide fractions, we need to know how to find the **reciprocal** of a fraction or whole number.

Reciprocal of a Number

Two numbers are **reciprocals** of each other if their product is 1.

For example,

$$\frac{2}{3} \cdot \frac{3}{2} = \frac{2 \cdot 3}{3 \cdot 2} = \frac{6}{6} = 1 \qquad \text{so } \frac{2}{3} \text{ and } \frac{3}{2} \text{ are reciprocals.}$$

$$4 \cdot \frac{1}{4} = \frac{4}{1} \cdot \frac{1}{4} = \frac{4 \cdot 1}{1 \cdot 4} = \frac{4}{4} = 1 \qquad \text{so } 4 \text{ and } \frac{1}{4} \text{ are reciprocals.}$$

Finding the Reciprocal of a Fraction

To find the reciprocal of a fraction, interchange its numerator and denominator.

For example, the reciprocal of $\frac{6}{11}$ is $\frac{11}{6}$.

EXAMPLES Find the reciprocal of each number.

1. The reciprocal of $\frac{5}{6}$ is $\frac{6}{5}$. $\qquad \frac{5}{6} \cdot \frac{6}{5} = \frac{5 \cdot 6}{6 \cdot 5} = \frac{30}{30} = 1$

2. The reciprocal of $\frac{11}{8}$ is $\frac{8}{11}$. $\qquad \frac{11}{8} \cdot \frac{8}{11} = \frac{11 \cdot 8}{8 \cdot 11} = \frac{88}{88} = 1$

3. The reciprocal of $\frac{1}{3}$ is $\frac{3}{1}$ or 3. $\qquad \frac{1}{3} \cdot \frac{3}{1} = \frac{1 \cdot 3}{3 \cdot 1} = \frac{3}{3} = 1$

4. The reciprocal of 5, or $\frac{5}{1}$, is $\frac{1}{5}$. $\qquad \frac{5}{1} \cdot \frac{1}{5} = \frac{5 \cdot 1}{1 \cdot 5} = \frac{5}{5} = 1$

⬛ Work Practice Problems 1–4

Helpful Hint
Every number except 0 has a reciprocal. The number 0 has no reciprocal because there is no number that when multiplied by 0 gives a result of 1.

PRACTICE PROBLEMS 1–4

Find the reciprocal of each number.

1. $\frac{4}{9}$ 2. $\frac{15}{7}$

3. 7 4. $\frac{1}{8}$

Answers

1. $\frac{9}{4}$, 2. $\frac{7}{15}$, 3. $\frac{1}{7}$, 4. 8

Objective B Dividing Fractions

Division of fractions has the same meaning as division of whole numbers. For example,

$10 \div 5$ means: How many 5s are there in 10?

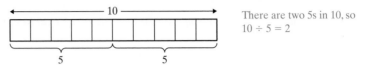

There are two 5s in 10, so $10 \div 5 = 2$

$\dfrac{3}{4} \div \dfrac{1}{8}$ means: How many $\dfrac{1}{8}$s are there in $\dfrac{3}{4}$?

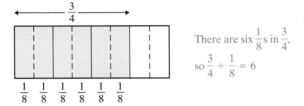

There are six $\dfrac{1}{8}$s in $\dfrac{3}{4}$, so $\dfrac{3}{4} \div \dfrac{1}{8} = 6$

We can use reciprocals to divide fractions.

Dividing Fractions

To divide two fractions, multiply the first fraction by the reciprocal of the second fraction.

If a, b, c, and d represent positive whole numbers, then

$$\frac{a}{b} \div \frac{c}{d} = \frac{a}{b} \cdot \underset{\text{reciprocal}}{\frac{d}{c}} = \frac{a \cdot d}{b \cdot c}$$

For example,

$$\frac{3}{4} \div \frac{1}{8} = \frac{3}{4} \cdot \overset{\text{multiply by reciprocal}}{\frac{8}{1}} = \frac{3 \cdot 8}{4 \cdot 1} = \frac{3 \cdot 2 \cdot \overset{1}{\cancel{4}}}{\underset{1}{\cancel{4}} \cdot 1} = \frac{6}{1} \text{ or } 6$$

Just as when you are multiplying fractions, always check to see whether your answer can be simplified when you divide fractions.

PRACTICE PROBLEMS 5–7

Divide and simplify.

5. $\dfrac{3}{2} \div \dfrac{14}{5}$ **6.** $\dfrac{8}{7} \div \dfrac{2}{9}$

7. $\dfrac{4}{9} \div \dfrac{1}{2}$

Answers

5. $\dfrac{15}{28}$, **6.** $\dfrac{36}{7}$ or $5\dfrac{1}{7}$, **7.** $\dfrac{8}{9}$

EXAMPLES Divide and simplify.

5. $\dfrac{7}{8} \div \dfrac{2}{9} = \dfrac{7}{8} \cdot \dfrac{9}{2} = \dfrac{7 \cdot 9}{8 \cdot 2} = \dfrac{63}{16}$

6. $\dfrac{5}{16} \div \dfrac{3}{4} = \dfrac{5}{16} \cdot \dfrac{4}{3} = \dfrac{5 \cdot 4}{16 \cdot 3} = \dfrac{5 \cdot \overset{1}{\cancel{4}}}{\underset{1}{\cancel{4}} \cdot 4 \cdot 3} = \dfrac{5}{12}$

7. $\dfrac{2}{5} \div \dfrac{1}{2} = \dfrac{2}{5} \cdot \dfrac{2}{1} = \dfrac{2 \cdot 2}{5 \cdot 1} = \dfrac{4}{5}$

■ **Work Practice Problems 5–7**

Helpful Hint

When dividing fractions, do *not* look for common factors to divide out until you rewrite the division as multiplication.

Do not try to divide out these two 2s.

$$\frac{1}{2} \div \frac{2}{3} = \frac{1}{2} \cdot \frac{3}{2} = \frac{3}{4}$$

Objective C Dividing Fractions and Mixed Numbers or Whole Numbers

Just as with multiplying, mixed or whole numbers should be written as fractions before you divide them.

Dividing Fractions and Mixed Numbers or Whole Numbers

To divide with a mixed number or a whole number, first write the mixed or whole number as a fraction and then divide as usual.

EXAMPLES Divide.

8. $\dfrac{3}{4} \div 5 = \dfrac{3}{4} \div \dfrac{5}{1} = \dfrac{3}{4} \cdot \dfrac{1}{5} = \dfrac{3 \cdot 1}{4 \cdot 5} = \dfrac{3}{20}$

9. $\dfrac{11}{18} \div 2\dfrac{5}{6} = \dfrac{11}{18} \div \dfrac{17}{6} = \dfrac{11}{18} \cdot \dfrac{6}{17} = \dfrac{11 \cdot 6}{18 \cdot 17} = \dfrac{11 \cdot \overset{1}{\cancel{6}}}{\underset{1}{\cancel{6}} \cdot 3 \cdot 17} = \dfrac{11}{51}$

10. $5\dfrac{2}{3} \div 2\dfrac{5}{9} = \dfrac{17}{3} \div \dfrac{23}{9} = \dfrac{17}{3} \cdot \dfrac{9}{23} = \dfrac{17 \cdot 9}{3 \cdot 23} = \dfrac{17 \cdot \overset{1}{\cancel{3}} \cdot 3}{\underset{1}{\cancel{3}} \cdot 23} = \dfrac{51}{23} \text{ or } 2\dfrac{5}{23}$

Work Practice Problems 8–10

Recall from Section 1.7 that the quotient of 0 and any number (except 0) is 0. This is true of fractions and mixed numbers also. For example,

$$0 \div \frac{7}{8} = \underbrace{0 \cdot \frac{8}{7}}_{} = 0 \qquad \text{Recall that 0 multiplied by any number is 0.}$$

Also recall from Section 1.7 that the quotient of any number and 0 is not a number. This is also true of fractions and mixed numbers. For example, to find $\dfrac{7}{8} \div 0$, or $\dfrac{7}{8} \div \dfrac{0}{1}$, we would need to find the reciprocal of 0 $\left(\text{or } \dfrac{0}{1}\right)$. As we mentioned in the helpful hint at the beginning of this section, 0 has no reciprocal because there is no number that when multiplied by 0 gives a result of 1. Thus,

$$\frac{7}{8} \div 0 \text{ is undefined.}$$

PRACTICE PROBLEMS 8–10

Divide.

8. $\dfrac{4}{9} \div 7$

9. $\dfrac{8}{15} \div 3\dfrac{4}{5}$

10. $3\dfrac{2}{7} \div 2\dfrac{3}{14}$

PRACTICE PROBLEMS 11–12

Divide.

11. $\dfrac{14}{17} \div 0$ **12.** $0 \div 2\dfrac{1}{8}$

EXAMPLES Divide.

11. $0 \div \dfrac{2}{21} = 0 \cdot \dfrac{21}{2} = 0$ **12.** $1\dfrac{3}{4} \div 0$ is undefined.

Work Practice Problems 11–12

✔ Concept Check   Which of the following is the correct way to divide $\dfrac{2}{5}$ by $\dfrac{3}{4}$? Or are both correct? Explain.

a. $\dfrac{5}{2} \cdot \dfrac{3}{4}$ **b.** $\dfrac{2}{5} \cdot \dfrac{4}{3}$

Objective D Solving Problems by Dividing Fractions

To solve real-life problems that involve dividing fractions, we continue to use our four problem-solving steps.

PRACTICE PROBLEM 13

A designer of women's clothing designs a woman's dress that requires $2\dfrac{1}{7}$ yards of material. How many dresses can be made from a 30-yard bolt of material?

EXAMPLE 13 Calculating Manufacturing Materials Needed

In a manufacturing process, a metal-cutting machine cuts strips $1\dfrac{3}{5}$ inches long from a piece of metal stock. How many such strips can be cut from a 48-inch piece of stock?

Solution:

1. UNDERSTAND the problem. To do so, read and reread the problem. Then draw a diagram:

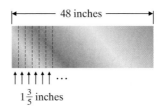

We want to know how many $1\dfrac{3}{5}$s there are in 48.

2. TRANSLATE.

In words:	Number of strips	is	48	divided by	$1\dfrac{3}{5}$
	↓	↓	↓	↓	↓
Translate:	Number of strips	$=$	48	$\div$	$1\dfrac{3}{5}$

3. SOLVE: Let's estimate a reasonable answer. The mixed number $1\dfrac{3}{5}$ rounds to 2 and $48 \div 2 = 24$.

$$48 \div 1\dfrac{3}{5} = 48 \div \dfrac{8}{5} = \dfrac{48}{1} \cdot \dfrac{5}{8} = \dfrac{48 \cdot 5}{1 \cdot 8} = \dfrac{\overset{1}{\cancel{8}} \cdot 6 \cdot 5}{1 \cdot \underset{1}{\cancel{8}}} = \dfrac{30}{1} \text{ or } 30$$

4. INTERPRET. *Check* your work. Since the exact answer of 30 is close to our estimate of 24, our answer is reasonable. *State* your conclusion: Thirty strips can be cut from the 48-inch piece of stock.

Work Practice Problem 13

Answers

11. undefined,   **12.** 0,   **13.** 14 dresses

✔ **Concept Check Answers**

a. incorrect,   **b.** correct

Objective *Find the reciprocal of each number. See Examples 1 through 4.*

1. $\dfrac{4}{7}$ **2.** $\dfrac{9}{10}$ **3.** $\dfrac{1}{11}$ **4.** $\dfrac{1}{20}$

5. 15   **6.** 13   **7.** $\dfrac{12}{7}$ **8.** $\dfrac{10}{3}$

Objective *Divide. Write each answer in simplest form. See Examples 5 through 7 and 11.*

9. $\dfrac{2}{3} \div \dfrac{5}{6}$ **10.** $\dfrac{5}{8} \div \dfrac{2}{3}$ **11.** $\dfrac{8}{9} \div \dfrac{1}{2}$ **12.** $\dfrac{10}{11} \div \dfrac{4}{5}$ **13.** $\dfrac{3}{7} \div \dfrac{5}{6}$

14. $\dfrac{16}{27} \div \dfrac{8}{15}$ **15.** $\dfrac{3}{5} \div \dfrac{4}{5}$ **16.** $\dfrac{11}{16} \div \dfrac{13}{16}$ **17.** $\dfrac{1}{10} \div \dfrac{10}{1}$ **18.** $\dfrac{3}{13} \div \dfrac{13}{3}$

19. $\dfrac{7}{9} \div \dfrac{7}{3}$ **20.** $\dfrac{6}{11} \div \dfrac{6}{5}$ **21.** $\dfrac{5}{8} \div \dfrac{3}{8}$ **22.** $\dfrac{7}{8} \div \dfrac{5}{6}$ **23.** $\dfrac{7}{45} \div \dfrac{4}{25}$

24. $\dfrac{14}{52} \div \dfrac{1}{13}$ **25.** $\dfrac{2}{37} \div \dfrac{1}{7}$ **26.** $\dfrac{100}{158} \div \dfrac{10}{79}$ **27.** $\dfrac{3}{25} \div \dfrac{27}{40}$ **28.** $\dfrac{6}{15} \div \dfrac{7}{10}$

29. $\dfrac{11}{12} \div \dfrac{11}{12}$ **30.** $\dfrac{7}{13} \div \dfrac{7}{13}$ **31.** $\dfrac{8}{13} \div 0$ **32.** $0 \div \dfrac{4}{11}$ **33.** $0 \div \dfrac{7}{8}$

34. $\dfrac{2}{3} \div 0$ **35.** $\dfrac{25}{126} \div \dfrac{125}{441}$ **36.** $\dfrac{65}{495} \div \dfrac{26}{231}$

Objective **C** *Divide. Write each answer in simplest form. See Examples 8 through 10 and 12.*

37. $\dfrac{2}{3} \div 4$ **38.** $\dfrac{5}{6} \div 10$ **39.** $8 \div \dfrac{3}{5}$ **40.** $7 \div \dfrac{2}{11}$ **41.** $2\dfrac{1}{2} \div \dfrac{1}{2}$

42. $4\dfrac{2}{3} \div \dfrac{2}{5}$ **43.** $\dfrac{5}{12} \div 2\dfrac{1}{3}$ **44.** $\dfrac{4}{15} \div 2\dfrac{1}{2}$ **45.** $3\dfrac{3}{7} \div 3\dfrac{1}{3}$ **46.** $2\dfrac{5}{6} \div 4\dfrac{6}{7}$

47. $1\dfrac{4}{9} \div 2\dfrac{5}{6}$ **48.** $3\dfrac{1}{10} \div 2\dfrac{1}{5}$ **49.** $0 \div 15\dfrac{4}{7}$ **50.** $\dfrac{33}{50} \div 1$ **51.** $1 \div \dfrac{13}{17}$

52. $0 \div 7\dfrac{9}{10}$ **53.** $1 \div \dfrac{18}{35}$ **54.** $\dfrac{17}{75} \div 1$ **55.** $10\dfrac{5}{9} \div 16\dfrac{2}{3}$ **56.** $20\dfrac{5}{6} \div 137\dfrac{1}{2}$

Objectives **B** **C** **Mixed Practice** *Divide. Write each answer in simplest form. See Examples 5 through 12.*

57. $\dfrac{6}{15} \div \dfrac{12}{5}$ **58.** $\dfrac{4}{15} \div \dfrac{8}{3}$ **59.** $\dfrac{11}{20} \div \dfrac{3}{11}$ **60.** $\dfrac{9}{20} \div \dfrac{2}{9}$

61. $12 \div \dfrac{1}{8}$ **62.** $9 \div \dfrac{1}{6}$ **63.** $\dfrac{3}{7} \div \dfrac{4}{7}$ **64.** $\dfrac{3}{8} \div \dfrac{5}{8}$

65. $2\dfrac{3}{8} \div 0$ **66.** $20\dfrac{1}{5} \div 0$ **67.** $\dfrac{11}{85} \div \dfrac{7}{5}$ **68.** $\dfrac{13}{84} \div \dfrac{3}{16}$

69. $4\dfrac{5}{11} \div 1\dfrac{2}{5}$ **70.** $8\dfrac{2}{7} \div 3\dfrac{1}{7}$ **71.** $\dfrac{27}{100} \div \dfrac{3}{20}$ **72.** $\dfrac{25}{128} \div \dfrac{5}{32}$

Objective **D** *Solve. Write each answer in simplest form. See Example 13.*

73. A patient is to take $3\dfrac{1}{3}$ tablespoons of medicine per day in 4 equally divided doses. How much medicine is to be taken in each dose?

74. If there are $13\dfrac{1}{3}$ grams of fat in 4 ounces of lean hamburger meat, how many grams of fat are in an ounce?

75. A heart attack patient in rehabilitation walked on a treadmill $12\frac{3}{4}$ miles over 4 days. How many miles is this per day?

76. A local restaurant is selling hamburgers from a booth on Memorial Day. A total of $27\frac{3}{4}$ pounds of hamburger have been ordered. How many quarter-pound hamburgers can this make?

77. The record for rainfall during a 24-hour period in Alaska is $15\frac{1}{5}$ inches. This record was set in Angoon, Alaska, in October 1982. How much rain fell per hour on average? (*Source:* National Climatic Data Center)

78. An order for 125 custom-made candle stands was placed with Mr. Levi, the manager of Just For You, Inc. The worker assigned to the job can produce $2\frac{3}{5}$ candle stands per hour. Using this worker, how many work hours will be required to complete the order?

79. In October, 2004, the average price of aluminum was $83\frac{1}{2}¢$ per pound. During that time, Severo Gutierrez received 1169¢ for aluminum cans that he sold for recycling at a scrap metal center. Assuming that he received the average price, how many pounds of aluminum cans did Severo recycle? (*Source:* London Metal Exchange)

80. Yoko's Fine Jewelry sells a $\frac{3}{4}$-carat gem for $450. At this price, what is the cost of one carat?

△ **81.** The area of the rectangle below is 12 square meters. If its width is $2\frac{4}{7}$ meters, find its length.

Rectangle	$2\frac{4}{7}$ meters

△ **82.** The perimeter of the square below is $23\frac{1}{2}$ feet. Find the length of each side.

Square

Mixed Practice (*Sections 2.4, 2.5*) *Perform the indicated operation.*

83. $\frac{2}{5} \cdot \frac{4}{7}$

84. $\frac{2}{5} \div \frac{4}{7}$

85. $2\frac{2}{3} \div 1\frac{1}{16}$

86. $2\frac{2}{3} \cdot 1\frac{1}{16}$

87. $5\frac{1}{7} \cdot \frac{2}{9} \cdot \frac{14}{15}$

88. $8\frac{1}{6} \cdot \frac{3}{7} \cdot \frac{18}{25}$

89. $\frac{11}{20} \div \frac{20}{11}$

90. $2\frac{1}{5} \div 1\frac{7}{10}$

Review

Perform each indicated operation. See Sections 1.3 and 1.4.

91.   27
    76
  + 98

92.   811
    42
  + 69

93.   968
  − 772

94.   882
  − 773

95.   2000
  − 431

96.   500
  − 92

Concept Extensions

Solve. See the Concept Check in this section.

97. A student asked you to check her work below. Is it correct? If not, where is the error?

$$20\frac{2}{3} \div 10\frac{1}{2} = 2\frac{1}{3}.$$

Choose the best estimate for each quotient.

98. $10\frac{1}{4} \div 2\frac{1}{16}$

    a. 8   **b.** 5   **c.** 20   **d.** 12

99. $20\frac{1}{4} \div \frac{5}{6}$

    a. 5   **b.** $5\frac{1}{8}$ **c.** 20   **d.** 10

100. $\frac{11}{12} \div 16\frac{1}{5}$

    a. $\frac{1}{16}$ **b.** 4   **c.** 8   **d.** 16

101. $12\frac{2}{13} \div 3\frac{7}{8}$

    a. 4   **b.** 9   **c.** 36   **d.** 3

102. In your own words, describe how to divide fractions.

Simplify.

103. $\frac{42}{25} \cdot \frac{125}{36} \div \frac{7}{6}$

104. $\left(\frac{8}{13} \cdot \frac{39}{16} \cdot \frac{8}{9}\right)^2 \div \frac{1}{2}$

105. The FedEx Express air fleet includes 258 Cessnas. These Cessnas make up $\frac{129}{320}$ of the FedEx fleet. How many aircraft make up the entire FedEx Express air fleet? (*Source:* FedEx Corporation)

106. One-third of all native flowering plant species in the United States are at risk of becoming extinct. That translates into 5144 at-risk flowering plant species. Based on this data, how many flowering plant species are native to the United States overall? (*Source:* The Nature Conservancy)

(*Hint:* How many $\frac{1}{3}$s are in 5144?)

THE BIGGER PICTURE **Operations on Sets of Numbers**

Continue your outline from Sections 1.7 and 1.9. Suggestions are once again written to help you complete this part of your outline, Section I.B. Fractions.

I. **Operations on Sets of Numbers**

   A. **Whole Numbers**

      1. **Add or Subtract** (Sections 1.3, 1.4)

      2. **Multiply or Divide** (Sections 1.6, 1.7)

      3. **Exponent** (Section 1.9)

      4. **Square Root** (Section 1.9)

      5. **Order of Operations** (Section 1.9)

   B. **Fractions**

      1. **Simplify:** Factor the numerator and denominator. Then divide out factors of 1 by dividing out common factors in the numerator and denominator.

$$\text{Simplify: } \frac{20}{28} = \frac{\overset{1}{\cancel{4}} \cdot 5}{\underset{1}{\cancel{4}} \cdot 7} = \frac{5}{7}$$

      2. **Multiply:** Numerator times numerator over denominator times denominator. $\dfrac{5}{9} \cdot \dfrac{2}{7} = \dfrac{10}{63}$

      3. **Divide:** First fraction times the reciprocal of the second fraction.

$$\frac{2}{11} \div \frac{3}{4} = \frac{2}{11} \cdot \frac{4}{3} = \frac{8}{33}$$

Perform the indicated operations.

1. $\dfrac{2}{3} \cdot \dfrac{8}{9}$ 2. $\dfrac{2}{3} \div \dfrac{8}{9}$

3. $12 \cdot \dfrac{1}{9}$ 4. $4\dfrac{1}{2} \div 1\dfrac{7}{8}$

5. $\sqrt{64}$ 6. $3^2 \cdot 2^3$

7. $\dfrac{11}{20} \cdot \dfrac{5}{8} \cdot \dfrac{4}{33}$ 8. $20 \div \dfrac{1}{2}$

9. $3 + 4(18 - 16)^3$ 10. $100 - 76$

 CHAPTER 2   **Group Activity**

Blood and Blood Donation (Sections 2.1, 2.2, 2.3)

Blood is the workhorse of the body. It carries to the body's tissues everything they need, from nutrients to antibodies to heat. Blood also carries away waste products like carbon dioxide. Blood contains three types of cells—red blood cells, white blood cells, and platelets—suspended in clear, watery fluid called plasma. Blood is $\dfrac{11}{20}$ plasma, and plasma itself is $\dfrac{9}{10}$ water. In the average healthy adult human, blood accounts for $\dfrac{1}{11}$ of a person's body weight.

Roughly every 2 seconds someone in the United States needs blood. Although only $\dfrac{1}{20}$ of eligible donors donate blood, the American Red Cross is still able to collect nearly 6 million volunteer donations of blood each year. This volume makes Red Cross Biomedical Services the largest blood supplier for blood transfusions in the United States.

Group Activity

Contact your local Red Cross Blood Service office. Find out how many people donated blood in your area in the past two months. Ask whether it is possible to get a breakdown of the blood donations by blood type. (For more on blood type, see Exercises 73 through 77 in Section 2.3.)

1. Research the population of the area served by your local Red Cross Blood Service office. Write the fraction of the local population who gave blood in the past two months.
2. Use the breakdown by blood type to write the fraction of donors giving each type of blood.

Chapter 2 Vocabulary Check

Fill in each blank with one of the words or phrases listed below.

mixed number	equivalent	0	undefined
composite number	improper fraction	simplest form	prime factorization
prime number	proper fraction	numerator	denominator
reciprocals			

1. Two numbers are _____ of each other if their product is 1.
2. A _____ is a natural number greater than 1 that is not prime.
3. Fractions that represent the same portion of a whole are called _____ fractions.
4. An _____ is a fraction whose numerator is greater than or equal to its denominator.
5. A _____ is a natural number greater than 1 whose only factors are 1 and itself.
6. A fraction is in _____ when the numerator and the denominator have no factors in common other than 1.
7. A _____ is one whose numerator is less than its denominator.
8. A _____ contains a whole number part and a fraction part.
9. In the fraction $\frac{7}{9}$, the 7 is called the _____ and the 9 is called the _____.
10. The _____ of a number is the factorization in which all the factors are prime numbers.
11. The fraction $\frac{3}{0}$ is _____.
12. The fraction $\frac{0}{5}$ = _____.

> **Helpful Hint**
>
> Are you preparing for your test? Don't forget to take the Chapter 2 Test on page 173. Then check your answers at the back of the text and use the Chapter Test Prep Video CD to see the fully worked-out solutions to any of the exercises you want to review.

2 Chapter Highlights

DEFINITIONS AND CONCEPTS	**EXAMPLES**
Section 2.1 Introduction to Fractions and Mixed Numbers	
A **fraction** is of the form $\underline{\text{numerator}}$ ← number of parts being considered denominator ← number of equal parts in the whole	Write a fraction to represent the shaded part of the figure. $\frac{3}{8}$ ← number of parts shaded ← number of equal parts

DEFINITIONS AND CONCEPTS	EXAMPLES

Section 2.1 Introduction to Fractions and Mixed Numbers (*continued*)

A fraction is called a **proper fraction** if its numerator is less than its denominator.

A fraction is called an **improper fraction** if its numerator is greater than or equal to its denominator.

A **mixed number** contains a whole number and a fraction.

$$\frac{1}{3}, \frac{2}{5}, \frac{7}{8}, \frac{100}{101}$$

$$\frac{5}{4}, \frac{2}{2}, \frac{9}{7}, \frac{101}{100}$$

$$1\frac{1}{2}, 5\frac{7}{8}, 25\frac{9}{10}$$

TO WRITE A MIXED NUMBER AS AN IMPROPER FRACTION

1. Multiply the denominator of the fraction by the whole number.

2. Add the numerator of the fraction to the product from step 1.

3. Write this sum from step 2 as the numerator of the improper fraction over the original denominator.

$$5\frac{2}{7} = \frac{5\cdot 7 + 2}{7} = \frac{35 + 2}{7} = \frac{37}{7}$$

TO WRITE AN IMPROPER FRACTION AS A MIXED NUMBER OR A WHOLE NUMBER

1. Divide the denominator into the numerator.

2. The whole number part of the mixed number is the quotient. The fraction is the remainder over the original denominator.

$$\quad\text{quotient}\,\dfrac{\text{remainder}}{\text{original denominator}}$$

$$\frac{17}{3} = 5\frac{2}{3}$$

$$\begin{array}{r} 5 \\ 3\overline{)17} \\ \underline{15} \\ 2 \end{array}$$

Section 2.2 Factors and Prime Factorization

A **prime number** is a natural number that has exactly two different factors, 1 and itself.

A **composite number** is any natural number other than 1 that is not prime.

The prime factorization of a number is the factorization in which all the factors are prime numbers.

$$2, 3, 5, 7, 11, 13, 17, \ldots$$

$$4, 6, 8, 9, 10, 12, 14, 15, 16, \ldots$$

Write the prime factorization of 60.

$$60 = 6\cdot 10$$
$$= 2\cdot 3\cdot 2\cdot 5 \quad\text{or}\quad 2^2\cdot 3\cdot 5$$

Section 2.3 Simplest Form of a Fraction

Fractions that represent the same portion of a whole are called **equivalent fractions.**

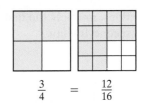

$$\frac{3}{4} \quad = \quad \frac{12}{16}$$

A fraction is in **simplest form** or **lowest terms** when the numerator and the denominator have no common factors other than 1.

The fraction $\frac{2}{3}$ is in simplest form.

continued

DEFINITIONS AND CONCEPTS	**EXAMPLES**

Section 2.3   Simplest Form of a Fraction (*continued*)

To write a fraction in simplest form, write the prime factorizations of the numerator and the denominator and then divide both by all common factors.	Write in simplest form: $\dfrac{30}{36}$ $$\frac{30}{36} = \frac{2 \cdot 3 \cdot 5}{2 \cdot 2 \cdot 3 \cdot 3} = \frac{2}{2} \cdot \frac{3}{3} \cdot \frac{5}{2 \cdot 3} = 1 \cdot 1 \cdot 1 \cdot \frac{5}{6} = \frac{5}{6}$$ or $\quad \dfrac{30}{36} = \dfrac{\overset{1}{\cancel{2}} \cdot \overset{1}{\cancel{3}} \cdot 5}{\underset{1}{\cancel{2}} \cdot 2 \cdot \underset{1}{\cancel{3}} \cdot 3} = \dfrac{5}{6}$
Two fractions are equivalent if **Method 1.** They simplify to the same fraction. **Method 2.** Their cross products are equal.	Determine whether $\dfrac{7}{8}$ and $\dfrac{21}{24}$ are equivalent. $\dfrac{7}{8}$ is in simplest form $\dfrac{21}{24} = \dfrac{\overset{1}{\cancel{3}} \cdot 7}{\underset{1}{\cancel{3}} \cdot 8} = \dfrac{1 \cdot 7}{1 \cdot 8} = \dfrac{7}{8}$ Since both simplify to $\dfrac{7}{8}$, then $\dfrac{7}{8} = \dfrac{21}{24}$.

$$\begin{array}{c} 24 \cdot 7 \\ = 168 \end{array} \qquad \dfrac{7}{8} \;=\; \dfrac{21}{24} \qquad \begin{array}{c} 8 \cdot 21 \\ = 168 \end{array}$$

Since $168 = 168$, $\dfrac{7}{8} = \dfrac{21}{24}$

Section 2.4   Multiplying Fractions

To multiply two fractions, multiply the numerators and multiply the denominators.	Multiply. $\dfrac{7}{8} \cdot \dfrac{3}{5} = \dfrac{7 \cdot 3}{8 \cdot 5} = \dfrac{21}{40}$ $\dfrac{3}{4} \cdot \dfrac{1}{6} = \dfrac{3 \cdot 1}{4 \cdot 6} = \dfrac{\overset{1}{\cancel{3}} \cdot 1}{4 \cdot \underset{1}{\cancel{3}} \cdot 2} = \dfrac{1}{8}$
To multiply with mixed numbers or whole numbers, first write any mixed or whole numbers as fractions and then multiply as usual.	$2\dfrac{1}{3} \cdot \dfrac{1}{9} = \dfrac{7}{3} \cdot \dfrac{1}{9} = \dfrac{7 \cdot 1}{3 \cdot 9} = \dfrac{7}{27}$

Section 2.5   Dividing Fractions

To find the **reciprocal** of a fraction, interchange its numerator and denominator. **To divide two fractions,** multiply the first fraction by the reciprocal of the second fraction.	The reciprocal of $\dfrac{3}{5}$ is $\dfrac{5}{3}$. Divide. $\dfrac{3}{10} \div \dfrac{7}{9} = \dfrac{3}{10} \cdot \dfrac{9}{7} = \dfrac{3 \cdot 9}{10 \cdot 7} = \dfrac{27}{70}$
To divide with mixed numbers or whole numbers, first write any mixed or whole numbers as fractions and then divide as usual.	$2\dfrac{5}{8} \div 3\dfrac{7}{16} = \dfrac{21}{8} \div \dfrac{55}{16} = \dfrac{21}{8} \cdot \dfrac{16}{55} = \dfrac{21 \cdot 16}{8 \cdot 55}$ $= \dfrac{21 \cdot 2 \cdot \overset{1}{\cancel{8}}}{\underset{1}{\cancel{8}} \cdot 55} = \dfrac{42}{55}$

CHAPTER REVIEW

(2.1) *Determine whether each number is an improper fraction, a proper fraction, or a mixed number.*

1. $\frac{11}{23}$

2. $\frac{9}{8}$

3. $\frac{1}{2}$

4. $2\frac{1}{4}$

Write a fraction to represent the shaded area.

5.

6.

7.

8.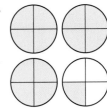

9. A basketball player made 11 free throws out of 12 during a game. What fraction of free throws did the player make?

10. A new car lot contained 23 blue cars out of a total of 131 cars.

   a. How many cars on the lot are not blue?

   b. What fraction of cars on the lot are not blue?

Write each improper fraction as a mixed number or a whole number.

11. $\frac{15}{4}$

12. $\frac{275}{6}$

13. $\frac{39}{13}$

14. $\frac{60}{12}$

Write each mixed number as an improper fraction.

15. $1\frac{1}{5}$

16. $1\frac{1}{21}$

17. $2\frac{8}{9}$

18. $3\frac{11}{12}$

(2.2) *Identify each number as prime or composite.*

19. 51

20. 17

List all factors of each number.

21. 42

22. 20

Find the prime factorization of each number.

23. 68   **24.** 90   **25.** 785   **26.** 255

(2.3) *Write each fraction in simplest form.*

27. $\dfrac{12}{28}$ **28.** $\dfrac{15}{27}$ **29.** $\dfrac{25}{75}$ **30.** $\dfrac{36}{72}$

31. $\dfrac{29}{32}$ **32.** $\dfrac{18}{23}$ **33.** $\dfrac{48}{6}$ **34.** $\dfrac{54}{9}$

Determine whether each two fractions are equivalent.

35. $\dfrac{10}{34}$ and $\dfrac{4}{14}$ **36.** $\dfrac{8}{12}$ and $\dfrac{12}{16}$ **37.** $\dfrac{20}{36}$ and $\dfrac{15}{18}$ **38.** $\dfrac{30}{50}$ and $\dfrac{9}{15}$

(2.4) *Multiply. Write each answer in simplest form. Estimate where noted.*

39. $\dfrac{3}{5} \cdot \dfrac{1}{2}$ **40.** $\dfrac{6}{7} \cdot \dfrac{5}{12}$ **41.** $\dfrac{24}{5} \cdot \dfrac{15}{8}$ **42.** $\dfrac{27}{21} \cdot \dfrac{7}{18}$

43. $5 \cdot \dfrac{7}{8}$ **44.** $6 \cdot \dfrac{5}{12}$ **45.** $\dfrac{39}{3} \cdot \dfrac{7}{13} \cdot \dfrac{5}{21}$ **46.** $\dfrac{42}{5} \cdot \dfrac{15}{6} \cdot \dfrac{7}{9}$

47. $1\dfrac{5}{8} \cdot 3\dfrac{1}{5}$ **48.** $3\dfrac{6}{11} \cdot 1\dfrac{7}{13}$ **49.** $\dfrac{3}{4} \cdot 8 \cdot 4\dfrac{1}{8}$ **50.** $2\dfrac{1}{9} \cdot 3 \cdot \dfrac{1}{38}$

Exact: _____   Exact: _____

Estimate: _____   Estimate: _____

51. There are $7\dfrac{1}{3}$ grams of fat in each ounce of hamburger. How many grams of fat are in a 5-ounce hamburger patty?

52. An art teacher needs 45 pieces of PVC piping for an art project. If each piece needs to be $\dfrac{3}{4}$ inch long, find the total length of piping she needs.

△ **53.** Find the area of each rectangle.

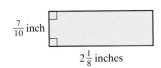

$\frac{7}{10}$ inch

$2\frac{1}{8}$ inches

△ **54.**

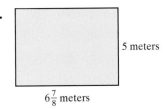

5 meters

$6\frac{7}{8}$ meters

(2.5) *Find the reciprocal of each number.*

55. 7

56. $\frac{1}{8}$

57. $\frac{14}{23}$

58. $\frac{17}{5}$

Divide. Write each answer in simplest form.

59. $\frac{3}{4} \div \frac{3}{8}$

60. $\frac{21}{4} \div \frac{7}{5}$

61. $\frac{5}{3} \div 2$

62. $5 \div \frac{15}{8}$

63. $6\frac{3}{4} \div 1\frac{2}{7}$

64. $5\frac{1}{2} \div 2\frac{1}{11}$

65. A truck traveled 341 miles on $15\frac{1}{2}$ gallons of gas. How many miles might we expect the truck to travel on 1 gallon of gas?

66. Herman Heltznutt walks 5 days a week for a total distance of $5\frac{1}{4}$ miles per week. If he walks the same distance each day, find the distance he walks each day.

Mixed Review

Determine whether each number is an improper fraction, a proper fraction, or a mixed number.

67. $\frac{0}{3}$

68. $\frac{12}{12}$

69. $5\frac{6}{7}$

70. $\frac{13}{9}$

Write each improper fraction as a mixed number or a whole number. Write each mixed number as an improper fraction.

71. $\frac{125}{4}$

72. $\frac{54}{9}$

73. $5\frac{10}{17}$

74. $7\frac{5}{6}$

Identify each number as prime or composite.

75. 27

76. 23

Find the prime factorization of each number.

77. 180

78. 98

Write each fraction in simplest form.

79. $\dfrac{45}{50}$

80. $\dfrac{30}{42}$

81. $\dfrac{140}{150}$

82. $\dfrac{84}{140}$

Multiply or divide as indicated. Write each answer in simplest form. Estimate where noted.

83. $\dfrac{7}{8} \cdot \dfrac{2}{3}$

84. $\dfrac{6}{15} \cdot \dfrac{5}{8}$

85. $\dfrac{18}{5} \div \dfrac{2}{5}$

86. $\dfrac{9}{2} \div \dfrac{1}{3}$

87. $4\dfrac{1}{6} \cdot 2\dfrac{2}{5}$

Exact:
Estimate:

88. $5\dfrac{2}{3} \cdot 2\dfrac{1}{4}$

Exact:
Estimate:

89. $\dfrac{7}{2} \div 1\dfrac{1}{2}$

90. $1\dfrac{3}{5} \div \dfrac{1}{4}$

△ **91.** A slab of natural granite is purchased and a rectangle with length $5\dfrac{1}{2}$ feet and width $7\dfrac{4}{11}$ feet is cut from it. Find the area of the rectangle.

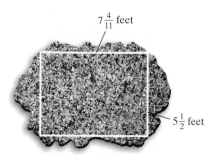

$7\dfrac{4}{11}$ feet

$5\dfrac{1}{2}$ feet

92. An area of Mississippi received $23\dfrac{1}{2}$ inches of rain in $30\dfrac{1}{2}$ hours. How many inches per 1 hour is this?

2 CHAPTER TEST

 Remember to use the Chapter Test Prep Video CD to see the fully worked-out solutions to any of the exercises you want to review.

Write a fraction to represent the shaded area.

1.

2.

Write each mixed number as an improper fraction.

3. $7\dfrac{2}{3}$

4. $3\dfrac{6}{11}$

Write each improper fraction as a mixed number or a whole number.

5. $\dfrac{23}{5}$

6. $\dfrac{75}{4}$

Write each fraction in simplest form.

7. $\dfrac{24}{210}$

8. $\dfrac{42}{70}$

Determine whether these fractions are equivalent.

9. $\dfrac{5}{7}$ and $\dfrac{8}{11}$

10. $\dfrac{6}{27}$ and $\dfrac{14}{63}$

Find the prime factorization of each number.

11. 84

12. 495

1. _____

2. _____

3. _____

4. _____

5. _____

6. _____

7. _____

8. _____

9. _____

10. _____

11. _____

12. _____

Perform each indicated operation. Write each answer in simplest form.

13. $\dfrac{4}{4} \div \dfrac{3}{4}$ **14.** $\dfrac{4}{3} \cdot \dfrac{4}{4}$ **15.** $2 \cdot \dfrac{1}{8}$ **16.** $\dfrac{2}{3} \cdot \dfrac{8}{15}$

17. $8 \div \dfrac{1}{2}$ **18.** $13\dfrac{1}{2} \div 3$ **19.** $\dfrac{3}{8} \cdot \dfrac{16}{6} \cdot \dfrac{4}{11}$ **20.** $5\dfrac{1}{4} \div \dfrac{7}{12}$

21. $\dfrac{16}{3} \div \dfrac{3}{12}$ **22.** $3\dfrac{1}{3} \cdot 6\dfrac{3}{4}$ **23.** $12 \div 3\dfrac{1}{3}$ **24.** $\dfrac{14}{5} \cdot \dfrac{25}{21} \cdot 2$

△ **25.** Find the area of the figure.

$\frac{2}{3}$ mile $\boxed{}$

$1\frac{8}{9}$ miles

26. During a 258-mile trip, a car used $10\dfrac{3}{4}$ gallons of gas. How many miles would we expect the car to travel on 1 gallon of gas?

27. How many square yards of artificial turf are necessary to cover a football field, *not* including the end zones and the sidelines? (*Hint:* A football field measures $100 \times 53\dfrac{1}{3}$ yards.)

$53\frac{1}{3}$ yards

100 yards

28. Prior to an oil spill, the stock in an oil company sold for \$120 per share. As a result of the liability that the company incurred from the spill, the price per share fell to $\dfrac{3}{4}$ of the price before the spill. What did the stock sell for after the spill?

13. _____

14. _____

15. _____

16. _____

17. _____

18. _____

19. _____

20. _____

21. _____

22. _____

23. _____

24. _____

25. _____

26. _____

27. _____

28. _____

Answers

1. Find the place value of the digit 4 in the whole number 48,761.

2. Write 2036 in words.

3. Write the number, eight hundred five, in standard form.

4. Add: $7 + 6 + 10 + 3 + 5$

5. Add: $34,285 + 149,761$

6. Find the average of 56, 18, and 43.

△ 7. Find the perimeter of the polygon shown.

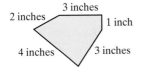

2 inches
3 inches
1 inch
4 inches
3 inches

8. Subtract 8 from 25.

9. The governor's salary in the state of Alabama was recently increased by $1706. If the old salary was $94,655, find the new salary. (*Source: The World Almanac and Book of Facts*, 2003 and 2005)

10. Find $\sqrt{25}$.

11. Subtract: $7826 - 505$
Check by adding.

12. Find 8^2.

13. The graph below shows the ratings of Best Picture nominees since PG-13 was introduced in 1984. On this graph, each bar represents a different rating, and the height of each bar represents the number of Best Picture nominees for that rating. (*Source: Academy of Motion Picture Arts and Sciences; Internet Movie Database*)

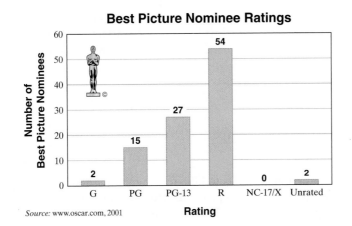

Best Picture Nominee Ratings

Source: www.oscar.com, 2001

a. Which rating did most Best Picture nominees have?
b. Find the total number of Best Picture nominees that were rated G, PG, or PG-13.

1. _____

2. _____

3. _____

4. _____

5. _____

6. _____

7. _____

8. _____

9. _____

10. _____

11. _____

12. _____

13. a. _____

b. _____

14. _____

15. _____

16. _____

17. _____

18. _____

19. a. _____

   b. _____

   c. _____

   d. _____

20. _____

21. a. _____

   b. _____

   c. _____

22. _____

23. a. _____

   b. _____

   c. _____

   d. _____

24. _____

25. _____

26. _____

27. _____

28. _____

29. _____

30. _____

14. Find $205 \div 8$.

15. Round 568 to the nearest ten.

16. Round 2366 to the nearest hundred.

17. Round each number to the nearest hundred to find an estimated difference.

$$4725$$
$$-2879$$

18. Round each number to the nearest ten to find an estimated sum.
$$38 + 43 + 126 + 92$$

19. Multiply.

  a. 6×1 **b.** $0(8)$

  c. $1 \cdot 45$ **d.** $(75)(0)$

20. Simplify: $30 \div 3 \cdot 2$

21. Rewrite each using the distributive property.

  a. $3(4 + 5)$ **b.** $10(6 + 8)$

  c. $2(7 + 3)$

22. Multiply: 12×15

23. Find each quotient. Check by multiplying.

  a. $9\overline{)0}$ **b.** $0 \div 12$

  c. $\dfrac{0}{5}$ **d.** $\dfrac{3}{0}$

24. Find the area.

7 miles	Rectangle

22 miles

25. Divide and check: $1872 \div 9$

26. Subtract: $5000 - 986$

27. How many boxes are needed to ship 56 pairs of Nikes to a shoe store in Texarkana if 9 pairs of shoes will fit in each shipping box?

28. Find the product of 9 and 7.

△ **29.** A gardener bought enough plants to fill a rectangular garden with length 30 feet and width 20 feet. Because of shading problems from a nearby tree, the gardener changed the width of the garden to 15 feet. If the area is to remain the same, what is the new length of the garden?

30. Find the sum of 9 and 7.

Write using exponential notation.

31. $4 \cdot 4 \cdot 4$

32. $7 \cdot 7 \cdot 7 \cdot 7$

33. $6 \cdot 6 \cdot 6 \cdot 8 \cdot 8 \cdot 8 \cdot 8 \cdot 8$

34. $2 \cdot 2 \cdot 3 \cdot 3 \cdot 3 \cdot 3$

35. Simplify: $2 \cdot 4 - 3 \div 3$

36. Simplify: $8 \cdot \sqrt{100} - 4^2 \cdot 5$

37. Write a fraction to represent the shaded part of the figure.

38. Write the prime factorization of 156.

39. Write as improper fractions.

  a. $4\dfrac{2}{9}$ **b.** $1\dfrac{8}{11}$

40. Write $7\dfrac{4}{5}$ as an improper fraction.

41. Find all the factors of 20.

42. Determine whether $\dfrac{8}{20}$ and $\dfrac{14}{35}$ are equivalent.

43. Write in simplest form: $\dfrac{42}{66}$

44. Write in simplest form: $\dfrac{70}{105}$

45. Multiply: $3\dfrac{1}{3} \cdot \dfrac{7}{8}$

46. Multiply: $\dfrac{2}{3} \cdot 4$

47. Find the reciprocal of $\dfrac{1}{3}$.

48. Find the reciprocal of 9.

49. Divide and simplify: $\dfrac{5}{16} \div \dfrac{3}{4}$

50. Divide: $1\dfrac{1}{10} \div 5\dfrac{3}{5}$

31. _____

32. _____

33. _____

34. _____

35. _____

36. _____

37. _____

38. _____

39. a. _____

   b. _____

40. _____

41. _____

42. _____

43. _____

44. _____

45. _____

46. _____

47. _____

48. _____

49. _____

50. _____

3

Adding and Subtracting Fractions

Having learned what fractions are and how to multiply and divide them in Chapter 2, we are ready to continue our study of fractions. In this chapter, we learn how to add and subtract fractions and mixed numbers. We then conclude this chapter with solving problems using fractions.

You may have heard before that the surface of the earth is about $\frac{1}{4}$ land and $\frac{3}{4}$ water, but what about the individual continents and oceans?

In Section 3.1, Exercises 45 through 48, and Section 3.3, Exercises 69 and 70, we use fractions to help us see the relative sizes of the continents and oceans.

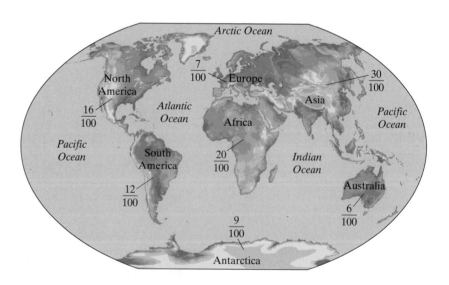

3.1 ADDING AND SUBTRACTING LIKE FRACTIONS

Fractions with the same denominator are called **like fractions.** Fractions that have different denominators are called **unlike fractions.**

Like Fractions

$\frac{2}{5}$ and $\frac{3}{5}$

└──┴── same denominator

$\frac{5}{21}, \frac{16}{21},$ and $\frac{7}{21}$

└──┴──┴── same denominator

Unlike Fractions

$\frac{2}{5}$ and $\frac{3}{4}$

└──┴── different denominator

$\frac{5}{7}$ and $\frac{5}{9}$

└──┴── different denominator

Objective **A** Adding Like Fractions

To see how we add like fractions (fractions with the same denominator), study the figures below:

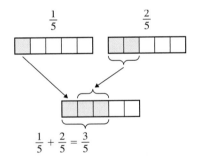

$$\frac{1}{5} + \frac{2}{5} = \frac{3}{5}$$

Adding Like Fractions

To add like fractions, add the numerators and write the sum over the common denominator.

If a, b, and c represent nonzero whole numbers, we have

$$\frac{a}{c} + \frac{b}{c} = \frac{a + b}{c}$$

For example,

$$\frac{1}{4} + \frac{2}{4} = \frac{1 + 2}{4} = \frac{3}{4}$$ ← Add the numerators.
← Keep the denominator.

Helpful Hint

As usual, don't forget to write all answers in simplest form.

PRACTICE PROBLEMS 1–3

Add and simplify.

1. $\dfrac{5}{9} + \dfrac{2}{9}$

2. $\dfrac{5}{8} + \dfrac{1}{8}$

3. $\dfrac{10}{11} + \dfrac{1}{11} + \dfrac{7}{11}$

EXAMPLES Add and simplify.

1. $\dfrac{2}{7} + \dfrac{3}{7} = \dfrac{2+3}{7} = \dfrac{5}{7}$ ← Add the numerators.
                  ← Keep the common denominator.

2. $\dfrac{3}{16} + \dfrac{7}{16} = \dfrac{3+7}{16} = \dfrac{10}{16} = \dfrac{\overset{1}{\cancel{2}} \cdot 5}{\underset{1}{\cancel{2}} \cdot 8} = \dfrac{5}{8}$

3. $\dfrac{7}{13} + \dfrac{6}{13} + \dfrac{3}{13} = \dfrac{7+6+3}{13} = \dfrac{16}{13}$ or $1\dfrac{3}{13}$

Work Practice Problems 1–3

✔ **Concept Check**   Find and correct the error in the following:

$$\dfrac{1}{5} + \dfrac{1}{5} = \dfrac{2}{10}$$

Objective B Subtracting Like Fractions

To see how we subtract like fractions (fractions with the same denominator), study the following figure:

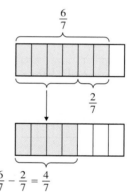

$$\dfrac{6}{7} - \dfrac{2}{7} = \dfrac{4}{7}$$

Subtracting Like Fractions

To subtract like fractions, subtract the numerators and write the difference over the common denominator.

If a, b, and c represent nonzero whole numbers, then

$$\dfrac{a}{c} - \dfrac{b}{c} = \dfrac{a-b}{c}$$

PRACTICE PROBLEMS 4–5

Subtract and simplify.

4. $\dfrac{7}{12} - \dfrac{2}{12}$ 5. $\dfrac{9}{10} - \dfrac{1}{10}$

For example,

$$\dfrac{4}{5} - \dfrac{2}{5} = \dfrac{4-2}{5} = \dfrac{2}{5}$$ ← Subtract the numerators.
                    ← Keep the denominator.

Answers

1. $\dfrac{7}{9}$,   2. $\dfrac{3}{4}$,   3. $\dfrac{18}{11}$ or $1\dfrac{7}{11}$,

4. $\dfrac{5}{12}$,   5. $\dfrac{4}{5}$

EXAMPLES Subtract and simplify.

4. $\dfrac{8}{9} - \dfrac{1}{9} = \dfrac{8-1}{9} = \dfrac{7}{9}$ ← Subtract the numerators.
                    ← Keep the common denominator.

✔ **Concept Check Answer**

We don't add denominators together; correct solution: $\dfrac{1}{5} + \dfrac{1}{5} = \dfrac{2}{5}$.

5. $\dfrac{7}{8} - \dfrac{5}{8} = \dfrac{7-5}{8} = \dfrac{2}{8} = \dfrac{\overset{1}{\cancel{2}}}{\underset{1}{\cancel{2}} \cdot 4} = \dfrac{1}{4}$

Work Practice Problems 4–5

Objective C Solving Problems by Adding or Subtracting Like Fractions

Many real-life problems involve finding the perimeters of square or rectangular areas such as pastures, swimming pools, and so on. We can use our knowledge of adding fractions to find perimeters.

EXAMPLE 6 Find the perimeter of the rectangle.

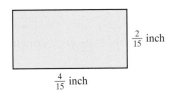

$\frac{2}{15}$ inch

$\frac{4}{15}$ inch

Solution: Recall that perimeter means distance around and that opposite sides of a rectangle are the same length.

$\frac{4}{15}$ inch

$\frac{2}{15}$ inch $\frac{2}{15}$ inch

$\frac{4}{15}$ inch

$$\text{Perimeter} = \frac{2}{15} + \frac{4}{15} + \frac{2}{15} + \frac{4}{15} = \frac{2+4+2+4}{15}$$

$$= \frac{12}{15} = \frac{\overset{1}{\cancel{3}} \cdot 4}{\underset{1}{\cancel{3}} \cdot 5} = \frac{4}{5}$$

The perimeter of the rectangle is $\frac{4}{5}$ inch.

■ **Work Practice Problem 6**

We can combine our skills in adding and subtracting fractions with our four problem-solving steps from Chapter 1 to solve many kinds of real-life problems.

EXAMPLE 7 **Total Amount of an Ingredient in a Recipe**

A recipe calls for $\frac{1}{3}$ of a cup of flour at the beginning and $\frac{2}{3}$ of a cup of flour later. How much total flour is needed to make the recipe?

$\frac{1}{3}$ cup $\frac{2}{3}$ cup

Solution:

1. UNDERSTAND the problem. To do so, read and reread the problem. Since we are finding total flour, we add. Continued on next page

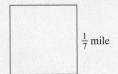

2. TRANSLATE.

In words:	total flour	is	flour at the beginning	added to	flour later
	↓	↓	↓	↓	↓
Translate:	total flour	=	$\frac{1}{3}$	+	$\frac{2}{3}$

3. SOLVE: $\frac{1}{3} + \frac{2}{3} = \frac{1+2}{3} = \frac{\cancel{3}^{1}}{\cancel{3}_{1}} = 1$

4. INTERPRET. *Check* your work. *State* your conclusion: The total flour needed for the recipe is 1 cup.

🔲 **Work Practice Problem 7**

PRACTICE PROBLEM 8

A jogger ran $\frac{13}{4}$ miles on Monday and $\frac{7}{4}$ miles on Wednesday. How much farther did he run on Monday than on Wednesday?

EXAMPLE 8 **Calculating Distance**

The distance from home to the World Gym is $\frac{7}{8}$ of a mile and from home to the post office is $\frac{3}{8}$ of a mile. How much farther is it from home to the World Gym than from home to the post office?

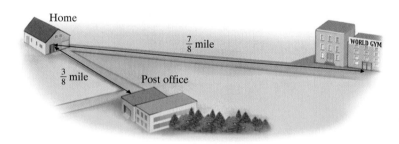

Solution:

1. UNDERSTAND. Read and reread the problem. The phrase "How much farther" tells us to subtract distances.

2. TRANSLATE.

In words:	distance farther	is	home to World Gym distance	minus	home to post office distance
	↓	↓	↓	↓	↓
Translate:	distance farther	=	$\frac{7}{8}$	−	$\frac{3}{8}$

3. SOLVE: $\frac{7}{8} - \frac{3}{8} = \frac{7-3}{8} = \frac{4}{8} = \frac{\cancel{4}^{1}}{2 \cdot \cancel{4}_{1}} = \frac{1}{2}$

4. INTERPRET. *Check* your work. *State* your conclusion: The distance from home to the World Gym is $\frac{1}{2}$ mile farther than from home to the post office.

🔲 **Work Practice Problem 8**

Answer

8. $\frac{3}{2}$ or $1\frac{1}{2}$ mi

Mental Math

State whether the fractions in each list are like or unlike fractions.

1. $\dfrac{7}{8}, \dfrac{7}{10}$

2. $\dfrac{2}{3}, \dfrac{4}{9}$

3. $\dfrac{9}{10}, \dfrac{1}{10}$

4. $\dfrac{8}{11}, \dfrac{2}{11}$

5. $\dfrac{2}{31}, \dfrac{30}{31}, \dfrac{19}{31}$

6. $\dfrac{3}{10}, \dfrac{3}{11}, \dfrac{3}{13}$

7. $\dfrac{5}{12}, \dfrac{7}{12}, \dfrac{12}{11}$

8. $\dfrac{1}{5}, \dfrac{2}{5}, \dfrac{4}{5}$

3.1 EXERCISE SET

FOR EXTRA HELP

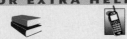

Student Solutions Manual   PH Math/Tutor Center   CD/Video for Review   MathXL   MathXL®   MyMathLab   MyMathLab

Objective A *Add and simplify. See Examples 1 through 3.*

1. $\dfrac{1}{7} + \dfrac{2}{7}$

2. $\dfrac{9}{17} + \dfrac{2}{17}$

3. $\dfrac{1}{10} + \dfrac{1}{10}$

4. $\dfrac{1}{4} + \dfrac{1}{4}$

5. $\dfrac{2}{9} + \dfrac{4}{9}$

6. $\dfrac{3}{10} + \dfrac{2}{10}$

7. $\dfrac{6}{20} + \dfrac{1}{20}$

8. $\dfrac{2}{8} + \dfrac{3}{8}$

9. $\dfrac{3}{14} + \dfrac{4}{14}$

10. $\dfrac{5}{24} + \dfrac{7}{24}$

11. $\dfrac{10}{11} + \dfrac{3}{11}$

12. $\dfrac{13}{17} + \dfrac{9}{17}$

13. $\dfrac{4}{13} + \dfrac{2}{13} + \dfrac{1}{13}$

14. $\dfrac{5}{11} + \dfrac{1}{11} + \dfrac{2}{11}$

15. $\dfrac{7}{18} + \dfrac{3}{18} + \dfrac{2}{18}$

16. $\dfrac{7}{15} + \dfrac{4}{15} + \dfrac{1}{15}$

Objective B *Subtract and simplify. See Examples 4 and 5.*

17. $\dfrac{10}{11} - \dfrac{4}{11}$

18. $\dfrac{9}{13} - \dfrac{5}{13}$

19. $\dfrac{4}{5} - \dfrac{1}{5}$

20. $\dfrac{7}{8} - \dfrac{4}{8}$

21. $\dfrac{7}{4} - \dfrac{3}{4}$

22. $\dfrac{18}{5} - \dfrac{3}{5}$

23. $\dfrac{7}{8} - \dfrac{1}{8}$

24. $\dfrac{5}{6} - \dfrac{1}{6}$

25. $\dfrac{25}{12} - \dfrac{15}{12}$

26. $\dfrac{30}{20} - \dfrac{15}{20}$

27. $\dfrac{11}{10} - \dfrac{3}{10}$

28. $\dfrac{14}{15} - \dfrac{4}{15}$

29. $\dfrac{27}{33} - \dfrac{8}{33}$

30. $\dfrac{37}{45} - \dfrac{18}{45}$

Objectives **A** **B** **Mixed Practice** *Perform the indicated operation. See Examples 1 through 5.*

31. $\dfrac{8}{21} + \dfrac{5}{21}$

32. $\dfrac{7}{37} + \dfrac{9}{37}$

33. $\dfrac{99}{100} - \dfrac{9}{100}$

34. $\dfrac{85}{200} - \dfrac{15}{200}$

35. $\dfrac{13}{28} - \dfrac{13}{28}$

36. $\dfrac{15}{26} - \dfrac{15}{26}$

37. $\dfrac{3}{16} + \dfrac{7}{16} + \dfrac{2}{16}$

38. $\dfrac{5}{18} + \dfrac{1}{18} + \dfrac{6}{18}$

Objective **C** *Find the perimeter of each figure. (Hint: Recall that perimeter means distance around.) See Example 6.*

39.
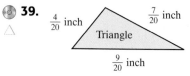

40.
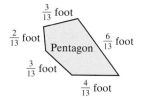

41.
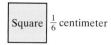

42.

Square $\dfrac{1}{6}$ centimeter

Solve. Write each answer in simplest form. See Examples 7 and 8.

43. Emil Vasquez, a bodybuilder, worked out $\dfrac{7}{8}$ of an hour one morning before school and $\dfrac{5}{8}$ of an hour that evening. How long did he work out that day?

44. A recipe for Heavenly Hash cake calls for $\dfrac{3}{4}$ cup of sugar and later $\dfrac{1}{4}$ cup of sugar. How much sugar is needed to make the recipe?

The map of the world below shows the fraction of the world's surface land area taken up by each continent. In other words, the continent of Africa makes up $\frac{20}{100}$ of the land in the world. Use this map for Exercises 45 through 48.

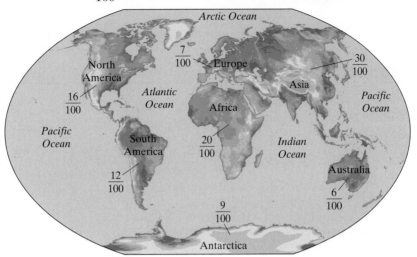

45. Find the fractional part of the world's land area within the continents of North America and South America.

46. Find the fractional part of the world's land area within the continents of Asia and Africa.

47. How much greater is the fractional part of the continent of Antarctica than the fractional part of the continent of Europe?

48. How much greater is the fractional part of the continent of Asia than the continent of Australia?

49. A railroad inspector must inspect $\frac{19}{20}$ of a mile of railroad track. If she has already inspected $\frac{5}{20}$ of a mile, how much more does she need to inspect?

50. Scott Davis has run $\frac{11}{8}$ miles already and plans to complete $\frac{16}{8}$ miles. To do this, how much farther must he run?

51. In the United States, about $\frac{7}{20}$ of all households own two television sets. Approximately $\frac{8}{20}$ of all households own 3 or more television sets. What fraction of U.S. households own 2 or more television sets? (*Source:* Neilsen Media Research)

52. In a recent survey, $\frac{55}{100}$ of people said that visiting family and friends would be their pleasure trip of choice while $\frac{29}{100}$ of people surveyed said that going to a beach resort would be their pleasure trip of choice. What fraction of people surveyed said visiting family and friends or going to a beach resort? (*Source:* American Express)

53. In 2004, the fraction of states in the United States with maximum interstate highway speed limits up to and including 70 mph was $\frac{37}{50}$. The fraction of states with 70 mph speed limits was $\frac{16}{50}$. What fraction of states had speed limits that were less than 70 mph? (*Source:* Insurance Institute for Highway Safety)

54. When people take aspirin, $\frac{31}{50}$ of the time it is used to treat some type of pain. Approximately $\frac{7}{50}$ of all aspirin use is for treating headaches. What fraction of aspirin use is for treating pain other than headaches? (*Source:* Bayer Market Research)

Review

Write the prime factorization of each number. See Section 2.2.

55. 10   **56.** 12   **57.** 8   **58.** 20   **59.** 55   **60.** 28

Concept Extensions

Perform each indicated operation.

61. $\dfrac{3}{8} + \dfrac{7}{8} - \dfrac{5}{8}$ **62.** $\dfrac{12}{20} - \dfrac{1}{20} - \dfrac{3}{20}$ **63.** $\dfrac{4}{11} + \dfrac{5}{11} - \dfrac{3}{11} + \dfrac{2}{11}$ **64.** $\dfrac{9}{12} + \dfrac{1}{12} - \dfrac{3}{12} - \dfrac{5}{12}$

Find and correct the error. See the Concept Check in this section.

65.
$$\dfrac{2}{7} + \dfrac{9}{7} = \dfrac{11}{14}$$

66.
$$\dfrac{3}{4} - \dfrac{1}{4} = \dfrac{2}{8} = \dfrac{1}{4}$$

Solve. Write each answer in simplest form.

67. In your own words, explain how to add like fractions.

68. In your own words, explain how to subtract like fractions.

69. Use the map of the world for Exercises 45 through 48 and find the sum of all the continents' fractions. Explain your answer.

70. Mike Cannon jogged $\dfrac{3}{8}$ of a mile from home and then rested. Then he continued jogging further from home for another $\dfrac{3}{8}$ of a mile until he discovered his watch had fallen off. He walked back along the same path for $\dfrac{4}{8}$ of a mile until he found his watch. Find how far he was from his home.

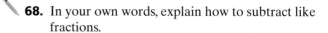

STUDY SKILLS BUILDER

How Well Do You Know Your Textbook?

The questions below will determine whether you are familiar with your textbook. For help, see Section 1.1 in this text.

1. What does the 💿 icon mean?

2. What does the ✏ icon mean?

3. What does the △ icon mean?

4. Where can you find a review for each chapter? What answers to this review can be found in the back of your text?

5. Each chapter contains an overview of the chapter along with examples. What is this feature called?

6. Each chapter contains a review of vocabulary. What is this feature called?

7. There is a CD in your text. What content is contained on this CD?

8. What is the location of the section that is entirely devoted to study skills?

9. There are Practice Problems that are contained in the margin of the text. What are they and how can they be used?

3.2 LEAST COMMON MULTIPLE

Objectives

A Find the Least Common Multiple (LCM) Using Multiples.

B Find the LCM Using Prime Factorization.

C Write Equivalent Fractions.

Objective **A** Finding the Least Common Multiple Using Multiples

A multiple of a number is the product of that number and a natural number. For example,
multiples of 5 are

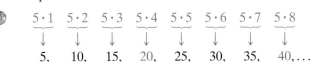

Multiples of 4 are

4, 8, 12, 16, 20, 24, 28, 32, 36, 40, 44, . . .

Common multiples of both 4 and 5 are numbers that are found in both lists above. If we study the lists of multiples and extend them we have

Common multiples of 4 and 5: 20, 40, 60, 80, . . .

We call the smallest number in the list of common multiples the **least common multiple (LCM).** From the list of common multiples of 4 and 5, we see that the LCM of 4 and 5 is 20.

EXAMPLE 1 Find the LCM of 6 and 8.

Solution: Multiples of 6: 6, 12, 18, 24, 30, 36, 42, 48, . . .

Multiples of 8: 8, 16, 24, 32, 40, 48, 56, . . .

The common multiples are 24, 48, ... The least common multiple (LCM) is 24.

▫ **Work Practice Problem 1**

Listing all the multiples of every number in a list can be cumbersome and tedious. We can condense the procedure shown in Example 1 with the following steps:

Method 1: Finding the LCM of a List of Numbers Using Multiples of the Largest Number

Step 1: Write the multiples of the largest number (starting with the number itself) until a multiple common to all numbers in the list is found.

Step 2: The multiple found in Step 1 is the LCM.

EXAMPLE 2 Find the LCM of 9 and 12.

Solution: We write the multiples of 12 until we find a number that is also a multiple of 9.

$12 \cdot 1 = 12$ Not a multiple of 9.

$12 \cdot 2 = 24$ Not a multiple of 9.

$12 \cdot 3 = 36$ A multiple of 9.

The LCM of 9 and 12 is 36.

▫ **Work Practice Problem 2**

PRACTICE PROBLEM 1

Find the LCM of 15 and 50.

PRACTICE PROBLEM 2

Find the LCM of 8 and 10.

Answers

1. 150, **2.** 40

PRACTICE PROBLEM 3

Find the LCM of 8 and 16.

EXAMPLE 3 Find the LCM of 7 and 14.

Solution: We write the multiples of 14 until we find one that is also a multiple of 7.

$14 \cdot 1 = 14$ A multiple of 7

The LCM of 7 and 14 is 14.

▣ **Work Practice Problem 3**

PRACTICE PROBLEM 4

Find the LCM of 25 and 30.

EXAMPLE 4 Find the LCM of 12 and 20.

Solution: We write the multiples of 20 until we find one that is also a multiple of 12.

$20 \cdot 1 = 20$ Not a multiple of 12
$20 \cdot 2 = 40$ Not a multiple of 12
$20 \cdot 3 = 60$ A multiple of 12

The LCM of 12 and 20 is 60.

▣ **Work Practice Problem 4**

Objective **B** Finding the LCM Using Prime Factorization

Method 1 for finding multiples works fine for smaller numbers, but may get tedious for larger numbers. A second method that uses prime factorization may be easier to use for larger numbers.

For example, to find the LCM of 270 and 84, let's look at the prime factorization of each.

$270 = 2 \cdot 3 \cdot 3 \cdot 3 \cdot 5$
$84 = 2 \cdot 2 \cdot 3 \cdot 7$

Recall that the LCM must be a multiple of both 270 and 84. Thus, to build the LCM, we will circle the greatest number of factors for each different prime number. The LCM is the product of the circled factors.

Prime Number Factors

$270 =$	$2 \cdot$	$(3 \cdot 3 \cdot 3) \cdot$	(5)
$84 =$	$(2 \cdot 2) \cdot$	$3 \cdot$	(7)

$$LCM = 2 \cdot 2 \cdot 3 \cdot 3 \cdot 3 \cdot 5 \cdot 7 = 3780$$

The number 3780 is the smallest number that both 270 and 84 divide into evenly.

This method 2 is summarized below:

Method 2: Finding the LCM of a List of Numbers Using Prime Factorization

Step 1: Write the prime factorization of each number.

Step 2: For each different prime factor in step 1, circle the greatest number of times that factor occurs in any one factorization.

Step 3: The LCM is the product of the circled factors.

Answers

3. 16, **4.** 150

EXAMPLE 5 Find the LCM of 72 and 60.

Solution: First we write the prime factorization of each number.

$$72 = 2 \cdot 2 \cdot 2 \cdot 3 \cdot 3$$
$$60 = 2 \cdot 2 \cdot 3 \cdot 5$$

For the prime factors shown, we circle the greatest number of factors found in either factorization.

$$72 = \boxed{2 \cdot 2 \cdot 2} \cdot \boxed{3 \cdot 3}$$
$$60 = 2 \cdot 2 \cdot 3 \cdot \boxed{5}$$

The LCM is the product of the circled factors.

$$\text{LCM} = 2 \cdot 2 \cdot 2 \cdot 3 \cdot 3 \cdot 5 = 360$$

The LCM is 360.

 Work Practice Problem 5

Helpful Hint

If you prefer working with exponents, circle the factor with the greatest exponent.

Example 5:

$$72 = \boxed{2^3} \cdot \boxed{3^2}$$
$$60 = 2^2 \cdot 3 \cdot \boxed{5}$$
$$\text{LCD} = 2^3 \cdot 3^2 \cdot 5 = 360$$

Helpful Hint

If the number of factors of a prime number are equal, circle either one, but not both. For example,

$$12 = \boxed{2 \cdot 2} \cdot \boxed{3}$$
$$15 = 3 \cdot \boxed{5}$$

Circle either 3 but not both.

The LCM is $2 \cdot 2 \cdot 3 \cdot 5 = 60$.

EXAMPLE 6 Find the LCM of 15, 18, and 54.

Solution: $15 = 3 \cdot \boxed{5}$
$18 = \boxed{2} \cdot 3 \cdot 3$
$54 = 2 \cdot \boxed{3 \cdot 3 \cdot 3}$

The LCM is $2 \cdot 3 \cdot 3 \cdot 3 \cdot 5$ or 270.

 Work Practice Problem 6

EXAMPLE 7 Find the LCM of 11 and 33.

Solution: $11 = \boxed{11}$
$33 = \boxed{3} \cdot 11$

It makes no difference which 11 is circled.

The LCM is $3 \cdot 11$ or 33.

Work Practice Problem 7

PRACTICE PROBLEM 5
Find the LCM of 40 and 108.

PRACTICE PROBLEM 6
Find the LCM of 20, 24, and 45.

PRACTICE PROBLEM 7
Find the LCM of 7 and 21.

Answers
5. 1080,   **6.** 360,   **7.** 21

Objective C Writing Equivalent Fractions

To add or subtract unlike fractions in the next section, we first write equivalent fractions with the LCM as the denominator. Recall from Section 2.3 that fractions that represent the same portion of a whole are called "equivalent fractions."

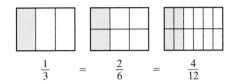

$$\frac{1}{3} \quad = \quad \frac{2}{6} \quad = \quad \frac{4}{12}$$

To write $\frac{1}{3}$ as an equivalent fraction with a denominator of 12, we multiply by 1 in the form of $\frac{4}{4}$.

$$\frac{1}{3} = \frac{1}{3} \cdot 1 = \frac{1}{3} \cdot \frac{4}{4} = \frac{1 \cdot 4}{3 \cdot 4} = \frac{4}{12}$$

$$\frac{4}{4} = 1$$

So $\frac{1}{3} = \frac{4}{12}$.

To Write an Equivalent Fraction,

$$\frac{a}{b} = \frac{a}{b} \cdot \frac{c}{c} = \frac{a \cdot c}{b \cdot c}$$

where a, b, and c are nonzero numbers.

✔ **Concept Check** Which of the following is not equivalent to $\frac{3}{4}$?

a. $\frac{6}{8}$ **b.** $\frac{18}{24}$ **c.** $\frac{9}{14}$ **d.** $\frac{30}{40}$

PRACTICE PROBLEM 8

Write an equivalent fraction with the indicated denominator: $\frac{7}{8} = \frac{}{56}$

Answer

8. $\frac{49}{56}$

✔ **Concept Check Answer**

c

EXAMPLE 8 Write an equivalent fraction with the indicated denominator.

$$\frac{3}{4} = \frac{}{20}$$

Solution: In the denominators, since $4 \cdot 5 = 20$, we will multiply by 1 in the form of $\frac{5}{5}$.

$$\frac{3}{4} = \frac{3}{4} \cdot \frac{5}{5} = \frac{3 \cdot 5}{4 \cdot 5} = \frac{15}{20}$$

Thus, $\frac{3}{4} = \frac{15}{20}$.

▣ **Work Practice Problem 8**

Helpful Hint

To check Example 8, write $\frac{15}{20}$ in simplest form.

$$\frac{15}{20} = \frac{3 \cdot \overset{1}{\cancel{5}}}{4 \cdot \underset{1}{\cancel{5}}} = \frac{3}{4}, \text{ the original fraction.}$$

If the original fraction is in lowest terms, we can check our work by writing the new equivalent fraction in simplest form. This form should be the original fraction.

EXAMPLE 9 Write an equivalent fraction with the indicated denominator.

$$\frac{1}{2} = \frac{}{14}$$

Solution: Since $2 \cdot 7 = 14$, we multiply by 1 in the form of $\frac{7}{7}$.

$$\frac{1}{2} = \frac{1}{2} \cdot \frac{7}{7} = \frac{1 \cdot 7}{2 \cdot 7} = \frac{7}{14}$$

Thus, $\frac{1}{2} = \frac{7}{14}$.

◻ **Work Practice Problem 9**

✔ **Concept Check** True or false? When the fraction $\frac{2}{9}$ is rewritten as an equivalent fraction with 27 as the denominator, the result is $\frac{2}{27}$.

PRACTICE PROBLEM 9

Write an equivalent fraction with the indicated denominator.
$$\frac{3}{5} = \frac{}{15}$$

Answer

9. $\frac{9}{15}$

✔ **Concept Check Answer**

false; the correct result would be $\frac{6}{27}$

3.2 EXERCISE SET

Objectives **A** **B** **Mixed Practice** *Find the LCM of each list of numbers. See Examples 1 through 7.*

1. 3, 4

2. 4, 6

3. 9, 15

4. 15, 20

5. 12, 18

6. 10, 15

7. 24, 36

8. 42, 70

9. 18, 21

10. 24, 45

11. 15, 25

12. 21, 14

13. 8, 24

14. 15, 90

15. 6, 7

16. 13, 8

17. 8, 6, 27

18. 6, 25, 10

19. 25, 15, 6

20. 4, 14, 20

21. 34, 68

22. 25, 175

23. 84, 294

24. 48, 54

25. 30, 36, 50

26. 21, 28, 42

27. 50, 72, 120

28. 70, 98, 100

29. 11, 33, 121

30. 10, 15, 100

31. 4, 6, 10, 15

32. 25, 3, 15, 10

Objective **C** *Write each fraction as an equivalent fraction with the given denominator. See Examples 8 and 9.*

33. $\dfrac{4}{7} = \dfrac{}{35}$

34. $\dfrac{3}{5} = \dfrac{}{20}$

35. $\dfrac{2}{3} = \dfrac{}{21}$

36. $\dfrac{5}{6} = \dfrac{}{24}$

37. $\dfrac{2}{5} = \dfrac{}{25}$

38. $\dfrac{9}{10} = \dfrac{}{70}$

39. $\dfrac{1}{2} = \dfrac{}{30}$

40. $\dfrac{1}{3} = \dfrac{}{30}$

41. $\dfrac{10}{7} = \dfrac{}{21}$

42. $\dfrac{5}{3} = \dfrac{}{21}$

43. $\dfrac{3}{4} = \dfrac{}{28}$

44. $\dfrac{4}{5} = \dfrac{}{45}$

45. $\dfrac{2}{3} = \dfrac{}{45}$

46. $\dfrac{2}{3} = \dfrac{}{75}$

47. $\dfrac{4}{9} = \dfrac{}{81}$

48. $\dfrac{5}{11} = \dfrac{}{88}$

49. $\dfrac{15}{13} = \dfrac{}{78}$

50. $\dfrac{9}{7} = \dfrac{}{84}$

51. $\dfrac{14}{17} = \dfrac{}{68}$

52. $\dfrac{19}{21} = \dfrac{}{126}$

Review

Add or subtract as indicated. See Section 3.1.

53. $\dfrac{7}{10} - \dfrac{2}{10}$

54. $\dfrac{8}{13} - \dfrac{3}{13}$

55. $\dfrac{1}{5} + \dfrac{1}{5}$

56. $\dfrac{1}{8} + \dfrac{3}{8}$

57. $\dfrac{23}{18} - \dfrac{15}{18}$

58. $\dfrac{36}{30} - \dfrac{12}{30}$

59. $\dfrac{2}{9} + \dfrac{1}{9} + \dfrac{6}{9}$

60. $\dfrac{2}{12} + \dfrac{7}{12} + \dfrac{3}{12}$

Concept Extensions

Write each fraction as an equivalent fraction with the indicated denominator.

61. $\dfrac{37}{165} = \dfrac{}{3630}$

62. $\dfrac{108}{215} = \dfrac{}{4085}$

63. In your own words, explain how to find the LCM of two numbers.

64. In your own words, explain how to write a fraction as an equivalent fraction with a given denominator.

Solve. See the Concept Checks in this section.

65. Which of the following are equivalent to $\dfrac{2}{3}$?

    a. $\dfrac{10}{15}$ **b.** $\dfrac{40}{60}$

    c. $\dfrac{16}{20}$ **d.** $\dfrac{200}{300}$

66. True or False? When the fraction $\dfrac{7}{12}$ is rewritten with a denominator of 48, the result is $\dfrac{11}{48}$. If false, give the correct fraction.

3.3 ADDING AND SUBTRACTING UNLIKE FRACTIONS

Objective A Adding Unlike Fractions

In this section we add and subtract fractions with unlike denominators. To add or subtract these unlike fractions, we first write the fractions as equivalent fractions with a common denominator and then add or subtract the like fractions. The common denominator that we use is the least common multiple (LCM) of the denominators. This denominator is called the **least common denominator (LCD)**.

To begin, let's add the unlike fractions $\frac{3}{4} + \frac{1}{6}$.

The LCM of denominators 4 and 6 is 12. This means that the number 12 is also the LCD. So we write each fraction as an equivalent fraction with a denominator of 12.

$$\frac{3}{4} = \frac{3}{4} \cdot \frac{3}{3} = \frac{9}{12} \quad \text{and} \quad \frac{1}{6} = \frac{1}{6} \cdot \frac{2}{2} = \frac{2}{12} \qquad \text{Remember } \frac{3}{3} = 1 \text{ and } \frac{2}{2} = 1.$$

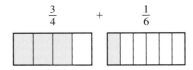

Now we can add, just as in Section 3.1.

$$\frac{3}{4} + \frac{1}{6} = \frac{9}{12} + \frac{2}{12} = \frac{11}{12}$$

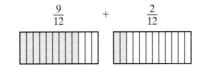

$$\frac{9}{12} + \frac{2}{12} = \frac{11}{12}$$

Adding or Subtracting Unlike Fractions

Step 1: Find the LCM of the denominators of the fractions. This number is the least common denominator (LCD).

Step 2: Write each fraction as an equivalent fraction whose denominator is the LCD.

Step 3: Add or subtract the like fractions.

Step 4: Write the sum or difference in simplest form.

EXAMPLE 1 Add: $\dfrac{2}{5} + \dfrac{4}{15}$

Solution:

Step 1: The LCM of the denominators 5 and 15 is 15. Thus, the LCD is 15. In later examples, we shall simply say, for example, that the LCD of 5 and 15 is 15.

Step 2: $\dfrac{2}{5} = \dfrac{2}{5} \cdot \dfrac{3}{3} = \dfrac{6}{15}, \quad \dfrac{4}{15} = \dfrac{4}{15}$ ← This fraction already has a denominator of 15.

                   └─ Multiply by 1 in the form $\dfrac{3}{3}$

Step 3: $\dfrac{2}{5} + \dfrac{4}{15} = \dfrac{6}{15} + \dfrac{4}{15} = \dfrac{10}{15}$

Step 4: Write in simplest form.

$$\dfrac{10}{15} = \dfrac{2 \cdot \overset{1}{\cancel{5}}}{3 \cdot \underset{1}{\cancel{5}}} = \dfrac{2}{3}$$

💿 **Work Practice Problem 1**

EXAMPLE 2 Add: $\dfrac{2}{15} + \dfrac{3}{10}$

Solution:

Step 1: The LCD of 15 and 10 is 30.

Step 2: $\dfrac{2}{15} = \dfrac{2}{15} \cdot \dfrac{2}{2} = \dfrac{4}{30} \qquad \dfrac{3}{10} = \dfrac{3}{10} \cdot \dfrac{3}{3} = \dfrac{9}{30}$

Step 3: $\dfrac{2}{15} + \dfrac{3}{10} = \dfrac{4}{30} + \dfrac{9}{30} = \dfrac{13}{30}$

Step 4: $\dfrac{13}{30}$ is in simplest form.

💿 **Work Practice Problem 2**

EXAMPLE 3 Add: $\dfrac{2}{3} + \dfrac{1}{7}$

Solution: The LCD of 3 and 7 is 21.

$$\dfrac{2}{3} + \dfrac{1}{7} = \dfrac{2}{3} \cdot \dfrac{7}{7} + \dfrac{1}{7} \cdot \dfrac{3}{3}$$

$$= \dfrac{14}{21} + \dfrac{3}{21}$$

$$= \dfrac{17}{21} \qquad \text{Simplest form.}$$

💿 **Work Practice Problem 3**

PRACTICE PROBLEM 4

Add: $\dfrac{1}{4} + \dfrac{4}{5} + \dfrac{9}{10}$

EXAMPLE 4 Add: $\dfrac{1}{2} + \dfrac{2}{3} + \dfrac{5}{6}$

Solution: The LCD of 2, 3, and 6 is 6.

$$\frac{1}{2} + \frac{2}{3} + \frac{5}{6} = \frac{1}{2} \cdot \frac{3}{3} + \frac{2}{3} \cdot \frac{2}{2} + \frac{5}{6}$$

$$= \frac{3}{6} + \frac{4}{6} + \frac{5}{6}$$

$$= \frac{12}{6} = 2$$

Work Practice Problem 4

✔**Concept Check** Find and correct the error in the following:

$$\frac{2}{9} + \frac{4}{11} = \frac{6}{20} = \frac{3}{10}$$

Objective B Subtracting Unlike Fractions

As indicated in the box on page 194, we follow the same steps when subtracting unlike fractions as when adding them.

PRACTICE PROBLEM 5

Subtract: $\dfrac{7}{12} - \dfrac{5}{24}$

EXAMPLE 5 Subtract: $\dfrac{2}{5} - \dfrac{3}{20}$

Solution:

Step 1: The LCD of 5 and 20 is 20.

Step 2: $\dfrac{2}{5} = \dfrac{2}{5} \cdot \dfrac{4}{4} = \dfrac{8}{20}$ $\dfrac{3}{20} = \dfrac{3}{20}$ ← The fraction already has a denominator of 20.

Step 3: $\dfrac{2}{5} - \dfrac{3}{20} = \dfrac{8}{20} - \dfrac{3}{20} = \dfrac{5}{20}$

Step 4: Write in simplest form.

$$\frac{5}{20} = \frac{\overset{1}{\cancel{5}}}{\underset{1}{\cancel{5}} \cdot 4} = \frac{1}{4}$$

Work Practice Problem 5

PRACTICE PROBLEM 6

Subtract: $\dfrac{9}{10} - \dfrac{3}{7}$

EXAMPLE 6 Subtract: $\dfrac{10}{11} - \dfrac{2}{3}$

Solution:

Step 1: The LCD of 11 and 3 is 33.

Step 2: $\dfrac{10}{11} = \dfrac{10}{11} \cdot \dfrac{3}{3} = \dfrac{30}{33}$ $\dfrac{2}{3} = \dfrac{2}{3} \cdot \dfrac{11}{11} = \dfrac{22}{33}$

Step 3: $\dfrac{10}{11} - \dfrac{2}{3} = \dfrac{30}{33} - \dfrac{22}{33} = \dfrac{8}{33}$

Step 4: $\dfrac{8}{33}$ is in simplest form.

Work Practice Problem 6

EXAMPLE 7 Subtract: $\dfrac{11}{12} - \dfrac{2}{9}$

Solution: The LCD of 12 and 9 is 36.

$$\dfrac{11}{12} - \dfrac{2}{9} = \dfrac{11}{12} \cdot \dfrac{3}{3} - \dfrac{2}{9} \cdot \dfrac{4}{4}$$

$$= \dfrac{33}{36} - \dfrac{8}{36}$$

$$= \dfrac{25}{36}$$

🔲 **Work Practice Problem 7**

Objective C Solving Problems by Adding or Subtracting Unlike Fractions

Very often, real-world problems involve adding or subtracting unlike fractions.

EXAMPLE 8 **Finding Total Weight**

A freight truck has $\dfrac{1}{4}$ ton of computers, $\dfrac{1}{3}$ ton of televisions, and $\dfrac{3}{8}$ ton of small appliances. Find the total weight of its load.

| | $\frac{1}{4}$ ton of computers | $\frac{1}{3}$ ton of televisions | $\frac{3}{8}$ ton of appliances |

Solution:

1. UNDERSTAND. Read and reread the problem. The phrase "total weight" tells us to add.

2. TRANSLATE.

In words:	total weight	is	weight of computers	plus	weight of televisions	plus	weight of appliances
	↓	↓	↓	↓	↓	↓	↓
Translate:	total weight	=	$\dfrac{1}{4}$	+	$\dfrac{1}{3}$	+	$\dfrac{3}{8}$

3. SOLVE: The LCD is 24.

$$\dfrac{1}{4} + \dfrac{1}{3} + \dfrac{3}{8} = \dfrac{1}{4} \cdot \dfrac{6}{6} + \dfrac{1}{3} \cdot \dfrac{8}{8} + \dfrac{3}{8} \cdot \dfrac{3}{3}$$

$$= \dfrac{6}{24} + \dfrac{8}{24} + \dfrac{9}{24}$$

$$= \dfrac{23}{24}$$

4. INTERPRET. *Check* the solution. *State* your conclusion: The total weight of the truck's load is $\dfrac{23}{24}$ ton.

🔲 **Work Practice Problem 8**

PRACTICE PROBLEM 7

Subtract: $\dfrac{7}{8} - \dfrac{5}{6}$

PRACTICE PROBLEM 8

To repair her sidewalk, a homeowner must pour small amounts of cement in three different locations. She needs $\dfrac{3}{5}$ of a cubic yard, $\dfrac{2}{10}$ of a cubic yard, and $\dfrac{2}{15}$ of a cubic yard for these locations. Find the total amount of cement the homeowner needs.

Answers

7. $\dfrac{1}{24}$, 8. $\dfrac{14}{15}$ cu yd

PRACTICE PROBLEM 9

Find the difference in length of two boards if one board is $\frac{4}{5}$ of a foot long and the other is $\frac{2}{3}$ of a foot long.

EXAMPLE 9 Calculating Flight Time

A flight from Tucson to Phoenix, Arizona, requires $\frac{5}{12}$ of an hour. If the plane has been flying $\frac{1}{4}$ of an hour, find how much time remains before landing.

Solution:

1. **UNDERSTAND.** Read and reread the problem. The phrase "how much time remains" tells us to subtract.

2. **TRANSLATE.**

In words:	time remaining	is	flight time from Tucson to Phoenix	minus	flight time already passed
	↓	↓	↓	↓	↓
Translate:	time remaining	=	$\frac{5}{12}$	−	$\frac{1}{4}$

3. **SOLVE:** The LCD is 12.

$$\frac{5}{12} - \frac{1}{4} = \frac{5}{12} - \frac{1}{4} \cdot \frac{3}{3}$$

$$= \frac{5}{12} - \frac{3}{12}$$

$$= \frac{2}{12} = \frac{\overset{1}{\cancel{2}}}{\underset{1}{\cancel{2}} \cdot 6} = \frac{1}{6}$$

4. **INTERPRET.** *Check* the solution. *State* your conclusion: The flight time remaining is $\frac{1}{6}$ of an hour.

■ **Work Practice Problem 9**

Answer

9. $\frac{2}{15}$ ft

Scientific Calculator

Many calculators have a fraction key, such as $\boxed{a\ b/c}$, that allows you to enter fractions, perform operations on fractions, and will give the result as a fraction. If your calculator has a fraction key, use it to calculate

$$\frac{3}{5} + \frac{4}{7}$$

Enter the keystrokes

$\boxed{3}\ \boxed{a\ b/c}\ \boxed{5}\ \boxed{+}\ \boxed{4}\ \boxed{a\ b/c}\ \boxed{7}\ \boxed{=}$

The display should read $\boxed{1\_6\ |\ 35}$

which represents the mixed number $1\frac{6}{35}$. Let's write the result as a fraction. To convert from mixed number notation to fractional notation, press

$\boxed{2^{\text{nd}}}\ \boxed{d/c}$

The display now reads $\boxed{41\ |\ 35}$

which represents $\frac{41}{35}$, the sum in fractional notation.

Graphing Calculator

Graphing calculators also allow you to perform operations on fractions and will give exact fractional results. The fraction option on a graphing calculator may be found under the $\boxed{\text{MATH}}$ menu. To perform the addition above, try the keystrokes.

$\boxed{3}\ \boxed{\div}\ \boxed{5}\ \boxed{+}\ \boxed{4}\ \boxed{\div}\ \boxed{7}\ \boxed{\text{MATH}}\ \boxed{\text{ENTER}}$
$\boxed{\text{ENTER}}$

The display should read

$\boxed{3/5\ +\ 4/7 \blacktriangleright \text{Frac } 41/35}$

Use a calculator to add the following fractions. Give each sum as a fraction.

1. $\dfrac{1}{16} + \dfrac{2}{5}$ **2.** $\dfrac{3}{20} + \dfrac{2}{25}$ **3.** $\dfrac{4}{9} + \dfrac{7}{8}$

4. $\dfrac{9}{11} + \dfrac{5}{12}$ **5.** $\dfrac{10}{17} + \dfrac{12}{19}$ **6.** $\dfrac{14}{31} + \dfrac{15}{21}$

3.3 EXERCISE SET

FOR EXTRA HELP

Student Solutions Manual   PH Math/Tutor Center   CD/Video for Review   MathXL®   MyMathLab

Objective A *Add and simplify. See Examples 1 through 4.*

1. $\dfrac{2}{3} + \dfrac{1}{6}$ **2.** $\dfrac{5}{6} + \dfrac{1}{12}$ **3.** $\dfrac{1}{2} + \dfrac{1}{3}$ **4.** $\dfrac{2}{3} + \dfrac{1}{4}$

5. $\dfrac{2}{11} + \dfrac{2}{33}$ **6.** $\dfrac{5}{9} + \dfrac{1}{3}$ **7.** $\dfrac{3}{14} + \dfrac{3}{7}$ **8.** $\dfrac{2}{5} + \dfrac{2}{15}$

9. $\dfrac{11}{35} + \dfrac{2}{7}$ **10.** $\dfrac{4}{5} + \dfrac{3}{40}$ **11.** $\dfrac{8}{25} + \dfrac{7}{35}$ **12.** $\dfrac{5}{14} + \dfrac{10}{21}$

13. $\dfrac{7}{15} + \dfrac{5}{12}$ **14.** $\dfrac{5}{8} + \dfrac{3}{20}$ **15.** $\dfrac{2}{28} + \dfrac{2}{21}$ **16.** $\dfrac{6}{25} + \dfrac{7}{35}$

17. $\dfrac{9}{44} + \dfrac{17}{36}$

18. $\dfrac{2}{33} + \dfrac{2}{21}$

19. $\dfrac{5}{11} + \dfrac{3}{13}$

20. $\dfrac{3}{7} + \dfrac{9}{17}$

21. $\dfrac{1}{3} + \dfrac{1}{9} + \dfrac{1}{27}$

22. $\dfrac{1}{4} + \dfrac{1}{16} + \dfrac{1}{64}$

23. $\dfrac{5}{7} + \dfrac{1}{8} + \dfrac{1}{2}$

24. $\dfrac{10}{13} + \dfrac{7}{10} + \dfrac{1}{5}$

25. $\dfrac{5}{11} + \dfrac{3}{9} + \dfrac{2}{3}$

26. $\dfrac{7}{18} + \dfrac{2}{9} + \dfrac{5}{6}$

27. $\dfrac{13}{20} + \dfrac{3}{5} + \dfrac{1}{3}$

28. $\dfrac{2}{7} + \dfrac{13}{28} + \dfrac{2}{5}$

Objective **B** *Subtract and simplify. See Examples 5 through 7.*

29. $\dfrac{7}{8} - \dfrac{3}{16}$

30. $\dfrac{5}{13} - \dfrac{3}{26}$

31. $\dfrac{5}{6} - \dfrac{3}{7}$

32. $\dfrac{3}{4} - \dfrac{1}{7}$

33. $\dfrac{5}{7} - \dfrac{1}{8}$

34. $\dfrac{10}{13} - \dfrac{7}{10}$

35. $\dfrac{5}{11} - \dfrac{3}{9}$

36. $\dfrac{7}{18} - \dfrac{2}{9}$

37. $\dfrac{11}{35} - \dfrac{2}{7}$

38. $\dfrac{2}{5} - \dfrac{3}{25}$

39. $\dfrac{5}{12} - \dfrac{1}{9}$

40. $\dfrac{7}{12} - \dfrac{5}{18}$

41. $\dfrac{7}{15} - \dfrac{5}{12}$

42. $\dfrac{5}{8} - \dfrac{3}{20}$

43. $\dfrac{3}{28} - \dfrac{2}{21}$

44. $\dfrac{6}{25} - \dfrac{7}{35}$

45. $\dfrac{1}{100} - \dfrac{1}{1000}$

46. $\dfrac{1}{50} - \dfrac{1}{500}$

47. $\dfrac{21}{44} - \dfrac{11}{36}$

48. $\dfrac{7}{18} - \dfrac{2}{45}$

Objectives **A** **B** **Mixed Practice** *Perform the indicated operation. See Examples 1 through 7.*

49. $\dfrac{5}{12} + \dfrac{1}{9}$

50. $\dfrac{7}{12} + \dfrac{5}{18}$

51. $\dfrac{17}{35} - \dfrac{2}{7}$

52. $\dfrac{13}{24} - \dfrac{1}{6}$

53. $\dfrac{9}{28} - \dfrac{3}{40}$

54. $\dfrac{10}{26} - \dfrac{3}{8}$

55. $\dfrac{2}{3} + \dfrac{4}{45} + \dfrac{4}{5}$

56. $\dfrac{3}{16} + \dfrac{1}{4} + \dfrac{1}{16}$

Objective **C** *Find the perimeter of each geometric figure. (Hint: Recall that perimeter means distance around.)*

57.

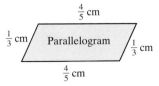

58.

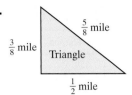

59.

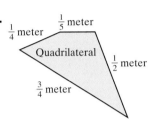

60.

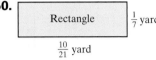

Solve. See Examples 8 and 9.

61. Killer bees have been known to chase people for up to $\frac{1}{4}$ of a mile, while domestic European honeybees will normally chase a person for no more than 100 feet, or $\frac{5}{264}$ of a mile. How much farther will a killer bee chase a person than a domestic honeybee? (*Source:* Coachella Valley Mosquito & Vector Control District)

62. The slowest mammal is the three-toed sloth from South America. The sloth has an average ground speed of $\frac{1}{10}$ mph. In the trees, it can accelerate to $\frac{17}{100}$ mph. How much faster can a sloth travel in the trees? (*Source: The Guiness Book of World Records*)

63. Given the following diagram, find its total length.

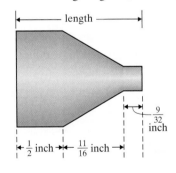

64. Given the following diagram, find its total width.

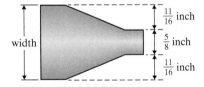

65. About $\frac{13}{20}$ of American students ages 10 to 17 name math, science, or art as their favorite subject in school. Art is the favorite subject for about $\frac{4}{25}$ of the American students ages 10 to 17. For what fraction of students this age is math or science their favorite subject? (*Source:* Peter D. Hart Research Associates for the National Science Foundation)

66. Together, the United States' and Japan's postal services handle $\frac{49}{100}$ of the world's mail volume. Japan's postal service alone handles $\frac{3}{50}$ of the world's mail. What fraction of the world's mail is handled by the postal service of the United States? (*Source:* United States Postal Service)

The table gives the fraction of Americans who eat pasta at various intervals. Use this table to answer Exercises 67 and 68.

How Often Americans Eat Pasta	
Frequency	**Fraction**
3 times per week	$\dfrac{31}{100}$
1 or 2 times per week	$\dfrac{23}{50}$
1 or 2 times per month	$\dfrac{17}{100}$
Less often	$\dfrac{3}{50}$
(*Source:* Princeton Survey Research)	

67. What fraction of Americans eat pasta 1, 2, or 3 times a week?

68. What fraction of Americans eat pasta 1 or 2 times a month or less often?

The map of the world, first shown in Section 3.1, now shows the fraction of the water's surface area taken up by each ocean. Use this map for Exercises 69 and 70.

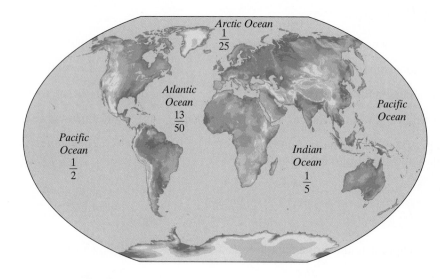

69. What fraction of the world's water surface area is accounted for by the Pacific and Atlantic Oceans?

70. What fraction of the world's water surface area is accounted for by the Arctic and Indian Oceans?

Review

Multiply or divide as indicated. See Sections 2.4 and 2.5.

71. $1\dfrac{1}{2} \cdot 3\dfrac{1}{3}$

72. $2\dfrac{5}{6} \div 5$

73. $4 \div 7\dfrac{1}{4}$

74. $4\dfrac{3}{4} \cdot 5\dfrac{1}{5}$

75. $3 \cdot 2\dfrac{1}{9}$

76. $6\dfrac{2}{7} \cdot 14$

Concept Extensions

For each sum below, do the following:

a. *Draw three rectangles of the same size and represent each fraction in the sum, one fraction per rectangle, by shading.*
b. *Using these rectangles as estimates, determine whether there is an error in the sum.*
c. *If there is an error, correctly calculate the sum.*

See the Concept Check in this section.

77. $\dfrac{3}{5} + \dfrac{4}{5} = \dfrac{7}{10}$

78. $\dfrac{5}{8} + \dfrac{3}{4} = \dfrac{8}{12}$

Subtract from left to right.

79. $\dfrac{2}{3} - \dfrac{1}{4} - \dfrac{2}{5}$

80. $\dfrac{9}{10} - \dfrac{7}{200} - \dfrac{1}{3}$

Perform each indicated operation.

 81. $\dfrac{30}{55} + \dfrac{1000}{1760}$

82. $\dfrac{19}{26} - \dfrac{968}{1352}$

83. In your own words, describe how to add or subtract two fractions with different denominators.

STUDY SKILLS BUILDER

Are You Organized?

Have you ever had trouble finding a completed assignment? When it's time to study for a test, are your notes neat and organized? Have you ever had trouble reading your own mathematics handwriting? (Be honest—I have.)

When any of these things happen, it's time to get organized. Here are a few suggestions:

Write your notes and complete your homework assignment in a notebook with pockets (spiral or ring binder.) Take class notes in this notebook, and then follow the notes with your completed homework assignment. When you receive graded papers or handouts, place them in the notebook pocket so that you will not lose them.

Remember to mark (possibly with an exclamation point) any note(s) that seem extra important to you. Also remember to mark (possibly with a question mark) any notes or homework that you are having trouble with. Don't forget to see your instructor or a math tutor to help you with the concepts or exercises that you are having trouble understanding.

Also, if you are having trouble reading your own handwriting, *slow down* and write your mathematics work clearly!

Exercises

1. Have you been completing your assignments on time?
2. Have you been correcting any exercises you may be having difficulty with?
3. If you are having trouble with a mathematical concept or correcting any homework exercises, have you visited your instructor, a tutor, or your campus math lab?
4. Are you taking lecture notes in your mathematics course? (By the way, these notes should include worked-out examples solved by your instructor.)
5. Is your mathematics course material (handouts, graded papers, lecture notes) organized?
6. If your answer to Exercise 5 is no, take a moment and review your course material. List at least two ways that you might better organize it. Then read the Study Skills Builder on organizing a notebook in Chapter 2.

Operations on Fractions and Mixed Numbers

Find the LCM of each list of numbers.

1. $5, 6$

2. $3, 7$

3. $2, 14$

4. $5, 25$

5. $4, 20, 25$

6. $6, 18, 30$

Write each fraction as an equivalent fraction with the indicated denominator.

7. $\dfrac{3}{8} = \dfrac{}{24}$

8. $\dfrac{7}{9} = \dfrac{}{36}$

9. $\dfrac{1}{4} = \dfrac{}{40}$

10. $\dfrac{2}{5} = \dfrac{}{30}$

11. $\dfrac{11}{15} = \dfrac{}{75}$

12. $\dfrac{5}{6} = \dfrac{}{48}$

Add or subtract as indicated. Simplify if necessary.

13. $\dfrac{3}{8} + \dfrac{1}{8}$

14. $\dfrac{7}{10} - \dfrac{3}{10}$

15. $\dfrac{17}{24} - \dfrac{3}{24}$

16. $\dfrac{4}{15} + \dfrac{9}{15}$

17. $\dfrac{1}{4} + \dfrac{1}{2}$

18. $\dfrac{1}{3} - \dfrac{1}{5}$

19. $\dfrac{7}{9} - \dfrac{2}{5}$

20. $\dfrac{3}{10} + \dfrac{2}{25}$

21. $\dfrac{7}{8} + \dfrac{1}{20}$

22. $\dfrac{5}{12} - \dfrac{2}{18}$ **23.** $\dfrac{1}{11} - \dfrac{1}{11}$ **24.** $\dfrac{3}{17} - \dfrac{2}{17}$

25. $\dfrac{9}{11} - \dfrac{2}{3}$ **26.** $\dfrac{1}{6} - \dfrac{1}{7}$ **27.** $\dfrac{2}{9} + \dfrac{1}{18}$

28. $\dfrac{4}{13} + \dfrac{2}{26}$ **29.** $\dfrac{2}{9} + \dfrac{1}{18} + \dfrac{1}{3}$ **30.** $\dfrac{3}{10} + \dfrac{1}{5} + \dfrac{6}{25}$

Mixed Practice (*Sections* 2.4, 2.5, 3.1, 3.2, 3.3)   *Perform the indicated operation.*

31. $\dfrac{9}{10} + \dfrac{2}{3}$ **32.** $\dfrac{9}{10} - \dfrac{2}{3}$ **33.** $\dfrac{9}{10} \cdot \dfrac{2}{3}$ **34.** $\dfrac{9}{10} \div \dfrac{2}{3}$

35. $\dfrac{21}{25} - \dfrac{3}{70}$ **36.** $\dfrac{21}{25} + \dfrac{3}{70}$ **37.** $\dfrac{21}{25} \div \dfrac{3}{70}$ **38.** $\dfrac{21}{25} \cdot \dfrac{3}{70}$

39. $3\dfrac{7}{8} \cdot 2\dfrac{2}{3}$ **40.** $3\dfrac{7}{8} \div 2\dfrac{2}{3}$ **41.** $\dfrac{2}{9} + \dfrac{5}{27} + \dfrac{1}{2}$ **42.** $\dfrac{3}{8} + \dfrac{11}{16} + \dfrac{2}{3}$

43. $11\dfrac{7}{10} \div 3\dfrac{3}{100}$ **44.** $7\dfrac{1}{4} \div 3\dfrac{3}{5}$ **45.** $\dfrac{14}{15} - \dfrac{4}{27}$ **46.** $\dfrac{9}{14} - \dfrac{11}{32}$

22. _____

23. _____

24. _____

25. _____

26. _____

27. _____

28. _____

29. _____

30. _____

31. _____

32. _____

33. _____

34. _____

35. _____

36. _____

37. _____

38. _____

39. _____

40. _____

41. _____

42. _____

43. _____

44. _____

45. _____

46. _____

3.4 ADDING AND SUBTRACTING MIXED NUMBERS

Objective **A** Adding Mixed Numbers

Recall that a mixed number has a whole number part and a fraction part.

$$2\frac{3}{8} \text{ means } 2 + \frac{3}{8}$$

✔ **Concept Check** Which of the following are equivalent to 7?

a. $6\frac{5}{5}$　　　　**b.** $6\frac{7}{7}$　　　　**c.** $5\frac{8}{4}$

d. $6\frac{17}{17}$　　　　**e.** all of these

Adding or Subtracting Mixed Numbers

To add or subtract mixed numbers, add or subtract the fractions and then add or subtract the whole numbers.

For example,

$$
\begin{array}{r}
2\frac{2}{7} \\
+\,6\frac{3}{7} \\
\hline
8\frac{5}{7}
\end{array}
$$
← Add the fractions; then add the whole numbers

PRACTICE PROBLEM 1

Add: $4\frac{2}{5} + 5\frac{1}{6}$

EXAMPLE 1 Add: $2\frac{1}{3} + 5\frac{3}{8}$. Check by estimating.

Solution: The LCD of 3 and 8 is 24.

$$
\begin{array}{r}
2\frac{1\cdot 8}{3\cdot 8} = 2\frac{8}{24} \\
+\,5\frac{3\cdot 3}{8\cdot 3} = 5\frac{9}{24} \\
\hline
7\frac{17}{24}
\end{array}
$$
← Add the fractions
　Add the whole numbers

To check by estimating, we round as usual. The fraction $2\frac{1}{3}$ rounds to 2, $5\frac{3}{8}$ rounds to 5, and $2 + 5 = 7$, our estimate.

Our exact answer is close to 7, so our answer is reasonable.

Work Practice Problem 1

Answer

1. $9\frac{17}{30}$

✔ **Concept Check Answer**

e

When adding or subtracting mixed numbers and whole numbers, it is a good idea to estimate to see if your answer is reasonable.

EXAMPLE 2 Add: $3\frac{4}{5} + 1\frac{4}{15}$

Solution: The LCD of 5 and 15 is 15.

$$3\frac{4}{5} = 3\frac{12}{15}$$
$$+1\frac{4}{15} = 1\frac{4}{15}$$

Add the fractions; then add the whole numbers.

$$4\frac{16}{15}$$

Notice that the fraction part is improper.

Since $\frac{16}{15}$ is $1\frac{1}{15}$ we can write the sum as

$$4\frac{16}{15} = 4 + 1\frac{1}{15} = 5\frac{1}{15}$$

Work Practice Problem 2

EXAMPLE 3 Add: $1\frac{4}{5} + 4 + 2\frac{1}{2}$

Solution: The LCD of 5 and 2 is 10.

$$1\frac{4}{5} = 1\frac{8}{10}$$
$$4 = 4$$
$$+2\frac{1}{2} = 2\frac{5}{10}$$
$$7\frac{13}{10} = 7 + 1\frac{3}{10} = 8\frac{3}{10}$$

Work Practice Problem 3

Objective B Subtracting Mixed Numbers

EXAMPLE 4 Subtract: $9\frac{3}{7} - 5\frac{2}{21}$. Check by estimating.

Solution: The LCD of 7 and 21 is 21.

$$9\frac{3}{7} = 9\frac{9}{21} \leftarrow \text{The LCD of 7 and 21 is 21.}$$
$$-5\frac{2}{21} = -5\frac{2}{21}$$
$$4\frac{7}{21} \leftarrow \text{Subtract the fractions.}$$

Subtract the whole numbers.

PRACTICE PROBLEM 2
Add: $2\frac{5}{14} + 5\frac{6}{7}$

PRACTICE PROBLEM 3
Add: $10 + 2\frac{6}{7} + 3\frac{1}{5}$

PRACTICE PROBLEM 4
Subtract: $29\frac{7}{9} - 13\frac{5}{18}$

Answers
2. $8\frac{3}{14}$, **3.** $16\frac{2}{35}$, **4.** $16\frac{1}{2}$

Continued on next page

Then $4\frac{7}{21}$ simplifies to $4\frac{1}{3}$. The difference is $4\frac{1}{3}$.

To check, $9\frac{3}{7}$ rounds to 9, $5\frac{2}{21}$ rounds to 5, and $9 - 5 = 4$, our estimate.

Our exact answer is close to 4, so our answer is reasonable.

▣ **Work Practice Problem 4**

When subtracting mixed numbers, borrowing may be needed, as shown in the next example.

PRACTICE PROBLEM 5

Subtract: $9\frac{7}{15} - 5\frac{3}{5}$

EXAMPLE 5 Subtract: $7\frac{3}{14} - 3\frac{6}{7}$

Solution: The LCD of 7 and 14 is 14.

$$7\frac{3}{14} = 7\frac{3}{14}$$
$$-3\frac{6}{7} = -3\frac{12}{14}$$

Notice that we cannot subtract $\frac{12}{14}$ from $\frac{3}{14}$, so we borrow from the whole number 7.

borrow 1 from 7

$$7\frac{3}{14} = 6 + 1\frac{3}{14} = 6 + \frac{17}{14} \text{ or } 6\frac{17}{14}$$

Now subtract.

$$7\frac{3}{14} = 7\frac{3}{14} = 6\frac{17}{14}$$
$$-3\frac{6}{7} = -3\frac{12}{14} = -3\frac{12}{14}$$
$$3\frac{5}{14} \leftarrow \text{Subtract the fractions.}$$

↑ Subtract the whole numbers.

▣ **Work Practice Problem 5**

✔**Concept Check** In the subtraction problem $5\frac{1}{4} - 3\frac{3}{4}$, $5\frac{1}{4}$ must be rewritten because $\frac{3}{4}$ cannot be subtracted from $\frac{1}{4}$. Why is it incorrect to rewrite $5\frac{1}{4}$ as $5\frac{5}{4}$?

PRACTICE PROBLEM 6

Subtract: $25 - 10\frac{2}{9}$

EXAMPLE 6 Subtract: $12 - 8\frac{3}{7}$

Solution:

$$12 = 11\frac{7}{7}$$ Borrow 1 from 12 and write it as $\frac{7}{7}$.
$$-8\frac{3}{7} = -8\frac{3}{7}$$
$$3\frac{4}{7} \leftarrow \text{Subtract the fractions.}$$

↑ Subtract the whole numbers.

▣ **Work Practice Problem 6**

Answers

5. $3\frac{13}{15}$, 6. $14\frac{7}{9}$

✔ **Concept Check Answer**

Rewrite $5\frac{1}{4}$ as $4\frac{5}{4}$ by borrowing from the 5.

Objective ⒞ Solving Problems by Adding or Subtracting Mixed Numbers

Now that we know how to add and subtract mixed numbers, we can solve real-life problems.

EXAMPLE 7 **Calculating Total Weight**

Sarah Grahamm purchases two packages of ground round. One package weighs $2\frac{3}{8}$ pounds and the other $1\frac{4}{5}$ pounds. What is the combined weight of the ground round?

Solution:

1. UNDERSTAND. Read and reread the problem. The phrase "combined weight" tells us to add.
2. TRANSLATE.

In words:	combined weight	is	weight of one package	plus	weight of second package
	↓	↓	↓	↓	↓
Translate:	combined weight	$=$	$2\frac{3}{8}$	$+$	$1\frac{4}{5}$

3. SOLVE: Before we solve, let's estimate. The fraction $2\frac{3}{8}$ rounds to 2, $1\frac{4}{5}$ rounds to 2, and $2 + 2 = 4$. The combined weight should be close to 4.

$$2\frac{3}{8} = 2\frac{15}{40}$$
$$+1\frac{4}{5} = 1\frac{32}{40}$$
$$3\frac{47}{40} = 4\frac{7}{40}$$

4. INTERPRET. *Check* your work. Our estimate of 4 tells us that the exact answer of $4\frac{7}{40}$ is reasonable. *State* your conclusion: The combined weight of the ground round is $4\frac{7}{40}$ pounds.

⬛ **Work Practice Problem 7**

EXAMPLE 8 **Finding Legal Lobster Size**

Lobster fisherman must measure the upper body shells of the lobsters they catch. Lobsters that are too small are thrown back into the ocean. Each state has its own size standard for lobsters to help control the breeding stock. In 1988, Massachusetts increased its legal

lobster size from $3\frac{3}{16}$ inches to $3\frac{7}{32}$ inches. How much of an increase was this? (*Source:* Peabody Essex Museum, Salem, Massachusetts)

Continued on next page

Solution:

1. UNDERSTAND. Read and reread the problem carefully. The word "increase" found in the problem might make you think that we add to solve the problem. But the phrase "how much of an increase" tells us to subtract to find the increase.

2. TRANSLATE.

In words:	increase	is	new lobster size	minus	old lobster size
	↓	↓	↓	↓	↓
Translate:	increase	=	$3\dfrac{7}{32}$	−	$3\dfrac{3}{16}$

3. SOLVE: Before we solve, let's estimate. The fraction $3\dfrac{7}{32}$ rounds to 3, $3\dfrac{3}{16}$ rounds to 3, and $3 - 3 = 0$. The increase is not 0, but will be very small.

$$3\dfrac{7}{32} = 3\dfrac{7}{32}$$
$$-3\dfrac{3}{16} = 3\dfrac{6}{32}$$
$$\dfrac{1}{32}$$

4. INTERPRET. *Check* your work. Our estimate tells us that the exact increase of $\dfrac{1}{32}$ inch is reasonable. *State* your conclusion: The increase in lobster size is $\dfrac{1}{32}$ of an inch.

⬛ **Work Practice Problem 8**

Mental Math

Choose the best estimate for each sum or difference.

1. $3\frac{7}{8} + 2\frac{1}{5}$

   a. 6 **b.** 5 **c.** 1 **d.** 2

2. $3\frac{7}{8} - 2\frac{1}{5}$

   a. 6 **b.** 5 **c.** 1 **d.** 2

3. $8\frac{1}{3} + 1\frac{1}{2}$

   a. 4 **b.** 10 **c.** 6 **d.** 16

4. $8\frac{1}{3} - 1\frac{1}{2}$

   a. 4 **b.** 10 **c.** 6 **d.** 16

3.4 EXERCISE SET

Objective A *Add. For those exercises marked, find an exact sum and an estimated sum. See Examples 1 through 3.*

1. $4\frac{7}{10}$
$+2\frac{1}{10}$

Exact:

Estimate:

2. $7\frac{4}{9}$
$+3\frac{2}{9}$

Exact:

Estimate:

3. $10\frac{3}{14}$
$+ 3\frac{4}{7}$

Exact:

Estimate:

4. $12\frac{5}{12}$
$+ 4\frac{1}{6}$

Exact:

Estimate:

5. $9\frac{1}{5}$
$+8\frac{2}{25}$

Exact:

Estimate:

6. $6\frac{2}{13}$
$+8\frac{7}{26}$

7. $3\frac{1}{2}$
$+4\frac{1}{8}$

8. $9\frac{3}{4}$
$+2\frac{1}{8}$

9. $1\frac{5}{6}$
$+5\frac{3}{8}$

10. $2\frac{5}{12}$
$+1\frac{5}{8}$

11. $8\frac{2}{5}$
$+11\frac{2}{3}$

12. $7\frac{3}{7}$
$+3\frac{3}{5}$

13. $11\frac{3}{5}$
$+7\frac{2}{5}$

14. $19\frac{7}{9}$
$+ 8\frac{2}{9}$

15. $40\frac{9}{10}$
$+15\frac{8}{27}$

16. $102\frac{5}{8}$
$+ 96\frac{21}{25}$

17. $3\frac{5}{8}$
$2\frac{1}{6}$
$+7\frac{3}{4}$

18. $4\frac{1}{3}$
$9\frac{2}{5}$
$+3\frac{1}{6}$

19. $12\frac{3}{14}$
10
$+25\frac{5}{12}$

20. $8\frac{2}{9}$
32
$+ 9\frac{10}{21}$

Objective **B** *Subtract. For those exercises marked, find an exact difference and an estimated difference. See Examples 4 through 6.*

21. $\quad 4\dfrac{7}{10}$

$\quad\underline{-2\dfrac{1}{10}}$

Exact:

Estimate:

22. $\quad 7\dfrac{4}{9}$

$\quad\underline{-3\dfrac{2}{9}}$

Exact:

Estimate:

23. $\quad 10\dfrac{13}{14}$

$\quad\underline{-\ 3\dfrac{4}{7}}$

Exact:

Estimate:

24. $\quad 12\dfrac{5}{12}$

$\quad\underline{-\ 4\dfrac{1}{6}}$

Exact:

Estimate:

25. $\quad 9\dfrac{1}{5}$

$\quad\underline{-8\dfrac{6}{25}}$

Exact:

Estimate:

26. $\quad 5\dfrac{2}{13}$

$\quad\underline{-4\dfrac{7}{26}}$

27. $\ 5\dfrac{2}{3} - 3\dfrac{1}{5}$

28. $\quad 23\dfrac{3}{5}$

$\quad\underline{-\ 8\dfrac{8}{15}}$

29. $\quad 15\dfrac{4}{7}$

$\quad\underline{-\ 9\dfrac{11}{14}}$

30. $\ 5\dfrac{3}{8} - 2\dfrac{13}{20}$

31. $47\dfrac{4}{18} - 23\dfrac{19}{24}$

32. $\ 6\dfrac{1}{6} - 5\dfrac{11}{14}$

33. $\quad 10$

$\quad\underline{-\ 8\dfrac{1}{5}}$

34. $\quad 23$

$\quad\underline{-17\dfrac{3}{4}}$

35. $\quad 11\dfrac{3}{5}$

$\quad\underline{-\ 9\dfrac{11}{15}}$

36. $\quad 9\dfrac{1}{10}$

$\quad\underline{-7\dfrac{2}{5}}$

⊙ 37. $\quad 6$

$\quad\underline{-2\dfrac{4}{9}}$

38. $\quad 8$

$\quad\underline{-1\dfrac{7}{10}}$

39. $\quad 63\dfrac{1}{6}$

$\quad\underline{-47\dfrac{5}{12}}$

40. $\quad 86\dfrac{2}{15}$

$\quad\underline{-27\dfrac{3}{10}}$

Objectives **A** **B** **Mixed Practice** *Perform the indicated operation. See Examples 1 through 6.*

41. $\quad 15\dfrac{1}{6}$

$\quad\underline{+13\dfrac{5}{12}}$

42. $\quad 21\dfrac{3}{10}$

$\quad\underline{+11\dfrac{3}{5}}$

43. $\quad 22\dfrac{7}{8}$

$\quad\underline{-\ 7}$

44. $\quad 27\dfrac{3}{21}$

$\quad\underline{-\ 9}$

45. $5\dfrac{8}{9} + 2\dfrac{1}{9}$

46. $12\dfrac{13}{16} + 7\dfrac{3}{16}$

47. $33\dfrac{11}{20} - 15\dfrac{19}{30}$

48. $54\dfrac{7}{30} - 38\dfrac{29}{50}$

Objective **C** *Solve. See Examples 7 and 8.*

△ **49.** To prevent intruding birds, birdhouses built for Eastern Bluebirds should have an entrance hole measuring $1\frac{1}{2}$ inches in diameter. Entrance holes in bird houses for Mountain Bluebirds should measure $1\frac{9}{16}$ inches in diameter. How much wider should entrance holes for Mountain Bluebirds be than for Eastern Bluebirds? (*Source:* North American Bluebird Society)

50. If the total weight allowable without overweight charges is 50 pounds and the traveler's luggage weighs $60\frac{5}{8}$ pounds, on how many pounds will the traveler's overweight charges be based?

51. Charlotte Dowlin has $15\frac{2}{3}$ feet of plastic pipe. She cuts off a $2\frac{1}{2}$-foot length and then a $3\frac{1}{4}$-foot length. If she now needs a 10-foot piece of pipe, will the remaining piece do? If not, by how much will the piece be short?

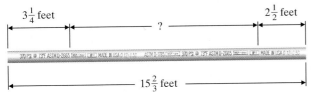

52. A trim carpenter cuts a board $3\frac{3}{8}$ feet long from one 6 feet long. How long is the remaining piece?

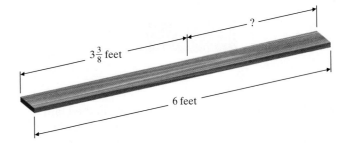

53. If Tucson's average annual rainfall is $11\frac{1}{4}$ inches and Yuma's is $3\frac{3}{5}$ inches, how much more rain, on average, does Tucson get than Yuma?

54. A pair of crutches needs adjustment. One crutch is 43 inches and the other is $41\frac{5}{8}$ inches. Find how much the short crutch should be lengthened to make both crutches the same length.

55. On four consecutive days, a concert pianist, practiced for $2\frac{1}{2}$ hours, $1\frac{2}{3}$ hours, $2\frac{1}{4}$ hours, and $3\frac{5}{6}$ hours. Find his total practice time.

56. A tennis coach was preparing her team for a tennis tournament and enforced this practice schedule: Monday, $2\frac{1}{2}$ hours; Tuesday, $2\frac{2}{3}$ hours; Wednesday, $1\frac{3}{4}$ hours; and Thursday, $1\frac{9}{16}$ hours. How long did the team practice that week before Friday's tournament?

57. Jerald Divis, a tax consultant, takes $3\frac{1}{2}$ hours to prepare a personal tax return and $5\frac{7}{8}$ hours to prepare a small business return. How much longer does it take him to prepare the small business return?

58. Jessica Callac takes $2\frac{3}{4}$ hours to clean her room. Her brother Matthew takes $1\frac{1}{3}$ hours to clean his room. If they start at the same time, how long does Matthew have to wait for Jessica to finish?

59. Located on an island in New York City's harbor, the Statue of Liberty is one of the largest statues in the world. The copper figure is $46\frac{1}{20}$ meters tall from feet to tip of torch. The figure stands on a pedestal that is $46\frac{47}{50}$ meters feet tall. What is the overall height of the Statue of Liberty from the base of the pedestal to the tip of the torch? (*Source:* National Park Service)

60. The record for largest rainbow trout ever caught is $42\frac{1}{8}$ pounds and was set in Alaska in 1970. The record for largest tiger trout ever caught is $20\frac{13}{16}$ pounds and was set in Michigan in 1978. How much more did the record-setting rainbow trout weigh than the record-setting tiger trout? (*Source:* International Game Fish Association)

61. The longest floating pontoon bridge in the United States is the Evergreen Point Bridge in Seattle, Washington. It is 2526 yards long. The second-longest pontoon bridge in the United States is the Hood Canal Bridge in Point Gamble, Washington, which is $2173\frac{2}{3}$ yards long. How much longer is the Evergreen Point Bridge than the Hood Canal Bridge? (*Source:* Federal Highway Administration)

62. What is the difference between interest rates of $11\frac{1}{2}\%$ and $9\frac{3}{4}\%$?

The following table lists some upcoming total eclipses of the Sun that will be visible in North America. The duration of each eclipse is listed in the table. Use the table to answer Exercises 63 through 66.

Total Solar Eclipses Visible from North America	
Date of Eclipse	**Duration (in Minutes)**
August 1, 2008	$2\frac{9}{20}$
August 21, 2017	$2\frac{2}{3}$
April 8, 2024	$4\frac{7}{15}$
(*Source:* NASA/Goddard Space Flight Center)	

63. What is the total duration for the three eclipses?

64. What is the total duration for the two eclipses occuring in even-numbered years?

65. How much longer will the April 8, 2024, eclipse be than the August 21, 2017, eclipse?

66. How much longer will the August 21, 2017, eclipse be than the August 1, 2008, eclipse?

Find the perimeter of each figure.

△ **67.**

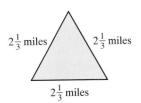

$2\frac{1}{3}$ miles $2\frac{1}{3}$ miles

$2\frac{1}{3}$ miles

△ **68.**

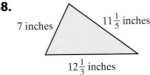

7 inches $11\frac{1}{5}$ inches

$12\frac{1}{3}$ inches

△ **69.**

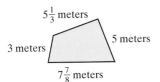

$5\frac{1}{3}$ meters

3 meters   5 meters

$7\frac{7}{8}$ meters

△ **70.**

$3\frac{1}{4}$ yards $3\frac{1}{4}$ yards

$3\frac{1}{4}$ yards $3\frac{1}{4}$ yards

$3\frac{1}{4}$ yards

Review

Evaluate each expression. See Section 1.9.

71. 2^3

72. 3^2

73. 5^2

74. 2^5

75. $20 \div 10 \cdot 2$

76. $36 - 5 \cdot 6 + 10$

77. $2 + 3(8 \cdot 7 - 1)$

78. $2(10 - 2 \cdot 5) + 13$

Simplify. Write any mixed number whose fraction part is not a proper fraction in simplest form.

79. $3\frac{5}{5}$

80. $10\frac{8}{7}$

81. $9\frac{10}{16}$

82. $6\frac{7}{14}$

Concept Extensions

Solve. See the Concept Checks in this section.

83. Which of the following are equivalent to 10?

    a. $9\frac{5}{5}$ **b.** $9\frac{100}{100}$ **c.** $6\frac{44}{11}$ **d.** $8\frac{13}{13}$

84. Which of the following are equivalent to $7\frac{3}{4}$?

    a. $6\frac{7}{4}$ **b.** $5\frac{11}{4}$ **c.** $7\frac{12}{16}$ **d.** all of them

Solve.

85. Explain in your own words why $9\frac{13}{9}$ is equal to $10\frac{4}{9}$.

86. In your own words, explain

    a. when to borrow when subtracting mixed numbers, and

    b. how to borrow when subtracting mixed numbers.

87. Carmen's Candy Clutch is famous for its "Nutstuff," a special blend of nuts and candy. A Supreme box of Nutstuff has $2\frac{1}{4}$ pounds of nuts and $3\frac{1}{2}$ pounds of candy. A Deluxe box has $1\frac{3}{8}$ pounds of nuts and $4\frac{1}{4}$ pounds of candy. Which box is heavier and by how much?

88. Willie Cassidie purchased three Supreme boxes and two Deluxe boxes of Nutstuff from Carmen's Candy Clutch. (See Exercise 87.) What is the total weight of his purchase?

 THE BIGGER PICTURE   Operations on Sets of Numbers

Continue your outline from Sections 1.7, 1.9, and 2.5. Suggestions are once again written to help you complete this part of your outline.

I. Some Operations on Sets of Numbers

  A. Whole Numbers

    1. Add or Subtract (Sections 1.3, 1.4)

    2. Multiply or Divide (Sections 1.6, 1.7)

    3. Exponent (Section 1.9)

    4. Square Root (Section 1.9)

    5. Order of Operations (Section 1.9)

  B. Fractions

    1. Simplify (Section 2.3)

    2. Multiply (Section 2.4)

    3. Divide (Section 2.5)

    4. Add or Subtract: Must have same denominators. If not, find the LCD, and write each fraction as an equivalent fraction with the LCD as denominator.

$$\frac{2}{5}+\frac{1}{15}=\frac{2}{5}\cdot\frac{3}{3}+\frac{1}{15}=\frac{6}{15}+\frac{1}{15}=\frac{7}{15}$$

Perform indicated operations.

1. $\frac{3}{17}+\frac{2}{17}$

2. $\frac{9}{10}-\frac{1}{10}$

3. $\frac{2}{3}+\frac{3}{10}$

4. $\frac{23}{24}-\frac{11}{12}$

5. $\frac{7}{8}+\frac{19}{20}$

6. $\frac{3^3}{4^3}$

7. $\begin{array}{r} 16 \\ -\ 3\frac{4}{7} \\ \hline \end{array}$

8. $\begin{array}{r} 2\frac{5}{8} \\ 1\frac{1}{6} \\ +5\frac{3}{4} \\ \hline \end{array}$

9. $\frac{6}{11}\cdot\frac{8}{9}$

10. $2\frac{4}{15}\div 1\frac{4}{5}$

3.5 ORDER, EXPONENTS, AND THE ORDER OF OPERATIONS

Objectives

A Compare Fractions.

B Evaluate Fractions Raised to Powers.

C Review Operations on Fractions.

D Use the Order of Operations.

Objective **A** Comparing Fractions

Recall that whole numbers can be shown on a number line using equally spaced distances.

From the number line, we can see the order of numbers. For example, we can see that 3 is less than 5 because 3 is to the left of 5.

For any two numbers on a number line, the number to the left is always the smaller number, and the number to the right is always the larger number.

We use the **inequality symbols** $<$ or $>$ to write the order of numbers.

Inequality Symbols

$<$ means *is less than.*

$>$ means *is greater than.*

For example,

3 is less than 5   or   5 is greater than 3

$$3 < 5 \qquad 5 > 3$$

We can compare fractions the same way. To see fractions on a number line, divide the spaces between whole numbers into equal parts.

For example, let's compare $\frac{2}{5}$ and $\frac{4}{5}$.

$$\frac{5}{5} = 1$$

Since $\frac{4}{5}$ is to the right of $\frac{2}{5}$,

$$\frac{2}{5} < \frac{4}{5}$$ Notice that $2 < 4$ also.

Comparing Fractions

To determine which of two fractions is greater,

Step 1: Write the fractions as like fractions.

Step 2: The fraction with the greater numerator is the greater fraction.

EXAMPLE 1 Insert $<$ or $>$ to form a true statement.

$$\frac{3}{10} \qquad \frac{2}{7}$$

Solution:

Step 1: The LCD of 10 and 7 is 70.

$$\frac{3}{10} = \frac{3}{10} \cdot \frac{7}{7} = \frac{21}{70}; \qquad \frac{2}{7} = \frac{2}{7} \cdot \frac{10}{10} = \frac{20}{70}$$

PRACTICE PROBLEM 1

Insert $<$ or $>$ to form a true statement.

$$\frac{8}{9} \qquad \frac{10}{11}$$

Answer

1. $<$

Continued on next page

Step 2: Since $21 > 20$, then $\dfrac{21}{70} > \dfrac{20}{70}$ or

$$\dfrac{3}{10} > \dfrac{2}{7}$$

🔲 **Work Practice Problem 1**

PRACTICE PROBLEM 2

Insert $<$ or $>$ to form a true statement.

$$\dfrac{3}{5} \quad \dfrac{2}{9}$$

EXAMPLE 2 Insert $<$ or $>$ to form a true statement.

$$\dfrac{9}{10} \quad \dfrac{11}{12}$$

Solution:

Step 1: The LCD of 10 and 12 is 60.

$$\dfrac{9}{10} = \dfrac{9}{10} \cdot \dfrac{6}{6} = \dfrac{54}{60} \qquad \dfrac{11}{12} = \dfrac{11}{12} \cdot \dfrac{5}{5} = \dfrac{55}{60}$$

Step 2: Since $54 < 55$, then $\dfrac{54}{60} < \dfrac{55}{60}$ or

$$\dfrac{9}{10} < \dfrac{11}{12}$$

🔲 **Work Practice Problem 2**

Helpful Hint

If we think of $<$ and $>$ as arrowheads, a true statement is always formed when the arrow points to the smaller number.

$$\dfrac{2}{3} > \dfrac{1}{3} \qquad\qquad \dfrac{5}{6} < \dfrac{7}{6}$$

↑ points to smaller number ↑ points to smaller number

Objective B Evaluating Fractions Raised to Powers

Recall from Section 1.9 that exponents indicate repeated multiplication.

$$5^{3} = \underbrace{5 \cdot 5 \cdot 5}_{\text{3 factors of 5}} = 125$$

exponent ↓ ↑ base

Exponents mean the same when the base is a fraction. For example,

$$\left(\dfrac{1}{3}\right)^{4} = \underbrace{\dfrac{1}{3} \cdot \dfrac{1}{3} \cdot \dfrac{1}{3} \cdot \dfrac{1}{3}}_{\text{4 factors of } \frac{1}{3}} = \dfrac{1}{81}$$

base ↑

PRACTICE PROBLEMS 3–5

Evaluate each expression.

3. $\left(\dfrac{1}{5}\right)^{2}$ **4.** $\left(\dfrac{2}{3}\right)^{3}$

5. $\left(\dfrac{1}{4}\right)^{2}\left(\dfrac{2}{3}\right)^{3}$

EXAMPLES Evaluate each expression.

3. $\left(\dfrac{1}{4}\right)^{2} = \dfrac{1}{4} \cdot \dfrac{1}{4} = \dfrac{1}{16}$

4. $\left(\dfrac{3}{5}\right)^{3} = \dfrac{3}{5} \cdot \dfrac{3}{5} \cdot \dfrac{3}{5} = \dfrac{27}{125}$

5. $\left(\dfrac{1}{6}\right)^{2} \cdot \left(\dfrac{3}{4}\right)^{3} = \left(\dfrac{1}{6} \cdot \dfrac{1}{6}\right) \cdot \left(\dfrac{3}{4} \cdot \dfrac{3}{4} \cdot \dfrac{3}{4}\right) = \dfrac{1 \cdot 1 \cdot \overset{1}{\cancel{3}} \cdot \overset{1}{\cancel{3}} \cdot 3}{2 \cdot \underset{1}{\cancel{3}} \cdot 2 \cdot \underset{1}{\cancel{3}} \cdot 4 \cdot 4 \cdot 4} = \dfrac{3}{256}$

🔲 **Work Practice Problems 3–5**

Answers

2. $>$, **3.** $\dfrac{1}{25}$, **4.** $\dfrac{8}{27}$, **5.** $\dfrac{1}{54}$

Objective C Reviewing Operations on Fractions

To get ready to use the order of operations with fractions, let's first review the operations on fractions that we have learned.

Review of Operations on Fractions		
Operation	**Procedure**	**Example**
Multiply	Multiply the numerators and multiply the denominators.	$\frac{5}{9} \cdot \frac{1}{2} = \frac{5 \cdot 1}{9 \cdot 2} = \frac{5}{18}$
Divide	Multiply the first fraction by the reciprocal of the second fraction.	$\frac{2}{3} \div \frac{11}{13} = \frac{2}{3} \cdot \frac{13}{11} = \frac{2 \cdot 13}{3 \cdot 11} = \frac{26}{33}$
Add or Subtract	1. Write each fraction as an equivalent fraction whose denominator is the LCD 2. Add or subtract numerators and write the result over the common denominator.	$\frac{3}{4} + \frac{1}{8} = \frac{3}{4} \cdot \frac{2}{2} + \frac{1}{8} = \frac{6}{8} + \frac{1}{8} = \frac{7}{8}$

EXAMPLES Perform each indicated operation.

6. $\frac{1}{2} \div \frac{8}{7} = \frac{1}{2} \cdot \frac{7}{8} = \frac{1 \cdot 7}{2 \cdot 8} = \frac{7}{16}$ To divide: multiply by the reciprocal.

7. $\frac{6}{35} + \frac{3}{7} = \frac{6}{35} + \frac{3}{7} \cdot \frac{5}{5} = \frac{6}{35} + \frac{15}{35} = \frac{21}{35}$ To add: need the LCD. The LCD is 35.

$$= \frac{\overset{1}{\cancel{7}} \cdot 3}{\underset{1}{\cancel{7}} \cdot 5} = \frac{3}{5}$$

8. $\frac{2}{9} \cdot \frac{3}{11} = \frac{2 \cdot 3}{9 \cdot 11} = \frac{2 \cdot \overset{1}{\cancel{3}}}{\underset{1}{\cancel{3}} \cdot 3 \cdot 11} = \frac{2}{33}$ To multiply: multiply numerators and multiply denominators.

9. $\frac{6}{7} - \frac{1}{3} = \frac{6}{7} \cdot \frac{3}{3} - \frac{1}{3} \cdot \frac{7}{7} = \frac{18}{21} - \frac{7}{21} = \frac{11}{21}$ To subtract: need the LCD. The LCD is 21.

🔲 **Work Practice Problems 6–9**

Objective D Using the Order of Operations

The order of operations that we use on whole numbers applies to expressions containing fractions and mixed numbers also.

Order of Operations

1. Perform all operations within parentheses ( ), brackets [ ], or other grouping symbols such as square roots or fraction bars.
2. Evaluate any expressions with exponents.
3. Multiply or divide in order from left to right.
4. Add or subtract in order from left to right.

PRACTICE PROBLEMS 6–9

Perform each indicated operation.

6. $\frac{3}{7} \div \frac{10}{11}$ **7.** $\frac{4}{15} + \frac{2}{5}$

8. $\frac{2}{3} \cdot \frac{9}{10}$ **9.** $\frac{11}{12} - \frac{2}{5}$

Answers

6. $\frac{33}{70}$,   **7.** $\frac{2}{3}$,   **8.** $\frac{3}{5}$,   **9.** $\frac{31}{60}$

PRACTICE PROBLEM 10

Simplify: $\dfrac{2}{9} \div \dfrac{4}{7} \cdot \dfrac{3}{10}$

EXAMPLE 10 Simplify: $\dfrac{1}{5} \div \dfrac{2}{3} \cdot \dfrac{4}{5}$

Solution: Multiply or divide *in order* from left to right. We divide first.

$$\dfrac{1}{5} \div \dfrac{2}{3} \cdot \dfrac{4}{5} = \underbrace{\dfrac{1}{5} \cdot \dfrac{3}{2}} \cdot \dfrac{4}{5}$$

To divide, multiply by the reciprocal.

$$= \dfrac{3}{10} \cdot \dfrac{4}{5}$$

$$= \dfrac{3 \cdot 4}{10 \cdot 5} \qquad \text{Multiply.}$$

$$= \dfrac{3 \cdot 2 \cdot \overset{1}{\cancel{2}}}{\underset{1}{\cancel{2}} \cdot 5 \cdot 5} \qquad \text{Simplify.}$$

$$= \dfrac{6}{25} \qquad \text{Simplify.}$$

▣ **Work Practice Problem 10**

PRACTICE PROBLEM 11

Simplify: $\left(\dfrac{2}{5}\right)^2 \div \left(\dfrac{3}{5} - \dfrac{11}{25}\right)$

EXAMPLE 11 Simplify: $\left(\dfrac{2}{3}\right)^2 \div \left(\dfrac{8}{27} + \dfrac{2}{3}\right)$

Solution: Start within the right set of parentheses. We add.

$$\left(\dfrac{2}{3}\right)^2 \div \left(\dfrac{8}{27} + \dfrac{2}{3}\right) = \left(\dfrac{2}{3}\right)^2 \div \left(\dfrac{8}{27} + \dfrac{18}{27}\right) \quad \text{The LCD is 27. Write } \dfrac{2}{3} \text{ as } \dfrac{18}{27}.$$

$$= \left(\dfrac{2}{3}\right)^2 \div \dfrac{26}{27} \qquad \text{Simplify inside the parentheses.}$$

$$= \dfrac{4}{9} \div \dfrac{26}{27} \qquad \text{Write } \left(\dfrac{2}{3}\right)^2 \text{ as } \dfrac{4}{9}.$$

$$= \dfrac{4}{9} \cdot \dfrac{27}{26}$$

$$= \dfrac{\overset{1}{\cancel{2}} \cdot 2 \cdot 3 \cdot \overset{1}{\cancel{9}}}{\underset{1}{\cancel{9}} \cdot \underset{1}{\cancel{2}} \cdot 13}$$

$$= \dfrac{6}{13}$$

▣ **Work Practice Problem 11**

✔ **Concept Check** What should be done first to simplify

$$3\left[\left(\dfrac{1}{4}\right)^2 + \dfrac{3}{2}\left(\dfrac{6}{7} - \dfrac{1}{3}\right)\right]?$$

Answers

10. $\dfrac{7}{60}$,   **11.** 1

✔ **Concept Check Answer**

$\dfrac{6}{7} - \dfrac{1}{3}$

Recall from Section 1.7 that the average of a list of numbers is their sum divided by the number of numbers in the list.

EXAMPLE 12 Find the average of $\frac{1}{3}, \frac{2}{5}$, and $\frac{2}{9}$.

Solution: The average is their sum, divided by 3.

$$\left(\frac{1}{3} + \frac{2}{5} + \frac{2}{9}\right) \div 3 = \left(\frac{15}{45} + \frac{18}{45} + \frac{10}{45}\right) \div 3 \quad \text{The LCD is 45.}$$

$$= \frac{43}{45} \div 3 \qquad\qquad \text{Add.}$$

$$= \frac{43}{45} \cdot \frac{1}{3}$$

$$= \frac{43}{135} \qquad\qquad \text{Multiply.}$$

🔲 **Work Practice Problem 12**

3.5 EXERCISE SET

FOR EXTRA HELP

Student Solutions Manual   PH Math/Tutor Center   CD/Video for Review   Math XL MathXL®   MyMathLab MyMathLab

Objective A *Insert $<$ or $>$ to form a true statement. See Examples 1 and 2.*

1. $\frac{7}{9}$ $\frac{6}{9}$ 2. $\frac{12}{17}$ $\frac{13}{17}$ 3. $\frac{3}{3}$ $\frac{5}{3}$ 4. $\frac{3}{23}$ $\frac{4}{23}$

5. $\frac{9}{42}$ $\frac{5}{21}$ 6. $\frac{17}{32}$ $\frac{5}{16}$ 7. $\frac{9}{8}$ $\frac{17}{16}$ 8. $\frac{3}{8}$ $\frac{14}{40}$

9. $\frac{3}{4}$ $\frac{2}{3}$ 10. $\frac{2}{5}$ $\frac{1}{3}$ 11. $\frac{3}{5}$ $\frac{9}{14}$ 12. $\frac{3}{10}$ $\frac{7}{25}$

13. $\frac{1}{10}$ $\frac{1}{11}$ 14. $\frac{1}{13}$ $\frac{1}{14}$ 15. $\frac{27}{100}$ $\frac{7}{25}$ 16. $\frac{37}{120}$ $\frac{9}{30}$

Objective B *Evaluate each expression. See Examples 3 through 5.*

17. $\left(\frac{1}{2}\right)^4$ 18. $\left(\frac{1}{7}\right)^2$ 19. $\left(\frac{2}{5}\right)^3$ 20. $\left(\frac{3}{4}\right)^3$

21. $\left(\frac{4}{7}\right)^3$ 22. $\left(\frac{2}{3}\right)^4$ 23. $\left(\frac{2}{9}\right)^2$ 24. $\left(\frac{7}{11}\right)^2$

25. $\left(\dfrac{3}{4}\right)^2 \cdot \left(\dfrac{2}{3}\right)^3$ **26.** $\left(\dfrac{1}{6}\right)^2 \cdot \left(\dfrac{9}{10}\right)^2$ **27.** $\dfrac{9}{10}\left(\dfrac{2}{5}\right)^2$ **28.** $\dfrac{7}{11}\left(\dfrac{3}{10}\right)^2$

Objective **C** **Mixed Practice** *Perform each indicated operation. See Examples 6 through 9.*

29. $\dfrac{2}{15} + \dfrac{3}{5}$ **30.** $\dfrac{5}{12} + \dfrac{5}{6}$ **31.** $\dfrac{3}{7} \cdot \dfrac{1}{5}$ **32.** $\dfrac{9}{10} \div \dfrac{2}{3}$ **33.** $1 - \dfrac{4}{9}$

34. $5 - \dfrac{2}{3}$ **35.** $4\dfrac{2}{9} + 5\dfrac{9}{11}$ **36.** $7\dfrac{3}{7} + 6\dfrac{3}{5}$ **37.** $\dfrac{5}{6} - \dfrac{3}{4}$ **38.** $\dfrac{7}{10} - \dfrac{3}{25}$

39. $\dfrac{6}{11} \div \dfrac{2}{3}$ **40.** $\dfrac{3}{8} \cdot \dfrac{1}{11}$ **41.** $0 \cdot \dfrac{9}{10}$ **42.** $\dfrac{5}{6} \cdot 0$ **43.** $0 \div \dfrac{9}{10}$

44. $\dfrac{5}{6} \div 0$ **45.** $\dfrac{20}{35} \cdot \dfrac{7}{10}$ **46.** $\dfrac{18}{25} \div \dfrac{3}{5}$ **47.** $\dfrac{4}{7} - \dfrac{6}{11}$ **48.** $\dfrac{11}{20} + \dfrac{7}{15}$

Objective **D** *Use the order of operations to simplify each expression. See Examples 10 and 11.*

49. $\dfrac{1}{5} + \dfrac{1}{3} \cdot \dfrac{1}{4}$ **50.** $\dfrac{1}{2} + \dfrac{1}{6} \cdot \dfrac{1}{3}$ **51.** $\dfrac{5}{6} \div \dfrac{1}{3} \cdot \dfrac{1}{4}$ **52.** $\dfrac{7}{8} \div \dfrac{1}{4} \cdot \dfrac{1}{7}$

53. $\dfrac{1}{5} \cdot \left(2\dfrac{5}{6} - \dfrac{1}{3}\right)$ **54.** $\dfrac{4}{7} \cdot \left(6 - 2\dfrac{1}{2}\right)$ **55.** $2 \cdot \left(\dfrac{1}{4} + \dfrac{1}{5}\right) + 2$ **56.** $\dfrac{2}{5} \cdot \left(5 - \dfrac{1}{2}\right) - 1$

57. $\left(\dfrac{3}{4}\right)^2 \div \left(\dfrac{3}{4} - \dfrac{1}{12}\right)$ **58.** $\left(\dfrac{8}{9}\right)^2 \div \left(2 - \dfrac{2}{3}\right)$ **59.** $\left(\dfrac{2}{3} - \dfrac{5}{9}\right)^2$ **60.** $\left(1 - \dfrac{2}{5}\right)^3$

61. $\dfrac{5}{9} \cdot \dfrac{1}{2} + \dfrac{2}{3} \cdot \dfrac{5}{6}$ **62.** $\dfrac{7}{10} \cdot \dfrac{1}{2} + \dfrac{3}{4} \cdot \dfrac{3}{5}$ **63.** $\dfrac{27}{16} \cdot \left(\dfrac{2}{3}\right)^2 - \dfrac{3}{20}$ **64.** $\dfrac{64}{27} \cdot \left(\dfrac{3}{4}\right)^2 - \dfrac{7}{10}$

65. $\dfrac{3}{13} \div \dfrac{9}{26} - \dfrac{7}{24} \cdot \dfrac{8}{14}$ **66.** $\dfrac{5}{11} \div \dfrac{15}{77} - \dfrac{7}{10} \cdot \dfrac{5}{14}$ **67.** $\dfrac{3}{14} + \dfrac{10}{21} \div \left(\dfrac{3}{7}\right)\left(\dfrac{9}{4}\right)$ **68.** $\dfrac{11}{15} + \dfrac{7}{9} \div \left(\dfrac{14}{3}\right)\left(\dfrac{2}{3}\right)$

69. $\left(\dfrac{3}{4} + \dfrac{1}{8}\right)^2 - \left(\dfrac{1}{2} + \dfrac{1}{8}\right)$ **70.** $\left(\dfrac{1}{6} + \dfrac{1}{3}\right)^3 + \left(\dfrac{2}{5} \cdot \dfrac{3}{4}\right)^2$

Find the average of each list of numbers. See Example 12.

71. $\dfrac{5}{6}$ and $\dfrac{2}{3}$ **72.** $\dfrac{1}{2}$ and $\dfrac{4}{7}$ **73.** $\dfrac{1}{5}, \dfrac{3}{10}$, and $\dfrac{3}{20}$ **74.** $\dfrac{1}{3}, \dfrac{1}{4}$, and $\dfrac{1}{6}$

Objectives Ⓐ Ⓓ **Mixed Practice** *The table shows the fraction of the population in each country that uses cell phones. Use this table to answer Exercises 75 through 80.*

75. Complete the table by writing each fraction as an equivalent fraction with a denominator of 100.

76. Which of these countries has the largest fraction of cell phone users?

77. Which of these countries has the smallest fraction of cell phone users?

78. In which of these countries do over $\dfrac{3}{4}$ of the population use cell phones? (*Hint*: Write $\dfrac{3}{4}$ as an equivalent fraction with a denominator of 100.)

Country	Fraction of Population Using Cell Phones	Equivalent Fraction with a Denominator of 100
Denmark	$\dfrac{22}{25}$	
Finland	$\dfrac{9}{10}$	
Israel	$\dfrac{24}{25}$	
Spain	$\dfrac{23}{25}$	
Japan	$\dfrac{17}{25}$	
Norway	$\dfrac{91}{100}$	
Singapore	$\dfrac{4}{5}$	
Macao	$\dfrac{41}{50}$	
Sweden	$\dfrac{89}{100}$	
United States	$\dfrac{7}{10}$	
(*Source: International Telecommunication and World Almanac*, 2005)		

79. Find the average fraction of all phone users in Denmark, Israel, and Sweden.

80. Find the average fraction of cell phone users in the United States, Japan, and Finland.

Review

Identify each key word with the operation it most likely translates to. After each word, write A for addition, S for subtraction, M for multiplication, and D for division. See Sections 1.3, 1.4, 1.6, and 1.7.

81. increased by   **82.** sum   **83.** triple   **84.** product

85. subtracted from   **86.** decreased by   **87.** quotient   **88.** divided by

89. times   **90.** difference   **91.** total   **92.** more than

Concept Extensions

Solve.

93. Calculate $\dfrac{2^3}{3}$ and $\left(\dfrac{2}{3}\right)^3$. Do both of these expressions simplify to the same number? Explain why or why not.

94. Calculate $\left(\dfrac{1}{2}\right)^2 \cdot \left(\dfrac{3}{4}\right)^2$ and $\left(\dfrac{1}{2} \cdot \dfrac{3}{4}\right)^2$. Do both of these expressions simplify to the same number? Explain why or why not.

Each expression contains one addition, one subtraction, one multiplication, and one division. Write the operations in the order that they should be performed. Do not actually simplify. See the Concept Check in this section.

95. $[9 + 3(4 - 2)] \div \dfrac{10}{21}$ **96.** $[30 - 4(3 + 2)] \div \dfrac{5}{2}$ **97.** $\dfrac{1}{3} \div \left(\dfrac{2}{3}\right)\left(\dfrac{4}{5}\right) - \dfrac{1}{4} + \dfrac{1}{2}$ **98.** $\left(\dfrac{5}{6} - \dfrac{1}{3}\right) \cdot \dfrac{1}{3} + \dfrac{1}{2} \div \dfrac{9}{8}$

Solve.

99. In 2000, about $\dfrac{11}{67}$ of the total weight of mail delivered by the United States Postal Service was first-class mail. That same year, about $\dfrac{75}{134}$ of the total weight of mail delivered by the United States Postal Service was standard mail. Which of these two categories account for a greater portion of the mail handled by weight? (*Source:* U.S. Postal Service)

100. The National Park System (NPS) in the United States includes a wide variety of park types. National military parks account for $\dfrac{3}{128}$ of all NPS parks, and $\dfrac{1}{24}$ of NPS parks are classified as national preserves. Which category, national military park or national preserve, is bigger? (*Source:* National Park Service)

101. Approximately $\dfrac{7}{10}$ of U.S. adults have a savings account. About $\dfrac{11}{25}$ of U.S. adults have a non-interest-bearing checking account. Which type of banking service, savings account or non-interest-bearing checking account, do adults in the United States use more? (*Source:* Scarborough Research/ US Data.com, Inc.)

102. About $\dfrac{127}{500}$ of U.S. adults rent one or two videos per month. Approximately $\dfrac{31}{200}$ of U.S. adults rent three or four videos per month. Which video rental category, 1–2 videos or 3–4 videos per month, is bigger? (*Source:* Telenation/Market Facts, Inc.)

3.6 FRACTIONS AND PROBLEM SOLVING

Objective **A** Solving Problems Containing Fractions or Mixed Numbers

Now that we know how to add, subtract, multiply, and divide fractions and mixed numbers, we can solve problems containing these numbers.

In the next example, we find the volume of a box. Volume measures the space enclosed by a region and is measured in cubic units. We study volume further in a later chapter.

Volume of a box = length · width · height

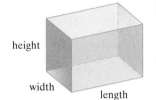

height
width
length

Helpful Hint

Remember:

Perimeter measures the distance around a figure. It is measured in **units.**

▢ Perimeter

Area measures the amount of surface of a figure. It is measured in **square units.**

▭ Area

Volume measures the amount of space enclosed by a region. It is measured in **cubic units.**

▱ Volume

EXAMPLE 1 Finding Volume of a Camcorder Box

Sony recently produced the smallest camcorder. It measures 5 inches by $2\frac{1}{2}$ inches by $1\frac{3}{4}$ inches and can store 30 minutes of moving images. Find the volume of a box with these dimensions. (*Source: Guinness World Records*)

Solution:

1. UNDERSTAND. Read and reread the problem. The phrase "volume of a box" tells us what to do. The volume of a box is the product of its length, width, and height. Since we are multiplying, it makes no difference which measurement we call length, width, or height.

2. TRANSLATE.

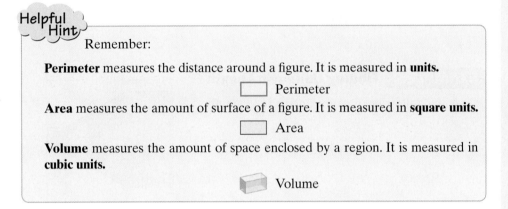

In words:

volume of a box	is	length	·	width	·	height
↓	↓	↓		↓		↓

Translate:

| volume of a box | = | 5 in. | · | $2\frac{1}{2}$ in. | · | $1\frac{3}{4}$ in. |

Continued on next page

PRACTICE PROBLEM 1

Find the volume of a box that measures $4\frac{1}{3}$ feet by $1\frac{1}{2}$ feet by $3\frac{1}{3}$ feet.

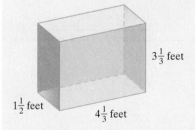

$3\frac{1}{3}$ feet

$1\frac{1}{2}$ feet

$4\frac{1}{3}$ feet

Answer

1. $21\frac{2}{3}$ cu ft

---

3. SOLVE: Before we multiply, let's estimate by rounding each dimension to a whole number. The number 5 rounds to 5, $2\frac{1}{2}$ rounds to 3, and $1\frac{3}{4}$ rounds to 2, so our estimate is $5 \cdot 3 \cdot 2$ or 30 cubic inches.

$$5\text{ in.}\cdot 2\frac{1}{2}\text{ in.}\cdot 1\frac{3}{4}\text{ in.} = \frac{5}{1}\cdot\frac{5}{2}\cdot\frac{7}{4} \quad \text{cubic inches}$$

$$= \frac{5\cdot 5\cdot 7}{1\cdot 2\cdot 4} \quad \text{cubic inches}$$

$$= \frac{175}{8}\text{ or } 21\frac{7}{8} \quad \text{cubic inches}$$

4. INTERPRET. *Check* your work. The exact answer is somewhat close to our estimate. If you'd like, round $2\frac{1}{2}$ down to 2, and our estimate is $5\cdot 2\cdot 2$ or 20 cubic inches. This estimate is also appropriate and closer to our exact answer, so it is reasonable. *State* your conclusion: The volume of a box that measures 5 inches by $2\frac{1}{2}$ inches by $1\frac{3}{4}$ inches is $21\frac{7}{8}$ cubic inches.

▣ **Work Practice Problem 1**

PRACTICE PROBLEM 2

Given the following diagram, find its total width.

EXAMPLE 2 **Finding Unknown Length**

Given the following diagram, find its total length.

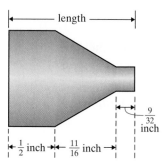

Solution:

1. UNDERSTAND. Read and reread the problem. Then study the diagram. The phrase "total length" tells us to add.

2. TRANSLATE. It makes no difference which length we call first, second, or third length.

In words:	total length	is	first length	+	second length	+	third length
	↓	↓	↓		↓		↓
Translate:	total length	$=$	$\frac{1}{2}$ in.	$+$	$\frac{11}{16}$ in.	$+$	$\frac{9}{32}$ in.

3. SOLVE:

$$\frac{1}{2} + \frac{11}{16} + \frac{9}{32} = \frac{1\cdot 16}{2\cdot 16} + \frac{11\cdot 2}{16\cdot 2} + \frac{9}{32}$$

$$= \frac{16}{32} + \frac{22}{32} + \frac{9}{32}$$

$$= \frac{47}{32}\text{ or } 1\frac{15}{32}$$

4. INTERPRET. *Check* your work. *State* your conclusion: The total length is $1\frac{15}{32}$ inches.

Many problems require more than one operation to solve as shown in the next application.

▣ **Work Practice Problem 2**

Answer

2. 2 in.

EXAMPLE 3 **Acreage for Single-Family Home Lots**

A contractor is considering buying land to develop a subdivision for single-family homes. Suppose she buys 44 acres and calculates that $4\frac{1}{4}$ acres of this land will be used for roads and a retention pond. How many $\frac{3}{4}$-acre lots can she sell using the rest of the acreage?

PRACTICE PROBLEM 3

Suppose that 25 acres of land are purchased, but because of roads and wetlands concerns, $6\frac{2}{3}$ acres cannot be developed into lots. How many $\frac{5}{6}$-acre lots can the rest of the land be divided into?

Solution:

1a. UNDERSTAND. Read and reread the problem. The phrase "using the rest of the acreage" tells is that initially we are to subtract.

2a. TRANSLATE. First, let's calculate the amount of acreage that can be used for lots.

In words:	acreage for lots	is	total acreage	minus	acreage for roads and a pond
	↓	↓	↓	↓	↓
Translate:	acreage for lots	=	44	−	$4\frac{1}{4}$

3a. SOLVE:

$$
\begin{array}{r}
44 = 43\frac{4}{4} \\
- 4\frac{1}{4} = - 4\frac{1}{4} \\
\hline
39\frac{3}{4}
\end{array}
$$

1b. UNDERSTAND. Now that we know $39\frac{3}{4}$ acres can be used for lots, we calculate how many $\frac{3}{4}$ acres are in $39\frac{3}{4}$. This means that we divide.

2b. TRANSLATE.

In words:	number of $\frac{3}{4}$-acre lots	is	acreage for lots	divided by	size of each lot
	↓	↓	↓	↓	↓
Translate:	number of $\frac{3}{4}$-acre lots	=	$39\frac{3}{4}$	÷	$\frac{3}{4}$

3b. SOLVE:

$$39\frac{3}{4} \div \frac{3}{4} = \frac{159}{4} \cdot \frac{4}{3} = \frac{\overset{53}{\cancel{159}} \cdot \overset{1}{\cancel{4}}}{\underset{1}{\cancel{4}} \cdot \underset{1}{\cancel{3}}} = \frac{53}{1} \text{ or } 53$$

4. INTERPRET. *Check* your work. *State* your conclusion: The contractor can sell $53\frac{3}{4}$-acre lots.

■ **Work Practice Problem 3**

Answer

3. 22 lots

Translate each to an expression. Then simplify the expression.

1. Find the sum of 11 and 2.

2. Find the product of 11 and 2.

3. Find the quotient of 20 and 6.

4. Find the difference of 20 and 6.

5. Subtract 8 from 35.

6. Find the total of 15 and 18.

7. Find 68 increased by 7.

8. Find 68 decreased by 7.

9. Multiply 21 and 9.

10. Find 37 divided by 9.

Objective **A** *Solve. See Examples 1 through 3.*

11. A recipe for brownies calls for $1\frac{2}{3}$ cups of sugar. If you are doubling the recipe, how much sugar do you need?

12. A nacho recipe calls for $\frac{1}{3}$ cup chedder cheese and $\frac{1}{2}$ cup jalapeño cheese. Find the total amount of cheese in the recipe.

13. A decorative wall in Ben and Joy Lander's garden is to be built using brick that is $2\frac{3}{4}$ inches wide and a mortar joint that is $\frac{1}{2}$ inch wide. Use the diagram to find the height of the wall.

14. Suppose that Ben and Joy Lander (from Exercise 13) decide that they want one more layer of bricks with a mortar joint below and above that layer. Find the new height of the wall.

height   Mortar joint

15. Doug and Claudia Scaggs recently drove $290\frac{1}{4}$ miles on $13\frac{1}{2}$ gallons of gas. Calculate how many miles per gallon they get in their vehicle.

16. A contractor is using 18 acres of his land to sell $\frac{3}{4}$-acre lots. How many lots can he sell?

 17. The life expectancy of a circulating coin is 30 years. The life expectancy of a circulating dollar bill is only $\frac{1}{20}$ as long. Find the life expectancy of circulating paper money. (*Source:* The U.S. Mint)

18. The Indian Head one-cent coin of 1859–1864 was made of copper and nickel only. If $\frac{3}{25}$ of the coin was nickel, what part of the whole coin was copper? (*Source:* The U.S. Mint)

19. The Gauge Act of 1846 set the standard gauge for U.S. railroads at $56\frac{1}{2}$ inches. (See figure.) If the standard gauge in Spain is $65\frac{9}{10}$ inches, how much wider is Spain's standard gauge than the U.S. standard gauge? (*Source:* San Diego Railroad Museum)

20. The standard railroad track gauge (see figure) in Spain is $65\frac{9}{10}$ inches, while in neighboring Portugal it is $65\frac{11}{20}$ inches. Which gauge is wider and by how much? (*Source:* San Diego Museum)

Track gauge (U.S. $56\frac{1}{2}$ inches)

$\frac{5}{8}$ inch

Point of measurement of gauge

21. Mark Nguyen is a tailor making costumes for a play. He needs enough material for 1 large shirt that requires $1\frac{1}{2}$ yards of material and 5 small shirts that each require $\frac{3}{4}$ yard of material. He finds a 5-yard remnant of material on sale. Is 5 yards of material enough to make all 6 shirts? If not, how much more material does he need?

22. A beanbag manufacturer makes a large beanbag requiring $4\frac{1}{3}$ yards of vinyl fabric and a smaller size requiring $3\frac{1}{4}$ yards. A 100-yard roll of fabric is to be used to make 12 large beanbags. How many smaller beanbags can be made from the remaining piece?

23. A plumber has a 10-foot piece of PVC pipe. How many $\frac{9}{5}$-foot pieces can be cut from the 10-foot piece?

24. A carpenter has a 12-foot board to be used to make windowsills. If each sill requires $2\frac{5}{16}$ feet, how many sills can be made from the 12-foot board?

25. Suppose that the cross section of a piece of pipe looks like the diagram shown. Find the total outer diameter.

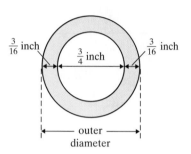

26. Suppose that the cross section of a piece of pipe looks like the diagram shown. Find the total inner diameter.

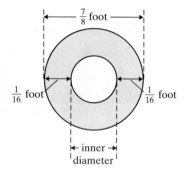

27. A recipe for chocolate chip cookies calls for $2\frac{1}{2}$ cups of flour. If you are making $1\frac{1}{2}$ recipes, how many cups of flour are needed?

28. A recipe for a homemade cleaning solution calls for $1\frac{3}{4}$ cups of vinegar. If you are tripling the recipe, how much vinegar is needed?

△ **29.** The Polaroid Pop Shot, the world's first disposable instant camera, can take color photographs measuring $4\frac{1}{2}$ inches by $2\frac{1}{2}$ inches. Find the area of a photograph. (*Source: Guinness World Records*)

△ **30.** A model for a proposed computer chip measures $\frac{3}{4}$ inch by $1\frac{1}{4}$ inches. Find its area.

31. A total solar eclipse on March 29, 2006 will last $4\frac{7}{60}$ minutes and can be viewed from Atlantic Ocean, Africa, and Asia. The next total solar eclipse on August 1, 2008, will last $2\frac{9}{20}$ minutes and can be viewed in parts of the Arctic Ocean and Asia. How much longer is the 2006 solar eclipse? (*Source: 2005 World Almanac*)

32. The pole vault record for the 1908 Summer Olympics was $12\frac{1}{6}$ feet. The record for the 2004 Summer Olympics was a little over $19\frac{1}{2}$ feet. Find the difference of these heights. (*Source: 2005 World Almanac*)

△ **33.** A small cell phone measures $3\frac{1}{5}$ inches by $1\frac{7}{10}$ inches by 1 inch. Find the volume of a box with those dimensions. (*Source: Guinness World Records*)

34. Early cell phones were large and heavy. One early model measured approximately 8 inches by $2\frac{1}{2}$ inches by $2\frac{1}{2}$ inches. Find the volume of a box with those dimensions.

35. A stack of $\frac{5}{8}$-inch-wide sheetrock has a height of $41\frac{7}{8}$ inches. How many sheets of sheetrock are in the stack?

36. A stack of $\frac{5}{4}$-inch-wide books has a height of $28\frac{3}{4}$ inches. How many books are in the stack?

37. William Arcencio is remodeling his home. In order to save money, he is upgrading the plumbing himself. He needs 12 pieces of copper tubing, each $\frac{3}{4}$ of a foot long.
  a. If he has a 10-foot piece of tubing, will that be enough?
  b. How much more does he need or how much tubing will he have left over?

38. Trishelle Dallam is building a bookcase. Each shelf will be $2\frac{3}{8}$ feet long, and she needs wood for 7 shelves.
  a. How many shelves can she cut from an 8-foot board?
  b. Based on your answer for part a, how many 8-foot boards will she need?

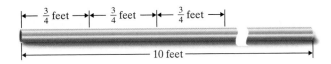

Recall that the average of a list of numbers is their sum divided by the number of numbers in the list. Use this procedure for Exercises 39 and 40.

39. A female lion had 4 cubs. They weighed $2\frac{1}{8}$, $2\frac{7}{8}$, $3\frac{1}{4}$, and $3\frac{1}{2}$ pounds. What is the average cub weight?

40. Three brook trout were caught, tagged, and then released. They weighed $1\frac{1}{2}$, $1\frac{3}{8}$, and $1\frac{7}{8}$ pounds. Find their average weight.

Find the area and perimeter of each figure.

△ **41.**
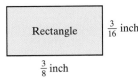

Rectangle $\frac{3}{16}$ inch

$\frac{3}{8}$ inch

△ **42.**

Square $1\frac{7}{10}$ mile

43.
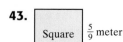
Square | $\frac{5}{9}$ meter

44.
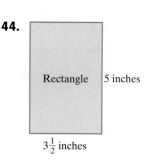
Rectangle | 5 inches

$3\frac{1}{2}$ inches

For Exercises 45 through 48, see the diagram. (Source: www.usflag.org)

45. The length of the U.S. flag is $1\frac{9}{10}$ its width. If a flag is being designed with a width of $2\frac{1}{2}$ feet, find its length.

46. The width of the Union portion the U.S. flag is $\frac{7}{13}$ of the width of the flag. If a flag is being designed with a width of $2\frac{1}{2}$ feet, find the width of the Union portion.

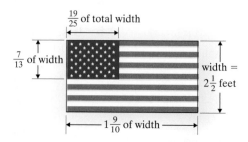

$\frac{19}{25}$ of total width

$\frac{7}{13}$ of width

width = $2\frac{1}{2}$ feet

$1\frac{9}{10}$ of width

47. There are 13 stripes of equal width in the flag. If the width of a flag is $2\frac{1}{2}$ feet, find the width of each stripe.

48. The length of the Union portion of the flag is $\frac{19}{25}$ of the total width. If the width of a flag is $2\frac{1}{2}$ feet, find the length of the Union portion.

Review

Simplify. See Section 1.9.

49. $\sqrt{9}$

50. $\sqrt{4}$

51. 9^2

52. 4^2

53. $8 \div 4 \cdot 2$

54. $20 \div 5 \cdot 2$

55. $3^2 - 2^2 + 5^2$

56. $8^2 - 6^2 + 7^2$

57. $5 + 3[14 - (12 \div 3)]$

58. $7 + 2[20 - (35 \div 5)]$

Concept Extensions

59. Suppose that you are finding the average of $1\frac{3}{4}$, $1\frac{1}{8}$, and $1\frac{9}{10}$. Can the average be $2\frac{1}{4}$? Can the average be $\frac{15}{16}$? Why or why not?

The figure shown is for Exercises 60 and 61.

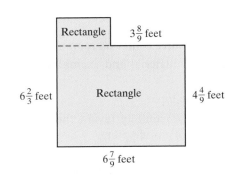

△ **60.** Find the area of the figure. (*Hint:* The area of the figure can be found by finding the sum of the areas of the rectangles shown in the figure.)

△ **61.** Find the perimeter of the figure.

62. On a particular day, 240 customers ate lunch at a local restaurant. If $\frac{3}{10}$ of them ordered a $7 lunch, $\frac{5}{12}$ of them ordered a $5 lunch, and the remaining customers ordered a $9 lunch, how many customers ordered a $9 lunch?

63. Scott purchased a case of 24 apples. He used $\frac{1}{3}$ of them to make an apple pie, $\frac{1}{4}$ of them to make apple crisp, and kept the rest for after-school snacks for his children. How many apples did Chris keep for snacks?

64. Coins were practically made by hand in the late 1700s. Back then, it took 3 years to produce our nation's first million coins. Today, it takes only $\frac{11}{13,140}$ as long to produce the same amount. Calculate how long it takes today in hours to produce one million coins. (*Hint:* First convert 3 years to equivalent hours.) (*Source:* The U.S. Mint)

65. The largest suitcase measures $13\frac{1}{3}$ feet by $8\frac{3}{4}$ feet by $4\frac{4}{25}$ feet. Find its volume. (*Source: Guinness World Records*)

STUDY SKILLS BUILDER

Tips for Studying for an Exam

To prepare for an exam, try the following study techniques:

- Start the study process days before your exam.
- Make sure that you are up-to-date on your assignments.
- If there is a topic that you are unsure of, use one of the many resources that are available to you. For example,

  See your instructor.

  Visit a learning resource center on campus.

  Read the textbook material and examples on the topic.

  View a video on the topic.

- Reread your notes and carefully review the Chapter Highlights at the end of any chapter.
- Work the review exercises at the end of the chapter. Check your answers and correct any mistakes. If you have trouble, use a resource listed above.
- Find a quiet place to take the Chapter Test found at the end of the chapter. Do not use any resources when taking this sample test. This way, you will have a clear indication of how prepared you are for your exam. Check your answers and make sure that you correct any missed exercises.
- Get lots of rest the night before the exam. It's hard to show how well you know the material if your brain is foggy from lack of sleep.

Good luck and keep a positive attitude.

Let's see how you did on your last exam.

1. How many days before your last exam did you start studying for that exam?
2. Were you up-to-date on your assignments at that time or did you need to catch up on assignments?

3. List the most helpful text supplement (if you used one).
4. List the most helpful campus supplement (if you used one).
5. List your process for preparing for a mathematics test.
6. Was this process helpful? In other words, were you satisfied with your performance on your exam?
7. If not, what changes can you make in your process that will make it more helpful to you?

Are You Prepared for a Test on Chapter 3?

Below I have listed some *common trouble areas* for students in Chapter 3. After studying for your test—but before taking your test—read these.

Make sure you remember how to perform different operations on fractions!!! Try to add, subtract, multiply, then divide $\frac{3}{5}$ and $\frac{7}{15}$. Check your results below.

$$\frac{3}{5} + \frac{7}{15} = \frac{3}{5} \cdot \frac{3}{3} + \frac{7}{15} = \frac{9}{15} + \frac{7}{15} = \frac{16}{15} \text{ or } 1\frac{1}{15}$$

To add or subtract, the fractions must have a common denominator.

$$\frac{3}{5} - \frac{7}{15} = \frac{3}{5} \cdot \frac{3}{3} - \frac{7}{15} = \frac{9}{15} - \frac{7}{15} = \frac{2}{15}$$

$$\frac{3}{5} \cdot \frac{7}{15} = \frac{3 \cdot 7}{5 \cdot 15} = \frac{\overset{1}{\cancel{3}} \cdot 7}{5 \cdot \cancel{3} \cdot 5} = \frac{7}{25}$$

To multiply, multiply numerators and multiply denominators.

$$\frac{3}{5} \div \frac{7}{15} = \frac{3}{5} \cdot \frac{15}{7} = \frac{3 \cdot 15}{5 \cdot 7} = \frac{3 \cdot 3 \cdot \overset{1}{\cancel{5}}}{\cancel{5} \cdot 7} = \frac{9}{7} \text{ or } 1\frac{2}{7}$$

To divide, multiply by the reciprocal.

CHAPTER 3   Group Activity

Sections 3.1–3.6

This activity may be completed by working in groups or individually.

Lobsters are normally classified by weight. Use the weight classification table to answer the questions in this activity.

Classification of Lobsters	
Class	**Weight (in Pounds)**
Chicken	1 to $1\frac{1}{8}$
Quarter	$1\frac{1}{4}$
Half	$1\frac{1}{2}$ to $1\frac{3}{4}$
Select	$1\frac{3}{4}$ to $2\frac{1}{2}$
Large select	$2\frac{1}{2}$ to $3\frac{1}{2}$
Jumbo	Over $3\frac{1}{2}$

(*Source:* The Maine Lobster Promotion Council)

1. A lobster fisher has kept four lobsters from a lobster trap. Classify each lobster if they have the following weights:

    a. $1\frac{7}{8}$ pounds

    b. $1\frac{9}{16}$ pounds

    c. $2\frac{3}{4}$ pounds

    d. $2\frac{3}{8}$ pounds

2. A recipe requires 5 pounds of lobster. Using the minimum weight for each class, decide whether a chicken, half, and select lobster will be enough for the recipe, and explain your reasoning. If not, suggest a better choice of lobsters to meet the recipe requirements.

3. A lobster market customer has selected two chickens, a select, and a large select. What is the most that these four lobsters could weigh? What is the least that these four lobsters could weigh?

4. A lobster market customer wishes to buy three quarters. If lobsters sell for $7 per pound, how much will the customer owe for her purchase?

5. Why do you think there is no classification for lobsters weighing under 1 pound?

Chapter 3 Vocabulary Check

Fill in each blank with one of the words or phrases listed below.

equivalent   least common multiple   like

mixed number   <   >   least common denominator

1. Fractions that have the same denominator are called _____ fractions.

2. The _____ is the smallest number that is a multiple of all numbers in a list of numbers.

3. _____ fractions represent the same portion of a whole.

4. A _____ has a whole number part and a fraction part.

5. The symbol _____ means is greater than.

6. The symbol _____ means is less than.

7. The LCM of the denominators in a list of fractions is called the _____.

> **Helpful Hint**
>
> Are you preparing for your test? Don't forget to take the Chapter 3 Test on page 244. Then check your answers at the back of the text and use the Chapter Test Prep Video CD to see the fully worked-out solutions to any of the exercises you want to review.

3 Chapter Highlights

DEFINITIONS AND CONCEPTS	EXAMPLES
Section 3.1 Adding and Subtracting Like Fractions	
Fractions that have the same denominator are called **like fractions.**	$\frac{1}{3}$ and $\frac{2}{3}$; $\frac{5}{7}$ and $\frac{6}{7}$
To add or subtract like fractions, combine the numerators and place the sum or difference over the common denominator.	$\frac{2}{7} + \frac{3}{7} = \frac{5}{7}$ ← Add the numerators. $\phantom{\frac{2}{7} + \frac{3}{7} = \frac{5}{7}}$ ← Keep the common denominator. $\frac{7}{8} - \frac{4}{8} = \frac{3}{8}$ ← Subtract the numerators. $\phantom{\frac{7}{8} - \frac{4}{8} = \frac{3}{8}}$ ← Keep the common denominator.
Section 3.2 Least Common Multiple	
The **least common multiple (LCM)** is the smallest number that is a multiple of all numbers in a list of numbers.	The LCM of 2 and 6 is 6 because 6 is the smallest number that is a multiple of both 2 and 6.
METHOD 1 FOR FINDING THE LCM OF A LIST OF NUMBERS USING MULTIPLES	Find the LCM of 4 and 6 using Method 1.
Step 1. Write the multiples of the largest number (starting with the number itself) until a multiple common to all numbers in the list is found. **Step 2.** The multiple found in step 1 is the LCM.	$6 \cdot 1 = 6$ Not a multiple of 4 $6 \cdot 2 = 12$ A multiple of 4 The LCM is 12.

DEFINITIONS AND CONCEPTS	**EXAMPLES**

Section 3.2   Least Common Multiple (*continued*)

METHOD 2 FOR FINDING THE LCM OF A LIST OF NUMBERS USING PRIME FACTORIZATION	Find the LCM of 6 and 20 using Method 2.
Step 1. Write the prime factorization of each number.	$6 = 2 \cdot ③$
Step 2. For each different prime factor in step 1, circle the greatest number of times that factor occurs in any one factorization.	$20 = ②\cdot②\cdot⑤$
Step 3. The LCM is the product of the circle factors.	The LCM is
	$2 \cdot 2 \cdot 3 \cdot 5 = 60$
Equivalent fractions represent the same portion of a whole.	Write an equivalent fraction with the indicated denominator.
	$\dfrac{2}{8} = \dfrac{}{16}$
	$\dfrac{2 \cdot 2}{8 \cdot 2} = \dfrac{4}{16}$

Section 3.3   Adding and Subtracting Unlike Fractions

TO ADD OR SUBTRACT FRACTIONS WITH UNLIKE DENOMINATORS	Add: $\dfrac{3}{20} + \dfrac{2}{5}$
Step 1. Find the LCD.	**Step 1.** The LCD of 20 and 5 is 20.
Step 2. Write each fraction as an equivalent fraction whose denominator is the LCD.	**Step 2.** $\dfrac{3}{20} = \dfrac{3}{20}; \dfrac{2}{5} = \dfrac{2}{5} \cdot \dfrac{4}{4} = \dfrac{8}{20}$
Step 3. Add or subtract the like fractions.	**Step 3.** $\dfrac{3}{20} + \dfrac{2}{5} = \dfrac{3}{20} + \dfrac{8}{20} = \dfrac{11}{20}$
Step 4. Write the sum or difference in simplest form.	**Step 4.** $\dfrac{11}{20}$ is in simplest form.

Section 3.4   Adding and Subtracting Mixed Numbers

To add or subtract with mixed numbers, add or subtract the fractions and then add or subtract the whole numbers.	Add: $2\dfrac{1}{2} + 5\dfrac{7}{8}$
	$2\dfrac{1}{2} = 2\dfrac{4}{8}$
	$+5\dfrac{7}{8} = 5\dfrac{7}{8}$
	$\rule{2cm}{0.4pt}$
	$7\dfrac{11}{8} = 7 + 1\dfrac{3}{8} = 8\dfrac{3}{8}$

Section 3.5   Order, Exponents, and the Order of Operations

To compare like fractions, compare the numerators. The order of the fractions is the same as the order of the numerators.	Compare $\dfrac{3}{10}$ and $\dfrac{4}{10}$.
	$\dfrac{3}{10} < \dfrac{4}{10}$ since $3 < 4$

continued

DEFINITIONS AND CONCEPTS	**EXAMPLES**

Section 3.5   Order, Exponents, and the Order of Operations (*continued*)

To compare unlike fractions, first write the fractions as like fractions. Then the fraction with the greater numerator is the greater fraction.

Compare $\frac{2}{5}$ and $\frac{3}{7}$.

$$\frac{2}{5} = \frac{2}{5} \cdot \frac{7}{7} = \frac{14}{35} \qquad \frac{3}{7} = \frac{3}{7} \cdot \frac{5}{5} = \frac{15}{35}$$

Since $14 < 15$, then

$$\frac{14}{35} < \frac{15}{35} \quad \text{or} \quad \frac{2}{5} < \frac{3}{7}$$

Exponents mean repeated multiplication when the base is a whole number or a fraction.

$$\left(\frac{1}{2}\right)^3 = \frac{1}{2} \cdot \frac{1}{2} \cdot \frac{1}{2} = \frac{1}{8}$$

ORDER OF OPERATIONS

Perform each indicated operation.

1. Perform all operations within parentheses ( ), brackets [ ], or other grouping symbols such as square roots or fraction bars.

2. Evaluate any expressions with exponents.

3. Multiply or divide in order from left to right.

4. Add or subtract in order from left to right.

$$\frac{1}{2} + \frac{2}{3} \cdot \frac{1}{5} = \frac{1}{2} + \frac{2}{15} \qquad \text{Multiply.}$$

$$= \frac{1}{2} \cdot \frac{15}{15} + \frac{2}{15} \cdot \frac{2}{2} \qquad \text{The LCD is 30.}$$

$$= \frac{15}{30} + \frac{4}{30}$$

$$= \frac{19}{30} \qquad \text{Add.}$$

Section 3.6   Fractions and Problem Solving

PROBLEM-SOLVING STEPS

A stack of $\frac{3}{4}$-inch plywood has a height of $50\frac{1}{4}$ inches. How many sheets of plywood are in the stack?

1. UNDERSTAND the problem.

1. UNDERSTAND. Read and reread the problem. We want to know how many $\frac{3}{4}$'s are in $50\frac{1}{4}$, so we divide.

2. TRANSLATE the problem.

2. TRANSLATE.

number of sheets in stack	is	height of stack	÷	height of a sheet

$$\text{number of sheets in stack} = 50\frac{1}{4} \div \frac{3}{4}$$

3. SOLVE the problem.

3. SOLVE. $50\frac{1}{4} \div \frac{3}{4} = \frac{201}{4} \cdot \frac{4}{3}$

$$= \frac{\overset{67}{\cancel{201}} \cdot \overset{1}{\cancel{4}}}{\underset{1}{\cancel{4}} \cdot \underset{1}{\cancel{3}}}$$

$$= 67$$

4. INTERPRET the results.

4. INTERPRET. *Check* your work and *state* your conclusion. There are 67 sheets of plywood in the stack.

3 CHAPTER REVIEW

(3.1) *Add or subtract as indicated. Simplify your answers.*

1. $\dfrac{7}{11} + \dfrac{3}{11}$

2. $\dfrac{4}{50} + \dfrac{2}{50}$

3. $\dfrac{11}{15} - \dfrac{1}{15}$

4. $\dfrac{4}{21} - \dfrac{1}{21}$

5. $\dfrac{4}{15} + \dfrac{3}{15} + \dfrac{2}{15}$

6. $\dfrac{3}{20} + \dfrac{7}{20} + \dfrac{2}{20}$

7. $\dfrac{1}{12} + \dfrac{11}{12}$

8. $\dfrac{3}{4} + \dfrac{1}{4}$

9. $\dfrac{11}{25} + \dfrac{6}{25} + \dfrac{2}{25}$

10. $\dfrac{4}{21} + \dfrac{1}{21} + \dfrac{11}{21}$

Solve.

11. One evening Mark Alorenzo did $\dfrac{3}{8}$ of his homework before supper, another $\dfrac{2}{8}$ of it while his children did their homework, and $\dfrac{1}{8}$ after his children went to bed. What part of his homework did he do that evening?

△ **12.** The Simpson's will be fencing in their land, which is in the shape of a rectangle. In order to do this, they need to find its perimeter. Find the perimeter of their land.

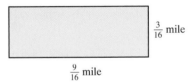

$\frac{3}{16}$ mile

$\frac{9}{16}$ mile

(3.2) *Find the LCM of each list of numbers.*

13. $5, 11$

14. $20, 30$

15. $20, 24$

16. $16, 5$

17. $12, 21, 63$

18. $6, 8, 18$

Write each fraction as an equivalent fraction with the given denominator.

19. $\dfrac{7}{8} = \dfrac{}{64}$

20. $\dfrac{2}{3} = \dfrac{}{30}$

21. $\dfrac{7}{11} = \dfrac{}{33}$

22. $\dfrac{10}{13} = \dfrac{}{26}$

23. $\dfrac{4}{15} = \dfrac{}{60}$

24. $\dfrac{5}{12} = \dfrac{}{60}$

(3.3) *Add or subtract as indicated. Simplify your answers.*

25. $\dfrac{7}{18} + \dfrac{2}{9}$

26. $\dfrac{4}{15} + \dfrac{1}{5}$

27. $\dfrac{4}{13} - \dfrac{1}{26}$

28. $\dfrac{7}{12} - \dfrac{1}{9}$

29. $\dfrac{1}{3} + \dfrac{9}{14}$

30. $\dfrac{7}{18} + \dfrac{5}{24}$

31. $\dfrac{11}{15} - \dfrac{4}{9}$

32. $\dfrac{9}{14} - \dfrac{3}{35}$

Find the perimeter of each figure.

△ **33.**

$\frac{2}{9}$ meter | Rectangle

$\frac{5}{6}$ meter

△ **34.** $\frac{1}{5}$ foot $\frac{3}{5}$ foot

$\frac{7}{10}$ foot

35. Find the difference in length of two scarves if one scarf is $\frac{5}{12}$ of a yard long and the other is $\frac{2}{3}$ of a yard long.

36. Truman Kalzote cleaned $\frac{3}{5}$ of his house yesterday and $\frac{1}{10}$ of it today. How much of the house has been cleaned?

(3.4) *Add or subtract as indicated. Simplify your answers.*

37. $31\frac{2}{7} + 14\frac{10}{21}$

38. $24\frac{4}{5} + 35\frac{1}{5}$

39. $69\frac{5}{22} - 36\frac{7}{11}$

40. $36\frac{3}{20} - 32\frac{5}{6}$

41. $\begin{array}{r} 29\frac{2}{9} \\ 27\frac{7}{18} \\ +54\frac{2}{3} \\ \hline \end{array}$

42. $\begin{array}{r} 7\frac{3}{8} \\ 9\frac{5}{6} \\ +3\frac{1}{12} \\ \hline \end{array}$

43. $\begin{array}{r} 9\frac{3}{5} \\ -4\frac{1}{7} \\ \hline \end{array}$

44. $\begin{array}{r} 8\frac{3}{11} \\ -5\frac{1}{5} \\ \hline \end{array}$

Solve.

45. The average annual snowfall at a certain ski resort is $62\frac{3}{10}$ inches. Last year it had $54\frac{1}{2}$ inches. How many inches below average was last year's snowfall?

△ **46.** Find the perimeter of a rectangular sheet of gift wrap that is $2\frac{1}{4}$ feet by $3\frac{1}{3}$ feet.

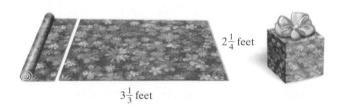

$2\frac{1}{4}$ feet

$3\frac{1}{3}$ feet

△ **47.** Find the perimeter of a sheet of shelf paper needed to fit exactly a square drawer $1\frac{1}{4}$ feet long on each side.

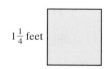

$1\frac{1}{4}$ feet

48. Dinah's homemade canned peaches contain $15\frac{3}{5}$ ounces per can. A can of Amy's brand contains $15\frac{5}{8}$ ounces per can. Amy's brand weighs how much more than Dinah's?

(3.5) *Insert < or > to form a true statement.*

49. $\dfrac{5}{11}$ $\quad$ $\dfrac{6}{11}$

50. $\dfrac{4}{35}$ $\quad$ $\dfrac{3}{35}$

51. $\dfrac{5}{14}$ $\quad$ $\dfrac{16}{42}$

52. $\dfrac{6}{35}$ $\quad$ $\dfrac{17}{105}$

53. $\dfrac{7}{8}$ $\quad$ $\dfrac{6}{7}$

54. $\dfrac{7}{10}$ $\quad$ $\dfrac{2}{3}$

Evaluate each expression. Use the order of operations to simplify.

55. $\left(\dfrac{3}{7}\right)^2$

56. $\left(\dfrac{4}{5}\right)^3$

57. $\left(\dfrac{1}{2}\right)^4 \cdot \left(\dfrac{3}{5}\right)^2$

58. $\left(\dfrac{1}{3}\right)^2 \cdot \left(\dfrac{9}{10}\right)^2$

59. $\dfrac{5}{13} \div \dfrac{1}{2} \cdot \dfrac{4}{5}$

60. $\dfrac{8}{11} \div \dfrac{1}{3} \cdot \dfrac{11}{12}$

61. $\left(\dfrac{6}{7} - \dfrac{3}{14}\right)^2$

62. $\dfrac{2}{7} \cdot \left(\dfrac{1}{5} + \dfrac{3}{10}\right)$

63. $\dfrac{8}{9} - \dfrac{1}{8} \div \dfrac{3}{4}$

64. $\dfrac{9}{10} - \dfrac{1}{9} \div \dfrac{2}{3}$

65. $\left(\dfrac{1}{3}\right)^2 - \dfrac{2}{27}$

66. $\dfrac{9}{10} \div \left(\dfrac{1}{5} + \dfrac{1}{20}\right)$

67. $\left(\dfrac{3}{4} + \dfrac{1}{2}\right) \div \left(\dfrac{4}{9} + \dfrac{1}{3}\right)$

68. $\left(\dfrac{3}{8} - \dfrac{1}{16}\right) \div \left(\dfrac{1}{2} - \dfrac{1}{8}\right)$

69. $\dfrac{6}{7} \cdot \dfrac{5}{2} - \dfrac{3}{4} \cdot \dfrac{1}{2}$

70. $\dfrac{9}{10} \cdot \dfrac{1}{3} - \dfrac{2}{5} \cdot \dfrac{1}{11}$

Find the average of each list of fractions.

71. $\dfrac{2}{3}, \dfrac{5}{6}, \dfrac{1}{9}$

72. $\dfrac{4}{5}, \dfrac{9}{10}, \dfrac{3}{20}$

(3.6)

73. Saturn has 28 moons. The planet Uranus has only $\frac{3}{4}$ as many. Find the number of moons for Uranus. (*Source:* NASA)

74. James Hardaway just bought $5\frac{7}{8}$ acres of land adjacent to the $9\frac{3}{4}$ acres he already owned. How much land does he now own?

Find the unknown measurements.

△ **75.**

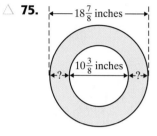

△ **76.**

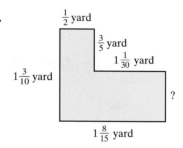

Find the perimeter and area of each rectangle. Attach the proper units to each. Remember that perimeter is measured in units and area is measured in square units.

△ **77.**

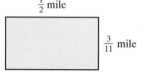

△ **78.**

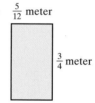

Mixed Review

Find the LCM of each list of numbers.

79. 15, 30, 45

80. 6, 15, 20

Write each fraction as an equivalent fraction with the given denominator.

81. $\frac{5}{6} = \frac{}{48}$

82. $\frac{7}{8} = \frac{}{72}$

Add or subtract as indicated. Simplify your answers.

83. $\frac{5}{12} - \frac{3}{12}$

84. $\frac{3}{10} - \frac{1}{10}$

85. $\frac{2}{3} + \frac{1}{4}$

86. $\frac{5}{11} + \frac{2}{55}$

87. $7\dfrac{3}{4}$

$+5\dfrac{2}{3}$

88. $2\dfrac{7}{8}$

$+9\dfrac{1}{2}$

89. $12\dfrac{3}{5}$

$-9\dfrac{1}{7}$

90. $32\dfrac{10}{21}$

$-24\dfrac{3}{7}$

Evaluate each expression. Use the order of operations to simplify.

91. $\dfrac{2}{5} + \left(\dfrac{2}{5}\right)^2 - \dfrac{3}{25}$

92. $\dfrac{1}{4} + \left(\dfrac{1}{2}\right)^2 - \dfrac{3}{8}$

93. $\left(\dfrac{5}{6} - \dfrac{3}{4}\right)^2$

94. $\left(2 - \dfrac{2}{3}\right)^3$

95. $\dfrac{2}{3} \div \left(\dfrac{3}{5} + \dfrac{5}{3}\right)$

96. $\dfrac{3}{8} \cdot \left(\dfrac{2}{3} - \dfrac{4}{9}\right)$

Insert $<$ or $>$ to form a true statement.

97. $\dfrac{3}{14}$ $\dfrac{2}{3}$

98. $\dfrac{7}{23}$ $\dfrac{3}{16}$

Solve.

99. Gregor Krowsky studied math for $\dfrac{3}{8}$ of an hour and geography for $\dfrac{1}{8}$ of an hour. How long did he study?

100. Two packages to be mailed weigh $3\dfrac{3}{4}$ pounds and $2\dfrac{3}{5}$ pounds. Find their combined weight.

101. A ribbon $5\dfrac{1}{2}$ yards long is cut from a reel of ribbon with 50 yards on it. Find the length of the piece remaining on the reel.

102. Linda Taneff has a board that is $10\dfrac{2}{3}$ feet in length. She plans to cut it into 5 equal lengths to use for a bookshelf. Find the length of each piece.

103. A recipe for pico de gallo calls for $1\dfrac{1}{2}$ tablespoons of cilantro. Five recipes will be made for a charity event. How much cilantro is needed?

104. Beryl Goldstein mixed $\dfrac{5}{8}$ of a gallon of water with $\dfrac{1}{8}$ of a gallon of punch concentrate. Then she and her friends drank $\dfrac{3}{8}$ of a gallon of the punch. How much of the punch was left?

Answers

3 CHAPTER TEST

 Remember to use the Chapter Test Prep Video CD to see the fully worked-out solutions to any of the exercises you want to review.

1. Find the LCM of 4 and 15.

2. Find the LCM of 8, 9, and 12.

Insert < or > to form a true statement.

3. $\dfrac{5}{6} \quad \dfrac{26}{30}$

4. $\dfrac{7}{8} \quad \dfrac{8}{9}$

Perform each indicated operation. Simplify your answers.

5. $\dfrac{7}{9} + \dfrac{1}{9}$

6. $\dfrac{8}{15} - \dfrac{2}{15}$

7. $\dfrac{9}{10} + \dfrac{2}{5}$

8. $\dfrac{1}{6} + \dfrac{3}{14}$

9. $\dfrac{7}{8} - \dfrac{1}{3}$

10. $\dfrac{6}{21} - \dfrac{1}{7}$

11. $\dfrac{9}{20} + \dfrac{2}{3}$

12. $\dfrac{16}{25} - \dfrac{1}{2}$

13. $\dfrac{11}{12} + \dfrac{3}{8} + \dfrac{5}{24}$

14. $\begin{array}{r} 3\frac{7}{8} \\ 7\frac{2}{5} \\ +2\frac{3}{4} \\ \hline \end{array}$

15. $\begin{array}{r} 8\frac{2}{9} \\ 12 \\ +10\frac{1}{15} \\ \hline \end{array}$

16. $\begin{array}{r} 5\frac{1}{6} \\ -3\frac{7}{8} \\ \hline \end{array}$

17. $\begin{array}{r} 19 \\ -2\frac{3}{11} \\ \hline \end{array}$

18. $\dfrac{2}{7} \cdot \left(6 - \dfrac{1}{6}\right)$

19. $\left(\dfrac{2}{3}\right)^4$

1. _____

2. _____

3. _____

4. _____

5. _____

6. _____

7. _____

8. _____

9. _____

10. _____

11. _____

12. _____

13. _____

14. _____

15. _____

16. _____

17. _____

18. _____

19. _____

20. $\dfrac{1}{2} \div \dfrac{2}{3} \cdot \dfrac{3}{4}$

21. $\left(\dfrac{4}{5}\right)^2 + \left(\dfrac{1}{2}\right)^3$

22. $\left(\dfrac{3}{4}\right)^2 \div \left(\dfrac{2}{3} + \dfrac{5}{6}\right)$

23. Find the average of $\dfrac{5}{6}, \dfrac{4}{3},$ and $\dfrac{7}{12}$.

Solve.

24. A carpenter cuts a piece $2\dfrac{3}{4}$ feet long from a cedar plank that is $6\dfrac{1}{2}$ feet long. How long is the remaining piece?

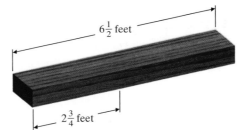

$6\frac{1}{2}$ feet

$2\frac{3}{4}$ feet

25. A small airplane used $58\dfrac{3}{4}$ gallons of fuel on a $7\dfrac{1}{2}$ hour trip. How many gallons of fuel were used for each hour?

The circle graph below shows us how the average consumer spends money. For example, $\dfrac{7}{50}$ of your spending goes for food. Use this information for Exercises 26 through 28.

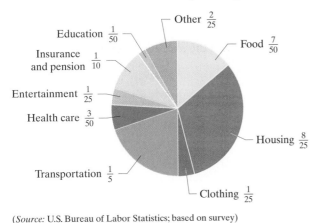

Consumer Spending

Other $\frac{2}{25}$

Education $\frac{1}{50}$

Insurance and pension $\frac{1}{10}$

Entertainment $\frac{1}{25}$

Health care $\frac{3}{50}$

Transportation $\frac{1}{5}$

Food $\frac{7}{50}$

Housing $\frac{8}{25}$

Clothing $\frac{1}{25}$

(*Source:* U.S. Bureau of Labor Statistics; based on survey)

26. What fraction of spending goes for housing and food combined?

27. What fraction of spending goes for education, transportation, and clothing?

28. Suppose your family spent $47,000 on the items in the graph above. How much might we expect was spent on health care?

Find the perimeter of each figure. For Exercise 29, find the area also.

△ **29.**

Rectangle $\frac{2}{3}$ foot

1 foot

△ **30.**

$\frac{4}{15}$ inch

$\frac{2}{15}$ inch

$\frac{6}{15}$ inch

Pentagon

$\frac{8}{15}$ inch

$\frac{1}{3}$ inch

20. _____

21. _____

22. _____

23. _____

24. _____

25. _____

26. _____

27. _____

28. _____

29. _____

30. _____

Write each number in words.

Answers

1. 85

2. 107

3. 126

4. 5026

5. Add: 23 + 136

6. Find the perimeter.

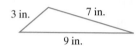

3 in.   7 in.

9 in.

7. Subtract: 543 − 29. Then check by adding.

8. Divide: 3268 ÷ 27

9. Round 278,362 to the nearest thousand.

10. Find all the factors of 30.

11. Multiply: 236 × 86

12. Multiply: 236 × 86 × 0

13. Find each quotient and then check the answer by multiplying.

a. $1\overline{)8}$

b. 11 ÷ 1

c. $\dfrac{9}{9}$

d. 7 ÷ 7

e. $\dfrac{10}{1}$

f. $6\overline{)6}$

14. Find the average of 25, 17, 19, and 39.

15. The Hudson River in New York State is 306 miles long. The Snake River, in the northwestern United States, is 732 miles longer than the Hudson River. How long is the Snake River? (*Source:* U.S. Department of the Interior)

16. Evaluate: $\sqrt{121}$

Answers

1. _____
2. _____
3. _____
4. _____
5. _____
6. _____
7. _____
8. _____
9. _____
10. _____
11. _____
12. _____
13. a. _____
    b. _____
    c. _____
    d. _____
    e. _____
    f. _____
14. _____
15. _____
16. _____

Evaluate.

17. 8^2 **18.** 5^3 **19.** 2^5 **20.** 10^3

Write the shaded part as an improper fraction and a mixed number.

21. 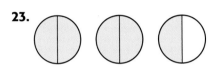   **22.**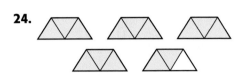

23.    **24.**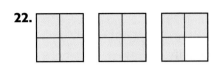

25. Of the numbers 3, 9, 11, 17, 26, which are prime and which are composite?

26. Simplify: $\dfrac{6^2 + 4 \cdot 4 + 2^3}{37 - 5^2}$

27. Find the prime factorization of 180.

28. Find the difference of 87 and 25.

29. Write $\dfrac{72}{26}$ in simplest form.

30. Write $9\dfrac{7}{8}$ as an improper fraction.

31. Determine whether $\dfrac{16}{40}$ and $\dfrac{10}{25}$ are equivalent.

32. Insert $<$ or $>$ to form a true statement. $\dfrac{4}{7} \quad \dfrac{5}{9}$

Multiply.

33. $\dfrac{2}{3} \cdot \dfrac{5}{11}$ **34.** $2\dfrac{5}{8} \cdot \dfrac{4}{7}$

35. $\dfrac{1}{4} \cdot \dfrac{1}{2}$ **36.** $7 \cdot 5\dfrac{2}{7}$

17. _____

18. _____

19. _____

20. _____

21. _____

22. _____

23. _____

24. _____

25. _____

26. _____

27. _____

28. _____

29. _____

30. _____

31. _____

32. _____

33. _____

34. _____

35. _____

36. _____

Divide.

37. _____

38. _____

39. _____

40. _____

41. _____

42. _____

43. _____

44. _____

45. _____

46. _____

47. _____

48. _____

49. _____

50. _____

37. $\dfrac{11}{18} \div 2\dfrac{5}{6}$

38. $\dfrac{15}{19} \div \dfrac{3}{5}$

39. $5\dfrac{2}{3} \div 2\dfrac{5}{9}$

40. $\dfrac{8}{11} \div \dfrac{1}{22}$

41. Add and simplify: $\dfrac{3}{16} + \dfrac{7}{16}$

42. Subtract and simplify: $\dfrac{11}{20} - \dfrac{7}{20}$

43. Find the LCM of 6 and 8.

44. Find the LCM of 7 and 5.

45. Add: $\dfrac{1}{2} + \dfrac{2}{3} + \dfrac{5}{6}$

46. Evaluate: $\left(\dfrac{5}{9}\right)^2$

47. Subtract: $9\dfrac{3}{7} - 5\dfrac{2}{21}$

48. Subtract: $\dfrac{31}{100} - \dfrac{5}{25}$

49. Simplify: $\left(\dfrac{2}{3}\right)^2 \div \left(\dfrac{8}{27} + \dfrac{2}{3}\right)$

50. $\dfrac{1}{10} \div \dfrac{7}{8} \cdot \dfrac{2}{5}$

4

Decimals

Decimal numbers represent parts of a whole, just like fractions. In this chapter, we learn to perform arithmetic operations using decimals and to analyze the relationship between factions and decimals. We also learn how decimals are used in the real world.

Video rental chains are suffering losses in revenue and this trend is predicted to continue. With many discount chains offering cheap DVDs, consumers are choosing to purchase rather than rent. There are also more rent-by-mail and video-on-demand companies competing for your business.

In Section 4.3, Exercise 65, we calculate the predicted loss of revenue for video rental stores.

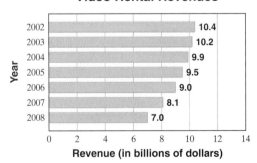

Video Rental Revenues

Year	Revenue
2002	10.4
2003	10.2
2004	9.9
2005	9.5
2006	9.0
2007	8.1
2008	7.0

Revenue (in billions of dollars)

Source: Forrester Research; Note: Many of these years are projections.

A Know the Meaning of Place Value for a Decimal Number, and Write Decimals in Words.

B Write Decimals in Standard Form.

C Write Decimals as Fractions.

D Write Fractions as Decimals.

4.1 INTRODUCTION TO DECIMALS

Objective **A** Decimal Notation and Writing Decimals in Words

Like fractional notation, decimal notation is used to denote a part of a whole. Numbers written in decimal notation are called **decimal numbers,** or simply **decimals.** The decimal 17.758 has three parts.

$$1\ 7\ .\ 7\ 5\ 8$$

Whole number part | Decimal part

Decimal point

In Section 1.2, we introduced place value for whole numbers. Place names and place values for the whole number part of a decimal number are exactly the same, as shown next. Place names and place values for the decimal part are also shown.

Helpful Hint

Notice that place values to the left of the decimal point end in "s." Place values to the right of the decimal point end in "ths."

Millions	Hundred-thousands	Ten-thousands	Thousands	Hundreds	Tens	Ones	Tenths	Hundredths	Thousandths	Ten-thousandths	Hundred-thousandths	Millionths
1,000,000	100,000	10,000	1000	100	10	1	$\frac{1}{10}$	$\frac{1}{100}$	$\frac{1}{1000}$	$\frac{1}{10,000}$	$\frac{1}{100,000}$	$\frac{1}{1,000,000}$

1 7.7 5 8

Notice that the value of each place is $\frac{1}{10}$ of the value of the place to its left. For example,

$$1 \cdot \frac{1}{10} = \frac{1}{10}$$
↑ ones   ↑ tenths

$$\frac{1}{10} \cdot \frac{1}{10} = \frac{1}{100}$$
↑ tenths   ↑ hundredths

The decimal number 17.758 means

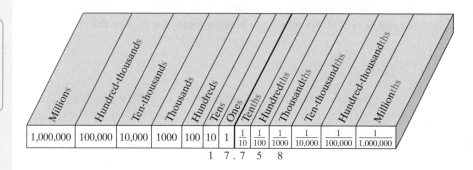

1 ten	+	7 ones	+	7 tenths	+	5 hundredths	+	8 thousandths
↓	↓	↓	↓	↓	↓	↓	↓	↓
or $1 \cdot 10$	+	$7 \cdot 1$	+	$7 \cdot \frac{1}{10}$	+	$5 \cdot \frac{1}{100}$	+	$8 \cdot \frac{1}{1000}$
or 10	+	7	+	$\frac{7}{10}$	+	$\frac{5}{100}$	+	$\frac{8}{1000}$

Writing (or Reading) a Decimal in Words

Step 1: Write the whole number part in words.

Step 2: Write "and" for the decimal point.

Step 3: Write the decimal part in words as though it were a whole number, followed by the place value of the last digit.

EXAMPLE 1 Write the decimal 1.3 in words.

Solution: one and three tenths

🔲 **Work Practice Problem 1**

PRACTICE PROBLEM 1

Write the decimal 8.7 in words.

EXAMPLE 2

Write the decimal in the following sentence in words: The Golden Jubilee Diamond is a 545.67 carat cut diamond. (*Source: The Guinness Book of Records*)

Solution: five hundred forty-five and sixty-seven hundredths

🔲 **Work Practice Problem 2**

PRACTICE PROBLEM 2

Write the decimal 97.28 in words.

EXAMPLE 3 Write the decimal 19.5023 in words.

Solution: nineteen and five thousand, twenty-three ten-thousandths

🔲 **Work Practice Problem 3**

PRACTICE PROBLEM 3

Write the decimal 302.1056 in words.

EXAMPLE 4

Write the decimal in the following sentence in words: The oldest known fragments of the Earth's crust are Zircon crystals; they were discovered in Australia and are thought to be 4.276 billion years old. (*Source: The Guinness Book of Records*)

PRACTICE PROBLEM 4

Write the decimal 72.1085 in words.

Solution: four and two hundred seventy-six thousandths

🔲 **Work Practice Problem 4**

Suppose that you are paying for a purchase of $368.42 at Circuit City by writing a check. Checks are usually written using the following format.

Answers

1. eight and seven tenths,
2. ninety-seven and twenty-eight hundredths, **3.** three hundred two and one thousand fifty-six ten-thousandths, **4.** seventy-two and one thousand eighty-five ten-thousandths

PRACTICE PROBLEM 5

Fill in the check to CLECO (Central Louisiana Electric Company) to pay for your monthly electric bill of $207.40.

EXAMPLE 5 Fill in the check to Camelot Music to pay for your purchase of $92.98.

Solution:

📝 **Work Practice Problem 5**

Objective **B** Writing Decimals in Standard Form

A decimal written in words can be written in standard form by reversing the preceding procedure.

EXAMPLES Write each decimal in standard form.

6. Forty-eight and twenty-six hundredths is

48.26

— hundredths place

7. Six and ninety-five thousandths is

6.095

— thousandths place

📝 **Work Practice Problems 6–7**

PRACTICE PROBLEMS 6–7

Write each decimal in standard form.

6. Three hundred and ninety-six hundredths

7. Thirty-nine and forty-two thousandths

Helpful Hint

When converting a decimal from words to decimal notation, make sure the last digit is in the correct place by inserting 0s if necessary. For example,

Two and thirty-eight thousandths is 2.038

thousandths place

Objective **C** Writing Decimals as Fractions

Once you master reading and writing decimals, writing a decimal as a fraction follows naturally.

Decimal	In Words	Fraction
0.7	seven tenths	$\dfrac{7}{10}$
0.51	fifty-one hundredths	$\dfrac{51}{100}$
0.009	nine thousandths	$\dfrac{9}{1000}$
0.05	five hundredths	$\dfrac{5}{100} = \dfrac{1}{20}$

Answers

5. CLECO; 207.40; Two hundred seven and $\dfrac{40}{100}$, **6.** 300.96, **7.** 39.042

Notice that the number of decimal places in a decimal number is the same as the number of zeros in the denominator of the equivalent fraction. We can use this fact to write decimals as fractions.

$$0.51 = \frac{51}{100}$$ $$0.009 = \frac{9}{1000}$$

2 decimal places   2 zeros   3 decimal places   3 zeros

EXAMPLE 8 Write 0.43 as a fraction.

Solution: $0.43 = \frac{43}{100}$

2 decimal places   2 zeros

⬛ **Work Practice Problem 8**

PRACTICE PROBLEM 8

Write 0.037 as a fraction.

EXAMPLE 9 Write 5.7 as a mixed number.

Solution: $5.7 = 5\frac{7}{10}$

1 decimal place   1 zero

⬛ **Work Practice Problem 9**

PRACTICE PROBLEM 9

Write 14.97 as a mixed number.

EXAMPLES Write each decimal as a fraction or a mixed number. Write your answer in simplest form.

10. $0.125 = \frac{125}{1000} = \frac{1}{8}$

11. $23.5 = 23\frac{5}{10} = 23\frac{\overset{1}{\cancel{5}}}{2\cdot\underset{1}{\cancel{5}}} = 23\frac{1}{2\cdot 1} = 23\frac{1}{2}$

12. $105.083 = 105\frac{83}{1000}$

⬛ **Work Practice Problems 10–12**

PRACTICE PROBLEMS 10–12

Write each decimal as a fraction or mixed number. Write your answer in simplest form.
10. 0.12
11. 57.8
12. 209.986

Objective D Writing Fractions as Decimals

If the denominator of a fraction is a power of 10, we can write it as a decimal by reversing the procedure above.

EXAMPLES Write each fraction as a decimal.

13. $\frac{8}{10} = 0.8$

1 zero   1 decimal place

14. $\frac{87}{10} = 8.7$

1 zero   1 decimal place

15. $\frac{18}{1000} = 0.018$

3 zeros   3 decimal places

16. $\frac{507}{100} = 5.07$

2 zeros   2 decimal places

⬛ **Work Practice Problems 13–16**

PRACTICE PROBLEMS 13–16

Write each fraction as a decimal.

13. $\frac{58}{100}$ **14.** $\frac{59}{100}$

15. $\frac{6}{1000}$ **16.** $\frac{172}{10}$

Answers

8. $\frac{37}{1000}$, **9.** $14\frac{97}{100}$, **10.** $\frac{3}{25}$,

11. $57\frac{4}{5}$, **12.** $209\frac{493}{500}$, **13.** 0.58,

14. 0.59, **15.** 0.006, **16.** 17.2

Mental Math

Determine the place value for the digit 7 in each number.

1. 70   **2.** 700   **3.** 0.7   **4.** 0.07

4.1 EXERCISE SET

FOR EXTRA HELP

 Student Solutions Manual   PH Math/Tutor Center   CD/Video for Review   Math XL MathXL®   MyMathLab MyMathLab

Objective **A** *Write each decimal number in words. See Examples 1 through 4.*

1. 6.52   **2.** 7.59   **3.** 16.23   **4.** 47.65

5. 0.205   **6.** 0.495   **7.** 167.009   **8.** 233.056

9. 200.005   **10.** 5000.02   **11.** 105.6   **12.** 410.30

13. The English Channel Tunnel is 31.04 miles long. (*Source: Railway Directory & Year Book*)

14. The Lake Pontchartrain Causeway bridge over Lake Pontchartrain in Louisiana is approximately 23.87 miles long.

15. The recommended daily allowance of riboflavin for teenage boys between the ages of 15 and 18 is 1.8 milligrams. (*Source:* Food and Nutrition Board of the Institute of Medicine, National Academy of Sciences)

16. Saturn makes a complete orbit of the Sun every 29.48 years. (*Source:* National Space Science Data Center)

17. The 2005 series finale of Everybody Loves Raymond received a Nielsen rating of 32.9. (*Source:* Nielsen Media Research)

18. The top-rated television series for the 2003–2004 viewing season was *CSI: Crime Scene Investigators,* which received a rating of 15.9. (*Source:* Nielsen Media Research)

Fill in each check for the described purchase. See Example 5.

19. Your monthly car loan of $321.42 to R. W. Financial.

Your Preprinted Name
Your Preprinted Address

60–8124/7233
1000613331

1407

DATE

PAY TO
THE ORDER OF

$

DOLLARS

FIRST STATE BANK
OF FARTHINGTON
FARTHINGTON, IL 64422

MEMO

⑆621497260⑆ 1000613331⑈ 1407

20. Your part of the monthly apartment rent, which is $213.70. You pay this to Amanda Dupre.

Your Preprinted Name
Your Preprinted Address

60–8124/7233
1000613331

1408

DATE

PAY TO
THE ORDER OF

$

DOLLARS

FIRST STATE BANK
OF FARTHINGTON
FARTHINGTON, IL 64422

MEMO

⑆621497260⑆ 1000613331⑈ 1408

21. Your cell phone bill of $59.68 to Bell South.

Your Preprinted Name
Your Preprinted Address

60–8124/7233
1000613331

1409

DATE

PAY TO
THE ORDER OF

$

DOLLARS

FIRST STATE BANK
OF FARTHINGTON
FARTHINGTON, IL 64422

MEMO

⑆621497260⑆ 1000613331⑈ 1409

22. Your grocery bill of $87.49 to Albertsons.

Your Preprinted Name
Your Preprinted Address

60–8124/7233
1000613331

1410

DATE

PAY TO
THE ORDER OF

$

DOLLARS

FIRST STATE BANK
OF FARTHINGTON
FARTHINGTON, IL 64422

MEMO

⑆621497260⑆ 1000613331⑈ 1410

Objective **B** *Write each decimal number in standard form. See Examples 6 and 7.*

23. Six and five tenths

24. Three and nine tenths

25. Nine and eight hundredths

26. Twelve and six hundredths

27. Seven hundred five and six hundred twenty-five thousandths

28. Eight hundred four and three hundred ninety-nine thousandths

29. Sixty-four ten-thousandths

30. Thirty-eight ten-thousandths

31. The record rainfall amount for a 24-hour period in Alabama is thirty-two and fifty-two hundredths inches. This record was set at Dauphin Island Sea Lab in 1997. (*Source:* National Climatic Data Center)

32. The United States Postal Service vehicle fleet averages nine and sixty-two hundredths miles per gallon of fuel. (*Source:* United States Postal Service)

33. Americans consume an average of fifteen and eight-tenths pounds of watermelon annually. (*Source:* Agricultural Marketing Service, U.S. Department of Agriculture)

34. Shaquille O'Neal of the NBA's Los Angeles Lakers scored an average of twenty-one and five tenths points per basketball game during the 2003–2004 regular season. (*Source:* National Basketball Association)

Objective Ⓒ *Write each decimal as a fraction or a mixed number. Write your answer in simplest form. See Examples 8 through 12.*

35. 0.3   **36.** 0.9   ⊙ **37.** 0.27   **38.** 0.39   **39.** 0.8

40. 0.4   **41.** 0.15   **42.** 0.64   **43.** 5.47   **44.** 6.3

45. 0.048   **46.** 0.082   **47.** 7.008   **48.** 9.005   ⊙ **49.** 15.802

50. 11.406   **51.** 0.3005   **52.** 0.2006   **53.** 487.32   **54.** 298.62

Objective Ⓓ *Write each fraction as a decimal. See Examples 13 through 16.*

⊙ **55.** $\dfrac{6}{10}$ **56.** $\dfrac{3}{10}$ ⊙ **57.** $\dfrac{45}{100}$ **58.** $\dfrac{75}{100}$

59. $\dfrac{37}{10}$ **60.** $\dfrac{28}{10}$ **61.** $\dfrac{268}{1000}$ **62.** $\dfrac{709}{1000}$

63. $\dfrac{9}{100}$ **64.** $\dfrac{7}{100}$ **65.** $\dfrac{4026}{1000}$ **66.** $\dfrac{3601}{1000}$

⊙ **67.** $\dfrac{28}{1000}$ **68.** $\dfrac{63}{1000}$ **69.** $\dfrac{563}{10}$ **70.** $\dfrac{206}{10}$

Objectives Ⓐ Ⓑ Ⓒ Ⓓ **Mixed Practice** *Fill in the chart. The first row is completed for you.*

	Decimal Number in Standard Form	In Words	Fraction
	0.37	thirty-seven hundredths	$\dfrac{37}{100}$
71.			$\dfrac{43}{100}$
72.			$\dfrac{89}{100}$
73.		eight tenths	
74.		five tenths	
75.	0.077		
76.	0.019		

Review

Round 47,261 to the indicated place value. See Section 1.5.

77. tens

78. hundreds

79. thousands

80. ten-thousands

Concept Extensions

 81. In your own words, describe how to write a decimal as a fraction or a mixed number.

82. In your own words, describe how to write a fraction as a decimal.

83. Write 0.00026849576 in words.

84. Write $7\dfrac{12}{100}$ as a decimal.

85. Write $17\dfrac{268}{1000}$ as a decimal.

86. Write 0.00026849576 as a fraction.

STUDY SKILLS BUILDER

Are You Getting All the Mathematics Help That You Need?

Remember that, in addition to your instructor, there are many places to get help with your mathematics course. For example,

- This text has an accompanying video lesson for every section and worked out solutions to every Chapter Test exercise on video.
- The back of the book contains answers to odd-numbered exercises and selected solutions.
- A student *Solutions Manual* is available that contains worked-out solutions to odd-numbered exercises as well as solutions to every exercise in the Integrated Reviews, Chapter Reviews, Chapter Tests, and Cumulative Reviews.

- Don't forget to check with your instructor for other local resources available to you, such as a tutor center.

Exercises

1. List items you find helpful in the text and all student supplements to this text.
2. List all the campus help that is available to you for this course.
3. List any help (besides the textbook) from Exercises 1 and 2 above that you are using.
4. List any help (besides the textbook) that you feel you should try.
5. Write a goal for yourself that includes trying anything you listed in Exercise 4 during the next week.

4.2 ORDER AND ROUNDING

Objective **A** Comparing Decimals

One way to compare decimals is to compare their graphs on a number line. Recall that for any two numbers on a number line, the number to the left is smaller and the number to the right is larger. The decimals 0.5 and 0.8 are graphed as follows:

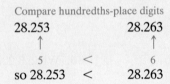

Comparing decimals by comparing their graphs on a number line can be time consuming. Another way to compare the size of decimals is to compare digits in corresponding places.

Comparing Two Decimals

Compare digits in the same places from left to right. When two digits are not equal, the number with the larger digit is the larger decimal. If necessary, insert 0s after the last digit to the right of the decimal point to continue comparing.

Compare hundredths-place digits

28.253   28.263
  ↑   ↑

  5   <   6

so 28.253   <   28.263

Before we continue, let's take a moment and convince ourselves that inserting a zero after the last digit to the right of a decimal point does not change the value of the number.

For example, let's show that

$0.7 = 0.70$

If we write 0.7 as a fraction, we have

$$0.7 = \frac{7}{10}$$

Let's now multiply by 1. Recall that multiplying a number by 1 does not change the value of the number.

$$0.7 = \frac{7}{10} = \frac{7}{10} \cdot 1 = \frac{7}{10} \cdot \frac{10}{10} = \frac{7 \cdot 10}{10 \cdot 10} = \frac{70}{100} = 0.70$$

Thus $0.7 = 0.70$ and so on.

☁ **Helpful Hint**

For any decimal, inserting 0s after the last digit to the right of the decimal point does not change the value of the number.

$7.6 = 7.60 = 7.600$, and so on

When a whole number is written as a decimal, the decimal point is placed to the right of the ones digit.

$25 = 25.0 = 25.00$, and so on

EXAMPLE 1 Insert $<$, $>$, or $=$ to form a true statement.

0.378   0.368

Solution:

0. 3 78   0. 3 68   The tenths places are the same.

0.3 7 8   0.3 6 8   The hundredths places are different.

Since $7 > 6$, then $0.378 > 0.368$.

◻ **Work Practice Problem 1**

EXAMPLE 2 Insert $<$, $>$, or $=$ to form a true statement.

0.052   0.236

Solution: 0. 0 52 $<$ 0. 2 36   0 is smaller than 2 in the tenths place.

◻ **Work Practice Problem 2**

EXAMPLE 3 Insert $<$, $>$, or $=$ to form a true statement.

0.52   0.063

Solution: 0. 5 2 $>$ 0. 0 63   0 is smaller than 5 in the tenths place.

◻ **Work Practice Problem 3**

EXAMPLE 4 Write the decimals in order from smallest to largest.

7.035, 8.12, 7.03, 7.1

Solution: By comparing the ones digits, the decimal 8.12 is the largest number. To write the rest of the decimals in order, we compare digits to the right of the decimal point. We will insert zeros to help us compare.

7.035   7.030   7.100

Helpful Hint You may also immediately notice that 7.1 is larger than both 7.035 and 7.03.

By comparing digits to the right of the decimal point, we can now arrange the decimals from smallest to largest.

7.030, 7.035, 7.100, 8.12   or

7.03, 7.035, 7.1, 8.12

◻ **Work Practice Problem 4**

Objective B Rounding Decimals

We **round the decimal part** of a decimal number in nearly the same way as we round whole numbers. The only difference is that we delete digits to the right of the rounding place, instead of replacing these digits by 0s. For example,

24.954   rounded to the nearest hundredth is   24.95

↑
hundredths place

PRACTICE PROBLEM 1

Insert $<$, $>$, or $=$ to form a true statement.

13.208   13.281

PRACTICE PROBLEM 2

Insert $<$, $>$, or $=$ to form a true statement.

0.124   0.086

PRACTICE PROBLEM 3

Insert $<$, $>$, or $=$ to form a true statement.

0.61   0.076

PRACTICE PROBLEM 4

Write the decimals in order from smallest to largest.

14.605, 14.65, 13.9, 14.006

Answers
1. $<$,   2. $>$,   3. $>$,
4. 13.9, 14.006, 14.605, 14.65

> ### Rounding Decimals to a Place Value to the Right of the Decimal Point
>
> **Step 1:** Locate the digit to the right of the given place value.
>
> **Step 2:** If this digit is 5 or greater, add 1 to the digit in the given place value and delete all digits to its right. If this digit is less than 5, delete all digits to the right of the given place value.

PRACTICE PROBLEM 5

Round 123.7814 to the nearest thousandth.

EXAMPLE 5 Round 736.2359 to the nearest tenth.

Solution:

Step 1: We locate the digit to the right of the tenths place.

```
                    ┌──── tenths place
                    ↓
        736.2③59
              └──→ digit to the right
```

Step 2: Since the digit to the right is less than 5, we delete it and all digits to its right.

Thus, 736.2359 rounded to the nearest tenth is 736.2.

🖳 **Work Practice Problem 5**

PRACTICE PROBLEM 6

Round 123.7817 to the nearest tenth.

EXAMPLE 6 Round 736.2359 to the nearest hundredth.

Solution:

Step 1: We locate the digit to the right of the hundredths place.

```
                  ┌──── hundredths place
                  ↓
        736.23⑤9
               └──→ digit to the right
```

Step 2: Since the digit to the right is 5, we add 1 to the digit in the hundredths place and delete all digits to the right of the hundredths place.

```
        736.23⑤9
             ↑  └Delete these digits.
          Add 1.
```

Thus, 736.2359 rounded to the nearest hundredth is 736.24.

🖳 **Work Practice Problem 6**

Rounding often occurs with money amounts. Since there are 100 cents in a dollar, each cent is $\frac{1}{100}$ of a dollar. This means that if we want to round to the nearest cent, we round to the nearest hundredth of a dollar.

PRACTICE PROBLEM 7

In Cititown, the price of a gallon of gasoline is $2.1589. Round this to the nearest cent.

EXAMPLE 7 The price of a gallon of gasoline in Aimsville is currently $2.1779. Round this to the nearest cent.

Solution:

```
    hundredths place ──┐  ┌── 7 is greater than 5
                       ↓  ↓
            $2.17⑦9
                  ↑  └── Delete these digits.
               Add 1.
```

Since the digit to the right is greater than 5, we add 1 to the hundredths digit and delete all digits to the right of the hundredths digit.

Thus, $2.1779 rounded to the nearest cent is $2.18.

🖳 **Work Practice Problem 7**

EXAMPLE 8 Round $0.098 to the nearest cent.

Solution:

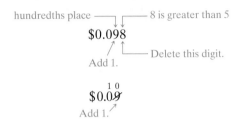

hundredths place ———⌐ ⌐——— 8 is greater than 5
$0.098
    ↗ ↑——— Delete this digit.
Add 1.

          1 0
$0.0~~9~~
Add 1. ↗

9 + 1 = 10, so replace the digit 9 by 0 and carry the 1 to the place value to the left. Thus, $0.098 rounded to the nearest cent is $0.10.

▣ **Work Practice Problem 8**

✔**Concept Check** 1756.0894 rounded to the nearest ten is

a. 1756.1   **b.** 1760.0894
c. 1760   **d.** 1750

EXAMPLE 9 **Determining State Taxable Income**

A high school teacher's taxable income is $41,567.72. The tax tables in the teacher's state use amounts to the nearest dollar. Round the teacher's income to the nearest whole dollar.

Solution: Rounding to the nearest whole dollar means rounding to the ones place.

ones place ———⌐ ⌐——— 7 is greater than 5
$41,567.72
    ↑ ↑‿——— Delete these digits.
Add 1.

Thus, the teacher's income rounded to the nearest dollar is $41,568.

▣ **Work Practice Problem 9**

PRACTICE PROBLEM 8

Round $1.095 to the nearest cent.

PRACTICE PROBLEM 9

Water bills in Gotham City are always rounded to the nearest dollar. Lois's water bill was $24.62. Round her bill to the nearest dollar.

Answers
8. $1.10,   **9.** $25

✔ **Concept Check Answer**
c

Objective A *Insert <, >, or = to form a true statement. See Examples 1 through 3.*

1. 0.15   0.16

2. 0.12   0.15

⊙ **3.** 0.57   0.54

4. 0.59   0.52

5. 0.098   0.1

6. 0.0756   0.2

7. 0.54900   0.549

8. 0.98400   0.984

⊙ **9.** 167.908   167.980

10. 519.3405   519.3054

11. 420,000   0.000042

12. 0.000987   987,000

Write the decimals in order from smallest to largest. See Example 4.

13. 0.006, 0.06, 0.0061

14. 0.082, 0.008, 0.080

15. 0.042, 0.36, 0.03

16. 0.21, 0.056, 0.065

17. 1.1, 1.16, 1.01, 1.09

18. 3.6, 3.069, 3.09, 3.06

19. 21.001, 20.905, 21.03, 21.12

20. 36.050, 35.72, 35.702, 35.072

Objective B *Round each decimal to the given place value. See Examples 5 and 6.*

21. 0.57, to the nearest tenth

22. 0.54, to the nearest tenth

⊙ **23.** 0.234, to the nearest hundredth

24. 0.452, to the nearest hundredth

25. 0.5942, to the nearest thousandth

26. 63.4523, to the nearest thousandth

27. 98,207.23, to the nearest ten

28. 68,934.543, to the nearest ten

29. 12.342, to the nearest tenth

30. 42.9878, to the nearest thousandth

⊙ **31.** 17.667, to the nearest hundredth

32. 0.766, to the nearest hundredth

33. 0.501, to the nearest tenth

34. 0.602, to the nearest tenth

35. 0.1295, to the nearest thousandth

36. 0.8295, to the nearest thousandth

37. 3829.34, to the nearest ten

38. 4520.876, to the nearest hundred

Round each monetary amount to the nearest cent or dollar as indicated. See Examples 7 through 9.

39. $0.067, to the nearest cent

40. $0.025, to the nearest cent

41. $42,650.14, to the nearest dollar

42. $768.45, to the nearest dollar

43. $26.95, to the nearest dollar

44. $14,769.52, to the nearest dollar

45. $0.1992, to the nearest cent

46. $0.7633, to the nearest cent

Round each number to the given place value.

47. At this writing, the disc of the smallest hard drive was created by Toshiba and measures 2.16 centimeters across. Round this number to the nearest tenth.

2.16 cm or 0.85 in.

48. A large tropical cockroach of the family Dictyoptera is the fastest-moving insect. This insect was clocked at a speed of 3.36 miles per hour. Round this number to the nearest tenth. (*Source:* University of California, Berkeley)

49. During the 2004 Boston Marathon, Catherine Ndereba of Kenya was the first woman to cross the finish line. Her time was 2.4075 hours. Round this time to the nearest hundredth. (*Source:* Boston Athletic Association)

50. The population density of the state of Louisiana is 102.5794 people per square mile. Round this population density to the nearest tenth. (*Source:* U.S. Census Bureau)

51. A used biology textbook is priced at $47.89. Round this price to the nearest dollar.

52. A used office desk is advertised at $19.95 by Drawley's Office Furniture. Round this price to the nearest dollar.

53. The length of a day on Mars is 24.6229 hours. Round this figure to the nearest thousandth. (*Source:* National Space Science Data Center)

54. Venus makes a complete orbit around the Sun every 224.695 days. Round this figure to the nearest whole day. (*Source:* National Space Science Data Center)

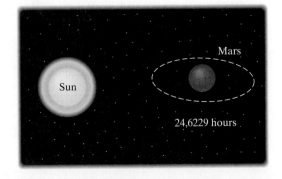

Sun · Mars

24,6229 hours

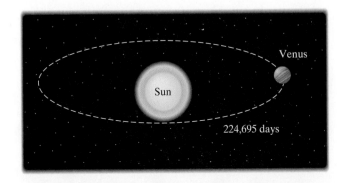

Sun · Venus

224,695 days

55. Millennium Force is a roller coaster at Cedar Point, an amusement park in Sandusky, Ohio. At the time of its debut, Millennium Force was the world's tallest and fastest roller coaster. A ride on the Millennium Force lasts about 2.75 minutes. Round this figure to the nearest tenth. (*Source:* Cedar Fair, L.P.)

56. During the 2003 NFL season, the average length of an Oakland Raiders' punt was 46.9 yards. Round this figure to the nearest whole yard. (*Source:* National Football League)

Review

Perform each indicated operation. See Sections 1.3 and 1.4.

57. $3452 + 2314$

58. $8945 + 4536$

59. $94 - 23$

60. $82 - 47$

61. $482 - 239$

62. $4002 - 3897$

Concept Extensions

Solve. See the Concept Check in this section.

63. 2849.1738 rounded to the nearest hundred is
   a. 2849.17
   b. 2800
   c. 2850
   d. 2849.174

64. 146.059 rounded to the nearest ten is
   a. 146.0
   b. 146.1
   c. 140
   d. 150

65. 2849.1738 rounded to the nearest hundredth is
   a. 2849.17
   b. 2800
   c. 2850
   d. 2849.174

66. 146.059 rounded to the nearest tenth is
   a. 146.0
   b. 146.1
   c. 140
   d. 150

Mixed Practice (*Sections 4.1, 4.2*) *The table gives the leading bowling averages for the Professional Bowlers Association for each of the years listed. Use the table to answer Exercises 67 through 69.*

67. What is the highest average score on the list? Write this score as a mixed number. Which bowler achieved that average?

Year	Bowler	Average Score
1996	Walter Ray Williams, Jr.	225.370
1997	Walter Ray Williams, Jr.	222.008
1998	Walter Ray Williams, Jr.	226.130
1999	Parker Bohn III	228.040
2000	Chris Barnes	220.930
2002	Parker Bohn III	221.546
2003	Walter Ray Williams, Jr	224.940
2004	Mike Koivuniemi	222.730
(*Source:* Professional Bowlers Association)		

68. What is the lowest average score on the list? Write this score as a mixed number. Which bowler had that average?

69. Make a list of the leading averages in order from greatest to least for the years shown in the table.

70. Write a 4-digit number that rounds to 26.3.

71. Write a 5-digit number that rounds to 1.7.

72. Explain how to identify the value of the 9 in the decimal 486.3297.

73. Write a decimal number that is greater than 48.1, but less than 48.2.

74. Which number(s) rounds to 0.26?

0.26559   0.26499   0.25786   0.25186

75. Which number(s) rounds to 0.06?

0.0612   0.066   0.0586   0.0506

STUDY SKILLS BUILDER

Are You Satisfied with Your Performance on a Particular Quiz or Exam?

If not, don't forget to analyze your quiz or exam and look for common errors. Were most of your errors a result of:

- *Carelessness?* Did you turn in your quiz or exam before the allotted time expired? If so, resolve next time to use the entire time allotted. Any extra time can be spent checking your work.

- *Running out of time?* If so, make a point to better manage your time on your next quiz or exam. Try completing any questions that you are unsure of last and delay checking your work until all questions have been answered.

- *Not understanding a concept?* If so, review that concept and correct your work. Try to understand how this happened so that you make sure it doesn't happen before the next quiz or exam.

- *Test conditions?* When studying for a quiz or exam, make sure you place yourself in conditions similar to test conditions. For example, before your next quiz or exam, use a few sheets of blank paper and take a sample test without the aid of your notes or text.

(See your instructor or use the Chapter Test at the end of each chapter.)

Exercises

1. Have you corrected all your previous quizzes and exams?

2. List any errors you have found common to two or more of your graded papers.

3. Is one of your common errors not understanding a concept? If so, are you making sure you understand all the concepts for the next quiz or exam?

4. Is one of your common errors making careless mistakes? If so, are you now taking all the time allotted to check over your work so that you can minimize the number of careless mistakes?

5. Are you satisfied with your grades thus far on quizzes and tests?

6. If your answer to Exercise 5 is no, are there any more suggestions you can make to your instructor or yourself to help? If so, list them here and share these with your instructor.

4.3 ADDING AND SUBTRACTING DECIMALS

Objective **A** Adding Decimals

Adding decimals is similar to adding whole numbers. We add digits in corresponding place values from right to left, carrying if necessary. To make sure that digits in corresponding place values are added, we line up the decimal points vertically.

Adding or Subtracting Decimals

Step 1: Write the decimals so that the decimal points line up vertically.

Step 2: Add or subtract as with whole numbers.

Step 3: Place the decimal point in the sum or difference so that it lines up vertically with the decimal points in the problem.

In this section, we will insert zeros in decimals numbers so that place value digits line up neatly. For instance, see Example 1.

PRACTICE PROBLEM 1

Add.

a. $15.52 + 2.371$

b. $20.06 + 17.612$

c. $0.125 + 122.8$

EXAMPLE 1 Add: $23.85 + 1.604$

Solution: First we line up the decimal points vertically.

$$
\begin{array}{r}
23.850 \\
+ \ 1.604 \\
\end{array}
$$
Insert one 0 so that digits line up neatly.

↑
line up decimal points

Then we add the digits from right to left as for whole numbers.

$$
\begin{array}{r}
\overset{1}{2}3.850 \\
+ \ 1.604 \\
\hline
25.454 \\
\end{array}
$$

Place the decimal point in the sum so that all decimal points line up.

Work Practice Problem 1

Helpful Hint

Recall that 0's may be placed after the last digit to the right of the decimal point without changing the value of the decimal. This may be used to help line up place values when adding decimals.

3.2	becomes	3.200	Insert two 0s.
15.567		15.567	
+ 0.11		+ 0.110	Insert one 0.
		18.877	Add.

Answers

1. a. 17.891, **b.** 37.672, **c.** 122.925

EXAMPLE 2 Add: 763.7651 + 22.001 + 43.89

Solution: First we line up the decimal points.

$$
\begin{array}{r}
\overset{\scriptstyle 1\ \ 1\ 1}{763.7651} \\
22.001\underline{0} \quad \text{Insert one 0.} \\
+\ \ 43.89\underline{00} \quad \text{Insert two 0s.} \\
\hline
829.6561 \quad \text{Add.}
\end{array}
$$

🖥 **Work Practice Problem 2**

> Don't forget that the decimal point in a whole number is after the last digit.

EXAMPLE 3 Add: 45 + 2.06

Solution: $\begin{array}{r} 45.00 \quad \text{Insert a decimal point and two 0s.} \\ +\ 2.06 \quad \text{Line up decimal points.} \\ \hline 47.06 \quad \text{Add.} \end{array}$

🖥 **Work Practice Problem 3**

✔ **Concept Check**   What is wrong with the following calculation of the sum of 7.03, 2.008, 19.16, and 3.1415?

$$
\begin{array}{r}
7.03 \\
2.008 \\
19.16 \\
+\ 3.1415 \\
\hline
3.6042
\end{array}
$$

Objective B Subtracting Decimals

Subtracting decimals is similar to subtracting whole numbers. We line up digits and subtract from right to left, borrowing when needed.

EXAMPLE 4 Subtract: 35.218 − 23.65. Check your answer.

Solution: First we line up the decimal points.

$$
\begin{array}{r}
\overset{\scriptstyle 4\ \ 1111}{3\cancel{5}.\cancel{2}\cancel{1}8} \\
-\ 23.650 \quad \text{Insert one 0.} \\
\hline
11.568 \quad \text{Subtract.}
\end{array}
$$

Recall that we can check a subtraction problem by adding.

$$
\begin{array}{r}
\overset{\scriptstyle 1\ 1}{11.568} \quad \text{Difference} \\
+\ 23.650 \quad \text{Subtrahend} \\
\hline
35.218 \quad \text{Minuend}
\end{array}
$$

🖥 **Work Practice Problem 4**

PRACTICE PROBLEM 2

Add.
a. 34.567 + 129.43 + 2.8903
b. 11.21 + 46.013 + 362.526

PRACTICE PROBLEM 3

Add: 26.072 + 119

PRACTICE PROBLEM 4

Subtract. Check your answers.
a. 82.75 − 15.9
b. 126.032 − 95.71

Answers
2. a. 166.8873,   **b.** 419.749,
3. 145.072,   **4. a.** 66.85,   **b.** 30.322

✔ **Concept Check Answer**

The decimal places are not lined up properly.

PRACTICE PROBLEM 5

Subtract. Check your answers.
a. $5.8 - 3.92$
b. $9.72 - 4.068$

EXAMPLE 5 Subtract: $3.5 - 0.068$. Check your answer.

Solution:

$$
\begin{array}{r}
\overset{9}{}\overset{4\;\;10\;10}{3.\cancel{5}\cancel{0}\cancel{0}} \\
3.5\,0\,0 \quad \text{Insert two 0s.}\\
-\,0.0\,6\,8 \quad \text{Line up decimal points.}\\
\hline
3.4\,3\,2 \quad \text{Subtract.}
\end{array}
$$

Check:
$$
\begin{array}{r}
3.432 \quad \text{Difference}\\
+\,0.068 \quad \text{Subtrahend}\\
\hline
3.500 \quad \text{Minuend}
\end{array}
$$

▣ **Work Practice Problem 5**

PRACTICE PROBLEM 6

Subtract. Check your answers.
a. $53 - 29.31$
b. $120 - 68.22$

EXAMPLE 6 Subtract: $85 - 17.31$. Check your answer.

Solution:
$$
\begin{array}{r}
\overset{9}{}\overset{7\;14\;10\;10}{8\cancel{5}.\cancel{0}\cancel{0}} \\
85.0\,0\\
-\,17.3\,1\\
\hline
67.6\,9
\end{array}
$$

Check:
$$
\begin{array}{r}
67.69 \quad \text{Difference}\\
+\,17.31 \quad \text{Subtrahend}\\
\hline
85.00 \quad \text{Minuend}
\end{array}
$$

▣ **Work Practice Problem 6**

Objective C Estimating When Adding or Subtracting Decimals

To help avoid errors, we can also estimate to see if our answer is reasonable when adding or subtracting decimals. Although only one estimate is needed per operation, we show two to show variety.

PRACTICE PROBLEM 7

Add or subtract as indicated. Then estimate to see if the answer is reasonable by rounding the given numbers and adding or subtracting the rounded numbers.
a. $48.1 + 326.97$
b. $18.09 - 0.746$

EXAMPLE 7 Add or subtract as indicated. Then estimate to see if the answer is reasonable by rounding the given numbers and adding or subtracting the rounded numbers.

a. $27.6 + 519.25$

Exact		Estimate 1		Estimate 2
$\overset{1}{2}7.60$	rounds to	30		30
$+\,519.25$	rounds to	$+\,500$	or	$+\,520$
546.85		530		550

Since the exact answer is close to either estimate, it is reasonable. (In the first estimate, each number is rounded to the place value of the leftmost digit. In the second estimate, each number is rounded to the nearest ten.)

b. $11.01 - 0.862$

Exact		Estimate 1		Estimate 2
$\overset{0\;\;9\;10\;10}{1\cancel{1}.\cancel{0}\cancel{1}\cancel{0}}$	rounds to	10		11
$-\,0.862$	rounds to	$-\,1$	or	$-\,1$
10.148		9		10

In the first estimate, we rounded the first number to the nearest ten and the second number to the nearest one. In the second estimate, we rounded both numbers to the nearest one. Both estimates show us that our answer is reasonable.

Remember: Estimates are for our convenience to quickly check the reasonableness of an answer.

■ **Work Practice Problem 7**

✔**Concept Check** Why shouldn't the sum 21.98 + 42.36 be estimated as 30 + 50 = 80?

Objective D Solving Problems by Adding or Subtracting Decimals

Decimals are very common in real-life problems.

EXAMPLE 8 **Calculating the Cost of Owning an Automobile**

Find the total monthly cost of owning and operating a certain automobile given the expenses shown.

Monthly car payment:	$256.63
Monthly insurance cost:	$47.52
Average gasoline bill per month:	$95.33

Solution:

1. **UNDERSTAND.** Read and reread the problem. The phrase "total monthly cost" tells us to add.

2. **TRANSLATE.**

In words: total monthly cost **is** car payment **plus** insurance cost **plus** gasoline bill

Translate: total monthly cost = $256.63 + $47.52 + $95.33

3. **SOLVE:** Let's also estimate by rounding each number to the nearest ten.

$$\begin{array}{ll}
\overset{111}{256.63} & \text{rounds to} \quad 260 \\
47.52 & \text{rounds to} \quad 50 \\
+\ 95.33 & \text{rounds to} \quad \underline{100} \\
\$399.48 \ \text{Exact.} & \quad\quad 410 \quad \text{Estimate.}
\end{array}$$

4. **INTERPRET.** *Check* your work. Since our estimate is close to our exact answer, our answer is reasonable. *State* your conclusion: The total monthly cost is $399.48.

■ **Work Practice Problem 8**

The next bar graph has horizontal bars. To visualize the value represented by a bar, see how far it extends to the right. The value of each bar is labeled and we will study bar graphs further in a later chapter.

EXAMPLE 9 **Comparing Average Heights**

The bar graph shows the current average heights for adults in various countries. How much greater is the average height in Denmark than the average height in the United States?

Continued on next page

PRACTICE PROBLEM 8

Find the total monthly cost of owning and operating a certain automobile given the expenses shown.

Monthly car payment:	$536.52
Monthly insurance cost:	$52.68
Average gasoline bill per month:	$87.50

Answer
8. $676.70

✔ **Concept Check Answer**
Each number is rounded incorrectly. The estimate is too high.

PRACTICE PROBLEM 9

Use the bar graph in Example 9. How much greater is the average height in the Netherlands than the average height in Czechoslovakia?

Average Adult Height

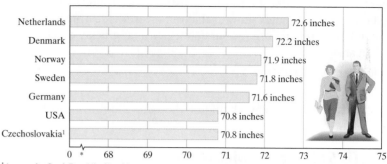

Netherlands 72.6 inches
Denmark 72.2 inches
Norway 71.9 inches
Sweden 71.8 inches
Germany 71.6 inches
USA 70.8 inches
Czechoslovakia[1] 70.8 inches

0 * 68 69 70 71 72 73 74 75

[1]Average for Czech Republic, Slovakia
Source: USA Today, 8/28/97

* The -√- means that some numbers are purposefully missing on the axis.

Solution:

1. **UNDERSTAND.** Read and reread the problem. Since we want to know "how much greater," we subtract.

2. **TRANSLATE.**

In words:	How much greater	is	Denmark's average height	minus	U.S. average height
	↓	↓	↓	↓	↓
Translate:	How much greater	=	72.2	−	70.8

3. **SOLVE:** We estimate by rounding each number to the nearest whole.

$$\begin{array}{r} \overset{1\ \ 12}{72.\cancel{2}} \text{ rounds to} \quad 72 \\ -\ 70.8 \text{ rounds to} \quad -71 \\ \hline 1.4 \text{ Exact.} \qquad 1 \text{ Estimate.} \end{array}$$

4. **INTERPRET.** *Check* your work. Since our estimate is close to our exact answer, 1.4 inches is reasonable. *State* your conclusion: The average height in Denmark is 1.4 inches greater than the average U.S. height.

Answer

9. 1.8 in.

📖 **Work Practice Problem 9**

🖩 **CALCULATOR EXPLORATIONS**

Entering Decimal Numbers

To enter a decimal number, find the key marked ⌶ ⋅ ⌶. To enter the number 2.56, for example, press the keys ⌶ 2 ⌶ ⌶ ⋅ ⌶ ⌶ 5 ⌶ ⌶ 6 ⌶. The display will read [2.56].

Operations on Decimal Numbers

Operations on decimal numbers are performed in the same way as operations on whole or signed numbers. For example, to find 8.625 − 4.29, press the keys ⌶ 8.625 ⌶ ⌶ − ⌶ ⌶ 4.29 ⌶ ⌶ = ⌶ or ⌶ ENTER ⌶. The display will read [4.335]. (Although entering 8.625, for example, requires pressing more than one key, we group numbers together here for easier reading.)

Use a calculator to perform each indicated operation.

1. 315.782 + 12.96
2. 29.68 + 85.902
3. 6.249 − 1.0076
4. 5.238 − 0.682

5.
$$\begin{array}{r} 12.555 \\ 224.987 \\ 5.2 \\ +\ 622.65 \end{array}$$

6.
$$\begin{array}{r} 47.006 \\ 0.17 \\ 313.259 \\ +\ 139.088 \end{array}$$

Mental Math

Find the sum or difference.

1. $\begin{aligned} 0.3 \\ +\,0.2 \end{aligned}$	**2.** $\begin{aligned} 0.4 \\ +\,0.5 \end{aligned}$	**3.** $\begin{aligned} 1.00 \\ +\,0.26 \end{aligned}$	**4.** $\begin{aligned} 3.00 \\ +\,0.19 \end{aligned}$
5. $\begin{aligned} 7.6 \\ +\,1.3 \end{aligned}$	**6.** $\begin{aligned} 4.5 \\ +\,3.2 \end{aligned}$	**7.** $\begin{aligned} 0.9 \\ -\,0.3 \end{aligned}$	**8.** $\begin{aligned} 0.6 \\ -\,0.2 \end{aligned}$

4.3 EXERCISE SET

FOR EXTRA HELP

Student Solutions Manual   PH Math/Tutor Center   CD/Video for Review   MathXL®   MyMathLab

Objectives Ⓐ Ⓒ **Mixed Practice** *Add. See Examples 1 through 3, and 7. For those exercises marked, also estimate to see if the answer is reasonable.*

1. $1.3 + 2.2$ **2.** $2.5 + 4.1$ **3.** $5.7 + 1.13$ **4.** $2.31 + 6.4$ **5.** $0.003 + 0.091$

6. $0.004 + 0.085$ **7.** $19.23 + 602.782$ **8.** $47.14 + 409.567$ **9.** $490 + 93.09$ **10.** $600 + 83.0062$

11. $\begin{aligned} 234.89 \\ +\,230.67 \end{aligned}$ Exact: _____ Estimate: _____

12. $\begin{aligned} 734.89 \\ +\,640.56 \end{aligned}$ Exact: _____ Estimate: _____

13. $\begin{aligned} 100.009 \\ 6.08 \\ +\ \ \ 9.034 \end{aligned}$ Exact: _____ Estimate: _____

14. $\begin{aligned} 200.89 \\ 7.49 \\ +\ \ 62.83 \end{aligned}$ Exact: _____ Estimate: _____

15. $24.6 + 2.39 + 0.0678$ **16.** $32.4 + 1.58 + 0.0934$

17. Find the sum of 45.023, 3.006, and 8.403   **18.** Find the sum of 65.0028, 5.0903, and 6.9003

Objectives Ⓑ Ⓒ **Mixed Practice** *Subtract and check. See Examples 4 through 7. For those exercises marked, also estimate to see if the answer is reasonable.*

19. $8.8 - 2.3$ **20.** $7.6 - 2.1$ **21.** $18 - 2.7$ **22.** $28 - 3.3$

23.   654.9
    − 56.67

24.   863.23
    − 39.453

25. $5.9 - 4.07$
    Exact:
    Estimate:

26. $6.4 - 3.04$
    Exact:
    Estimate:

27. $923.5 - 61.9$

28. $845.93 - 45.8$

29. $500.34 - 123.45$

30. $600.74 - 463.98$

31.   1000
    − 123.4
    Exact:

    Estimate:

32.   2000
    − 327.47
    Exact:

    Estimate:

33. $200 - 5.6$

34. $800 - 8.9$

35. $3 - 0.0012$

36. $7 - 0.097$

37. Subtract 6.7 from 23.

38. Subtract 9.2 from 45.

Objectives **A** **B** **Mixed Practice** *Perform the indicated operation. See Examples 1 through 6.*

39. $86.05 + 1.978$

40. $95.07 + 4.216$

41. $86.05 - 1.978$

42. $95.07 - 4.216$

43. Add 150 and 93.17.

44. Add 250 and 86.07.

45. $150 - 93.17$

46. $250 - 86.07$

47. Subtract 8.94 from 12.1.

48. Subtract 6.73 from 20.2.

Objective **D** *Solve. See Examples 8 and 9.*

49. Find the total monthly cost of owning and maintaining a car given the information shown.

Monthly car payment:	$275.36
Monthly insurance cost:	$ 83.00
Average cost of gasoline per month:	$ 81.60
Average maintenance cost per month:	$ 14.75

50. Find the total monthly cost of owning and maintaining a car given the information shown.

Monthly car payment:	$306.42
Monthly insurance cost:	$ 53.50
Average cost of gasoline per month:	$123.00
Average maintenance cost per month:	$ 23.50

51. Gasoline was $1.739 per gallon on one day and $1.879 per gallon the next day. By how much did the price change?

52. A pair of eyeglasses costs a total of $347.89. The frames of the glasses are $97.23. How much do the lenses of the eyeglasses cost?

53. Find the perimeter.

Square   7.14 meters

54. Find the perimeter.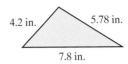

4.2 in.   5.78 in.   7.8 in.

The iPod mini is a miniture version of Apple Computer's popular iPod portable audio player. This mini was introduced in January 2004 with a storage capacity of 4 gigabytes. (This is about 1000 3-minute or 3-megabyte songs.)

55. The top face of the iPod mini shown measures 3.6 inches by 2.0 inches. Find the perimeter of the rectangular face.

56. The face of the larger Apple iPod measures 4.1 inches by 2.4 inches. Find the perimeter of this rectangular face.

57. Ann-Margaret Tober bought a book for $32.48. If she paid with two $20 bills, what was her change?

58. Phillip Guillot bought a car part for $18.26. If he paid with two $10 bills, what was his change?

59. Americans' consumption of sugar is on the decline. During 2000, Americans consumed an average of 150.1 pounds of sugar in its various forms such as refined white sugar, honey, and corn sweeteners. By 2002, the average American was consuming 146 pounds of sugar products per year. How much less sugar was the average American consuming annually in 2002 than in 2000? (*Source:* Economic Research Service, U.S. Department of Agriculture)

60. In 2001, the average wage for U.S. production workers was $14.29 per hour. One year later in 2002, this average wage had climbed to $14.95 per hour. How much of an increase was this? (*Source:* Bureau of Labor Statistics)

61. The average wind speed at the weather station on Mt. Washington in New Hampshire is 35.2 miles per hour. The highest speed ever recorded at the station is 321.0 miles per hour. How much faster is the highest speed than the average wind speed? (*Source:* National Climatic Data Center)

62. The average annual rainfall in Omaha, Nebraska, is 30.22 inches. The average annual rainfall in New Orleans, Louisiana, is 61.88 inches. On average, how much more rain does New Orleans receive annually than Omaha? (*Source:* National Climatic Data Center)

63. In October 1997, Andy Green set a new one-mile land speed record. This record was 129.567 miles per hour faster than a previous record of 633.468 set in 1983. What was Green's record-setting speed? (*Source:* United States Auto Club)

64. It costs $3.13 to send a 2-pound package locally via parcel post at a U.S. Post Office. To send the same package as Priority Mail, it costs $3.95. How much more does it cost to send a package as Priority Mail? (*Source:* USPS)

This bar graph shows the predicted decrease in home video rental revenue for chains such as Blockbuster and Hollywood Video. Use this graph for Exercise 65.

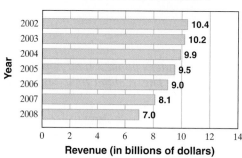

Video Rental Revenues

Source: Forrester Research; Note: Many of these years are projections.

65. Find the decrease in video rental revenue from the year 2002 to 2008.

66. It is predicted that home video *sales* (not shown on the bar graph) will increase from $15.3 billion in 2002 to $24.6 billion in 2008. Find the amount of increase.

67. The snowiest city in the United States is Blue Canyon, California, which receives an average of 111.6 more inches of snow than the second-snowiest city. The second-snowiest city in the United States is Marquette, Michigan. Marquette receives an average of 129.2 inches of snow annually. How much snow does Blue Canyon receive on average each year? (*Source:* National Climatic Data Center)

68. The driest city in the world is Aswan, Egypt, which receives an average of only 0.02 inches of rain per year. Yuma, Arizona, is the driest city in the United States. Yuma receives an average of 2.63 more inches of rain each year than Aswan. What is the average annual rainfall in Yuma? (*Source:* National Climatic Data Center)

△ **69.** A landscape architect is planning a border for a flower garden that's shaped like a triangle. The sides of the garden measure 12.4 feet, 29.34 feet, and 25.7 feet. Find the amount of border material needed.

△ **70.** A contractor needs to buy railing to completely enclose a newly built rectangular deck. If the deck has a length of 15.7 feet and a width of 10.6 feet, find the amount of railing needed.

The table shows the average retail price of a gallon of gasoline (all grades and formulations) in the United States in May of each of the years shown. Use this table to answer Exercises 71 and 72.

Year	Gasoline Price (dollars per gallon)
2000	1.563
2001	1.531
2002	1.441
2003	1.638
2004	1.861

(*Source:* Energy Information Administration)

71. How much more was the average cost of a gallon of gasoline in 2000 than in 2002?

72. How much more was the average cost of a gallon of gasoline in 2004 than in 2001?

The following table shows spaceflight information for astronaut James A. Lovell. Use this table to answer Exercises 73 and 74.

Spaceflights of James A. Lovell		
Year	Mission	Duration (in hours)
1965	Gemini 6	330.583
1966	Gemini 12	94.567
1968	Apollo 8	147.0
1970	Apollo 13	142.9
(*Source:* NASA)		

73. Find the total time spent in spaceflight by astronaut James A. Lovell.

74. Find the total time James A. Lovell spent in spaceflight on all Apollo missions.

The bar graph shows the top five chocolate-consuming nations in the world. Use this table to answer Exercises 75 through 79.

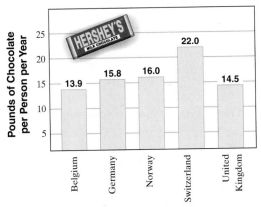

The World's Top Chocolate-Consuming Countries

Source: Hershey Foods Corporation

75. Which country in the table has the greatest chocolate consumption per person?

76. Which country in the table has the least chocolate consumption per person?

77. How much more is the greatest chocolate consumption than the least chocolate consumption shown in the table?

78. How much more chocolate does the average German consume than the average citizen of the United Kingdom?

79. Make a new chart listing the countries and their corresponding chocolate consumptions in order from greatest to least.

Review

Multiply. See Sections 1.6 and 2.4.

80. $23 \cdot 2$

81. $46 \cdot 3$

82. $43 \cdot 90$

83. $30 \cdot 32$

84. $\left(\dfrac{2}{3}\right)^2$

85. $\left(\dfrac{1}{5}\right)^3$

86. $\dfrac{12}{7} \cdot \dfrac{14}{3}$

87. $\dfrac{25}{36} \cdot \dfrac{24}{40}$

Concept Extensions

Solve. See the first Concept Check in this section.

88. A friend asks you to check his calculation to the right. Is it correct? If not, explain your friends' error and correct the calculation.

$$\begin{array}{r} \overset{1}{9}.2 \\ \overset{1}{8}.63 \\ +\,4.005 \\ \hline 4.960 \end{array}$$

Find the unknown length in each figure.

△ **89.**

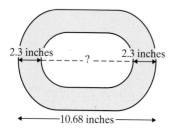

2.3 inches   ?   2.3 inches

10.68 inches

△ **90.**

←5.26→ ←7.82→ ? meters meters meters

17.67 meters

Let's review the values of these common U.S. coins in order to answer the following exercises.

Penny	Nickel	Dime	Quarter

$0.01 $0.05 $0.10 $0.25

Write the value of each group of coins. To do so, it is usually easiest to start with the coin(s) of greatest value and end with the coin(s) of least value.

91.

92.

93. Name the different ways that coins can have a value of $0.17 given that you may use no more than 10 coins.

94. Name the different ways that coin(s) can have a value of $0.25 given that there are no pennies.

95. Why shouldn't the sum

82.95 + 51.26

be estimated as 90 + 60 = 150? See the Concept Check in this section.

96. Explain how adding or subtracting decimals is similar to adding or subtracting whole numbers.

97. Laser beams can be used to measure the distance to the moon. One measurement showed the distance to the moon to be 256,435.235 miles. A later measurement showed that the distance is 256,436.012 miles. Find how much farther away the moon is in the second measurement as compared to the first.

4.4 MULTIPLYING DECIMALS AND CIRCUMFERENCE OF A CIRCLE

Objectives

A Multiply Decimals.

B Estimate When Multiplying Decimals.

C Multiply by Powers of 10.

D Find the Circumference of a Circle.

E Solve Problems by Multiplying Decimals.

Objective **A** Multiplying Decimals

Multiplying decimals is similar to multiplying whole numbers. The only difference is that we place a decimal point in the product. To discover where a decimal point is placed in the product, let's multiply 0.6×0.03. We first write each decimal as an equivalent fraction and then multiply.

$$0.6 \times 0.03 = \frac{6}{10} \times \frac{3}{100} = \frac{18}{1000} = 0.018$$

1 decimal place   2 decimal places   3 decimal places

Notice that $1 + 2 = 3$, the number of decimal places in the product. Now let's multiply 0.03×0.002.

$$0.03 \times 0.002 = \frac{3}{100} \times \frac{2}{1000} = \frac{6}{100,000} = 0.00006$$

2 decimal places   3 decimal places   5 decimal places

Again, we see that $2 + 3 = 5$, the number of decimal places in the product.

Instead of writing decimals as fractions each time we want to multiply, we notice a pattern from these examples and state a rule that we can use:

Multiplying Decimals

Step 1: Multiply the decimals as though they are whole numbers.

Step 2: The decimal point in the product is placed so that the number of decimal places in the product is equal to the *sum* of the number of decimal places in the factors.

EXAMPLE 1 Multiply: 23.6×0.78

Solution:

```
     23.6    1 decimal place
  × 0.78     2 decimal places
  ------
    1888
   16520
  ------
  18.408    Since 1 + 2 = 3, insert the
            decimal point in the product so
            that there are 3 decimal places.
```

PRACTICE PROBLEM 1

Multiply: 45.9×0.42

■ **Work Practice Problem 1**

EXAMPLE 2 Multiply: 0.283×0.3

Solution:

```
   0.283    3 decimal places
  ×  0.3    1 decimal place
  ------
  0.0849    Since 3 + 1 = 4, insert the
            decimal point in the product so
            that there are 4 decimal places.

            Insert one 0 since the product
            must have 4 decimal places.
```

PRACTICE PROBLEM 2

Multiply: 0.112×0.6

Answers
1. 19.278, **2.** 0.0672

■ **Work Practice Problem 2**

PRACTICE PROBLEM 3

Multiply: 0.0721×48

EXAMPLE 3 Multiply: 0.0531×16

Solution:

$$
\begin{array}{r}
0.0531 \quad \text{4 decimal places} \\
\times \quad 16 \quad \text{0 decimal places} \\
\hline
3186 \\
5310 \\
\hline
0.8496 \\
\end{array}
$$

4 decimal places $(4 + 0 = 4)$

■ **Work Practice Problem 3**

✔ **Concept Check** True or false? The number of decimal places in the product of 0.261 and 0.78 is 6. Explain.

Objective B Estimating When Multiplying Decimals

Just as for addition and subtraction, we can estimate when multiplying decimals to check the reasonableness of our answer.

PRACTICE PROBLEM 4

Multiply: 30.26×2.98. Then estimate to see whether the answer is reasonable.

EXAMPLE 4 Multiply: 28.06×1.95. Then estimate to see whether the answer is reasonable by rounding each factor, then multiplying the rounded numbers.

Solution:

Exact:	Estimate 1	Estimate 2

$$
\begin{array}{r}
28.06 \\
\times \quad 1.95 \\
\hline
14030 \\
252540 \\
280600 \\
\hline
54.7170 \\
\end{array}
\qquad
\begin{array}{r}
28 \quad \text{Rounded to ones or} \\
\times \quad 2 \\
\hline
56 \\
\end{array}
\qquad
\begin{array}{r}
30 \quad \text{Rounded to tens} \\
\times \quad 2 \\
\hline
60 \\
\end{array}
$$

The answer 54.7170 is reasonable.

■ **Work Practice Problem 4**

As shown in Example 4, estimated results will vary depending on what estimates are used. Notice that estimating results is a good way to see whether the decimal point has been correctly placed.

Objective C Multiplying by Powers of 10

There are some patterns that occur when we multiply a number by a power of 10 such as 10, 100, 1000, 10,000, and so on.

$23.6951 \times 10 = 236.951$ Move the decimal point *1 place* to the *right*.
1 zero

$23.6951 \times 100 = 2369.51$ Move the decimal point *2 places* to the *right*.
2 zeros

$23.6951 \times 100,000 = 2,369,510.$ Move the decimal point *5 places* to the *right* (insert a 0).
5 zeros

Answers

3. 3.4608, **4.** 90.1748

✔ **Concept Check Answer**

false: 3 decimal places and 2 decimal places means 5 decimal places in the product

Notice that we move the decimal point the same number of places as there are zeros in the power of 10.

Multiplying Decimals by Powers of 10 such as 10, 100, 1000, 10,000 . . .

Move the decimal point to the *right* the same number of places as there are *zeros* in the power of 10.

EXAMPLES Multiply.

5. $7.68 \times 10 = 76.8$ 7.68

6. $23.702 \times 100 = 2370.2$ 23.702

7. $76.3 \times 1000 = 76{,}300$ 76.300

Work Practice Problems 5–7

PRACTICE PROBLEMS 5–7
Multiply.
5. 23.7×10
6. 203.004×100
7. 1.15×1000

There are also powers of 10 that are less than 1. The decimals 0.1, 0.01, 0.001, 0.0001, and so on are examples of powers of 10 less than 1. Notice the pattern when we multiply by these powers of 10:

$569.2 \times 0.1 = 56.92$ Move the decimal point *1 place* to the *left.*

    1 decimal place

$569.2 \times 0.01 = 5.692$ Move the decimal point *2 places* to the *left.*

    2 decimal places

$569.2 \times 0.0001 = 0.05692$ Move the decimal point *4 places* to the *left* (insert one 0).

    4 decimal places

Multiplying Decimals by Powers of 10 such as 0.1, 0.01, 0.001, 0.0001 . . .

Move the decimal point to the *left* the same number of places as there are *decimal places* in the power of 10.

EXAMPLES Multiply.

8. $42.1 \times 0.1 = 4.21$ 42.1

9. $76{,}805 \times 0.01 = 768.05$ $76{,}805.$

10. $9.2 \times 0.001 = 0.0092$ 0009.2

Work Practice Problems 8–10

PRACTICE PROBLEMS 8–10
Multiply.
8. 7.62×0.1
9. 1.9×0.01
10. 7682×0.001

Many times we see large numbers written, for example, in the form 295.3 million rather than in the longer standard notation. The next example shows us how to interpret these numbers.

Answers
5. 237,   **6.** 20,300.4,   **7.** 1150,
8. 0.762,   **9.** 0.019,   **10.** 7.682.

PRACTICE PROBLEM 11

According to the 2000 Census, there were 115.9 million households in the United States. Write this number in standard notation. (*Source:* U.S. Census Bureau)

EXAMPLE 11 At the beginning of 2005, the population of the United States was projected to be 295.3 million. Write this number in standard notation. (*Source:* U.S. Census Bureau)

295.3 million

Solution: 295.3 million = 295.3 × 1 million

= 295.3 × 1,000,000 = 295,300,000

☐ **Work Practice Problem 11**

Objective D Finding the Circumference of a Circle

Recall that the distance around a polygon is called its **perimeter.** The distance around a circle is given a special name called the **circumference,** and this distance depends on the radius or the diameter of the circle.

Circumference of a Circle

radius

diameter

Circumference = 2 · π · radius   or   Circumference = π · diameter

---

The symbol π is the Greek letter pi, pronounced "pie." It is a number between 3 and 4. The number π rounded to two decimal places is 3.14, and a fraction approximation for π is $\frac{22}{7}$.

EXAMPLE 12 Find the circumference of a circle whose radius is 5 inches. Then use the approximation 3.14 for π to approximate the circumference.

Solution: Circumference $= 2 \cdot \pi \cdot \text{radius}$

$$= 2 \cdot \pi \cdot 5 \text{ inches}$$

$$= 10\pi \text{ inches}$$

5 inches

Next, we replace π with the approximation 3.14.

Circumference $= 10\pi$ inches

("is approximately") $\rightarrow$ $\approx 10(3.14)$ inches

$$= 31.4 \text{ inches}$$

The *exact* circumference or distance around the circle is 10π inches, which is *approximately* 31.4 inches.

🔲 **Work Practice Problem 12**

PRACTICE PROBLEM 12

Find the circumference of a circle whose radius is 11 meters. Then use the approximation 3.14 for π to approximate this circumference.

Objective E Solving Problems by Multiplying Decimals

The solutions to many real-life problems are found by multiplying decimals. We continue using our four problem-solving steps to solve such problems.

EXAMPLE 13 Finding the Total Cost of Materials for a Job

A college student is hired to paint a billboard with paint costing $2.49 per quart. If the job requires 3 quarts of paint, what is the total cost of the paint?

Solution:

1. **UNDERSTAND.** Read and reread the problem. The phrase "total cost" might make us think addition, but since this problem requires repeated addition, let's multiply.

2. **TRANSLATE.**

In words:	Total cost	is	cost per quart of paint	times	number of quarts
	↓	↓	↓	↓	↓
Translate:	Total cost	=	2.49	×	3

3. **SOLVE.** We can estimate to check our calculations. The number 2.49 rounds to 2 and $2 \times 3 = 6$.

$$\begin{array}{r} \overset{1\ 2}{2.49} \\ \times \quad 3 \\ \hline 7.47 \end{array}$$

4. **INTERPRET.** *Check* your work. Since 7.47 is close to our estimate of 6, our answer is reasonable. *State* your conclusion: The total cost of the paint is $7.47.

🔲 **Work Practice Problem 13**

PRACTICE PROBLEM 13

Elaine Rehmann is fertilizing her garden. She uses 5.6 ounces of fertilizer per square yard. The garden measures 60.5 square yards. How much fertilizer does she need?

Mental Math

Do not multiply. Just give the number of decimal places in the product. See the Concept Check in this section.

1. $\begin{array}{r} 0.46 \\ \times\,0.81 \\ \hline \end{array}$	**2.** $\begin{array}{r} 57.9 \\ \times\,0.36 \\ \hline \end{array}$	**3.** $\begin{array}{r} 0.428 \\ \times\,\ \ 0.2 \\ \hline \end{array}$	**4.** $\begin{array}{r} 0.0073 \\ \times\,\ \ \ \ 21 \\ \hline \end{array}$	**5.** $\begin{array}{r} 0.028 \\ \times\,1.36 \\ \hline \end{array}$	**6.** $\begin{array}{r} 5.1296 \\ \times\,7.3987 \\ \hline \end{array}$

4.4 EXERCISE SET

FOR EXTRA HELP

Student Solutions Manual · PH Math/Tutor Center · CD/Video for Review · MathXL® · MyMathLab

Objectives Ⓐ Ⓑ **Mixed Practice** *Multiply. See Examples 1 through 4. For those exercises marked, also estimate to see if the answer is reasonable.*

1. $\begin{array}{r} 0.2 \\ \times\,0.6 \\ \hline \end{array}$	**2.** $\begin{array}{r} 0.7 \\ \times\,0.9 \\ \hline \end{array}$	**3.** $\begin{array}{r} 1.2 \\ \times\,0.5 \\ \hline \end{array}$	**4.** $\begin{array}{r} 6.8 \\ \times\,0.3 \\ \hline \end{array}$

5. 0.26×5 **6.** 0.19×6 **7.** 5.3×4.2
Exact:
Estimate: **8.** 6.2×3.8
Exact:
Estimate:

9. $\begin{array}{r} 0.576 \\ \times\,\ \ 0.7 \\ \hline \end{array}$	**10.** $\begin{array}{r} 0.971 \\ \times\,\ \ 0.5 \\ \hline \end{array}$	**11.** $\begin{array}{r} 1.0047 \\ \times\,\ \ \ \ 8.2 \\ \hline \end{array}$ Exact:　　　　Estimate:	**12.** $\begin{array}{r} 2.0005 \\ \times\,\ \ \ \ 5.5 \\ \hline \end{array}$ Exact:　　　　Estimate:

13. $\begin{array}{r} 490.2 \\ \times\,0.023 \\ \hline \end{array}$ **14.** $\begin{array}{r} 300.9 \\ \times\,0.032 \\ \hline \end{array}$ **15.** Multiply 16.003 and 5.31   **16.** Multiply 31.006 and 3.71

Objective Ⓒ *Multiply. See Examples 5 through 10.*

17. 6.5×10 **18.** 7.2×100 **19.** 6.5×0.1 **20.** 4.7×0.1

21. 7.2×0.01 **22.** 0.06×0.01 **23.** 7.093×100 **24.** 0.5×100

25. 6.046×1000 **26.** 9.1×1000 **27.** 37.62×0.001 **28.** 14.3×0.001

Objectives Ⓐ Ⓑ Ⓒ **Mixed Practice** *Multiply. See Examples 1 through 10.*

29. 0.123×0.4 **30.** 0.216×0.3 **31.** 0.123×100 **32.** 0.216×100

33. 8.6×0.15 **34.** 0.42×5.7 **35.** 9.6×0.01 **36.** 5.7×0.01

37. 562.3×0.001 **38.** 993.5×0.001 **39.** $\begin{array}{r} 5.62 \\ \times\ 7.7 \\ \hline \end{array}$ **40.** $\begin{array}{r} 8.03 \\ \times\ 5.5 \\ \hline \end{array}$

Write each number in standard notation. See Example 11.

41. The storage silos at the main Hershey chocolate factory in Hershey, Pennsylvania, can hold enough cocoa beans to make 5.5 billion Hershey's milk chocolate bars. (*Source:* Hershey Foods Corporation)

42. The total value of works from Pablo Picasso (if sold) is $1.5 billion. (*Source: Top 10 of Everything*, 2005)

43. The Blue Streak is the oldest roller coaster at Cedar Point, an amusement park in Sandusky, Ohio. Since 1964, it has given more than 49.8 million rides. (*Source:* Cedar Fair, L.P.)

44. About 36.4 million American households own at least one dog. (*Source:* American Pet Products Manufacturers Association)

45. The most-visited national park in the United States is the Blue Ridge Parkway in Virginia and North Carolina. An estimated 353 thousand people visited the park each week in 2003. (*Source:* National Park Service)

46. There are 844 thousand places to eat out in the United States. (*Source:* National Restaurant Association)

Objective D *Find the circumference of each circle. Then use the approximation 3.14 for π and approximate each circumference. See Example 12.*

47.

4 meters

48.

8 feet

49.

10 centimeters

50.

22 inches

51.

9.1 yards

52.

5.9 kilometers

Objectives D E Mixed Practice *Solve. See Examples 12 and 13. For circumference applications find the exact circumference and then use 3.14 for π to approximate the circumference.*

53. A 1-ounce serving of cream cheese contains 6.2 grams of saturated fat. How much saturated fat is in 4 ounces of cream cheese? (*Source: Home and Garden Bulletin No. 72;* U.S. Department of Agriculture)

54. A 3.5-ounce serving of lobster meat contains 0.1 gram of saturated fat. How much saturated fat do 3 servings of lobster meat contain? (*Source:* The National Institute of Health)

55. The average cost of driving a car in 2003 was $0.52 per mile. How much would it have cost to drive a car 8750 miles in 2003? (*Source:* American Automobile Association)

56. In 2003, a U.S. airline passenger paid $0.1174, on average, to fly 1 mile. How much would it have cost to fly from Atlanta, Georgia, to Minneapolis, Minnesota, a distance of 905 miles? Round to the nearest cent. (*Source:* Air Transport Association of America, Inc.)

△ **57.** In 1893, the first ride called a Ferris wheel was constructed by Washington Gale Ferris. Its diameter was 250 feet. Find its circumference. Give an exact answer and an approximation using 3.14 for π. (*Source: The Handy Science Answer Book*, Visible Ink Press, 1994)

△ **58.** The radius of Earth is approximately 3950 miles. Find the distance around Earth at the equator. Give an exact answer and an approximation using 3.14 for π. (*Hint:* Find the circumference of a circle with radius 3950 miles.)

△ **59.** The London Eye, built for the Millennium celebration in London, resembles a gigantic ferris wheel with a diameter of 135 meters. If Adam Hawn rides the Eye for one revolution, find how far he travels. (Give an exact answer and an approximation using 3.14 for π. (*Source:* Londoneye.com)

△ **60.** The world's longest suspension bridge is the Akashi Kaikyo Bridge in Japan. This bridge has two circular caissons, which are underwater foundations. If the diameter of a caisson is 80 meters, find its circumference. Give an exact answer and an approximation using 3.14 for π. (*Source: Scientific American; How Things Work Today*)

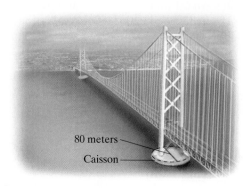

61. A meter is a unit of length in the metric system that is approximately equal to 39.37 inches. Sophia Wagner is 1.65 meters tall. Find her approximate height in inches.

62. The doorway to a room is 2.15 meters tall. Approximate this height in inches. (*Hint:* See Exercise 61.)

63. Jose Severos, an electrician for Central Power and Light, worked 40 hours last week. Calculate his pay before taxes for last week if his hourly wage is $13.88.

64. Maribel Chin, an assembly line worker, worked 20 hours last week. Her hourly rate is $8.52 per hour. Calculate Maribel's pay before taxes.

△ **65. a.** Approximate the circumference of each circle.

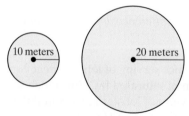

b. If the radius of a circle is doubled, is its corresponding circumference doubled?

△ **66. a.** Approximate the circumference of each circle.

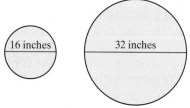

b. If the diameter of a circle is doubled, is its corresponding circumference doubled?

67. Recall that the top face of the Apple iPod mini (see Section 4.3) measures 3.6 inches by 2.0 inches. Find the area of the face of the iPod mini.

68. Recall that the face of the regular Apple iPod measures 4.1 inches by 2.4 inches. Find the area of the face of this iPod.

Review

Divide. See Sections 1.7 and 2.5.

69. $130 \div 5$

70. $495 \div 27$

71. $2016 \div 56$

72. $1863 \div 69$

73. $2920 \div 365$

74. $2916 \div 6$

75. $\dfrac{24}{7} \div \dfrac{8}{21}$

76. $\dfrac{162}{25} \div \dfrac{9}{75}$

Concept Extensions

Mixed Practice (Sections 4.3, 4.4) *Perform the indicated operations.*

77. $3.6 + 0.04$

78. 3.6×0.04

79. $3.6 - 0.04$

80. $100 - 48.6$

81. 0.221×0.5

82. $7.2 + 0.14 + 98.6$

83. Find how far radio waves travel in 20.6 seconds. (Radio waves travel at a speed of $1.86 \times 100,000$ miles per second.)

84. If it takes radio waves approximately 8.3 minutes to travel from the Sun to the Earth, find approximately how far it is from the Sun to the Earth. (*Hint:* See Exercise 83.)

85. In your own words, explain how to find the number of decimal places in a product of decimal numbers.

86. In your own words, explain how to multiply by a power of 10.

87. Write down two decimal numbers whose product will contain 5 decimal places. Without multiplying, explain how you know your answer is correct.

INTEGRATED REVIEW — Sections 4.1–4.4

Operations on Decimals

1. _____

2. _____

3. _____

4. _____

5. _____

6. _____

7. _____

8. _____

9. _____

10. _____

11. _____

12. _____

13. _____

14. _____

15. _____

16. _____

17. _____

18. _____

19. _____

20. _____

21. _____

22. _____

23. _____

24. _____

25. _____

26. _____

Perform the indicated operations.

1. $1.6 + 0.97$

2. $3.2 + 0.85$

3. $9.8 - 0.9$

4. $10.2 - 6.7$

5.
$$\begin{array}{r} 0.8 \\ \times\, 0.2 \\ \hline \end{array}$$

6.
$$\begin{array}{r} 0.6 \\ \times\, 0.4 \\ \hline \end{array}$$

7. $8 + 2.16 + 0.9$

8. $6 + 3.12 + 0.6$

9.
$$\begin{array}{r} 9.6 \\ \times\, 0.5 \\ \hline \end{array}$$

10.
$$\begin{array}{r} 8.7 \\ \times\, 0.7 \\ \hline \end{array}$$

11.
$$\begin{array}{r} 123.6 \\ -\ 48.04 \\ \hline \end{array}$$

12.
$$\begin{array}{r} 325.2 \\ -\ 36.08 \\ \hline \end{array}$$

13. $25 + 0.026$

14. $0.125 + 44$

15. $100 - 17.3$

16. $300 - 26.1$

17. 2.8×100

18. 1.6×1000

19.
$$\begin{array}{r} 96.21 \\ 7.028 \\ +\ 121.7 \\ \hline \end{array}$$

20.
$$\begin{array}{r} 0.268 \\ 1.93 \\ +\ 142.881 \\ \hline \end{array}$$

21. Find the product of 1.2 and 5.

22. Find the sum of 1.2 and 5.

23.
$$\begin{array}{r} 12.004 \\ \times\ \ \ \ 2.3 \\ \hline \end{array}$$

24.
$$\begin{array}{r} 28.006 \\ \times\ \ \ \ 5.2 \\ \hline \end{array}$$

25. Subtract 4.6 from 10.

26. Subtract 0.26 from 18.

27.   268.19
        $\underline{+\,146.25}$

28.   860.18
        $\underline{+\,434.85}$

29. $160 - 43.19$

30. $120 - 101.21$

31. 15.62×10

32. $15.62 + 10$

33. $15.62 - 10$

34. 117.26×2.6

35. $117.26 - 2.6$

36. $117.26 + 2.6$

37. 0.0072×0.06

38. 0.0025×0.03

39. $0.0072 + 0.06$

40. $0.03 - 0.0025$

41. 0.862×1000

42. 2.93×0.01

43. Estimate the distance in miles between Garden City, Kansas, and Wichita, Kansas, by rounding each given distance to the nearest ten.

Garden City
53.7 miles
Dodge City
79.2 miles   Pratt   71.2 miles   Wichita

Kansas

27. _____

28. _____

29. _____

30. _____

31. _____

32. _____

33. _____

34. _____

35. _____

36. _____

37. _____

38. _____

39. _____

40. _____

41. _____

42. _____

43. _____

A Divide Decimals.

B Estimate When Dividing Decimals.

C Divide Decimals by Powers of 10.

D Solve Problems by Dividing Decimals.

E Review Order of Operations to Simplify Expressions Containing Decimals.

4.5 DIVIDING DECIMALS AND ORDER OF OPERATIONS

Objective **A** Dividing Decimals

Dividing decimal numbers is similar to dividing whole numbers. The only difference is that we place a decimal point in the quotient. If the divisor is a whole number, we place the decimal point in the quotient directly above the decimal point in the dividend, and then divide as with whole numbers. Recall that division can be checked by multiplication.

$$
\begin{array}{r}
0.26 \leftarrow \text{quotient} \\
\text{divisor} \rightarrow 32\overline{)8.32} \leftarrow \text{dividend} \\
-6\ 4 \\
\hline
1\ 92 \\
-1\ 92 \\
\hline
0
\end{array}
$$

Check:
$$
\begin{array}{r}
0.26 \quad \text{Quotient} \\
\times \quad 32 \quad \text{Divisor} \\
\hline
52 \\
7\ 80 \\
\hline
8.32 \quad \text{Dividend}
\end{array}
$$

Dividing by a Whole Number

Step 1: Place the decimal point in the quotient directly above the decimal point in the dividend.

Step 2: Divide as with whole numbers.

PRACTICE PROBLEM 1

Divide: $517.2 \div 6$. Check your answer.

EXAMPLE 1 Divide: $270.2 \div 7$. Check your answer.

Solution:

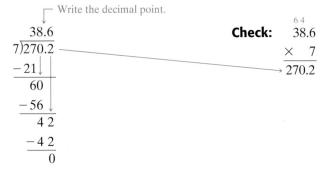

The quotient is 38.6.

☐ **Work Practice Problem 1**

PRACTICE PROBLEM 2

Divide: $26.19 \div 9$. Check your answer.

EXAMPLE 2 Divide: $60.24 \div 8$. Check your answer.

Solution:

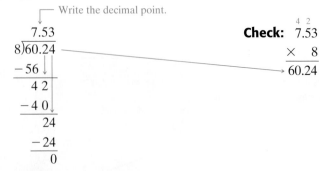

☐ **Work Practice Problem 2**

Answers

1. 86.2,   **2.** 2.91

Sometimes to continue dividing we need to insert zeros after the last digit in the dividend.

EXAMPLE 3 Divide and Check: $0.5 \div 4$.

Solution:

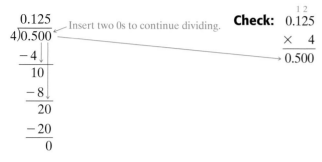

$$\begin{array}{r} 0.125 \\ 4\overline{)0.500} \\ -4 \\ \hline 10 \\ -8 \\ \hline 20 \\ -20 \\ \hline 0 \end{array}$$

Insert two 0s to continue dividing.

Check: $\overset{1\ 2}{0.125}$
$\underline{\times\quad 4}$
0.500

⬛ **Work Practice Problem 3**

Divide and check.
a. $0.4 \div 8$
b. $13.62 \div 12$

If the divisor is not a whole number, before we divide we need to move the decimal point to the right until the divisor is a whole number.

$$1.5\overline{)64.85}$$

divisor ⌐ └ dividend

To understand how this works, let's rewrite

$1.5\overline{)64.85}$ as $\dfrac{64.85}{1.5}$

and then multiply by 1 in the form of $\dfrac{10}{10}$. We use the form $\dfrac{10}{10}$ so that the denominator (divisor) becomes a whole number.

$$\frac{64.85}{1.5} = \frac{64.85}{1.5} \cdot 1 = \frac{64.85}{1.5} \cdot \frac{10}{10} = \frac{64.85 \cdot 10}{1.5 \cdot 10} = \frac{648.5}{15}$$

which can be written as $15.\overline{)648.5}$. Notice that

$1.5\overline{)64.85}$ is equivalent to $15.\overline{)648.5}$

The decimal points in the dividend and the divisor were both moved one place to the right, and the divisor is now a whole number. This procedure is summarized next:

Dividing by a Decimal

Step 1: Move the decimal point in the divisor to the right until the divisor is a whole number.

Step 2: Move the decimal point in the dividend to the right the *same number of places* as the decimal point was moved in Step 1.

Step 3: Divide. Place the decimal point in the quotient directly over the moved decimal point in the dividend.

PRACTICE PROBLEM 4
Divide: 166.88 ÷ 5.6

EXAMPLE 4 Divide: $10.764 \div 2.3$

Solution: We move the decimal points in the divisor and the dividend one place to the right so that the divisor is a whole number.

$$2.3\overline{)10.764}$$ becomes

$$
\begin{array}{r}
4.68 \\
23\overline{)107.64} \\
-92 \\
\hline
15\,6 \\
-13\,8 \\
\hline
1\,84 \\
-1\,84 \\
\hline
0
\end{array}
$$

■ **Work Practice Problem 4**

PRACTICE PROBLEM 5
Divide: 1.976 ÷ 0.16

EXAMPLE 5 Divide: $5.264 \div 0.32$

Solution:

$$0.32\overline{)5.264}$$ becomes

$$
\begin{array}{r}
16.45 \\
32\overline{)526.40} \quad \text{Insert one 0.} \\
-32 \\
\hline
206 \\
-192 \\
\hline
14\,4 \\
-12\,8 \\
\hline
1\,60 \\
-1\,60 \\
\hline
0
\end{array}
$$

■ **Work Practice Problem 5**

✔ **Concept Check** Is it always true that the number of decimal places in a quotient equals the sum of the decimal places in the dividend and divisor?

PRACTICE PROBLEM 6
Divide 23.4 ÷ 0.57. Round the quotient to the nearest hundredth.

EXAMPLE 6 Divide: 17.5 ÷ 0.48. Round the quotient to the nearest hundredth.

Solution: First we move the decimal points in the divisor and the dividend two places. Then we divide and round the quotient to the nearest hundredth.

— hundredths place

$$
\begin{array}{r}
36.458 \approx 36.46 \\
48\overline{)1750.000} \\
-144 \\
\hline
310 \\
-288 \\
\hline
22\,0 \\
-19\,2 \\
\hline
2\,80 \\
-2\,40 \\
\hline
400 \\
-384 \\
\hline
16
\end{array}
$$

"is approximately"

When rounding to the nearest hundredth, carry the division process out to one more decimal place, the thousandths place.

■ **Work Practice Problem 6**

Objective B Estimating When Dividing Decimals

Just as for addition, subtraction, and multiplication of decimals, we can estimate when dividing decimals to check the reasonableness of our answer.

EXAMPLE 7 Divide: $272.356 \div 28.4$. Then estimate to see whether the proposed result is reasonable.

Solution:

Exact:	Estimate 1		Estimate 2

$$
\begin{array}{r}
9.59 \\
284.\overline{)2723.56} \\
-2556 \\
\hline
1675 \\
-1420 \\
\hline
2556 \\
-2556 \\
\hline
0
\end{array}
$$

Estimate 1:
$$
\begin{array}{r}
9 \\
30\overline{)270}
\end{array}
$$
or
Estimate 2:
$$
\begin{array}{r}
10 \\
30\overline{)300}
\end{array}
$$

The estimate is 9 or 10, so 9.59 is reasonable.

Work Practice Problem 7

PRACTICE PROBLEM 7
Divide: $713.7 \div 91.5$. Then estimate to see whether the proposed answer is reasonable.

✔ **Concept Check** If a quotient is to be rounded to the nearest thousandth, to what place should the division be carried out? (Assume that the division carries out to your answer.)

Objective C Dividing Decimals by Powers of 10

As with multiplication, there are patterns that occur when we divide decimals by powers of 10 such as 10, 100, 1000, and so on.

$$\frac{569.2}{10} = 56.92 \quad \text{Move the decimal point } 1 \text{ place to the left.}$$
— 1 zero

$$\frac{569.2}{10,000} = 0.05692 \quad \text{Move the decimal point } 4 \text{ places to the left.}$$
— 4 zeros

This pattern suggests the following rule:

Dividing Decimals by Powers of 10 such as 10, 100, or 1000

Move the decimal point of the dividend to the *left* the same number of places as there are *zeros* in the power of 10.

EXAMPLES Divide.

8. $\frac{786.1}{1000} = 0.7861$ Move the decimal point *3 places* to the *left.*
— 3 zeros

9. $\frac{0.12}{10} = 0.012$ Move the decimal point *1 place* to the *left.*
— 1 zero

Work Practice Problems 8–9

PRACTICE PROBLEMS 8–9
Divide.
8. $\frac{128.3}{1000}$ **9.** $\frac{0.56}{10}$

Answers
7. 7.8, **8.** 0.1283, **9.** 0.056

✔ **Concept Check Answer**
ten-thousandths place

Objective D Solving Problems by Dividing Decimals

Many real-life problems involve dividing decimals.

A bag of fertilizer covers 1250 square feet of lawn. Tim Parker's lawn measures 14,800 square feet. How many bags of fertilizer does he need? If he can buy only whole bags of fertilizer, how many whole bags does he need?

EXAMPLE 10 Calculating Materials Needed for a Job

A gallon of paint covers a 250-square-foot area. If Betty Adkins wishes to paint a wall that measures 1450 square feet, how many gallons of paint does she need? If she can buy only gallon containers of paint, how many gallon containers does she need?

Solution:

1. UNDERSTAND. Read and reread the problem. We need to know how many 250s are in 1450, so we divide.

2. TRANSLATE.

In words:	number of gallons	is	square feet	divided by	square feet per gallon
	↓	↓	↓	↓	↓
Translate:	number of gallons	=	1450	÷	250

3. SOLVE. Let's see if our answer is reasonable by estimating. The dividend 1450 rounds to 1500 and divisor 250 rounds to 300. Then $1500 \div 300 = 5$.

$$
\begin{array}{r}
5.8 \\
250\overline{)1450.0} \\
-1250 \\
\hline
200\,0 \\
-200\,0 \\
\hline
0
\end{array}
$$

4. INTERPRET. *Check* your work. Since our estimate is close to our answer of 5, our answer is reasonable. *State* your conclusion: Betty needs 5.8 gallons of paint. If she can buy only gallon containers of paint, she needs 6 gallon containers of paint to complete the job.

Work Practice Problem 10

Objective E Simplifying Expressions with Decimals

In the remaining examples, we will review the order of operations by simplifying expressions that contain decimals.

Order of Operations

1. Perform all operations within parentheses ( ), brackets [ ], or other grouping symbols such as square roots or fraction bars.
2. Evaluate any expressions with exponents.
3. Multiply or divide in order from left to right.
4. Add or subtract in order from left to right.

Answer

10. 11.84 bags; 12 bags

EXAMPLE 11 Simplify: $723.6 \div 1000 \times 10$

Solution: Multiply or divide in order from left to right.

$$723.6 \div 1000 \times 10 = 0.7236 \times 10 \quad \text{Divide.}$$
$$= 7.236 \quad \text{Multipiy.}$$

Work Practice Problem 11

PRACTICE PROBLEM 11
Simplify: $897.8 \div 100 \times 10$

EXAMPLE 12 Simplify: $0.5(8.6 - 1.2)$

Solution: According to the order of operations, we simplify inside the parentheses first.

$$0.5(8.6 - 1.2) = 0.5(7.4) \quad \text{Subtract.}$$
$$= 3.7 \quad \text{Multiply.}$$

Work Practice Problem 12

PRACTICE PROBLEM 12
Simplify: $8.69(3.2 - 1.8)$

EXAMPLE 13 Simplify: $\dfrac{5.68 + (0.9)^2 \div 100}{0.2}$

Solution: First we simplify the numerator of the fraction. Then we divide.

$$\frac{5.68 + (0.9)^2 \div 100}{0.2} = \frac{5.68 + 0.81 \div 100}{0.2} \quad \text{Simplify } (0.9)^2.$$
$$= \frac{5.68 + 0.0081}{0.2} \quad \text{Divide.}$$
$$= \frac{5.6881}{0.2} \quad \text{Add.}$$
$$= 28.4405 \quad \text{Divide.}$$

Work Practice Problem 13

PRACTICE PROBLEM 13
Simplify: $\dfrac{20.06 - (1.2)^2 \div 10}{0.02}$

Answers
11. 89.78, **12.** 12.166, **13.** 995.8

CALCULATOR EXPLORATIONS

Calculator errors can easily be made by pressing an incorrect key or by not pressing a correct key hard enough. Estimation is a valuable tool that can be used to check calculator results.

EXAMPLE Use estimation to determine whether the calculator result is reasonable or not. (For example, a result that is not reasonable can occur if proper keys are not pressed.)

Simplify: $82.064 \div 23$
Calculator display: $\boxed{\quad 35.68 \quad}$

Solution: Round each number to the nearest 10. Since $80 \div 20 = 4$, the calculator display 35.68 is not reasonable.

Use estimation to determine whether each result is reasonable or not.

1. 102.62×41.8 Result: 428.9516

2. $174.835 \div 47.9$ Result: 3.65

3. $1025.68 - 125.42$ Result: 900.26

4. $562.781 + 2.96$ Result: 858.781

Mental Math

Recall properties of division and simplify.

1. $\dfrac{5.9}{1}$ **2.** $\dfrac{0.7}{0.7}$ **3.** $\dfrac{0}{9.86}$ **4.** $\dfrac{2.36}{0}$

5. $\dfrac{7.261}{7.261}$ **6.** $\dfrac{8.25}{1}$ **7.** $\dfrac{11.1}{0}$ **8.** $\dfrac{0}{89.96}$

4.5 EXERCISE SET

FOR EXTRA HELP

Student Solutions Manual   PH Math/Tutor Center   CD/Video for Review   MathXL®   MyMathLab

Objectives A B Mixed Practice *Divide. See Examples 1 through 5 and 7. For those exercises marked, also estimate to see if the answer is reasonable.*

1. $3\overline{)13.8}$ **2.** $2\overline{)11.8}$  **3.** $5\overline{)0.47}$ **4.** $6\overline{)0.51}$ **5.** $0.06\overline{)18}$

6. $0.04\overline{)20}$ **7.** $0.82\overline{)4.756}$ **8.** $0.92\overline{)3.312}$ **9.** $5.5\overline{)36.3}$

Exact:

Estimate: **10.** $2.2\overline{)21.78}$

Exact:

Estimate:

11. $6.195 \div 15$ **12.** $8.823 \div 17$ **13.** $0.54 \div 12$ **14.** $1.35 \div 18$ **15.** Divide 4.2 by 0.6.

16. Divide 3.6 by 0.9.   **17.** $0.27\overline{)1.296}$ **18.** $0.34\overline{)2.176}$ **19.** $0.02\overline{)42}$ **20.** $0.03\overline{)24}$

21. $0.6\overline{)18}$ **22.** $0.4\overline{)20}$ **23.** $0.005\overline{)35}$ **24.** $0.0007\overline{)35}$ **25.** $7.2\overline{)70.56}$

Exact:

Estimate:

26. $6.3\overline{)54.18}$ **27.** $5.4\overline{)51.84}$ **28.** $7.7\overline{)33.88}$ **29.** $\dfrac{1.215}{0.027}$ **30.** $\dfrac{3.213}{0.051}$

Exact:

Estimate:

31. $0.25\overline{)13.648}$ **32.** $0.75\overline{)49.866}$ **33.** $3.78\overline{)0.02079}$ **34.** $2.96\overline{)0.01332}$

Divide. Round the quotients as indicated. See Example 6.

35. Divide 429.34 by 2.4 and round the quotient to the nearest whole number.

36. Divide 54.8 by 2.6 and round the quotient to the nearest whole number.

37. Divide 0.549 by 0.023 and round the quotient to the nearest hundredth.

38. Divide 0.0453 by 0.98 and round the quotient to the nearest thousandth.

39. Divide 45.23 by 0.4 and round the quotient to the nearest tenth.

40. Divide 83.32 by 0.063 and round the quotient to the nearest tenth.

Objective **C** *Divide. See Examples 8 and 9.*

41. $\dfrac{54.982}{100}$ **42.** $\dfrac{342.54}{100}$ **43.** $\dfrac{26.87}{10}$ **44.** $\dfrac{13.49}{10}$ **45.** $\dfrac{12.9}{1000}$ **46.** $\dfrac{0.27}{1000}$

Objectives **A** **C** **Mixed Practice** *Divide. See Examples 1 through 6.*

47. $7\overline{)88.2}$ **48.** $9\overline{)130.5}$ **49.** $\dfrac{13.1}{10}$ **50.** $\dfrac{17.7}{10}$

51. $6.8\overline{)83.13}$ **52.** $4.8\overline{)123.72}$ **53.** $\dfrac{456.25}{10,000}$ **54.** $\dfrac{986.11}{10,000}$

Objective **D** *Solve. See Example 10.*

55. Dorren Schmidt pays $73.86 per month to pay back a loan of $1772.64. In how many months will the loan be paid off?

56. Josef Jones is painting the walls of a room. The walls have a total area of 546 square feet. A quart of paint covers 52 square feet. If he must buy paint in whole quarts, how many quarts does he need?

57. The leading monetary winner in men's professional golf in 2003 was Vijay Singh. He earned $7,573,907. Suppose he had earned this working 40 hours per week for a year. Determine his hourly wage to the nearest cent. (*Note:* There are 52 weeks in a year.) (*Source:* 2005 *World Almanac*)

58. Juanita Gomez bought unleaded gasoline for her car at $1.169 per gallon. She wanted to keep a record of how many gallons her car is using but forgot to write down how many gallons she purchased. She wrote a check for $27.71 to pay for it. How many gallons, to the nearest tenth of a gallon, did she buy?

59. A pound of fertilizer covers 39 square feet of lawn. Vivian Bulgakov's lawn measures 7883.5 square feet. How much fertilizer, to the nearest tenth of a pound, does she need to buy?

60. A page of a book contains about 1.5 kilobytes of information. If a computer disk can hold 740 kilobytes of information, how many pages of a book can be stored on one computer disk? Round to the nearest tenth of a page.

61. There are approximately 39.37 inches in 1 meter. How many meters, to the nearest tenth of a meter, are there in 200 inches?

←——1 meter——→
←— ≈39.37 inches —→

62. There are 2.54 centimeters in 1 inch. How many inches are there in 50 centimeters? Round to the nearest tenth.

←—— 1 inch ——→
←— 2.54 cm —→

63. In the United States, an average child will wear down 730 crayons by his or her tenth birthday. Find the number of boxes of 64 crayons this is equivalent to. Round to the nearest tenth. (*Source:* Binney & Smith Inc.)

64. American farmers receive an average of $238 per 100 chickens. What is the average price per chicken? (*Source:* National Agricultural Statistics Service)

A child is to receive a dose of 0.5 teaspoon of cough medicine every 4 hours. If the bottle contains 4 fluid ounces, answer Exercises 65 through 68.

65. A fluid ounce equals 6 teaspoons. How many teaspoons are in 4 fluid ounces?

66. The bottle of medicine contains how many doses for the child?

67. If the child takes a dose every four hours, how many days will the medicine last?

68. If the child takes a dose every six hours, how many days will the medicine last?

69. During the 24 Hours of the Le Mans endurance auto race in 2004, the winning team of Seiji Ara, Tom Kristensen, and Rinaldo Capello drove a total of 3211.2 miles in 24 hours. What was their average speed in miles per hour? (*Source:* Automobile Club de l'Ouest)

70. In 2000, Kenyan runner Tegla Loroupe set a new world record for the women's 20,000-meter event. Her time for the event was 3926.6 seconds. What was her average speed in meters per second? Round to the nearest tenth. (*Source:* 2005 *Guinness World Record.*)

71. Lauren Jackson of the WNBA's Seattle Storm scored a total of 634 points during the 31 basketball games she played in the 2004 regular season. What was the average number of points she scored per game? Round to the nearest hundredth. (*Source:* Women's National Basketball Association)

72. During the 2004 Major League Soccer season, the Metro Stars was the top-scoring team with a total of 47 goals throughout the season. The Metro Stars played 30 games. What was the average number of goals the team scored per game? Round to the nearest hundredth. (*Source:* Major League Soccer)

Objective E *Simplify each expression. See Examples 11 through 13.*

73. $0.7(6 - 2.5)$

74. $1.4(2 - 1.8)$

75. $\dfrac{0.29 + 1.69}{3}$

76. $\dfrac{1.697 - 0.29}{0.7}$

77. $30.03 + 5.1 \times 9.9$

78. $60 - 6.02 \times 8.97$

79. $7.8 - 4.83 \div 2.1 + 9.2$

80. $90 - 62.1 \div 2.7 + 8.6$

81. $93.07 \div 10 \times 100$

82. $35.04 \div 100 \times 10$

83. $\dfrac{7.8 + 1.1 \times 100 - 3.6}{0.2}$

84. $\dfrac{9.6 - 7.8 \div 10 + 1.2}{0.02}$

85. $5(20.6 - 2.06) - (0.8)^2$

86. $(10.6 - 9.8)^2 \div 0.01 + 8.6$

87. $6 \div 0.1 + 8.9 \times 10 - 4.6$

88. $8 \div 10 + 7.6 \times 0.1 - (0.1)^2$

Review

Write each decimal as a fraction.

89. 0.9

90. 0.7

91. 0.05

92. 0.08

Concept Extensions

Mixed Practice (Sections 4.3, 4.4, 4.5) *Perform the indicated operation.*

93. $1.278 \div 0.3$

94. 1.278×0.3

95. $1.278 + 0.3$

96. $1.278 - 0.3$

97.
$$\begin{array}{r} 8.6 \\ \times\ 3.1 \\ \hline \end{array}$$

98. $7.2 + 0.05 + 49.1$

99.
$$\begin{array}{r} 1000 \\ -\ \ 95.71 \\ \hline \end{array}$$

100. $\dfrac{87.2}{10{,}000}$

Choose the best estimate.

101. 8.62×41.7
 a. 36
 b. 32
 c. 360
 d. 3.6

102. $1.437 + 20.69$
 a. 34
 b. 22
 c. 3.4
 d. 2.2

103. $78.6 \div 97$
 a. 7.86
 b. 0.786
 c. 786
 d. 7860

104. $302.729 - 28.697$
 a. 270
 b. 20
 c. 27
 d. 300

Recall from Section 1.7 that the average of a list of numbers is their total divided by how many numbers there are in the list. Use this procedure to find the average of the test scores listed in Exercises 105 and 106. If necessary, round to the nearest tenth.

105. $86, 78, 91, 87$

106. $56, 75, 80$

107. In 2003, American manufacturers shipped approximately 745.94 million music CDs to retailers. How many music CDs were shipped per week on average? (*Source:* Recording Industry Association of America)

△ **108.** The area of a rectangle is 38.7 square feet. If its width is 4.5 feet, find its length.

△ **109.** The perimeter of a square is 180.8 centimeters. Find the length of a side.

△ **110.** Don Larson is building a horse corral that's shaped like a rectangle with dimensions of 24.28 meters by 15.675 meters. He plans to make a four-wire fence; that is, he will string four wires around the corral. How much wire will he need?

111. When dividing decimals, describe the process you use to place the decimal point in the quotient.

112. In your own words, describe how to quickly divide a number by a power of 10 such as 10, 100, 1000, etc.

To convert wind speeds in miles per hour to knots, divide by 1.15. Use this information and the Saffir-Simpson Hurricane Intensity chart below to answer Exercises 113–114. Round to the nearest tenth.

113. The chart gives wind speeds in miles per hour. What is the range of wind speeds for a Category 1 hurricane in knots?

114. What is the range of wind speeds for a Category 4 hurricane in knots?

Saffir-Simpson Hurricane Intensity Scale

Category	Wind Speed	Barometric Pressure [inches of mercury (Hg)]	Storm Surge	Damage Potential
1 (Weak)	75–95 mph	≥28.94 in.	4–5 ft	Minimal damage to vegetation
2 (Moderate)	96–110 mph	28.50–28.93 in.	6–8 ft	Moderate damage to houses
3 (Strong)	111–130 mph	27.91–28.49 in.	9–12 ft	Extensive damage to small buildings
4 (Very Strong)	131–155 mph	27.17–27.90 in.	13–18 ft	Extreme structural damage
5 (Devastating)	>155 mph	<27.17 in.	>18 ft	Catastrophic building failures possible

 THE BIGGER PICTURE   **Operations on Sets of Numbers**

Continue your outline from Sections 1.7, 1.9, 2.5, and 3.4. Suggestions are once again written to help you complete this part of your outline.

I. Some Operations on Sets of Numbers

  A. Whole Numbers

    1. Add or Subtract (Sections 1.3, 1.4)

    2. Multiply or Divide (Sections 1.6, 1.7)

    3. Exponent (Section 1.9)

    4. Square Root (Section 1.9)

    5. Order of Operations (Section 1.9)

  B. Fractions

    1. Simplify (Section 2.3)

    2. Multiply (Section 2.4)

    3. Divide (Section 2.5)

    4. Add or Subtract (Section 3.4)

  C. Decimals

    1. Add or Subtract: Line up decimal points.

$$\begin{array}{r} 1.27 \\ +0.6 \\ \hline 1.87 \end{array}$$

    2. Multiply:

$$\begin{array}{r} 2.56 \\ \times\ 3.2 \\ \hline 512 \\ 7680 \\ \hline 8.192 \end{array}$$

    2 decimal places
    1 decimal place
    2 + 1 = 3
    3 decimal places

3. Divide:

$$8\overline{)5.6} = 0.7 \qquad 0.6\overline{)0.786} = 1.31$$

Perform indicated operations.

1. $3.6 + 8.092 + 10.48$

2. $7 - 3.049$

3. 91.332×100

4. $\dfrac{68}{10}$

5. $\begin{array}{r} 5.2 \\ \times\ 0.27 \end{array}$

6. $9\overline{)77.94}$

7. $0.35\overline{)0.01785}$

8. $2.3 - (0.4)^2$

9. $\dfrac{8}{15} - \dfrac{2}{5}$

10. $\dfrac{8}{15} \cdot \dfrac{2}{5}$

4.6 FRACTIONS AND DECIMALS

Objectives

A Write Fractions as Decimals.

B Compare Fractions and Decimals.

C Solve Area Problems Containing Fractions and Decimals.

Objective **A** Writing Fractions as Decimals

To write a fraction as a decimal, we interpret the fraction bar to mean division and find the quotient.

Writing Fractions as Decimals

To write a fraction as a decimal, divide the numerator by the denominator.

EXAMPLE 1 Write $\frac{1}{4}$ as a decimal.

Solution: $\frac{1}{4} = 1 \div 4$

$$
\begin{array}{r}
0.25 \\
4\overline{)1.00} \\
-8 \\
\hline
20 \\
-20 \\
\hline
0
\end{array}
$$

Thus, $\frac{1}{4}$ written as a decimal is 0.25.

■ **Work Practice Problem 1**

PRACTICE PROBLEM 1

a. Write $\frac{2}{5}$ as a decimal.

b. Write $\frac{9}{40}$ as a decimal.

EXAMPLE 2 Write $\frac{2}{3}$ as a decimal.

Solution:

$$
\begin{array}{r}
0.666\ldots \\
3\overline{)2.000} \\
-18 \\
\hline
20 \\
-18 \\
\hline
20 \\
-18 \\
\hline
2
\end{array}
$$

This pattern will continue because $\frac{2}{3} = 0.6666\ldots$

Remainder is 2, then 0 is brought down.

Remainder is 2, then 0 is brought down.

Remainder is 2.

Notice the digit 2 keeps occurring as the remainder. This will continue so that the digit 6 will keep repeating in the quotient. We place a bar over the digit 6 to indicate that it repeats.

$$\frac{2}{3} = 0.666\ldots = 0.\overline{6}$$

We can also write a decimal approximation for $\frac{2}{3}$. For example, $\frac{2}{3}$ rounded to the nearest hundredth is 0.67. This can be written as $\frac{2}{3} \approx 0.67$.

■ **Work Practice Problem 2**

PRACTICE PROBLEM 2

a. Write $\frac{5}{6}$ as a decimal.

b. Write $\frac{2}{9}$ as a decimal.

Answers
1. a. 0.4, **b.** 0.225,
2. a. $0.8\overline{3}$, **b.** $0.\overline{2}$

Write $\dfrac{28}{13}$ as a decimal. Round to the nearest thousandth.

EXAMPLE 3 Write $\dfrac{22}{7}$ as a decimal. (The fraction $\dfrac{22}{7}$ is an approximation for π.) Round to the nearest hundredth.

Solution:

$$3.142 \approx 3.14$$

Carry the division out to the thousandths place.

$$
\begin{array}{r}
3.142 \\
7\overline{)22.000} \\
-21 \\
\hline
1\,0 \\
-\ 7 \\
\hline
30 \\
-28 \\
\hline
20 \\
-14 \\
\hline
6
\end{array}
$$

The fraction $\dfrac{22}{7}$ in decimal form is approximately 3.14.

Work Practice Problem 3

PRACTICE PROBLEM 4

Write $3\dfrac{5}{16}$ as a decimal.

EXAMPLE 4 Write $2\dfrac{3}{16}$ as a decimal.

Solution:

Option 1. Write the fractional part only as a decimal.

$$\frac{3}{16} \longrightarrow 16\overline{)3.0000}$$

$$
\begin{array}{r}
0.1875 \\
16\overline{)3.0000} \\
-1\,6 \\
\hline
1\,40 \\
-1\,28 \\
\hline
120 \\
-112 \\
\hline
80 \\
-80 \\
\hline
0
\end{array}
$$

Thus $2\dfrac{3}{16} = 2.1875$

Option 2. Write $2\dfrac{3}{16}$ as an improper fraction, and divide.

$$2\frac{3}{16} = \frac{35}{16} \longrightarrow 16\overline{)35.0000}$$

$$
\begin{array}{r}
2.1875 \\
16\overline{)35.0000} \\
-32 \\
\hline
3\,0 \\
-1\,6 \\
\hline
1\,40 \\
-1\,28 \\
\hline
120 \\
-112 \\
\hline
80 \\
-80 \\
\hline
0
\end{array}
$$

Thus $2\dfrac{3}{16} = 2.1875$

Work Practice Problem 4

Some fractions may be written as decimals using our knowledge of decimals. From Section 4.1, we know that if the denominator of a fraction is 10, 100, 1000, or so on, we can immediately write the fraction as a decimal. For example,

$$\frac{4}{10} = 0.4, \qquad \frac{12}{100} = 0.12, \text{ and so on.}$$

EXAMPLE 5   Write $\frac{4}{5}$ as a decimal.

Solution: Let's write $\frac{4}{5}$ as an equivalent fraction with a denominator of 10.

$$\frac{4}{5} = \frac{4}{5} \cdot \frac{2}{2} = \frac{8}{10} = 0.8$$

◻ **Work Practice Problem 5**

EXAMPLE 6   Write $\frac{1}{25}$ as a decimal.

Solution: $\frac{1}{25} = \frac{1}{25} \cdot \frac{4}{4} = \frac{4}{100} = 0.04$

◻ **Work Practice Problem 6**

✔ **Concept Check**   Suppose you are writing the fraction $\frac{9}{16}$ as a decimal. How do you know you have made a mistake if your answer is 1.735?

Objective B Comparing Decimals and Fractions

Now we can compare decimals and fractions by writing fractions as equivalent decimals.

EXAMPLE 7   Insert $<$, $>$, or $=$ to form a true statement.

$$\frac{1}{8} \qquad 0.12$$

Solution: First we write $\frac{1}{8}$ as an equivalent decimal. Then we compare decimal places.

$$\begin{array}{r} 0.125 \\ 8\overline{)1.000} \\ \underline{-8} \\ 20 \\ \underline{-16} \\ 40 \\ \underline{-40} \\ 0 \end{array}$$

Original numbers	$\frac{1}{8}$	0.12
Decimals	0.125	0.120
Compare	0.125 > 0.12	

Thus, $\dfrac{1}{8} > 0.12$

◻ **Work Practice Problem 7**

EXAMPLE 8   Insert $<$, $>$, or $=$ to form a true statement.

$$0.\overline{7} \qquad \frac{7}{9}$$

Solution: We write $\frac{7}{9}$ as a decimal and then compare.

$$\begin{array}{r} 0.77\ldots = 0.\overline{7} \\ 9\overline{)7.00} \\ \underline{-6\ 3} \\ 70 \\ \underline{-63} \\ 7 \end{array}$$

Original numbers	$0.\overline{7}$	$\frac{7}{9}$
Decimals	$0.\overline{7}$	$0.\overline{7}$
Compare	$0.\overline{7} = 0.\overline{7}$	

Thus, $0.\overline{7} = \dfrac{7}{9}$

◻ **Work Practice Problem 8**

PRACTICE PROBLEM 5

Write $\frac{3}{5}$ as a decimal.

PRACTICE PROBLEM 6

Write $\frac{3}{50}$ as a decimal.

PRACTICE PROBLEM 7

Insert $<$, $>$, or $=$ to form a true statement.

$$\frac{1}{5} \qquad 0.25$$

PRACTICE PROBLEM 8

Insert $<$, $>$, or $=$ to form a true statement.

a. $\dfrac{1}{2}$ 0.54   **b.** $0.\overline{4}$ $\dfrac{4}{9}$

c. $\dfrac{5}{7}$ 0.72

Answers

5. 0.6,   **6.** 0.06,   **7.** <,
8. a. <,   **b.** =,   **c.** <

✔ **Concept Check Answer**

$\dfrac{9}{16}$ is less than 1 while 1.735 is greater than 1.

PRACTICE PROBLEM 9

Write the numbers in order from smallest to largest.

a. $\frac{1}{3}, 0.302, \frac{3}{8}$ **b.** $1.26, 1\frac{1}{4}, 1\frac{2}{5}$

c. $0.4, 0.41, \frac{5}{7}$

EXAMPLE 9 Write the numbers in order from smallest to largest.

$$\frac{9}{20}, \frac{4}{9}, 0.456$$

Solution:

Original numbers	$\frac{9}{20}$	$\frac{4}{9}$	0.456
Decimals	0.450	0.444...	0.456
Compare in order	2nd	1st	3rd

Written in order, we have

1st 2nd 3rd

$$\frac{4}{9}, \frac{9}{20}, 0.456$$

Work Practice Problem 9

Objective C Solving Area Problems Containing Fractions and Decimals

Sometimes real-life problems contain both fractions and decimals. In this section, we solve such problems concerning area. In the next example, we review the area of a triangle. This concept will be studied more in depth in a later chapter.

PRACTICE PROBLEM 10

Find the area of the triangle.

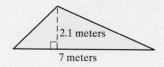

EXAMPLE 10 The area of a triangle is Area $= \frac{1}{2} \cdot$ base $\cdot$ height. Find the area of the triangle shown.

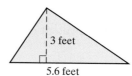

Solution:

$$\text{Area} = \frac{1}{2} \cdot \text{base} \cdot \text{height}$$
$$= \frac{1}{2} \cdot 5.6 \cdot 3$$
$$= 0.5 \cdot 5.6 \cdot 3 \quad \text{Write } \frac{1}{2} \text{ as the decimal 0.5.}$$
$$= 8.4$$

The area of the triangle is 8.4 square feet.

Work Practice Problem 10

Answers

9. a. $0.302, \frac{1}{3}, \frac{3}{8}$, **b.** $1\frac{1}{4}, 1.26, 1\frac{2}{5}$,

c. $0.4, 0.41, \frac{5}{7}$, **10.** 7.35 sq m

4.6 EXERCISE SET

FOR EXTRA HELP

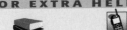
Student Solutions Manual

PH Math/Tutor Center

CD/Video for Review

Math XL
MathXL®

MyMathLab
MyMathLab

Objective **A** *Write each number as a decimal. See Examples 1 through 6.*

1. $\dfrac{1}{5}$ **2.** $\dfrac{1}{20}$ **3.** $\dfrac{17}{25}$ **4.** $\dfrac{13}{25}$ **5.** $\dfrac{3}{4}$ **6.** $\dfrac{3}{8}$

7. $\dfrac{2}{25}$ **8.** $\dfrac{3}{25}$ **9.** $\dfrac{6}{5}$ **10.** $\dfrac{5}{4}$ **11.** $\dfrac{11}{12}$ **12.** $\dfrac{5}{12}$

13. $\dfrac{17}{40}$ **14.** $\dfrac{19}{25}$ **15.** $\dfrac{9}{20}$ **16.** $\dfrac{31}{40}$ **17.** $\dfrac{1}{3}$ **18.** $\dfrac{7}{9}$

19. $\dfrac{7}{16}$ **20.** $\dfrac{9}{16}$ **21.** $\dfrac{7}{11}$ **22.** $\dfrac{9}{11}$ **23.** $5\dfrac{17}{20}$ **24.** $4\dfrac{7}{8}$

25. $\dfrac{78}{125}$ **26.** $\dfrac{159}{375}$

Round each number as indicated.

27. Round your decimal answer to Exercise 17 to the nearest hundredth.

28. Round your decimal answer to Exercise 18 to the nearest hundredth.

29. Round your decimal answer to Exercise 19 to the nearest hundredth.

30. Round your decimal answer to Exercise 20 to the nearest hundredth.

31. Round your decimal answer to Exercise 21 to the nearest tenth.

32. Round your decimal answer to Exercise 22 to the nearest tenth.

Write each fraction as a decimal. If necessary, round to the nearest hundredth.

33. During a recent Boston Marathon, $\dfrac{17}{25}$ of the starting runners over the age of 70 finished the race. (*Source:* Boston Athletic Association)

34. About $\dfrac{21}{50}$ of all blood donors have type A blood. (*Source:* American Red Cross Biomedical Services)

35. Of the U.S. mountains that are over 14,000 feet in elevation, $\frac{56}{91}$ are located in Colorado. (*Source:* U.S. Geological Survey)

36. By October 2000, $\frac{29}{46}$ of all individuals who had flown in space were citizens of the United States. (*Source:* Congressional Research Service)

37. The United States contains the greatest fraction of people who use the internet, with about $\frac{67}{94}$ people using it. (*Source:* UCLA Center for Communication Policy)

38. Hungary has the lowest fraction of people using the Internet, with only $\frac{7}{40}$ people using it. (*Source:* UCLA Center for Communication Policy)

Objective **B** *Insert* <, >, *or* = *to form a true statement. See Examples 7 and 8.*

39. 0.562   0.569

40. 0.983   0.988

41. 0.215 $\frac{43}{200}$

42. $\frac{29}{40}$ 0.725

43. $\frac{9}{100}$ 0.0932

44. $\frac{1}{200}$ 0.00563

45. $0.\overline{6}$ $\frac{5}{6}$

46. $0.\overline{1}$ $\frac{2}{17}$

47. $\frac{51}{91}$ $0.56\overline{4}$

48. $0.58\overline{3}$ $\frac{6}{11}$

49. $\frac{4}{7}$ 0.14

50. $\frac{5}{9}$ 0.557

51. 1.38 $\frac{18}{13}$

52. 0.372 $\frac{22}{59}$

53. 7.123 $\frac{456}{64}$

54. 12.713 $\frac{89}{7}$

Write the numbers in order from smallest to largest. See Example 9.

55. 0.34, 0.35, 0.32

56. 0.47, 0.42, 0.40

57. 0.49, 0.491, 0.498

58. 0.72, 0.727, 0.728

59. $\frac{3}{4}$, 0.78, 0.73

60. $\frac{2}{5}$, 0.49, 0.42

61. $\frac{4}{7}$, 0.453, 0.412

62. $\frac{6}{9}$, 0.663, 0.668

63. $5.23, \dfrac{42}{8}, 5.34$ **64.** $7.56, \dfrac{67}{9}, 7.562$ **65.** $\dfrac{12}{5}, 2.37, \dfrac{17}{8}$ **66.** $\dfrac{29}{16}, 1.75, \dfrac{59}{32}$

Objective **C** *Find the area of each triangle or rectangle. See Example 10.*

△ **67.**

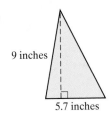

9 inches

5.7 inches

△ **68.**

4.4 feet

17 feet

△ **69.**

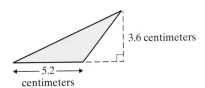

3.6 centimeters

5.2 centimeters

△ **70.**

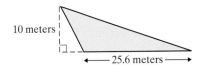

10 meters

25.6 meters

△ **71.**

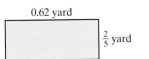

0.62 yard

$\dfrac{2}{5}$ yard

△ **72.**

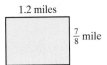

1.2 miles

$\dfrac{7}{8}$ mile

Review

Simplify. See Sections 1.9 and 3.5.

73. 2^3 **74.** 5^4 **75.** $6^2 \cdot 2$ **76.** $4 \cdot 3^4$ **77.** $\left(\dfrac{1}{3}\right)^4$

78. $\left(\dfrac{4}{5}\right)^3$ **79.** $\left(\dfrac{3}{5}\right)^2$ **80.** $\left(\dfrac{7}{2}\right)^2$ **81.** $\left(\dfrac{2}{5}\right)\left(\dfrac{5}{2}\right)^2$ **82.** $\left(\dfrac{2}{3}\right)^2\left(\dfrac{3}{2}\right)^3$

Concept Extensions

Without calculating, describe each number as < 1, $= 1$, or > 1. See the Concept Check in this section.

83. 1.0 **84.** 1.0000 **85.** 1.00001 **86.** $\dfrac{101}{99}$ **87.** $\dfrac{99}{100}$ **88.** $\dfrac{99}{99}$

In 2004, there were 10,649 commercial radio stations in the United States. The most popular formats are listed in the table along with their counts. Use this graph to answer Exercises 89–92.

89. Write the fraction of radio stations with a country music format as a decimal. Round to the nearest thousandth.

90. Write the fraction of radio stations with a news/talk format as a decimal. Round to the nearest hundredth.

91. Estimate, by rounding each number in the table to the nearest hundred, the total number of stations with the top six formats in 2004.

92. Use your estimate from Exercise 91 to write the fraction of radio stations accounted for by the top six formats as a decimal. Round to the nearest hundredth.

Top Commercial Radio Station Formats in 2004

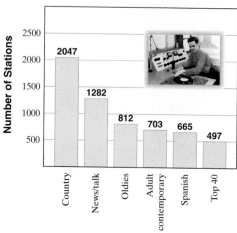

Format (Total stations: 10,649)

93. Describe 2 ways to determine the larger of two fractions.

94. Describe two ways to write fractions as decimals.

95. Describe two ways to write mixed numbers as decimals.

Find the value of each expression. Give the result as a decimal.

96. $2(7.8) - \dfrac{1}{5}$

97. $(9.6)(5) - \dfrac{3}{4}$

98. $8.25 - \left(\dfrac{1}{2}\right)^2$

99. $\left(\dfrac{1}{10}\right)^2 + (1.6)(2.1)$

100. $\dfrac{1}{4}(9.6 + 5.2)$

101. $\dfrac{3}{8}(5.9 - 4.7)$

CHAPTER 4   Group Activity

Maintaining a Checking Account
(Sections 4.1, 4.2, 4.3, 4.4)

This activity may be completed by working in groups or individually.

A checking account is a convenient way of handling money and paying bills. To open a checking account, the bank or savings and loan association requires a customer to make a deposit. Then the customer receives a checkbook that contains checks, deposit slips, and a register for recording checks written and deposits made. It is important to record all payments and deposits that affect the account. It is also important to keep the checkbook balance current by subtracting checks written and adding deposits made.

About once a month checking customers receive a statement from the bank listing all activity that the account has had in the last month. The statement lists a beginning balance, all checks and deposits, any service charges made against the account, and an ending balance. Because it may take several days for checks that a customer has written to clear the banking system, the check register may list checks that do not appear on the monthly bank statement. These checks are called **outstanding checks.** Deposits that are recorded in the check register but do not appear on the statement are called **deposits in transit.** Because of these differences, it is important to balance, or reconcile, the checkbook against the monthly statement. The steps for doing so are listed below.

Balancing or Reconciling a Checkbook

Step 1: Place a check mark in the checkbook register next to each check and deposit listed on the monthly bank statement. Any entries in the register without a check mark are outstanding checks or deposits in transit.

Step 2: Find the ending checkbook register balance and add to it any outstanding checks and any interest paid on the account.

Step 3: From the total in Step 2, subtract any deposits in transit and any service charges.

Step 4: Compare the amount found in Step 3 with the ending balance listed on the bank statement. If they are the same, the checkbook balances with the bank statement. Be sure to update the check register with service charges and interest.

Step 5: If the checkbook does not balance, recheck the balancing process. Next, make sure that the running checkbook register balance was calculated correctly. Finally, compare the checkbook register with the statement to make sure that each check was recorded for the correct amount.

For the checkbook register and monthly bank statement given:

a. *update the checkbook register*   **b.** *list the outstanding checks and deposits in transit*
c. *balance the checkbook—be sure to update the register with any interest or service fees*

Checkbook Register						Balance
#	Date	Description	Payment	✔	Deposit	425.86
114	4/1	Market Basket	30.27			
115	4/3	May's Texaco	8.50			
	4/4	Cash at ATM	50.00			
116	4/6	UNO Bookstore	121.38			
	4/7	Deposit			100.00	
117	4/9	MasterCard	84.16			
118	4/10	Blockbuster	6.12			
119	4/12	Kroger	18.72			
120	4/14	Parking sticker	18.50			
	4/15	Direct deposit			294.36	
121	4/20	Rent	395.00			
122	4/25	Student fees	20.00			
	4/28	Deposit			75.00	

First National Bank Monthly Statement 4/30		
BEGINNING BALANCE:		425.86
Date	Number	Amount
CHECKS AND ATM WITHDRAWALS		
4/3	114	30.27
4/4	ATM	50.00
4/11	117	84.16
4/13	115	8.50
4/15	119	18.72
4/22	121	395.00
DEPOSITS		
4/7		100.00
4/15	Direct deposit	294.36
SERVICE CHARGES		
Low balance fee		7.50
INTEREST		
Credited 4/30		1.15
ENDING BALANCE:		227.22

Chapter 4 Vocabulary Check

Fill in each blank with one of the words listed below.

vertically	decimal	and
sum	denominator	numerator

1. Like fractional notation, _____ notation is used to denote a part of a whole.
2. To write fractions as decimals, divide the _____ by the _____.
3. To add or subtract decimals, write the decimals so that the decimal points line up _____.
4. When writing decimals in words, write "_____" for the decimal point.
5. When multiplying decimals, the decimal point in the product is placed so that the number of decimal places in the product is equal to the _____ of the number of decimal places in the factors.

Helpful Hint

Are you preparing for your test? Don't forget to take the Chapter 4 Test on page 315. Then check your answers at the back of the text and use the Chapter Test Prep Video CD to see the fully worked-out solutions to any of the exercises you want to review.

4 Chapter Highlights

DEFINITIONS AND CONCEPTS	EXAMPLES

Section 4.1   Introduction to Decimals

PLACE-VALUE CHART

hundreds	tens	ones		tenths	hundredths	thousandths	ten-thousandths	hundred-thousandths
		4	.	2	6	5		
100	10	1	decimal point	$\frac{1}{10}$	$\frac{1}{100}$	$\frac{1}{1000}$	$\frac{1}{10,000}$	$\frac{1}{100,000}$

4.265 means

$$4 \cdot 1 + 2 \cdot \frac{1}{10} + 6 \cdot \frac{1}{100} + 5 \cdot \frac{1}{1000}$$

or

$$4 + \frac{2}{10} + \frac{6}{100} + \frac{5}{1000}$$

WRITING (OR READING) A DECIMAL IN WORDS

Step 1. Write the whole number part in words.

Step 2. Write "and" for the decimal point.

Step 3. Write the decimal part in words as though it were a whole number, followed by the place value of the last digit.

A decimal written in words can be written in standard form by reversing the above procedure.

Write 3.08 in words.
Three and eight hundredths

Write "four and twenty-one thousandths" in standard form.

4.021

DEFINITIONS AND CONCEPTS	**EXAMPLES**

Section 4.2 Order and Rounding

To **compare decimals,** compare digits in the same place from left to right. When two digits are not equal, the number with the larger digit is the larger decimal.

$3.0261 > 3.0186$ because

$$2 > 1$$

TO ROUND DECIMALS TO A PLACE VALUE TO THE RIGHT OF THE DECIMAL POINT

Step 1. Locate the digit to the right of the given place value.

Step 2. If this digit is 5 or greater, add 1 to the digit in the given place value and delete all digits to its right. If this digit is less than 5, delete all digits to the right of the given place value.

Round 86.1256 to the nearest hundredth.

hundredths place

Step 1. 86.12⑤6

digit to the right

Step 2. Since the digit to the right is 5 or greater, we add 1 to the digit in the hundredths place and delete all digits to its right.

86.1256 rounded to the nearest hundredth is 86.13.

Section 4.3 Adding and Subtracting Decimals

TO ADD OR SUBTRACT DECIMALS

Step 1. Write the decimals so that the decimal points line up vertically.

Step 2. Add or subtract as with whole numbers.

Step 3. Place the decimal point in the sum or difference so that it lines up vertically with the decimal points in the problem.

Add: $4.6 + 0.28$ Subtract: $2.8 - 1.04$

$$
\begin{array}{r}
4.60 \\
+\,0.28 \\
\hline
4.88
\end{array}
\qquad
\begin{array}{r}
{}^{7\ 10} \\
2.8\cancel{0} \\
-\,1.04 \\
\hline
1.76
\end{array}
$$

Section 4.4 Multiplying Decimals and Circumference of a Circle

TO MULTIPLY DECIMALS

Step 1. Multiply the decimals as though they are whole numbers.

Step 2. The decimal point in the product is placed so that the number of decimal places in the product is equal to the *sum* of the number of decimal places in the factors.

The **circumference** of a circle is the distance around the circle.

$C = 2 \cdot \pi \cdot \text{radius}$ or
$C = \pi \cdot \text{diameter}$,

where $\pi \approx 3.14$ or $\dfrac{22}{7}$.

Multiply: 1.48×5.9

$$
\begin{array}{r}
1.4\,8 \leftarrow \text{2 decimal places} \\
\times\ \ 5.9 \leftarrow \text{1 decimal place} \\
\hline
1\,3\,3\,2 \\
7\,4\,0\,0 \\
\hline
8.7\,3\,2 \leftarrow \text{3 decimal places}
\end{array}
$$

Find the exact circumference of a circle with radius 5 miles and an approximation by using 3.14 for π.

$$
\begin{aligned}
C &= 2 \cdot \pi \cdot \text{radius} \\
&= 2 \cdot \pi \cdot 5 \\
&= 10\pi \\
&\approx 10(3.14) \\
&= 31.4
\end{aligned}
$$

The circumference is exactly 10π miles and *approximately* 31.4 miles.

continued

DEFINITIONS AND CONCEPTS	**EXAMPLES**
Section 4.5 Dividing Decimals and Order of Operations	

<table>
<tr>
<td>

TO DIVIDE DECIMALS

Step 1. If the divisor is not a whole number, move the decimal point in the divisor to the right until the divisor is a whole number.

Step 2. Move the decimal point in the dividend to the right the *same number of places* as the decimal point was moved in step 1.

Step 3. Divide. The decimal point in the quotient is directly over the moved decimal point in the dividend.

ORDER OF OPERATIONS

1. Perform all operations within parentheses ( ), brackets [ ], or grouping symbols such as square roots or fraction bars.

2. Evaluate any expressions with exponents.

3. Multiply or divide in order from left to right.

4. Add or subtract in order from left to right.

</td>
<td>

Divide: $1.118 \div 2.6$

$$
\begin{array}{r}
0.43 \\
2.6\overline{)1.118} \\
-1\,04 \\
\hline
78 \\
-78 \\
\hline
0
\end{array}
$$

Simplify.

$$1.9(12.8 - 4.1) = 1.9(8.7) \quad \text{Subtract.}$$
$$= 16.53 \quad \text{Multiply.}$$

</td>
</tr>
</table>

Section 4.6 Fractions and Decimals	

<table>
<tr>
<td>

To **write fractions as decimals,** divide the numerator by the denominator.

</td>
<td>

Write $\dfrac{3}{8}$ as a decimal.

$$
\begin{array}{r}
0.375 \\
8\overline{)3.000} \\
-2\,4 \\
\hline
60 \\
-56 \\
\hline
40 \\
-40 \\
\hline
0
\end{array}
$$

</td>
</tr>
</table>

 STUDY SKILLS BUILDER

Are You Prepared for a Test on Chapter 4?

Below I have listed some *common trouble areas* for students in Chapter 4. After studying for your test—but before taking your test—read these.

- Don't forget the order of operations. To simplify $0.7 + 1.3(5 - 0.1)$, should you add, subtract, or multiply first? First, perform the subtraction within parentheses, then multiply, and finally add.

$$0.7 + 1.3(5 - 0.1) = 0.7 + 1.3(4.9) \quad \text{Subtract.}$$
$$= 0.7 + 6.37 \quad \text{Multiply.}$$
$$= 7.07 \quad \text{Add.}$$

- If you are having trouble with ordering or operations on decimals, don't forget that you can insert 0s after

the last digit to the right of the decimal point as needed.

Addition	Addition with zeros inserted	Subtraction	Subtraction with zeros inserted
8.1	8.100	7	7.00
0.6	0.600	$-\,0.28$	$-\,0.28$
$+\,23.003$	$+\,23.003$		6.72
	31.703		

Place in order from smallest to largest: 0.108, 0.18, 0.0092
If we insert zeros, we have: 0.1080, 0.1800, 0.0092
The decimals in order are: 0.0092, 0.1080, 0.1800 or 0.0092, 0.108, 0.18

4 CHAPTER REVIEW

(4.1) Determine the place value of the digit 4 in each decimal.

1. 23.45

2. 0.000345

Write each decimal in words.

3. 0.45

4. 0.00345

5. 109.23

6. 46.007

Write each decimal in standard form.

7. Two and fifteen hundredths

8. Five hundred three and one hundred two thousandths

Write the decimal as a fraction or a mixed number. Write your answer in simplest form.

9. 0.16

10. 12.023

11. 1.0045

12. 25.25

Write each fraction as a decimal.

13. $\dfrac{9}{10}$

14. $\dfrac{25}{100}$

15. $\dfrac{45}{1000}$

16. $\dfrac{261}{10}$

(4.2) Insert $<$, $>$, or $=$ to make a true statement.

17. 0.49   0.43

18. 0.973   0.9730

Write the decimals in order from smallest to largest.

19. 8.6, 8.09, 0.92

20. 0.09, 0.1, 0.091

Round each decimal to the given place value.

21. 0.623, nearest tenth

22. 0.9384, nearest hundredth

Round each money amount to the nearest cent.

23. $0.259

24. $12.461

Solve.

25. Every day in America an average of 13,490.5 people get married. Round this number to the nearest whole.

26. A certain kind of chocolate candy bar contains 10.75 teaspoons of sugar. Write this number as a mixed number.

(4.3) *Add or subtract as indicated.*

27. 2.4 + 7.12

28. 3.9 − 1.2

29. 6.4 + 0.88

30. 19.02 + 6.98 + 0.007

31. 892.1 − 432.4

32. 100.342 − 0.064

33. Subtract 34.98 from 100.

34. Subtract 10.02 from 200.

35. Find the total distance between Grove City and Jerome.

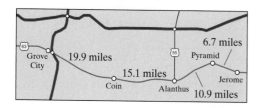

36. The price of oil was $49.02 per barrel on October 23. It was $51.46 on October 24. Find by how much the price of oil increased from the 23rd to the 24th.

△ **37.** Find the perimeter.

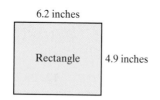

38. Find the perimeter.

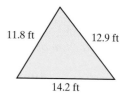

(4.4) *Multiply.*

39.   3.7
      × 5

40.   9.1
      × 6

41. 7.2 × 10

42. 9.345 × 1000

43.   4.02
      × 2.3

44.   39.02
      × 87.3

Solve.

△ **45.** Find the exact circumference of the circle. Then use the approximation 3.14 for π and approximate the circumference.

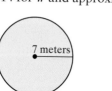

46. A kilometer is approximately 0.625 mile. It is 102 kilometers from Hays to Colby. Write 102 kilometers in miles to the nearest tenth of a mile.

Write each number in standard notation.

47. Saturn is a distance of about 887 million miles from the Sun.

48. The tail of a comet can be over 600 thousand miles long.

(4.5) *Divide. Round the quotient to the nearest thousandth if necessary.*

49. 3)0.2631

50. 20)316.5

51. 21 ÷ 0.3

52. 0.0063 ÷ 0.03

53. $0.34\overline{)2.74}$

54. $19.8\overline{)601.92}$

55. $\dfrac{2.67}{100}$

56. $\dfrac{93}{10}$

57. There are approximately 3.28 feet in 1 meter. Find how many meters are in 24 feet to the nearest tenth of a meter.

```
←—— 1 meter ——→
├———————————————┤
←—— ≈3.28 feet ——→
```

58. George Strait pays \$69.71 per month to pay back a loan of \$3136.95. In how many months will the loan be paid off?

Simplify each expression.

59. $7.6 \times 1.9 + 2.5$

60. $(2.3)^2 - 1.4$

61. $\dfrac{7 + 0.74}{0.06}$

62. $0.9(6.5 - 5.6)$

63. $\dfrac{(1.5)^2 + 0.5}{0.05}$

64. $0.0726 \div 10 \times 1000$

(4.6) *Write each fraction as a decimal. Round to the nearest thousandth if necessary.*

65. $\dfrac{4}{5}$

66. $\dfrac{12}{13}$

67. $2\dfrac{1}{3}$

68. $\dfrac{13}{60}$

Insert $<$, $>$, or $=$ to make a true statement.

69. $0.392 \quad 0.392$

70. $\dfrac{4}{7} \quad 0.625$

71. $0.293 \quad \dfrac{5}{17}$

Write the numbers in order from smallest to largest.

72. $0.837, 0.839, \dfrac{17}{20}$

73. $\dfrac{3}{7}, 0.42, 0.43$

74. $\dfrac{18}{11}, 1.63, \dfrac{19}{12}$

Find each area.

△ **75.**

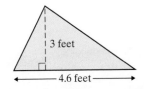

△ **76.**

Mixed Review

77. Write 200.0032 in words.

78. Write sixteen thousand twenty-five and fourteen thousandths in standard form.

79. Write 0.00231 as a fraction or a mixed number.

80. Write the numbers $\dfrac{6}{7}, \dfrac{8}{9}, 0.75$ in order from smallest to largest.

Write each fraction as a decimal. Round to the nearest thousandth, if necessary.

81. $\dfrac{7}{100}$

82. $\dfrac{9}{80}$ (Do not round.)

83. $\dfrac{8935}{175}$

Insert $<, >,$ *or* $=$ *to make a true statement.*

84. 402.00032   402.000032

85. 0.230505   0.23505

86. $\dfrac{6}{11}$ 0.55

Round each decimal to the given place value.

87. 42.895, nearest hundredth

88. 16.34925, nearest thousandth

Round each money amount to the nearest dollar.

89. $123.46, nearest dollar

90. $3645.52, nearest dollar

Add or subtract as indicated.

91. $4.9 - 3.2$

92. $5.23 - 2.74$

93. $200.49 + 16.82 + 103.002$

94. $0.00236 + 100.45 + 48.29$

Multiply or divide as indicated. Round to the nearest thousandth, if necessary.

95. $\begin{array}{r} 2.54 \\ \times\ 3.2 \\ \hline \end{array}$

96. $\begin{array}{r} 3.45 \\ \times\ 2.1 \\ \hline \end{array}$

97. $0.005\overline{)24.5}$

98. $2.3\overline{)54.98}$

Solve.

△ **99.** Tomaso is going to fertilize his lawn, a rectangle that measures 77.3 feet by 115.9 feet. Approximate the area of the lawn by rounding each measurement to the nearest ten feet.

100. Estimate the cost of the items to see whether the groceries can be purchased with a $5 bill.

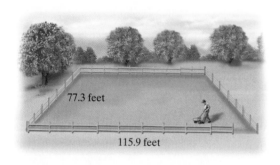

77.3 feet

115.9 feet

$1.89

$1.07

3 cans for $0.99

Simplify each expression.

101. $\dfrac{(3.2)^2}{100}$

102. $(2.6 + 1.4)(4.5 - 3.6)$

CHAPTER TEST

Answers

 Use the Chapter Test Prep Video CD to see the fully worked-out solutions to any of the exercises you want to review.

Write the decimal as indicated.

1. 45.092, in words

2. Three thousand and fifty-nine thousandths, in standard form

Round the decimal to the indicated place value.

3. 34.8923, nearest tenth

4. 0.8623, nearest thousandth

5. Insert $<$, $>$, or $=$ to make a true statement. 25.0909   25.9090

6. Write the numbers in order from smallest to largest. $\dfrac{4}{9}$ 0.454   0.445

Write the decimal as a fraction or a mixed number in simplest form.

7. 0.345

8. 24.73

Write the fraction or mixed number as a decimal. If necessary, round to the nearest thousandth.

9. $\dfrac{13}{20}$

10. $5\dfrac{8}{9}$

11. $\dfrac{16}{17}$

Perform the indicated operations. Round the result to the nearest thousandth if necessary.

12. $2.893 + 4.2 + 10.49$

13. Subtract 8.6 from 20.

14. $\begin{array}{r} 10.2 \\ \times\ \ 4.3 \\ \hline \end{array}$

15. $0.23\overline{)12.88}$

16. $\begin{array}{r} 0.165 \\ \times\ 0.47 \\ \hline \end{array}$

17. $7\overline{)46.71}$

1. _____

2. _____

3. _____

4. _____

5. _____

6. _____

7. _____

8. _____

9. _____

10. _____

11. _____

12. _____

13. _____

14. _____

15. _____

16. _____

17. _____

18. _____

19. _____

20. _____

21. _____

22. _____

23. _____

24. _____

25. a. _____

b. _____

26. _____

18. 126.9×100

19. $\dfrac{47.3}{10}$

20. $0.3[1.57 - (0.6)^2]$

21. $\dfrac{0.23 + 1.63}{0.3}$

22. At its farthest, Pluto is 4,583 million miles from the Sun. Write this number using standard notation.

△ **23.** Find the area.

1.1 miles
4.2 miles

△ **24.** Find the exact circumference of the circle. Then use the approximation 3.14 for π and approximate the circumference.

9 miles

25. Vivian Thomas is going to put insecticide on her lawn to control grubworms. The lawn is a rectangle that measures 123.8 feet by 80 feet. The amount of insecticide required is 0.02 ounces per square foot.

a. Find the area of her lawn.

b. Find how much insecticide Vivian needs to purchase.

26. Find the total distance from Bayette to Center City.

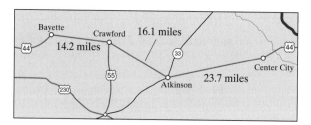
Bayette
Crawford   16.1 miles
14.2 miles
Atkinson   23.7 miles
Center City

1. Write 106,052,447 in words.

2. Write two hundred seventy-six thousand, four in standard form.

3. The governor's salary in the state of Alabama was recently increased by $1706. If the old salary was $94,655, find the new salary. (*Source: The World Almanac and Book of Facts,* 2003 and 2005)

4. There are 12 fluid ounces of soda in a can. How many fluid ounces of soda are in a case (24 cans) of soda?

5. Subtract: $900 - 174$. Then check by adding.

6. Simplify: $5^2 \cdot 2^3$

7. Round each number to the nearest hundred to find an estimated sum.

$$
\begin{array}{r}
294 \\
625 \\
1071 \\
+\ 349 \\
\end{array}
$$

8. Simplify: $7 \cdot \sqrt{144}$

9. A digital video disc (DVD) can hold about 4800 megabytes (MB) of information. How many megabytes can 12 DVDs hold?

10. Find the perimeter and area of the square.

7 feet

11. Divide: $6819 \div 17$

12. Write $2\frac{5}{8}$ as an improper fraction.

13. Simplify: $4^3 + [3^2 - (10 \div 2)] - 7 \cdot 3$

14. Write $\frac{64}{5}$ as a mixed number.

15. Identify the numerator and the denominator: $\frac{3}{7}$

16. Simplify: $24 \div 8 \cdot 3$

17. Write $\frac{6}{60}$ in simplest form.

18. Simplify: $(8 - 5)^2 + (10 - 8)^3$

Answers

1. _____

2. _____

3. _____

4. _____

5. _____

6. _____

7. _____

8. _____

9. _____

10. _____

11. _____

12. _____

13. _____

14. _____

15. _____

16. _____

17. _____

18. _____

19. Multiply: $\dfrac{3}{4} \cdot 20$

20. Simplify: $1 + 2[30 \div (7 - 2)]$

21. Divide: $\dfrac{7}{8} \div \dfrac{2}{9}$

22. Find the average of 117, 125, and 142.

23. Multiply: $1\dfrac{2}{3} \cdot 2\dfrac{1}{4}$

24. A total of \$324 is paid for 36 tickets to the Audubon Zoo. How much did each ticket cost?

25. Divide: $\dfrac{3}{4} \div 5$

26. Simplify: $\left(\dfrac{3}{4} \div \dfrac{1}{2}\right) \cdot \dfrac{9}{10}$

Simplify.

27. $\dfrac{8}{9} - \dfrac{1}{9}$

28. $\dfrac{4}{15} + \dfrac{2}{15}$

29. $\dfrac{7}{8} - \dfrac{5}{8}$

30. $\dfrac{1}{20} + \dfrac{3}{20} + \dfrac{4}{20}$

Write an equivalent fraction with the indicated denominator.

31. $\dfrac{3}{4} = \dfrac{}{20}$

32. $\dfrac{7}{9} = \dfrac{}{45}$

Perform the indicated operations.

33. $\dfrac{2}{15} + \dfrac{3}{10}$

34. $\dfrac{7}{30} - \dfrac{2}{9}$

35. Sarah Grahamm purchases two packages of ground round. One package weighs $2\dfrac{3}{8}$ pounds and the other $1\dfrac{4}{5}$ pounds. What is the combined weight of the ground round?

36. A color cartridge for a business printer weights $2\dfrac{5}{16}$ pounds. How much do 12 cartridges weigh?

Evaluate each expression.

37. $\left(\dfrac{1}{4}\right)^2$

38. $\left(\dfrac{7}{11}\right)^2$

19. _____

20. _____

21. _____

22. _____

23. _____

24. _____

25. _____

26. _____

27. _____

28. _____

29. _____

30. _____

31. _____

32. _____

33. _____

34. _____

35. _____

36. _____

37. _____

38. _____

39. $\left(\dfrac{1}{6}\right)^2 \cdot \left(\dfrac{3}{4}\right)^3$

40. $\left(\dfrac{1}{2}\right)^3 \cdot \left(\dfrac{4}{9}\right)^2$

41. Write 0.43 as a fraction.

42. Write $\dfrac{3}{4}$ as a decimal.

43. Insert $<$, $>$, or $=$ to form a true statement.
0.378   0.368

44. Write "five and six hundredths" in standard form.

45. Subtract: $35.218 - 23.65$
Check your answer.

46. Add: $75.1 + 0.229$

Multiply.

47. 23.702×100

48. 1.7×0.07

49. $76,805 \times 0.01$

50. Divide: $0.1157 \div 0.013$

39. _____

40. _____

41. _____

42. _____

43. _____

44. _____

45. _____

46. _____

47. _____

48. _____

49. _____

50. _____

5

Ratio and Proportion

Having studied fractions in Chapters 2 and 3, we are ready to explore the useful notations of ratio and proportion. Ratio is another name for quotient and is usually written in fraction form. A proportion is an equation with 2 equal ratios.

The Olympic Games originated in 776 B.C. in Greece. After the Romans conquered Greece, the Olympic games were eventually banned in 393 A.D. The games resumed in modern times in Athens, Greece, in 1896. Each event awards three medals to the top finishers: gold, silver, and bronze. The award ceremony, which features the national anthem of the country of the gold medal winner, is one of the most moving ceremonies in modern sports. In Exercise 51, Section 5.1, we will see how ratios can be used to compare the success of different countries in the Olympic games.

Future Olympic Sites

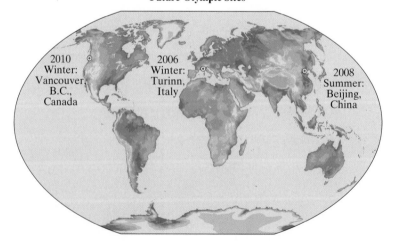

5.1 RATIOS

Objective **A** Writing Ratios as Fractions

A **ratio** is the quotient of two quantities. A ratio, in fact, is no different from a fraction, except that a ratio is sometimes written using notation other than fractional notation. For example, the ratio of 1 to 2 can be written as

$$1 \text{ to } 2 \quad \text{or} \quad \frac{1}{2} \quad \text{or} \quad 1 : 2$$

fractional notation   colon notation

These ratios are all read as, "the ratio of 1 to 2."

✔**Concept Check** How should each ratio be read aloud?

a. $\dfrac{8}{5}$ **b.** $\dfrac{5}{8}$

In this section, we write ratios using fractional notation. If the fraction happens to be an improper fraction, do not write the fraction as a mixed number, why? The mixed number form is not a ratio or quotient of two quantities.

Writing a Ratio as a Fraction

The order of the quantities is important when writing ratios. To write a ratio as a fraction, write the *first number* of the ratio as the *numerator* of the fraction and the *second number* as the *denominator*.

For example, the ratio of 6 to 11 is $\dfrac{6}{11}$, *not* $\dfrac{11}{6}$.

EXIMPLE 1 Write the ratio of 12 to 17 using fractional notation.

Solution: The ratio is $\dfrac{12}{17}$.

> **Helpful Hint**
> Don't forget that order is important when writing ratios. The ratio $\dfrac{17}{12}$ is *not* the same as the ratio $\dfrac{12}{17}$.

▣ **Work Practice Problem 1**

EXAMPLES Write each ratio using fractional notation.

2. The ratio of 2.6 to 3.1 is $\dfrac{2.6}{3.1}$.

3. The ratio of $1\dfrac{1}{2}$ to $7\dfrac{3}{4}$ is $\dfrac{1\frac{1}{2}}{7\frac{3}{4}}$.

▣ **Work Practice Problems 2-3**

PRACTICE PROBLEM 1

Write the ratio of 20 to 23 using fractional notation.

PRACTICE PROBLEMS 2-3

Write each ratio using fractional notation.

2. The ratio of 10.3 to 15.1

3. The ratio of $3\dfrac{1}{3}$ to $12\dfrac{1}{5}$

Answers

1. $\dfrac{20}{23}$, **2.** $\dfrac{10.3}{15.1}$, **3.** $\dfrac{3\frac{1}{3}}{12\frac{1}{5}}$

✔ **Concept Check Answers**
a. "eight to five," **b.** "five to eight"

321

Objective B Writing Ratios in Simplest Form

To simplify a ratio, we just write the fraction in simplest form. Common factors as well as common units can be divided out.

PRACTICE PROBLEM 4

Write the ratio of $8 to $6 as a fraction in simplest form.

EXAMPLE 4 Write the ratio of $15 to $10 as a fraction in simplest form.

Solution:

$$\frac{\$15}{\$10} = \frac{15}{10} = \frac{3 \cdot \overset{1}{\cancel{5}}}{2 \cdot \underset{1}{\cancel{5}}} = \frac{3}{2}$$

▨ **Work Practice Problem 4**

Helpful Hint

In the example above, although $\frac{3}{2} = 1\frac{1}{2}$, a ratio is a quotient of *two* quantities. For that reason, ratios are not written as mixed numbers.

If a ratio contains decimal numbers or mixed numbers, we simplify by writing the ratio as a ratio of whole numbers.

PRACTICE PROBLEM 5

Write the ratio of 1.71 to 4.56 as a fraction in simplest form.

EXAMPLE 5 Write the ratio of 2.6 to 3.1 as a fraction in simplest form.

Solution: The ratio in fraction form is

$$\frac{2.6}{3.1}$$

Now let's clear the ratio of decimals.

$$\frac{2.6}{3.1} = \frac{2.6}{3.1} \cdot 1 = \frac{2.6}{3.1} \cdot \frac{10}{10} = \frac{2.6 \cdot 10}{3.1 \cdot 10} = \frac{26}{31} \quad \text{Simplest form}$$

▨ **Work Practice Problem 5**

PRACTICE PROBLEM 6

Write the ratio of $2\frac{2}{3}$ to $1\frac{13}{15}$ as a fraction in simplest form.

EXAMPLE 6 Write the ratio of $1\frac{1}{5}$ to $2\frac{7}{10}$ as a fraction in simplest form.

Solution: The ratio in fraction form is $\dfrac{1\frac{1}{5}}{2\frac{7}{10}}$.

To simplify, remember that the fraction bar means division.

$$\frac{1\frac{1}{5}}{2\frac{7}{10}} = 1\frac{1}{5} \div 2\frac{7}{10} = \frac{6}{5} \div \frac{27}{10} = \frac{6}{5} \cdot \frac{10}{27} = \frac{6 \cdot 10}{5 \cdot 27} = \frac{2 \cdot \overset{1}{\cancel{3}} \cdot 2 \cdot \overset{1}{\cancel{5}}}{\underset{1}{\cancel{5}} \cdot \underset{1}{\cancel{3}} \cdot 3 \cdot 3} = \frac{4}{9} \quad \text{Simplest form.}$$

▨ **Work Practice Problem 6**

Answers

4. $\frac{4}{3}$, 5. $\frac{3}{8}$, 6. $\frac{10}{7}$

EXAMPLE 7 Writing a Ratio from a Circle Graph

The circle graph in the margin shows the part of a car's total mileage that falls into a particular category. Write the ratio of medical miles to total miles as a fraction in simplest form.

Solution:

$$\frac{\text{medical miles}}{\text{total miles}} = \frac{150 \text{ miles}}{15,000 \text{ miles}} = \frac{150}{15,000} = \frac{\overset{1}{\cancel{150}}}{\underset{1}{\cancel{150} \cdot 100}} = \frac{1}{100}$$

🔲 **Work Practice Problem 7**

⚠ **EXAMPLE 8** Given the rectangle shown:

a. Find the ratio of its width to its length.
b. Find the ratio of its length to its perimeter.

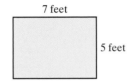

7 feet

5 feet

Solution:

a. The ratio of its width to its length is

$$\frac{\text{width}}{\text{length}} = \frac{5 \text{ feet}}{7 \text{ feet}} = \frac{5}{7}$$

b. Recall that the perimeter of the rectangle is the distance around the rectangle: $7 + 5 + 7 + 5 = 24$ feet. The ratio of its length to its perimeter is

$$\frac{\text{length}}{\text{perimeter}} = \frac{7 \text{ feet}}{24 \text{ feet}} = \frac{7}{24}$$

🔲 **Work Practice Problem 8**

✔ **Concept Check** Explain why the answer $\frac{7}{5}$ would be incorrect for part (a) of Example 7.

PRACTICE PROBLEM 7

Use the circle graph below to write the ratio of work miles to total miles as a fraction in simplest form.

Work
4800 miles

Medical
150 miles

Vacation/
other
900 miles

Visit friends
1800 miles

Shopping
1800 miles

School/
church
600 miles

Social/
recreational
1950 miles

Family business
3000 miles

Total yearly mileage: 15,000

Sources: The American Automobile Manufacturers Association and The National Automobile Dealers Association.

⚠ **PRACTICE PROBLEM 8**

Given the triangle shown:

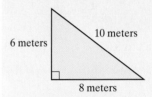

10 meters

6 meters

8 meters

a. Find the ratio of the length of the shortest side to the length of the longest side.
b. Find the ratio of the length of the longest side to the perimeter of the triangle.

Answers

7. $\frac{8}{25}$,   **8. a.** $\frac{3}{5}$,   **b.** $\frac{5}{12}$

✔ **Concept Check Answer**

$\frac{7}{5}$ would be the ratio of the rectangle's length to its width.

5.1 EXERCISE SET

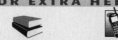
Objective **A** *Write each ratio using fractional notation. Do not simplify. See Examples 1 through 3.*

1. 11 to 14

2. 7 to 12

3. 23 to 10

4. 14 to 5

5. 151 to 201

6. 673 to 1000

7. 2.8 to 7.6

8. 3.9 to 4.2

9. 5 to $7\frac{1}{2}$

10. $5\frac{3}{4}$ to 3

11. $3\frac{3}{4}$ to $1\frac{2}{3}$

12. $2\frac{2}{5}$ to $6\frac{1}{2}$

Objectives **A** **B** **Mixed Practice** *Write each ratio as a ratio of whole numbers using fractional notation. Write the fraction in simplest form. See Examples 1 through 6.*

13. 16 to 24

14. 25 to 150

15. 7.7 to 10

16. 8.1 to 10

17. 4.63 to 8.21

18. 9.61 to 7.62

19. 9 inches to 12 inches

20. 14 centimeters to 20 centimeters

21. 10 hours to 24 hours

22. 18 quarts to 30 quarts

23. \$32 to \$100

24. \$46 to \$102

25. 24 days to 14 days

26. 80 miles to 120 miles

27. 32,000 bytes to 46,000 bytes

28. 600 copies to 150 copies

29. 8 inches to 20 inches

30. 9 yards to 2 yards

31. $3\frac{1}{2}$ to $12\frac{1}{4}$

32. $3\frac{1}{3}$ to $4\frac{1}{6}$

33. $7\frac{3}{5}$ hours to $1\frac{9}{10}$ hours

34. $25\frac{1}{2}$ days to $2\frac{5}{6}$ days

Find the ratio described in each exercise as a fraction in simplest form. For Exercises 35 and 36, use the circle graph by Practice Problem 7. See Examples 7 and 8.

35. Write the ratio of vacation/other miles to total miles as a fraction in simplest form.

36. Write the ratio of shopping miles to total miles as a fraction in simplest form.

△ **37.** Find the ratio of the length to the width of a regulation size basketball court.

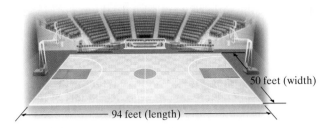

50 feet (width)

94 feet (length)

△ **38.** Find the ratio of the base to the height of the triangular mainsail.

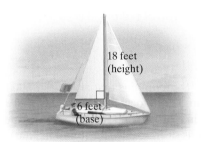

18 feet (height)

6 feet (base)

△ **39.** Find the ratio of the longest side to the perimeter of the right-triangular-shaped billboard.

8 feet   15 feet

17 feet

△ **40.** Find the ratio of the width to the perimeter of the rectangular vegetable garden.

4.5 meters   2 meters

41. A large order of McDonald's french fries has 450 calories. Of this total, 200 calories are from fat. Find the ratio of calories from fat to total calories in a large order of McDonald's french fries. (*Source:* McDonald's Corporation)

42. A McDonald's Quarter Pounder® with Cheese contains 30 grams of fat. A McDonald's Grilled Chicken™ sandwich contains 20 grams of fat. Find the ratio of the amount of fat in a Quarter Pounder with Cheese to the amount of fat in a Grilled Chicken sandwich. (*Source:* McDonald's Corporation)

At the Honey Island Parent Teacher Organization meeting one night, there were 125 women and 100 men present.

43. Find the ratio of women to men.

44. Find the ratio of men to the total number of people present.

A poll at State University revealed that 4500 students out of 6000 students are single, and the rest are married.

45. Find the ratio of single students to married students.

46. Find the ratio of married students to the total student population.

Blood contains three types of cells: red blood cells, white blood cells, and platelets. For approximately every 600 red blood cells in healthy humans, there are 40 platelets and 1 white blood cell. (Source: American Red Cross Biomedical Services)

47. Write the ratio of red blood cells to platelet cells.

48. Write the ratio of white blood cells to red blood cells.

49. Of the U.S. mountains that are over 14,000 feet in elevation, 57 are located in Colorado and 19 are located in Alaska. Find the ratio of the number of mountains over 14,000 feet found in Alaska to the number of mountains over 14,000 feet found in Colorado. (*Source:* U.S. Geological Survey)

50. Citizens of the United States eat an average of 25 pints of ice cream per year. Residents of the New England states eat an average of 39 pints of ice cream per year. Find the ratio of the amount of ice cream eaten by New Englanders to the amount eaten by the average U.S. citizen. (*Source:* International Dairy Foods Association)

51. At the Summer Olympics in Athens, Greece, a total of 301 gold medals were awarded, and Russian Federation athletes won a total of 27 gold medals. German athletes won a total of 14 gold medals. Find the ratio of gold medals won by the German athletes to the total gold medals awarded. (*Source:* International Olympic Committee)

52. For the 2004 Boston Marathon, 10,496 males and 6237 females finished the race. Find the ratio of female finishers to male finishers. (*Source:* Boston Athletic Association)

53. As of 2004, Target stores operate in 49 states. Find the ratio of states without Target stores to states with Target stores. (*Source:* Target Corporation)

54. A total of 32 states have 200 or more public libraries. Find the ratio of states with 200 or more public libraries to states with fewer than 200 public libraries. (*Source:* U.S. Department of Education)

Review

Divide. See Section 4.5.

55. $9\overline{)20.7}$ **56.** $7\overline{)60.2}$ **57.** $3.7\overline{)0.555}$ **58.** $4.6\overline{)1.15}$

Concept Extensions

Solve. See the Concept Checks in this section. Write how each should be read as a ratio.

59. $\dfrac{7}{9}$

60. $\dfrac{12}{5}$

61. $30 : 1$

62. 5 to 4

63. Is the ratio $\dfrac{11}{15}$ the same as the ratio of $\dfrac{15}{11}$? Explain your answer.

64. Explain why the ratio $\dfrac{40}{17}$ is incorrect for Exercise 39.

Decide whether each value is a ratio written as a fraction in simplest form. If not, write it as a fraction in simplest form.

65. $\dfrac{\$3}{\$2}$

66. $\dfrac{6 \text{ inches}}{15 \text{ inches}}$

67. $\dfrac{7.1}{4.3}$

68. $\dfrac{2\frac{1}{10}}{3\frac{3}{14}}$

69. $4\dfrac{1}{2}$

70. A panty hose manufacturing machine will be repaired if the ratio of defective panty hose to good panty hose is at least 1 to 20. A quality control engineer found 10 defective panty hose in a batch of 200. Determine whether the machine should be repaired.

71. A grocer will refuse a shipment of tomatoes if the ratio of bruised tomatoes to the total batch is at least 1 to 10. A sample is found to contain 3 bruised tomatoes and 33 good tomatoes. Determine whether the shipment should be refused.

72. In 2005, 19 states have mandatory helmet laws. (*Source:* Bicycle Helmet Safety Institute)

  a. Find the ratio of states with mandatory helmet laws to total U.S. states.

  b. Find the ratio of states with mandatory helmet laws to states without mandatory helmet laws.

    c. Are your ratios for parts **a** and **b** the same? Explain why or why not.

STUDY SKILLS BUILDER

Is Your Notebook Still Organized?

It's never too late to organize your material in a course. Let's see how you are doing.

1. Are all your graded papers in one place in your math notebook or binder?

2. Flip through the pages of your notebook. Are your notes neat and readable?

3. Are your notes complete with no sections missing?

4. Are important notes marked in some way (like an exclamation point) so that you will know to review them before a quiz or test?

5. Are your assignments complete?

6. Do exercises that have given you trouble have a mark (like a question mark) so that you will remember to talk to your instructor or a tutor about them?

7. Describe your attitude toward this course.

8. List ways your attitude can improve and make a commitment to work on at least one of these during the next week.

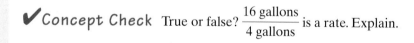
5.2 RATES

Objective **A** Writing Rates as Fractions

A special type of ratio is a rate. **Rates** are used to compare *different* kinds of quantities. For example, suppose that a recreational runner can run 3 miles in 33 minutes. If we write this rate as a fraction, we have

$$\frac{3 \text{ miles}}{33 \text{ minutes}} = \frac{1 \text{ mile}}{11 \text{ minutes}} \quad \text{In simplest form}$$

> **Helpful Hint**
>
> When comparing quantities with different units, write the units as part of the comparison. They do not divide out.
>
> **Same Units:** $\dfrac{3 \text{ \cancel{inches}}}{12 \text{ \cancel{inches}}} = \dfrac{1}{4}$
>
> **Different Units:** $\dfrac{2 \text{ miles}}{20 \text{ minutes}} = \dfrac{1 \text{ mile}}{10 \text{ minutes}}$ Units are still written.

PRACTICE PROBLEM 1

Write the rate as a fraction in simplest form: 12 commercials every 45 minutes

EXAMPLE 1 Write the rate as a fraction in simplest form: 10 nails every 6 feet

Solution:

$$\frac{10 \text{ nails}}{6 \text{ feet}} = \frac{5 \text{ nails}}{3 \text{ feet}}$$

⬛ **Work Practice Problem 1**

PRACTICE PROBLEMS 2–3

Write each rate as a fraction in simplest form.

2. $1680 for 8 weeks

3. 236 miles on 12 gallons of gasoline

EXAMPLES Write each rate as a fraction in simplest form.

2. $2160 for 12 weeks is $\dfrac{2160 \text{ dollars}}{12 \text{ weeks}} = \dfrac{180 \text{ dollars}}{1 \text{ week}}$

3. 360 miles on 16 gallons of gasoline is $\dfrac{360 \text{ miles}}{16 \text{ gallons}} = \dfrac{45 \text{ miles}}{2 \text{ gallons}}$

⬛ **Work Practice Problems 2–3**

✔ **Concept Check** True or false? $\dfrac{16 \text{ gallons}}{4 \text{ gallons}}$ is a rate. Explain.

Objective **B** Finding Unit Rates

A **unit rate** is a rate with a denominator of 1. A familiar example of a unit rate is 55 mph, read as "55 **miles per hour.**" This means 55 miles per 1 hour or

$$\frac{55 \text{ miles}}{1 \text{ hour}} \quad \text{Denominator of 1}$$

> **Helpful Hint**
>
> In this context, the word "per" translates to division.

Answers

1. $\dfrac{4 \text{ commercials}}{15 \text{ min}}$,   **2.** $\dfrac{\$210}{1 \text{ wk}}$,

3. $\dfrac{59 \text{ mi}}{3 \text{ gal}}$

✔ **Concept Check Answer**

false; a rate compares different kinds of quantities

328

Writing a Rate as a Unit Rate

To write a rate as a unit rate, divide the numerator of the rate by the denominator.

EXAMPLE 4 Write as a unit rate: $27,000 every 6 months

Solution:

$$\frac{27,000 \text{ dollars}}{6 \text{ months}} \qquad 6\overline{)27,000} \;\; 4,500$$

The unit rate is

$$\frac{4500 \text{ dollars}}{1 \text{ month}} \text{ or } 4500 \text{ dollars/month}$$ Read as, "4500 dollars per month."

■ **Work Practice Problem 4**

PRACTICE PROBLEM 4

Write as a unit rate: 3600 feet every 12 seconds

EXAMPLE 5 Write as a unit rate: 318.5 miles every 13 gallons of gas

Solution:

$$\frac{318.5 \text{ miles}}{13 \text{ gallons}} \qquad 13\overline{)318.5} \;\; 24.5$$

The unit rate is

$$\frac{24.5 \text{ miles}}{1 \text{ gallon}} \text{ or } 24.5 \text{ miles/gallon}$$ Read as, "24.5 miles per gallon."

■ **Work Practice Problem 5**

PRACTICE PROBLEM 5

Write as a unit rate:
52 bushels of fruit from 8 trees

Objective C Finding Unit Prices

Rates are used extensively in sports, business, medicine, and science. One of the most common uses of rates is in consumer economics. When a unit rate is "money per item," it is also called a **unit price.**

$$\text{unit price} = \frac{\text{price}}{\text{number of units}}$$

EXAMPLE 6 Finding Unit Price

A store charges $3.36 for a 16-ounce jar of picante sauce. What is the unit price in dollars per ounce?

Solution:

$$\frac{\text{unit}}{\text{price}} = \frac{\text{price}}{\text{number of units}} = \frac{\$3.36}{16 \text{ ounces}} = \frac{\$0.21}{1 \text{ ounce}} \text{ or } \$0.21 \text{ per ounce}$$

■ **Work Practice Problem 6**

PRACTICE PROBLEM 6

An automobile rental agency charges $170 for 5 days for a certain model car. What is the unit price in dollars per day?

Answers

4. $\dfrac{300 \text{ ft}}{1 \text{ sec}}$ or 300 ft/sec,

5. $\dfrac{6.5 \text{ bushels}}{1 \text{ tree}}$ or 6.5 bushels/tree,

6. $34 per day

PRACTICE PROBLEM 7

Approximate each unit price to decide which is the better buy for a bag of nacho chips: 11 ounces for $2.32 or 16 ounces for $3.59.

EXAMPLE 7 Finding the Best Buy

Approximate each unit price to decide which is the better buy: 4 bars for $0.99 of soap or 5 bars of soap for $1.19.

Solution:

$$\frac{\text{unit}}{\text{price}} = \frac{\text{price}}{\text{no. of units}} = \frac{\$0.99}{4 \text{ bars}} \approx \frac{\$0.25 \text{ per bar}}{\text{of soap}} \qquad 4\overline{)0.990} \approx 0.25$$

("is approximately")

$$\frac{\text{unit}}{\text{price}} = \frac{\text{price}}{\text{no. of units}} = \frac{\$1.19}{5 \text{ bars}} \approx \frac{\$0.24 \text{ per bar}}{\text{of soap}} \qquad 5\overline{)1.190} \approx 0.24$$

Thus, the 5-bar package is the better buy.

Work Practice Problem 7

Answer

7. 11-oz bag

5.2 EXERCISE SET

Student Solutions Manual   PH Math/Tutor Center   CD/Video for Review   MathXL   MathXL®   MyMathLab   MyMathLab

Objective A *Write each rate as a fraction in simplest form. See Examples 1 through 3.*

1. 5 shrubs every 15 feet

2. 14 lab tables for 28 students

3. 15 returns for 100 sales

4. 150 graduate students for 8 advisors

5. 8 phone lines for 36 employees

6. 6 laser printers for 28 computers

7. 18 gallons of pesticide for 4 acres of crops

8. 4 inches of rain in 18 hours

9. 6 flight attendants for 200 passengers

10. 240 pounds of grass seed for 9 lawns

11. 355 calories in a 10-fluid-ounce chocolate milkshake (*Source: Home and Garden Bulletin No. 72*, U.S. Department of Agriculture)

12. 160 calories in an 8-fluid-ounce serving of cream of tomato soup (*Source: Home and Garden Bulletin No. 72*, U.S. Department of Agriculture)

Objective B *Write each rate as a unit rate. See Examples 4 and 5.*

13. 375 riders in 5 subway cars

14. 18 campaign yard signs in 6 blocks

15. 330 calories in a 3-ounce serving

16. 275 miles in 11 hours

17. A hummingbird moves its wings at a rate of 5400 wingbeats a minute write this rate in wingbeats per second.

18. A bat moves its wings at a rate of 1200 wingbeats a minute. Write this rate in wingbeats per second.

19. $1,000,000 lottery winnings paid over 20 years

20. 400,000 library books for 8000 students

21. In 1999, the manned balloon *Breitling Orbiter* completed the first round-the-world flight. The balloon flew 26,600 miles in 20 days. Write this rate in miles per day. (*Source: Fantastic Book of Comparisons*)

22. A bullet fired from a rifle moves at a rate of 1620 miles per 1 hour. Write this rate in miles per *minute*.

23. The state of Arizona has approximately 114,000 square miles of land for 15 counties. (*Source:* U.S. Bureau of the Census)

24. The state of Louisiana has approximately 4,468,800 residents for 64 parishes. (*Note:* Louisiana is the only U.S. state with parishes instead of counties. *Source:* U.S. Bureau of the Census)

25. 12,000 good assembly line products to 40 defective products

26. 5,000,000 lottery tickets for 4 lottery winners

27. 12,000,000 tons of dust and dirt are trapped by the 25,000,000 acres of lawns in the United States each year. (*Source:* Professional Lawn Care Association of America)

28. Approximately 65,000,000,000 checks are written each year by a total of approximately 260,000,000 Americans. (*Source:* Board of Governors of the Federal Reserve System)

29. The National Zoo in Washington, D.C., has an annual budget of $28,595,000 for its 475 different species. (*Source:* Smithsonian Institution)

30. On average, the operating costs for 5 hours of flight in a B747-200 aircraft is $45,765. (*Source:* Air Transport Association of America)

31. On average, it costs $1,165,000 to build 25 Habitat for Humanity houses in the United States. (*Source:* Habitat for Humanity International)

32. The top-grossing concert tour in North America was the 1994 Rolling Stones tour, which grossed $121,200,000 for 60 shows. (*Source:* Pollstar)

Find each unit rate.

33. The record number of tornados in the U.S. for one 24-hour period is 148. Write this as a unit rate of tornadoes per hour rounded to the nearest tenth.

34. Sammy Joe Wingfield from Arlington, Texas, is the fastest bricklayer on record. On May 20, 1994, he laid 1048 bricks in 60 minutes. Find his unit rate of bricks per minute rounded to the nearest tenth. (*Source: The Guinness Book of Records*)

35. Greer Krieger can assemble 250 computer boards in an 8-hour shift while Lamont Williams can assemble 402 computer boards in a 12-hour shift.
  a. Find the unit rate of Greer.

  b. Find the unit rate of Lamont.

  c. Who can assemble computer boards faster, Greer or Lamont?

36. Jerry Stein laid 713 bricks in 46 minutes while his associate, Bobby Burns, laid 396 bricks in 30 minutes.
  a. Find the unit rate of Jerry.

  b. Find the unit rate of Bobby.

  c. Who is the faster bricklayer?

For Exercises 37 and 38, round the rates to the nearest tenth.

37. One student drove 400 miles in his car on 14.5 gallons of gasoline. His sister drove 270 miles in her truck on 9.25 gallons of gasoline.
  a. Find the unit rate of the car.
  b. Find the unit rate of the truck.
  c. Which vehicle gets better gas mileage?

38. Charlotte Leal is a grocery scanner who can scan an average of 100 items in 3.5 minutes while her cousin Leo can scan 148 items in 5.5 minutes.
  a. Find the unit rate of Charlotte.
  b. Find the unit rate of Leo.
  c. Who is the faster scanner?

Objective C *Find each unit price. See Example 6.*

39. $57.50 for 5 compact discs

40. $0.87 for 3 apples

41. 7 bananas for $1.19

42. 6 lawn chairs for $73.50

Find each unit price and decide which is the better buy. Round to 3 decimal places. Assume that we are comparing different sizes of the same brand. See Examples 6 and 7.

43. Crackers:
  $1.19 for 8 ounces
  $1.59 for 12 ounces

44. Pickles:
  $1.89 for 32 ounces
  $0.89 for 18 ounces

45. Frozen orange juice:
  $1.69 for 16 ounces
  $0.69 for 6 ounces

46. Eggs:
  $0.69 for a dozen
  $2.10 for a flat $\left(2\frac{1}{2}\text{ dozen}\right)$

47. Soy sauce:
12 ounces for $2.29
8 ounces for $1.49

48. Shampoo:
20 ounces for $1.89
32 ounces for $3.19

49. Napkins:
100 for $0.59
180 for $0.93

50. Crackers:
20 ounces for $2.39
8 ounces for $0.99

Review

Multiply or divide as indicated. See Sections 4.4 and 4.5.

51.
$$\begin{array}{r} 1.7 \\ \times\ 6 \\ \hline \end{array}$$

52.
$$\begin{array}{r} 2.3 \\ \times\ 9 \\ \hline \end{array}$$

53.
$$\begin{array}{r} 3.7 \\ \times 1.2 \\ \hline \end{array}$$

54.
$$\begin{array}{r} 6.6 \\ \times 2.5 \\ \hline \end{array}$$

55. $2.3\overline{)4.37}$

56. $3.5\overline{)22.75}$

Concept Extensions

57. Fill in the table to calculate miles per gallon.

Beginning Odometer Reading	Ending Odometer Reading	Miles Driven	Gallons of Gas Used	Miles per Gallon (round to the nearest tenth)
79,286	79,543		13.4	
79,543	79,895		15.8	
79,895	80,242		16.1	

Find each unit rate.

58. The longest stairway is the service stairway for the Niesenbahn Cable railway near Spiez, Switzerland. It has 11,674 steps and rises to a height of 7759 feet. Find the unit rate of steps per foot rounded to the nearest tenth of a step. (*Source: The Guinness Book of Records*)

59. In the United States, the total number of students enrolled in public schools is 48,000,000. There are 88,300 public schools. Write a unit rate in students per school. Round to the nearest whole. (*Source: National Center for Education Statistics*)

60. Suppose that the amount of a product decreases, say from an 80-ounce container to a 70-ounce container, but the price of the container remains the same. Does the unit price increase or decrease? Explain why.

61. In your own words, define the phrase unit rate.

62. In your own words, defined the phrase unit price.

63. Should the rate $\dfrac{3 \text{ lights}}{2 \text{ feet}}$ be written as $\dfrac{3}{2}$? Explain why or why not?

64. Find an item in the grocery store and calculate its unit price.

Ratio and Rate

Answers

Write each ratio as a ratio of whole numbers using fractional notation. Write the fraction in simplest form.

1. 18 to 20

2. 36 to 100

3. 8.6 to 10

4. 1.6 to 4.6

5. $8.65 to $6.95

6. 7.2 ounces to 8.4 ounces

7. $3\frac{1}{2}$ to 13

8. $1\frac{2}{3}$ to $2\frac{3}{4}$

9. 8 inches to 12 inches

10. 3 hours to 24 hours

Find the ratio described in each problem.

11. In 2003, a full college professor earned $84.1 thousand, while an associate professor earned $61.5 thousand. Find the ratio of full professor salary to associate professor salary. (*Source:* American Association of University Professors)

12. At the end of 2003, Eastman Kodak had $14,818 million in assets and $2304 million in long-term debt. Find the ratio of assets to long-term debt. (*Source:* Eastman Kodak Company)

13. The circle graph below shows how the top 20 movies of 2004 were rated. Use this graph to answer the questions.

   a. How many top 20 movies were rated PG-13?

   b. Find the ratio of top 20 PG-13 movies to total movies for that year.

14. Find the ratio of the width to the length of the sign below.

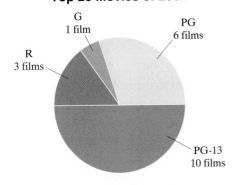

Top 20 Movies of 2004

G 1 film

PG 6 films

R 3 films

PG-13 10 films

Source: Internet search and Bryan Gay

12 inches

18 inches

RESERVED PARKING

---

1. _____

2. _____

3. _____

4. _____

5. _____

6. _____

7. _____

8. _____

9. _____

10. _____

11. _____

12. _____

13. a. _____

   b. _____

14. _____

Write each rate as a fraction in simplest form.

15. 5 offices for every 20 graduate assistants   **16.** 6 lights every 15 feet

17. 100 U.S. senators for 50 states   **18.** 5 teachers for every 140 students

19. 64 computers every 100 households   **20.** 45 students for every 10 computers

Write each rate as a unit rate.

21. 165 miles in 3 hours   **22.** 560 feet in 4 seconds

23. 63 employees for 3 fax lines   **24.** 85 phone calls for 5 teenagers

25. 115 miles every 5 gallons   **26.** 112 teachers for 7 computers

27. 7524 books for 1254 college students   **28.** 2002 pounds for 13 adults

Write each unit price, rounded to the nearest hundredths, and decide which is the better buy.

29. Dog food:
    $2.16 for 8 pounds
    $4.99 for 18 pounds

30. Paper plates:
    $1.98 for 100
    $8.99 for 500
    (Round to the nearest thousandths.)

31. Microwave popcorn:
    3 packs for $2.39
    8 packs for $5.99

32. AA Batteries:
    4 for $3.69
    10 for $9.89

15. _____

16. _____

17. _____

18. _____

19. _____

20. _____

21. _____

22. _____

23. _____

24. _____

25. _____

26. _____

27. _____

28. _____

29. _____

30. _____

31. _____

32. _____

5.3 PROPORTIONS

Objectives

A Write Sentences as Proportions.

B Determine Whether Proportions Are True.

C Find An Unknown Number in a Proportion.

Objective **A** Writing Proportions

A **proportion** is a statement that 2 ratios or rates are equal. For example,

$$\frac{5}{6} = \frac{10}{12}$$

is a proportion. We can read this as, "5 is to 6 as 10 is to 12."

EXAMPLE 1 Write each sentence as a proportion.

a. 12 diamonds is to 15 rubies as 4 diamonds is to 5 rubies.

b. 5 hits is to 9 at bats as 20 hits is to 36 at bats.

Solution:

a. diamonds $\rightarrow$ $\dfrac{12}{15} = \dfrac{4}{5}$ $\leftarrow$ diamonds
      rubies $\rightarrow$ $\leftarrow$ rubies

b.   hits $\rightarrow$ $\dfrac{5}{9} = \dfrac{20}{36}$ $\leftarrow$ hits
      at bats $\rightarrow$ $\leftarrow$ at bats

▢ **Work Practice Problem 1**

> **Helpful Hint**
>
> Notice in the above examples of proportions that the numerators contain the same units and the denominators contain the same units. In this text, proportions will be written so that this is the case.

Objective **B** Determining Whether Proportions Are True

Like other mathematical statements, a proportion may be either true or false. A proportion is true if its ratios are equal. Since ratios are fractions, one way to determine whether a proportion is true is to write both fractions in simplest form and compare them.

Another way is to compare cross products as we did in Section 2.3.

Using Cross Products to Determine Whether Proportions Are True or False

$$\overset{a \cdot d}{\underset{\displaystyle \frac{a}{b} = \frac{c}{d}}{\nearrow\nwarrow}} \quad b \cdot c$$

If cross products are *equal*, the proportion is *true*.
If $ad = bc$, then the proportion is true.
If cross products are *not equal*, the proportion is *false*.
If $ad \neq bc$, then the proportion is false.

PRACTICE PROBLEM 1

Write each sentence as a proportion.

a. 24 right is to 6 wrong as 4 right is to 1 wrong.

b. 32 Cubs fans is to 18 Mets fans as 16 Cubs fans is to 9 Mets fans.

Answers

1. a. $\dfrac{24}{6} = \dfrac{4}{1}$,   **b.** $\dfrac{32}{18} = \dfrac{16}{9}$

PRACTICE PROBLEM 2

Is $\dfrac{3}{6} = \dfrac{4}{8}$ a true proportion?

EXAMPLE 2 Is $\dfrac{2}{3} = \dfrac{4}{6}$ a true proportion?

Solution:

Cross products

$2 \cdot 6$ $3 \cdot 4$

$$\dfrac{2}{3} = \dfrac{4}{6}$$

$2 \cdot 6 \overset{?}{=} 3 \cdot 4$ Are cross products equal?
$12 = 12$ Equal, so proportion is true.

Since the cross products are equal, the proportion is true.

■ **Work Practice Problem 2**

PRACTICE PROBLEM 3

Is $\dfrac{3.6}{6} = \dfrac{5.4}{8}$ a true proportion?

EXAMPLE 3 Is $\dfrac{4.1}{7} = \dfrac{2.9}{5}$ a true proportion?

Solution:

Cross products

$4.1 \cdot 5$ $7 \cdot 2.9$

$$\dfrac{4.1}{7} = \dfrac{2.9}{5}$$

$4.1 \cdot 5 \overset{?}{=} 7 \cdot 2.9$ Are cross products equal?
$20.5 \neq 20.3$ Not equal, so proportion is false.

Since the cross products are not equal, $\dfrac{4.1}{7} \neq \dfrac{2.9}{5}$. The proportion is false.

■ **Work Practice Problem 3**

PRACTICE PROBLEM 4

Is $\dfrac{4\frac{1}{5}}{2\frac{1}{3}} = \dfrac{3\frac{3}{10}}{1\frac{5}{6}}$ a true proportion?

EXAMPLE 4 Is $\dfrac{1\frac{1}{6}}{10\frac{1}{2}} = \dfrac{\frac{1}{2}}{4\frac{1}{2}}$ a true proportion?

Solution:

$$\dfrac{1\frac{1}{6}}{10\frac{1}{2}} = \dfrac{\frac{1}{2}}{4\frac{1}{2}}$$

$1\frac{1}{6} \cdot 4\frac{1}{2} \overset{?}{=} 10\frac{1}{2} \cdot \frac{1}{2}$ Are cross products equal?

$\dfrac{7}{6} \cdot \dfrac{9}{2} \overset{?}{=} \dfrac{21}{2} \cdot \dfrac{1}{2}$ Write mixed numbers as improper fractions.

$\dfrac{21}{4} = \dfrac{21}{4}$ Equal, so proportion is true.

Since the cross products are equal, the proportion is true.

■ **Work Practice Problem 4**

Answers
2. yes, 3. no, 4. yes

✔ **Concept Check Answer**

possible answers: $\dfrac{8}{5} = \dfrac{16}{10}$ and $\dfrac{5}{10} = \dfrac{8}{16}$

✔ **Concept Check** Think about cross products and write the true proportion $\dfrac{5}{8} = \dfrac{10}{16}$ in two other ways so that each result is also a true proportion.
(*Note:* There are no units attached in this proportion.)

Copyright 2006 Pearson Education, Inc.

Objective C Finding Unknown Numbers in Proportions

When one number of a proportion is unknown, we can use cross products to find the unknown number. For example, to find the unknown number n in the proportion $\frac{n}{30} = \frac{2}{3}$, we first find the cross products.

$$n \cdot 3 \qquad\qquad 30 \cdot 2 \quad \text{Find the cross products.}$$
$$\frac{n}{30} = \frac{2}{3}$$

If the proportion is true, then cross products are equal.

$n \cdot 3 = 30 \cdot 2$ Set the cross products equal to each other.
$n \cdot 3 = 60$ Write $2 \cdot 30$ as 60.

To find the unknown number n, we ask ourselves, "What number times 3 is 60?" The number is 20 and can be found by dividing 60 by 3.

$n = \dfrac{60}{3}$ Divide 60 by the number multiplied by n.

$n = 20$ Simplify.

Thus, the unknown number is 20.

To *check*, let's replace n with this value, 20, and verify that a true proportion results.

$\dfrac{20}{30} \stackrel{?}{=} \dfrac{2}{3}$ ← Replace n with 20.

$$\frac{2}{3} \stackrel{?}{=} \frac{20}{30}$$

$2 \cdot 30 \stackrel{?}{=} 3 \cdot 20$
$60 = 60$ Cross products are equal.

Finding an Unknown Value n in a Proportion

Step 1: Set the cross products equal to each other.

Step 2: Divide the number not multiplied by n by the number multiplied by n.

EXAMPLE 5 Find the value of the unknown number n.

$$\frac{51}{34} = \frac{3}{n}$$

Solution:
Step 1:

$$\frac{51}{34} = \frac{3}{n}$$

$51 \cdot n = 34 \cdot 3$ Set cross products equal.
$51 \cdot n = 102$ Multiply.

Step 2:

$n = \dfrac{102}{51}$ Divide 102 by 51, the number multiplied by n.

$n = 2$ Simplify.

Continued on next page

PRACTICE PROBLEM 5
Find the value of the unknown number n.

$$\frac{15}{2} = \frac{60}{n}$$

Answer
5. $n = 8$

Check: $\dfrac{34}{51} \stackrel{?}{=} \dfrac{2}{3}$ Replace n with its value, 2.

$$\dfrac{51}{34} \stackrel{?}{=} \dfrac{3}{2}$$

$51 \cdot 2 \stackrel{?}{=} 34 \cdot 3$ Cross products are equal, so the
$102 = 102$ proportion is true.

■ **Work Practice Problem 5**

PRACTICE PROBLEM 6

Find the unknown number n.

$$\dfrac{8}{n} = \dfrac{5}{9}$$

EXAMPLE 6   Find the unknown number n.

$$\dfrac{7}{n} = \dfrac{6}{5}$$

Solution:

Step 1:

$$\dfrac{7}{n} = \dfrac{6}{5}$$

$7 \cdot 5 = n \cdot 6$ Set the cross products equal to each other.
$35 = n \cdot 6$ Multiply.

Step 2:

$$\dfrac{35}{6} = n \quad \text{Divide 35 by 6, the number multiplied by } n.$$

$$5\dfrac{5}{6} = n$$

Check to see that $5\dfrac{5}{6}$ is the unknown number.

■ **Work Practice Problem 6**

PRACTICE PROBLEM 7

Find the unknown number n.

$$\dfrac{n}{6} = \dfrac{0.7}{1.2}$$

EXAMPLE 7   Find the unknown number n.

$$\dfrac{n}{3} = \dfrac{0.8}{1.5}$$

Solution:

Step 1:

$$\dfrac{n}{3} = \dfrac{0.8}{1.5}$$

$n \cdot 1.5 = 3 \cdot 0.8$ Set the cross products equal to each other.
$n \cdot 1.5 = 2.4$ Multiply.

Step 2:

$$n = \dfrac{2.4}{1.5} \quad \text{Divide 2.4 by 1.5, the number multiplied by } n.$$

$n = 1.6$ Simplify.

Check to see that 1.6 is the unknown number.

■ **Work Practice Problem 7**

Answers

6. $n = 14\dfrac{2}{5}$,   **7.** $n = 3.5$

EXAMPLE 8 Find the unknown number n.

$$\frac{1\frac{2}{3}}{3\frac{1}{4}} = \frac{n}{2\frac{3}{5}}$$

PRACTICE PROBLEM 8

Find the unknown number n.

$$\frac{n}{4\frac{1}{3}} = \frac{4\frac{1}{2}}{1\frac{3}{4}}$$

Solution:

Step 1:

$1\frac{2}{3} \cdot 2\frac{3}{5} = 3\frac{1}{4} \cdot n$ Set the cross products equal to each other.

$\frac{13}{3} = 3\frac{1}{4} \cdot n$ Multiply. $1\frac{2}{3} \cdot 2\frac{3}{5} = \frac{5}{3} \cdot \frac{13}{5} = \frac{\overset{1}{\cancel{5}} \cdot 13}{3 \cdot \cancel{5}} = \frac{13}{3}$

$\frac{13}{3} = \frac{13}{4} \cdot n$ Write $3\frac{1}{4}$ as $\frac{13}{4}$.

Step 2:

$\frac{13}{3} \div \frac{13}{4} = n$ Divide $\frac{13}{3}$ by $\frac{13}{4}$, the number multiplied by n.

or

$n = \frac{13}{3} \cdot \frac{4}{13} = \frac{4}{3}$ or $1\frac{1}{3}$ Divide by multiplying by the reciprocal.

Check to see that $1\frac{1}{3}$ is the unknown number.

Work Practice Problem 8

Answer

8. $n = 11\frac{1}{7}$

Mental Math

Objective B *State whether each proportion is true or false.*

1. $\dfrac{2}{1} = \dfrac{6}{3}$ **2.** $\dfrac{3}{1} = \dfrac{15}{5}$ **3.** $\dfrac{1}{2} = \dfrac{3}{5}$ **4.** $\dfrac{2}{11} = \dfrac{1}{5}$ **5.** $\dfrac{2}{3} = \dfrac{40}{60}$ **6.** $\dfrac{3}{4} = \dfrac{6}{8}$

5.3 EXERCISE SET

FOR EXTRA HELP

Student Solutions Manual   PH Math/Tutor Center   CD/Video for Review   Math XL MathXL®   MyMathLab MyMathLab

Objective A *Write each sentence as a proportion. See Example 1.*

1. 10 diamonds is to 6 opals as 5 diamonds is to 3 opals.

2. 8 books is to 6 courses as 4 books is to 3 courses.

3. 3 printers is to 12 computers as 1 printer is to 4 computers.

4. 4 hit songs is to 16 releases as 1 hit song is to 4 releases.

5. 6 eagles is to 58 sparrows as 3 eagles is to 29 sparrows.

6. 12 errors is to 8 pages as 1.5 errors is to 1 page.

7. $2\dfrac{1}{4}$ cups of flour is to 24 cookies as $6\dfrac{3}{4}$ cups of flour is to 72 cookies.

8. $1\dfrac{1}{2}$ cups milk is to 10 bagels as $\dfrac{3}{4}$ cup milk is to 5 bagels.

9. 22 vanilla wafers is to 1 cup of cookie crumbs as 55 vanilla wafers is to 2.5 cups of cookie crumbs. (*Source:* Based on data from *Family Circle* magazine)

10. 1 cup of instant rice is to 1.5 cups cooked rice as 1.5 cups of instant rice is to 2.25 cups of cooked rice. (*Source:* Based on data from *Family Circle* magazine)

Objective B *Determine whether each proportion is a true proportion. See Examples 2 through 4.*

11. $\dfrac{15}{9} = \dfrac{5}{3}$ **12.** $\dfrac{8}{6} = \dfrac{20}{15}$ **13.** $\dfrac{8}{6} = \dfrac{9}{7}$ **14.** $\dfrac{7}{12} = \dfrac{4}{7}$ **15.** $\dfrac{9}{36} = \dfrac{2}{8}$ **16.** $\dfrac{8}{24} = \dfrac{3}{9}$

17. $\dfrac{5}{8} = \dfrac{625}{1000}$

18. $\dfrac{30}{50} = \dfrac{600}{1000}$

19. $\dfrac{0.8}{0.3} = \dfrac{0.2}{0.6}$

20. $\dfrac{0.7}{0.4} = \dfrac{0.3}{0.1}$

21. $\dfrac{8}{10} = \dfrac{5.6}{0.7}$

22. $\dfrac{4.2}{8.4} = \dfrac{5}{10}$

23. $\dfrac{\frac{3}{4}}{\frac{4}{3}} = \dfrac{\frac{1}{2}}{\frac{8}{9}}$

24. $\dfrac{\frac{2}{5}}{\frac{2}{7}} = \dfrac{\frac{1}{10}}{\frac{1}{3}}$

25. $\dfrac{2\frac{2}{5}}{\frac{2}{3}} = \dfrac{1\frac{1}{9}}{\frac{1}{4}}$

26. $\dfrac{5\frac{5}{8}}{\frac{5}{3}} = \dfrac{4\frac{1}{2}}{1\frac{1}{5}}$

27. $\dfrac{\frac{4}{5}}{\frac{5}{6}} = \dfrac{\frac{6}{5}}{\frac{6}{9}}$

28. $\dfrac{\frac{6}{7}}{\frac{6}{3}} = \dfrac{\frac{10}{7}}{\frac{10}{5}}$

Objectives Ⓐ Ⓑ **Mixed Practice** *Write each sentence as a proportion. Then determine whether the proportion is a true proportion. See Examples 1 through 4.*

29. eight is to twelve as four is to six

30. six is to eight as nine is to twelve

31. five is to two as thirteen is to five

32. four is to three as seven is to five

33. one and eight tenths is to two as four and five tenths is to five

34. fifteen hundredths is to three as thirty-five hundredths is to seven

35. two thirds is to one fifth as two fifths is to one ninth

36. ten elevenths is to three fourths as one fourth is to one half

Objective Ⓒ *For each proportion, find the unknown number n. See Examples 5 through 8.*

37. $\dfrac{n}{5} = \dfrac{6}{10}$

38. $\dfrac{n}{3} = \dfrac{12}{9}$

39. $\dfrac{18}{54} = \dfrac{3}{n}$

40. $\dfrac{25}{100} = \dfrac{7}{n}$

41. $\dfrac{n}{8} = \dfrac{50}{100}$

42. $\dfrac{n}{21} = \dfrac{12}{18}$

43. $\dfrac{8}{15} = \dfrac{n}{6}$

44. $\dfrac{12}{10} = \dfrac{n}{16}$

45. $\dfrac{24}{n} = \dfrac{60}{96}$

46. $\dfrac{26}{n} = \dfrac{28}{49}$

47. $\dfrac{3.5}{12.5} = \dfrac{7}{n}$

48. $\dfrac{0.2}{0.7} = \dfrac{8}{n}$

49. $\dfrac{0.05}{12} = \dfrac{n}{0.6}$

50. $\dfrac{7.8}{13} = \dfrac{n}{2.6}$

51. $\dfrac{8}{\frac{1}{3}} = \dfrac{24}{n}$

52. $\dfrac{12}{\frac{3}{4}} = \dfrac{48}{n}$

53. $\dfrac{\frac{1}{3}}{\frac{3}{8}} = \dfrac{\frac{2}{5}}{n}$

54. $\dfrac{\frac{7}{9}}{\frac{8}{27}} = \dfrac{\frac{1}{4}}{n}$

55. $\dfrac{12}{n} = \dfrac{\frac{2}{3}}{\frac{6}{9}}$

56. $\dfrac{24}{n} = \dfrac{\frac{8}{15}}{\frac{5}{9}}$

57. $\dfrac{n}{1\frac{1}{5}} = \dfrac{4\frac{1}{6}}{6\frac{2}{3}}$

58. $\dfrac{n}{3\frac{1}{8}} = \dfrac{7\frac{3}{5}}{2\frac{3}{8}}$

59. $\dfrac{25}{n} = \dfrac{3}{\frac{7}{30}}$

60. $\dfrac{9}{n} = \dfrac{5}{\frac{11}{15}}$

Review

Insert $<$ or $>$ to form a true statement. See Sections 3.5 and 4.2.

61. 8.01 8.1

62. 7.26 7.026

63. $2\frac{1}{2}$ $2\frac{1}{3}$

64. $9\frac{1}{5}$ $9\frac{1}{4}$

65. $5\frac{1}{3}$ $6\frac{2}{3}$

66. $1\frac{1}{2}$ $2\frac{1}{2}$

Concept Extensions

Think about cross products and write each proportion in two other ways so that each result is also a true proportion. See the Concept Check in this section.

67. $\dfrac{9}{15} = \dfrac{3}{5}$

68. $\dfrac{1}{4} = \dfrac{5}{20}$

69. $\dfrac{6}{18} = \dfrac{1}{3}$

70. $\dfrac{2}{7} = \dfrac{4}{14}$

71. If the proportion $\dfrac{a}{b} = \dfrac{c}{d}$ is a true proportion, write two other true proportions using the same letters.

72. Write a true proportion.

73. Explain the difference between a ratio and a proportion.

74. Explain how to find the unknown number in a proportion such as $\dfrac{n}{18} = \dfrac{12}{8}$.

For each proportion, find the unknown number n.

75. $\dfrac{n}{7} = \dfrac{0}{8}$

76. $\dfrac{0}{2} = \dfrac{n}{3.5}$

77. $\dfrac{n}{1150} = \dfrac{588}{483}$

78. $\dfrac{585}{n} = \dfrac{117}{474}$

79. $\dfrac{222}{1515} = \dfrac{37}{n}$

80. $\dfrac{1425}{1062} = \dfrac{n}{177}$

THE BIGGER PICTURE Operations on Sets of Numbers and Solving Equations

Continue your outline from Sections 1.7, 1.9, 2.5, 3.4, and 4.5. Suggestions are once again written to help you complete this part of your outline. Notice that this part of the outline has to do with solving a certain type of equation, proportions.

I. Some Operations on Sets of Numbers

  A. Whole Numbers

    1. Add or Subtract (Sections 1.3, 1.4)

    2. Multiply or Divide (Sections 1.6, 1.7)

    3. Exponent (Section 1.9)

    4. Square Root (Section 1.9)

    5. Order of Operations (Section 1.9)

  B. Fractions

    1. Simplify (Section 2.3)

    2. Multiply (Section 2.4)

    3. Divide (Section 2.5)

    4. Add or Subtract (Section 3.4)

  C. Decimals

    1. Add or Subtract (Section 4.3)

    2. Multiply (Section 4.4)

    3. Divide (Section 4.5)

II. Solving Equations

  A. Proportions: Set cross products equal to each other. Then solve.

$$\frac{14}{3} = \frac{2}{n}, \text{ or } 14 \cdot n = 3 \cdot 2, \text{ or } 14 \cdot n = 6, \text{ or } n = \frac{6}{14} = \frac{3}{7}$$

Perform indicated operations.

1. $\dfrac{7}{20} - \dfrac{1}{10}$

2. $\dfrac{7}{20} \cdot \dfrac{1}{10}$

3. $\dfrac{7}{20} \div \dfrac{1}{10}$

4. $\dfrac{7}{20} + \dfrac{1}{10}$

5. $7.6 + 0.02$

6. $7.6(0.02)$

For each proportion, find the unknown number, n.

7. $\dfrac{4}{n} = \dfrac{50}{100}$

8. $\dfrac{60}{10} = \dfrac{15}{n}$

9. $\dfrac{n}{0.8} = \dfrac{0.06}{12}$

10. $\dfrac{\frac{7}{8}}{\frac{1}{4}} = \dfrac{n}{\frac{5}{6}}$

5.4 PROPORTIONS AND PROBLEM SOLVING

Objective **A** Solving Problems by Writing Proportions

Writing proportions is a powerful tool for solving problems in almost every field, including business, chemistry, biology, health sciences, and engineering, as well as in daily life. Given a specified ratio (or rate) of two quantities, a proportion can be used to determine an unknown quantity.

In this section, we use the same problem solving steps that we have used earlier in this text.

EXAMPLE 1 **Determining Distances from a Map**

On a chamber of commerce map of Abita Springs, 5 miles corresponds to 2 inches. How many miles correspond to 7 inches?

PRACTICE PROBLEM 1

On an architect's blueprint, 1 inch corresponds to 12 feet. How long is a wall represented by a $3\frac{1}{2}$-inch line on the blueprint?

Solution:

1. UNDERSTAND. Read and reread the problem. You may want to draw a diagram.

15 miles			between 15 and 20 miles
			20 miles
5 miles	5 miles	5 miles	5 miles	= a little over 15 miles
2 inches	2 inches	2 inches	2 inches	= 7 inches
6 inches			8 inches
		7 inches	

From the diagram we can see that a reasonable solution should be between 15 and 20 miles.

2. TRANSLATE. We will let n represent our unknown number. Since 5 miles corresponds to 2 inches as n miles corresponds to 7 inches, we have the proportion

$$\begin{array}{ll} \text{miles} \rightarrow \\ \text{inches} \rightarrow \end{array} \frac{5}{2} = \frac{n}{7} \begin{array}{ll} \leftarrow \text{miles} \\ \leftarrow \text{inches} \end{array}$$

3. SOLVE: In earlier sections, we estimated to obtain a reasonable answer. Notice we did this in Step 1 above.

$$\frac{5}{2} = \frac{n}{7}$$

$$5 \cdot 7 = 2 \cdot n \qquad \text{Set the cross products equal to each other.}$$
$$35 = 2 \cdot n \qquad \text{Multiply.}$$
$$\frac{35}{2} = n \qquad \text{Divide 35 by 2, the number multiplied by } n.$$
$$n = 17\frac{1}{2} \text{ or } 17.5 \quad \text{Simplify.}$$

4. INTERPRET. *Check* your work. This result is reasonable since it is between 15 and 20 miles. *State* your conclusion: 7 inches corresponds to 17.5 miles.

Answer

1. 42 ft

■ **Work Practice Problem 1**

Helpful Hint

We can also solve Example 1 by writing the proportion

$$\frac{2 \text{ inches}}{5 \text{ miles}} = \frac{7 \text{ inches}}{n \text{ miles}}$$

Although other proportions may be used to solve Example 1, we will solve by writing proportions so that the numerators have the same unit measures and the denominators have the same unit measures.

EXAMPLE 2 Finding Medicine Dosage

The standard dose of an antibiotic is 4 cc (cubic centimeters) for every 25 pounds (lb) of body weight. At this rate, find the standard dose for a 140-lb woman.

Solution:

1. UNDERSTAND. Read and reread the problem. You may want to draw a diagram to estimate a reasonable solution.

140–pound woman

25 pounds ⟶ 4 cc
25 pounds ⟶ 4 cc
25 pounds ⟶ 4 cc
25 pounds ⟶ 4 cc
25 pounds ⟶ 4 cc
15 pounds ⟶ ?

140 pounds over 20 cc

From the diagram, we can see that a reasonable solution is a little over 20 cc.

2. TRANSLATE. We will let n represent the unknown number. From the problem, we know that 4 cc is to 25 pounds as n cc is to 140 pounds, or

cubic centimeters ⟶ $\dfrac{4}{25} = \dfrac{n}{140}$ ⟵ cubic centimeters
pounds ⟶ ⟵ pounds

3. SOLVE:

$$\frac{4}{25} = \frac{n}{140}$$

$4 \cdot 140 = 25 \cdot n$ Set the cross products equal to each other.

$560 = 25 \cdot n$ Multiply.

$\dfrac{560}{25} = n$ Divide 560 by 25, the number multiplied by n.

$n = 22\dfrac{2}{5}$ or 22.4   Simplify.

4. INTERPRET. *Check* your work. This result is reasonable since it is a little over 20 cc. *State* your conclusion: The standard dose for a 140-lb woman is 22.4 cc.

Work Practice Problem 2

PRACTICE PROBLEM 2

An auto mechanic recommends that 3 ounces of isopropyl alcohol be mixed with a tankful of gas (14 gallons) to increase the octane of the gasoline for better engine performance. At this rate, how many gallons of gas can be treated with a 16-ounce bottle of alcohol?

Answer

2. $74\dfrac{2}{3}$ or $74.\overline{6}$ gal

PRACTICE PROBLEM 3

If a gallon of paint covers 400 square feet, how many gallons are needed to paint a retaining wall that is 260 feet long and 4 feet high? Round the answer up to the nearest whole gallon.

 EXAMPLE 3 **Calculating Supplies Needed to Fertilize a Lawn**

A 50-pound bag of fertilizer covers 2400 square feet of lawn. How many bags of fertilizer are needed to cover a town square containing 15,360 square feet of lawn? Round the answer up to the nearest whole bag.

Solution:

1. UNDERSTAND. Read and reread the problem. Draw a picture.

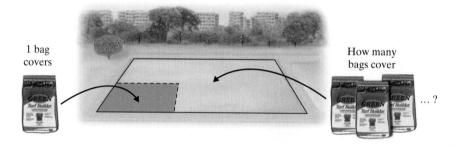

1 bag covers

How many bags cover

... ?

Since one bag covers 2400 square feet, let's see how many 2400's there are in 15,360. We will estimate. The number 15,360 rounded to the nearest thousand is 15,000 and 2400 rounded to the nearest thousand is 2000. Then

$$15,000 \div 2000 = 7\frac{1}{2} \text{ or } 7.5.$$

2. TRANSLATE. We'll let n represent the unknown number. From the problem, we know that 1 bag is to 2400 square feet as n bags is to 15,360 square feet.

$$\begin{array}{ccc} \text{bags} & \rightarrow & \dfrac{1}{2400} = \dfrac{n}{15,360} & \leftarrow & \text{bags} \\ \text{square feet} & \rightarrow & & \leftarrow & \text{square feet} \end{array}$$

Answer

3. 3 gal

3. SOLVE:

$$\frac{1}{2400} = \frac{n}{15,360}$$

$1 \cdot 15,360 = 2400 \cdot n$ Set the cross products equal to each other.

$15,360 = 2400 \cdot n$ Multiply.

$\frac{15,360}{2400} = n$ Divide 15,360 by 2400, the number multiplied by n.

$n = 6.4$ Simplify.

4. INTERPRET. *Check* that replacing n with 6.4 makes the proportion true. Is the answer reasonable? Yes, since it's close to $7\frac{1}{2}$ or 7.5. Since we must buy whole bags of fertilizer, 7 bags are needed. *State* your conclusion: To cover 15,360 square feet of lawn, 7 bags are needed.

Work Practice Problem 3

✔**Concept Check** You are told that 12 ounces of ground coffee will brew enough coffee to serve 20 people. How could you estimate how much ground coffee will be needed to serve 95 people?

5.4 EXERCISE SET

FOR EXTRA HELP

 Student Solutions Manual

 PH Math/Tutor Center

 CD/Video for Review

 Math XL MathXL®

MyMathLab MyMathLab

Objective **A** *Solve. See Examples 1 through 3.*

The ratio of a quarterback's completed passes to attempted passes is 4 to 9.

1. If he attempted 27 passes, find how many passes he completed.

2. If he completed 20 passes, find how many passes he attempted.

It takes Sandra Hallahan 30 minutes to word process and spell check 4 pages.

3. Find how long it takes her to word process and spell check 22 pages.

4. Find how many pages she can word process and spell check in 4.5 hours.

University Law School accepts 2 out of every 7 applicants.

5. If the school accepted 180 students, find how many applications they received.

6. If the school accepted 150 students, find how many applications were received.

On an architect's blueprint, 1 inch corresponds to 8 feet.

7. Find the length of a wall represented by a line $2\frac{7}{8}$ inches long on the blueprint.

8. Find the length of a wall represented by a line $5\frac{1}{4}$ inches on the blueprint.

A human-factors expert recommends that there be at least 9 square feet of floor space in a college classroom for every student in the class.

△ **9.** Find the minimum floor space that 30 students require.

△ **10.** Due to a lack of space, a university converts a 21-by-15-foot conference room into a classroom. Find the maximum number of students the room can accommodate.

A Honda Civic averages 450 miles on a 12-gallon tank of gas.

11. If Dave Smythe runs out of gas in a Honda Civic and AAA comes to his rescue with $1\frac{1}{2}$ gallons of gas, determine how far he can go. Round to the nearest mile.

12. Find how many gallons of gas Denise Wolcott can expect to burn on a 2000-mile vacation trip in a Honda Civic. Round to the nearest gallon.

The scale on an Italian map states that 1 centimeter corresponds to 30 kilometers.

13. Find how far apart Milan and Rome are if their corresponding points on the map are 15 centimeters apart.

14. On the map, a small Italian village is located 0.4 centimeter from the Mediterranean Sea. Find the actual distance.

A drink called Sea Breeze Punch is made by mixing 3 parts of grapefruit juice with 4 parts of cranberry juice.

15. Find how much grapefruit juice should be mixed with 32 ounces of cranberry juice.

16. For a party, 6 quarts of grapefruit juice have been purchased to make Sea Breeze Punch. Find how much cranberry juice should be purchased.

A bag of Scott fertilizer covers 3000 square feet of lawn.

17. Find how many bags of fertilizer should be purchased to cover a rectangular lawn 260 feet by 180 feet.

△ **18.** Find how many bags of fertilizer should be purchased to cover a square lawn measuring 160 feet on each side.

Yearly homeowner property taxes are figured at a rate of $1.45 tax for every $100 of house value.

19. If Janet Blossom pays $2349 in property taxes, find the value of her home.

20. Find the property taxes on a condominium valued at $72,000.

A Cubs baseball player gets 3 hits in every 8 times at bat.

21. If this Cubs player comes up to bat 40 times in the World Series, find how many hits he would be expected to get.

22. At this rate, if he got 12 hits, find how many times he batted.

A survey reveals that 2 out of 3 people prefer Coke to Pepsi.

23. In a room of 40 people, how many people are likely to prefer Coke? Round the answer to the nearest person.

24. In a college class of 36 students, find how many students are likely to prefer Pepsi.

An office uses 5 boxes of envelopes every 3 weeks.

25. Find how long a gross of envelope boxes is likely to last. (A gross of boxes is 144 boxes.) Round to the nearest week.

26. Find how many boxes should be purchased to last a year. Round to the nearest box.

27. The daily supply of oxygen for one person is provided by 625 square feet of lawn. A total of 3750 square feet of lawn would provide the daily supply of oxygen for how many people? (*Source:* Professional Lawn Care Association of America)

28. In the United States, approximately 71 million of the 200 million cars and light trucks in service have driver-side air bags. In a parking lot containing 800 cars and light trucks, how many would be expected to have driver-side air bags? (*Source:* Insurance Institute for Highway Safety)

29. A student would like to estimate the height of the Statue of Liberty in New York City's harbor. The length of the Statue of Liberty's right arm is 42 feet. The student's right arm is 2 feet long and her height is $5\frac{1}{3}$ feet. Use this information to estimate the height of the Statue of Liberty. How close is your estimate to the statue's actual height of 111 feet, 1 inch from heel to top of head? (*Source:* National Park Service)

30. The length of the Statue of Liberty's index finger is 8 feet while the height to the top of the head is about 111 feet. Suppose your measurements are proportionaly the same as this statue and your height is 5 feet.

  a. Use this information to find the proposed length of your index finger. Give an exact measurement and then a decimal rounded to the nearest hundredth.

  b. Measure your index finger and write it as decimal in feet rounded to the nearest hundredth. How close is the length of your index finger to the answer to **a**? Explain why.

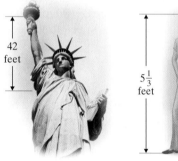

31. There are 72 milligrams of cholesterol in a 3.5 ounce serving of lobster. How much cholesterol is in 5 ounces of lobster? Round to the nearest tenth of a milligram. (*Source:* The National Institute of Health)

32. There are 76 milligrams of cholesterol in a 3-ounce serving of skinless chicken. How much cholesterol is in 8 ounces of chicken? (*Source:* USDA)

33. Trump World Tower in New York City is 881 feet tall and contains 72 stories. The Empire State Building contains 102 stories. If the Empire State Building has the same number of feet per floor as the Trump World Tower, approximate its height rounded to the nearest foot. (*Source:* skyscrapers.com)

34. Two out of every 5 men blame their poor eating habits on too much fast food. In a room of 40 men, how many would you expect to blame their not eating well on fast food? (*Source:* Healthy Choice Mixed Grills survey)

35. Medication is prescribed in 7 out of every 10 hospital emergency room visits that involve an injury. If a large urban hospital had 620 emergency room visits involving an injury in the past month, how many of these visits would you expect included a prescription for medication? (*Source:* National Center for Health Statistics)

36. Currently in the American population of people aged 65 years old and older, there are 145 women for every 100 men. In a nursing home with 280 male residents over the age of 65, how many female residents over the age of 65 would be expected? (*Source:* U.S. Bureau of the Census)

37. McDonald's four-piece Chicken McNuggets® has 190 calories. How many calories are in a nine-piece Chicken McNuggets? (*Source:* McDonald's Corporation)

38. A small order of McDonald's french fries weighs 68 grams and contains 10 grams of fat. McDonald's Super Size® french fries weighs 176 grams. How many grams of fat are in McDonald's SuperSize french fries? Round to the nearest tenth. (*Source:* McDonald's Corporation)

39. One pound of firmly-packed brown sugar yields $2\frac{1}{4}$ cups. How many pounds of brown sugar will be required in a recipe that calls for 6 cups of firmly packed brown sugar? (*Source:* Based on data from *Family Circle* magazine)

40. One out of 3 American adults has worked in the restaurant industry at some point during his or her life. In an office of 84 workers, how many of these people would you expect to have worked in the restaurant industry at some point? (*Source:* National Restaurant Association)

When making homemade ice cream in a hand-cranked freezer, the tub containing the ice cream mix is surrounded by a brine (water/salt) solution. To freeze the ice cream mix rapidly so that smooth and creamy ice cream results, the brine solution should combine crushed ice and rock salt in a ratio of 5 to 1. Use this for Exercises 41 and 42. (Source: White Mountain Freezers, The Rival Company)

41. A small ice cream freezer requires 12 cups of crushed ice. How much rock salt should be mixed with the ice to create the necessary brine solution?

42. A large ice cream freezer requires $18\frac{3}{4}$ cups of crushed ice. How much rock salt will be needed?

43. The gas/oil ratio for a certain chainsaw is 50 to 1.
   a. How much oil (in gallons) should be mixed with 5 gallons of gasoline?
   b. If 1 gallon equals 128 fluid ounces, write the answer to part **a** in fluid ounces. Round to the nearest whole ounce.

44. The gas/oil ratio for a certain tractor mower is 20 to 1.
   a. How much oil (in gallons) should be mixed with 10 gallons of gas?
   b. If 1 gallon equals 4 quarts, write the answer to part **a** in quarts.

45. The adult daily dosage for a certain medicine is 150 mg (milligrams) of medicine for every 20 pounds of body weight.
   a. At this rate, find the daily dose for a man who weighs 275 pounds.
   b. If the man is to receive 500 mg of this medicine every 8 hours, is he receiving the proper dosage?

46. The adult daily dosage for a certain medicine is 80 mg (milligrams) for every 25 pounds of body weight.
   a. At this rate, find the daily dose for a woman who weighs 190 pounds.
   b. If she is to receive this medicine every 6 hours, find the amount to be given every 6 hours.

Review

Find the prime factorization of each number. See Section 2.2.

47. 15   **48.** 21   **49.** 20   **50.** 24

51. 200   **52.** 300   **53.** 32   **54.** 81

Concept Extensions

As we have seen earlier, proportions are often used in medicine dosage calculations. The exercises below have to do with liquid drug preparations, where the weight of the drug is contained in a volume of solution. The description of mg and ml below will help. We will study metric units further in Chapter 7.

   mg means milligrams (A paper clip weighs about a gram. A milligram is about the weight of $\frac{1}{1000}$ of a paper clip.)

   ml means milliliter (A liter is about a quart, A milliliter is about the amount of liquid in $\frac{1}{1000}$ of a quart.)

One way to solve the applications below is to set up the proportion $\frac{mg}{ml} = \frac{mg}{ml}$.

A solution strength of 15 mg of medicine in 1 ml of solution is available.

55. If a patient needs 12 mg of medicine, how many ml do you administer?

56. If a patient need 33 mg of medicine, how many ml do you administer?

A solution strength of 8 mg of medicine in 1 ml of solution is available.

57. If a patient needs 10 mg of medicine, how many ml do you administer?

58. If a patient needs 6 mg of medicine, how many ml do you administer?

Estimate the following. See the Concept Check in this section.

59. It takes 1.5 cups of milk to make 11 muffins. Estimate the amount of milk needed to make 8 dozen muffins. Explain your calculation.

60. A favorite chocolate chip recipe calls for $2\frac{1}{2}$ cups of flour to make 2 dozen cookies. Estimate the amount of flour needed to make 50 cookies. Explain your calculation.

A board such as the one pictured below will balance if the following proportion is true:

$$\frac{\text{first weight}}{\text{second distance}} = \frac{\text{second weight}}{\text{first distance}}$$

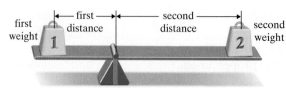

Use this proportion to solve Exercises 61 and 62.

61. Find the distance *n* that will allow the board to balance.

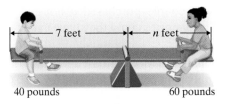

7 feet

n feet

40 pounds

60 pounds

62. Find the length *n* needed to lift the weight below.

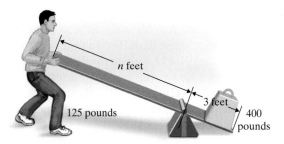

n feet

125 pounds

3 feet

400 pounds

63. Describe a situation in which writing a proportion might solve a problem related to driving a car.

STUDY SKILLS BUILDER

How Are You Doing?

If you haven't done so yet, take a few moments and think about how you are doing in this course. Are you working toward your goal of successfully completing this course? Is your performance on homework, quizzes, and tests satisfactory? If not, you might want to see your instructor to see if he/she has any suggestions on how you can improve your performance. Reread Section 1.1 for ideas on places to get help with your mathematics course.

Answer the following.

1. List any textbook supplements you are using to help you through this course.

2. List any campus resources you are using to help you through this course.

3. Write a short paragraph describing how you are doing in your mathematics course.

4. If improvement is needed, list ways that you can work toward improving your situation as described in Exercise 3.

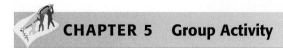

CHAPTER 5   Group Activity

Sections 5.1–5.4

Consumer Price Index

Do you remember when the regular price of a candy bar was 5¢, 10¢, or 25¢? It is certainly difficult to find a candy bar for that price these days. The reason is inflation: The tendency for the price of a given product to increase over time. Businesses and government agencies use the Consumer Price Index (CPI) to track inflation. The CPI measures the change in prices over time of basic consumer goods and services.

The CPI is very useful for comparing the prices of fixed items in various years. For instance, suppose an insurance company customer submits a claim for the theft of a fishing boat purchased in 1975. Because the customer's policy includes replacement cost coverage, the insurance company must calculate how much it would cost to replace the boat at the time of the theft. (Let's assume the theft took place in 2003.) The customer has a receipt for the boat showing that it cost $598 in 1975. The insurance company can use the following proportion to calculate the replacement cost:

$$\frac{\text{price in earlier year}}{\text{price in later year}} = \frac{\text{CPI value in earlier year}}{\text{CPI value in later year}}$$

Because the CPI value is 53.8 for 1975 and 184.0 for 2003, the insurance company would use the following proportion for this situation. (We will let n represent the unknown price in 2003).

$$\frac{\text{price in 1975}}{\text{price in 2003}} = \frac{\text{CPI value in 1975}}{\text{CPI value in 2003}}$$

$$\frac{598}{n} = \frac{53.8}{184.0}$$

$$53.8 \cdot n = 598(184.0)$$

$$53.8 \cdot n = 110{,}032$$

$$\frac{53.8 \cdot n}{53.8} = \frac{110{,}032}{53.8}$$

$$n \approx 2045$$

The replacement cost of the fishing boat at 2003 prices is $2045.

Critical Thinking

1. What trends do you see in the CPI values in the table? Do you think these trends make sense? Explain.

2. A piece of jewelry cost $800 in 1985. What is its 2000 replacement value?

3. In 2000, the cost of a loaf of bread was about $1.89. What would an equivalent loaf of bread cost in 1950?

4. Suppose a couple purchased a house for $22,000 in 1920. At what price could they have expected to sell the house in 1990?

5. An original Ford Model T cost about $850 in 1915. What is the equivalent cost of a Model T in 2000 dollars?

Consumer Price Index	
Year	CPI
1915	10.1
1920	20.0
1925	17.5
1930	16.7
1935	13.7
1940	14.0
1945	18.0
1950	24.1
1955	26.8
1960	29.6
1965	31.5
1970	38.8
1975	53.8
1980	82.4
1985	107.6
1990	130.7
1995	152.4
1997	160.5
1998	163.0
1999	166.6
2000	172.2
2001	177.1
2002	179.9
2003	184.0

(*Source:* Bureau of Labor Statistics, U.S. Department of Labor)

Chapter 5 Vocabulary Check

Fill in each blank with one of the words or phrases listed below.

    not equal   equal   cross products   rate

    unit rate   ratio   unit price   proportion

1. A _____ is the quotient of two numbers. It can be written as a fraction, using a colon, or using the word *to*.

2. $\frac{x}{2} = \frac{7}{16}$ is an example of a _____.

3. A _____ is a rate with a denominator of 1.

4. A _____ is a "money per item" unit rate.

5. A _____ is used to compare different kinds of quantities.

6. In the proportion $\frac{x}{2} = \frac{7}{16}$, $x \cdot 16$ and $2 \cdot 7$ are called _____.

7. If cross products are _____ the proportion is true.

8. If cross products are _____ the proportion is false.

> **Helpful Hint**
>
> Are you preparing for your test? Don't forget to take the Chapter 5 Test on page 364. Then check your answers at the back of the text and use the Chapter Test Prep Video CD to see the fully worked-out solutions to any of the exercises you want to review.

5 Chapter Highlights

DEFINITIONS AND CONCEPTS	EXAMPLES
Section 5.1 Ratios	
A **ratio** is the quotient of two quantities.	The ratio of 3 to 4 can be written as $$\frac{3}{4} \qquad \text{or} \qquad 3:4$$ $\uparrow$ fraction notation $\qquad\qquad$ $\uparrow$ colon notation
Section 5.2 Rates	
Rates are used to compare different kinds of quantities.	Write the rate 12 spikes every 8 inches as a fraction in simplest form. $$\frac{12 \text{ spikes}}{8 \text{ inches}} = \frac{3 \text{ spikes}}{2 \text{ inches}}$$
A **unit rate** is a rate with a denominator of 1.	Write as a unit rate: 117 miles on 5 gallons of gas $$\frac{117 \text{ miles}}{5 \text{ gallons}} = \frac{23.4 \text{ miles}}{1 \text{ gallon}}$$ or 23.4 miles per gallon or 23.4 miles/gallon
A **unit price** is a "money per item" unit rate.	Write as a unit price: $5.88 for 42 ounces of detergent $$\frac{\$5.88}{42 \text{ ounces}} = \frac{\$0.14}{1 \text{ ounce}} = \$0.14 \text{ per ounce}$$

DEFINITIONS AND CONCEPTS	EXAMPLES

Section 5.3   Proportions

A **proportion** is a statement that two ratios or rates are equal.

$\dfrac{1}{2} = \dfrac{4}{8}$ is a proportion.

Is $\dfrac{6}{10} = \dfrac{9}{15}$ a true proportion?

USING CROSS PRODUCTS TO DETERMINE WHETHER PROPORTIONS ARE TRUE OR FALSE

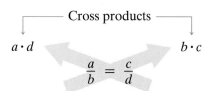

Cross products

$a \cdot d \qquad b \cdot c$

$$\dfrac{a}{b} = \dfrac{c}{d}$$

Cross products

$6 \cdot 15 \qquad 10 \cdot 9$

$$\dfrac{6}{10} = \dfrac{9}{15}$$

$6 \cdot 15 \overset{?}{=} 10 \cdot 9$ Are cross products equal?

$90 = 90$

Since cross products are equal, the proportion is a true proportion.

If cross products are equal, the proportion is true.
If $ad = bc$, then the proportion is true.
If cross products are not equal, the proportion is false.
If $ad \neq bc$, then the proportion is false.

FINDING AN UNKNOWN VALUE N IN A PROPORTION

Step 1. Set the cross products equal to each other.

Find n: $\dfrac{n}{7} = \dfrac{5}{8}$

Step 1.

$$\dfrac{n}{7} = \dfrac{5}{8}$$

$n \cdot 8 = 7 \cdot 5$ Set the cross products equal to each other.

$n \cdot 8 = 35$ Multiply.

Step 2. Divide the number not multiplied by n by the number multiplied by n.

Step 2.

$$n = \dfrac{35}{8}$$ Divide 35 by 8, the number multiplied by n.

$$n = 4\dfrac{3}{8}$$

Section 5.4   Proportions and Problem Solving

Given a specified ratio (or rate) of two quantities, a proportion can be used to determine an unknown quantity.

On a map, 50 miles corresponds to 3 inches. How many miles correspond to 10 inches?

1. UNDERSTAND. Read and reread the problem.

2. TRANSLATE. We let n represent the unknown number. We are given that 50 miles is to 3 inches as n miles is to 10 inches.

miles → $\dfrac{50}{3} = \dfrac{n}{10}$ ← miles
inches → $\phantom{\dfrac{50}{3}}$ ← inches

DEFINITIONS AND CONCEPTS	**EXAMPLES**
Section 5.4 Proportions and Problem Solving	

3. SOLVE:

$$\frac{50}{3} = \frac{n}{10}$$

$50 \cdot 10 = 3 \cdot n$ Set the cross products equal to each other.

$500 = 3 \cdot n$ Multiply.

$\dfrac{500}{3} = n$ Divide 500 by 3, the number multiplied by n.

$n = 166\dfrac{2}{3}$

4. INTERPRET. *Check* your work. *State* your conclusion:

On the map, $166\dfrac{2}{3}$ miles corresponds to 10 inches.

5 CHAPTER REVIEW

(5.1) *Write each ratio as a fraction in simplest form.*

1. 23 to 37

2. 14 to 51

3. 6000 people to 4800 people

4. $121 to $143

5. 3.5 centimeters to 7.5 centimeters

6. 4.25 yards to 8.75 yards

7. $2\dfrac{1}{4}$ to $4\dfrac{3}{8}$

8. $3\dfrac{1}{2}$ to $2\dfrac{7}{10}$

The circle graph below shows how the top 20 movies (or films) of 2004 were rated, use this graph to answer the questions.

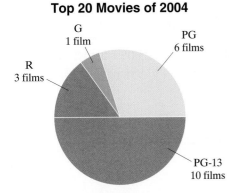

Top 20 Movies of 2004

G — 1 film
PG — 6 films
R — 3 films
PG-13 — 10 films

Source: Internet search and Bryan Gay

9. a. How many top 20 movies were rated PG?

b. Find the ratio of top 20 PG-rated movies to total movies for that year.

10. a. How many top 20 movies were rated R?

b. Find the ratio of top 20 R-rated movies to total movies for that year.

(5.2) *Write each rate as a fraction in simplest form.*

11. 8 stillborn births to 1000 live births

12. 6 professors for 20 graduate research assistants

13. 15 word processing pages printed in 6 minutes

14. 8 computers assembled in 6 hours

Write each rate as a unit rate.

15. 468 miles in 9 hours

16. 180 feet in 12 seconds

17. $6.96 for 4 diskettes

18. 8 gallons of pesticide for 6 acres of crops

19. $234 for books for 5 college courses

20. 104 bushels of fruit from 8 trees

Find each unit price and decide which is the better buy. Round to 3 decimal places. Assume that we are comparing different sizes of the same brand.

21. Taco sauce: 8 ounces for $0.99 or 12 ounces for $1.69

22. Peanut butter: 18 ounces for $1.49 or 28 ounces for $2.39

23. 2% milk: $0.59 for 16 ounces, $1.69 for 64 ounces, or $2.29 for 1 gallon (1 gallon = 128 fluid ounces)

24. Coca-Cola: $0.59 for 12 ounces, $0.79 for 16 ounces, or $1.19 for 32 ounces

(5.3) *Write each sentence as a proportion.*

25. 20 men is to 14 women as 10 men is to 7 women.

26. 50 tries is to 4 successes as 25 tries is to 2 successes.

27. 16 sandwiches is to 8 players as 2 sandwiches is to 1 player.

28. 12 tires is to 3 cars as 4 tires is to 1 car.

Determine whether each proportion is true.

29. $\dfrac{21}{8} = \dfrac{14}{6}$

30. $\dfrac{3}{5} = \dfrac{60}{100}$

31. $\dfrac{3.75}{3} = \dfrac{7.5}{6}$

32. $\dfrac{3.1}{6.2} = \dfrac{0.8}{0.16}$

Find the unknown number n in each proportion.

33. $\dfrac{n}{6} = \dfrac{15}{18}$

34. $\dfrac{n}{9} = \dfrac{5}{3}$

35. $\dfrac{4}{13} = \dfrac{10}{n}$

36. $\dfrac{8}{5} = \dfrac{9}{n}$

37. $\dfrac{8}{\frac{3}{2}} = \dfrac{n}{6}$

38. $\dfrac{9}{2} = \dfrac{n}{\frac{3}{2}}$

39. $\dfrac{27}{\frac{9}{4}} = \dfrac{n}{5}$

40. $\dfrac{6}{\frac{5}{2}} = \dfrac{n}{3}$

41. $\dfrac{0.4}{n} = \dfrac{2}{4.7}$

42. $\dfrac{7.2}{n} = \dfrac{6}{0.3}$

43. $\dfrac{n}{4\frac{1}{2}} = \dfrac{2\frac{1}{10}}{8\frac{2}{5}}$

44. $\dfrac{n}{4\frac{2}{7}} = \dfrac{3\frac{1}{9}}{9\frac{1}{3}}$

(5.4) *Solve.*

The ratio of a quarterback's completed passes to attempted passes is 3 to 7.

45. If he attempts 32 passes, find how many passes he completed. Round to the nearest whole pass.

46. If he completed 15 passes, find how many passes he attempted.

One bag of pesticide covers 4000 square feet of garden.

47. Find how many bags of pesticide should be purchased to cover a rectangular garden that is 180 feet by 175 feet.

△ **48.** Find how many bags of pesticide should be purchased to cover a square garden that is 250 feet on each side.

An owner of a Ford Escort can drive 420 miles on 11 gallons of gas.

49. If Tom Aloiso runs out of gas in an Escort and AAA comes to his rescue with $1\frac{1}{2}$ gallons of gas, determine whether Tom can then drive to a gas station 65 miles away.

50. Find how many gallons of gas Tom can expect to burn on a 3000-mile trip. Round to the nearest gallon.

Yearly homeowner property taxes are figured at a rate of $1.15 tax for every $100 of house value.

51. If a homeowner pays $627.90 in property taxes, find the value of his home.

52. Find the property taxes on a town house valued at $89,000.

On an architect's blueprint, 1 inch = 12 feet.

53. Find the length of a wall represented by a $3\frac{3}{8}$-inch line on the blueprint.

54. If an exterior wall is 99 feet long, find how long the blueprint measurement should be.

Mixed Review

Write each ratio as a fraction in simplest form.

55. 15 to 25

56. 16 to 36

57. 14 feet to 28 feet

58. 25 feet to 60 feet

59. 3 pints to 81 pints

60. 6 pints to 48 pints

Write each rate as a fraction in simplest form.

61. 2 teachers for 18 students

62. 6 nurses for 24 patients

Write each rate as a unit rate.

63. 24 cups for 6 people

64. 18 toys for 3 children

65. 136 miles in 4 hours

66. 12 gallons of milk from 6 cows

Find each unit price and decide which is the better buy. Round to 3 decimal places. Assume that we are comparing different sizes of the same brand.

67. cold medicine:
$4.94 for 4 oz.
$9.98 for 8 oz.

68. juice:
12 oz for $0.65.
64 oz for $2.98.

Write each sentence as a proportion.

69. 2 cups of cookie dough is to 30 cookies as 4 cups of cookie dough is to 60 cookies

70. 5 nickels is to 3 dollars as 20 nickels is to 12 dollars

Determine whether each proportion is a true proportion.

71. $\dfrac{3}{4} = \dfrac{87}{116}$

72. $\dfrac{2}{3} = \dfrac{4}{9}$

Find the unknown number n in each proportion.

73. $\dfrac{3}{n} = \dfrac{15}{8}$

74. $\dfrac{6}{n} = \dfrac{30}{24}$

75. $\dfrac{42}{5} = \dfrac{n}{10}$

76. $\dfrac{5}{4} = \dfrac{n}{20}$

Solve. The monthly loan payment for a car is $39.75 for each $1500 borrowed.

77. Find the monthly payment for a $23,000 car loan.

78. Find the monthly payment for a $18,000 car loan.

An investment of $1,200 yields $152 each year.

79. At the same rate, how much will an investment of $1350 yield in one year?

80. At the same rate, how much will an investment of $750 yield in one year?

5 CHAPTER TEST

Use the Chapter Test Prep Video CD to see the fully worked-out solutions to any of the exercises you want to review.

Write each ratio or rate as a fraction in simplest form.

1. $75 to $10

2. 4500 trees to 6500 trees

3. 28 men to every 4 women

4. 9 inches of rain in 30 days

5. 8.6 to 10

6. $5\frac{7}{8}$ to $9\frac{3}{4}$

7. The world's largest yacht, the Octopus, measures in at 414 feet long. A Boeing 747-400 jumbo jet measures 231 feet long. Find the ratio of the length of the Octopus to a 747–400. (*Source: Power & Motoryacht* magazine)

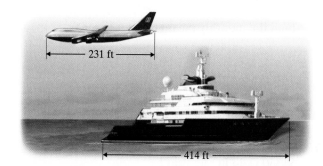

Find each unit rate.

8. 650 kilometers in 8 hours

9. 8 inches of rain in 12 hours

10. 140 students for 5 teachers

11. QR10 (Quest for Curiosity) is the world's first bipedal robot capable of running (moving with both legs off the ground at the same time) at a rate of 108 inches each 12 seconds. (*Source: Guinness World Records*)

Find each unit price and decide which is the better buy.

12. Steak sauce:
8 ounces for $1.19
12 ounces for $1.89

13. Jelly:
$1.49 for 16 ounces
$2.39 for 24 ounces

1. _____

2. _____

3. _____

4. _____

5. _____

6. _____

7. _____

8. _____

9. _____

10. _____

11. _____

12. _____

13. _____

Determine whether each proportion is true.

14. $\dfrac{28}{16} = \dfrac{14}{8}$

15. $\dfrac{3.6}{2.2} = \dfrac{1.9}{1.2}$

16. Write the sentence as a proportion.

25 computers is to 600 students as 1 computer is to 24 students.

Find the unknown number n in each proportion.

17. $\dfrac{n}{3} = \dfrac{15}{9}$

18. $\dfrac{8}{n} = \dfrac{11}{6}$

19. $\dfrac{\dfrac{15}{12}}{\dfrac{3}{7}} = \dfrac{n}{\dfrac{4}{5}}$

20. $\dfrac{1.5}{5} = \dfrac{2.4}{n}$

21. $\dfrac{n}{2\dfrac{5}{8}} = \dfrac{1\dfrac{1}{6}}{3\dfrac{1}{2}}$

Solve.

22. On an architect's drawing, 2 inches corresponds to 9 feet. Find the length of a home represented by a line that is 11 inches long.

23. If a car can be driven 80 miles in 3 hours, how long will it take to travel 100 miles?

24. The standard dose of medicine for a dog is 10 grams for every 15 pounds of body weight. What is the standard dose for a dog that weighs 80 pounds?

25. Jerome Grant worked 6 hours and packed 86 cartons of books. At this rate, how many cartons can he pack in 8 hours?

26. Currently 27 out of every 50 American adults drink coffee every day. In a town with a population of 7900 adults, how many of these adults would you expect to drink coffee every day? (*Source: National Coffee Association*)

14. _____

15. _____

16. _____

17. _____

18. _____

19. _____

20. _____

21. _____

22. _____

23. _____

24. _____

25. _____

26. _____

Answers

1a. _____

b. _____

c. _____

d. _____

2a. _____ b. _____

c. _____ d. _____

3. _____

4. _____

5a. _____

b. _____

6. _____

7. _____

8. _____

9. _____

10. _____

11. _____

12. _____

13. _____

14. _____

15. _____

16. _____

1. Subtract. Check each answer by adding.
  a. $12 - 9$
  b. $11 - 6$
  c. $5 - 5$
  d. $7 - 0$

2. Multiply
  a. $20 \cdot 0$
  b. $20 \cdot 1$
  c. $0 \cdot 20$
  d. $1 \cdot 20$

3. Round 248,982 to the nearest hundred.

4. Round 248,982 to the nearest thousand.

5. Multiply:
  a. $\begin{array}{r} 25 \\ \times\ 8 \\ \hline \end{array}$
  b. $\begin{array}{r} 246 \\ \times\ 5 \\ \hline \end{array}$

6. Divide: $10,468 \div 28$

7. The director of a learning lab at a local community college is working on next year's budget. Thirty-three new DVD players are needed at a cost of $187 each. What is the total cost of these DVD players?

8. A study is being conducted for erecting soundproof walls along the interstate of a metropolitan area. The following feet of walls are part of the proposal. Find their total: 4800 feet, 3270 feet, 2761 feet, 5760 feet.

9. Find the prime factorization of 45.

10. Find $\sqrt{64}$.

11. Write $\dfrac{12}{20}$ in simplest form.

12. Find $9^2 \cdot \sqrt{9}$.

Multiply.

13. $\dfrac{3}{4} \cdot \dfrac{8}{5}$

14. $3\dfrac{3}{8} \cdot 4\dfrac{5}{9}$

15. $\dfrac{6}{13} \cdot \dfrac{26}{30}$

16. $\dfrac{2}{11} \cdot \dfrac{5}{8} \cdot \dfrac{22}{27}$

Perform the indicated operation and simplify.

17. $\dfrac{2}{7} + \dfrac{3}{7}$

18. $\dfrac{26}{30} - \dfrac{7}{30}$

19. $\dfrac{7}{13} + \dfrac{6}{13} + \dfrac{3}{13}$

20. $\dfrac{7}{10} - \dfrac{3}{10} + \dfrac{4}{10}$

21. Find the LCM of 9 and 12.

22. Add: $\dfrac{17}{25} + \dfrac{3}{10}$

23. Write an equivalent fraction with the indicated denominator. $\dfrac{1}{2} = \dfrac{}{14}$

24. Determine whether these fractions are equivalent.

$\dfrac{10}{55}, \dfrac{6}{33}$

25. Subtract: $\dfrac{10}{11} - \dfrac{2}{3}$

26. Subtract: $17\dfrac{5}{24} - 9\dfrac{5}{9}$

27. A flight from Tucson to Phoenix, Arizona, requires $\dfrac{5}{12}$ of an hour. If the plane has been flying $\dfrac{1}{4}$ of an hour, find how much time remains before landing.

Arizona

Phoenix

$\dfrac{5}{12}$ hour

Tucson

28. Simplify: $80 \div 8 \cdot 2 + 7$

29. Add: $2\dfrac{1}{3} + 5\dfrac{3}{8}$

30. Find the average of $\dfrac{3}{5}, \dfrac{4}{9}$, and $\dfrac{11}{15}$.

31. Insert $<$ or $>$ to form a true statement.

$\dfrac{3}{10} \quad \dfrac{2}{7}$

32. Multiply: $28{,}000 \times 500$

33. Write the decimal 1.3 in words.

34. Write "seventy-five thousandths" in standard form.

35. Round 736.2359 to the nearest tenth.

17. _____

18. _____

19. _____

20. _____

21. _____

22. _____

23. _____

24. _____

25. _____

26. _____

27. _____

28. _____

29. _____

30. _____

31. _____

32. _____

33. _____

34. _____

35. _____

36. _____

37. _____

38. _____

39. _____

40. _____

41. _____

42. _____

43. _____

44. _____

45. _____

46. _____

47. _____

48. _____

49. _____

50. _____

36. Round 736.2359 to the nearest thousandth.

37. Add: 23.85 + 1.604

38. Subtract: 700 − 18.76

39. Multiply: 0.283 × 0.3

40. Write $\dfrac{3}{8}$ as a decimal.

41. Divide and check: 0.5 ÷ 4

42. Write 7.9 as an improper fraction.

43. Simplify: 0.5(8.6 − 1.2)

44. Find the unknown number n.
$$\frac{n}{4} = \frac{12}{16}$$

45. Write the numbers in order from smallest to largest.
$$\frac{9}{20}, \frac{4}{9}, 0.456$$

46. Write the rate as a unit rate.
700 meters in 5 seconds

Write each ratio using fractional notation. Simplify Exercises 48 and 50 only.

47. The ratio of 2.6 to 3.1

48. The ratio of 7 to 21

49. The ratio of $1\dfrac{1}{2}$ to $7\dfrac{3}{4}$

50. The ratio of 900 to 9000

6
Percent

This chapter is devoted to percent, a concept used virtually every day in ordinary and business life. Understanding percent and using it efficiently depends on understanding ratios because a percent is a ratio whose denominator is 100. We present techniques to write percents as fractions and as decimals and then solve problems relating to sales tax, commission, discounts, interest, and other real-life situations that use percents.

The Nutrition Labeling and Education Act (NLEA) was signed into law on November 8, 1990. It requires food manufacturers to include nutrition information on their product labels. The NLEA provides specific guidelines concerning the use of terms such as "low fat," or "high fiber." Labels contain information about portion sizes, vitamins and minerals, and sodium, fat, and cholesterol content of foods. The result of this important legislation is to help consumers make more informed and healthier food choices. In Exercises 13 and 14 of Section 6.5, we will determine what percent of some foods' total calories is from fat.

Nutrition Facts

Serving Size 18 crackers (29g)
Servings Per Container About 9

Amount Per Serving

Calories 120   Calories from Fat 35

	% Daily Value*
Total Fat 4g	**6%**
Saturated Fat 0.5g	**3%**
Polyunsaturated Fat 0g	
Monounsaturated Fat 1.5g	
Cholesterol 0mg	**0%**
Sodium 220mg	**9%**
Total Carbohydrate 21g	**7%**
Dietary Fiber 2g	**7%**
Sugars 3g	
Protein 2g	

Vitamin A 0% • Vitamin C 0%

Calcium 2% • Iron 4%

Phosphorus 10%

6.1 INTRODUCTION TO PERCENT

Objective **A** Understanding Percent

The word **percent** comes from the Latin phrase *per centum*, which means **"per 100."** For example, 53% (percent) means 53 per 100. In the square below, 53 of the 100 squares are shaded. Thus, 53% of the figure is shaded.

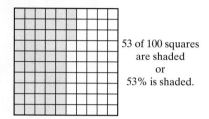
53 of 100 squares are shaded
or
53% is shaded.

Since 53% means 53 per 100, 53% is the ratio of 53 to 100, or $\frac{53}{100}$.

$$53\% = \frac{53}{100}$$

Also,

$$7\% = \frac{7}{100} \qquad \text{7 parts per 100 parts}$$

$$73\% = \frac{73}{100} \qquad \text{73 parts per 100 parts}$$

$$109\% = \frac{109}{100} \qquad \text{109 parts per 100 parts}$$

Percent

Percent means **per one hundred.** The "%" symbol is used to denote percent.

Percent is used in a variety of everyday situations. For example:

- The interest rate is 5.7%.
- 50.5% of U.S. homes have Internet access.
- The store is having a 25%-off sale.
- 78% of us trust our local fire department.
- The enrollment in community colleges has increased 141% in the last 30 years.

PRACTICE PROBLEM 1

Of 100 students in a club, 23 are freshmen. What percent of the students are freshmen?

Answer

1. 23%

EXAMPLE 1

In a survey of 100 people, 17 people drive blue cars. What percent of people drive blue cars?

Solution: Since 17 people out of 100 drive blue cars, the fraction is $\frac{17}{100}$. Then

$$\frac{17}{100} = 17\%$$

▪ **Work Practice Problem 1**

EXAMPLE 2 46 out of every 100 college students live at home. What percent of students live at home? (*Source:* Independent Insurance Agents of America)

Solution:

$$\frac{46}{100} = 46\%$$

■ **Work Practice Problem 2**

PRACTICE PROBLEM 2

29 out of 100 executives are in their forties. What percent of executives are in their forties?

Objective B Writing Percents as Decimals

Since percent means "per hundred," we have that

$$1\% = \frac{1}{100} = 0.01$$

In other words, the percent symbol means "per hundred" or, equivalently, "$\frac{1}{100}$" or "0.01." Thus

$$87\% = 87 \times \frac{1}{100} = \frac{87}{100}$$

or

$$87\% = 87 \times (0.01) = 0.87$$

Of course, we know that the end results are the same, that is,

$$\frac{87}{100} = 0.87$$

The above gives us two options for converting percents. We can replace the percent symbol, %, by $\frac{1}{100}$ or 0.01 and then multiply.

For consistency, when we

- convert from a percent to a *decimal,* we will drop the % symbol and multiply by 0.01. (this section)
- convert from a percent to a *fraction,* we will drop the % symbol and multiply by $\frac{1}{100}$. (next section)

Thus, to write 53.% as a decimal,

$$53\% = 53(0.01) = 0.53 \quad \text{Replace the percent symbol with 0.01. Then multiply.}$$

Writing a Percent as a Decimal

Replace the percent symbol with its decimal equivalent, 0.01; then multiply.

$$43\% = 43(0.01) = 0.43$$

Helpful Hint

If it helps, think of writing a percent as a decimal by

Percent → | Remove the % symbol and move decimal point 2 places to the left | → Decimal

Answer

2. 29%

PRACTICE PROBLEM 3

Write 89% as a decimal.

EXAMPLE 3 Write 23% as a decimal.

Solution:

$$23\% = 23(0.01) \quad \text{Replace the percent symbol with 0.01.}$$
$$= 0.\underset{\smile}{23} \quad \text{Multiply.}$$

■ **Work Practice Problem 3**

PRACTICE PROBLEMS 4–7

Write each percent as a decimal.

4. 2.7%   **5.** 150%
6. 0.69% **7.** 500%

EXAMPLES Write each percent as a decimal.

4. $4.6\% = 4.6(0.01) = 0.\underset{\smile}{046}$ Replace the percent symbol with 0.01. Then multiply.

5. $190\% = 190(0.01) = 1.\underset{\smile}{90}$ or 1.9

6. $0.74\% = 0.74(0.01) = 0.\underset{\smile}{0074}$

7. $100\% = 100(0.01) = 1.\underset{\smile}{00}$ or 1

We just learned that

$$100\% = 1$$

■ **Work Practice Problems 4–7**

✔ **Concept Check** Why is it incorrect to write the percent 0.033% as 3.3 in decimal form?

Objective **C** Writing Decimals as Percents

To write a decimal as a percent, we use the result of Example 7 above. In this example, we found that $1 = 100\%$.

$$0.38 = 0.38(1) = 0.38(100\%) = 38\%$$

Notice that the result is

$$0.38 = 0.38(100\%) = \underset{\curvearrowright}{38.}\%$$ Multiply by 1 in the form of 100%.

Writing a Decimal as a Percent

Multiply by 1 in the form of 100%.

$$0.27 = 0.27(100\%) = \underset{\curvearrowright}{27.}\%$$

Helpful Hint

If it helps, think of writing a decimal as a percent by reversing the steps in the Helpful Hint on the previous page.

Percent ← | Move the decimal point 2 places to the right and attach a % symbol. | ← Decimal

EXAMPLE 8 Write 0.65 as a percent.

Solution:

$$0.65 = 0.65(100\%) = 65.\%$$ Multiply by 100%.

$$= 65\%$$

☐ **Work Practice Problem 8**

PRACTICE PROBLEM 8

Write 0.19 as a percent.

EXAMPLES Write each decimal as a percent.

9. $1.25 = 1.25(100\%) = 125.\%$ or 125%

10. $0.012 = 0.012(100\%) = 001.2\%$ or 1.2%

11. $0.6 = 0.6(100\%) = 060.\%$ or 60%

Helpful Hint
A zero was inserted as a placeholder.

☐ **Work Practice Problems 9–11**

PRACTICE PROBLEMS 9–11

Write each decimal as a percent.

9. 1.75 **10.** 0.044 **11.** 0.7

✔ **Concept Check** Why is it incorrect to write the decimal 0.0345 as 34.5% in percent form?

Answers

8. 19%, **9.** 175%, **10.** 4.4%,
11. 70%

✔ Concept Check Answer

To change a decimal to a percent, multiply by 100%, or move the decimal point *only* two places to the right. So the correct answer is 3.45%.

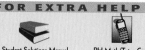
Objective A *Solve. See Examples 1 and 2.*

1. A basketball player makes 81 out of 100 attempted free throws. What percent of free throws was made?

2. In a survey of 100 people, 54 preferred chocolate syrup on their ice cream. What percent preferred chocolate syrup?

3. Michigan leads the United States in tart cherry production, producing 75 out of every 100 tart cherries each year.
   a. What percent of tart cherries are produced in Michigan?
   b. What percent of tart cherries are *not* produced in Michigan? (*Source:* Cherry Marketing Institute)

4. 51 out of 100 adults ages 30 to 49 say the best way to meet a potential date is through volunteer activities.
   a. What percent of adults ages 30 to 49 say the best way to meet a potential date is through volunteer activities?
   b. What percent of adults ages 30 to 49 say the best way to meet a potential date is *not* through volunteer activities? (*Source:* NFO Research for Combe)

Adults were asked what type of cookie was their favorite. The circle graph below shows the average results for every 100 people. Use this graph to answer Exercises 5 through 8. See Examples 1 and 2.

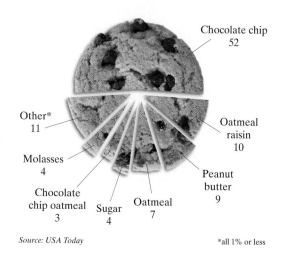

Chocolate chip
52

Other*
11

Oatmeal
raisin
10

Molasses
4

Chocolate
chip oatmeal
3

Sugar
4

Oatmeal
7

Peanut
butter
9

Source: USA Today

*all 1% or less

5. What percent preferred peanut butter cookies?

6. What percent preferred oatmeal raisin cookies?

7. What type of cookie was preferred by most adults? What percent preferred this type of cookie?

8. What two types of cookies were preferred by the same number of adults? What percent preferred each type?

Objective B *Write each percent as a decimal. See Examples 3 through 7.*

9. 48%

10. 64%

11. 6%

12. 9%

13. 100%

14. 136%

15. 61.3%

16. 52.7%

17. 2.8%

18. 1.7%

19. 0.6%

20. 0.9%

21. 300%

22. 700%

23. 32.58%

24. 72.18%

Write each percent as a decimal. See Examples 3 through 7.

25. 67% of American men are happy with their current weight. (*Source:* Gallup for Wheat Foods Council)

26. About 95% of tableservice restaurants in the United States include appetizers on their menus. (*Source:* National Restaurant Association)

27. Video games made up 21.2% of the total toy market in the United States in 2000. (*Source:* The NPD Group Worldwide)

28. In 2003, 50.3% of all paper used was recycled. (*Source:* American Forest & Paper Association)

29. At the beginning of 2005, the U.S. unemployment rate was 5.7%. (*Source:* NH Economic and Labor Market Unemployment Bureau)

30. In 2003, rock music accounted for 25.2% of recorded music sales in the United States. (*Source:* Recording Industry Association of America)

Objective **C** *Write each decimal as a percent. See Examples 8 through 11.*

31. 0.98

32. 0.75

33. 3.1

34. 4.8

35. 29.00

36. 56.00

37. 0.003

38. 0.006

39. 0.22

40. 0.45

41. 5.3

42. 1.6

43. 0.056

44. 0.027

45. 0.3328

46. 0.1115

47. 3.00

48. 5.00

49. 0.7

50. 0.8

Write each decimal as a percent. See Examples 8 through 11.

51. The Munoz family saves 0.10 of their take-home pay.

52. The cost of an item for sale is 0.7 of the sale price.

53. People take aspirin for a variety of reasons. The most common use of aspirin is to prevent heart disease, accounting for 0.38 of all aspirin use. (*Source:* Bayer Market Research)

54. About 0.25 of the world's automobiles are produced in North America. (*Source:* Automotive Intelligence)

55. Nearly 0.093 of people in the United States are affected by pollen allergies. (*Source:* National Institute of Allergy and Infectious Diseases)

56. According to the 2000 census, 0.509 of the American population is female. (*Source:* U.S. Census Bureau)

Review

Write each fraction as a decimal. See Section 4.6.

57. $\dfrac{1}{4}$ **58.** $\dfrac{3}{5}$ **59.** $\dfrac{13}{20}$ **60.** $\dfrac{11}{40}$ **61.** $\dfrac{9}{10}$ **62.** $\dfrac{7}{10}$

Solve. See the Concept Checks in this section.

63. Which of the following are correct?
  a. 6.5% = 0.65 **b.** 7.8% = 0.078
  c. 120% = 0.12 **d.** 0.35% = 0.0035

64. Which of the following are correct?
  a. 0.231 = 23.1% **b.** 5.12 = 0.0512%
  c. 3.2 = 320% **d.** 0.0175 = 0.175%

Recall that 1 = 100%. This means that 1 whole is 100%. Use this for Exercises 65 through 66. (Source: Some Body by Dr. Pete Rowen)

65. The four blood types are A, B, O, and AB. (Each blood type can also be further classified as Rh-positive or Rh-negative depending upon whether your blood contains protein or not.) Given the percent blood types for the U.S. below, calculate the percent of U.S. population with AB blood type.

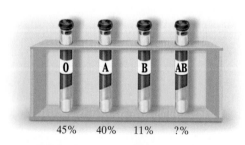

66. The top four components of bone are below. Find the missing percent.
  1. Minerals—45%
  2. Living tissue—30%
  3. Water—20%
  4. Other—?

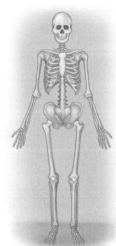

Concept Extensions

The bar graph shows the predicted fastest-growing occupations. Use this graph for Exercises 67 through 70.

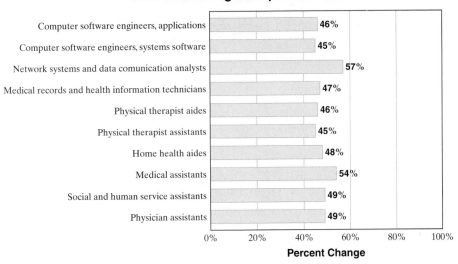

Fastest-Growing Occupations 2002–2012

Occupation	Percent Change
Computer software engineers, applications	46%
Computer software engineers, systems software	45%
Network systems and data comunication analysts	57%
Medical records and health information technicians	47%
Physical therapist aides	46%
Physical therapist assistants	45%
Home health aides	48%
Medical assistants	54%
Social and human service assistants	49%
Physician assistants	49%

Percent Change

Source: Bureau of Labor Statistics

67. What occupation is predicted to be the fastest growing?

68. What occupation is predicted to be the second fastest growing?

69. Write the percent change for physician assistants as a decimal.

70. Write the percent change for medical assistants as a decimal.

 71. In your own words, explain how to write a percent as a decimal.

72. In your own words, explain how to write a decimal as a percent.

STUDY SKILLS BUILDER

Are You Satisfied with Your Performance in this Course thus Far?

To see if there is room for improvement, answer these questions:

1. Am I attending all classes and arriving on time?

2. Am I working and checking my homework assignments on time?

3. Am I getting help (from my instructor or a campus learning resource lab) when I need it?

4. In addition to my instructor, am I using the text supplements that might help me?

5. Am I satisfied with my performance on quizzes and exams?

If you answered no to any of these questions, read or reread Section 1.1 for suggestions in these areas. Also, you might want to contact your instructor for additional feedback.

6.2 PERCENTS AND FRACTIONS

Objective **A** Writing Percents as Fractions

Recall from 6.1 that percent means per hundred. Thus

$$1\% = \frac{1}{100} = 0.01$$

For example,

$$87\% = 87 \times \frac{1}{100} = \frac{87}{100} \quad \text{Writing 87\% as a fraction.}$$

or

$$87\% = 87 \times 0.01 = 0.87 \quad \text{Writing 87\% as a decimal.}$$

In this section we are writing percents as fractions, so we do the following.

Writing a Percent as a Fraction

Replace the percent symbol with its fraction equivalent, $\frac{1}{100}$; then multiply. Don't forget to simplify the fraction if possible.

$$7\% = 7 \cdot \frac{1}{100} = \frac{7}{100}$$

PRACTICE PROBLEMS 1–5

Write each percent as a fraction or mixed number in simplest form.

1. 25%

2. 2.3%

3. 175%

4. $66\frac{2}{3}\%$

5. 8%

EXAMPLES Write each percent as a fraction or mixed number in simplest form.

1. $40\% = 40 \cdot \frac{1}{100} = \frac{40}{100} = \frac{2 \cdot \cancel{20}^{1}}{5 \cdot \cancel{20}_{1}} = \frac{2}{5}$

2. $1.9\% = 1.9 \cdot \frac{1}{100} = \frac{1.9}{100}$. We don't want the numerator of the fraction to contain a decimal, so we multiply by 1 in the form of $\frac{10}{10}$.

$$= \frac{1.9}{100} \cdot \frac{10}{10} = \frac{1.9 \cdot 10}{100 \cdot 10} = \frac{19}{1000}$$

3. $125\% = 125 \cdot \frac{1}{100} = \frac{125}{100} = \frac{5 \cdot \cancel{25}^{1}}{4 \cdot \cancel{25}_{1}} = \frac{5}{4} \text{ or } 1\frac{1}{4}$

4. $33\frac{1}{3}\% = \underbrace{33\frac{1}{3}}_{\substack{\llcorner\; \text{Write as} \;\lrcorner \\ \text{an improper fraction.}}} \cdot \frac{1}{100} = \frac{100}{3} \cdot \frac{1}{100} = \frac{\cancel{100}^{1} \cdot 1}{3 \cdot \cancel{100}_{1}} = \frac{1}{3}$

5. $100\% = 100 \cdot \frac{1}{100} = \frac{100}{100} = 1$

> **Helpful Hint**
> Just as in the previous section, we confirm that 100% = 1

Work Practice Problems 1–5

Answers

1. $\frac{1}{4}$, **2.** $\frac{23}{1000}$, **3.** $\frac{7}{4}$ or $1\frac{3}{4}$,

4. $\frac{2}{3}$, **5.** $\frac{2}{25}$

Objective B Writing Fractions as Percents

Recall that to write a percent as a fraction, we replace the percent symbol by its fraction equivalent, $\frac{1}{100}$. We reverse these steps to write a fraction as a percent.

Writing a Fraction as a Percent

Multiply by 1 in the form of 100%.

$$\frac{1}{8} = \frac{1}{8} \cdot 100\% = \frac{1}{8} \cdot \frac{100}{1}\% = \frac{100}{8}\% = 12\frac{1}{2}\% \quad \text{or} \quad 12.5\%$$

Helpful Hint

From Example 5, we know that

$$100\% = 1$$

Recall that when we multiply a number by 1, we are not changing the value of that number. This means that when we multiply a number by 100%, we are not changing its value but rather writing the number as an equivalent percent.

 EXAMPLES Write each fraction or mixed number as a percent.

6. $\frac{9}{20} = \frac{9}{20} \cdot 100\% = \frac{9}{20} \cdot \frac{100}{1}\% = \frac{900}{20}\% = 45\%$

7. $\frac{2}{3} = \frac{2}{3} \cdot 100\% = \frac{2}{3} \cdot \frac{100}{1}\% = \frac{200}{3}\% = 66\frac{2}{3}\%$

Helpful Hint

$\frac{200}{3} = 66.\overline{6}$. Thus, another way to write $\frac{200}{3}\%$ is $66.\overline{6}\%$.

8. $1\frac{1}{2} = \frac{3}{2} \cdot 100\% = \frac{3}{2} \cdot \frac{100}{1}\% = \frac{300}{2}\% = 150\%$

☐ **Work Practice Problems 6–8**

✔ **Concept Check** Which digit in the percent 76.4582% represents

a. A tenth percent?

b. A thousandth percent?

c. A hundredth percent?

d. A whole percent?

PRACTICE PROBLEMS 6–8

Write each fraction or mixed number as a percent.

6. $\frac{1}{2}$ **7.** $\frac{7}{40}$ **8.** $2\frac{1}{4}$

Answers

6. 50%, **7.** $17\frac{1}{2}\%$, **8.** 225%

✔ **Concept Check Answers**

a. 4, **b.** 8, **c.** 5, **d.** 6

PRACTICE PROBLEM 9

Write $\frac{3}{17}$ as a percent. Round to the nearest hundredth percent.

EXAMPLE 9 Write $\frac{1}{12}$ as a percent. Round to the nearest hundredth percent.

Solution:

"approximately"

$$\frac{1}{12} = \frac{1}{12} \cdot 100\% = \frac{1}{12} \cdot \frac{100\%}{1} = \frac{100}{12}\% \approx 8.33\%$$

$$\begin{array}{r} 8.333 \approx 8.33 \\ 12\overline{)100.000} \\ \underline{-96} \\ 4\,0 \\ \underline{-3\,6} \\ 40 \\ \underline{-36} \\ 40 \\ \underline{-36} \\ 4 \end{array}$$

Thus, $\frac{1}{12}$ is approximately 8.33%.

◻ **Work Practice Problem 9**

Objective C Converting Percents, Decimals, and Fractions

Let's summarize what we have learned so far about percents, decimals, and fractions.

Summary of Converting Percents, Decimals, and Fractions

- *To write a percent as a decimal*, replace the % symbol with its decimal equivalent, 0.01; then multiply.
- *To write a percent as a fraction*, replace the % symbol with its fraction equivalent, $\frac{1}{100}$; then multiply.
- *To write a decimal or fraction as a percent*, multiply by 100%.

If we let p represent a number, below we summarize using symbols.

Write a percent as a decimal:	Write a percent as a fraction:	Write a number as a percent:
$p\% = p(0.01)$	$p\% = p \cdot \frac{1}{100}$	$p = p \cdot 100\%$

Answer

9. 17.65%

EXAMPLE 10 17.8% of automobile thefts in the continental United States occur in the Midwest. Write this percent as a decimal and as a fraction. (*Source:* The American Automobile Manufacturers Association)

Solution:

As a decimal: $17.8\% = 17.8(0.01) = 0.178.$

As a fraction: $17.8\% = 17.8 \cdot \dfrac{1}{100} = \dfrac{17.8}{100} = \dfrac{17.8}{100} \cdot \dfrac{10}{10} = \dfrac{178}{1000} = \dfrac{\overset{1}{\cancel{2}} \cdot 89}{\underset{1}{\cancel{2}} \cdot 500} = \dfrac{89}{500}.$

Thus, 17.8% written as a decimal is 0.178, and written as a fraction is $\dfrac{89}{500}$.

▣ **Work Practice Problem 10**

EXAMPLE 11 An advertisement for a stereo system reads "$\dfrac{1}{4}$ off." What percent off is this?

Solution: Write $\dfrac{1}{4}$ as a percent.

$$\frac{1}{4} = \frac{1}{4} \cdot 100\% = \frac{1}{4} \cdot \frac{100\%}{1} = \frac{100}{4}\% = 25\%$$

Thus, "$\dfrac{1}{4}$ off" is the same as "25% off."

▣ **Work Practice Problem 11**

Note: It is helpful to know a few basic percent conversions. Appendix A4 contains a handy reference of percent, decimal, and fraction equivalencies.
   Also, Appendix A4 shows how to find common percents of a number.

PRACTICE PROBLEM 10
A family decides to spend no more than 22.5% of its monthly income on rent. Write 22.5% as a decimal and as a fraction.

PRACTICE PROBLEM 11
Provincetown's budget for waste disposal increased by $1\dfrac{1}{4}$ times over the budget from last year. What percent increase is this?

Answers

10. $0.225, \dfrac{9}{40}$,   **11.** 125%

Mental Math

Write each fraction as a percent.

1. $\dfrac{13}{100}$

2. $\dfrac{92}{100}$

3. $\dfrac{87}{100}$

4. $\dfrac{71}{100}$

5. $\dfrac{1}{100}$

6. $\dfrac{2}{100}$

6.2 EXERCISE SET

FOR EXTRA HELP

Student Solutions Manual   PH Math/Tutor Center   CD/Video for Review   MathXL MathXL®   MyMathLab MyMathLab

Objective **A** *Write each percent as a fraction or mixed number in simplest form. See Examples 1 through 5.*

1. 12%

2. 24%

 3. 4%

4. 2%

5. 4.5%

6. 7.5%

 7. 175%

8. 250%

9. 73%

10. 86%

11. 12.5%

12. 62.5%

13. 6.25%

14. 3.75%

15. 6%

16. 16%

 17. $10\dfrac{1}{3}\%$

18. $7\dfrac{3}{4}\%$

19. $22\dfrac{3}{8}\%$

20. $15\dfrac{5}{8}\%$

Objective **B** *Write each fraction or mixed number as a percent. See Examples 6 through 8.*

21. $\dfrac{3}{4}$

22. $\dfrac{5}{8}$

 23. $\dfrac{7}{10}$

24. $\dfrac{3}{10}$

25. $\dfrac{2}{5}$

26. $\dfrac{4}{5}$

27. $\dfrac{59}{100}$

28. $\dfrac{73}{100}$

29. $\dfrac{17}{50}$

30. $\dfrac{47}{50}$

 31. $\dfrac{3}{8}$

32. $\dfrac{5}{16}$

33. $\dfrac{5}{16}$ **34.** $\dfrac{7}{16}$ **35.** $1\dfrac{3}{5}$ **36.** $1\dfrac{3}{4}$ **37.** $\dfrac{7}{9}$ **38.** $\dfrac{1}{3}$

39. $\dfrac{13}{20}$ **40.** $\dfrac{3}{20}$ **41.** $2\dfrac{1}{2}$ **42.** $2\dfrac{1}{5}$ **43.** $1\dfrac{9}{10}$ **44.** $2\dfrac{7}{10}$

Write each fraction as a percent. Round to the nearest hundredth percent. See Example 9.

45. $\dfrac{7}{11}$ **46.** $\dfrac{5}{12}$ **47.** $\dfrac{4}{15}$ **48.** $\dfrac{10}{11}$

49. $\dfrac{1}{7}$ **50.** $\dfrac{1}{9}$ **51.** $\dfrac{11}{12}$ **52.** $\dfrac{5}{6}$

Objective **C** *Complete each table. See Examples 10 and 11.*

53.

Percent	Decimal	Fraction
35%		
		$\dfrac{1}{5}$
	0.5	
70%		
		$\dfrac{3}{8}$

54.

Percent	Decimal	Fraction
50%		
		$\dfrac{2}{5}$
	0.25	
12.5%		
		$\dfrac{5}{8}$
		$\dfrac{7}{50}$

55.

Percent	Decimal	Fraction
40%		
	0.235	
		$\dfrac{4}{5}$
$33\dfrac{1}{3}\%$		
		$\dfrac{7}{8}$
7.5%		

56.

Percent	Decimal	Fraction
	0.525	
		$\dfrac{3}{4}$
$66\dfrac{2}{3}\%$		
		$\dfrac{5}{6}$
100%		

57.

Percent	Decimal	Fraction
200%		
	2.8	
705%		
		$4\frac{27}{50}$

58.

Percent	Decimal	Fraction
800%		
	3.2	
608%		
		$9\frac{13}{50}$

Solve. See Examples 10 and 11.

 59. Approximately 14.8% of new luxury cars are silver, making silver the most popular new vehicle color for that class. Write this percent as a decimal and a fraction. (*Source:* Ward's Communications)

60. In 1950, the United States produced 75.7% of all motor vehicles made worldwide. Write this percent as a decimal and a fraction. (*Source:* American Automobile Manufacturers Association)

61. At this writing, 23% of Americans surveyed are in favor of abolishing the penny. Write this percent as a decimal and a fraction.

62. 52% of Americans say that their ideal family size is fewer than three children. Write this percent as a decimal and a fraction. (*Source:* Gallup)

63. In 2003, $\frac{137}{500}$ of all new cars sold in the United States were imports. Write this fraction as a percent. (*Source:* Ward's AutoInfoBank)

64. In 1997, $\frac{41}{250}$ of all new cars sold in the United States were imports. Write this fraction as a percent. (*Source:* Ward's Communications)

65. The sales tax in Slidell, Louisiana, is 8.75%. Write this percent as a decimal.

66. A real estate agent receives a commission of 3% of the sale price of a house. Write this percent as a decimal.

67. In the 2003/2004 television season, the top-rated show was *CSI: Crime Scene Investigation,* which had an average audience share of $\frac{6}{25}$ of all those watching television during that time slot. Write this fraction as a percent. (*Source:* Nielsen Media Research)

68. The 2003 National Assessment of Educational Progress showed that $\frac{8}{25}$ of U.S. fourth-graders were proficient in math. Write this fraction as a percent. (*Source:* National Center for Education Statistics)

In Exercises 69 through 74, you are asked to write each percent in this circle graph as a decimal and a fraction.

World Population by Continent

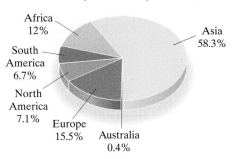

69. 0.4%   **70.** 58.3%   **71.** 12%

72. 6.7%   **73.** 7.1%   **74.** 15.5%

Review

Find the value of n. See Section 5.3.

75. $3 \cdot n = 45$ **76.** $7 \cdot n = 48$ **77.** $8 \cdot n = 80$

78. $2 \cdot n = 16$ **79.** $6 \cdot n = 72$ **80.** $5 \cdot n = 35$

Concept Extensions

Solve. See the Concept Check in this section.

81. Given the percent 52.8647%, round as indicated.
   a. Round to a tenth of a percent.
   b. Round to a hundredth of a percent.

82. Given the percent 0.5269%, round as indicated.
   a. Round to a tenth of a percent.
   b. Round to a hundredth of a percent.

83. Write 1.07835 as a percent rounded to the nearest tenth of a percent.

84. Write 1.25348 as a percent rounded to the nearest tenth of a percent.

85. Write 0.65794 as a percent rounded to the nearest hundredth of a percent.

86. Write 0.92571 as a percent rounded to the nearest hundredth of a percent.

87. Write 0.7682 as a percent rounded to the nearest percent.

88. Write 0.2371 as a percent rounded to the nearest percent.

What percent of the figure is shaded?

89.   **90.**   **91.**   **92.**

Fill in the blanks.

93. A fraction written as a percent is greater than 100% when the numerator is _____ than the denominator. (greater/less)

94. A decimal written as a percent is less than 100% when the decimal is _____ than 1. (greater/less)

95. In your own words, explain how to write a percent as a fraction.

96. In your own words, explain how to write a fraction as a decimal.

Write each fraction as a decimal and then write each decimal as a percent. Round the decimal to three decimal places (nearest thousandth) and the percent to the nearest tenth of a percent.

97. $\frac{21}{79}$ **98.** $\frac{56}{102}$ **99.** $\frac{850}{736}$ **100.** $\frac{506}{248}$

STUDY SKILLS BUILDER

What to Do the Day of an Exam

On the day of an exam, don't forget to try the following:

- Allow yourself plenty of time to arrive.
- Read the directions on the test carefully.
- Read each problem carefully as you take your test. Make sure that you answer the question asked.
- Watch your time and pace yourself so that you may attempt each problem on your test.
- Check your work and answers.
- ***Do not turn your test in early.*** If you have extra time, spend it double-checking your work.

Good luck!

Answer the following questions based on your most recent mathematics exam, whenever that was.

1. How soon before class did you arrive?
2. Did you read the directions on the test carefully?
3. Did you make sure you answered the question asked for each problem on the exam?
4. Were you able to attempt each problem on your exam?
5. If your answer to Question 4 is no, list reasons why.
6. Did you have extra time on your exam?
7. If your answer to Question 6 is yes, describe how you spent that extra time.

6.3 SOLVING PERCENT PROBLEMS USING EQUATIONS

Note: Sections 6.3 and 6.4 introduce two methods for solving percent problems. It is not necessary that you study both sections. You may want to check with your instructor for further advice.

Throughout this text, we have written mathematical statements such as $3 + 10 = 13$, or area = length · width. These statements are called "equations." An **equation** is a mathematical statement that contains an equal sign. To solve percent problems in this section, we translate the problems into such mathematical statements, or equations.

Objective **A** Writing Percent Problems as Equations

Recognizing key words in a percent problem is helpful in writing the problem as an equation. Three key words in the statement of a percent problem and their meanings are as follows:

of means **multiplication** (·)

is means **equals** (=)

what (or some equivalent) means **the unknown number**

In our examples, we let the letter n stand for the unknown number.

> **Helpful Hint**
> Any letter of the alphabet can be used to represent the unknown number. In this section, we use the letter n.

EXAMPLE 1 Translate to an equation.

5 is what percent of 20?

Solution: 5 is what percent of 20?

$$5 = n \cdot 20$$

⬛ **Work Practice Problem 1**

> **Helpful Hint**
> Remember that an equation is simply a mathematical statement that contains an equal sign (=).
>
> $$5 = n \cdot 20$$
>
> ↑
> equal sign

EXAMPLE 2 Translate to an equation.

1.2 is 30% of what number?

Solution: 1.2 is 30% of what number?

$$1.2 = 30\% \cdot n$$

⬛ **Work Practice Problem 2**

PRACTICE PROBLEM 1

Translate: 6 is what percent of 24?

PRACTICE PROBLEM 2

Translate: 1.8 is 20% of what number?

Answers
1. $6 = n \cdot 24$,   **2.** $1.8 = 20\% \cdot n$

PRACTICE PROBLEM 3

Translate: What number is 40% of 3.6?

EXAMPLE 3 Translate to an equation.

What number is 25% of 0.008?

Solution: What number is 25% of 0.008?

$$n = 25\% \cdot 0.008$$

📖 **Work Practice Problem 3**

PRACTICE PROBLEMS 4–6

Translate each to an equation.
4. 42% of 50 is what number?
5. 15% of what number is 9?
6. What percent of 150 is 90?

EXAMPLES Translate each of the following to an equation:

4. 38% of 200 is what number?

$$38\% \cdot 200 = n$$

5. 40% of what number is 80?

$$40\% \cdot n = 80$$

6. What percent of 85 is 34?

$$n \cdot 85 = 34$$

📖 **Work Practice Problems 4–6**

✔**Concept Check** In the equation $2 \cdot n = 10$, what step should be taken to solve the equation for n?

Objective **B** Solving Percent Problems

You may have noticed by now that each percent problem has contained three numbers—in our examples, two are known and one is unknown. Each of these numbers is given a special name.

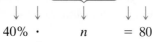

15% of 60 is 9

| 15% percent | · | 60 base | = | 9 amount |

We call this equation the **percent equation.**

Percent Equation

percent · base = amount

Helpful Hint

Notice that the percent equation given above is a true statement. To see this, simplify the left side as shown:

$$15\% \cdot 60 = 9$$
$$0.15 \cdot 60 = 9 \quad \text{Write 15\% as 0.15.}$$
$$9 = 9 \quad \text{Multiply.}$$

The statement $9 = 9$ is true.

Answers

3. $n = 40\% \cdot 3.6$, 4. $42\% \cdot 50 = n$,
5. $15\% \cdot n = 9$, 6. $n \cdot 150 = 90$

✔ **Concept Check Answer**

If $2 \cdot n = 10$, then $n = \dfrac{10}{2}$, or $n = 5$.

After a percent problem has been written as a percent equation, we can use the equation to find the unknown number. This is called **solving** the equation.

Solving Percent Equations for the Amount

EXAMPLE 7

What number is 35% of 40?

Solution:

$$n = 35\% \cdot 40 \quad \text{Translate to an equation.}$$
$$n = 0.35 \cdot 40 \quad \text{Write 35\% as 0.35.}$$
$$n = 14 \quad \text{Multiply } 0.35 \cdot 40 = 14.$$

Thus, 14 is 35% of 40.

Work Practice Problem 7

PRACTICE PROBLEM 7
What number is 20% of 85?

Helpful Hint

When solving a percent equation, write the percent as a decimal (or fraction).

EXAMPLE 8

85% of 300 is what number?

Solution:

$$85\% \cdot 300 = n \quad \text{Translate to an equation.}$$
$$0.85 \cdot 300 = n \quad \text{Write 85\% as 0.85.}$$
$$255 = n \quad \text{Multiply } 0.85 \cdot 300 = 255.$$

Thus, 85% of 300 is 255.

Work Practice Problem 8

PRACTICE PROBLEM 8
90% of 150 is what number?

Solving Percent Equations for the Base

EXAMPLE 9

12% of what number is 0.6?

Solution:

$$12\% \cdot n = 0.6 \quad \text{Translate to an equation.}$$
$$0.12 \cdot n = 0.6 \quad \text{Write 12\% as 0.12.}$$

Recall from Section 5.3 that if "0.12 times some number is 0.6," then the number is 0.6 divided by 0.12.

$$n = \frac{0.6}{0.12} \quad \text{Divide 0.6 by 0.12, the number multiplied by } n.$$
$$n = 5$$

Thus, 12% of 5 is 0.6.

Work Practice Problem 9

PRACTICE PROBLEM 9
15% of what number is 1.2?

Answers
7. 17,   **8.** 135,   **9.** 8

PRACTICE PROBLEM 10

27 is $4\frac{1}{2}$ % of what number?

EXAMPLE 10

$$
\begin{array}{ccccc}
13 & \text{is} & 6\frac{1}{2}\% & \text{of} & \underbrace{\text{what number?}} \\
\downarrow & \downarrow & \downarrow & \downarrow & \downarrow
\end{array}
$$

Solution:
$$13 = 6\frac{1}{2}\% \cdot n \quad \text{Translate to an equation.}$$
$$13 = 0.065 \cdot n \quad 6\frac{1}{2}\% = 6.5\% = 0.065.$$
$$\frac{13}{0.065} = n \quad \text{Divide 13 by 0.065, the number multiplied by } n.$$
$$200 = n$$

Thus, 13 is $6\frac{1}{2}$% of 200.

⬛ **Work Practice Problem 10**

Solving Percent Equations for Percent

EXAMPLE 11

$$
\begin{array}{ccccc}
\underbrace{\text{What percent}} & \text{of} & 12 & \text{is} & 9? \\
\downarrow & & \downarrow & \downarrow & \downarrow
\end{array}
$$

Solution:
$$n \cdot 12 = 9 \quad \text{Translate to an equation.}$$
$$n = \frac{9}{12} \quad \text{Divide 9 by 12, the number multiplied by } n.$$
$$n = 0.75$$

Next, since we are looking for percent, we write 0.75 as a percent.

$$n = 75\%$$

So, 75% of 12 is 9.

⬛ **Work Practice Problem 11**

PRACTICE PROBLEM 11

What percent of 80 is 8?

> **Helpful Hint**
> If your unknown in the percent equation is the percent, don't forget to convert your answer to a percent.

PRACTICE PROBLEM 12

35 is what percent of 25?

EXAMPLE 12

$$
\begin{array}{ccccc}
78 & \text{is} & \underbrace{\text{What percent}} & \text{of} & 65? \\
\downarrow & \downarrow & \downarrow & & \downarrow \downarrow
\end{array}
$$

Solution:
$$78 = n \cdot 65 \quad \text{Translate to an equation.}$$
$$\frac{78}{65} = n \quad \text{Divide 78 by 65, the number multiplied by } n.$$
$$1.2 = n$$
$$120\% = n \quad \text{Write 1.2 as a percent.}$$

So, 78 is 120% of 65.

⬛ **Work Practice Problem 12**

Answers

10. 600, **11.** 10%, **12.** 140%

✔**Concept Check** Consider these problems

1. 75% of 50 =

   a. 50

   b. a number greater than 50

   c. a number less than 50

2. 40% of a number is 10. Is the number

   a. 10

   b. less than 10

   c. greater than 10?

3. 800 is 120% of what number? Is the number

   a. 800

   b. less than 800

   c. greater than 800?

Helpful Hint

Use the following to see if your answers are reasonable.

$$(100\%) \text{ of a number} = \text{the number}$$

$$\left(\begin{array}{c}\text{a percent} \\ \text{greater than} \\ 100\%\end{array}\right) \text{ of a number} = \begin{array}{l}\text{a number larger} \\ \text{than the original number}\end{array}$$

$$\left(\begin{array}{c}\text{a percent} \\ \text{less than } 100\%\end{array}\right) \text{ of a number} = \begin{array}{l}\text{a number less} \\ \text{than the original number}\end{array}$$

Mental Math

Identify the percent, the base, and the amount in each equation. Recall that percent · base = amount.

1. $42\% \cdot 50 = 21$

2. $30\% \cdot 65 = 19.5$

3. $107.5 = 125\% \cdot 86$

4. $99 = 110\% \cdot 90$

6.3 EXERCISE SET

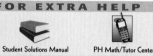
Objective A *Translate each to an equation. Do not solve. See Examples 1 through 6.*

1. 15% of 72 is what number?

2. 72% of 63 is what number?

3. 30% of what number is 80?

4. 50% of what number is 8?

5. 1.9 is 40% of what number?

6. 0.5 is 20% of what number?

7. What percent of 90 is 20?

8. 4.5 is what percent of 45?

9. What number is 9% of 43?

10. What number is 25% of 55?

Objective B *Solve. See Examples 7 and 8.*

11. 10% of 35 is what number?

12. 25% of 60 is what number?

13. What number is 14% of 52?

14. What number is 30% of 17?

Solve. See Examples 9 and 10.

15. 5% of what number is 30?

16. 25% of what number is 25?

17. 1.2 is 12% of what number?

18. 0.22 is 44% of what number?

Solve. See Examples 11 and 12.

19. What percent of 60 is 66?

20. What percent of 20 is 30?

21. 16 is what percent of 50?

22. 27 is what percent of 50?

Objectives A B Mixed Review *Solve. See Examples 1 through 12.*

23. 0.1 is 10% of what number?

24. 0.5 is 5% of what number?

25. 125% of 36 is what number?

26. 200% of 13.5 is what number?

27. 82.5 is $16\frac{1}{2}\%$ of what number?

28. 7.2 is $6\frac{1}{4}\%$ of what number?

29. 126 is what percent of 31.5?

30. 264 is what percent of 33?

31. What number is 42% of 60?

32. What number is 36% of 80?

33. What percent of 150 is 67.5?

34. What percent of 105 is 88.2?

35. 120% of what number is 42?

36. 160% of what number is 40?

37. 2.4% of 26 is what number?

38. 4.8% of 32 is what number?

39. What percent of 600 is 3?

40. What percent of 500 is 2?

41. 6.67 is 4.6% of what number?

42. 9.75 is 7.5% of what number?

43. 1575 is what percent of 2500?

44. 2520 is what percent of 3500?

Review

Find the value of n in each proportion. See Section 5.3.

45. $\dfrac{27}{n} = \dfrac{9}{10}$

46. $\dfrac{35}{n} = \dfrac{7}{5}$

47. $\dfrac{n}{5} = \dfrac{8}{11}$

48. $\dfrac{n}{3} = \dfrac{6}{13}$

Write each phrase as a proportion.

49. 17 is to 12 as n is to 20

50. 20 is to 25 as n is to 10

51. 8 is to 9 as 14 is to n

52. 5 is to 6 as 15 is to n

Concept Extensions

For each equation, determine the next step taken to find the value of n. See the first Concept Check in this section.

53. $5 \cdot n = 32$

    a. $n = 5 \cdot 32$ **b.** $n = \dfrac{5}{32}$ **c.** $n = \dfrac{32}{5}$ **d.** none of these

54. $n = 0.7 \cdot 12$

    a. $n = 8.4$ **b.** $n = \dfrac{12}{0.7}$ **c.** $n = \dfrac{0.7}{12}$ **d.** none of these

55. $0.06 = n \cdot 7$

    a. $n = 0.06 \cdot 7$ **b.** $n = \dfrac{0.06}{7}$ **c.** $n = \dfrac{7}{0.06}$ **d.** none of these

56. Write a word statement for the equation $20\% \cdot n = 18.6$. Use the phrase "some number" for "n".

57. Write a word statement for the equation $n = 33\frac{1}{3}\% \cdot 24$. Use the phrase "some number" for "n".

For each exercise, determine whether the percent, n, is (a) 100%, (b) greater than 100%, or (c) less than 100%. See the last Concept Check in this section.

58. $n\%$ of 20 is 30

59. $n\%$ of 98 is 98

60. $n\%$ of 120 is 85

For each exercise, determine whether the number, n, is (a) equal to 45, (b) greater than 45, or (c) less than 45.

61. 55% of 45 is n

62. 230% of 45 is n

63. 100% of 45 is n

64. 30% of n is 45

65. 100% of n is 45

66. 180% of n is 45

Solve.

67. In your own words, explain how to solve a percent equation.

68. Write a percent problem that uses the percent 50%.

69. 1.5% of 45,775 is what number?

70. What percent of 75,528 is 27,945.36?

71. 22,113 is 180% of what number?

 THE BIGGER PICTURE Operations on Sets of Numbers and Solving Equations

Continue your outline from Sections 1.7, 1.9, 2.5, 3.4, 4.5, and 5.3. Suggestions are once again written to help you complete this part of your outline. Notice that this part of the outline has to do with solving equations.

I. Some Operations on Sets of Numbers
  A. Whole Numbers
    1. Add or Subtract (Sections 1.3, 1.4)
    2. Multiply or Divide (Sections 1.6, 1.7)
    3. Exponent (Section 1.9)
    4. Square Root (Section 1.9)
    5. Order of Operations (Section 1.9)
  B. Fractions
    1. Simplify (Section 2.3)
    2. Multiply (Section 2.4)
    3. Divide (Section 2.5)
    4. Add or Subtract (Section 3.4)
  C. Decimals
    1. Add or Subtract (Section 4.3)
    2. Multiply (Section 4.4)
    3. Divide (Section 4.5)

II. Solving Equations
  A. Proportions (Section 5.3)
  B. Percent Problems
    1. Solved by Equations: Remember that "of" means multiplication and "is" means equals.

12% of some number is 6 translates to

$$12\% \cdot n = 6 \ or \ 0.12 \cdot n = 6 \ or \ n = \frac{6}{0.12} \ or \ n = 50$$

Perform the indicated operations.

1. $\dfrac{2}{9} + \dfrac{1}{5}$
    2. $42 \div 2 \cdot 3$

3. $0.03(0.7)$
    4. $\sqrt{49} + \sqrt{1}$

Solve.

5. $\dfrac{3}{8} = \dfrac{n}{128}$
    6. $\dfrac{7.2}{n} = \dfrac{36}{8}$

7. 215 is what percent of 86?

8. 95% of 48 is what number?

9. 4.2 is what percent of 15?

10. 93.6 is 52% of what number?

6.4 SOLVING PERCENT PROBLEMS USING PROPORTIONS

There is more than one method that can be used to solve percent problems. (See the note at the beginning of Section 6.3.) In the last section, we used the percent equation. In this section, we will use proportions.

Objective A Writing Percent Problems as Proportions

To understand the proportion method, recall that 70% means the ratio of 70 to 100, or $\frac{70}{100}$.

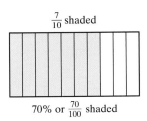

$\frac{7}{10}$ shaded

70% or $\frac{70}{100}$ shaded

$$70\% = \frac{70}{100} = \frac{7}{10}$$

Since the ratio $\frac{70}{100}$ is equal to the ratio $\frac{7}{10}$, we have the proportion

$$\frac{7}{10} = \frac{70}{100}.$$

We call this proportion the "percent proportion." In general, we can name the parts of this proportion as follows:

Percent Proportion

$$\frac{\text{amount}}{\text{base}} = \frac{\text{percent}}{100} \quad \leftarrow \text{always } 100$$

or

$$\text{amount} \rightarrow \frac{a}{b} = \frac{p}{100} \quad \leftarrow \text{percent}$$
$$\text{base} \rightarrow$$

When we translate percent problems to proportions, the **percent,** p, can be identified by looking for the symbol % or the word *percent*. The **base,** b, usually follows the word *of*. The **amount,** a, is the part compared to the whole.

Helpful Hint

Part of Proportion	How It's Identified
Percent	% or percent
Base	Appears after *of*
Amount	Part compared to whole

PRACTICE PROBLEM 1

Translate to a proportion.
15% of what number is 55?

EXAMPLE 1 Translate to a proportion.

12% of what number is 47?

Solution:

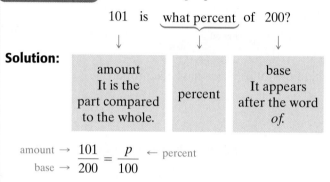

percent	base It appears after the word *of*.	amount It is the part compared to the whole.

$$\text{amount} \to \frac{47}{b} = \frac{12}{100} \leftarrow \text{percent}$$
$$\text{base} \to$$

◻ **Work Practice Problem 1**

PRACTICE PROBLEM 2

Translate to a proportion.
35 is what percent of 70?

EXAMPLE 2 Translate to a proportion.

101 is what percent of 200?

Solution:

amount It is the part compared to the whole.	percent	base It appears after the word *of.*

$$\text{amount} \to \frac{101}{200} = \frac{p}{100} \leftarrow \text{percent}$$
$$\text{base} \to$$

◻ **Work Practice Problem 2**

PRACTICE PROBLEM 3

Translate to a proportion.
What number is 25% of 68?

EXAMPLE 3 Translate to a proportion.

What number is 90% of 45?

Solution:

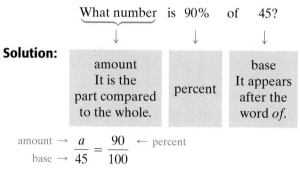

amount It is the part compared to the whole.	percent	base It appears after the word *of.*

$$\text{amount} \to \frac{a}{45} = \frac{90}{100} \leftarrow \text{percent}$$
$$\text{base} \to$$

◻ **Work Practice Problem 3**

PRACTICE PROBLEM 4

Translate to a proportion.
520 is 65% of what number?

EXAMPLE 4 Translate to a proportion.

238 is 40% of what number?

Solution:

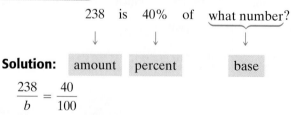

amount	percent	base

$$\frac{238}{b} = \frac{40}{100}$$

◻ **Work Practice Problem 4**

Answers

1. $\dfrac{55}{b} = \dfrac{15}{100}$, 2. $\dfrac{35}{70} = \dfrac{p}{100}$,

3. $\dfrac{a}{68} = \dfrac{25}{100}$, 4. $\dfrac{520}{b} = \dfrac{65}{100}$

EXAMPLE 5 Translate to a proportion.

What percent of 30 is 75?

↓ ↓ ↓

Solution: percent | base amount

$$\frac{75}{30} = \frac{p}{100}$$

▣ **Work Practice Problem 5**

EXAMPLE 6 Translate to a proportion.

45% of 105 is what number?

↓ ↓ ↓

Solution: percent base | amount

$$\frac{a}{105} = \frac{45}{100}$$

▣ **Work Practice Problem 6**

Objective B Solving Percent Problems

The proportions that we have written in this section contain three values that can change: The percent, the base, and the amount. If any two of these values are known, we can find the third (the unknown value). To do this, we write a percent proportion and find the unknown value as we did in Section 5.3.

EXAMPLE 7 Solving Percent Proportion for the Amount

What number is 30% of 9?

↓ ↓ ↓

Solution: amount percent base

$$\frac{a}{9} = \frac{30}{100}$$

To solve, we set cross products equal to each other.

$$\frac{a}{9} = \frac{30}{100}$$

$a \cdot 100 = 9 \cdot 30$ Set cross products equal.

$a \cdot 100 = 270$ Multiply.

Recall from Section 5.3 that if "some number times 100 is 270," then the number is 270 divided by 100.

$$a = \frac{270}{100}$$ Divide 270 by 100, the number multiplied by a.

$a = 2.7$ Simplify.

Thus, 2.7 is 30% of 9.

▣ **Work Practice Problem 7**

PRACTICE PROBLEM 5

Translate to a proportion.
What percent of 50 is 65?

PRACTICE PROBLEM 6

Translate to a proportion.
36% of 80 is what number?

PRACTICE PROBLEM 7

What number is 8% of 120?

Helpful Hint   The proportion in Example 7 contains the ratio $\frac{30}{100}$. A ratio in a proportion may be simplified before solving the proportion. The unknown number in both

$$\frac{a}{9} = \frac{30}{100} \text{ and } \frac{a}{9} = \frac{3}{10} \text{ is } 2.7$$

Answers

5. $\frac{65}{50} = \frac{p}{100}$, 6. $\frac{a}{80} = \frac{36}{100}$,

7. 9.6

✔**Concept Check** Consider the statement 78 is what percent of 350?
Which part of the percent proportion is unknown?

   a. the amount   **b.** the base   **c.** the percent

Consider another statement: "14 is 10% of some number."
Which part of the percent proportion is unknown?

   a. the amount   **b.** the base   **c.** the percent

PRACTICE PROBLEM 8

75% of what number is 60?

EXAMPLE 8 **Solving Percent Problems for the Base**

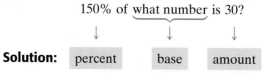

$$150\% \text{ of } \underbrace{\text{what number}}_{} \text{ is } 30?$$

Solution: percent   base   amount

$$\frac{30}{b} = \frac{150}{100} \quad \text{Write the proportion.}$$

$$\frac{30}{b} = \frac{3}{2} \qquad \text{Write } \frac{150}{100} \text{ as } \frac{3}{2}.$$

$$30 \cdot 2 = b \cdot 3 \qquad \text{Set cross products equal.}$$
$$60 = b \cdot 3 \qquad \text{Multiply.}$$
$$\frac{60}{3} = b \qquad \text{Divide 60 by 3, the number multiplied by } b.$$
$$20 = b \qquad \text{Simplify.}$$

Thus, 150% of 20 is 30.

◻ **Work Practice Problem 8**

✔**Concept Check** When solving a percent problem by using a proportion, describe how you can check the result.

PRACTICE PROBLEM 9

15.2 is 5% of what number?

EXAMPLE 9

$$20.8 \text{ is } 40\% \text{ of } \underbrace{\text{what number?}}_{}$$

Solution: amount   percent   base

$$\frac{20.8}{b} = \frac{40}{100} \quad \text{or} \quad \frac{20.8}{b} = \frac{2}{5} \quad \text{Write the proportion and simplify } \frac{40}{100}.$$
$$20.8 \cdot 5 = b \cdot 2 \qquad \text{Set cross products equal.}$$
$$104 = b \cdot 2 \qquad \text{Multiply.}$$
$$\frac{104}{2} = b \qquad \text{Divide 104 by 2, the number multiplied by } b.$$
$$52 = b \qquad \text{Simplify.}$$

So, 20.8 is 40% of 52.

◻ **Work Practice Problem 9**

Answers
8. 80,   **9.** 304

✔ **Concept Check Answers**
c, b;
By putting the result into the proportion and checking that the proportion is true

EXAMPLE 10 Solving Percent Problems for the Percent

What percent of 50 is 8?

Solution: percent base amount

$$\frac{8}{50} = \frac{p}{100} \quad \text{or} \quad \frac{4}{25} = \frac{p}{100} \qquad \text{Write the proportion and simplify } \frac{8}{50}.$$

$$4 \cdot 100 = 25 \cdot p \qquad \text{Set cross products equal.}$$

$$400 = 25 \cdot p \qquad \text{Multiply.}$$

$$\frac{400}{25} = p \qquad \text{Divide 400 by 25, the number multiplied by } p.$$

$$16 = p \qquad \text{Simplify.}$$

So, 16% of 50 is 8.

▣ **Work Practice Problem 10**

PRACTICE PROBLEM 10
What percent of 40 is 6?

Helpful Hint

Recall from our percent proportion that this number already is a percent. Just keep the number as is and attach a % symbol.

EXAMPLE 11

504 is what percent of 360?

Solution: amount percent base

$$\frac{504}{360} = \frac{p}{100}$$

Let's choose not to simplify the ratio $\frac{504}{360}$.

$$504 \cdot 100 = 360 \cdot p \qquad \text{Set cross products equal.}$$

$$50,400 = 360 \cdot p \qquad \text{Multiply.}$$

$$\frac{50,400}{360} = p \qquad \text{Divide 50,400 by 360, the number multiplied by } p.$$

$$140 = p \qquad \text{Simplify.}$$

Notice that by choosing not to simplify $\frac{504}{360}$, we had larger numbers in our equation. Either way, we find that 504 is 140% of 360.

▣ **Work Practice Problem 11**

You may have noticed the following while working examples.

PRACTICE PROBLEM 11
336 is what percent of 160?

Helpful Hint

Use the following to see whether your answers are reasonable.

100% of a number = the number

$$\left(\begin{array}{c}\text{a percent} \\ \text{greater than} \\ 100\%\end{array}\right) \text{of a number} = \begin{array}{l}\text{a number larger} \\ \text{than the original number}\end{array}$$

$$\left(\begin{array}{c}\text{a percent} \\ \text{less than } 100\%\end{array}\right) \text{of a number} = \begin{array}{l}\text{a number less} \\ \text{than the original number}\end{array}$$

Answers
10. 15%, **11.** 210%

Mental Math

Identify the amount, the base, and the percent in each equation. Recall that $\dfrac{\text{amount}}{\text{base}} = \dfrac{\text{percent}}{100}$.

1. $\dfrac{12.6}{42} = \dfrac{30}{100}$

2. $\dfrac{201}{300} = \dfrac{67}{100}$

3. $\dfrac{20}{100} = \dfrac{102}{510}$

4. $\dfrac{40}{100} = \dfrac{248}{620}$

6.4 EXERCISE SET

Objective A *Translate each to a proportion. Do not solve. See Examples 1 through 6.*

1. 32% of 65 is what number?

2. 92% of 30 is what number?

3. What number is 19% of 130?

4. What number is 5% of 125?

5. 2.3 is 58% of what number?

6. 1.2 is 47% of what number?

7. 40% of what number is 75?

8. 520 is 85% of what number?

9. What percent of 200 is 70?

10. 8.2 is what percent of 82?

Objective B *Solve. See Example 7.*

11. 10% of 55 is what number?

12. 25% of 84 is what number?

13. What number is 18% of 105?

14. What number is 40% of 29?

Solve. See Examples 8 and 9.

15. 15% of what number is 60?

16. 75% of what number is 75?

17. 7.8 is 78% of what number?

18. 1.1 is 44% of what number?

Solve. See Examples 10 and 11.

19. 105 is what percent of 84?

20. 77 is what percent of 44?

21. 14 is what percent of 50?

22. 37 is what percent of 50?

Objectives **A** **B** **Mixed Practice** *Solve. See Examples 1 through 11.*

23. 2.9 is 10% of what number?

24. 6.2 is 5% of what number?

25. 2.4% of 80 is what number?

26. 6.5% of 120 is what number?

27. 160 is 16% of what number?

28. 30 is 6% of what number?

29. 348.6 is what percent of 166?

30. 262.4 is what percent of 82?

31. What number is 89% of 62?

32. What number is 53% of 130?

33. What percent of 8 is 3.6?

34. What percent of 5 is 1.6?

35. 140% of what number is 119?

36. 170% of what number is 221?

37. 1.8% of 48 is what number?

38. 7.8% of 24 is what number?

39. What percent of 500 is 3?

40. What percent of 800 is 4?

41. 3.5 is 2.5% of what number?

42. 9.18 is 6.8% of what number?

43. 2486 is what percent of 2200?

44. 9310 is what percent of 3800?

Review

Add or subtract the fractions. See Sections 3.1, 3.3, and 3.4.

45. $\frac{11}{16} + \frac{3}{16}$

46. $\frac{5}{8} - \frac{7}{12}$

47. $3\frac{1}{2} - \frac{11}{30}$

48. $2\frac{2}{3} + 4\frac{1}{2}$

Add or subtract the decimals. See Section 4.3.

49. $\begin{array}{r} 0.41 \\ + 0.29 \\ \hline \end{array}$

50. $\begin{array}{r} 10.78 \\ 4.3 \\ + 0.21 \\ \hline \end{array}$

51. $\begin{array}{r} 2.38 \\ - 0.19 \\ \hline \end{array}$

52. $\begin{array}{r} 16.37 \\ - 2.61 \\ \hline \end{array}$

Concept Extensions

53. Write a word statement for the proportion $\frac{n}{28} = \frac{25}{100}$. Use the phrase "the number" for "n."

Solve. See the Concept Checks in this section.

Suppose you have finished solving three percent problems using proportions that you set up correctly. Check each answer to see if each makes the proportion a true proportion. If any proportion is not true, solve it to find the correct solution.

54. $\frac{a}{64} = \frac{25}{100}$
Is the amount equal to 17?

55. $\frac{520}{b} = \frac{65}{100}$
Is the base equal to 800?

56. $\frac{36}{12} = \frac{P}{100}$
Is the percent equal to 50 (50%)?

57. Write a percent statement that translates to
$\frac{16}{80} = \frac{20}{100}$

58. In your own words, explain how to use a proportion to solve a percent problem.

Solve. Round to the nearest tenth, if necessary.

59. What number is 22.3% of 53,862?

60. What percent of 110,736 is 88,542?

61. 8652 is 119% of what number?

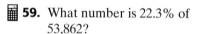 **THE BIGGER PICTURE** Operations on Sets of Numbers and Solving Equations

Continue your outline from Sections 1.7, 1.9, 2.5, 3.4, 4.5, and 5.3. (If you did not cover Section 6.3, pay no attention to the part of the outline numbered II.B.1.) Suggestions are once again written to help you complete this part of your outline. Notice that this part of the outline has to do with solving equations.

I. **Some Operations on Sets of Numbers**
   A. **Whole Numbers**
      1. **Add or Subtract** (Sections 1.3, 1.4)
      2. **Multiply or Divide** (Sections 1.6, 1.7)
      3. **Exponent** (Section 1.9)
      4. **Square Root** (Section 1.9)
      5. **Order of Operations** (Section 1.9)
   B. **Fractions**
      1. **Simplify** (Section 2.3)
      2. **Multiply** (Section 2.4)
      3. **Divide** (Section 2.5)
      4. **Add or Subtract** (Section 3.4)
   C. **Decimals**
      1. **Add or Subtract** (Section 4.3)
      2. **Multiply** (Section 4.4)
      3. **Divide** (Section 4.5)
II. **Solving Equations**
   A. **Proportions** (Section 5.3)

B. **Percent Problems**
   1. **Solved by Equations** (Section 6.3—you may not have covered this section)
   2. **Solved by Proportions:** Remember that percent, p, is identified by % or percent, base, b, usually appears after "of" and amount, a, is the part compared to the whole.
   12% of some number is 6 translates to
   $\frac{6}{b} = \frac{12}{100}$ or $6 \cdot 100 = b \cdot 12$ or $\frac{600}{12} = b$ or $50 = b$

Perform the indicated operations.

1. $\frac{2}{9} + \frac{1}{5}$

2. $42 \div 2 \cdot 3$

3. $0.03\,(0.7)$

4. $\sqrt{49} + \sqrt{1}$

Solve.

5. $\frac{3}{8} = \frac{n}{128}$

6. $\frac{7.2}{n} = \frac{36}{8}$

7. 215 is what percent of 86?

8. 95% of 48 is what number?

9. 4.2 is what percent of 15?

10. 93.6 is 52% of what number?

Percent and Percent Problems

Write each number as a percent.

1. 0.12

2. 0.68

3. $\frac{1}{8}$

4. $\frac{5}{2}$

5. 5.2

6. 8

7. $\frac{3}{50}$

8. $\frac{11}{25}$

9. $7\frac{1}{2}$

10. $3\frac{1}{4}$

11. 0.03

12. 0.05

Write each percent as a decimal.

13. 65%

14. 31%

15. 8%

16. 7%

17. 142%

18. 400%

19. 2.9%

20. 6.6%

Write each percent as a decimal and as a fraction or mixed number in simplest form. (If necessary when writing as a decimal, round to the nearest thousandth.)

21. 3%

22. 5%

23. 5.25%

24. 12.75%

1. _____

2. _____

3. _____

4. _____

5. _____

6. _____

7. _____

8. _____

9. _____

10. _____

11. _____

12. _____

13. _____

14. _____

15. _____

16. _____

17. _____

18. _____

19. _____

20. _____

21. _____

22. _____

23. _____

24. _____

25. 38% **26.** 45% **27.** $12\frac{1}{3}\%$ **28.** $16\frac{2}{3}\%$

25. _____

26. _____

27. _____

28. _____

29. _____

30. _____

31. _____

32. _____

33. _____

34. _____

35. _____

36. _____

37. _____

38. _____

39. _____

40. _____

Solve each percent problem.

29. 12% of 70 is what number?　　　　　**30.** 36 is 36% of what number?

31. 212.5 is 85% of what number?　　　　**32.** 66 is what percent of 55?

33. 23.8 is what percent of 85?　　　　　**34.** 38% of 200 is what number?

35. What number is 25% of 44?　　　　　**36.** What percent of 99 is 128.7?

37. What percent of 250 is 215?　　　　　**38.** What number is 45% of 84?

39. 42% of what number is 63?　　　　　**40.** 95% of what number is 58.9?

6.5 APPLICATIONS OF PERCENT

Objective **A** Solving Applications Involving Percent

Percent is used in a variety of everyday situations. The next examples show just a few ways that percent occurs in real-life settings. (Each of these examples shows two ways of solving these problems. If you studied Section 6.3 only, see *Method 1*. If you studied Section 6.4 only, see *Method 2*.)

EXAMPLE 1 Finding Percent of Nursing Schools with Increases in Enrollment

There is a world wide shortage of nurses that is projected to be 20% below requirements by 2020. Until 2001, there has also been a continual decline in enrollment in nursing schools. That has recently changed.

In 2003, 2178 of the total 2593 nursing schools in the U.S. had an increase in applications or enrollment. What percent of nursing schools had an increase? Round to the nearest whole percent. (*Source:* CNN and *Nurse Week*)

Solution: *Method 1.* First, we state the problem in words.

In words: 2178   is   what percent   of   2593?

Translate: 2178   = n ·   2593

Next, solve for n.

$\dfrac{2178}{2593} = n$ Divide 2178 by 2593, the number multiplied by n.

$0.84 \approx n$ Divide and round to the nearest hundredth.

$84\% \approx n$ Write as a percent.

In 2003, about 84% of nursing schools had an increase in applications or enrollment.

Method 2.

In words: 2178   is   what percent   of   2593?

amount   percent   base

Translate: amount → $\dfrac{2178}{2593}$ $=$ $\dfrac{p}{100}$ ← percent
base →

Next, solve for p.

$2178 \cdot 100 = 2593 \cdot p$ Set cross products equal.

$217{,}800 = 2593 \cdot p$ Multiply.

$\dfrac{217{,}800}{2593} = p$ Divide 217,800 by 2593, the number multiplied by p.

$84 \approx p$

In 2003, about 84% of nursing schools had an increase in applications or enrollment.

📖 **Work Practice Problem 1**

PRACTICE PROBLEM 1

There are 106 nursing schools in Ohio. Of these schools, 61 offer RN (registered nurse) degrees. What percent of nursing schools in Ohio offer RN degrees? Round to the nearest whole percent.

Answer
1. 58%

405

PRACTICE PROBLEM 2

The freshmen class of 775 students is 31% of all students at Euclid University. How many students go to Euclid University?

EXAMPLE 2 **Finding the Base Number of Absences**

Mr. Buccaran, the principal at Slidell High School, counted 31 freshmen absent during a particular day. If this is 4% of the total number of freshmen, how many freshmen are there at Slidell High School?

Solution: *Method 1.* First we state the problem in words; then we translate.

In words: 31   is   4%   of   what number?

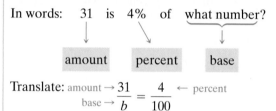

Translate: 31   =   4%   ·   n

Next, we solve for *n*.

$$31 = 0.04 \cdot n \quad \text{Write 4\% as a decimal.}$$

$$\frac{31}{0.04} = n \quad \text{Divide 31 by 0.04, the number multiplied by } n.$$

$$775 = n \quad \text{Simplify.}$$

There are 775 freshmen at Slidell High School.

Method 2. First we state the problem in words; then we translate.

In words: 31   is   4%   of   what number?

amount   percent   base

Translate: amount → $\dfrac{31}{b} = \dfrac{4}{100}$ ← percent
base →

Next, we solve for *b*.

$$31 \cdot 100 = b \cdot 4 \quad \text{Set cross products equal.}$$

$$3100 = b \cdot 4 \quad \text{Multiply.}$$

$$\frac{3100}{4} = b \quad \text{Divide 3100 by 4, the number multiplied by } b.$$

$$775 = b \quad \text{Simplify.}$$

There are 775 freshmen at Slidell High School.

▢ **Work Practice Problem 2**

PRACTICE PROBLEM 3

The nutrition label below is from a can of cashews. Find what percent of total calories are from fat. Round to the nearest tenth of a percent.

Nutrition Facts

Serving Size ¼ cup (33g)
Servings Per Container About 9

Amount Per Serving

Calories 190 **Calories from Fat** 130

	% Daily Value
Total Fat 16g	**24%**
Saturated Fat 3g	**16%**
Cholesterol 0mg	**0%**
Sodium 135mg	**6%**
Total Carbohydrate 9g	**3%**
Dietary Fiber 1g	**5%**
Sugars 2g	
Protein 5g	

Vitamin A 0% • Vitamin C 0%
Calcium 0% • Iron 8%

EXAMPLE 3 **Finding Nutrition Label Percents**

Standardized nutrition labels like the one shown at the right have been on foods since 1994. It is recommended that no more than 30% of your calorie intake be from fat. Find what percent of the total calories shown are fat.

Solution: *Method 1.*

In words: 10   is   what percent   of   80?

Translate: 10   =   n   ·   80

Nutrition Facts

Serving Size 1 pouch (20g)
Servings Per Container 6

Amount Per Serving

Calories	80
Calories from fat	10

	% Daily Value*
Total Fat 1g	**2%**
Sodium 45mg	**2%**
Total Carbohydrate 17g	**6%**
Sugars 9g	
Protein 0g	
Vitamin C	25%

Not a significant source of saturated fat, cholesterol, dietary fiber, vitamin A, calcium and iron.

*Percent Daily Values are based on a 2,000 calorie diet.

Fruit snacks nutrition label

Answers

2. 2500,   **3.** 68.4%

Next, we solve for n.

$$\frac{10}{80} = n \quad \text{Divide 10 by 80, the number multiplied by } n.$$

$$0.125 = n \quad \text{Simplify.}$$

$$12.5\% = n \quad \text{Write 0.125 as a percent.}$$

12.5% of this food's total calories are from fat.

Method 2.
In words:　　10 is what percent of 80?

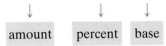

Translate: $\quad$ amount → $\dfrac{10}{80} = \dfrac{p}{100}$ ← percent
$\qquad\qquad$ base →

Next, we solve for p.

$$10 \cdot 100 = 80 \cdot p \quad \text{Set cross products equal.}$$

$$1000 = 80 \cdot p \quad \text{Multiply.}$$

$$\frac{1000}{80} = p \quad \text{Divide 1000 by 80, the number multiplied by } p.$$

$$12.5 = p \quad \text{Simplify.}$$

12.5% of this food's total calories are from fat.

■ **Work Practice Problem 3**

EXAMPLE 4 **Finding the Base Increase in Population**

The state of Nevada had the largest percent increase in population, about 66%, from the 1990 census to the 2000 census. In 1990, the population of Nevada was about 1202 thousand.

a. Find the increase in population from 1990 to 2000.
b. Find the population of Nevada in 2000.

(*Source:* U.S. Census Bureau)

Solution:　*Method 1.* First we find the increase in population.

In words:　What number is 66% of 1202?

Translate:　　　$n \quad = 66\% \cdot 1202$
Next, we solve for n.

$$n = 0.66 \cdot 1202 \quad \text{Write 66\% as a decimal.}$$

$$n = 793.32 \quad \text{Multiply.}$$

Continued on next page

PRACTICE PROBLEM 4

The state of Arizona had the second-largest percent increase in population, 40%, from the 1990 census to the 2000 census. In 1990, the population of Arizona was about 3665 thousand. (*Source:* U.S. Census Bureau)

a. Find the increase in population from 1990 to 2000.

b. Find the population of Arizona in 2000.

Answers
4. a. 1466 thousand, **b.** 5131 thousand

The increase in population is 793.32 thousand. This means that the

$$
\begin{matrix}
\text{Nevada} \\
\text{population} \\
\text{in 2000}
\end{matrix}
=
\begin{matrix}
\text{Population} \\
\text{in 1990}
\end{matrix}
+
\begin{matrix}
\text{Increase} \\
\text{in population}
\end{matrix}
$$

$$= 1202 \text{ thousand} + 793.32 \text{ thousand}$$

$$= 1995.32 \text{ thousand}$$

Method 2. First we find the increase in population.

In words: What number is 66% of 1202?

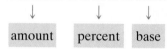

amount   percent   base

Translate: amount → $\dfrac{a}{1202} = \dfrac{66}{100}$ ← percent
base →

Next, we solve for a.

$a \cdot 100 = 1202 \cdot 66$ Set cross products equal.

$a \cdot 100 = 79{,}332$ Multiply.

$a = \dfrac{79{,}332}{100}$ Divide 79,332 by 100, the number multiplied by a.

$a = 793.32$ Simplify.

The increase in population is 793.32 thousand. This means that the population of Nevada in 2000 was

$$
\begin{matrix}
\text{Nevada} \\
\text{population} \\
\text{in 2000}
\end{matrix}
=
\begin{matrix}
\text{Population} \\
\text{in 1990}
\end{matrix}
+
\begin{matrix}
\text{Increase} \\
\text{in population}
\end{matrix}
$$

$$= 1202 \text{ thousand} + 793.32 \text{ thousand}$$

$$= 1995.32 \text{ thousand}$$

▢ **Work Practice Problem 4**

Objective ▣ Finding Percent Increase and Percent Decrease

We often use percents to show how much an amount has increased or decreased.

Suppose that the population of a town is 10,000 people and then it increases by 2000 people. The **percent of increase** is

amount of increase → $\dfrac{2000}{10{,}000} = 0.2 = 20\%$
original amount →

In general, we have the following.

Percent of Increase

$$\text{percent of increase} = \frac{\text{amount of increase}}{\text{original amount}}$$

Then write the quotient as a percent.

EXAMPLE 5 Finding Percent Increase

The number of applications for a mathematics scholarship at Yale increased from 34 to 45 in one year. What is the percent increase? Round to the nearest whole percent.

Solution: First we find the amount of increase by subtracting the original number of applicants from the new number of applicants.

$$\text{amount of increase} = 45 - 34 = 11$$

The amount of increase is 11 applicants. To find the percent of increase,

$$\text{percent of increase} = \frac{\text{amount of increase}}{\text{original amount}} = \frac{11}{34} \approx 0.32 = 32\%$$

The number of applications increased by about 32%.

⬛ **Work Practice Problem 5**

✔**Concept Check** A student is calculating the percent increase in enrollment from 180 students one year to 200 students the next year. Explain what is wrong with the following calculations:

$$\frac{\text{Amount}}{\text{of increase}} = 200 - 180 = 20$$

$$\frac{\text{Percent of}}{\text{increase}} = \frac{20}{200} = 0.1 = 10\%$$

Suppose that your income was $300 a week and then it decreased by $30. The **percent of decrease** is

$$\begin{array}{c}\text{amount of decrease} \rightarrow \\ \text{original amount} \rightarrow \end{array} \frac{\$30}{\$300} = 0.1 = 10\%$$

Percent of Decrease

$$\text{percent of decrease} = \frac{\text{amount of decrease}}{\text{original amount}}$$

Then write the quotient as a percent.

EXAMPLE 6 Finding Percent Decrease

In response to a decrease in sales, a company with 1500 employees reduces the number of employees to 1230. What is the percent decrease?

Solution: First we find the amount of decrease by subtracting 1230 from 1500.

$$\text{amount of decrease} = 1500 - 1230 = 270$$

The amount of decrease is 270. To find the percent of decrease,

$$\frac{\text{percent of}}{\text{decrease}} = \frac{\text{amount of decrease}}{\text{original amount}} = \frac{270}{1500} = 0.18 = 18\%$$

The number of employees decreased by 18%.

⬛ **Work Practice Problem 6**

6.5 EXERCISE SET

Student Solutions Manual   PH Math/Tutor Center   CD/Video for Review   MathXL®   MyMathLab

Objective A *Solve. See Examples 1 and 2.*

1. An inspector found 24 defective bolts during an inspection. If this is 1.5% of the total number of bolts inspected, how many bolts were inspected?

2. A day care worker found 28 children absent one day during an epidemic of chicken pox. If this was 35% of the total number of children attending the day care center, how many children attend this day care center?

3. 18% of Frank's wages are withheld for income tax. Find the amount withheld from Frank's wages of $3680 per month.

4. The Hodder family paid 20% of the purchase price of a $75,000 home as a down payment. Determine the amount of the down payment.

5. Vera Faciane earns $2000 per month and budgets $300 per month for food. What percent of her monthly income is spent on food?

6. Last year, Mai Toberlan bought a share of stock for $83. She was paid a dividend of $4.15. Determine what percent of the stock price is the dividend.

7. A manufacturer of electronic components expects 1.04% of its products to be defective. Determine the number of defective components expected in a batch of 28,350 components. Round to the nearest whole component.

8. An owner of a repair service company estimates that for every 40 hours a repairperson is on the job, he can bill for only 78% of the hours. The remaining hours, the repairperson is idle or driving to or from a job. Determine the number of hours per 40-hour week the owner can bill for a repairperson.

9. Of the 535 members of the 108th U.S. Congress, 73 have attended a community college. What percent of the members of the 108th Congress is this? Round to the nearest tenth of a percent. (*Source:* American Association of Community Colleges)

10. The Los Angeles County courts excused 775,130 prospective jurors from jury duty in a recent year. This represented 28% of all juror qualification affidavits sent out that year. How many juror qualification affidavits were sent out that year? Round to the nearest whole affidavit. (*Source:* Los Angeles Superior Court)

11. There are about 98,400 female dental hygienists registered in the United States. If this represents about 98.3% of the nation's dental hygienists, find the approximate number of dental hygienists in the United States. (*Source:* The American Dental Hygienists' Association)

12. 31.6% of all households in the United States own at least one pet dog. There are 11,250 households in Anytown. How many of these households would you expect own a dog? (*Source:* American Veterinary Medical Association)

For each food described, find what percent of total calories is from fat. If necessary, round to the nearest tenth of a percent. See Example 3.

13. Ranch dressing serving size of 2 tablespoons

	Calories
Total	40
From fat	20

14. Unsweetened cocoa powder serving size of 1 tablespoon

	Calories
Total	20
From fat	5

15.

Nutrition Facts

Serving Size 18 crackers (29g)
Servings Per Container About 9

Amount Per Serving

Calories 120 Calories from Fat 35

	% Daily Value*
Total Fat 4g	**6%**
Saturated Fat 0.5g	3%
Polyunsaturated Fat 0g	
Monounsaturated Fat 1.5g	
Cholesterol 0mg	**0%**
Sodium 220mg	**9%**
Total Carbohydrate 21g	**7%**
Dietary Fiber 2g	7%
Sugars 3g	
Protein 2g	

Vitamin A 0% • Vitamin C 0%

Calcium 2% • Iron 4%

Phosphorus 10%

Snack Crackers

16.

Nutrition Facts

Serving Size 28 crackers (31g)
Servings Per Container About 6

Amount Per Serving

Calories 130 Calories from Fat 35

	% Daily Value*
Total Fat 4g	**6%**
Saturated Fat 2g	**10%**
Polyunsaturated Fat 1g	
Monounsaturated Fat 1g	
Cholesterol 0mg	**0%**
Sodium 470mg	**20%**
Total Carbohydrate 23g	**8%**
Dietary Fiber 1g	4%
Sugars 4g	
Protein 2g	

Vitamin A 0% • Vitamin C 0%

Calcium 0% • Iron 2%

Snack Crackers

Solve. Round money amounts to the nearest cent and all other amounts to the nearest tenth. See Example 4.

17. Ace Furniture Company currently produces 6200 chairs per month. If production decreases by 8%, find the decrease and the new number of chairs produced each month.

18. The enrollment at a local college decreased by 5% over last year's enrollment of 7640. Find the decrease in enrollment and the current enrollment.

19. By carefully planning their meals, a family was able to decrease their weekly grocery bill by 20%. Their weekly grocery bill used to be $170. What is their new weekly grocery bill?

20. The profit of Ramone Company last year was $175,000. This year's profit decreased by 11%. Find this year's profit.

21. A car manufacturer announced that next year the price of a certain model of car would increase by 4.5%. This year the price is $19,286. Find the increase in price and the new price.

22. A union contract calls for a 6.5% salary increase for all employees. Determine the increase and the new salary that a worker currently making $38,500 under this contract can expect.

23. From 2002 to 2012, the number of people employed as physician assistants in the United States is expected to increase by 49%. The number of people employed as physician assistants in 2002 was 63,000. Find the predicted number of physician assistants in 2012. (*Source:* Bureau of Labor Statistics)

24. The state of North Dakota had the smallest percent increase in population, 0.5%, from the 1990 census to the 2000 census. In 1990, the population of North Dakota was 638,800. What was the population of North Dakota in 2000? (*Source:* U.S. Census Bureau)

North Dakota

25. The population of Americans aged 65 and older was 35 million in 2000. That population is projected to increase by 80% by 2025. Find the increase and the projected 2025 population. (*Source:* Bureau of the Census)

26. The from 2000 to 2010, the number of masters degrees awarded to women is projected to increase by 8.3%. The number of women who received masters degrees in 2000 was 265,000. Find the predicted number of women to be awarded masters degrees in 2010. (*Source:* U.S. National Center for Education Statistics)

Objective **B** *Find the amount of increase and the percent increase. See Example 5.*

	Original Amount	New Amount	Amount of Increase	Percent Increase
27.	40	50		
28.	10	15		
29.	85	187		
30.	78	351		

Find the amount of decrease and the percent decrease. See Example 6.

	Original Amount	New Amount	Amount of Decrease	Percent Decrease
31.	8	6		
32.	25	20		
33.	160	40		
34.	200	162		

Solve. Round percents to the nearest tenth, if necessary. See Examples 5 and 6.

35. There are 150 calories in a cup of whole milk and only 84 in a cup of skim milk. In switching to skim milk, find the percent decrease in number of calories per cup.

36. In reaction to a slow economy, the number of employees at a soup company decreased from 530 to 477. What was the percent decrease in the number of employees?

37. By changing his driving routines, Alan Miller increased his car's rate of miles per gallon from 19.5 to 23.7. Find the percent increase.

38. John Smith decided to decrease the number of calories in his diet from 3250 to 2100. Find the percent decrease.

39. The number of cable TV systems recently decreased from 10,845 to 10,700. Find the percent decrease.

40. Before taking a typing course, Geoffry Landers could type 32 words per minute. By the end of the course, he was able to type 76 words per minute. Find the percent increase.

41. In 1940, the average size of a U.S. farm was 174 acres. By 2003, the average size of a U.S. farm had increased to 441 acres. What was the percent increase? (*Source:* National Agricultural Statistics Service)

42. In 1995, 272.6 million recorded music cassettes were shipped to retailers in the United States. By 2000, this number had decreased to 76.0 million cassettes. What was the percent decrease? (*Source:* Recording Industry Association of America)

43. In 1994, approximately 16,000,000 Americans subscribed to cellular phone service. By 2003, this number had increased to about 159,000,000 American subscribers. What was the percent increase? (*Source:* Network World, Inc.)

44. In 1970, there were 1754 deaths from boating accidents in the United States. By 2003, the number of deaths from boating accidents had decreased to 703. What was the percent decrease? (*Source:* U.S. Coast Guard)

45. In 1994, approximately 16,000 occupational therapy assistants and aides were employed in the United States. According to one survey, by 2005, this number is expected to increase to 29,000 assistants and aides. What is the percent increase? (*Source:* Bureau of Labor Statistics)

46. In 1994, approximately 206,000 medical assistants were employed in the United States. By 2005, this number is expected to increase to 327,000 medical assistants. What is the percent increase? (*Source:* Bureau of Labor Statistics)

47. In 1999, discarded electronics, including obsolete computer equipment, accounted for 75,000 tons of solid waste per year in Massachusetts. By 2006, discarded electronic waste is expected to increase to 300,000 tons of waste per year in the state. Find the percent increase. (*Source:* Massachusetts Department of Environmental Protection)

48. The average soft-drink size has increased from 13.1 oz to 19.9 oz over the past two decades. Find the percent increase. (*Source:* University of North Carolina at Chapel Hill, *Journal for American Medicine*)

19.9 oz   13.1 oz

49. The population of Tokyo is expected to decrease from 127,333 thousand in 2004 to 99,887 thousand in 2050. Find the percent decrease. (*Source:* International Programs Center, Bureau of the Census, U.S. Dept. of Commerce)

50. In 2002, approximately 394,000 computer application software engineers were employed in the United States. By 2012, this number is expected to increase to 573,000. What is the percent increase? (*Source:* Bureau of Labor Statistics)

Japan

Tokyo

Review

Perform each indicated operation. See Sections 4.3 and 4.4.

51. 0.12
$\times$ 38

52.   42
$\times$ 0.7

53. 9.20 + 1.98

54. 46 + 7.89

55. 78 − 19.46

56. 64.80 − 10.72

Concept Extensions

57. If a number is increased by 100%, how does the increased number compare with the original number? Explain your answer.

58. In your own words, explain what is wrong with the following statement. "Last year we had 80 students attend. This year we have a 50% increase or a total of 160 students attend."

59. Explain what errors were made by each student when solving percent of increase or decrease problems and then correct the errors. *"The population of a certain rural town was 150 in 1980, 180 in 1990, and 150 in 2000."*

   a. Find the percent of increase in population from 1980 to 1990.

   Miranda's solution: Percent of increase $= \dfrac{30}{180} = 0.1\overline{6} \approx 16.7\%$

   b. Find the percent of decrease in population from 1990 to 2000.

   Jeremy's solution: Percent of decrease $= \dfrac{30}{150} = 0.20 = 20\%$

   c. The percent of increase from 1980 to 1990 is the same as the percent of decrease from 1990 to 2000. True or false.

   Chris's answer: True because they had the same amount of increase as the amount of decrease.

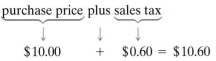

6.6 PERCENT AND PROBLEM SOLVING: SALES TAX, COMMISSION, AND DISCOUNT

Objectives

A Calculate Sales Tax and Total Price.

B Calculate Commissions.

C Calculate Discount and Sale Price.

Objective **A** Calculating Sales Tax and Total Price

Percents are frequently used in the retail trade. For example, most states charge a tax on certain items when purchased. This tax is called a **sales tax,** and retail stores collect it for the state. Sales tax is almost always stated as a percent of the purchase price.

A 6% sales tax rate on a purchase of a $10 item gives a sales tax of

$$\text{sales tax} = 6\% \text{ of } \$10 = 0.06 \cdot \$10.00 = \$0.60$$

The total price to the customer would be

purchase price plus sales tax

$$\$10.00 \quad + \quad \$0.60 = \$10.60$$

This example suggests the following equations:

Sales Tax and Total Price

$$\text{sales tax} = \text{tax rate} \cdot \text{purchase price}$$
$$\text{total price} = \text{purchase price} + \text{sales tax}$$

In this section we round dollar amounts to the nearest cent.

EXAMPLE 1 Finding Sales Tax and Purchase Price

Find the sales tax and the total price on the purchase of an $85.50 trench coat in a city where the sales tax rate is 7.5%.

Solution: The purchase price is $85.50 and the tax rate is 7.5%.

$$\text{sales tax} = \text{tax rate} \cdot \text{purchase price}$$

$$\begin{aligned} \text{sales tax} &= 7.5\% \cdot \$85.50 \\ &= 0.075 \cdot \$85.5 \quad \text{Write 7.5\% as a decimal.} \\ &\approx \$6.41 \quad \text{Rounded to the nearest cent.} \end{aligned}$$

Thus, the sales tax is $6.41. Next find the total price.

$$\text{total price} = \text{purchase price} + \text{sales tax}$$

$$\begin{aligned} \text{total price} &= \$85.50 + \$6.41 \\ &= \$91.91 \end{aligned}$$

The sales tax on $85.50 is $6.41, and the total price is $91.91.

■ **Work Practice Problem 1**

PRACTICE PROBLEM 1

If the sales tax rate is 6%, what is the sales tax and the total amount due on a $29.90 Goodgrip tire?

Answer
1. tax: $1.79; total: $31.69

415

PRACTICE PROBLEM 2

The sales tax on a $13,500 automobile is $1080. Find the sales tax rate.

✔**Concept Check** The purchase price of a textbook is $50 and sales tax is 10%. If you are told by the cashier that the total price is $75, how can you tell that a mistake has been made?

EXAMPLE 2 **Finding a Sales Tax Rate**

The sales tax on a $300 printer is $22.50. Find the sales tax rate.

Solution: Let r represent the unknown sales tax rate. Then

$$\boxed{\text{sales tax}} = \boxed{\text{tax rate}} \cdot \boxed{\text{purchase price}}$$

$$\$22.50 = r \cdot \$300$$

$$\frac{22.50}{300} = r \qquad \text{Divide 22.50 by 300, the number multiplied by } r.$$

$$0.075 = r \qquad \text{Simplify.}$$

$$7.5\% = r \qquad \text{Write 0.075 as a percent.}$$

The sales tax rate is 7.5%.

▣ **Work Practice Problem 2**

Objective **B** **Calculating Commissions**

A **wage** is payment for performing work. Hourly wage, commissions, and salary are some of the ways wages can be paid. Many people who work in sales are paid a commission. An employee who is paid a **commission** is paid a percent of his or her total sales.

Commission

commission = commission rate · sales

PRACTICE PROBLEM 3

Mr. Olsen is a sales representative for Miko Copiers. Last month he sold $37,632 worth of copy equipment and supplies. What is his commission for the month if he is paid a commission of 6.6% of his total sales for the month?

EXAMPLE 3 **Finding the Amount of Commission**

Sherry Souter, a real estate broker for Wealth Investments, sold a house for $114,000 last week. If her commission is 1.5% of the selling price of the home, find the amount of her commission.

Solution:

$$\boxed{\text{commission}} = \boxed{\text{commission rate}} \cdot \boxed{\text{sales}}$$

commission	=	1.5%	· $114,000	
	=	0.015	· $114,000	Write 1.5% as 0.015.
	=	$1710		Multiply.

Answers

2. 8%, **3.** $2483.71

✔ **Concept Check Answer**

Since $10\% = \frac{1}{10}$, the sales tax is $\frac{\$50}{10} = \$5$. The total price should have been $55.

Her commission on the house is $1710.

■ **Work Practice Problem 3**

EXAMPLE 4 **Finding a Commission Rate**

A salesperson earned $1560 for selling $13,000 worth of television and stereo systems. Find the commission rate.

Solution: Let r stand for the unknown commission rate. Then

$$\text{commission} = \text{commission rate} \cdot \text{sales}$$

$$\$1560 = r \cdot \$13,000$$

$$\frac{1560}{13,000} = r \quad \text{Divide 1560 by 13,000, the number multiplied by } r.$$

$$0.12 = r \quad \text{Simplify.}$$

$$12\% = r \quad \text{Write 0.12 as a percent.}$$

The commission rate is 12%.

■ **Work Practice Problem 4**

Objective C Calculating Discount and Sale Price

Suppose that an item that normally sells for $40 is on sale for 25% off. This means that the **original price** of $40 is reduced, or **discounted,** by 25% of $40, or $10. The **discount rate** is 25%, the **amount of discount** is $10, and the **sale price** is $40 − $10, or $30. Study the diagram below to visualize these terms.

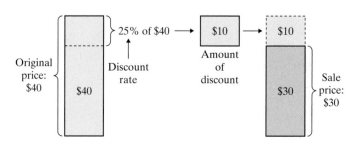

PRACTICE PROBLEM 4

A salesperson earns $1290 for selling $8600 worth of appliances. Find the commission rate.

Answer
4. 15%

To calculate discounts and sale prices, we can use the following equations:

Discount and Sale Price

$$\text{amount of discount} = \text{discount rate} \cdot \text{original price}$$
$$\text{sale price} = \text{original price} - \text{amount of discount}$$

PRACTICE PROBLEM 5

A Panasonic TV is advertised on sale for 15% off the regular price of $700. Find the discount and the sale price.

EXAMPLE 5 **Finding a Discount and a Sale Price**

A speaker that normally sells for $65 is on sale for 25% off. What is the discount and what is the sale price?

Solution: First we find the discount.

amount of discount	=	discount rate	·	original price
↓		↓		↓
amount of discount	=	25%	·	$65

$$= 0.25 \cdot \$65 \quad \text{Write 25\% as 0.25.}$$
$$= \$16.25 \quad \text{Multiply.}$$

The discount is $16.25. Next, find the sale price.

sale price	=	original price	−	discount
↓		↓		↓
sale price	=	$65	−	$16.25

$$= \$48.75 \quad \text{Subtract.}$$

The sale price is $48.75.

☐ **Work Practice Problem 5**

Answer
5. $105; $595

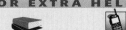
Objective Ⓐ *Solve. See Examples 1 and 2.*

1. What is the sales tax on a suit priced at $150 if the sales tax rate is 5%?

2. If the sales tax rate is 6%, find the sales tax on a microwave oven priced at $188.

3. The purchase price of a camcorder is $799. What is the total price if the sales tax rate is 7.5%?

4. A stereo system has a purchase price of $426. What is the total price if the sales tax rate is 8%?

5. A chair and ottoman have a purchase price of $600. If the sales tax on this purchase is $57, find the sales tax rate.

6. The sales tax on the purchase of a $2500 computer is $162.50. Find the sales tax rate.

7. The sales tax on a table saw is $10.20.
  a. What is the purchase price of the table saw (before tax) if the sales tax rate is 8.5%?
  b. Find the total price of the table saw.

8. The sales tax on a one-half-carat diamond ring is $76.
  a. Find the purchase price of the ring (before tax) if the sales tax rate is 9.5%.
  b. Find the total price of the ring.

9. A gold and diamond bracelet sells for $1800. Find the total price if the sales tax rate is 6.5%.

10. The purchase price of a personal computer is $1890. If the sales tax rate is 8%, what is the total price?

11. The sales tax on the purchase of a truck is $920. If the tax rate is 8%, find the purchase price of the truck.

12. The sales tax on the purchase of a desk is $27.50. If the tax rate is 5%, find the purchase price of the desk.

13. The sales tax is $98.70 on a stereo sound system purchase of $1645. Find the sales tax rate.

14. The sales tax is $103.50 on a necklace purchase of $1150. Find the sales tax rate.

15. A cell phone costs $90 and a battery recharger costs $15. What is the total price for purchasing these items if the sales tax rate is 7%?

16. Ms. Warner bought a blouse for $35, a skirt for $55, and a blazer for $95. Find the total price she paid, given a sales tax rate of 6.5%.

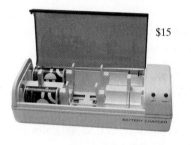
$15

$90

Objective **B** *Solve. See Examples 3 and 4.*

17. Jane Moreschi, a sales representative for a large furniture warehouse, is paid a commission rate of 4%. Find her commission if she sold $1,236,856 worth of furniture last year.

18. Rosie Davis-Smith is a beauty consultant for a home cosmetic business. She is paid a commission rate of 4.8%. Find her commission if she sold $1638 in cosmetics last month.

19. A salesperson earned a commission of $1380.40 for selling $9860 worth of paper products. Find the commission rate.

20. A salesperson earned a commission of $3575 for selling $32,500 worth of books to various bookstores. Find the commission rate.

21. How much commission will Jack Pruet make on the sale of a $125,900 house if he receives 1.5% of the selling price?

22. Frankie Lopez sold $9638 of jewelry this week. Find her commission for the week if she receives a commission rate of 5.6%.

23. A real estate agent earned a commission of $2565 for selling a house. If his rate is 3%, find the selling price of the house.

24. A salesperson earned $1750 for selling fertilizer. If her commission rate is 7%, find the selling price of the fertilizer.

Objective **C** *Find the amount of discount and the sale price. See Example 5.*

	Original Price	Discount Rate	Amount of Discount	Sale Price
25.	$68	10%		
26.	$47	20%		
27.	$96.50	50%		
28.	$110.60	40%		
29.	$215	35%		
30.	$370	25%		
31.	$21,700	15%		
32.	$17,800	12%		

33. A $300 fax machine is on sale for 15% off. Find the discount and the sale price.

34. A $2000 designer dress is on sale for 30% off. Find the discount and the sale price.

Objectives **A** **B** **Mixed Practice** Complete each table.

	Purchase Price	Tax Rate	Sales Tax	Total Price
35.	$586	9%		
36.	$243	8%		
37.	$82	5.5%		
38.	$65	8.4%		

	Sale	Commission Rate	Commission
39.	$235,800	3%	
40.	$195,450	5%	
41.	$17,900		$1432
42.	$25,600		$2304

Review

Multiply. See Sections 4.4 and 4.6.

43. $2000 \cdot 0.3 \cdot 2$

44. $500 \cdot 0.08 \cdot 3$

45. $400 \cdot 0.03 \cdot 11$

46. $1000 \cdot 0.05 \cdot 5$

47. $600 \cdot 0.04 \cdot \dfrac{2}{3}$

48. $6000 \cdot 0.06 \cdot \dfrac{3}{4}$

Concept Extensions

Solve. See the Concept Check in this section.

49. Your purchase price is $68 and the sales tax rate is 9.5%. Round each amount and use the rounded amounts to estimate the total price. Choose the best estimate.

a. $105   **b.** $58   **c.** $93   **d.** $77

50. Your purchase price is $200 and the tax rate is 10%. Choose the best estimate.

a. $190   **b.** $210   **c.** $220   **d.** $300

One very useful application of percent is mentally calculating a tip. Recall that to find 10% of a number, simply move the decimal point one place to the left. To find 20% of a number, just double 10% of the number. To find 15% of a number, find 10% and then add to that number half of the 10% amount. Mentally fill in the chart below. To do so, start by rounding the bill amount to the nearest dollar.

Tipping Chart			
Bill Amount	10%	15%	20%
51. $40.21			
52. $15.89			
53. $72.17			
54. $9.33			

55. Suppose that the original price of a shirt is $50. Which is better, a 60% discount or a discount of 30% followed by a discount of 35% of the reduced price. Explain your answer.

56. Which is better, a 30% discount followed by an additional 25% off or a 20% discount followed by an additional 40% off? To see, suppose an item costs $100 and calculate each discounted price. Explain your answer.

57. A diamond necklace sells for $24,966. If the tax rate is 7.5%, find the total price.

58. A house recently sold for $562,560. The commission rate on the sale is 5.5%. If the real estate agent is to receive 60% of the commission, find the amount received by the agent.

STUDY SKILLS BUILDER

Are You Familiar with Your Textbook Supplements?

Below is a review of some of the student supplements available for additional study. Check to see if you are using the ones most helpful to you.

- Chapter Test Prep Videos on CD. This material is found with your textbook and is fully explained there. The CD contains video clip solutions to the Chapter Test exercises in this text and are excellent help when studying for chapter tests.
- Lecture Videos on CD-ROM. These video segments are keyed to each section of the text. The material is presented by me, Elayn Martin-Gay, and I have placed a ⊚ by the exercises in the text that I have worked on the video.
- The *Student Solutions Manual*. This contains worked out solutions to odd-numbered exercises as well as every exercise in the Integrated Reviews, Chapter Reviews, Chapter Tests, and Cumulative Reviews.
- Prentice Hall Tutor Center. Mathematic questions may be phoned, faxed, or emailed to this center.

- MyMathLab, MathXL, and Interact Math. These are computer and Internet tutorials. This supplement may already be available to you somewhere on campus, for example at your local learning resource lab. Take a moment and find the name and location of any such lab on campus.

As usual, your instructor is your best source of information.

Let's see how you are doing with textbook supplements.

1. Name one way the Lecture Videos can be helpful to you.
2. Name one way the Chapter Test Prep Video can help you prepare for a chapter test.
3. List any textbook supplements that you have found useful.
4. Have you located and visited a learning resource lab located on your campus?
5. List the textbook supplements that are currently housed in your campus' learning resource lab.

6.7 PERCENT AND PROBLEM SOLVING: INTEREST

Objectives

Ⓐ Calculate Simple Interest.

Ⓑ Calculate Compound Interest.

Ⓒ Calculate Monthly Payments.

Objective Ⓐ Calculating Simple Interest

Interest is money charged for using other people's money. When you borrow money, you pay interest. When you loan or invest money, you earn interest. The money borrowed, loaned, or invested is called the **principal amount,** or simply **principal.** Interest is normally stated in terms of a percent of the principal for a given period of time. The **interest rate** is the percent used in computing the interest. Unless stated otherwise, *the rate is understood to be per year.* When the interest is computed on the original principal, it is called **simple interest.** Simple interest is calculated using the following equation:

Simple Interest

$$\text{simple interest} = \text{principal} \cdot \text{rate} \cdot \text{time}$$

where the rate is understood to be per year and time is in years.

EXAMPLE 1 Finding Simple Interest

Find the simple interest after 2 years on $500 at an interest rate of 12%.

Solution: In this example, the principal is $500, the rate is 12%, and the time is 2 years.

simple interest	=	principal	·	rate	·	time
↓		↓		↓		↓
simple interest	=	$500	·	12%	·	2
	=	$500	·	0.12	·	2	Write 12% as 0.12.
	=	$120					Multiply.

The simple interest is $120.

▢ **Work Practice Problem 1**

If time is not given in years, we need to convert the given time to years.

EXAMPLE 2 Finding Simple Interest

Ivan Borski borrowed $2400 at 10% simple interest for 8 months to buy a used Chevy S-10. Find the simple interest he paid.

Solution: Since there are 12 months in a year, we first find what part of a year 8 months is.

$$8 \text{ months} = \frac{8}{12} \text{ year} = \frac{2}{3} \text{ year}$$

Now we find the simple interest.

simple interest	=	principal	·	rate	·	time
↓		↓		↓		↓
simple interest	=	$2400	·	10%	·	$\frac{2}{3}$
	=	$2400	·	0.10	·	$\frac{2}{3}$
	=	$160				

The interest on Ivan's loan is $160.

▢ **Work Practice Problem 2**

PRACTICE PROBLEM 1

Find the simple interest after 3 years on $750 at an interest rate of 8%.

PRACTICE PROBLEM 2

Juanita Lopez borrowed $800 for 9 months at a simple interest rate of 20%. How much interest did she pay?

Answers
1. $180, **2.** $120

When money is borrowed, the borrower pays the original amount borrowed, or the principal, as well as the interest. When money is invested, the investor receives the original amount invested, or the principal, as well as the interest. In either case, the **total amount** is the sum of the principal and the interest.

> ### Finding the Total Amount of a Loan or Investment
>
> total amount (paid or received) = principal + interest

PRACTICE PROBLEM 3

If $500 is borrowed at a simple interest rate of 12% for 6 months, find the total amount paid.

EXAMPLE 3 **Finding the Total Amount of an Investment**

An accountant invested $2000 at a simple interest rate of 10% for 2 years. What total amount of money will she have from her investment in 2 years?

Solution: First we find her interest.

$$\text{simple interest} = \text{principal} \cdot \text{rate} \cdot \text{time}$$

$$\text{simple interest} = \$2000 \cdot 10\% \cdot 2$$
$$= \$2000 \cdot 0.10 \cdot 2$$
$$= \$400$$

The interest is $400.

Next, we add the interest to the principal.

$$\text{total amount} = \text{principal} + \text{interest}$$

$$\text{total amount} = \$2000 + \$400$$
$$= \$2400$$

After 2 years, she will have a total amount of $2400.

Work Practice Problem 3

✔ **Concept Check** Which investment would earn more interest: An amount of money invested at 8% interest for 2 years, or the same amount of money invested at 8% for 3 years? Explain.

Objective **B** Calculating Compound Interest

Recall that simple interest depends on the original principal only. Another type of interest is compound interest. **Compound interest** is computed on not only the principal, but also on the interest already earned in previous compounding periods. Compound interest is used more often than simple interest.

Let's see how compound interest differs from simple interest. Suppose that $2000 is invested at 7% interest **compounded annually** for 3 years. This means that interest is added to the principal at the end of each year and that next year's interest is computed on this new amount. In this section, we round dollar amounts to the nearest cent.

Answer

3. $530

✔ **Concept Check Answer**

8% for 3 years. Since the interest rate is the same, the longer you keep the money invested, the more interest you earn.

	Amount at Beginning of Year	Principal	·	Rate	·	Time	= Interest	Amount at End of Year
1st year	$2000	$2000	·	0.07	·	1	= $140	$2000 + 140 = $2140
2nd year	$2140	$2140	·	0.07	·	1	= $149.80	$2140 + 149.80 = $2289.80
3rd year	$2289.80	$2289.80	·	0.07	·	1	= $160.29	$2289.80 + 160.29 = $2450.09

The compound interest earned can be found by

total amount	−	original principal	=	compound interest
↓		↓		↓
$2450.09	−	$2000	=	$450.09

The simple interest earned would have been

principal	·	rate	·	time	=	interest
↓		↓		↓		↓
$2000	·	0.07	·	3	=	$420

Since compound interest earns "interest on interest," compound interest earns more than simple interest.

Computing compound interest using the method above can be tedious. We can use a **compound interest table** to compute interest more quickly. The compound interest table in this textbook is found in Appendix A7. This table gives the total compound interest and principal paid on $1 for given rates and numbers of years. Then we can use the following equation to find the total amount of interest and principal:

Finding Total Amounts with Compound Interest

total amount = original principal · compound interest factor (from table)

EXAMPLE 4 **Finding Total Amount Received on an Investment**

$4000 is invested at 8% compounded semiannually for 10 years. Find the total amount at the end of 10 years.

Solution: Look in Appendix A7. The compound interest factor for 10 years at 8% in the Compounded Semiannually section is 2.19112.

total amount	=	original principal	·	compound interest factor
↓		↓		↓
total amount	=	$4000	·	2.19112
		= $8764.48		

Therefore, the total amount at the end of 10 years is $8764.48.

🔲 **Work Practice Problem 4**

EXAMPLE 5 **Finding Compound Interest Earned**

In Example 4 we found that the total amount for $4000 invested at 8% compounded semiannually for 10 years is $8764.48. Find the compound interest earned.

Solution:

interest earned	=	total amount	−	original principal
↓		↓		↓
interest earned	=	$8764.48	−	$4000
		= $4764.48		

The compound interest earned is $4764.48.

🔲 **Work Practice Problem 5**

PRACTICE PROBLEM 4

$5500 is invested at 7% compounded daily for 5 years. Find the total amount at the end of 5 years. Use 1 year = 365 days.

PRACTICE PROBLEM 5

If the total amount is $9933.14 when $5500 is invested, find the compound interest earned.

Answers

4. $7804.61, **5.** $4433.14

Objective C Calculating a Monthly Payment

We conclude this section with a method to find the monthly payment on a loan.

> ### Finding the Monthly Payment of a Loan
>
> $$\text{monthly payment} = \frac{\text{principal} + \text{interest}}{\text{total number of payments}}$$

PRACTICE PROBLEM 6

Find the monthly payment on a $3000 3-year loan if the interest on the loan is $1123.58.

EXAMPLE 6 Finding a Monthly Payment

Find the monthly payment on a $2000 loan for 2 years. The interest on the 2-year loan is $435.88.

Solution: First we determine the total number of monthly payments. The loan is for 2 years. Since there are 12 months per year, the number of payments is $2 \cdot 12$, or 24. Now we calculate the monthly payment.

$$\text{monthly payment} = \boxed{\frac{\text{principal} + \text{interest}}{\text{total number of payments}}}$$

$$\text{monthly payment} = \frac{\$2000 + \$435.88}{24}$$

$$\approx \$101.50$$

The monthly payment is about $101.50.

☐ **Work Practice Problem 6**

🖩 CALCULATOR EXPLORATIONS Compound Interest Factor

A compound interest factor may be found by using your calculator and evaluating the formula

$$\textbf{compound interest factor} = \left(1 + \frac{r}{n}\right)^{nt}$$

where r is the interest rate, t is the time in years, and n is the number of times compounded per year. For example, we stated earlier that the compound interest factor for 10 years at 8% compounded semiannually is 2.19112. Let's find this factor by evaluating the compound interest factor formula when $r = 8\%$ or 0.08, $t = 10$, and $n = 2$ (compounded semiannually means 2 times per year). Thus,

$$\text{compound interest factor} = \left(1 + \frac{0.08}{2}\right)^{2 \cdot 10}$$

$$\text{or} \quad \left(1 + \frac{0.08}{2}\right)^{20}$$

To evaluate, press the keys

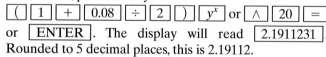

or ENTER . The display will read 2.1911231 . Rounded to 5 decimal places, this is 2.19112.

Find the compound interest factors. Use the table in the Appendix A.7 to check your answers.

1. 5 years, 9%, compounded quarterly
2. 15 years, 14%, compounded daily
3. 20 years, 11%, compounded annually
4. 1 year, 7%, compounded semiannually
5. Find the total amount after 4 years when $500 is invested at 6% compounded quarterly.
6. Find the total amount for 19 years when $2500 is invested at 5% compounded daily.

Answer
6. $114.54

6.7 EXERCISE SET

Student Solutions Manual   PH Math/Tutor Center   CD/Video for Review   MathXL MathXL®   MyMathLab MyMathLab

Objective A *Find the simple interest. See Examples 1 and 2.*

	Principal	Rate	Time
1.	$200	8%	2 years
3.	$160	11.5%	4 years
5.	$5000	10%	$1\frac{1}{2}$ years
7.	$375	18%	6 months
9.	$2500	16%	21 months

	Principal	Rate	Time
2.	$800	9%	3 years
4.	$950	12.5%	5 years
6.	$1500	14%	$2\frac{1}{4}$ years
8.	$775	15%	8 months
10.	$1000	10%	18 months

Solve. See Examples 1 through 3.

11. A company borrows $62,500 for 2 years at a simple interest of 12.5% to buy an airplane. Find the total amount paid on the loan.

12. $65,000 is borrowed to buy a house. If the simple interest rate on the 30-year loan is 10.25%, find the total amount paid on the loan.

13. A money market fund advertises a simple interest rate of 9%. Find the total amount received on an investment of $5000 for 15 months.

14. The Real Service Company takes out a 270-day (9-month) short-term, simple interest loan of $4500 to finance the purchase of some new equipment. If the interest rate is 14%, find the total amount that the company pays back.

15. Marsha Waide borrows $8500 and agrees to pay it back in 4 years. If the simple interest rate is 12%, find the total amount she pays back.

16. Ms. Lapchinski gives her 18-year-old daughter a graduation gift of $2000. If this money is invested at 8% simple interest for 5 years, find the total amount.

Objective B *Find the total amount in each compound interest account. See Example 4.*

17. $6150 is compounded semiannually at a rate of 14% for 15 years.

18. $2060 is compounded annually at a rate of 15% for 10 years.

19. $1560 is compounded daily at a rate of 8% for 5 years.

20. $1450 is compounded quarterly at a rate of 10% for 15 years.

21. $10,000 is compounded semiannually at a rate of 9% for 20 years.

22. $3500 is compounded daily at a rate of 8% for 10 years.

Find the total amount of compound interest earned. See Example 5.

23. $2675 is compounded annually at a rate of 9% for 1 year.

24. $6375 is compounded semiannually at a rate of 10% for 1 year.

25. $2000 is compounded annually at a rate of 8% for 5 years.

26. $2000 is compounded semiannually at a rate of 8% for 5 years.

27. $2000 is compounded quarterly at a rate of 8% for 5 years.

28. $2000 is compounded daily at a rate of 8% for 5 years.

Objective C *Solve. See Example 6.*

29. A college student borrows $1500 for 6 months to pay for a semester of school. If the interest is $61.88, find the monthly payment.

30. Jim Tillman borrows $1800 for 9 months. If the interest is $148.90, find his monthly payment.

31. $20,000 is borrowed for 4 years. If the interest on the loan is $10,588.70, find the monthly payment.

32. $105,000 is borrowed for 15 years. If the interest on the loan is $181,125, find the monthly payment.

Review

Find the perimeter of each figure. See Section 1.3.

33.

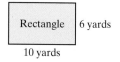

Rectangle — 6 yards, 10 yards

34.

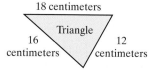

18 centimeters, Triangle, 16 centimeters, 12 centimeters

35.

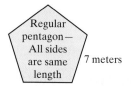

Regular pentagon— All sides are same length — 7 meters

36.

Square — 21 miles

Concept Extensions

37. Explain how to look up a compound interest factor in the compound interest table.

38. Explain how to find the amount of interest in a compounded account.

39. Compare the following accounts: Account 1: $1000 is invested for 10 years at a simple interest rate of 6%. Account 2: $1000 is compounded semiannually at a rate of 6% for 10 years. Discuss how the interest is computed for each account. Determine which account earns more interest. Why?

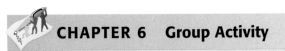

CHAPTER 6   Group Activity

Sections 6.1, 6.2, 6.7

How Much Can You Afford for a House?

When a home buyer takes out a mortgage to buy a house, the loan is generally repaid on a monthly basis with a monthly mortgage payment. (Some banks also offer biweekly payment programs.) An important consideration in choosing a house is the amount of the monthly payment. Usually, the amount that a home buyer can afford to make as a monthly payment will dictate the house purchase price that can be afforded.

The first step in deciding how much can be afforded for a house is finding out how much income the household has each month before taxes. The Mortgage Bankers Association of American (MBAA) suggests that the monthly mortgage payment be between 25% and 28% of the total monthly income. If other long-term debts exist (such as car or education loans and long-term credit card debt repayment), the MBAA further recommends that the total of housing costs and other monthly debt payments not exceed 36% of the total monthly income.

Once the size of the monthly payment that can be afforded has been found, a mortgage payment calculator can be used to work backward to estimate the mortgage amount that will give that desired monthly payment. For example, the Interest.com Web site includes a mortgage payment calculator at http://www.interest.com/calculators/monthlypayment.shtml. (Alternatively, visit www.interest.com and navigate to "Use our mortgage calculators.") Look for the calculator to calculate the monthly payment for a particular mortgage loan. With this mortgage payment calculator, the user can input the interest rate (as a percent), the term of the loan (in years), and total home loan amount (in dollars). This information is then used to calculate the associated monthly payment. To work backward with this mortgage payment calculator to find the total loan amount that can be afforded:

- Enter the interest rate that is likely for your loan and the term of the loan in which you are interested.

- Then make a guess (perhaps $100,000?) for the total home loan amount that can be afforded.
- Have the mortgage calculator calculate the monthly payment.
- If the monthly payment that is calculated is higher than the range that can be afforded, repeat the calculation using the same interest rate and loan term but a lower value for the total home loan amount.
- If the monthly payment that is calculated is lower than the range that can be afforded, repeat the calculation using the same interest rate and loan term but a higher value for the total home loan amount.
- Repeat these calculations methodically until a monthly payment is obtained that is in the range that can be afforded. The initial principal value that gave this monthly payment amount is an estimate of the mortgage amount that can be afforded to buy a home.

Group Activity

1. Research current interest rates on 30-year mortgages.
2. Use the method described above to find the size of mortgages that can be afforded by households with the following total monthly incomes before taxes. (Assume in each case that the household has no other debts.) Use a loan term of 30 years and a current interest rate on a 30-year mortgage.

   a. $3000   **b.** $3500   **c.** $4000
   d. $4500   **e.** $5000   **f.** $5500
3. Create a table of your results.

Chapter 6 Vocabulary Check

Fill in each blank with one of the words or phrases listed below.

percent	of	amount	100%	compound interest
base	is	0.01	$\frac{1}{100}$	

1. In a mathematical statement, _____ usually means "multiplication."

2. In a mathematical statement, _____ means "equals."

3. _____ means "per hundred."

4. _____ is computed not only on the principal, but also on interest already earned in previous compounding periods.

5. In the percent proportion $\dfrac{\rule{2cm}{0.4pt}}{\rule{2cm}{0.4pt}} = \dfrac{\text{percent}}{100}$

6. To write a decimal or fraction as a percent, multiply by _____.

7. The decimal equivalent of the % symbol is _____.

8. The fraction equivalent of the % symbol is _____.

Helpful Hint

Are you preparing for your test? Don't forget to take the Chapter 6 Test on page 437. Then check your answers at the back of the text and use the Chapter Test Prep Video CD to see the fully worked-out solutions to any of the exercises you want to review.

6 Chapter Highlights

DEFINITIONS AND CONCEPTS	EXAMPLES
Section 6.1 Introduction to Percent	
Percent means "per hundred." The % symbol denotes percent.	$51\% = \dfrac{51}{100}$ 51 per 100 $7\% = \dfrac{7}{100}$ 7 per 100
To write a percent as a decimal, replace the % symbol with its decimal equivalent, 0.01, and multiply. **To write a decimal as a percent,** multiply by 100%.	$32\% = 32(0.01) = 0.32$ $0.08 = 0.08(100\%) = 08.\% = 8\%$
Section 6.2 Percents and Fractions	
To write a percent as a fraction, replace the % symbol with its fraction equivalent, $\dfrac{1}{100}$, and multiply. **To write a fraction as a percent,** multiply by 100%.	$25\% = \dfrac{25}{100} = \dfrac{\overset{1}{\cancel{25}}}{4 \cdot \cancel{25}} = \dfrac{1}{4}$ $\dfrac{1}{6} = \dfrac{1}{6} \cdot 100\% = \dfrac{1}{6} \cdot \dfrac{100}{1}\% = \dfrac{100}{6}\% = 16\dfrac{2}{3}\%$

DEFINITIONS AND CONCEPTS	EXAMPLES

Section 6.3 Solving Percent Problems Using Equations

Three key words in the statement of a percent problem are **of,** which means **multiplication** ($\cdot$) **is,** which means **equals** ($=$) **what** (or some equivalent word or phrase), which stands for **the unknown number**	Solve: $\quad$ 6 $\quad$ is $\;$ 12% $\;$ of what number? $\quad\downarrow\quad\downarrow\quad\downarrow\quad\downarrow\quad\downarrow$ $\quad 6 \;=\; 12\% \;\cdot\; n$ $\quad 6 \;=\; 0.12 \;\cdot\; n$ $\quad$ Write 12% as a decimal. $\quad \dfrac{6}{0.12} = n$ $\quad$ Divide 6 by 0.12, the number multiplied by n. $\quad 50 \;=\; n$ Thus, 6 is 12% of 50.

Section 6.4 Solving Percent Problems Using Proportions

PERCENT PROPORTION $\quad \dfrac{\text{amount}}{\text{base}} = \dfrac{\text{percent}}{100} \; \leftarrow$ always 100 or $\quad \text{amount} \rightarrow \dfrac{a}{b} = \dfrac{p}{100} \; \leftarrow$ percent $\quad \text{base} \rightarrow$	Solve: $\quad$ 20.4 is what percent of 85? $\quad\quad\downarrow\quad\quad\quad\downarrow\quad\quad\quad\downarrow$ $\quad$ amount $\quad$ percent $\;$ base $\quad \text{amount} \rightarrow \dfrac{20.4}{85} = \dfrac{p}{100} \leftarrow$ percent $\quad \text{base} \rightarrow$ $\quad 20.4 \cdot 100 = 85 \cdot p$ $\quad$ Set cross products equal. $\quad 2040 = 85 \cdot p$ $\quad$ Multiply. $\quad \dfrac{2040}{85} = p$ $\quad$ Divide 2040 by 85, the number multiplied by p. $\quad 24 = p$ $\quad$ Simplify. Thus, 20.4 is 24% of 85.

Section 6.5 Applications of Percent

PERCENT OF INCREASE $\quad \text{percent of increase} = \dfrac{\text{amount of increase}}{\text{original amount}}$ **PERCENT OF DECREASE** $\quad \text{percent of decrease} = \dfrac{\text{amount of decrease}}{\text{original amount}}$	A town with a population of 16,480 decreased to 13,870 over a 12-year period. Find the percent decrease. Round to the nearest whole percent. $\quad$ amount of decrease $= 16{,}480 - 13{,}870$ $\quad\quad\quad\quad\quad\quad\quad\quad = 2610$ $\quad \text{percent of decrease} = \dfrac{\text{amount of decrease}}{\text{original amount}}$ $\quad\quad\quad\quad\quad\quad\quad = \dfrac{2610}{16{,}480} \approx 0.16$ $\quad\quad\quad\quad\quad\quad\quad = 16\%$ The town's population decreased by 16%.

Section 6.6 Percent and Problem Solving: Sales Tax, Commission, and Discount

SALES TAX AND TOTAL PRICE $\quad$ sales tax $=$ sales tax rate $\cdot$ purchase price $\quad$ total price $=$ purchase price $+$ sales tax	Find the sales tax and the total price of a purchase of $42 if the sales tax rate is 9%. $\quad$ sales tax $\;=\;$ sales tax rate $\;\cdot\;$ purchase price $\quad\quad\quad\downarrow\quad\quad\quad\quad\quad\downarrow\quad\quad\quad\quad\downarrow$ $\quad$ sales tax $\;=\;$ 9% $\;\cdot\;$ $42 $\quad\quad\quad\quad = 0.09 \cdot \$42$ $\quad\quad\quad\quad = \$3.78$

continued

DEFINITIONS AND CONCEPTS	EXAMPLES

Section 6.6   Percent and Problem Solving: Sales Tax, Commission, and Discount (*continued*)

The total price is

$$\text{total price} = \text{purchase price} + \text{sales tax}$$

$$\text{total price} = \$42 + \$3.78$$
$$= \$45.78$$

COMMISSION

$$\text{commission} = \text{commission rate} \cdot \text{total sales}$$

A salesperson earns a commission of 3%. Find the commission from sales of $12,500 worth of appliances.

$$\text{commission} = \text{commission rate} \cdot \text{sales}$$

$$\text{commission} = 3\% \cdot \$12,500$$
$$= 0.03 \cdot 12,500$$
$$= \$375$$

DISCOUNT AND SALE PRICE

$$\text{amount of discount} = \text{discount rate} \cdot \text{original price}$$
$$\text{sale price} = \text{original price} - \text{amount of discount}$$

A suit is priced at $320 and is on sale today for 25% off. What is the sale price?

$$\text{amount of discount} = \text{discount rate} \cdot \text{original price}$$

$$\text{amount of discount} = 25\% \cdot \$320$$

$$= 0.25 \cdot 320$$
$$= \$80$$

$$\text{sale price} = \text{original price} - \text{amount of discount}$$

$$\text{sale price} = \$320 - \$80$$
$$= \$240$$

The sale price is $240.

Section 6.7   Percent and Problem Solving: Interest

SIMPLE INTEREST

$$\text{interest} = \text{principal} \cdot \text{rate} \cdot \text{time}$$

where the rate is understood to be per year.

Find the simple interest after 3 years on $800 at an interest rate of 5%.

$$\text{interest} = \text{principal} \cdot \text{rate} \cdot \text{time}$$

$$\text{interest} = \$800 \cdot 5\% \cdot 3$$
$$= \$800 \cdot 0.05 \cdot 3 \quad \text{Write 5\% as 0.05.}$$
$$= \$120 \quad \text{Multiply.}$$

The interest is $120.

Compound interest is computed not only on the principal, but also on interest already earned in previous compounding periods. (See Appendix A7.)

$$\text{total amount} = \text{original principal} \cdot \begin{array}{c}\text{compound} \\ \text{interest} \\ \text{factor}\end{array}$$

$800 is invested at 5% compounded quarterly for 10 years. Find the total amount at the end of 10 years.

$$\text{total amount} = \text{original principal} \cdot \begin{array}{c}\text{compound} \\ \text{interest} \\ \text{factor}\end{array}$$

$$\text{total amount} = \$800 \cdot 1.64362$$
$$\approx \$1314.90$$

STUDY SKILLS BUILDER

Are You Prepared for a Test on Chapter 6?

Below I have listed some *common trouble areas* for students in Chapter 6. After studying for your test—but before taking your test—read these.

- Can you convert from percents to fractions or decimals and from fractions or decimals to percents?

  Percent to decimal: $7.5\% = 7.5(0.01) = 0.075$

  Percent to fraction: $11\% = 11 \cdot \dfrac{1}{100} = \dfrac{11}{100}$

  Decimal to percent: $0.36 = 0.36(100\%) = 36\%$

  Fraction to percent: $\dfrac{6}{7} = \dfrac{6}{7} \cdot 100\% = \dfrac{6}{7} \cdot \dfrac{100}{1}\%$

  $$= \dfrac{600}{7}\% = 85\dfrac{5}{7}\%$$

- Do you remember how to find percent increase or percent decrease? The number of CDs increased from 40 to 48. Find the percent increase.

  $$\dfrac{\text{percent}}{\text{increase}} = \dfrac{\text{increase}}{\text{original number}} = \dfrac{8}{40} = 0.20 = 20\%$$

6 CHAPTER REVIEW

(6.1) *Solve.*

1. In a survey of 100 adults, 37 preferred pepperoni on their pizzas. What percent preferred pepperoni?

2. A basketball player made 77 out 100 attempted free throws. What percent of free throws was made?

Write each percent as a decimal.

3. 83%

4. 75%

5. 73.5%

6. 1.5%

7. 125%

8. 145%

9. 0.5%

10. 0.7%

11. 200%

12. 400%

13. 26.25%

14. 85.34%

Write each decimal as a percent.

15. 2.6

16. 0.055

17. 0.35

18. 1.02

19. 0.725

20. 0.252

21. 0.076

22. 0.085

23. 0.71

24. 0.65

25. 4

26. 9

(6.2) *Write each percent as a fraction or mixed number in simplest form.*

27. 1%

28. 10%

29. 25%

30. 8.5%

31. 10.2%

32. $16\frac{2}{3}\%$

33. $33\frac{1}{3}\%$

34. 110%

Write each fraction or mixed number as a percent.

35. $\frac{1}{5}$

36. $\frac{7}{10}$

37. $\frac{5}{6}$

38. $1\frac{2}{3}$

39. $1\frac{1}{4}$

40. $\frac{3}{5}$

41. $\frac{1}{16}$

42. $\frac{5}{8}$

(6.3) *Translate each to an equation and solve.*

43. 1250 is 1.25% of what number?

44. What number is $33\frac{1}{3}\%$ of 24,000?

45. 124.2 is what percent of 540?

46. 22.9 is 20% of what number?

47. What number is 40% of 7500?

48. 693 is what percent of 462?

(6.4) *Translate each to a proportion and solve.*

49. 104.5 is 25% of what number?

50. 16.5 is 5.5% of what number?

51. What number is 36% of 180?

52. 63 is what percent of 35?

53. 93.5 is what percent of 85?

54. What number is 33% of 500?

(6.5) *Solve.*

55. In a survey of 2000 people, it was found that 1320 have a microwave oven. Find the percent of people who own microwaves.

56. Of the 12,360 freshmen entering County College, 2000 are enrolled in basic college mathematics. Find the percent of entering freshmen who are enrolled in basic college mathematics. Round to the nearest whole percent.

57. The number of violent crimes in a city decreased from 675 to 534. Find the percent decrease. Round to the nearest tenth of a percent.

58. The current charge for dumping waste in a local landfill is $16 per cubic foot. To cover new environmental costs, the charge will increase to $33 per cubic foot. Find the percent increase.

59. This year the fund drive for a charity collected $215,000. Next year, a 4% decrease is expected. Find how much is expected to be collected in next year's drive.

60. A local union negotiated a new contract that increases the hourly pay 15% over last year's pay. The old hourly rate was $11.50. Find the new hourly rate rounded to the nearest cent.

(6.6) *Solve.*

61. If the sales tax rate is 5.5%, what is the total amount charged for a $250 coat?

62. Find the sales tax paid on a $25.50 purchase if the sales tax rate is 4.5%.

63. Russ James is a sales representative for a chemical company and is paid a commission rate of 5% on all sales. Find his commission if he sold $100,000 worth of chemicals last month.

64. Carol Sell is a sales clerk in a clothing store. She receives a commission of 7.5% on all sales. Find her commission for the week if her sales for the week were $4005. Round to the nearest cent.

65. A $3000 mink coat is on sale for 30% off. Find the discount and the sale price.

66. A $90 calculator is on sale for 10% off. Find the discount and the sale price.

(6.7) *Solve.*

67. Find the simple interest due on $4000 loaned for 4 months at 12% interest.

68. Find the simple interest due on $6500 loaned for 3 months at 20%.

69. Find the total amount in an account if $5500 is compounded annually at 12% for 15 years.

70. Find the total amount in an account if $6000 is compounded semiannually at 11% for 10 years.

71. Find the compound interest earned if $100 is compounded quarterly at 12% for 5 years.

72. Find the compound interest earned if $1000 is compounded quarterly at 18% for 20 years.

Mixed Review

Write each percent as a decimal.

73. 3.8%

74. 24.5%

75. 0.9%

Write each decimal as a percent.

76. 0.54

77. 95.2

78. 0.3

Write each percent as a fraction or mixed number in simplest form.

79. 47%   **80.** $6\frac{2}{5}\%$ **81.** 5.6%

Write each fraction or mixed number as a percent.

82. $\frac{3}{8}$ **83.** $\frac{2}{13}$ **84.** $\frac{6}{5}$

Translate each into an equation and solve.

85. 43 is 16% of what number?   **86.** 27.5 is what percent of 25?

87. What number is 36% of 1968?   **88.** 67 is what percent of 50?

Translate each into a proportion and solve.

89. 75 is what percent of 25?   **90.** What number is 16% of 240?

91. 28 is 5% of what number?   **92.** 52 is what percent of 16?

Solve.

93. The total number of cans in a soft drink machine is 300. If 78 soft drinks have been sold, find the percent of soft drink cans that have been sold.

94. A home valued at $96,950 last year has lost 7% of its value this year. Find the loss in value.

95. A dinette set sells for $568.00. If the sales tax rate is 8.75%, find the purchase price of the dinette set.

96. The original price of a video game is $23.00. It is on sale for 15% off. What is the amount of the discount?

97. A candy salesman makes a commission of $1.60 from each case of candy he sells. If a case of candy costs $12.80, what is his rate of commission?

98. Find the total amount due on a 6 month loan of $1400 at a simple interest rate of 13%.

99. Find the total amount due on a loan of $5,500 for 9 years at 12.5% simple interest.

6 CHAPTER TEST

 Use the Chapter Test Prep Video CD to see the fully worked-out solutions to any of the exercises you want to review.

Write each percent as a decimal.

1. 85%   **2.** 500%   **3.** 0.8%

Write each decimal as a percent.

4. 0.056   **5.** 6.1   **6.** 0.39

Write each percent as a fraction or mixed number in simplest form.

7. 120%   **8.** 38.5%   **9.** 0.2%

Write each fraction or mixed number as a percent.

10. $\dfrac{11}{20}$ **11.** $\dfrac{3}{8}$ **12.** $1\dfrac{5}{9}$

Solve.

13. What number is 42% of 80?   **14.** 0.6% of what number is 7.5?

15. 567 is what percent of 756?

1. _____

2. _____

3. _____

4. _____

5. _____

6. _____

7. _____

8. _____

9. _____

10. _____

11. _____

12. _____

13. _____

14. _____

15. _____

16. _____

17. _____

18. _____

19. _____

20. _____

21. _____

22. _____

23. _____

24. _____

25. _____

Solve. Round all dollar amounts to the nearest cent.

16. An alloy is 12% copper. How much copper is contained in 320 pounds of this alloy?

17. A farmer in Nebraska estimates that 20% of his potential crop, or $11,350, has been lost to a hard freeze. Find the total value of his potential crop.

18. If the local sales tax rate is 1.25%, find the total amount charged for a stereo system priced at $354.

19. A town's population increased from 25,200 to 26,460. Find the percent increase.

20. A $120 framed picture is on sale for 15% off. Find the discount and the sale price.

21. Randy Nguyen is paid a commission rate of 4% on all sales. Find Randy's commission if his sales were $9875.

22. A sales tax of $1.53 is added to an item's price of $152.99. Find the sales tax rate. Round to the nearest whole percent.

23. Find the simple interest earned on $2000 saved for $3\frac{1}{2}$ years at an interest rate of 9.25%.

24. $1365 is compounded annually at 8%. Find the total amount in the account after 5 years.

25. A couple borrowed $400 from a bank at 13.5% for 6 months for car repairs. Find the total amount due the bank at the end of the 6-month period.

1. How many cases can be filled with 9900 cans of jalapeños if each case holds 48 cans? How many cans will be left over? Will there be enough cases to fill an order for 200 cases?

2. Multiply: 409×76

3. Write each fraction as a mixed number or a whole number.

   a. $\dfrac{30}{7}$ **b.** $\dfrac{16}{15}$ **c.** $\dfrac{84}{6}$

4. Write each mixed number as an improper fraction.

   a. $2\dfrac{5}{7}$ **b.** $10\dfrac{1}{10}$ **c.** $5\dfrac{3}{8}$

5. Use a factor tree to find the prime factorization of 24.

6. Find the area of the rectangle.

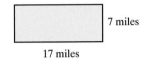

7 miles

17 miles

7. Write $\dfrac{10}{27}$ in simplest form.

8. Find the average of 28, 34, and 70.

9. Multiply and simplify: $\dfrac{23}{32} \cdot \dfrac{4}{7}$

10. Round 76,498 to the nearest ten.

11. Find the reciprocal of $\dfrac{11}{8}$.

12. Write the shaded part of the figure as an improper fraction and as a mixed number.

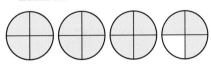

13. Find the perimeter of the rectangle.

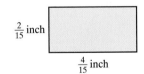

$\frac{2}{15}$ inch

$\frac{4}{15}$ inch

14. Find $2 \cdot 5^2$

15. Find the LCM of 12 and 20.

16. Subtract $\dfrac{7}{9}$ from $\dfrac{10}{9}$.

17. Add: $\dfrac{2}{5} + \dfrac{4}{15}$

18. Find $\dfrac{2}{3}$ of 510.

19. Subtract: $7\dfrac{3}{14} - 3\dfrac{6}{7}$

20. Simplify: $9 \cdot \sqrt{25} - 6 \cdot \sqrt{4}$

Perform each indicated operation.

21. $\dfrac{1}{2} \div \dfrac{8}{7}$

22. $20\dfrac{4}{5} + 12\dfrac{7}{8}$

Answers

1. _____

2. _____

3. a. _____

   b. _____

   c. _____

4. a. _____

   b. _____

   c. _____

5. _____

6. _____

7. _____

8. _____

9. _____

10. _____

11. _____

12. _____

13. _____

14. _____

15. _____

16. _____

17. _____

18. _____

19. _____

20. _____

21. _____

22. _____

23. _____

24. _____

25. _____

26. _____

27. _____

28. _____

29. _____

30. _____

31. _____

32. _____

33. _____

34. _____

35. _____

36. _____

37. _____

38. _____

39. _____

40. _____

41. _____

42. _____

43. _____

44. _____

45. _____

46. _____

47. _____

48. a. _____

   b. _____

   c. _____

49. _____

50. _____

23. $\dfrac{2}{9} \cdot \dfrac{3}{11}$

24. $1\dfrac{7}{8} \cdot 3\dfrac{2}{5}$

Write each fraction as a decimal.

25. $\dfrac{8}{10}$

26. $\dfrac{9}{100}$

27. $\dfrac{87}{10}$

28. $\dfrac{48}{10,000}$

29. The price of a gallon of gasoline in Aimsville is currently $2.1779. Round this to the nearest cent.

30. Subtract: $38 - 10.06$

31. Add: $763.7651 + 22.001 + 43.89$

32. 12.483×100

33. Multiply: 23.6×0.78

34. 76.3×1000

Divide.

35. $\dfrac{786.1}{1000}$

36. $0.5\overline{)0.638}$

37. $\dfrac{0.12}{10}$

38. $0.23\overline{)11.6495}$

39. Simplify: $723.6 \div 1000 \times 10$

40. Simplify: $\dfrac{3.19 - 0.707}{13}$

41. Write $\dfrac{1}{4}$ as a decimal.

42. Write $\dfrac{5}{9}$ as a decimal. Give an exact answer and a three-decimal-place approximation.

Write the following rate as a fraction in simplest form.

43. 10 nails every 6 feet

44. 115 miles every 5 gallons

45. Is $\dfrac{4.1}{7} = \dfrac{2.9}{5}$ a true proportion?

46. Find each unit rate and decide on the better buy.

$0.93 for 18 flour tortillas

$1.40 for 24 flour tortillas

47. On a chamber of commerce map of Abita Springs, 5 miles corresponds to 2 inches. How many miles correspond to 7 inches?

48. Write each percent as a decimal.

   a. 7%   **b.** 200%   **c.** 0.5%

49. Translate to an equation: What number is 25% of 0.008?

50. Write $\dfrac{3}{8}$ as a percent.

7

Measurement

The use of measurements is common in everyday life. A sales representative records the number of miles she has driven when she submits her travel expense report. A respiratory therapist measures the volume of air exhaled by a patient. A measurement is necessary in each case.

The Statue of Liberty, standing on Liberty Island in New York City's harbor, is a symbol of freedom and was a gift from the people of France. After the pedestal had been prepared in 1885, the statue arrived dismantled in 214 packing cases of iron framework and copper sheeting and was assembled using rivets. Over a year later it was dedicated by President Grover Cleveland. Throughout this chapter, we explore some of the measurements of the Statue of Liberty.

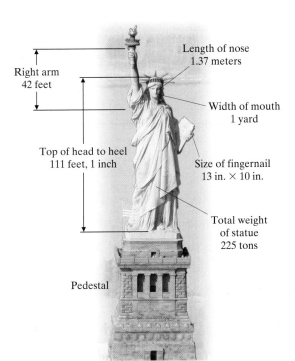

Right arm
42 feet

Length of nose
1.37 meters

Width of mouth
1 yard

Top of head to heel
111 feet, 1 inch

Size of fingernail
13 in. × 10 in.

Total weight
of statue
225 tons

Pedestal

7.1 LENGTH: U.S. AND METRIC SYSTEMS OF MEASUREMENT

Objectives

A Define U.S. Units of Length and Convert from One Unit to Another.

B Use Mixed Units of Length.

C Perform Arithmetic Operations on U.S. Units of Length.

D Define Metric Units of Length and Convert from One Unit to Another.

E Perform Arithmetic Operations on Metric Units of Length.

Objective **A** Defining and Converting U.S. System Units of Length

In the United States, two systems of measurement are commonly used. They are the **United States (U.S.), or English, measurement system** and the **metric system.** The U.S. measurement system is familiar to most Americans. Units such as feet, miles, ounces, and gallons are used. However, the metric system is also commonly used in fields such as medicine, sports, international marketing, and certain physical sciences. We are accustomed to buying 2-liter bottles of soft drinks, watching televised coverage of the 100-meter dash at the Olympic Games, or taking a 200-milligram dose of pain reliever.

The U.S. system of measurement uses the **inch, foot, yard,** and **mile** to measure **length.** The following is a summary of equivalencies between units of length:

U.S. Units of Length

$$12 \text{ inches (in.)} = 1 \text{ foot (ft)}$$
$$3 \text{ feet} = 1 \text{ yard (yd)}$$
$$36 \text{ inches} = 1 \text{ yard}$$
$$5280 \text{ feet} = 1 \text{ mile (mi)}$$

To convert from one unit of length to another, we will use **unit fractions.** We define a unit fraction to be a fraction that is equivalent to 1. Examples of unit fractions are as follows:

Unit Fractions

$$\frac{12 \text{ in.}}{1 \text{ ft}} = 1 \text{ or } \frac{1 \text{ ft}}{12 \text{ in.}} = 1 \text{ (since 12 in.} = 1 \text{ ft)}$$

$$\frac{3 \text{ ft}}{1 \text{ yd}} = 1 \text{ or } \frac{1 \text{ yd}}{3 \text{ ft}} = 1 \text{ (since 3 ft} = 1 \text{ yd)}$$

$$\frac{5280 \text{ ft}}{1 \text{ mi}} = 1 \text{ or } \frac{1 \text{ mi}}{5280 \text{ ft}} = 1 \text{ (since 5280 ft} = 1 \text{ mi)}$$

Remember that multiplying a number by 1 does not change the value of the number.

PRACTICE PROBLEM 1

Convert 5 feet to inches.

EXAMPLE 1 Convert 8 feet to inches.

Solution: We multiply 8 feet by a unit fraction that uses the equality 12 inches = 1 foot. The unit fraction should be in the form $\frac{\text{units to convert to}}{\text{original units}}$ or in this case $\frac{12 \text{ inches}}{1 \text{ foot}}$. We do this so that like units divide out, as shown.

$$8 \text{ ft} = \frac{8 \text{ ft}}{1} \cdot 1 \qquad \text{Multiply by 1 in the form of } \frac{12 \text{ in.}}{1 \text{ ft}}.$$

$$= \frac{8 \cancel{\text{ ft}}}{1} \cdot \frac{12 \text{ in.}}{1 \cancel{\text{ ft}}}$$

$$= 8 \cdot 12 \text{ in.}$$

$$= 96 \text{ in.} \qquad \text{Multiply.}$$

Answer

1. 60 in.

Thus, 8 ft = 96 in., as shown in the diagram:

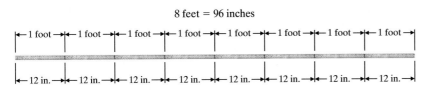

8 feet = 96 inches

| ←1 foot→ | ←1 foot→ | ←1 foot→ | ←1 foot→ | ←1 foot→ | ←1 foot→ | ←1 foot→ | ←1 foot→ |

| ←12 in.→ | ←12 in.→ | ←12 in.→ | ←12 in.→ | ←12 in.→ | ←12 in.→ | ←12 in.→ | ←12 in.→ |

🔲 **Work Practice Problem 1**

EXAMPLE 2 Convert 7 feet to yards.

PRACTICE PROBLEM 2

Convert 7 yards to feet.

Solution: We multiply by a unit fraction that compares 1 yard to 3 feet.

$$7 \text{ ft} = \frac{7 \text{ ft}}{1} \cdot 1$$

$$= \frac{7 \text{ ft}}{1} \cdot \frac{1 \text{ yd}}{3 \text{ ft}} \quad \leftarrow \text{Units to convert to} \\ \leftarrow \text{Original units}$$

$$= \frac{7}{3} \text{ yd}$$

$$= 2\frac{1}{3} \text{ yd} \qquad \text{Divide.}$$

Thus, $7 \text{ ft} = 2\frac{1}{3} \text{ yd}$, as shown in the diagram.

7 feet = $2\frac{1}{3}$ yards

| ←1 foot→ | ←1 foot→ | ←1 foot→ | ←1 foot→ | ←1 foot→ | ←1 foot→ | ←1 foot→ |

| ←————— 1 yard —————→ | ←————— 1 yard —————→ | ←$\frac{1}{3}$ yard→ |

🔲 **Work Practice Problem 2**

EXAMPLE 3 Finding Length of Pelican's Bill

PRACTICE PROBLEM 3

Suppose the bill in the photo measures 18 inches. Convert 18 inches to feet, using decimals.

The Australian pelican has the longest bill, measuring from 13 to 18.5 inches long. The pelican in the photo has a 15-inch bill. Convert 15 inches to feet, using decimals.

Solution:

$$15 \text{ in.} = \frac{15 \text{ in.}}{1} \cdot \frac{1 \text{ ft}}{12 \text{ in.}} \quad \leftarrow \text{Units to convert to} \\ \leftarrow \text{Original units}$$

$$= \frac{15}{12} \text{ ft}$$

$$= \frac{5}{4} \text{ ft} \qquad \text{Simplify } \frac{15}{12}.$$

$$= 1.25 \text{ ft} \qquad \text{Divide.}$$

Thus, 15 in. = 1.25 ft, as shown in the diagram.

15 inches = 1.25 ft

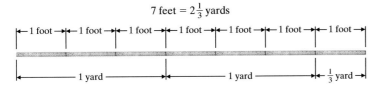

| ←————— 1 ft —————→ | $\frac{1}{4}$ or 0.25 ft |

🔲 **Work Practice Problem 3**

Answers

2. 21 ft, **3.** 1.5 ft

Objective B Using Mixed U.S. System Units of Length

Sometimes it is more meaningful to express a measurement of length with mixed units such as 1 ft and 5 in. We usually condense this and write 1 ft 5 in.

In Example 2, we found that 7 feet was the same as $2\frac{1}{3}$ yards. The measurement can also be written as a mixture of yards and feet. That is,

$$7 \text{ ft} = \underline{\quad} \text{ yd} \underline{\quad} \text{ ft}$$

Because 3 ft = 1 yd, we divide 3 into 7 to see how many whole yards are in 7 feet. The quotient is the number of yards, and the remainder is the number of feet.

$$\begin{array}{r} 2 \text{ yd } 1 \text{ ft} \\ 3\overline{)7} \\ -6 \\ \hline 1 \end{array}$$

Thus, 7 ft = 2 yd 1 ft, as seen in the diagram:

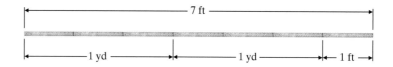

PRACTICE PROBLEM 4

Convert:
68 in. = _____ ft _____ in.

EXAMPLE 4 Convert: 134 in. = _____ ft _____ in.

Solution: Because 12 in. = 1 ft, we divide 12 into 134. The quotient is the number of feet. The remainder is the number of inches. To see why we divide 12 into 134, notice that

$$134 \text{ in.} = \frac{134 \text{ in.}}{1} \cdot \frac{1 \text{ ft}}{12 \text{ in.}} = \frac{134}{12} \text{ ft}$$

$$\begin{array}{r} 11 \text{ ft } 2 \text{ in.} \\ 12\overline{)134} \\ -12 \\ \hline 14 \\ -12 \\ \hline 2 \end{array}$$

Thus, 134 in. = 11 ft 2 in.

▣ **Work Practice Problem 4**

PRACTICE PROBLEM 5

Convert 5 yards 2 feet to feet.

EXAMPLE 5 Convert 3 feet 7 inches to inches.

Solution: First, we convert 3 feet to inches. Then we add 7 inches.

$$3 \text{ ft} = \frac{3 \text{ ft}}{1} \cdot \frac{12 \text{ in.}}{1 \text{ ft}} = 36 \text{ in.}$$

Then

$$3 \text{ ft } 7 \text{ in.} = 36 \text{ in.} + 7 \text{ in.} = 43 \text{ in.}$$

▣ **Work Practice Problem 5**

Answers
4. 5 ft 8 in., **5.** 17 ft

Objective Ⓒ **Performing Operations on U.S. System Units of Length**

Finding sums or differences of measurements often involves converting units, as shown in the next example. Just remember that, as usual, only like units can be added or subtracted.

EXAMPLE 6 Add 3 ft 2 in. and 5 ft 11 in.

Solution: To add, we line up the similar units.

$$\begin{array}{r} 3 \text{ ft } 2 \text{ in.} \\ + 5 \text{ ft } 11 \text{ in.} \\ \hline 8 \text{ ft } 13 \text{ in.} \end{array}$$

Since 13 inches is the same as 1 ft 1 in., we have

$$8 \text{ ft } 13 \text{ in.} = 8 \text{ ft } + \overbrace{1 \text{ ft } 1 \text{ in.}}$$
$$= 9 \text{ ft } 1 \text{ in.}$$

▢ **Work Practice Problem 6**

✔ **Concept Check** How could you estimate the following sum?

$$\begin{array}{r} 7 \text{ yd } 4 \text{ in.} \\ + 3 \text{ yd } 27 \text{ in.} \\ \hline \end{array}$$

EXAMPLE 7 Multiply 8 ft 9 in. by 3.

Solution: By the distributive property, we multiply 8 ft by 3 and 9 in. by 3.

$$\begin{array}{r} 8 \text{ ft } 9 \text{ in.} \\ \times \quad\quad 3 \\ \hline 24 \text{ ft } 27 \text{ in.} \end{array}$$

Since 27 in. is the same as 2 ft 3 in., we simplify the product as

$$24 \text{ ft } 27 \text{ in.} = 24 \text{ ft } + \overbrace{2 \text{ ft } 3 \text{ in.}}$$
$$= 26 \text{ ft } 3 \text{ in.}$$

▢ **Work Practice Problem 7**

EXAMPLE 8 Divide 24 yd 6 in. by 3.

Solution: We divide each of the units by 3.

$$\begin{array}{r} 8 \text{ yd } 2 \text{ in.} \\ 3\overline{)24 \text{ yd } 6 \text{ in.}} \\ \underline{-24 \text{ yd}} \\ 6 \text{ in.} \\ \underline{-6 \text{ in.}} \\ 0 \end{array}$$

The quotient is 8 yd 2 in.

To check, see that 8 yd 2 in. multiplied by 3 is 24 yd 6 in.

▢ **Work Practice Problem 8**

PRACTICE PROBLEM 6
Add 4 ft 8 in. to 8 ft 11 in.

PRACTICE PROBLEM 7
Multiply 4 ft 7 in. by 4.

PRACTICE PROBLEM 8
Divide 18 ft 6 in. by 2.

Answers
6. 13 ft 7 in.,   **7.** 18 ft 4 in.,
8. 9 ft 3 in.

✔ **Concept Check Answer**
round each to the nearest yard:
7 yd + 4 yd = 11 yd

PRACTICE PROBLEM 9

A carpenter cuts 1 ft 9 in. from a board of length 5 ft 8 in. Find the remaining length of the board.

EXAMPLE 9 **Finding the Length of a Piece of Rope**

A rope of length 6 yd 1 ft has 2 yd 2 ft cut from one end. Find the length of the remaining rope.

Solution: Subtract 2 yd 2 ft from 6 yd 1 ft.

$$
\begin{array}{rl}
\text{beginning length} \;\rightarrow & 6 \text{ yd } 1 \text{ ft} \\
- \quad \text{amount cut} \;\rightarrow & -2 \text{ yd } 2 \text{ ft} \\
\hline
\text{remaining length} &
\end{array}
$$

We cannot subtract 2 ft from 1 ft, so we borrow 1 yd from the 6 yd. One yard is converted to 3 ft and combined with the 1 ft already there.

Borrow 1 yd = 3 ft

5 yd + (1 yd) (3 ft)

$$
\begin{array}{rcl}
\cancel{6 \text{ yd }} 1 \text{ ft} & = & 5 \text{ yd } 4 \text{ ft} \\
- 2 \text{ yd } 2 \text{ ft} & = & -2 \text{ yd } 2 \text{ ft} \\
\hline
& & 3 \text{ yd } 2 \text{ ft}
\end{array}
$$

The remaining rope is 3 yd 2 ft long.

Work Practice Problem 9

Objective **D** **Defining and Converting Metric System Units of Length**

The basic unit of length in the metric system is the **meter.** A meter is slightly longer than a yard. It is approximately 39.37 inches long. Recall that a yard is 36 inches long.

1 yard = 36 inches

1 meter ≈ 39.37 inches

All units of length in the metric system are based on the meter. The following is a summary of the prefixes used in the metric system. Also shown are equivalencies between units of length. Like the decimal system, the metric system uses powers of 10 to define units.

Metric Unit of Length
1 **kilo**meter (km) = 1000 meters (m)
1 **hecto**meter (hm) = 100 m
1 **deka**meter (dam) = 10 m
1 **meter (m)** = 1 m
1 **deci**meter (dm) = 1/10 m or 0.1 m
1 **centi**meter (cm) = 1/100 m or 0.01 m
1 **milli**meter (mm) = 1/1000 m or 0.001 m

The figure below will help you with decimeters, centimeters, and millimeters.

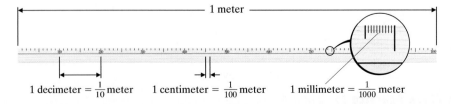

1 meter

1 decimeter = $\frac{1}{10}$ meter   1 centimeter = $\frac{1}{100}$ meter   1 millimeter = $\frac{1}{1000}$ meter

Answer

9. 3 ft 11 in.

Study the figure above for other equivalencies between metric units of length.

10 decimeters = 1 meter   10 millimeters = 1 centimeter
100 centimeters = 1 meter   10 centimeters = 1 decimeter
1000 millimeters = 1 meter

These same prefixes are used in the metric system for mass and capacity. The most commonly used measurements of length in the metric system are the **meter, millimeter, centimeter,** and **kilometer.**

Being comfortable with the metric units of length means gaining a "feeling" for metric lengths, just as you have a "feeling" for the length of an inch, a foot, and a mile. To help you accomplish this, study the following examples:

A millimeter is about the thickness of a large paper clip.

A centimeter is about the width of a large paper clip.

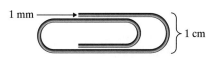

A meter is slightly longer than a yard.

A kilometer is about two-thirds of a mile.

The length of this book is approximately 27.5 centimeters.

The width of this book is approximately 21.5 centimeters.

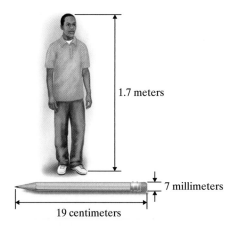

1.7 meters

7 millimeters

19 centimeters

New York

Philadelphia   160 km

As with the U.S. system of measurement, unit fractions may be used to convert from one unit of length to another. For example, let's convert 1200 meters to kilometers. To do so, we will multiply by 1 in the form of the unit fraction

$$\frac{1 \text{ km}}{1000 \text{ m}}$$ ← Units to convert to
                  ← Original units

Unit fraction

$$1200 \text{ m} = \frac{1200 \text{ m}}{1} \cdot 1 = \frac{1200 \text{ m}}{1} \cdot \frac{1 \text{ km}}{1000 \text{ m}} = \frac{1200 \text{ km}}{1000} = 1.2 \text{ km}$$

Thus, 1200 m = 1.2 km as shown in the diagram.

1200 m = 1.200 km	1000 m	200 m

3 places to the left   ← 1 km →   ← 0.2 km →

The metric system does, however, have a distinct advantage over the U.S. system of measurement: The ease of converting from one unit of length to another. Since all units of length are powers of 10 of the meter, converting from one unit of length to another is as simple as moving the decimal point. Listing units of length in order from largest to smallest helps to keep track of how many places to move the decimal point when converting.

Let's again convert 1200 meters to kilometers. This time, to convert from meters to kilometers, we move along the chart shown 3 units to the left, from meters to kilometers. This means that we move the decimal point 3 places to the left.

km   hm   dam   **m**   dm   cm   mm

3 units to the left

PRACTICE PROBLEM 10
Convert 2.5 m to millimeters.

EXAMPLE 10   Convert 2.3 m to centimeters.

Solution: First we will convert by using a unit fraction.

Unit fraction

$$2.3 \text{ m} = \frac{2.3 \text{ m}}{1} \cdot \frac{100 \text{ cm}}{1 \text{ m}} = 230 \text{ cm}$$

Now we will convert by listing the units of length in order from left to right and moving from meters to centimeters.

km   hm   dam   m   dm   cm   mm

2 units to the right

$$2.30 \text{ m} = 230. \text{ cm}$$

2 places to the right

With either method, we get 230 cm.

■ **Work Practice Problem 10**

PRACTICE PROBLEM 11
Convert 3500 m to kilometers.

EXAMPLE 11   Convert 450,000 mm to meters.

Solution: We list the units of length in order from left to right and move from millimeters to meters.

km   hm   dam   m   dm   cm   mm

3 units to the left

$$450,000 \text{ mm} = 450.000 \text{ m or } 450 \text{ m}$$

■ **Work Practice Problem 11**

✔**Concept Check**   What is wrong with the following conversion of 150 cm to meters?

$$150.00 \text{ cm} = 15,000 \text{ m}$$

Objective E Performing Operations on Metric System Units of Length

To add, subtract, multiply, or divide with metric measurements of length, we write all numbers using the same unit of length and then add, subtract, multiply, or divide as with decimals.

Answers
10. 2500 mm, **11.** 3.5 km

✔ **Concept Check Answer**
decimal should be moved to the left:
1.5 m

EXAMPLE 12 Subtract 430 m from 1.3 km.

Solution: First we convert both measurements to kilometers or both to meters.

$$430 \text{ m} = 0.43 \text{ km}$$

$$\begin{array}{r} 1.30 \text{ km} \\ - 0.43 \text{ km} \\ \hline 0.87 \text{ km} \end{array}$$

or

$$1.3 \text{ km} = 1300 \text{ m}$$

$$\begin{array}{r} 1300 \text{ m} \\ - 430 \text{ m} \\ \hline 870 \text{ m} \end{array}$$

The difference is 0.87 km or 870 m.

◉ **Work Practice Problem 12**

EXAMPLE 13 Multiply 5.7 mm by 4.

Solution: Here we simply multiply the two numbers. Note that the unit of measurement remains the same.

$$\begin{array}{r} 5.7 \text{ mm} \\ \times \quad 4 \\ \hline 22.8 \text{ mm} \end{array}$$

◉ **Work Practice Problem 13**

EXAMPLE 14 Finding a Crocodile's Length

A newly hatched Nile crocodile averages 26 centimeters in length. This type of crocodile normally grows 4.74 meters to reach its adult length. What is the adult length of this type of crocodile?

Solution:

$$\begin{array}{ll} \text{original length} & \rightarrow \quad 0.26 \text{ m} \quad \text{(since 26 cm = 0.26 m)} \\ + \quad \text{length grown} & \rightarrow \quad + 4.74 \text{ m} \\ \hline \text{adult length} & \quad\quad 5.00 \text{ m} \end{array}$$

The adult length is 5 meters.

◉ **Work Practice Problem 14**

PRACTICE PROBLEM 12

Subtract 640 m from 2.1 km.

PRACTICE PROBLEM 13

Multiply 18.3 hm by 5.

PRACTICE PROBLEM 14

Doris Blackwell is knitting a scarf that is currently 0.8 meter long. If she knits an additional 45 centimeters, how long will the scarf be?

Answers

12. 1.46 km or 1460 m,   **13.** 91.5 hm,
14. 125 cm or 1.25 m

Mental Math

Convert as indicated.

1. 12 inches to feet

2. 6 feet to yards

3. 24 inches to feet

4. 36 inches to feet

5. 36 inches to yards

6. 2 yards to inches

Determine whether the measurement in each statement is reasonable.

7. The screen of a home television set has a 30-meter diagonal.

8. A window measures 1 meter by 0.5 meter.

9. A drinking glass is made of glass 2 millimeters thick.

10. A paper clip is 4 kilometers long.

11. The distance across the Colorado River is 50 kilometers.

12. A model's hair is 30 centimeters long.

7.1 EXERCISE SET

FOR EXTRA HELP

Student Solutions Manual   PH Math/Tutor Center   CD/Video for Review   Math XL MathXL®   MyMathLab MyMathLab

Objective A *Convert each measurement as indicated. See Examples 1 through 3.*

 1. 60 in. to feet

2. 84 in. to feet

 3. 12 yd to feet

4. 18 yd to feet

5. 42,240 ft to miles

6. 36,960 ft to miles

7. 102 in. to feet

8. 150 in. to feet

9. 10 ft to yards

10. 25 ft to yards

11. 6.4 mi to feet

12. 3.8 mi to feet

13. 162 in. to yd (Write answer as a decimal.)

14. 7216 yd to mi (Write answer as a decimal.)

15. 3 in. to ft (Write answer as a decimal.)

16. 129 in. to ft (Write answer as a decimal.)

Objective B *Convert each measurement as indicated. See Examples 4 and 5.*

17. 40 ft = _____ yd _____ ft

18. 100 ft = _____ yd _____ ft

19. 41 in. = _____ ft _____ in.

20. 75 in. = _____ ft _____ in.

21. 10,000 ft = _____ mi _____ ft

22. 25,000 ft = _____ mi _____ ft

23. 5 ft 2 in. = _____ in.

24. 4 ft 11 in. = _____ in.

25. 7 yd 2 ft = _____ ft

26. 7 yd 1 ft = _____ ft

27. 2 yd 1 ft = _____ in.

28. 1 yd 2 ft = _____ in.

Objective **C** *Perform each indicated operation. Simplify the result if possible. See Examples 6 through 8.*

29. 5 ft 8 in. + 6 ft 7 in.

30. 9 ft 10 in. + 8 ft 4 in.

31. 12 yd 2 ft + 9 yd 2 ft

32. 16 yd 2 ft + 8 yd 1 ft

33. 24 ft 8 in. − 16 ft 3 in.

34. 15 ft 5 in. − 8 ft 2 in.

35. 16 ft 3 in. − 10 ft 9 in.

36. 14 ft 8 in. − 3 ft 11 in.

37. 6 ft 8 in. ÷ 2

38. 26 ft 10 in. ÷ 2

39. 12 yd 2 ft × 4

40. 15 yd 1 ft × 8

Objective **D** *Convert as indicated. See Examples 10 and 11.*

41. 40 m to centimeters

42. 18 m to centimeters

43. 40 mm to centimeters

44. 18 mm to centimeters

45. 300 m to kilometers

46. 400 m to kilometers

47. 1400 mm to meters

48. 6400 mm to meters

49. 1500 cm to meters

50. 6400 cm to meters

51. 0.42 km to centimeters

52. 0.95 km to centimeters

53. 7 km to meters

54. 5 km to meters

55. 8.3 cm to millimeters

56. 4.6 cm to millimeters

57. 20.1 mm to decimeters

58. 140.2 mm to decimeters

59. 0.04 m to millimeters

60. 0.2 m to millimeters

Objective **E** *Perform each indicated operation. See Examples 12 and 13.*

61. 8.6 m + 0.34 m

62. 14.1 cm + 3.96 cm

63. 2.9 m + 40 mm

64. 30 cm + 8.9 m

65. 24.8 mm − 1.19 cm

66. 45.3 m − 2.16 dam

67. 15 km − 2360 m

68. 14 cm − 15 mm

69. 18.3 m × 3

70. 14.1 m × 4

71. 6.2 km ÷ 4

72. 9.6 m ÷ 5

Objectives **A** **C** **D** **E** **Mixed Practice** *Solve. Remember to insert units when writing your answers. For Exercises 73–82, complete the charts. See Examples 3, 9 through 11, and 14.*

		Yards	Feet	Inches
73.	Crysler Building in New York City		1046	
74.	4-story building			792
75.	Python length		35	
76.	Ostrich height			108

Complete the chart.

		Meters	Millimeters	Kilometers	Centimeters
77.	Length of elephant	5			
78.	Height of grizzly bear	3			
79.	Tennis ball diameter				6.5
80.	Golf ball diameter				4.6
81.	Distance from London to Paris			342	
82.	Distance from Houston to Dallas			396	

83. The National Zoo maintains a small patch of bamboo, which it grows as a food supply for its pandas. Two weeks ago, the bamboo was 6 ft 10 in. tall. Since then, the bamboo has grown 3 ft 8 in. How tall is the bamboo now?

84. While exploring in the Marianas Trench, a submarine probe was lowered to a point 1 mile 1400 feet below the ocean's surface. Later it was lowered an additional 1 mile 4000 feet below this point. How far is the probe below the surface of the Pacific?

85. The length of one of the Statue of Liberty's hands is 16 ft 5 in. One of the Statue's eyes is 2 ft 6 in. across. How much longer is a hand than the width of an eye? (*Source:* National Park Service)

86. The width of the Statue of Liberty's head from ear to ear is 10 ft. The height of the Statue's head from chin to cranium is 17 ft 3 in. How much taller is the Statue's head than its width? (*Source:* National Park Service)

87. A 3.4-m rope is attached to a 5.8-m rope. However, when the ropes are tied, 8 cm of length is lost to form the knot. What is the length of the tied ropes?

88. A 2.15-m-long sash cord has become frayed at both ends so that 1 cm is trimmed from each end. How long is the remaining cord?

89. The ice on a pond is 5.33 cm thick. For safe skating, the owner of the pond insists that it must be 80 mm thick. How much thicker must the ice be before skating is allowed?

90. The sediment on the bottom of the Towamencin Creek is normally 14 cm thick, but the recent flood washed away 22 mm of sediment. How thick is it now?

91. The Amana Corporation stacks up its microwave ovens in a distribution warehouse. Each stack is 1 ft 9 in. wide. How far from the wall would 9 of these stacks extend?

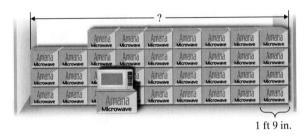

1 ft 9 in.

92. The highway commission is installing concrete sound barriers along a highway. Each barrier is 1 yd 2 ft long. Find the total length of 25 barriers placed end to end.

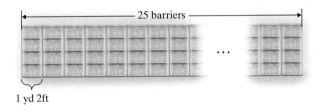

25 barriers

1 yd 2ft

93. A carpenter needs to cut a board into thirds. If the board is 9 ft 3 in. long originally, how long will each cut piece be?

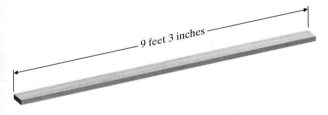

9 feet 3 inches

94. A wall is erected exactly halfway between two buildings that are 192 ft 8 in. apart. If the wall is 8 in. wide, how far is it from the wall to either of the buildings?

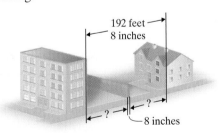

192 feet 8 inches

? ?

8 inches

95. An art class is learning how to make kites. The two sticks used for each kite have lengths of 1 m and 65 cm. What total length of wood must be ordered for the sticks if 25 kites are to be built?

96. The total pages of a hardbound economics text are 3.1 cm thick. The front and back covers are each 2 mm thick. How high would a stack of 10 of these texts be?

97. A logging firm needs to cut a 67-m-long redwood log into 20 equal pieces before loading it onto a truck for shipment. How long will each piece be?

98. An 18.3-m-tall flagpole is mounted on a 65-cm-high pedestal. How far is the top of the flagpole from the ground?

△ **99.** Evelyn Pittman plans to erect a fence around her garden to keep the rabbits out. If the garden is a rectangle 24 ft 9 in. long by 18 ft 6 in. wide, what is the length of the fencing material she must purchase?

△ **100.** Ronnie Hall needs new gutters for the front and *both sides* of his home. The front of the house is 50 ft. 8 in., and each side is 22 ft 9 in. wide. What length of gutter must he buy?

101. The world's longest Coca-Cola truck is in Sweden and is 79 feet long. How many *yards* long are 4 of these trucks? (*Source: Coca-Cola Today*)

△ **102.** The world's largest Coca-Cola sign is in Arica, Chile. It is in the shape of a rectangle whose length is $133\frac{1}{3}$ yards and whose width is 131 feet. Find the area of the sign in square feet. (*Source: Coca-Cola Today*) (*Hint:* Recall that area of a rectangle is the product: length times width.)

103. At one time it was believed that the fort of Basasi, on the Indian-Tibetan border, was the highest located structure at an elevation of 5.988 km above sea level. However, a settlement has been located that is 21 m higher than the fort. What is the elevation of this settlement?

104. The average American male at age 35 is 1.75 m tall. The average 65-year-old male is 48 mm shorter. How tall is the average 65-year-old male?

105. A floor tile is 22.86 cm wide. How many tiles in a row are needed to cross a room 3.429 m wide?

△ **106.** A standard postcard is 1.6 times longer than it is wide. If it is 9.9 cm wide, what is its length?

Review

Write each decimal or fraction as a percent. See Sections 6.1 and 6.2.

107. 0.21   **108.** 0.86   **109.** $\frac{13}{100}$ **110.** $\frac{47}{100}$ **111.** $\frac{1}{4}$ **112.** $\frac{3}{20}$

Concept Extensions

Estimate each sum or difference. See the Concept Check in this section.

113.   5 yd   2 in.
   + 7 yd 30 in.

114.   45 ft   1 in.
   − 10 ft 11 in.

115. Using a unit other than the foot, write a length that is equivalent to 4 feet. (*Hint:* There are many possibilities.)

116. Using a unit other than the meter, write a length that is equivalent to 7 meters. (*Hint:* There are many possibilities.)

117. To convert from meters to centimeters, the decimal point is moved two places to the right. Explain how this relates to the fact that the prefix *centi* means $\frac{1}{100}$.

118. Explain why conversions in the metric system are easier to make than conversions in the U.S. system of measurement.

7.2 WEIGHT AND MASS: U.S. AND METRIC SYSTEMS OF MEASUREMENT

Objectives

A Define U.S. Units of Weight and Convert from One Unit to Another.

B Perform Arithmetic Operations on Units of Weight.

C Define Metric Units of Mass and Convert from One Unit to Another.

D Perform Arithmetic Operations on Units of Mass.

Objective **A** Defining and Converting U.S. System Units of Weight

Whenever we talk about how heavy an object is, we are concerned with the object's **weight.** We discuss weight when we refer to a 12-ounce box of Rice Krispies, a 15-pound tabby cat, or a barge hauling 24 tons of garbage.

12 ounces

15 pounds

24 tons of garbage

The most common units of weight in the U.S. measurement system are the **ounce,** the **pound,** and the **ton.** The following is a summary of equivalencies between units of weight:

U.S. Units of Weight	Unit Fractions
16 ounces (oz) = 1 pound (lb)	$\dfrac{16\ oz}{1\ lb} = \dfrac{1\ lb}{16\ oz} = 1$
2000 pounds = 1 ton	$\dfrac{2000\ lb}{1\ ton} = \dfrac{1\ ton}{2000\ lb} = 1$

✔ **Concept Check** If you were describing the weight of a fully-loaded semi-trailer, which type of unit would you use: ounce, pound, or ton? Why?

Unit fractions that equal 1 are used to convert between units of weight in the U.S. system. When converting using unit fractions, recall that the numerator of a unit fraction should contain the units we are converting to and the denominator should contain the original units.

EXAMPLE 1 Convert 9000 pounds to tons.

Solution: We multiply 9000 lb by a unit fraction that uses the equality

2000 pounds = 1 ton.

Remember, the unit fraction should be $\dfrac{\text{units to convert to}}{\text{original units}}$ or $\dfrac{1\ ton}{2000\ lb}$.

Continued on next page

PRACTICE PROBLEM 1

Convert 4500 pounds to tons.

Answer

1. $2\dfrac{1}{4}$ tons

✔ **Concept Check Answer**

ton

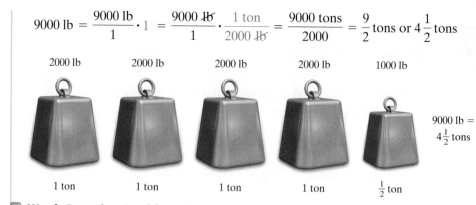

$$9000 \text{ lb} = \frac{9000 \text{ lb}}{1} \cdot 1 = \frac{9000 \text{ lb}}{1} \cdot \frac{1 \text{ ton}}{2000 \text{ lb}} = \frac{9000 \text{ tons}}{2000} = \frac{9}{2} \text{ tons or } 4\frac{1}{2} \text{ tons}$$

2000 lb   2000 lb   2000 lb   2000 lb   1000 lb

$9000 \text{ lb} = 4\frac{1}{2} \text{ tons}$

1 ton   1 ton   1 ton   1 ton $\frac{1}{2}$ ton

▣ **Work Practice Problem 1**

PRACTICE PROBLEM 2

Convert 56 ounces to pounds.

EXAMPLE 2 Convert 3 pounds to ounces.

Solution: We multiply by the unit fraction $\frac{16 \text{ oz}}{1 \text{ lb}}$ to convert from pounds to ounces.

$$3 \text{ lb} = \frac{3 \text{ lb}}{1} \cdot 1 = \frac{3 \text{ lb}}{1} \cdot \frac{16 \text{ oz}}{1 \text{ lb}} = 3 \cdot 16 \text{ oz} = 48 \text{ oz}$$

1 pound   1 pound   1 pound

3 lb = 48 oz

16 ounces   16 ounces   16 ounces

▣ **Work Practice Problem 2**

As with length, it is sometimes useful to simplify a measurement of weight by writing it in terms of mixed units.

PRACTICE PROBLEM 3

Convert:
45 ounces = _____ lb _____ oz

EXAMPLE 3 Convert: 33 ounces = _____ lb _____ oz

Solution: Because 16 oz = 1 lb, divide 16 into 33 to see how many pounds are in 33 ounces. The quotient is the number of pounds, and the remainder is the number of ounces. To see why we divide 16 into 33, notice that

$$33 \text{ oz} = 33 \text{ oz} \cdot \frac{1 \text{ lb}}{16 \text{ oz}} = \frac{33}{16} \text{ lb}$$

$$\begin{array}{r} 2 \text{ lb } 1 \text{ oz} \\ 16\overline{)33} \\ -32 \\ \hline 1 \end{array}$$

Thus, 33 ounces is the same as 2 lb 1 oz.

16 ounces   16 ounces   1 ounce

33 oz = 2 lb 1 oz

1 pound   1 pound   1 ounce

▣ **Work Practice Problem 3**

Answers

2. $3\frac{1}{2}$ lb,   **3.** 2 lb 13 oz

Objective **B** **Performing Operations on U.S. System Units of Weight**

Performing arithmetic operations on units of weight works the same way as performing arithmetic operations on units of length.

EXAMPLE 4 Subtract 3 tons 1350 lb from 8 tons 1000 lb.

Solution: To subtract, we line up similar units.

$$\begin{array}{r} 8 \text{ tons } 1000 \text{ lb} \\ - 3 \text{ tons } 1350 \text{ lb} \\ \hline \end{array}$$

Since we cannot subtract 1350 lb from 1000 lb, we borrow 1 ton from the 8 tons. To do so, we write 1 ton as 2000 lb and combine it with the 1000 lb.

$$\overbrace{7 \text{ tons } + \boxed{1 \text{ ton}}}\ \overset{\frown}{2000} \text{ lb}$$

$$\begin{array}{r} \cancel{8} \text{ tons } 1000 \text{ lb} \\ - 3 \text{ tons } 1350 \text{ lb} \\ \end{array} \quad \begin{array}{l} = \\ = \end{array} \quad \begin{array}{r} 7 \text{ tons } 3000 \text{ lb} \\ - 3 \text{ tons } 1350 \text{ lb} \\ \hline 4 \text{ tons } 1650 \text{ lb} \end{array}$$

To check, see that the sum of 4 tons 1650 lb and 3 tons 1350 lb is 8 tons 1000 lb.

 **Work Practice Problem 4**

EXAMPLE 5 Multiply 5 lb 9 oz by 6.

Solution: We multiply 5 lb by 6 and 9 oz by 6.

$$\begin{array}{r} 5 \text{ lb } 9 \text{ oz} \\ \times \qquad 6 \\ \hline 30 \text{ lb } 54 \text{ oz} \end{array}$$

To write 54 oz as pounds and ounces, divide by 16 (1 lb = 16 oz). Since 54 oz is the same as 3 lb 6 oz, we have

$$30 \text{ lb } 54 \text{ oz} = 30 \text{ lb} + 3 \text{ lb } 6 \text{ oz} = 33 \text{ lb } 6 \text{ oz}$$

Work Practice Problem 5

EXAMPLE 6 Divide 9 lb 6 oz by 2.

Solution: We divide each of the units by 2.

$$\begin{array}{r} 4 \text{ lb} \qquad 11 \text{ oz} \\ 2{\overline{\smash{\big)}\,9 \text{ lb} \qquad 6 \text{ oz}}} \\ \underline{-8} \qquad\qquad \\ 1 \text{ lb} = 16 \text{ oz} \\ \overline{\qquad 22 \text{ oz}} \end{array}$$

Convert 1 lb to 16 oz and add to 6 oz before continuing.
Divide 2 into 22 oz to get 11 oz in quotient.

To check, multiply 4 pounds 11 ounces by 2. The result will be 9 pounds 6 ounces.

Work Practice Problem 6

PRACTICE PROBLEM 4

Subtract 5 tons 1200 lb from 8 tons 100 lb.

PRACTICE PROBLEM 5

Multiply 4 lb 11 oz by 8.

PRACTICE PROBLEM 6

Divide 5 lb 8 oz by 4.

Answers
4. 2 tons 900 lb,   **5.** 37 lb 8 oz,
6. 1 lb 6 oz

EXAMPLE 7 Finding the Weight of a Child

Bryan weighed 8 lb 8 oz at birth. By the time he was 1 year old, he had gained 11 lb 14 oz. Find his weight at age 1 year.

Solution:

birth weight	→	8 lb 8 oz
+ weight gained	→	+ 11 lb 14 oz
total weight	→	19 lb 22 oz

Since 22 oz equals 1 lb 6 oz,

$$19 \text{ lb } 22 \text{ oz} = 19 \text{ lb} + 1 \text{ lb } 6 \text{ oz}$$
$$= 20 \text{ lb } 6 \text{ oz}$$

Bryan weighed 20 lb 6 oz on his first birthday.

■ Work Practice Problem 7

Objective C Defining and Converting Metric System Units of Mass

In scientific and technical areas, a careful distinction is made between **weight** and **mass**. **Weight** is really a measure of the pull of gravity. The farther from Earth an object gets, the less it weighs. However, **mass** is a measure of the amount of substance in the object and does not change. Astronauts orbiting Earth weigh much less than they weigh on Earth, but they have the same mass in orbit as they do on Earth. Here on Earth weight and mass are the same, so either term may be used.

The basic unit of mass in the metric system is the **gram.** It is defined as the mass of water contained in a cube 1 centimeter (cm) on each side.

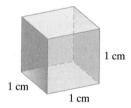

The following examples may help you get a feeling for metric masses:

A tablet contains 200 milligrams of ibuprofen.

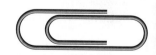

A large paper clip weighs approximately 1 gram.

A box of crackers weighs 453 grams.

A kilogram is slightly over 2 pounds. An adult woman may weigh 60 kilograms.

The prefixes for units of mass in the metric system are the same as for units of length, as shown in the following table:

Metric Unit of Mass
1 **kilo**gram (kg) = 1000 grams (g)
1 **hecto**gram (hg) = 100 g
1 **deka**gram (dag) = 10 g
1 gram (g) = 1 g
1 **deci**gram (dg) = 1/10 g or 0.1 g
1 **centi**gram (cg) = 1/100 g or 0.01 g
1 **milli**gram (mg) = 1/1000 g or 0.001 g

✔ **Concept Check** True or false? A decigram is larger than a dekagram. Explain.

The **milligram,** the **gram,** and the **kilogram** are the three most commonly used units of mass in the metric system.

As with lengths, all units of mass are powers of 10 of the gram, so converting from one unit of mass to another involves moving only the decimal point. To convert from one unit of mass to another in the metric system, list the units of mass in order from largest to smallest.

Let's convert 4300 milligrams to grams. To convert from milligrams to grams, we move along the table 3 units to the left.

kg   hg   dag   **g**   dg   cg   **mg**

3 units to the left

This means that we move the decimal point 3 places to the left to convert from milligrams to grams.

4300 mg = 4.3 g

Don't forget, the same conversion can be done with unit fractions.

$$4300 \text{ mg} = \frac{4300 \text{ mg}}{1} \cdot 1 = \frac{4300 \text{ mg}}{1} \cdot \frac{0.001 \text{ g}}{1 \text{ mg}}$$

$$= 4300 \cdot 0.001 \text{ g}$$

$$= 4.3 \text{ g} \quad \text{To multiply by 0.001, move the decimal point 3 places to the left.}$$

To see that this is reasonable, study the diagram:

Thus, 4300 mg = 4.3 g

PRACTICE PROBLEM 8

Convert 3.41 g to milligrams.

EXAMPLE 8 Convert 3.2 kg to grams.

Solution: First we convert by using a unit fraction.

$$3.2 \text{ kg} = 3.2 \text{ kg} \cdot 1 = 3.2 \text{ kg} \cdot \overbrace{\frac{1000 \text{ g}}{1 \text{ kg}}}^{\text{Unit fraction}} = 3200 \text{ g}$$

Now let's list the units of mass in order from left to right and move from kilograms to grams.

kg   hg   dag   g   dg   cg   mg

3 units to the right

$$3.200 \text{ kg} = 3200. \text{ g}$$

3 places to the right

1 kg	1 kg	1 kg	0.2 kg

3.2 kg = 3200 g

1000 g	1000 g	1000 g	200 g

■ **Work Practice Problem 8**

PRACTICE PROBLEM 9

Convert 56.2 cg to grams.

EXAMPLE 9 Convert 2.35 cg to grams.

Solution: We list the units of mass in a chart and move from centigrams to grams.

kg   hg   dag   g   dg   cg   mg

2 units to the left

$$02.35 \text{ cg} = 0.0235 \text{ g}$$

2 places to the left

■ **Work Practice Problem 9**

Objective D Performing Operations on Metric System Units of Mass

Arithmetic operations can be performed with metric units of mass just as we performed operations with metric units of length. We convert each number to the same unit of mass and add, subtract, multiply, or divide as with decimals.

PRACTICE PROBLEM 10

Subtract 3.1 dg from 2.5 g.

EXAMPLE 10 Subtract 5.4 dg from 1.6 g.

Solution: We convert both numbers to decigrams or to grams before subtracting.

$$5.4 \text{ dg} = 0.54 \text{ g} \qquad \text{or} \qquad 1.6 \text{ g} = 16 \text{ dg}$$

$$\begin{array}{r} 1.60 \text{ g} \\ - 0.54 \text{ g} \\ \hline 1.06 \text{ g} \end{array} \qquad\qquad \begin{array}{r} 16.0 \text{ dg} \\ - 5.4 \text{ dg} \\ \hline 10.6 \text{ dg} \end{array}$$

The difference is 1.06 g or 10.6 dg.

■ **Work Practice Problem 10**

Answers

8. 3410 mg, **9.** 0.562 g,
10. 2.19 g or 21.9 dg

EXAMPLE 11 Multiply 15.4 kg by 5.

Solution: We multiply the two numbers together.

$$\begin{array}{r} 15.4 \text{ kg} \\ \times \quad 5 \\ \hline 77.0 \text{ kg} \end{array}$$

The result is 77.0 kg.

⬜ **Work Practice Problem 11**

EXAMPLE 12 **Calculating Allowable Weight in an Elevator**

An elevator has a weight limit of 1400 kg. A sign posted in the elevator indicates that the maximum capacity of the elevator is 17 persons. What is the average allowable weight for each passenger, rounded to the nearest kilogram?

Solution: To solve, notice that the total weight of 1400 kilograms ÷ 17 = average weight

$$\begin{array}{r} 82.3 \text{ kg} \approx 82 \text{ kg} \\ 17\overline{)1400.0 \text{ kg}} \\ \underline{-136} \\ 40 \\ \underline{-34} \\ 6\,0 \\ \underline{-5\,1} \\ 9 \end{array}$$

Each passenger can weigh an average of 82 kg. (Recall that a kilogram is slightly over 2 pounds, so 82 kilograms is over 164 pounds.

⬜ **Work Practice Problem 12**

PRACTICE PROBLEM 11
Multiply 12.6 kg by 4.

PRACTICE PROBLEM 12
Twenty-four bags of cement weigh a total of 550 kg. Find the average weight of 1 bag, rounded to the nearest kilogram.

Answers
11. 50.4 kg, **12.** 23 kg

Mental Math

Convert.

1. 16 ounces to pounds

2. 32 ounces to pounds

3. 1 ton to pounds

4. 3 tons to pounds

5. 1 pound to ounces

6. 3 pounds to ounces

7. 2000 pounds to tons

8. 4000 pounds to tons

Determine whether the measurement in each statement is reasonable.

9. The doctor prescribed a pill containing 2 kg of medication.

10. A full-grown cat weighs approximately 15 g.

11. A bag of flour weighs 4.5 kg.

12. A staple weighs 15 mg.

13. A professor weighs less than 150 g.

14. A car weighs 2000 mg.

FOR EXTRA HELP

7.2 EXERCISE SET

 Student Solutions Manual   PH Math/Tutor Center   CD/Video for Review Math XL MathXL® MyMathLab MyMathLab

Objective A *Convert as indicated. See Examples 1 through 3.*

1. 2 pounds to ounces

2. 5 pounds to ounces

3. 5 tons to pounds

4. 7 tons to pounds

5. 12,000 pounds to tons

6. 32,000 pounds to tons

7. 60 ounces to pounds

8. 90 ounces to pounds

9. 3500 pounds to tons

10. 11,000 pounds to tons

11. 16.25 pounds to ounces

12. 14.5 pounds to ounces

13. 4.9 tons to pounds

14. 8.3 tons to pounds

15. $4\frac{3}{4}$ pounds to ounces

16. $9\frac{1}{8}$ pounds to ounces

17. 2950 pounds to the nearest tenth of a ton

18. 51 ounces to the nearest tenth of a pound

19. $\frac{4}{5}$ oz to pounds

20. $\frac{1}{4}$ oz to pounds

21. $5\frac{3}{4}$ lb to ounces

22. $2\frac{1}{4}$ lb to ounces

23. 10 lb 1 oz to ounces

24. 7 lb 6 oz to ounces

25. 89 oz to _____ lb _____ oz

26. 100 oz = _____ lb _____ oz

Objective **B** *Perform each indicated operation. See Examples 4 through 6.*

27. 34 lb 12 oz + 18 lb 14 oz

28. 6 lb 10 oz + 10 lb 8 oz

29. 6 tons 1540 lb + 2 tons 850 lb

30. 2 tons 1575 lb + 1 ton 480 lb

31. 5 tons 1050 lb − 2 tons 875 lb

32. 4 tons 850 lb − 1 ton 260 lb

33. 12 lb 4 oz − 3 lb 9 oz

34. 45 lb 6 oz − 26 lb 10 oz

35. 5 lb 3 oz × 6

36. 2 lb 5 oz × 5

37. 6 tons 1500 lb ÷ 5

38. 5 tons 400 lb ÷ 4

Objective **C** *Convert as indicated. See Examples 8 and 9.*

39. 500 g to kilograms

40. 650 g to kilograms

41. 4 g to milligrams

42. 9 g to milligrams

43. 25 kg to grams

44. 18 kg to grams

45. 48 mg to grams

46. 112 mg to grams

47. 6.3 g to kilograms

48. 4.9 g to kilograms

49. 15.14 g to milligrams

50. 16.23 g to milligrams

51. 4.01 kg to grams

52. 3.16 kg to grams

53. 35 hg to centigrams

54. 4.26 cg to dekagrams

Objective **D** *Perform each indicated operation. See Examples 10 and 11.*

55. 3.8 mg + 9.7 mg

56. 41.6 g + 9.8 g

57. 205 mg + 5.61 g

58. 2.1 g + 153 mg

59. 9 g − 7150 mg

60. 4 kg − 2410 g

61. 1.61 kg − 250 g

62. 6.13 g − 418 mg

63. 5.2 kg × 2.6   **64.** 4.8 kg × 9.3   **65.** 17 kg ÷ 8   **66.** 8.25 g ÷ 6

Objectives A B C D **Mixed Practice** *Solve. Remember to insert units when writing your answers. See Examples 1 through 11. For Exercises 67 through 74, complete the chart.*

	Object	Tons	Pounds	Ounces
67.	Statue of Liberty—weight of copper sheeting	100		
68.	Statue of Liberty—weight of steel	125		
69.	A 12-inch cube of osmium (heaviest metal)		1,345	
70.	A 12-inch cube of lithium (lightest metal)		32	

	Object	Grams	Kilograms	Milligrams	Centigrams
71.	Capsule of Amoxicillin (Antibiotic)			500	
72.	Tablet of Topamax (Epilepsy and Migraine uses)			25	
73.	A six-year-old boy		21		
74.	A golf ball	45			

75. A can of 7-Up weighs 336 grams. Find the weight in kilograms of 24 cans.

76. Guy Green normally weighs 73 kg, but he lost 2800 grams after being sick with the flu. Find Guy's new weight.

77. Sudafed is a decongestant that comes in two strengths. Regular strength contains 60 mg of medication. Extra strength contains 0.09 g of medication. How much extra medication is in the extra-strength tablet?

78. A small can of Planters sunflower seeds weighs 177 g. If each can contains 6 servings, find the weight of one serving.

79. Doris Johnson has two open containers of Uncle Ben's rice. If she combines 1 lb 10 oz from one container with 3 lb 14 oz from the other container, how much total rice does she have?

80. Dru Mizel maintains the records of the amount of coal delivered to his department in the steel mill. In January, 3 tons 1500 lb were delivered. In February, 2 tons 1200 lb were delivered. Find the total amount delivered in these two months.

81. Carla Hamtini was amazed when she grew a 28 lb 10 oz zucchini in her garden, but later she learned that the heaviest zucchini ever grown weighed 64 lb 8 oz in Llanharry, Wales, by B. Lavery in 1990. How far below the record weight was Carla's zucchini? (*Source: The Guinness Book of Records*)

82. The heaviest baby born in good health weighed an incredible 22 lb 8 oz. He was born in Italy in September, 1955. How much heavier is this than a 7 lb 12 oz baby? (*Source: The Guinness Book of Records*)

83. Tim Caucutt's doctor recommends that Tim limit his daily intake of sodium to 0.6 gram. A one-ounce serving of Cheerios with $\frac{1}{2}$ cup of fortified skim milk contains 350 mg of sodium. How much more sodium can Tim have after he eats a bowl of Cheerios for breakfast, assuming he intends to follow the doctor's orders?

84. A large bottle of Hire's Root Beer weighs 1900 grams. If a carton contains 6 large bottles of root beer, find the weight in kilograms of 5 cartons.

85. Three milligrams of preservatives are added to a 0.5-kg box of dried fruit. How many milligrams of preservatives are in 3 cartons of dried fruit if each carton contains 16 boxes?

86. One box of Swiss Miss Cocoa Mix weighs 0.385 kg, but 39 grams of this weight is the packaging. Find the actual weight of the cocoa in 8 boxes.

87. A carton of 12 boxes of Quaker Oats Oatmeal weighs 6.432 kg. Each box includes 26 grams of packaging material. What is the actual weight of the oatmeal in the carton?

88. The supermarket prepares hamburger in 85-gram market packages. When Leo Gonzalas gets home, he divides the package in half before refrigerating the meat. How much will each package weigh?

89. The Shop 'n Bag supermarket chain ships hamburger meat by placing 10 packages of hamburger in a box, with each package weighing 3 lb 4 oz. How much will 4 boxes of hamburger weigh?

90. The Quaker Oats Company ships its 1-lb 2-oz boxes of oatmeal in cartons containing 12 boxes of oatmeal. How much will 3 such cartons weigh?

91. A carton of Del Monte Pineapple weighs 55 lb 4 oz, but 2 lb 8 oz of this weight is due to packaging. Subtract the weight of the packaging to find the actual weight of the pineapple in 4 cartons.

92. The Hormel Corporation ships cartons of canned ham weighing 43 lb 2 oz each. Of this weight, 3 lb 4 oz is due to packaging. Find the actual weight of the ham found in 3 cartons.

93. One bag of Pepperidge Farm Bordeaux cookies weighs $6\frac{3}{4}$ ounces. How many pounds will a dozen bags weigh?

94. One can of Payless Red Beets weighs $8\frac{1}{2}$ ounces. How much will eight cans weigh? Give your answer in pounds and ounces.

95. A package of Trailway's Gorp, a high-energy hiking trail mix, contains 0.3 kg of nuts, 0.15 kg of chocolate bits, and 400 grams of raisins. Find the total weight of the package.

96. The manufacturer of Anacin wants to reduce the caffeine content of its aspirin by $\frac{1}{4}$. Currently, each regular tablet contains 32 mg of caffeine. How much caffeine should be removed from each tablet?

97. A regular-size bag of Lay's potato chips weighs 198 grams. Find the weight of a dozen bags, rounded to the nearest hundredth of a kilogram.

98. A cat weighs a hefty 9 kg. The vet has recommended that the cat lose 1500 grams. How much should the cat weigh?

Review

Write each fraction as a decimal. See Section 4.6.

99. $\frac{1}{4}$ **100.** $\frac{1}{20}$ **101.** $\frac{4}{25}$ **102.** $\frac{3}{5}$ **103.** $\frac{7}{8}$ **104.** $\frac{3}{16}$

Concept Extensions

105. Use a unit other than centigram and write a mass that is equivalent to 25 centigrams. (*Hint:* There are many possibilities.)

106. Use a unit other than pound and write a weight that is equivalent to 4000 pounds. (*Hint:* There are many possibilities.)

True or False? See the Concept Check in the section.

107. A kilogram is larger than a gram.

108. A decigram is larger than a milligram.

 109. Why is the decimal point moved to the right when grams are converted to milligrams?

110. To change 8 pounds to ounces, multiply by 16. Why is this the correct procedure?

📖 STUDY SKILLS BUILDER

How Are Your Homework Assignments Going?

Remember that it is important to keep up with homework. Why? Many concepts in mathematics build on each other. Often, your understanding of a day's lecture depends on an understanding of the previous day's material.

To complete a homework assignment, remember these 4 things:

- Attempt all of it.
- Check it.
- Correct it.
- If needed, ask questions about it.

Take a moment and review your completed homework assignments. Answer the exercises below based on this review.

1. Approximate the fraction of your homework you have attempted.
2. Approximate the fraction of your homework you have checked (if possible).
3. If you are able to check your homework, have you corrected it when errors have been found?
4. When working homework, if you do not understand a concept, what do you personally do?

7.3 CAPACITY: U.S. AND METRIC SYSTEMS OF MEASUREMENT

Objectives

A Define U.S. Units of Capacity and Convert from One Unit to Another.

B Perform Arithmetic Operations on U.S. Units of Capacity.

C Define Metric Units of Capacity and Convert from One Unit to Another.

D Perform Arithmetic Operations on Metric Units of Capacity.

Objective **A** Defining and Converting U.S. System Units of Capacity

Units of **capacity** are generally used to measure liquids. The number of gallons of gasoline needed to fill a gas tank in a car, the number of cups of water needed in a bread recipe, and the number of quarts of milk sold each day at a supermarket are all examples of using units of capacity. The following summary shows equivalencies between units of capacity:

U.S. Units of Capacity

$$8 \text{ fluid ounces (fl oz)} = 1 \text{ cup (c)}$$
$$2 \text{ cups} = 1 \text{ pint (pt)}$$
$$2 \text{ pints} = 1 \text{ quart (qt)}$$
$$4 \text{ quarts} = 1 \text{ gallon (gal)}$$

Just as with units of length and weight, we can form unit fractions to convert between different units of capacity. For instance,

$$\frac{2 \text{ c}}{1 \text{ pt}} = \frac{1 \text{ pt}}{2 \text{ c}} = 1 \quad \text{and} \quad \frac{2 \text{ pt}}{1 \text{ qt}} = \frac{1 \text{ qt}}{2 \text{ pt}} = 1$$

EXAMPLE 1 Convert 9 quarts to gallons.

Solution: We multiply by the unit fraction $\frac{1 \text{ gal}}{4 \text{ qt}}$.

$$9 \text{ qt} = \frac{9 \text{ qt}}{1} \cdot 1$$

$$= \frac{9 \text{ qt}}{1} \cdot \frac{1 \text{ gal}}{4 \text{ qt}}$$

$$= \frac{9 \text{ gal}}{4}$$

$$= 2\frac{1}{4} \text{ gal}$$

Thus, 9 quarts is the same as $2\frac{1}{4}$ gallons, as shown in the diagram:

1 gallon + 1 gallon + $\frac{1}{4}$ gallon

9 quarts = $2\frac{1}{4}$ gal

■ Work Practice Problem 1

PRACTICE PROBLEM 1

Convert 43 pints to quarts.

Answer

1. $21\frac{1}{2}$ qt

PRACTICE PROBLEM 2

Convert 26 quarts to cups.

EXAMPLE 2 Convert 14 cups to quarts.

Solution: Our equivalency table contains no direct conversion from cups to quarts. However, from this table we know that

$$1 \text{ qt} = 2 \text{ pt} = \frac{2 \text{ pt}}{1} \cdot 1 = \frac{2 \text{ pt}}{1} \cdot \frac{2 \text{ c}}{1 \text{ pt}} = 4 \text{ c}$$

so 1 qt = 4 c. Now we have the unit fraction $\dfrac{1 \text{ qt}}{4 \text{ c}}$. Thus,

$$14 \text{ c} = \frac{14 \text{ c}}{1} \cdot 1 = \frac{14 \text{ c}}{1} \cdot \frac{1 \text{ qt}}{4 \text{ c}} = \frac{14 \text{ qt}}{4} = \frac{7}{2} \text{ qt} \quad \text{or} \quad 3\frac{1}{2} \text{ qt}$$

$$\underbrace{\qquad}_{1 \text{ quart}} + \underbrace{\qquad}_{1 \text{ quart}} + \underbrace{\qquad}_{1 \text{ quart}} + \underbrace{\qquad}_{\frac{1}{2} \text{ quart}} \quad \begin{array}{l} 14 \text{ cups} \\ = 3\frac{1}{2} \text{ qt} \end{array}$$

■ **Work Practice Problem 2**

✔ **Concept Check** If 50 cups are converted to quarts, will the equivalent number of quarts be less than or greater than 50? Explain.

Objective B Performing Operations on U.S. System Units of Capacity

As is true of units of length and weight, units of capacity can be added, subtracted, multiplied, and divided.

PRACTICE PROBLEM 3

Subtract 2 qt from 1 gal 1 qt.

EXAMPLE 3 Subtract 3 qt from 4 gal 2 qt.

Solution: To subtract, we line up similar units.

$$\begin{array}{r} 4 \text{ gal } 2 \text{ qt} \\ - \quad\quad 3 \text{ qt} \\ \hline \end{array}$$

We cannot subtract 3 qt from 2 qt. We need to borrow 1 gallon from the 4 gallons, convert it to 4 quarts, and then combine it with the 2 quarts.

$$\underbrace{3 \text{ gal} + \overbrace{(1 \text{ gal})}^{}}_{} \, 4 \text{ qt}$$

$$\begin{array}{rcl} 4 \text{ gal } 2 \text{ qt} & = & 3 \text{ gal } 6 \text{ qt} \\ - \quad\quad 3 \text{ qt} & = & - \quad\quad 3 \text{ qt} \\ \hline & & 3 \text{ gal } 3 \text{ qt} \end{array}$$

To check, see that the sum of 3 gal 3 qt and 3 qt is 4 gal 2 qt.

■ **Work Practice Problem 3**

PRACTICE PROBLEM 4

Multiply 2 gal 3 qt by 2.

EXAMPLE 4 Multiply 3 qt 1 pt by 3.

Solution: We multiply each of the units of capacity by 3.

$$\begin{array}{r} 3 \text{ qt } 1 \text{ pt} \\ \times \quad\quad 3 \\ \hline 9 \text{ qt } 3 \text{ pt} \end{array}$$

Since 3 pints is the same as 1 quart and 1 pint, we have

$$9 \text{ qt } 3 \text{ pt} = 9 \text{ qt} + 1 \text{ qt } 1 \text{ pt} = 10 \text{ qt } 1 \text{ pt}$$

Answers

2. 104 c, **3.** 3 qt, **4.** 5 gal 2 qt

✔ **Concept Check Answer**

less than 50

If you'd like, the 10 quarts can be changed to gallons by dividing by 4, since there are 4 quarts in a gallon. To see why we divide, notice that

$$10 \text{ qt} = \frac{10 \text{ qt}}{1} \cdot \frac{1 \text{ gal}}{4 \text{ qt}} = \frac{10}{4} \text{ gal}$$

$$
\begin{array}{r}
2 \text{ gal } 2 \text{ qt} \\
4\overline{)10 \text{ qt}} \\
-8 \phantom{\text{ qt}} \\
\hline
2 \phantom{\text{ qt}}
\end{array}
$$

Thus, the product is 10 qt 1 pt or 2 gal 2 qt 1 pt.

🔲 **Work Practice Problem 4**

EXAMPLE 5 Divide 3 gal 2 qt by 2.

Solution: We divide each unit of capacity by 2.

$$
\begin{array}{r}
1 \text{ gal} \quad 3 \text{ qt} \\
2\overline{)3 \text{ gal}} \quad 2 \text{ qt} \\
-2 \phantom{\text{ gal}} \\
\hline
1 \text{ gal} = 4 \text{ qt} \quad \text{Convert 1 gallon to 4 qt and add to 2 qt before continuing.} \\
6 \text{ qt} \quad 6 \text{ qt} \div 2 = 3 \text{ qt}
\end{array}
$$

🔲 **Work Practice Problem 5**

EXAMPLE 6 Finding the Amount of Water in an Aquarium

An aquarium contains 6 gal 3 qt of water. If 2 gal 2 qt of water is added, what is the total amount of water in the aquarium?

Solution:

$$
\begin{array}{rcl}
\text{beginning water} & \rightarrow & 6 \text{ gal } 3 \text{ qt} \\
+ \quad \text{water added} & \rightarrow & +\ 2 \text{ gal } 2 \text{ qt} \\
\hline
\text{total water} & \rightarrow & 8 \text{ gal } 5 \text{ qt}
\end{array}
$$

Since 5 qt = 1 gal 1 qt, we have

$$
\begin{array}{c}
\overbrace{8 \text{ gal}} \quad \overbrace{5 \text{ qt}} \\
= \quad 8 \text{ gal} \ + \ 1 \text{ gal } 1 \text{ qt} \\
= \quad 9 \text{ gal } 1 \text{ qt}
\end{array}
$$

The total amount of water is 9 gal 1 qt.

🔲 **Work Practice Problem 6**

Objective 🄲 Defining and Converting Metric System Units of Capacity

Thus far, we know that the basic unit of length in the metric system is the meter and that the basic unit of mass in the metric system is the gram. What is the basic unit of capacity? The **liter.** By definition, a **liter** is the capacity or volume of a cube measuring 10 centimeters on each side.

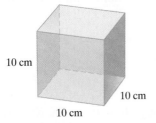

10 cm
10 cm
10 cm

PRACTICE PROBLEM 5

Divide 6 gal 3 qt by 2.

PRACTICE PROBLEM 6

A large oil drum contains 15 gal 3 qt of oil. How much will be in the drum if an additional 4 gal 3 qt of oil is poured into it?

Answers
5. 3 gal 1 qt 1 pt, **6.** 20 gal 2 qt

The following examples may help you get a feeling for metric capacities:

One liter of liquid is slightly more than one quart.

1 quart   1 liter

Many soft drinks are packaged in 2-liter bottles.

The metric system was designed to be a consistent system. Once again, the prefixes for metric units of capacity are the same as for metric units of length and mass, as summarized in the following table:

Metric Unit of Capacity
1 **kilo**liter (kl) = 1000 liters (L)
1 **hecto**liter (hl) = 100 L
1 **deka**liter (dal) = 10 L
1 liter (L) = 1 L
1 **deci**liter (dl) = 1/10 L or 0.1 L
1 **centi**liter (cl) = 1/100 L or 0.01 L
1 **milli**liter (ml) = 1/1000 L or 0.001 L

The **milliliter** and the **liter** are the two most commonly used metric units of capacity.

Converting from one unit of capacity to another involves multiplying by powers of 10 or moving the decimal point to the left or to the right. Listing units of capacity in order from largest to smallest helps to keep track of how many places to move the decimal point when converting.

Let's convert 2.6 liters to milliliters. To convert from liters to milliliters, we move along the chart 3 units to the right.

kl   hl   dal   **L**   dl   cl   **ml**

3 units to the right

This means that we move the decimal point 3 places to the right to convert from liters to milliliters.

2.600 L = 2600. ml

This same conversion can be done with unit fractions.

$$2.6\text{ L} = \frac{2.6\text{ L}}{1} \cdot 1$$
$$= \frac{2.6\text{ L}}{1} \cdot \frac{1000\text{ ml}}{1\text{ L}}$$
$$= 2.6 \cdot 1000\text{ ml}$$
$$= 2600\text{ ml} \quad \text{To multiply by 1000, move the decimal point 3 places to the right.}$$

To visualize the result, study the diagram below:

2.6 L

1000 ml   1000 ml   600 ml = 2600 ml

Thus, 2.6 L = 2600 ml.

EXAMPLE 7 Convert 3210 ml to liters.

Solution: Let's use the unit fraction method first.

$$3210 \text{ ml} = \frac{3210 \text{ ml}}{1} \cdot 1 = 3210 \cancel{\text{ml}} \cdot \frac{\overbrace{1 \text{ L}}^{\text{Unit fraction}}}{1000 \cancel{\text{ml}}} = 3.21 \text{ L}$$

Now let's list the unit measures in order from left to right and move from milliliters to liters.

kl   hl   dal   L   dl   cl   ml

3 units to the left

3210 ml = 3.210 L, the same results as before and
shown below in the diagram.

3 places to the left

1000 ml   1000 ml   1000 ml

210 ml

3210 ml

1 L   1 L   1 L   0.210 L = 3.210 L

▣ **Work Practice Problem 7**

EXAMPLE 8 Convert 0.185 dl to milliliters.

Solution: We list the unit measures in order from left to right and move from deciliters to milliliters.

kl   hl   dal   L   dl   cl   ml

2 units to the right

0.185 dl = 18.5 ml

2 places to the right

▣ **Work Practice Problem 8**

Objective ▣ **Performing Operations on Metric System Units of Capacity**

As was true for length and weight, arithmetic operations involving metric units of capacity can also be performed. Make sure that the metric units of capacity are the same before adding, subtracting, multiplying, or dividing.

PRACTICE PROBLEM 9

Add 1250 ml to 2.9 L.

EXAMPLE 9 Add 2400 ml to 8.9 L.

Solution: We must convert both to liters or both to milliliters before adding the capacities together.

$$2400 \text{ ml} = 2.4 \text{ L} \quad\text{or}\quad 8.9 \text{ L} = 8900 \text{ ml}$$

$$\begin{array}{r} 2.4 \text{ L} \\ + \ 8.9 \text{ L} \\ \hline 11.3 \text{ L} \end{array} \qquad \begin{array}{r} 2400 \text{ ml} \\ + \ 8900 \text{ ml} \\ \hline 11{,}300 \text{ ml} \end{array}$$

The total is 11.3 L or 11,300 ml. They both represent the same capacity.

■ **Work Practice Problem 9**

✔ **Concept Check** How could you estimate the following operation? Subtract 950 ml from 7.5 L.

EXAMPLE 10 Divide 18.08 ml by 16.

Solution:

$$\begin{array}{r} 1.13 \text{ ml} \\ 16\overline{)18.08 \text{ ml}} \\ -16 \\ \hline 2\,0 \\ -1\,6 \\ \hline 48 \\ -48 \\ \hline 0 \end{array}$$

The solution is 1.13 ml.

■ **Work Practice Problem 10**

PRACTICE PROBLEM 10

Divide 146.9 L by 13.

PRACTICE PROBLEM 11

If 28.6 L of water can be pumped every minute, how much water can be pumped in 85 minutes?

EXAMPLE 11 **Finding the Amount of Medication a Person Has Received**

A patient hooked up to an IV unit in the hospital is to receive 12.5 ml of medication every hour. How much medication does the patient receive in 3.5 hours?

Solution: We multiply 12.5 ml by 3.5.

$$\begin{array}{ll} \text{medication per hour} \rightarrow & 12.5 \text{ ml} \\ \underline{\times \qquad\qquad\quad \text{hours}} \rightarrow & \underline{\times \ 3.5} \\ \text{total medication} & 625 \\ & \underline{3750} \\ & 43.75 \text{ ml} \end{array}$$

The patient receives 43.75 ml of medication.

■ **Work Practice Problem 11**

Answers

9. 4150 ml or 4.15 L, **10.** 11.3 L, **11.** 2431 L

✔ **Concept Check Answer**

950 ml = 0.95 L; round 0.95 to 1; 7.5 − 1 = 6.5 L

Mental Math

Convert as indicated.

1. 2 c to pints

2. 4 c to pints

3. 4 qt to gallons

4. 8 qt to gallons

5. 2 pt to quarts

6. 6 pt to quarts

7. 8 fl oz to cups

8. 24 fl oz to cups

9. 1 pt to cups

10. 3 pt to cups

11. 1 gal to quarts

12. 2 gal to quarts

Determine whether the measurement in each statement is reasonable.

13. Clair took a dose of 2 L of cough medicine to cure her cough.

14. John drank 250 ml of milk for lunch.

15. Jeannie likes to relax in a tub filled with 3000 ml of hot water.

16. Sarah pumped 20 L of gasoline into her car yesterday.

7.3 EXERCISE SET

FOR EXTRA HELP

Student Solutions Manual · PH Math/Tutor Center · CD/Video for Review · MathXL® · MyMathLab

Objective A *Convert each measurement as indicated. See Examples 1 and 2.*

1. 32 fluid ounces to cups

2. 16 quarts to gallons

3. 8 quarts to pints

4. 9 pints to quarts

5. 10 quarts to gallons

6. 15 cups to pints

 7. 80 fluid ounces to pints

8. 18 pints to gallons

9. 2 quarts to cups

10. 3 pints to fluid ounces

11. 120 fluid ounces to quarts

12. 20 cups to gallons

13. 6 gallons to fluid ounces

14. 5 quarts to cups

15. $4\frac{1}{2}$ pints to cups

16. $6\frac{1}{2}$ gallons to quarts

17. 5 gal 3 qt to quarts   **18.** 4 gal 1 qt to quarts   **19.** $\frac{1}{2}$ cup to pint   **20.** $\frac{1}{2}$ pint to quarts

21. 58 qt = _____ gal _____ qt   **22.** 70 qt = _____ gal _____ qt

23. 39 pt = _____ gal _____ qt _____ pt   **24.** 29 pt = _____ gal _____ qt _____ pt

25. $2\frac{3}{4}$ gallons to pints   **26.** $3\frac{1}{4}$ quarts to cups

Objective B *Perform each indicated operation. See Examples 3 through 5.*

27. 4 gal 3 qt + 5 gal 2 qt   **28.** 2 gal 3 qt + 8 gal 3 qt   **29.** 1 c 5 fl oz + 2 c 7 fl oz

30. 2 c 3 fl oz + 2 c 6 fl oz   **31.** 3 gal − 1 gal 3 qt   **32.** 2 pt − 1 pt 1 c

33. 3 gal 1 qt − 1 qt 1 pt   **34.** 3 qt 1 c − 1 c 4 fl oz   **35.** 1 pt 1 c × 3

36. 1 qt 1 pt × 2   **37.** 8 gal 2 qt × 2   **38.** 6 gal 1 pt × 2

39. 9 gal 2 qt ÷ 2   **40.** 5 gal 6 fl oz ÷ 2

Objective C *Convert as indicated. See Examples 7 and 8.*

41. 5 L to milliliters   **42.** 8 L to milliliters   **43.** 4500 ml to liters   **44.** 3100 ml to liters

45. 3.2 L to centiliters   **46.** 1.7 L to centiliters   **47.** 410 L to kiloliters   **48.** 250 L to kiloliters

49. 64 ml to liters   **50.** 39 ml to liters   **51.** 0.16 kl to liters   **52.** 0.48 kl to liters

53. 3.6 L to milliliters   **54.** 1.9 L to milliliters   **55.** 0.16 L to kiloliters   **56.** 0.127 L to kiloliters

Objective **D** *Perform each indicated operation. See Examples 9 and 10.*

57. 2.9 L + 19.6 L

58. 18.5 L + 4.6 L

59. 2700 ml + 1.8 L

60. 4.6 L + 1600 ml

61. 8.6 L − 190 ml

62. 4.8 L − 283 ml

63. 11,400 ml − 0.8 L

64. 6850 ml − 0.3 L

65. 480 ml × 8

66. 290 ml × 6

67. 81.2 L ÷ 0.5

68. 5.4 L ÷ 3.6

Objectives **A** **B** **C** **D** **Mixed Practice** *Solve. Remember to insert units when writing your answers. See Examples 1 through 11. For Exercises 69 through 72, complete the chart.*

	Capacity	Cups	Gallons	Quarts	Pints
69.	An average-size bath of water		21		
70.	A dairy cow's daily milk yield				38
71.	Your kidneys filter about this amount of blood every minute	4			
72.	The amount of water needed in a punch recipe	2			

73. A can of Hawaiian Punch holds $1\frac{1}{2}$ quarts of liquid. How many fluid ounces is this?

74. Weight Watchers Double Fudge bars contain 21 fluid ounces of ice cream. How many cups of ice cream is this?

75. Many diet experts advise individuals to drink 64 ounces of water each day. How many quarts of water is this?

76. A recipe for walnut fudge cake calls for $1\frac{1}{4}$ cups of water. How many fluid ounces is this?

77. Mike Schaferkotter drank 410 ml of Mountain Dew from a 2-liter bottle. How much Mountain Dew remains in the bottle?

78. The Werners' Volvo has a 54.5-L gas tank. Only 3.8 liters of gasoline still remain in the tank. How much is needed to fill it?

79. Margie Phitts added 354 ml of Prestone dry gas to the 18.6 L of gasoline in her car's tank. Find the total amount of gasoline in the tank.

80. Chris Peckaitis wishes to share a 2-L bottle of Coca Cola equally with 7 of his friends. How much will each person get?

81. Can 5 pt 1 c of fruit punch and 2 pt 1 c of ginger ale be poured into a 1-gal container without it overflowing?

82. Three cups of prepared Jell-O are poured into 6 dessert dishes. How many fluid ounces of Jell-O are in each dish?

83. How much punch has been prepared if 1 qt 1 pt of Ocean Spray Cranapple drink is mixed with 1 pt 1 c of ginger ale?

84. Henning's Supermarket sells homemade soup in 1-qt-1-pt containers. How much soup is contained in three such containers?

85. Stanley Fisher paid $14 to fill his car with 44.3 liters of gasoline. Find the price per liter of gasoline to the nearest thousandth of a dollar.

86. A student carelessly misread the scale on a cylinder in the chemistry lab and added 40 cl of water to a mixture instead of 40 ml. Find the excess amount of water.

87. A large bottle of Ocean Spray Cranicot drink contains 1.42 L of beverage. The smaller bottle contains only 946 ml. How much more is in the larger bottle?

88. In a lab experiment, Melissa Martin added 400 ml of salt water to 1.65 L of water. Later 320 ml of the solution was drained off. How much of the solution still remained?

Review

Write each decimal as a fraction. See section 4.6.

89. 0.7

90. 0.9

91. 0.03

92. 0.007

93. 0.006

94. 0.08

Concept Extensions

Solve. See the Concept Checks in the section.

95. If 70 pints are converted to gallons, will the equivalent number of gallons be less than or greater than 70? Explain why.

96. If 30 gallons are converted to quarts, will the equivalent number of quarts be less than or greater than 30? Explain why.

97. Explain how to estimate the following operation: Add 986 ml to 6.9 L.

98. Find the number of fluid ounces in 1 gallon.

99. Explain how to borrow in order to subtract 1 gal 2 qt from 3 gal 1 qt.

A cubic centimeter (cc) is the amount of space that a volume of 1 mL occupies. Because of this, we will say that 1 cc = 1 mL.

A common syringe is one with a capacity of 3 cc. Use the diagram and give the measurement indicated by each arrow.

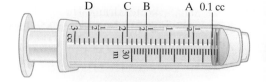

100. A

101. B

102. C

103. D

In order to measure small dosages, such as for insulin, u-100 syringes are used. For these syringes, 1 cc has been divided into 100 equal units (u). Use the diagram and give the measurement indicated by each arrow in units (u) and then cubic centimeters. Use 100 u = 1 cc and round to the nearest hundredth.

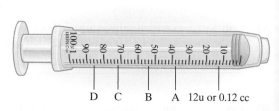

104. A

105. B

106. C

107. D

Length, Weight, and Capacity

Convert each measurement as indicated.

Length

1. 36 in. = _____ ft

2. 10,560 ft = _____ mi

3. 20 ft = _____ yd

4. $6\frac{1}{3}$ yd = _____ ft

5. 2.1 mi = _____ ft

6. 3.2 ft = _____ in.

7. 30 m = _____ cm

8. 24 mm = _____ cm

9. 2000 mm = _____ m

10. 1800 cm = _____ m

11. 7.2 cm = _____ mm

12. 600 m = _____ km

Weight or Mass

13. $7\frac{1}{2}$ tons = _____ lb

14. 11,000 lb = _____ tons

15. 8.5 lb = _____ oz

16. 72 oz = _____ lb

Answers

1. _____

2. _____

3. _____

4. _____

5. _____

6. _____

7. _____

8. _____

9. _____

10. _____

11. _____

12. _____

13. _____

14. _____

15. _____

16. _____

17. _____

18. _____

19. _____

20. _____

21. _____

22. _____

23. _____

24. _____

25. _____

26. _____

27. _____

28. _____

29. _____

30. _____

31. _____

32. _____

33. _____

34. _____

35. _____

36. _____

37. _____

38. _____

17. 104 oz = _____ lb

18. 5 lb = _____ oz

19. 28 kg = _____ g

20. 1400 mg = _____ g

21. 5.6 g = _____ kg

22. 6 kg = _____ g

23. 670 mg = _____ g

24. 3.6 g = _____ kg

Capacity

25. 6 qt = _____ pt

26. 5 pt = _____ qt

27. 14 qt = _____ gal

28. 17 c = _____ pt

29. $3\frac{1}{2}$ pt = _____ c

30. 26 qt = _____ gal

31. 7 L = _____ ml

32. 350 L = _____ kl

33. 47 ml = _____ L

34. 0.97 kl = _____ L

35. 0.126 kl = _____ L

36. 75 ml = _____ L

37. $\frac{1}{2}$ c = _____ fl oz

38. $\frac{3}{4}$ gal = _____ c

7.4 CONVERSIONS BETWEEN THE U.S. AND METRIC SYSTEMS

Objective A Converting Between the U.S. and Metric Systems

The metric system probably had its beginnings in France in the 1600s, but it was the Metric Act of 1866 that made the use of this system legal (but not mandatory) in the United States. Other laws have followed that allow for a slow, but deliberate, transfer to the modernized metric system. In April, 2001, for example, the U.S. Stock Exchanges completed their change to decimal trading instead of fractions. By the end of 2009, all products sold in Europe (with some exceptions) will be required to have only metric units on their labels. (*Source:* U.S. Metric Association and National Institute of Standards and Technology)

You may be surprised at the number of everyday items we use that are already manufactured in metric units. We easily recognize 1L and 2L soda bottles, but what about the following?

Pencil leads (0.5 mm or 0.7 mm)
Camera film (35 mm)
Sporting events (5 km or 10 km races)
Medicines (500 mg capsules)
Labels on retail goods (dual-labeled since 1994)

Since the United States has not completely converted to the metric system, we need to practice converting from one system to the other. Below is a table of mostly approximate conversions.

Length:

metric	U.S. System
1 m	≈ 1.09 yd
1 m	≈ 3.28 ft
1 km	≈ 0.62 mi
2.54 cm	= 1 in.
0.30 m	≈ 1 ft
1.61 km	≈ 1 mi

1 yard

1 meter

Capacity:

metric	U.S. System
1 L	≈ 1.06 qt
1 L	≈ 0.26 gal
3.79 L	≈ 1 gal
0.95 L	≈ 1 qt
29.57 ml	≈ 1 fl oz

1 quart   1 liter

Weight (mass):

metric	U.S. System
1 kg	≈ 2.20 lb
1 g	≈ 0.04 oz
0.45 kg	≈ 1 lb
28.35 g	≈ 1 oz

1 pound   1 kilogram

There are many ways to perform these metric to U.S. Conversions. We will do so by using unit fractions.

PRACTICE PROBLEM 1

The center hole of a compact disc is 1.5 centimeters in diameter. Convert this length to inches. Round the result to 2 decimal places.

EXAMPLE 1 Compact Discs

Compact discs are 12 centimeters in diameter. Convert this length to inches. Round the result to two decimal places. (*Source:* usByte.com)

Solution: From our length conversion table, we know that 2.54 cm = 1 in. This fact gives us two unit fractions: $\frac{2.54 \text{ cm}}{1 \text{ in.}}$ and $\frac{1 \text{ in.}}{2.54 \text{ cm}}$. We use the unit fraction with cm in the denominator so that these units divide out.

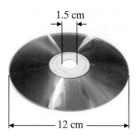

1.5 cm

12 cm

$$12 \text{ cm} = \frac{12 \text{ cm}}{1} \cdot 1 = \frac{12 \text{ c\!\!\!/m}}{1} \cdot \overbrace{\frac{1 \text{ in.}}{2.54 \text{ c\!\!\!/m}}}^{\text{Unit fraction}} \quad \begin{matrix} \leftarrow & \text{Units to convert to} \\ \leftarrow & \text{Original units} \end{matrix}$$

$$= \frac{12 \text{ in.}}{2.54}$$

$$\approx 4.72 \text{ in.} \quad \text{Divide.}$$

Thus, the diameter of a compact disc is exactly 12 cm or approximately 4.72 inches. For a dimension this size, you can use a ruler to check. Another method is to approximate. Our result, 4.72 in., is close to 5 inches. Since 1 in. is about 2.5 cm, then 5 in. is about 5(2.5 cm) = 12.5 cm, which is close to 12 cm.

 Work Practice Problem 1

PRACTICE PROBLEM 2

A full-grown human heart weighs about 8 ounces. Convert this weight to grams. If necessary, round your result to the nearest tenth of a gram.

EXAMPLE 2 Liver

The liver is your largest internal organ. It weighs about 3.5 pounds in a grown man. Convert this weight to kilograms. Round to the nearest tenth. (*Source: Some Body!* by Dr. Pete Rowan)

Solution: $3.5 \text{ lb} \approx \frac{3.5 \text{ l\!\!\!/b}}{1} \cdot \overbrace{\frac{0.45 \text{ kg}}{1 \text{ l\!\!\!/b}}}^{\text{Unit fraction}} = 3.5(0.45 \text{ kg}) \approx 1.6 \text{ kg}$

Thus 3.5 pounds are approximately 1.6 kilograms. From the table of conversions, we know that 1 kg ≈ 2.2 lb. So that 0.5 kg ≈ 1.1 lb and adding, we have 1.5 kg ≈ 3.3 lb. Our result is reasonable.

 Work Practice Problem 2

Answers

1. 0.59 in.,   **2.** 226.8 g

EXAMPLE 3 Postage Stamp

Australia converted to the metric system in 1973. In that year, four postage stamps were issued to publicize this conversion. One such stamp is shown below. Let's check the mathematics on the stamp by converting 7 fluid ounces to milliliters. Round to the nearest hundred.

Unit fraction

Solution: $7 \text{ fl oz} \approx \dfrac{7 \ \cancel{\text{fl oz}}}{1} \cdot \dfrac{\overbrace{29.57 \text{ ml}}}{1 \ \cancel{\text{fl oz}}} = 7(29.57 \text{ ml}) = 206.99 \text{ ml}$

Rounded to the nearest hundred, 7 fl oz $\approx$ 200 ml.

⬛ **Work Practice Problem 3**

PRACTICE PROBLEM 3

Convert 237 ml to fluid ounces. Round to the nearest whole fluid ounce.

Answer

3. 8 fl oz

Note: Because approximations are used, your answers may vary slightly from the answers given in the back of the book.

Objective [A] *Convert as indicated. If necessary, round answers to two decimal places. See Examples 1 through 3.*

1. 578 milliliters to fluid ounces

2. 5 liters to quarts

3. 86 inches to centimeters

4. 86 miles to kilometers

5. 1000 grams to ounces

6. 100 kilograms to pounds

7. 93 kilometers to miles

8. 9.8 meters to feet

9. 14.5 liters to gallons

10. 150 milliliters to fluid ounces

11. 30 pounds to kilograms

12. 15 ounces to grams

Fill in the chart. Give exact answers or round to 1 decimal place.

		Meters	Yards	Centimeters	Feet	Inches
13.	The Height of a Woman				5	
14.	Statue of Liberty Length of Nose	1.37				
15.	Leaning Tower of Pisa		60			
16.	Blue Whale		36			

Solve. If necessary, round answers to two decimal places. See Examples 1 through 3.

17. The balance beam for female gymnasts is 10 centimeters wide. Convert this width to inches.

18. In men's gymnastics, the rings are 250 centimeters from the floor. Convert this height to inches, then to feet.

19. The speed limit is 70 miles per hour. Convert this to kilometers per hour.

20. The speed limit is 40 kilometers per hour. Convert this to miles per hour.

21. Ibuprofen comes in 200 milligram tablets. Convert this to ounces. (Round your answer to this exercise to 3 decimal places.)

22. Vitamin C tablets come in 500 milligram caplets. Convert this to ounces.

23. A stone is a unit in the British customary system. Use the conversion: 14 pounds = 1 stone to check the equivalencies in this 1973 Australian stamp. Is 100 kilograms approximately 15 stone 10 pounds?

24. Convert 5 feet 11 inches to centimeters and check the conversion on this 1973 Australian stamp. Is it correct?

25. You find two soda sizes at the store. One is 12 fluid ounces and the other is 380 milliliters. Which is larger?

26. A punch recipe calls for 2 gallons of pineapple juice. You have 8 liters of pineapple juice. Do you have enough for the recipe?

27. A $3\frac{1}{2}$-inch diskette is not really $3\frac{1}{2}$ inches. To find its actual width, convert this measurement to centimeters, then to millimeters. Round the result to the nearest ten.

28. The average two-year-old is 84 centimeters tall. Convert this to feet and inches.

84 cm

29. For an average adult, the weight of a right lung is greater than the weight of a left lung. If the right lung weighs 1.5 pounds and the left lung weighs 1.25 pounds, find the difference in grams. (*Source: Some Body!*)

30. The skin of an average adult weighs 9 pounds and is the heaviest organ. Find the weight in grams. (*Source: Some Body!*)

31. A fast sneeze has been clocked at about 167 kilometers per hour. Convert this to miles per hour. Round to the nearest whole.

32. A Boeing 747 has a cruising speed of about 980 kilometers per hour. Convert this to miles per hour. Round to the nearest whole.

33. The General Sherman giant sequoia tree has a diameter of about 8 meters at its base. Convert this to feet. (*Source: Fantastic Book of Comparisions*)

34. The largest crater on the near side of the moon is Billy Crater. It has a diameter of 303 kilometers. Convert this to miles. (*Source: Fantastic Book of Comparisions*)

35. The total length of the track on a CD is about 4.5 kilometers. Convert this to miles. Round to the nearest whole mile.

36. The distance between Mackinaw City, Michigan, and Cheyenne, Wyoming, is 2079 kilometers. Convert this to miles. Round to the nearest whole mile.

37. A doctor orders a dosage of 5 ml of medicine every 4 hours for 1 week. How many fluid ounces of medicine should be purchased? Round up to the next whole fluid ounce.

38. A doctor orders a dosage of 12 ml of medicine every 6 hours for 10 days. How many fluid ounces of medicine should be purchased? Round up to the next whole fluid ounce.

Without actually converting, choose the most reasonable answer.

39. A twin mattress has a width of about _____.
 a. 1 m   **b.** 100 m
 c. 10 m   **d.** 1000 m

40. A pie plate has a diameter of about _____.
 a. 22 m   **b.** 22 km
 c. 22 cm   **d.** 22 g

41. A liter has _____ capacity than a quart.
 a. less   **b.** greater   **c.** the same

42. A foot is _____ a meter.
 a. shorter than   **b.** longer than
 c. the same length as

43. A kilogram weighs _____ a pound.
 a. the same as   **b.** less than
 c. greater than

44. A football field is 100 yards, which is about _____.
 a. 9 m   **b.** 90 m
 c. 900 m   **d.** 9000 m

45. An $8\frac{1}{2}$ ounce glass of water has a capacity of about _____.
 a. 250 L   **b.** 25 L
 c. 2.5 L   **d.** 250 ml

46. A 5-gallon gasoline can has a capacity of about _____.
 a. 19 L   **b.** 1.9 L
 c. 19 ml   **d.** 1.9 ml

47. The weight of an average man is about _____.
 a. 700 kg   **b.** 7 kg
 c. 0.7 kg   **d.** 70 kg

48. The weight of a pill is about _____.
 a. 200 kg   **b.** 20 kg
 c. 2 kg   **d.** 200 mg

Review

Perform the indicated operations. See Section 1.9.

49. $6 \cdot 4 + 5 \div 1$

50. $10 \div 2 + 9(8)$

51. $\dfrac{10 + 8}{10 - 8}$

52. $\dfrac{14 + 1}{5(3)}$

53. $3 + 5(19 - 17) - 8$

54. $1 + 4(19 - 9) + 5$

55. $3[(1 + 5) \cdot (8 - 6)]$

56. $5[(18 - 8) - 9]$

Concept Extensions

Body surface area (BSA) is often used to calculate dosages for some drugs. BSA is calculated in square meters using a person's weight and height.

$$BSA = \sqrt{\frac{(\text{weight in kg}) \times (\text{height in cm})}{3600}}$$

For Exercises 57 through 62, calculate the BSA for each person. Round to the nearest hundredth. You will need to use the square root key on your calculator.

57. An adult whose height is 182 cm and weight is 90 kg.

58. An adult whose height is 157 cm and weight is 63 kg.

59. A child whose height is 40 in. and weight is 50 kg. (*Hint:* Don't forget to first convert inches to centimeters)

60. A child whose height is 26 in. and weight is 13 kg.

61. An adult whose height is 60 in. and weight is 150 lb.

62. An adult whose height is 69 in. and weight is 172 lb.

Solve.

63. Suppose the adult from Exercise 57 is to receive a drug that has a recommended dosage range of 10–12 mg per sq meter. Find the dosage range for the adult.

64. Suppose the child from Exercise 60 is to receive a drug that has a recommended dosage of 30 mg per sq meter. Find the dosage for the child.

65. A handball court is a rectangle that measures 20 meters by 40 meters. Find its area in square meters and square feet.

66. A backpack measures 16 inches by 13 inches by 5 inches. Find the volume of a box with these dimensions. Find the volume in cubic inches and cubic centimeters. Round the cubic centimeters to the nearest whole cubic centimeter.

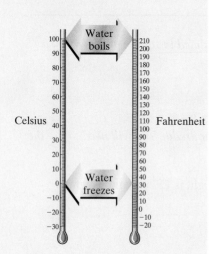

7.5 TEMPERATURE: U.S. AND METRIC SYSTEMS OF MEASUREMENT

When Gabriel Fahrenheit and Anders Celsius independently established units for temperature scales, each based his unit on the heat of water the moment it boils compared to the moment it freezes. One degree Celsius is 1/100 of the difference in heat. One degree Fahrenheit is 1/180 of the difference in heat. Celsius arbitrarily labeled the temperature at the freezing point at 0°C, making the boiling point 100°C; Fahrenheit labeled the freezing point 32°F, making the boiling point 212°F. Water boils at 212°F and 100°C.

By comparing the two scales in the figure, we see that a 20°C day is as warm as a 68°F day. Similarly, a sweltering 104°F day in the Mojave Desert corresponds to a 40°C day.

✔ **Concept Check** Which of the following statements is correct? Explain.

a. 6°C is below the freezing point of water.

b. 6°F is below the freezing point of water.

Objective **A** Converting Degrees Celsius to Degrees Fahrenheit

To convert from Celsius temperatures to Fahrenheit temperatures, we can use either of the equations in the box below.

Converting Celsius to Fahrenheit

$$F = \frac{9}{5} \cdot C + 32 \quad \text{or} \quad F = 1.8 \cdot C + 32$$

(To convert to Fahrenheit temperature, multiply the Celsius temperature by $\frac{9}{5}$ or 1.8, and then add 32.)

In these equations, we use the symbol F to represent degrees Fahrenheit and the symbol C to represent degrees Celsius.

EXAMPLE 1 Convert 15°C to degrees Fahrenheit.

Solution:
$$F = \frac{9}{5} \cdot C + 32$$
$$= \frac{9}{5} \cdot 15 + 32 \quad \text{Replace C with 15.}$$
$$= 27 + 32 \quad \text{Simplify.}$$
$$= 59 \quad \text{Add.}$$

Thus, 15°C is equivalent to 59°F.

▣ **Work Practice Problem 1**

EXAMPLE 2 Convert 29°C to degrees Fahrenheit.

Solution:
$$F = 1.8 \cdot C + 32$$
$$= 1.8 \cdot 29 + 32 \quad \text{Replace C with 29.}$$
$$= 52.2 + 32 \quad \text{Multiply 1.8 by 29.}$$
$$= 84.2 \quad \text{Add.}$$

Therefore, 29°C is the same as 84.2°F.

▣ **Work Practice Problem 2**

PRACTICE PROBLEM 1

Convert 50°C to degrees Fahrenheit.

PRACTICE PROBLEM 2

Convert 18°C to degrees Fahrenheit.

Answers
1. 122°F, **2.** 64.4°F

✔ **Concept Check Answer**

b

Objective **B** **Converting Degrees Fahrenheit to Degrees Celsius**

To convert from Fahrenheit temperatures to Celsius temperatures, we can use the equation in the box below.

Converting Fahrenheit to Celsius

$$C = \frac{5}{9} \cdot (F - 32)$$

(To convert to Celsius temperature, subtract 32 from the Fahrenheit temperature, and then multiply by $\frac{5}{9}$.)

In this equation, the symbol C represents degrees Celsius, and the symbol F represents degrees Fahrenheit.

EXAMPLE 3 Convert 59°F to degrees Celsius.

Solution: We evaluate the formula $C = \frac{5}{9} \cdot (F - 32)$ when F is 59.

$C = \frac{5}{9} \cdot (F - 32)$

$\quad = \frac{5}{9} \cdot (59 - 32)$ Replace F with 59.

$\quad = \frac{5}{9} \cdot (27)$ Subtract inside parentheses.

$\quad = 15$ Multiply.

Therefore, 59°F is the same temperature as 15°C.

◻ **Work Practice Problem 3**

PRACTICE PROBLEM 3

Convert 86°F to degrees Celsius.

EXAMPLE 4 Convert 114°F to degrees Celsius. If necessary, round to the nearest tenth of a degree.

Solution:

$C = \frac{5}{9} \cdot (F - 32)$

$\quad = \frac{5}{9} \cdot (114 - 32)$ Replace F with 114.

$\quad = \frac{5}{9} \cdot (82)$ Subtract inside parentheses.

$\quad \approx 45.6$ Multiply.

Therefore, 114°F is approximately 45.6°C.

◻ **Work Practice Problem 4**

PRACTICE PROBLEM 4

Convert 113°F to degrees Celsius. If necessary, round to the nearest tenth of a degree.

Answers
3. 30°C, **4.** 45°C

PRACTICE PROBLEM 5

During a bout with the flu, Albert's temperature reaches 102.2°F. What is his temperature measured in degrees Celsius?

EXAMPLE 5 Normal body temperature is 98.6°F. What is this temperature in degrees Celsius?

Solution: We evaluate the formula $C = \frac{5}{9} \cdot (F - 32)$ when F is 98.6.

$$C = \frac{5}{9} \cdot (F - 32)$$

$$= \frac{5}{9} \cdot (98.6 - 32) \quad \text{Replace F with 98.6.}$$

$$= \frac{5}{9} \cdot (66.6) \qquad \text{Subtract inside parentheses.}$$

$$= 37 \qquad\qquad \text{Multiply.}$$

Therefore, normal body temperature is 37°C.

Work Practice Problem 5

✔**Concept Check** Clarissa must convert 40°F to degrees Celsius. What is wrong with her work shown below?

$$F = 1.8 \cdot C + 32$$
$$F = 1.8 \cdot 40 + 32$$
$$F = 72 + 32$$
$$F = 104$$

Answer

5. 39°C

✔**Concept Check Answer**

She used the conversion for Celsius to Fahrenheit instead of Fahrenheit to Celsius.

Mental Math

Determine whether the measurement in each statement is reasonable.

1. A 72°F room feels comfortable.

2. Water heated to 110°F will boil.

3. Josiah has a fever if a thermometer shows his temperature to be 40°F.

4. An air temperature of 20°F on a Vermont ski slope can be expected in the winter.

5. When the temperature is 30°C outside, an overcoat is needed.

6. An air-conditioned room at 60°C feels quite chilly.

7. Barbara has a fever when a thermometer records her temperature at 40°C.

8. Water cooled to 32°C will freeze.

7.5 EXERCISE SET

Objectives A B **Mixed Practice** *Convert as indicated. When necessary, round to the nearest tenth of a degree. See Examples 1 through 5.*

1. 41°F to degrees Celsius

2. 68°F to degrees Celsius

 3. 104°F to degrees Celsius

4. 95°F to degrees Celsius

5. 60°C to degrees Fahrenheit

6. 80°C to degrees Fahrenheit

7. 115°C to degrees Fahrenheit

8. 35°C to degrees Fahrenheit

9. 62°F to degrees Celsius

10. 182°F to degrees Celsius

11. 142.1°F to degrees Celsius

12. 43.4°F to degrees Celsius

13. 92°C to degrees Fahrenheit

14. 75°C to degrees Fahrenheit

15. 16.3°C to degrees Fahrenheit

16. 48.6°C to degrees Fahrenheit

17. The hottest temperature ever recorded in New Mexico was 122°F. Convert this temperature to degrees Celsius. (*Source:* National Climatic Data Center)

18. The hottest temperature ever recorded in Rhode Island was 104°F. Convert this temperature to degrees Celsius. (*Source:* National Climatic Data Center)

19. A weather forecaster in Caracas predicts a high temperature of 27°C. Find this measurement in degrees Fahrenheit.

20. While driving to work, Alan Olda notices a temperature of 22°C flash on the local bank's temperature display. Find the corresponding temperature in degrees Fahrenheit.

21. Water boils at 212°F. Find this temperature in degrees Celsius.

22. Water freezes at 0°C. Find this temperature in degrees Fahrenheit.

23. Najib Tan is running a fever of 100.2°F. Find his temperature as it would be shown on a Celsius thermometer.

24. William Saylor generally has a subnormal temperature of 98.2°F. Find what this temperature would be on a Celsius thermometer.

25. In a European cookbook, a recipe requires the ingredients for caramels to be heated to 118°C, but the cook has access only to a Fahrenheit thermometer. Find the temperature in degrees Fahrenheit that should be used to make the caramels.

26. The ingredients for divinity should be heated to 127°C, but the candy thermometer that Myung Kim has is calibrated to degrees Fahrenheit. Find how hot he should heat the ingredients.

27. The surface temperature of Venus can reach 864°F. Find this temperature in degrees Celsius.

28. The temperature of Earth's core is estimated to be 4000°C. Find the corresponding temperature in degrees Fahrenheit.

29. At Mack Trucks' headquarters, the room temperature is to be set at 70°F, but the thermostat is calibrated in degrees Celsius. Find the temperature to be set.

30. The computer room at Merck, Sharp, and Dohm is normally cooled to 66°F. Find the corresponding temperature in degrees Celsius.

Review

Find the perimeter of each figure. See Sections 1.3 and 7.1.

△ **31.**

3 in.

3 in. | Square

△ **32.**

25 m

6 m Rectangle

△ **33.**

4 cm   3 cm
   Triangle
5 cm

△ **34.**

3 ft   3 ft
  Pentagon
3 ft   3 ft
    3 ft

△ **35.**

2 ft 8 in.

1 ft 6 in. Rectangle

△ **36.**

2.6 m

2.6 m Square

Concept Extensions

Solve. See the first Concept Check in this section. True or False.

37. 10°F is above the freezing point of water.

38. 10°C is above the freezing point of water.

39. 102°C is above the boiling point of water.

40. 102°F is above the boiling point of water.

41. On July 19, 1996, at the Naka Fusion Research Establishment in Nakamachi, Ibaraki, Japan, the highest temperature produced in a laboratory was achieved. This temperature was approximately 936,000,000°F. Convert this temperature to degrees Celsius. (*Note:* This is almost 30 times the temperature at the center of the sun.) (*Source: Guinness Book of Records*)

 42. The hottest-burning substance known is carbon subnitride. Its flame at one atmospheric pressure reaches 9010°F. Convert this temperature to degrees Celsius. (*Source: Guinness Book of Records*)

43. In your own words, describe how to convert from degrees Celsius to degrees Fahrenheit.

📖 STUDY SKILLS BUILDER

Have You Decided to Successfully Complete this Course?

Hopefully by now, one of your current goals is to successfully complete this course.

   If it is not a goal of yours, ask yourself why? One common reason is fear of failure. Amazingly enough, fear of failure alone can be strong enough to keep many of us from doing our best in any endeavor. Another common reason is that you simply haven't taken the time to make successfully completing this course one of your goals.

   Anytime you are registered for a course, successfully completing this course should probably be a goal. How do you do this? Start by writing this goal in your mathematics notebook. Then list steps you will take to ensure success. A great first step is to read or reread Section 1.1 and make a commitment to try the suggestions in this section.

   Good luck and don't forget that a positive attitude will make a big difference.

Let's see how you are doing.

1. Have you made the decision to make "successfully completing this course" a goal of yours? If no, please list reasons that this has not happened. Study your list and talk to your instructor about this.

2. If your answer to Exercise 1 is yes, take a moment and list, in your notebook, further specific goals that will help you achieve this major goal of successfully completing this course. (For example, my goal this semester is not to miss any of my mathematics classes.)

3. Rate your commitment to this course with a number between 1 and 5. Use the diagram below to help.

High Commitment		Average Commitment		Not committed at all
5	4	3	2	1

4. If you have rated your personal commitment level (from the exercise above) as a 1, 2, or 3, list the reasons why this is so. Then determine whether it is possible to increase your commitment level to a 4 or 5.

A Define and Use U.S. Units of
Energy and Convert from One Unit
to Another.

B Define and Use Metric Units
of Energy.

7.6 ENERGY: U.S. AND METRIC SYSTEMS OF MEASUREMENT

Many people think of energy as a concept that involves movement or activity. However, **energy** is defined as "the capacity to do work." Often energy is stored, awaiting use at some later point in time.

Objective **A** Defining and Using the U.S. System Units of Energy

In the U.S. system of measurement, energy is commonly measured in foot-pounds. One **foot-pound (ft-lb)** is the amount of energy needed to lift a 1-pound object a distance of 1 foot. To determine the amount of energy necessary to move a 50-pound weight a distance of 100-feet, we simply multiply these numbers. That is,

$$50 \text{ pounds} \cdot 100 \text{ feet} = 5000 \text{ ft-lb of energy}$$

PRACTICE PROBLEM 1

Three bales of cardboard must be lifted 340 feet. If each bale weighs 63 pounds, find the amount of work required to lift the cardboard.

EXAMPLE 1 Finding the Amount of Energy Needed to Move a Carton

An employee for the Jif Peanut Butter company must lift a carton of peanut butter jars 16 feet to the top of the warehouse. In the carton are 24 jars, each of which weighs 1.125 pounds. How much energy is required to lift the carton?

Solution: First we determine the weight of the carton.

$$\begin{aligned} \text{weight of carton} &= \text{weight of a jar} \cdot \text{number of jars} \\ &= 1.125 \text{ pounds} \cdot 24 \\ &= 27 \text{ pounds} \end{aligned}$$

Thus, the carton weighs 27 pounds.
To find the energy needed to lift the 27-pound carton, we multiply the weight times the distance.

$$\text{energy} = 27 \text{ pounds} \cdot 16 \text{ feet} = 432 \text{ ft-lb}$$

Thus, 432 ft-lb of energy are required to lift the carton.

Work Practice Problem 1

✔ **Concept Check** Suppose you would like to find how many foot-pounds of energy are needed to lift an object weighing 12 ounces a total of 14 yards. What adjustments should you make before computing the answer?

Another form of energy is heat. In the U.S. system of measurement, heat is measured in **British Thermal Units (BTU).** A BTU is the amount of heat required to raise the temperature of 1 pound of water 1 degree Fahrenheit. To relate British Thermal Units to foot-pounds, we need to know that

$$1 \text{ BTU} = 778 \text{ ft-lb}$$

Answer
1. 64,260 ft-lb

✔ **Concept Check Answer**
convert 12 ounces to 0.75 pound and 14 yards to 42 feet; 31.5 ft-lb

EXAMPLE 2 Converting BTU to Foot-Pounds

The Raywall Company produces several different furnace models. Their FC-4 model requires 13,652 BTU every hour to operate. Convert the required energy to foot-pounds.

Solution:

To convert BTU to foot-pounds, we multiply by the unit fraction $\dfrac{778 \text{ ft-lb}}{1 \text{ BTU}}$.

$$13{,}652 \text{ BTU} = 13{,}652 \text{ } \overline{\text{BTU}} \cdot \overset{\text{Unit fraction}}{\dfrac{778 \text{ ft-lb}}{1 \text{ } \overline{\text{BTU}}}}$$

$$= 10{,}621{,}256 \text{ ft-lb}$$

Thus, 13,652 BTU is equivalent to 10,621,256 ft-lb.

⬛ **Work Practice Problem 2**

Objective B Defining and Using the Metric System Units of Energy

In the metric system, heat is measured in calories. A **calorie (cal)** is the amount of heat required to raise the temperature of 1 kilogram of water 1 degree Celsius.

    The fact that an apple contains 70 calories means that 70 calories of heat energy are stored in our bodies whenever we eat an apple. This energy is stored in fat tissue and is burned (or "oxidized") by our bodies when we require energy to do work. We need 20 calories each hour just to stand still. This means that 20 calories of heat energy will be burned by our bodies each hour that we spend standing.

EXAMPLE 3 Finding the Number of Calories Needed

It takes 20 calories for Jim to stand for 1 hour. How many calories does he use when standing for 3 hours at a crowded party?

Solution: We multiply the number of calories used in 1 hour by the number of hours spent standing.

$$\text{total calories} = 20 \cdot 3 = 60 \text{ calories}$$

Therefore, Jim uses 60 calories to stand for 3 hours at the party.

⬛ **Work Practice Problem 3**

EXAMPLE 4 Finding the Number of Calories Needed

It takes 115 calories for Kathy to walk slowly for 1 hour. How many calories does she use walking slowly for 1 hour a day for 6 days?

Solution: We multiply the total number of calories used in 1 hour each day by the number of days.

$$\text{total calories} = 115 \cdot 6 = 690 \text{ calories}$$

Therefore, Kathy uses 690 calories walking slowly for 1 hour for 6 days.

⬛ **Work Practice Problem 4**

PRACTICE PROBLEM 2

The FC-5 model furnace produced by Raywall uses 17,065 BTU every hour. Convert this energy requirement to foot-pounds.

70 calories

PRACTICE PROBLEM 3

It takes 30 calories each hour for Alan to fly a kite. How many calories will he use if he flies his kite for 2 hours?

PRACTICE PROBLEM 4

It takes 200 calories for Melanie to play Frisbee for an hour. How many calories will she use playing Frisbee for an hour each day for 5 days?

Answers

2. 13,276,570 ft-lb, **3.** 60 cal,
4. 1000 cal

To play volleyball for an hour requires 300 calories. If Martha plays volleyball 1.25 hours each day for 4 days, how many calories does Martha use?

EXAMPLE 5 **Finding the Number of Calories Needed**

It requires 100 calories to play a game of cards for an hour. If Jason plays poker for 1.5 hours each day for 5 days, how many calories are required?

Solution: We first determine the number of calories Jason uses each day to play poker.

calories used each day $= 100(1.5) = 150$ calories

Then we multiply the number of calories used each day by the number of days.

calories used for 5 days $= 150 \cdot 5 = 750$ calories

Thus, Jason uses 750 calories to play poker for 1.5 hours each day for 5 days.

Work Practice Problem 5

Answer

5. 1500 cal

Mental Math

Solve.

1. How many foot-pounds of energy are needed to lift a 6-pound object 5 feet?

2. How many foot-pounds of energy are needed to lift a 10-pound object 4 feet?

3. How many foot-pounds of energy are needed to lift a 3-pound object 20 feet?

4. How many foot-pounds of energy are needed to lift a 5-pound object 9 feet?

5. If 30 calories are burned by the body in 1 hour, how many calories are burned in 3 hours?

6. If 15 calories are burned by the body in 1 hour, how many calories are burned in 2 hours?

7. If 20 calories are burned by the body in 1 hour, how many calories are burned in $\frac{1}{4}$ of an hour?

8. If 50 calories are burned by the body in 1 hour, how many calories are burned in $\frac{1}{2}$ of an hour?

7.6 EXERCISE SET

FOR EXTRA HELP

 Student Solutions Manual   PH Math/Tutor Center   CD/Video for Review   *Math*XL MathXL®   MyMathLab MyMathLab

Objective A *Solve. See Examples 1 and 2.*

1. How much energy is required to lift a 3-pound math textbook 380 feet up a hill?

2. How much energy is required to lift a 20-pound sack of potatoes 55 feet?

3. How much energy is required to lift a 168-pound person 22 feet?

4. How much energy is needed to lift a 2250-pound car a distance of 45 feet?

5. How many foot-pounds of energy are needed to take 2.5 tons of topsoil 85 feet from the pile delivered by the nursery to the garden?

6. How many foot-pounds of energy are needed to lift 4.25 tons of coal 16 feet into a new coal bin?

7. Convert 30 BTU to foot-pounds.

8. Convert 50 BTU to foot-pounds.

9. Convert 1000 BTU to foot-pounds.

10. Convert 10,000 BTU to foot-pounds.

11. A 20,000 BTU air conditioner requires how many foot-pounds of energy to operate?

12. A 24,000 BTU air conditioner requires how many foot-pounds of energy to operate?

13. The Raywall model FC-10 heater uses 34,130 BTU each hour to operate. How many foot-pounds of energy does it use each hour?

14. The Raywall model FC-12 heater uses 40,956 BTU each hour to operate. How many foot-pounds of energy does it use each hour?

15. 8,000,000 ft-lb is equivalent to how many BTU, rounded to the nearest whole number?

16. 450,000 ft-lb is equivalent to how many BTU, rounded to the nearest whole number?

Objective **B** *Solve. See Examples 3 through 5.*

17. While walking slowly, Janie Gaines burns 115 calories each hour. How many calories does she burn if she walks slowly for an hour every day of the week?

18. Dancing burns 270 calories per hour. How many calories are needed to go dancing an hour a night for 3 nights?

19. Approximately 300 calories are burned each hour skipping rope. How many calories are required to skip rope $\frac{1}{2}$ of an hour each day for 5 days?

20. Ebony Jordan burns 360 calories per hour while riding her stationary bike. How many calories does she burn when she rides her bicycle $\frac{1}{4}$ of an hour each day for 6 days?

21. Julius Davenport goes through a rigorous exercise routine each day. He burns calories at a rate of 720 calories per hour. How many calories does he need to exercise 20 minutes per day, 6 days a week?

22. A roller skater can easily use 325 calories per hour while skating. How many calories are needed to roller skate 75 minutes per day for 3 days?

23. A casual stroll burns 165 calories per hour. How long will it take to stroll off the 425 calories contained in a hamburger, to the nearest tenth of an hour?

24. Even when asleep, the body burns 15 calories per hour. How long must a person sleep to burn off the calories in an 80-calorie orange, to the nearest tenth of an hour?

25. One pound of body weight is lost whenever 3500 calories are burned off. If walking briskly burns 200 calories for each mile walked, how far must Sheila Osby walk to lose 1 pound?

26. Bicycling can burn as much as 500 calories per hour. How long must a person ride a bicycle at this rate to use up the 3500 calories needed to lose 1 pound?

Review

Write each fraction in simplest form. See Section 2.3.

27. $\frac{20}{25}$ **28.** $\frac{75}{100}$ **29.** $\frac{27}{45}$ **30.** $\frac{56}{60}$ **31.** $\frac{72}{80}$ **32.** $\frac{18}{20}$

Concept Extensions

33. A 123.9-pound pile of prepacked canned goods must be lifted 9 inches to permit a door to close. How much energy is needed to do the job?

34. A 14.3-pound framed picture must be lifted 6 feet 3 inches. How much energy is required to move the picture?

35. 6400 ft-lb of energy were needed to lift an anvil 25 feet. Find the weight of the anvil.

36. 825 ft-lb of energy were needed to lift 40 pounds of apples to a new container. How far were the apples moved?

37. In your own words, define calorie.

CHAPTER 7   Group Activity

Speeds

Section 7.1

A speed measures how far something travels in a given unit of time. You already learned in Section 5.2 that the speed 55 miles per hour is a rate that can be written as $\frac{55 \text{ miles}}{1 \text{ hour}}$. Just as there are different units of measurement for length or distance, there are different units of measurement for speed as well. It is also possible to perform unit conversions on speeds. Before we learn about converting speeds, we will review units of time. The following is a summary of equivalencies between various units of time.

Units of Time	Unit Fractions
60 seconds (s) = 1 minute (min)	$\dfrac{60 \text{ s}}{1 \text{ min}} = \dfrac{1 \text{ min}}{60 \text{ s}} = 1$
60 minutes = 1 hour (h)	$\dfrac{60 \text{ min}}{1 \text{ h}} = \dfrac{1 \text{ h}}{60 \text{ min}} = 1$
3600 seconds = 1 hour	$\dfrac{3600 \text{ s}}{1 \text{ h}} = \dfrac{1 \text{ h}}{3600 \text{ s}}$

Here are some common speeds.

Speeds

Miles per hour (mph)
Miles per minute (mi/min)
Miles per second (mi/s)
Feet per second (ft/s)
Feet per minute (ft/min)
Kilometers per hour (kmph or km/h)
Kilometers per second (kmps or km/s)
Meters per second (m/s)
Knots

To convert from one speed to another, unit fractions may be used. To convert from mph to ft/s first write the original speed as a unit rate. Then multiply by a unit fraction that relates miles to feet and by a unit fraction that relates hours to seconds. The unit fractions should be written so that like units will divide out. For example, to convert 55 mph to ft/s:

$$55 \text{ mph} = \frac{55 \text{ miles}}{1 \text{ hour}} = \frac{55 \cancel{\text{ miles}}}{1 \cancel{\text{ hour}}} \cdot \frac{5280 \text{ ft}}{1 \cancel{\text{ mile}}} \cdot \frac{1 \cancel{\text{ hour}}}{3600 \text{ s}}$$

$$= \frac{55 \cdot 5280 \text{ ft}}{3600 \text{ s}}$$

$$= \frac{290{,}400 \text{ ft}}{3600 \text{ s}}$$

$$= 80\frac{2}{3} \text{ ft/s}$$

Group Activity

1. Research the current world land speed record. Convert the speed from mph to feet per second.

2. Research the current world water speed record. Convert from mph to knots.

3. Research and then describe the Beaufort Wind Scale, its origins, and how it is used. Give the scale keyed to both miles per hour and knots. Why would both measures be useful?

> **Helpful Hint**   A **knot** is 1 nautical mile per hour and is a measure of speed used for ships.
>
> 1 nautical mile (nmi) ≈ 1.15 miles (mi)
>
> 1 nautical mile (nmi) ≈ 6076.12 feet (ft)

Chapter 7 Vocabulary Check

Fill in each blank with one of the words or phrases listed below.

mass	unit fractions	gram	energy	weight
meter	liter	calorie	British Thermal Unit	

1. _____ is a measure of the pull of gravity.
2. _____ is a measure of the amount of substance in an object. This measure does not change.
3. The basic unit of length in the metric system is the _____.
4. To convert from one unit of length to another, _____ may be used.
5. A _____ is the basic unit of mass in the metric system.
6. _____ is the capacity to do work.
7. In the U.S. system of measurement, a _____ is the amount of heat required to raise the temperature of 1 pound of water 1 degree Fahrenheit.
8. The _____ is the basic unit of capacity in the metric system.
9. In the metric system, a _____ is the amount of heat required to raise the temperature of 1 kilogram of water 1 degree Celsius.

Helpful Hint

Are you preparing for your test? Don't forget to take the Chapter 7 Test on page 506. Then check your answers at the back of the text and use the Chapter Test Prep Video CD to see the fully worked-out solutions to any of the exercises you want to review.

7 Chapter Highlights

DEFINITIONS AND CONCEPTS	EXAMPLES
Section 7.1 Length: U.S. and Metric Systems of Measurement	

DEFINITIONS AND CONCEPTS	EXAMPLES
To convert from one unit of length to another, multiply by a **unit fraction** in the form $$\frac{\text{units to convert to}}{\text{original units}}.$$	$$\frac{12 \text{ inches}}{1 \text{ foot}}, \frac{1 \text{ foot}}{12 \text{ inches}}, \frac{3 \text{ feet}}{1 \text{ yard}}$$ Convert 6 feet to inches. $$6 \text{ ft} = \frac{6 \text{ ft}}{1} \cdot 1$$ $$= \frac{6 \text{ ft}}{1} \cdot \frac{12 \text{ in.}}{1 \text{ ft}} \quad \leftarrow \text{units to convert to} \\ \quad\quad\quad\quad\quad\quad \leftarrow \text{original units}$$ $$= 6 \cdot 12 \text{ in.}$$ $$= 72 \text{ in.}$$
LENGTH: U.S. SYSTEM OF MEASUREMENT 12 inches (in.) = 1 foot (ft) 3 feet = 1 yard (yd) 5280 feet = 1 mile (mi)	Convert 3650 centimeters to meters. $$3650 \text{ cm} = 3650 \text{ cm} \cdot 1$$ $$= \frac{3650 \text{ cm}}{1} \cdot \frac{0.01 \text{ m}}{1 \text{ cm}} = 36.5 \text{ m}$$
The basic unit of length in the metric system is the **meter.** A meter is slightly longer than a yard.	or

LENGTH: METRIC SYSTEM OF MEASUREMENT

Metric Unit of Length
1 **kilo**meter (km) = 1000 meters (m)
1 **hecto**meter (hm) = 100 m
1 **deka**meter (dam) = 10 m
1 meter (m) = 1 m
1 **deci**meter (dm) = 1/10 m or 0.1 m
1 **centi**meter (cm) = 1/100 m or 0.01 m
1 **milli**meter (mm) = 1/1000 m or 0.001 m

km   hm   dam   m   dm   cm   mm

2 units to the left

$$3650 \text{ cm} = 36.5 \text{ m}$$

2 places to the left

DEFINITIONS AND CONCEPTS	EXAMPLES

Section 7.2   Weight and Mass: U.S. and Metric Systems of Measurement

Weight is really a measure of the pull of gravity. **Mass** is a measure of the amount of substance in an object and does not change.	Convert 5 pounds to ounces. $$5 \text{ lb} = 5 \text{ lb} \cdot 1 = \frac{5 \text{ lb}}{1} \cdot \frac{16 \text{ oz}}{1 \text{ lb}} = 80 \text{ oz}$$

WEIGHT: U.S. SYSTEM OF MEASUREMENT

$$16 \text{ ounces (oz)} = 1 \text{ pound (1b)}$$
$$2000 \text{ pounds} = 1 \text{ ton}$$

A **gram** is the basic unit of mass in the metric system. It is the mass of water contained in a cube 1 centimeter on each side. A paper clip weighs about 1 gram.

Convert 260 grams to kilograms.

$$260 \text{ g} = \frac{260 \text{ g}}{1} \cdot 1 = \frac{260 \text{ g}}{1} \cdot \frac{1 \text{ kg}}{1000 \text{ g}} = 0.26 \text{ kg}$$

or

MASS: METRIC SYSTEM OF MEASUREMENT

Metric Unit of Mass
1 kilogram (kg) = 1000 grams (g)
1 hectogram (hg) = 100 g
1 dekagram (dag) = 10 g
1 gram (g) = 1 g
1 decigram (dg) = 1/10 g or 0.1 g
1 centigram (cg) = 1/100 g or 0.01 g
1 milligram (mg) = 1/1000 g or 0.001 g

kg   hg   dag   g   dg   cg   mg

3 units to the left

260 g = 0.260 kg

3 places to the left

Section 7.3   Capacity: U.S. and Metric Systems of Measurement

CAPACITY: U.S. SYSTEM OF MEASUREMENT

$$8 \text{ fluid ounces (fl oz)} = 1 \text{ cup (c)}$$
$$2 \text{ cups} = 1 \text{ pint (pt)}$$
$$2 \text{ pints} = 1 \text{ quart (qt)}$$
$$4 \text{ quarts} = 1 \text{ gallon (gal)}$$

Convert 5 pints to gallons.

$$1 \text{ gal} = 4 \text{ qt} = 8 \text{ pt}$$

$$5 \text{ pt} = 5 \text{ pt} \cdot 1 = \frac{5 \text{ pt}}{1} \cdot \frac{1 \text{ gal}}{8 \text{ pt}} = \frac{5}{8} \text{ gal}$$

The **liter** is the basic unit of capacity in the metric system. It is the capacity or volume of a cube measuring 10 centimeters on each side. A liter of liquid is slightly more than 1 quart.

Convert 1.5 liters to milliliters.

$$1.5 \text{ L} = \frac{1.5 \text{ L}}{1} \cdot 1 = \frac{1.5 \text{ L}}{1} \cdot \frac{1000 \text{ ml}}{1 \text{ L}} = 1500 \text{ ml}$$

or

CAPACITY: METRIC SYSTEM OF MEASUREMENT

Metric Unit of Capacity
1 kiloliter (kl) = 1000 liters (L)
1 hectoliter (hl) = 100 L
1 dekaliter (dal) = 10 L
1 liter (L) = 1 L
1 deciliter (dl) = 1/10 L or 0.1 L
1 centiliter (cl) = 1/100 L or 0.01 L
1 milliliter (ml) = 1/1000 L or 0.001 L

kl   hl   dal   L   dl   cl   ml

3 units to the right

1.500 L = 1500 ml

3 places to the right

DEFINITIONS AND CONCEPTS	EXAMPLES

Section 7.4   Conversions Between the U.S. and Metric Systems

To convert between systems, use approximate unit fractions from Section 7.4.	Convert 7 feet to meters. $$7 \text{ ft} \approx \frac{7 \cancel{\text{ft}}}{1} \cdot \frac{0.30 \text{ m}}{1 \cancel{\text{ft}}} = 2.1 \text{ m}$$ Convert 8 liters to quarts. $$8 \text{ L} \approx \frac{8 \cancel{\text{L}}}{1} \cdot \frac{1.06 \text{ qt}}{1 \cancel{\text{L}}} = 8.48 \text{ qt}$$ Convert 363 grams to ounces. $$363 \text{ g} \approx \frac{363 \cancel{\text{g}}}{1} \cdot \frac{0.04 \text{ oz}}{1 \cancel{\text{g}}} = 14.52 \text{ oz}$$

Section 7.5   Temperature: U.S. and Metric Systems of Measurement

TO CONVERT FROM CELSIUS TEMPERATURE TO FAHRENHEIT TEMPERATURE $$F = \frac{9}{5} \cdot C + 32 \quad \text{or} \quad F = 1.8 \cdot C + 32$$ **TO CONVERT FROM FAHRENHEIT TEMPERATURE TO CELSIUS TEMPERATURE** $$C = \frac{5}{9} \cdot (F - 32)$$	Convert $35°C$ to degrees Fahrenheit. $$F = \frac{9}{5} \cdot 35 + 32 = 63 + 32 = 95$$ $35°C = 95°F$ Convert $50°F$ to degrees Celsius. $$C = \frac{5}{9} \cdot (50 - 32) = \frac{5}{9} \cdot 18 = 10$$ $50°F = 10°C$

Section 7.6   Energy: U.S. and Metric Systems of Measurement

Energy is the capacity to do work. In the U.S. system of measurement, a **foot-pound** (ft-lb) is the amount of energy needed to lift a 1-pound object a distance of 1 foot. In the U.S. system of measurement, a **British Thermal Unit** (BTU) is the amount of heat required to raise the temperature of 1 pound of water 1 degree Fahrenheit. (1 BTU = 778 ft-lb) In the metric system, a **calorie** is the amount of heat required to raise the temperature of 1 kilogram of water 1 degree Celsius.	How much energy is needed to lift a 20-pound object 35 feet? 20 pounds $\cdot$ 35 feet = 700 foot-pounds of energy Convert 50 BTU to foot-pounds. $$50 \text{ BTU} = 50 \cancel{\text{BTU}} \cdot \frac{778 \text{ ft-lb}}{1 \cancel{\text{BTU}}} = 38,900 \text{ ft-lb}$$ A stationary bicyclist uses 350 calories in 1 hour. How many calories will the bicyclist use in $\frac{1}{2}$ of an hour? $$\text{calories used} = 350 \cdot \frac{1}{2} = 175 \text{ calories}$$

7 CHAPTER REVIEW

(7.1) *Convert.*

1. 108 in. to feet

2. 72 ft to yards

3. 1.5 mi to feet

4. $\frac{1}{2}$ yd to inches

5. 52 ft = _____ yd _____ ft

6. 46 in. = _____ ft _____ in.

7. 42 m to centimeters

8. 82 cm to millimeters

9. 12.18 mm to meters

10. 2.31 m to kilometers

Perform each indicated operation.

11. 4 yd 2 ft + 16 yd 2 ft

12. 12 ft 1 in. − 4 ft 8 in.

13. 8 ft 3 in. × 5

14. 7 ft 4 in. ÷ 2

15. 8 cm + 15 mm

16. 4 m − 126 cm

17. 8.62 m × 4

18. 19.6 km ÷ 8

Solve.

19. A bolt of cloth contains 333 yd 1 ft of cotton ticking. Find the amount of material that remains after 163 yd 2 ft is removed from the bolt.

20. The local ambulance corps plans to award 20 framed certificates of valor to some of its outstanding members. If each frame requires 6 ft 4 in. of framing material, how much material is needed for all the frames?

21. The trip from Philadelphia to Washington, D.C., is 217 km each way. Four friends agree to share the driving equally. How far must each drive on this round-trip vacation?

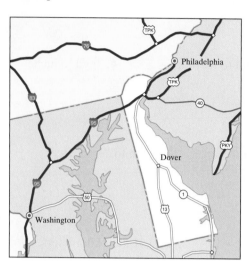

△ **22.** The college has ordered that NO SMOKING signs be placed above the doorway of each classroom. Each sign is 0.8 m long and 30 cm wide. Find the area of each sign. (*Hint:* Recall that the area of a rectangle = width · length.)

0.8 meter

NO SMOKING

30 centimeters

(7.2) *Convert.*

23. 66 oz to pounds

24. 2.3 tons to pounds

25. 52 oz = _____ lb _____ oz.

26. 10,300 lb = _____ tons _____ lb

27. 27 mg to grams

28. 40 kg to grams

29. 2.1 hg to dekagrams

30. 0.03 mg to decigrams

Perform each indicated operation.

31. 6 lb 5 oz − 2 lb 12 oz

32. 5 tons 1600 lb + 4 tons 1200 lb

33. 6 tons 2250 lb ÷ 3

34. 8 lb 6 oz × 4

35. 4.3 mg × 5

36. 4.8 kg − 4200 g

Solve.

37. Donshay Berry ordered 1 lb 12 oz of soft-center candies and 2 lb 8 oz of chewy-center candies for his party. Find the total weight of the candy ordered.

38. Four local townships jointly purchase 38 tons 300 lb of cinders to spread on their roads during an ice storm. Determine the weight of the cinders each township receives if they share the purchase equally.

39. Linda Holden ordered 8.3 kg of whole wheat flour from the health-food store, but she received 450 g less. How much flour did she actually receive?

40. Eight friends spent a weekend in the Poconos tapping maple trees and preparing 9.3 kg of maple syrup. Find the weight each friend receives if they share the syrup equally.

(7.3) *Convert.*

41. 16 pints to quarts

42. 40 fluid ounces to cups

43. 3 qt 1 pt to pints

44. 18 quarts to cups

45. 9 pt = _____ qt _____ pt

46. 15 qt = _____ gal _____ qt

47. 3.8 L to milliliters

48. 4.2 ml to deciliters

49. 14 hl to kiloliters

50. 30.6 L to centiliters

Perform each indicated operation.

51. 1 qt 1 pt + 3 qt 1 pt

52. 3 gal 2 qt × 2

53. 0.946 L − 210 ml

54. 6.1 L + 9400 ml

Solve.

55. Carlos Perez prepares 4 gal 2 qt of iced tea for a block party. During the first 30 minutes of the party, 1 gal 3 qt of the tea is consumed. How much iced tea remains?

56. A recipe for soup stock calls for 1 c 4 fl oz of beef broth. How much should be used if the recipe is cut in half?

57. Each bottle of Kiwi liquid shoe polish holds 85 ml of the polish. Find the number of liters of shoe polish contained in 8 boxes if each box contains 16 bottles.

58. Ivan Miller wants to pour three separate containers of saline solution into a single vat with a capacity of 10 liters. Will 6 liters of solution in the first container combined with 1300 milliliters in the second container and 2.6 liters in the third container fit into the larger vat?

(7.4) *Note: Because approximations are used in this section, your answers may vary slightly from the answers given in the back of the book.*

Convert as indicated. If necessary, round to two decimal places.

59. 7 meters to feet.

60. 11.5 yards to meters.

61. 17.5 liters to gallons

62. 7.8 liters to quarts

63. 15 ounces to grams

64. 23 pounds to kilograms

65. A 100-meter dash is being held today. How many yards is this?

66. If a person weighs 82 kilograms, how many pounds is this?

67. How many quarts are contained in a 3-liter bottle of cola?

68. A compact disc is 1.2 mm thick. Find the height (in inches) of 50 discs.

(7.5) *Convert. Round to the nearest tenth of a degree, if necessary.*

69. 245°C to degrees Fahrenheit

70. 160°C to degrees Fahrenheit

71. 42°C to degrees Fahrenheit

72. 93.2°F to degrees Celsius

73. 41.3°F to degrees Celsius

74. 80°F to degrees Celsius

Solve. Round to the nearest tenth of a degree, if necessary.

75. A sharp dip in the jet stream caused the temperature in New Orleans to drop to 35°F. Find the corresponding temperature in degrees Celsius.

76. The recipe for meat loaf calls for a 165°C oven. Find the setting used if the oven has a Fahrenheit thermometer.

(7.6) *Solve.*

77. How many foot-pounds of energy are needed to lift a 5.6-pound radio a distance of 12 feet?

78. How much energy is required to lift a 21-pound carton of Rice-A-Roni a distance of 6.5 feet?

79. How much energy is used when a 1.2-ton pile of sand is lifted 15 yards?

80. The energy required to operate a 12,000-BTU air conditioner is equivalent to how many foot-pounds?

81. Convert 2,000,000 foot-pounds to BTU, rounded to the nearest hundred.

82. Kip Yates burns off 450 calories each hour he plays handball. How many calories does he use to play handball for $2\frac{1}{2}$ hours?

83. Qwanetta Sesson uses 210 calories each hour she spends mowing the grass. Find the number of calories needed to mow the grass if she spends 3 hours mowing each week for 24 weeks.

84. Four ounces of sirloin steak contain 420 calories. If Edith Lutrell uses 180 calories each hour she walks, how long must she walk to burn off the calories from this steak?

Mixed Review

Convert the following.

85. 2.5 mi to feet

86. 6.25 ft to inches

87. 23,760 ft to miles

88. 129 in. to feet

89. 8200 lb = _____ tons _____ lb

90. 4300 lb = _____ tons _____ lb

91. 5 m to centimeters

92. 286 mm to kilometers

93. 1400 mg to grams

94. 240 mg to grams

95. 6.75 gallons to quarts

96. 5.25 gallons to quarts

97. 8.5 pints to cups

98. 6.25 pints to cups

99. 86°C to degrees Fahrenheit

100. 15°C to degrees Fahrenheit

101. 51.8°F to degrees Celsius

102. 82.4°F to degrees Celsius

Perform the indicated operations and simplify.

103. 9.3 km − 183 m

104. 8.6 km − 247 m

105. 7.4 L + 6500 ml

106. 35 L + 700 ml

107. 9.3 g − 1200 mg

108. 3.4 g − 1800 mg

109. 6.3 kg × 8

110. 3.2 kg × 4

111. 3 gal 1 qt + 4 gal 2 qt

112. 6 gal 1 qt + 2 gal 1 qt

113. 4100 mm − 3 dm

114. 6300 mm − 5 dm

115. 4.5 tons ÷ 2

116. 6.75 tons ÷ 3

7 CHAPTER TEST

 Use the Chapter Test Prep Video CD to see the fully worked-out solutions to any of the exercises you want to review.

Convert.

1. 280 in. = _____ ft _____ in.

2. $2\frac{1}{2}$ gal to quarts

3. 30 oz to pounds

4. 2.8 tons to pounds

5. 38 pt to gallons

6. 40 mg to grams

7. 2.4 kg to grams

8. 3.6 cm to millimeters

9. 4.3 dg to grams

10. 0.83 L to milliliters

Perform each indicated operation.

11. 3 qt 1 pt + 2 qt 1 pt

12. 8 lb 6 oz − 4 lb 9 oz

13. 2 ft 9 in. × 3

14. 5 gal 2 qt ÷ 2

15. 8 cm − 14 mm

16. 1.8 km + 456 m

Convert. Round to the nearest tenth of a degree, if necessary.

17. 84°F to degrees Celsius

18. 12.6°C to degrees Fahrenheit

19. The sugar maples in front of Bette MacMillan's house are 8.4 meters tall. Because they interfere with the phone lines, the telephone company plans to remove the top third of the trees. How tall will the maples be after they are shortened?

20. A total of 15 gal 1 qt of oil has been removed from a 20-gallon drum. How much oil still remains in the container?

21. The engineer in charge of bridge construction said that the span of a certain bridge would be 88 m. But the actual construction required it to be 340 cm longer. Find the span of the bridge, in meters.

22. If 2 ft 9 in. of material is used to manufacture one scarf, how much material is needed for 6 scarves?

1. _____

2. _____

3. _____

4. _____

5. _____

6. _____

7. _____

8. _____

9. _____

10. _____

11. _____

12. _____

13. _____

14. _____

15. _____

16. _____

17. _____

18. _____

19. _____

20. _____

21. _____

22. _____

23. The Vietnam Veterans Memorial, inscribed with the names of 58,226 deceased and missing U.S. soldiers from the Vietnam War, is located on the National Mall in Washington, D.C. This memorial is formed from two straight sections of wall that meet at an angle at the center of the monument. Each wall is 246 ft 9 in. long. What is the total length of the Vietnam Veterans Memorial's wall? (*Source:* National Park Service)

24. Each panel making up the wall of the Vietnam Veterans Memorial is 101.6 cm wide. There are a total of 148 panels making up the wall. What is the total length of the wall in meters? (*Source:* National Park Service)

25. The hottest temperature ever recorded was 136°F in El Azizia, Libya, on September 13, 1922. Convert this temperature to degrees Celsius. Round your answer to the nearest tenth of a degree. (*Source:* National Climatic Data Center)

26. The doctors are quite concerned about Lucia Gillespie, who is running a 41°C fever. Find Lucia's temperature in degrees Fahrenheit.

27. The largest ice cream sundae ever made in the U.S. was assembled in Anaheim, California, in 1985. This giant sundae used 4667 gallons of ice cream. How many pints of ice cream were used?

28. A piece of candy weighs 5 grams. How many ounces is this?

29. A 5-kilometer race is being held today. How many miles is this?

30. A 5-gallon container holds how many liters?

31. Phillipe Jordaine must lift a 48.5-pound carton of canned tomatoes a distance of 14 feet. Find the energy required to move the carton.

32. Energy used by a 26,000-BTU heater is equivalent to how many foot-pounds?

33. Robin Nestle burns 180 calories each hour when she swims. How many calories does she use if she swims 1 hour per day for 5 days?

23. ___
24. ___
25. ___
26. ___
27. ___
28. ___
29. ___
30. ___
31. ___
32. ___
33. ___

1. Add: $1647 + 246 + 32 + 85$

2. Subtract: $2000 - 469$

Answers

1. _____

2. _____

3. Find the prime factorization of 945.

4. Find the area of the rectangle.

17 in.

9 in.

3. _____

4. _____

5. Find the LCM of 11 and 33.

6. Subtract: $\dfrac{8}{21} - \dfrac{2}{9}$

5. _____

7. Add: $3\dfrac{4}{5} + 1\dfrac{4}{15}$

8. Multiply: $2\dfrac{1}{2} \cdot 4\dfrac{2}{15}$

6. _____

7. _____

Write each decimal as a fraction or mixed number in simplest form.

8. _____

9. 0.125

10. 1.2

9. _____

10. _____

11. 105.083

12. Evaluate: $\left(\dfrac{2}{3}\right)^3$

11. _____

13. Insert $<$, $>$, or $=$ to form a true statement.

$0.052 \quad 0.236$

14. Evaluate: $30 \div 6 \cdot 5$

12. _____

13. _____

14. _____

15. _____

15. Subtract $85 - 17.31$. Check your answer.

16. Add: $27.9 + 8.07 + 103.261$

16. _____

17. _____

18. _____

Multiply.

17. 42.1×0.1

18. 186.04×1000

19. _____

20. _____

21. _____

19. 9.2×0.001

20. Find the average of 6.8, 9.7, and 0.9.

22. _____

21. Divide: $60.24 \div 8$. Check your answer.

22. Add: $\dfrac{3}{10} + \dfrac{3}{4}$

23. _____

24. _____

23. Write $2\dfrac{3}{16}$ as a decimal.

24. Round 7.2846 to the nearest tenth.

25. _____

26. _____

25. Write $\dfrac{2}{3}$ as a decimal.

26. Simplify: $\dfrac{0.12 + 0.96}{0.5}$

27. Write the ratio of 12 to 17 using fractional notation.

28. Write the ratio of $2\frac{2}{3}$ to $5\frac{1}{9}$ as a ratio of whole numbers using fractional notation.

29. Write "318.5 miles every 13 gallons of gas" as a unit rate.

30. A square is 9 inches by 9 inches. Find the ratio of a side to its perimeter.

31. Find the unknown number n. $\frac{7}{n} = \frac{6}{5}$

32. A recipe that makes 2 pie crusts call for 3 cups of flour. How much flour is needed to make 5 pie crusts?

33. A 50-pound bag of fertilizer covers 2400 square feet of lawn. How many bags of fertilizer are needed to cover a town square containing 15,360 square feet of lawn? Round the answer up to the nearest whole bag.

34. Write 23% as a fraction.

35. Write 23% as a decimal.

36. Write $\frac{7}{8}$ as a percent.

37. Write $\frac{1}{12}$ as a percent. Round to the nearest hundredth percent.

38. 108 is what percent of 450?

39. What number is 35% of 40?

40. Convert 4 gallons to pints.

41. Translate to a proportion. What percent of 30 is 75?

42. Convert 8.6 meters to centimeters.

43. In response to a decrease in sales, a company with 1500 employees reduces the number of employees to 1230. What is the percent decrease?

44. Convert 13,000 pounds to tons.

45. A speaker that normally sells for $65 is on sale for 25% off. What is the discount and what is the sale price?

46. Convert $3\frac{1}{4}$ pounds to ounces.

47. Find the simple interest after 2 years on $500 at an interest rate of 12%.

48. The number of faculty at a local community college was recently increased from 240 to 276. What is the percent increase?

49. Convert 9000 pounds to tons.

50. Convert 25° Celsius to degrees Fahrenheit.

27. _____

28. _____

29. _____

30. _____

31. _____

32. _____

33. _____

34. _____

35. _____

36. _____

37. _____

38. _____

39. _____

40. _____

41. _____

42. _____

43. _____

44. _____

45. _____

46. _____

47. _____

48. _____

49. _____

50. _____

8

Geometry

The word *geometry* is formed from the Greek words *geo*, meaning Earth, and *metron*, meaning measure. Geometry literally means to measure the Earth. In this chapter we learn about various geometric figures and their properties such as perimeter, area, and volume. Knowledge of geometry can help us solve practical problems in real-life situations. For instance, knowing certain measures of a circular swimming pool allows us to calculate how much water it can hold.

Modern soccer may have its origins as far back as 3000 years. Although soccer (called football in England) was originally banned in England for its vulgarity, perhaps Eton College had the earliest known rules of the game in 1815. Today soccer is undisputed as the most watched and played sport. This past World Cup was watched by 33 billion people around the world.

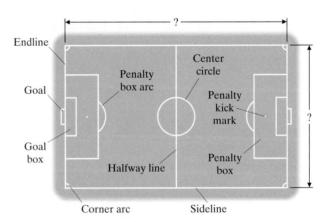

Dimensions of soccer playing fields are determined by many factors, including the ages of the players. In Exercises 69, 70, Section 8.3, and 37, 38, Section 8.5, we calculate the perimeter and area of various-sized fields.

9

Statistics and Probability

We often need to make decisions based on known statistics or the probability of an event occurring. For example, we decide whether or not to bring an umbrella to work based on the probability of rain. We choose an investment based on its mean, or average, return. We can predict which football team will win based on the trend in its previous wins and losses. This chapter reviews presenting data in a usable form on a graph and the basic ideas of statistics and probability.

A tornado is a violent, whirling column of air that is often spawned by the unstable weather conditions that occur during thunderstorms. Although tornadoes are capable of sustaining wind speeds of 250 to more than 300 mph, most tornadoes have wind speeds under 110 mph. The average forward speed of a tornado is 30 mph, but some tornadoes have been known to travel over land at speeds up to 70 mph. The path of a tornado can extend anywhere from a few feet to 100 miles long. Each year in the United States, an average of 800 tornadoes occur, causing an average of 80 deaths. The deadliest tornado in the United States was the Tri-State Tornado Outbreak on March 18, 1925, which killed 689 people and injured over 2000 more in Missouri, Illinois, and Indiana. In Exercises 19–24 on page 599 and the Chapter Highlights on page 627, we will see how graphs can be used to summarize data about tornadoes.

9.1 READING PICTOGRAPHS, BAR GRAPHS, HISTOGRAMS, AND LINE GRAPHS

Often data is presented visually in a graph. In this section, we practice reading several kinds of graphs including pictographs, bar graphs, and line graphs.

Objective **A** Reading Pictographs

A **pictograph** such as the one below is a graph in which pictures or symbols are used. This type of graph contains a key that explains the meaning of the symbol used. An advantage of using a pictograph to display information is that comparisons can easily be made. A disadvantage of using a pictograph is that it is often hard to tell what fractional part of a symbol is shown. For example, in the pictograph below, Sweden shows a part of a symbol, but it's hard to read with any accuracy what fractional part of a symbol is shown.

PRACTICE PROBLEM 1

Use the pictograph shown in Example 1 to answer the following questions:

a. Approximate the amount of nuclear energy that was generated in Japan.

b. Approximate the total nuclear energy generated in Japan and Russia.

EXAMPLE 1 Calculating Nuclear Energy Generated

The following pictograph shows the approximate amount of nuclear energy generated by selected countries in the year 2002. Use this pictograph to answer the questions.

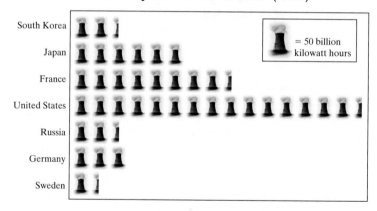

Nuclear Energy Generated by Selected Countries (2002)

Source: Energy Information Administration

a. Approximate the amount of nuclear energy that was generated in Germany.

b. Approximate how much more nuclear energy was generated in France than in Germany.

Solution:

a. Germany corresponds to 3 symbols, and each symbol represents 50 billion kilowatt hours of energy. This means that Germany generated approximately $3 \cdot (50 \text{ billion})$ or 150 billion kilowatt hours of energy.

b. France shows $5\frac{1}{2}$ more symbols than Germany. This means that France generated $5\frac{1}{2} \cdot (50 \text{ billion})$ or 275 billion more kilowatt hours of nuclear energy than Germany.

Answers

1. a. 300 billion kilowatt hours,
b. 425 billion kilowatt hours

Work Practice Problem 1

Objective B Reading Bar Graphs

Another way to visually present data is with a **bar graph.** Bar graphs can appear with vertical bars or horizontal bars. Although we have studied bar graphs in previous sections, we now practice reading the height of the bars contained in a bar graph. An advantage to using bar graphs is that a scale is usually included for greater accuracy. Care must be taken when reading bar graphs, as well as other types of graphs—they may be misleading, as shown later in this section.

EXAMPLE 2 Finding Number of Endangered Species

The following bar graph shows the number of endangered species in the U.S. in 2001. Use this graph to answer the questions.

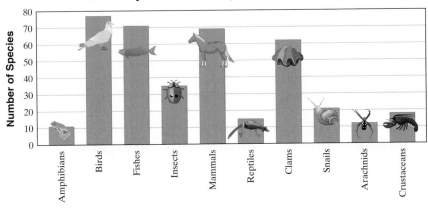

How Many U.S. Animal Species Are Endangered?

Source: U.S. Fish and Wildlife Service

a. Approximate the number of endangered species that are reptiles.
b. Which category has the most endangered species?

Solution:

a. To approximate the number of endangered species that are reptiles, we go to the top of the bar that represents reptiles. From the top of this bar, we move horizontally to the left until the scale is reached. We read the height of the bar on the scale as approximately 15. There are approximately 15 reptile species that are endangered, as shown.

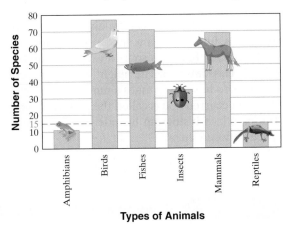

How Many Species Are Endangered?

Source: U.S. Fish and Wildlife Service

b. The most endangered species is represented by the tallest (longest) bar. The tallest bar corresponds to birds.

■ **Work Practice Problem 2**

PRACTICE PROBLEM 2

Use the bar graph in Example 2 to answer the following questions:

a. Approximate the number of endangered species that are insects.

b. Which category shows the fewest endangered species?

Answers
2. a. 35, **b.** amphibians

As mentioned previously, graphs can be misleading. Both graphs below show the same information, but with different scales. Special care should be taken when forming conclusions from the appearance of a graph.

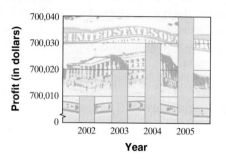

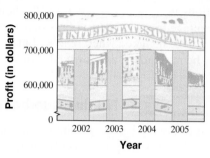

Are profits shown in the graphs above greatly increasing, or are they remaining about the same?

> **Helpful Hint**
>
> Notice the ⩳ symbol on each vertical scale on the previous graphs. Remember that this symbol alerts us that numbers are missing on that scale.

Objective C Reading and Constructing Histograms

Suppose that the test scores of 36 students are summarized in the table below:

Student Scores	Frequency (Number of Students)
40–49	1
50–59	3
60–69	2
70–79	10
80–89	12
90–99	8

The results in the table can be displayed in a histogram. A **histogram** is a special bar graph. The width of each bar represents a range of numbers called a **class interval.** The height of each bar corresponds to how many times a number in the class interval occurred and is called the **class frequency.** The bars in a histogram lie side by side with no space between them.

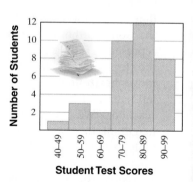

Student Test Scores

PRACTICE PROBLEM 3

Use the histogram on the right to determine how many students scored 70–79 on the test.

Answer

3. 10

EXAMPLE 3 Reading a Histogram on Student Test Scores

Use the preceding histogram to determine how many students scored 50–59 on the test.

Solution: We find the bar representing 50–59. The height of this bar is 3, which means 3 students scored 50–59 on the test.

◻ **Work Practice Problem 3**

EXAMPLE 4   Reading a Histogram on Student Test Scores

Use the preceding histogram to determine how many students scored 80 or above on the test.

Solution: We see that two different bars fit this description. There are 12 students who scored 80–89 and 8 students who scored 90–99. The sum of these two categories is 12 + 8 or 20 students. Thus, 20 students scored 80 or above on the test.

☐ **Work Practice Problem 4**

Now we will look at a way to construct histograms.

The daily high temperatures for 1 month in New Orleans, Louisiana, are recorded in the following list:

85°	90°	95°	89°	88°	94°
87°	90°	95°	92°	95°	94°
82°	92°	96°	91°	94°	92°
89°	89°	90°	93°	95°	91°
88°	90°	88°	86°	93°	89°

The data in this list have not been organized and can be hard to interpret. One way to organize the data is to place it in a **frequency distribution table.** We will do this in Example 5.

EXAMPLE 5   Completing a Frequency Distribution on Temperature

Complete the frequency distribution table for the preceding temperature data.

Solution: Go through the data and place a tally mark in the second column of the table next to the class interval. Then count the tally marks and write each total in the third column of the table.

Class Intervals (Temperatures)	Tally	Class Frequency (Number of Days)
82°–84°	I	1
85°–87°	III	3
88°–90°	⅂⅂⅂⅂ ⅂⅂⅂⅂ I	11
91°–93°	⅂⅂⅂⅂ II	7
94°–96°	⅂⅂⅂⅂ III	8

☐ **Work Practice Problem 5**

EXAMPLE 6   Constructing a Histogram

Construct a histogram from the frequency distribution table in Example 5.

Solution:

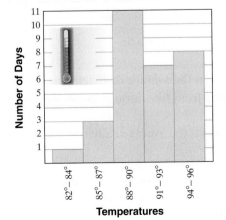

☐ **Work Practice Problem 6**

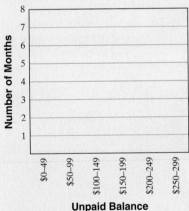
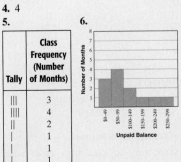

✔**Concept Check** Which of the following sets of data is better suited to representation by a histogram? Explain.

Set 1		Set 2	
Grade on Final	# of Students	Section Number	Avg. Grade on Final
51–60	12	150	78
61–70	18	151	83
71–80	29	152	87
81–90	23	153	73
91–100	25		

Objective D Reading Line Graphs

Another common way to display information with a graph is by using a **line graph.** An advantage of a line graph is that it can be used to visualize relationships between two quantities. A line graph can also be very useful in showing a change over time.

PRACTICE PROBLEM 7

Use the temperature graph in Example 7 to answer the following questions:

a. During what month is the average daily temperature the lowest?

b. During what month is the average daily temperature 25°F?

c. During what months is the average daily temperature greater than 70°F?

EXAMPLE 7 **Reading Temperatures from Line Graph**

The following line graph shows the average daily temperature for each month for Omaha, Nebraska. Use this graph to answer the questions.

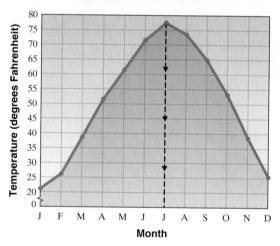

Average Daily Temperature for Omaha, Nebraska

Source: National Climatic Data Center

a. During what month is the average daily temperature the highest?

b. During what month, from July through December, is the average daily temperature 65°F?

c. During what months is the average daily temperature less than 30°F?

Solution:

a. The month with the highest temperature corresponds to the highest point. This is the red point shown on the graph above. We follow this highest point downward to the horizontal month scale and see that this point corresponds to July.

Answers

7. **a.** January, **b.** December,
c. June, July, and August

✔ **Concept Check Answer**

Set 1; the grades are arranged in range of scores.

b. The months July through December correspond to the right side of the graph. We find the 65°F mark on the vertical temperature scale and move to the right until a point on the right side of the graph is reached. From that point, we move downward to the horizontal month scale and read the corresponding month. During the month of September, the average daily temperature was 65°F.

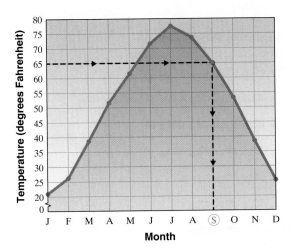

Source: National Climatic Data Center

c. To see what months the temperature is less than 30°F, we find what months correspond to points that fall below the 30°F mark on the vertical scale. These months are January, February, and December.

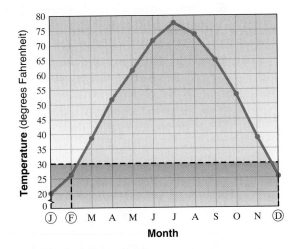

Source: National Climatic Data Center

■ **Work Practice Problem 7**

9.1 EXERCISE SET

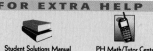
Student Solutions Manual

PH Math/Tutor Center

CD/Video for Review

Math XL
MathXL®

MyMathLab
MyMathLab

Objective **A** *The following pictograph shows the annual automobile production by one plant for the years 1999–2005. Use this graph to answer Exercises 1 through 10. See Example 1.*

Automobile Production

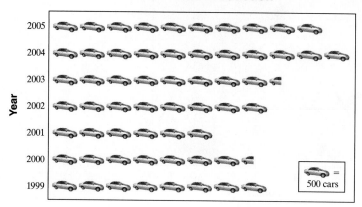

1. In what year was the greatest number of cars manufactured?

2. In what year was the least number of cars manufactured?

3. Approximate the number of cars manufactured in 2002.

4. Approximate the number of cars manufactured in 2003.

5. Approximate the total number of cars manufactured in 2004 and 2005.

6. Approximate the total number of cars manufactured in 2002 and 2003.

7. a. In what year(s) did the production of cars decrease from the previous year?

   b. Find the amount of automobile production decrease for each of these years.

8. a. In what year(s) did the production of cars increase from the previous year?

   b. Find the amount of automobile production increase for each of these years.

9. In what year(s) were 4000 cars manufactured?

10. In what year(s) were 5500 cars manufactured?

The following pictograph shows the average number of ounces of chicken consumed per person per week in the United States. Use this graph to answer Exercises 11 through 18. See Example 1.

Chicken Consumption

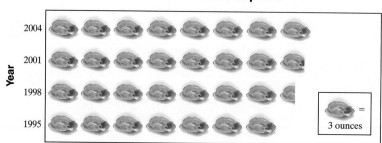

Source: National Agricultural Statistics Service

11. Approximate the number of ounces of chicken consumed per week in 1998.

12. Approximate the number of ounces of chicken consumed per week in 2004.

13. In what year(s) was the number of ounces of chicken consumed per week greater than 21 ounces?

14. In what year(s) was the number of ounces of chicken consumed per week 21 ounces or less?

15. What was the increase in average chicken consumption from 1995 to 2004?

16. What was the increase in average chicken consumption from 1998 to 2004?

17. Suppose that you need to represent 17 ounces on this pictograph. How many symbols represent 17 ounces?

18. Describe a trend in eating habits shown by this graph.

Objective **B** *The following bar graph shows the average number of people killed by tornadoes during the months of the year. Use this graph to answer Exercises 19 through 24. See Example 2.*

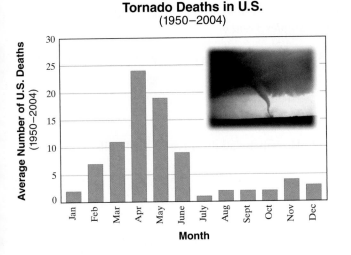

Tornado Deaths in U.S.
(1950–2004)

Source: Storm Prediction Center

19. In which month(s) did the most tornado-related deaths occur?

20. In which month(s) did the fewest tornado-related deaths occur?

21. Approximate the average number of tornado-related deaths that occurred in May.

22. Approximate the average number of tornado-related deaths that occurred in April.

23. In which month(s) did more than 5 deaths occur?

24. In which month(s) did more than 15 deaths occur?

The following horizontal bar graph shows the 2004 population of the world's largest agglomerations (cities plus their suburbs). Use this graph to answer Exercises 25 through 32. See Example 2.

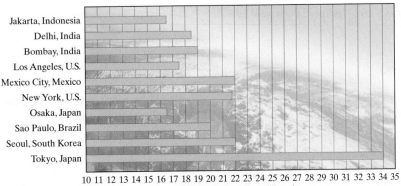

World's Largest Agglomerations

Population (in millions)

Source: Thomas Brinkhoff: *The Principal Agglomerations of the World*, http://www.citypopulation.de, 8/17/2004

25. Estimate the population of Delhi, India.

26. Estimate the population of Seoul, South Korea.

27. Name the city with the largest population and estimate its population.

28. Name the city whose population is between 17 and 18 million and estimate its population.

29. Name the city in the United States with the largest population and estimate its population.

30. Name the city in the graph with the smallest population and estimate its population.

31. How much larger is the population of Tokyo than the population of Sao Paulo?

32. How much larger is the population of Mexico City than the population of Bombay?

Objective C *The following histogram shows the number of miles that each adult, from a survey of 100 adults, drives per week. Use this histogram to answer Exercises 33 through 42. See Examples 3 and 4.*

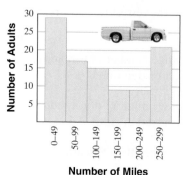

33. How many adults drive 100–149 miles per week?

34. How many adults drive 200–249 miles per week?

35. How many adults drive fewer than 150 miles per week?

36. How many adults drive 200 miles or more per week?

37. How many adults drive 100–199 miles per week?

38. How many adults drive 150–249 miles per week?

39. How many more adults drive 250–299 miles per week than 200–249 miles per week?

40. How many more adults drive 0–49 miles per week than 50–99 miles per week?

41. What is the ratio of adults who drive 150–199 miles per week to the total number of adults surveyed?

42. What is the ratio of adults who drive 50–99 miles per week to the total number of adults surveyed?

The following histogram shows the projected ages of householders for the year 2010. Use this histogram to answer Exercises 43 through 50. For Exercises 45 through 48, estimate to the nearest whole million. See Examples 3 and 4.

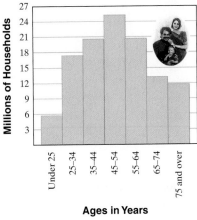

Ages in Years

Source: U.S. Bureau of the Census, *Current Population Reports*

43. The most householders will be in what age range?

44. The least number of householders will be in what age range?

45. How many householders will be 55–64 years old?

46. How many householders will be 35–44 years old?

47. How many householders will be 44 years old or younger?

48. How many householders will be 55 years old or older?

49. Which bar represents the household you expect to be in during the year 2010?

50. How many more householders will be 45–54 years old than 55–64 years old?

The following list shows the golf scores for an amateur golfer. Use this list to complete the frequency distribution table to the right. See Example 5.

78	84	91	93	97
97	95	85	95	96
101	89	92	89	100

	Class Intervals (Scores)	Tally	Class Frequency (Number of Games)
51.	70–79		
52.	80–89		
53.	90–99		
54.	100–109		

Twenty-five people in a survey were asked to give their current checking account balances. Use the balances shown in the following list to complete the frequency distribution table to the right. See Example 5.

$53	$105	$162	$443	$109
$468	$47	$259	$316	$228
$207	$357	$15	$301	$75
$86	$77	$512	$219	$100
$192	$288	$352	$166	$292

	Class Intervals (Account Balances)	Tally	Class Frequency (Number of People)
55.	$0–$99		
56.	$100–$199		
57.	$200–$299		
58.	$300–$399		
59.	$400–$499		
60.	$500–$599		

61. Use the frequency distribution table from Exercises 51 through 54 to construct a histogram. See Example 6.

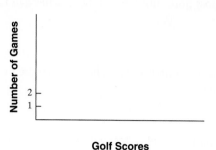

Golf Scores

62. Use the frequency distribution table from Exercises 55 through 60 to construct a histogram. See Example 6.

Account Balances

Objective D *The following line graph shows the World Cup goals per game average during the years shown. Use this graph to answer Exercises 63 through 70. See Example 7.*

63. Find the average number of goals per game in 1994.

64. Find the average number of goals per game in 2002.

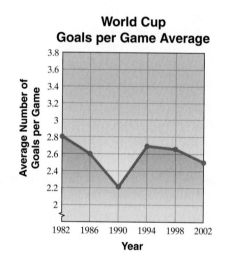

World Cup Goals per Game Average

Source: Soccer America Magazine

65. During what year shown was the average number of goals per game the highest?

66. During what year shown was the average number of goals per game the lowest?

67. Between 1998 and 2002, did the average number of goals per game increase or decrease?

68. Between 1990 and 1994, did the average number of goals per game increase or decrease?

69. During what year(s) was the average goals per game less than 2.5?

70. During what year(s) was the average goals per game greater than 2.6?

Review

Find each percent. See Sections 6.3 and 6.4.

71. 30% of 12

72. 45% of 120

73. 10% of 62

74. 95% of 50

Write each fraction as a percent. See Section 6.2.

75. $\dfrac{1}{4}$

76. $\dfrac{2}{5}$

77. $\dfrac{17}{50}$

78. $\dfrac{9}{10}$

Concept Extensions

The following double-line graph shows temperature highs and lows for a week. Use this graph to answer Exercises 79 through 84.

79. What was the high temperature reading on Thursday?

80. What was the low temperature reading on Thursday?

81. What day was the temperature the lowest? What was this low temperature?

82. What day of the week was the temperature the highest? What was this high temperature?

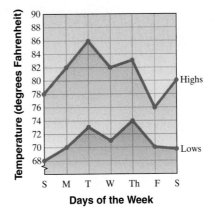

83. On what day of the week was the difference between the high temperature and the low temperature the greatest? What was this difference in temperature?

84. On what day of the week was the difference between the high temperature and the low temperature the least? What was this difference in temperature?

85. True or false? With a bar graph, the width of the bar is just as important as the height of the bar. Explain your answer.

9.2 READING CIRCLE GRAPHS

Objective **A** Reading Circle Graphs

In Section 6.1, the following **circle graph** was shown. This particular graph shows the average favorite cookie for every 100 people.

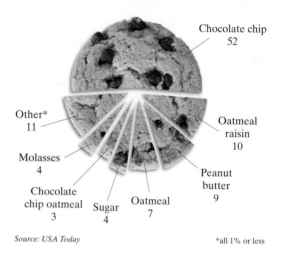

Source: USA Today   *all 1% or less

Each sector of the graph (shaped like a piece of pie) shows a category and the relative size of the category. In other words, the most popular cookie is the chocolate chip cookie, and it is represented by the largest sector.

PRACTICE PROBLEM 1

Find the ratio of people preferring oatmeal raisin cookies to total people. Write the ratio as a fraction in simplest form.

EXAMPLE 1 Find the ratio of people preferring chocolate chip cookies to total people. Write the ratio as a fraction in simplest form.

Solution: The ratio is

$$\frac{\text{people preferring chocolate chip}}{\text{total people}} = \frac{52}{100} = \frac{13}{25}$$

◻ **Work Practice Problem 1**

A circle graph is often used to show percents in different categories, with the whole circle representing 100%.

PRACTICE PROBLEM 2

Using the circle graph shown in Example 2, determine the percent of Americans that have two or more working computers at home.

EXAMPLE 2 Using a Circle Graph

The following circle graph shows the percent of Americans with various numbers of working computers at home. Using the circle graph shown, determine the percent of Americans that have one or more working computers at home.

Number of Working Computers at Home

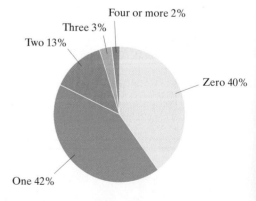

Source: UCLA Center for Communication Policy

Answers

1. $\frac{1}{10}$, **2.** 18%

Solution: To find this percent, we add the percents corresponding to one, two, three, and four or more working computers at home. The percent of Americans that have one or more working computers at home is

$$42\% + 13\% + 3\% + 2\% = 60\%$$

◼ **Work Practice Problem 2**

> **Helpful Hint**
>
> Since a circle graph represents a whole, the percents should add to 100% or 1. Notice this is true for Example 2.

EXAMPLE 3 **Finding Percent of Population**

In 2005, the population of the United States is approximately 295,500,000. Using the circle graph from Example 2, find the number of Americans that have no working computers at home.

Solution: We use the percent equation.

amount	=	percent	·	base

$$\text{amount} = 0.40 \cdot 295,500,000$$
$$= 0.40(295,500,000) = 118,200,000$$

Thus, 118,200,000 Americans have no working computer at home.

◼ **Work Practice Problem 3**

✔ **Concept Check** Can the following data be represented by a circle graph? Why or why not?

Responses to the Question, "In Which Activities Are You Involved?"	
Intramural sports	60%
On-campus job	42%
Fraternity/sorority	27%
Academic clubs	21%
Music programs	14%

Objective **B** **Drawing Circle Graphs**

To draw a circle graph, we use the fact that a whole circle contains 360° (degrees).

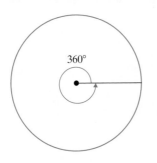

360°

PRACTICE PROBLEM 3

Using the circle graph from Example 2, find the number of Americans that have four or more working computers at home.

Answer

3. 5,910,000 Americans

✔ **Concept Check Answer**

no; the percents add up to more than 100%

Use the data shown to draw a circle graph.

Freshmen	30%
Sophomores	27%
Juniors	25%
Seniors	18%

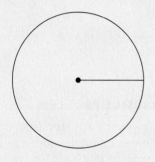

EXAMPLE 4 Drawing Circle Graph for U.S. Armed Forces Personnel

The following table shows the percent of U.S. armed forces personnel that are in each branch of service. (*Source:* U.S. Department of Defense)

Branch of Service	Percent
Army	33
Navy	27
Marine Corps	12
Air Force	25
Coast Guard	3

Draw a circle graph showing this data.

Solution: First we find the number of degrees in each sector representing each branch of service. Remember that the whole circle contains 360°. (We will round degrees to the nearest whole.)

Sector	Degrees in Each Sector
Army	$33\% \times 360° = 0.33 \times 360° = 118.8° \approx 119°$
Navy	$27\% \times 360° = 0.27 \times 360° = 97.2° \approx 97°$
Marine Corps	$12\% \times 360° = 0.12 \times 360° = 43.2° \approx 43°$
Air Force	$25\% \times 360° = 0.25 \times 360° = 90° = 90°$
Coast Guard	$3\% \times 360° = 0.03 \times 360° = 10.8° \approx 11°$

Next we draw a circle and mark its center. Then we draw a line from the center of the circle to the circle itself.

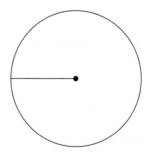

To construct the sectors, we will use a **protractor.** We place the hole in the protractor over the center of the circle. Then we adjust the protractor so that 0° on the protractor is aligned with the line that we drew.

It makes no difference which sector we draw first. To construct the "Army" sector, we find 119° on the protractor and mark our circle. Then we remove the protractor and use this mark to draw a second line from the center to the circle itself.

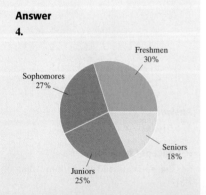

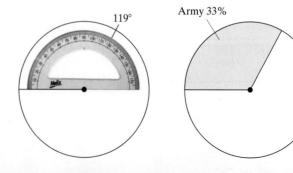

To construct the "Navy" sector, we follow the same procedure as above, except that we line up 0° with the second line we drew and mark the protractor at 97°.

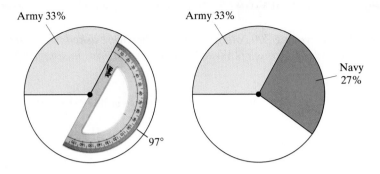

We continue in this manner until the circle graph is complete.

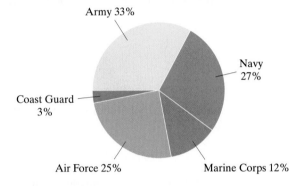

■ **Work Practice Problem 4**

✔ **Concept Check** True or false? The larger a sector in a circle graph, the larger the percent of the total it represents. Explain your answer.

FOR EXTRA HELP

Student Solutions Manual

PH Math/Tutor Center

CD/Video for Review

Math XL
MathXL®

MyMathLab
MyMathLab

Objective A *The following circle graph is a result of surveying 700 college students. They were asked where they live while attending college. Use this graph to answer Exercises 1 through 6. Write all ratios as fractions in simplest form. See Example 1.*

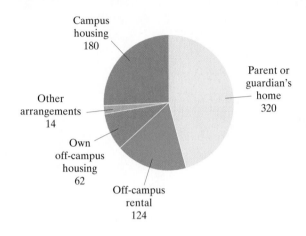

Campus housing 180
Parent or guardian's home 320
Other arrangements 14
Own off-campus housing 62
Off-campus rental 124

1. Where do most of these college students live?

2. Besides the category "Other Arrangements," where do least of these college students live?

3. Find the ratio of students living in campus housing to total students.

4. Find the ratio of students living in off-campus rentals to total students.

5. Find the ratio of students living in campus housing to students living in a parent or guardian's home.

6. Find the ratio of students living in off-campus rentals to students living in a parent or guardian's home.

The following circle graph shows the percent of the land area of the continents of Earth. Use this graph for Exercises 7 through 14. See Examples 2 and 3.

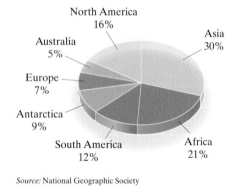

North America 16%
Australia 5%
Europe 7%
Antarctica 9%
South America 12%
Africa 21%
Asia 30%

Source: National Geographic Society

7. Which continent is the largest?

8. Which continent is the smallest?

9. What percent of the land on Earth is accounted for by Asia and Europe together?

10. What percent of the land on Earth is accounted for by North and South America?

The total amount of land on Earth is approximately 57,000,000 square miles. Use the graph to find the area of the continents given in Exercises 11 through 14.

11. Asia   **12.** South America   **13.** Australia   **14.** Europe

608

The following circle graph shows the percent of the types of books available at Midway Memorial Library. Use this graph for Exercises 15 through 24. See Examples 2 and 3.

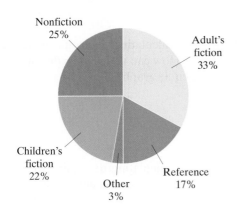

Nonfiction 25%

Adult's fiction 33%

Children's fiction 22%

Other 3%

Reference 17%

🔘 **15.** What percent of books are classified as some type of fiction?

16. What percent of books are nonfiction or reference?

🔘 **17.** What is the second-largest category of books?

18. What is the third-largest category of books?

If this library has 125,600 books, find how many books are in each category given in Exercises 19 through 24.

19. Nonfiction

20. Reference

21. Children's fiction

22. Adult's fiction

23. Reference or other

24. Nonfiction or other

Objective Ⓑ *Draw a circle graph to represent the information given in each table. See Example 4.*

25.

2004 Light Vehicle Sales by Vehicle Origin	
Country of Origin	**Percent**
United States	58
Asia	36
Europe	6
(*Source:* Ward's AutoInfoBank)	

26.

Number of Times the "Are We There Yet?" Question Is Asked to Parents During Road Trips:	
Never	20%
Once	11%
2–5 times	36%
6–10 times	14%
More than 10 times	19%
(*Source:* KRC Research for Goodyear Tire & Rubber Co.)	

Review

Write the prime factorization of each number. See Section 2.2.

27. 20   **28.** 25   **29.** 40   **30.** 16   **31.** 85   **32.** 105

Concept Extensions

The following circle graph shows the relative sizes of the great oceans.

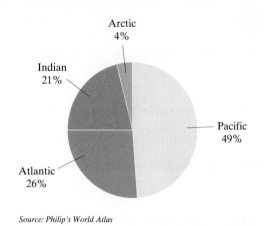

Source: *Philip's World Atlas*

33. Without calculating, determine which ocean is the largest. How can you answer this question by looking at the circle graph?

34. Without calculating, determine which ocean is the smallest. How can you answer this question by looking at the circle graph?

These oceans together make up 264,489,800 square kilometers of the Earth's surface. Find the square kilometers for each ocean.

35. Pacific Ocean   **36.** Atlantic Ocean   **37.** Indian Ocean   **38.** Arctic Ocean

Answer the question. See the Concept Check in the section.

39. True or false? The smaller a sector in a circle graph, the smaller the percent of the total it represents.

40. Can the data below be represented by a circle graph?

Type of Ice Cream Preferred:	
Vanilla	50%
Chocolate	46%

Explain.

INTEGRATED REVIEW Sections 9.1–9.2

Reading Graphs

The following pictograph shows the average number of pounds of beef and veal consumed per person per year in the United States. Use this graph to answer Exercises 1 through 4.

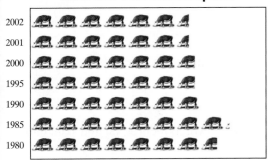

Beef and Veal Consumption

2002, 2001, 2000, 1995, 1990, 1985, 1980

Each  represents 10 pounds

Source: U.S. Department of Agriculture

1. Approximate the number of pounds of beef and veal consumed per person in 1995.

2. Approximate the number of pounds of beef and veal consumed per person in 1980.

3. How much more beef was consumed in 1980 than in 2002?

4. In what year(s) was the number of pounds consumed the least?

The following bar graph shows the highest U.S. dams. Use this graph to answer Exercises 5 through 8.

5. Name the U.S. dam with the greatest height and estimate its height.

6. Name the U.S. dam whose height is between 625 and 650 feet and estimate its height.

7. Estimate how much higher the Hoover Dam is than the Glen Canyon Dam.

8. How many U.S. dams have heights over 700 feet?

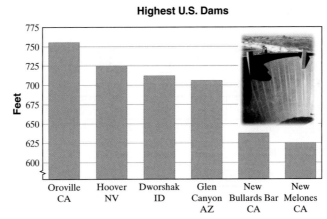

Highest U.S. Dams

Feet

Oroville CA, Hoover NV, Dworshak ID, Glen Canyon AZ, New Bullards Bar CA, New Melones CA

Source: Committee on Register of Dams

The following line graph shows the daily high temperatures for 1 week in Annapolis, Maryland. Use this graph to answer Exercises 9 through 12.

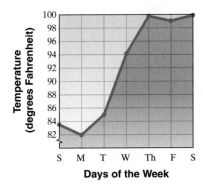

Temperature (degrees Fahrenheit)

S M T W Th F S

Days of the Week

9. Name the day(s) of the week with the highest temperature and give that high temperature.

10. Name the day(s) of the week with the lowest temperature and give that low temperature.

11. On what days of the week was the temperature less than 90° Fahrenheit?

12. On what days of the week was the temperature greater than 90° Fahrenheit?

Answers

1.

2.

3.

4.

5.

6.

7.

8.

9.

10.

11.

12.

611

13. _____

14. _____

15. _____

16. _____

17. see table

18. see table

19. see table

20. see table

21. see table

22. see graph

The following circle graph shows the type of beverage milk consumed in the United States. Use this graph for Exercises 13 through 16. If a store in Kerrville, Texas, sells 200 quart containers of milk per week, estimate how many quart containers are sold in each category below.

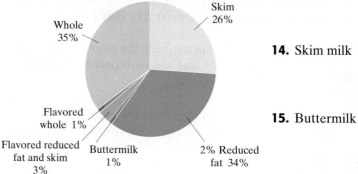

Types of Beverage Milk Consumed

Skim 26%

Whole 35%

Flavored whole 1%

Flavored reduced fat and skim 3%

Buttermilk 1%

2% Reduced fat 34%

Source: U.S. Department of Agriculture

13. Whole milk

14. Skim milk

15. Buttermilk

16. Flavored reduced fat and skim milk

The following list shows weekly quiz scores for a student in basic college mathematics. Use this list to complete the frequency distribution table.

50	80	71	83	86
67	89	93	88	97
	53	90		
75	80	78	93	99

	Class Intervals (Scores)	Tally	Class Frequency (Number of Quizzes)
17.	50–59		
18.	60–69		
19.	70–79		
20.	80–89		
21.	90–99		

22. Use the table from Exercises 17 through 21 to construct a histogram.

Number of Quizzes

2

1

Quiz Scores

9.3 MEAN, MEDIAN, AND MODE

Objectives

A Find the Mean of a List of Numbers.

B Find the Median of a List of Numbers.

C Find the Mode of a List of Numbers.

Objective **A** Finding the Mean

Sometimes we want to summarize data by displaying them in a graph, but sometimes it is also desirable to be able to describe a set of data, or a set of numbers, by a single "middle" number. Three such **measures of central tendency** are the **mean,** the **median,** and the **mode.**

The most common measure of central tendency is the mean (sometimes called the "arithmetic mean" or the "average"). Recall that we first introduced finding the average of a list of numbers in Section 1.7.

The **mean (average)** of a set of number items is the sum of the items divided by the number of items.

$$\text{mean} = \frac{\text{sum of items}}{\text{number of items}}$$

EXAMPLE 1 Finding the Mean Time in an Experiment

Seven students in a psychology class conducted an experiment on mazes. Each student was given a pencil and asked to successfully complete the same maze. The timed results are below:

Student	Ann	Thanh	Carlos	Jesse	Melinda	Ramzi	Dayni
Time (Seconds)	13.2	11.8	10.7	16.2	15.9	13.8	18.5

a. Who completed the maze in the shortest time? Who completed the maze in the longest time?

b. Find the mean time.

c. How many students took longer than the mean time? How many students took shorter than the mean time?

Solution:

a. Carlos completed the maze in 10.7 seconds, the shortest time. Dayni completed the maze in 18.5 seconds, the longest time.

b. To find the mean (or average), we find the sum of the number items and divide by 7, the number of items.

$$\text{mean} = \frac{13.2 + 11.8 + 10.7 + 16.2 + 15.9 + 13.8 + 18.5}{7}$$

$$= \frac{100.1}{7} = 14.3$$

c. Three students, Jesse, Melinda, and Dayni, had times longer than the mean time. Four students, Ann, Thanh, Carlos, and Ramzi, had times shorter than the mean time.

■ Work Practice Problem 1

✔ **Concept Check** Estimate the mean of the following set of data:

5, 10, 10, 10, 10, 15

Often in college, the calculation of a **grade point average** (GPA) is a **weighted mean** and is calculated as shown in Example 2.

PRACTICE PROBLEM 1

Find the mean of the following test scores: 77, 85, 86, 91, and 88.

Answer
1. 85.4

✔ **Concept Check Answer**
10

613

PRACTICE PROBLEM 2

Find the grade point average if the following grades were earned in one semester.

Grade	Credit Hours
A	2
C	4
B	5
D	2
A	2

EXAMPLE 2 Calculating Grade Point Average (GPA)

The following grades were earned by a student during one semester. Find the student's grade point average.

Course	Grade	Credit Hours
College mathematics	A	3
Biology	B	3
English	A	3
PE	C	1
Social studies	D	2

Solution: To calculate the grade point average, we need to know the point values for the different possible grades. The point values of grades commonly used in colleges and universities are given below:

A: 4,   B: 3,   C: 2,   D: 1,   F: 0

Now, to find the grade point average, we multiply the number of credit hours for each course by the point value of each grade. The grade point average is the sum of these products divided by the sum of the credit hours.

Course	Grade	Point Value of Grade	Credit Hours	Point Value · Credit Hours
College mathematics	A	4	3	12
Biology	B	3	3	9
English	A	4	3	12
PE	C	2	1	2
Social studies	D	1	2	2
		Totals:	12	37

$$\text{grade point average} = \frac{37}{12} \approx 3.08 \text{ rounded to two decimal places}$$

The student earned a grade point average of 3.08.

■ **Work Practice Problem 2**

Objective B Finding the Median

You may have noticed that a very low number or a very high number can affect the mean of a list of numbers. Because of this, you may sometimes want to use another measure of central tendency. A second measure of central tendency is called the **median.** The median of a list of numbers is not affected by a low or high number in the list.

The **median** of a set of numbers in numerical order is the middle number. If the number of items is odd, the median is the middle number. If the number of items is even, the median is the mean of the two middle numbers.

PRACTICE PROBLEM 3

Find the median of the list of numbers: 7, 9, 13, 23, 24, 35, 38, 41, 43

EXAMPLE 3 Find the median of the following list of numbers:

25, 54, 56, 57, 60, 71, 98

Solution: Because this list is in numerical order, the median is the middle number, 57.

■ **Work Practice Problem 3**

Answers
2. 2.73, 3. 24

EXAMPLE 4 Find the median of the following list of scores: 67, 91, 75, 86, 55, 91

Solution: First we list the scores in numerical order and then find the middle number.

55, 67, 75, 86, 91, 91

Since there is an even number of scores, there are two middle numbers, 75 and 86. The median is the mean of the two middle numbers.

$$\text{median} = \frac{75 + 86}{2} = 80.5$$

The median is 80.5.

Work Practice Problem 4

Helpful Hint
Don't forget to write the numbers in order from smallest to largest before finding the median.

Objective **C** **Finding the Mode**

The last common measure of central tendency is called the **mode.**

The **mode** of a set of numbers is the number that occurs most often. (It is possible for a set of numbers to have more than one mode or to have no mode.)

EXAMPLE 5 Find the mode of the list of numbers:

11, 14, 14, 16, 31, 56, 65, 77, 77, 78, 79

Solution: There are two numbers that occur the most often. They are 14 and 77. This list of numbers has two modes, 14 and 77.

Work Practice Problem 5

EXAMPLE 6 Find the median and the mode of the following set of numbers. These numbers were high temperatures for 14 consecutive days in a city in Montana.

76, 80, 85, 86, 89, 87, 82, 77, 76, 79, 82, 89, 89, 92

Solution: First we write the numbers in numerical order.

76, 76, 77, 79, 80, 82, 82, 85, 86, 87, 89, 89, 89, 92

Since there is an even number of items, the median is the mean of the two middle numbers, 82 and 85.

$$\text{median} = \frac{82 + 85}{2} = 83.5$$

The mode is 89, since 89 occurs most often.

Work Practice Problem 6

✔**Concept Check** True or false? Every set of numbers *must* have a mean, median, and mode. Explain your answer.

Helpful Hint
Don't forget that it is possible for a list of numbers to have no mode. For example, the list

2, 4, 5, 6, 8, 9

has no mode. There is no number or numbers that occur more often than the others.

PRACTICE PROBLEM 4
Find the median of the list of scores:

43, 89, 78, 65, 95, 95, 88, 71

PRACTICE PROBLEM 5
Find the mode of the list of numbers:

9, 10, 10, 13, 15, 15, 15, 17, 18, 18, 20

PRACTICE PROBLEM 6
Find the median and the mode of the list of numbers:

26, 31, 15, 15, 26, 30, 16, 18, 15, 35

Answers
4. 83,   **5.** 15,   **6.** median: 22; mode: 15

✔ **Concept Check Answer**
false; a set of numbers may have no mode.

Mental Math

State the mean for each list of numbers.

1. 3, 5   **2.** 10, 20   **3.** 1, 3, 5   **4.** 7, 7, 7

9.3 EXERCISE SET

FOR EXTRA HELP

Student Solutions Manual   PH Math/Tutor Center   CD/Video for Review   Math XL MathXL®   MyMathLab MyMathLab

Objectives A B C **Mixed Practice** *For each set of numbers, find the mean, the median, and the mode. If necessary, round the mean to one decimal place. See Examples 1 and 3 through 6.*

1. 21, 28, 16, 42, 38

2. 42, 35, 36, 40, 50

 3. 7.6, 8.2, 8.2, 9.6, 5.7, 9.1

4. 4.9, 7.1, 6.8, 6.8, 5.3, 4.9

5. 0.2, 0.3, 0.5, 0.6, 0.6, 0.9, 0.2, 0.7, 1.1

6. 0.6, 0.6, 0.8, 0.4, 0.5, 0.3, 0.7, 0.8, 0.1

7. 231, 543, 601, 293, 588, 109, 334, 268

8. 451, 356, 478, 776, 892, 500, 467, 780

The eight tallest buildings in the world are listed in the following table. Use this table to answer Exercises 9 through 12. If necessary, round results to one decimal place. See Examples 1 and 3 through 6.

9. Find the mean height of the five tallest buildings.

10. Find the median height of the five tallest buildings.

11. Find the median height of the eight tallest buildings.

12. Find the mean height of the eight tallest buildings.

Building	Height (in Feet)
Petronas Tower 1, Kuala Lumpur	1483
Petronas Tower 2, Kuala Lumpur	1483
Sears Tower, Chicago	1450
Jin Mao Building, Shanghai	1381
Citic Plaza, Guangzhou	1283
Shun Hing Square, Shenzhen	1260
Empire State Building, New York	1250
Central Plaza, Hong Kong	1227
(*Source:* Council on Tall Buildings and Urban Habitat)	

13. Given the building heights, explain how you know, without calculating, that the answer to Exercise 10 is more than the answer to Exercise 11.

14. Given the building heights, explain how you know, without calculating, that the answer to Exercise 12 is less than the answer to Exercise 9.

For Exercises 15 through 18, the grades are given for a student for a particular semester. Find the grade point average. If necessary, round the grade point average to the nearest hundredth. See Example 2.

15.

Grade	Credit Hours
B	3
C	3
A	4
C	4

16.

Grade	Credit Hours
D	1
F	1
C	4
B	5

17.

Grade	Credit Hours
A	3
A	3
B	4
B	1
B	2

18.

Grade	Credit Hours
B	2
B	2
A	3
C	3
B	3

During an experiment, the following times (in seconds) were recorded:

   7.8, 6.9, 7.5, 4.7, 6.9, 7.0

19. Find the mean. Round to the nearest tenth.

20. Find the median.

21. Find the mode.

In a mathematics class, the following test scores were recorded for a student: 86, 95, 91, 74, 77, 85.

22. Find the mean. Round to the nearest hundredth.

23. Find the median.

24. Find the mode.

The following pulse rates were recorded for a group of 15 students: 78, 80, 66, 68, 71, 64, 82, 71, 70, 65, 70, 75, 77, 86, 72.

25. Find the mean.

26. Find the median.

27. Find the mode.

28. How many rates were higher than the mean?

29. How many rates were lower than the mean?

Review

Write each fraction in simplest form. See Section 2.3.

30. $\dfrac{12}{20}$

31. $\dfrac{6}{18}$

32. $\dfrac{4}{36}$

33. $\dfrac{18}{30}$

34. $\dfrac{35}{100}$

35. $\dfrac{55}{75}$

Concept Extensions

Find the missing numbers in each set of numbers.

36. 16, 18, _____, _____, _____. The mode is 21. The median is 20.

37. _____, _____, _____, 40, _____. The mode is 35. The median is 37. The mean is 38.

 38. Write a list of numbers for which you feel the median would be a better measure of central tendency than the mean.

STUDY SKILLS BUILDER

Tips for Studying for an Exam

To prepare for an exam, try the following study techniques.

- Start the study process days before your exam.
- Make sure that you are up-to-date on your assignments.
- If there is a topic that you are unsure of, use one of the many resources that are available to you. For example,

  See your instructor.

  Visit a learning resource center on campus.

  Read the textbook material and examples on the topic.

  View a video on the topic.

- Reread your notes and carefully review the Chapter Highlights at the end of any chapter.
- Work the review exercises at the end of the chapter. Check your answers and correct any mistakes. If you have trouble, use a resource listed above.
- Find a quiet place to take the Chapter Test found at the end of the chapter. Do not use any resources when taking this sample test. This way, you will have a clear indication of how prepared you are for your exam.

Check your answers and make sure that you correct any missed exercises.

- Get lots of rest the night before the exam. It's hard to show how well you know the material if your brain is foggy from lack of sleep.

Good luck and keep a positive attitude.

Let's see how you did on your last exam.

1. How many days before your last exam did you start studying?

2. Were you up-to-date on your assignments at that time or did you need to catch up on assignments?

3. List the most helpful text supplement (if you used one).

4. List the most helpful campus supplement (if you used one).

5. List your process for preparing for a mathematics test.

6. Was this process helpful? In other words, were you satisfied with your performance on your exam?

7. If not, what changes can you make in your process that will make it more helpful to you?

9.4 COUNTING AND INTRODUCTION TO PROBABILITY

Objectives

A Use a Tree Diagram to Count Outcomes.

B Find the Probability of an Event.

Objective A Using a Tree Diagram

In our daily conversations, we often talk about the likelihood or the **probability** of a given result occurring. For example:

The *chance* of thundershowers is 70 percent.

What are the *odds* that the Saints will go to the Super Bowl?

What is the *probability* that you will finish cleaning your room today?

Each of these chance happenings—thundershowers, the New Orleans Saints playing in the Super Bowl, and cleaning your room today—is called an **experiment.** The possible results of an experiment are called **outcomes.** For example, flipping a coin is an experiment, and the possible outcomes are heads (H) or tails (T).

One way to picture the outcomes of an experiment is to draw a **tree diagram.** Each outcome is shown on a separate branch. For example, the outcomes of flipping a coin are

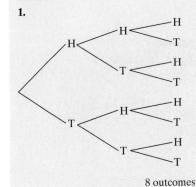

Heads   Tails

EXAMPLE 1 Draw a tree diagram for tossing a coin twice. Then use the diagram to find the number of possible outcomes.

Solution: There are 4 possible outcomes when tossing a coin twice.

Work Practice Problem 1

PRACTICE PROBLEM 1

Draw a tree diagram for tossing a coin three times. Then use the diagram to find the number of possible outcomes.

Answer

1.

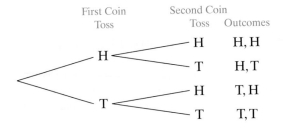

8 outcomes

619

PRACTICE PROBLEM 2

Draw a tree diagram for an experiment consisting of tossing a coin and then rolling a die. Then use the diagram to find the number of possible outcomes.

EXAMPLE 2 Draw a tree diagram for an experiment consisting of rolling a die and then tossing a coin. Then use the diagram to find the number of possible outcomes.

Die

Solution: Recall that a die has six sides and that each side represents a number, 1 through 6.

Roll a Die	Toss a coin	Outcomes
1	H	1, H
	T	1, T
2	H	2, H
	T	2, T
3	H	3, H
	T	3, T
4	H	4, H
	T	4, T
5	H	5, H
	T	5, T
6	H	6, H
	T	6, T

There are 12 possible outcomes for rolling a die and then tossing a coin.

🔲 **Work Practice Problem 2**

Any number of outcomes considered together are called an **event.** For example, when tossing a coin twice, H, H is an event. The event is tossing heads first and tossing heads second. Another event would be tossing tails first and then heads (T, H), and so on.

Objective B Finding the Probability of an Event

As we mentioned earlier, the **probability of an event is a measure of the chance or likelihood of it occurring.** For example, if a coin is tossed, what is the probability that heads occurs? Since one of two equally likely possible outcomes is heads, the probability is $\frac{1}{2}$.

The Probability of an Event

$$\text{probability of an event} = \frac{\text{number of ways that the event can occur}}{\text{number of possible outcomes}}$$

Answer

2.

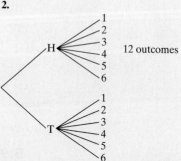

12 outcomes

Helpful Hint

Note from the definition of probability that the probability of an event is always between 0 and 1, inclusive (i.e., including 0 and 1). A probability of 0 means that an event won't occur, and a probability of 1 means that an event is certain to occur.

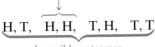 If a coin is tossed twice, find the probability of tossing heads and then heads (H, H).

Solution: 1 way the event can occur

$$\underbrace{\text{H,T, } \overbrace{\text{H,H,}}^{\downarrow} \text{ T,H, T,T}}_{\text{4 possible outcomes}}$$

probability $= \dfrac{1}{4}$ Number of ways the event can occur / Number of possible outcomes

The probability of tossing heads and then heads is $\dfrac{1}{4}$.

■ **Work Practice Problem 3**

EXAMPLE 4 If a die is rolled one time, find the probability of rolling a 3 or a 4.

Solution: Recall that there are 6 possible outcomes when rolling a die.

2 ways that the event can occur

$$\text{possible outcomes: } \underbrace{1, \quad 2, \quad \overset{\downarrow}{3}, \quad \overset{\downarrow}{4}, \quad 5, \quad 6}_{\text{6 possible outcomes}}$$

probability of a 3 or a 4 $= \dfrac{2}{6}$ Number of ways the event can occur / Number of possible outcomes

$= \dfrac{1}{3}$ Simplest form

■ **Work Practice Problem 4**

✔ **Concept Check** Suppose you have calculated a probability of $\dfrac{11}{9}$. How do you know that you have made an error in your calculation?

EXAMPLE 5 Find the probability of choosing a red marble from a box containing 1 red, 1 yellow, and 2 blue marbles.

Solution: 1 way that event can occur

probability $= \dfrac{1}{4}$

■ **Work Practice Problem 5**

PRACTICE PROBLEM 3

If a coin is tossed three times, find the probability of tossing heads, then tails, then tails (H, T, T).

PRACTICE PROBLEM 4

If a die is rolled one time, find the probability of rolling a 1 or a 2.

PRACTICE PROBLEM 5

Use the diagram from Example 5 and find the probability of choosing a blue marble from the box.

Answers

3. $\dfrac{1}{8}$,   4. $\dfrac{1}{3}$,   5. $\dfrac{1}{2}$

✔ **Concept Check Answer**

The number of ways an event can occur can't be larger than the number of possible outcomes.

Mental Math

If a coin is tossed once, find the probability of each event.

1. The coin lands heads up.

2. The coin lands tails up.

If the spinner shown is spun once, find the probability of each event.

3. The spinner stops on red.

4. The spinner stops on blue.

9.4 EXERCISE SET

Objective A *Draw a tree diagram for each experiment. Then use the diagram to find the number of possible outcomes. See Examples 1 and 2.*

1. Choosing a vowel (a, e, i, o, u) and then a number (1, 2, or 3)

2. Choosing a number (1 or 2) and then a vowel (a, e, i, o, u)

3. Spinning Spinner A once

4. Spinning Spinner B once

Spinner A

Spinner B

5. Spinning Spinner B twice

6. Spinning Spinner A twice

7. Spinning Spinner A and then Spinner B

8. Spinning Spinner B and then Spinner A

9. Tossing a coin and then spinning Spinner B

10. Tossing a coin and then spinning Spinner A

Objective **B** *If a single die is tossed once, find the probability of each event. See Examples 3 through 5.*

11. A 5

12. A 7

13. A 1 or a 4

14. A 2 or a 3

15. An even number

16. An odd number

17. A number greater than 1

18. A number less than 5

Suppose the spinner shown is spun once. Find the probability of each event. See Examples 3 through 5.

19. The result of the spin is 2.

20. The result of the spin is 3.

21. The result of a spin is 1, 2, or 3.

22. The result of a spin is not 3.

23. The result of the spin is an odd number.

24. The result of the spin is an even number.

If a single choice is made from the bag of marbles shown, find the probability of each event. See Examples 3 through 5.

25. A red marble is chosen.

26. A blue marble is chosen.

27. A yellow marble is chosen.

28. A green marble is chosen.

29. A blue or red marble is chosen.

30. A red or yellow marble is chosen.

A new drug is being tested that is supposed to lower blood pressure. This drug was given to 200 people and the results are below.

Lower Blood Pressure	Higher Blood Pressure	Blood Pressure Not Changed
152	38	10

31. If a person is testing this drug, what is the probability that their blood pressure will be higher?

32. If a person is testing this drug, what is the probability that their blood pressure will be lower?

33. If a person is testing this drug, what is the probability that their blood pressure will not change?

34. What is the sum of the answers to exercises 25, 26, and 27? In your own words, explain why.

Review

Perform each indicated operation. See Sections 2.4, 2.5, and 3.3.

35. $\dfrac{1}{2} + \dfrac{1}{3}$

36. $\dfrac{7}{10} - \dfrac{2}{5}$

37. $\dfrac{1}{2} \cdot \dfrac{1}{3}$

38. $\dfrac{7}{10} \div \dfrac{2}{5}$

39. $5 \div \dfrac{3}{4}$

40. $\dfrac{3}{5} \cdot 10$

Concept Extensions

Recall that a deck of cards contains 52 cards. These cards consist of four suits (hearts, spades, clubs, and diamonds) of each of the following: 2, 3, 4, 5, 6, 7, 8, 9, 10, jack, queen, king, and ace. If a card is chosen from a deck of cards, find the probability of each event.

41. The king of hearts

42. The 10 of spades

43. A king

44. A 10

45. A heart

46. A club

47. A red card

48. A king or queen

Two dice are tossed. Find the probability of each sum of the dice. (Hint: Draw a tree diagram of the possibilities of two tosses of a die, and then find the sum of the numbers on each branch.)

49. A sum of 4

50. A sum of 11

51. A sum of 13

52. A sum of 2

Solve. See the Concept Check in this section.

53. In your own words, explain why the probability of an event cannot be greater than 1.

54. In your own words, explain when the probability of an event is 0.

 CHAPTER 9   Group Activity

Sections 9.1, 9.3

This activity may be completed by working in groups or individually.

How often have you read an article in a newspaper or in a magazine that included results from a survey or poll? Surveys seem to have become very popular ways of getting feedback on anything from a political candidate, to a new product, to services offered by a health club. In this activity, you will conduct a survey and analyze the results.

1. Conduct a survey of 30 students in one of your classes. Ask each student to report his or her age.

2. Classify each age according to the following categories: under 20, 20 to 24, 25 to 29, 30 to 39, 40 to 49, and 50 or over. Tally the number of your survey respondents that fall into each category. Make a bar graph of your results. What does this graph tell you about the ages of your survey respondents?

3. Find the average age of your survey respondents.

4. Find the median age of your survey respondents.

5. Find the mode of the ages of your survey respondents.

6. Compare the mean, median, and mode of your age data. Are these measures similar? Which is largest? Which is smallest? If there is a noticeable difference between any of these measures, can you explain why?

Chapter 9 Vocabulary Check

Fill in each blank with one of the words or phrases listed below.

outcomes	bar	experiment	mean	tree diagram
pictograph	line	class interval	median	probability
histogram	circle	class frequency	mode	

1. A _____ graph presents data using vertical or horizontal bars.

2. The _____ of a set of number items is $\dfrac{\text{sum of items}}{\text{number of items}}$.

3. The possible results of an experiment are the _____.

4. A _____ is a graph in which pictures or symbols are used to visually present data.

5. The _____ of a set of numbers is the number that occurs most often.

6. A _____ graph displays information with a line that connects data points.

7. The _____ of an ordered set of numbers is the middle number.

8. A _____ is one way to picture and count outcomes.

9. An _____ is an activity being considered, such as tossing a coin or rolling a die.

10. In a _____ graph, each section (shaped like a piece of pie) shows a category and the relative size of the category.

11. The _____ of an event is $\dfrac{\text{the number of ways that the event can occur}}{\text{number of possible outcomes}}$.

12. A _____ is a special bar graph in which the width of each bar represents a _____ and the height of each bar represents the _____.

> **Helpful Hint**
>
> Are you preparing for your test? Don't forget to take the Chapter Test on page 634. Then check your answers at the back of your text and use the Chapter Test Prep Video CD to see the fully worked-out solutions to any of the exercises you want to review.

9 Chapter Highlights

DEFINITIONS AND CONCEPTS	EXAMPLES

Section 9.1   Reading Pictographs, Bar Graphs, Histograms, and Line Graphs

A **pictograph** is a graph in which pictures or symbols are used to visually present data.

A **line graph** displays information with a line that connects data points.

A **bar graph** presents data using vertical or horizontal bars.

The bar graph on the right shows the number of acres of wheat harvested in 1996 for leading states.

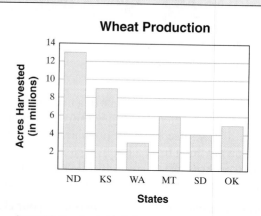

Source: U.S. Department of Agriculture

1. Approximately how many acres of wheat were harvested in Kansas?

9,000,000 acres

DEFINITIONS AND CONCEPTS	**EXAMPLES**

Section 9.1   Reading Pictographs, Bar Graphs, Histograms, and Line Graphs (*continued*)

A **histogram** is a special bar graph in which the width of each bar represents a **class interval** and the height of each bar represents the **class frequency.** The histogram on the right shows student quiz scores.	**2.** About how many more acres of wheat were harvested in North Dakota than South Dakota? $\begin{array}{r} 13 \text{ million} \\ - 4 \text{ million} \\ \hline 9 \text{ million} \end{array}$ or 9,000,000 acres 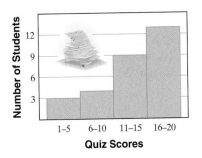 **1.** How many students received a score of 6–10? 4 students **2.** How many students received a score of 11–20? $9 + 13 = 22$ students

Section 9.2   Reading Circle Graphs

In a **circle graph,** each section (shaped like a piece of pie) shows a category and the relative size of the category. The circle graph on the right classifies tornadoes by wind speed.	**Tornado Wind Speeds** 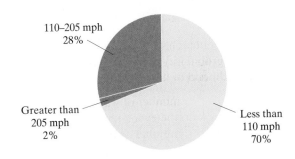 *Source:* National Oceanic and Atmospheric Administration **1.** What percent of tornadoes have wind speeds of 110 mph or greater? $28\% + 2\% = 30\%$ **2.** If there were 1235 tornadoes in the United States in 1995, how many of these might we expect to have had wind speeds less than 110 mph? Find 70% of 1235. $70\%(1235) = 0.70(1235) = 864.5 \approx 865$ Around 865 tornadoes would be expected to have had wind speeds of less than 110 mph.

DEFINITIONS AND CONCEPTS	EXAMPLES

Section 9.3 Mean, Median, and Mode

The **mean** (or **average**) of a set of number items is

$$\text{mean} = \frac{\text{sum of items}}{\text{number of items}}$$

The **median** of a set of numbers in numerical order is the middle number. If the number of items is even, the median is the mean of the two middle numbers.

The **mode** of a set of numbers is the number that occurs most often. (A set of numbers may have no mode or more than one mode.)

Find the mean, median, and mode of the following set of numbers: 33, 35, 35, 43, 68, 68

$$\text{mean} = \frac{33 + 35 + 35 + 43 + 68 + 68}{6} = 47$$

The median is the mean of the two middle numbers, 35 and 43

$$\text{median} = \frac{35 + 43}{2} = 39$$

There are two modes because there are two numbers that occur twice:

35 and 68

Section 9.4 Counting and Introduction to Probability

An **experiment** is an activity being considered, such as tossing a coin or rolling a die. The possible results of an experiment are the **outcomes**. A **tree diagram** is one way to picture and count outcomes.

Draw a tree diagram for tossing a coin and then choosing a number from 1 to 4.

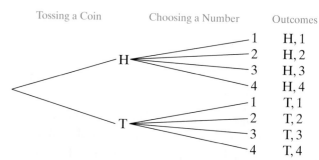

Any number of outcomes considered together is called an **event**. The **probability** of an event is a measure of the chance or likelihood of it occurring.

$$\begin{array}{c} \text{probability of} \\ \text{an event} \end{array} = \frac{\begin{array}{c}\text{number of ways that} \\ \text{the event can occur}\end{array}}{\begin{array}{c}\text{number of possible} \\ \text{outcomes}\end{array}}$$

Find the probability of tossing a coin twice and tails occurring each time.

1 way the event can occur

HH, HT, TH, TT

4 possible outcomes

$$\text{probability} = \frac{1}{4}$$

📖 STUDY SKILLS BUILDER

Are You Prepared for a Test on Chapter 9?

Below I have listed some *common trouble areas* for students in chapter 9. After studying for your test—but before taking your test—read these.

- Do you remember that a set of numbers can have no mode, 1 mode, or even more than 1 mode?

  2, 5, 8, 9   no mode

  2, 2, 8, 9   mode: 2

  2, 2, 3, 3, 5, 7, 7   mode: 2, 3, 7

- Do you remember how to find the median of an even-numbered set of numbers?

  2, 5, 8, 9 $\frac{5 + 8}{2} = 6.5$ The median is the average of the two "middle" numbers.

- Don't forget that the probability of an event is always between 0 and 1 inclusive (including 0 and 1).
- What is the probability of an event that won't occur? 0
- What is the probability of an event that is certain to occur? 1

(9.1) *The following pictograph shows the number of new homes constructed in 2003, by region. Use this graph to answer Exercises 1 through 6.*

2003 Housing Starts by Region of United States

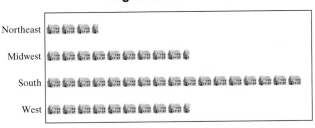

Northeast

Midwest

South

West

Each 🏠 represents 50,000 homes

Source: U.S. Census Bureau

1. How many housing starts were there in the Midwest in 2003?

2. How many housing starts were there in the Northeast in 2003?

3. Find the total housing starts in the Midwest and Northeast.

4. How many more housing starts were in the South than in the West?

5. Which region(s) had 400,000 or more housing starts?

6. Which region(s) had fewer than 400,000 housing starts?

The following bar graph shows the percent of persons age 25 or over who completed four or more years of college. Use this graph to answer Exercises 7 through 10.

Four or More Years of College by Persons Age 25 or Over

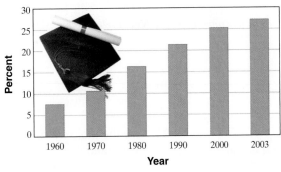

Source: U.S. Census Bureau

7. Approximate the percent of persons who completed four or more years of college in 1960.

8. What year shown had the greatest percent of persons completing four or more years of college?

9. What years shown had 15% or more of persons completing four or more years of college?

10. Describe any patterns you notice in this graph.

The following line graph shows the average price of a 30-second television advertisement during the Super Bowl for the years shown. Use this graph to answer Exercises 11 through 15.

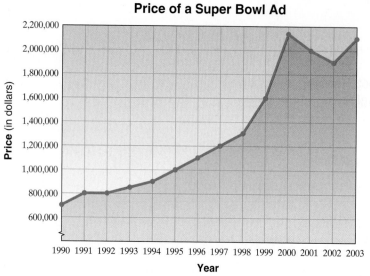

Price of a Super Bowl Ad

Sources: Nielsen Media Research and *Advertising Age* research

11. Approximate the price of a Super Bowl ad in 2003.

12. Approximate the price of a Super Bowl ad in 1997.

13. Between which two years did the price of a Super Bowl ad *not* increase?

14. Between which two years did the price of a Super Bowl ad increase the most?

15. During which years was the price of a Super Bowl ad *less than* $1,000,000?

The following histogram shows the hours worked per week by the employees of Southern Star Furniture. Use this histogram to answer Exercises 16 through 19.

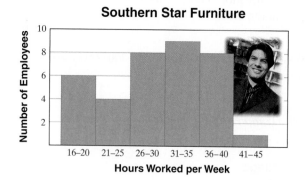

Southern Star Furniture

16. How many employees work 21–25 hours per week?

17. How many employees work 41–45 hours per week?

18. How many employees work 36 hours or more per week?

19. How many employees work 30 hours or less per week?

Following is a list of monthly record high temperatures for New Orleans, Louisiana. Use this list to complete the frequency distribution table below.

83	96	101	92
85	100	92	102
89	101	87	84

	Class Intervals (Temperatures)	Tally	Class Frequency (Number of Months)
20.	80°–89°		
21.	90°–99°		
22.	100°–109°		

23. Use the table from Exercises 20, 21, and 22 to draw a histogram.

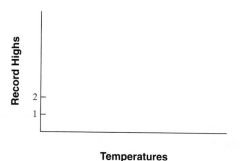

Record Highs

Temperatures

(9.2) *The following circle graph shows a family's $4000 monthly budget. Use this graph to answer Exercises 24 through 30. Write all ratios as fractions in simplest form.*

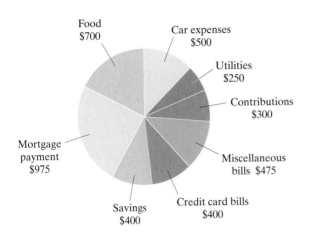

24. What is the largest budget item?

25. What is the smallest budget item?

26. How much money is budgeted for the mortgage payment and utilities?

27. How much money is budgeted for savings and contributions?

28. Find the ratio of the mortgage payment to the total monthly budget.

29. Find the ratio of food to the total monthly budget.

30. Find the ratio of car expenses to food.

The following circle graph shows the percent of the 50 states with various rural interstate highway speed limits in 2000. Use this graph to determine the number of states with each speed limit in Exercises 31 through 34.

Percent of States with Rural Interstate Highway Speed Limit

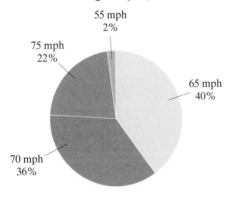

Source: Insurance Institute for Highway Safety

31. How many states had a rural interstate highway speed limit of 65 mph?

32. How many states had a rural interstate highway speed limit of 75 mph?

33. How many states had a rural interstate highway speed limit of 55 mph?

34. How many states had a rural interstate highway speed limit of 70 mph or 75 mph?

(9.3) *Find the mean, median, and any mode(s) for each list of numbers. If necessary, round to the nearest tenth.*

35. 13, 23, 33, 14, 6

36. 45, 86, 21, 60, 86, 64, 45

37. 14,000, 20,000, 12,000, 20,000, 36,000, 45,000

38. 560, 620, 123, 400, 410, 300, 400, 780, 430, 450

For Exercises 39 and 40, the grades are given for a student for a particular semester. Find each grade point average. If necessary, round the grade point average to the nearest hundredth.

39.

Grade	Credit Hours
A	3
A	3
C	2
B	3
C	1

40.

Grade	Credit Hours
B	3
B	4
C	2
D	2
B	3

(9.4) *Draw a tree diagram for each experiment. Then use the diagram to determine the number of outcomes.*

Spinner 1   Spinner 2

41. Tossing a coin and then spinning Spinner 1

42. Spinning Spinner 2 and then tossing a coin

43. Spinning Spinner 1 twice

44. Spinning Spinner 2 twice

45. Spinning Spinner 1 and then Spinner 2

Find the probability of each event.

46. Rolling a 4 on a die

47. Rolling a 3 on a die

48. Spinning a 4 on the spinner

49. Spinning a 3 on the spinner

50. Spinning either a 1, 3, or 5 on the spinner

51. Spinning either a 2 or a 4 on the spinner

52. Rolling an even number on a die

53. Rolling a number greater than 3 on a die

Mixed Review

Find the mean, median, and any mode(s) for each list of numbers. If needed round answers to two decimal places.

54. 73, 82, 95, 68, 54

55. 25, 27, 32, 98, 62

56. 750, 500, 427, 322, 500, 225

57. 952, 327, 566, 814, 327, 729

Given a bag containing 2 red marbles, 2 blue marbles, 3 yellow marbles, and 1 green marble, find the following:

58. The probability of choosing a blue marble from the bag

59. The probability of choosing a yellow marble from the bag

60. The probability of choosing a red marble from the bag

61. The probability of choosing a green marble from the bag

9 CHAPTER TEST

 Remember to use the Chapter Test Prep Video CD to see the fully worked-out solutions to any of the exercises you want to review.

The following pictograph shows the money collected each week from a wrapping paper fundraiser. Use this graph to answer Exercises 1 through 3.

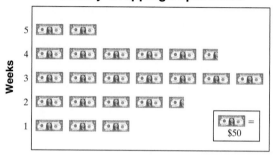

Weekly Wrapping Paper Sales

1. How much money was collected during the second week?

2. During which week was the most money collected? How much money was collected during that week?

3. What was the total money collected for the fundraiser?

The bar graph shows the normal monthly precipitation in centimeters for Chicago, Illinois. Use this graph to answer Exercises 4 through 6.

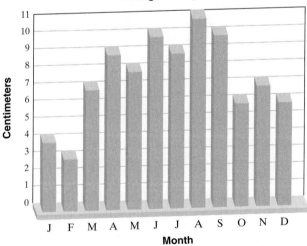

Chicago Precipitation

Source: U.S. National Oceanic and Atmospheric Administration, *Climatography of the United States,* No. 81

4. During which month(s) does Chicago normally have more than 9 centimeters of precipitation?

5. During which month does Chicago normally have the least amount of precipitation? How much precipitation occurs during that month?

6. During which month(s) does 7 centimeters of precipitation normally occur?

6. _____

7. Use the information in the table to draw a bar graph. Clearly label each bar.

Countries with the Highest Newspaper Circulations	
Country	**Average Daily Circulation (in millions)**
Japan	72
US	56
China	50
India	31
Germany	24
Russia	24
UK	19

(*Source:* World Association of Newspapers)

Countries with the Highest Newspaper Circulations

Average Daily Circulation (in millions)

20
10

7. see graph _____

8. _____

The following line graph shows the annual inflation rate in the United States for the years 1990–2003. Use this graph to answer Exercises 8 through 10.

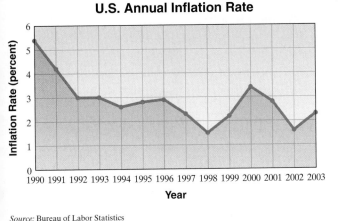

U.S. Annual Inflation Rate

Inflation Rate (percent)

6
5
4
3
2
1
0

1990 1991 1992 1993 1994 1995 1996 1997 1998 1999 2000 2001 2002 2003

Year

Source: Bureau of Labor Statistics

8. Approximate the annual inflation rate in 2002.

9. During which of the years shown was the inflation rate greater than 3%?

10. During which sets of years was the inflation rate increasing?

9. _____

10. _____

The result of a survey of 200 people is shown in the following circle graph. Each person was asked to tell his or her favorite type of music. Use this graph to answer Exercises 11 and 12.

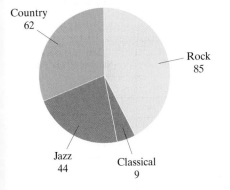

Country 62

Rock 85

Jazz 44

Classical 9

11. Find the ratio of those who prefer rock music to the total number surveyed.

12. Find the ratio of those who prefer country music to those who prefer jazz.

11. _____

12. _____

13. _____

The following circle graph shows the U.S. labor force employment by industry for 2000. There were approximately 132,000,000 people employed by these industries in the United States in 2000. Use the graph to find how many people were employed by the industries given in Exercises 13 and 14.

U.S. Labor Force Employment by Industry

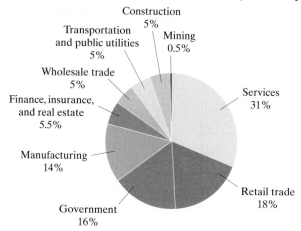

Source: Bureau of Labor Statistics

14. _____

13. Services

14. Government

A professor measures the heights of the students in her class. The results are shown in the following histogram. Use this histogram to answer Exercises 15 and 16.

15. _____

Student Heights

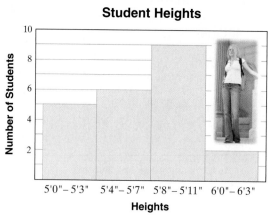

15. How many students are 5′8″–5′11″ tall?

16. How many students are 5′7″ or shorter?

16. _____

17. The history test scores of 25 students are shown below. Use these scores to complete the frequency distribution table.

70	86	81	65	92
43	72	85	69	97
82	51	75	50	68
88	83	85	77	99
77	63	59	84	90

Class Intervals (Scores)	Tally	Class Frequency (Number of Students)
40–49		
50–59		
60–69		
70–79		
80–89		
90–99		

17. see table

18. Use the results of Exercise 17 to draw a histogram.

Find the mean, median, and mode of each list of numbers.

19. 26, 32, 42, 43, 49

20. 8, 10, 16, 16, 14, 12, 12, 13

Find the grade point average. If necessary, round to the nearest hundredth.

21.

Grade	Credit Hours
A	3
B	3
C	3
B	4
A	1

22. Draw a tree diagram for the experiment of spinning the spinner twice. State the number of outcomes.

23. Draw a tree diagram for the experiment of tossing a coin twice. State the number of outcomes.

Suppose that the numbers 1 to 10 are each written on a scrap of paper and placed in a bag. You then select one number from the bag.

24. What is the probability of choosing a 6 from the bag?

25. What is the probability of choosing a 3 or a 4 from the bag?

18. see graph

19. _____

20. _____

21. _____

22. _____

23. _____

24. _____

25. _____

1. Simplify: $(8 - 6)^2 + 2^3 \cdot 3$

2. Simplify: $48 \div 8 \cdot 2$

Answers

1. _____

2. _____

3. Write $\dfrac{30}{108}$ in simplest form.

4. Subtract: $\dfrac{19}{40} - \dfrac{3}{10}$

3. _____

4. _____

5. Add: $1\dfrac{4}{5} + 4 + 2\dfrac{1}{2}$

6. Multiply: $5\dfrac{1}{3} \cdot 2\dfrac{1}{8}$

5. _____

6. _____

△ **7.** The formula for finding the area of a triangle is Area $= \dfrac{1}{2} \cdot$ base $\cdot$ height. Find the area of a triangle with height 3 feet and length 5.6 feet.

8. Find the perimeter of a rectangle with length $3\dfrac{1}{2}$ meters and width $1\dfrac{1}{2}$ meters.

7. _____

8. _____

9. _____

9. Write the ratio of $10 to $15 as a fraction in simplest form.

10. Write the ratio 14 inches to 3 feet as a fraction in simplest form.

10. _____

11. _____

Write each rate as a fraction in simplest form.

12. _____

11. $2160 for 12 weeks

12. 340 miles every 5 hours

13. _____

14. _____

13. 360 miles on 16 gallons of gasoline

14. 78 files every 4 hours

15. Is $\dfrac{1\frac{1}{6}}{10\frac{1}{2}} = \dfrac{\frac{1}{2}}{4\frac{1}{2}}$ a true proportion?

16. Is $\dfrac{7.8}{3} = \dfrac{5.2}{2}$ a true proportion?

17. The standard dose of an antibiotic is 4 cc (cubic centimeters) for every 25 pounds (lb) of body weight. At this rate, find the standard dose for a 140-lb woman.

18. On a certain map, 2 inches represents 75 miles. How many miles are represented by 7 inches?

Write each percent as a decimal.

19. 4.6%

20. 0.29%

21. 190%

22. 452%

Write each percent as a fraction in simplest form.

23. 40%

24. 27%

25. $33\frac{1}{3}$ %

26. $61\frac{1}{7}$ %

27. Translate to an equation: Five is what percent of 20?

28. Translate to a proportion: Five is what percent of 20?

29. Find the sales tax and the total price on the purchase of an $85.50 trench coat in a city where the sales tax rate is 7.5%.

30. A salesperson makes a 7% commission rate on her total sales. If her total sales are $23,000, what is her commission?

31. An accountant invested $2000 at a simple interest rate of 10% for 2 years. What total amount of money will she have from her investment in 2 years?

32. Find the mean (or average) of 28, 35, 40, and 32.

15. _____
16. _____
17. _____
18. _____
19. _____
20. _____
21. _____
22. _____
23. _____
24. _____
25. _____
26. _____
27. _____
28. _____
29. _____
30. _____
31. _____
32. _____

33. _____

34. _____

35. _____

36. _____

37. _____

38. _____

39. _____

40. _____

41. _____

42. _____

43. _____

44. _____

45. _____

46. _____

47. _____

48. _____

49. _____

50. _____

33. Convert 7 feet to yards.

34. Convert 2.5 tons to pounds.

35. Divide 9 lb 6 oz by 2.

36. Find: $1 + 3(10 - 8)$

37. Convert 2.35 cg to grams.

38. Convert 106 cm to millimeters.

39. Convert 3210 ml to liters.

40. Convert 5 m to centimeters.

41. Convert 15°C to degrees Fahrenheit.

42. Convert 41°F to degrees Celsius.

43. Find the complement of a 48° angle.

44. Find the supplement of a 48° angle.

45. Find $\sqrt{\dfrac{1}{36}}$.

46. Find: $\sqrt{\dfrac{1}{25}}$

47. Find the mode of the list of numbers:
11, 14, 14, 16, 31, 56, 65, 77, 77, 78, 79

48. Find the median of the numbers in Exercise 47.

49. If a coin is tossed twice, find the probability of tossing heads and then heads.

50. A bag contains 3 red marbles and 2 blue marbles. Find the probability of choosing a red marble.

10

Signed Numbers

Thus far, we have studied whole numbers, fractions, and decimals. However, these numbers are not sufficient for representing many situations in real life. For example, to express 5 degrees below zero or $100 in debt, numbers less than 0 are needed. This chapter is devoted to signed numbers, which include numbers less than 0, and to operations on these numbers.

H ave you ever wondered about the weather on other planets? Scientists do! Information from satellites, probes, and telescopes tells of extreme atmospheric conditions of our Solar System neighbors. Pluto's distance from the Sun contributes to its frigid temperatures, some recorded as low as 338°F *below zero.* Compare that to the extreme heat of Venus, where temperatures on the surface are in excess of 800°F. In Exercises 51–54 on page 663, we will see how signed numbers can be used to compare average daily temperatures of several planets in our Solar System.

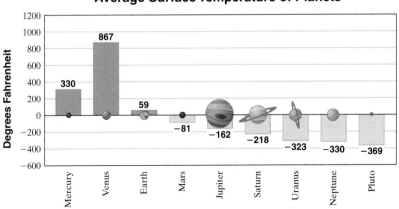

Average Surface Temperature of Planets*

*(For some planets, the temperature given is the temperature where the atmosphere pressure equals 1 Earth atmosphere; *Source: The World Almanac*, 2005)

A Represent Real-Life Situations with Signed Numbers.

B Graph Signed Numbers on a Number Line.

C Compare Signed Numbers.

D Find the Absolute Value of a Number.

E Find the Opposite of a Number.

F Read Bar Graphs Containing Signed Numbers.

10.1 SIGNED NUMBERS

Objective **A** Representing Real-Life Situations

Thus far in this text, all numbers have been 0 or greater than 0. Numbers greater than 0 are called **positive numbers.** However, sometimes situations exist that cannot be represented by a number greater than 0. For example,

5 degrees below 0°

Sea level

20 feet below sea level

To represent these situations, we need numbers less than 0.

Extending the number line to the left of 0 allows us to picture **negative numbers,** which are numbers that are less than 0.

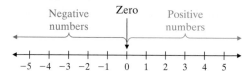

Negative numbers   Zero   Positive numbers

−5 −4 −3 −2 −1   0   1   2   3   4   5

When a single + sign or no sign is in front of a number, the number is a positive number. When a single − sign is in front of a number, the number is a negative number. Together, we call positive numbers, negative numbers, and zero the **signed numbers.**

−5 indicates "negative five."

5 and +5 both indicate "positive five."

The number 0 is neither positive nor negative.

Now we have numbers to represent the situations previously mentioned.

5 degrees below 0   −5°

20 feet below sea level   −20 feet

> **Helpful Hint**
>
> A − sign, such as the one in −1, tells us that the number is to the left of 0 on the number line.
>
> −1 is read "negative one."
>
> A + sign or no sign tells us that a number lies to the right of 0 on the number line. For example, 3 and +3 both mean positive three.

EXAMPLE 1 **Representing Depth with a Signed Number**

Jack Mayfield, a miner for the Molly Kathleen Gold Mine, is presently 150 feet below the surface of the Earth. Represent this position using a signed number.

Solution: If 0 represents the surface of the Earth, then 150 feet below the surface can be represented by −150.

▦ **Work Practice Problem 1**

PRACTICE PROBLEM 1

a. A deep-sea diver is 800 feet below the surface of the ocean. Represent this position using a signed number.

b. A company reports a $2 million loss for the year. Represent this amount using a signed number.

Answers

1. a. −800,   **b.** −2 million

Objective B Graphing Signed Numbers

EXAMPLE 2 Graph the signed numbers $-2\frac{1}{4}$, -2, $-\frac{1}{2}$, 4, and -3.8 on a number line.

Solution:

■ Work Practice Problem 2

Some signed numbers are integers. The **integers** consist of 0, the natural numbers, and the opposites of the natural numbers. The integers are $\ldots, -3, -2, -1, 0, 1, 2, 3, \ldots$ and are graphed below.

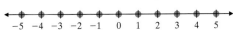

In Example 2 above we graphed the signed numbers $-2\frac{1}{4}$, -2, $-\frac{1}{2}$, 4, -3.8. Of these signed numbers, -2 and 4 are integers; the rest are not integers.

Objective C Comparing Signed Numbers

For any two numbers graphed on a number line, the number to the **right** is the **greater number,** and the number to the **left** is the **smaller number.** Recall that the symbol $>$ means "is greater than" and the symbol $<$ means "is less than."

To illustrate, both -5 and -2 are graphed on the number line shown:

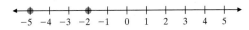

The graph of -5 is **to the left of** -2, so -5 **is less than** -2. We can write this as

$$-5 < -2$$

We can also write

$$-2 > -5$$

since -2 is **to the right** of -5, so -2 **is greater than** -5.

✔ **Concept Check** Is there a smallest negative number? Is there a largest positive number? Explain.

EXAMPLES Insert $<$ or $>$ between each pair of numbers to make a true statement.

3. -7 7 $\quad$ -7 is to the left of 7, so $-7 < 7$.
4. 0 -4 $\quad$ 0 is to the right of -4, so $0 > -4$.
5. -9 -11 $\quad$ -9 is to the right of -11, so $-9 > -11$.
6. -2.9 -1 $\quad$ -2.9 is to the left of -1, so $-2.9 < -1$.
7. -6 0 $\quad$ -6 is to the left of 0, so $-6 < 0$.
8. 8.6 -8.6 $\quad$ 8.6 is to the right of -8.6, so $8.6 > -8.6$.
9. $-\frac{1}{4}$ $-2\frac{1}{2}$ $\quad$ $-\frac{1}{4}$ is to the right of $-2\frac{1}{2}$, so $-1\frac{1}{4} > -2\frac{1}{2}$.

■ Work Practice Problems 3–9

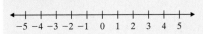

Helpful
Hint

> Helpful
> Hint
>
> If you think of $<$ and $>$ as arrowheads, notice that in a true statement the arrow always points to the smaller number.
>
> $$5 > -4 \qquad -3 < -1$$
> $\qquad$ ↑ $\qquad\qquad$ ↑
> $\quad$ smaller $\qquad$ smaller
> $\quad$ number $\qquad$ number

Objective D Finding the Absolute Value of a Number

The **absolute value** of a number is the number's distance from 0 on a number line. The symbol for absolute value is | |. For example, $|3|$ is read as "the absolute value of 3."

$|3| = 3$ because 3 is 3 units from 0.

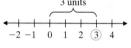

$|-3| = 3$ because -3 is 3 units from 0.

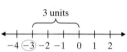

PRACTICE PROBLEMS 10–14

Find each absolute value.

10. $|6|$

11. $|-4|$

12. $|0|$

13. $\left|\dfrac{7}{8}\right|$

14. $|-3.4|$

EXAMPLES Find each absolute value.

10. $|-2| = 2$ $\quad$ because -2 is 2 units from 0.

11. $|5| = 5$ $\quad$ because 5 is 5 units from 0.

12. $|0| = 0$ $\quad$ because 0 is 0 units from 0.

13. $\left|-\dfrac{3}{4}\right| = \dfrac{3}{4}$ $\quad$ because $-\dfrac{3}{4}$ is $\dfrac{3}{4}$ unit from 0.

14. $|1.2| = 1.2$ $\quad$ because 1.2 is 1.2 units from 0.

▪ **Work Practice Problems 10–14**

> Helpful
> Hint
>
> Since the absolute value of a number is that number's *distance* from 0, the absolute value of a number is always 0 or positive. It is never negative.
>
> $$|0| = 0 \qquad |-6| = 6$$
> $\qquad$ ↑ $\qquad\qquad\quad$ ↑
> $\quad$ zero $\qquad$ a positive number

Objective E Finding the Opposite of a Number

Two numbers that are the same distance from 0 on the number line but are on opposite sides of 0 are called **opposites.**

4 and -4 are opposites.

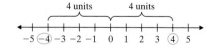

Answers

10. 6, 11. 4, 12. 0, 13. $\dfrac{7}{8}$, 14. 3.4

When two numbers are opposites, we say that each is the opposite of the other. Thus, **4 is the opposite of −4** and **−4 is the opposite of 4.**

The phrase "the opposite of" is written in symbols as "−". For example,

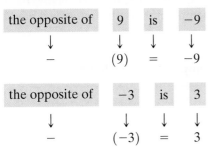

the opposite of   9   is   −9

       −   (9)   =   −9

the opposite of   −3   is   3

       −   (−3)   =   3

Notice we just stated that

$$-(-3) = 3$$

In general, we have the following:

Opposites

If a is a number, then $-(-a) = a$.

Notice that because "the opposite of" is written as "−", to find the opposite of a number we place a "−" sign in front of the number.

EXAMPLES Find the opposite of each number.

15. 12   The opposite of 12 is -12.

16. 1.7   The opposite of 1.7 is -1.7.

17. −1   The opposite of −1 is $-(-1)$ or 1.

18. 0   The opposite of 0 is -0 or 0.

19. $-\dfrac{10}{13}$ The opposite of $-\dfrac{10}{13}$ is $-\left(-\dfrac{10}{13}\right)$ or $\dfrac{10}{13}$.

Helpful Hint

Remember that 0 is neither positive nor negative.

🖳 **Work Practice Problems 15–19**

✔ **Concept Check**   True or false? The number 0 is the only number that is its own opposite.

EXAMPLES Simplify.

20. $-(-4) = 4$ The opposite of negative 4 is 4.

21. $-|6| = -6$ The opposite of the absolute value of 6 is the opposite of 6, which is −6.

22. $-|-5| = -5$ The opposite of the absolute value of −5 is the opposite of 5, which is −5.

🖳 **Work Practice Problems 20–22**

PRACTICE PROBLEMS 15–19

Find the opposite of each number.

15. −7   **16.** 0

17. $\dfrac{11}{15}$ **18.** −9.6

19. 4

PRACTICE PROBLEMS 20–22

Simplify.

20. $-(-11)$

21. $-|7|$

22. $-|-2|$

Answers

15. 7,   **16.** 0,   **17.** $-\dfrac{11}{15}$,   **18.** 9.6,

19. −4,   **20.** 11,   **21.** −7,   **22.** −2

✔ **Concept Check Answer**

true

Objective F Reading Bar Graphs Containing Signed Numbers

The bar graph below shows the average temperature (in Fahrenheit) of the known planets. Notice that a negative temperature is illustrated by a bar below the horizontal line representing 0°F, and a positive temperature is illustrated by a bar above the horizontal line representing 0°F.

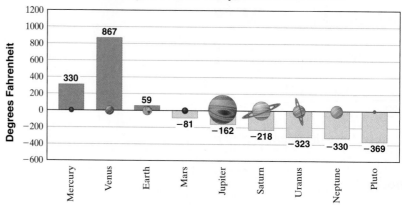

Average Surface Temperature of Planets*

*(For some planets, the temperature given is the temperature where the atmosphere pressure equals 1 Earth atmosphere; *Source: The World Almanac*, 2005)

PRACTICE PROBLEM 23

Which planet has the highest average temperature?

EXAMPLE 23 Which planet has the lowest average temperature?

Solution The planet with the lowest average temperature is the one that corresponds to the bar that extends the furthest in the negative direction (downward.) Pluto has the lowest average temperature of −369°F.

◻ **Work Practice Problem 23**

Objective **A** *Represent each quantity by a signed number. See Example 1.*

1. A worker in a silver mine in Nevada works 1445 feet underground.

2. A scuba diver is swimming 35 feet below the surface of the water in the Gulf of Mexico.

3. The peak of Mount Elbert in Colorado is 14,433 feet above sea level. (*Source:* U.S. Geological Survey)

4. The lowest elevation in the United States is found at Death Valley, California, at an elevation of 282 feet below sea level. (*Source:* U.S. Geological Survey)

5. The record high temperature in Nevada is 118 degrees above zero Fahrenheit. (*Source:* National Climatic Data Center)

6. The Minnesota Viking football team lost 15 yards on a play.

7. The average depth of the Atlantic Ocean is 11,730 feet below the surface of the ocean. (*Source:* 2005 *World Almanac*)

8. The Dow Jones stock market average fell 317 points in one day.

9. Gateway, Inc., manufactures personal computers. In the second quarter of fiscal year 2004, Gateway posted a net loss of $339 million. (*Source:* Gateway, Inc.)

10. For the second quarter of fiscal year 2004, Gateway reported a loss of 91¢ per share.

11. Two divers are exploring the bottom of a trench in the Pacific Ocean. Joe is at 135 feet below the surface of the ocean and Sara is at 157 feet below the surface. Represent each quantity by an integer and determine who is deeper in the water.

12. The temperature on one January day in Chicago was 10° below 0° Celsius. Represent this quantity by an integer and tell whether this temperature is cooler or warmer than 5° below 0° Celsius.

13. In 2003, the number of music cassette singles shipped to retailers reflected a 45 percent loss from the previous year. Write a signed number to represent the percent loss in cassette singles shipped. (*Source:* Recording Industry Association of America)

14. In 2003, the number of music CDs shipped to retailers reflected a 7 percent loss from the previous year. Write a signed number to represent the percent loss in CDs shipped. (*Source:* Recording Industry Association of America)

Objective [B] *Graph the signed numbers in each list on a number line. See Example 2.*

15. $-3, 0, 4, -1\frac{1}{2}$

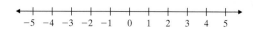

16. $-4, 0, 2, -3\frac{1}{4}$

17. $5, -2, -4.7$

18. $3, -1, -4, -2.1$

Objective [C] *Insert < or > between each pair of numbers to make a true statement. See Examples 3 through 9.*

19. 5   7

20. 16   10

21. 4   0

22. 8   0

23. -5 -7

24. -12 -10

25. 0 -3

26. 0 -7

27. -4.6 -2.7

28. -8.4 -1.6

29. $-1\frac{3}{4}$ 0

30. 0 $-\frac{7}{8}$

31. $\frac{1}{4}$ $-\frac{8}{11}$

32. $-\frac{1}{5}$ 6

33. $-2\frac{1}{2}$ $-\frac{9}{10}$

34. $-1\frac{1}{5}$ $-3\frac{1}{9}$

Objective [D] *Find each absolute value. See Examples 10 through 14.*

35. $|9|$

36. $|7|$

37. $|-8|$

38. $|-19|$

39. $|0|$

40. $|100|$

41. $|-5|$

42. $|-10|$

43. $|-8.1|$

44. $|-31.6|$

45. $\left|-\frac{1}{2}\right|$

46. $\left|\frac{9}{10}\right|$

47. $\left|-\frac{3}{8}\right|$

48. $\left|\frac{20}{23}\right|$

49. $|7.6|$

50. $|-0.6|$

Objective [E] *Find the opposite of each number. See Examples 15 through 19.*

51. 5

52. 8

53. -4

54. -6

55. 23.6

56. 123.9

57. $-\frac{9}{16}$

58. $-\frac{4}{9}$

59. -0.7

60. -4.4

61. $\frac{17}{18}$

62. $\frac{2}{3}$

Simplify. See Examples 20 through 22.

63. $|-7|$ **64.** $|-11|$ **65.** $-|20|$ **66.** $-|43|$ ⊙ **67.** $-|-3|$ **68.** $-|-18|$

69. $-(-8)$ **70.** $-(-7)$ **71.** $|-14|$ **72.** $-(-14)$ **73.** $-(-29)$ **74.** $-|-29|$

Objectives Ⓓ Ⓔ **Mixed Practice** *Fill in the chart. See Examples 10 through 19.*

	Number	Absolute Value of Number	Opposite of Number
75.	25		
76.	-13		
77.	-8.4		
78.	$\dfrac{11}{18}$		

Objective Ⓕ *The bar graph shows elevation of selected lakes. Use this graph For Exercises 79 through 82.* (*Source:* U.S. Geological Survey). *See Example 8.*

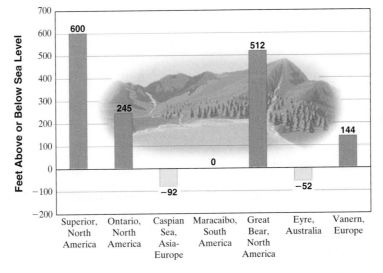

79. Which lake has an elevation at sea level?

80. Which lake shown has the lowest elevation?

81. Which lake shown has the second lowest elevation?

82. Which lake shown has the highest elevation?

Use the bar graph from Example 23 to answer Exercises 83 through 86.

83. Which planet has an average temperature closest to 0°F?

84. Which planet has a negative average temperature closest to 0°F?

85. Which planet has an average temperature closest to −200°F?

86. Which planet has an average temperature closest to −300°F?

Review

Add. See Section 1.3.

87. $0 + 13$

88. $9 + 0$

89. $15 + 20$

90. $20 + 15$

91. $47 + 236 + 77$

92. $362 + 37 + 90$

Concept Extensions

Write the given numbers in order from least to greatest.

93. $2^2, -|3|, -(-5), -|-8|$

94. $|10|, 2^3, -|-5|, -(-4)$

95. $|-1|, -|-6|, -(-6), -|1|$

96. $1^4, -(-3), -|7|, |-20|$

97. $-(-2), 5^2, -10, -|-9|, |-12|$

98. $3^3, -|-11|, -(-10), -4, -|2|$

Choose all numbers for x from each given list that make each statement true.

99. $|x| > 8$
   a. 0 **b.** -5 **c.** 8 **d.** -12

100. $|x| > 4$
   a. 0 **b.** 4 **c.** -1 **d.** -100

101. Evaluate: $-(-|-5|)$

102. Evaluate: $-(-|-(-7)|)$

Answer true or false for Exercises 103 through 107.

103. If $a > b$, then a must be a positive number.

104. The absolute value of a number is *always* a positive number.

105. A positive number is always greater than a negative number.

106. Zero is always less than a positive number.

107. The number $-a$ is always a negative number. (*Hint:* Read "$-$" as "the opposite of.")

108. Given the number line , is it true that $b < a$?

109. Write in your own words how to find the absolute value of a signed number.

110. Explain how to determine which of two signed numbers is larger.

For Exercises 111 and 112, see the first Concept Check in this section.

111. Is there a largest negative number? If so, what is it?

112. Is there a smallest positive number? If so, what is it?

10.2 ADDING SIGNED NUMBERS

Objective **A** Adding Signed Numbers

Adding signed numbers can be visualized by using a number line. A positive number can be represented on the number line by an arrow of appropriate length pointing to the right, and a negative number by an arrow of appropriate length pointing to the left.

Both arrows represent 2 or +2.

They both point to the right, and they are both 2 units long.

Both arrows represent −3.

They both point to the left, and they are both 3 units long.

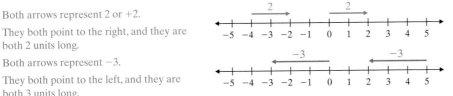

To add signed numbers such as $5 + (-2)$ on a number line, we start at 0 on the number line and draw an arrow representing 5. From the tip of this arrow, we draw another arrow representing −2. The tip of the second arrow ends at their sum, 3.

$5 + (-2) = 3$

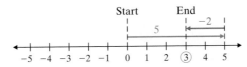

To add $-1 + (-4)$ on the number line, we start at 0 and draw an arrow representing −1. From the tip of this arrow, we draw another arrow representing −4. The tip of the second arrow ends at their sum, −5.

$-1 + (-4) = -5$

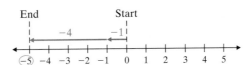

EXAMPLE 1 Add using a number line: $-3 + (-4)$

Solution:

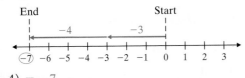

$-3 + (-4) = -7$

 Work Practice Problem 1

EXAMPLE 2 Add using a number line: $-7 + 3$

Solution:

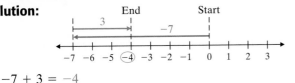

$-7 + 3 = -4$

 Work Practice Problem 2

Using a number line each time we add two numbers can be time consuming. Instead, we can notice patterns in the previous examples and write rules for adding signed numbers.

PRACTICE PROBLEM 1

Add using a number line:
$-5 + (-3)$

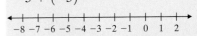

PRACTICE PROBLEM 2

Add using a number line:
$5 + (-1)$

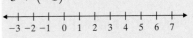

Answers

1.
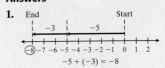
$-5 + (-3) = -8$

2.
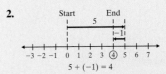
$5 + (-1) = 4$

651

Rules for adding signed numbers depend on whether we are adding numbers with the same sign or different signs. When adding two numbers with the same sign, notice that the sign of the sum is the same as the sign of the addends.

> ### Adding Two Numbers with the Same Sign
>
> **Step 1:** Add their absolute values.
>
> **Step 2:** Use their common sign as the sign of the sum.

PRACTICE PROBLEM 3

Add: $(-3) + (-9)$

EXAMPLE 3 Add: $-2 + (-21)$

Solution:

Step 1: $|-2| = 2, |-21| = 21$, and $2 + 21 = 23$.

Step 2: Their common sign is negative, so the sum is negative:

$$-2 + (-21) = -23$$

Work Practice Problem 3

PRACTICE PROBLEMS 4–7

Add.

4. $-12 + (-3)$
5. $9 + 5$
6. $-\dfrac{3}{7} + \left(-\dfrac{2}{7}\right)$
7. $-8.3 + (-5.7)$

EXAMPLES Add.

4. $-5 + (-11) = -16$
5. $2 + 6 = 8$
6. $-\dfrac{3}{8} + \left(-\dfrac{1}{8}\right) = -\dfrac{4}{8} = -\dfrac{\overset{1}{\cancel{4}}}{2 \cdot \underset{1}{\cancel{4}}} = -\dfrac{1}{2}$
7. $-1.2 + (-7.1) = -8.3$

Work Practice Problems 4–7

The rule for adding two numbers with different signs follows:

> ### Adding Two Numbers with Different Signs
>
> **Step 1:** Find the larger absolute value minus the smaller absolute value.
>
> **Step 2:** Use the sign of the number with the larger absolute value as the sign of the sum.

PRACTICE PROBLEM 8

Add: $-3 + 9$

EXAMPLE 8 Add: $-2 + 20$

Solution:

Step 1: $|-2| = 2, |20| = 20$, and $20 - 2 = 18$.

Step 2: 20 has the larger absolute value and its sign is an understood + so the sum is positive.

$$-2 + 20 = +18 \text{ or } 18$$

Work Practice Problem 8

EXAMPLE 9 Add: $3 + (-7)$

Solution:

Step 1: $|3| = 3, |-7| = 7$, and $7 - 3 = 4$.
Step 2: -7 has the larger absolute value and its sign is $-$ so the sum is negative.

$$3 + (-7) = -4$$

■ **Work Practice Problem 9**

PRACTICE PROBLEM 9
Add: $2 + (-8)$

EXAMPLES Add.

10. $-18 + 10 = -8$
11. $12.9 + (-8.6) = 4.3$
12. $-\dfrac{1}{2} + \dfrac{1}{6} = -\dfrac{3}{6} + \dfrac{1}{6} = -\dfrac{2}{6} = -\dfrac{1}{3}$
13. $0 + (-5) = -5$ The sum of 0 and any number is the number.

■ **Work Practice Problems 10–13**

PRACTICE PROBLEMS 10–13
Add.
10. $-46 + 20$ **11.** $8.6 + (-6.2)$
12. $-\dfrac{3}{4} + \dfrac{1}{8}$ **13.** $-2 + 0$

✔ **Concept Check** What is wrong with the following calculation?

$$5 + (-13) = 8$$

When we add three or more numbers, we follow the order of operations and add from left to right. That is, we start at the left and add the first two numbers. Then we add their sum to the next number. We continue this process until the addition is completed.

EXAMPLE 14 Add: $(-3) + 4 + (-11)$

Solution:

$$(-3) + 4 + (-11) = 1 + (-11)$$
$$= -10$$

■ **Work Practice Problem 14**

PRACTICE PROBLEM 14
Add: $8 + (-3) + (-13)$

EXAMPLE 15 Add: $1 + (-10) + (-8) + 9$

Solution:

$$1 + (-10) + (-8) + 9 = -9 + (-8) + 9 \quad 1 + (-10) = -9$$
$$= -17 + 9 \quad -9 + (-8) = -17$$
$$= -8$$

■ **Work Practice Problem 15**

PRACTICE PROBLEM 15
Add: $5 + (-3) + 12 + (-14)$

Answers
9. -6, **10.** -26, **11.** 2.4, **12.** $-\dfrac{5}{8}$,
13. -2, **14.** -8, **15.** 0

✔ **Concept Check Answer**
$5 + (-13) = -8$

Objective **B** **Solving Problems by Adding Signed Numbers**

Next, we practice solving problems that require adding signed numbers.

PRACTICE PROBLEM 16

If the temperature was −8° Fahrenheit at 6 a.m., and it rose 4 degrees by 7 a.m., and then rose another 7 degrees in the hour from 7 a.m. to 8 a.m., what was the temperature at 8 a.m.?

EXAMPLE 16 **Calculating Temperature**

On January 6 the temperature in Caribou, Maine, at 8 a.m. was −12° Fahrenheit. By 9 a.m., the temperature had risen by 4 degrees, and by 10 a.m. it had risen 6 degrees from the 9 a.m. temperature. What was the temperature at 10 a.m.?

Solution:

1. UNDERSTAND. Read and reread the problem.
2. TRANSLATE.

In words:

temperature at 10 a.m.	=	8 a.m. temperature	+	rise of 4°	+	rise of 6°
↓		↓		↓		↓

Translate:

$$\text{temperature at 10 a.m.} = -12 + (+4) + (+6)$$

3. SOLVE:

$$\text{temperature at 10 a.m.} = -12 + (+4) + (+6)$$
$$= -8 + (+6)$$
$$= -2$$

4. INTERPRET. Check and state your conclusion: The temperature was −2°F at 10 a.m.

▣ **Work Practice Problem 16**

▦ **CALCULATOR EXPLORATIONS** Entering Negative Numbers

To enter a negative number on a calculator, find the key marked $\boxed{+/-}$. (Some calculators have a key marked $\boxed{\text{CHS}}$, and some calculators have a special key $\boxed{(-)}$ for entering a negative sign.) To enter the number −2, for example, press the keys $\boxed{2}$ $\boxed{+/-}$. The display will read $\boxed{-2}$. (Some calculators require the change of sign or negative key to be pressed before the digit.)

To find −32 + (−131), press the keys
$\boxed{32}$ $\boxed{+/-}$ $\boxed{+}$ $\boxed{131}$ $\boxed{+/-}$ $\boxed{=}$ or $\boxed{\text{ENTER}}$.

The display will read $\boxed{-163}$. Thus,
−32 + (−131) = −163.

Use a calculator to perform each indicated operation.

1. −256 + 97
2. 811 + (−1058)
3. 6(15) + (−46)
4. −129 + 10(48)
5. −108.65 + (−786.205)
6. −196.662 + (−129.856)

Answer

16. 3°F

Mental Math

Add.

1. $5 + 0$ **2.** $(-7) + 0$ **3.** $0 + (-35)$ **4.** $0 + 3$

FOR EXTRA HELP

Student Solutions Manual   PH Math/Tutor Center   CD/Video for Review   MathXL®   MyMathLab

Objective **A** *Add using a number line. See Examples 1 and 2.*

1. $8 + 2$

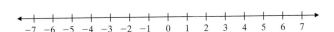

2. $9 + (-4)$

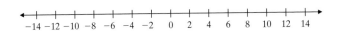

3. $-4 + 7$

4. $10 + (-3)$

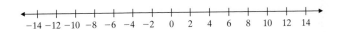

5. $-13 + 7$

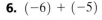

6. $(-6) + (-5)$

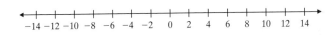

Add. See Examples 3 through 13.

7. $23 + 12$ **8.** $15 + 42$ **9.** $-6 + (-2)$ **10.** $-5 + (-4)$ **11.** $-43 + 43$

12. $-62 + 62$ **13.** $6 + (-2)$ **14.** $8 + (-3)$ **15.** $-6 + 8$ **16.** $-8 + 12$

17. $3 + (-5)$ **18.** $5 + (-9)$ **19.** $-2 + (-9)$ **20.** $-6 + (-1)$ **21.** $-7 + 7$

22. $-10 + 10$ **23.** $12 + (-5)$ **24.** $24 + (-10)$ **25.** $-6 + 3$ **26.** $-10 + 2$

27. $-12 + 3$ **28.** $-15 + 5$ **29.** $-12 + (-12)$ **30.** $-23 + (-23)$ **31.** $-25 + (-32)$

32. $-45 + (-90)$ **33.** $56 + (-26)$ **34.** $89 + (-37)$ **35.** $-37 + 57$ **36.** $-25 + 65$

37. $-123 + (-100)$ **38.** $-500 + (-230)$ **39.** $-42 + 193$ **40.** $-64 + 164$

41. $-6.3 + (-2.2)$ **42.** $-9.1 + (-4.6)$ **43.** $-10.7 + 15.3$ **44.** $-19.6 + 23.1$

45. $-\dfrac{7}{11} + \left(-\dfrac{1}{11}\right)$ **46.** $-\dfrac{9}{13} + \left(-\dfrac{1}{13}\right)$ **47.** $-\dfrac{2}{3} + \left(-\dfrac{1}{6}\right)$ **48.** $-\dfrac{3}{8} + \left(-\dfrac{1}{4}\right)$

49. $-\dfrac{4}{5} + \dfrac{1}{10}$ **50.** $-\dfrac{9}{16} + \dfrac{3}{8}$ **51.** $-2\dfrac{1}{4} + 7\dfrac{7}{8}$ **52.** $-4\dfrac{1}{5} + 6\dfrac{9}{10}$

Add. See Examples 14 and 15.

53. $-4 + 2 + (-5)$ **54.** $-1 + 5 + (-8)$ **55.** $-5.2 + (-7.7) + (-11.7)$

56. $-10.3 + (-3.2) + (-2.7)$ **57.** $12 + (-4) + (-4) + 12$ **58.** $18 + (-9) + 5 + (-2)$

59. $(-10) + 14 + 25 + (-16)$ **60.** $34 + (-12) + (-11) + 213$

Objective **B** *Solve. See Example 16.*

61. Find the sum of -8 and 25.   **62.** Find the sum of -30 and 10.

63. Find the sum of -31, -9, and 30.   **64.** Find the sum of -49, -2, and 40.

65. Suppose a deep-sea diver dives from the surface to 165 feet below the surface. He then dives down 16 more feet. Use positive and negative numbers to represent this situation. Then find the diver's present depth.

66. Suppose a diver dives from the surface to 248 meters below the surface and then swims up 6 meters, down 17 meters, down another 24 meters, and then up 23 meters. Use positive and negative numbers to represent this situation. Then find the diver's depth after these movements.

In some card games, it is possible to have positive and negative scores. The table shows the scores for two teams playing a series of four card games. Use this table to answer Exercises 67 and 68.

	Game 1	Game 2	Game 3	Game 4
Team 1	-2	-13	20	2
Team 2	5	11	-7	-3

67. Find each team's total score after four games. If the winner is the team with the greater score, find the winning team.

68. Find each team's total score after three games. If the winner is the team with the greater score, which team was winning after three games?

The bar graph below shows the yearly net income for Apple, Inc. Net income is one indication of a company's health. It measures revenue (money taken in) minus cost (money spent). Use this graph for Exercises 69 through 72. (Source: Apple, Inc.)

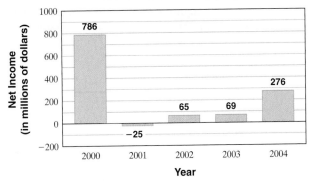

Net Income for Apple, Inc.

69. What was the net income (in dollars) for Apple, Inc. in 2000?

70. What was the net income (in dollars) for Apple, Inc. in 2001?

71. Find the total net income for years 2001 and 2002.

72. Find the total net income for all the years shown.

73. The temperature at 4 p.m. on February 2 was $-10°$ Celsius. By 11 p.m. the temperature had risen 12 degrees. Find the temperature at 11 p.m.

74. Scores in golf can be positive or negative integers. For example, a score of 3 *over* par can be represented by $+3$ and a score of 5 *under* par can be represented by -5. If Fred Couples had scores of 3 over par, 6 under par, and 7 under par for three games of golf, what was his total score?

A small business company reports the following net incomes. Use this table for Exercises 75 and 76.

Year	Net Income (in Dollars)
2001	$75,083
2002	$-$10,412
2003	$-$1,786
2004	$96,398

75. Find the sum of the net incomes for 2002 and 2003.

76. Find the net income sum for all four years shown.

77. The all-time record low temperature for Wyoming is $-66°$F, which was recorded on February 9, 1933. Kansas's all-time record low temperature is $26°$F higher than Wyoming's record low. What is Kansas's record low temperature? (*Source:* National Climatic Data Center)

78. The all-time record low temperature for New York is $-52°$F, which occurred on February 13, 1905. In Mississippi, the lowest temperature ever recorded is $33°$F higher than New York's all-time low temperature. What is the all-time record low temperature for Mississippi? (*Source:* National Climatic Data Center)

79. The deepest spot in the Pacific Ocean is the Mariana Trench, which has an elevation of 10,924 meters below sea level. The bottom of the Pacific's Aleutian Trench has an elevation 3245 meters higher than that of the Mariana Trench. Use a negative number to represent the depth of the Aleutian Trench. (*Source:* Defense Mapping Agency)

80. The deepest spot in the Atlantic Ocean is the Puerto Rico Trench, which has an elevation of 8605 meters below sea level. The bottom of the Atlantic's Cayman Trench has an elevation 1070 meters above the level of the Puerto Rico Trench. Use a negative number to represent the depth of the Cayman Trench. (*Source:* Defense Mapping Agency)

Review

Subtract. See Sections 1.4 and 4.3.

81. $44 - 0$ **82.** $91 - 0$ **83.** $76.1 - 4.09$ **84.** $93.7 - 10.08$ **85.** $200 - 59$ **86.** $400 - 18$

Concept Extensions

87. Name 2 numbers whose sum is -17.

88. Name 2 numbers whose sum is -30.

Each calculation below is incorrect. Find the error and correct. See the Concept Check in this section.

89. $7 + (-10) \stackrel{?}{=} 17$ **90.** $-10 + (-12) \stackrel{?}{=} -120$ **91.** $-4 + 14 \stackrel{?}{=} -18$ **92.** $-15 + (-17) \stackrel{?}{=} 32$

For Exercises 93 through 96, determine whether each statement is true or false.

93. The sum of two negative numbers is always a negative number.

94. The sum of two positive numbers is always a positive number.

95. The sum of a positive number and a negative number is always a negative number.

96. The sum of zero and a negative number is always a negative number.

 97. In your own words, explain how to add two negative numbers.

98. In your own words, explain how to add a positive number and a negative number.

📖 **STUDY SKILLS BUILDER**

Are You Preparing for Your Final Exam?

To prepare for your final exam, try the following study techniques.

- Review the material that you will be responsible for on your exam. This includes material from your textbook, your notebook, and any handouts from your instructor.
- Review any formulas that you may need to memorize.
- Check to see if your instructor or mathematics department will be conducting a final exam review.
- Check with your instructor to see whether final exams from previous semesters/quarters are available to students for review.

- Use your previously taken exams as a practice final exam. To do so, rewrite the test questions in mixed order on blank sheets of paper. This will help you prepare for exam conditions.
- If you are unsure of a few concepts, see your instructor or visit a learning lab for assistance. Also, view the video segment on any troublesome sections.
- If you need further exercises to work, try the Cumulative Reviews at the end of the chapters.

Good luck! I hope you have enjoyed this textbook and your mathematics course.

10.3 SUBTRACTING SIGNED NUMBERS

Objectives

A Subtract Signed Numbers.

B Add and Subtract Signed Numbers.

C Solve Problems by Subtracting Signed Numbers.

In Section 10.1 we discussed the opposite of a number.

The opposite of 3 is −3.
The opposite of −6.7 is 6.7.
Notice the pattern when we find the sum of these opposites.

$$3 + (-3) = 0 \quad \text{and} \quad -6.7 + 6.7 = 0$$

This pattern is always true. That is, the sum of a number and its opposite is always 0. Because of this, the opposite of a number is also called the **additive inverse** of a number. In this section, we use opposites (or additive inverses) to subtract signed numbers.

Objective **A** Subtracting Signed Numbers

To subtract signed numbers, we write the subtraction problem as an addition problem. To see how we do this, study the examples below:

$$10 - 4 = 6$$
$$10 + (-4) = 6$$

Since both expressions simplify to 6, this means that

$$10 - 4 = 10 + (-4) = 6$$

Also,

$$3 - 2 = 3 + (-2) = 1$$
$$15 - 1 = 15 + (-1) = 14$$

Thus, to subtract two numbers, we add the first number to the opposite (also called the **additive inverse**) of the second number.

Subtracting Two Numbers

If a and b are numbers, then $a - b = a + (-b)$.

EXAMPLES Subtract.

subtraction	=	first number	+	opposite of the second number		
1. $8 - 5$	=	8	+	(-5)	=	3
2. $-4 - 10$	=	−4	+	(-10)	=	−14
3. $6 - (-5)$	=	6	+	5	=	11
4. $-11 - (-7)$	=	−11	+	7	=	−4

■ **Work Practice Problems 1–4**

PRACTICE PROBLEMS 1–4

Subtract.
1. $12 - 7$ **2.** $-6 - 4$
3. $11 - (-14)$ **4.** $-9 - (-1)$

Answers
1. 5, **2.** −10, **3.** 25, **4.** −8

659

PRACTICE PROBLEMS 5–9

Subtract.

5. $5 - 9$ **6.** $-12 - 4$

7. $-2 - (-7)$ **8.** $-10.5 - 14.3$

9. $\dfrac{5}{13} - \dfrac{12}{13}$

EXAMPLES Subtract.

5. $-10 - 5 = -10 + (-5) = -15$

6. $8 - 15 = 8 + (-15) = -7$

7. $-4 - (-5) = -4 + 5 = 1$

8. $-1.7 - 6.2 = -1.7 + (-6.2) = -7.9$

9. $-\dfrac{10}{11} - \left(-\dfrac{3}{11}\right) = -\dfrac{10}{11} + \dfrac{3}{11} = -\dfrac{7}{11}$

🔲 **Work Practice Problems 5–9**

Helpful Hint

To visualize subtraction, try the following:

The difference between $5°F$ and $-2°F$ can be found by subtracting. That is,

$$5 - (-2) = 5 + 2 = 7$$

Can you visually see from the thermometer on the right that there are actually 7 degrees between $5°F$ and $-2°F$?

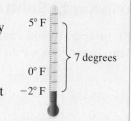

✔**Concept Check** What is wrong with the following calculation?

$$-7 - (-3) = -10$$

PRACTICE PROBLEM 10

Subtract 5 from -10.

EXAMPLE 10 Subtract 7 from -3.

Solution: To subtract 7 *from* -3, we find

$$-3 - 7 = -3 + (-7) = -10$$

🔲 **Work Practice Problem 10**

Objective B Adding and Subtracting Signed Numbers

If a problem involves adding or subtracting more than two signed numbers, we rewrite differences as sums and add. Recall that by associative and commutative properties, we may add numbers in any order. In Examples 11 and 12, we will add from left to right.

PRACTICE PROBLEM 11

Simplify: $-4 - 3 - 7 - (-5)$

EXAMPLE 11 Simplify: $7 - 8 - (-5) - 1$

Solution:

$$
\begin{aligned}
7 - 8 - (-5) - 1 &= 7 + (-8) + 5 + (-1) \\
&= -1 + 5 + (-1) \\
&= 4 + (-1) \\
&= 3
\end{aligned}
$$

🔲 **Work Practice Problem 11**

Answers

5. -4, **6.** -16, **7.** 5, **8.** -24.8,

9. $-\dfrac{7}{13}$, **10.** -15, **11.** -9

EXAMPLE 12 Simplify: $7 + (-12) - 3 - (-8)$

Solution:

$$7 + (-12) - 3 - (-8) = \underbrace{7 + (-12)} + (-3) + 8$$
$$= \underbrace{-5 + (-3)} + 8$$
$$= -8 + 8$$
$$= 0$$

Work Practice Problem 12

PRACTICE PROBLEM 12

Simplify:
$3 + (-5) - 6 - (-4)$

Objective **C** **Solving Problems by Subtracting Signed Numbers**

Solving problems often requires subtraction of signed numbers.

EXAMPLE 13 **Finding a Change in Elevation**

The highest point in the United States is the top of Mount McKinley, at a height of 20,320 feet above sea level. The lowest point is Death Valley, California, which is 282 feet below sea level. How much higher is Mount McKinley than Death Valley? (*Source:* U.S. Geological Survey)

PRACTICE PROBLEM 13

The highest point in Asia is the top of Mount Everest, at a height of 29,028 feet above sea level. The lowest point is the Dead Sea, which is 1312 feet below sea level. How much higher is Mount Everest than the Dead Sea? (*Source:* National Geographic Society)

Solution:

1. UNDERSTAND. Read and reread the problem. To find "how much higher," we subtract. Don't forget that since Death Valley is 282 feet *below* sea level, we represent its height by -282. Draw a diagram to help visualize the problem.

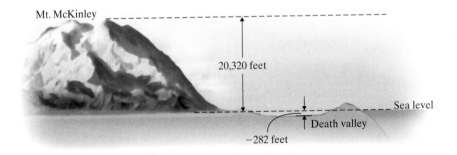

2. TRANSLATE.

In words:	how much higher is Mt. McKinley	=	height of Mt. McKinley	minus	height of Death Valley
	↓	↓	↓	↓	↓
Translate:	how much higher is Mt. McKinley	=	20,320	−	(−282)

3. SOLVE:

$$20,320 - (-282) = 20,320 + 282 = 20,602$$

4. INTERPRET. Check and state your conclusion: Mount McKinley is 20,602 feet higher than Death Valley.

Work Practice Problem 13

Answers
12. −4,   **13.** 30,340 ft

Mental Math

Subtract.

1. $5 - 5$ **2.** $7 - 7$ **3.** $6.2 - 6.2$ **4.** $1.9 - 1.9$

10.3 EXERCISE SET

Objective *Subtract. See Examples 1 through 9.*

1. $-5 - (-5)$ **2.** $-6 - (-6)$ **3.** $8 - 3$ **4.** $5 - 2$ **5.** $3 - 8$

6. $2 - 5$ **7.** $7 - (-7)$ **8.** $12 - (-12)$ **9.** $-5 - (-8)$ **10.** $-25 - (-25)$

11. $-14 - 4$ **12.** $-2 - 42$ **13.** $2 - 16$ **14.** $8 - 9$ **15.** $2.2 - 5.5$

16. $1.7 - 6.3$ **17.** $3.62 - (-0.4)$ **18.** $8.44 - (-0.2)$ **19.** $-\dfrac{3}{10} - \left(-\dfrac{7}{10}\right)$ **20.** $-\dfrac{2}{11} - \left(-\dfrac{5}{11}\right)$

21. $\dfrac{2}{5} - \dfrac{7}{10}$ **22.** $\dfrac{3}{16} - \dfrac{7}{8}$ **23.** $\dfrac{1}{2} - \left(-\dfrac{1}{3}\right)$ **24.** $\dfrac{1}{7} - \left(-\dfrac{1}{4}\right)$

Solve. See Example 10.

25. Subtract 18 from -20.   **26.** Subtract 10 from -22.   **27.** Find the difference of -20 and -3.

28. Find the difference of -8 and -13.   **29.** Subtract -11 from 2.   **30.** Subtract -50 from -50.

Mixed Practice (*Sections 10.2, 10.3*) *Add or subtract as indicated.*

31. $-21 + (-17)$ **32.** $-35 + (-11)$ **33.** $9 - 20$ **34.** $7 - 30$

35. $-4.9 - 7.8$ **36.** $-10.5 - 6.8$ **37.** $\dfrac{4}{7} + \left(-\dfrac{1}{7}\right)$ **38.** $\dfrac{9}{13} + \left(-\dfrac{5}{13}\right)$

Objective B *Simplify. See Examples 11 and 12.*

39. $7 - 3 - 2$

40. $8 - 4 - 1$

41. $12 - 5 - 7$

42. $30 - 7 - 12$

43. $-5 - 8 - (-12)$

44. $-10 - 6 - (-9)$

45. $-10 + (-5) - 12$

46. $-15 + (-8) - 4$

47. $12 - (-34) + (-6)$

48. $23 - (-17) + (-9)$

49. $19 - 14 + (-6) + (-50)$

50. $28 - 16 + (-14) + (-1)$

Objective C *Solve. See Example 13.*

The bar graph from Section 10.1 showing the average temperature in Fahrenheit of known planets is reprinted below. Notice that a negative temperature is illustrated by a bar below the horizontal line representing 0°F, and a positive temperature is illustrated by a bar above the horizontal line representing 0°F.

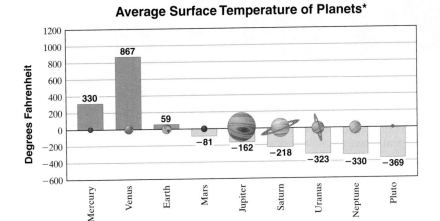

Average Surface Temperature of Planets*

*(For some planets, the temperature given is the temperature where the atmosphere pressure equals 1 Earth atmosphere; *Source: The World Almanac,* 2005)

51. Find the difference in temperature between Earth and Pluto.

52. Find the difference in temperature between Venus and Mars.

53. Find the difference in temperature between the two plants with the lowest temperature.

54. Find the difference in temperature between Jupiter and Saturn.

55. The coldest temperature ever recorded on Earth was −129°F in Antarctica. The warmest temperature ever recorded was 136°F in the Sahara Desert. How many degrees warmer is 136°F than −129°F? (*Source: Questions Kids Ask,* Grolier Limited, 1991, and *The World Almanac,* 2005)

56. The coldest temperature ever recorded in the United States was −80°F in Alaska. The warmest temperature ever recorded was 134°F in California. How many degrees warmer is 134°F than −80°F? (*Source: The World Almanac,* 2005)

57. Aaron Aiken has $125 in his checking account. He writes a check for $117, makes a deposit of $45, and then writes another check for $69. Find the balance in his account. (Write the amount as an integer.)

58. In the card game canasta, it is possible to have a negative score. If Juan Santanilla's score is 15, what is his new score if he loses 20 points?

59. The temperature on a February morning is −6° Celsius at 6 a.m. If the temperature drops 3 degrees by 7 a.m., rises 4 degrees between 7 a.m. and 8 a.m., and then drops 7 degrees between 8 a.m. and 9 a.m., find the temperature at 9 a.m.

60. Mauna Kea in Hawaii has an elevation of 13,796 feet above sea level. The Mid-America Trench in the Pacific Ocean has an elevation of 21,857 feet below sea level. Find the difference in elevation between those two points. (*Source:* National Geographic Society and Defense Mapping Agency)

Some places on Earth lie below sea level, which is the average level of the surface of the oceans. Use this diagram to answer Exercises 61 through 64. (Source: Fantastic Book of Comparisons, Russell Ash, 1999)

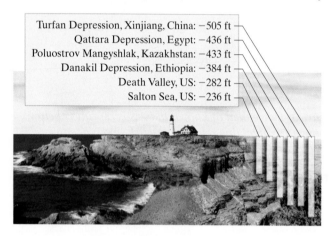

Turfan Depression, Xinjiang, China: −505 ft
Qattara Depression, Egypt: −436 ft
Poluostrov Mangyshlak, Kazakhstan: −433 ft
Danakil Depression, Ethiopia: −384 ft
Death Valley, US: −282 ft
Salton Sea, US: −236 ft

61. Find the difference in elevation between Death Valley and Quattâra Depression.

62. Find the difference in elevation between Danakil and Turfan Depressions.

63. Find the difference in elevation between the two lowest elevations shown.

64. Find the difference in elevation between the highest elevation shown and the lowest elevation shown.

The bar graph shows heights of selected lakes. For Exercises 65 through 68, find the difference in elevation for the lakes listed. (Source: U.S. Geological Survey)

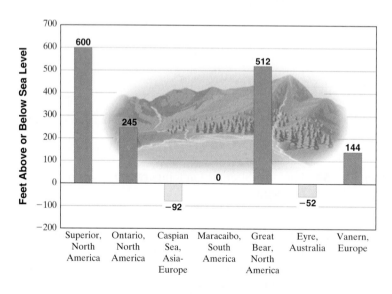

Feet Above or Below Sea Level

700
600 — 600
500 — 512
400
300 — 245
200
100 — 144
0 — 0
−100 — −92   −52
−200

Superior, North America | Ontario, North America | Caspian Sea, Asia-Europe | Maracaibo, South America | Great Bear, North America | Eyre, Australia | Vanern, Europe

65. Lake Superior and Lake Eyre

66. Great Bear Lake and Caspian Sea

67. Lake Maracaibo and Lake Vanern

68. Lake Eyre and Caspian Sea

69. The difference between a country's exports and imports is called the country's *trade balance.* In 2003, the United States had $725 billion in exports and $1257 billion in imports. What was the U.S. trade balance in 2001? (*Source:* U.S. Department of Commerce)

70. In 2003, the United States exported 375 million barrels of petroleum products and imported 4476 million barrels of petroleum products. What was the U.S. trade balance for petroleum products in 1997? (*Source:* U.S. Energy Information Administration)

Review

Multiply. See Section 1.6.

71. $8 \cdot 0$

72. $0 \cdot 8$

73. $1 \cdot 8$

74. $8 \cdot 1$

75. $\begin{array}{r} 23 \\ \times\ 46 \\ \hline \end{array}$

76. $\begin{array}{r} 51 \\ \times\ 89 \\ \hline \end{array}$

Concept Extensions

77. Name two numbers whose difference is -3.

78. Name two numbers whose difference is -10.

Each calculation below is incorrect. Find the error and correct. See the Concept Check in this section.

79. $9 - (-7) \overset{?}{=} 2$

80. $-4 - 8 \overset{?}{=} 4$

81. $10 - 30 \overset{?}{=} 20$

82. $-3 - (-10) \overset{?}{=} -13$

Simplify. (Hint: Find the absolute values first.)

83. $|-3| - |-7|$

84. $|-12| - |-5|$

85. $|-6| - |6|$

86. $|-9| - |9|$

87. $|-17| - |-29|$

88. $|-23| - |-42|$

For Exercises 89 and 90, determine whether each statement is true or false.

89. $|-8 - 3| = 8 - 3$

90. $|-2 - (-6)| = |-2| - |-6|$

91. In your own words, explain how to subtract one signed number from another.

92. A student explains to you that the first step to simplify $8 + 12 \cdot 5 - 100$ is to add 8 and 12. Is the student correct? Explain why or why not.

Signed Numbers

Answers

1. _____

2. _____

3. _____

4. _____

5. see number line

6. _____

7. _____

8. _____

9. _____

10. _____

11. _____

12. _____

13. _____

14. _____

15. _____

16. _____

17. _____

18. _____

19. _____

20. _____

21. _____

Represent each quantity by a signed number.

1. The peak of Mount Everest in Asia is 29,028 feet above sea level. (*Source:* U.S. Geological Survey)

2. The Mariana Trench in the Pacific Ocean is 35,840 feet below sea level. (*Source: The World Almanac,* 1998)

3. The deepest hole ever drilled in the Earth's crust is in Russia and its depth is over 7 miles below sea level. (*Source: Fantastic Book of Comparisons,* 1999)

Surface of the earth

Over 7 miles

4. The peak of K2 in Asia is 28,250 feet above sea level. (*Source:* National Geographic Society)

5. Graph the signed numbers on the given number line. $-4, 0, -1.5, 3\frac{1}{4}$

$$\begin{array}{c} \longleftrightarrow \\ -5\ -4\ -3\ -2\ -1\ \ 0\ \ 1\ \ 2\ \ 3\ \ 4\ \ 5 \end{array}$$

Insert $<$ or $>$ between each pair of numbers to make a true statement.

6. $0 \quad -3$

7. $-15 \quad -5$

8. $-1\frac{1}{2} \quad 1\frac{1}{4}$

9. $-2 \quad -7.6$

10. $7 \quad 0$

11. $-4 \quad -40$

12. $3.9 \quad -3.9$

13. $-\frac{1}{2} \quad -\frac{1}{3}$

Simplify.

14. $|-1|$

15. $|1|$

16. $|0|$

17. $-|-4|$

18. $|-8.6|$

19. $|100.3|$

20. $-\left(-\frac{3}{4}\right)$

21. $-\left|-\frac{3}{4}\right|$

Find the opposite of each number.

22. 6

23. −13

24. 89.1

25. $-\dfrac{2}{9}$

Add or subtract as indicated.

26. −7 + 12

27. −9.2 + (−11.6)

28. $\dfrac{5}{9} + \left(-\dfrac{1}{3}\right)$

29. 1 − 3

30. $\dfrac{3}{8} - \left(-\dfrac{3}{8}\right)$

31. −2.6 − 1.4

32. −7 + (−2.6)

33. −14 + 8

34. −8 − (−20)

35. 18 − (−102)

36. 8.65 − 12.09

37. $-\dfrac{4}{5} - \dfrac{3}{10}$

38. −8 + (−6) + 20

39. −11 − 7 − (−19)

40. −4 + (−8) − 16 − (−9)

41. Subtract 26 from 14.

42. Subtract −8 from −12.

43. Find the sum of −17 and −27.

44. The coldest temperature ever recorded in Europe was −67°F in Ust'Shchugor, Russia. The warmest temperature ever recorded in Europe was 122°F in Seville, Spain. How many degrees warmer is 122°F than −67°F? (*Source:* National Climatic Data Center)

22. _____

23. _____

24. _____

25. _____

26. _____

27. _____

28. _____

29. _____

30. _____

31. _____

32. _____

33. _____

34. _____

35. _____

36. _____

37. _____

38. _____

39. _____

40. _____

41. _____

42. _____

43. _____

44. _____

10.4 MULTIPLYING AND DIVIDING SIGNED NUMBERS

Multiplying and dividing signed numbers is similar to multiplying and dividing whole numbers. One difference is that we need to determine whether the result is a positive number or a negative number.

Objective **A** Multiplying Signed Numbers

Consider the following pattern of products:

First factor decreases by 1 each time.

$3 \cdot 2 = 6$
$2 \cdot 2 = 4$
$1 \cdot 2 = 2$
$0 \cdot 2 = 0$

Product decreases by 2 each time.

This pattern can be continued, as follows:

$-1 \cdot 2 = -2$
$-2 \cdot 2 = -4$
$-3 \cdot 2 = -6$

This suggests that the product of a negative number and a positive number is a negative number.

What is the sign of the product of two negative numbers? To find out, we form another pattern of products. Again, we decrease the first factor by 1 each time, but this time the second factor is negative.

$2 \cdot (-3) = -6$
$1 \cdot (-3) = -3$
$0 \cdot (-3) = 0$

Product increases by 3 each time.

This pattern continues as

$-1 \cdot (-3) = 3$
$-2 \cdot (-3) = 6$
$-3 \cdot (-3) = 9$

This suggests that the product of two negative numbers is a positive number. Thus, we can determine the sign of a product when we know the signs of the factors.

Multiplying Numbers

The product of two numbers having the same sign is a positive number.

The product of two numbers having different signs is a negative number.

Product of Like Signs

$(+)(+) = +$
$(-)(-) = +$

Product of Different Signs

$(-)(+) = -$
$(+)(-) = -$

EXAMPLES Multiply.

1. $-7 \cdot 3 = -21$
2. $-2(-5) = 10$
3. $0 \cdot (-4) = 0$
4. $\left(-\dfrac{1}{2}\right)\left(-\dfrac{2}{3}\right) = \dfrac{1 \cdot \overset{1}{\cancel{2}}}{\underset{1}{\cancel{2}} \cdot 3} = \dfrac{1}{3}$
5. $-3(1.2) = -3.6$

▢ **Work Practice Problems 1–5**

Recall that by the associative and commutative properties for multiplication, we may multiply numbers in any order that we wish. In Examples 6 and 7, we multiply from left to right.

EXAMPLES Multiply.

6. $\overbrace{7(-6)}(-2) = -42(-2)$
   $= 84$
7. $\overbrace{(-2)(-3)}(-4) = 6(-4)$
   $= -24$
8. $(-1)(-2)(-3)(-4) = -1(-24)$ We have -24 from Example 6.
   $= 24$

▢ **Work Practice Problems 6–8**

✔ **Concept Check** What is the sign of the product of five negative numbers? Explain.

Helpful Hint

Have you noticed a pattern when multiplying signed numbers?
If we let $(-)$ represent a negative number and $(+)$ represent a positive number, then

The product of an even number of negative numbers is a positive result.
$(-)(-) = (+)$
$(-)(-)(-) = (-)$
$(-)(-)(-)(-) = (+)$
$(-)(-)(-)(-)(-) = (-)$
The product of an odd number of negative numbers is a negative result.

Recall from our study of exponents that $2^3 = 2 \cdot 2 \cdot 2 = 8$. We can now work with bases that are negative numbers. For example,

$(-2)^3 = \underbrace{(-2)(-2)(-2)}_{3 \text{ factors of } -2} = -8$

EXAMPLE 9 Evaluate: $(-5)^2$

Solution: Remember that $(-5)^2$ means 2 factors of -5.

$(-5)^2 = (-5)(-5) = 25$

▢ **Work Practice Problem 9**

PRACTICE PROBLEMS 1–5
Multiply.
1. $-2 \cdot 6$
2. $-4(-3)$
3. $0 \cdot (-10)$
4. $\left(\dfrac{3}{7}\right)\left(-\dfrac{1}{3}\right)$
5. $-4(-3.2)$

PRACTICE PROBLEMS 6–8
Multiply.
6. $7(-2)(-4)$
7. $(-5)(-6)(-1)$
8. $(-2)(-5)(-6)(-1)$

PRACTICE PROBLEM 9
Evaluate: $(-3)^4$

Answers
1. -12, 2. 12, 3. 0, 4. $-\dfrac{1}{7}$,
5. 12.8, 6. 56, 7. -30, 8. 60,
9. 81

✔ **Concept Check Answer**
negative

Notice in Example 9 the parentheses around -5 in $(-5)^2$. With these parentheses, -5 is the base that is squared. Without parentheses, such as -7^2, only the 7 is squared, as shown next.

PRACTICE PROBLEM 10

Evaluate: -9^2

EXAMPLE 10 Evaluate: -7^2

Solution: Remember that without parentheses, only the 7 is squared.

$$-7^2 = -(7 \cdot 7) = -49$$

■ Work Practice Problem 10

Helpful Hint

Make sure you understand the difference between Examples 9 and 10.

$\rightarrow$ parentheses, so -5 is squared

$$\overbrace{(-5)^2} = (-5)(-5) = 25$$

$\rightarrow$ no parentheses, so only the 7 is squared

$$-7^2 = -(7 \cdot 7) = -49$$

Objective B Dividing Signed Numbers

Division of signed numbers is related to multiplication of signed numbers. The sign rules for division can be discovered by writing a related multiplication problem. For example,

$$\frac{6}{2} = 3 \qquad \text{because } 3 \cdot 2 = 6$$

Helpful Hint

Just as for whole numbers, division can be checked by multiplication.

$$\frac{-6}{2} = -3 \qquad \text{because } -3 \cdot 2 = -6$$

$$\frac{6}{-2} = -3 \qquad \text{because } -3 \cdot (-2) = 6$$

$$\frac{-6}{-2} = 3 \qquad \text{because } 3 \cdot (-2) = -6$$

Dividing Numbers

The quotient of two numbers having the same sign is a positive number.

Quotient of Like Signs

$$\frac{(+)}{(+)} = + \qquad \frac{(-)}{(-)} = +$$

The quotient of two numbers having different signs in a negative number.

Quotient of Different Signs

$$\frac{(+)}{(-)} = - \qquad \frac{(-)}{(+)} = -$$

PRACTICE PROBLEMS 11–14

Divide.

11. $\dfrac{28}{-7}$ **12.** $-18 \div (-2)$

13. $\dfrac{-4.6}{0.2}$ **14.** $\dfrac{3}{5} \div \left(-\dfrac{2}{7}\right)$

Answers

10. -81, **11.** -4, **12.** 9, **13.** -23,

14. $-\dfrac{21}{10}$ or $-2\dfrac{1}{10}$

EXAMPLES Divide.

11. $\dfrac{-12}{6} = -2$

12. $-20 \div (-4) = 5$

13. $\dfrac{1.2}{-0.6} = -2$ $0.6\overline{)1.2}$ (quotient 2)

14. $\dfrac{7}{9} \div \left(-\dfrac{2}{5}\right) = \dfrac{7}{9} \cdot \left(-\dfrac{5}{2}\right) = -\dfrac{7 \cdot 5}{9 \cdot 2} = -\dfrac{35}{18}$ or $-1\dfrac{17}{18}$

■ Work Practice Problems 11–14

✔ Concept Check Find the error in the following computation:

$$\cancel{\frac{1}{2} \div (-3) = \frac{1}{2} \cdot \frac{1}{3} = \frac{1}{6}}$$

EXAMPLES Divide, if possible.

15. $\dfrac{0}{-5} = 0$ because $0 \cdot -5 = 0$

16. $\dfrac{-7}{0}$ is undefined because there is no number that gives a product of -7 when multiplied by 0

▣ **Work Practice Problems 15–16**

PRACTICE PROBLEMS 15–16

Divide, if possible.

15. $\dfrac{-1}{0}$ **16.** $\dfrac{0}{-2}$

Let's take a moment and notice a pattern from earlier work in this section.

$$\frac{-6}{2} = -3, \quad \frac{6}{-2} = -3, \quad \text{and} \quad -\frac{6}{2} = -3$$

Since $\dfrac{-6}{2}, \dfrac{6}{-2}$, and $-\dfrac{6}{2}$ all equal -3, then they must equal each other. Thus,

$$\frac{-6}{2} = \frac{6}{-2} = -\frac{6}{2}.$$

In general, this shows us three equivalent ways to write a negative fraction.

> The fraction $-\dfrac{a}{b} = \dfrac{-a}{b} = \dfrac{a}{-b}$

✔ Concept Check Write $-\dfrac{4}{7}$ in two other equivalent ways.

Objective C Solving Problems by Multiplying and Dividing Signed Numbers

Many real-life problems involve multiplication and division of signed numbers.

PRACTICE PROBLEM 17

A card player had a score of -12 for each of four games. Find her total score.

EXAMPLE 17 **Calculating Total Golf Score**

A professional golfer finished seven strokes under par (-7) for each of three days of a tournament. What was his total score for the tournament?

Solution:

1. UNDERSTAND. Read and reread the problem. Although the key word is "total," since this is repeated addition of the same number we multiply.

2. TRANSLATE.

In words:	golfer's total score	=	number of day	·	score each day
	↓	↓	↓	↓	↓
Translate:	golfer's total	=	3	·	(-7)

3. SOLVE: $3 \cdot (-7) = -21$

4. INTERPRET. Check and state your conclusion: The golfer's total score is -21, or 21 strokes under par.

▣ **Work Practice Problem 17**

Answers
15. undefined, **16.** 0, **17.** -48

✔ **Concept Check Answers**
$\dfrac{1}{2} \div (-3) = \dfrac{1}{2} \cdot \left(-\dfrac{1}{3}\right) = -\dfrac{1}{6}; \quad \dfrac{-4}{7}, \dfrac{4}{-7}$

Objective A *Multiply. See Examples 1 through 5.*

1. $-2(-3)$

2. $5(-3)$

3. $-4(9)$

4. $-7(-2)$

5. $(2.6)(-1.2)$

6. $-0.3(5.6)$

7. $0(-14)$

8. $-6(0)$

9. $-\dfrac{3}{5}\left(-\dfrac{2}{7}\right)$

10. $-\dfrac{3}{4}\left(\dfrac{9}{10}\right)$

Multiply. See Examples 6 through 8.

11. $6(-4)(2)$

12. $8(-3)(3)$

13. $-1(-2)(-4)$

14. $-2(-5)(-4)$

15. $-4(4)(-5)$

16. $-2(3)(-7)$

17. $10(-5)(-1)(-3)$

18. $2(-1)(3)(-2)$

Evaluate. See Examples 9 and 10.

19. $(-2)^2$

20. $(-2)^4$

21. -5^2

22. -3^2

23. $(-3)^3$

24. $(-1)^4$

25. -2^3

26. -1^3

27. $(-9)^2$

28. $(-4)^3$

29. $\left(-\dfrac{5}{11}\right)^2$

30. $\left(-\dfrac{3}{7}\right)^2$

Objective B *Divide. See Examples 11 through 16.*

31. $-24 \div 6$

32. $90 \div (-9)$

33. $\dfrac{-30}{6}$

34. $\dfrac{56}{-8}$

35. $\dfrac{-88}{-11}$

36. $\dfrac{-32}{4}$

37. $\dfrac{0}{14}$

38. $\dfrac{-13}{0}$

39. $\dfrac{39}{-3}$

40. $\dfrac{-24}{-12}$

41. $\dfrac{7.8}{-0.3}$

42. $\dfrac{1.21}{-1.1}$

43. $-\dfrac{5}{12} \div \left(-\dfrac{1}{5}\right)$

44. $-\dfrac{3}{8} \div \left(-\dfrac{2}{7}\right)$

45. $\dfrac{100}{-20}$

46. $450 \div (-9)$

47. $\dfrac{240}{-40}$

48. $480 \div (-8)$

49. $\dfrac{-12}{-4}$

50. $\dfrac{-36}{-3}$

51. $\dfrac{-120}{0.4}$

52. $\dfrac{-200}{2.5}$

53. $-\dfrac{8}{15} \div \dfrac{2}{3}$

54. $-\dfrac{1}{6} \div \dfrac{7}{18}$

Objectives Ⓐ Ⓑ **Mixed Practice** *Perform the indicated operation.*

55. $-12(0)$

56. $0(-100)$

57. $(-5)^3$

58. $(-3)^2$

59. $\dfrac{430}{-8.6}$

60. $\dfrac{-423}{4.7}$

61. $-1(2)(7)(-3.1)$

62. $-2(3)(5)(-6.2)$

63. $\dfrac{4}{3}\left(-\dfrac{8}{9}\right)$

64. $-\dfrac{1}{9}\left(-\dfrac{1}{3}\right)$

65. $\dfrac{4}{3} \div \left(-\dfrac{8}{9}\right)$

66. $-\dfrac{1}{9} \div \left(-\dfrac{1}{3}\right)$

Objective Ⓒ *Solve. See Example 17.*

67. Find the quotient of -27 and 9.

68. Find the quotient of -63 and -3.

69. Find the product of -51 and -6.

70. Find the product of -49 and 5.

71. A football team lost four yards on each of three consecutive plays. Represent the total loss as a product of signed numbers and find the total loss.

72. Joe Norstrom lost \$400 on each of seven consecutive days in the stock market. Represent his total loss as a product of signed numbers and find his total loss.

73. A deep-sea diver must move up or down in the water in short steps in order to keep from getting a physical condition called the "bends." Suppose a diver moves down from the surface in five steps of 20 feet each. Represent his total movement as a product of signed numbers and find the product.

74. A weather forecaster predicts that the temperature will drop five degrees each hour for the next six hours. Represent this drop as a product of signed numbers and find the total drop in temperature.

75. During the third quarter of 2004, Delta Airlines posted a net income of $-\$646$ million. If this continued, what would Delta's net income have been after four quarters? (*Source:* Delta Airlines)

76. During the third quarter of 2004, AMR Corporation, the parent company of American Airlines, Inc., posted a net income of $-\$214$ million. If this continued, what would AMR's net income have been after four quarters? (*Source:* AMR Corporation)

77. In 1987, there were only 27 California Condors in the entire world. Thanks to conservation efforts, in 2004 there were 221 California Condors. (*Source:* California Department of Fish and Game)

    a. Find the change in the number of California Condors from 1987 to 2004.

    b. Find the average change per year in the California Condor population over the period in part a. Round to the nearest whole.

78. In 2000, a total of 76 million music cassettes were shipped to retailers in the United States. In 2004, this number had dropped to 17.2 music cassettes. (*Source:* Recording Industry Association of America)

    a. Find the change in the number of music cassettes shipped to retailers from 2000 to 2004.

    b. Find the average change per year in the number of music cassettes shipped to retailers over this period.

The graph shows melting points in degrees Celsius of selected elements. Use this graph to answer Exercises 79 through 82.

79. The melting point of nitrogen is 3 times the melting point of radon. Find the melting point of nitrogen.

80. The melting point of rubidium is −1 times the melting point of mercury. Find the melting point of rubidium.

81. The melting point of argon is −3 times the melting point of potassium. Find the melting point of argon.

82. The melting point of strontium is −11 times the melting point of radon. Find the melting point of strontium.

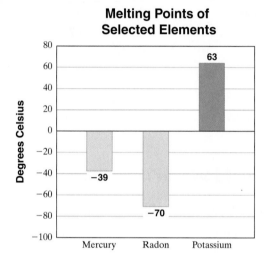

Melting Points of Selected Elements

Recall that the average of a list of numbers is the sum of the numbers divided by how many numbers are in the list. Use this for Exercises 83 and 84.

83. During the 2004 U.S. Women's Open golf tournament, the winner, Meg Mallon, had scores of +2, −2, −4, and −6 in four rounds of golf. Find her average score per round. (*Source:* Ladies Professional Golf Association)

84. During the 2004 Washovia LPGA Classic golf tournament, the winner, Lorena Ochoa, had scores of −7, −3, −4, and −5 in four rounds of golf. Find her average score per round. (*Source:* Ladies Professional Golf Association)

Review

Perform each indicated operation. See Section 1.9.

85. $(3 \cdot 5)^2$

86. $(12 - 3) \cdot (18 - 10)$

87. $90 + 12^2 - 5^3$

88. $3 \cdot (7 - 4) + 2 \cdot 5^2$

89. $12 \div 4 - 2 + 7$

90. $12 \div (4 - 2) + 7$

Concept Extensions

Mixed Practice (*Sections 10.2, 10.3, 10.4*) *Perform indicated operations.*

91. $-87 \div 3$

92. $-9(-10)$

93. $-9 - 10$

94. $-4 + (-3) + 21$

95. $-4 - 15 - (-11)$

96. $-16 - (-2)$

In Exercises 97 through 100, determine whether each statement is true or false.

97. The product of two negative numbers is always a negative number.

98. The product of a positive number and a negative number is always a negative number.

99. The quotient of two negative numbers is always a positive number.

100. The quotient of zero and a negative number is always zero.

Solve. For Exercises 101 through 103, see the first Concept Check in this section.

101. What is the sign of the product of seven negative numbers?

102. What is the sign of the product of ten negative numbers?

103. Write the fractions in two other equivalent ways by different placements of the negative sign.

    a. $-\dfrac{20}{41}$

    b. $-\dfrac{8}{17}$

Without actually finding the product, write the list of numbers in Exercises 104 and 105 in order from least to greatest. For help, see a helpful hint box in this section.

104. $(-2)^{12}, (-2)^{17}, (-5)^{12}, (-5)^{17}$

105. $(-1)^{50}, (-1)^{55}, 0^{15}, (-7)^{20}, (-7)^{23}$

106. In your own words, explain how to divide two signed numbers.

107. In your own words, explain how to multiply two signed numbers.

THE BIGGER PICTURE   **Operations on Sets of Numbers and Solving Equations**

Continue your outline from Sections 1.7, 1.9, 2.5, 3.4, 4.5, 5.3, and 6.3 or 6.4. Suggestions are once again written to help you complete this part of your outline. Notice that this part of the outline has to do with operations on signed numbers.

I. **Some Operations on Sets of Numbers**

   A. **Whole Numbers**

     1. **Add or Subtract** (Sections 1.3, 1.4)

     2. **Multiply or Divide** (Sections 1.6, 1.7)

     3. **Exponent** (Section 1.9)

     4. **Square Root** (Section 1.9)

     5. **Order of Operations** (Section 1.9)

   B. **Fractions**

     1. **Simplify** (Section 2.3)

     2. **Multiply** (Section 2.4)

     3. **Divide** (Section 2.5)

     4. **Add or Subtract** (Section 3.4)

   C. **Decimals**

     1. **Add or Subtract** (Section 4.3)

     2. **Multiply** (Section 4.4)

     3. **Divide** (Section 4.5)

   D. **Signed Numbers**

     1. **Add:**

$$-5 + (-2) = -7$$

Adding like signs. Add absolute value. Attach the common sign.

$$-5 + 2 = -3$$

Adding unlike signs. Subtract absolute values. Attach the sign of the number with the larger absolute value.

     2. **Subtract:** Add the first number to the opposite of the second number.

$$7 - 10 = 7 + (-10) = -3$$

     3. **Multiply or Divide:** Multiply or divide as usual. If the signs of the two numbers are the same, the answer is positive. If the signs of the two numbers are different, the answer is negative.

$$-5 \cdot 5 = -25, \quad \frac{-32}{-8} = 4$$

II. **Solving Equations**

   A. **Proportions** (Section 5.3)

   B. **Percent Problems**

     1. **Solved by Equations** (Section 6.3)

     2. **Solved by Proportions** (Section 6.4)

Perform the indicated operations.

1. $-9 + 14$

2. $-5(-11)$

3. $5 - 11$

4. $58 - |-70|$

5. $18 + (-30)$

6. $(-9)^2$

7. -9^2

8. $-10 + (-24)$

9. $1 - (-9)$

10. $-15 - 15$

11. $-\dfrac{7}{27}\left(\dfrac{9}{14}\right)$

12. $\dfrac{|-88|}{-|-8|}$

13. $2 + 4(7 - 9)^3$

14. $-100 - (-20)$

15. $-3\dfrac{1}{3} \div \left(-2\dfrac{5}{6}\right)$

16. $\left(\dfrac{3}{4} - \dfrac{7}{8}\right)^2 + \left(-\dfrac{5}{8}\right)$

10.5 ORDER OF OPERATIONS

Objective **A** Simplifying Expressions

We first discussed the order of operations in Chapter 1. In this section, you are given an opportunity to practice using the order of operations when expressions contain signed numbers. The rules for the order of operations from Section 1.9 are repeated here.

Order of Operations

1. Perform all operations within parentheses ( ), brackets [ ], or other grouping symbols such as square roots or fraction bars.
2. Evaluate any expressions with exponents.
3. Multiply or divide in order from left to right.
4. Add or subtract in order from left to right.

EXAMPLE 1 Simplify: $\dfrac{-6(2)}{-3}$

Solution: First we multiply -6 and 2. Then we divide.

$$\frac{-6(2)}{-3} = \frac{-12}{-3}$$
$$= 4$$

Work Practice Problem 1

PRACTICE PROBLEM 1

Simplify: $\dfrac{25}{5(-1)}$

EXAMPLE 2 Simplify: $\dfrac{12 - 16}{-1 + 3}$

Solution: We simplify above and below the fraction bar separately. Then we divide.

$$\frac{12 - 16}{-1 + 3} = \frac{-4}{2}$$
$$= -2$$

Work Practice Problem 2

PRACTICE PROBLEM 2

Simplify: $\dfrac{-18 + 6}{-3 - 1}$

EXAMPLE 3 Simplify: $60 + 30 + (-2)^3$

Solution: $60 + 30 + (-2)^3 = 60 + 30 + (-8)$ Write $(-2)^3$ as -8.
$$= 90 + (-8) \qquad \text{Add from left to right.}$$
$$= 82$$

Work Practice Problem 3

PRACTICE PROBLEM 3

Simplify: $20 + 50 + (-4)^3$

EXAMPLE 4 Simplify: $-4^2 + (-3)^2 - 1^3$

Solution:

$$-4^2 + (-3)^2 - 1^3 = -16 + 9 - 1 \quad \text{Simplify expressions with exponents.}$$
$$= -7 - 1 \qquad \text{Add or subtract from left to right.}$$
$$= -8$$

Work Practice Problem 4

PRACTICE PROBLEM 4

Simplify: $-2^3 + (-4)^2 + 1^5$

Answers
1. -5,   2. 3,   3. 6,   4. 9

PRACTICE PROBLEM 5
Simplify:
$2(2 - 8) + (-12) - \sqrt{9}$

EXAMPLE 5 Simplify: $3(4 - 7) + (-2) - \sqrt{25}$

Solution:
$$3(4 - 7) + (-2) - \sqrt{25} = 3(-3) + (-2) - 5 \quad \text{Simplify inside parentheses and}$$
$$\text{replace } \sqrt{25} \text{ with 5.}$$
$$= -9 + (-2) - 5 \quad \text{Multiply.}$$
$$= -11 - 5 \quad \text{Add or subtract from left to right.}$$
$$= -16$$

◻ **Work Practice Problem 5**

PRACTICE PROBLEM 6
Simplify:
$(-5) \cdot |-4| + (-3) + 2^3$

EXAMPLE 6 Simplify: $(-3) \cdot |-5| - (-2) + 4^2$

Solution:
$$(-3) \cdot |-5| - (-2) + 4^2 = (-3) \cdot 5 - (-2) + 4^2 \quad \text{Write } |-5| \text{ as 5.}$$
$$= (-3) \cdot 5 - (-2) + 16 \quad \text{Write } 4^2 \text{ as 16.}$$
$$= -15 - (-2) + 16 \quad \text{Multiply.}$$
$$= -13 + 16 \quad \text{Add or subtract from left to right.}$$
$$= 3$$

◻ **Work Practice Problem 6**

PRACTICE PROBLEM 7
Simplify:
$-4[-2 + 5(-3 + 5)] - 7.9$

EXAMPLE 7 Simplify: $-2[-3 + 2(-1 + 6)] - 5.3$

Solution: Here we begin with the innermost set of parentheses.
$$-2[-3 + 2(-1 + 6)] - 5.3 = -2[-3 + 2(5)] - 5.3 \quad \text{Write } -1 + 6 \text{ as 5.}$$
$$= -2[-3 + 10] - 5.3 \quad \text{Multiply.}$$
$$= -2(7) - 5.3 \quad \text{Add.}$$
$$= -14 - 5.3 \quad \text{Multiply.}$$
$$= -19.3 \quad \text{Subtract.}$$

◻ **Work Practice Problem 7**

✔**Concept Check** True or false? Explain your answer. The result of
$$-4(3 - 7) - 8(9 - 6)$$
is positive because there are four negative signs.

PRACTICE PROBLEM 8
Simplify: $\dfrac{5}{8} \div \left(\dfrac{1}{4} - \dfrac{3}{4}\right)$

EXAMPLE 8 Simplify: $\left(\dfrac{1}{6} - \dfrac{5}{6}\right) \cdot \dfrac{3}{7}$

Solution:
$$\left(\frac{1}{6} - \frac{5}{6}\right) \cdot \frac{3}{7} = -\frac{2}{3} \cdot \frac{3}{7} \quad \frac{1}{6} - \frac{5}{6} = -\frac{4}{6} = -\frac{2}{3}$$

$$= -\frac{2 \cdot \overset{1}{\cancel{3}}}{\underset{1}{\cancel{3}} \cdot 7} \quad \text{Multiply.}$$

$$= -\frac{2}{7} \quad \text{Simplify.}$$

◻ **Work Practice Problem 8**

Even though most calculators follow the order of operations, parentheses must sometimes be inserted. For example, to simplify $\dfrac{-8 + 6}{-2}$ on a calculator, enter parentheses around the expression above the fraction bar so that it is simplified separately.

To simplify $\dfrac{-8 + 6}{-2}$, press the keys

| (| 8 | +/− | + | 6 |) | ÷ | 2 | +/− | = |

or | ENTER |.

The display will read | 1 |.

Thus, $\dfrac{-8 + 6}{-2} = 1$.

Use a calculator to simplify.

1. $\dfrac{-12 - 36}{-10}$

2. $\dfrac{475}{-0.2 + (-1.7)}$

3. $\dfrac{-316 + (-458)}{28 + (-25)}$

4. $\dfrac{-234 + 86}{-18 + 16}$

10.5 EXERCISE SET

Objective A *Simplify. See Examples 1 through 8.*

1. $-1(-2) + 1$

2. $3 + (-8) \div 2$

3. $\dfrac{-8(-5)}{10}$

4. $\dfrac{-9(-6)}{18}$

5. $9 - 12 - 4$

6. $10 - 23 - 12$

7. $4 + 3(-6)$

8. $8 + 4(-3)$

9. $\dfrac{4}{9}\left(\dfrac{2}{10} - \dfrac{7}{10}\right)$

10. $\dfrac{2}{5}\left(\dfrac{3}{8} - \dfrac{4}{8}\right)$

11. $-10 + 4 \div 2$

12. $-12 + 6 \div 3$

13. $25 \div (-5) + \sqrt{81}$

14. $28 \div (-7) + \sqrt{25}$

15. $\dfrac{-|-5| + 3}{7 - 9}$

16. $\dfrac{-|-11| + 7}{7 - 9}$

17. $\dfrac{24}{10 + (-4)}$

18. $\dfrac{88}{-8 - 3}$

19. $5(-3) - (-12)$

20. $7(-4) - (-6)$

21. $-19 - 12(3)$

22. $-24 - 14(2)$

23. $\dfrac{-23 + 7}{14 + (-10)}$

24. $\dfrac{-27 + 6}{13 + (-10)}$

25. $[8 + (-4)]^2$

26. $[9 + (-2)]^3$

27. $3^3 - 12$

28. $5^2 - 100$

29. $(3 - 12) \div 3$

30. $(12 - 19) \div 7$

31. $5 + 2^3 - 4^2$

32. $12 + 5^2 - 2^4$

33. $(5 - 9)^2 \div (4 - 2)^2$

34. $(2 - 7)^2 \div (4 - 3)^4$

35. $|8 - 24| \cdot (-2) \div (-2)$

36. $|3 - 15| \cdot (-4) \div (-16)$

37. $(-12 - 20) \div 16 - 25$

38. $(-20 - 5) \div 5 - 15$

39. $5(5 - 2) + (-5)^2 - \sqrt{36}$

40. $3(8 - 3) + (-4)^2 - \sqrt{100}$

41. $(0.2 - 0.7)(0.6 - 1.9)$

42. $(0.4 - 1.2)(0.8 - 1.7)$

43. $2 - 7 \cdot 6 - 19$

44. $4 - 12 \cdot 8 - 17$

45. $(-36 \div 6) - (4 \div 4)$

46. $(-4 \div 4) - (8 \div 8)$

47. $\left(\dfrac{1}{2}\right)^2 - \left(\dfrac{1}{3}\right)^2$

48. $\left(\dfrac{1}{4}\right)^2 - \left(\dfrac{1}{2}\right)^2$

49. $(-5)^2 - 6^2$

50. $(-4)^4 - (5)^4$

51. $(10 - 4^2)^2$

52. $(11 - 3^2)^3$

53. $2(8 - 10)^2 - 5(1 - 6)^2$

54. $-3(4 - 8)^2 + 5(14 - 16)^3$

55. $3(-10) \div [5(-3) - 7(-2)]$

56. $12 - [7 - (3 - 6)] + (2 - 3)^3$

57. $\dfrac{(-7)(-3) - 4(3)}{3[7 \div (3 - 10)]}$

58. $\dfrac{10(-1) - (-2)(-3)}{2[-8 \div (-2 - 2)]}$

59. $(0.2)^2 - (1.5)^2$

60. $(1.3)^2 - (2.2)^2$

61. $-3^2 + (-2)^3 - 4^2$

62. $-4^2 + (-3)^2 - 2^2$

63. $\dfrac{|8 - 13| + \sqrt{81}}{-5(3) - (-5)}$

64. $\dfrac{|10 - 6| + \sqrt{36}}{-4(5) - (-12)}$

Review

Perform each indicated operation. See Sections 1.3, 1.4, 1.6, and 1.7.

65. $45 \cdot 90$

66. $90 \div 45$

67. $90 - 45$

68. $45 + 90$

Find the perimeter of each figure. See Section 8.3.

69. Square

8 in.

△ **70.** Parallelogram

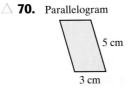

5 cm

3 cm

△ **71.** Rectangle

6 ft

9 ft

△ **72.** Triangle

17 m   23 m

32 m

Concept Extensions

Recall that the average of a list of numbers is

$$average = \frac{sum\ of\ numbers}{number\ of\ numbers}$$

Use this for Exercises 73 and 74.

The graph shows some monthly normal temperatures for Barrow, Alaska.

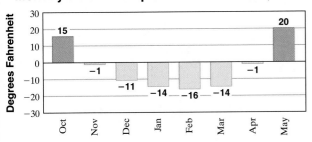

Monthly Normal Temperatures for Barrow, Alaska

73. Use this graph to find the average of the temperatures for months January through May.

74. Find the average of the temperatures for the months October through April.

Insert parentheses where needed so that each expression evaluates to the given number.

75. $2 \cdot 7 - 5 \cdot 3$; evaluates to 12

76. $7 \cdot 3 - 4 \cdot 2$; evaluates to 34

77. $-6 \cdot 10 - 4$; evaluates to -36

78. $2 \cdot 8 \div 4 - 20$; evaluates to -36

79. Are parentheses necessary in the expression $3 + (4 \cdot 5)$? Explain your answer.

80. Are parentheses necessary in the expression $(3 + 4) \cdot 5$? Explain your answer.

81. Discuss the effect parentheses have in an exponential expressions. For example, what is the difference between $(-6)^2$ and -6^2.

82. Discuss the effect parentheses have in an exponential expression. For example, what is the difference between $(2 \cdot 4)^2$ and $2 \cdot 4^2$?

Evaluate.

83. $(-12)^4$

84. $(-17)^6$

CHAPTER 10   Group Activity

Magic Squares

Sections 10.1–10.3

A magic square is a set of numbers arranged in a square table so that the sum of the numbers in each column, row, and diagonal is the same. For instance, in the magic square below, the sum of each column, row, and diagonal is 15. Notice that no number is used more than once in the magic square.

2	9	4
7	5	3
6	1	8

The properties of magic squares have been known for a very long time and once were thought to be good luck charms. The ancient Egyptians and Greeks understood their patterns. A magic square even made it into a famous work of art. The engraving titled *Melencolia I*, created by German artist Albrecht Dürer in 1514, features the following four-by-four magic square on the building behind the central figure.

16	3	2	13
5	10	11	8
9	6	7	12
4	15	14	1

Exercises

1. Verify that what is shown in the Dürer engraving is, in fact, a magic square. What is the common sum of the columns, rows, and diagonals?

2. Negative numbers can also be used in magic squares. Complete the following magic square:

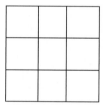

		−2
	−1	
0		−4

3. Use the numbers −16, −12, −8, −4, 0, 4, 8, 12, and 16 to form a magic square:

Chapter 10 Vocabulary Check

Fill in each blank with one of the words or phrases listed below.

| signed | positive | opposites | negative | absolute value | additive inverse | integers |

1. Two numbers that are the same distance from 0 on the number line but are on opposite sides of 0 are called
   _____.

2. Together, positive numbers, negative numbers, and 0 are called _____ numbers.

3. The _____ of a number is that number's distance from 0 on a number line.

4. The _____ are $\ldots, -3, -2, -1, 0, 1, 2, 3, \ldots$.

5. The opposite of a number is also called its _____.

6. The _____ numbers are numbers less than zero.

7. The _____ numbers are numbers greater than zero.

Helpful Hint

Are you preparing for your test? Don't forget to take the Chapter 10 Test on page 689. Then check your answers at the back of the text and use the Chapter Test Prep Video CD to see the fully worked-out solutions to any of the exercises you want to review.

10 Chapter Highlights

DEFINITIONS AND CONCEPTS	EXAMPLES
Section 10.1 Signed Numbers	
Together, positive numbers, negative numbers, and 0 are called **signed numbers.**	$-432, -10, 0, 15$
The **integers** are $\ldots, -3, -2, -1, 0, 1, 2, 3, \ldots$.	
The **absolute value** of a number is that number's distance from 0 on a number line. The symbol for absolute value is $\mid\ \mid$.	$\lvert -2 \rvert = 2$ 2 units $\quad -3\ -2\ -1\ \ 0\ \ 1\ \ 2\ \ 3$ $\lvert 2 \rvert = 2$ 2 units $\quad -3\ -2\ -1\ \ 0\ \ 1\ \ 2\ \ 3$
Two numbers that are the same distance from 0 on the number line but are on opposite sides of 0 are called **opposites.**	5 and -5 are opposites. 5 units 5 units $\quad -5\ -4\ -3\ -2\ -1\ \ 0\ \ 1\ \ 2\ \ 3\ \ 4\ \ 5$
If a is a number, then $-(-a) = a$.	$-(-11) = 11$. Do not confuse with 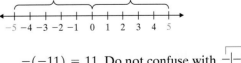

continued

DEFINITIONS AND CONCEPTS	**EXAMPLES**

Section 10.2   Adding Signed Numbers (*continued*)

ADDING TWO NUMBERS WITH THE SAME SIGN

Step 1. Add their absolute values.

Step 2. Use their common sign as the sign of the sum.

ADDING TWO NUMBERS WITH DIFFERENT SIGNS

Step 1. Find the larger absolute value minus the smaller absolute value.

Step 2. Use the sign of the number with the larger absolute value as the sign of the sum.

Add:

$$-3 + (-2) = -5$$
$$-7 + (-15) = -22$$
$$-1.2 + (-5.7) = -6.9$$
$$-6 + 4 = -2$$
$$17 + (-12) = 5$$
$$-\frac{4}{11} + \frac{1}{11} = -\frac{3}{11}$$
$$-32 + (-2) + 14 = -34 + 14$$
$$= -20$$

Section 10.3   Subtracting Signed Numbers

SUBTRACTING TWO NUMBERS

If a and b are numbers, then $a - b = a + (-b)$.

Subtract:

$$-35 - 4 = -35 + (-4) = -39$$
$$3 - 8 = 3 + (-8) = -5$$
$$-7.8 - (-10.2) = -7.8 + 10.2 = 2.4$$
$$7 - 20 - 18 - (-3) = 7 + (-20) + (-18) + 3$$
$$= -13 + (-18) + 3$$
$$= -31 + 3$$
$$= -28$$

Section 10.4   Multiplying and Dividing Signed Numbers

MULTIPLYING SIGNED NUMBERS

The product of two numbers having the same sign is a positive number.
The product of two numbers having different signs is a negative number.

Multiply:

$$(-7)(-6) = 42$$
$$9(-4) = -36$$
$$-3(0.7) = -2.1$$

Evaluate:

$$(-3)^2 = (-3)(-3) = 9$$
$$\left(-\frac{2}{3}\right)^2 = \left(-\frac{2}{3}\right)\left(-\frac{2}{3}\right) = \frac{4}{9}$$
$$-3^2 = -(3 \cdot 3) = -9$$

DIVIDING SIGNED NUMBERS

The quotient of two numbers having the same sign is a positive number.
The quotient of two numbers having different signs is a negative number.

Divide:

$$-100 \div (-10) = 10$$
$$\frac{14}{-2} = -7, \frac{-3.6}{-0.3} = 12, \frac{0}{-3} = 0, \frac{22}{0} \text{ is undefined.}$$

DEFINITIONS AND CONCEPTS	**EXAMPLES**
Section 10.5 Order of Operations	

ORDER OF OPERATIONS

1. Perform all operations within parentheses ( ), brackets [ ], or other grouping symbols such as square roots or fraction bars.
2. Evaluate any expressions with exponents.
3. Multiply or divide in order from left to right.
4. Add or subtract in order from left to right.

Simplify:

$$3 + 2 \cdot (-5) = 3 + (-10)$$
$$= -7$$

$$\frac{-2(5-7)}{-7 + |-3|} = \frac{-2(-2)}{-7+3}$$
$$= \frac{4}{-4}$$
$$= -1$$

 STUDY SKILLS BUILDER

Are You Prepared for a Test on Chapter 10?

Below I have listed some *common trouble areas* for students in Chapter 10. After studying for your test—but before taking your test—read these.

- Don't forget the difference between $-(-5)$ and $-|-5|$.

  $-(-5) = 5$ The opposite of -5 is 5.

  $-|-5| = -5$ The opposite of the absolute value of -5 is the opposite of 5, which is -5.

- Remember how to simplify $(-7)^2$ and -7^2.

  $(-7)^2 = (-7)(-7) = 49$

  $-7^2 = -(7)(7) = -49$

- Don't forget order of operations.

  $1 + 3(4 - 6) = 1 + 3(-2)$ Simplify inside parentheses.
  $= 1 + (-6)$ Multiply.
  $= -5$ Add.

Remember: This is simply a checklist of common trouble spots. For a review of Chapter 10, see the Highlights and Chapter Review at the end of this chapter.

10 CHAPTER REVIEW

(10.1) *Represent each quantity by a signed number.*

1. A gold miner is working 1435 feet below the surface of Earth.

2. A mountain peak is 7562 meters above sea level.

Graph each number on a number line.

3. $-2, 4, -3.5, 0$

4. $-7, -1.6, 3, -4\frac{1}{3}$

Insert < or > between each pair of numbers to form a true statement.

5. $-18 \quad -20$

6. $-5\frac{1}{3} \quad -4\frac{7}{8}$

7. $-12.3 \quad -19.8$

Find each absolute value.

8. $|-12|$

9. $|0|$

10. $\left|-\frac{7}{8}\right|$

Find the opposite of each number.

11. -12

12. $\frac{1}{2}$

Simplify.

13. $-(-3.9)$

14. $-|-7|$

Determine whether each statement is true or false.

15. A negative number is always less than a positive number.

16. The absolute value of a number is always 0 or a positive number.

(10.2) *Add.*

17. $5 + (-3)$

18. $18 + (-4)$

19. $-12 + 16$

20. $-23 + 40$

21. $-8 + (-15)$

22. $-5 + (-17)$

23. $-2.4 + 0.3$

24. $-8.9 + 1.9$

25. $\frac{2}{3} + \left(-\frac{2}{5}\right)$

26. $-\frac{8}{9} + \frac{1}{3}$

27. $-43 + (-108)$

28. $-100 + (-506)$

29. The temperature at 5 a.m. on a day in January was $-15°$ Celsius. By 6 a.m. the temperature had fallen 5 degrees. Use a signed number to represent the temperature at 6 a.m.

30. A diver starts out at 127 feet below the surface and then swims downward another 23 feet. Use a signed number to represent the diver's current depth.

31. During the 2004 PGA Masters Tournament, the winner, Phil Mickelson, had scores of 0, -3, -3, and -3 over four rounds of golf. What was his total score for the tournament? (*Source:* Professional Golfer's Association)

32. During the 2004 U.S. Open golf tournament, the winner, Retief Goosen, had a score of -4. The third-place finisher, Jeff Maggert, had a score that was 5 points more than the winning score. What was Jeff Maggert's score in the U.S. Open? (*Source:* Professional Golfer's Association)

(10.3) *Subtract.*

33. $4 - 12$

34. $-12 - 14$

35. $-\dfrac{3}{4} - \dfrac{1}{2}$

36. $-\dfrac{2}{5} - \dfrac{7}{10}$

37. $7 - (-13)$

38. $-6 - (-14)$

39. $-(-5) - 12 - (-3)$

40. $-16 - 16 - (-4) - (-12)$

41. $-1.7 - (-2.9)$

42. $-0.5 - (-1.2)$

43. $\dfrac{4}{9} - \dfrac{7}{9} - \left(-\dfrac{1}{18}\right)$

44. $\dfrac{3}{7} - \dfrac{5}{7} - \left(-\dfrac{1}{14}\right)$

45. Josh Weidner has $142 in his checking account. He writes a check for $125, makes a deposit for $43, and then writes another check for $85. Represent the balance in his account by a signed number.

46. If the elevation of Lake Superior is 600 feet above sea level and the elevation of the Caspian Sea is 92 feet below sea level, find their difference in elevation. Represent the difference by a signed number.

(10.4) *Perform the indicated operations.*

47. $(-11)^2$

48. $(-3)^4$

49. -3^4

50. -11^2

51. $\left(-\dfrac{4}{5}\right)^3$

52. $\left(-\dfrac{2}{3}\right)^3$

53. $(-3)(-7)$

54. $-6 \cdot 3$

55. $\dfrac{-78}{3}$

56. $\dfrac{38}{-2}$

57. $(-4)(-1)(-9)$

58. $(-2)(-2)(-10)$

59. $-\dfrac{2}{3} \cdot \dfrac{7}{8}$

60. $-0.5(-12)$

61. $-2 \div 0$

62. $0 \div (-61)$

63. $\dfrac{-0.072}{-0.06}$

64. $-\dfrac{8}{25} \div \left(-\dfrac{2}{5}\right)$

65. A football team lost five yards on each of two consecutive plays. Represent the total loss by a product of signed numbers and find the total loss.

66. Find the average of -20, -17, 5, 9, and -12.

(10.5) *Simplify.*

67. $-10 + 3(-2)$

68. $3(-12) - \sqrt{64}$

69. $5.2 + \sqrt{36} \div (-0.3)$

70. $-6 + (-10) \div (-0.2)$

71. $|-16| + (-3) \cdot 12 \div 4$

72. $-(-4) \cdot |-3| - 5$

73. $4^3 - (8 - 3)^2$

74. $2^3 - (9 - 2)^2$

75. $\left(-\dfrac{1}{3}\right)^2 - \dfrac{8}{3}$

76. $\left(-\dfrac{1}{10}\right)^2 - \dfrac{9}{10}$

77. $\dfrac{(-4)(-3) - (-2)(-1)}{-10 + 5}$

78. $\dfrac{4(12 - 18)}{-10 \div (-2 - 3)}$

Mixed Review

Perform the indicated operations.

79. $(-4)^2$

80. -4^2

81. $-6 + (-9)$

82. $-16 - 3$

83. $-4(-12)$

84. $\dfrac{84}{-4}$

85. $-7.6 - (-9.7)$

86. $-\dfrac{9}{20} + \dfrac{4}{20}$

87. $-\dfrac{15}{14} \div \left(-\dfrac{25}{28}\right)$

88. $\dfrac{3}{11} \cdot \left(-\dfrac{22}{4}\right)$

89. $\dfrac{7}{8} - \dfrac{9}{10}$

90. $5(-0.27)$

91. Joe owed his mother \$32. He gave her \$23. Write his financial situation as a signed number.

92. The temperature at noon on a Monday in December was $-11°C$. By noon on Tuesday, it had warmed by $17°C$. What was the temperature at noon on Tuesday?

93. The top of the mountain has an altitude of 12,923 feet. The bottom of the valley is 195 feet below sea level. Find the difference between these two elevations.

94. Wednesday's lowest temperature was $-18°C$. The cold weather continued and by Friday it had dropped another $9°C$. What was the temperature on Friday?

Simplify.

95. $(3 - 7)^2 \div (6 - 4)^3$

96. $(4 + 6)^2 \div (2 - 7)^2$

97. $3(4 + 2) + (-6) - 3^2$

98. $4(5 - 3) - (-2) + 3^3$

99. $2 - 4 \cdot 3 + \sqrt{25}$

100. $4 - 6 \cdot 5 + \sqrt{1}$

101. $\dfrac{-|-14| - 6}{7 + 2(-3)}$

102. $5(7 - 6)^3 - 4(2 - 3)^2 + 2^4$

10 CHAPTER TEST

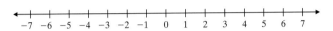 *Remember to use the Chapter Test Prep Video CD to see the fully worked-out solutions to any of the exercises you want to review.*

1. Graph each number on a number line.

$-5, 0, 2, -6.5, -1\dfrac{2}{3}$

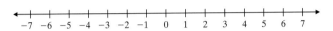

1. see number line

2. Find the opposite of $\dfrac{2}{3}$.

2. _____

3. _____

4. _____

5. _____

Simplify.

3. $|-2.9|$ **4.** $-(-98)$ **5.** $-|-98|$

6. _____

7. _____

Insert $<$ or $>$ between each pair of numbers to form a true statement.

6. $-17 \quad -19$ **7.** $0 \quad -2.5$

8. _____

9. _____

10. _____

Simplify each expression.

8. $-5 + 8$ **9.** $18 - 24$ **10.** $0.5(-20)$

11. _____

12. _____

11. $-16 \div (-4)$ **12.** $-\dfrac{3}{11} + \left(-\dfrac{5}{22}\right)$ **13.** $-7 - (-19)$

13. _____

14. _____

15. _____

14. $-5(-13)$ **15.** $\dfrac{-2.5}{-0.5}$ **16.** $|-25| + (-13)$

16. _____

17. _____

17. $-8 + 9 \div (-3)$ **18.** $-7 + (-32) - 12 + \sqrt{25}$

18. _____

19. _____

19. $(-5)^3 - 24 \div (-3)$ **20.** $(5 - 9)^2 \cdot (8 - 6)^3$

20. _____

689

21. _____

22. _____

23. _____

24. _____

25. _____

26. _____

27. _____

28. _____

29. _____

30. _____

31. _____

32. _____

21. $\dfrac{-3(-2) + 12}{-1(-4 - 5)}$

22. $\dfrac{|25 - 30|^2}{2(-6) + 7}$

23. $\left(\dfrac{5}{9} - \dfrac{7}{9}\right)^2 + \left(-\dfrac{2}{9}\right)$

24. Find the sum of -7, -9, and 35.

25. Subtract 43 from 40.

26. Find the product of $-\dfrac{1}{10}$ and $\dfrac{2}{9}$.

27. Find the quotient of $-\dfrac{1}{10}$ and $\dfrac{2}{9}$.

28. A diver starts at sea level and then makes 4 successive descents of 22 feet. After the descents, what is her elevation?

29. Aaron Hawn has $129 in his checking account. He writes a check for $79, withdraws $40 from an ATM, and then deposits $35. Represent the new balance in his account by an integer.

30. Mt. Washington in New Hampshire has an elevation of 6288 feet above sea level. The Romanche Gap in the Atlantic Ocean has an elevation of 25,354 feet below sea level. Represent the difference in elevation between these two points by an integer. (*Source:* National Geographic Society and Defense Mapping Agency)

31. Lake Baykal in Siberian Russia is the deepest lake in the world with a maximum depth of 5315 feet. The elevation of the lake's surface is 1495 feet above sea level. What is the elevation (with respect to sea level) of the deepest point in the lake? (*Source:* U.S. Geological Survey)

1495 feet above sea level

Sea level

1495 feet

5315 feet

? elevation

32. Find the average of -12, -13, 0, 9.

Chapters 1–10

Answers

1. Multiply: 631×125

2. Multiply: $\dfrac{5}{8} \cdot \dfrac{10}{11}$

3. Divide: $\dfrac{2}{5} \div \dfrac{1}{2}$

4. Divide: $2124 \div 9$

5. Add: $\dfrac{2}{3} + \dfrac{1}{7}$

6. Subtract: $9\dfrac{2}{7} - 7\dfrac{1}{2}$

For Exercises 7 through 9, write each decimal in standard form.

7. Forty-eight and twenty-six hundredths

8. Eight hundredths

9. Six and ninety-five thousandths

10. Multiply: 563.21×100

11. Subtract: $3.5 - 0.068$

12. Divide: $0.27 \div 0.02$

13. Simplify: $\dfrac{5.68 + (0.9)^2 \div 100}{0.2}$

14. Simplify: $50 \div 5 \cdot 2$

15. Write "$27,000 every 6 months" as a unit rate.

16. Write "300 miles every 5 hours" as a unit rate.

Find the value of the unknown number n.

17. $\dfrac{51}{34} = \dfrac{3}{n}$

18. $\dfrac{7}{8} = \dfrac{6}{n}$

19. 46 out of every 100 college students live at home. What percent of students live at home? (*Source:* Independent Insurance Agents of America)

20. A basketball player made 4 out of 5 free throws. What percent of free throws were made?

1. _____

2. _____

3. _____

4. _____

5. _____

6. _____

7. _____

8. _____

9. _____

10. _____

11. _____

12. _____

13. _____

14. _____

15. _____

16. _____

17. _____

18. _____

19. _____

20. _____

21. _____

22. _____

23. _____

24. _____

25. _____

26. _____

27. _____

28. _____

29. _____

30. _____

31. _____

32. _____

33. _____

34. _____

35. _____

36. _____

37. _____

38. _____

Write each fraction, mixed, or whole number as a percent.

21. $\dfrac{9}{20}$

22. $\dfrac{53}{50}$

23. $1\dfrac{1}{2}$

24. 5

Solve.

25. 13 is $6\dfrac{1}{2}$% of what number?

26. What is 110% of 220?

27. Translate to a proportion. 101 is what percent of 200?

28. Translate to an equation. 101 is what percent of 200?

29. Ivan Borski borrowed $2400 at 10% simple interest for 8 months to buy a used Chevy S-10. Find the simple interest he paid.

30. C. J. Dufour wants to buy a digital camera. She has $762 in her savings account. If the camera costs $237, how much money will she have in her account after buying the camera?

31. Add 3 ft 2 in. and 5 ft 11 in.

32. Find the perimeter of the square.

17 meters

33. The normal body temperature is 98.6°F. What is this temperature in degrees Celsius?

34. Convert 7.2 meters to centimeters.

35. Find the supplement of a 107° angle.

36. Find the complement of a 34° angle.

△ **37.** Find the measure of ∠b.

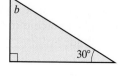

△ **38.** Find the measure of ∠a.

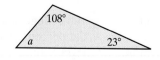

39. Find the area of the parallelogram:

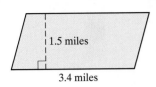

1.5 miles

3.4 miles

△ **40.** Find the area of the circle. Give an exact area, then use 3.14 for π to approximate the area.

5 m

△ **41.** Approximate the volume of a ball of radius 3 inches. Use the approximation $\dfrac{22}{7}$ for π. Give an exact answer and an approximate answer.

3 inches

△ **42.** Find the volume of the box.

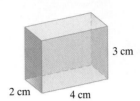

3 cm

2 cm   4 cm

43. Find the median of the list of numbers: $25, 54, 56, 57, 60, 71, 98$

44. Find the mean or average of $36, 25, 18,$ and 19.

45. If a die is rolled, find the probability of rolling a 3 or a 4.

46. Subtract: $-9 - (-4.1)$

47. Add: $-2 + (-21)$

48. Simplify:
    a. $(-10)^3$
    b. -10^3

49. Simplify: $60 + 30 + (-2)^3$

50. Simplify: $\dfrac{\sqrt{16} - (-8)}{9 - 12}$

39. _____

40. _____

41. _____

42. _____

43. _____

44. _____

45. _____

46. _____

47. _____

48. a. _____

    b. _____

49. _____

50. _____

11

Introduction to Algebra

In this chapter we make the transition from arithmetic to algebra. In algebra, letters are used to stand for unknown quantities. Using variables is a very powerful tool for solving problems that cannot be solved with arithmetic alone. This chapter introduces variables, algebraic expressions, and solving variable equations.

The double-line graph given shows the projected shortage of registered nurses. The red line shows the expected demand for nurses while the blue line shows the expected supply of nurses. Since the red line is above the blue line, we project there to be a shortage of nurses, since red is above blue. In Exercises 57 and 58 of Section 11.5, we calculate the actual shortage in percent and number of nurses for a few particular years.

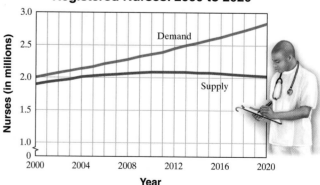

National Supply and Demand Projections for Full-Time Equivalent Registered Nurses: 2000 to 2020

Source: Bureau of Health Professions, RN Suppy and Demand Projections

Find each absolute value.

31. $|-2|$ **32.** $\left|\dfrac{5}{6}\right|$ **33.** $|1.2|$ **34.** $|0|$

Add.

35. $-5 + (-11)$ **36.** $-8.2 + 4.6$

37. $-\dfrac{3}{8} + \left(-\dfrac{1}{8}\right)$ **38.** $\dfrac{2}{5} + \left(-\dfrac{3}{10}\right)$

Subtract.

39. $8 - 15$ **40.** $4.6 - (-1.2)$

41. $-4 - (-5)$ **42.** $\dfrac{7}{10} - \dfrac{23}{24}$

Multiply.

43. $-2(-5)$ **44.** $-8(1.2)$

45. $\left(-\dfrac{1}{2}\right)\left(-\dfrac{2}{3}\right)$ **46.** $-2\dfrac{2}{9}\left(1\dfrac{4}{5}\right)$

47. Simplify: $(-3) \cdot |-5| - (-2) + 4^2$ **48.** Solve: $4x - 7.1 = 3x + 2.6$

49. Solve: $3(2x - 6) + 6 = 0$ **50.** Solve: $6(x - 5) = 4(x + 4) - 6$

31. _____

32. _____

33. _____

34. _____

35. _____

36. _____

37. _____

38. _____

39. _____

40. _____

41. _____

42. _____

43. _____

44. _____

45. _____

46. _____

47. _____

48. _____

49. _____

50. _____

A Tables

A.1 ADDITION TABLE AND ONE HUNDRED ADDITION FACTS

+	0	1	2	3	4	5	6	7	8	9
0	0	1	2	3	4	5	6	7	8	9
1	1	2	3	4	5	6	7	8	9	10
2	2	3	4	5	6	7	8	9	10	11
3	3	4	5	6	7	8	9	10	11	12
4	4	5	6	7	8	9	10	11	12	13
5	5	6	7	8	9	10	11	12	13	14
6	6	7	8	9	10	11	12	13	14	15
7	7	8	9	10	11	12	13	14	15	16
8	8	9	10	11	12	13	14	15	16	17
9	9	10	11	12	13	14	15	16	17	18

One Hundred Addition Facts

Knowledge of the basic addition facts found above is an important prerequisite for a course in prealgebra. Study the table above and then perform the additions. Check your answers either by comparing them with those found in the back-of-the-book answer section or by using the table. Review any facts that you missed.

1. $\begin{array}{r} 1 \\ +4 \\ \hline \end{array}$ **2.** $\begin{array}{r} 5 \\ +6 \\ \hline \end{array}$ **3.** $\begin{array}{r} 2 \\ +3 \\ \hline \end{array}$ **4.** $\begin{array}{r} 7 \\ +8 \\ \hline \end{array}$ **5.** $\begin{array}{r} 3 \\ +9 \\ \hline \end{array}$ **6.** $\begin{array}{r} 6 \\ +1 \\ \hline \end{array}$

7. $\begin{array}{r} 4 \\ +4 \\ \hline \end{array}$ **8.** $\begin{array}{r} 0 \\ +6 \\ \hline \end{array}$ **9.** $\begin{array}{r} 9 \\ +5 \\ \hline \end{array}$ **10.** $\begin{array}{r} 8 \\ +2 \\ \hline \end{array}$ **11.** $\begin{array}{r} 5 \\ +7 \\ \hline \end{array}$ **12.** $\begin{array}{r} 3 \\ +2 \\ \hline \end{array}$

13. $\begin{array}{r} 5 \\ +5 \\ \hline \end{array}$ **14.** $\begin{array}{r} 1 \\ +1 \\ \hline \end{array}$ **15.** $\begin{array}{r} 8 \\ +1 \\ \hline \end{array}$ **16.** $\begin{array}{r} 6 \\ +6 \\ \hline \end{array}$ **17.** $\begin{array}{r} 2 \\ +9 \\ \hline \end{array}$ **18.** $\begin{array}{r} 3 \\ +5 \\ \hline \end{array}$

19. $\begin{array}{r} 9 \\ +9 \\ \hline \end{array}$ **20.** $\begin{array}{r} 5 \\ +2 \\ \hline \end{array}$ **21.** $\begin{array}{r} 6 \\ +4 \\ \hline \end{array}$ **22.** $\begin{array}{r} 0 \\ +0 \\ \hline \end{array}$ **23.** $\begin{array}{r} 1 \\ +9 \\ \hline \end{array}$ **24.** $\begin{array}{r} 3 \\ +7 \\ \hline \end{array}$

25. 9
    +8

26. 0
    +8

27. 4
    +9

28. 3
    +0

29. 7
    +5

30. 8
    +9

31. 9
    +7

32. 2
    +6

33. 4
    +3

34. 8
    +5

35. 3
    +1

36. 0
    +3

37. 7
    +1

38. 3
    +4

39. 8
    +0

40. 6
    +3

41. 2
    +4

42. 0
    +9

43. 8
    +8

44. 5
    +3

45. 3
    +6

46. 6
    +9

47. 4
    +8

48. 0
    +1

49. 2
    +5

50. 6
    +0

51. 2
    +0

52. 4
    +2

53. 8
    +3

54. 7
    +4

55. 1
    +7

56. 4
    +6

57. 0
    +5

58. 9
    +1

59. 8
    +6

60. 5
    +1

61. 6
    +7

62. 4
    +0

63. 1
    +6

64. 4
    +5

65. 0
    +7

66. 5
    +8

67. 7
    +6

68. 7
    +0

69. 4
    +1

70. 5
    +4

71. 0
    +4

72. 1
    +2

73. 7
    +9

74. 3
    +8

75. 7
    +7

76. 9
    +4

77. 1
    +0

78. 4
    +7

79. 2
    +2

80. 1
    +3

81. 2
    +8

82. 5
    +9

83. 6
    +2

84. 9
    +6

85. 5
    +0

86. 8
    +7

87. 7
    +3

88. 0
    +2

89. 9
    +2

90. 3
    +3

91. 9
    +3

92. 1
    +5

93. 2
    +7

94. 6
    +5

95. 7
    +2

96. 1
    +8

97. 6
    +8

98. 8
    +4

99. 9
    +0

100. 2
    +1

A.2 MULTIPLICATION TABLE AND ONE HUNDRED MULTIPLICATION FACTS

×	1	2	3	4	5	6	7	8	9
1	1	2	3	4	5	6	7	8	9
2	2	4	6	8	10	12	14	16	18
3	3	6	9	12	15	18	21	24	27
4	4	8	12	16	20	24	28	32	36
5	5	10	15	20	25	30	35	40	45
6	6	12	18	24	30	36	42	48	54
7	7	14	21	28	35	42	49	56	63
8	8	16	24	32	40	48	56	64	72
9	9	18	27	36	45	54	63	72	81

One Hundred Multiplication Facts

Knowledge of the basic multiplication facts found above is an important prerequisite for a course in prealgebra. Study the table above and then perform the multiplications. Check your answers either by comparing them with those found in the back-of-the-book answer section or by using the table. Review any facts that you missed.

1. $\begin{array}{r} 1 \\ \times\, 1 \\ \hline \end{array}$ 2. $\begin{array}{r} 5 \\ \times\, 7 \\ \hline \end{array}$ 3. $\begin{array}{r} 7 \\ \times\, 8 \\ \hline \end{array}$ 4. $\begin{array}{r} 3 \\ \times\, 3 \\ \hline \end{array}$ 5. $\begin{array}{r} 8 \\ \times\, 4 \\ \hline \end{array}$ 6. $\begin{array}{r} 9 \\ \times\, 5 \\ \hline \end{array}$

7. $\begin{array}{r} 4 \\ \times\, 7 \\ \hline \end{array}$ 8. $\begin{array}{r} 7 \\ \times\, 1 \\ \hline \end{array}$ 9. $\begin{array}{r} 2 \\ \times\, 2 \\ \hline \end{array}$ 10. $\begin{array}{r} 0 \\ \times\, 5 \\ \hline \end{array}$ 11. $\begin{array}{r} 9 \\ \times\, 7 \\ \hline \end{array}$ 12. $\begin{array}{r} 8 \\ \times\, 8 \\ \hline \end{array}$

13. $\begin{array}{r} 3 \\ \times\, 2 \\ \hline \end{array}$ 14. $\begin{array}{r} 6 \\ \times\, 0 \\ \hline \end{array}$ 15. $\begin{array}{r} 5 \\ \times\, 6 \\ \hline \end{array}$ 16. $\begin{array}{r} 2 \\ \times\, 5 \\ \hline \end{array}$ 17. $\begin{array}{r} 4 \\ \times\, 6 \\ \hline \end{array}$ 18. $\begin{array}{r} 0 \\ \times\, 7 \\ \hline \end{array}$

19. $\begin{array}{r} 6 \\ \times\, 3 \\ \hline \end{array}$ 20. $\begin{array}{r} 8 \\ \times\, 9 \\ \hline \end{array}$ 21. $\begin{array}{r} 5 \\ \times\, 8 \\ \hline \end{array}$ 22. $\begin{array}{r} 7 \\ \times\, 2 \\ \hline \end{array}$ 23. $\begin{array}{r} 4 \\ \times\, 8 \\ \hline \end{array}$ 24. $\begin{array}{r} 1 \\ \times\, 2 \\ \hline \end{array}$

25. $\begin{array}{r} 9 \\ \times\, 6 \\ \hline \end{array}$ 26. $\begin{array}{r} 3 \\ \times\, 1 \\ \hline \end{array}$ 27. $\begin{array}{r} 8 \\ \times\, 7 \\ \hline \end{array}$ 28. $\begin{array}{r} 2 \\ \times\, 8 \\ \hline \end{array}$ 29. $\begin{array}{r} 6 \\ \times\, 9 \\ \hline \end{array}$ 30. $\begin{array}{r} 5 \\ \times\, 5 \\ \hline \end{array}$

31. $\begin{array}{r} 2 \\ \times\, 1 \\ \hline \end{array}$ 32. $\begin{array}{r} 8 \\ \times\, 0 \\ \hline \end{array}$ 33. $\begin{array}{r} 4 \\ \times\, 9 \\ \hline \end{array}$ 34. $\begin{array}{r} 8 \\ \times\, 3 \\ \hline \end{array}$ 35. $\begin{array}{r} 6 \\ \times\, 2 \\ \hline \end{array}$ 36. $\begin{array}{r} 4 \\ \times\, 5 \\ \hline \end{array}$

37. 9
$\times 4$

38. 2
$\times 9$

39. 3
$\times 4$

40. 1
$\times 6$

41. 8
$\times 6$

42. 9
$\times 8$

43. 1
$\times 8$

44. 5
$\times 1$

45. 9
$\times 0$

46. 7
$\times 4$

47. 9
$\times 3$

48. 0
$\times 3$

49. 3
$\times 5$

50. 6
$\times 8$

51. 5
$\times 9$

52. 2
$\times 6$

53. 1
$\times 0$

54. 3
$\times 9$

55. 9
$\times 9$

56. 5
$\times 4$

57. 0
$\times 6$

58. 1
$\times 9$

59. 5
$\times 0$

60. 6
$\times 1$

61. 9
$\times 2$

62. 1
$\times 7$

63. 1
$\times 3$

64. 7
$\times 3$

65. 6
$\times 6$

66. 4
$\times 0$

67. 7
$\times 9$

68. 4
$\times 3$

69. 7
$\times 5$

70. 2
$\times 0$

71. 6
$\times 7$

72. 0
$\times 8$

73. 8
$\times 5$

74. 2
$\times 4$

75. 0
$\times 1$

76. 3
$\times 8$

77. 9
$\times 1$

78. 7
$\times 0$

79. 5
$\times 3$

80. 4
$\times 4$

81. 1
$\times 5$

82. 6
$\times 5$

83. 3
$\times 0$

84. 1
$\times 4$

85. 3
$\times 7$

86. 4
$\times 2$

87. 0
$\times 2$

88. 7
$\times 7$

89. 8
$\times 2$

90. 6
$\times 4$

91. 0
$\times 0$

92. 2
$\times 7$

93. 4
$\times 1$

94. 0
$\times 4$

95. 2
$\times 3$

96. 8
$\times 1$

97. 3
$\times 6$

98. 5
$\times 2$

99. 0
$\times 9$

100. 7
$\times 6$

A.3 TABLE OF GEOMETRIC FIGURES

Plane Figures Have Length and Width but No Thickness or Depth		
Name	**Description**	**Figure**
Polygon	Union of three or more coplanar line segments that intersect with each other only at each endpoint, with each endpoint shared by two segments.	
Triangle	Polygon with three sides (sum of measures of three angles is 180°).	
Scalene Triangle	Triangle with no sides of equal length.	
Isosceles Triangle	Triangle with two sides of equal length.	
Equilateral Triangle	Triangle with all sides of equal length.	
Right Triangle	Triangle that contains a right angle.	leg, hypotenuse, leg
Quadrilateral	Polygon with four sides (sum of measures of four angles is 360°).	
Trapezoid	Quadrilateral with exactly one pair of opposite sides parallel.	base, leg, parallel sides, leg, base
Isosceles Trapezoid	Trapezoid with legs of equal length.	
Parallelogram	Quadrilateral with both pairs of opposite sides parallel.	
Rhombus	Parallelogram with all sides of equal length.	

(Continued)

Name	Description	Figure
Rectangle	Parallelogram with four right angles.	
Square	Rectangle with all sides of equal length.	
Circle	All points in a plane the same distance from a fixed point called the **center.**	

Solid Figures Have Length, Width, and Height or Depth		
Name	**Description**	**Figure**
Rectangular Solid	A solid with six sides, all of which are rectangles.	
Cube	A rectangular solid whose six sides are squares.	
Sphere	All points the same distance from a fixed point, called the **center.**	
Right Circular Cylinder	A cylinder having two circular bases that are perpendicular to its altitude.	
Right Circular Cone	A cone with a circular base that is perpendicular to its altitude.	

Percent	Decimal	Fraction
1%	0.01	$\frac{1}{100}$
5%	0.05	$\frac{1}{20}$
10%	0.1	$\frac{1}{10}$
12.5% or $12\frac{1}{2}$%	0.125	$\frac{1}{8}$
$16.\overline{6}$% or $16\frac{2}{3}$%	$0.1\overline{6}$	$\frac{1}{6}$
20%	0.2	$\frac{1}{5}$
25%	0.25	$\frac{1}{4}$
30%	0.3	$\frac{3}{10}$
$33.\overline{3}$% or $33\frac{1}{3}$%	$0.\overline{3}$	$\frac{1}{3}$
37.5% or $37\frac{1}{2}$%	0.375	$\frac{3}{8}$
40%	0.4	$\frac{2}{5}$
50%	0.5	$\frac{1}{2}$
60%	0.6	$\frac{3}{5}$
62.5% or $62\frac{1}{2}$%	0.625	$\frac{5}{8}$
$66.\overline{6}$% or $66\frac{2}{3}$%	$0.\overline{6}$	$\frac{2}{3}$
70%	0.7	$\frac{7}{10}$
75%	0.75	$\frac{3}{4}$
80%	0.8	$\frac{4}{5}$
$83.\overline{3}$% or $83\frac{1}{3}$%	$0.8\overline{3}$	$\frac{5}{6}$
87.5% or $87\frac{1}{2}$%	0.875	$\frac{7}{8}$
90%	0.9	$\frac{9}{10}$
100%	1.0	1
110%	1.1	$1\frac{1}{10}$
125%	1.25	$1\frac{1}{4}$
$133.\overline{3}$% or $133\frac{1}{3}$%	$1.\overline{3}$	$1\frac{1}{3}$
150%	1.5	$1\frac{1}{2}$
$166.\overline{6}$% or $166\frac{2}{3}$%	$1.\overline{6}$	$1\frac{2}{3}$
175%	1.75	$1\frac{3}{4}$
200%	2.0	2

A.5 TABLE ON FINDING COMMON PERCENTS OF A NUMBER

Common Percent Equivalences*	Shortcut Method for Finding Percent	Example
$1\% = 0.01 \left(\text{or } \frac{1}{100}\right)$	To find 1% of a number, multiply by 0.01. To do so, move the decimal point 2 places to the left.	1% of 210 is 2.10 or 2.1. 1% of 1500 is 15. 1% of 8.6 is 0.086.
$10\% = 0.1 \left(\text{or } \frac{1}{10}\right)$	To find 10% of a number, multiply by 0.1, or move the decimal point of the number one place to the left.	10% of 140 is 14. 10% of 30 is 3. 10% of 17.6 is 1.76.
$25\% = \frac{1}{4}$	To find 25% of a number, find $\frac{1}{4}$ of the number, or divide the number by 4.	25% of 20 is $\frac{20}{4}$ or 5. 25% of 8 is 2. 25% of 10 is $\frac{10}{4}$ or $2\frac{1}{2}$.
$50\% = \frac{1}{2}$	To find 50% of a number, find $\frac{1}{2}$ of the number, or divide the number by 2.	50% of 64 is $\frac{64}{2}$ or 32. 50% of 1000 is 500. 50% of 9 is $\frac{9}{2}$ or $4\frac{1}{2}$.
$100\% = 1$	To find 100% of a number, multiply the number by 1. In other words, 100% of a number is the number.	100% of 98 is 98. 100% of 1407 is 1407. 100% of 18.4 is 18.4.
$200\% = 2$	To find 200% of a number, multiply the number by 2.	200% of 31 is $31 \cdot 2$ or 62. 200% of 750 is 1500. 200% of 6.5 is 13.

*See Appendix A4.

n	n^2	$\sqrt{n}$	n	n^2	$\sqrt{n}$
1	1	1.000	51	2601	7.141
2	4	1.414	52	2704	7.211
3	9	1.732	53	2809	7.280
4	16	2.000	54	2916	7.348
5	25	2.236	55	3025	7.416
6	36	2.449	56	3136	7.483
7	49	2.646	57	3249	7.550
8	64	2.828	58	3364	7.616
9	81	3.000	59	3481	7.681
10	100	3.162	60	3600	7.746
11	121	3.317	61	3721	7.810
12	144	3.464	62	3844	7.874
13	169	3.606	63	3969	7.937
14	196	3.742	64	4096	8.000
15	225	3.873	65	4225	8.062
16	256	4.000	66	4356	8.124
17	289	4.123	67	4489	8.185
18	324	4.243	68	4624	8.246
19	361	4.359	69	4761	8.307
20	400	4.472	70	4900	8.367
21	441	4.583	71	5041	8.426
22	484	4.690	72	5184	8.485
23	529	4.796	73	5329	8.544
24	576	4.899	74	5476	8.602
25	625	5.000	75	5625	8.660
26	676	5.099	76	5776	8.718
27	729	5.196	77	5929	8.775
28	784	5.292	78	6084	8.832
29	841	5.385	79	6241	8.888
30	900	5.477	80	6400	8.944
31	961	5.568	81	6561	9.000
32	1024	5.657	82	6724	9.055
33	1089	5.745	83	6889	9.110
34	1156	5.831	84	7056	9.165
35	1225	5.916	85	7225	9.220
36	1296	6.000	86	7396	9.274
37	1369	6.083	87	7569	9.327
38	1444	6.164	88	7744	9.381
39	1521	6.245	89	7921	9.434
40	1600	6.325	90	8100	9.487
41	1681	6.403	91	8281	9.539
42	1764	6.481	92	8464	9.592
43	1849	6.557	93	8649	9.644
44	1936	6.633	94	8836	9.695
45	2025	6.708	95	9025	9.747
46	2116	6.782	96	9216	9.798
47	2209	6.856	97	9409	9.849
48	2304	6.928	98	9604	9.899
49	2401	7.000	99	9801	9.950
50	2500	7.071	100	10,000	10.000

A.7 COMPOUND INTEREST TABLE

Compounded Annually

	5%	6%	7%	8%	9%	10%	11%	12%	13%	14%	15%	16%	17%	18%
1 year	1.05000	1.06000	1.07000	1.08000	1.09000	1.10000	1.11000	1.12000	1.13000	1.14000	1.15000	1.16000	1.17000	1.18000
5 years	1.27628	1.33823	1.40255	1.46933	1.53862	1.61051	1.68506	1.76234	1.84244	1.92541	2.01136	2.10034	2.19245	2.28776
10 years	1.62889	1.79085	1.96715	2.15892	2.36736	2.59374	2.83942	3.10585	3.39457	3.70722	4.04556	4.41144	4.80683	5.23384
15 years	2.07893	2.39656	2.75903	3.17217	3.64248	4.17725	4.78459	5.47357	6.25427	7.13794	8.13706	9.26552	10.53872	11.97375
20 years	2.65330	3.20714	3.86968	4.66096	5.60441	6.72750	8.06231	9.64629	11.52309	13.74349	16.36654	19.46076	23.10560	27.39303

Compounded Semiannually

	5%	6%	7%	8%	9%	10%	11%	12%	13%	14%	15%	16%	17%	18%
1 year	1.05063	1.06090	1.07123	1.08160	1.09203	1.10250	1.11303	1.12360	1.13423	1.14490	1.15563	1.16640	1.17723	1.18810
5 years	1.28008	1.34392	1.41060	1.48024	1.55297	1.62889	1.70814	1.79085	1.87714	1.96715	2.06103	2.15892	2.26098	2.36736
10 years	1.63862	1.80611	1.98979	2.19112	2.41171	2.65330	2.91776	3.20714	3.52365	3.86968	4.24785	4.66096	5.11205	5.60441
15 years	2.09757	2.42726	2.80679	3.24340	3.74532	4.32194	4.98395	5.74349	6.61437	7.61226	8.75496	10.06266	11.55825	13.26768
20 years	2.68506	3.26204	3.95926	4.80102	5.81636	7.03999	8.51331	10.28572	12.41607	14.97446	18.04424	21.72452	26.13302	31.40942

Compounded Quarterly

	5%	6%	7%	8%	9%	10%	11%	12%	13%	14%	15%	16%	17%	18%
1 year	1.05095	1.06136	1.07186	1.08243	1.09308	1.10381	1.11462	1.12551	1.13648	1.14752	1.15865	1.16986	1.18115	1.19252
5 years	1.28204	1.34686	1.41478	1.48595	1.56051	1.63862	1.72043	1.80611	1.89584	1.98979	2.08815	2.19112	2.29891	2.41171
10 years	1.64362	1.81402	2.00160	2.20804	2.43519	2.68506	2.95987	3.26204	3.59420	3.95926	4.36038	4.80102	5.28497	5.81636
15 years	2.10718	2.44322	2.83182	3.28103	3.80013	4.39979	5.09225	5.89160	6.81402	7.87809	9.10513	10.51963	12.14965	14.02741
20 years	2.70148	3.29066	4.00639	4.87544	5.93015	7.20957	8.76085	10.64089	12.91828	15.67574	19.01290	23.04980	27.93091	33.83010

Compounded Daily

	5%	6%	7%	8%	9%	10%	11%	12%	13%	14%	15%	16%	17%	18%
1 year	1.05127	1.06183	1.07250	1.08328	1.09416	1.10516	1.11626	1.12747	1.13880	1.15024	1.16180	1.17347	1.18526	1.19716
5 years	1.28400	1.34983	1.41902	1.49176	1.56823	1.64861	1.73311	1.82194	1.91532	2.01348	2.11667	2.22515	2.33918	2.45906
10 years	1.64866	1.82203	2.01362	2.22535	2.45933	2.71791	3.00367	3.31946	3.66845	4.05411	4.48031	4.95130	5.47178	6.04696
15 years	2.11689	2.45942	2.85736	3.31968	3.85678	4.48077	5.20569	6.04786	7.02625	8.16288	9.48335	11.01738	12.79950	14.86983
20 years	2.71810	3.31979	4.05466	4.95216	6.04831	7.38703	9.02202	11.01883	13.45751	16.43582	20.07316	24.51533	29.94039	36.56577

B The Bigger Picture

I. Some Operations on Sets of Numbers

A. Whole Numbers

1. Add or Subtract:

$$\begin{array}{r} 14 \\ + 39 \\ \hline 53 \end{array} \qquad \begin{array}{r} 300 \\ - 27 \\ \hline 273 \end{array}$$

2. Multiply or Divide:

$$\begin{array}{r} 238 \\ \times 47 \\ \hline 1666 \\ 9520 \\ \hline 11,186 \end{array} \qquad \begin{array}{r} 127 \text{ R2} \\ 7\overline{)891} \\ -7 \\ \hline 19 \\ -14 \\ \hline 51 \\ -49 \\ \hline 2 \end{array}$$

3. Exponent:

$$3^4 = \overbrace{3 \cdot 3 \cdot 3 \cdot 3}^{4 \text{ factors of } 3} = 81$$

4. Square Root:

$$\sqrt{25} = 5 \text{ } because \text{ } 5 \cdot 5 = 25 \text{ and } 5 \text{ is a positive number.}$$

5. Order of Operations:

$$\begin{aligned} 24 \div 3 \cdot 2 - (2 + 8) &= 24 \div 3 \cdot 2 - (10) && \text{Parentheses.} \\ &= 8 \cdot 2 - 10 && \text{Multiply or divide from left to right.} \\ &= 16 - 10 && \text{Multiply or divide from left to right.} \\ &= 6 && \text{Add or subtract from left to right.} \end{aligned}$$

B. Fractions

1. Simplify: Factor the numerator and denominator. Then divide out factors of 1 by dividing out common factors in the numerator and denominator.

Simplify: $\dfrac{20}{35} = \dfrac{4 \cdot 5}{4 \cdot 7} = \dfrac{5}{7}$

2. Multiply: Numerator times numerator over denominator times denominator.

$$\frac{5}{9} \cdot \frac{2}{7} = \frac{10}{63}$$

3. Divide: First fraction times the reciprocal of the second fraction.

$$\frac{2}{11} \div \frac{3}{4} = \frac{2}{11} \cdot \frac{4}{3} = \frac{8}{33}$$

4. Add or Subtract: Must have same denominators. If not, find the LCD, and write each fraction as an equivalent fraction with the LCD as denominator.

$$\frac{2}{5} + \frac{1}{15} = \frac{2}{5} \cdot \frac{3}{3} + \frac{1}{15} = \frac{6}{15} + \frac{1}{15} = \frac{7}{15}$$

C. Decimals

1. Add or Subtract: Line up decimal points.

$$\begin{array}{r} 1.27 \\ +\ 0.6 \\ \hline 1.87 \end{array}$$

2. Multiply:

$$\begin{array}{r} 2.56 \quad \text{2 decimal places} \\ \times\ 3.2 \quad \text{1 decimal place} \\ \hline 512 \qquad 2 + 1 = 3 \\ 768 \qquad\quad \\ \hline 8.192 \quad \text{3 decimal places} \end{array}$$

3. Divide: $8)\overline{5.6}$ gives $.7$ $\qquad$ $0.6)\overline{0.786}$ gives 1.31

D. Signed Numbers

1. Add: $-5 + (-2) = -7$ $\quad$ Adding like signs.
Add absolute value. Attach the common sign.

$-5 + 2 = -3$ $\quad$ Adding unlike signs.
Subtract absolute values. Attach the sign of the number with the larger absolute value.

2. Subtract: Add the first number to the opposite of the second number.

$$7 - 10 = 7 + (-10) = -3$$

3. Multiply or Divide: Multiply or divide as usual. If the signs of the two numbers are the same, the answer is positive. If the signs of the two numbers are different, the answer is negative.

$$-5 \cdot 5 = -25, \quad \frac{-32}{-8} = 4$$

II. Solving Equations

A. Proportions:
Set cross products equal to each other. Then solve.

$$\frac{14}{3} = \frac{2}{n}, \text{ or } 14 \cdot n = 3 \cdot 2, \text{ or } 14 \cdot n = 6, \text{ or } n = \frac{6}{14} = \frac{3}{7}$$

B. Percent Problems

1. Solved by Equations: Remember that "of" means multiplication and "is" means equals.

"12% of some number is 6" translates to

$$12\% \cdot n = 6 \text{ or } 0.12 \cdot n = 6 \text{ or } n = \frac{6}{0.12} \text{ or } n = 50$$

2. Solved by Proportions: Remember that percent, p, is identified by % or percent, base, b, usually appears after "of" and amount, a, is the part compared to the whole.

"12% of some number is 6" translates to

$$\frac{6}{b} = \frac{12}{100} \text{ or } 6 \cdot 100 = b \cdot 12 \text{ or } \frac{600}{12} = b \text{ or } 50 = b$$

C. Equations in General:
Simplify both sides of the equation by removing parentheses and adding any like terms. Then use the Addition Property to write variable terms on one side, constants (or numbers) on the other side. Then use the Multiplication Property to solve for the variable by dividing both sides of the equation by the coefficient of the variable.

Solve: $2(x - 5) = 80$

$$\begin{aligned} 2x - 10 &= 80 & \text{Use the distributive property.} \\ 2x - 10 + 10 &= 80 + 10 & \text{Add 10 to both sides.} \\ 2x &= 90 & \text{Simplify.} \\ \frac{2x}{2} &= \frac{90}{2} & \text{Divide both sides by 2.} \\ x &= 45 & \text{Simplify.} \end{aligned}$$

Appendix

C Unit Analysis

Let's suppose that you are traveling at a rate of 60 miles per hour. This means that

in 1 hour, your distance traveled is 60 miles;
in 2 hours, your distance traveled is $2 \cdot 60$ or 120 miles.

The rate 60 miles per hour can also be written as

$$60 \text{ mph}, \qquad 60 \text{ miles per 1 hour}, \qquad \text{or} \qquad \frac{60 \text{ miles}}{1 \text{ hour}}.$$

We can use rates such as $\dfrac{60 \text{ miles}}{1 \text{ hour}}$ to help us solve problems. Before we do this, notice that if 60 miles are traveled in 1 hour, then in 1 hour a distance of 60 miles is traveled and we also have the rate $\dfrac{1 \text{ hour}}{60 \text{ miles}}$, if needed.

Let's practice writing the fraction form of rates once again. The rate of 30 drops of medicine per liter of saline solution can be written as:

$$\frac{30 \text{ drops}}{1 \text{ liter}}. \text{ If needed, we also have the rate } \frac{1 \text{ liter}}{30 \text{ drops}}.$$

How do we know which version to use when solving a problem? As you will see in the examples, we use the rate that has *units to be divided out* in the *denominator* and *units asked to find* in the *numerator*.

EXAMPLE 1 If you are traveling in a car at a rate of 60 miles per hour, how many miles do you travel in 21 hours?

Solution: Let's use a form of the given rate to help us answer this question. Since we are asked to find miles, we will multiply 21 hours by a version of the rate that has units to be divided out (hours) in the denominator and units asked to find (miles) in the numerator.

$$\begin{aligned} \text{miles traveled in 21 hours} &= \frac{21 \text{ hours}}{1} \cdot \frac{60 \text{ miles}}{1 \text{ hour}} \\ &= \frac{21 \cdot 60}{1 \cdot 1} \text{ miles} \\ &= 1260 \text{ miles} \end{aligned}$$

You travel 1260 miles in 21 hours.

Helpful Hint

Pay careful attention to units and how they divide out.

EXAMPLE 2 If you are traveling at the rate of 60 miles per hour, how many hours does it take to travel 900 miles in the car?

Solution: Let's use a form of the given rate again. For this example, we are asked to find hours, so we will write a rate so that units to be divided out (miles) are in the denominator and units needed in the answer (hours) are in the numerator.

$$\text{hours taken to travel 900 miles} = \frac{900 \text{ miles}}{1} \cdot \frac{1 \text{ hour}}{60 \text{ miles}}$$

$$= \frac{900 \cdot 1}{1 \cdot 60} \text{ hours}$$

$$= 15 \text{ hours}$$

It takes 15 hours to travel 900 miles.

Helpful Hint

Remember: The rate you use depends on the exercise. A general rule is to use a factor that has units needed to divide out in the denominator and units asked to find in the numerator.

To solve some unit applications, it may be necessary to multiply by 2 or more rates. (More exercises involving unit conversions on length, weight, or mass can be found in the chapter on measurement, Chapter 7.)

EXAMPLE 3 A telemarketer makes an average of 24 calls per hour. He is paid $0.50 per call. If he worked 25 hours last week, calculate his earnings (before deductions).

Solution: To calculate his earnings, notice we multiply by two different rates.

$$\text{earnings for 25 hours} = \frac{25 \text{ hours}}{1} \cdot \frac{24 \text{ calls}}{1 \text{ hour}} \cdot \frac{\$0.50}{1 \text{ call}}$$

$$= \frac{25 \cdot 24 \cdot \$0.50}{1 \cdot 1 \cdot 1}$$

$$= \$300$$

He made $300 last week.

C EXERCISE SET

FOR EXTRA HELP

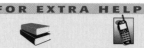
Student Solutions Manual

PH Math/Tutor Center

CD/Video for Review

Math XL
MathXL®

MyMathLab
MyMathLab

1. Suppose you make $16 per hour.

   a. Calculate your earnings (before deductions) for 40 hours.
   b. How many hours of work are required to earn $240 (before deductions)?

2. A lab technician needs a solution containing 20 drops of concentrated medicine per liter of saline solution.

   a. How many drops are needed for 17 liters of solution?
   b. How many drops are needed for 280 liters of saline solution?
   c. If you are told to make a solution using an entire container of 520 drops of medicine, how many liters of saline solution are needed?

3. A hummingbird's wings beat an average of 90 beats per second.

   a. How many beats occur during 14 seconds?
   b. How much time (in seconds) has elapsed after 5400 wing beats? How much time is your answer in minutes?
   c. How much time (in seconds) has elapsed after 8100 wing beats? How much time is your answer in minutes?

4. In a recent year, Noah Wyle (on "ER") was the highest paid TV drama actor per episode. He earned $400,000 per episode.

   a. How much money did he make for 12 episodes?
   b. How many episodes did he need to tape in order to earn $6,800,000?

5. Switzerland has an average of one hospital bed per 155 people (in population).

   a. Suppose there is a city in Switzerland with a population of 31,000. At this rate, how many hospital beds are there in this city?
   b. Suppose the only hospital in a city in Switzerland has 73 beds. Using the given rate, estimate the population of the city.

6. Niger has an average of one hospital bed per 2000 people (in population).

   a. Suppose there is a city in Niger with a population of 16,000. At this rate, how many hospital beds are there in this city?
   b. Suppose the only hospital in a city in Niger has 21 beds. Using the given rate, estimate the population of the city.

7. A recipe calls for 3 cups of water for every 2 cups of flour.

   a. If 9 cups of water are added, how many cups of flour are needed?
   b. If 20 cups of water are added, how many cups of flour are needed?
   c. If 15 cups of flour are added, how many cups of water are needed?

8. A recipe calls for 4 cups of sugar for every 3 cups of water.

   a. If 12 cups of sugar are added, how many cups of water are needed?
   b. If 14 cups of sugar are added, how many cups of water are needed?
   c. If 20 cups of water are added, how many cups of sugar are needed?

9. A computer technician on an assembly line makes $0.75 for her completion of each computer component. She can complete 26 components in an hour. If she worked 33 hours last week, what was her pay before deductions?

10. A cockroach is traveling at a rate of 3 miles per hour. Convert this speed to feet per second.

11. A lab technician needs a solution containing 15 drops of concentrated medicine per liter of saline solution.

    a. How many drops will be needed for 17.5 liters of solution?

    b. How many liters will be needed for 300 drops of saline solution?

12. A car travels at a rate of 57 miles per hour.

    a. How many miles does the car traveled in $5\frac{1}{2}$ hours?

    b. At this rate, how many hours does it take to travel 627 miles in the car?

13. A tortilla-making machine makes 16 tortillas per minute.

    a. How many tortillas can be made in 7.5 hours?

    b. How long will it take to make 200 tortillas?

14. During a flood watch in New Orleans, Louisiana, an average of 0.5 inch of rain fell per hour for 48 hours.

    a. How much water fell during the first 21 hours?

    b. At this given rate, how long did it take for 15.5 inches of rain to fall?

15. At this writing, Ray Romano (of "Everybody Loves Raymond") is the world's highest paid TV actor. He earns $1.8 million per episode.

    a. How much money does he earn for 6 episodes?

    b. How many episodes must be taped for him to earn $8.1 million?

16. Suppose a supporting actor of a television series makes $18,000 per episode.

    a. How much money does she make for 8 episodes?

    b. How many episodes did she perform in to earn $486,000?

    c. According to this actor's contract, it is possible to pay her for fractional portions of episodes. How much money does she make for 12.5 episodes?

17. A cheetah is the fastest known land animal and has been recorded traveling at speeds of 65 miles per hour. Suppose a particular cheetah is traveling at a speed of 45 miles per hour.

    a. How far has the cheetah traveled in $\frac{1}{4}$ hour?

    b. How long does it take the cheetah to travel 5 miles? Give your answer in hours and then in minutes.

18. The Gentoo penguin has a maximum speed of 27 kilometers per hour.

    a. Convert this to miles per hour. (Round to the nearest hundredth.) (*Hint:* 1 mile = 1.61 km)

    b. How far can the penguin travel in 10 minutes? Give your answer in miles.

ANSWERS TO SELECTED EXERCISES

CHAPTER 1   The Whole Numbers

Exercise Set 1.2 **1.** tens **3.** thousands **5.** hundred-thousands **7.** millions **9.** five hundred forty-two
11. seven thousand, eight hundred ninety-six **13.** twenty-six thousand, nine hundred ninety **15.** one million, six hundred twenty thousand
17. fifty-three million, five hundred twenty thousand, one hundred seventy **19.** sixty-four thousand, four hundred eighty-two
21. one thousand, six hundred seventy-nine **23.** thirteen million, six hundred thousand **25.** twelve thousand, six hundred sixty-two
27. two hundred two thousand, seven hundred **29.** 6587 **31.** 29,900 **33.** 16,504,019 **35.** 3,000,014 **37.** 220 **39.** 440,276
41. 70,251,710 **43.** 1815 **45.** 755 **47.** $400 + 6$ **49.** $5000 + 200 + 90$ **51.** $60,000 + 2000 + 400 + 7$ **53.** $30,000 + 600 + 80$
55. $30,000,000 + 9,000,000 + 600,000 + 80,000$ **57.** 5532; five thousand, five hundred thirty-two **59.** $5000 + 400 + 90 + 2$
61. Mt. Washington **63.** Golden retriever **65.** Labrador retriever; one hundred forty-four thousand, nine hundred thirty-four
67. 25 pounds **69.** 7632 **71.** no; one hundred five **73.** answers may vary **75.** Canton

Calculator Explorations **1.** 134 **3.** 340 **5.** 2834

Mental Math **1.** 16 **3.** 9000 **5.** 1620

Exercise Set 1.3 **1.** 36 **3.** 292 **5.** 49 **7.** 5399 **9.** 117 **11.** 512 **13.** 209,078 **15.** 25 **17.** 62 **19.** 212 **21.** 94
23. 910 **25.** 8273 **27.** 11,926 **29.** 1884 **31.** 16,717 **33.** 1110 **35.** 8999 **37.** 35,901 **39.** 632,389 **41.** 42 in. **43.** 25 ft
45. 24 in. **47.** 8 yd **49.** 29 in. **51.** 2093 **53.** 266 **55.** 544 **57.** 3452 **59.** 6684 ft **61.** 340 ft **63.** 291,147 motorcycles
65. 2425 ft **67.** 13,255 mi **69.** 124 ft **71.** 767,312 **73.** 8867 **75.** California **77.** 366 stores **79.** Florida and Georgia
81. answers may vary **83.** answers may vary **85.** 40 ft **87.** 1,044,473,765 **89.** correct **91.** incorrect; 933

Calculator Explorations **1.** 770 **3.** 109 **5.** 8978

Mental Math **1.** 7 **3.** 5 **5.** 0 **7.** 400 **9.** 500

Exercise Set 1.4 **1.** 44 **3.** 265 **5.** 135 **7.** 2254 **9.** 5545 **11.** 600 **13.** 25 **15.** 45 **17.** 146 **19.** 288 **21.** 168
23. 106 **25.** 447 **27.** 5723 **29.** 504 **31.** 89 **33.** 79 **35.** 39,914 **37.** 32,711 **39.** 5041 **41.** 31,213 **43.** 4 **45.** 20
47. 7 **49.** 72 **51.** 88 **53.** 264 pages **55.** 4 million sq km **57.** 6065 ft **59.** 23 points **61.** $409 **63.** 358 mi **65.** $389
67. 3,044,452 people **69.** 19,036 cocker spaniels **71.** 5920 sq ft **73.** Hartsfield Atlanta International **75.** 32 million
77. General Motors Corp., Time Warner, Procter & Gamble Co. **79.** $1112 million or $1,112,000,000 **81.** 1034 **83.** 9 **85.** 8515
87. 22,876 **89.** minuend: 48; subtrahend: 1 **91.** minuend: 70; subtrahend: 7 **93.** Jo; by 271 votes **95.** incorrect; 685 **97.** correct
99. $5269 - 2385 = 2884$ **101.** answers may vary **103.** no; 1089 more pages

Exercise Set 1.5 **1.** 630 **3.** 640 **5.** 1800 **7.** 400 **9.** 51,000 **11.** 43,000 **13.** 248,700 **15.** 36,000 **17.** 100,000
19. 60,000,000 **21.** 5280; 5300; 5000 **23.** 9440; 9400; 9000 **25.** 14,880; 14,900; 15,000 **27.** 380,000 **29.** 10,800 **31.** 70,000,000,000
33. 2,500,000 **35.** 159,000,000; 7,000,000 **37.** 130 **39.** 380 **41.** 5500 **43.** 300 **45.** 8500 **47.** correct **49.** incorrect
51. correct **53.** $3100 **55.** 80 mi **57.** 6000 ft **59.** 1,400,000 people **61.** 14,000,000 votes **63.** 52,000 children
65. $3,430,000,000; $3,400,000,000; $3,000,000,000 **67.** $2,234,000,000; $2,200,000,000; $2,000,000,000 **69.** 4618, for example
71. a. 8550 **b.** 8649 **73.** answers may vary **75.** 140 m

Calculator Explorations **1.** 3456 **3.** 15,322 **5.** 272,291

Mental Math **1.** 24 **3.** 0 **5.** 0 **7.** 87

Exercise Set 1.6 **1.** $4 \cdot 3 + 4 \cdot 9$ **3.** $2 \cdot 4 + 2 \cdot 6$ **5.** $10 \cdot 11 + 10 \cdot 7$ **7.** 252 **9.** 1872 **11.** 1662 **13.** 5310 **15.** 1372
17. 10,857 **19.** 11,326 **21.** 24,800 **23.** 0 **25.** 5900 **27.** 59,232 **29.** 142,506 **31.** 1,821,204 **33.** 3,949,935 **35.** 64,790
37. 800 **39.** 11,000 **41.** 74,060 **43.** 24,000 **45.** 45,000 **47.** 3,280,000 **49.** 240,000 **51.** 300,000 **53.** c **55.** c
57. 63 sq m **59.** 390 sq ft **61.** 770 **63.** 5400 **65.** 4480 **67.** 375 cal **69.** $1890 **71. a.** 192 cans **b.** 96 cans
73. 900 sq ft **75.** 56,000 sq ft **77.** 5828 pixels **79.** 1500 characters **81.** 1280 cal **83.** 71,343 mi
85. $10, $50; $10, $100; $12, $24; $12, $24; $228 **87.** 21,700,000 qt **89.** 134 **91.** 1008 **93.** 24 **95.** 12
97. $5 \cdot 3$ or $3 \cdot 5$ **99. a.** $7 + 7 + 7 + 7$ or $4 + 4 + 4 + 4 + 4 + 4 + 4$ **b.** answers may vary

101.
$$
\begin{array}{r}
203 \\
\times \ \ 14 \\
\hline
812 \\
2030 \\
\hline
2842
\end{array}
$$
103. 2; 9 **105.** answers may vary **107.** 506 windows

Calculator Explorations **1.** 53 **3.** 62 **5.** 261 **7.** 0

Mental Math **1.** 5 **3.** 9 **5.** 0 **7.** 9 **9.** 1 **11.** 5 **13.** undefined **15.** 7 **17.** 0 **19.** 8

Exercise Set 1.7 **1.** 26 **3.** 37 **5.** 338 **7.** undefined **9.** 8 **11.** 25 **13.** 65 R 4 **15.** 225 R 4 **17.** 37 R 1 **19.** 265 R 5
21. 49 **23.** 13 **25.** 97 R 40 **27.** 206 R 10 **29.** 506 **31.** 202 R 7 **33.** 45 **35.** 98 R 100 **37.** 202 R 15 **39.** 579 R 72
41. 19 **43.** 513 R 1 **45.** 2082 R 26 **47.** 5030 **49.** 21 R 1 **51.** 2 R 30 **53.** 20 R 2 **55.** 58 students **57.** $252,000

59. 415 bushels   **61.** 105 lane dividers   **63.** yes, she needs 176 ft; she has 9 ft left over   **65.** 27 touchdowns   **67.** 1760 yd   **69.** 26
71. 498   **73.** 79   **75.** 16°   **77.** 8862   **79.** 29,210   **81.** 589   **83.** undefined   **85.** 7 R 15   **87.** d   **89.** a   **91.** $3,376,500,000
93. increase; answers may vary   **95.** no; answers may vary   **97.** answers may vary

The Bigger Picture   1. 118   **2.** 28   **3.** 3285   **4.** 89 R 11   **5.** 0   **6.** 0   **7.** 19   **8.** undefined   **9.** 64   **10.** 1844

Integrated Review   1. 148   **2.** 6555   **3.** 1620   **4.** 562   **5.** 79   **6.** undefined   **7.** 9   **8.** 1   **9.** 0   **10.** 0   **11.** 0   **12.** 3
13. 2433   **14.** 9826   **15.** 213 R 3   **16.** 79,317   **17.** 27   **18.** 9   **19.** 138   **20.** 276   **21.** 1099 R 2   **22.** 111 R 1   **23.** 663 R 6
24. 1076 R 60   **25.** 1024   **26.** 9899   **27.** 30,603   **28.** 47,500   **29.** 65   **30.** 456   **31.** 7 R 1   **32.** 49   **33.** 86   **34.** 22
35. 8630; 8600; 9000   **36.** 1550; 1600; 2000   **37.** 10,900; 10,909; 11,000   **38.** 432,200; 432,200; 432,000   **39.** perimeter: 20 ft; area: 25 sq ft
40. perimeter: 42 in.; area: 98 sq in.   **41.** 26 mi   **42.** 26 m   **43.** 24   **44.** 124   **45.** Lake Pontchartrain; 2175 ft   **46.** $5904

Exercise Set 1.8   1. 49   **3.** 237   **5.** 42   **7.** 600   **9. a.** 400 ft   **b.** 9600 sq ft   **11.** $15,500   **13.** 168 hr   **15.** 5758   **17.** 129 yr
19. 312 billion bricks   **21.** 719 towns   **23.** $21   **25.** 55 cal   **27.** 24   **29.** $33,506,850   **31.** 38,034,000 students   **33.** 3987 mi
35. 13 paychecks   **37.** $239   **39.** $1045   **41.** b will be cheaper by $3   **43.** IBM Corporation   **45.** 2113 patents   **47.** 99 patents
49. 2433   **51.** $14,754   **53.** 16,800 mg   **55. a.** 3750 sq ft   **b.** 375 sq ft   **c.** 3375 sq ft
57. $240   **59.** answers may vary

Calculator Explorations   1. 729   **3.** 1024   **5.** 2048   **7.** 2526   **9.** 4295   **11.** 8

Exercise Set 1.9   1. 3^4 **3.** 7^8 **5.** 12^3 **7.** $6^2 \cdot 5^3$ **9.** $9^3 \cdot 8$ **11.** $3 \cdot 2^5$ **13.** $3 \cdot 2^2 \cdot 5^3$ **15.** 49   **17.** 125   **19.** 64   **21.** 1
23. 7   **25.** 243   **27.** 256   **29.** 64   **31.** 81   **33.** 729   **35.** 100   **37.** 20   **39.** 729   **41.** 48   **43.** 54   **45.** 3   **47.** 8
49. 12   **51.** 4   **53.** 21   **55.** 11   **57.** 4   **59.** 17   **61.** 46   **63.** 10   **65.** 126   **67.** 105   **69.** 2   **71.** 35   **73.** 4
75. undefined   **77.** 30   **79.** 52   **81.** 44   **83.** 12   **85.** 21   **87.** 24   **89.** 28   **91.** 3   **93.** 25   **95.** 23   **97.** 13
99. 400 sq mi   **101.** 64 sq cm   **103.** false   **105.** false   **107.** $(2 + 3) \cdot 6 - 2$ **109.** $24 \div (3 \cdot 2) + 2 \cdot 5$ **111.** 1260 ft
113. 6,384,814   **115.** answers may vary; $(20 - 10) \cdot 5 \div 25 + 3$

The Bigger Picture   1. 64   **2.** 48   **3.** 9   **4.** 15   **5.** 22   **6.** 50   **7.** 688   **8.** 2160   **9.** 10 R 46   **10.** 27

Chapter 1 Vocabulary Check   1. whole numbers   **2.** perimeter   **3.** place value   **4.** exponent   **5.** area   **6.** square root
7. digits   **8.** sum   **9.** divisor   **10.** dividend   **11.** quotient   **12.** factor   **13.** product   **14.** minuend   **15.** subtrahend
16. difference   **17.** addend

Chapter 1 Review   1. hundreds   **2.** ten-millions   **3.** five thousand, four hundred eighty
4. forty-six million, two hundred thousand, one hundred twenty   **5.** $6000 + 200 + 70 + 9$
6. $400,000,000 + 3,000,000 + 200,000 + 20,000 + 5000$ **7.** 59,800   **8.** 6,304,000,000   **9.** 1,630,553   **10.** 2,968,528
11. San Antonio, TX   **12.** New York, NY   **13.** 63   **14.** 67   **15.** 48   **16.** 77   **17.** 956   **18.** 840   **19.** 7950   **20.** 7250
21. 4211   **22.** 1967   **23.** 1326   **24.** 886   **25.** 27,346   **26.** 39,300   **27.** 8032 mi   **28.** $197,699   **29.** 276 ft   **30.** 66 km
31. 14   **32.** 34   **33.** 65   **34.** 304   **35.** 3914   **36.** 7908   **37.** 17,897   **38.** 34,658   **39.** 531,341   **40.** 76,704   **41.** 397 pages
42. $25,626   **43.** May   **44.** August   **45.** $110   **46.** $240   **47.** 90   **48.** 50   **49.** 470   **50.** 500   **51.** 4800   **52.** 58,000
53. 50,000,000   **54.** 800,000   **55.** 73,000,000   **56.** 571,000   **57.** 7400   **58.** 4100   **59.** 2500 mi   **60.** 2,500,000   **61.** 1911
62. 1396   **63.** 1410   **64.** 2898   **65.** 800   **66.** 900   **67.** 3696   **68.** 1694   **69.** 0   **70.** 0   **71.** 16,994   **72.** 8954
73. 113,634   **74.** 44,763   **75.** 411,426   **76.** 636,314   **77.** 375,000   **78.** 108,000   **79.** 12,000   **80.** 35,000   **81.** 5,100,000
82. 7,600,000   **83.** 1150   **84.** 4920   **85.** 108   **86.** 112   **87.** 24 g   **88.** $4,897,341   **89.** 60 sq mi   **90.** 500 sq cm   **91.** 3
92. 4   **93.** 6   **94.** 7   **95.** 5 R 2   **96.** 4 R 2   **97.** undefined   **98.** 0   **99.** 1   **100.** 10   **101.** undefined   **102.** 0
103. 33 R 2   **104.** 19 R 7   **105.** 24 R 2   **106.** 35 R 15   **107.** 506 R 10   **108.** 907 R 40   **109.** 2793 R 140   **110.** 2012 R 60
111. 18 R 2   **112.** 21 R 2   **113.** 458 ft   **114.** 13 mi   **115.** 51   **116.** 59   **117.** 27 boxes   **118.** $192   **119.** 7 billion   **120.** 75¢
121. $898   **122.** 23,150 sq ft   **123.** 49   **124.** 125   **125.** 45   **126.** 400   **127.** 13   **128.** 10   **129.** 15   **130.** 7   **131.** 12
132. 9   **133.** 42   **134.** 33   **135.** 9   **136.** 2   **137.** 1   **138.** 0   **139.** 6   **140.** 29   **141.** 40   **142.** 72   **143.** 5
144. 7   **145.** 49 sq m   **146.** 9 sq in.   **147.** 307   **148.** 682   **149.** 2160   **150.** 2516   **151.** 901   **152.** 1411   **153.** 458 R 8
154. 237 R 1   **155.** 70,848   **156.** 95,832   **157.** 1644   **158.** 8481   **159.** 740   **160.** 258,000   **161.** 2000   **162.** 40,000
163. thirty-six thousand, nine hundred eleven   **164.** one hundred fifty-four thousand, eight hundred sixty-three   **165.** 70,943   **166.** 43,401
167. 64   **168.** 125   **169.** 12   **170.** 10   **171.** 12   **172.** 1   **173.** 2   **174.** 6   **175.** 4   **176.** 24   **177.** 24   **178.** 14
179. $59,452,000   **180.** $582,140,000   **181.** 53 full boxes with 18 left over   **182.** $86

Chapter 1 Test   1. eighty-two thousand, four hundred twenty-six   **2.** 402,550   **3.** 141   **4.** 113   **5.** 14,880   **6.** 766 R 42   **7.** 200
8. 10   **9.** 0   **10.** undefined   **11.** 33   **12.** 21   **13.** 8   **14.** 36   **15.** 5,698,000   **16.** 11,200,000   **17.** 52,000   **18.** 13,700
19. 1600   **20.** 92   **21.** 122   **22.** 1605   **23.** 7 R 2   **24.** $17   **25.** $126   **26.** 360 cal   **27.** $7905   **28.** 20 cm; 25 sq cm
29. 60 yd; 200 sq yd

CHAPTER 2   Multiplying and Dividing Fractions

Mental Math   1. numerator: 1; denominator: 2; proper   **3.** numerator: 10; denominator: 3; improper
5. numerator: 15; denominator: 15; improper

Exercise Set 2.1   1. 1   **3.** undefined   **5.** 13   **7.** 0   **9.** undefined   **11.** 16   **13.** $\frac{5}{6}$ **15.** $\frac{7}{12}$ **17.** $\frac{3}{7}$ **19.** $\frac{4}{9}$ **21.** $\frac{1}{6}$

23. $\frac{5}{8}$ **25.**   **27.**   **29.**   **31.**

33. $\frac{42}{131}$ **35. a.** 89 **b.** $\frac{89}{131}$ **37.** $\frac{8}{43}$ **39.** $\frac{27}{70}$ of the hard drive **41.** $\frac{11}{31}$ of the month **43.** $\frac{10}{31}$ of the class

45. a. $\frac{33}{50}$ of the states **b.** 17 states **c.** $\frac{17}{50}$ of the states **47. a.** $\frac{21}{50}$ **b.** 29 **c.** $\frac{29}{50}$ **49. a.** $\frac{11}{4}$ **b.** $2\frac{3}{4}$ **51. a.** $\frac{23}{6}$ **b.** $3\frac{5}{6}$

53. a. $\frac{4}{3}$ **b.** $1\frac{1}{3}$ **55. a.** $\frac{11}{2}$ **b.** $5\frac{1}{2}$ **57.** $\frac{7}{3}$ **59.** $\frac{18}{5}$ **61.** $\frac{53}{8}$ **63.** $\frac{41}{15}$ **65.** $\frac{83}{7}$ **67.** $\frac{84}{13}$ **69.** $\frac{109}{24}$ **71.** $\frac{211}{12}$ **73.** $\frac{187}{20}$

75. $\frac{265}{107}$ **77.** $\frac{500}{3}$ **79.** $3\frac{2}{5}$ **81.** $4\frac{5}{8}$ **83.** $3\frac{2}{15}$ **85.** $2\frac{4}{21}$ **87.** 33 **89.** 15 **91.** $66\frac{2}{3}$ **93.** $10\frac{17}{23}$ **95.** $17\frac{13}{18}$

97. $1\frac{7}{175}$ **99.** $6\frac{65}{112}$ **101.** 9 **103.** 125 **105.** 7^5 **107.** $2^3\cdot3$ **109.** answers may vary **111.** $\frac{2}{3}$

113. ⬤ ⬤ ⬤ ⬤ ◯ ◯ ◯ ◯ ◯ **115.** $\frac{6253}{8851}$ of the restaurants **117.** $\frac{1651}{2285}$ of the affiliates

Exercise Set 2.2 **1.** 1, 2, 4, 8 **3.** 1, 5, 25 **5.** 1, 2, 4 **7.** 1, 2, 3, 6, 9, 18 **9.** 1, 29 **11.** 1, 2, 4, 5, 8, 10, 16, 20, 40, 80 **13.** 1, 2, 3, 4, 6, 12
15. 1, 2, 17, 34 **17.** prime **19.** composite **21.** prime **23.** composite **25.** prime **27.** composite **29.** prime **31.** composite
33. composite **35.** 2^5 **37.** $3\cdot5$ **39.** $2^3\cdot5$ **41.** $2^2\cdot3^2$ **43.** $3\cdot13$ **45.** $2^2\cdot3\cdot5$ **47.** $2\cdot5\cdot11$ **49.** $5\cdot17$ **51.** 2^7
53. $2\cdot7\cdot11$ **55.** $2^2\cdot3\cdot5^2$ **57.** $2^4\cdot3\cdot5$ **59.** $2^2\cdot3^2\cdot23$ **61.** $2\cdot3^2\cdot7^2$ **63.** $7^2\cdot13$ **65.** $3\cdot11$ **67.** $2\cdot7^2$ **69.** prime
71. $3^3\cdot17$ **73.** prime **75.** $2^2\cdot5^2\cdot7$ **77.** 4300 **79.** 4,286,340 **81.** 10,000,000 **83.** $\frac{19}{130}$ **85.** $2^2\cdot3^5\cdot5\cdot7$ **87.** answers may vary
89. answers may vary

Calculator Explorations **1.** $\frac{4}{7}$ **3.** $\frac{20}{27}$ **5.** $\frac{15}{8}$ **7.** $\frac{9}{2}$

Exercise Set 2.3 **1.** $\frac{1}{4}$ **3.** $\frac{2}{21}$ **5.** $\frac{7}{8}$ **7.** $\frac{2}{3}$ **9.** $\frac{7}{10}$ **11.** $\frac{7}{9}$ **13.** $\frac{3}{5}$ **15.** $\frac{27}{64}$ **17.** $\frac{5}{8}$ **19.** $\frac{5}{8}$ **21.** $\frac{14}{17}$ **23.** $\frac{3}{2}$ or $1\frac{1}{2}$

25. $\frac{3}{4}$ **27.** $\frac{5}{14}$ **29.** $\frac{3}{14}$ **31.** $\frac{11}{17}$ **33.** $\frac{3}{14}$ **35.** $\frac{7}{8}$ **37.** $\frac{3}{5}$ **39.** 14 **41.** equivalent **43.** not equivalent **45.** equivalent

47. equivalent **49.** not equivalent **51.** not equivalent **53.** $\frac{1}{4}$ of a shift **55.** $\frac{1}{2}$ mi **57. a.** $\frac{3}{10}$ **b.** 35 states **c.** $\frac{7}{10}$

59. $\frac{5}{12}$ of the wall **61. a.** 22 **b.** $\frac{11}{25}$ **63.** 364 **65.** 2322 **67.** 2520 **69.** answers may vary **71.** $\frac{3}{5}$ **73.** $\frac{9}{25}$ **75.** $\frac{1}{25}$

77. $\frac{3}{20}$ **79.** $\frac{2}{25}$ **81.** answers may vary

Integrated Review **1.** $\frac{3}{6}$ **2.** $\frac{7}{4}$ or $1\frac{3}{4}$ **3.** $\frac{73}{85}$ **4.** [bar model: 9 of 13 shaded] **5.** 1 **6.** 17

7. 0 **8.** undefined **9.** $\frac{25}{8}$ **10.** $\frac{28}{5}$ **11.** $\frac{69}{7}$ **12.** $\frac{141}{7}$ **13.** $2\frac{6}{7}$ **14.** 5 **15.** $4\frac{7}{8}$ **16.** $8\frac{10}{11}$ **17.** 1, 5, 7, 35

18. 1, 2, 4, 5, 8, 10, 20, 40 **19.** composite **20.** prime **21.** $5\cdot13$ **22.** $2\cdot5\cdot7$ **23.** $2^5\cdot3$ **24.** $2^2\cdot3\cdot11$ **25.** $2^2\cdot3^2\cdot7$ **26.** prime

27. $3^2\cdot5\cdot7$ **28.** $3^2\cdot7^2$ **29.** $2\cdot11\cdot13$ **30.** prime **31.** $\frac{1}{7}$ **32.** $\frac{6}{5}$ or $1\frac{1}{5}$ **33.** $\frac{9}{19}$ **34.** $\frac{21}{55}$ **35.** $\frac{14}{15}$ **36.** $\frac{9}{10}$ **37.** $\frac{2}{5}$ **38.** $\frac{3}{8}$

39. $\frac{11}{14}$ **40.** $\frac{7}{11}$ **41.** not equivalent **42.** equivalent **43. a.** $\frac{1}{25}$ **b.** 48 **c.** $\frac{24}{25}$ **44. a.** $\frac{55}{92}$ **b.** 185 **c.** $\frac{37}{92}$

Mental Math **1.** 8 **3.** 6 **5.** 8 **7.** 20

Exercise Set 2.4 **1.** $\frac{2}{15}$ **3.** $\frac{6}{35}$ **5.** $\frac{9}{80}$ **7.** $\frac{5}{28}$ **9.** $\frac{12}{5}$ or $2\frac{2}{5}$ **11.** $\frac{1}{70}$ **13.** 0 **15.** $\frac{1}{110}$ **17.** $\frac{18}{55}$ **19.** $\frac{27}{80}$ **21.** $\frac{1}{56}$

23. $\frac{2}{105}$ **25.** 0 **27.** $\frac{1}{90}$ **29.** 3 **31.** $\frac{5}{2}$ or $2\frac{1}{2}$ **33.** $\frac{1}{5}$ **35.** $\frac{5}{3}$ or $1\frac{2}{3}$ **37.** $\frac{2}{3}$ **39.** Exact: $\frac{77}{10}$ or $7\frac{7}{10}$; Estimate: 8

41. Exact: $\frac{836}{35}$ or $23\frac{31}{35}$; Estimate: 24 **43.** $\frac{25}{2}$ or $21\frac{1}{2}$ **45.** 15 **47.** 6 **49.** $\frac{45}{4}$ or $11\frac{1}{4}$ **51.** $\frac{49}{3}$ or $16\frac{1}{3}$ **53.** $\frac{1}{30}$ **55.** 0

57. $\frac{16}{5}$ or $3\frac{1}{5}$ **59.** $\frac{7}{2}$ or $3\frac{1}{2}$ **61.** $\frac{1}{8}$ **63.** $\frac{1}{56}$ **65.** $\frac{55}{3}$ or $18\frac{1}{3}$ **67.** 0 **69.** $\frac{208}{7}$ or $29\frac{5}{7}$ **71.** 50 **73.** 20 **75.** $\frac{3}{2}$ or $1\frac{1}{2}$ in.

77. 868 mi **79.** $\frac{17}{2}$ or $8\frac{1}{2}$ in. **81.** $\frac{3}{16}$ in. **83.** 600 cal **85.** $1838 **87.** $\frac{39}{2}$ or $19\frac{1}{2}$ in. **89.** $3\frac{367}{625}$ sq in. **91.** $\frac{1}{14}$ sq ft

93. $\frac{7}{2}$ or $3\frac{1}{2}$ sq yd **95.** 3840 mi **97.** 2400 mi **99.** 206 **101.** 56 R 12 **103.** answers may vary

105. Incorrect; $3\frac{2}{3}\cdot1\frac{1}{7}=\frac{11}{3}\cdot\frac{8}{7}=\frac{11\cdot8}{3\cdot7}=\frac{88}{21}=4\frac{4}{21}$ **107.** c **109.** d **111.** 15,660,000 Americans

Exercise Set 2.5   **1.** $\frac{7}{4}$ **3.** 11   **5.** $\frac{1}{15}$ **7.** $\frac{7}{12}$ **9.** $\frac{4}{5}$ **11.** $\frac{16}{9}$ or $1\frac{7}{9}$ **13.** $\frac{18}{35}$ **15.** $\frac{3}{4}$ **17.** $\frac{1}{100}$ **19.** $\frac{1}{3}$ **21.** $\frac{5}{3}$ or $1\frac{2}{3}$

23. $\frac{35}{36}$ **25.** $\frac{14}{37}$ **27.** $\frac{8}{45}$ **29.** 1   **31.** undefined   **33.** 0   **35.** $\frac{7}{10}$ **37.** $\frac{1}{6}$ **39.** $\frac{40}{3}$ or $13\frac{1}{3}$ **41.** 5   **43.** $\frac{5}{28}$

45. $\frac{36}{35}$ or $1\frac{1}{35}$ **47.** $\frac{26}{51}$ **49.** 0   **51.** $\frac{17}{13}$ or $1\frac{4}{13}$ **53.** $\frac{35}{18}$ or $1\frac{17}{18}$ **55.** $\frac{19}{30}$ **57.** $\frac{1}{6}$ **59.** $\frac{121}{60}$ or $2\frac{1}{60}$ **61.** 96   **63.** $\frac{3}{4}$

65. undefined   **67.** $\frac{11}{119}$ **69.** $\frac{35}{11}$ or $3\frac{2}{11}$ **71.** $\frac{9}{5}$ or $1\frac{4}{5}$ **73.** $\frac{5}{6}$ Tbsp   **75.** $3\frac{3}{16}$ miles   **77.** $\frac{19}{30}$ in.   **79.** 14 lb   **81.** $4\frac{2}{3}$ m

83. $\frac{8}{35}$ **85.** $\frac{17}{6}$ or $2\frac{5}{6}$ **87.** $\frac{16}{15}$ or $1\frac{1}{15}$ **89.** $\frac{121}{400}$ **91.** 201   **93.** 196   **95.** 1569

97. Incorrect; to divide mixed numbers, first write each mixed number as an improper fraction.   **99.** c   **101.** d   **103.** 5   **105.** 640

The Bigger Picture   **1.** $\frac{16}{27}$ **2.** $\frac{3}{4}$ **3.** $1\frac{1}{3}$ **4.** $2\frac{2}{5}$ **5.** 8   **6.** 72   **7.** $\frac{1}{24}$ **8.** 40   **9.** 35   **10.** 24

Vocabulary Check   **1.** reciprocals   **2.** composite number   **3.** equivalent   **4.** improper fraction   **5.** prime number   **6.** simplest form   **7.** proper fraction   **8.** mixed number   **9.** numerator; denominator   **10.** prime factorization   **11.** undefined   **12.** 0

Chapter 2 Review   **1.** proper   **2.** improper   **3.** proper   **4.** mixed number   **5.** $\frac{2}{6}$ **6.** $\frac{4}{7}$ **7.** $\frac{7}{3}$ **8.** $\frac{13}{4}$ **9.** $\frac{11}{12}$

10. a. 108   **b.** $\frac{108}{131}$ **11.** $3\frac{3}{4}$ **12.** $45\frac{5}{6}$ **13.** 3   **14.** 5   **15.** $\frac{6}{5}$ **16.** $\frac{22}{21}$ **17.** $\frac{26}{9}$ **18.** $\frac{47}{12}$ **19.** composite   **20.** prime

21. 1, 2, 3, 6, 7, 14, 21, 42   **22.** 1, 2, 4, 5, 10, 20   **23.** $2^2 \cdot 17$ **24.** $2 \cdot 3^2 \cdot 5$ **25.** $5 \cdot 157$ **26.** $3 \cdot 5 \cdot 17$ **27.** $\frac{3}{7}$ **28.** $\frac{5}{9}$ **29.** $\frac{1}{3}$

30. $\frac{1}{2}$ **31.** $\frac{29}{32}$ **32.** $\frac{18}{23}$ **33.** 8   **34.** 6   **35.** no   **36.** no   **37.** no   **38.** yes   **39.** $\frac{3}{10}$ **40.** $\frac{5}{14}$ **41.** 9   **42.** $\frac{1}{2}$

43. $\frac{35}{8}$ or $4\frac{3}{8}$ **44.** $\frac{5}{2}$ or $2\frac{1}{2}$ **45.** $\frac{5}{3}$ or $1\frac{2}{3}$ **46.** $\frac{49}{3}$ or $16\frac{1}{3}$ **47.** Exact: $\frac{26}{5}$ or $5\frac{1}{5}$; Estimate: 6   **48.** Exact: $\frac{60}{11}$ or $5\frac{5}{11}$; Estimate: 8

49. $\frac{99}{4}$ or $24\frac{3}{4}$ **50.** $\frac{1}{6}$ **51.** $\frac{110}{3}$ or $36\frac{2}{3}$ g   **52.** $\frac{135}{4}$ or $33\frac{3}{4}$ in.   **53.** $\frac{119}{80}$ or $1\frac{39}{80}$ sq in.   **54.** $\frac{275}{8}$ or $34\frac{3}{8}$ sq m   **55.** $\frac{1}{7}$ **56.** 8

57. $\frac{23}{14}$ **58.** $\frac{5}{17}$ **59.** 2   **60.** $\frac{15}{4}$ or $3\frac{3}{4}$ **61.** $\frac{5}{6}$ **62.** $\frac{8}{3}$ or $2\frac{2}{3}$ **63.** $\frac{21}{4}$ or $5\frac{1}{4}$ **64.** $\frac{121}{46}$ or $2\frac{29}{46}$ **65.** 22 mi   **66.** $\frac{21}{20}$ or $1\frac{1}{20}$ mi

67. proper   **68.** improper   **69.** mixed number   **70.** improper   **71.** $31\frac{1}{4}$ **72.** 6   **73.** $\frac{95}{17}$ **74.** $\frac{47}{6}$ **75.** composite   **76.** prime

77. $2^2 \cdot 3^2 \cdot 5$ **78.** $2 \cdot 7^2$ **79.** $\frac{9}{10}$ **80.** $\frac{5}{7}$ **81.** $\frac{14}{15}$ **82.** $\frac{3}{5}$ **83.** $\frac{7}{12}$ **84.** $\frac{1}{4}$ **85.** 9   **86.** $\frac{27}{2}$ or $13\frac{1}{2}$ **87.** Exact: 10; Estimate: 8

88. Exact: $\frac{51}{4}$ or $12\frac{3}{4}$; Estimate: 12   **89.** $\frac{7}{3}$ or $2\frac{1}{3}$ **90.** $\frac{32}{5}$ or $6\frac{2}{5}$ **91.** $\frac{81}{2}$ or $40\frac{1}{2}$ sq ft   **92.** $\frac{47}{61}$ in.

Chapter 2 Test   **1.** $\frac{7}{16}$ **2.** $\frac{13}{5}$ **3.** $\frac{23}{3}$ **4.** $\frac{39}{11}$ **5.** $4\frac{3}{5}$ **6.** $18\frac{3}{4}$ **7.** $\frac{4}{35}$ **8.** $\frac{3}{5}$ **9.** not equivalent   **10.** equivalent

11. $2^2 \cdot 3 \cdot 7$ **12.** $3^2 \cdot 5 \cdot 11$ **13.** $\frac{4}{3}$ or $1\frac{1}{3}$ **14.** $\frac{4}{3}$ or $1\frac{1}{3}$ **15.** $\frac{1}{4}$ **16.** $\frac{16}{45}$ **17.** 16   **18.** $\frac{9}{2}$ or $4\frac{1}{2}$ **19.** $\frac{4}{11}$ **20.** 9   **21.** $\frac{64}{3}$ or $21\frac{1}{3}$

22. $\frac{45}{2}$ or $22\frac{1}{2}$ **23.** $\frac{18}{5}$ or $3\frac{3}{5}$ **24.** $\frac{20}{3}$ or $6\frac{2}{3}$ **25.** $\frac{34}{27}$ or $1\frac{7}{27}$ sq mi   **26.** 24 mi   **27.** $\frac{16,000}{3}$ or $5333\frac{1}{3}$ sq yd   **28.** $90 per share

Cumulative Review   **1.** ten-thousands (Sec. 1.2, Ex. 1)   **2.** two thousand thirty-six   **3.** 805 (Sec. 1.2, Ex. 9)   **4.** 31
5. 184,046 (Sec. 1.3, Ex. 2)   **6.** 39   **7.** 13 in. (Sec. 1.3, Ex. 5)   **8.** 17   **9.** $96,351 (Sec. 1.3, Ex. 7)   **10.** 5   **11.** 7321 (Sec. 1.4, Ex. 2)
12. 64   **13. a.** R   **b.** 44 (Sec. 1.3, Ex. 8)   **14.** 25 R 5   **15.** 570 (Sec. 1.5, Ex. 1)   **16.** 2400   **17.** 1800 (Sec. 1.5, Ex. 5)   **18.** 300
19. a. 6   **b.** 0   **c.** 45   **d.** 0 (Sec. 1.6, Ex. 1)   **20.** 20   **21. a.** $3 \cdot 4 + 3 \cdot 5$ **b.** $10 \cdot 6 + 10 \cdot 8$ **c.** $2 \cdot 7 + 2 \cdot 3$ (Sec. 1.6, Ex. 2)   **22.** 180
23. a. 0   **b.** 0   **c.** 0   **d.** undefined (Sec. 1.7, Ex. 3)   **24.** 154 sq mi   **25.** 208 (Sec. 1.7, Ex. 5)   **26.** 4014   **27.** 7 boxes (Sec. 1.7, Ex. 11)
28. 63   **29.** 40 ft (Sec. 1.8, Ex. 5)   **30.** 16   **31.** 4^3 (Sec. 1.9, Ex. 1)   **32.** 7^4 **33.** $6^3 \cdot 8^5$ (Sec. 1.9, Ex. 4)   **34.** $2^2 \cdot 3^4$
35. 7 (Sec. 1.9, Ex. 12)   **36.** 0   **37.** $\frac{2}{5}$ (Sec. 2.1, Ex. 7)   **38.** $2^2 \cdot 3 \cdot 13$ **39. a.** $\frac{38}{9}$ **b.** $\frac{19}{11}$ (Sec. 2.1, Ex. 17)   **40.** $\frac{39}{5}$
41. 1, 2, 4, 5, 10, 20 (Sec. 2.2, Ex. 1)   **42.** yes   **43.** $\frac{7}{11}$ (Sec. 2.3, Ex. 2)   **44.** $\frac{2}{3}$ **45.** $\frac{35}{12}$ or $2\frac{11}{12}$ (Sec. 2.4, Ex. 8)   **46.** $\frac{8}{3}$ or $2\frac{2}{3}$
47. $\frac{3}{1}$ or 3 (Sec. 2.5, Ex. 3)   **48.** $\frac{1}{9}$ **49.** $\frac{5}{12}$ (Sec. 2.5, Ex. 6)   **50.** $\frac{11}{56}$

CHAPTER 3　Adding and Subtracting Fractions

Mental Math　**1.** unlike　**3.** like　**5.** like　**7.** unlike

Exercise Set 3.1　**1.** $\frac{3}{7}$　**3.** $\frac{1}{5}$　**5.** $\frac{2}{3}$　**7.** $\frac{7}{20}$　**9.** $\frac{1}{2}$　**11.** $\frac{13}{11}$ or $1\frac{2}{11}$　**13.** $\frac{7}{13}$　**15.** $\frac{2}{3}$　**17.** $\frac{6}{11}$　**19.** $\frac{3}{5}$　**21.** 1　**23.** $\frac{3}{4}$　**25.** $\frac{5}{6}$　**27.** $\frac{4}{5}$　**29.** $\frac{19}{33}$　**31.** $\frac{13}{21}$　**33.** $\frac{9}{10}$　**35.** 0　**37.** $\frac{3}{4}$　**39.** 1 in.　**41.** 2 m　**43.** $\frac{3}{2}$ or $1\frac{1}{2}$ h　**45.** $\frac{7}{25}$　**47.** $\frac{1}{50}$　**49.** $\frac{7}{10}$ of a mi　**51.** $\frac{3}{4}$　**53.** $\frac{21}{50}$　**55.** $2 \cdot 5$　**57.** 2^3　**59.** $5 \cdot 11$　**61.** $\frac{5}{8}$　**63.** $\frac{8}{11}$　**65.** $\frac{2}{7} + \frac{9}{7} = \frac{11}{7}$　**67.** answers may vary　**69.** 1; answers may vary

Exercise Set 3.2　**1.** 12　**3.** 45　**5.** 36　**7.** 72　**9.** 126　**11.** 75　**13.** 24　**15.** 42　**17.** 216　**19.** 150　**21.** 68　**23.** 588　**25.** 900　**27.** 1800　**29.** 363　**31.** 60　**33.** 20　**35.** 14　**37.** 10　**39.** 15　**41.** 30　**43.** 21　**45.** 30　**47.** 36　**49.** 90　**51.** 56　**53.** $\frac{1}{2}$　**55.** $\frac{2}{5}$　**57.** $\frac{4}{9}$　**59.** 1　**61.** 814　**63.** answers may vary　**65.** a, b, and d

Calculator Explorations　**1.** $\frac{37}{80}$　**3.** $\frac{95}{72}$　**5.** $\frac{394}{323}$

Exercise Set 3.3　**1.** $\frac{5}{6}$　**3.** $\frac{5}{6}$　**5.** $\frac{8}{33}$　**7.** $\frac{9}{14}$　**9.** $\frac{3}{5}$　**11.** $\frac{13}{25}$　**13.** $\frac{53}{60}$　**15.** $\frac{1}{6}$　**17.** $\frac{67}{99}$　**19.** $\frac{98}{143}$　**21.** $\frac{13}{27}$　**23.** $\frac{75}{56}$ or $1\frac{19}{56}$　**25.** $\frac{16}{11}$ or $1\frac{5}{11}$　**27.** $\frac{19}{12}$ or $1\frac{7}{12}$　**29.** $\frac{11}{16}$　**31.** $\frac{17}{42}$　**33.** $\frac{33}{56}$　**35.** $\frac{4}{33}$　**37.** $\frac{1}{35}$　**39.** $\frac{11}{36}$　**41.** $\frac{1}{20}$　**43.** $\frac{1}{84}$　**45.** $\frac{9}{1000}$　**47.** $\frac{17}{99}$　**49.** $\frac{19}{36}$　**51.** $\frac{1}{5}$　**53.** $\frac{69}{280}$　**55.** $\frac{14}{9}$ or $1\frac{5}{9}$　**57.** $\frac{34}{15}$ or $2\frac{4}{15}$ cm　**59.** $\frac{17}{10}$ or $1\frac{7}{10}$ m　**61.** $\frac{61}{264}$ mi　**63.** $\frac{11}{8}$ or $1\frac{3}{8}$ in.　**65.** $\frac{49}{100}$ of students　**67.** $\frac{77}{100}$ of Americans　**69.** $\frac{19}{25}$　**71.** 5　**73.** $\frac{16}{29}$　**75.** $\frac{19}{3}$ or $6\frac{1}{3}$　**77.** $\frac{3}{5} + \frac{4}{5} = \frac{7}{5}$ or $1\frac{2}{5}$　**79.** $\frac{1}{60}$　**81.** $\frac{49}{44}$ or $1\frac{5}{44}$　**83.** answers may vary

Integrated Review　**1.** 30　**2.** 21　**3.** 14　**4.** 25　**5.** 100　**6.** 90　**7.** $\frac{9}{24}$　**8.** $\frac{28}{36}$　**9.** $\frac{10}{40}$　**10.** $\frac{12}{30}$　**11.** $\frac{55}{75}$　**12.** $\frac{40}{48}$　**13.** $\frac{1}{2}$　**14.** $\frac{2}{5}$　**15.** $\frac{7}{12}$　**16.** $\frac{13}{15}$　**17.** $\frac{3}{4}$　**18.** $\frac{2}{15}$　**19.** $\frac{17}{45}$　**20.** $\frac{19}{50}$　**21.** $\frac{37}{40}$　**22.** $\frac{11}{36}$　**23.** 0　**24.** $\frac{1}{17}$　**25.** $\frac{5}{33}$　**26.** $\frac{1}{42}$　**27.** $\frac{5}{18}$　**28.** $\frac{5}{13}$　**29.** $\frac{11}{18}$　**30.** $\frac{37}{50}$　**31.** $\frac{47}{30}$ or $1\frac{17}{30}$　**32.** $\frac{7}{30}$　**33.** $\frac{3}{5}$　**34.** $\frac{27}{20}$ or $1\frac{7}{20}$　**35.** $\frac{279}{350}$　**36.** $\frac{309}{350}$　**37.** $\frac{98}{5}$ or $19\frac{3}{5}$　**38.** $\frac{9}{250}$　**39.** $\frac{31}{3}$ or $10\frac{1}{3}$　**40.** $\frac{93}{64}$ or $1\frac{29}{64}$　**41.** $\frac{49}{54}$　**42.** $\frac{83}{48}$ or $1\frac{35}{48}$　**43.** $\frac{390}{101}$ or $3\frac{87}{101}$　**44.** $\frac{145}{72}$ or $2\frac{1}{72}$　**45.** $\frac{106}{135}$　**46.** $\frac{67}{224}$

Mental Math　**1.** a　**3.** b

Exercise Set 3.4　**1.** Exact: $6\frac{4}{5}$; Estimate: 7　**3.** Exact: $13\frac{11}{14}$; Estimate: 14　**5.** Exact: $17\frac{7}{25}$; Estimate: 17　**7.** $7\frac{5}{8}$　**9.** $7\frac{5}{24}$　**11.** $20\frac{1}{15}$　**13.** 19　**15.** $56\frac{53}{270}$　**17.** $13\frac{13}{24}$　**19.** $47\frac{53}{84}$　**21.** Exact: $2\frac{3}{5}$; Estimate: 3　**23.** Exact: $7\frac{5}{14}$; Estimate: 7　**25.** Exact: $\frac{24}{25}$; Estimate: 1　**27.** $2\frac{7}{15}$　**29.** $5\frac{11}{14}$　**31.** $23\frac{31}{72}$　**33.** $1\frac{4}{5}$　**35.** $1\frac{13}{15}$　**37.** $3\frac{5}{9}$　**39.** $15\frac{3}{4}$　**41.** $28\frac{7}{12}$　**43.** $15\frac{7}{8}$　**45.** 8　**47.** $17\frac{11}{12}$　**49.** $\frac{1}{16}$ in.　**51.** no; she will be $\frac{1}{12}$ of a foot short　**53.** $7\frac{13}{20}$ in.　**55.** $10\frac{1}{4}$ hr　**57.** $2\frac{3}{8}$ hr　**59.** $92\frac{99}{100}$ m　**61.** $352\frac{1}{3}$ yd　**63.** $9\frac{7}{12}$ min　**65.** $1\frac{4}{5}$ min　**67.** 7 mi　**69.** $21\frac{5}{24}$ m　**71.** 8　**73.** 25　**75.** 4　**77.** 167　**79.** 4　**81.** $9\frac{5}{8}$　**83.** a, b, c　**85.** answers may vary　**87.** Supreme is heavier by $\frac{1}{8}$ lb

The Bigger Picture　**1.** $\frac{5}{17}$　**2.** $\frac{4}{5}$　**3.** $\frac{29}{30}$　**4.** $\frac{1}{24}$　**5.** $1\frac{33}{40}$　**6.** $\frac{27}{64}$　**7.** $12\frac{3}{7}$　**8.** $9\frac{13}{24}$　**9.** $\frac{16}{33}$　**10.** $\frac{34}{27}$ or $1\frac{7}{27}$

Exercise Set 3.5　**1.** >　**3.** <　**5.** <　**7.** >　**9.** >　**11.** <　**13.** >　**15.** <　**17.** $\frac{1}{16}$　**19.** $\frac{8}{125}$　**21.** $\frac{64}{343}$　**23.** $\frac{4}{81}$　**25.** $\frac{1}{6}$　**27.** $\frac{18}{125}$　**29.** $\frac{11}{15}$　**31.** $\frac{3}{35}$　**33.** $\frac{5}{9}$　**35.** $\frac{994}{99}$ or $10\frac{4}{99}$　**37.** $\frac{1}{12}$　**39.** $\frac{9}{11}$　**41.** 0　**43.** 0　**45.** $\frac{2}{5}$　**47.** $\frac{2}{77}$　**49.** $\frac{17}{60}$　**51.** $\frac{5}{8}$　**53.** $\frac{1}{2}$　**55.** $\frac{29}{10}$ or $2\frac{9}{10}$　**57.** $\frac{27}{32}$　**59.** $\frac{1}{81}$　**61.** $\frac{5}{6}$　**63.** $\frac{3}{5}$　**65.** $\frac{1}{2}$　**67.** $\frac{19}{7}$ or $2\frac{5}{7}$　**69.** $\frac{9}{64}$　**71.** $\frac{3}{4}$　**73.** $\frac{13}{60}$

75. $\frac{88}{100}, \frac{90}{100}, \frac{96}{100}, \frac{92}{100}, \frac{68}{100}, \frac{91}{100}, \frac{80}{100}, \frac{82}{100}, \frac{89}{100}, \frac{70}{100}$ **77.** Japan   **79.** $\frac{91}{100}$ **81.** A   **83.** M   **85.** S   **87.** D   **89.** M   **91.** A
93. no; answers may vary   **95.** subtraction, multiplication, addition, division   **97.** division, multiplication, subtraction, addition
99. standard mail   **101.** savings account

Exercise Set 3.6   **1.** $11 + 2 = 13$ **3.** $6\overline{)20}$ $\;^{3\ R\ 2}$ **5.** $35 - 8 = 27$ **7.** $68 + 7 = 75$ **9.** $21 \cdot 9 = 189$ **11.** $3\frac{1}{3}$ c   **13.** $12\frac{1}{2}$ in.

15. $21\frac{1}{2}$ mi per gal   **17.** $1\frac{1}{2}$ yr   **19.** $9\frac{2}{5}$ in.   **21.** no; $\frac{1}{4}$ yd   **23.** 5 pieces   **25.** $\frac{9}{8}$ or $1\frac{1}{8}$ in.   **27.** $3\frac{3}{4}$ c   **29.** $11\frac{1}{4}$ sq in.   **31.** $1\frac{2}{3}$ min

33. $5\frac{11}{25}$ cu in.   **35.** 67 sheets   **37. a.** yes **b.** 1 ft left over   **39.** $2\frac{15}{16}$ lb   **41.** area: $\frac{9}{128}$ sq in.; perimeter: $1\frac{1}{8}$ in.

43. area: $\frac{25}{81}$ sq m; perimeter: $2\frac{2}{9}$ m   **45.** $4\frac{3}{4}$ ft   **47.** $\frac{5}{26}$ ft   **49.** 3   **51.** 81   **53.** 4   **55.** 30   **57.** 35

59. no; no; answers may vary   **61.** $26\frac{8}{9}$ ft   **63.** 10 apples   **65.** $485\frac{1}{3}$ cu ft

Vocabulary Check   **1.** like   **2.** least common multiple   **3.** equivalent   **4.** mixed number   **5.** >   **6.** <
7. least common denominator

Chapter 3 Review   **1.** $\frac{10}{11}$ **2.** $\frac{3}{25}$ **3.** $\frac{2}{3}$ **4.** $\frac{1}{7}$ **5.** $\frac{3}{5}$ **6.** $\frac{3}{5}$ **7.** 1   **8.** 1   **9.** $\frac{19}{25}$ **10.** $\frac{16}{21}$ **11.** $\frac{3}{4}$ of his homework

12. $\frac{3}{2}$ or $1\frac{1}{2}$ mi   **13.** 55   **14.** 60   **15.** 120   **16.** 80   **17.** 252   **18.** 72   **19.** $\frac{56}{64}$ **20.** $\frac{20}{30}$ **21.** $\frac{21}{33}$ **22.** $\frac{20}{26}$

23. $\frac{16}{60}$ **24.** $\frac{25}{60}$ **25.** $\frac{11}{18}$ **26.** $\frac{7}{15}$ **27.** $\frac{7}{26}$ **28.** $\frac{17}{36}$ **29.** $\frac{41}{42}$ **30.** $\frac{43}{72}$ **31.** $\frac{13}{45}$ **32.** $\frac{39}{70}$ **33.** $2\frac{1}{9}$ m   **34.** $1\frac{1}{2}$ ft

35. $\frac{1}{4}$ of a yd   **36.** $\frac{7}{10}$ has been cleaned   **37.** $45\frac{16}{21}$ **38.** 60   **39.** $32\frac{13}{22}$ **40.** $3\frac{19}{60}$ **41.** $111\frac{5}{18}$ **42.** $20\frac{7}{24}$ **43.** $5\frac{16}{35}$

44. $3\frac{4}{55}$ **45.** $7\frac{4}{5}$ in.   **46.** $11\frac{1}{6}$ ft   **47.** 5 ft   **48.** $\frac{1}{40}$ oz   **49.** <   **50.** >   **51.** <   **52.** >   **53.** >

54. >   **55.** $\frac{9}{49}$ **56.** $\frac{64}{125}$ **57.** $\frac{9}{400}$ **58.** $\frac{9}{100}$ **59.** $\frac{8}{13}$ **60.** 2   **61.** $\frac{81}{196}$ **62.** $\frac{1}{7}$ **63.** $\frac{13}{18}$ **64.** $\frac{11}{15}$ **65.** $\frac{1}{27}$

66. $\frac{18}{5}$ or $3\frac{3}{5}$ **67.** $\frac{45}{28}$ or $1\frac{17}{28}$ **68.** $\frac{5}{6}$ **69.** $\frac{99}{56}$ or $1\frac{43}{56}$ **70.** $\frac{29}{110}$ **71.** $\frac{29}{54}$ **72.** $\frac{37}{60}$ **73.** 21 moons   **74.** $15\frac{5}{8}$ acres

75. each measurement is $4\frac{1}{4}$ in.   **76.** $\frac{7}{10}$ yd   **77.** perimeter: $1\frac{6}{11}$ mi; area: $\frac{3}{22}$ sq mi   **78.** perimeter: $2\frac{1}{3}$ m; area: $\frac{5}{16}$ sq m   **79.** 90

80. 60   **81.** 40   **82.** 63   **83.** $\frac{1}{6}$ **84.** $\frac{1}{5}$ **85.** $\frac{11}{12}$ **86.** $\frac{27}{55}$ **87.** $13\frac{5}{12}$ **88.** $12\frac{3}{8}$ **89.** $3\frac{16}{35}$ **90.** $8\frac{1}{21}$ **91.** $\frac{11}{25}$ **92.** $\frac{1}{8}$

93. $\frac{1}{144}$ **94.** $\frac{64}{27}$ **95.** $\frac{5}{17}$ **96.** $\frac{1}{12}$ **97.** <   **98.** >   **99.** $\frac{1}{2}$ hr   **100.** $6\frac{7}{20}$ lb   **101.** $44\frac{1}{2}$ yd   **102.** $2\frac{2}{15}$ ft

103. $7\frac{1}{2}$ tablespoons   **104.** $\frac{3}{8}$ of a gallon

Chapter 3 Test   **1.** 60   **2.** 72   **3.** <   **4.** <   **5.** $\frac{8}{9}$ **6.** $\frac{2}{5}$ **7.** $\frac{13}{10}$ or $1\frac{3}{10}$ **8.** $\frac{8}{21}$ **9.** $\frac{13}{24}$ **10.** $\frac{1}{7}$ **11.** $\frac{67}{60}$ or $1\frac{7}{60}$ **12.** $\frac{7}{50}$

13. $\frac{3}{2}$ or $1\frac{1}{2}$ **14.** $14\frac{1}{40}$ **15.** $30\frac{13}{45}$ **16.** $1\frac{7}{24}$ **17.** $16\frac{8}{11}$ **18.** $\frac{5}{3}$ or $1\frac{2}{3}$ **19.** $\frac{16}{81}$ **20.** $\frac{9}{16}$ **21.** $\frac{153}{200}$ **22.** $\frac{3}{8}$ **23.** $\frac{11}{12}$

24. $3\frac{3}{4}$ ft   **25.** $7\frac{5}{6}$ gal   **26.** $\frac{23}{50}$ **27.** $\frac{13}{50}$ **28.** $2820   **29.** perimeter: $3\frac{1}{3}$ ft; area: $\frac{2}{3}$ sq ft   **30.** $1\frac{2}{3}$ in.

Cumulative Review   **1.** eighty-five (Sec. 1.2, Ex. 4)   **2.** one hundred seven   **3.** one hundred twenty-six (Sec. 1.2, Ex. 5)
4. five thousand, twenty-six   **5.** 159 (Sec. 1.3, Ex. 1)   **6.** 19 in.   **7.** 514 (Sec. 1.4, Ex. 3)   **8.** 121 R 1   **9.** 278,000 (Sec. 1.5, Ex. 2)
10. 1, 2, 3, 5, 6, 10, 15, 30   **11.** 20,296 (Sec. 1.6, Ex. 4)   **12.** 0   **13. a.** 8 **b.** 11 **c.** 1 **d.** 1 **e.** 10 **f.** 1 (Sec. 1.7, Ex. 2)   **14.** 25
15. 1038 mi (Sec. 1.8, Ex. 1)   **16.** 11   **17.** 64 (Sec. 1.9, Ex. 5)   **18.** 125   **19.** 32 (Sec. 1.9, Ex. 7)   **20.** 1000

21. $\frac{4}{3}$ or $1\frac{1}{3}$ (Sec. 2.1, Ex. 15)   **22.** $\frac{11}{4}$ or $2\frac{3}{4}$ **23.** $\frac{5}{2}$ or $2\frac{1}{2}$ (Sec. 2.1, Ex. 16)   **24.** $\frac{14}{3}$ or $4\frac{2}{3}$

25. 3, 11, 17 are prime; 9, 26 are composite; (Sec. 2.2, Ex. 2)   **26.** 5   **27.** $2^2 \cdot 3^2 \cdot 5$ (Sec. 2.2, Ex. 4)   **28.** 62   **29.** $\frac{36}{13}$ or $2\frac{10}{13}$ (Sec. 2.3, Ex. 5)

30. $\frac{79}{8}$ **31.** equivalent (Sec. 2.3, Ex. 8)   **32.** >   **33.** $\frac{10}{33}$ (Sec. 2.4, Ex. 1)   **34.** $\frac{3}{2}$ or $1\frac{1}{2}$ **35.** $\frac{1}{8}$ (Sec. 2.4, Ex. 2)   **36.** 37

37. $\frac{11}{51}$ (Sec. 2.5, Ex. 9)   **38.** $\frac{25}{19}$ or $1\frac{6}{19}$ **39.** $\frac{51}{23}$ or $2\frac{5}{23}$ (Sec. 2.5, Ex. 10)   **40.** 16   **41.** $\frac{5}{8}$ (Sec. 3.1, Ex. 2)   **42.** $\frac{1}{5}$

43. 24 (Sec. 3.2, Ex. 1)   **44.** 35   **45.** 2 (Sec. 3.3, Ex. 4)   **46.** $\frac{25}{81}$ **47.** $4\frac{1}{3}$ (Sec. 3.4, Ex. 4)   **48.** $\frac{11}{100}$ **49.** $\frac{6}{13}$ (Sec. 3.5, Ex. 11)

50. $\frac{8}{175}$

CHAPTER 4   Decimals

Mental Math   1. tens   **3.** tenths

Exercise Set 4.1   1. six and fifty-two hundredths   **3.** sixteen and twenty-three hundredths   **5.** two hundred five thousandths
7. one hundred sixty-seven and nine thousandths   **9.** two hundred and five thousandths   **11.** one hundred five and six tenths
13. thirty-one and four hundredths   **15.** one and eight tenths   **17.** thirty-two and nine tenths
19. R. W. Financial; 321.42; Three hundred twenty-one and 42/100   **21.** Bell South; 59.68; Fifty-nine and 68/100   **23.** 6.5   **25.** 9.08
27. 705.625   **29.** 0.0064   **31.** 32.52   **33.** 15.8   **35.** $\frac{3}{10}$ **37.** $\frac{27}{100}$ **39.** $\frac{4}{5}$ **41.** $\frac{3}{20}$ **43.** $5\frac{47}{100}$ **45.** $\frac{6}{125}$ **47.** $7\frac{1}{125}$
49. $15\frac{401}{500}$ **51.** $\frac{601}{2000}$ **53.** $487\frac{8}{25}$ **55.** 0.6   **57.** 0.45   **59.** 3.7   **61.** 0.268   **63.** 0.09   **65.** 4.026   **67.** 0.028   **69.** 56.3
71. 0.43; forty-three hundredths   **73.** 0.8; $\frac{8}{10}$ or $\frac{4}{5}$ **75.** seventy-seven thousandths; $\frac{77}{1000}$ **77.** 47,260   **79.** 47,000
81. answers may vary   **83.** twenty-six million, eight hundred forty-nine thousand, five hundred seventy-six hundred-billionths   **85.** 17.268

Exercise Set 4.2   1. <   **3.** >   **5.** <   **7.** =   **9.** <   **11.** >   **13.** 0.006, 0.0061, 0.06   **15.** 0.03, 0.042, 0.36   **17.** 1.01, 1.09, 1.1, 1.16
19. 20.905, 21.001, 21.03, 21.12   **21.** 0.6   **23.** 0.23   **25.** 0.594   **27.** 98,210   **29.** 12.3   **31.** 17.67   **33.** 0.5   **35.** 0.130
37. 3830   **39.** $0.07   **41.** $42,650   **43.** $27   **45.** $0.20   **47.** 2.2 cm   **49.** 2.41 hr   **51.** $48.00   **53.** 24.623 hr   **55.** 2.8 min
57. 5766   **59.** 71   **61.** 243   **63.** b   **65.** a   **67.** 228.040; $228\frac{1}{25}$; Parker Bohn III
69. 228.040, 226.130, 225.370, 224.940, 222.730, 222.008, 2221.546, 220.930   **71.** answers may vary   **73.** answers may vary   **75.** 0.0612; 0.0586

Calculator Explorations   1. 328.742   **3.** 5.2414   **5.** 865.392

Mental Math   1. 0.5   **3.** 1.26   **5.** 8.9   **7.** 0.6

Exercise Set 4.3   1. 3.5   **3.** 6.83   **5.** 0.094   **7.** 622.012   **9.** 583.09   **11.** Exact: 465.56; Estimate: $\begin{array}{r} 230 \\ +\,230 \\ \hline 460 \end{array}$

13. Exact: 115.123; Estimate: $\begin{array}{r} 100 \\ 6 \\ +\ 9 \\ \hline 115 \end{array}$ **15.** 27.0578   **17.** 56.432   **19.** 6.5   **21.** 15.3   **23.** 598.23   **25.** Exact: 1.83; Estimate: $6 - 4 = 2$

27. 861.6   **29.** 376.89   **31.** Exact: 876.6; Estimate: $\begin{array}{r} 1000 \\ -\ 100 \\ \hline 900 \end{array}$ **33.** 194.4   **35.** 2.9988   **37.** 16.3   **39.** 88.028   **41.** 84.072

43. 243.17   **45.** 56.83   **47.** 3.16   **49.** $454.71   **51.** $0.14   **53.** 28.56 m   **55.** 11.2 in.   **57.** $7.52   **59.** 4.1 lb
61. 285.8 mph   **63.** 763.035 mph   **65.** $3.4 billion   **67.** 240.8 in.   **69.** 67.44 ft   **71.** $0.122   **73.** 715.05 hr
75. Switzerland   **77.** 8.1 lb
79.

Country	Pounds of Chocolate per Person
Switzerland	22.0
Norway	16.0
Germany	15.8
United Kingdom	14.5
Belgium	13.9

81. 138   **83.** 960   **85.** $\frac{1}{125}$ **87.** $\frac{5}{12}$ **89.** 6.08 in.   **91.** $1.20
93. 1 nickel, 1 dime, and 2 pennies; 3 nickels and 2 pennies; 1 dime and 7 pennies
95. answers may vary   **97.** 0.777 mi

Mental Math   1. 4   **3.** 4   **5.** 5

Exercise Set 4.4 **1.** 0.12 **3.** 0.6 **5.** 1.3 **7.** Exact: 22.26; Estimate: $5 \times 4 = 20$ **9.** 0.4032 **11.** Exact: 8.23854; Estimate: $\begin{array}{r} 1 \\ \times\,8 \\ \hline 8 \end{array}$

13. 11.2746 **15.** 84.97593 **17.** 65 **19.** 0.65 **21.** 0.072 **23.** 709.3 **25.** 6046 **27.** 0.03762 **29.** 0.0492 **31.** 12.3 **33.** 1.29 **35.** 0.096 **37.** 0.5623 **39.** 43.274 **41.** 5,500,000,000 **43.** 49,800,000 **45.** 353,000 **47.** $8\pi \approx 25.12$ m **49.** $10\pi \approx 31.4$ cm **51.** $18.2\pi \approx 57.148$ yd **53.** 24.8 g **55.** $4550 **57.** 250π ft ≈ 785 ft **59.** 135π m ≈ 423.9 m **61.** 64.9605 in. **63.** $555.20 **65. a.** 62.8 m and 125.6 m **b.** yes **67.** 7.2 sq in. **69.** 26 **71.** 36 **73.** 8 **75.** 9 **77.** 3.64 **79.** 3.56 **81.** 0.1105 **83.** 3,831,600 mi **85.** answers may vary **87.** answers may vary

Integrated Review—Operations on Decimals **1.** 2.57 **2.** 4.05 **3.** 8.9 **4.** 3.5 **5.** 0.16 **6.** 0.24 **7.** 11.06 **8.** 9.72 **9.** 4.8 **10.** 6.09 **11.** 75.56 **12.** 289.12 **13.** 25.026 **14.** 44.125 **15.** 82.7 **16.** 273.9 **17.** 280 **18.** 1600 **19.** 224.938 **20.** 145.079 **21.** 6 **22.** 6.2 **23.** 27.6092 **24.** 145.6312 **25.** 5.4 **26.** 17.74 **27.** 414.44 **28.** 1295.03 **29.** 116.81 **30.** 18.79 **31.** 156.2 **32.** 25.62 **33.** 5.62 **34.** 304.876 **35.** 114.66 **36.** 119.86 **37.** 0.000432 **38.** 0.000075 **39.** 0.0672 **40.** 0.0275 **41.** 862 **42.** 0.0293 **43.** 200 mi

Calculator Explorations **1.** not reasonable **3.** reasonable

Mental Math **1.** 5.9 **3.** 0 **5.** 1 **7.** undefined

Exercise Set 4.5 **1.** 4.6 **3.** 0.094 **5.** 300 **7.** 5.8 **9.** Exact: 6.6; Estimate: $6\overline{)36}$ with 6 on top **11.** 0.413 **13.** 0.045 **15.** 7 **17.** 4.8 **19.** 2100 **21.** 30 **23.** 7000 **25.** Exact: 9.8; Estimate: $7\overline{)70}$ with 10 on top **27.** 9.6 **29.** 45 **31.** 54.592 **33.** 0.0055 **35.** 179 **37.** 23.87 **39.** 113.1 **41.** 0.54982 **43.** 2.687 **45.** 0.0129 **47.** 12.6 **49.** 1.31 **51.** 12.225 **53.** 0.045625 **55.** 24 mo **57.** $3641.30 **59.** 202.1 lb **61.** 5.1 m **63.** 11.4 boxes **65.** 24 tsp **67.** 8 days **69.** 133.8 mph **71.** 20.45 points **73.** 2.45 **75.** 0.66 **77.** 80.52 **79.** 14.7 **81.** 930.7 **83.** 571 **85.** 92.06 **87.** 144.4 **89.** $\frac{9}{10}$ **91.** $\frac{1}{20}$ **93.** 4.26 **95.** 1.578 **97.** 26.66 **99.** 904.29 **101.** c **103.** b **105.** 85.5 **107.** 14.345 million, or 14,345,000 CDs **109.** 45.2 cm **111.** answers may vary **113.** 65.2–82.6 knots

The Bigger Picture **1.** 22.172 **2.** 3.951 **3.** 9133.2 **4.** 6.8 **5.** 1.404 **6.** 8.66 **7.** 0.051 **8.** 2.14 **9.** $\frac{2}{15}$ **10.** $\frac{16}{75}$

Exercise Set 4.6 **1.** 0.2 **3.** 0.68 **5.** 0.75 **7.** 0.08 **9.** 1.2 **11.** $0.91\overline{6}$ **13.** 0.425 **15.** 0.45 **17.** $0.\overline{3}$ **19.** 0.4375 **21.** $0.\overline{63}$ **23.** 5.85 **25.** 0.624 **27.** 0.33 **29.** 0.44 **31.** 0.6 **33.** 0.68 **35.** 0.62 **37.** 0.71 **39.** $<$ **41.** $=$ **43.** $<$ **45.** $<$ **47.** $<$ **49.** $>$ **51.** $<$ **53.** $<$ **55.** 0.32, 0.34, 0.35 **57.** 0.49, 0.491, 0.498 **59.** 0.73, $\frac{3}{4}$, 0.78 **61.** 0.412, 0.453, $\frac{4}{7}$ **63.** 5.23, $\frac{42}{8}$, 5.34 **65.** $\frac{17}{8}$, 2.37, $\frac{12}{5}$ **67.** 25.65 sq in. **69.** 9.36 sq cm **71.** 0.248 sq yd **73.** 8 **75.** 72 **77.** $\frac{1}{81}$ **79.** $\frac{9}{25}$ **81.** $\frac{5}{2}$ **83.** $=1$ **85.** >1 **87.** <1 **89.** 0.192 **91.** 6000 stations **93.** answers may vary **95.** answers may vary **97.** 47.25 **99.** 3.37 **101.** 0.45

Chapter 4 Vocabulary Check **1.** decimal **2.** numerator; denominator **3.** vertically **4.** and **5.** sum

Chapter 4 Review **1.** tenths **2.** hundred-thousandths **3.** forty-five hundredths **4.** three hundred forty-five hundred-thousandths **5.** one hundred nine and twenty-three hundredths **6.** forty-six and seven thousandths **7.** 2.15 **8.** 503.102 **9.** $\frac{4}{25}$ **10.** $12\frac{23}{1000}$ **11.** $1\frac{9}{2000}$ **12.** $25\frac{1}{4}$ **13.** 0.9 **14.** 0.25 **15.** 0.045 **16.** 26.1 **17.** $>$ **18.** $=$ **19.** 0.92, 8.09, 8.6 **20.** 0.09, 0.091, 0.1 **21.** 0.6 **22.** 0.94 **23.** $0.26 **24.** $12.46 **25.** 13.491 **26.** $10\frac{3}{4}$ **27.** 9.52 **28.** 2.7 **29.** 7.28 **30.** 26.007 **31.** 459.7 **32.** 100.278 **33.** 65.02 **34.** 189.98 **35.** 52.6 mi **36.** $2.44 **37.** 22.2 in. **38.** 38.9 ft **39.** 18.5 **40.** 54.6 **41.** 72 **42.** 9345 **43.** 9.246 **44.** 3406.446 **45.** 14π m, 43.96 m **46.** 63.8 mi **47.** 887,000,000 **48.** 600,000 **49.** 0.0877 **50.** 15.825 **51.** 70 **52.** 0.21 **53.** 8.059 **54.** 30.4 **55.** 0.0267 **56.** 9.3 **57.** 7.3 m **58.** 45 mo **59.** 16.94 **60.** 3.89 **61.** 129 **62.** 0.81 **63.** 55 **64.** 7.26 **65.** 0.8 **66.** 0.923 **67.** $2.\overline{3}$ or 2.333 **68.** $0.21\overline{6}$ or 0.217 **69.** $=$ **70.** $<$ **71.** $<$ **72.** 0.837, 0.839, $\frac{17}{20}$ **73.** 0.42, $\frac{3}{7}$, 0.43 **74.** $\frac{19}{12}$, 1.63, $\frac{18}{11}$ **75.** 6.9 sq ft **76.** 5.46 sq in. **77.** two hundred and thirty-two ten-thousandths **78.** 16,025.014 **79.** $\frac{231}{100,000}$ **80.** 0.75, $\frac{6}{7}$, $\frac{8}{9}$ **81.** 0.07 **82.** 0.1125 **83.** 51.057 **84.** $>$ **85.** $<$ **86.** $<$ **87.** 42.90 **88.** 16.349 **89.** $123.00 **90.** $3646.00 **91.** 1.7 **92.** 2.49 **93.** 320.312 **94.** 148.74236 **95.** 8.128 **96.** 7.245 **97.** 4900 **98.** 23.904 **99.** 9600 sq ft **100.** yes **101.** 0.1024 **102.** 3.6

Chapter 4 Test **1.** forty-five and ninety-two thousandths **2.** 3000.059 **3.** 34.9 **4.** 0.862 **5.** $<$ **6.** $\frac{4}{9}$, 0.445, 0.454 **7.** $\frac{69}{200}$ **8.** $24\frac{73}{100}$ **9.** 0.65 **10.** $5.\overline{8}$ or 5.889 **11.** 0.941 **12.** 17.583 **13.** 11.4 **14.** 43.86 **15.** 56 **16.** 0.07755 **17.** 6.673 **18.** 12,690 **19.** 4.73 **20.** 0.363 **21.** 6.2 **22.** 4,583,000,000 **23.** 2.31 sq mi **24.** 18π mi, 56.52 mi **25. a.** 9904 sq ft **b.** 198.08 oz **26.** 54 mi

Cumulative Review **1.** one hundred six million, fifty-two thousand, four hundred forty-seven (Sec. 1.2, Ex. 7) **2.** 276,004 **3.** $96,361 (Sec. 1.3, Ex. 7) **4.** 288 **5.** 726 (Sec. 1.4, Ex. 4) **6.** 200 **7.** 2300 (Sec. 1.5, Ex. 4) **8.** 84 **9.** 57,600 megabytes (Sec. 1.6, Ex. 11) **10.** perimeter: 28 ft; area: 49 sq ft **11.** 401 R 2 (Sec. 1.7, Ex. 8) **12.** $\frac{21}{8}$ **13.** 47 (Sec. 1.9, Ex. 15)

14. $12\frac{4}{5}$ **15.** numerator: 3; denominator: 7 (Sec. 2.1, Ex. 1)   **16.** 9   **17.** $\frac{1}{10}$ (Sec. 2.3, Ex. 6)   **18.** 17   **19.** $\frac{15}{1}$ or 15 (Sec. 2.4, Ex. 9)

20. 13   **21.** $\frac{63}{16}$ (Sec. 2.5, Ex. 5)   **22.** 128   **23.** $\frac{15}{4}$ or $3\frac{3}{4}$ (Sec. 2.4, Ex. 10)   **24.** \$9   **25.** $\frac{3}{20}$ (Sec. 2.5, Ex. 8)   **26.** $\frac{27}{20}$ or $1\frac{7}{20}$

27. $\frac{7}{9}$ (Sec. 3.1, Ex. 4)   **28.** $\frac{2}{5}$ **29.** $\frac{1}{4}$ (Sec. 3.1, Ex. 5)   **30.** $\frac{2}{5}$ **31.** $\frac{15}{20}$ (Sec. 3.2, Ex. 8)   **32.** $\frac{35}{45}$ **33.** $\frac{13}{30}$ (Sec. 3.3, Ex. 2)

34. $\frac{1}{90}$ **35.** $4\frac{7}{40}$ lb (Sec. 3.4, Ex. 7)   **36.** $27\frac{3}{4}$ lb   **37.** $\frac{1}{16}$ (Sec. 3.5, Ex. 3)   **38.** $\frac{49}{121}$ **39.** $\frac{3}{256}$ (Sec. 3.5, Ex. 5)   **40.** $\frac{2}{81}$

41. $\frac{43}{100}$ (Sec. 4.1, Ex. 8)   **42.** 0.75   **43.** > (Sec. 4.2, Ex. 1)   **44.** 5.06   **45.** 11.568 (Sec. 4.3, Ex. 4)   **46.** 75.329

47. 2370.2 (Sec. 4.4, Ex. 6)   **48.** 0.119   **49.** 768.05 (Sec. 4.4, Ex. 9)   **50.** 8.9

CHAPTER 5   Ratio and Proportion

Exercise Set 5.1   1. $\frac{11}{4}$ **3.** $\frac{23}{10}$ **5.** $\frac{151}{201}$ **7.** $\frac{2.8}{7.6}$ **9.** $\frac{5}{7\frac{1}{2}}$ **11.** $\frac{3\frac{3}{4}}{1\frac{2}{3}}$ **13.** $\frac{2}{3}$ **15.** $\frac{77}{100}$ **17.** $\frac{463}{821}$ **19.** $\frac{3}{4}$ **21.** $\frac{5}{12}$ **23.** $\frac{8}{25}$

25. $\frac{12}{7}$ **27.** $\frac{16}{23}$ **29.** $\frac{2}{5}$ **31.** $\frac{2}{7}$ **33.** $\frac{4}{1}$ **35.** $\frac{3}{50}$ **37.** $\frac{47}{25}$ **39.** $\frac{17}{40}$ **41.** $\frac{4}{9}$ **43.** $\frac{5}{4}$ **45.** $\frac{3}{1}$ **47.** $\frac{15}{1}$ **49.** $\frac{1}{3}$ **51.** $\frac{2}{43}$

53. $\frac{1}{49}$ **55.** 2.3   **57.** 0.15   **59.** the ratio of seven to nine   **61.** the ratio of thirty to one   **63.** no; answers may vary   **65.** no; $\frac{3}{2}$

67. no; $\frac{71}{43}$ **69.** no; $\frac{9}{2}$ **71.** no, the shipment should not be refused

Exercise Set 5.2   1. $\frac{1 \text{ shrub}}{3 \text{ ft}}$ **3.** $\frac{3 \text{ returns}}{20 \text{ sales}}$ **5.** $\frac{2 \text{ phone lines}}{9 \text{ employees}}$ **7.** $\frac{9 \text{ gal}}{2 \text{ acres}}$ **9.** $\frac{3 \text{ flight attendants}}{100 \text{ passengers}}$ **11.** $\frac{71 \text{ cal}}{2 \text{ fl oz}}$ **13.** 75 riders/car

15. 110 cal/oz   **17.** 90 wingbeats/sec   **19.** \$50,000/yr   **21.** 1330 mi/day   **23.** 7600 sq mi/county   **25.** 300 good/defective

27. 0.48 tons of dust and dirt/acre   **29.** \$60,200 species   **31.** \$46,600/house   **33.** 6.2 tornadoes/hr

35. a. 31.25 computer boards/hr   **b.** 33.5 computer boards/hr   **c.** Lamont   **37. a.** $\approx$ 27.6 miles/gal   **b.** $\approx$ 29.2 miles/gal   **c.** the truck

39. \$11.50 per compact disc   **41.** \$0.17 per banana   **43.** 8 oz: \$0.149 per oz; 12 oz: \$0.133 per oz; 12 oz

45. 16 oz: \$0.106 per oz; 6 oz: \$0.115 per oz; 16 oz   **47.** 12 oz: \$0.191 per oz; 8 oz: \$0.186 per oz; 8 oz

49. 100: \$0.006 per napkin; 180: \$0.005 per napkin; 180 napkins   **51.** 10.2   **53.** 4.44   **55.** 1.9

57. miles driven: 257, 352, 347; miles per gallon: 19.2, 22.3, 21.6   **59.** 544 students/school   **61.** answers may vary

63. no; answers may vary

Integrated Review—Ratio and Rate   1. $\frac{9}{10}$ **2.** $\frac{9}{25}$ **3.** $\frac{43}{50}$ **4.** $\frac{8}{23}$ **5.** $\frac{173}{139}$ **6.** $\frac{6}{7}$ **7.** $\frac{7}{26}$ **8.** $\frac{20}{33}$ **9.** $\frac{2}{3}$ **10.** $\frac{1}{8}$ **11.** $\frac{841}{615}$

12. $\frac{7409}{1152}$ **13. a.** 10   **b.** $\frac{1}{2}$ **14.** $\frac{2}{3}$ **15.** $\frac{1 \text{ office}}{4 \text{ graduate assistants}}$ **16.** $\frac{2 \text{ lights}}{5 \text{ ft}}$ **17.** $\frac{2 \text{ senators}}{1 \text{ state}}$ **18.** $\frac{1 \text{ teacher}}{28 \text{ students}}$ **19.** $\frac{16 \text{ computers}}{25 \text{ households}}$

20. $\frac{9 \text{ students}}{2 \text{ computers}}$ **21.** 55 mi/hr   **22.** 140 ft/sec   **23.** 21 employees/fax line   **24.** 17 phone calls/teenager   **25.** 23 mi/gal

26. 16 teachers/computer   **27.** 6 books/student   **28.** 154 lb/adult   **29.** 8 lb: \$0.27 per lb; 18 lb: \$0.28 per lb; 8 lb

30. 100: \$0.020 per plate; 500: \$0.018 per plate; 500 paper plates   **31.** 3 packs: \$0.80 per pack; 8 packs: \$0.75 per pack; 8 packs

32. 4: \$0.92 per battery; 10: \$0.99 per battery; 4 batteries

Mental Math   1. true   **3.** false   **5.** true

Exercise Set 5.3   1. $\frac{10 \text{ diamonds}}{6 \text{ opals}} = \frac{5 \text{ diamonds}}{3 \text{ opals}}$ **3.** $\frac{3 \text{ printers}}{12 \text{ computers}} = \frac{1 \text{ printer}}{4 \text{ computers}}$ **5.** $\frac{6 \text{ eagles}}{58 \text{ sparrows}} = \frac{3 \text{ eagles}}{29 \text{ sparrows}}$

7. $\frac{2\frac{1}{4} \text{ cups flour}}{24 \text{ cookies}} = \frac{6\frac{3}{4} \text{ cups flour}}{72 \text{ cookies}}$ **9.** $\frac{22 \text{ vanilla wafers}}{1 \text{ cup cookie crumbs}} = \frac{55 \text{ vanilla wafers}}{2.5 \text{ cups cookie crumbs}}$ **11.** true   **13.** false   **15.** true   **17.** true

19. false   **21.** false   **23.** true   **25.** false   **27.** true   **29.** $\frac{8}{12} = \frac{4}{6}$; true   **31.** $\frac{5}{2} = \frac{13}{5}$; false   **33.** $\frac{1.8}{2} = \frac{4.5}{5}$; true

35. $\frac{\frac{2}{3}}{\frac{1}{5}} = \frac{\frac{2}{5}}{\frac{1}{9}}$; false   **37.** 3   **39.** 9   **41.** 4   **43.** 3.2   **45.** 38.4   **47.** 25   **49.** 0.0025   **51.** 1   **53.** $\frac{9}{20}$ **55.** 12   **57.** $\frac{3}{4}$

59. $\frac{35}{18}$ **61.** <   **63.** >   **65.** <   **67.** $\frac{9}{3} = \frac{15}{5}$; $\frac{5}{15} = \frac{3}{9}$; $\frac{15}{9} = \frac{5}{3}$ **69.** $\frac{6}{1} = \frac{18}{3}$; $\frac{3}{18} = \frac{1}{6}$; $\frac{18}{6} = \frac{3}{1}$ **71.** $\frac{d}{b} = \frac{c}{a}$; $\frac{a}{c} = \frac{b}{d}$; $\frac{b}{a} = \frac{d}{c}$

73. answers may vary   **75.** 0   **77.** 1400   **79.** 252.5

The Bigger Picture   1. $\frac{1}{4}$ **2.** $\frac{7}{200}$ **3.** $\frac{7}{2}$ or $3\frac{1}{2}$ **4.** $\frac{9}{20}$ **5.** 7.62   **6.** 0.152   **7.** 8   **8.** $\frac{5}{2}$ or $2\frac{1}{2}$ **9.** 0.004   **10.** $\frac{35}{12}$ or $2\frac{11}{12}$

Exercise Set 5.4   1. 12 passes   **3.** 165 min   **5.** 630 applications   **7.** 23 ft   **9.** 270 sq ft   **11.** 56 mi   **13.** 450 km   **15.** 24 oz

17. 16 bags   **19.** \$162,000   **21.** 15 hits   **23.** 27 people   **25.** 86 wk   **27.** 6 people   **29.** 112 ft; 11-in. difference   **31.** 102.9 mg

33. 1248 feet; coincidentally; this is the actual height of the Empire State Building   **35.** 434 emergency room visits   **37.** 427.5 cal

39. $2\frac{2}{3}$ lb   **41.** 2.4 c   **43. a.** 0.1 gal   **b.** 13 fl oz   **45. a.** 2062.5 mg   **b.** no   **47.** $3 \cdot 5$ **49.** $2^2 \cdot 5$ **51.** $2^3 \cdot 5^2$ **53.** 2^5

55. 0.8 ml   **57.** 1.25 ml   **59.** $11 \approx 12$ or 1 dozen; $1.5 \times 8 = 12$; 12 cups of milk   **61.** $4\frac{2}{3}$ ft   **63.** answers may vary

Vocabulary Check   1. ratio   **2.** proportion   **3.** unit rate   **4.** unit price   **5.** rate   **6.** cross products   **7.** equal   **8.** not equal

Chapter 5 Review   1. $\frac{23}{37}$ **2.** $\frac{14}{51}$ **3.** $\frac{5}{4}$ **4.** $\frac{11}{13}$ **5.** $\frac{7}{15}$ **6.** $\frac{17}{35}$ **7.** $\frac{18}{35}$ **8.** $\frac{35}{27}$ **9. a.** 6   **b.** $\frac{3}{10}$ **10. a.** 3   **b.** $\frac{3}{20}$

11. $\frac{1 \text{ stillborn birth}}{125 \text{ live births}}$ **12.** $\frac{3 \text{ professors}}{10 \text{ assistants}}$ **13.** $\frac{5 \text{ pages}}{2 \text{ min}}$ **14.** $\frac{4 \text{ computers}}{3 \text{ hr}}$ **15.** 52 mi/hr   **16.** 15 ft/sec   **17.** $1.74/diskette

18. $1\frac{1}{3}$ gal/acre   **19.** $46.80/course   **20.** 13 bushels/tree   **21.** 8 oz; $0.124 per oz: 12 oz; $0.141 per oz: 8-oz size   **22.** 18 oz; $0.083: 28 oz; $0.085: 18-oz size   **23.** 16 oz; $0.037: 64 oz; $0.026: 128 oz; $0.018: 1-gal size

24. 12 oz; $0.049: 16 oz; $0.049: 32 oz; $0.037: 32-oz size   **25.** $\frac{20 \text{ men}}{14 \text{ women}} = \frac{10 \text{ men}}{7 \text{ women}}$ **26.** $\frac{50 \text{ tries}}{4 \text{ successes}} = \frac{25 \text{ tries}}{2 \text{ successes}}$ **27.** $\frac{16 \text{ sandwiches}}{8 \text{ players}} = \frac{2 \text{ sandwiches}}{1 \text{ player}}$ **28.** $\frac{12 \text{ tries}}{3 \text{ cars}} = \frac{4 \text{ tires}}{1 \text{ car}}$

29. no   **30.** yes   **31.** yes   **32.** no   **33.** 5   **34.** 15   **35.** 32.5   **36.** 5.625   **37.** 32   **38.** $6\frac{3}{4}$ **39.** 60   **40.** $7\frac{1}{5}$ **41.** 0.94

42. 0.36   **43.** $1\frac{1}{8}$ **44.** $1\frac{3}{7}$ **45.** 14   **46.** 35   **47.** 8 bags   **48.** 16 bags   **49.** no   **50.** 79 gal   **51.** $54,600   **52.** $1023.50

53. $40\frac{1}{2}$ ft   **54.** $8\frac{1}{4}$ in.   **55.** $\frac{3}{5}$ **56.** $\frac{4}{9}$ **57.** $\frac{1}{2}$ **58.** $\frac{5}{12}$ **59.** $\frac{1}{27}$ **60.** $\frac{1}{8}$ **61.** $\frac{1 \text{ teacher}}{9 \text{ students}}$ **62.** $\frac{1 \text{ nurse}}{4 \text{ patients}}$ **63.** 4 cups/person

64. 6 toys/child   **65.** 34 miles/hour   **66.** 2 gallons/cow   **67.** 4 oz; $1.235: 8 oz; $1.248: 4-oz size   **68.** 12 oz; $0.054: 64 oz; $0.047: 64-oz size   **69.** $\frac{2 \text{ cups cookie dough}}{30 \text{ cookies}} = \frac{4 \text{ cups cookie dough}}{60 \text{ cookies}}$

70. $\frac{5 \text{ nickels}}{3 \text{ dollars}} = \frac{20 \text{ nickels}}{12 \text{ dollars}}$ **71.** yes   **72.** no   **73.** 1.6   **74.** 4.8   **75.** 84   **76.** 25   **77.** $609.50   **78.** $477   **79.** $171   **80.** $95

Chapter 5 Test   1. $\frac{15}{2}$ **2.** $\frac{9}{13}$ **3.** $\frac{7 \text{ men}}{1 \text{ woman}}$ **4.** $\frac{13 \text{ in.}}{10 \text{ days}}$ **5.** $\frac{43}{50}$ **6.** $\frac{47}{78}$ **7.** $\frac{138}{77}$ **8.** 81.25 km/hr   **9.** $\frac{2}{3}$ in./hr

10. 28 students/teacher   **11.** 9 inches/sec   **12.** 8-oz size   **13.** 16-oz size   **14.** true   **15.** false   **16.** $\frac{25 \text{ computers}}{600 \text{ students}} = \frac{1 \text{ computer}}{24 \text{ students}}$

17. 5   **18.** $4\frac{4}{11}$ **19.** $\frac{7}{3}$ **20.** 8   **21.** $\frac{7}{8}$ **22.** $49\frac{1}{2}$ ft   **23.** $3\frac{3}{4}$ hr   **24.** $53\frac{1}{3}$ g   **25.** $114\frac{2}{3}$ cartons   **26.** 4266 adults

Cumulative Review   1. a. 3 (Sec. 1.4, Ex. 1)   **b.** 5 (Sec. 1.4, Ex. 1)   **c.** 0 (Sec. 1.4, Ex. 1)   **d.** 7 (Sec. 1.4, Ex. 1)   **2. a.** 0   **b.** 20   **c.** 0   **d.** 20
3. 249,000 (Sec. 1.5, Ex. 3)   **4.** 249,000   **5. a.** 200   **b.** 1230 (Sec. 1.6, Ex. 3)   **6.** 373 R 24   **7.** $6171 (Sec. 1.8, Ex. 3)

8. 16,591 feet   **9.** $3 \cdot 3 \cdot 5$ or $3^2 \cdot 5$ (Sec. 2.2, Ex. 3)   **10.** 8   **11.** $\frac{3}{5}$ (Sec. 2.3, Ex. 1)   **12.** 243   **13.** $\frac{6}{5}$ (Sec. 2.4, Ex. 5)   **14.** $\frac{123}{8}$ or $15\frac{3}{8}$

15. $\frac{2}{5}$ (Sec. 2.4, Ex. 6)   **16.** $\frac{5}{54}$ **17.** $\frac{5}{7}$ (Sec. 3.1, Ex. 1)   **18.** $\frac{19}{30}$ **19.** $\frac{16}{13}$ or $1\frac{3}{13}$ (Sec. 3.1, Ex. 3)   **20.** $\frac{4}{5}$ **21.** 36 (Sec. 3.2, Ex. 2)

22. $\frac{49}{50}$ **23.** $\frac{7}{14}$ (Sec. 3.2, Ex. 9)   **24.** yes   **25.** $\frac{8}{33}$ (Sec. 3.3, Ex. 6)   **26.** $7\frac{47}{72}$ **27.** $\frac{1}{6}$ of an hour (Sec. 3.3, Ex. 9)   **28.** 27

29. $7\frac{17}{24}$ (Sec. 3.4, Ex. 1)   **30.** $\frac{16}{27}$ **31.** $>$ (Sec. 3.5, Ex. 1)   **32.** 14,000,000   **33.** one and three tenths (Sec. 4.1, Ex. 1)   **34.** 0.075
35. 736.2 (Sec. 4.2, Ex. 5)   **36.** 736.236   **37.** 25.454 (Sec. 4.3, Ex. 1)   **38.** 681.24   **39.** 0.0849 (Sec. 4.4, Ex. 2)   **40.** 0.375
41. 0.125 (Sec. 4.5, Ex. 3)   **42.** $\frac{79}{10}$ **43.** 3.7 (Sec. 4.5, Ex. 12)   **44.** 3   **45.** $\frac{4}{9}, \frac{9}{20}$, 0.456 (Sec. 4.6, Ex. 9)   **46.** 140 m/sec

47. $\frac{2.6}{3.1}$ (Sec. 5.1, Ex. 2)   **48.** $\frac{1}{3}$ **49.** $\frac{1\frac{1}{2}}{7\frac{3}{4}}$ (Sec. 5.1, Ex. 3)   **50.** $\frac{1}{10}$

CHAPTER 6   Percent

Exercise Set 6.1   1. 81%   **3. a.** 75%   **b.** 25%   **5.** 9%   **7.** chocolate chip; 52%   **9.** 0.48   **11.** 0.06   **13.** 1.00 or 1   **15.** 0.613
17. 0.028   **19.** 0.006   **21.** 3.00 or 3   **23.** 0.3258   **25.** 0.67   **27.** 0.212   **29.** 0.057   **31.** 98%   **33.** 310%   **35.** 2900%
37. 0.3%   **39.** 22%   **41.** 530%   **43.** 5.6%   **45.** 33.28%   **47.** 300%   **49.** 70%   **51.** 10%   **53.** 38%   **55.** 9.3%   **57.** 0.25
59. 0.65   **61.** 0.9   **63.** b, d   **65.** 4%   **67.** network systems and data communication analysts   **69.** 0.49   **71.** answers may vary

Mental Math   1. 13%   **3.** 87%   **5.** 1%

Exercise Set 6.2   1. $\frac{3}{25}$ **3.** $\frac{1}{25}$ **5.** $\frac{9}{200}$ **7.** $\frac{7}{4}$ or $1\frac{3}{4}$ **9.** $\frac{73}{100}$ **11.** $\frac{1}{8}$ **13.** $\frac{1}{16}$ **15.** $\frac{3}{50}$ **17.** $\frac{31}{300}$ **19.** $\frac{179}{800}$ **21.** 75%

23. 70%   **25.** 40%   **27.** 59%   **29.** 34%   **31.** $37\frac{1}{2}$%   **33.** $31\frac{1}{4}$%   **35.** 160%   **37.** $77\frac{7}{9}$%   **39.** 65%   **41.** 250%

43. 190%   **45.** 63.64%   **47.** 26.67%   **49.** 14.29%   **51.** 91.67%   **53.** $0.35, \frac{7}{20}$; 20%, 0.2; 50%, $\frac{1}{2}$; 0.7, $\frac{7}{10}$; 37.5%, 0.375

55. $0.4, \frac{2}{5}$; $23\frac{1}{2}$%, $\frac{47}{200}$; 80%, 0.8; $0.333\overline{3}, \frac{1}{3}$; 87.5%, 0.875; 0.075, $\frac{3}{40}$ **57.** 2, 2; 280%, $2\frac{4}{5}$; 7.05, $7\frac{1}{20}$; 454%, 4.54   **59.** 0.148; $\frac{37}{250}$

61. 0.23; $\frac{23}{100}$ **63.** 27.4%   **65.** 0.0875   **67.** 24%   **69.** 0.004; $\frac{1}{250}$ **71.** 0.12; $\frac{3}{25}$ **73.** 0.071; $\frac{71}{1000}$ **75.** $n = 15$ **77.** $n = 10$

79. $n = 12$ **81. a.** 52.9%   **b.** 52.86%   **83.** 107.8%   **85.** 65.79%   **87.** 77%   **89.** 75%   **91.** 80%   **93.** greater

95. answers may vary   **97.** 0.266; 26.6%   **99.** 1.155; 115.5%

Mental Math   **1.** percent: 42%; base: 50; amount: 21   **3.** percent: 125%; base: 86; amount: 107.5

Exercise Set 6.3   **1.** $15\% \cdot 72 = n$ **3.** $30\% \cdot n = 80$ **5.** $1.9 = 40\% \cdot n$ **7.** $n \cdot 90 = 20$ **9.** $n = 9\% \cdot 43$ **11.** 3.5   **13.** 7.28
15. 600   **17.** 10   **19.** 110%   **21.** 32%   **23.** 1   **25.** 45   **27.** 500   **29.** 400%   **31.** 25.2   **33.** 45%   **35.** 35
37. 0.624   **39.** 0.5%   **41.** 145   **43.** 63%   **45.** $n = 30$ **47.** $n = 3\frac{7}{11}$ **49.** $\frac{17}{12} = \frac{n}{20}$ **51.** $\frac{8}{9} = \frac{14}{n}$ **53.** c   **55.** b

57. some number equals thirty-three and one-third percent of twenty-four   **59.** a   **61.** c   **63.** a   **65.** a   **67.** answers may vary
69. 686.625   **71.** 12,285

The Bigger Picture   **1.** $\frac{19}{45}$ **2.** 63   **3.** 0.021   **4.** 8   **5.** 48   **6.** 1.6   **7.** 250%   **8.** 45.6 or $45\frac{3}{5}$ **9.** 28%   **10.** 180

Mental Math   **1.** amount: 12.6; base: 42; percent: 30   **3.** amount: 102; base: 510; percent: 20

Exercise Set 6.4   **1.** $\frac{a}{65} = \frac{32}{100}$ **3.** $\frac{a}{130} = \frac{19}{100}$ **5.** $\frac{2.3}{b} = \frac{58}{100}$ **7.** $\frac{75}{b} = \frac{40}{100}$ **9.** $\frac{70}{200} = \frac{p}{100}$ **11.** 5.5   **13.** 18.9   **15.** 400
17. 10   **19.** 125%   **21.** 28%   **23.** 29   **25.** 1.92   **27.** 1000   **29.** 210%   **31.** 55.18   **33.** 45%   **35.** 85   **37.** 0.864
39. 0.6%   **41.** 140   **43.** 113%   **45.** $\frac{7}{8}$ **47.** $3\frac{2}{15}$ **49.** 0.7   **51.** 2.19   **53.** answers may vary   **55.** yes   **57.** answers may vary
59. 12,011.2   **61.** 7270.6

The Bigger Picture 1. $\frac{19}{45}$ **2.** 63   **3.** 0.021   **4.** 8   **5.** 48   **6.** 1.6   **7.** 250%   **8.** $45\frac{3}{5}$ or 45.6   **9.** 28%   **10.** 180

Integrated Review   **1.** 12%   **2.** 68%   **3.** 12.5%   **4.** 250%   **5.** 520%   **6.** 800%   **7.** 6%   **8.** 44%   **9.** 750%   **10.** 325%
11. 3%   **12.** 5%   **13.** 0.65   **14.** 0.31   **15.** 0.08   **16.** 0.07   **17.** 1.42   **18.** 4   **19.** 0.029   **20.** 0.066   **21.** 0.03; $\frac{3}{100}$

22. 0.05; $\frac{1}{20}$ **23.** 0.0525; $\frac{21}{400}$ **24.** 0.1275; $\frac{51}{400}$ **25.** 0.38; $\frac{19}{50}$ **26.** 0.45; $\frac{9}{20}$ **27.** 0.123; $\frac{37}{300}$ **28.** 0.167; $\frac{1}{6}$ **29.** 8.4   **30.** 100
31. 250   **32.** 120%   **33.** 28%   **34.** 76   **35.** 11   **36.** 130%   **37.** 86%   **38.** 37.8   **39.** 150   **40.** 62

Exercise Set 6.5   **1.** 1600 bolts   **3.** \$662.40   **5.** 15%   **7.** 295 components   **9.** 13.6%   **11.** 100, 102 dental hygienists   **13.** 50%
15. 29.2%   **17.** 496 chairs; 5704 chairs   **19.** \$136   **21.** \$867.87; \$20,153.87   **23.** 93,870 physician assistants   **25.** 28 million; 63 million
27. 10; 25%   **29.** 102; 120%   **31.** 2; 25%   **33.** 120; 75%   **35.** 44%   **37.** 21.5%   **39.** 1.3%   **41.** 153.4%   **43.** 893.8%
45. 81.3%   **47.** 300%   **49.** 21.6%   **51.** 4.56   **53.** 11.18   **55.** 58.54   **57.** The increased number is double the original number.
59. a. percent increase $= \frac{30}{150} = 20\%$ **b.** percent decrease $= \frac{30}{180} = 16\frac{2}{3}\%$ **c.** False; the percents are different.

Exercise Set 6.6   **1.** \$7.50   **3.** \$858.93   **5.** 9.5%   **7. a.** \$120   **b.** \$130.20   **9.** \$1917   **11.** \$11,500   **13.** 6%   **15.** \$112.35
17. \$49,474.24   **19.** 14%   **21.** \$1888.50   **23.** \$85,500   **25.** \$6.80; \$61.20   **27.** \$48.25; \$48.25   **29.** \$75.25; \$139.75
31. \$3255; \$18,445   **33.** \$45; \$255   **35.** \$52.74; \$638.74   **37.** \$4.51; \$86.51   **39.** \$7074   **41.** 8%   **43.** 1200   **45.** 132   **47.** 16
49. d   **51.** \$4.00; \$6.00; \$8.00   **53.** \$7.20; \$10.80; \$14.40   **55.** A discount of 60% is better; answers may vary   **57.** \$26,838.45

Calculator Explorations   **1.** 1.56051   **3.** 8.06231   **5.** \$634.49

Exercise Set 6.7   **1.** \$32   **3.** \$73.60   **5.** \$750   **7.** \$33.75   **9.** \$700   **11.** \$78,125   **13.** \$5562.50   **15.** \$12,580   **17.** \$46,815.40
19. \$2327.15   **21.** \$58,163.60   **23.** \$240.75   **25.** \$938.66   **27.** \$971.90   **29.** \$260.31   **31.** \$637.26   **33.** 32 yd   **35.** 35 m
37. answers may vary   **39.** answers may vary

Chapter 6 Vocabulary Check   **1.** of   **2.** is   **3.** percent   **4.** compound interest   **5.** $\frac{amount}{base}$ **6.** 100%   **7.** 0.01   **8.** $\frac{1}{100}$

Chapter 6 Review   **1.** 37%   **2.** 77%   **3.** 0.83   **4.** 0.75   **5.** 0.735   **6.** 0.015   **7.** 1.25   **8.** 1.45   **9.** 0.005   **10.** 0.007
11. 2.00 or 2   **12.** 4.00 or 4   **13.** 0.2625   **14.** 0.8534   **15.** 260%   **16.** 5.5%   **17.** 35%   **18.** 102%   **19.** 72.5%   **20.** 25.2%
21. 7.6%   **22.** 8.5%   **23.** 71%   **24.** 65%   **25.** 400%   **26.** 900%   **27.** $\frac{1}{100}$ **28.** $\frac{1}{10}$ **29.** $\frac{1}{4}$ **30.** $\frac{17}{200}$ **31.** $\frac{51}{500}$ **32.** $\frac{1}{6}$

33. $\frac{1}{3}$ **34.** $1\frac{1}{10}$ **35.** 20%   **36.** 70%   **37.** $83\frac{1}{3}\%$ **38.** $166\frac{2}{3}\%$ **39.** 125%   **40.** 60%   **41.** 6.25%   **42.** 62.5%
43. 100,000   **44.** 8000   **45.** 23%   **46.** 114.5   **47.** 3000   **48.** 150%   **49.** 418   **50.** 300   **51.** 64.8   **52.** 180%   **53.** 110%
54. 165   **55.** 66%   **56.** 16%   **57.** 20.9%   **58.** 106.25%   **59.** \$206,400   **60.** \$13.23   **61.** \$263.75   **62.** \$1.15   **63.** \$5000
64. \$300.38   **65.** discount: \$900; sale price: \$2100   **66.** discount: \$9; sale price: \$81   **67.** \$160   **68.** \$325   **69.** \$30,104.64
70. \$17,506.56   **71.** \$80.61   **72.** \$32,830.10   **73.** 0.038   **74.** 0.245   **75.** 0.009   **76.** 54%   **77.** 9520%   **78.** 30%

79. $\frac{47}{100}$ **80.** $\frac{8}{125}$ **81.** $\frac{7}{125}$ **82.** $37\frac{1}{2}\%$ **83.** $15\frac{5}{13}\%$ **84.** 120%   **85.** 268.75   **86.** 110%   **87.** 708.48   **88.** 134%   **89.** 300%

90. 38.4   **91.** 560   **92.** 325%   **93.** 26%   **94.** \$6786.50   **95.** \$617.70   **96.** \$3.45   **97.** 12.5%   **98.** \$1491   **99.** \$11,687.50

Chapter 6 Test   **1.** 0.85   **2.** 5   **3.** 0.008   **4.** 5.6%   **5.** 610%   **6.** 39%   **7.** $\frac{6}{5}$ **8.** $\frac{77}{200}$ **9.** $\frac{1}{500}$ **10.** 55%   **11.** 37.5%
12. $155\frac{5}{9}\%$ **13.** 33.6   **14.** 1250   **15.** 75%   **16.** 38.4 lb   **17.** \$56,750   **18.** \$358.43   **19.** 5%   **20.** discount: \$18; sale price: \$102
21. \$395   **22.** 1%   **23.** \$647.50   **24.** \$2005.64   **25.** \$427

Cumulative Review   **1.** 206 cases; 12 cans; yes (Sec. 1.8, Ex. 2)   **2.** 31,084   **3. a.** $4\frac{2}{7}$ **b.** $1\frac{1}{15}$ **c.** 14 (Sec. 2.1, Ex. 18)   **4. a.** $\frac{19}{7}$ **b.** $\frac{101}{10}$ **c.** $\frac{43}{8}$
5. $2\cdot2\cdot2\cdot3$ or $2^3\cdot3$ (Sec. 2.2, Ex. 7)   **6.** 119 sq mi   **7.** $\frac{10}{27}$ (Sec. 2.3, Ex. 3)   **8.** 44   **9.** $\frac{23}{56}$ (Sec. 2.4, Ex. 4)   **10.** 76,500
11. $\frac{8}{11}$ (Sec. 2.5, Ex. 2)   **12.** $\frac{15}{4}$ or $3\frac{3}{4}$ **13.** $\frac{4}{5}$ in. (Sec. 3.1, Ex. 6)   **14.** 50   **15.** 60 (Sec. 3.2, Ex. 4)   **16.** $\frac{1}{3}$ **17.** $\frac{2}{3}$ (Sec. 3.3, Ex. 1)
18. 340   **19.** $3\frac{5}{14}$ (Sec. 3.4, Ex. 5)   **20.** 33   **21.** $\frac{7}{16}$ (Sec. 3.5, Ex. 6)   **22.** $33\frac{27}{40}$ **23.** $\frac{2}{33}$ (Sec. 3.5, Ex. 8)   **24.** $6\frac{3}{8}$
25. 0.8 (Sec. 4.1, Ex. 13)   **26.** 0.09   **27.** 8.7 (Sec. 4.1, Ex. 14)   **28.** 0.0048   **29.** \$2.18 (Sec. 4.2, Ex. 7)   **30.** 27.94
31. 829.6561 (Sec. 4.3, Ex. 2)   **32.** 1248.3   **33.** 18.408 (Sec. 4.4, Ex. 1)   **34.** 76,300   **35.** 0.7861 (Sec. 4.5, Ex. 8)   **36.** 1.276
37. 0.012 (Sec. 4.5, Ex. 9)   **38.** 50.65   **39.** 7.236 (Sec. 4.5, Ex. 11)   **40.** 0.191   **41.** 0.25 (Sec. 4.6, Ex. 1)   **42.** $0.\overline{5} \approx 0.556$
43. $\frac{5 \text{ nails}}{3 \text{ ft}}$ (Sec. 5.2, Ex. 1)   **44.** 23 miles/gal   **45.** no (Sec. 5.3, Ex. 3)   **46.** 0.052 per tortilla; 0.058 per tortilla; 18 tortilla pkg is better buy.
47. $17\frac{1}{2}$ mi (Sec. 5.4, Ex. 1)   **48. a.** 0.07 **b.** 2 **c.** 0.005   **49.** $n = 25\% \cdot 0.008$ (Sec. 6.3, Ex. 3)   **50.** 37.5% or $37\frac{1}{2}\%$

CHAPTER 7   Measurement

Mental Math   **1.** 1 ft   **3.** 2 ft   **5.** 1 yd   **7.** no   **9.** yes   **11.** no

Exercise Set 7.1   **1.** 5 ft   **3.** 36 ft   **5.** 8 mi   **7.** $8\frac{1}{2}$ ft   **9.** $3\frac{1}{3}$ yd   **11.** 33,792 ft   **13.** 4.5 yd   **15.** 0.25 ft   **17.** 13 yd 1 ft
19. 3 ft 5 in.   **21.** 1 mi 4720 ft   **23.** 62 in.   **25.** 23 ft   **27.** 84 in.   **29.** 12 ft 3 in.   **31.** 22 yd 1 ft   **33.** 8 ft 5 in.   **35.** 5 ft 6 in.
37. 3 ft 4 in.   **39.** 50 yd 2 ft   **41.** 4000 cm   **43.** 4.0 cm   **45.** 0.3 km   **47.** 1.4 m   **49.** 15 m   **51.** 42,000 cm   **53.** 7000 m
55. 83 mm   **57.** 0.201 dm   **59.** 40 mm   **61.** 8.94 m   **63.** 2.94 m or 2940 mm   **65.** 1.29 cm or 12.9 mm   **67.** 12.640 km or 12,640 m
69. 54.9 m   **71.** 1.55 km   **73.** $348\frac{2}{3}$ yd; 12,552 in.   **75.** $11\frac{2}{3}$ yd; 140 in.   **77.** 5000 mm; 0.005 km; 500 cm   **79.** 0.065 m; 65 mm; 0.000065 km
81. 342,000 m; 342,000,000 mm; 34,200,000 cm   **83.** 10 ft 6 in.   **85.** 13 ft 11 in.   **87.** 9.12 m   **89.** 26.7 mm   **91.** 15 ft 9 in.   **93.** 3 ft 1 in.
95. 41.25 m or 4125 cm   **97.** 3.35 m   **99.** 86 ft 6 in.   **101.** $105\frac{1}{3}$ yd   **103.** 6.009 km or 6009 m   **105.** 15 tiles   **107.** 21%
109. 13%   **111.** 25%   **113.** Estimate: 13 yd   **115.** answers may vary: for example, $1\frac{1}{3}$ yd or 48 in.   **117.** answers may vary

Mental Math   **1.** 1 lb   **3.** 2000 lb   **5.** 16 oz   **7.** 1 ton   **9.** no   **11.** yes   **13.** no

Exercise Set 7.2   **1.** 32 oz   **3.** 10,000 lb   **5.** 6 tons   **7.** $3\frac{3}{4}$ lb   **9.** $1\frac{3}{4}$ tons   **11.** 260 oz   **13.** 9800 lb   **15.** 76 oz   **17.** 1.5 tons
19. $\frac{1}{20}$ lb   **21.** 92 oz   **23.** 161 oz   **25.** 5 lb 9 oz   **27.** 53 lb 10 oz   **29.** 9 tons 390 lb   **31.** 3 tons 175 lb   **33.** 8 lb 11 oz
35. 31 lb 2 oz   **37.** 1 ton 700 lb   **39.** 0.5 kg   **41.** 4000 mg   **43.** 25,000 g   **45.** 0.048 g   **47.** 0.0063 kg   **49.** 15,140 mg
51. 4010 g   **53.** 350,000 cg   **55.** 13.5 mg   **57.** 5.815 g or 5815 mg   **59.** 1850 mg or 1.850 g   **61.** 1360 g or 1.360 kg
63. 13.52 kg   **65.** 2.125 kg   **67.** 200,000 lb; 3,200,000 oz   **69.** $\frac{269}{400}$ or 0.6725 ton; 21,520 oz   **71.** 0.5 g; 0.0005 kg; 50 cg
73. 21,000 g; 21,000,000 mg; 2,100,000 cg   **75.** 8.064 kg   **77.** 30 mg   **79.** 5 lb 8 oz   **81.** 35 lb 14 oz   **83.** 250 mg   **85.** 144 mg
87. 6.12 kg   **89.** 130 lb   **91.** 211 lb   **93.** 5 lb 1 oz   **95.** 850 g or 0.85 kg   **97.** 2.38 kg   **99.** 0.25   **101.** 0.16   **103.** 0.875
105. answers may vary   **107.** true   **109.** answers may vary

Mental Math   **1.** 1 pt   **3.** 1 gal   **5.** 1 qt   **7.** 1 c   **9.** 2 c   **11.** 4 qt   **13.** no   **15.** no

Exercise Set 7.3   **1.** 4 c   **3.** 16 pt   **5.** $2\frac{1}{2}$ gal   **7.** 5 pt   **9.** 8 c   **11.** $3\frac{3}{4}$ qt   **13.** 768 fl oz   **15.** 9 c   **17.** 23 qt   **19.** $\frac{1}{4}$ pt
21. 14 gal 2 qt   **23.** 4 gal 3 qt 1 pt   **25.** 22 pt   **27.** 10 gal 1 qt   **29.** 4 c 4 fl oz   **31.** 1 gal 1 qt   **33.** 2 gal 3 qt 1 pt   **35.** 2 qt 1 c
37. 17 gal   **39.** 4 gal 3 qt   **41.** 5000 ml   **43.** 4.5 L   **45.** 320 cl   **47.** 0.41 kl   **49.** 0.064 L   **51.** 160 L   **53.** 3600 ml
55. 0.00016 kl   **57.** 22.5 L   **59.** 4.5 L or 4500 ml   **61.** 8410 ml or 8.41 L   **63.** 10,600 ml or 10.6 L   **65.** 3840 ml   **67.** 162.4 L
69. 336 c; 84 qt; 168 pt   **71.** $\frac{1}{4}$ gal; 1 qt; 2 pt   **73.** 48 fl oz   **75.** 2 qt   **77.** 1.59 L   **79.** 18.954 L   **81.** yes   **83.** 2 qt 1 c
85. \$0.316   **87.** 474 ml   **89.** $\frac{7}{10}$ **91.** $\frac{3}{100}$ **93.** $\frac{3}{500}$ **95.** answers may vary   **97.** answers may vary   **99.** answers may vary
101. 1.5 cc   **103.** 2.7 cc   **105.** 54 u or 0.54 cc   **107.** 86 u or 0.86 cc

Integrated Review   **1.** 3 ft   **2.** 2 mi   **3.** $6\frac{2}{3}$ yd   **4.** 19 ft   **5.** 11,088 ft   **6.** 38.4 in.   **7.** 3000 cm   **8.** 2.4 cm   **9.** 2 m   **10.** 18 m
11. 72 mm   **12.** 0.6 km   **13.** 15,000 lb   **14.** 5.5 tons   **15.** 136 oz   **16.** 4.5 lb   **17.** 6.5 lb   **18.** 80 oz   **19.** 28,000 g   **20.** 1.4 g
21. 0.0056 kg   **22.** 6000 g   **23.** 0.67 g   **24.** 0.0036 kg   **25.** 12 pt   **26.** 2.5 qt   **27.** 3.5 gal   **28.** 8.5 pt   **29.** 7 c   **30.** 6.5 gal
31. 7000 ml   **32.** 0.35 kl   **33.** 0.047 L   **34.** 970 L   **35.** 126 L   **36.** 0.075 L   **37.** 4 fl oz   **38.** 12 c

Exercise Set 7.4   **1.** 19.55 fl oz   **3.** 218.44 cm   **5.** 40 oz   **7.** 57.66 mi   **9.** 3.77 gal   **11.** 13.5 kg   **13.** 1.5 m; $1\frac{2}{3}$ yd; 150 cm; 60 in.
15. 54.9 m; 5486.4 cm; 180 ft; 2160 in.   **17.** 3.94 in.   **19.** 112.7 kph   **21.** 0.008 oz   **23.** yes   **25.** 380 ml   **27.** 90 mm   **29.** 112.5 g

31. 104 mph   **33.** 26.24 ft   **35.** 3 mi   **37.** 8 oz   **39.** a   **41.** b   **43.** c   **45.** d   **47.** d   **49.** 29   **51.** 2   **53.** 5
55. 36   **57.** 2.13 sq m   **59.** 1.19 sq m   **61.** 1.69 sq m   **63.** 21.3 mg–25.56 mg   **65.** 800 sq m or 8606.72 sq ft

Mental Math   **1.** yes   **3.** no   **5.** no   **7.** yes

Exercise Set 7.5   **1.** 5°C   **3.** 40°C   **5.** 140°F   **7.** 239°F   **9.** 16.7°C   **11.** 61.2°C   **13.** 197.6°F   **15.** 61.3°F   **17.** 50°C
19. 80.6°F   **21.** 100°C   **23.** 37.9°C   **25.** 244.4°F   **27.** 462.2°C   **29.** 21.1°C   **31.** 12 in.   **33.** 12 cm   **35.** 8 ft 4 in.   **37.** false
39. true   **41.** $\approx$ 520,000,000°C   **43.** answers may vary

Mental Math   **1.** 30 ft-lb   **3.** 60 ft-lb   **5.** 90 cal   **7.** 5 cal

Exercise Set 7.6   **1.** 1140 ft-lb   **3.** 3696 ft-lb   **5.** 425,000 ft-lb   **7.** 23,340 ft-lb   **9.** 778,000 ft-lb   **11.** 15,560,000 ft-lb
13. 26,553,140 ft-lb   **15.** 10,283 BTU   **17.** 805 cal   **19.** 750 cal   **21.** 1440 cal   **23.** 2.6 hr   **25.** 17.5 mi   **27.** $\frac{4}{5}$ **29.** $\frac{3}{5}$
31. $\frac{9}{10}$ **33.** 92.925 ft-lb   **35.** 256 lb   **37.** answers may vary

Vocabulary Check   **1.** weight   **2.** mass   **3.** meter   **4.** unit fractions   **5.** gram   **6.** energy   **7.** British Thermal Unit   **8.** liter
9. calorie

Chapter 7 Review   **1.** 9 ft   **2.** 24 yd   **3.** 7920 ft   **4.** 18 in.   **5.** 17 yd 1 ft   **6.** 3 ft 10 in.   **7.** 4200 cm   **8.** 820 mm   **9.** 0.01218 m
10. 0.00231 km   **11.** 21 yd 1 ft   **12.** 7 ft 5 in.   **13.** 41 ft 3 in.   **14.** 3 ft 8 in.   **15.** 9.5 cm or 95 mm   **16.** 2.74 m or 274 cm
17. 34.48 m   **18.** 2.45 km   **19.** 169 yd 2 ft   **20.** 126 ft 8 in.   **21.** 108.5 km   **22.** 0.24 sq m   **23.** 4.125 lb   **24.** 4600 lb
25. 3 lb 4 oz   **26.** 5 tons 300 lb   **27.** 0.027 g   **28.** 40,000 g   **29.** 21 dag   **30.** 0.0003 dg   **31.** 3 lb 9 oz   **32.** 10 tons 800 lb
33. 2 tons 750 lb   **34.** 33 lb 8 oz   **35.** 21.5 mg   **36.** 0.6 kg or 600 g   **37.** 4 lb 4 oz   **38.** 9 tons 1075 lb   **39.** 7.85 kg   **40.** 1.1625 kg
41. 8 qt   **42.** 5 c   **43.** 7 pt   **44.** 72 c   **45.** 4 qt 1 pt   **46.** 3 gal 3 qt   **47.** 3800 ml   **48.** 0.042 dl   **49.** 1.4 kl   **50.** 3060 cl
51. 1 gal 1 qt   **52.** 7 gal   **53.** 736 ml or 0.736 L   **54.** 15.5 L or 15,500 ml   **55.** 2 gal 3 qt   **56.** 6 fl oz   **57.** 10.88 L   **58.** yes
59. 22.96 ft   **60.** 10.55 m   **61.** 4.55 gal   **62.** 8.27 qt   **63.** 425.25 g   **64.** 10.35 kg   **65.** 109 yd   **66.** 180.4 lb   **67.** 3.18 qt
68. 2.36 in.   **69.** 473°F   **70.** 320°F   **71.** 107.6°F   **72.** 34°C   **73.** 5.2°C   **74.** 26.7°C   **75.** 1.7°C   **76.** 329°C   **77.** 67.2 ft-lb
78. 136.5 ft-lb   **79.** 108,000 ft-lb   **80.** 9,336,000 ft-lb   **81.** 2600 BTU   **82.** 1125 cal   **83.** 15,120 cal   **84.** $2\frac{1}{3}$ hr   **85.** 13,200 ft
86. 75 in.   **87.** 4.5 mi   **88.** 10.75 ft   **89.** 4 tons 200 lb   **90.** 2 tons 300 lb   **91.** 500 cm   **92.** 0.000286 km   **93.** 1.4 g   **94.** 0.24 g
95. 27 qt   **96.** 21 qt   **97.** 17 c   **98.** $12\frac{1}{2}$ c   **99.** 186.8°F   **100.** 59°F   **101.** 11°C   **102.** 28°C   **103.** 9117 m or 9.117 km
104. 8.353 km or 8353 m   **105.** 13.9 L or 13,900 ml   **106.** 35.7 L or 35,700 ml   **107.** 8.1 g or 8100 mg   **108.** 1.6 g or 1,600 mg
109. 50.4 kg   **110.** 12.8 kg   **111.** 7 gal 3 qt   **112.** 8 gal 2 qt   **113.** 38 dm or 3800 mm   **114.** 58 dm or 5800 mm   **115.** 2.25 tons
116. 2.25 tons

Chapter 7 Test   **1.** 23 ft 4 in.   **2.** 10 qt   **3.** 1.875 lb   **4.** 5600 lb   **5.** $4\frac{3}{4}$ gal   **6.** 0.04 g   **7.** 2400 g   **8.** 36 mm   **9.** 0.43 g
10. 830 ml   **11.** 1 gal 2 qt   **12.** 3 lb 13 oz   **13.** 8 ft 3 in.   **14.** 2 gal 3 qt   **15.** 66 mm or 6.6 cm   **16.** 2.256 km or 2256 m
17. 28.9°C   **18.** 54.7°F   **19.** 5.6 m   **20.** 4 gal 3 qt   **21.** 91.4 m   **22.** 16 ft 6 in.   **23.** 493 ft 6 in.   **24.** 150.368 m   **25.** 57.8°C
26. 105.8°F   **27.** 37,336 pt   **28.** 0.2 oz   **29.** 3.1 mi   **30.** 18.95 L   **31.** 679 ft-lb   **32.** 20,228,000 ft-lb   **33.** 900 cal

Cumulative Review   **1.** 2010 (Sec. 1.3, Ex. 4)   **2.** 1531   **3.** $3 \cdot 3 \cdot 3 \cdot 5 \cdot 7$ or $3^3 \cdot 5 \cdot 7$ (Sec. 2.2, Ex. 5)   **4.** 153 sq in.
5. 33 (Sec. 3.2, Ex. 7)   **6.** $\frac{10}{63}$ **7.** $5\frac{1}{15}$ (Sec. 3.4, Ex. 2)   **8.** $10\frac{1}{3}$ **9.** $\frac{1}{8}$ (Sec. 4.1, Ex. 10)   **10.** $1\frac{1}{5}$ **11.** $105\frac{83}{1000}$ (Sec. 4.1, Ex. 12)
12. $\frac{8}{27}$ **13.** < (Sec. 4.2, Ex. 2)   **14.** 25   **15.** 67.69 (Sec. 4.3, Ex. 6)   **16.** 139.231   **17.** 4.21 (Sec. 4.4, Ex. 8)   **18.** 186,040
19. 0.0092 (Sec. 4.4, Ex. 10)   **20.** 5.8   **21.** 7.53 (Sec. 4.5, Ex. 2)   **22.** $\frac{21}{20}$ or $1\frac{1}{20}$ **23.** 2.1875 (Sec. 4.6, Ex. 4)   **24.** 7.3
25. $0.\overline{6}$ (Sec. 4.6, Ex. 2)   **26.** 2.16   **27.** $\frac{12}{17}$ (Sec. 5.1, Ex. 1)   **28.** $\frac{12}{23}$ **29.** 24.5 mi/gal (Sec. 5.2, Ex. 5)   **30.** $\frac{1}{4}$
31. $n = \frac{35}{6}$ or $5\frac{5}{6}$ (Sec. 5.3, Ex. 6)   **32.** 7.5 cups   **33.** 7 bags (Sec. 5.4, Ex. 3)   **34.** $\frac{23}{100}$ **35.** 0.23 (Sec. 6.1, Ex. 3)   **36.** 87.5% or $87\frac{1}{2}$%
37. 8.33% (Sec. 6.2, Ex. 9)   **38.** 24%   **39.** 14 (Sec. 6.3, Ex. 7)   **40.** 32 pints   **41.** $\frac{75}{30} = \frac{p}{100}$ (Sec. 6.4, Ex. 5)   **42.** 860 cm
43. 18% (Sec. 6.5, Ex. 6)   **44.** 6.5 tons   **45.** discount: $16.25; sale price: $48.75 (Sec. 6.6, Ex. 5)   **46.** 52 oz   **47.** $120 (Sec. 6.7, Ex. 1)
48. 15%   **49.** $4\frac{1}{2}$ tons (Sec. 7.2, Ex. 1)   **50.** 77°F

CHAPTER 8   Geometry

Exercise Set 8.1   **1.** line; line YZ or $\overleftrightarrow{YZ}$ **3.** line segment; line segment LM or $\overline{LM}$ **5.** line segment; line segment PQ or $\overline{PQ}$
7. ray; ray UW or $\overrightarrow{UW}$ **9.** 90°   **11.** 0°; 90°   **13.** straight   **15.** right   **17.** obtuse   **19.** right   **21.** 73°   **23.** 163°   **25.** 32°
27. 75°   **29.** $\angle MNP$ and $\angle RNO$; $\angle PNQ$ and $\angle QNR$ **31.** $\angle SPT$ and $\angle TPQ$; $\angle SPR$ and $\angle RPQ$; $\angle SPT$ and $\angle SPR$; $\angle TPQ$ and $\angle QPR$
33. 32°   **35.** 132°   **37.** $m\angle x = 35°$; $m\angle y = 145°$; $m\angle z = 145°$ **39.** $m\angle x = 77°$; $m\angle y = 103°$; $m\angle z = 77°$
41. $m\angle x = 100°$; $m\angle y = 80°$; $m\angle z = 100°$ **43.** $m\angle x = 134°$; $m\angle y = 46°$; $m\angle z = 134°$ **45.** $\angle ABC$ or $\angle CBA$ **47.** $\angle DBE$ or $\angle EBD$
49. 15°   **51.** 50°   **53.** 65°   **55.** 95°   **57.** $\frac{9}{8}$ or $1\frac{1}{8}$ **59.** $\frac{7}{32}$ **61.** $\frac{5}{6}$ **63.** $\frac{4}{3}$ or $1\frac{1}{3}$ **65.** 54.8°   **67.** false   **69.** true
71. $m\angle a = 60°$; $m\angle b = 50°$; $m\angle c = 110°$; $m\angle d = 70°$; $m\angle e = 120°$ **73.** 45°, 45°

Exercise Set 8.2 **1.** pentagon **3.** hexagon **5.** quadrilateral **7.** pentagon **9.** equilateral **11.** scalene; right **13.** isosceles **15.** 25° **17.** 13° **19.** 40° **21.** diameter **23.** rectangle **25.** parallelogram **27.** hypotenuse **29.** 14 m **31.** 14.5 cm **33.** 40.6 cm **35.** 36 in. **37.** cylinder **39.** rectangular solid **41.** cone **43.** cube **45.** rectangular solid **47.** sphere **49.** pyramid **51.** 14.8 in. **53.** 13 mi **55.** 72,368 mi **57.** 108 **59.** 12.56 **61.** true **63.** true **65.** false **67.** yes; answers may vary **69.** answers may vary

Exercise Set 8.3 **1.** 64 ft **3.** 120 cm **5.** 21 in. **7.** 48 ft **9.** 12 in. **11.** 105 cm **13.** 21 ft **15.** 60 ft **17.** 346 yd **19.** 22 ft **21.** $66 **23.** 36 in. **25.** 28 in. **27.** $24.08 **29.** 96 m **31.** 66 ft **33.** 128 mi **35.** 17π cm; 53.38 cm

37. 16π mi; 50.24 mi **39.** 26π m; 81.64 m **41.** $31\frac{3}{7}$ ft $\approx$ 31.43 ft **43.** 12,560 ft **45.** 30.7 mi **47.** $14\pi \approx 43.96$ cm **49.** 40 mm

51. 84 ft **53.** 23 **55.** 1 **57.** 10 **59.** 216 **61.** perimeter **63.** area **65.** area **67.** perimeter **69. a.** width: 30 yd; length: 40 yd **b.** 140 yd **71.** b **73. a.** 62.8 m; 125.6 m **b.** yes **75.** $44 + 10\pi \approx 75.4$ m **77.** 6 ft **79.** 27.4 m

Exercise Set 8.4 **1.** 7 sq m **3.** $9\frac{3}{4}$ sq yd **5.** 15 sq yd **7.** 2.25π sq in. ≈ 7.065 sq in. **9.** 17.64 sq ft **11.** 28 sq m **13.** 22 sq yd

15. $36\frac{3}{4}$ sq ft **17.** $22\frac{1}{2}$ sq in. **19.** 25 sq cm **21.** 86 sq mi **23.** 24 sq cm **25.** 36π sq in. $\approx 113\frac{1}{7}$ sq in. **27.** 168 sq ft

29. 113,625 sq ft **31.** $4\pi \approx 12.56$ sq ft **33.** 128 sq in.; $\frac{8}{9}$ sq ft **35.** 510 sq in. **37.** 168 sq ft **39.** 9200 sq ft **41.** 381 sq ft

43. 14π in. ≈ 43.96 in. **45.** 25 ft **47.** $12\frac{3}{4}$ ft **49.** 12-in. pizza **51.** $1\frac{1}{3}$ sq ft; 192 sq in. **53.** 7.74 sq in. **55.** $1296\pi \approx 4069.404$ sq in. **57.** 298.5 sq m **59.** no; answers may vary

Exercise Set 8.5 **1.** 72 cu in. **3.** 512 cu cm **5.** $12\frac{4}{7}$ cu yd **7.** $523\frac{17}{21}$ cu in. **9.** $28\frac{2}{7}$ cu in. **11.** 75 cu cm **13.** $2\frac{10}{27}$ cu in.

15. 8.4 cu ft **17.** $10\frac{5}{6}$ cu in. **19.** 960 cu cm **21.** $\frac{1372}{3}\pi$ cu in. or $457\frac{1}{3}\pi$ cu in. **23.** $7\frac{1}{2}$ cu ft **25.** $12\frac{4}{7}$ cu cm

27. 36π cu in. ≈ 113.04 cu in. **29.** 25 **31.** 9 **33.** 5 **35.** 20 **37. a.** width: 40 yd; length: 60 yd **b.** 2400 sq yd **39.** 2,583,283 cu m **41.** 2,583,669 cu m **43.** 26,696.5 cu ft **45.** answers may vary

Integrated Review **1.** 153°; 63° **2.** $m\angle x = 75°$; $m\angle y = 105°$; $m\angle z = 75°$ **3.** $m\angle x = 128°$; $m\angle y = 52°$; $m\angle z = 128°$ **4.** $m\angle x = 52°$ **5.** 4.6 in. **6.** $4\frac{1}{4}$ in. **7.** 20 m; 25 sq m **8.** 12 ft; 6 sq ft **9.** 10π cm ≈ 31.4 cm; 25π sq cm ≈ 78.5 sq cm **10.** 32 mi; 44 sq mi **11.** 54 cm; 143 sq cm **12.** 62 ft; 238 sq ft **13.** 64 cu in. **14.** 30.6 cu ft **15.** 400 cu cm **16.** $4\frac{1}{2}\pi$ cm mi $\approx 14\frac{1}{7}$ cu mi

Calculator Explorations **1.** 32 **3.** 3.873 **5.** 9.849

Exercise Set 8.6 **1.** 2 **3.** 8 **5.** $\frac{1}{9}$ **7.** $\frac{4}{8} = \frac{1}{2}$ **9.** 1.732 **11.** 3.873 **13.** 6.856 **15.** 5.099 **17.** 16 **19.** 3.742 **21.** $\frac{7}{12}$ **23.** 8.426 **25.** 13 in. **27.** 6.633 cm **29.** 52.802 m **31.** 117 mm **33.** 5 **35.** 12 **37.** 17.205 **39.** 44.822 **41.** 42.426 **43.** 1.732 **45.** 8.5 **47.** 141.42 yd **49.** 25.0 ft **51.** 340 ft **53.** $n = 4$ **55.** $n = 45$ **57.** $n = 6$ **59.** 6, 7 **61.** 10, 11 **63.** answers may vary **65.** no

Mental Math **1.** $\angle A$ and $\angle D$, $\angle B$ and $\angle E$, $\angle C$ and $\angle F$, $\frac{a}{d} = \frac{b}{e} = \frac{c}{f}$

Exercise Set 8.7 **1.** congruent **3.** not congruent **5.** congruent **7.** congruent **9.** $\frac{2}{1}$ **11.** $\frac{3}{2}$ **13.** 4.5 **15.** 6 **17.** 5 **19.** 13.5 **21.** 17.5 **23.** 8 **25.** 21.25 **27.** 10 **29.** 500 ft **31.** 60 ft **33.** 14.4 ft **35.** 200 ft, 300 ft, 425 ft **37.** 17.5 **39.** 81 **41.** $3\frac{8}{9}$ in.; no **43.** 32.7

Chapter 8 Vocabulary Check **1.** right triangle; hypotenuse; legs **2.** line segment **3.** complementary **4.** line **5.** perimeter **6.** angle; vertex **7.** congruent **8.** area **9.** ray **10.** square root **11.** transversal **12.** straight **13.** volume **14.** vertical **15.** adjacent **16.** obtuse **17.** right **18.** acute **19.** supplementary **20.** similar

Chapter 8 Review **1.** right **2.** straight **3.** acute **4.** obtuse **5.** 65° **6.** 75° **7.** 58° **8.** 98° **9.** 90° **10.** 25° **11.** $\angle a$ and $\angle b$; $\angle b$ and $\angle c$; $\angle c$ and $\angle d$; $\angle d$ and $\angle a$ **12.** $\angle x$ and $\angle w$; $\angle y$ and $\angle z$ **13.** $m\angle x = 100°$; $m\angle y = 80°$; $m\angle z = 80°$ **14.** $m\angle x = 155°$; $m\angle y = 155°$; $m\angle z = 25°$ **15.** $m\angle x = 53°$; $m\angle y = 53°$; $m\angle z = 127°$ **16.** $m\angle x = 42°$; $m\angle y = 42°$; $m\angle z = 138°$ **17.** 103° **18.** 60° **19.** 60° **20.** 65° **21.** $4\frac{2}{10}$ m or $4\frac{1}{5}$ m **22.** 7 ft **23.** 9.5 m **24.** $15\frac{1}{5}$ cm **25.** cube **26.** cylinder **27.** pyramid **28.** rectangular solid **29.** 18 in. **30.** 2.35 m **31.** pentagon **32.** hexagon **33.** equilateral **34.** isosceles, right **35.** 89 m **36.** 30.6 cm **37.** 36 m **38.** 90 ft **39.** 32 ft **40.** 440 ft **41.** 5.338 in. **42.** 31.4 yd **43.** 240 sq ft **44.** 140 sq m **45.** 600 sq cm **46.** 189 sq yd **47.** 49π sq ft ≈ 153.86 sq ft **48.** 82.81 sq m **49.** 119 sq in. **50.** 1248 sq cm **51.** 144 sq m **52.** 432 sq ft **53.** 130 sq ft **54.** $15\frac{5}{8}$ cu in. **55.** 84 cu ft **56.** $20,000\pi$ cu cm $\approx 62,800$ cu cm **57.** $\frac{1}{6}\pi$ cu km $\approx \frac{11}{21}$ cu km **58.** $2\frac{2}{3}$ cu ft **59.** 307.72 cu in. **60.** $7\frac{1}{2}$ cu ft **61.** 0.5π cu ft or $\frac{1}{2}\pi$ cu ft **62.** 8 **63.** 12 **64.** $\frac{2}{5}$ **65.** $\frac{1}{10}$ **66.** 13 **67.** 29 **68.** 10.7 **69.** 93 **70.** 127.3 ft **71.** 88.2 ft **72.** $37\frac{1}{2}$ **73.** $13\frac{1}{3}$ **74.** 17.4 **75.** approximately 33 ft **76.** $x = \frac{5}{6}$ in.; $y = 2\frac{1}{6}$ in. **77.** 108° **78.** 89° **79.** 82° **80.** 78° **81.** 95° **82.** 57° **83.** 13 m **84.** 12.6 in. **85.** 22 dm **86.** 27.3 in. **87.** 194 ft

88. 1624 sq m   **89.** 9π sq m $\approx$ 28.26 sq m   **90.** $346\frac{1}{2}$ cu in.   **91.** 140 cubic in.   **92.** 1260 cu ft   **93.** 28.728 cu ft   **94.** 1   **95.** 6

96. $\frac{4}{9}$ **97.** 86.6   **98.** 20.8   **99.** 48.1   **100.** 19.7   **101.** 12   **102.** $6\frac{1}{2}$

Chapter 8 Test   1. 12°   **2.** 56°   **3.** 57°   **4.** $m\angle x = 118°; m\angle y = 62°; m\angle z = 118°$ **5.** $m\angle x = 73°; m\angle y = 73°; m\angle z = 73°$

6. 6.2 m   **7.** $10\frac{1}{4}$ in.   **8.** 26°   **9.** circumference $= 18\pi \approx 56.52$ in.; area $= 81\pi \approx 254.34$ sq in.

10. perimeter $= 24.6$ yd; area $= 37.1$ sq yd   **11.** perimeter $= 68$ in.; area $= 185$ sq in.   **12.** $62\frac{6}{7}$ cu in.   **13.** 30 cu ft   **14.** 7   **15.** 8.888

16. $\frac{8}{10} = \frac{4}{5}$ **17.** 16 in.   **18.** 18 cu ft   **19.** 62 ft; $115.94   **20.** 5.66 cm   **21.** 198.08 oz   **22.** 7.5   **23.** approximately 69 ft

Cumulative Review   1. nineteen and five thousand twenty-three ten-thousandths (Sec. 4.1, Ex. 3)   **2.** $\frac{53}{66}$ **3.** 736.2 (Sec. 4.2, Ex. 5)   **4.** 700

5. 47.06 (Sec. 4.3, Ex. 3)   **6.** $\frac{20}{11}$ or $1\frac{9}{11}$ **7.** 76.8 (Sec. 4.4, Ex. 5)   **8.** $\frac{7}{66}$ **9.** 76,300 (Sec. 4.4, Ex. 7)   **10.** $\frac{23}{2}$ or $11\frac{1}{2}$

11. 38.6 (Sec. 4.5, Ex. 1)   **12.** 0.567   **13.** 3.7 (Sec. 4.5, Ex. 12)   **14.** $\frac{3}{5}$ or 0.6   **15.** > (Sec. 4.6, Ex. 7)   **16.** <   **17.** $\frac{26}{31}$ (Sec. 5.1, Ex. 5)

18. $\frac{16}{45}$ **19.** yes (Sec. 5.3, Ex. 2)   **20.** $\frac{35}{2}$ or $17\frac{1}{2}$ **21.** 17% (Sec. 6.1, Ex. 1)   **22.** 68%   **23.** $\frac{19}{1000}$ (Sec. 6.2, Ex. 2)   **24.** $\frac{13}{50}$

25. $\frac{5}{4}$ or $1\frac{1}{4}$ (Sec. 6.2, Ex. 3)   **26.** $5\frac{3}{5}$ **27.** 255 (Sec. 6.3, Ex. 8)   **28.** 15%   **29.** 52 (Sec. 6.4, Ex. 9)   **30.** 9

31. 775 freshmen (Sec. 6.5, Ex. 2)   **32.** $2.25/sq ft   **33.** $1710 (Sec. 6.6, Ex. 3)   **34.** 35 exercises   **35.** 96 in. (Sec. 7.1, Ex. 1)

36. 2 yd 2 ft 4 in.   **37.** 3200 g (Sec. 7.2, Ex. 8)   **38.** 0.07 m   **39.** 3 gal 3 qt (Sec. 7.3, Ex. 3)   **40.** 70,052   **41.** 84.2°F (Sec. 7.5, Ex. 2)

42. 12.5%   **43.** 50° (Sec. 8.2, Ex. 1)   **44.** 33 m   **45.** 28 in. (Sec. 8.3, Ex. 1)   **46.** 45 sq in.   **47.** $\frac{2}{5}$ (Sec. 8.6, Ex. 3)   **48.** $\frac{3}{4}$

49. $\frac{12}{17}$ (Sec. 8.7, Ex. 2)   **50.** $14\frac{1}{6}$

CHAPTER 9 Statistics and Probability

Exercise Set 9.1   1. 2004   **3.** 4000 cars   **5.** 10,500 cars   **7. a.** 2000, 2001, 2005   **b.** 250 fewer cars in 2000, 750 fewer cars in 2001, 500 fewer cars in 2005   **9.** 1999, 2002   **11.** 22.5 oz   **13.** 1998, 2001, 2004   **15.** 3 oz/wk   **17.** $5\frac{2}{3}$ symbols   **19.** April

21. 19 deaths   **23.** February, March, April, May, June   **25.** 18.5 million or 18,500,000   **27.** Tokyo: 34 million or 34,000,000

29. New York: 21.7 million or 21,700,000   **31.** 14 million or 14,000,000   **33.** 15 adults   **35.** 61 adults   **37.** 24 adults

39. 12 adults   **41.** $\frac{9}{100}$ **43.** 45–54   **45.** 21 million householders   **47.** 44 million householders

49. answers may vary   **51.** |; 1   **53.** ||||| |||; 8   **55.** ||||| |; 6   **57.** ||||| |; 6   **59.** ||; 2   **61.**

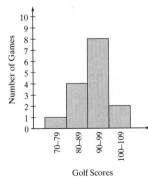

Golf Scores

63. 2.7 goals   **65.** 1982   **67.** decrease   **69.** 1990   **71.** 3.6   **73.** 6.2

75. 25%   **77.** 34%   **79.** 83°F   **81.** Sunday; 68°F   **83.** Tuesday: 13°F

85. answers may vary

Exercise Set 9.2   1. parent or guardian's home   **3.** $\frac{9}{35}$ **5.** $\frac{9}{16}$ **7.** Asia   **9.** 37%   **11.** 17,100,000 sq mi   **13.** 2,850,000 sq mi

15. 55%   **17.** nonfiction   **19.** 31,400 books   **21.** 27,632 books   **23.** 25,120 books   **25.**   **27.** $2^2 \times 5$

29. $2^3 \times 5$ **31.** 5×17 **33.** answers may vary   **35.** 129,600,002 sq km

37. 55,542,858 sq km   **39.** true

Europe 6%
Asia 36%
United States 58%

Integrated Review   1. 69 lb   **2.** 78 lb   **3.** 10 lb   **4.** 2001 and 2002   **5.** Oroville Dam; 755 ft   **6.** New Bullards Bar Dam; 635 ft

7. 15 ft   **8.** 4 dams   **9.** Thursday and Saturday; 100°F   **10.** Monday; 82°F   **11.** Sunday, Monday, and Tuesday

12. Wednesday, Thursday, Friday, and Saturday   **13.** 70 qt containers   **14.** 52 qt containers   **15.** 2 qt containers   **16.** 6 qt containers
17. ‖; 2   **18.** |; 1   **19.** |||; 3   **20.** ₶₶|; 6   **21.** ₶₶; 5   **22.**

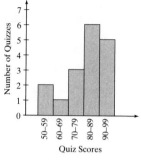

Mental Math   **1.** 4   **3.** 3

Exercise Set 9.3   **1.** mean: 29; median: 28; no mode   **3.** mean: 8.1; median: 8.2; mode: 8.2   **5.** mean: 0.6; median: 0.6; mode: 0.2 and 0.6
7. mean: 370.9; median: 313.5; no mode   **9.** 1416 ft   **11.** 1332 ft   **13.** answers may vary   **15.** 2.79   **17.** 3.46   **19.** 6.8   **21.** 6.9
23. 85.5   **25.** 73   **27.** 70 and 71   **29.** 9 rates   **31.** $\frac{1}{3}$ **33.** $\frac{3}{5}$ **35.** $\frac{11}{15}$ **37.** 35, 35, 37, 43

Mental Math   **1.** $\frac{1}{2}$ **3.** $\frac{1}{2}$

Exercise Set 9.4   **1.**

Outcomes

a — 1 a, 1
   2 a, 2
   3 a, 3
e — 1 e, 1
   2 e, 2
   3 e, 3
i — 1 i, 1
   2 i, 2
   3 i, 3
o — 1 o, 1
   2 o, 2
   3 o, 3
u — 1 u, 1
   2 u, 2
   3 u, 3

15 outcomes

3.

Outcomes

Red   Red
Blue   Blue
Yellow Yellow

3 outcomes

5.

Outcomes

1 — 1 1, 1
   2 1, 2
   3 1, 3
   4 1, 4
2 — 1 2, 1
   2 2, 2
   3 2, 3
   4 2, 4
3 — 1 3, 1
   2 3, 2
   3 3, 3
   4 3, 4
4 — 1 4, 1
   2 4, 2
   3 4, 3
   4 4, 4

16 outcomes

7.

Outcomes

Red — 1 Red, 1
     2 Red, 2
     3 Red, 3
     4 Red, 4
Blue — 1 Blue, 1
      2 Blue, 2
      3 Blue, 3
      4 Blue, 4
Yellow — 1 Yellow, 1
        2 Yellow, 2
        3 Yellow, 3
        4 Yellow, 4

12 outcomes

9.

Outcomes

H — 1 H, 1
   2 H, 2
   3 H, 3
   4 H, 4
T — 1 T, 1
   2 T, 2
   3 T, 3
   4 T, 4

8 outcomes

11. $\frac{1}{6}$ **13.** $\frac{1}{3}$ **15.** $\frac{1}{2}$ **17.** $\frac{5}{6}$ **19.** $\frac{1}{3}$ **21.** 1   **23.** $\frac{2}{3}$
25. $\frac{1}{7}$ **27.** $\frac{2}{7}$ **29.** $\frac{2}{7}$ **31.** $\frac{19}{100}$ **33.** $\frac{1}{20}$ **35.** $\frac{5}{6}$ **37.** $\frac{1}{6}$
39. $\frac{20}{3}$ or $6\frac{2}{3}$ **41.** $\frac{1}{52}$ **43.** $\frac{1}{13}$ **45.** $\frac{1}{4}$ **47.** $\frac{1}{2}$ **49.** $\frac{1}{12}$ **51.** 0
53. answers may vary

Chapter 9 Vocabulary Check   **1.** bar   **2.** mean   **3.** outcomes   **4.** pictograph   **5.** mode   **6.** line   **7.** median   **8.** tree diagram
9. experiment   **10.** circle   **11.** probability   **12.** histogram; class interval; class frequency

Chapter 9 Review   **1.** 475,000   **2.** 175,000   **3.** 650,000   **4.** 375,000   **5.** Midwest, South, and West   **6.** Northeast   **7.** 7.5%
8. 2003   **9.** 1980, 1990, 2000, 2003   **10.** answers may vary   **11.** $2,100,000   **12.** $1,200,000
13. 1991 and 1992, 2000 and 2001, 2001 and 2002   **14.** 1999 and 2000   **15.** 1990, 1991, 1992, 1993, 1994   **16.** 4 employees   **17.** 1 employee

18. 9 employees   **19.** 18 employees   **20.** ꀀꀀꀀꀀꀀ; 5   **21.** |||; 3   **22.** ||||; 4   **23.**   **24.** mortgage payment

25. utilities   **26.** $1225   **27.** $700   **28.** $\dfrac{39}{160}$ **29.** $\dfrac{7}{40}$ **30.** $\dfrac{5}{7}$

31. 20 states   **32.** 11 states   **33.** 1 state   **34.** 29 states

35. mean: 17.8; median: 14; no mode   **36.** mean: 58.1; median: 60; mode: 45 and 86

37. mean: $24,500; median: $20,000; mode: $20,000

38. mean: 447.3; median: 420; mode: 400

39. 3.25   **40.** 2.57   **41.**

Outcomes

H — 1 H, 1
2 H, 2
3 H, 3
4 H, 4
5 H, 5

T — 1 T, 1
2 T, 2
3 T, 3
4 T, 4
5 T, 5

10 outcomes

42.

Outcomes

Red — H Red, H
T Red, T

Blue — H Blue, H
T Blue, T

4 outcomes

43.

Outcomes

1 — 1, 1
2 1, 2
3 1, 3
4 1, 4
5 1, 5

2 — 2, 1
2, 2
3 2, 3
4 2, 4
5 2, 5

3 — 3, 1
3, 2
3, 3
4 3, 4
5 3, 5

4 — 4, 1
4, 2
4, 3
4, 4
5 4, 5

5 — 5, 1
5, 2
5, 3
5, 4
5, 5

25 outcomes

44.

Outcomes

Red < Red Red, Red
Blue Red, Blue

Blue < Red Blue, Red
Blue Blue, Blue

4 outcomes

45.

Outcomes

1 < Red 1, Red
Blue 1, Blue

2 < Red 2, Red
Blue 2, Blue

3 < Red 3, Red
Blue 3, Blue

4 < Red 4, Red
Blue 4, Blue

5 < Red 5, Red
Blue 5, Blue

10 outcomes

46. $\dfrac{1}{6}$ **47.** $\dfrac{1}{6}$ **48.** $\dfrac{1}{5}$ **49.** $\dfrac{1}{5}$ **50.** $\dfrac{3}{5}$ **51.** $\dfrac{2}{5}$ **52.** $\dfrac{1}{2}$ **53.** $\dfrac{1}{2}$ **54.** mean: 74.4; median: 73; mode: none

55. mean: 48.8; median: 32; mode: none   **56.** mean: $454; median: $463.5; mode: $500   **57.** mean: $619.17; median: $647.5; mode: $327

58. $\dfrac{1}{4}$ **59.** $\dfrac{3}{8}$ **60.** $\dfrac{1}{4}$ **61.** $\dfrac{1}{8}$

Chapter 9 Test   1. $225   **2.** 3rd week; $350   **3.** $1100   **4.** June, August, September   **5.** February; 3 cm   **6.** March and November

7.

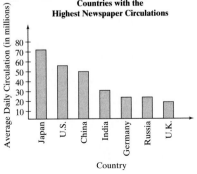

8. 1.5%   **9.** 1990, 1991, 2000   **10.** 1994–1995, 1995–1996, 1998–1999, 1999–2000, 2002–2003

11. $\dfrac{17}{40}$ **12.** $\dfrac{31}{22}$ **13.** 40,920,000 people   **14.** 21,120,000 people   **15.** 9 students

16. 11 students   **17.**

Class Interval (Scores)	Tally	Class Frequency (Number of Students)
40–49	|	1
50–59	|||	3
60–69	||||	4
70–79	ꀀꀀꀀꀀꀀ	5
80–89	ꀀꀀꀀꀀꀀ |||	8
90–99	||||	4

18.

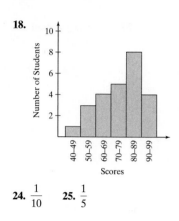

19. mean: 38.4; median: 42; no mode   **20.** mean: 12.625; median: 12.5; mode: 12 and 16

21. 3.07   **22.**

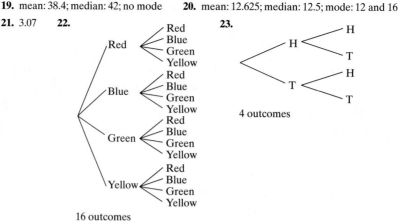

16 outcomes

23.

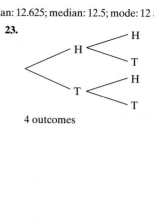

4 outcomes

24. $\dfrac{1}{10}$ **25.** $\dfrac{1}{5}$

Cumulative Review   1. 28 (Sec. 1.9, Ex. 14)   **2.** 12   **3.** $\dfrac{5}{18}$ (Sec. 2.3, Ex. 4)   **4.** $\dfrac{7}{40}$ **5.** $8\dfrac{3}{10}$ (Sec. 3.4, Ex. 3)   **6.** $\dfrac{34}{3}$ or $11\dfrac{1}{3}$

7. 8.4 sq ft (Sec. 4.6, Ex. 10)   **8.** 10 m   **9.** $\dfrac{2}{3}$ (Sec. 5.1, Ex. 4)   **10.** $\dfrac{7}{18}$ **11.** $\dfrac{\$180}{1\ \text{week}}$ (Sec. 5.2, Ex. 2)   **12.** $\dfrac{68\ \text{mi}}{1\ \text{hr}}$ or 68 mi/hr

13. $\dfrac{45\ \text{mi}}{2\ \text{gal}}$ (Sec. 5.2, Ex. 3)   **14.** $\dfrac{39\ \text{files}}{2\ \text{hours}}$ **15.** yes (Sec. 5.3, Ex. 4)   **16.** yes   **17.** 22.4 cc (Sec. 5.4, Ex. 2)   **18.** 262.5 mi

19. 0.046 (Sec. 6.1, Ex. 4)   **20.** 0.0029   **21.** 1.9 (Sec. 6.1, Ex. 5)   **22.** 4.52   **23.** $\dfrac{2}{5}$ (Sec. 6.2, Ex. 1)   **24.** $\dfrac{27}{100}$ **25.** $\dfrac{1}{3}$ (Sec. 6.2, Ex. 4)

26. $\dfrac{107}{175}$ **27.** $5 = n \cdot 20$; (Sec. 6.3, Ex. 1)   **28.** $\dfrac{5}{20} = \dfrac{p}{100}$ **29.** sales tax: $6.41; total price: $91.91 (Sec. 6.6, Ex. 1)   **30.** $1610

31. $2400 (Sec. 6.7, Ex. 3)   **32.** 33.75   **33.** $2\dfrac{1}{3}$ yd (Sec. 7.1, Ex. 2)   **34.** 5000 pounds   **35.** 4 lb 11 oz (Sec. 7.2, Ex. 6)   **36.** 7

37. 0.0235g (Sec. 7.2, Ex. 9)   **38.** 1060 mm   **39.** 3.21 L (Sec. 7.3, Ex. 7)   **40.** 500 cm   **41.** 59°F (Sec. 7.5, Ex. 1)   **42.** 5°C

43. 42° (Sec. 8.1, Ex. 4)   **44.** 132°   **45.** $\dfrac{1}{6}$ (Sec. 8.6, Ex. 2)   **46.** $\dfrac{1}{5}$ **47.** 14, 77 (Sec. 9.3, Ex. 5)   **48.** 56   **49.** $\dfrac{1}{4}$ (Sec. 9.4, Ex. 3)

50. $\dfrac{3}{5}$

CHAPTER 10   Signed Numbers

Exercise Set 10.1   1. −1445   **3.** +14,433   **5.** +118   **7.** −11,730   **9.** −339 million   **11.** −135; −157; Sara   **13.** −45

15. (number line, point at $-1\frac{1}{2}$)   **17.** (number line, point at −4.7)   **19.** <   **21.** >   **23.** >   **25.** >   **27.** <

29. <   **31.** >   **33.** <   **35.** 9   **37.** 8   **39.** 0   **41.** 5   **43.** 8.1   **45.** $\dfrac{1}{2}$ **47.** $\dfrac{3}{8}$ **49.** 7.6   **51.** −5   **53.** 4

55. −23.6   **57.** $\dfrac{9}{16}$ **59.** 0.7   **61.** $-\dfrac{17}{18}$ **63.** 7   **65.** −20   **67.** −3   **69.** 8   **71.** 14   **73.** 29   **75.** 25; −25   **77.** 8.4; 8.4

79. Lake Maracaibo   **81.** Lake Eyre   **83.** Earth   **85.** Saturn   **87.** 13   **89.** 35   **91.** 360   **93.** $-|-8|, -|3|, 2^2, -(-5)$

95. $-|-6|, -|1|, |-1|, -(-6)$ **97.** $-10, -|-9|, -(-2), |-12|, 5^2$ **99.** d   **101.** 5   **103.** false   **105.** true   **107.** false

109. answers may vary   **111.** no; answers may vary

Calculator Explorations   1. −159   **3.** 44   **5.** −894.855

Mental Math   1. 5   **3.** −35

Exercise Set 10.2   1.

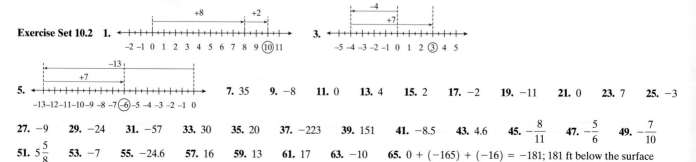

7. 35   **9.** −8   **11.** 0   **13.** 4   **15.** 2   **17.** −2   **19.** −11   **21.** 0   **23.** 7   **25.** −3

27. −9   **29.** −24   **31.** −57   **33.** 30   **35.** 20   **37.** −223   **39.** 151   **41.** −8.5   **43.** 4.6   **45.** $-\dfrac{8}{11}$ **47.** $-\dfrac{5}{6}$ **49.** $-\dfrac{7}{10}$

51. $5\dfrac{5}{8}$ **53.** −7   **55.** −24.6   **57.** 16   **59.** 13   **61.** 17   **63.** −10   **65.** $0 + (-165) + (-16) = -181$; 181 ft below the surface

67. Team 1: 7; Team 2: 6; winning team: Team 1   **69.** $786,000,000   **71.** $761,000,000   **73.** 2°C   **75.** −$12,198   **77.** −40°F

79. -7679 m **81.** 44 **83.** 72.01 **85.** 141 **87.** answers may vary **89.** -3 **91.** 10 **93.** true **95.** false
97. answers may vary

Mental Math 1. 0 **3.** 0

Exercise Set 10.3 1. 0 **3.** 5 **5.** -5 **7.** 14 **9.** 3 **11.** -18 **13.** -14 **15.** -3.3 **17.** 4.02 **19.** $\frac{2}{5}$ **21.** $-\frac{3}{10}$ **23.** $\frac{5}{6}$

25. -38 **27.** -17 **29.** 13 **31.** -38 **33.** -11 **35.** -12.7 **37.** $\frac{3}{7}$ **39.** 2 **41.** 0 **43.** -1 **45.** -27 **47.** 40

49. -51 **51.** 428 degrees **53.** 39 degrees **55.** 265°F **57.** $-\$16$ **59.** -12°C **61.** 154 ft **63.** 69 ft **65.** 652 ft **67.** 144 ft
69. $-\$532$ billion **71.** 0 **73.** 8 **75.** 1058 **77.** answers may vary **79.** 16 **81.** -20 **83.** -4 **85.** 0 **87.** -12 **89.** false
91. answers may vary

Integrated Review 1. $+29{,}028$ **2.** $-35{,}840$ **3.** -7 **4.** $+28{,}250$ **5.** **6.** $>$ **7.** $<$ **8.** $<$
9. $>$ **10.** $>$ **11.** $>$ **12.** $>$ **13.** $<$ **14.** 1 **15.** 1

16. 0 **17.** -4 **18.** 8.6 **19.** 100.3 **20.** $\frac{3}{4}$ **21.** $-\frac{3}{4}$ **22.** -6 **23.** 13 **24.** -89.1 **25.** $\frac{2}{9}$ **26.** 5 **27.** -20.8 **28.** $\frac{2}{9}$

29. -2 **30.** $\frac{3}{4}$ **31.** -4 **32.** -9.6 **33.** -6 **34.** 12 **35.** 120 **36.** -3.44 **37.** $-\frac{11}{10}$ or $-1\frac{1}{10}$ **38.** 6 **39.** 1 **40.** -19

41. -12 **42.** -4 **43.** -44 **44.** 189°F

Exercise Set 10.4 1. 6 **3.** -36 **5.** -3.12 **7.** 0 **9.** $\frac{6}{35}$ **11.** -48 **13.** -8 **15.** 80 **17.** -150 **19.** 4 **21.** -25

23. -27 **25.** -8 **27.** 81 **29.** $\frac{25}{121}$ **31.** -4 **33.** -5 **35.** 8 **37.** 0 **39.** -13 **41.** -26 **43.** $\frac{25}{12}$ or $2\frac{1}{12}$

45. -5 **47.** -6 **49.** 3 **51.** -300 **53.** $-\frac{4}{5}$ **55.** 0 **57.** -125 **59.** -50 **61.** 43.4 **63.** $-\frac{32}{27}$ **65.** $-\frac{3}{2}$ **67.** -3

69. 306 **71.** $3\cdot(-4)=-12$ yd; a loss of 12 yards **73.** $5\cdot(-20)=-100$; a depth of 100 feet **75.** $-\$2584$ million
77. a. 194 condors **b.** 11 condors per year **79.** -210°C **81.** -189°C **83.** -2.5 **85.** 225 **87.** 109 **89.** 8 **91.** -29
93. -19 **95.** -8 **97.** false **99.** true **101.** negative **103. a.** $\frac{-20}{41},\frac{20}{-41}$ **b.** $\frac{-8}{17},\frac{8}{-17}$
105. $(-7)^{23},(-1)^{55},0^{15},(-1)^{50},(-7)^{20}$ **107.** answers may vary

The Bigger Picture 1. 5 **2.** 55 **3.** -6 **4.** -12 **5.** -12 **6.** 81 **7.** -81 **8.** -34 **9.** 10 **10.** -30 **11.** $-\frac{1}{6}$
12. -11 **13.** -30 **14.** -80 **15.** $\frac{20}{17}$ or $1\frac{3}{17}$ **16.** $-\frac{39}{64}$

Calculator Explorations 1. 4.8 **3.** -258

Exercise Set 10.5 1. 3 **3.** 4 **5.** -7 **7.** -14 **9.** $-\frac{2}{9}$ **11.** -8 **13.** 4 **15.** 1 **17.** 4 **19.** -3 **21.** -55 **23.** -4

25. 16 **27.** 15 **29.** -3 **31.** -3 **33.** 4 **35.** 16 **37.** -27 **39.** 34 **41.** 0.65 **43.** -59 **45.** -7 **47.** $\frac{5}{36}$ **49.** -11

51. 36 **53.** -117 **55.** 30 **57.** -3 **59.** -2.21 **61.** -33 **63.** $-\frac{7}{5}$ **65.** 4050 **67.** 45 **69.** 32 in. **71.** 30 ft **73.** -5°F

75. $2\cdot(7-5)\cdot3$ **77.** $-6\cdot(10-4)$ **79.** answers may vary **81.** answers may vary **83.** 20,736

Chapter 10 Vocabulary Check 1. opposites **2.** signed **3.** absolute value **4.** integers **5.** additive inverse **6.** negative
7. positive

Chapter 10 Review 1. -1435 **2.** $+7562$ **3.** **4.** **5.** $>$ **6.** $<$

7. $>$ **8.** 12 **9.** 0 **10.** $\frac{7}{8}$ **11.** 12 **12.** $-\frac{1}{2}$ **13.** 3.9 **14.** -7 **15.** true **16.** true **17.** 2 **18.** 14 **19.** 4 **20.** 17

21. -23 **22.** -22 **23.** -2.1 **24.** -7 **25.** $\frac{4}{15}$ **26.** $-\frac{5}{9}$ **27.** -151 **28.** -606 **29.** -20°C **30.** -150 ft **31.** -9

32. $+1$ or 1 **33.** -8 **34.** -26 **35.** $-\frac{5}{4}$ or $-1\frac{1}{4}$ **36.** $-\frac{11}{10}$ or $-1\frac{1}{10}$ **37.** 20 **38.** 8 **39.** -4 **40.** -16 **41.** 1.2 **42.** 0.7

43. $-\frac{5}{18}$ **44.** $-\frac{3}{14}$ **45.** $-\$25$ **46.** $+692$ ft **47.** 121 **48.** 81 **49.** -81 **50.** -121 **51.** $-\frac{64}{125}$ **52.** $-\frac{8}{27}$ **53.** 21

54. -18 **55.** -26 **56.** -19 **57.** -36 **58.** -40 **59.** $-\frac{7}{12}$ **60.** 6 **61.** undefined **62.** 0 **63.** 1.2 **64.** $\frac{4}{5}$

65. $(-5)(2)=-10$; a loss of 10 yards **66.** -7 **67.** -16 **68.** -44 **69.** -14.8 **70.** 44 **71.** 7 **72.** 7 **73.** 39 **74.** -41

75. $-\frac{23}{9}$ **76.** $-\frac{89}{100}$ **77.** -2 **78.** -12 **79.** 16 **80.** -16 **81.** -15 **82.** -19 **83.** 48 **84.** -21 **85.** 2.1 **86.** $-\frac{1}{4}$

87. $\frac{6}{5}$ **88.** $-\frac{3}{2}$ **89.** $-\frac{1}{40}$ **90.** -1.35 **91.** $-\$9$ **92.** 6°C **93.** 13,118 ft **94.** -27°C **95.** 2 **96.** 4 **97.** 3 **98.** 37

99. -5 **100.** -25 **101.** -20 **102.** 17

Chapter 10 Test **1.**

2. $-\dfrac{2}{3}$ **3.** 2.9 **4.** 98 **5.** -98 **6.** $>$ **7.** $>$ **8.** 3

9. -6 **10.** -10 **11.** 4 **12.** $-\dfrac{1}{2}$ **13.** 12 **14.** 65 **15.** 5 **16.** 12 **17.** -11 **18.** -46 **19.** -117 **20.** 128 **21.** 2

22. -5 **23.** $-\dfrac{14}{81}$ **24.** 19 **25.** -3 **26.** $-\dfrac{1}{45}$ **27.** $-\dfrac{9}{20}$ **28.** 88 feet below sea level **29.** 45 **30.** 31,642

31. 3820 ft below sea level **32.** -4

Cumulative Review **1.** 78,875 (Sec. 1.6, Ex. 5) **2.** $\dfrac{25}{44}$ **3.** $\dfrac{4}{5}$ (Sec. 2.5, Ex. 7) **4.** 236 **5.** $\dfrac{17}{21}$ (Sec. 3.3, Ex. 3) **6.** $1\dfrac{11}{14}$

7. 48.26 (Sec. 4.1, Ex. 6) **8.** 0.08 **9.** 6.095 (Sec. 4.1, Ex. 7) **10.** 56,321 **11.** 3.432 (Sec. 4.3, Ex. 5) **12.** 13.5

13. 28.4405 (Sec. 4.5, Ex. 13) **14.** 20 **15.** $\dfrac{4500 \text{ dollars}}{1 \text{ month}}$ or 4500 dollars/month (Sec. 5.2, Ex. 4) **16.** $\dfrac{60 \text{ miles}}{1 \text{ hour}}$ or 60 miles/hour

17. $n = 2$ (Sec. 5.3, Ex. 5) **18.** $n = \dfrac{48}{7}$ **19.** 46% (Sec. 6.1, Ex. 2) **20.** 80% **21.** 45% (Sec. 6.2, Ex. 6) **22.** 106%

23. 150% (Sec. 6.2, Ex. 8) **24.** 500% **25.** 200 (Sec. 6.3, Ex. 10) **26.** 242 **27.** $\dfrac{101}{200} = \dfrac{p}{100}$ (Sec. 6.4, Ex. 2) **28.** $101 = n \cdot 200$

29. \$160 (Sec. 6.7, Ex. 2) **30.** \$525 **31.** 9 ft 1 in. (Sec. 7.1, Ex. 6) **32.** 68 m **33.** 37°C (Sec. 7.5, Ex. 5) **34.** 720 cm

35. 73° (Sec. 8.1, Ex. 5) **36.** 56° **37.** 60° (Sec. 8.2, Ex. 2) **38.** 49° **39.** 5.1 sq mi (Sec. 8.4, Ex. 2) **40.** $25\pi \approx 78.5$ sq m

41. $36\pi \approx 113\dfrac{1}{7}$ cu in. (Sec. 8.5, Ex. 2) **42.** 24 cu cm **43.** 57 (Sec. 9.3, Ex. 3) **44.** 24.5 **45.** $\dfrac{1}{3}$ (Sec. 9.4, Ex. 4) **46.** -4.9

47. -23 (Sec. 10.2, Ex. 3) **48. a.** -1000 **b.** -1000 **49.** 82 (Sec. 10.5, Ex. 3) **50.** -4

CHAPTER 11 Introduction to Algebra

Mental Math **1.** unlike **3.** like **5.** unlike **7.** like

Exercise Set 11.1 **1.** -3 **3.** -2 **5.** 4 **7.** -3 **9.** -10 **11.** 133 **13.** -15 **15.** -4 **17.** $-\dfrac{4}{3}$ or $-1\dfrac{1}{3}$ **19.** -12

21. $\dfrac{3}{2}$ or $1\dfrac{1}{2}$ **23.** -10.6 **25.** $8x$ **27.** $-4n$ **29.** $-2c$ **31.** $-4x$ **33.** $13a - 8$ **35.** $-0.9x + 11.2$ **37.** $2x - 7$

39. $-5x + 4y - 5$ **41.** $\dfrac{1}{2} - \dfrac{53}{60}x$ **43.** $-4.8m - 4.1$ **45.** $30x$ **47.** $-22y$ **49.** $-4.2a$ **51.** $-4a$ **53.** $2y + 4$ **55.** $15a - 40$

57. $-12x - 28$ **59.** $6x - 0.12$ **61.** $-4x - \dfrac{3}{2}$ **63.** $2x - 9$ **65.** $27n - 20$ **67.** $7w + 15$ **69.** $-11x + 8$ **71.** 2000 sq ft

73. 64 ft **75.** \$360 **77.** $16y^2$ sq cm **79.** 78.5 sq ft **81.** $(3x + 6)$ ft **83.** 23°F **85.** 288 cu in. **87.** $91.2x$ cu in. **89.** -3
91. 8 **93.** 0 **95.** incorrect; $5(3x - 2) = 15x - 10$ **97.** correct **99.** distributive **101.** associative **103.** answers may vary
105. $(20x + 16)$ sq mi **107.** 45,996.2 sq in. **109.** $4824q + 12,274$

Mental Math **1.** 2 **3.** -1

Exercise Set 11.2 **1.** yes **3.** no **5.** yes **7.** yes **9.** 18 **11.** -8 **13.** 9 **15.** -16 **17.** 3 **19.** $\dfrac{1}{8}$ **21.** 6 **23.** 8

25. 5.3 **27.** -1 **29.** -20.1 **31.** 2 **33.** 0 **35.** -28 **37.** 1 **39.** 1 **41.** 1 **43.** subtract $\dfrac{2}{3}$ from both sides

45. add $\dfrac{4}{5}$ to both sides **47.** answers may vary **49.** 162,964 **51.** 1949 yd **53.** \$23,842,000,000

Exercise Set 11.3 **1.** 4 **3.** -4 **5.** -30 **7.** -17 **9.** 50 **11.** 25 **13.** -30 **15.** $\dfrac{1}{3}$ **17.** $-\dfrac{2}{3}$ **19.** -4 **21.** 8 **23.** 1.3

25. 2 **27.** 0 **29.** -0.05 **31.** $-\dfrac{15}{64}$ **33.** $\dfrac{2}{3}$ **35.** 6 **37.** 0 **39.** -2 **41.** -8 **43.** 1 **45.** 72 **47.** 25 **49.** 1

51. -10 **53.** addition **55.** division **57.** answers may vary **59.** -3648 **61.** 6.5 hr **63.** 58.8 mph

Integrated Review **1.** 4 **2.** -6 **3.** 1 **4.** -4 **5.** $8x$ **6.** $-4y$ **7.** $-2a - 2$ **8.** $-2x + 3y - 7$ **9.** $-20x$ **10.** $5y + 10$

11. $3x + 12$ **12.** $11x + 16$ **13.** $(12x - 6)$ sq m **14.** $25y^2$ sq in. **15.** 13 **16.** -9 **17.** $\dfrac{7}{10}$ **18.** 0 **19.** -4 **20.** 25

21. -1 **22.** -3 **23.** 6 **24.** 8 **25.** $-\dfrac{9}{11}$ **26.** 5

Calculator Explorations **1.** yes **3.** no **5.** yes

Exercise Set 11.4 **1.** 3 **3.** 1.9 **5.** −4 **7.** 100 **9.** −3.9 **11.** −4 **13.** −12 **15.** −3 **17.** −1 **19.** −45 **21.** 5 **23.** −5 **25.** 8 **27.** 0 **29.** −22 **31.** 6 **33.** 5 **35.** −3 **37.** 5 **39.** 2 **41.** −4 **43.** −1 **45.** 4 **47.** −2 **49.** 3 **51.** −1 **53.** 8 **55.** 4 **57.** 3 **59.** 64 **61.** $\frac{1}{9}$ **63.** $\frac{3}{2}$ **65.** −54 **67.** 2 **69.** $\frac{9}{5}$ **71.** $-42 + 16 = -26$ **73.** $-5(-29) = 145$ **75.** $3(-14 - 2) = -48$ **77.** $\frac{100}{2(50)} = 1$ **79.** 97 million returns **81.** 20 million returns **83.** b **85.** a

87. $6x - 10 = 5x - 7$
$6x = 5x + 3$
$x = 3$

89. 136.04°F **91.** −81.4°F

The Bigger Picture **1.** −5 **2.** 11 **3.** −35 **4.** 103 **5.** 75 **6.** −11 **7.** 11.4 **8.** 150% **9.** −6 **10.** 2.7

Exercise Set 11.5 **1.** $x + 5$ **3.** $x + 8$ **5.** $20 - x$ **7.** $512x$ **9.** $\frac{x}{2}$ **11.** $17 + x + 5x$ **13.** $-5 + x = -7$ **15.** $3x = 27$ **17.** $-20 - x = 104$ **19.** $5x$ **21.** $11 - x$ **23.** $2x = 108$ **25.** $50 - 8x$ **27.** $5(-3 + x) = -20$ **29.** $9 + 3x = 33; 8$ **31.** $3 + 4 + x = 16; 9$ **33.** $x - 3 = \frac{10}{5}; 5$ **35.** $30 - x = 3(x + 6); 3$ **37.** $5x - 40 = x + 8; 12$ **39.** $3(x - 5) = \frac{108}{12}; 8$ **41.** $4x = 30 - 2x; 5$ **43.** Bush: 286 votes; Kerry: 252 votes **45.** bamboo: 36 inches; kelp: 18 inches **47.** India: 8407; US: 5758 **49.** Gamecube: $150; games: $450 **51.** Michigan Stadium: 107,501; Neyland Stadium: 102,854 **53.** California: 309 thousand; Washington: 103 thousand **55.** crow: 9 oz; finch: 4 oz **57.** 2010: 275,215; 2020: 808,416 **59.** $225 **61.** 70 points **63.** 590 **65.** 1000 **67.** 3000 **69.** answers may vary **71.** $8250 **73.** $5

Chapter 11 Vocabulary Check **1.** simplified; combined **2.** like **3.** variable **4.** algebraic expression **5.** terms **6.** numerical coefficient **7.** evaluating the expression

Chapter 11 Review **1.** −5 **2.** 17 **3.** undefined **4.** 0 **5.** 129 **6.** −2 **7.** 8 cu ft **8.** 64 cu ft **9.** $1800 **10.** $300 **11.** $-15x$ **12.** $-\frac{7}{30}x$ **13.** $-6y - 10$ **14.** $-6a - 7$ **15.** $-8y + 2$ **16.** $4.6x - 11.9$ **17.** $-8y$ **18.** $15y - 24$ **19.** $11x - 12$ **20.** $4x - 7$ **21.** $-5a + 4$ **22.** $12y - 9$ **23.** $(6x - 3)$ sq yd **24.** $25y^2$ sq m **25.** yes **26.** no **27.** −2 **28.** 7 **29.** $-\frac{1}{2}$ **30.** $-\frac{6}{11}$ **31.** −6 **32.** −20 **33.** 1.3 **34.** 2.4 **35.** 7 **36.** −9 **37.** 1 **38.** −5 **39.** $-\frac{4}{5}$ **40.** −24 **41.** −120 **42.** 13 **43.** 4 **44.** 3 **45.** 5 **46.** 12 **47.** 63 **48.** 33 **49.** −2.25 **50.** 1.3 **51.** 2 **52.** 6 **53.** 11 **54.** −5 **55.** 6 **56.** 8 **57.** $20 - (-8) = 28$ **58.** $5(-2 + 6) = -20$ **59.** $\frac{-75}{5 + 20} = -3$ **60.** $-2 - 19 = -21$ **61.** $\frac{70}{x}$ **62.** $x - 13$ **63.** $85 - x$ **64.** $2x + 11$ **65.** $x + 8 = 40$ **66.** $2x - 12 = 10$ **67.** 5 **68.** −16 **69.** incumbent: 14,752 votes; challenger: 3546 votes **70.** 42 CDs **71.** 29 **72.** $-\frac{1}{4}$ **73.** $-11x$ **74.** $-35x$ **75.** $22x - 19$ **76.** $-9x - 32$ **77.** $x - 17$ **78.** $3(x + 5)$ **79.** $x - 3 = \frac{x}{4}$ **80.** $6x = x + 2$ **81.** no **82.** yes **83.** −1 **84.** −25 **85.** 13 **86.** −6 **87.** 17 **88.** 7 **89.** −22 **90.** −6 **91.** $-\frac{3}{4}$ **92.** −4 **93.** 2 **94.** $-\frac{8}{3}$ **95.** 12 **96.** −8 **97.** 0 **98.** 0 **99.** 5 **100.** 1

Chapter 11 Test **1.** −1 **2.** $-5x + 5$ **3.** $-6y - 14$ **4.** $14z - 8$ **5.** $(12x - 4)$ sq m **6.** 7 **7.** $-\frac{1}{2}$ **8.** −12 **9.** 40 **10.** 24 **11.** 3 **12.** −2 **13.** −2 **14.** 4.5 **15.** 0 **16.** −2 **17.** $\frac{22}{3}$ **18.** 4 **19.** 0 **20.** 6000 sq ft **21.** 30 sq ft **22.** a. $17x$ b. $20 - 2x$ **23.** −2 **24.** 34 points **25.** 244 women

Chapter 11 Cumulative Review **1.** 0.8496 (Sec. 4.4, Ex. 3) **2.** 53.1 **3.** a. $\frac{5}{7}$ b. $\frac{7}{24}$ (Sec. 5.1, Ex. 8) **4.** $\frac{23}{36}$ **5.** 5 (Sec. 6.3, Ex. 9) **6.** $\frac{7}{12}$ **7.** 75% (Sec. 6.3, Ex. 11) **8.** $\frac{18}{23}$ **9.** 48 oz (Sec. 7.2, Ex. 2) **10.** 24,000 **11.** 1.13 ml (Sec. 7.3, Ex. 10) **12.** 0.024 **13.** a. line b. line segment c. angle d. ray (Sec. 8.1, Ex. 1) **14.** 168° **15.** 10 cm (Sec. 8.2, Ex. 3) **16.** 34° **17.** 50 ft (Sec. 8.3, Ex. 6) **18.** 132 sq ft **19.** 56 sq cm (Sec. 8.4, Ex. 1) **20.** 18 **21.** 5.657 (Sec. 8.6, Ex. 5) **22.** 5.78 **23.** 46 ft (Sec. 8.7, Ex. 4) **24.** 24% **25.** a. 15 reptile species b. birds (Sec. 9.1, Ex. 2) **26.** mean: 8; median: 9; mode: 11 **27.** < (Sec. 10.1, Ex. 6) **28.** > **29.** > (Sec. 10.1, Ex. 5) **30.** < **31.** 2 (Sec. 10.1, Ex. 10) **32.** $\frac{5}{6}$ **33.** 1.2 (Sec. 10.1, Ex. 14) **34.** 0 **35.** −16 (Sec. 10.2, Ex. 4) **36.** −3.6 **37.** $-\frac{1}{2}$ (Sec. 10.2, Ex. 6) **38.** $\frac{1}{10}$ **39.** −7 (Sec. 10.3, Ex. 6) **40.** 5.8 **41.** 1 (Sec. 10.3, Ex. 7) **42.** $-\frac{31}{120}$ **43.** 10 (Sec. 10.4, Ex. 2) **44.** −9.6 **45.** $\frac{1}{3}$ (Sec. 10.4, Ex. 4) **46.** 4 **47.** 3 (Sec. 10.5, Ex. 6) **48.** 9.7 **49.** 2 (Sec. 11.4, Ex. 7) **50.** 20

APPENDIX A   Tables

A1: One Hundred Addition Facts   **1.** 5   **3.** 5   **5.** 12   **7.** 8   **9.** 14   **11.** 12   **13.** 10   **15.** 9   **17.** 11   **19.** 18   **21.** 10
23. 10   **25.** 17   **27.** 13   **29.** 12   **31.** 16   **33.** 7   **35.** 4   **37.** 8   **39.** 8   **41.** 6   **43.** 16   **45.** 9   **47.** 12   **49.** 7
51. 2   **53.** 11   **55.** 8   **57.** 5   **59.** 14   **61.** 13   **63.** 7   **65.** 7   **67.** 13   **69.** 5   **71.** 4   **73.** 16   **75.** 14   **77.** 1
79. 4   **81.** 10   **83.** 8   **85.** 5   **87.** 10   **89.** 11   **91.** 12   **93.** 9   **95.** 9   **97.** 14   **99.** 9

A2: One Hundred Multiplication Facts   **1.** 1   **3.** 56   **5.** 32   **7.** 28   **9.** 4   **11.** 63   **13.** 6   **15.** 30   **17.** 24   **19.** 18   **21.** 40
23. 32   **25.** 54   **27.** 56   **29.** 54   **31.** 2   **33.** 36   **35.** 12   **37.** 36   **39.** 12   **41.** 48   **43.** 8   **45.** 0   **47.** 27   **49.** 15
51. 45   **53.** 0   **55.** 81   **57.** 0   **59.** 0   **61.** 18   **63.** 3   **65.** 36   **67.** 63   **69.** 35   **71.** 42   **73.** 40   **75.** 0   **77.** 9
79. 15   **81.** 5   **83.** 0   **85.** 21   **87.** 0   **89.** 16   **91.** 0   **93.** 4   **95.** 6   **97.** 18   **99.** 0

APPENDIX C   Unit Analysis

Exercise Set C.1   **1. a.** \$640   **b.** 15 hr   **3. a.** 1260 beats   **b.** 60 sec or 1 min   **c.** 90 sec or $1\frac{1}{2}$ min   **5. a.** 200 beds   **b.** 11,315

7. a. 6 c   **b.** $13\frac{1}{3}$ c   **c.** $22\frac{1}{2}$ c   **9.** \$643.50   **11. a.** 262.5 drops   **b.** 20 liters   **13. a.** 7200 tortillas   **b.** $12\frac{1}{2}$ min

15. a. \$10.8 million   **b.** 4.5 episodes   **17. a.** $11\frac{1}{4}$ mi   **b.** $\frac{1}{9}$ hr or $6\frac{2}{3}$ min

SOLUTIONS TO SELECTED EXERCISES

CHAPTER 1

Exercise Set 1.2

1. The place value of the 5 in 352 is tens.
5. The place value of the 5 in 62,500,000 is hundred-thousands.
9. 542 is written as five hundred forty-two.
13. 26,990 is written as twenty-six thousand, nine hundred ninety.
17. 53,520,170 is written as fifty-three million, five hundred twenty thousand, one hundred seventy.
21. 1679 is written as one thousand, six hundred seventy-nine.
25. 12,662 is written as twelve thousand, six hundred sixty-two.
29. Six thousand, five hundred eighty-seven in standard form is 6587.
33. Sixteen million, five hundred four thousand, nineteen in standard form is 16,504,019.
37. Two hundred twenty in standard form is 220.
41. Seventy million, two hundred fifty-one thousand, seven hundred ten in standard form is 70,251,710.
45. Seven hundred fifty-five in standard form is 755.
49. $5290 = 5000 + 200 + 90$
53. $30,680 = 30,000 + 600 + 80$
57. 5532 is written as five thousand, five hundred thirty-two.
61. The tallest mountain in New England is Mt. Washington.
65. The Labrador retriever breed has the most American Kennel Club registrations. 144,934 is written as one hundred forty-four thousand, nine hundred thirty-four.
69. The largest number results when the largest digit available is used for each place value when reading from left to right. Thus, the largest number possible is 7632.
73. answers may vary

Exercise Set 1.3

1.
$$\begin{array}{r} 14 \\ + 22 \\ \hline 36 \end{array}$$

5.
$$\begin{array}{r} 12 \\ 13 \\ + 24 \\ \hline 49 \end{array}$$

9.
$$\begin{array}{r} \overset{1}{5}3 \\ + 64 \\ \hline 117 \end{array}$$

13.
$$\begin{array}{r} \overset{1}{2}\overset{1}{2},\overset{1}{7}81 \\ + 186,297 \\ \hline 209,078 \end{array}$$

17.
$$\begin{array}{r} \overset{2}{6} \\ 21 \\ 14 \\ 9 \\ + 12 \\ \hline 62 \end{array}$$

21.
$$\begin{array}{r} \overset{1}{6}2 \\ 18 \\ + 14 \\ \hline 94 \end{array}$$

25.
$$\begin{array}{r} \overset{111}{7}542 \\ 49 \\ + 682 \\ \hline 8273 \end{array}$$

29.
$$\begin{array}{r} \overset{1}{6}\overset{2}{2}7 \\ 628 \\ + 629 \\ \hline 1884 \end{array}$$

33.
$$\begin{array}{r} \overset{11}{5}07 \\ 593 \\ + 10 \\ \hline 1110 \end{array}$$

37.
$$\begin{array}{r} \overset{11}{}\overset{22}{4}9 \\ 628 \\ 5\,762 \\ + 29,462 \\ \hline 35,901 \end{array}$$

41.
$$\begin{array}{r} \overset{2}{9} \\ 12 \\ 9 \\ + 12 \\ \hline 42 \end{array}$$
The perimeter is 42 inches.

45. Opposite sides of a rectangle have the same length.
$$\begin{array}{r} \overset{2}{4} \\ 8 \\ 4 \\ + 8 \\ \hline 24 \end{array}$$
The perimeter is 24 inches.

49. $8 + 3 + 5 + 7 + 5 + 1 = 8 + 1 + 3 + 7 + 5 + 5$
$$= 9 + 10 + 10$$
$$= 29$$
The perimeter is 29 inches.

53.
$$\begin{array}{r} \overset{13}{7}6 \\ 39 \\ 8 \\ 17 \\ + 126 \\ \hline 266 \end{array}$$

57.
$$\begin{array}{r} \overset{121}{2}686 \\ 686 \\ + 80 \\ \hline 3452 \end{array}$$

61.
$$\begin{array}{r} \overset{21}{78} \\ 90 \\ 102 \\ +\ 70 \\ \hline 340 \end{array}$$

He needs 340 feet of wiring.

65.
$$\begin{array}{r} \overset{11}{1430} \\ 675 \\ +\ 320 \\ \hline 2425 \end{array}$$

The total height of Yosemite Falls is 2425 feet.

69. The sides of a square are all the same length.
$$\begin{array}{r} \overset{1}{31} \\ 31 \\ 31 \\ +\ 31 \\ \hline 124 \end{array}$$

The perimeter of the board is 124 feet.

73. To find the number of Blockbusters worldwide, we add.
$$\begin{array}{r} \overset{1}{5670} \\ +\ 3197 \\ \hline 8867 \end{array}$$

There are 8867 Blockbuster stores worldwide.

77. The states with the most Target stores are California, Texas, and Florida.
$$\begin{array}{r} \overset{11}{184} \\ 104 \\ +\ 78 \\ \hline 366 \end{array}$$

There are 366 Target stores in these states.

81. answers may vary

85.
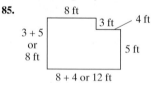

$p = (8 + 12 + 5 + 4 + 3 + 8)$ ft

    $= 40$ ft

89.
$$\begin{array}{r} \overset{121}{773} \\ 659 \\ +\ 481 \\ \hline 1913 \end{array}$$

The given answer is correct.

Exercise Set 1.4

1.
$$\begin{array}{r} 67 \\ -\ 23 \\ \hline 44 \end{array}$$

Check:
$$\begin{array}{r} 44 \\ +\ 23 \\ \hline 67 \end{array}$$

5.
$$\begin{array}{r} 167 \\ -\ 32 \\ \hline 135 \end{array}$$

Check:
$$\begin{array}{r} 135 \\ +\ 32 \\ \hline 167 \end{array}$$

9.
$$\begin{array}{r} 6998 \\ -\ 1453 \\ \hline 5545 \end{array}$$

Check:
$$\begin{array}{r} 5545 \\ +\ 1453 \\ \hline 6998 \end{array}$$

13.
$$\begin{array}{r} 62 \\ -\ 37 \\ \hline 25 \end{array}$$

Check:
$$\begin{array}{r} \overset{1}{25} \\ +\ 37 \\ \hline 62 \end{array}$$

17.
$$\begin{array}{r} 938 \\ -\ 792 \\ \hline 146 \end{array}$$

Check:
$$\begin{array}{r} \overset{1}{146} \\ +\ 792 \\ \hline 938 \end{array}$$

21.
$$\begin{array}{r} 600 \\ -\ 432 \\ \hline 168 \end{array}$$

Check:
$$\begin{array}{r} \overset{11}{168} \\ +\ 432 \\ \hline 600 \end{array}$$

25.
$$\begin{array}{r} 923 \\ -\ 476 \\ \hline 447 \end{array}$$

Check:
$$\begin{array}{r} \overset{11}{447} \\ +\ 476 \\ \hline 923 \end{array}$$

29.
$$\begin{array}{r} 533 \\ -\ 29 \\ \hline 504 \end{array}$$

Check:
$$\begin{array}{r} \overset{1}{504} \\ +\ 29 \\ \hline 533 \end{array}$$

33.
$$\begin{array}{r} 1983 \\ -\ 1904 \\ \hline 79 \end{array}$$

Check:
$$\begin{array}{r} \overset{1}{79} \\ +\ 1904 \\ \hline 1983 \end{array}$$

37.
$$\begin{array}{r} 50,000 \\ -\ 17,289 \\ \hline 32,711 \end{array}$$

Check:
$$\begin{array}{r} \overset{11\ \ 11}{32,711} \\ +\ 17,289 \\ \hline 50,000 \end{array}$$

41. 51,111
$-$ 19,898
31,213

Check:

$\overset{1\,1\,\,1\,1}{31,213}$
$+$ 19,898
51,111

45. 41
$-$ 21
20

The difference of 41 and 21 is 20.

49. 108
$-$ 36
72

108 less 36 is 72.

53. 503
$-$ 239
264

Dyllis has 264 more pages to read.

57. 20,320
$-$ 14,255
6 065

The peak of Mt. McKinley is 6065 feet higher than the peak of Long's Peak.

61. 538
$-$ 129
409

There will be $409 left in his account.

65. 914
$-$ 525
389

She will have $389 left in her savings account after buying the VCR.

69. 29,393
$-$ 10,357
19,036

There were 19,036 cocker spaniels registered with the AKC in 2003.

73. The tallest bar corresponds to Hartsfield Atlanta International, so that is the busiest airport.

77. The companies that spent more than $3000 million on advertising in 2003 were General Motors Corp., Time Warner, and Procter & Gamble Co.

81. $\overset{1\,1}{986}$
$+$ 48
1034

85. 9000
$-$ 482
8518

89. In $\begin{array}{r} 48 \\ -\,1 \end{array}$, 48 is the minuend and 1 is the subtrahend.

93. Votes for Jo:

$\overset{1\,2\,1}{276}$
362
201
$+$ 179
1018

Votes for Trudy:

$\overset{1\,1}{295}$
122
312
$+$ 18
747

Since Jo received more votes, she won the election.

1018
$-$ 747
271

Jo won the election by 271 votes.

97. $\overset{1\,1}{141}$
$+$ 888
1029

The given answer is correct.

101. answers may vary.

Exercise Set 1.5

1. To round 632 to the nearest ten, observe that the digit in the ones place is 2. Since this digit is less than 5, we do not add 1 to the digit in the tens place. The number 632 rounded to the nearest ten is 630.

5. To round 1792 to the nearest hundred, observe that the digit in the tens place is 9. Since this digit is at least 5, we need to add 1 to the digit in the hundreds place. The number 1792 rounded to the nearest hundred is 1800.

9. To round 51,096 to the nearest thousand, observe that the digit in the hundreds place is 0. Since this digit is less than 5, we do not add 1 to the digit in the thousands place. The number 51,096 rounded to the nearest thousand is 51,000.

13. To round 248,695 to the nearest hundred, observe that the digit in the tens place is 9. Since this digit is at least 5, we need to add 1 to the digit in the hundreds place. The number 248,695 rounded to the nearest hundred is 248,700.

17. To round 99,995 to the nearest ten, observe that the digit in the ones place is 5. Since this digit is at least 5, we need to add 1 to the digit in the hundreds place. The number 99,995 rounded to the nearest ten is 100,000.

		Tens	Hundreds	Thousands
21.	5281	5280	5200	5000
25.	14,876	14,880	14,900	15,000

29. To round 10,759 to the nearest hundred, observe that the digit in the tens place is 5. Since this digit is at least 5, we need to add 1 to the digit in the hundreds place. The number 10,759 rounded to the nearest hundred is 10,800.

33. To round 2,486,609 to the nearest hundred-thousand, observe that the digit in the ten-thousands place is 8. Since this digit is at least 5, we need to add 1 to the digit in the hundred-thousands place. The number 2,486,609 rounded to the nearest hundred-thousand is 2,500,000.

37. 29 rounds to   30
35 rounds to   40
42 rounds to   40
$+$ 16 rounds to $+$ 20
130

The estimated sum is 130.

41.

1812	rounds to	1800
1776	rounds to	1800
+ 1945	rounds to	+ 1900
		5500

The estimated sum is 5500.

45.

2995	rounds to	3000
1649	rounds to	1600
+ 3940	rounds to	+ 3900
		8500

The estimated sum is 8500.

49. 432 + 679 + 198 is approximately
400 + 700 + 200 = 1300.
The answer of 1139 is incorrect.

53.

799	rounds to	800
1299	rounds to	1300
+ 999	rounds to	+ 1000
		3100

The total cost is approximately $3100.

57.

20,320	rounds to	20,000
− 14,410	rounds to	− 14,000
		6 000

The difference in elevation is approximately 6000 feet.

61.

41,126,233	rounds to	41,000,000
− 27,174,898	rounds to	− 27,000,000
		14,000,000

Lyndon Johnson won the election by approximately 14,000,000 votes.

65. 3430 million dollars = 3430 × $1,000,000 = $3,430,000,000;
rounded to the nearest hundred-million is $3,400,000,000; rounded to the nearest billion is $3,000,000,000.

69. Any number between 4550 and 4649, when rounded to the nearest hundred, will round to 4600. 4618 is one example.

73. answers may vary

Exercise Set 1.6

1. $4(3 + 9) = 4 \cdot 3 + 4 \cdot 9$

5. $10(11 + 7) = 10 \cdot 11 + 10 \cdot 7$

9.
$$\begin{array}{r} 624 \\ \times\ \ \ 3 \\ \hline 1872 \end{array}$$

13.
$$\begin{array}{r} 1062 \\ \times\ \ \ 5 \\ \hline 5310 \end{array}$$

17.
$$\begin{array}{r} 231 \\ \times\ \ \ 47 \\ \hline 1\ 617 \\ 9\ 240 \\ \hline 10,857 \end{array}$$

21.
$$\begin{array}{r} 620 \\ \times\ \ \ 40 \\ \hline 0 \\ 24\ 800 \\ \hline 24,800 \end{array}$$

25. $(590)(1)(10$ 5900

29.
$$\begin{array}{r} 609 \\ \times\ \ \ 234 \\ \hline 2\ 436 \\ 18\ 270 \\ 121\ 800 \\ \hline 142,506 \end{array}$$

33.
$$\begin{array}{r} 1941 \\ \times\ \ \ 2035 \\ \hline 9\ 705 \\ 58\ 230 \\ 3\ 882\ 000 \\ \hline 3,949,935 \end{array}$$

37. $8 \times 100 = 800$

41. $7406 \cdot 10 = 74,060$

45. $50 \cdot 900 = 45,000$

49.

576	rounds to	600
× 354	rounds to	× 400
		240,000

576 × 354 is approximately 240,000.

53. The best estimate is c, 1600, since 38 × 42 is approximately 40 × 40.

57. Area = length · width
= (9 meters)(7 meters)
= 63 square meters
The area is 63 square meters.

61. $70 \times 11 = 770$

65. $2 \times 2240 = 4480$

69.
$$\begin{array}{r} 54 \\ \times 35 \\ \hline 270 \\ 1620 \\ \hline 1890 \end{array}$$

The total cost of the books for the class is $1890.

73. $90 \times 110 = 9900$
The area is 9900 square feet.

77.
$$\begin{array}{r} 62 \\ \times\ \ 94 \\ \hline 248 \\ 5580 \\ \hline 5828 \end{array}$$

There are 5828 pixels on the screen.

81.
$$\begin{array}{r} 160 \\ \times\ \ 8 \\ \hline 1280 \end{array}$$

There are 1280 calories in 8 ounces of the peanuts.

85.

T-Shirt Size	Number of Shirts Ordered	Cost per Shirt	Cost per Size Ordered
S	3	$10	$30
M	5	$10	$50
L	10	$10	$100
XL	2	$12	$24
XXL	2	$12	$24
		Total Cost:	$228

89.
$$\begin{array}{r} \overset{1}{1}26 \\ +\ \ \ 8 \\ \hline 134 \end{array}$$

93.
$$\begin{array}{r} \overset{1}{1}8 \\ +\ 6 \\ \hline 24 \end{array}$$

97. $3 + 3 + 3 + 3 + 3 = 5 \cdot 3$ or $3 \cdot 5$

101.
$$\begin{array}{r} 203 \\ \times\ 14 \\ \hline 812 \\ 2030 \\ \hline 2842 \end{array}$$

105. answers may vary

Exercise Set 1.7

1.
$$\begin{array}{r} 26 \\ 3{\overline{)\,78}} \\ -6 \\ \hline 18 \\ -18 \\ \hline 0 \end{array}$$
Check: $26 \cdot 3 = 78$

5.
$$\begin{array}{r} 338 \\ 3{\overline{)1014}} \\ -9 \\ \hline 11 \\ -9 \\ \hline 24 \\ -24 \\ \hline 0 \end{array}$$
Check: $338 \cdot 3 = 1014$

9.
$$\begin{array}{r} 8 \\ 6{\overline{)\,48}} \\ -48 \\ \hline 0 \end{array}$$
Check: $8 \cdot 6 = 48$

13.
$$\begin{array}{r} 65 \text{ R } 4 \\ 9{\overline{)\,589}} \\ -54 \\ \hline 49 \\ -45 \\ \hline 4 \end{array}$$
Check: $65 \cdot 9 + 4 = 585 + 4 = 589$

17.
$$\begin{array}{r} 37 \text{ R } 1 \\ 5{\overline{)\,186}} \\ -15 \\ \hline 36 \\ -35 \\ \hline 1 \end{array}$$
Check: $37 \cdot 5 + 1 = 185 + 1 = 186$

21.
$$\begin{array}{r} 49 \\ 23{\overline{)1127}} \\ -92 \\ \hline 207 \\ -207 \\ \hline 0 \end{array}$$
Check: $49 \cdot 23 = 1127$

25.
$$\begin{array}{r} 97 \text{ R } 40 \\ 97{\overline{)\,9449}} \\ -873 \\ \hline 719 \\ -679 \\ \hline 40 \end{array}$$
Check: $97 \cdot 97 + 40 = 9409 + 40 = 9449$

29.
$$\begin{array}{r} 506 \\ 13{\overline{)\,6578}} \\ -65 \\ \hline 07 \\ -0 \\ \hline 78 \\ -78 \\ \hline 0 \end{array}$$
Check: $506 \cdot 13 = 6578$

33.
$$\begin{array}{r} 45 \\ 236{\overline{)10620}} \\ -944 \\ \hline 1180 \\ -1180 \\ \hline 0 \end{array}$$
Check: $45 \cdot 236 = 10{,}620$

37.
$$\begin{array}{r} 202 \text{ R } 15 \\ 102{\overline{)\,20619}} \\ -204 \\ \hline 21 \\ -0 \\ \hline 219 \\ -204 \\ \hline 15 \end{array}$$
Check: $202 \cdot 102 + 15 = 20{,}604 + 15 = 20{,}619$

41.
$$\begin{array}{r} 19 \\ 7{\overline{)133}} \\ -7 \\ \hline 63 \\ -63 \\ \hline 0 \end{array}$$

45.
$$\begin{array}{r} 2082 \text{ R } 26 \\ 30{\overline{)\,62486}} \\ -60 \\ \hline 24 \\ -0 \\ \hline 248 \\ -240 \\ \hline 86 \\ -60 \\ \hline 26 \end{array}$$

49.
$$\begin{array}{r} 21 \text{ R } 1 \\ 4{\overline{)\,85}} \\ -8 \\ \hline 05 \\ -4 \\ \hline 1 \end{array}$$
The quotient of 85 and 4 is 21 R 1.

53.
$$\begin{array}{r} 20 \text{ R } 2 \\ 3{\overline{)\,62}} \\ -6 \\ \hline 02 \\ -0 \\ \hline 2 \end{array}$$
The quotient of 62 and 3 is 20 R 2.

57.

$$
\begin{array}{r}
252000 \\
21\overline{)\,5292000} \\
-42 \\
\hline
109 \\
-105 \\
\hline
42 \\
42 \\
\hline
0
\end{array}
$$

Each person won $252,000.

61. A white stripe and the space after it (one lane divider) takes up 50 feet.

$$
\begin{array}{r}
105 \\
50\overline{)\,5280} \\
-50 \\
\hline
28 \\
-0 \\
\hline
280 \\
250 \\
\hline
30
\end{array}
$$

There are 105 whole lane dividers in 1 mile.

65.

$$
\begin{array}{r}
27 \\
6\overline{)\,162} \\
-12 \\
\hline
42 \\
-42 \\
\hline
0
\end{array}
$$

Priest Homes scored 27 touchdowns in the 2003 season.

69. There are six numbers,

$$
\begin{array}{r}
\overset{2}{1}4 \\
22 \\
45 \\
18 \\
30 \\
+27 \\
\hline
156
\end{array}
\qquad
\begin{array}{r}
26 \\
6\overline{)\,156} \\
-12 \\
\hline
36 \\
-36 \\
\hline
0
\end{array}
$$

The average is 26.

73. There are five numbers.

$$
\begin{array}{r}
\overset{2}{8}6 \\
79 \\
81 \\
69 \\
+80 \\
\hline
395
\end{array}
\qquad
\begin{array}{r}
79 \\
5\overline{)\,395} \\
-35 \\
\hline
45 \\
-45 \\
\hline
0
\end{array}
$$

The average is 79.

77.

$$
\begin{array}{r}
\overset{1\,2}{7}8 \\
236 \\
42 \\
+8506 \\
\hline
8862
\end{array}
$$

81.

$$
\begin{array}{r}
635 \\
-46 \\
\hline
589
\end{array}
$$

85.

$$
\begin{array}{r}
7\ R\ 15 \\
28\overline{)\,211} \\
-196 \\
\hline
15
\end{array}
$$

89. 100 divided by 10 is written as $100 \div 10$, b.

93. The average will increase; answers may vary.

97. answers may vary

Exercise Set 1.8

1.

41	increased by	8	is	some number
↓	↓	↓	↓	↓
41	+	8	=	some number

$$
\begin{array}{r}
41 \\
+8 \\
\hline
49
\end{array}
$$

5.

The total of	35	and	7	is	some number
	↓	↓	↓	↓	↓
	35	+	7	=	some number

$$
\begin{array}{r}
35 \\
+7 \\
\hline
42
\end{array}
$$

9. a.

Perimeter	is	two	times	length	plus	two	times	width
↓	↓	↓	↓	↓	↓	↓	↓	↓
Perimeter	=	2	·	120	+	2	·	80

$$
\begin{aligned}
&= 2 \cdot 120 + 2 \cdot 80 \\
&= 240 + 160 \\
&= 400
\end{aligned}
$$

The perimeter is 400 feet.

b.

Area	is	length	times	width
↓	↓	↓	↓	↓
Area	=	120	×	80

$$
\begin{array}{r}
120 \\
\times\ 80 \\
\hline
9600
\end{array}
$$

The area is 9600 square feet.

13.

Hours per week	is	hours per day	times	day per week
↓	↓	↓	↓	↓
Hours per week	=	24	×	7

$$
\begin{array}{r}
24 \\
\times\ 7 \\
\hline
168
\end{array}
$$

There are 168 hours in a week.

17.

Difference in years	is	Governors Island National Monument	minus	Yellowstone National Park
↓	↓	↓	↓	↓
Difference	=	2001	−	1872

$$
\begin{array}{r}
2001 \\
-1872 \\
\hline
129
\end{array}
$$

Yellowstone is 129 years older than Governors Island.

21.

Total	is	number of Fairview	plus	number of Midway	plus	number of Riverside
↓	↓	↓	↓	↓	↓	↓
Total	=	287	+	252	+	180

$$
= 287 + 252 + 180 = 719
$$

There are a total of 719 towns named Fairview, Midway, or Riverside.

25.

Calories in 1 ounce	is	calories	per	ounces
↓	↓	↓	↓	↓

Calories in 1 ounce $= 165 \div 3$

$$
\begin{array}{r}
55 \\
3\overline{)\ 165} \\
-15 \\
\hline
15 \\
-15 \\
\hline
0
\end{array}
$$

There are 55 calories in 1 ounce of canned tuna.

29.

Average	is	total sales	divided by	number of stores
↓	↓	↓	↓	↓

Average $= 2{,}446{,}000{,}050 \div 73$

$$
\begin{array}{r}
33506850 \\
73\overline{)\ 2446000050} \\
-219 \\
\hline
256 \\
-219 \\
\hline
370 \\
-365 \\
\hline
500 \\
-438 \\
\hline
620 \\
-584 \\
\hline
365 \\
-365 \\
\hline
00
\end{array}
$$

The average sales by each store is \$33,506,850.

33.

Northern length	is	Southern length	plus	2054
↓	↓	↓	↓	↓

Length $= 1933 + 2054$
$= 1933 + 2054 = 3987$

The northern boundary of the conterminous United States is 3987 miles long.

37.

Total cost	is	number of sweaters	times	cost of sweater	plus	number of shirts	times	cost of shirt
↓	↓	↓	↓	↓	↓	↓	↓	↓
Total	=	3	·	38	+	5	·	25

$= 3 \cdot 38 + 5 \cdot 25 = 114 + 125 = 239$

The total cost is \$239.

41. Option a: a hamburger, onion rings, a candy bar, and a soda cost
\$4 + \$3 + \$2 + \$1 = \$10.

Option b: a hot dog, an apple, french fries, and a soda cost
\$3 + \$1 + \$2 + \$1 = \$7

Thus option b is cheaper by \$10 − \$7 or \$3.

45. The most patents received was 3415, the fewest received was 1302.

$$
\begin{array}{r}
3415 \\
-1302 \\
\hline
2113
\end{array}
$$

The company with the most patents received 2113 more than the company with the fewest patents.

49. The three largest numbers of patents received are 3415, 1992, and 1893.

$(3415 + 1992 + 1893) \div 3 = 7300 \div 3 = 2433$ R 1. The whole number average is 2433 patents.

53. There are 7 days in a week.

$7 \cdot 2400 = 16{,}800$

No more than 16,800 milligrams of sodium should be consumed in one week.

57. 48,551,700,000 rounded to the nearest hundred-million is 48,600,000,000.

$48{,}600{,}000{,}000 \div 202{,}500{,}000 = 240$

The average value of each money order was \$240.

Exercise Set 1.9

1. $3 \cdot 3 \cdot 3 \cdot 3 = 3^4$

5. $12 \cdot 12 \cdot 12 = 12^3$

9. $9 \cdot 9 \cdot 9 \cdot 8 = 9^3 \cdot 8$

13. $3 \cdot 2 \cdot 2 \cdot 5 \cdot 5 \cdot 5 = 3 \cdot 2^2 \cdot 5^3$

17. $5^3 = 5 \cdot 5 \cdot 5 = 125$

21. $1^{10} = 1 \cdot 1 \cdot 1 \cdot 1 \cdot 1 \cdot 1 \cdot 1 \cdot 1 \cdot 1 \cdot 1 = 1$

25. $3^5 = 3 \cdot 3 \cdot 3 \cdot 3 \cdot 3 = 243$

29. $4^3 = 4 \cdot 4 \cdot 4 = 64$

33. $9^3 = 9 \cdot 9 \cdot 9 = 729$

37. $20^1 = 20$

41. $3 \cdot 2^4 = 3 \cdot 2 \cdot 2 \cdot 2 \cdot 2 = 48$

45. $\sqrt{9} = 3$ since $3 \cdot 3 = 9$.

49. $\sqrt{144} = 12$ since $12 \cdot 12 = 144$.

53. $15 + 3 \cdot 2 = 15 + 6 = 21$

57. $28 \div 4 - 3 = 7 - 3 = 4$

61. $6 \cdot 5 + 8 \cdot 2 = 30 + 8 \cdot 2 = 30 + 16 = 46$

65. $(3 + 5^2) \div 2 \cdot 3^2 = (3 + 25) \div 2 \cdot 3^2$
$= 28 \div 2 \cdot 3^2$
$= 28 \div 2 \cdot 9$
$= 14 \cdot 9$
$= 126$

69. $\dfrac{18 + 6}{2^4 - 2^2} = \dfrac{24}{16 - 4} = \dfrac{24}{12} = 2$

73. $\dfrac{7(9 - 6) + 3}{3^2 - 3} = \dfrac{7(3) + 3}{9 - 3} = \dfrac{21 + 3}{6} = \dfrac{24}{6} = 4$

77. $2^3 \cdot 4 - (10 \div 5) = 2^3 \cdot 4 - 2$
$= 8 \cdot 4 - 2$
$= 32 - 2$
$= 30$

81. $(7 \cdot 5) + [9 \div (3 \div 3)] = (7 \cdot 5) + [9 \div 1]$
$= 35 + [9 \div 1]$
$= 35 + 9$
$= 44$

85. $\dfrac{9^2 + 2^2 - 1^2}{8 \div 2 \cdot 3 \cdot 1 \div 3} = \dfrac{81 + 4 - 1}{4 \cdot 3 \cdot 1 \div 3}$
$= \dfrac{85 - 1}{12 \cdot 1 \div 3}$
$= \dfrac{84}{12 \div 3}$
$= \dfrac{84}{4}$
$= 21$

89. $4 \cdot \sqrt{49} - 0 \div \sqrt{100} = 4 \cdot 7 - 0 \div 10$
$= 28 - 0 \div 10$
$= 28 - 0$
$= 28$

93. $\sqrt{81} \div \sqrt{9} + 4^2 \cdot 2 - 10 = 9 \div 3 + 16 \cdot 2 - 10$
$= 3 + 16 \cdot 2 - 10$
$= 3 + 32 - 10$
$= 35 - 10$
$= 25$

97. $7^2 - \left\{18 - \left[40 \div (4 \cdot 2) + \sqrt{4}\right] + 5^2\right\}$
$= 7^2 - \left\{18 - \left[40 \div 8 + \sqrt{4}\right] + 5^2\right\}$
$= 7^2 - \left\{18 - [40 \div 8 + 2] + 5^2\right\}$
$= 7^2 - \left\{18 - [5 + 2] + 5^2\right\}$
$= 7^2 - \left\{18 - 7 + 5^2\right\}$
$= 7^2 - \left\{18 - 7 + 25\right\}$
$= 7^2 - \left\{11 + 25\right\}$
$= 7^2 - 36$
$= 49 - 36$
$= 13$

101. Area $= (\text{side})^2$
$= (8 \text{ centimeters})^2$
$= 64 \text{ square centimeters}$

105. False; 2^5 is $2 \cdot 2 \cdot 2 \cdot 2 \cdot 2 = 32$ while $5 \cdot 5 = 25$.

109. $24 \div (3 \cdot 2) + 2 \cdot 5 = 24 \div 6 + 2 \cdot 5$
$= 4 + 2 \cdot 5$
$= 4 + 10$
$= 14$

113. $(7 + 2^4)^5 - (3^5 - 2^4)^2 = (7 + 16)^5 - (243 - 16)^2$
$= 23^5 - 227^2$
$= 6{,}436{,}343 - 51{,}529$
$= 6{,}384{,}814$

Chapter 1 Test

1. 82,426 is written as eighty-two thousand, four hundred twenty-six.

5.
$$\begin{array}{r} 496 \\ \times\ \ 30 \\ \hline 0 \\ 14\ 880 \\ \hline 14{,}880 \end{array}$$

9. $0 \div 49 = 0$

13.
$$\frac{64 \div 8 \cdot 2}{\left(\sqrt{9} - \sqrt{4}\right)^2 + 1} = \frac{8 \cdot 2}{(3 - 2)^2 + 1}$$
$$= \frac{16}{1^2 + 1}$$
$$= \frac{16}{1 + 1}$$
$$= \frac{16}{2}$$
$$= 8$$

17. To round 52,369 to the nearest thousand, observe that the digit in the hundreds place is 3. Since this digit is less than 5, we do not add 1 to the digit in the thousands place. The number 52,369 rounded to the nearest thousand is 52,000.

21.
$$\begin{array}{r} \overset{1}{15} \\ +\ 107 \\ \hline 122 \end{array}$$
The sum of 15 and 107 is 122.

25.
$$\begin{array}{r} 725 \\ -\ 599 \\ \hline 126 \end{array}$$
The more expensive refrigerator costs $126 more than the less expensive one.

29. Perimeter $= 2(\text{length}) + 2(\text{width})$
$= 2(20 \text{ yards}) + 2(10 \text{ yards})$
$= 40 \text{ yards} + 20 \text{ yards}$
$= 60 \text{ yards}$
The perimeter is 60 yards.
Area $= (\text{length}) \cdot (\text{width})$
$= (20 \text{ yards}) \cdot (10 \text{ yards})$
$= 200 \text{ square yards}$
The area is 200 square yards.

CHAPTER 2

Exercise Set 2.1

1. $\dfrac{21}{21} = 1$

5. $\dfrac{13}{1} = 13$

9. $\dfrac{10}{0}$ is undefined.

13. 5 of the 6 equal parts are shaded: $\dfrac{5}{6}$

17. 3 of the 7 equal parts are shaded: $\dfrac{3}{7}$

21. 1 of the 6 equal parts is shaded: $\dfrac{1}{6}$

25.

29.

33. freshmen $\rightarrow \overline{42}$
students $\rightarrow 131$
$\dfrac{42}{131}$ of the students are freshmen.

37. born in Virginia $\rightarrow \overline{8}$
U.S. presidents $\rightarrow 43$
$\dfrac{8}{43}$ of U.S. presidents were born in Virginia.

41. 11 of the 31 days of March is $\dfrac{11}{31}$ of the month.

45. There are 50 states total. 33 states contain federal Indian reservations.
a. $\dfrac{33}{50}$ of the states contain Indian reservations.
b. $50 - 33 = 17$
17 states do not contain Indian reservations.
c. $\dfrac{17}{50}$ of the states do not contain Indian reservations.

49. Each part is $\dfrac{1}{4}$ of a whole and there are 11 parts shaded, or 2 wholes and 3 more parts.
a. $\dfrac{11}{4}$ **b.** $2\dfrac{3}{4}$

53. Each part is $\dfrac{1}{3}$ of a whole and there are 4 parts shaded, or 1 whole and 1 more part.
a. $\dfrac{4}{3}$ **b.** $1\dfrac{1}{3}$

57. $2\dfrac{1}{3} = \dfrac{3 \cdot 2 + 1}{3} = \dfrac{7}{3}$

61. $6\dfrac{5}{8} = \dfrac{8 \cdot 6 + 5}{8} = \dfrac{53}{8}$

65. $11\dfrac{6}{7} = \dfrac{7 \cdot 11 + 6}{7} = \dfrac{83}{7}$

69. $4\dfrac{13}{24} = \dfrac{24 \cdot 4 + 13}{24} = \dfrac{109}{24}$

73. $9\dfrac{7}{20} = \dfrac{20 \cdot 9 + 7}{20} = \dfrac{187}{20}$

77. $166\dfrac{2}{3} = \dfrac{3 \cdot 166 + 2}{3} = \dfrac{500}{3}$

81.
$$\begin{array}{r} 4\ \text{R}\ 5 \\ 8)\overline{37} \\ 32 \\ \hline 5 \end{array}$$
$$\dfrac{37}{8} = 4\dfrac{5}{8}$$

85.
$$\begin{array}{r} 2\ \text{R}\ 4 \\ 21)\overline{46} \\ 42 \\ \hline 4 \end{array}$$
$$\dfrac{46}{21} = 2\dfrac{4}{21}$$

89.
$$15\overline{)225}$$
$$\underline{15}$$
$$75$$
$$\underline{75}$$
$$0$$

$$\frac{225}{15} = 15$$

93.
$$23\overline{)247} \quad \text{10 R 17}$$
$$\underline{23}$$
$$17$$
$$\underline{0}$$
$$17$$

$$\frac{247}{23} = 10\frac{17}{23}$$

97.
$$175\overline{)182} \quad \text{1 R 7}$$
$$\underline{175}$$
$$7$$

$$\frac{182}{175} = 1\frac{7}{175}$$

101. $3^2 = 3 \cdot 3 = 9$

105. $7 \cdot 7 \cdot 7 \cdot 7 \cdot 7 = 7^5$

109. answers may vary

113.

117. $1651 + 634 = 2285$

There are a total of 2285 affiliates, of which 1651 are in the United States. $\frac{1651}{2285}$ of the affiliates are in the United States.

Exercise Set 2.2

1. $1 \cdot 8 = 8$
$2 \cdot 4 = 8$
The factors of 8 are 1, 2, 4, and 8.

5. $1 \cdot 4 = 4$
$2 \cdot 2 = 4$
The factors of 4 are 1, 2, and 4.

9. $1 \cdot 29 = 29$
The factors of 29 are 1 and 29.

13. $1 \cdot 12 = 12$
$2 \cdot 6 = 12$
$3 \cdot 4 = 12$
The factors of 12 are 1, 2, 3, 4, 6, and 12.

17. Prime, since its only factors are 1 and 7.

21. Prime, since its only factors are 1 and 23.

25. Prime, since its only factors are 1 and 67.

29. Prime, since its only factors are 1 and 31.

33. Composite, since its factors are 1, 7, 17, and 119.

37.
$$3\overline{)15} \quad 5$$
$$15 = 3 \cdot 5$$

41.
$$3\overline{)9} \quad 3$$
$$2\overline{)18}$$
$$2\overline{)36}$$
$$36 = 2^2 \cdot 3^2$$

45.
$$3\overline{)15} \quad 5$$
$$2\overline{)30}$$
$$2\overline{)60}$$
$$60 = 2^2 \cdot 3 \cdot 5$$

49.
$$5\overline{)85} \quad 17$$
$$85 = 5 \cdot 17$$

53.
$$7\overline{)77} \quad 11$$
$$2\overline{)154}$$
$$154 = 2 \cdot 7 \cdot 11$$

57.
$$3\overline{)15} \quad 5$$
$$2\overline{)30}$$
$$2\overline{)60}$$
$$2\overline{)120}$$
$$2\overline{)240}$$
$$240 = 2^4 \cdot 3 \cdot 5$$

61.
$$7\overline{)49} \quad 7$$
$$3\overline{)147}$$
$$3\overline{)441}$$
$$2\overline{)882}$$
$$882 = 2 \cdot 3^2 \cdot 7^2$$

65.
$$3\overline{)33} \quad 11$$
$$33 = 3 \cdot 11$$

69. 67 is prime, since its only factors are 1 and 67.

73. 97 is prime, since its only factors are 1 and 97.

77. To round 4267 to the nearest hundred, observe that the digit in the tens place is 6. Since this digit is at least 5, we need to add 1 to the digit in the hundreds place. The number 4267 rounded to the nearest hundred is 4300.

81. To round 10,292,876 to the nearest million, observe that the digit in the hundred-thousands place is 2. Since this digit is less than 5, we do not add 1 to the digit in the millions place. The number 10,292,876 rounded to the nearest million is 10,000,000.

85.
$$5\overline{)35} \quad 7$$
$$3\overline{)105}$$
$$3\overline{)315}$$
$$3\overline{)945}$$
$$3\overline{)2835}$$
$$3\overline{)8505}$$
$$2\overline{)17,010}$$
$$2\overline{)34,020}$$
$$34,020 = 2^2 \cdot 3^5 \cdot 5 \cdot 7$$

89. answers may vary

Exercise Set 2.3

1. $\dfrac{3}{12} = \dfrac{3}{3 \cdot 4} = \dfrac{1 \cdot 3}{4 \cdot 3} = \dfrac{1}{4}$

5. $\dfrac{14}{16} = \dfrac{2 \cdot 7}{2 \cdot 8} = \dfrac{7}{8}$

9. $\dfrac{35}{50} = \dfrac{5 \cdot 7}{5 \cdot 10} = \dfrac{7}{10}$

13. $\dfrac{24}{40} = \dfrac{8 \cdot 3}{8 \cdot 5} = \dfrac{3}{5}$

17. $\dfrac{25}{40} = \dfrac{5 \cdot 5}{5 \cdot 8} = \dfrac{5}{8}$

21. $\dfrac{56}{68} = \dfrac{4 \cdot 14}{4 \cdot 17} = \dfrac{14}{17}$

25. $\dfrac{90}{120} = \dfrac{30 \cdot 3}{30 \cdot 4} = \dfrac{3}{4}$

29. $\dfrac{66}{308} = \dfrac{22 \cdot 3}{22 \cdot 14} = \dfrac{3}{14}$

33. $\dfrac{75}{350} = \dfrac{25 \cdot 3}{25 \cdot 14} = \dfrac{3}{14}$

37. $\dfrac{288}{480} = \dfrac{96 \cdot 3}{96 \cdot 5} = \dfrac{3}{5}$

41. Equivalent, since the cross products are equal: $6 \cdot 4 = 24$ and $8 \cdot 3 = 24$

45. Equivalent, since the cross products are equal: $15 \cdot 6 = 90$ and $9 \cdot 10 = 90$

49. Not equivalent, since the cross products are not equal: $13 \cdot 12 = 156$ and $15 \cdot 10 = 150$

53. $\dfrac{2 \text{ hours}}{8 \text{ hours}} = \dfrac{2 \cdot 1}{2 \cdot 4} = \dfrac{1}{4}$

2 hours represents $\dfrac{1}{4}$ of a work shift.

57. a. $\dfrac{15 \text{ states}}{50 \text{ states}} = \dfrac{5 \cdot 3}{5 \cdot 10} = \dfrac{3}{10}$

$\dfrac{3}{10}$ of the states can claim at least one Ritz-Carlton hotel.

b. $50 - 15 = 35$

35 states do not have a Ritz-Carlton hotel.

c. $\dfrac{35}{50} = \dfrac{5 \cdot 7}{5 \cdot 10} = \dfrac{7}{10}$

$\dfrac{7}{10}$ of the states do not have a Ritz-Carlton hotel.

61. a. $50 - 28 = 22$

22 states do not have this type of Web site.

b. $\dfrac{22 \text{ states}}{50 \text{ states}} = \dfrac{2 \cdot 11}{2 \cdot 25} = \dfrac{11}{25}$

$\dfrac{11}{25}$ of the states do not have this type of Web site.

65. $\begin{array}{r} 387 \\ \times\ \ \ 6 \\ \hline 2322 \end{array}$

69. answers may vary

73. $\dfrac{36 \text{ donors}}{100 \text{ donors}} = \dfrac{4 \cdot 9}{4 \cdot 25} = \dfrac{9}{25}$

$\dfrac{9}{25}$ of blood donors have blood type A/Rh-positive.

77. $7 + 6 + 1 + 1 = 15$

$\dfrac{15 \text{ donors}}{100 \text{ donors}} = \dfrac{5 \cdot 3}{5 \cdot 20} = \dfrac{3}{20}$

$\dfrac{3}{20}$ of blood donors have the negative Rh-factor.

81. answers may vary

Exercise Set 2.4

1. $\dfrac{1}{3} \cdot \dfrac{2}{5} = \dfrac{1 \cdot 2}{3 \cdot 5} = \dfrac{2}{15}$

5. $\dfrac{3}{10} \cdot \dfrac{3}{8} = \dfrac{3 \cdot 3}{10 \cdot 8} = \dfrac{9}{80}$

9. $\dfrac{16}{5} \cdot \dfrac{3}{4} = \dfrac{16 \cdot 3}{5 \cdot 4} = \dfrac{4 \cdot 4 \cdot 3}{5 \cdot 4} = \dfrac{3 \cdot 4}{5} = \dfrac{12}{5}$ or $2\dfrac{2}{5}$

13. $0 \cdot \dfrac{8}{9} = 0$

17. $\dfrac{18}{20} \cdot \dfrac{36}{99} = \dfrac{18 \cdot 36}{20 \cdot 99} = \dfrac{9 \cdot 2 \cdot 4 \cdot 9}{4 \cdot 5 \cdot 9 \cdot 11} = \dfrac{2 \cdot 9}{5 \cdot 11} = \dfrac{18}{55}$

21. $\dfrac{11}{20} \cdot \dfrac{1}{7} \cdot \dfrac{5}{22} = \dfrac{11 \cdot 1 \cdot 5}{20 \cdot 7 \cdot 22}$

$= \dfrac{11 \cdot 1 \cdot 5}{5 \cdot 4 \cdot 7 \cdot 11 \cdot 2}$

$= \dfrac{1}{4 \cdot 7 \cdot 2}$

$= \dfrac{1}{56}$

25. $\dfrac{9}{20} \cdot 0 \cdot \dfrac{4}{19} = 0$

29. $12 \cdot \dfrac{1}{4} = \dfrac{12}{1} \cdot \dfrac{1}{4} = \dfrac{12 \cdot 1}{1 \cdot 4} = \dfrac{4 \cdot 3 \cdot 1}{1 \cdot 4} = \dfrac{3}{1} = 3$

33. $1\dfrac{1}{4} \cdot \dfrac{4}{25} = \dfrac{5}{4} \cdot \dfrac{4}{25} = \dfrac{5 \cdot 4}{4 \cdot 25} = \dfrac{5 \cdot 4}{4 \cdot 5 \cdot 5} = \dfrac{1}{5}$

37. $\dfrac{2}{3} \cdot 1 = \dfrac{2}{3}$

41. Exact: $3\dfrac{4}{5} \cdot 6\dfrac{2}{7} = \dfrac{19}{5} \cdot \dfrac{44}{7} = \dfrac{19 \cdot 44}{5 \cdot 7} = \dfrac{836}{35}$ or $23\dfrac{31}{35}$

Estimate: $3\dfrac{4}{5}$ rounds to 4, $6\dfrac{2}{7}$ rounds to 6.

$4 \cdot 6 = 24$, so the answer is reasonable.

45. $1\dfrac{1}{5} \cdot 12\dfrac{1}{2} = \dfrac{6}{5} \cdot \dfrac{25}{2} = \dfrac{6 \cdot 25}{5 \cdot 2} = \dfrac{2 \cdot 3 \cdot 5 \cdot 5}{5 \cdot 2} = \dfrac{3 \cdot 5}{1} = 15$

49. $\dfrac{3}{10} \cdot 15 \cdot 2\dfrac{1}{2} = \dfrac{3}{10} \cdot \dfrac{15}{1} \cdot \dfrac{5}{2}$

$= \dfrac{3 \cdot 15 \cdot 5}{10 \cdot 1 \cdot 2}$

$= \dfrac{3 \cdot 15 \cdot 5}{5 \cdot 2 \cdot 1 \cdot 2}$

$= \dfrac{3 \cdot 15}{2 \cdot 2}$

$= \dfrac{45}{4}$ or $11\dfrac{1}{4}$

53. $\dfrac{1}{4} \cdot \dfrac{2}{15} = \dfrac{1 \cdot 2}{4 \cdot 15} = \dfrac{1 \cdot 2}{2 \cdot 2 \cdot 15} = \dfrac{1}{2 \cdot 15} = \dfrac{1}{30}$

57. $2\dfrac{4}{5} \cdot 1\dfrac{1}{7} = \dfrac{14}{5} \cdot \dfrac{8}{7}$

$= \dfrac{14 \cdot 8}{5 \cdot 7}$

$= \dfrac{2 \cdot 7 \cdot 8}{5 \cdot 7} = \dfrac{2 \cdot 8}{5}$

$= \dfrac{16}{5}$ or $3\dfrac{1}{5}$

61. $\dfrac{6}{15} \cdot \dfrac{5}{16} = \dfrac{6 \cdot 5}{15 \cdot 16} = \dfrac{2 \cdot 3 \cdot 5}{3 \cdot 5 \cdot 2 \cdot 8} = \dfrac{1}{8}$

65. $20 \cdot \dfrac{11}{12} = \dfrac{20}{1} \cdot \dfrac{11}{12}$

$= \dfrac{20 \cdot 11}{1 \cdot 12}$

$= \dfrac{4 \cdot 5 \cdot 11}{1 \cdot 4 \cdot 3}$

$= \dfrac{5 \cdot 11}{3}$

$= \dfrac{55}{3}$ or $18\dfrac{1}{3}$

69. $12\dfrac{4}{5} \cdot 6\dfrac{7}{8} \cdot \dfrac{26}{77} = \dfrac{64}{5} \cdot \dfrac{55}{8} \cdot \dfrac{26}{77}$

$= \dfrac{64 \cdot 55 \cdot 26}{5 \cdot 8 \cdot 77}$

$= \dfrac{8 \cdot 8 \cdot 5 \cdot 11 \cdot 26}{5 \cdot 8 \cdot 11 \cdot 7}$

$= \dfrac{8 \cdot 26}{7}$

$= \dfrac{208}{7}$ or $29\dfrac{5}{7}$

73. $\dfrac{5}{6} \cdot 24 = \dfrac{5}{6} \cdot \dfrac{24}{1} = \dfrac{5 \cdot 24}{6 \cdot 1} = \dfrac{5 \cdot 6 \cdot 4}{6 \cdot 1} = \dfrac{5 \cdot 4}{1} = 20$

$\dfrac{5}{6}$ of 24 is 20.

77. $\dfrac{2}{5} \cdot 2170 = \dfrac{2}{5} \cdot \dfrac{2170}{1}$

$= \dfrac{2 \cdot 2170}{5 \cdot 1}$

$= \dfrac{2 \cdot 5 \cdot 434}{5 \cdot 1}$

$= \dfrac{2 \cdot 434}{1}$

$= 868$

He has hiked 868 miles.

81. $\dfrac{1}{2} \cdot \dfrac{3}{8} = \dfrac{1 \cdot 3}{2 \cdot 8} = \dfrac{3}{16}$

The radius is $\dfrac{3}{16}$ inch.

85. $\dfrac{2}{3} \cdot 2757 = \dfrac{2}{3} \cdot \dfrac{2757}{1}$

$= \dfrac{2 \cdot 2757}{3 \cdot 1}$

$= \dfrac{2 \cdot 3 \cdot 919}{3 \cdot 1}$

$= \dfrac{2 \cdot 919}{1}$

$= 1838$

The sale price of the cruise is $1838.

89. $2\dfrac{9}{25} \cdot 1\dfrac{13}{25} = \dfrac{59}{25} \cdot \dfrac{38}{25} = \dfrac{59 \cdot 38}{25 \cdot 25} = \dfrac{2242}{625}$ or $3\dfrac{367}{625}$

The area of the face of the camera is $\dfrac{2242}{625}$ or $3\dfrac{367}{625}$ square inches.

93. $1\dfrac{3}{4} \cdot 2 = \dfrac{7}{4} \cdot \dfrac{2}{1} = \dfrac{7 \cdot 2}{4 \cdot 1} = \dfrac{7 \cdot 2}{2 \cdot 2 \cdot 1} = \dfrac{7}{2}$

The area is $\dfrac{7}{2}$ or $3\dfrac{1}{2}$ square yards.

97. $\dfrac{1}{5} \cdot 12{,}000 = \dfrac{1}{5} \cdot \dfrac{12{,}000}{1}$

$= \dfrac{1 \cdot 12{,}000}{5 \cdot 1}$

$= \dfrac{1 \cdot 5 \cdot 2400}{5 \cdot 1}$

$= 2400$

The family drove 2400 miles on family business.

101. $23\overline{)1300}$ 56 R 12

$\underline{115}$
150
$\underline{138}$
12

105. Incorrect

$3\dfrac{2}{3} \cdot 1\dfrac{1}{7} = \dfrac{11}{3} \cdot \dfrac{8}{7} = \dfrac{11 \cdot 8}{3 \cdot 7} = \dfrac{88}{21}$ or $4\dfrac{4}{21}$

109. $7\dfrac{1}{4}$ rounds to 7

$4\dfrac{1}{5}$ rounds to 4

$7 \cdot 4 = 28$

The best estimate is d.

Exercise Set 2.5

1. The reciprocal of $\dfrac{4}{7}$ is $\dfrac{7}{4}$.

5. The reciprocal of $15 = \dfrac{15}{1}$ is $\dfrac{1}{15}$.

9. $\dfrac{2}{3} \div \dfrac{5}{6} = \dfrac{2}{3} \cdot \dfrac{6}{5} = \dfrac{2 \cdot 6}{3 \cdot 5} = \dfrac{2 \cdot 3 \cdot 2}{3 \cdot 5} = \dfrac{2 \cdot 2}{5} = \dfrac{4}{5}$

13. $\dfrac{3}{7} \div \dfrac{5}{6} = \dfrac{3}{7} \cdot \dfrac{6}{5} = \dfrac{3 \cdot 6}{7 \cdot 5} = \dfrac{18}{35}$

17. $\dfrac{1}{10} \div \dfrac{10}{1} = \dfrac{1}{10} \cdot \dfrac{1}{10} = \dfrac{1 \cdot 1}{10 \cdot 10} = \dfrac{1}{100}$

21. $\dfrac{5}{8} \div \dfrac{3}{8} = \dfrac{5}{8} \cdot \dfrac{8}{3} = \dfrac{5 \cdot 8}{8 \cdot 3} = \dfrac{5}{3}$ or $1\dfrac{2}{3}$

25. $\dfrac{2}{37} \div \dfrac{1}{7} = \dfrac{2}{37} \cdot \dfrac{7}{1} = \dfrac{2 \cdot 7}{37 \cdot 1} = \dfrac{14}{37}$

29. $\dfrac{11}{12} \div \dfrac{11}{12} = \dfrac{11}{12} \cdot \dfrac{12}{11} = \dfrac{11 \cdot 12}{12 \cdot 11} = 1$

33. $0 \div \dfrac{7}{8} = 0 \cdot \dfrac{8}{7} = 0$

37. $\dfrac{2}{3} \div 4 = \dfrac{2}{3} \div \dfrac{4}{1} = \dfrac{2}{3} \cdot \dfrac{1}{4} = \dfrac{2 \cdot 1}{3 \cdot 4} = \dfrac{2 \cdot 1}{3 \cdot 2 \cdot 2} = \dfrac{1}{3 \cdot 2} = \dfrac{1}{6}$

41. $2\dfrac{1}{2} \div \dfrac{1}{2} = \dfrac{5}{2} \div \dfrac{1}{2} = \dfrac{5}{2} \cdot \dfrac{2}{1} = \dfrac{5 \cdot 2}{2 \cdot 1} = \dfrac{5}{1} = 5$

45. $3\dfrac{3}{7} \div 3\dfrac{1}{3} = \dfrac{24}{7} \div \dfrac{10}{3}$

$= \dfrac{24}{7} \cdot \dfrac{3}{10}$

$= \dfrac{24 \cdot 3}{7 \cdot 10}$

$= \dfrac{2 \cdot 12 \cdot 3}{7 \cdot 2 \cdot 5}$

$= \dfrac{12 \cdot 3}{7 \cdot 5}$

$= \dfrac{36}{35}$ or $1\dfrac{1}{35}$

49. $0 \div 15\dfrac{4}{7} = 0 \div \dfrac{109}{7} = 0 \cdot \dfrac{7}{109} = 0$

53. $1 \div \dfrac{18}{35} = 1 \cdot \dfrac{35}{18} = \dfrac{35}{18}$ or $1\dfrac{17}{18}$

57. $\dfrac{6}{15} \div \dfrac{12}{5} = \dfrac{6}{15} \cdot \dfrac{5}{12} = \dfrac{6 \cdot 5}{15 \cdot 12} = \dfrac{6 \cdot 5}{5 \cdot 3 \cdot 6 \cdot 2} = \dfrac{1}{3 \cdot 2} = \dfrac{1}{6}$

61. $12 \div \dfrac{1}{8} = 12 \cdot \dfrac{8}{1} = 12 \cdot 8 = 96$

65. $2\dfrac{3}{8} \div 0$ is undefined.

69. $4\dfrac{5}{11} \div 1\dfrac{2}{5} = \dfrac{49}{11} \div \dfrac{7}{5}$

$= \dfrac{49}{11} \cdot \dfrac{5}{7}$

$= \dfrac{49 \cdot 5}{11 \cdot 7}$

$= \dfrac{7 \cdot 7 \cdot 5}{11 \cdot 7}$

$= \dfrac{7 \cdot 5}{11}$

$= \dfrac{35}{11}$ or $3\dfrac{2}{11}$

73. $3\dfrac{1}{3} \div 4 = \dfrac{10}{3} \div \dfrac{4}{1}$

$= \dfrac{10}{3} \cdot \dfrac{1}{4}$

$= \dfrac{10 \cdot 1}{3 \cdot 4}$

$= \dfrac{2 \cdot 5 \cdot 1}{3 \cdot 2 \cdot 2}$

$= \dfrac{5 \cdot 1}{3 \cdot 2}$

$= \dfrac{5}{6}$

Each dose should be $\dfrac{5}{6}$ tablespoon.

77. $15\dfrac{1}{5} \div 24 = \dfrac{76}{5} \div \dfrac{24}{1}$

$= \dfrac{76}{5} \cdot \dfrac{1}{24}$

$= \dfrac{76 \cdot 1}{5 \cdot 24}$

$= \dfrac{4 \cdot 19 \cdot 1}{5 \cdot 4 \cdot 6}$

$= \dfrac{19 \cdot 1}{5 \cdot 6}$

$= \dfrac{19}{30}$

On average, $\dfrac{19}{30}$ inch of rain fell per hour.

81. $12 \div 2\dfrac{4}{7} = \dfrac{12}{1} \div \dfrac{18}{7}$

$= \dfrac{12}{1} \cdot \dfrac{7}{18}$

$= \dfrac{12 \cdot 7}{1 \cdot 18}$

$= \dfrac{6 \cdot 2 \cdot 7}{1 \cdot 6 \cdot 3}$

$= \dfrac{2 \cdot 7}{1 \cdot 3}$

$= \dfrac{14}{3}$ or $4\dfrac{2}{3}$

The length of the rectangle is $4\dfrac{2}{3}$ meters.

85. $2\dfrac{2}{3} \div 1\dfrac{1}{16} = \dfrac{8}{3} \div \dfrac{17}{16} = \dfrac{8}{3} \cdot \dfrac{16}{17} = \dfrac{8 \cdot 16}{3 \cdot 17} = \dfrac{128}{51}$ or $2\dfrac{26}{51}$.

89. $\dfrac{11}{20} \div \dfrac{20}{11} = \dfrac{11}{20} \cdot \dfrac{11}{20} = \dfrac{11 \cdot 11}{20 \cdot 20} = \dfrac{121}{400}$

93. $\begin{array}{r} 968 \\ -772 \\ \hline 196 \end{array}$

97. The work is incorrect. To divide mixed numbers, first write each mixed number as an improper fraction.

$20\dfrac{2}{3} \div 10\dfrac{1}{2} = \dfrac{62}{3} \div \dfrac{21}{2} = \dfrac{62}{3} \cdot \dfrac{2}{21} = \dfrac{62 \cdot 2}{3 \cdot 21} = \dfrac{124}{63}$

101. $12\dfrac{2}{13}$ rounds to 12.

$3\dfrac{7}{8}$ rounds to 4.

$12 \div 4 = 3$

The best estimate is d.

105. $258 \div \dfrac{129}{320} = \dfrac{258}{1} \cdot \dfrac{320}{129}$

$= \dfrac{258 \cdot 320}{1 \cdot 129}$

$= \dfrac{129 \cdot 2 \cdot 320}{1 \cdot 129}$

$= \dfrac{2 \cdot 320}{1}$

$= 640$

The FedEx Express air fleet is 640 planes.

Chapter 2 Test

1. 7 of the 16 equal parts are shaded: $\dfrac{7}{16}$

5. $\begin{array}{r} 4\ \text{R}\ 3 \\ 5\overline{)23} \\ \underline{20} \\ 3 \end{array}$

$\dfrac{23}{5} = 4\dfrac{3}{5}$

9. Not equivalent, since the cross products are not equal: $7 \cdot 8 = 56$ and $11 \cdot 5 = 55$

13. $\dfrac{4}{4} \div \dfrac{3}{4} = \dfrac{4}{4} \cdot \dfrac{4}{3} = \dfrac{4 \cdot 4}{4 \cdot 3} = \dfrac{4}{3}$ or $1\dfrac{1}{3}$

17. $8 \div \dfrac{1}{2} = \dfrac{8}{1} \cdot \dfrac{2}{1} = \dfrac{8 \cdot 2}{1 \cdot 1} = 16$

21. $\dfrac{16}{3} \div \dfrac{3}{12} = \dfrac{16}{3} \cdot \dfrac{12}{3}$

$= \dfrac{16 \cdot 12}{3 \cdot 3}$

$= \dfrac{16 \cdot 3 \cdot 4}{3 \cdot 3}$

$= \dfrac{16 \cdot 4}{3}$

$= \dfrac{64}{3}$ or $21\dfrac{1}{3}$

25. $\dfrac{2}{3} \cdot 1\dfrac{8}{9} = \dfrac{2}{3} \cdot \dfrac{17}{9} = \dfrac{2 \cdot 17}{3 \cdot 9} = \dfrac{34}{27}$ or $1\dfrac{7}{27}$

The area is $\dfrac{34}{27}$ or $1\dfrac{7}{27}$ square miles.

CHAPTER 3

Exercise Set 3.1

1. $\dfrac{1}{7} + \dfrac{2}{7} = \dfrac{1 + 2}{7} = \dfrac{3}{7}$

5. $\dfrac{2}{9} + \dfrac{4}{9} = \dfrac{2 + 4}{9} = \dfrac{6}{9} = \dfrac{3 \cdot 2}{3 \cdot 3} = \dfrac{2}{3}$

9. $\dfrac{3}{14} + \dfrac{4}{14} = \dfrac{3 + 4}{14} = \dfrac{7}{14} = \dfrac{7 \cdot 1}{7 \cdot 2} = \dfrac{1}{2}$

13. $\dfrac{4}{13} + \dfrac{2}{13} + \dfrac{1}{13} = \dfrac{4 + 2 + 1}{13} = \dfrac{7}{13}$

17. $\dfrac{10}{11} - \dfrac{4}{11} = \dfrac{10 - 4}{11} = \dfrac{6}{11}$

21. $\dfrac{7}{4} - \dfrac{3}{4} = \dfrac{7 - 3}{4} = \dfrac{4}{4} = 1$

25. $\dfrac{25}{12} - \dfrac{15}{12} = \dfrac{25 - 15}{12} = \dfrac{10}{12} = \dfrac{2 \cdot 5}{2 \cdot 6} = \dfrac{5}{6}$

29. $\dfrac{27}{33} - \dfrac{8}{33} = \dfrac{27 - 8}{33} = \dfrac{19}{33}$

33. $\dfrac{99}{100} - \dfrac{9}{100} = \dfrac{99 - 9}{100} = \dfrac{90}{100} = \dfrac{10 \cdot 9}{10 \cdot 10} = \dfrac{9}{10}$

37. $\dfrac{3}{16} + \dfrac{7}{16} + \dfrac{2}{16} = \dfrac{3 + 7 + 2}{16} = \dfrac{12}{16} = \dfrac{4 \cdot 3}{4 \cdot 4} = \dfrac{3}{4}$

41. The perimeter is the distance around. Opposite sides of a rectangle have equal length.

$$\text{Perimeter} = \frac{7}{12} + \frac{5}{12} + \frac{7}{12} + \frac{5}{12}$$

$$= \frac{7 + 5 + 7 + 5}{12}$$

$$= \frac{24}{12}$$

$$= \frac{12 \cdot 2}{12 \cdot 1}$$

$$= \frac{2}{1}$$

$$= 2$$

The perimeter is 2 meters.

45. North America takes up $\frac{16}{100}$ of the world's land area, while South America takes up $\frac{12}{100}$ of the land area.

$$\frac{16}{100} + \frac{12}{100} = \frac{16 + 12}{100} = \frac{28}{100} = \frac{4 \cdot 7}{4 \cdot 25} = \frac{7}{25}$$

$\frac{7}{25}$ of the world's land area is within North America and South America.

49. To find the remaining amount of track to be inspected, subtract the $\frac{5}{20}$ mile that has already been inspected from the $\frac{19}{20}$ mile total that must be inspected.

$$\frac{19}{20} - \frac{5}{20} = \frac{19 - 5}{20} = \frac{14}{20} = \frac{2 \cdot 7}{2 \cdot 10} = \frac{7}{10}$$

$\frac{7}{10}$ of a mile of track remains to be inspected.

53. To find the fraction of states that had maximum speed limits less than 70 mph, subtract the fraction that had speed limits of 70 mph $\left(\frac{16}{50}\right)$ from the fraction that had speed limits up to and including 70 mph $\left(\frac{37}{50}\right)$.

$$\frac{37}{50} - \frac{16}{50} = \frac{37 - 16}{50} = \frac{21}{50}$$

$\frac{21}{50}$ of the states had maximum speed limits less than 70 mph.

57.
$$2\overline{)4}$$
$$2\overline{)8}$$
$$8 = 2 \cdot 2 \cdot 2 = 2^3$$

61. $\dfrac{3}{8} + \dfrac{7}{8} - \dfrac{5}{8} = \dfrac{3 + 7 - 5}{8} = \dfrac{10 - 5}{8} = \dfrac{5}{8}$

65. $\dfrac{2}{7} + \dfrac{9}{7} = \dfrac{2 + 9}{7} = \dfrac{11}{7}$

69. $\dfrac{16}{100} + \dfrac{12}{100} + \dfrac{9}{100} + \dfrac{7}{100} + \dfrac{20}{100} + \dfrac{30}{100} + \dfrac{6}{100}$

$$= \frac{16 + 12 + 9 + 7 + 20 + 30 + 6}{100}$$

$$= \frac{100}{100}$$

$$= 1$$

answers may vary

Exercise Set 3.2

1. Multiplies of 3: 3, 6, 9, $\boxed{12}$, 15, ...
Multiplies of 4: 4, 8, $\boxed{12}$, 16, ...
LCM: 12

5. Multiples of 12: 12, 24, $\boxed{36}$, 48, ...
Multiplies of 18: 18, $\boxed{36}$, 54, ...
LCM: 36

9. $18 = \boxed{2} \cdot \boxed{3 \cdot 3}$
$21 = 3 \cdot \boxed{7}$
LCM: $2 \cdot 3 \cdot 3 \cdot 7 = 126$

13. $8 = \boxed{2 \cdot 2 \cdot 2}$
$24 = 2 \cdot 2 \cdot 2 \cdot \boxed{3}$
LCM: $2 \cdot 2 \cdot 2 \cdot 3 = 24$

17. $8 = \boxed{2 \cdot 2 \cdot 2}$
$6 = 2 \cdot 3$
$27 = \boxed{3 \cdot 3 \cdot 3}$
LCM: $2 \cdot 2 \cdot 2 \cdot 3 \cdot 3 \cdot 3 = 216$

21. $34 = 2 \cdot \boxed{17}$
$68 = \boxed{2 \cdot 2} \cdot 17$
LCM: $2 \cdot 2 \cdot 17 = 68$

25. $30 = 2 \cdot 3 \cdot 5$
$36 = \boxed{2 \cdot 2} \cdot \boxed{3 \cdot 3}$
$50 = 2 \cdot \boxed{5 \cdot 5}$
LCM: $2 \cdot 2 \cdot 3 \cdot 3 \cdot 5 \cdot 5 = 900$

29. $11 = 11$
$33 = \boxed{3} \cdot 11$
$121 = \boxed{11 \cdot 11}$
LCM: $3 \cdot 11 \cdot 11 = 363$

33. $\dfrac{4}{7} = \dfrac{4 \cdot 5}{7 \cdot 5} = \dfrac{20}{35}$

37. $\dfrac{2}{5} = \dfrac{2 \cdot 5}{5 \cdot 5} = \dfrac{10}{25}$

41. $\dfrac{10}{7} = \dfrac{10 \cdot 3}{7 \cdot 3} = \dfrac{30}{21}$

45. $\dfrac{2}{3} = \dfrac{2 \cdot 15}{3 \cdot 15} = \dfrac{30}{45}$

49. $\dfrac{15}{13} = \dfrac{15 \cdot 6}{13 \cdot 6} = \dfrac{90}{78}$

53. $\dfrac{7}{10} - \dfrac{2}{10} = \dfrac{7 - 2}{10} = \dfrac{5}{10} = \dfrac{5 \cdot 1}{5 \cdot 2} = \dfrac{1}{2}$

57. $\dfrac{23}{18} - \dfrac{15}{18} = \dfrac{23 - 15}{18} = \dfrac{8}{18} = \dfrac{2 \cdot 4}{2 \cdot 9} = \dfrac{4}{9}$

61. $\dfrac{37}{165} = \dfrac{37 \cdot 22}{165 \cdot 22} = \dfrac{814}{3630}$

65. a. $\dfrac{10}{15} = \dfrac{5 \cdot 2}{5 \cdot 3} = \dfrac{2}{3}$

b. $\dfrac{40}{60} = \dfrac{20 \cdot 2}{20 \cdot 3} = \dfrac{2}{3}$

c. $\dfrac{16}{20} = \dfrac{4 \cdot 4}{4 \cdot 5} = \dfrac{4}{5}$

d. $\dfrac{200}{300} = \dfrac{100 \cdot 2}{100 \cdot 3} = \dfrac{2}{3}$

a, b, and d are equivalent to $\dfrac{2}{3}$.

Exercise Set 3.3

1. The LCD of 3 and 6 is 6.

$$\frac{2}{3} + \frac{1}{6} = \frac{2}{3} \cdot \frac{2}{2} + \frac{1}{6} = \frac{4}{6} + \frac{1}{6} = \frac{5}{6}$$

5. The LCD of 11 and 33 is 33.

$$\frac{2}{11} + \frac{2}{33} = \frac{2}{11} \cdot \frac{3}{3} + \frac{2}{33} = \frac{6}{33} + \frac{2}{33} = \frac{8}{33}$$

9. The LCD of 35 and 7 is 35.

$$\frac{11}{35} + \frac{2}{7} = \frac{11}{35} + \frac{2}{7} \cdot \frac{5}{5}$$
$$= \frac{11}{35} + \frac{10}{35}$$
$$= \frac{21}{35}$$
$$= \frac{7 \cdot 3}{7 \cdot 5}$$
$$= \frac{3}{5}$$

13. The LCD of 15 and 12 is 60.

$$\frac{7}{15} + \frac{5}{12} = \frac{7}{15} \cdot \frac{4}{4} + \frac{5}{12} \cdot \frac{5}{5}$$
$$= \frac{28}{60} + \frac{25}{60}$$
$$= \frac{53}{60}$$

17. The LCD of 44 and 36 is 396.

$$\frac{9}{44} \cdot \frac{9}{9} + \frac{17}{36} \cdot \frac{11}{11} = \frac{81}{396} + \frac{187}{396}$$
$$= \frac{268}{396}$$
$$= \frac{4 \cdot 67}{4 \cdot 99}$$
$$= \frac{67}{99}$$

21. The LCD of 3, 9, and 27 is 27.

$$\frac{1}{3} + \frac{1}{9} + \frac{1}{27} = \frac{1}{3} \cdot \frac{9}{9} + \frac{1}{9} \cdot \frac{3}{3} + \frac{1}{27}$$
$$= \frac{9}{27} + \frac{3}{27} + \frac{1}{27}$$
$$= \frac{13}{27}$$

25. The LCD of 11, 9, and 3 is 99.

$$\frac{5}{11} + \frac{3}{9} + \frac{2}{3} = \frac{5}{11} \cdot \frac{9}{9} + \frac{3}{9} \cdot \frac{11}{11} + \frac{2}{3} \cdot \frac{33}{33}$$
$$= \frac{45}{99} + \frac{33}{99} + \frac{66}{99}$$
$$= \frac{144}{99}$$
$$= \frac{9 \cdot 16}{9 \cdot 11}$$
$$= \frac{16}{11} \text{ or } 1\frac{5}{11}$$

29. The LCD of 8 and 16 is 16.

$$\frac{7}{8} - \frac{3}{16} = \frac{7}{8} \cdot \frac{2}{2} - \frac{3}{16} = \frac{14}{16} - \frac{3}{16} = \frac{11}{16}$$

33. The LCD of 7 and 8 is 56.

$$\frac{5}{7} - \frac{1}{8} = \frac{5}{7} \cdot \frac{8}{8} - \frac{1}{8} \cdot \frac{7}{7} = \frac{40}{56} - \frac{7}{56} = \frac{33}{56}$$

37. The LCD of 35 and 7 is 35.

$$\frac{11}{35} - \frac{2}{7} = \frac{11}{35} - \frac{2}{7} \cdot \frac{5}{5} = \frac{11}{35} - \frac{10}{35} = \frac{1}{35}$$

41. The LCD of 15 and 12 is 60.

$$\frac{7}{15} - \frac{5}{12} = \frac{7}{15} \cdot \frac{4}{4} - \frac{5}{12} \cdot \frac{5}{5}$$
$$= \frac{28}{60} - \frac{25}{60}$$
$$= \frac{3}{60}$$
$$= \frac{3 \cdot 1}{3 \cdot 20}$$
$$= \frac{1}{20}$$

45. The LCD of 100 and 1000 is 1000.

$$\frac{1}{100} - \frac{1}{1000} = \frac{1}{100} \cdot \frac{10}{10} - \frac{1}{1000}$$
$$= \frac{10}{1000} - \frac{1}{1000}$$
$$= \frac{9}{1000}$$

49. The LCD of 12 and 9 is 36.

$$\frac{5}{12} + \frac{1}{9} = \frac{5}{12} \cdot \frac{3}{3} + \frac{1}{9} \cdot \frac{4}{4} = \frac{15}{36} + \frac{4}{36} = \frac{19}{36}$$

53. The LCD of 28 and 40 is 280.

$$\frac{9}{28} - \frac{3}{40} = \frac{9}{28} \cdot \frac{10}{10} - \frac{3}{40} \cdot \frac{7}{7} = \frac{90}{280} - \frac{21}{280} = \frac{69}{280}$$

57. Add the lengths of the four sides. The LCD of 3 and 5 is 15.

$$\frac{4}{5} + \frac{1}{3} + \frac{4}{5} + \frac{1}{3} = \frac{4}{5} \cdot \frac{3}{3} + \frac{1}{3} \cdot \frac{5}{5} + \frac{4}{5} \cdot \frac{3}{3} + \frac{1}{3} \cdot \frac{5}{5}$$
$$= \frac{12}{15} + \frac{5}{15} + \frac{12}{15} + \frac{5}{15}$$
$$= \frac{34}{15} \text{ or } 2\frac{4}{15}$$

The perimeter is $\frac{34}{15}$ or $2\frac{4}{15}$ cm.

61. Subtract the distance domestic European honeybees will chase a person from the distance killer bees will chase a person.
The LCD of 4 and 264 is 264.

$$\frac{1}{4} - \frac{5}{264} = \frac{1}{4} \cdot \frac{66}{66} - \frac{5}{264} = \frac{66}{264} - \frac{5}{264} = \frac{61}{264}$$

Killer bees will chase a person $\frac{61}{264}$ mile farther.

65. Subtract the fraction of students who name art as their favorite subject from the fraction that name math, science, or art as their favorite subject.
The LCD of 20 and 25 is 100.

$$\frac{13}{20} - \frac{4}{25} = \frac{13}{20} \cdot \frac{5}{5} - \frac{4}{25} \cdot \frac{4}{4} = \frac{65}{100} - \frac{16}{100} = \frac{49}{100}$$

$\frac{49}{100}$ of American students age 10 to 17 name math or science as their favorite subject.

69. The Pacific Ocean takes up $\frac{1}{2}$ of the world's water area, while the Atlantic Ocean takes up $\frac{13}{50}$ of the water area.
The LCD of 2 and 50 is 50.

$$\frac{1}{2} + \frac{13}{50} = \frac{1}{2} \cdot \frac{25}{25} + \frac{13}{50}$$
$$= \frac{25}{50} + \frac{13}{50}$$
$$= \frac{38}{50}$$
$$= \frac{2 \cdot 19}{2 \cdot 25}$$
$$= \frac{19}{25}$$

$\frac{19}{25}$ of the world's water area is within the Pacific Ocean and the Atlantic Ocean.

73. $4 \div 7\frac{1}{4} = \frac{4}{1} \div \frac{29}{4} = \frac{4}{1} \cdot \frac{4}{29} = \frac{4 \cdot 4}{1 \cdot 29} = \frac{16}{29}$

77. a.

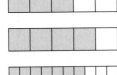

b. Yes, there is an error.

c. $\dfrac{3}{5} + \dfrac{4}{5} = \dfrac{3+4}{5} = \dfrac{7}{5}$ or $1\dfrac{2}{5}$

81. The LCD of 55 and 1760 is 1760.

$$\dfrac{30}{55} + \dfrac{1000}{1760} = \dfrac{30}{55} \cdot \dfrac{32}{32} + \dfrac{1000}{1760}$$

$$= \dfrac{960}{1760} + \dfrac{1000}{1760}$$

$$= \dfrac{1960}{1760} = \dfrac{49 \cdot 40}{44 \cdot 40}$$

$$= \dfrac{49}{44} \text{ or } 1\dfrac{5}{44}$$

Exercise Set 3.4

1. Exact:
$$\begin{array}{r} 4\dfrac{7}{10} \\[2mm] + 2\dfrac{1}{10} \\ \hline 6\dfrac{8}{10} = 6\dfrac{4}{5} \end{array}$$

Estimate: $4\dfrac{7}{10}$ rounds to 5. $2\dfrac{1}{10}$ rounds to 2.

$5 + 2 = 7$

5. The LCD of 5 and 25 is 25.

Exact:
$$\begin{array}{cc} 9\dfrac{1}{5} & 9\dfrac{5}{25} \\[2mm] +8\dfrac{2}{25} & +8\dfrac{2}{25} \\ \hline & 17\dfrac{7}{25} \end{array}$$

Estimate: $9\dfrac{1}{5}$ rounds to 9. $8\dfrac{2}{25}$ rounds to 8.

$9 + 8 = 17$

9. The LCD of 6 and 8 is 24.

$$\begin{array}{cc} 1\dfrac{5}{6} & 1\dfrac{20}{24} \\[2mm] +5\dfrac{3}{8} & +5\dfrac{9}{24} \\ \hline & 6\dfrac{29}{24} = 6 + 1\dfrac{5}{24} = 7\dfrac{5}{24} \end{array}$$

13.
$$\begin{array}{r} 11\dfrac{3}{5} \\[2mm] +7\dfrac{2}{5} \\ \hline 18\dfrac{5}{5} = 18 + 1 = 19 \end{array}$$

17. The LCD of 8, 6, and 4 is 24.

$$\begin{array}{cc} 3\dfrac{5}{8} & 3\dfrac{15}{24} \\[2mm] 2\dfrac{1}{6} & 2\dfrac{4}{24} \\[2mm] +7\dfrac{3}{4} & +7\dfrac{18}{24} \\ \hline & 12\dfrac{37}{24} = 12 + 1\dfrac{13}{24} = 13\dfrac{13}{24} \end{array}$$

21. Exact:
$$\begin{array}{r} 4\dfrac{7}{10} \\[2mm] -2\dfrac{1}{10} \\ \hline 2\dfrac{6}{10} = 2\dfrac{3}{5} \end{array}$$

Estimate: $4\dfrac{7}{10}$ rounds to 5. $2\dfrac{1}{10}$ rounds to 2.

$5 - 2 = 3$

25. The LCD of 5 and 25 is 25.

Exact:
$$\begin{array}{ccc} 9\dfrac{1}{5} & 9\dfrac{5}{25} & 8\dfrac{30}{25} \\[2mm] -8\dfrac{6}{25} & -8\dfrac{6}{25} & -8\dfrac{6}{25} \\ \hline & & \dfrac{24}{25} \end{array}$$

Estimate: $9\dfrac{1}{5}$ rounds to 9. $8\dfrac{6}{25}$ rounds to 8.

$9 - 8 = 1$

29. The LCD of 7 and 14 is 14.

$$\begin{array}{ccc} 15\dfrac{4}{7} & 15\dfrac{8}{14} & 14\dfrac{22}{14} \\[2mm] -9\dfrac{11}{14} & -9\dfrac{11}{14} & -9\dfrac{11}{14} \\ \hline & & 5\dfrac{11}{14} \end{array}$$

33.
$$\begin{array}{cc} 10 & 9\dfrac{5}{5} \\[2mm] -8\dfrac{1}{5} & -8\dfrac{1}{5} \\ \hline & 1\dfrac{4}{5} \end{array}$$

37.
$$\begin{array}{cc} 6 & 5\dfrac{9}{9} \\[2mm] -2\dfrac{4}{9} & -2\dfrac{4}{9} \\ \hline & 3\dfrac{5}{9} \end{array}$$

41. The LCD of 6 and 12 is 12.

$$\begin{array}{cc} 15\dfrac{1}{6} & 15\dfrac{2}{12} \\[2mm] +13\dfrac{5}{12} & +13\dfrac{5}{12} \\ \hline & 28\dfrac{7}{12} \end{array}$$

45.
$$\begin{array}{r} 5\dfrac{8}{9} \\[2mm] +2\dfrac{1}{9} \\ \hline 7\dfrac{9}{9} = 7 + 1 = 8 \end{array}$$

49. Subtract the diameter for Eastern Bluebirds from the diameter for Mountain Bluebirds.
The LCD of 2 and 16 is 16.

$$\begin{array}{cc} 1\dfrac{9}{16} & 1\dfrac{9}{16} \\[2mm] -1\dfrac{1}{2} & -1\dfrac{8}{16} \\ \hline & \dfrac{1}{16} \end{array}$$

The entrance holes for Mountain Bluebirds should be $\dfrac{1}{16}$ inch wider.

53. Subtract Yuma's average annual rainfall from Tucson's average annual rainfall. The LCD of 4 and 5 is 20.

$$11\frac{1}{4} \qquad 11\frac{5}{20} \qquad 10\frac{25}{20}$$
$$-\,3\frac{3}{5} \qquad -\,3\frac{12}{20} \qquad -\,3\frac{12}{20}$$
$$\overline{} \qquad \overline{} \qquad 7\frac{13}{20}$$

On average, Tucson gets $7\frac{13}{20}$ inches more rain annually than Yuma.

57. Subtract the time for a personal return from the time for a small business return.
The LCD of 2 and 8 is 8.

$$5\frac{7}{8} \qquad 5\frac{7}{8}$$
$$-\,3\frac{1}{2} \qquad -\,3\frac{4}{8}$$
$$\overline{} \qquad 2\frac{3}{8}$$

It takes him $2\frac{3}{8}$ hours longer to prepare a small business return.

61. Subtract the length of the Hood Canal Bridge from the length of the Evergreen Point Bridge.

$$2526 \qquad 2525\frac{3}{3}$$
$$-\,2173\frac{2}{3} \qquad -\,2173\frac{2}{3}$$
$$\overline{} \qquad 352\frac{1}{3}$$

The Evergreen Point Bridge is $352\frac{1}{3}$ yards longer than the Hood Canal Bridge.

65. Subtract the length of the August 21, 2017 eclipse from the length of the April 8, 2024 eclipse. The LCD of 3 and 15 is 15.

$$4\frac{7}{15} \qquad 4\frac{7}{15} \qquad 3\frac{22}{15}$$
$$-\,2\frac{2}{3} \qquad -\,2\frac{10}{15} \qquad -\,2\frac{10}{15}$$
$$\overline{} \qquad \overline{} \qquad 1\frac{12}{15} = 1\frac{4}{5}$$

The April 8, 2024 eclipse will be $1\frac{4}{5}$ minutes longer than the August 21, 2017 eclipse.

69. Add the lengths of the sides. The LCD of 3 and 8 is 24.

$$\begin{array}{cc} 3 & 3 \\ 5\frac{1}{3} & 5\frac{8}{24} \\ 5 & 5 \\ +\,7\frac{7}{8} & +\,7\frac{21}{24} \\ \hline & 20\frac{29}{24} = 20 + 1\frac{5}{24} = 21\frac{5}{24} \end{array}$$

The perimeter is $21\frac{5}{24}$ meters.

73. $5^2 = 5 \cdot 5 = 25$

77. $2 + 3(8 \cdot 7 - 1) = 2 + 3(56 - 1)$
$$= 2 + 3(55)$$
$$= 2 + 165$$
$$= 167$$

81. $9\frac{10}{16} = 9 + \frac{2 \cdot 5}{2 \cdot 8} = 9\frac{5}{8}$

85. answers may vary

Exercise Set 3.5

1. Since $7 > 6$, then $\frac{7}{9} > \frac{6}{9}$.

5. The LCD of 42 and 21 is 42.

$\frac{9}{42}$ has a denominator of 42.

$$\frac{5}{21} = \frac{5}{21} \cdot \frac{2}{2} = \frac{10}{42}$$

Since $9 < 10$, then $\frac{9}{42} < \frac{10}{42}$, so $\frac{9}{42} < \frac{5}{21}$.

9. The LCD of 4 and 3 is 12.

$$\frac{3}{4} = \frac{3}{4} \cdot \frac{3}{3} = \frac{9}{12}$$
$$\frac{2}{3} = \frac{2}{3} \cdot \frac{4}{4} = \frac{8}{12}$$

Since $9 > 8$, then $\frac{9}{12} > \frac{8}{12}$, so $\frac{3}{4} > \frac{2}{3}$.

13. The LCD of 10 and 11 is 110.

$$\frac{1}{10} = \frac{1}{10} \cdot \frac{11}{11} = \frac{11}{110}$$
$$\frac{1}{11} = \frac{1}{11} \cdot \frac{10}{10} = \frac{10}{110}$$

Since $11 > 10$, then $\frac{11}{110} > \frac{10}{110}$, so $\frac{1}{10} > \frac{1}{11}$.

17. $\left(\frac{1}{2}\right)^4 = \frac{1}{2} \cdot \frac{1}{2} \cdot \frac{1}{2} \cdot \frac{1}{2} = \frac{1}{16}$

21. $\left(\frac{4}{7}\right)^3 = \frac{4}{7} \cdot \frac{4}{7} \cdot \frac{4}{7} = \frac{64}{343}$

25. $\left(\frac{3}{4}\right)^2 \cdot \left(\frac{2}{3}\right)^3 = \left(\frac{3}{4} \cdot \frac{3}{4}\right) \cdot \left(\frac{2}{3} \cdot \frac{2}{3} \cdot \frac{2}{3}\right)$
$$= \frac{3 \cdot 3 \cdot 2 \cdot 2 \cdot 2}{4 \cdot 4 \cdot 3 \cdot 3 \cdot 3}$$
$$= \frac{3 \cdot 3 \cdot 2 \cdot 2 \cdot 2}{2 \cdot 2 \cdot 2 \cdot 2 \cdot 3 \cdot 3 \cdot 3}$$
$$= \frac{1}{2 \cdot 3}$$
$$= \frac{1}{6}$$

29. The LCD of 15 and 5 is 15.

$$\frac{2}{15} + \frac{3}{5} = \frac{2}{15} + \frac{3}{5} \cdot \frac{3}{3} = \frac{2}{15} + \frac{9}{15} = \frac{11}{15}$$

33. $1 - \frac{4}{9} = \frac{9}{9} - \frac{4}{9} = \frac{5}{9}$

37. The LCD of 6 and 4 is 24.

$$\frac{5}{6} - \frac{3}{4} = \frac{5}{6} \cdot \frac{4}{4} - \frac{3}{4} \cdot \frac{6}{6} = \frac{20}{24} - \frac{18}{24} = \frac{2}{24} = \frac{2 \cdot 1}{2 \cdot 12} = \frac{1}{12}$$

41. $0 \cdot \frac{9}{10} = 0$

45. $\frac{20}{35} \cdot \frac{7}{10} = \frac{20 \cdot 7}{35 \cdot 10} = \frac{10 \cdot 2 \cdot 7}{7 \cdot 5 \cdot 10} = \frac{2}{5}$

49. $\frac{1}{5} + \frac{1}{3} \cdot \frac{1}{4} = \frac{1}{5} + \frac{1 \cdot 1}{3 \cdot 4} = \frac{1}{5} + \frac{1}{12}$

The LCD of 5 and 12 is 60.

$$\frac{1}{5} + \frac{1}{12} = \frac{1}{5} \cdot \frac{12}{12} + \frac{1}{12} \cdot \frac{5}{5} = \frac{12}{60} + \frac{5}{60} = \frac{17}{60}$$

53. $\frac{1}{5}\left(2\frac{5}{6} - \frac{1}{3}\right) = \frac{1}{5}\left(\frac{17}{6} - \frac{1}{3}\cdot\frac{2}{2}\right)$

$= \frac{1}{5}\left(\frac{17}{6} - \frac{2}{6}\right)$

$= \frac{1}{5}\left(\frac{15}{6}\right)$

$= \frac{1\cdot 15}{5\cdot 6}$

$= \frac{1\cdot 5\cdot 3}{5\cdot 3\cdot 2}$

$= \frac{1}{2}$

57. $\left(\frac{3}{4}\right)^2 \div \left(\frac{3}{4} - \frac{1}{12}\right) = \left(\frac{3}{4}\right)^2 \div \left(\frac{3}{4}\cdot\frac{3}{3} - \frac{1}{12}\right)$

$= \left(\frac{3}{4}\right)^2 \div \left(\frac{9}{12} - \frac{1}{12}\right)$

$= \left(\frac{3}{4}\right)^2 \div \left(\frac{8}{12}\right)$

$= \left(\frac{3}{4}\right)^2 \div \left(\frac{4\cdot 2}{4\cdot 3}\right)$

$= \left(\frac{3}{4}\right)^2 \div \left(\frac{2}{3}\right)$

$= \left(\frac{3}{4}\cdot\frac{3}{4}\right) \div \left(\frac{2}{3}\right)$

$= \frac{9}{16} \div \frac{2}{3}$

$= \frac{9}{16}\cdot\frac{3}{2}$

$= \frac{9\cdot 3}{16\cdot 2}$

$= \frac{27}{32}$

61. $\frac{5}{9}\cdot\frac{1}{2} + \frac{2}{3}\cdot\frac{5}{6} = \frac{5\cdot 1}{9\cdot 2} + \frac{2\cdot 5}{3\cdot 6}$

$= \frac{5}{18} + \frac{10}{18}$

$= \frac{15}{18}$

$= \frac{3\cdot 5}{3\cdot 6}$

$= \frac{5}{6}$

65. $\frac{3}{13} \div \frac{9}{26} - \frac{7}{24}\cdot\frac{8}{14} = \frac{3}{13}\cdot\frac{26}{9} - \frac{7}{24}\cdot\frac{8}{14}$

$= \frac{3\cdot 26}{13\cdot 9} - \frac{7\cdot 8}{24\cdot 14}$

$= \frac{3\cdot 13\cdot 2}{13\cdot 3\cdot 3} - \frac{7\cdot 8}{8\cdot 3\cdot 7\cdot 2}$

$= \frac{2}{3} - \frac{1}{6}$

$= \frac{2}{3}\cdot\frac{2}{2} - \frac{1}{6}$

$= \frac{4}{6} - \frac{1}{6}$

$= \frac{3}{6}$

$= \frac{1}{2}$

69. $\left(\frac{3}{4} + \frac{1}{8}\right)^2 - \left(\frac{1}{2} + \frac{1}{8}\right) = \left(\frac{3}{4}\cdot\frac{2}{2} + \frac{1}{8}\right)^2 - \left(\frac{1}{2}\cdot\frac{4}{4} + \frac{1}{8}\right)$

$= \left(\frac{6}{8} + \frac{1}{8}\right)^2 - \left(\frac{4}{8} + \frac{1}{8}\right)$

$= \left(\frac{7}{8}\right)^2 - \left(\frac{5}{8}\right)$

$= \left(\frac{7}{8}\cdot\frac{7}{8}\right) - \frac{5}{8}$

$= \frac{49}{64} - \frac{5}{8}$

$= \frac{49}{64} - \frac{5}{8}\cdot\frac{8}{8}$

$= \frac{49}{64} - \frac{40}{64}$

$= \frac{9}{64}$

73. The average is the sum, divided by 3.

$\left(\frac{1}{5} + \frac{3}{10} + \frac{3}{20}\right) \div 3 = \left(\frac{1}{5}\cdot\frac{4}{4} + \frac{3}{10}\cdot\frac{2}{2} + \frac{3}{20}\right) \div 3$

$= \left(\frac{4}{20} + \frac{6}{20} + \frac{3}{20}\right) \div 3$

$= \frac{13}{20} \div 3$

$= \frac{13}{20}\cdot\frac{1}{3}$

$= \frac{13}{60}$

77. The fraction for Japan has the smallest numerator when written with a denominator of 100, so Japan has the smallest fraction of cell phone users.

81. "Increased by" is most likely to translate to addition.

85. "Subtracted from" is most likely to translate to subtraction.

89. "Times" is most likely to translate to multiplication.

93. $\frac{2^3}{3} = \frac{2\cdot 2\cdot 2}{3} = \frac{8}{3}$

$\left(\frac{2}{3}\right)^3 = \frac{2}{3}\cdot\frac{2}{3}\cdot\frac{2}{3} = \frac{8}{27}$

$\frac{2^3}{3}$ and $\left(\frac{2}{3}\right)^3$ do not simplify to the same value.

answers may vary

97. The operations should be done in the order: division, multiplication, subtraction, addition

101. The LCD of 10 and 25 is 50.

$\frac{7}{10} = \frac{7}{10}\cdot\frac{5}{5} = \frac{35}{50}$

$\frac{11}{25} = \frac{11}{25}\cdot\frac{2}{2} = \frac{22}{50}$

Since $35 > 22$, then $\frac{35}{50} > \frac{22}{50}$, so $\frac{7}{10} > \frac{11}{25}$.

Adults in the U.S. use savings accounts more.

Exercise Set 3.6

1. "Find the sum" translates as addition.
$11 + 2 = 13$

5. "Subtract" indicates subtraction.
$35 - 8 = 27$

9. "Multiply" indicates multiplication.
$21\cdot 9 = 189$

13.

Wall height	is	number of bricks	times	brick width	plus	layers of mortar	times	mortar width
↓	↓	↓	↓	↓	↓	↓	↓	↓
Height	=	4	·	$2\frac{3}{4}$	+	3	·	$\frac{1}{2}$

$$= 4\cdot\frac{11}{4} + 3\cdot\frac{1}{2} = 11 + \frac{3}{2} = 11 + 1 + \frac{1}{2} = 12\frac{1}{2}$$

The wall is $12\frac{1}{2}$ inches high.

17.

Bill life	is	$\frac{1}{20}$	times	coin life
↓	↓	↓	↓	↓
Life	=	$\frac{1}{20}$	·	30

$$= \frac{30}{20} = \frac{10\cdot 3}{10\cdot 2} = \frac{3}{2} \text{ or } 1\frac{1}{2}$$

The life expectancy of circulating paper money is $1\frac{1}{2}$ years.

21.

Total needed	is	amount for large shirt	plus	number of small shirts	times	amount for small shirt
↓	↓	↓	↓	↓	↓	↓
Total	=	$1\frac{1}{2}$	+	5	·	$\frac{3}{4}$

$$= 1\frac{1}{2} + 5\cdot\frac{3}{4} = \frac{3}{2} + \frac{15}{4} = \frac{3}{2}\cdot\frac{2}{2} + \frac{15}{4} = \frac{6}{4} + \frac{15}{4}$$
$$= \frac{21}{4} \text{ or } 5\frac{1}{4}$$

The amount of cloth needed is $5\frac{1}{4}$ yards, so the 5-yard remnant is not enough. Another $\frac{1}{4}$ yard of material is required.

25.

Outer diameter	is	left thickness	plus	inner diameter	plus	right thickness
↓	↓	↓	↓	↓	↓	↓
outer diameter	=	$\frac{3}{16}$	+	$\frac{3}{4}$	+	$\frac{3}{16}$

$$= \frac{3}{16} + \frac{3}{4} + \frac{3}{16} = \frac{3}{16} + \frac{3}{4}\cdot\frac{4}{4} + \frac{3}{16} = \frac{3}{16} + \frac{12}{16} + \frac{3}{16} = \frac{18}{16}$$
$$= \frac{2\cdot 9}{2\cdot 8} = \frac{9}{8} \text{ or } 1\frac{1}{8}$$

The outer diameter is $\frac{9}{8}$ or $1\frac{1}{8}$ inches.

29.

Area of photograph	is	length	times	width
↓		↓	↓	↓
Area	=	$4\frac{1}{2}$	·	$2\frac{1}{2}$

$$= 4\frac{1}{2}\cdot 2\frac{1}{2} = \frac{9}{2}\cdot\frac{5}{2} = \frac{9\cdot 5}{2\cdot 2} = \frac{45}{4} \text{ or } 11\frac{1}{4}$$

The area of the photograph is $11\frac{1}{4}$ square inches.

33.

Volume of cell phone	is	length	times	width	times	height
↓		↓	↓	↓	↓	↓
Volume	=	$3\frac{1}{5}$	·	$1\frac{7}{10}$	·	1

$$= 3\frac{1}{5}\cdot 1\frac{7}{10}\cdot 1 = \frac{16}{5}\cdot\frac{17}{10}\cdot 1 = \frac{16\cdot 17}{5\cdot 10} = \frac{272}{50}$$
$$= \frac{2\cdot 136}{2\cdot 25} = \frac{136}{25} \text{ or } 5\frac{11}{25}$$

The volume of the cell phone is $5\frac{11}{25}$ cubic inches.

37. a.

Length needed	is	number of pieces	times	length of each pieces
↓	↓	↓	↓	↓
Length	=	12	·	$\frac{3}{4}$

$$= 12\cdot\frac{3}{4} = \frac{12}{1}\cdot\frac{3}{4} = \frac{4\cdot 3\cdot 3}{1\cdot 4} = \frac{3\cdot 3}{1} = 9$$

Since he needs a total of 9 feet of tubing, the 10-foot piece is enough.

b. $10 - 9 = 1$

He will have 1 foot of tubing left over.

41.

Area	is	length	times	width
↓	↓	↓	↓	↓
Area	=	$\frac{3}{16}$	·	$\frac{3}{8}$

$$= \frac{3\cdot 3}{16\cdot 8} = \frac{9}{128}$$

The area is $\frac{9}{128}$ square inch.

Perimeter	is	two	times	length	plus	two	times	width
↓	↓	↓	↓	↓	↓	↓	↓	↓
Perimeter	=	2	·	$\frac{3}{16}$	+	2	·	$\frac{3}{8}$

$$= \frac{2\cdot 3}{16} + \frac{2\cdot 3}{8} = \frac{6}{16} + \frac{6}{8} = \frac{6}{16} + \frac{12}{16} = \frac{18}{16} = \frac{9}{8} \text{ or } 1\frac{1}{8}$$

The perimeter is $1\frac{1}{8}$ inches.

45.

New length	is	$1\frac{9}{10}$	times	new width
↓	↓	↓	↓	↓
Length	=	$1\frac{9}{10}$	·	$2\frac{1}{2}$

$$= 1\frac{9}{10}\cdot 2\frac{1}{2} = \frac{19}{10}\cdot\frac{5}{2} = \frac{19\cdot 5}{10\cdot 2} = \frac{19\cdot 5}{5\cdot 2\cdot 2} = \frac{19}{2\cdot 2} = \frac{19}{4} \text{ or } 4\frac{3}{4}$$

The length of the new flag is $4\frac{3}{4}$ feet.

49. $\sqrt{9} = 3$, because $3\cdot 3 = 9$.

53. $8 \div 4\cdot 2 = 2\cdot 2 = 4$

57. $5 + 3[14 - (12 \div 3)] = 5 + 3[14 - 4] = 5 + 3[10]$
$$= 5 + 30 = 35$$

61. The unmarked horizontal edge of the figure has length

$6\frac{7}{9}$ feet $- 3\frac{8}{9}$ feet.

$$6\frac{7}{9} - 3\frac{8}{9} = 5\frac{16}{9} - 3\frac{8}{9} = 2\frac{8}{9}$$

The unmarked vertical edge of the figure has length

$6\frac{2}{3}$ feet $- 4\frac{4}{9}$ feet.

$$6\frac{2}{3} - 4\frac{4}{9} = 6\frac{6}{9} - 4\frac{4}{9} = 2\frac{2}{9}$$

Perimeter $= 3\frac{8}{9} + 4\frac{4}{9} + 6\frac{7}{9} + 6\frac{2}{3} + 2\frac{8}{9} + 2\frac{2}{9}$

$$= 3\frac{8}{9} + 4\frac{4}{9} + 6\frac{7}{9} + 6\frac{6}{9} + 2\frac{8}{9} + 2\frac{2}{9}$$

$$= 3 + 4 + 6 + 6 + 2 + 2 + \frac{8}{9} + \frac{4}{9} + \frac{7}{9} + \frac{6}{9} + \frac{8}{9} + \frac{2}{9}$$

$$= 23 + \frac{35}{9} = 23 + 3 + \frac{8}{9} = 26\frac{8}{9}$$

The perimeter is $26\frac{8}{9}$ feet.

65. Volume $= 13\frac{1}{3} \cdot 8\frac{3}{4} \cdot 4\frac{4}{25}$

$$= \frac{40}{3} \cdot \frac{35}{4} \cdot \frac{104}{25}$$

$$= \frac{40 \cdot 35 \cdot 104}{3 \cdot 4 \cdot 25}$$

$$= \frac{4 \cdot 5 \cdot 2 \cdot 5 \cdot 7 \cdot 104}{3 \cdot 4 \cdot 5 \cdot 5}$$

$$= \frac{2 \cdot 7 \cdot 104}{3}$$

$$= \frac{1456}{3} \text{ or } 485\frac{1}{3}$$

The volume of the suitcase is $485\frac{1}{3}$ cubic feet.

Chapter 3 Test

1. $4 = \boxed{2 \cdot 2}$

$15 = \boxed{3} \cdot \boxed{5}$

LCM: $2 \cdot 2 \cdot 3 \cdot 5 = 60$

5. $\frac{7}{9} + \frac{1}{9} = \frac{7+1}{9} = \frac{8}{9}$

9. The LCD of 8 and 3 is 24.

$\frac{7}{8} = \frac{7}{8} \cdot \frac{3}{3} = \frac{21}{24}$

$\frac{1}{3} = \frac{1}{3} \cdot \frac{8}{8} = \frac{8}{24}$

$\frac{7}{8} - \frac{1}{3} = \frac{21}{24} - \frac{8}{24} = \frac{13}{24}$

13. The LCD of 12, 8, and 24 is 24.

$\frac{11}{12} = \frac{11}{12} \cdot \frac{2}{2} = \frac{22}{24}$

$\frac{3}{8} = \frac{3}{8} \cdot \frac{3}{3} = \frac{9}{24}$

$\frac{11}{12} + \frac{3}{8} + \frac{5}{24} = \frac{22}{24} + \frac{9}{24} + \frac{5}{24}$

$$= \frac{36}{24}$$

$$= \frac{12 \cdot 3}{12 \cdot 2}$$

$$= \frac{3}{2} \text{ or } 1\frac{1}{2}$$

17. $\begin{array}{r} 19 \\ -2\frac{3}{11} \\ \hline \end{array} \quad \begin{array}{r} 18\frac{11}{11} \\ -2\frac{3}{11} \\ \hline 16\frac{8}{11} \end{array}$

21. $\left(\frac{4}{5}\right)^2 + \left(\frac{1}{2}\right)^3 = \left(\frac{4}{5} \cdot \frac{4}{5}\right) + \left(\frac{1}{2} \cdot \frac{1}{2} \cdot \frac{1}{2}\right)$

$$= \frac{16}{25} + \frac{1}{8}$$

$$= \frac{16}{25} \cdot \frac{8}{8} + \frac{1}{8} \cdot \frac{25}{25}$$

$$= \frac{128}{200} + \frac{25}{200}$$

$$= \frac{153}{200}$$

25. Divide the number of gallons of fuel by the number of hours.

$58\frac{3}{4} \div 7\frac{1}{2} = \frac{235}{4} \div \frac{15}{2} = \frac{235}{4} \cdot \frac{2}{15} = \frac{235 \cdot 2}{4 \cdot 15} = \frac{5 \cdot 47 \cdot 2}{2 \cdot 2 \cdot 5 \cdot 3}$

$$= \frac{47}{2 \cdot 3} = \frac{47}{6} \text{ or } 7\frac{5}{6}$$

$7\frac{5}{6}$ gallons of fuel were used each hour.

29. Perimeter $= 2 \cdot 1 + 2 \cdot \frac{2}{3}$

$$= 2 + \frac{2}{1} \cdot \frac{2}{3}$$

$$= 2 + \frac{4}{3}$$

$$= 2 + 1 + \frac{1}{3}$$

$$= 3\frac{1}{3}$$

The perimeter is $3\frac{1}{3}$ feet.

Area $= 1 \cdot \frac{2}{3} = \frac{2}{3}$

The area is $\frac{2}{3}$ square foot.

CHAPTER 4

Exercise Set 4.1

1. 6.52 in words is six and fifty-two hundredths.

5. 0.205 in words is two hundred five thousandths.

9. 200.005 in words is two hundred and five thousandths.

13. 31.04 in words is thirty one and four hundredths

17. 32.9 in words is thirty-two and nine tenths

21. The check should be paid to "Bell South," for the amount of "59.68," which is written in words as "Fifty-nine and $\frac{68}{100}$."

25. Nine and eight hundredths is 9.08.

29. Sixty-four ten-thousandths is 0.0064.

33. Fifteen and eight tenths is 15.8.

37. $0.27 = \frac{27}{100}$

41. $0.15 = \frac{15}{100} = \frac{3}{20}$

45. $0.048 = \frac{48}{1000} = \frac{6}{125}$

49. $15.802 = 15\frac{802}{1000} = 15\frac{401}{500}$

53. $487.32 = 487\frac{32}{100} = 487\frac{8}{25}$

57. $\frac{45}{100} = 0.45$

61. $\frac{268}{1000} = 0.268$

65. $\frac{4026}{1000} = 4.026$

69. $\frac{563}{10} = 56.3$

73. In standard form, eight tenths is 0.8, while as a fraction it is $\frac{8}{10}$ or $\frac{4}{5}$.

77. To round 47,261 to the nearest ten, observe that the digit in the ones place is 1. Since the digit is less than 5, we do not add 1 to the digit in the tens place. The number 47,261 rounded to the nearest ten is 47,260.

81. answers may vary

85. $17\frac{268}{1000} = 17.268$

Exercise Set 4.2

1. 0.15 0.16
  ↑   ↑
  5 < 6 so
  0.15 < 0.16

5. 0.098 0.1
  ↑   ↑
  0 < 1 so
  0.098 < 0.1

9. 167.908 167.980
     ↑   ↑
     0 < 8 so
     167.908 < 167.980

13. Smallest to largest: 0.006, 0.0061, 0.06

17. Smallest to largest: 1.01, 1.09, 1.1, 1.16

21. To round 0.57 to the nearest tenth, observe that the digit in the hundredths place is 7. Since this digit is at least 5, we need to add 1 to the digit in the tenths place. The number 0.57 rounded to the nearest tenth is 0.6.

25. To round 0.5942 to the nearest thousandth, observe that the digit in the ten-thousandths place is 2. Since this digit is less than 5, we do not add to the digit in the thousandths place. The number 0.5942 rounded to the nearest thousandth is 0.594.

29. To round 12.342 to the nearest tenth, observe that the digit in the hundredths place is 4. Since this digit is less than 5, we do not add 1 to digit in the tenths place. The number 12.342 rounded to the nearest tenth is 12.3.

33. To round 0.501 to the nearest tenth, observe that the digit in the hundredths place is 0. Since this digit is less than 5, we do not add 1 to the digit in the tenths place. The number 0.501 rounded to the nearest tenth is 0.5.

37. To round 3829.34 to the nearest ten, observe that the digit in the ones place is 9. Since this digit is at least 5, we need to add 1 to the digit in the tens place. The number 3829.34 rounded to the nearest ten is 3830.

41. To round 42,650.14 to the nearest one, observe that the digit in the tenths is 1. Since this digit is less than 5, we do not add 1 to the digit in the ones place. The number 42,650.14 rounded to the nearest one is 42,650. The amount is $42,650.

45. To round 0.1992 to the nearest hundredth, observe that the digit in the thousandths place is 9. Since this digit is at least 5, we need to add 1 to the digit in the hundredths place. The number 0.1992 rounded to the nearest hundredth is 0.2. The amount is $0.20.

49. To round 2.4075 to the nearest hundredth, observe that the digit in the thousandths place is 7. Since this digit is at least 5, we need to add 1 to the digit in the hundredths place. The number 2.4075 rounded to the nearest hundredth is 2.41. The time is 2.41 hours.

53. To round 24.6229 to the nearest thousandth, observe that the digit in the ten-thousandths place is 9. Since this digit is at least 5, we need to add 1 to the digit in the thousandths place. 24.6229 rounded to the nearest thousandth is 24.623. The day length is 24.623 hours.

57.   3452
   + 2314
   5766

61.   482
   − 239
   243

65. To round 2849.1738 to the nearest hundredth, observe that the digit in the thousandths place is 3. Since this digit is less than 5, we do not add 1 to the digit in the hundredths place. 2849.1738 rounded to the nearest hundredth is 2849.17, which is choice a.

69. Comparing each place value and listing from greatest to least yields: 228.040, 226.130, 225.370, 224.940, 222.730, 222.008, 221.546, 220.930.

73. answers may vary

Exercise Set 4.3

1.   1.3
   + 2.2
   3.5

5.   0.003
   + 0.091
   0.094

9. $\overset{1}{4}$90.00
   + 93.09
   583.09

13. Exact: $10\overset{1}{0}.\overset{1}{0}\overset{1}{0}9$ Estimate: $\overset{1}{1}00$
     6.080   6
   + 9.034   + 9
   115.123   115

17. $4\overset{1}{5}.\overset{1}{0}23$
   3.006
   + 8.403
   56.432

21. 18.0   Check: $1\overset{1}{5}.3$
   − 2.7   + 2.7
   15.3   18.0

25. Exact: 5.90 Estimate: 6   Check: $\overset{1}{1}.83$
   − 4.07   − 4   + 4.07
   1.83   2   5.90

29. 500.34   Check: $\overset{1}{3}\overset{1}{7}\overset{1}{6}.\overset{1}{8}9$
   − 123.45   + 123.45
   376.89   500.34

33. 200.0   Check: $\overset{1}{1}\overset{1}{9}\overset{1}{4}.4$
   − 5.6   + 5.6
   194.4   200.0

37. 23.0   Check: $\overset{1}{1}\overset{1}{6}.3$
   − 6.7   + 6.7
   16.3   23.0

41. 86.050
   − 1.978
   84.072

45. 150.00
   − 93.17
   56.83

49. The phrase "Find the total" indicates that we should add the amounts.
   $\overset{2}{2}\overset{1}{7}\overset{1}{5}.\overset{1}{3}6$
   83.00
   81.60
   + 14.75
   454.71
The total is $454.71.

53. The perimeter is the distance around. The sides of a square have the same length.
   $\overset{1}{7}.14$
   7.14
   7.14
   + 7.14
   28.56
The perimeter is 28.56 meters.

57. Two $20 bills total $40.
   40.00
   − 32.48
   7.52
Her change was $7.52.

61. The phrase "How much faster" indicates that we should subtract the average wind speed from the record speed.

$$\begin{array}{r} 321.0 \\ -\ 35.2 \\ \hline 285.8 \end{array}$$

the highest wind speed is 285.8 miles per hour faster than the average wind speed.

65. The phrase "Find the decrease" indicates that we should subtract the 2008 revenue amount from the 2002 revenue amount.

$$\begin{array}{r} 10.4 \\ -\ 7.0 \\ \hline 3.4 \end{array}$$

The decrease from 2002 to 2008 is predicted to be $3.4 billion.

69. The amount of border material needed is the perimeter of the triangle. Add the lengths of the sides.

$$\begin{array}{r} {}^{1\ 1}\ \\ 12.40 \\ 29.34 \\ +\ 25.70 \\ \hline 67.44 \end{array}$$

67.44 feet of border material are needed.

73. The phrase "Find the total" indicates that we should add durations of the flights.

$$\begin{array}{r} {}^{2\ 1\ 2\ \ 1\ 1}\ \\ 330.583 \\ 94.567 \\ 147.000 \\ +\ 142.900 \\ \hline 715.050 \end{array}$$

James A. Lovell spent 715.05 hours in spaceflight.

77. The phrase "How much more" indicates that we should subtract the least amount from the greatest.

$$\begin{array}{r} 22.0 \\ -\ 13.9 \\ \hline 8.1 \end{array}$$

The greatest consumption is 8.1 pounds per year greater than the least.

81.
$$\begin{array}{r} 46 \\ \times\ 3 \\ \hline 138 \end{array}$$

85. $\left(\dfrac{1}{5}\right)^3 = \dfrac{1}{5}\cdot\dfrac{1}{5}\cdot\dfrac{1}{5} = \dfrac{1}{125}$

89. The unknown length, plus the sum of 2.3 and 2.3, totals 10.68.

$$\begin{array}{r} 2.3 \\ +\ 2.3 \\ \hline 4.6 \end{array} \qquad \begin{array}{r} 10.68 \\ -\ 4.60 \\ \hline 6.08 \end{array}$$

The unknown length is 6.08 inches.

93. 1 nickel, 1 dime, and 2 pennies = 0.05 + 0.10 + 0.01 + 0.01 = $0.17; also, 3 nickels and 2 pennies = 0.05 + 0.05 + 0.05 + 0.01 + 0.01 = $0.17; also, 1 dime and 7 pennies = 0.10 + 0.01 + 0.01 + 0.01 + 0.01 + 0.01 + 0.01 + 0.01 = $0.17

97.
$$\begin{array}{r} 256{,}436.012 \\ -\ 256{,}435.235 \\ \hline 0.777 \end{array}$$

The moon is 0.777 miles farther in the second measurement.

Exercise Set 4.4

1.
$$\begin{array}{r} 0.2 \\ 0.6 \\ \hline 0.12 \end{array}$$

5.
$$\begin{array}{r} 0.26 \\ \times\ 5 \\ \hline 1.30 \text{ or } 1.3 \end{array}$$

9.
$$\begin{array}{r} 0.576 \\ 0.7 \\ \hline 0.4032 \end{array}$$

13.
$$\begin{array}{r} 490.2 \\ 0.023 \\ \hline 14706 \\ 98040 \\ \hline 11.2746 \end{array}$$

17. $6.5 \times 10 = 65$

21. $7.2 \times 0.01 = 0.072$

25. $6.046 \times 1000 = 6046$

29.
$$\begin{array}{r} 0.123 \\ \times\ 0.4 \\ \hline 0.0492 \end{array}$$

33.
$$\begin{array}{r} 8.6 \\ \times\ 0.15 \\ \hline 430 \\ 860 \\ \hline 1.290 \text{ or } 1.29 \end{array}$$

37. $526.3 \times 0.001 = 0.5263$

41. 5.5 billion = 5.5×1 billion
$\qquad\qquad = 5.5 \times 1{,}000{,}000{,}000$
$\qquad\qquad = 5{,}500{,}000{,}000$
The silos hold enough to make 5,500,000,000 bars.

45. 353 thousand = 353×1 thousand
$\qquad\qquad = 353 \times 1000$
$\qquad\qquad = 353{,}000$
353,000 people visited the park each week.

49. Circumference = $\pi \cdot$ diameter
$C = \pi \cdot 10 = 10\pi$
$C \approx 10(3.14) = 31.4$
The circumference is 10π centimeters, which is approximately 31.4 centimeters.

53. Multiply the number of ounces by the number of grams of saturated fat in 1 ounce.

$$\begin{array}{r} 6.2 \\ \times\ 4 \\ \hline 24.8 \end{array}$$

There are 24.8 grams of saturated fat in a 4-ounce serving of cream cheese.

57. Circumference = $\pi \cdot$ diameter
$C = \pi \cdot 250 = 250\pi$

$$\begin{array}{r} 250 \\ \times\ 3.14 \\ \hline 1000 \\ 2500 \\ 75000 \\ \hline 785.00 \end{array}$$

The circumference is 250π feet, which is approximately 785 feet.

61. Multiply her height in meters by the number of inches in 1 meter.

$$\begin{array}{r} 39.37 \\ \times\ 1.65 \\ \hline 19685 \\ 236220 \\ 393700 \\ \hline 64.9605 \end{array}$$

She is approximately 64.9605 inches tall.

65. a. Circumference = $2 \cdot \pi \cdot$ radius
Smaller circle:
$C = 2 \cdot \pi \cdot 10 = 20\pi$
$C \approx 20(3.14) = 62.8$
The circumference of the smaller circle is approximately 62.8 meters.
Larger circle:
$C = 2 \cdot \pi \cdot 20 = 40\pi$
$C \approx 40(3.14) = 125.6$
The circumference of the larger circle is approximately 125.6 meters.

b. Yes, the circumference gets doubled when the radius is doubled.

69.
$$
\begin{array}{r}
26 \\
5\overline{)\ 130} \\
-10 \\
\hline
30 \\
-30 \\
\hline
6
\end{array}
$$

73.
$$
\begin{array}{r}
8 \\
365\overline{)\ 2920} \\
-2920 \\
\hline
0
\end{array}
$$

77.
$$
\begin{array}{r}
3.60 \\
+\ 0.04 \\
\hline
3.64
\end{array}
$$

81.
$$
\begin{array}{r}
0.221 \\
\times\ \ 0.5 \\
\hline
0.1105
\end{array}
$$

85. answers may vary

Exercise Set 4.5

1.
$$
\begin{array}{r}
4.6 \\
3\overline{)\ 13.8} \\
-12 \\
\hline
1\ 8 \\
1\ 8 \\
\hline
0
\end{array}
$$

5. $0.06\overline{)18}$ becomes
$$
\begin{array}{r}
300 \\
6\overline{)\ 1800} \\
-18 \\
\hline
000
\end{array}
$$

9. Exact: $5.5\overline{)36.3}$ becomes
$$
\begin{array}{r}
6.6 \\
55\overline{)\ 363.0} \\
-330 \\
\hline
33\ 0 \\
-33\ 0 \\
\hline
0
\end{array}
$$

Estimate:
$$
\begin{array}{r}
6 \\
6\overline{)36}
\end{array}
$$

13.
$$
\begin{array}{r}
0.045 \\
12\overline{)0.540} \\
-48 \\
\hline
60 \\
-60 \\
\hline
0
\end{array}
$$

17. $0.27\overline{)1.296}$ becomes
$$
\begin{array}{r}
4.8 \\
27\overline{)\ 129.6} \\
-108 \\
\hline
21\ 6 \\
-21\ 6 \\
\hline
0
\end{array}
$$

21. $0.6\overline{)18}$ becomes
$$
\begin{array}{r}
30. \\
6\overline{)\ 180.} \\
-18 \\
\hline
00
\end{array}
$$

25. Exact: $7.2\overline{)70.56}$ becomes
$$
\begin{array}{r}
9.8 \\
72\overline{)\ 705.6} \\
-648 \\
\hline
57\ 6 \\
-57\ 6 \\
\hline
0
\end{array}
$$

Estimate:
$$
\begin{array}{r}
10 \\
7\overline{)\ 70}
\end{array}
$$

29. $0.027\overline{)1.215}$ becomes
$$
\begin{array}{r}
45 \\
27\overline{)\ 1215} \\
-108 \\
\hline
135 \\
-135 \\
\hline
0
\end{array}
$$

$$\frac{1.215}{0.027} = 45$$

33. $3.78\overline{)0.02079}$ becomes
$$
\begin{array}{r}
0.0055 \\
378\overline{)\ 2.0790} \\
-1\ 890 \\
\hline
1890 \\
-1890 \\
\hline
0
\end{array}
$$

37. $0.023\overline{)0.549}$ becomes
$$
\begin{array}{r}
23.869 \approx 23.87 \\
23\overline{)\ 549.000} \\
-46 \\
\hline
89 \\
-69 \\
\hline
20\ 0 \\
-18\ 4 \\
\hline
1\ 60 \\
-1\ 38 \\
\hline
220 \\
-207 \\
\hline
13
\end{array}
$$

41. $\dfrac{54.982}{100} = 0.54982$

45. $\dfrac{12.9}{1000} = 0.0129$

49. $\dfrac{13.1}{10} = 1.31$

53. $\dfrac{456.25}{10,000} = 0.045625$

57. There are 52 weeks in one year. Therefore, there are $40 \times 52 = 2080$ hours per year.
$$
\begin{array}{r}
3641.301 \approx 3641.30 \\
2080\overline{)\ 7573907.000} \\
-6240 \\
\hline
13339 \\
-12480 \\
\hline
8590 \\
-8320 \\
\hline
2707 \\
-2080 \\
\hline
6270 \\
-6240 \\
\hline
300 \\
-0 \\
\hline
3000 \\
-2080 \\
\hline
920
\end{array}
$$

His hourly wage was $3641.30.

61. $39.37\overline{)200}$ becomes
$$
\begin{array}{r}
5.08 \approx 5.1 \\
3937\overline{)\ 20000.00} \\
-19685 \\
\hline
315\ 0 \\
-0 \\
\hline
315\ 00 \\
314\ 96 \\
\hline
4
\end{array}
$$

There are approximately 5.1 meters in 200 inches.

65. Multiply the number of teaspoons in 1 fluid ounce by the number of fluid ounces.

$$
\begin{array}{r}
6 \\
\times\ 4 \\
\hline
24
\end{array}
$$

There are 24 teaspoons in 4 fluid ounces.

69. Divide the number of miles by the number of hours.

$$
\begin{array}{r}
133.8 \\
24\overline{)\ 3211.2} \\
\underline{-\ 24} \\
81 \\
\underline{-\ 72} \\
91 \\
\underline{-\ 72} \\
19\,2 \\
\underline{-\ 19\,2} \\
0
\end{array}
$$

The average speed was 133.8 miles per hour.

73. $0.7(6 - 2.5) = 0.7(3.5) = 2.45$

77. $30.03 + 5.1 \times 9.9 = 30.03 + 50.49 = 80.52$

81. $93.07 \div 10 \times 100 = 9.307 \times 100 = 930.7$

85. $5(20.6 - 2.06) - (0.8)^2 = 5(18.54) - (0.8)^2$
$= 5(18.54) - 0.64$
$= 92.70 - 0.64$
$= 92.06$

89. $0.9 = \dfrac{9}{10}$

93. $0.3\overline{)1.278}$ becomes
$$
\begin{array}{r}
4.26 \\
3\overline{)\ 12.78} \\
\underline{-\ 12} \\
0\,7 \\
\underline{-\ 6} \\
18 \\
\underline{-\ 18} \\
0
\end{array}
$$

$1.278 \div 0.3 = 4.26$

97.
$$
\begin{array}{r}
8.6 \\
\times\ 3.1 \\
\hline
86 \\
2580 \\
\hline
26.66
\end{array}
$$

101. 8.62×41.7 is approximately $9 \times 40 = 360$, which is choice c.

105. Add the numbers, then divide by 4.

$$
\begin{array}{r}
\overset{2}{8}6 \\
78 \\
91 \\
+\ 87 \\
\hline
342
\end{array}
$$

$$
\begin{array}{r}
85.5 \\
4\overline{)\ 342.0} \\
\underline{-\ 32} \\
22 \\
\underline{-\ 20} \\
2\,0 \\
\underline{2\,0} \\
0
\end{array}
$$

The average is 85.5.

109.
$$
\begin{array}{r}
45.2 \\
4\overline{)\ 180.8} \\
\underline{-\ 16} \\
20 \\
\underline{-\ 20} \\
0\,8 \\
\underline{-\ 8} \\
0
\end{array}
$$

Each side has length 45.2 centimeters.

113. $1.15\overline{)75}$ becomes
$$
\begin{array}{r}
65.21 \approx 65.2 \\
115\overline{)\ 7500.00} \\
\underline{-\ 690} \\
600 \\
\underline{-\ 575} \\
25\,0 \\
\underline{-\ 23\,0} \\
2\,00 \\
\underline{-\ 1\,15} \\
85
\end{array}
$$

$1.15\overline{)95}$ becomes
$$
\begin{array}{r}
82.60 \approx 82.6 \\
115\overline{)\ 9500.00} \\
\underline{-\ 920} \\
300 \\
\underline{-\ 230} \\
70\,0 \\
\underline{-\ 69\,0} \\
1\,00 \\
\underline{-\ 0} \\
1\,00
\end{array}
$$

The range of wind speeds is 65.2–82.6 knots.

Exercise Set 4.6

1.
$$
\begin{array}{r}
0.2 \\
5\overline{)\ 1.0} \\
\underline{-\ 1\,0} \\
0
\end{array}
\qquad \frac{1}{5} = 0.2
$$

5.
$$
\begin{array}{r}
0.75 \\
4\overline{)\ 3.00} \\
\underline{-\ 2\,8} \\
20 \\
\underline{-\ 20} \\
0
\end{array}
\qquad \frac{3}{4} = 0.75
$$

9.
$$
\begin{array}{r}
1.2 \\
5\overline{)\ 6.0} \\
\underline{-\ 5} \\
1\,0 \\
\underline{-\ 1\,0} \\
0
\end{array}
\qquad \frac{6}{5} = 1.2
$$

13.
$$
\begin{array}{r}
0.425 \\
40\overline{)\ 17.000} \\
\underline{-\ 16\,0} \\
1\,00 \\
\underline{-\ 80} \\
200 \\
\underline{200} \\
0
\end{array}
\qquad \frac{17}{40} = 0.425
$$

17.
$$
\begin{array}{r}
0.333\ldots \\
3\overline{)1.000} \\
-9 \\
\hline
10 \\
-9 \\
\hline
10 \\
9 \\
\hline
1
\end{array}
$$
$\dfrac{1}{3} = 0.\overline{3}$

21.
$$
\begin{array}{r}
0.636363\ldots \\
11\overline{)7.000000} \\
-66 \\
\hline
40 \\
-33 \\
\hline
70 \\
-66 \\
\hline
40 \\
-33 \\
\hline
70 \\
-60 \\
\hline
40 \\
-33 \\
\hline
7
\end{array}
$$
$\dfrac{7}{11} = 0.\overline{63}$

25.
$$
\begin{array}{r}
0.624 \\
125\overline{)78.000} \\
-75\,0 \\
\hline
3\,00 \\
-2\,50 \\
\hline
500 \\
-500 \\
\hline
0
\end{array}
$$
$\dfrac{78}{125} = 0.624$

29. $\dfrac{7}{16} = 0.4375 \approx 0.44$

33.
$$
\begin{array}{r}
0.68 \\
25\overline{)17.00} \\
-15\,0 \\
\hline
2\,00 \\
2\,00 \\
\hline
0
\end{array}
$$
$\dfrac{17}{25} = 0.68$

37.
$$
\begin{array}{r}
0.712 \approx 0.71 \\
94\overline{)67.000} \\
-65\,8 \\
\hline
1\,20 \\
-94 \\
\hline
260 \\
-188 \\
\hline
12
\end{array}
$$
$\dfrac{67}{94} \approx 0.71$

41.
$$
\begin{array}{r}
0.215 \\
200\overline{)43.000} \\
-40\,0 \\
\hline
3\,00 \\
-2\,00 \\
\hline
1\,000 \\
-1\,000 \\
\hline
0
\end{array}
$$
$0.215 = \dfrac{43}{200}$

45.
$$
\begin{array}{r}
0.833\ldots \\
6\overline{)5.000} \\
-4\,8 \\
\hline
20 \\
-18 \\
\hline
20 \\
-18 \\
\hline
2
\end{array}
$$
$\dfrac{5}{6} = 0.8\overline{3}$ and $0.\overline{6} < 0.8\overline{3}$, so $0.\overline{6} < \dfrac{5}{6}$.

49.
$$
\begin{array}{r}
0.571 \\
7\overline{)4.000} \\
-3\,5 \\
\hline
50 \\
-49 \\
\hline
10 \\
-7 \\
\hline
3
\end{array}
$$
$\dfrac{4}{7} \approx 0.57$ and $0.57 > 0.14$, so $\dfrac{4}{7} > 0.14$.

53.
$$
\begin{array}{r}
7.125 \\
64\overline{)456.000} \\
-448 \\
\hline
8\,0 \\
-6\,4 \\
\hline
1\,60 \\
-1\,28 \\
\hline
320 \\
-320 \\
\hline
0
\end{array}
$$
$\dfrac{456}{64} = 7.125$ and $7.123 < 7.125$, so

$7.123 < \dfrac{456}{64}$

57. $0.49 = 0.490$

$0.49, 0.491, 0.498$

61. $\dfrac{4}{7} \approx 0.571$

$0.412, 0.453, \dfrac{4}{7}$

65. $\dfrac{12}{5} = 2.400$

$2.37 = 2.370$

$\dfrac{17}{8} = 2.125$

$\dfrac{17}{8}, 2.37, \dfrac{12}{5}$

69. Area $= \dfrac{1}{2} \times$ base $\times$ height

$ = \dfrac{1}{2} \times 5.2 \times 3.6$

$ = 0.5 \times 5.2 \times 3.6$

$ = 9.36$

73. $2^3 = 2 \cdot 2 \cdot 2 = 8$

77. $\left(\dfrac{1}{3}\right)^4 = \dfrac{1}{3} \cdot \dfrac{1}{3} \cdot \dfrac{1}{3} \cdot \dfrac{1}{3} = \dfrac{1}{81}$

81. $\left(\dfrac{2}{5}\right)\left(\dfrac{5}{2}\right)^2 = \dfrac{2}{5} \cdot \dfrac{5}{2} \cdot \dfrac{5}{2} = \dfrac{5}{2}$

85. $1.00001 > 1$

89. The fraction of stations with a country music format is $\dfrac{2047}{10,649}$.

$$
\begin{array}{r}
0.1922 \approx 0.192 \\
10649\overline{)2047.0000} \\
-1064\,9 \\
\hline
982\,10 \\
-958\,41 \\
\hline
23\,690 \\
-21\,298 \\
\hline
2\,3920 \\
-2\,1298 \\
\hline
2622
\end{array}
$$

$\dfrac{2047}{10,649} \approx 0.192$

93. answers may vary

97. $(9.6)(5) - \dfrac{3}{4} = (9.6)(5) - 0.75$

$= 48 - 0.75$

$= 47.25$

101. $\dfrac{3}{8}(5.9 - 4.7) = 0.375(5.9 - 4.7)$

$= 0.375(1.2)$

$= 0.45$

Chapter 4 Test

1. 45.092 in words is forty-five and ninety-two thousandths.

5. $25.0909 < 25.9090$

9.
```
      0.65
20) 13.00
  − 12 0
     1 00
   − 1 00
        0
```

$\dfrac{13}{20} = 0.65$

13.
```
  20.0
− 8.6
  11.4
```

17.
```
         6.6728 ≈ 6.673
7) 46.7100
 − 42
    47
  − 4 2
     51
   − 49
      20
    − 14
       60
     − 56
        4
```

21. $\dfrac{0.23 + 1.63}{0.3} = \dfrac{1.86}{0.3}$

```
                    6.2
0.3)1.86  becomes 3) 18.6
                  − 18
                    0 6
                  − 6
                     0
```

$\dfrac{0.23 + 1.63}{0.3} = 6.2$

25. a.
```
    123.8
×      80
  9904.0
```
The area of the lawn is 9904 square feet.

b. Multiply the number of square feet by the number of ounces per square foot.
```
  9904
  0.02
198.08
```
198.08 ounces of insecticide are needed.

CHAPTER 5

Exercise Set 5.1

1. The ratio of 11 to 14 is $\dfrac{11}{14}$.

5. The ratio of 151 to 201 is $\dfrac{151}{201}$.

9. The ratio of 5 to $7\dfrac{1}{2}$ is $\dfrac{5}{7\dfrac{1}{2}}$.

13. The ratio of 16 to 24 is $\dfrac{16}{24} = \dfrac{8 \cdot 2}{8 \cdot 3} = \dfrac{2}{3}$.

17. The ratio of 4.63 to 8.21 is $\dfrac{4.63}{8.21} = \dfrac{4.63 \cdot 100}{8.21 \cdot 100} = \dfrac{463}{821}$.

21. The ratio of 10 hours to 24 hours is $\dfrac{10\text{ hours}}{24\text{ hours}} = \dfrac{10}{24} = \dfrac{2 \cdot 5}{2 \cdot 12} = \dfrac{5}{12}$.

25. The ratio of 24 days to 14 days is $\dfrac{24\text{ days}}{14\text{ days}} = \dfrac{24}{14} = \dfrac{2 \cdot 12}{2 \cdot 7} = \dfrac{12}{7}$.

29. The ratio of 8 inches to 20 inches is $\dfrac{8\text{ inches}}{20\text{ inches}} = \dfrac{8}{20} = \dfrac{4 \cdot 2}{4 \cdot 5} = \dfrac{2}{5}$.

33. The ratio of $7\dfrac{3}{5}$ hours to $1\dfrac{9}{10}$ hours is

$\dfrac{7\dfrac{3}{5}\text{ hours}}{1\dfrac{9}{10}\text{ hours}} = \dfrac{7\dfrac{3}{5}}{1\dfrac{9}{10}}$

$= 7\dfrac{3}{5} \div 1\dfrac{9}{10}$

$= \dfrac{38}{5} \div \dfrac{19}{10}$

$= \dfrac{38}{5} \cdot \dfrac{10}{19}$

$= \dfrac{19 \cdot 2 \cdot 5 \cdot 2}{5 \cdot 19}$

$= \dfrac{2 \cdot 2}{1}$

$= \dfrac{4}{1}$

37. The ratio of length to width is $\dfrac{94\text{ feet}}{50\text{ feet}} = \dfrac{94}{50} = \dfrac{2 \cdot 47}{2 \cdot 25} = \dfrac{47}{25}$.

41. The ratio of calories from fat to total fat is
$\dfrac{200\text{ calories}}{450\text{ calories}} = \dfrac{200}{450} = \dfrac{50 \cdot 4}{50 \cdot 9} = \dfrac{4}{9}$.

45. There are $6000 - 4500 = 1500$ married students. The ratio of single students to married students is
$\dfrac{4500\text{ students}}{1500\text{ students}} = \dfrac{4500}{1500} = \dfrac{1500 \cdot 3}{1500 \cdot 1} = \dfrac{3}{1}$.

49. The ratio of mountains over 14,000 feet tall found in Alaska to those found in Colorado is $\dfrac{19\text{ mountains}}{57\text{ mountains}} = \dfrac{19}{57} = \dfrac{19 \cdot 1}{19 \cdot 3} = \dfrac{1}{3}$.

53. There is $50 - 49 = 1$ state without Target stores. The ratio of states without Target stores to states with Target stores is
$\dfrac{1\text{ state}}{49\text{ states}} = \dfrac{1}{49}$.

57.
```
                      0.15
3.7)0.555  becomes 37) 5.55
                     − 3 7
                      1 85
                    − 1 85
                         0
```

61. 30 : 1 should be read as "the ratio of thirty to one."

65. $\dfrac{\$3}{\$2}$ is not in simplest form: $\dfrac{\$3}{\$2} = \dfrac{3}{2}$.

69. $4\dfrac{1}{2}$ is not in simplest form: $4\dfrac{1}{2} = \dfrac{9}{2}$.

Exercise Set 5.2

1. The rate of 5 shrubs every 15 feet is $\dfrac{5 \text{ shrubs}}{15 \text{ feet}} = \dfrac{1 \text{ shrub}}{3 \text{ feet}}$.

5. The rate of 8 phone lines for 36 employees is
$\dfrac{8 \text{ phone lines}}{36 \text{ employees}} = \dfrac{2 \text{ phone lines}}{9 \text{ employees}}$.

9. The rate of 6 flight attendants for 200 passengers is
$\dfrac{6 \text{ flight attendants}}{200 \text{ passengers}} = \dfrac{3 \text{ flight attendants}}{100 \text{ passengers}}$.

13.
$$
\begin{array}{r}
75 \\
5\overline{)\,375} \\
-35 \\
\hline
25 \\
-25 \\
\hline
0
\end{array}
$$

$\dfrac{375 \text{ riders}}{5 \text{ subway cars}} = \dfrac{75 \text{ riders}}{1 \text{ car}} = 75 \text{ riders/car}$

17. 1 minute = 60 seconds
$$
\begin{array}{r}
90 \\
60\overline{)\,5400} \\
-540 \\
\hline
00 \\
-0 \\
\hline
0
\end{array}
$$

$\dfrac{5400 \text{ wingbeats}}{1 \text{ minute}} = \dfrac{5400 \text{ wingbeats}}{60 \text{ seconds}}$
$= \dfrac{90 \text{ wingbeats}}{1 \text{ second}}$
$= 90 \text{ wingbeats/second}$

21.
$$
\begin{array}{r}
1330 \\
20\overline{)\,26600} \\
-20 \\
\hline
66 \\
-60 \\
\hline
60 \\
-60 \\
\hline
00 \\
-0 \\
\hline
0
\end{array}
$$

$\dfrac{26{,}600 \text{ miles}}{20 \text{ days}} = \dfrac{1330 \text{ miles}}{1 \text{ day}} = 1330 \text{ miles/day}$

25.
$$
\begin{array}{r}
300 \\
40\overline{)\,12000} \\
-120 \\
\hline
00 \\
-0 \\
\hline
00 \\
-0 \\
\hline
0
\end{array}
$$

$\dfrac{12{,}000 \text{ good products}}{40 \text{ defective products}} = \dfrac{300 \text{ good products}}{1 \text{ defective product}}$
$= 300 \text{ good/defective}$

29.
$$
\begin{array}{r}
60200 \\
475\overline{)\,28595000} \\
-2850 \\
\hline
95 \\
-0 \\
\hline
950 \\
-950 \\
\hline
00 \\
-0 \\
\hline
00 \\
-0 \\
\hline
0
\end{array}
$$

$\dfrac{\$28{,}595{,}000}{475 \text{ species}} = \dfrac{\$60{,}200}{1 \text{ species}} = \$60{,}200\text{/species}$

33.
$$
\begin{array}{r}
6.16 \approx 6.2 \\
24\overline{)\,148.00} \\
-144 \\
\hline
4\,0 \\
-2\,4 \\
\hline
1\,60 \\
-1\,44 \\
\hline
16
\end{array}
$$

$\dfrac{148 \text{ tornadoes}}{24 \text{ hours}} \approx \dfrac{6.2 \text{ tornadoes}}{1 \text{ hour}}$
$= 6.2 \text{ tornadoes/hour}$

37. a. $14.5\overline{)400}$ becomes
$$
\begin{array}{r}
27.58 \approx 27.6 \\
145\overline{)\,4000.00} \\
-290 \\
\hline
1100 \\
-1015 \\
\hline
85\,0 \\
-72\,5 \\
\hline
12\,50 \\
-11\,60 \\
\hline
90
\end{array}
$$

The unit rate for the car is approximately 27.6 miles/gallon.

b. $9.25\overline{)270}$ becomes
$$
\begin{array}{r}
29.18 \approx 29.2 \\
925\overline{)\,27000.00} \\
-1850 \\
\hline
8500 \\
-8325 \\
\hline
175\,0 \\
-92\,5 \\
\hline
82\,50 \\
-74\,00 \\
\hline
8\,50
\end{array}
$$

The unit rate for the truck is approximately 29.2 miles/gallon.

c. Since the unit rate of the truck is larger, the truck gets better gas mileage.

41.
$$
\begin{array}{r}
0.17 \\
7\overline{)\,1.19} \\
-7 \\
\hline
49 \\
-49 \\
\hline
0
\end{array}
$$

The unit price is \$0.17 per banana.

45.
$$16\overline{)}\begin{array}{l}0.1056 \approx 0.106 \\ \overline{1.6900}\end{array}$$
$$\begin{array}{r}-16 \\ \hline 09 \\ -0 \\ \hline 90 \\ -80 \\ \hline 100 \\ -96 \\ \hline 4\end{array}$$
The 16-ounce size costs about $0.106 per ounce.

$$6\overline{)}\begin{array}{l}0.115 \\ \overline{0.690}\end{array}$$
$$\begin{array}{r}-6 \\ \hline 09 \\ -6 \\ \hline 30 \\ -30 \\ \hline 0\end{array}$$
The 6-ounce size costs $0.115 per ounce.
The 16-ounce size is the better buy.

49.
$$100\overline{)}\begin{array}{l}0.0059 \approx 0.006 \\ \overline{0.5900}\end{array}$$
$$\begin{array}{r}-500 \\ \hline 900 \\ -900 \\ \hline 0\end{array}$$
The 100-count napkins cost about $0.006 per napkin.

$$180\overline{)}\begin{array}{l}0.0051 \approx 0.005 \\ \overline{0.9300}\end{array}$$
$$\begin{array}{r}-900 \\ \hline 300 \\ -180 \\ \hline 120\end{array}$$
The 180-count napkins cost about $0.005 per napkin.
The 180-count package is the better buy.

53.
$$\begin{array}{r}3.7 \\ \times 1.2 \\ \hline 74 \\ 37 \\ \hline 4.44\end{array}$$

57. Fill in the "Miles Driven" column by subtracting "Beginning Odometer Reading" from "Ending Odometer Reading." Fill in the "Miles per Gallon" column by dividing "Miles Driven" by "Gallons of Gas Used," and rounding to the nearest tenth.

Miles Driven	Miles per Gallon
257	19.2
352	22.3
347	21.6

61. answers may vary

Exercise Set 5.3

1. $\dfrac{10 \text{ diamonds}}{6 \text{ opals}} = \dfrac{5 \text{ diamonds}}{3 \text{ opals}}$

5. $\dfrac{6 \text{ eagles}}{58 \text{ sparrows}} = \dfrac{3 \text{ eagles}}{29 \text{ sparrows}}$

9. $\dfrac{22 \text{ vanilla wafers}}{1 \text{ cup cookie crumbs}} = \dfrac{55 \text{ vanilla wafers}}{2.5 \text{ cups cookie crumbs}}$

13. $\dfrac{8}{6} \overset{?}{=} \dfrac{9}{7}$
$8 \cdot 7 \overset{?}{=} 9 \cdot 6$
$56 \neq 54$
false

17. $\dfrac{5}{8} \overset{?}{=} \dfrac{625}{1000}$
$5 \cdot 1000 \overset{?}{=} 8 \cdot 625$
$5000 = 5000$
true

21. $\dfrac{8}{10} \overset{?}{=} \dfrac{5.6}{0.7}$
$8(0.7) \overset{?}{=} 10(5.6)$
$5.6 \neq 56$
false

25. $\dfrac{2\frac{2}{5}}{\frac{2}{3}} \overset{?}{=} \dfrac{1\frac{1}{9}}{\frac{1}{4}}$
$2\dfrac{2}{5} \cdot \dfrac{1}{4} \overset{?}{=} 1\dfrac{1}{9} \cdot \dfrac{2}{3}$
$\dfrac{12}{5} \cdot \dfrac{1}{4} \overset{?}{=} \dfrac{10}{9} \cdot \dfrac{2}{3}$
$\dfrac{3}{5} \neq \dfrac{20}{27}$
false

29. $\dfrac{8}{12} \overset{?}{=} \dfrac{4}{6}$
$8 \cdot 6 \overset{?}{=} 12 \cdot 4$
$48 = 48$
true

33. $\dfrac{1.8}{2} \overset{?}{=} \dfrac{4.5}{5}$
$1.8(5) \overset{?}{=} 4.5(2)$
$9 = 9$
true

37. $\dfrac{n}{5} = \dfrac{6}{10}$
$10n = 6 \cdot 5$
$10n = 30$
$n = 3$

41. $\dfrac{n}{8} = \dfrac{50}{100}$
$100n = 8 \cdot 50$
$100n = 400$
$n = 4$

45. $\dfrac{24}{n} = \dfrac{60}{96}$
$24 \cdot 96 = 60n$
$2304 = 60n$
$38.4 = n$

49. $\dfrac{0.05}{12} = \dfrac{n}{0.6}$
$0.05(0.6) = 12n$
$0.03 = 12n$
$0.0025 = n$

53. $\dfrac{\frac{1}{3}}{\frac{3}{8}} = \dfrac{\frac{2}{5}}{n}$
$\dfrac{1}{3}n = \dfrac{3}{8} \cdot \dfrac{2}{5}$
$\dfrac{1}{3}n = \dfrac{3}{20}$
$n = \dfrac{3}{20} \div \dfrac{1}{3}$
$n = \dfrac{3}{20} \cdot \dfrac{3}{1}$
$n = \dfrac{9}{20}$

57.
$$\frac{n}{1\frac{1}{5}} = \frac{4\frac{1}{6}}{6\frac{2}{3}}$$

$$\left(6\frac{2}{3}\right)n = \left(1\frac{1}{5}\right)\left(4\frac{1}{6}\right)$$

$$\frac{20}{3}n = \frac{6}{5} \cdot \frac{25}{6}$$

$$\frac{20}{3}n = \frac{5}{1}$$

$$n = \frac{5}{1} \div \frac{20}{3}$$

$$n = \frac{5}{1} \cdot \frac{3}{20}$$

$$n = \frac{3}{4}$$

61. $8.01 \quad 8.1$
$$\uparrow \qquad \uparrow$$
$$0 \; < \; 1 \text{ so}$$
$$8.01 < 8.1$$

65. $5\frac{1}{3} = \frac{16}{3}$

$6\frac{2}{3} = \frac{20}{3}$

$16 < 20$, so $5\frac{1}{3} < 6\frac{2}{3}$

69. $\frac{6}{18} = \frac{1}{3}$

$\frac{6}{1} = \frac{18}{3}$

$\frac{3}{18} = \frac{1}{6}$

$\frac{18}{6} = \frac{3}{1}$

73. answers may vary

77. $\frac{n}{1150} = \frac{588}{483}$

$483n = 1150 \cdot 588$

$483n = 676{,}200$

$n = 1400$

Exercise Set 5.4

1. Let n = number of passes completed.

completed → $\dfrac{n}{27} = \dfrac{4}{9}$ ← completed
attempted →   ← attempted

$$9n = 4 \cdot 27$$
$$9n = 108$$
$$n = 12$$

12 passes were completed.

5. Let n = number of applications received.

applications → $\dfrac{n}{180} = \dfrac{7}{2}$ ← applications
accepted →   ← accepted

$$2n = 7 \cdot 180$$
$$2n = 1260$$
$$n = 630$$

630 applications were received.

9. Let n = square feet of floor space needed.

floor space → $\dfrac{n}{30} = \dfrac{9}{1}$ ← floor space
students →   ← students

$$1 \cdot n = 9 \cdot 30$$
$$n = 270$$

270 square feet of floor space are needed.

13. Let n = number of kilometers between Milan and Rome.

kilometers → $\dfrac{n}{15} = \dfrac{30}{1}$ ← kilometers
cm on map →   ← cm on map

$$1 \cdot n = 15 \cdot 30$$
$$n = 450$$

Milan and Rome are 450 kilometers apart.

17. Let n = number of bags of fertilizer. The area of the lawn is $260 \cdot 180 = 46{,}800$ square feet.

bags → $\dfrac{n}{46{,}800} = \dfrac{1}{3000}$ ← bags
square feet →   ← square feet

$$3000n = 1 \cdot 46{,}800$$
$$300n = 46{,}800$$
$$n = 15.6$$

Since only whole bags of fertilizer can be purchased, 16 bags should be purchased.

21. Let n = the number of hits the player is expected to get.

hits → $\dfrac{n}{40} = \dfrac{3}{8}$ ← hits
times at bat →   ← times at bat

$$8n = 3 \cdot 40$$
$$8n = 120$$
$$n = 15$$

The Cubs player would be expected to get 15 hits.

25. Let n = the number of weeks the envelopes are expected to last.

weeks → $\dfrac{n}{144} = \dfrac{3}{5}$ ← weeks
boxes →   ← boxes

$$5n = 3 \cdot 144$$
$$5n = 432$$
$$n = 86.4$$

A gross of boxes of envelopes would be expected to last 86 weeks.

29. Let n = estimated head-to-toe height of the Statue of Liberty.

height → $\dfrac{n}{42} = \dfrac{5\frac{1}{3}}{2}$ ← height
arm length →   ← arm length

$$2n = 5\frac{1}{3} \cdot 42$$

$$2n = \frac{16}{3} \cdot 42$$

$$2n = 224$$
$$n = 112$$

The head-to-toe height of the Statue of Liberty is estimated to be 112 feet.

$$112 - 111\frac{1}{12} = \frac{11}{12}$$

The difference is $\dfrac{11}{12}$ foot, or 11 inches.

33. Let n = the estimated height of the Empire State Building.

height → $\dfrac{n}{102} = \dfrac{881}{72}$ ← height
stories →   ← stories

$$72n = 102 \cdot 881$$
$$72n = 89{,}862$$
$$n \approx 1248$$

The height of the Empire State Building is approximately 1248 feet.

37. Let n = the number of calories in a nine-piece order.

calories → $\dfrac{n}{9} = \dfrac{190}{4}$ ← calories
pieces →   ← pieces

$$4n = 9(190)$$
$$4n = 1710$$
$$n = 427.5$$

There are 427.5 calories in a 9-piece order.

41. Let n = the amount of rock salt to be used.

salt → $\dfrac{n}{12} = \dfrac{1}{5}$ ← salt
ice →   ← ice

$$5n = 12 \cdot 1$$
$$5n = 12$$
$$n = 2.4$$

2.4 cups of rock salt should be used.

45. a. Let n = the number of milligrams in a daily dose.

milligrams → $\dfrac{n}{275} = \dfrac{150}{20}$ ← milligrams
pounds →   ← pounds

$$20n = 275 \cdot 150$$
$$20n = 41{,}250$$
$$n = 2062.5$$

The man should receive 2062.5 milligrams daily.

b. One day is 24 hours, so the man receives 3 500-milligram doses, for a total of 1500 milligrams, daily. Since his daily dose should be 2062.5 milligrams, the dosage is not correct.

49.
$$2\overline{)10}\quad^{5}$$
$$2\overline{)20}$$
$$20 = 2 \cdot 2 \cdot 5 = 2^2 \cdot 5$$

53.
$$2\overline{)\,4}\quad^{2}$$
$$2\overline{)\,8}$$
$$2\overline{)16}$$
$$2\overline{)32}$$
$$32 = 2 \cdot 2 \cdot 2 \cdot 2 \cdot 2 = 2^5$$

57. Let n = the number of ml of medicine to be administered.
$$\text{mg} \rightarrow \frac{10}{n} = \frac{8}{1} \leftarrow \text{mg}$$
$$\text{ml} \rightarrow \quad\quad\quad \leftarrow \text{ml}$$
$$10 = 8n$$
$$\frac{1}{8} \cdot 10 = n$$
$$1.25 = n$$
1.25 ml of medicine should be administered.

61.
$$\text{first weight} \rightarrow \frac{40}{n} = \frac{60}{7} \leftarrow \text{second weight}$$
$$\text{second distance} \rightarrow \quad\quad\quad \leftarrow \text{first distance}$$
$$40 \cdot 7 = 60n$$
$$280 = 60n$$
$$\frac{1}{60} \cdot 280 = n$$
$$\frac{14}{3} = n$$
The distance should be $\frac{14}{3}$ or $4\frac{2}{3}$ feet.

Chapter 5 Test

1. $\dfrac{\$75}{\$10} = \dfrac{75}{10} = \dfrac{5 \cdot 15}{5 \cdot 2} = \dfrac{15}{2}$

5. $\dfrac{8.6}{10} = \dfrac{8.6 \cdot 10}{10 \cdot 10} = \dfrac{86}{100} = \dfrac{2 \cdot 43}{2 \cdot 50} = \dfrac{43}{50}$

9. $\dfrac{8 \text{ inches}}{12 \text{ hours}} = \dfrac{8}{12} \text{ inch/hour} = \dfrac{2}{3} \text{ inch/hour}$

13.
$$16\overline{)\,1.4900}\quad^{0.0931 \approx 0.093}$$
$$\underline{-1\,44}$$
$$\quad\;50$$
$$\quad\underline{-48}$$
$$\quad\quad 20$$
$$\quad\;\underline{-16}$$
$$\quad\quad\; 4$$
The 16-ounce size costs approximately \$0.093/ounce.

$$24\overline{)\,2.3900}\quad^{0.0995 \approx 0.100}$$
$$\underline{-2\,16}$$
$$\quad 230$$
$$\underline{-216}$$
$$\quad\; 140$$
$$\;\underline{-120}$$
$$\quad\quad 20$$
The 24-ounce size costs approximately \$0.100/ounce. The 16-ounce size is the better buy.

17.
$$\frac{n}{3} = \frac{15}{9}$$
$$9n = 3 \cdot 15$$
$$9n = 45$$
$$n = \frac{45}{9}$$
$$n = 5$$

21.
$$\frac{n}{2\frac{5}{8}} = \frac{1\frac{1}{6}}{3\frac{1}{2}}$$
$$\left(3\frac{1}{2}\right)n = \left(1\frac{1}{6}\right)\left(2\frac{5}{8}\right)$$
$$\frac{7}{2}n = \frac{7}{6} \cdot \frac{21}{8}$$
$$\frac{7}{2}n = \frac{49}{16}$$
$$n = \frac{49}{16} \div \frac{7}{2}$$
$$n = \frac{49}{16} \cdot \frac{2}{7}$$
$$n = \frac{7}{8}$$

25. Let n = the number of cartons.
$$\text{cartons} \rightarrow \frac{n}{8} = \frac{86}{6} \leftarrow \text{cartons}$$
$$\text{hours} \rightarrow \quad\quad\quad \leftarrow \text{hours}$$
$$6n = 8 \cdot 86$$
$$6n = 688$$
$$n = \frac{688}{6}$$
$$n = 114\frac{2}{3}$$
He can pack $114\frac{2}{3}$ cartons in 8 hours.

CHAPTER 6

Exercise Set 6.1

1. $\dfrac{81}{100} = 81\%$

5. $\dfrac{9}{100} = 9\%$

9. $48\% = 48(0.01) = 0.48$

13. $100\% = 100(0.01) = 1.00 \text{ or } 1$

17. $2.8\% = 2.8(0.01) = 0.028$

21. $300\% = 300(0.01) = 3.00 \text{ or } 3$

25. $67\% = 67(0.01) = 0.67$

29. $5.7\% = 5.7(0.01) = 0.057$

33. $3.1 = 3.1(100\%) = 310\%$

37. $0.003 = 0.003(100\%) = 0.3\%$

41. $5.3 = 5.3(100\%) = 530\%$

45. $0.3328 = 0.3328(100\%) = 33.28\%$

49. $0.7 = 0.7(100\%) = 70\%$

53. $0.38 = 0.38(100\%) = 38\%$

57. $\dfrac{1}{4} = \dfrac{1}{4} \cdot \dfrac{25}{25} = \dfrac{25}{100} = 0.25$

61. $\dfrac{9}{10} = \dfrac{9}{10} \cdot \dfrac{10}{10} = \dfrac{90}{100} = 0.9$

65. If the percentages of the four blood types are added, the total will be 100%, since the blood types cover the whole population.
$45\% + 40\% + 11\% = (45 + 40 + 11)\% = 96\%$
$100\% - 96\% = (100 - 96)\% = 4\%$
4% of the U.S. population has the blood type AB.

69. $49\% = 49(0.01) = 0.49$

Exercise Set 6.2

1. $12\% = 12 \cdot \dfrac{1}{100} = \dfrac{12}{100} = \dfrac{3 \cdot 4}{25 \cdot 4} = \dfrac{3}{25}$

5. $4.5\% = 4.5 \cdot \dfrac{1}{100}$

$= \dfrac{4.5}{100}$

$= \dfrac{4.5}{100} \cdot \dfrac{10}{10}$

$= \dfrac{45}{1000}$

$= \dfrac{9 \cdot 5}{200 \cdot 5}$

$= \dfrac{9}{200}$

9. $73\% = 73 \cdot \dfrac{1}{100} = \dfrac{73}{100}$

13. $6.25\% = 6.25 \cdot \dfrac{1}{100}$

$= \dfrac{6.25}{100}$

$= \dfrac{6.25}{100} \cdot \dfrac{100}{100}$

$= \dfrac{625}{10,000}$

$= \dfrac{1 \cdot 625}{16 \cdot 625}$

$= \dfrac{1}{16}$

17. $10\dfrac{1}{3}\% = \dfrac{31}{3}\% = \dfrac{31}{3} \cdot \dfrac{1}{100} = \dfrac{31}{300}$

21. $\dfrac{3}{4} = \dfrac{3}{4}(100\%) = \dfrac{300}{4}\% = 75\%$

25. $\dfrac{2}{5} = \dfrac{2}{5}(100\%) = \dfrac{200}{5}\% = 40\%$

29. $\dfrac{17}{50} = \dfrac{17}{50}(100\%) = \dfrac{1700}{50}\% = 34\%$

33. $\dfrac{5}{16} = \dfrac{5}{16}(100\%) = \dfrac{500}{16}\% = \dfrac{125}{4}\% = 31\dfrac{1}{4}\%$

37. $\dfrac{7}{9} = \dfrac{7}{9}(100\%) = \dfrac{700}{9}\% = 77\dfrac{7}{9}\%$

41. $2\dfrac{1}{2} = \dfrac{5}{2} = \dfrac{5}{2}(100\%) = \dfrac{500}{2}\% = 250\%$

45. $\dfrac{7}{11} = \dfrac{7}{11}(100\%) = \dfrac{700}{11}\% \approx 63.64\%$

$$\begin{array}{r} 63.636\ldots \approx 63.64 \\ 11\overline{)\,700.000} \\ \underline{-66} \\ 40 \\ \underline{-33} \\ 7\,0 \\ \underline{-6\,6} \\ 40 \\ \underline{-33} \\ 70 \\ \underline{-66} \\ 4 \end{array}$$

49. $\dfrac{1}{7} = \dfrac{1}{7}(100\%) = \dfrac{100}{7}\% \approx 14.29\%$

$$\begin{array}{r} 14.285 \approx 14.29 \\ 7\overline{)\,100.000} \\ \underline{-7} \\ 30 \\ \underline{-28} \\ 2\,0 \\ \underline{-1\,4} \\ 60 \\ \underline{-56} \\ 40 \\ \underline{-35} \\ 5 \end{array}$$

53.

Percent	Decimal	Fraction
35%	$35\% = 0.35$	$35\% = \dfrac{35}{100} = \dfrac{7}{20}$
$\dfrac{1}{5} = \dfrac{20}{100} = 20\%$	$\dfrac{1}{5} = \dfrac{2}{10} = 0.2$	$\dfrac{1}{5}$
$0.5 = 0.50 = 50\%$	0.5	$0.5 = \dfrac{5}{10} = \dfrac{1}{2}$
70%	$70\% = 0.7$	$70\% = \dfrac{70}{100} = \dfrac{7}{10}$
$\dfrac{3}{8} = \dfrac{375}{1000} = \dfrac{37.5}{100}$ $= 37.5\%$	$\dfrac{3}{8} = \dfrac{375}{1000} = 0.375$	$\dfrac{3}{8}$

57.

Percent	Decimal	Fraction
200%	$200\% = 2.00 = 2$	$200\% = \dfrac{200}{100} = 2$
$2.8 = \dfrac{28}{10} = \dfrac{280}{100}$ $= 280\%$	2.8	$2.8 = 2\dfrac{8}{10} = 2\dfrac{4}{5}$
705%	$705\% = 7.05$	$705\% = \dfrac{705}{100}$ $= 7\dfrac{5}{100} = 7\dfrac{1}{20}$
$4\dfrac{27}{50} = 4\dfrac{54}{100}$ $= \dfrac{454}{100} = 454\%$	$4\dfrac{27}{50} = 4\dfrac{54}{100} = 4.54$	$4\dfrac{27}{50}$

61. $23\% = 0.23$

$23\% = \dfrac{23}{100}$

65. $8.75\% = 0.0875$

69. $0.4\% = 0.004$

$0.4\% = \dfrac{0.4}{100} = \dfrac{40}{100} = \dfrac{1}{250}$

73. $7.1\% = 0.071$

$7.1\% = \dfrac{7.1}{100} = \dfrac{71}{1000}$

77. $8 \cdot n = 80$

$\dfrac{8 \cdot n}{8} = \dfrac{80}{8}$

$n = 10$

81. a. To round 52.8647 to the nearest tenth observe that the digit in the hundredths place is 6. Since this digit is at least 5, we need to add 1 to the digit in the tenths place. The number 52.8647 rounded to the nearest tenth is 52.9. Thus 52.8647% ≈ 52.9%.

b. To round 52.8647 to the nearest hundredth observe that the digit in the thousandths place is 4. Since this digit is less than 5, we do not add 1 to the digit in the hundredths place. The number 52.8647 rounded to the nearest hundredth is 52.86. Thus 52.8647% ≈ 52.86%.

85. 0.65794 = 65.794%

To round 65.794 to the nearest hundredth observe that the digit in the thousandths place is 4. Since this digit is less than 5, we do not add 1 to the digit in the hundredths place. The number 65.794 to the nearest hundredth is 65.79. Thus,
0.65794 = 65.794% ≈ 65.79%.

89. 3 of the 4 equal parts are shaded.
$$\frac{3}{4} = \frac{3}{4} \cdot \frac{25}{25} = \frac{75}{100} = 75\%$$
75% of the figure is shaded.

93. A fraction written as a percent is greater than 100% when the numerator is *greater* than the denominator.

97.
$$
\begin{array}{r}
0.2658 \approx 0.266 \\
79\overline{)21.0000} \\
-15\,8 \\
\hline
5\,20 \\
-4\,74 \\
\hline
460 \\
-395 \\
\hline
650 \\
-632 \\
\hline
18
\end{array}
$$

$$\frac{21}{79} \approx 0.266 \text{ or } 26.6\%$$

Exercise Set 6.3

1. 15% of 72 is what number?

↓ ↓ ↓ ↓   ↓
15% · 72 = n

5. 1.9 is 40% of what number?

↓ ↓ ↓ ↓   ↓
1.9 = 40% · n

9. What number is 9% of 43?

↓   ↓ ↓ ↓ ↓
n = 9% · 43

13. $n = 14\% \cdot 52$
$n = 0.14 \cdot 52$
$n = 7.28$
7.28 is 14% of 52.

17. $1.2 = 12\% \cdot n$
$1.2 = 0.12n$
$\frac{1.2}{0.12} = n$
$10 = n$
1.2 is 12% of 10.

21. $16 = n \cdot 50$
$\frac{16}{50} = n$
$0.32 = n$
$32\% = n$
16 is 32% of 50.

25. $125\% \cdot 36 = n$
$1.25 \cdot 36 = n$
$45 = n$
125% of 36 is 45.

29. $126 = n \cdot 31.5$
$\frac{126}{31.5} = n$
$4 = n$
$400\% = n$
126 is 400% of 31.5.

33. $n \cdot 150 = 67.5$
$n = \frac{67.5}{150}$
$n = 0.45$
$n = 45\%$
45% of 150 is 67.5.

37. $2.4\% \cdot 26 = n$
$0.024 \cdot 26 = n$
$0.624 = n$
2.4% of 26 is 0.624.

41. $6.67 = 4.6\% \cdot n$
$6.67 = 0.046 \cdot n$
$\frac{6.67}{0.046} = n$
$145 = n$
6.67 is 4.6% of 145.

45. $\frac{27}{n} = \frac{9}{10}$
$27 \cdot 10 = 9 \cdot n$
$270 = 9n$
$\frac{270}{9} = n$
$30 = n$

49. $\frac{17}{12} = \frac{n}{20}$

53. In the equation $5 \cdot n = 32$, the step that should be taken to find the value of n is to divide by 5, obtaining $n = \frac{32}{5}$, which is choice c.

57. $n = 33\frac{1}{3}\% \cdot 24$ in words is "some number is thirty-three and one third percent of twenty-four."

61. Since 55% is less than 100%, which is 1, 55% of 45 is less than 45; c.

65. Since 100% is 1, and 100% of n is 45, then n is 45; a.

69. $1.5\% \cdot 45,775 = n$
$0.015 \cdot 45,775 = n$
$686.625 = n$
1.5% of 45,775 is 686.625.

Exercise Set 6.4

1. 32% of 65 is what number?

↓   ↓   ↓
percent base   amount = a
$$\frac{a}{65} = \frac{32}{100}$$

5. 2.3 is 58% of what number?

↓   ↓   ↓
amount percent   base = b
$$\frac{2.3}{b} = \frac{58}{100}$$

9. What percent of 200 is 70?

↓   ↓   ↓
percent = p base amount
$$\frac{70}{200} = \frac{p}{100}$$

13.
$$\frac{a}{105} = \frac{18}{100}$$
$$\frac{a}{105} = \frac{9}{50}$$
$$a \cdot 50 = 9 \cdot 105$$
$$50a = 945$$
$$a = \frac{945}{50}$$
$$a = 18.9$$
Therefore, 18.9 is 18% of 105.

17.
$$\frac{7.8}{b} = \frac{78}{100}$$
$$7.8 \cdot 100 = 78 \cdot b$$
$$780 = 78b$$
$$\frac{780}{78} = b$$
$$10 = b$$
Therefore, 7.8 is 78% of 10.

21.
$$\frac{14}{50} = \frac{p}{100}$$
$$\frac{7}{25} = \frac{p}{100}$$
$$7 \cdot 100 = p \cdot 25$$
$$700 = 25p$$
$$\frac{700}{25} = p$$
$$28 = p$$
Therefore, 14 is 28% of 50.

25.
$$\frac{a}{80} = \frac{2.4}{100}$$
$$a \cdot 100 = 2.4 \cdot 80$$
$$100a = 192$$
$$a = \frac{192}{100}$$
$$a = 1.92$$
Therefore, 2.4% of 80 is 1.92.

29.
$$\frac{348.6}{166} = \frac{p}{100}$$
$$348.6 \cdot 100 = p \cdot 166$$
$$34{,}860 = 166p$$
$$\frac{34{,}860}{166} = p$$
$$210 = p$$
Therefore, 348.6 is 210% of 166.

33.
$$\frac{3.6}{8} = \frac{p}{100}$$
$$3.6 \cdot 100 = p \cdot 8$$
$$360 = 8p$$
$$\frac{360}{8} = p$$
$$45 = p$$
Therefore, 45% of 8 is 3.6.

37.
$$\frac{a}{48} = \frac{1.8}{100}$$
$$a \cdot 100 = 1.8 \cdot 48$$
$$100a = 86.4$$
$$a = \frac{86.4}{100}$$
$$a = 0.864$$
Therefore, 1.8% of 48 is 0.864.

41.
$$\frac{3.5}{b} = \frac{2.5}{100}$$
$$3.5 \cdot 100 = 2.5 \cdot b$$
$$350 = 2.5b$$
$$\frac{350}{2.5} = b$$
$$140 = b$$
Therefore, 3.5 is 2.5% of 140.

45. $\dfrac{11}{16} + \dfrac{3}{16} = \dfrac{11 + 3}{16} = \dfrac{14}{16} = \dfrac{7 \cdot 2}{8 \cdot 2} = \dfrac{7}{8}$

49.
$$\overset{1}{0.41}$$
$$\underline{+0.29}$$
$$0.70$$

53. answers may vary

57. answers may vary

61.
$$\frac{8652}{b} = \frac{119}{100}$$
$$8652 \cdot 100 = 119 \cdot b$$
$$865{,}200 = 119b$$
$$\frac{865{,}200}{119} = b$$
$$7270.6 \approx b$$

Exercise Set 6.5

1. 24 is 1.5% of what number?
Method 1
$$24 = 1.5\% \cdot n$$
$$24 = 0.015n$$
$$\frac{24}{0.015} = n$$
$$1600 = n$$
1600 bolts were inspected.
Method 2
$$\frac{24}{b} = \frac{1.5}{100}$$
$$24 \cdot 100 = 1.5 \cdot b$$
$$2400 = 1.5b$$
$$\frac{2400}{1.5} = b$$
$$1600 = b$$
1600 bolts were inspected.

5. 300 is what percent of 2000?
Method 1
$$300 = n \cdot 2000$$
$$300 = 2000n$$
$$\frac{300}{2000} = n$$
$$\frac{15}{100} = n$$
$$15\% = n$$
Vera spends 15% of her monthly income on food.
Method 2
$$\frac{300}{2000} = \frac{p}{100}$$
$$\frac{3}{20} = \frac{p}{100}$$
$$3 \cdot 100 = p \cdot 20$$
$$300 = 20p$$
$$\frac{300}{20} = p$$
$$15 = p$$
Vera spends 15% of her monthly income on food.

9. 73 is what percent of 535?
Method 1
$$73 = n \cdot 535$$
$$73 = 535n$$
$$\frac{73}{535} = n$$
$$0.136 \approx n$$
13.6% of the members of the 108th U.S. Congress have attended a community college.

Method 2

$$\frac{73}{535} = \frac{p}{100}$$

$$73 \cdot 100 = 535p$$

$$7300 = 535p$$

$$\frac{7300}{535} = p$$

$$13.6 \approx p$$

13.6% of the members of the 108th U.S. Congress have attended a community college.

13. 20 is what percent of 40?

Method 1

$$20 = n \cdot 40$$

$$20 = 40n$$

$$\frac{20}{40} = n$$

$$0.5 = n$$

$$50\% = n$$

50% of the total calories come from fat.

Method 2

$$\frac{20}{40} = \frac{p}{100}$$

$$20 \cdot 100 = p \cdot 40$$

$$2000 = 40p$$

$$\frac{2000}{40} = p$$

$$50 = p$$

50% of the total calories come from fat.

17. What number is 8% of 6200?

Method 1

$$n = 8\% \cdot 6200$$

$$n = 0.08 \cdot 620$$

$$n = 496$$

The decrease was 496 chairs. The new number of chairs produced each month is $6200 - 496 = 5704$ chairs.

Method 2

$$\frac{a}{6200} = \frac{8}{100}$$

$$a \cdot 100 = 8 \cdot 6200$$

$$100a = 49,600$$

$$a = \frac{49,600}{100}$$

$$a = 496$$

The decrease was 496 chairs. The new number of chairs produced each month is $6200 - 496 = 5704$ chairs.

21. What number is 4.5% of 19,286?

Method 1

$$n = 4.5\% \cdot 19,286$$

$$n = 0.045 \cdot 19,286$$

$$n = 867.87$$

The price of the car will increase by $867.87. The new price of that model will be $19,286 + \$867.87 = \$20,153.87$.

Method 2

$$\frac{a}{19,286} = \frac{4.5}{100}$$

$$a \cdot 100 = 4.5 \cdot 19,286$$

$$100a = 86,787$$

$$a = \frac{86,787}{100}$$

$$a = 867.87$$

The price of the car will increase by $867.87. The new price of that model will be $19,286 + \$867.87 = \$20,153.87$.

25. What number is 80% of 35?

Method 1

$$n = 80\% \cdot 35$$

$$n = 0.80 \cdot 35$$

$$n = 28$$

The increase is projected to be 28 million. The population is projected to be $(35 + 28)$ million = 63 million.

Method 2

$$\frac{a}{35} = \frac{80}{100}$$

$$a \cdot 100 = 80 \cdot 35$$

$$100a = 2800$$

$$a = \frac{2800}{100}$$

$$a = 28$$

The increase is projected to be 28 million. The population is projected to be $(35 + 28)$ million = 63 million.

29.

Original Amount	New Amount	Amount of Increase	Percent Increase
85	187	$187 - 85 = 102$	$\dfrac{102}{85} = 1.2 = 120\%$

33.

Original Amount	New Amount	Amount of Decrease	Percent Decrease
160	40	$160 - 40 = 120$	$\dfrac{120}{160} = 0.75 = 75\%$

37. percent increase $= \dfrac{\text{amount of increase}}{\text{original amount}} = \dfrac{23.7 - 19.5}{19.5}$

$$= \frac{4.2}{19.5} \approx 0.215$$

The miles per gallon increased by 21.5%.

41. percent increase $= \dfrac{\text{amount of increase}}{\text{original amount}} = \dfrac{441 - 174}{174}$

$$= \frac{267}{174} \approx 1.534$$

The farm size increased by 153.4%.

45. percent increase $= \dfrac{\text{amount of increase}}{\text{original amount}} = \dfrac{29,000 - 16,000}{16,000}$

$$= \frac{13,000}{16,000} = 0.8125$$

The number is expected to increase by 81.25%.

49. percent decrease $= \dfrac{\text{amount of decrease}}{\text{original amount}} = \dfrac{127,333 - 99,887}{127,333}$

$$= \frac{27,446}{127,333} \approx 0.216$$

The population is expected to decrease by 21.6%.

53.
$$\begin{array}{r} \overset{1\,1}{9.20} \\ + 1.98 \\ \hline 11.18 \end{array}$$

57. The increased number is double the original number, since
$n + (100\%)n = n + 1 \cdot n = n + n = 2n$.

Exercise Set 6.6

1. sales tax $= 5\% \cdot \$150 = 0.05 \cdot \$150 = \$7.50$
The sales tax is $7.50.

5. $\$57 = r \cdot \$600$

$$\frac{\$57}{\$600} = r$$

$$0.095 = r$$

The sales tax rate is 9.5%.

9. sales tax $= 6.5\% \cdot \$1800 = 0.065 \cdot \$1800 = \$117$
total price $= \$1800 + \$117 = \$1917$
The total price of the bracelet is $1917.

13. $\$98.70 = r \cdot \$1645$

$$\frac{\$98.70}{\$1645} = r$$

$$0.06 = r$$

The sales tax rate is 6%.

17. commission $= 4\% \cdot \$1{,}236{,}856 = 0.04 \cdot \$1{,}236{,}856 = \$49{,}474.24$
Her commission was $49,474.24.

21. commission $= 1.5\% \cdot \$125{,}900 = 0.015 \cdot \$125{,}900 = \$1888.50$
His commission will be $1888.50.

	Original Price	Discount Rate	Amount of Discount	Sale Price
25.	$68	10%	$10\% \cdot \$68$ $= \$6.80$	$\$68 - \$6.80$ $= \$61.20$
29.	$215	35%	$35\% \cdot \$215$ $= \$73.25$	$\$215 - \$73.25$ $= \$139.75$

33. discount $= 15\% \cdot \$300 = 0.15 \cdot \$300 = \$45$
sale price $= \$300 - \$45 = \$255$
The discount is $45 and the sale price is $255.

37.	Purchase Price	Tax Rate	Sales Tax	Total Price
	$82	5.5%	$5.5\% \cdot \$82 = \$4.51$	$\$82 + \$4.51$ $= \$86.51$

41.	Sale	Commission Rate	Commission
	$17,900	$\dfrac{\$1432}{\$17{,}900} = 0.08 = 8\%$	$1432

45. $400 \cdot 0.03 \cdot 11 = 12 \cdot 11 = 132$

49. Round $68 to $70 and 9.5% to 10%.
$10\% \cdot \$70 = 0.10 \cdot \$70 = \$7$
$\$70 + \$7 = \$77$
The best estimate of the total price is $77; d.

53.	Bill Amount	10%	15%	20%
	$\$72.17 \approx \$72.00$	$7.20	$\$7.20 + \dfrac{1}{2}(\$7.20)$ $= \$7.20 + \$3.60$ $= \$10.80$	$2(\$7.20)$ $= \$14.40$

57. $7.5\% \cdot \$24{,}966 = 0.075 \cdot \$24{,}966 = \$1872.45$
$\$24{,}966 + \$1872.45 = \$26{,}838.45$
The total price of the necklace is $26,838.45.

Exercise Set 6.7

1. simple interest $=$ principal $\cdot$ rate $\cdot$ time $= (\$200)(8\%)(2)$
$= (\$200)(0.08)(2) = \$32$

5. simple interest $=$ principal $\cdot$ rate $\cdot$ time $= (\$5000)(10\%)\left(1\dfrac{1}{2}\right)$
$= (\$5000)(0.10)(1.5) = \$750$

9. simple interest $=$ principal $\cdot$ rate $\cdot$ time $= (\$2500)(16\%)\left(\dfrac{21}{12}\right)$
$= (\$2500)(0.16)(1.75) = \$700$

13. simple interest $=$ principal $\cdot$ rate $\cdot$ time $= \$5000(9\%)\left(\dfrac{15}{12}\right)$
$= \$5000(0.09)(1.25) = \$562.50$
Total $= \$5000 + \$562.50 = \$5562.50$

17. Total amount $=$ original principal $\cdot$ compound interest factor
$= \$6150(7.61226) = \$46{,}815.399$
The total amount is $46,815.40.

21. Total amount $=$ original principal $\cdot$ compound interest factor
$= \$10{,}000(5.81636) = \$58{,}163.60$
The total amount is $58,163.60.

25. Total amount $=$ original principal $\cdot$ compound interest factor
$= \$2000(1.46933) = \$2938.66$
Compound interest $=$ total amount $-$ original principal
$= \$2938.66 - \$2000 = \$938.66$

29. monthly payment $= \dfrac{\text{principal} + \text{simple interest}}{\text{number of payments}}$
$= \dfrac{\$1500 + \$61.88}{6}$
$= \dfrac{\$1561.88}{6}$
$\approx \$260.31$
The monthly payment is $260.31.

33. perimeter $= 10 + 6 + 10 + 6 = 32$
The perimeter is 32 yards.

37. answers may vary

Chapter 6 Test

1. $85\% = 85(0.01) = 0.85$

5. $6.1 = 6.1(100\%) = 610\%$

9. $0.2\% = \dfrac{0.2}{100} = \dfrac{2}{1000} = \dfrac{1}{500}$

13. $n = 42\% \cdot 80$
$n = 0.42 \cdot 80$
$n = 33.6$
Therefore, 42% of 80 is 33.6.

17. 20% of what number is $11,350?
$0.20n = \$11{,}350$
$n = \dfrac{\$11{,}350}{0.20}$
$n = \$56{,}750$
The value is $56,750.

21. commission $= 4\% \cdot \$9875 = 0.04 \cdot \$9875 = \$395$
His commission is $395.

25. simple interest $=$ principal $\cdot$ rate $\cdot$ time
$= (\$400)(13.5\%)\left(\dfrac{6}{12}\right)$
$= (\$400)(0.135)(0.5)$
$= \$27.00$
Total amount due the bank $= \$400 + \$27 = \$427$

CHAPTER 7

Exercise Set 7.1

1. $60 \text{ in.} = \dfrac{60 \text{ in.}}{1} \cdot \dfrac{1 \text{ ft}}{12 \text{ in.}} = \dfrac{60}{12} \text{ ft} = 5 \text{ ft}$

5. $42{,}240 \text{ ft} = \dfrac{42{,}240 \text{ ft}}{1} \cdot \dfrac{1 \text{ mi}}{5280 \text{ ft}}$
$= \dfrac{42{,}240}{5280} \text{ mi}$
$= 8 \text{ mi}$

9. $10 \text{ ft} = \dfrac{10 \text{ ft}}{1} \cdot \dfrac{1 \text{ yd}}{3 \text{ ft}} = \dfrac{10}{3} \text{ yd} = 3\dfrac{1}{3} \text{ yd}$

13. $162 \text{ in.} = \dfrac{162 \text{ in.}}{1} \cdot \dfrac{1 \text{ ft}}{12 \text{ in.}} \cdot \dfrac{1 \text{ yd}}{3 \text{ ft}}$
$= \dfrac{162}{36} \text{ yd}$
$= 4.5 \text{ yd}$

17. $40 \text{ ft} = \dfrac{40 \text{ ft}}{1} \cdot \dfrac{1 \text{ yd}}{3 \text{ ft}} = \dfrac{40}{3} \text{ yd}$

$$
\begin{array}{r}
13 \text{ yd } 1 \text{ ft} \\
3{\overline{\smash{)}\,40}} \\
\underline{-3} \\
10 \\
\underline{-9} \\
1
\end{array}
$$

21. $10{,}000 \text{ ft} = \dfrac{10{,}000 \text{ ft}}{1} \cdot \dfrac{1 \text{ mi}}{5280 \text{ ft}} = \dfrac{10{,}000}{5280} \text{ mi}$

$$1 \text{ mi } 4720 \text{ ft}$$

$$5280 \overline{)\ 10{,}000}$$
$$\underline{-\ 5\,280}$$
$$4\,720$$

25. $7 \text{ yd } 2 \text{ ft} = \dfrac{7 \text{ yd}}{1} \cdot \dfrac{3 \text{ ft}}{1 \text{ yd}} + 2 \text{ ft}$

$$= 21 \text{ ft} + 2 \text{ ft}$$
$$= 23 \text{ ft}$$

29. 5 ft 8 in. + 6 ft 7 in. = 11 ft 15 in.
$$= 11 \text{ ft} + 1 \text{ ft } 3 \text{ in.}$$
$$= 12 \text{ ft } 3 \text{ in.}$$

33. 24 ft 8 in.
$$\underline{-\ 16 \text{ ft } 3 \text{ in.}}$$
$$8 \text{ ft } 5 \text{ in.}$$

37. 6 ft 8 in. ÷ 2 = 3 ft 4 in.

41. $40 \text{ m} = \dfrac{40 \text{ m}}{1} \cdot \dfrac{100 \text{ cm}}{1 \text{ m}} = 4000 \text{ cm}$

45. $300 \text{ m} = \dfrac{300 \text{ m}}{1} \cdot \dfrac{1 \text{ km}}{1000 \text{ m}} = \dfrac{300}{1000} \text{ km} = 0.3 \text{ km}$

49. $1500 \text{ cm} = \dfrac{1500 \text{ cm}}{1} \cdot \dfrac{1 \text{ m}}{100 \text{ cm}} = \dfrac{1500}{100} \text{ m} = 15 \text{ m}$

53. $7 \text{ km} = \dfrac{7 \text{ km}}{1} \cdot \dfrac{1000 \text{ m}}{1 \text{ km}} = 7000 \text{ m}$

57. $20.1 \text{ mm} = \dfrac{20.1 \text{ mm}}{1} \cdot \dfrac{1 \text{ dm}}{100 \text{ mm}}$

$$= \dfrac{20.1}{100} \text{ dm}$$
$$= 0.201 \text{ dm}$$

61. 8.6 m
$$\underline{+\ 0.34 \text{ m}}$$
$$8.94 \text{ m}$$

65. 24.8 mm $\qquad$ 24.8 mm $\qquad\qquad$ 2.48 cm
$$\underline{-\ 1.19 \text{ cm}} \quad \underline{-\ 11.9 \text{ mm}} \quad \text{or} \quad \underline{-\ 1.19 \text{ cm}}$$
$$12.9 \text{ m} \qquad\qquad\qquad 1.29 \text{ cm}$$

69. 18.3 m × 3 = 54.9 m

73.

	Yards	Feet	Inches
Chrysler Building in New York City	$348\dfrac{2}{3}$	1046	12,552

	meters	millimeters	kilometers	centimeters
77. Length of elephant	5	5000	0.005	500
81. Distance from London to Paris	342,000	342,000,000	342	34,200,000

85. 16 ft 5 in. $\qquad$ 15 ft 17 in.
$$\underline{-\ 2 \text{ ft } 6 \text{ in.}} \quad \underline{-\ 2 \text{ ft }\ 6 \text{ in.}}$$
$$13 \text{ ft } 11 \text{ in.}$$
A hand of the Statue of Liberty is 13 ft 11 in. longer than the width of an eye.

89. 80 mm $\qquad$ 80.0 mm
$$\underline{-\ 5.33 \text{ cm}} \quad \underline{-\ 53.3 \text{ mm}}$$
$$26.7 \text{ mm}$$
The ice must be 26.7 mm thicker before skating is allowed.

93. 9 ft 3 in. ÷ 3 = 3 ft 1 in.
Each cut piece will be 3 ft 1 in. long.

97.
$$\begin{array}{r} 3.35 \\ 20 \overline{)\ 67.00} \\ \underline{-\ 60} \\ 7\,0 \\ \underline{-\ 6\,0} \\ 1\,00 \\ \underline{-\ 1\,00} \\ 0 \end{array}$$
Each piece will be 3.35 meters long.

101. 79 ft × 4 = 316 ft
4 trucks are 316 feet long.
$$\begin{array}{r} 105 \\ 3 \overline{)\ 316} \\ \underline{-\ 3} \\ 01 \\ \underline{-\ 0} \\ 16 \\ \underline{-\ 15} \\ 1 \end{array}$$
The four trucks are $105\dfrac{1}{3}$ yards long.

105. 3.429 m = 342.9 cm
$$22.86 \overline{)342.90} \text{ becomes } 2286 \overline{)\ 34290}$$
$$\begin{array}{r} 15 \\ \underline{-\ 2286} \\ 11430 \\ \underline{-\ 11430} \\ 0 \end{array}$$
15 tiles are needed to cross the room.

109. $\dfrac{13}{100} = 13\%$

113. To estimate, round each measurement to the nearest yard.
$$\begin{array}{r} 5 \text{ yd } 2 \text{ in.} \approx 5 \text{ yd} \\ \underline{+\ 7 \text{ yd } 30 \text{ in.} \approx +8 \text{ yd}} \\ 13 \text{ yd estimate} \end{array}$$

117. answers may vary

Exercise Set 7.2

1. $2 \text{ lb} = \dfrac{2 \text{ lb}}{1} \cdot \dfrac{16 \text{ oz}}{1 \text{ lb}} = 2 \cdot 16 \text{ oz} = 32 \text{ oz}$

5. $12{,}000 \text{ lb} = \dfrac{12{,}000 \text{ lb}}{1} \cdot \dfrac{1 \text{ ton}}{2000 \text{ lb}}$

$$= \dfrac{12{,}000}{2000} \text{ tons}$$
$$= 6 \text{ tons}$$

9. $3500 \text{ lb} = \dfrac{3500 \text{ lb}}{1} \cdot \dfrac{1 \text{ ton}}{2000 \text{ lb}}$

$$= \dfrac{3500}{2000} \text{ tons}$$
$$= \dfrac{7}{4} \text{ tons}$$
$$= 1\dfrac{3}{4} \text{ tons}$$

13. $4.9 \text{ tons} = \dfrac{4.9 \text{ tons}}{1} \cdot \dfrac{2000 \text{ lb}}{1 \text{ ton}}$

$$= 4.9 \cdot 2000 \text{ lb}$$
$$= 9800 \text{ lb}$$

17. $2950 \text{ lb} = \dfrac{2950 \text{ lb}}{1} \cdot \dfrac{1 \text{ ton}}{2000 \text{ lb}}$

$$= \dfrac{2950}{2000} \text{ tons}$$
$$= \dfrac{59}{40} \text{ tons}$$
$$\approx 1.5 \text{ tons}$$

21. $5\frac{3}{4}$ lb $= \frac{23}{4}$ lb $= \frac{\frac{23}{4} \text{ lb}}{1} \cdot \frac{16 \text{ oz}}{1 \text{ lb}}$

$= \frac{23}{4} \cdot 16 \text{ oz} = 23 \cdot 4 \text{ oz} = 92 \text{ oz}$

25. 89 oz $= \frac{89 \text{ oz}}{1} \cdot \frac{1 \text{ lb}}{16 \text{ oz}} = \frac{89}{16}$ lb

$$16\overline{)89} \quad \begin{array}{l} 5 \text{ lb } 9 \text{ oz} \\ \\ \underline{-80} \\ 9 \end{array}$$

89 oz $= 5$ lb 9 oz

29. 6 tons 1540 lb $+$ 2 tons 850 lb
$= 8$ tons 2390 lb
$= 8$ tons $+$ 1 ton 390 lb
$= 9$ tons 390 lb

33. $\begin{array}{cc} 12 \text{ lb } 4 \text{ oz} & 11 \text{ lb } 20 \text{ oz} \\ \underline{-3 \text{ lb } 9 \text{ oz}} & \underline{-3 \text{ lb } 9 \text{ oz}} \\ & 8 \text{ lb } 11 \text{ oz} \end{array}$

37. 6 tons 1500 lb $\div 5 = \frac{6}{5}$ tons 300 lb

$= 1\frac{1}{5}$ tons 300 lb

$= 1 \text{ ton} + \frac{2000 \text{ lb}}{5} + 300 \text{ lb}$

$= 1 \text{ ton} + 400 \text{ lb} + 300 \text{ lb}$

$= 1 \text{ ton } 700 \text{ lb}$

41. $4 \text{ g} = \frac{4 \text{ g}}{1} \cdot \frac{1000 \text{ mg}}{1 \text{ g}} = 4 \cdot 1000 \text{ mg} = 4000 \text{ mg}$

45. $48 \text{ mg} = \frac{48 \text{ mg}}{1} \cdot \frac{1 \text{ g}}{1000 \text{ mg}} = \frac{48}{1000} \text{ g} = 0.048 \text{ g}$

49. $15.14 \text{ g} = \frac{15.14 \text{ g}}{1} \cdot \frac{1000 \text{ mg}}{1 \text{ g}}$

$= 15.14 \cdot 1000 \text{ mg}$

$= 15,140 \text{ mg}$

53. $35 \text{ hg} = \frac{35 \text{ hg}}{1} \cdot \frac{10,000 \text{ cg}}{1 \text{ hg}}$

$= 35 \cdot 10,000 \text{ cg}$

$= 350,000 \text{ cg}$

57. $205 \text{ mg} + 5.61 \text{ g} = 0.205 \text{ g} + 5.61 \text{ g} = 5.815 \text{ g}$
or
$205 \text{ mg} + 5.61 \text{ g} = 205 \text{ mg} + 5610 \text{ mg}$
$= 5815 \text{ mg}$

61. $1.61 \text{ kg} - 250 \text{ g} = 1.61 \text{ kg} - 0.250 \text{ kg} = 1.36 \text{ kg}$
or
$1.61 \text{ kg} - 250 \text{ g} = 1610 \text{ g} - 250 \text{ g} = 1360 \text{ g}$

65. $17 \text{ kg} \div 8 = \frac{17}{8}$ kg

$$8\overline{)17.000} \quad \begin{array}{l} 2.125 \\ \\ \underline{-16} \\ 1 \ 0 \\ \underline{-8} \\ 20 \\ \underline{-16} \\ 40 \\ \underline{-40} \\ 0 \end{array}$$

$17 \text{ kg} \div 8 = 2.125 \text{ kg}$

69.

Object	Tons	Pounds	Ounces
A 12-inch cube of osmium	$\frac{269}{400}$ or 0.6725	1345	21,520

73.

Object	Grams	Kilograms	Milligrams	Centigrams
A six-year-old boy	21,000	21	21,000,000	2,100,000

77. $0.09 \text{ g} = \frac{0.09 \text{ g}}{1} \cdot \frac{1000 \text{ mg}}{1 \text{ g}} = 0.09 \cdot 1000 \text{ mg} = 90 \text{ mg}$

$90 \text{ mg} - 60 \text{ mg} = 30 \text{ mg}$
The extra-strength tablet contains 30 mg more medication.

81. $\begin{array}{cc} 64 \text{ lb } 8 \text{ oz} & 63 \text{ lb } 24 \text{ oz} \\ \underline{-28 \text{ lb } 10 \text{ oz}} & \underline{-28 \text{ lb } 10 \text{ oz}} \\ & 35 \text{ lb } 14 \text{ oz} \end{array}$

Carla's zucchini was 35 lb 14 oz lighter than the record weight.

85. $3 \times 16 = 48$
3 cartons contain 48 boxes of fruit.
$3 \text{ mg} \times 48 = 144 \text{ mg}$
3 cartons contain 144 mg of preservatives.

89. 3 lb 4 oz $\times 10 = 30$ lb 40 oz
$= 30 \text{ lb} + 2 \text{ lb } 8 \text{ oz}$
$= 32 \text{ lb } 8 \text{ oz}$
Each box weighs 32 lb 8 oz.
32 lb 8 oz $\times 4 = 128$ lb 32 oz
$= 128 \text{ lb} + 2 \text{ lb}$
$= 130 \text{ lb}$
4 boxes of meat weigh 130 lb.

93. $6\frac{3}{4} \text{ oz} \times 12 = 72\frac{36}{4} \text{ oz}$

$= 72 \text{ oz} + 9 \text{ oz}$
$= 81 \text{ oz}$
$= 5 \text{ lb } 1 \text{ oz}$
A dozen bags of cookies weighs 5 lb 1 oz.

97. $198 \text{ g} = 0.198 \text{ kg}$
$0.198 \text{ kg} \times 12 = 2.376 \text{ kg} \approx 2.38 \text{ kg}$
A dozen bags of chips weigh approximately 2.38 kg.

101. $\frac{4}{25} = \frac{4}{25} \cdot \frac{4}{4} = \frac{16}{100} = 0.16$

105. answers may vary

109. answers may vary

Exercise Set 7.3

1. $32 \text{ fl oz} = \frac{32 \text{ fl oz}}{1} \cdot \frac{1 \text{ c}}{8 \text{ fl oz}} = \frac{32}{8} \text{ c} = 4 \text{ c}$

5. $10 \text{ qt} = \frac{10 \text{ qt}}{1} \cdot \frac{1 \text{ gal}}{4 \text{ qt}} = \frac{10}{4} \text{ gal} = 2\frac{1}{2} \text{ gal}$

9. $2 \text{ qt} = \frac{2 \text{ qt}}{1} \cdot \frac{2 \text{ pt}}{1 \text{ qt}} \cdot \frac{2 \text{ c}}{1 \text{ pt}} = 2 \cdot 2 \cdot 2 \text{ c} = 8 \text{ c}$

13. $6 \text{ gal} = \frac{6 \text{ gal}}{1} \cdot \frac{4 \text{ qt}}{1 \text{ gal}} \cdot \frac{2 \text{ pt}}{1 \text{ qt}} \cdot \frac{2 \text{ c}}{1 \text{ pt}} \cdot \frac{8 \text{ fl oz}}{1 \text{ c}}$
$= 6 \cdot 4 \cdot 2 \cdot 2 \cdot 8 \text{ fl oz}$
$= 768 \text{ fl oz}$

17. $5 \text{ gal } 3 \text{ qt} = \frac{5 \text{ gal}}{1} \cdot \frac{4 \text{ qt}}{1 \text{ gal}} + 3 \text{ qt}$
$= 5 \cdot 4 \text{ qt} + 3 \text{ qt}$
$= 20 \text{ qt} + 3 \text{ qt}$
$= 23 \text{ qt}$

21. $58 \text{ qt} = 56 \text{ qt} + 2 \text{ qt}$
$= \frac{56 \text{ qt}}{1} \cdot \frac{1 \text{ gal}}{4 \text{ qt}} + 2 \text{ qt}$
$= \frac{56}{4} \text{ gal} + 2 \text{ qt}$
$= 14 \text{ gal } 2 \text{ qt}$

25. $2\dfrac{3}{4}\,\text{gal} = \dfrac{11}{4}\,\text{gal}$

$= \dfrac{\frac{11}{4}\,\text{gal}}{1} \cdot \dfrac{4\,\text{qt}}{1\,\text{gal}} \cdot \dfrac{2\,\text{pt}}{1\,\text{qt}}$

$= \dfrac{11}{4} \cdot 4 \cdot 2\,\text{pt}$

$= 22\,\text{pt}$

29. $1\,\text{c}\,5\,\text{fl oz} + 2\,\text{c}\,7\,\text{fl oz} = 3\,\text{c}\,12\,\text{fl oz}$

$\qquad\qquad\qquad\qquad = 3\,\text{c} + 1\,\text{c}\,4\,\text{fl oz}$

$\qquad\qquad\qquad\qquad = 4\,\text{c}\,4\,\text{fl oz}$

33.
$$\begin{array}{ccc} 3\,\text{gal}\,1\,\text{qt} & 2\,\text{gal}\,5\,\text{qt} & 2\,\text{gal}\,4\,\text{qt}\,2\,\text{pt} \\ \underline{-\,1\,\text{qt}\,1\,\text{pt}} & \underline{-\,1\,\text{qt}\,1\,\text{pt}} & \underline{-\,1\,\text{qt}\,1\,\text{pt}} \\ & & 2\,\text{gal}\,3\,\text{qt}\,1\,\text{pt} \end{array}$$

37. $8\,\text{gal}\,2\,\text{qt} \times 2 = 16\,\text{gal}\,4\,\text{qt}$

$\qquad\qquad\qquad\quad = 16\,\text{gal} + 1\,\text{gal}$

$\qquad\qquad\qquad\quad = 17\,\text{gal}$

41. $5\,\text{L} = \dfrac{5\,\text{L}}{1} \cdot \dfrac{1000\,\text{ml}}{1\,\text{L}} = 5000\,\text{ml}$

45. $3.2\,\text{L} = \dfrac{3.2\,\text{L}}{1} \cdot \dfrac{100\,\text{cl}}{1\,\text{L}} = 320\,\text{cl}$

49. $64\,\text{ml} = \dfrac{64\,\text{ml}}{1} \cdot \dfrac{1\,\text{L}}{1000\,\text{ml}} = \dfrac{64}{1000}\,\text{L} = 0.064\,\text{L}$

53. $3.6\,\text{L} = \dfrac{3.6\,\text{L}}{1} \cdot \dfrac{1000\,\text{ml}}{1\,\text{L}} = 3600\,\text{ml}$

57. $2.9\,\text{L} + 19.6\,\text{L} = 22.5\,\text{L}$

61.
$$\begin{array}{ccc} 8.6\,\text{L} & 8600\,\text{ml} & 8.60\,\text{L} \\ \underline{-\,190\,\text{ml}} & \underline{-\,190\,\text{ml}} \quad\text{or} & \underline{-\,0.19\,\text{L}} \\ & 8410\,\text{ml} & 8.41\,\text{L} \end{array}$$

65. $480\,\text{ml} \times 8 = 3840\,\text{ml}$

69.

Capacity	Cups	Gallons	Quarts	Pints
An average-size bath of water	336	21	84	168

73. $1\dfrac{1}{2}\,\text{qt} = \dfrac{3}{2}\,\text{qt}$

$= \dfrac{\frac{3}{2}\,\text{qt}}{1} \cdot \dfrac{2\,\text{pt}}{1\,\text{qt}} \cdot \dfrac{2\,\text{c}}{1\,\text{pt}} \cdot \dfrac{8\,\text{fl oz}}{1\,\text{c}}$

$= \dfrac{3}{2} \cdot 2 \cdot 2 \cdot 8\,\text{fl oz}$

$= 48\,\text{fl oz}$

A can of Hawaiian Punch holds 48 fl oz.

77.
$$\begin{array}{cc} 2\,\text{L} & 2.000\,\text{L} \\ \underline{-\,410\,\text{ml}} & \underline{-\,0.410\,\text{L}} \\ & 1.590\,\text{L} \end{array}$$

There was 1.59 L left in the bottle.

81. $5\,\text{pt}\,1\,\text{c} + 2\,\text{pt}\,1\,\text{c} = 7\,\text{pt}\,2\,\text{c}$

$\qquad\qquad\qquad\qquad = 7\,\text{pt} + 1\,\text{pt}$

$\qquad\qquad\qquad\qquad = 8\,\text{pt}$

$\qquad\qquad\qquad\qquad = \dfrac{8\,\text{pt}}{1} \cdot \dfrac{1\,\text{qt}}{2\,\text{pt}}$

$\qquad\qquad\qquad\qquad = \dfrac{8}{2}\,\text{qt}$

$\qquad\qquad\qquad\qquad = \dfrac{4\,\text{qt}}{1} \cdot \dfrac{1\,\text{gal}}{4\,\text{qt}}$

$\qquad\qquad\qquad\qquad = \dfrac{4}{4}\,\text{gal}$

$\qquad\qquad\qquad\qquad = 1\,\text{gal}$

Yes, the liquid can be poured into the container without causing it to overflow.

85. $44.3\overline{)14.0}$ becomes

$$\begin{array}{r} 0.3160 \\ 443\overline{)\,140.0000} \\ \underline{-\,132\,9} \\ 7\,10 \\ \underline{-\,4\,43} \\ 2\,670 \\ \underline{-\,2\,658} \\ 120 \\ \underline{-\quad 0} \\ 120 \end{array}$$

$\dfrac{\$14}{44.3\,\text{L}} \approx \dfrac{\$0.316}{1\,\text{L}}$

The price is \$0.316 per liter.

89. $0.7 = \dfrac{7}{10}$

93. $0.006 = \dfrac{6}{1000} = \dfrac{3}{500}$

97. answers may vary

101. B indicates 1.5 cc.

105. B indicates 54 u or 0.54 cc.

Exercise Set 7.4

1. $578\,\text{ml} \approx \dfrac{578\,\text{ml}}{1} \cdot \dfrac{1\,\text{fl oz}}{29.57\,\text{ml}} \approx 19.55\,\text{fl oz}$

5. $1000\,\text{g} \approx \dfrac{1000\,\text{g}}{1} \cdot \dfrac{0.04\,\text{oz}}{1\,\text{g}} \approx 40\,\text{oz}$

9. $14.5\,\text{L} \approx \dfrac{14.5\,\text{L}}{1} \cdot \dfrac{0.26\,\text{gal}}{1\,\text{L}} \approx 3.77\,\text{gal}$

13.

	Meters	Yards	Centimeters	Feet	Inches
The height of a woman	1.5	$1\dfrac{2}{3}$	150	5	60

17. $10\,\text{cm} = \dfrac{10\,\text{cm}}{1} \cdot \dfrac{1\,\text{in.}}{2.54\,\text{cm}} \approx 3.94\,\text{in.}$

The balance beam is approximately 3.94 inches wide.

21. $200\,\text{mg} = 0.2\,\text{g} \approx \dfrac{0.2\,\text{g}}{1} \cdot \dfrac{0.04\,\text{oz}}{1\,\text{g}} \approx 0.008\,\text{oz}$

25. $12\,\text{fl oz} \approx \dfrac{12\,\text{fl oz}}{1} \cdot \dfrac{29.57\,\text{ml}}{1\,\text{fl oz}} \approx 355\,\text{ml}$

The 380-ml size is larger.

29. $1.5\,\text{lb} - 1.25\,\text{lb} = 0.25\,\text{lb}$

$0.25\,\text{lb} \approx \dfrac{0.25\,\text{lb}}{1} \cdot \dfrac{0.45\,\text{kg}}{1\,\text{lb}} \cdot \dfrac{1000\,\text{g}}{1\,\text{kg}} \approx 112.5\,\text{g}$

The difference is approximately 112.5 g.

33. $8\,\text{m} \approx \dfrac{8\,\text{m}}{1} \cdot \dfrac{3.28\,\text{ft}}{1\,\text{m}} \approx 26.24\,\text{ft}$

The base diameter is approximately 26.24 ft.

37. One dose every 4 hours results in $\dfrac{24}{4} = 6$ doses per day and

$6 \times 7 = 42$ doses per week.

$5\,\text{ml} \times 42 = 210\,\text{ml}$

$210\,\text{ml} \approx \dfrac{210\,\text{ml}}{1} \cdot \dfrac{1\,\text{fl oz}}{29.57\,\text{ml}} \approx 7.1\,\text{fl oz}$

8 fluid ounces of medicine should be purchased.

41. A liter has greater capacity than a quart; b.

45. An $8\dfrac{1}{2}$ ounce glass of water has a capacity of about $250\,\text{ml}\left(\dfrac{1}{4}\,\text{L}\right)$; d.

49. $6 \cdot 4 + 5 \div 1 = 24 + 5 = 29$

SOLUTIONS TO SELECTED EXERCISES

53. $3 + 5(19 - 17) - 8 = 3 + 5(2) - 8$
$$= 3 + 10 - 8$$
$$= 13 - 8$$
$$= 5$$

57. $\text{BSA} = \sqrt{\dfrac{90 \times 182}{3600}} \approx 2.13$

The BSA is approximately 2.13 sq m.

61. $60 \text{ in.} = \dfrac{60 \text{ in.}}{1} \cdot \dfrac{2.54 \text{ cm}}{1 \text{ in.}} = 152.4 \text{ cm}$

$150 \text{ lb} \approx \dfrac{150 \text{ lb}}{1} \cdot \dfrac{0.45 \text{ kg}}{1 \text{ lb}} = 67.5 \text{ kg}$

$\text{BSA} \approx \sqrt{\dfrac{67.5 \times 152.4}{3600}} \approx 1.690$

The BSA is approximately 1.69 sq m.

65. $20 \text{ m} \times 40 \text{ m} = 800 \text{ sq m}$

$20 \text{ m} \approx \dfrac{20 \text{ m}}{1} \cdot \dfrac{3.28 \text{ ft}}{1 \text{ m}} \approx 65.6 \text{ ft}$

$40 \text{ m} \approx \dfrac{40 \text{ m}}{1} \cdot \dfrac{3.28 \text{ ft}}{1 \text{ m}} = 131.2 \text{ ft}$

$20 \text{ m} \times 40 \text{ m} \approx 65.6 \text{ ft} \times 131.2 \text{ ft} \approx 8606.72 \text{ sq ft}$

The area is 800 sq m or approximately 8606.72 sq ft.

Exercise Set 7.5

1. $C = \dfrac{5}{9}(F - 32)$
$$= \dfrac{5}{9}(41 - 32)$$
$$= \dfrac{5}{9}(9)$$
$$= 5$$
41°F is 5°C.

5. $F = \dfrac{9}{5}C + 32$
$$= \dfrac{9}{5}(60) + 32$$
$$= 108 + 32$$
$$= 140$$
60°C is 140°F.

9. $C = \dfrac{5}{9}(F - 32)$
$$= \dfrac{5}{9}(62 - 32)$$
$$= \dfrac{5}{9}(30)$$
$$\approx 16.7$$
62°F is 16.7°C.

13. $F = 1.8C + 32$
$$= 1.8(92) + 32$$
$$= 165.6 + 32$$
$$= 197.6$$
92°C is 197.6°F.

17. $C = \dfrac{5}{9}(F - 32)$
$$= \dfrac{5}{9}(122 - 32)$$
$$= \dfrac{5}{9}(90)$$
$$= 50$$
122°F is 50°C.

21. $C = \dfrac{5}{9}(F - 32)$
$$= \dfrac{5}{9}(212 - 32)$$
$$= \dfrac{5}{9}(180)$$
$$= 100$$
212°F is 100°C.

25. $F = 1.8C + 32$
$$= 1.8(118) + 32$$
$$= 212.4 + 32$$
$$= 244.4$$
118°C is 244.4°F.

29. $C = \dfrac{5}{9}(F - 32)$
$$= \dfrac{5}{9}(70 - 32)$$
$$= \dfrac{5}{9}(38)$$
$$\approx 21.1$$
70°F is 21.1°C.

33. $4 \text{ cm} + 3 \text{ cm} + 5 \text{ cm} = (4 + 3 + 5) \text{ cm} = 12 \text{ cm}$

37. False; the freezing point of water is 32°F.

41. $C = \dfrac{5}{9}(F - 32)$
$$= \dfrac{5}{9}(936,000,000 - 32)$$
$$= \dfrac{5}{9}(935,999,968)$$
$$\approx 520,000,000$$
936,000,000°F is approximately 520,000,000°C.

Exercise Set 7.6

1. energy $= 3 \text{ pounds} \cdot 380 \text{ feet} = 1140 \text{ foot-pounds}$

5. energy $= \dfrac{2.5 \text{ tons}}{1} \cdot \dfrac{2000 \text{ pounds}}{1 \text{ ton}} \cdot 85 \text{ feet}$
$$= 425,000 \text{ foot-pounds}$$

9. $1000 \text{ BTU} = 1000 \text{ BTU} \cdot \dfrac{778 \text{ foot-pounds}}{1 \text{ BTU}}$
$$= 778,000 \text{ foot-pounds}$$

13. $34,130 \text{ BTU} = 34,130 \text{ BTU} \cdot \dfrac{778 \text{ foot-pounds}}{1 \text{ BTU}}$
$$= 26,553,140 \text{ foot-pounds}$$

17. total hours $= 1 \cdot 7 = 7$ hours
calories $= 7 \cdot 115 = 805$ calories

21. total hours $= \dfrac{1}{3} \cdot 6 = 2$ hours
calories $= 2 \cdot 720 = 1440$ calories

25. miles $= \dfrac{3500}{200} = 17.5$ miles

29. $\dfrac{27}{45} = \dfrac{3 \cdot 3 \cdot 3}{3 \cdot 3 \cdot 5} = \dfrac{3}{5}$

33. energy $= 123.9 \text{ pounds} \cdot \dfrac{9 \text{ inches}}{1} \cdot \dfrac{1 \text{ foot}}{12 \text{ inches}}$
$$= 92.925 \text{ foot-pounds}$$

37. answers may vary

Chapter 7 Test

1.
$$\begin{array}{r} 23 \\ 12\overline{)\,280} \\ \underline{-24} \\ 40 \\ \underline{-36} \\ 4 \end{array}$$
280 inches = 23 feet 4 inches

5. $38 \text{ pt} = \dfrac{38 \text{ pt}}{1} \cdot \dfrac{1 \text{ qt}}{2 \text{ pt}} \cdot \dfrac{1 \text{ gal}}{4 \text{ qt}}$
$$= \dfrac{38}{8} \text{ gal}$$
$$= \dfrac{19}{4} \text{ gal}$$
$$= 4\dfrac{3}{4} \text{ gal}$$

9. $4.3 \text{ dg} = \dfrac{4.3 \text{ dg}}{1} \cdot \dfrac{1 \text{ g}}{10 \text{ dg}} = \dfrac{4.3}{10} \text{ g} = 0.43 \text{ g}$

13. 2 ft 9 in. $\times$ 3 = 6 ft 27 in.
$\qquad\qquad\quad$ = 6 ft + 2 ft 3 in.
$\qquad\qquad\quad$ = 8 ft 3 in.

17. $C = \dfrac{5}{9}(F - 32)$

$\quad = \dfrac{5}{9}(84 - 32)$

$\quad = \dfrac{5}{9}(52)$

$\quad \approx 28.9$

84°F is 28.9°C.

21. 88 m + 340 cm = 88 m + 3.40 m = 91.4 m
The span is 91.4 meters

25. $C = \dfrac{5}{9}(F - 32)$

$\quad = \dfrac{5}{9}(136 - 32)$

$\quad = \dfrac{5}{9}(104)$

$\quad \approx 57.8$

136°F is 57.8°C.

29. $5 \text{ km} \approx \dfrac{5 \text{ km}}{1} \cdot \dfrac{0.62 \text{ mi}}{1 \text{ km}} \approx 3.1 \text{ mi}$
5 km is about 3.1 mi.

33. $\dfrac{180 \text{ cal}}{1 \text{ hour}} \cdot \dfrac{1 \text{ hour}}{1 \text{ day}} \cdot \dfrac{5 \text{ days}}{1} = 180 \cdot 5 \text{ cal} = 900 \text{ cal}$
She burns 900 calories.

CHAPTER 8

Exercise Set 8.1

1. The figure extends indefinitely in two directions. It is line YZ, or $\overleftrightarrow{YZ}$.

5. The figure has two endpoints. It is line segment PQ or $\overline{PQ}$.

9. A right angle has a measure of 90°.

13. $\angle S$ measures 180°. It is a straight angle.

17. $\angle Q$ measures between 90° and 180°. It is an obtuse angle.

21. The complement of an angle that measures 17° is an angle that measures 90° − 17° = 73°.

25. The complement of an angle that measures 58° is an angle that measures 90° − 58° = 32°.

29. 52° + 38° = 90°, so $\angle PNQ$ and $\angle QNR$ are complementary. 60° + 30° = 90°, so $\angle MNP$ and $\angle RNO$ are complementary.

33. $m\angle x = 120° - 88° = 32°$

37. $\angle x$ and the angle marked 35° are vertical angles, so $m\angle x = 35°$. $\angle x$ and $\angle y$ are supplementary, so $m\angle y = 180° - m\angle x = 180° - 35° = 145°$. $\angle y$ and $\angle z$ are vertical angles so $m\angle z = m\angle y = 145°$.

41. $\angle x$ and the angle marked 80° are supplementary, so $m\angle x = 180° - 80° = 100°$. $\angle y$ and the angle marked 80° are alternate interior angles, so $m\angle y = 80°$. $\angle x$ and $\angle z$ are corresponding angles, so $m\angle z = m\angle x = 100°$.

45. $\angle x$ can also be named $\angle ABC$ or $\angle CBA$.

49. $m\angle ABC = 15°$

53. $m\angle DBA = m\angle DBC + m\angle CBA$
$\qquad\qquad\; = 50° + 15°$
$\qquad\qquad\; = 65°$

57. $\dfrac{7}{8} + \dfrac{1}{4} = \dfrac{7}{8} + \dfrac{2}{8} = \dfrac{9}{8}$ or $1\dfrac{1}{8}$

61. $3\dfrac{1}{3} - 2\dfrac{1}{2} = \dfrac{10}{3} - \dfrac{5}{2} = \dfrac{20}{6} - \dfrac{15}{6} = \dfrac{5}{6}$

65. The supplement of an angle that measures 125.2° is an angle with measure 180° − 125.2° = 54.8°.

69. True; since 120° is less than 180°, it is possible to find the supplement of a 120° angle.

73. Two angles are complementary if their sum is 90°. If two complementary angles have the same measure, then the measure of each must be $\dfrac{1}{2}(90°) = 45°$.

Exercise Set 8.2

1. The figure has five sides, so it is a pentagon.

5. The figure has four sides, so it is a quadrilateral.

9. All three sides of the triangle have the same length, therefore the triangle is equilateral.

13. Two sides of the triangle have the same length, therefore the triangle is isosceles.

17. $m\angle x = 180° - 95° - 72° = 13°$

21. Twice the radius of a circle is its diameter.

25. A quadrilateral with opposite sides parallel is a parallelogram.

29. $d = 2 \cdot r = 2 \cdot 7 = 14$ m

33. $d = 2 \cdot r = 2 \cdot 20.3 = 40.6$ cm

37. The solid is a cylinder.

41. The solid is a cone.

45. The object has the shape of a rectangular solid.

49. The object has the shape of a pyramid.

53. $r = \dfrac{1}{2}d = \dfrac{1}{2} \cdot 26 = 13$ miles

57. 2(18) + 2(36) = 36 + 72 = 108

61. True; since all four sides of a square are equal in length, a square is also a rhombus.

65. False; a pentagon has five sides, so it cannot be a quadrilateral, which has four sides.

69. answers may vary

Exercise Set 8.3

1. $P = 2 \cdot l + 2 \cdot w$
$\quad = 2 \cdot 17 \text{ ft} + 2 \cdot 15 \text{ ft}$
$\quad = 34 \text{ ft} + 30 \text{ ft}$
$\quad = 64 \text{ ft}$
The perimeter is 64 feet.

5. $P = a + b + c$
$\quad = 5 \text{ in.} + 7 \text{ in.} + 9 \text{ in.}$
$\quad = 21 \text{ in.}$
The perimeter is 21 inches.

9. All sides of a regular triangle have the same length.
$P = a + b + c = 4 \text{ in.} + 4 \text{ in.} + 4 \text{ in.} = 12 \text{ in.}$
The perimeter is 12 inches.

13. Sum the lengths of the sides.
$P = 5 \text{ ft} + 3 \text{ ft} + 2 \text{ ft} + 7 \text{ ft} + 4 \text{ ft}$
$\quad = 21 \text{ ft}$
The perimeter is 21 feet.

17. $P = 2 \cdot l + 2 \cdot w$
$\quad = 2 \cdot 120 \text{ yd} + 2 \cdot 53 \text{ yd}$
$\quad = 240 \text{ yd} + 106 \text{ yd}$
$\quad = 346 \text{ yd}$
The perimeter of the football field is 346 yards.

21. The amount of stripping needed is 22 feet.
22 feet · \$3 per foot = \$66
The total cost of the stripping is \$66.

25. $P = 4 \cdot s = 4 \cdot 7$ in. = 28 in.
The perimeter is 28 inches.

29. The unmarked vertical side must have length 28 m − 20 m = 8 m.
The unmarked horizontal side must have length
20 m − 17 m = 3 m.
Sum the lengths of the sides.
$P = 17$ m + 8 m + 3 m + 20 m + 20 m + 28 m
= 96 m
The perimeter is 96 meters.

33. The unmarked vertical side must have length
10 mi + 12 mi = 22 mi.
The unmarked horizontal side must have length
8 mi + 34 mi = 42 mi.
Sum the lengths of the sides.
$P = 42$ mi + 12 mi + 34 mi + 10 mi + 8 mi + 22 mi
= 128 mi
The perimeter is 128 miles.

37. $C = 2 \cdot \pi \cdot r$
$= 2 \cdot \pi \cdot 8$ mi
$= 16\pi$ mi
≈ 50.24 mi

41. $C = 2 \cdot \pi \cdot r$
$= 2 \cdot \pi \cdot 5$ ft
$= 10\pi$ ft
$\approx 10 \cdot \dfrac{22}{7}$ ft

The distance around is about $\dfrac{220}{7} = 31\dfrac{3}{7}$ feet or 31.43 feet.

45. Sum the lengths of the sides.
$P = 9$ mi + 6 mi + 11 mi + 4.7 mi
= 30.7 mi
The perimeter is 30.7 miles.

49. The sides of a regular pentagon all have the same length. Sum the lengths of the sides.
$P = 8$ mm + 8 mm + 8 mm + 8 mm + 8 mm
= 40 mm
The perimeter is 40 millimeters.

53. $5 + 6 \cdot 3 = 5 + 18 = 23$

57. $(18 + 8) - (12 + 4) = 26 - 16 = 10$

61. A fence goes around the edge of a yard, thus the situation involves perimeter.

65. Paint covers the surface of a wall, thus the situation involves area.

69. a. The first age category that 8-year-old children fit into is "Under 9," thus the minimum width is 30 yards and the minimum length is 40 yards.
b. $P = 2 \cdot l + 2 \cdot w$
$= 2 \cdot 40$ yd + $2 \cdot 30$ yd
= 80 yd + 60 yd
= 140 yd
The perimeter of the field is 140 yards.

73. a. Smaller circle:
$C = 2 \cdot \pi \cdot r$
$= 2 \cdot \pi \cdot 10$ m
$= 20\pi$ m
≈ 62.8 m
Larger circle:
$C = 2 \cdot \pi \cdot r$
$= 2 \cdot \pi \cdot 20$ m
$= 40\pi$ m
≈ 125.6 m
b. Yes, when the radius of a circle is doubled, the circumference is also doubled.

77. $P = 2 \cdot l + 2 \cdot w$
30 ft = $2 \cdot 9$ ft + $2 \cdot w$
30 ft = 18 ft + $2 \cdot w$
12 ft = $2 \cdot w$
6 ft = w
The width is 6 feet.

Exercise Set 8.4

1. $A = l \cdot w = 2$ m $\cdot 3.5$ m = 7 sq m

5. $A = \dfrac{1}{2} \cdot b \cdot h = \dfrac{1}{2} \cdot 6$ yd $\cdot 5$ yd = 15 sq yd

9. $A = s^2 = (4.2 \text{ ft})^2 = 17.64$ sq ft

13. $A = \dfrac{1}{2}(b + B) \cdot h$
$= \dfrac{1}{2}(7 \text{ yd} + 4 \text{ yd}) \cdot 4$ yd
$= \dfrac{1}{2}(11 \text{ yd}) \cdot 4$ yd
$= 22$ sq yd

17. $A = b \cdot h$
$= 5$ in. $\cdot 4\dfrac{1}{2}$ in.
$= 5$ in. $\cdot \dfrac{9}{2}$ in.
$= \dfrac{45}{2}$ sq in.
$= 22\dfrac{1}{2}$ sq in.

21.

Rectangle 1: $A = l \cdot w = 10$ mi $\cdot 5$ mi = 50 sq mi
Rectangle 2: $A = l \cdot w = 12$ mi $\cdot 3$ mi = 36 sq mi
The area of the figure is 50 sq mi + 36 sq mi = 86 sq mi.

25. $A = \pi r^2 = \pi(6 \text{ in.})^2 = 36\pi$ sq in. $\approx 113\dfrac{1}{7}$ sq in.

29. $A = l \cdot w = 505$ ft $\cdot 225$ ft = 113,625 sq ft
The area of the flag is 113,625 square feet.

33. $A = l \cdot w = 16$ in. $\cdot 8$ in. = 128 sq in.
128 sq in. $\cdot \dfrac{1 \text{ sq ft}}{144 \text{ sq in.}} = \dfrac{128}{144}$ sq ft $= \dfrac{8}{9}$ sq ft
The side has area 128 square inches, which is $\dfrac{8}{9}$ square foot.

37. $A = l \cdot w = 7$ ft $\cdot 6$ ft = 42 sq ft
$4 \cdot 42$ sq ft = 168 sq ft
Four panels have an area of 168 square feet.

41. $A = \dfrac{1}{2}(b + B)h$
$= \dfrac{1}{2}(25 \text{ ft} + 36 \text{ ft}) \cdot 12\dfrac{1}{2}$ ft
$= \dfrac{1}{2} \cdot 61$ ft $\cdot 12\dfrac{1}{2}$ ft
$= 381\dfrac{1}{4}$ sq ft
To the nearest square foot, the area is 381 square feet.

45. Sum the lengths of the sides.

$$3 \text{ ft} + 3\frac{1}{2} \text{ ft} + 6 \text{ ft} + 8\frac{1}{2} \text{ ft} + 4 \text{ ft} = 25 \text{ ft}$$

49. Note that the dimensions given are the diameters of the pizzas.
12-inch pizza:

$$r = \frac{1}{2} \cdot d = \frac{1}{2} \cdot 12 \text{ in.} = 6 \text{ in.}$$

$$A = \pi \cdot r^2 = \pi (6 \text{ in.})^2 = 36\pi \text{ sq in.}$$

Price per square inch $= \dfrac{\$10}{36\pi \text{ sq in.}} \approx \$0.0884$

8-inch pizzas:

$$r = \frac{1}{2} \cdot d = \frac{1}{2} \cdot 8 \text{ in.} = 4 \text{ in.}$$

$$A = \pi \cdot r^2 = \pi (4 \text{ in.})^2 = 16\pi \text{ sq in.}$$

$$2 \cdot A = 2 \cdot 16\pi \text{ sq in.} = 32\pi \text{ sq in.}$$

Price per square inch: $\dfrac{\$9}{32\pi \text{ sq in.}} \approx \$0.0895$

Since the price per square inch for the 12-inch pizza is less, the 12-inch pizza is the better deal.

53. The area of the shaded region is the area of the square minus the area of the circle.

Square: $A = s^2 = (6 \text{ in.})^2 = 36 \text{ sq in.}$

Circle: $r = \frac{1}{2} \cdot d = \frac{1}{2} (6 \text{ in.}) = 3 \text{ in.}$

$$A = \pi \cdot r^2 = \pi (3 \text{ in.})^2 = 9\pi \text{ sq in.} \approx 28.26 \text{ sq in.}$$

$$36 \text{ sq in.} - 28.26 \text{ sq in.} = 7.74 \text{ sq in.}$$

The shaded region has area of approximately 7.74 square inches.

57. The skating area is a rectangle with a half circle on each end.

Rectangle: $A = l \cdot w = 22 \text{ m} \cdot 10 \text{ m} = 220 \text{ sq m}$

Half circles: $A = 2 \cdot \dfrac{1}{2} \cdot \pi \cdot r^2$

$$= \pi (5 \text{ m})^2$$

$$= 25\pi \text{ sq m} \approx 78.5 \text{ sq m}$$

$$220 \text{ sq m} + 78.5 \text{ sq m} = 298.5 \text{ sq m}$$

The skating surface has area of 298.5 square meters.

Exercise Set 8.5

1. $V = l \cdot w \cdot h = 6 \text{ in.} \cdot 4 \text{ in.} \cdot 3 \text{ in.} = 72 \text{ cu in.}$

5. $V = \dfrac{1}{3} \pi \cdot r^2 \cdot h = \dfrac{1}{3} \pi \cdot (2 \text{ yd})^2 \cdot 3 \text{ yd} = 4\pi \text{ cu yd} \approx 12\dfrac{4}{7} \text{ cu yd}$

9. $V = \pi \cdot r^2 \cdot h$

$$= \pi (1 \text{ in.})^2 \cdot 9 \text{ in.}$$

$$= 9\pi \text{ cu in.} \approx 28\frac{2}{7} \text{ cu in.}$$

13. $V = s^3 = \left(1\dfrac{1}{3} \text{ in.}\right)^3$

$$= \left(\frac{4}{3} \text{ in.}\right)^3$$

$$= \frac{64}{27} \text{ cu in.}$$

$$= 2\frac{10}{27} \text{ cu in.}$$

17. Note: $1\dfrac{3}{10} \text{ in.} = \dfrac{13}{10} \text{ in.}$

$$V = \frac{1}{3} s^2 h$$

$$= \frac{1}{3} (5 \text{ in.})^2 \cdot \frac{13}{10} \text{ in.}$$

$$= \frac{1}{3} \cdot 25 \cdot \frac{13}{10} \text{ cu in.}$$

$$= 10\frac{5}{6} \text{ cu in.}$$

21. $V = \dfrac{4}{3} \pi r^3$

$$= \frac{4}{3} \pi (7 \text{ in.})^3$$

$$= \frac{1372}{3} \pi \text{ cu in. or } 457\frac{1}{3} \pi \text{ cu in.}$$

25. $r = \dfrac{1}{2} \cdot d = \dfrac{1}{2} \cdot 4 \text{ cm} = 2 \text{ cm}$

$$V = \frac{1}{3} \pi \cdot r^2 \cdot h$$

$$= \frac{1}{3} \pi \cdot (2 \text{ cm})^2 \cdot 3 \text{ cm}$$

$$= 4\pi \text{ cu cm}$$

$$\approx 12\frac{4}{7} \text{ cu cm}$$

There are approximately $12\dfrac{4}{7}$ cubic centimeters of ice cream in the cone.

29. $5^2 = 5 \cdot 5 = 25$

33. $1^2 + 2^2 = 1 \cdot 1 + 2 \cdot 2 = 1 + 4 = 5$

37. a. The first age category that 9-year-old children fit into is "Under 10," thus the minimum width is 40 yards and the minimum length is 60 yards.

 b. $A = l \cdot w = 40 \text{ yd} \cdot 60 \text{ yd} = 2400 \text{ sq yd}$
 The area of the field is 2400 square yards.

41. $V = \dfrac{1}{3} \cdot s^2 \cdot h$

$$= \frac{1}{3} \cdot (344 \text{ m})^2 \cdot 65.5 \text{ m}$$

$$\approx 2{,}583{,}669 \text{ cu m}$$

The original volume of the pyramid was about 2,583,669 cubic meters.

45. answers may vary

Exercise Set 8.6

1. $\sqrt{4} = 2$ because $2^2 = 4$.

5. $\sqrt{\dfrac{1}{81}} = \dfrac{1}{9}$ because $\dfrac{1}{9} \cdot \dfrac{1}{9} = \dfrac{1}{81}$.

9. $\sqrt{3} \approx 1.732$

13. $\sqrt{47} \approx 6.856$

17. $\sqrt{256} = 16$ because $16^2 = 256$.

21. $\sqrt{\dfrac{49}{144}} = \dfrac{7}{12}$ because $\dfrac{7}{12} \cdot \dfrac{7}{12} = \dfrac{49}{144}$.

25. hypotenuse $= \sqrt{(\text{leg})^2 + (\text{other leg})^2}$

$$= \sqrt{(5)^2 + (12)^2}$$

$$= \sqrt{25 + 144}$$

$$= \sqrt{169}$$

$$= 13$$

The hypotenuse is 13 inches.

29. hypotenuse $= \sqrt{(\text{leg})^2 + (\text{other leg})^2}$

$$= \sqrt{(22)^2 + (48)^2}$$

$$= \sqrt{484 + 2304}$$

$$= \sqrt{2788}$$

$$\approx 52.802$$

The hypotenuse is about 52.802 meters.

33.

hypotenuse $= \sqrt{(\text{leg})^2 + (\text{other leg})^2}$
$= \sqrt{(3)^2 + (4)^2}$
$= \sqrt{9 + 16}$
$= \sqrt{25}$
$= 5$

The hypotenuse has length 5 units.

37.

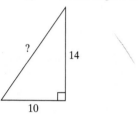

hypotenuse $= \sqrt{(\text{leg})^2 + (\text{other leg})^2}$
$= \sqrt{(10)^2 + (14)^2}$
$= \sqrt{100 + 196}$
$= \sqrt{296}$
≈ 17.205

The hypotenuse is about 17.205 units.

41.

hypotenuse $= \sqrt{(\text{leg})^2 + (\text{other leg})^2}$
$= \sqrt{(30)^2 + (30)^2}$
$= \sqrt{900 + 900}$
$= \sqrt{1800}$
≈ 42.426

The hypotenuse is about 42.426 units.

45.

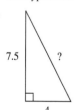

hypotenuse $= \sqrt{(\text{leg})^2 + (\text{other leg})^2}$
$= \sqrt{(7.5)^2 + (4)^2}$
$= \sqrt{56.25 + 16}$
$= \sqrt{72.25}$
$= 8.5$

The hypotenuse has length 8.5 units.

49. leg $= \sqrt{(\text{hypotenuse})^2 - (\text{other leg})^2}$
$= \sqrt{(32)^2 - (20)^2}$
$= \sqrt{1024 - 400}$
$= \sqrt{624}$
≈ 25.0

The tree is about 25 feet tall.

53. $\dfrac{n}{6} = \dfrac{2}{3}$
$3 \cdot n = 2 \cdot 6$
$3n = 12$
$n = \dfrac{12}{3}$
$n = 4$

57. $\dfrac{3}{n} = \dfrac{7}{14}$
$3 \cdot 14 = 7 \cdot n$
$42 = 7n$
$\dfrac{42}{7} = n$
$6 = n$

61. Since 101 is between $100 = 10 \cdot 10$ and $121 = 11 \cdot 11$, $\sqrt{101}$ is between 10 and 11; $\sqrt{101} \approx 10.05$.

65. $\sqrt{(20)^2 + (45)^2} = \sqrt{400 + 2025}$
$= \sqrt{2425}$
≈ 49.244

Since $\sqrt{(20)^2 + (45)^2} \neq 50$, the set does not form the sides of a right triangle.

Exercise Set 8.7

1. The triangles are congruent by Side-Side-Side.

5. The triangles are congruent by Angle-Side-Angle.

9. $\dfrac{22}{11} = \dfrac{14}{7} = \dfrac{12}{6} = \dfrac{2}{1}$

The ratio of corresponding sides is $\dfrac{2}{1}$.

13. $\dfrac{n}{3} = \dfrac{9}{6}$
$6 \cdot n = 3 \cdot 9$
$6n = 27$
$n = \dfrac{27}{6}$
$n = 4.5$

17. $\dfrac{n}{3.75} = \dfrac{12}{9}$
$9 \cdot n = 12 \cdot 3.75$
$9n = 45$
$n = \dfrac{45}{9}$
$n = 5$

21. $\dfrac{n}{3.25} = \dfrac{17.5}{3.25}$
$3.25 \cdot n = 17.5 \cdot 3.25$
$3.25n = 56.875$
$n = \dfrac{56.875}{3.25}$
$n = 17.5$

25. $\dfrac{n}{34} = \dfrac{10}{16}$
$16 \cdot n = 10 \cdot 34$
$16n = 340$
$n = \dfrac{340}{16}$
$n = 21.25$

29. $\dfrac{n}{25} = \dfrac{40}{2}$
$2 \cdot n = 40 \cdot 25$
$2n = 1000$
$n = \dfrac{1000}{2}$
$n = 500$

The building is 500 feet tall.

33. $\dfrac{n}{18} = \dfrac{24}{30}$

$\dfrac{n}{18} = \dfrac{4}{5}$

$5 \cdot n = 4 \cdot 18$

$5 \cdot n = 72$

$n = \dfrac{72}{5}$

$n = 14.4$

The shadow of the tree is 14.4 feet long.

37. Average $= \dfrac{14 + 17 + 21 + 18}{4} = \dfrac{70}{4} = 17.5$

41. $\dfrac{n}{7} = \dfrac{5}{9}$

$9 \cdot n = 5 \cdot 7$

$9n = 35$

$n = \dfrac{35}{9} = 3\dfrac{8}{9}$

The print is $3\dfrac{8}{9}$ inches wide, so it is too wide to fit on a 3-by-5-inch index card.

Chapter 8 Test

1. The complement of an angle that measures 78° is an angle that measures $90° - 78° = 12°$.

5. $\angle x$ and the angle marked 73° are vertical angles, so $m\angle x = 73°$. $\angle x$ and $\angle y$ are alternate interior angles, so $m\angle y = m\angle x = 73°$. $\angle x$ and $\angle z$ are corresponding angles, so $m\angle z = m\angle x = 73°$.

9. Circumference:
$C = 2 \cdot \pi \cdot r$
$\quad = 2 \cdot \pi \cdot 9$ in.
$\quad = 18\pi$ in.
$\quad \approx 56.52$ in.
Area:
$A = \pi r^2$
$\quad = \pi (9 \text{ in.})^2$
$\quad = 81\pi$ sq in.
$\quad \approx 254.34$ sq in.

13. $V = l \cdot w \cdot h = 5 \text{ ft} \cdot 3 \text{ ft} \cdot 2 \text{ ft} = 30$ cu ft

17. $P = 4 \cdot s = 4 \cdot 4$ in. $= 16$ in.
The perimeter of the photo is 16 inches.

21. First find the area of the lawn.
$A = l \cdot w = 123.8 \text{ ft} \cdot 80 \text{ ft} = 9904$ sq ft
0.02 ounce per square foot is $\dfrac{0.02 \text{ oz}}{1 \text{ sq ft}}$.

$\dfrac{0.02 \text{ ox}}{1 \text{ sq ft}} \cdot 9904 \text{ sq ft} = 198.08$ oz

Vivian needs to purchase 198.08 ounces of insecticide.

CHAPTER 9

Exercise Set 9.1

1. The year with the most car symbols is 2004, so the greatest number of cars was manufactured in 2004.

5. There are 10 car symbols for 2005 and 11 car symbols for 2004, for a total of 21 car symbols. Each symbol represents 500 cars.
$500 \cdot 21 = 10,500$
Approximately 10,500 cars were manufactured in 2004 and 2005.

9. Since $\dfrac{4000}{500} = 8$, 4000 cars would be represented by 8 car symbols. Both 1999 and 2002 have 8 car symbols, so 4000 cars were manufactured in 1999 and 2002.

13. Since $\dfrac{21}{3} = 7$, 21 ounces of chicken would be represented by 7 chicken symbols. 1997, 2001, and 2004 have more than 7 chicken symbols, so more than 21 ounces of chicken were consumed per person per week in 1997, 2001, and 2004.

17. To represent 17 ounces, divide 17 by 3, the number of ounces represented by a chicken symbol. $\dfrac{17}{3} = 5\dfrac{2}{3}$, so $5\dfrac{2}{3}$ symbols represent 17 ounces.

21. The bar for May is between 15 and 20, and closer to 20, so the average number of tornadoes for May is about 19.

25. The bar for Delhi, India, ends about halfway between the lines for 18 million and 19 million, so the population is about 18.5 million or 18,500,000.

29. The U.S. cities in the graph are Los Angeles and New York. The New York bar is longer and ends closer to 22 than 21, so New York City has the largest population at about 21.7 million or 21,700,000.

33. The height of the bar for 100–149 miles per week is 15, so 15 of the adults drive 100–149 miles per week.

37. 15 of the adults drive 100–149 miles per week and 9 of the adults drive 150–199 miles per week, so $15 + 9 = 24$ of the adults drive 100–199 miles per week.

41. 9 of the 100 adults surveyed drive 150–199 miles per week, so the ratio is $\dfrac{9}{100}$.

45. According to the bar graph, approximately 21 million householders will be 55–64 years old.

49. answers may vary

53.

Class Interval (Scores)	Tally	Class Frequency (Number of Games)
90–99	ⅢⅢ III	8

57.

Class Interval (Account Balances)	Tally	Class Frequency (Number of People)
$200–$299	ⅢⅢ I	6

61.

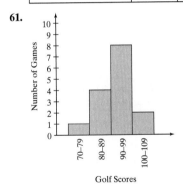

Golf Scores

65. The highest point on the graph corresponds to 1982, so the average number of goals per game was the greatest in 1982.

69. The dot for 1990 is below the 2.5-level, so the average number of goals per game was less than 2.5 in 1990.

73. 10% of 62 is $0.10 \cdot 62 = 6.2$

77. $\dfrac{17}{50} = \dfrac{17 \cdot 2}{50 \cdot 2} = \dfrac{34}{100} = 34\%$

81. The lowest point on the graph of low temperatures corresponds to Sunday. The low temperature on Sunday was 68°F.

85. answer may vary.

Exercise Set 9.2

1. The largest sector corresponds to the category "parent or guardian's home," thus most of the students live in a parent or guardian's home.

5. 180 of the students live in campus housing while 320 live in a parent or guardian's home.
$\dfrac{180}{320} = \dfrac{9}{16}$
The ratio is $\dfrac{9}{16}$.

9. 30% + 7% = 37%

37% of the land on Earth is accounted for by Europe and Asia.

13. Australia accounts for 5% of the land on Earth.

5% of 57,000,000 = 0.05 · 57,000,000

= 2,850,000

Australia is 2,850,000 square miles.

17. The second-largest sector corresponds to nonfiction, so the second-largest category of books is nonfiction.

21. Children's fiction accounts for 22% of the books.

22% of 125,600 = 0.22 · 125,600

= 27,632

The library has 27,632 children's fiction books.

25.

Sector	Degrees in Each Sector
United States	58% × 360° = 0.58 × 360° = 208.8° ≈ 209°
Asia	36% × 360° = 0.36 × 360° = 129.6° ≈ 130°
Europe	6% × 360° = 0.06 × 360° = 21.6° ≈ 22°

29.
$$2\overline{)\begin{array}{c}5\\10\end{array}}$$
$$2\overline{)20}$$
$$2\overline{)40}$$

40 = 2 · 2 · 2 · 5 = 2^3 × 5

33. answers may vary

37. The Indian Ocean accounts for 21% of Earth's oceans.
21% of 264,489,800 = 0.21 · 264,489,800 = 55,542,858.
The Indian Ocean covers 55,542,858 square kilometers.

Exercise Set 9.3

1. Mean: $\dfrac{21 + 28 + 16 + 42 + 38}{5} = \dfrac{145}{5} = 29$

Median:
Write the numbers in order. 16, 21, 28, 38, 42
The middle number is 28.
Mode: There is no mode, since each number occurs once.

5. Mean: $\dfrac{0.2 + 0.3 + 0.5 + 0.6 + 0.6 + 0.9 + 0.2 + 0.7 + 1.1}{9} = \dfrac{5.1}{9}$
$$\approx 0.6$$

Median:
Write the numbers in order. 0.2, 0.2, 0.3, 0.5, 0.6, 0.6, 0.7, 0.9, 1.1
The middle number is 0.6.
Mode: Since 0.2 and 0.6 occur twice, there are two modes, 0.2 and 0.6.

9. Mean: $\dfrac{1483 + 1483 + 1450 + 1381 + 1283}{5} = \dfrac{7080}{5}$
$$= 1416 \text{ feet}$$

13. answers may vary

17. gpa = $\dfrac{4 \cdot 3 + 4 \cdot 3 + 3 \cdot 4 + 3 \cdot 1 + 3 \cdot 2}{3 + 3 + 4 + 1 + 2}$

$= \dfrac{45}{13} \approx 3.46$

21. Mode: 6.9 since this number appears twice.

25. Mean: $\dfrac{\text{sum of 15 scores}}{15} = \dfrac{1095}{15} = 73$

29. There are 9 scores (rates) lower than the mean. They are 66, 68, 71, 64, 71, 70, 65, 70, and 72.

33. $\dfrac{18}{30} = \dfrac{2 \cdot 3 \cdot 3}{5 \cdot 2 \cdot 3} = \dfrac{3}{5}$

37. Since the mode is 35, we use 35 twice. Since there are an odd number of items in the list and the median is 37, then 37 must be in the list. Let the last missing number be n. Then

$\dfrac{35 + 35 + 37 + 40 + n}{5} = 38$, the mean, or

35 + 35 + 37 + 40 + n = 38 · 5   or

147 + n = 190   or   n = 43.

The missing numbers are 35, 35, 37, and 43.

Exercise Set 9.4

1.

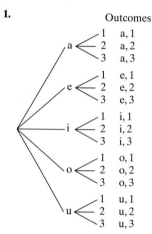

15 outcomes

5.

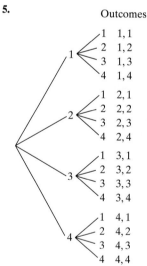

16 outcomes

9.

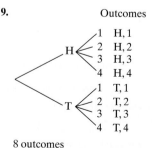

8 outcomes

13. A 1 or a 4 are two of the six possible outcomes. The probability is $\frac{2}{6} = \frac{1}{3}$.

17. Five of the six possible outcomes are numbers greater than 1. The probability is $\frac{5}{6}$.

21. A 1, a 2, or a 3 are three of three possible outcomes. The probability is $\frac{3}{3} = 1$.

25. One of the seven marbles is red. The probability is $\frac{1}{7}$.

29. Two of the seven marbles are either blue or red. The probability is $\frac{2}{7}$.

33. The blood pressure did not change for 10 of the 200 people. The probability is $\frac{10}{200} = \frac{1}{20}$.

37. $\frac{1}{2} \cdot \frac{1}{3} = \frac{1 \cdot 1}{2 \cdot 3} = \frac{1}{6}$

41. One of the 52 cards is the king of hearts. The probability is $\frac{1}{52}$.

45. Thirteen of the 52 cards are hearts. The probability is $\frac{13}{52} = \frac{1}{4}$.

49.

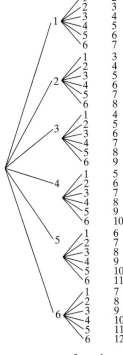

probability $= \frac{3}{36} = \frac{1}{12}$

53. answers may vary

Chapter 9 Test

1. There are $4\frac{1}{2}$ dollar symbols for the second week. Each dollar symbol corresponds to $50. $4\frac{1}{2} \cdot \$50 = \frac{9}{2} \cdot \$50 = \frac{\$450}{2} = \$225$

$225 was collected during the second week.

5. The shortest bar corresponds to February. The normal monthly precipitation in February in Chicago is 3 centimeters.

9. The line graph is above the 3 level for 1990, 1991, and 2000. Thus the inflation rate was greater than 3% in 1990, 1991, and 2000.

13. Services employed 31% of the labor force.
31% of 132,000,000 = 0.31 × 132,000,000
= 40,920,000
40,920,000 people were employed in the service industry.

17.

Class Interval (Scores)	Tally	Class Frequency (Number of Students)
40–49	I	1
50–59	III	3
60–69	IIII	4
70–79	ℍ҄	5
80–89	ℍ҄ III	8
90–99	IIII	4

21.

Grade	Point Value	Credit Hours	(Point Value) · (Credit Hours)
A	4	3	12
B	3	3	9
C	2	3	6
B	3	4	12
A	4	1	4
	Totals	14	43

25. A 3 or a 4 are two of the ten possible outcomes. The probability is $\frac{2}{10} = \frac{1}{5}$.

$\frac{43}{14} \approx 3.07$

The grade point average is about 3.07.

CHAPTER 10

Exercise Set 10.1

1. If 0 represents ground level, then 1445 feet underground can be represented by −1445.

5. 118 degrees above zero Fahrenheit can be represented by +118.

9. A net loss of $339 million can be represented by −339 million.

13. A 45 percent loss can be represented by −45.

17.
$$\overset{-4.7}{\longleftarrow} \begin{array}{ccccccccccc} \bullet & | & + & | & + & \blacklozenge & + & | & + & | & + & | & + & | & + & | & + & \blacklozenge & \longrightarrow \\ -5 & -4 & -3 & -2 & -1 & 0 & 1 & 2 & 3 & 4 & 5 \end{array}$$

21. The graph of 4 is to the right of 0 on a number line so 4 is greater than 0, or $4 > 0$.

25. The graph of 0 is to the right of −3 on a number line, so 0 is greater than −3, or $0 > -3$.

29. The graph o $-1\frac{3}{4}$ is to the left of 0 on a number line, so $-1\frac{3}{4}$ is less than 0, or $-1\frac{3}{4} < 0$.

33. The graph of $-2\frac{1}{2}$ is to the left of $-\frac{9}{10}$ on a number line, so $-2\frac{1}{2}$ is less than $-\frac{9}{10}$, or $-2\frac{1}{2} < -\frac{9}{10}$.

37. $|-8| = 8$ since -8 is 8 units from 0.

41. $|-5| = 5$ since -5 is 5 units from 0.

45. $\left|-\frac{1}{2}\right| = \frac{1}{2}$ since $-\frac{1}{2}$ is $\frac{1}{2}$ unit from 0.

49. $|7.6| = 7.6$ since 7.6 is 7.6 units from 0.

53. The opposite of -4 is $-(-4)$ or 4.

57. The opposite of $-\dfrac{9}{16}$ is $-\left(-\dfrac{9}{16}\right)$ or $\dfrac{9}{16}$.

61. The opposite of $\dfrac{17}{18}$ is $-\dfrac{17}{18}$.

65. $-|20| = -20$

69. $-(-8) = 8$

73. $-(-29) = 29$

77.

Number	Absolute Value of Number	Opposite of Number
-8.4	$\|-8.4\| = 8.4$	$-(-8.4) = 8.4$

81. The lake with the second-lowest elevation corresponds to the second-smallest number on the graph, which is -52. The lake with the second-lowest elevation is Lake Eyre.

85. The number on the graph that is closest to $-200°F$ is -218. Thus the planet that has an average temperature closest to $-200°F$ is Saturn.

89. $\begin{array}{r} 15 \\ + 20 \\ \hline 35 \end{array}$

93. $2^2 = 2 \cdot 2 = 4$
$-|3| = -3$
$-(-5) = 5$
$-|-8| = -8$
In order from least to greatest:
$-|-8|, -|3|, 2^2, -(-5)$

97. $-(-2) = 2$
$5^2 = 5 \cdot 5 = 25$
$-10 = -10$
$-|-9| = -9$
$|-12| = 12$
In order from least to greatest:
$-10, -|-9|, -(-2), |-12|, 5^2$

101. $-(-|-5|) = -(-5) = 5$

105. True; since every positive number is to the right of 0 on a number line and every negative number is to the left of 0, a positive number is always greater than a negative number.

109. answers may vary

Exercise Set 10.2

1.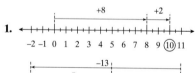

5.

9. $-6 + (-2) = -8$

13. $6 + (-2) = 4$

17. $3 + (-5) = -2$

21. $-7 + 7 = 0$

25. $-6 + 3 = -3$

29. $-12 + (-12) = -24$

33. $56 + (-26) = 30$

37. $-123 + (-100) = -223$

41. $-6.3 + (-2.2) = -8.5$

45. $-\dfrac{7}{11} + \left(-\dfrac{1}{11}\right) = -\dfrac{8}{11}$

49. $-\dfrac{4}{5} + \dfrac{1}{10} = -\dfrac{8}{10} + \dfrac{1}{10} = -\dfrac{7}{10}$

53. $-4 + 2 + (-5) = -2 + (-5) = -7$

57. $12 + (-4) + (-4) + 12 = 8 + (-4) + 12$
$\hspace{3.2cm} = 4 + 12$
$\hspace{3.2cm} = 16$

61. $-8 + 25 = 17$

65. $0 + (-165) + (-16) = -165 + (-16) = -181$
The diver is 181 feet below the surface.

69. The height of the bar for 2000 is marked as 786, so the net income for Apple, Inc. in 2000 was $786,000,000.

73. $-10 + 12 = 2$
The temperature at 11 p.m. was 2°C.

77. $-66 + 26 = -40$
Kansas's record low temperature is $-40°F$.

81. $44 - 0 = 44$

85. $\begin{array}{r} \overset{\scriptscriptstyle 9}{} \\ \overset{1}{2}\ \overset{10}{\cancel{0}}\ \overset{10}{\cancel{0}} \\ -\ \ 5\ \ 9 \\ \hline 1\ \ 4\ \ 1 \end{array}$

89. Since the signs are different, the absolute values should be subtracted, rather than added.
$7 + (-10) = -3$

93. True; since two negative numbers have the same sign, the sum will have the common sign. That is, the sum will be negative.

97. answers may vary

Exercise Set 10.3

1. $-5 - (-5) = -5 + 5 = 0$

5. $3 - 8 = 3 + (-8) = -5$

9. $-5 - (-8) = -5 + 8 = 3$

13. $2 - 16 = 2 + (-16) = -14$

17. $3.62 - (-0.4) = 3.62 + 0.4 = 4.02$

21. $\dfrac{2}{5} - \dfrac{7}{10} = \dfrac{2}{5} + \left(-\dfrac{7}{10}\right) = \dfrac{4}{10} + \left(-\dfrac{7}{10}\right) = -\dfrac{3}{10}$

25. $-20 - 18 = -20 + (-18) = -38$

29. $2 - (-11) = 2 + 11 = 13$

33. $9 - 20 = 9 + (-20) = -11$

37. $\dfrac{4}{7} + \left(-\dfrac{1}{7}\right) = \dfrac{3}{7}$

41. $12 - 5 - 7 = 12 + (-5) + (-7)$
$\hspace{2.5cm} = 7 + (-7)$
$\hspace{2.5cm} = 0$

45. $-10 + (-5) - 12 = -10 + (-5) + (-12)$
$\hspace{3.2cm} = -15 + (-12)$
$\hspace{3.2cm} = -27$

49. $19 - 14 + (-6) + (-50) = 19 + (-14) + (-6) + (-50)$
$\hspace{4.5cm} = 5 + (-6) + (-50)$
$\hspace{4.5cm} = -1 + (-50)$
$\hspace{4.5cm} = -51$

53. The planets with the lowest temperatures are Neptune $(-330°F)$ and Pluto $(-369°F)$. $-330 - (-369) = -330 + 369 = 39$
The difference is 39 degrees.

57. Represent checks with negative numbers and deposits with positive numbers.
$125 - 117 + 45 - 69 = 125 + (-117) + 45 + (-69)$
$\hspace{4.3cm} = 8 + 45 + (-69)$
$\hspace{4.3cm} = 53 + (-69)$
$\hspace{4.3cm} = -16$
His balance is $-\$16$.

61. $-282 - (-436) = -282 + 436 = 154$
The difference in elevations is 154 feet.

65. The elevation of Lake Superior is 600 feet. The elevation of Lake Eyre is -52 feet.
$600 - (-52) = 600 + 52 = 652$
The difference in elevation is 652 feet.

69. $725 - 1257 = 725 + (-1257) = -532$
The U.S. trade balance in 2001 was $-\$532$ billion.

73. $1 \cdot 8 = 8$

77. answers may vary

81. $10 - 30 = 10 + (-30)$
Since $|-30| > |10|$, the sign of the difference should be the same as the sign of -30.
$10 - 30 = 10 + (-30) = -20$

85. $|-6| - 6 = 6 + (-6) = 0$

89. False
$|-8 - 3| = |-8 + (-3)| = |-11| = 11$
$8 - 3 = 8 + (-3) = 5$

Exercise Set 10.4

1. $-2(-3) = 6$

5. $(2.6)(-1.2) = -3.12$

9. $-\dfrac{3}{5}\left(-\dfrac{2}{7}\right) = \dfrac{6}{35}$

13. $(-1)(-2)(-4) = 2(-4) = -8$

17. $10(-5)(-1)(-3) = -50(-1)(-3)$
$= 50(-3)$
$= -150$

21. $-5^2 = -(5 \cdot 5) = -25$

25. $-2^3 = -(2 \cdot 2 \cdot 2) = -8$

29. $\left(-\dfrac{5}{11}\right)^2 = \left(-\dfrac{5}{11}\right)\left(-\dfrac{5}{11}\right) = \dfrac{25}{121}$

33. $\dfrac{-30}{6} = -5$ because $6 \cdot -5 = -30$.

37. $\dfrac{0}{14} = 0$ because $14 \cdot 0 = 0$

41. $\dfrac{7.8}{-0.3} = -26$ because $-0.3 \cdot -26 = 7.8$

45. $\dfrac{100}{-20} = -5$ because $-20 \cdot -5 = 100$

49. $\dfrac{-12}{-4} = 3$ because $-4 \cdot 3 = -12$.

53. $-\dfrac{8}{15} \div \dfrac{2}{3} = -\dfrac{8}{15} \cdot \dfrac{3}{2} = -\dfrac{8 \cdot 3}{15 \cdot 2} = -\dfrac{2 \cdot 4 \cdot 3}{3 \cdot 5 \cdot 2} = -\dfrac{4}{5}$

57. $(-5)^3 = (-5)(-5)(-5) = 25(-5) = -125$

61. $-1(2)(7)(-3.1) = -2(7)(-3.1)$
$= -14(-3.1)$
$= 43.4$

65. $\dfrac{4}{3} \div \left(-\dfrac{8}{9}\right) = \dfrac{4}{3} \cdot \left(-\dfrac{9}{8}\right) = -\dfrac{4 \cdot 9}{3 \cdot 8} = -\dfrac{4 \cdot 3 \cdot 3}{3 \cdot 4 \cdot 2} = -\dfrac{3}{2}$

69. $-51(-6) = 306$

73. Moving down 20 feet can be represented by -20.
$5 \cdot (-20) = -100$
The diver reached a depth of 100 feet below the surface.

77. **a.** $221 - 27 = 221 + (-27) = 194$
The number of California condors changed by 194 from 1987 to 2004.

    b. 1987 to 2004 is 17 years.
$\dfrac{194}{17} \approx 11$
The average change was 11 condors per year.

81. $-3 \cdot 63 = -189$
The melting point of argon is $-189°$C.

85. $(3 \cdot 5)^2 = (15)^2 = 15 \cdot 15 = 225$

89. $12 \div 4 - 2 + 7 = 3 - 2 + 7$
$= 1 + 7$
$= 8$

93. $-9 - 10 = -9 + (-10) = -19$

97. False; since the product of two numbers having the same sign is positive, the product of two negative numbers is always a positive number.

101. The product of an odd number of negative numbers is negative, so the product of seven negative numbers is negative.

105. Note that a negative number raised to an even power is positive, while a negative number raised to an odd power is negative, and 0 raised to any power is 0. In order from least to greatest, the numbers are: $(-7)^{23}, (-1)^{55}, 0^{15}, (-1)^{50}, (-7)^{20}$.

Exercise Set 10.5

1. $-1(-2) + 1 = 2 + 1 = 3$

5. $9 - 12 - 4 = -3 - 4 = -7$

9. $\dfrac{4}{9}\left(\dfrac{2}{10} - \dfrac{7}{10}\right) = \dfrac{4}{9}\left(-\dfrac{5}{10}\right)$
$= \dfrac{4}{9}\left(-\dfrac{1}{2}\right)$
$= -\dfrac{2}{9}$

13. $25 \div (-5) + \sqrt{81} = 25 \div (-5) + 9$
$= -5 + 9$
$= 4$

17. $\dfrac{24}{10 + (-4)} = \dfrac{24}{6} = 4$

21. $-19 - 12(3) = -19 - 36 = -55$

25. $[8 + (-4)]^2 = [4]^2 = 16$

29. $(3 - 12) \div 3 = (-9) \div 3 = -3$

33. $(5 - 9)^2 \div (4 - 2)^2 = (-4)^2 \div (2)^2$
$= 16 \div 4$
$= 4$

37. $(-12 - 20) \div 16 - 25 = (-32) \div 16 - 25$
$= -2 - 25$
$= -27$

41. $(0.2 - 0.7)(0.6 - 1.9) = (-0.5)(-1.3)$
$= 0.65$

45. $(-36 \div 6) - (4 \div 4) = (-6) - (1) = -7$

49. $(-5)^2 - 6^2 = 25 - 36 = -11$

53. $2(8 - 10)^2 - 5(1 - 6)^2 = 2(-2)^2 - 5(-5)^2$
$= 2(4) - 5(25)$
$= 8 - 125$
$= -117$

57. $\dfrac{(-7)(-3) - 4(3)}{3[7 \div (3 - 10)]} = \dfrac{21 - 12}{3[7 \div (-7)]}$
$= \dfrac{9}{3[-1]}$
$= \dfrac{9}{-3}$
$= -3$

61. $-3^2 + (-2)^3 - 4^2 = -9 + (-8) - 16$
$= -17 - 16$
$= -33$

65. $45 \cdot 90 = 4050$

69. $P = 4 \cdot s = 4 \cdot 8 \text{ in.} = 32 \text{ in.}$
The perimeter is 32 inches.

73. $\dfrac{\text{sum of temperatures}}{\text{number of temperatures}}$

$= \dfrac{-14 + (-16) + (-14) + (-1) + 20}{5}$

$= \dfrac{-30 + (-14) + (-1) + 20}{5}$

$= \dfrac{-44 + (-1) + 20}{5}$

$= \dfrac{-45 + 20}{5}$

$= \dfrac{-25}{5}$

$= -5$

The average temperature for January through May is $-5°$F.

77. $-6 \cdot (10 - 4) = -6 \cdot (6) = -36$

81. answers may vary

Chapter 10 Test

1.

5. $-|-98| = -98$

9. $18 - 24 = 18 + (-24) = -6$

13. $-7 - (-19) = -7 + 19 = 12$

17. $-8 + 9 \div (-3) = -8 + (-3) = -11$

21. $\dfrac{-3(-2) + 12}{-1(-4 - 5)} = \dfrac{6 + 12}{-1(-9)} = \dfrac{18}{9} = 2$

25. $40 - 43 = 40 + (-43) = -3$

29. Checks and withdrawals are represented by negative numbers, while deposits are represented by positive numbers.

$129 - 79 - 40 + 35 = 50 - 40 + 35$

$= 10 + 35$

$= 45$

His balance is $45, which can be represented by the number 45.

CHAPTER 11

Exercise Set 11.1

1. $3 + 2z = 3 + 2(-3)$

$= 3 + (-6)$

$= -3$

5. $z - x + y = -3 - (-2) + 5$

$= -3 + 2 + 5$

$= -1 + 5$

$= 4$

9. $8 - (5y - 7) = 8 - (5 \cdot 5 - 7)$

$= 8 - (25 - 7)$

$= 8 - 18$

$= -10$

13. $\dfrac{6xy}{4} = \dfrac{6(-2)(5)}{4}$

$= \dfrac{-12(5)}{4}$

$= \dfrac{-60}{4}$

$= -15$

17. $\dfrac{x + 2y}{2z} = \dfrac{-2 + 2 \cdot 5}{2(-3)}$

$= \dfrac{-2 + 10}{-6}$

$= \dfrac{8}{-6}$

$= -\dfrac{4}{3}$ or $-1\dfrac{1}{3}$

21. $\dfrac{xz}{y} + \dfrac{3}{10} = \dfrac{-2(-3)}{5} + \dfrac{3}{10}$

$= \dfrac{6}{5} + \dfrac{3}{10}$

$= \dfrac{12}{10} + \dfrac{3}{10}$

$= \dfrac{15}{10}$

$= \dfrac{3}{2}$ or $1\dfrac{1}{2}$

25. $3x + 5x = (3 + 5)x = 8x$

29. $4c + c - 7c = (4 + 1 - 7)c$

$= (5 - 7)c$

$= -2c$

33. $4a + 3a + 6a - 8 = (4 + 3 + 6)a - 8$

$= (7 + 6)a - 8$

$= 13a - 8$

37. $3x + 7 - x - 14 = 3x - x + 7 - 14$

$= (3 - 1)x + (7 - 14)$

$= 2x + (-7)$

$= 2x - 7$

41. $\dfrac{5}{6} - \dfrac{7}{12}x - \dfrac{1}{3} - \dfrac{3}{10}x = \dfrac{5}{6} - \dfrac{1}{3} - \dfrac{7}{12}x - \dfrac{3}{10}x$

$= \left(\dfrac{5}{6} - \dfrac{1}{3}\right) + \left(-\dfrac{7}{12} - \dfrac{3}{10}\right)x$

$= \left(\dfrac{5}{6} - \dfrac{2}{6}\right) + \left(-\dfrac{35}{60} - \dfrac{18}{60}\right)x$

$= \dfrac{3}{6} + \left(-\dfrac{53}{60}\right)x$

$= \dfrac{1}{2} - \dfrac{53}{60}x$

45. $6(5x) = (6 \cdot 5)x = 30x$

49. $-0.6(7a) = (-0.6 \cdot 7)a = -4.2a$

53. $2(y + 2) = 2 \cdot y + 2 \cdot 2 = 2y + 4$

57. $-4(3x + 7) = -4 \cdot 3x + (-4) \cdot 7$

$= (-4 \cdot 3)x + (-28)$

$= -12x - 28$

61. $\dfrac{1}{2}(-8x - 3) = \dfrac{1}{2}(-8x) - \dfrac{1}{2}(3)$

$= \left(\dfrac{1}{2} \cdot -8\right)x - \dfrac{3}{2}$

$= -4x - \dfrac{3}{2}$

65. $4(6n - 5) + 3n = 4 \cdot 6n - 4 \cdot 5 + 3n$

$= 24n - 20 + 3n$

$= 24n + 3n - 20$

$= (24 + 3)n - 20$

$= 27n - 20$

69. $-2(3x + 1) - 5(x - 2)$

$= -2 \cdot 3x + (-2) \cdot 1 - 5 \cdot x - (-5) \cdot 2$

$= (-2 \cdot 3)x + (-2) - 5x - (-10)$

$= -6x - 2 - 5x + 10$

$= -6x - 5x - 2 + 10$

$= (-6 - 5)x + (-2 + 10)$

$= -11x + 8$

73. Let $l = 18$ and $w = 14$.

$P = 2l + 2w$

$= 2 \cdot 18 + 2 \cdot 14$

$= 36 + 28$

$= 64$

The perimeter is 64 feet.

77. $A = s^2 = (4y)^2 = 4y \cdot 4y = 4 \cdot 4 \cdot y \cdot y = 16y^2$
The area is $16y^2$ square centimeters.

81. $P = a + b + c = 5 + x + (2x + 1)$
$\quad = 5 + x + 2x + 1 = 3x + 6.$
The perimeter is $(3x + 6)$ feet.

85. Let $l = 12$, $w = 6$, and $h = 4$.
$V = lwh = 12 \cdot 6 \cdot 4 = 72 \cdot 4 = 288$
The volume is 288 cubic inches.

89. $-13 + 10 = -3$

93. $-4 + 4 = 0$

97. The given result is correct.
$7x - (x + 2) = 7x - 1(x + 2)$
$\qquad\qquad = 7x - 1 \cdot x + (-1)(2)$
$\qquad\qquad = 7x - x - 2$

101. The order of the terms is not changed, only the grouping within parentheses. Thus,
$-7 + (4 + y) = (-7 + 4) + y$
demonstrates the associative property of addition.

105. Add the area of the left-hand rectangle and the right-hand rectangle.
$7(2x + 1) + 3(2x + 3) = 7 \cdot 2x + 7 \cdot 1 + 3 \cdot 2x + 3 \cdot 3$
$\qquad\qquad\qquad\qquad = (7 \cdot 2)x + 7 + (3 \cdot 2)x + 9$
$\qquad\qquad\qquad\qquad = 14x + 7 + 6x + 9$
$\qquad\qquad\qquad\qquad = 14x + 6x + 7 + 9$
$\qquad\qquad\qquad\qquad = (14 + 6)x + 7 + 9$
$\qquad\qquad\qquad\qquad = 20x + 16$
The area is $(20x + 16)$ square miles.

109. $9684q - 686 - 4860q + 12{,}960$
$\quad = 9684q - 4860q - 686 + 12{,}960$
$\quad = (9684 - 4860)q + (-686 + 12{,}960)$
$\quad = 4824q + 12{,}274$

Exercise Set 11.2

1. $x - 8 = 2$
$10 - 8 \overset{?}{=} 2$
$\quad 2 \overset{?}{=} 2 \quad$ True
Yes, 10 is a solution of the equation.

5. $-9f = 64 - f$
$-9(-8) \overset{?}{=} 64 - (-8)$
$\quad 72 \overset{?}{=} 64 + 8$
$\quad 72 \overset{?}{=} 72 \quad$ True
Yes, -8 is a solution of the equation.

9. $a + 5 = 23$
$a + 5 - 5 = 23 - 5$
$\qquad a = 18$

Check:
$a + 5 = 23$
$18 + 5 \overset{?}{=} 23$
$\quad 23 \overset{?}{=} 23 \quad$ True
The solution of the equation is 18.

13. $7 = y - 2$
$7 + 2 = y - 2 + 2$
$\quad 9 = y$

Check:
$7 = y - 2$
$7 \overset{?}{=} 9 - 2$
$7 \overset{?}{=} 7 \quad$ True
The solution of the equation is 9.

17. $x + \dfrac{1}{2} = \dfrac{7}{2}$
$x + \dfrac{1}{2} - \dfrac{1}{2} = \dfrac{7}{2} - \dfrac{1}{2}$
$\qquad x = \dfrac{6}{2}$
$\qquad x = 3$

Check:
$x + \dfrac{1}{2} = \dfrac{7}{2}$
$3 + \dfrac{1}{2} \overset{?}{=} \dfrac{7}{2}$
$\dfrac{6}{2} + \dfrac{1}{2} \overset{?}{=} \dfrac{7}{2}$
$\quad \dfrac{7}{2} \overset{?}{=} \dfrac{7}{2} \quad$ True
The solution of the equation is 3.

21. $x - 3 = -1 + 4$
$x - 3 = 3$
$x - 3 + 3 = 3 + 3$
$\qquad x = 6$

Check:
$x - 3 = -1 + 4$
$6 - 3 \overset{?}{=} -1 + 4$
$\quad 3 \overset{?}{=} 3 \quad$ True
The solution of the equation is 6.

25. $x - 0.6 = 4.7$
$x - 0.6 + 0.6 = 4.7 + 0.6$
$\qquad x = 5.3$

Check:
$x - 0.6 = 4.7$
$5.3 - 0.6 \overset{?}{=} 4.7$
$\quad 4.7 \overset{?}{=} 4.7 \quad$ True
The solution of the equation is 5.3.

29. $y + 2.3 = -9.2 - 8.6$
$y + 2.3 = -17.8$
$y + 2.3 - 2.3 = -17.8 - 2.3$
$\qquad y = -20.1$

Check:
$y + 2.3 = -9.2 - 8.6$
$-20.1 + 2.3 \overset{?}{=} -9.2 - 8.6$
$\quad -17.8 \overset{?}{=} -17.8 \quad$ True
The solution of the equation is -20.1.

33. $5 + (-12) = 5x - 7 - 4x$
$5 + (-12) = 5x - 4x - 7$
$\qquad -7 = x - 7$
$-7 + 7 = x - 7 + 7$
$\qquad 0 = x$

Check:
$5 + (-12) = 5x - 7 - 4x$
$5 + (-12) \overset{?}{=} 5(0) - 7 - 4(0)$
$5 + (-12) \overset{?}{=} 0 - 7 - 0$
$\qquad -7 \overset{?}{=} -7 \quad$ True
The solution of the equation is 0.

37. $\dfrac{-7}{-7} = 1$ because $-7 \cdot 1 = -7$.

41. $-\dfrac{2}{3} \cdot -\dfrac{3}{2} = \dfrac{2 \cdot 3}{3 \cdot 2} = \dfrac{6}{6} = 1$

45. To solve $-\dfrac{1}{7} = -\dfrac{4}{5} + x$, $\dfrac{4}{5}$ should be added to both sides of the equation.

49. $x - 76{,}862 = 86{,}102$
$x - 76{,}862 + 76{,}862 = 86{,}102 + 76{,}862$
$\qquad\qquad x = 162{,}964$

53. Use $I = R - E$ where $I = 705{,}000{,}000$ and $R = 24{,}547{,}000{,}000$.
$I = R - E$
$705{,}000{,}000 = 24{,}547{,}000{,}000 - E$
$705{,}000{,}000 - 24{,}547{,}000{,}000 = 24{,}547{,}000{,}000 - 24{,}547{,}000{,}000 - E$
$-23{,}842{,}000{,}000 = -E$
$23{,}842{,}000{,}000 = E$
Best Buy's total expenses for the year were \$23,842,000,000.

Exercise Set 11.3

1. $5x = 20$

$$\frac{5x}{5} = \frac{20}{5}$$

$$x = 4$$

5. $0.4y = -12$

$$\frac{0.4y}{0.4} = \frac{-12}{0.4}$$

$$y = -30$$

9. $-0.3x = -15$

$$\frac{-0.3x}{-0.3} = \frac{-15}{-0.3}$$

$$x = 50$$

13. $\frac{1}{6}y = -5$

$$\frac{6}{1} \cdot \frac{1}{6}y = \frac{6}{1} \cdot -5$$

$$y = -30$$

17. $-\frac{2}{9}z = \frac{4}{27}$

$$-\frac{9}{2} \cdot -\frac{2}{9}z = -\frac{9}{2} \cdot \frac{4}{27}$$

$$z = -\frac{2}{3}$$

21. $16 = 10t - 8t$

$$16 = 2t$$

$$\frac{16}{2} = \frac{2t}{2}$$

$$8 = t$$

25. $4 - 10 = -3z$

$$-6 = -3z$$

$$\frac{-6}{-3} = \frac{-3z}{-3}$$

$$2 = z$$

29. $0.4 = -8z$

$$\frac{0.4}{-8} = \frac{-8z}{-8}$$

$$-0.05 = z$$

33. $-\frac{3}{5}x = -\frac{6}{15}$

$$-\frac{5}{3} \cdot -\frac{3}{5}x = -\frac{5}{3} \cdot -\frac{6}{15}$$

$$x = \frac{2}{3}$$

37. $5 - 5 = 2x + 7x$

$$0 = 9x$$

$$\frac{0}{9} = \frac{9x}{9}$$

$$0 = x$$

41. $-3x - 3x = 50 - 2$

$$-6x = 48$$

$$\frac{-6x}{-6} = \frac{48}{-6}$$

$$x = -8$$

45. $\frac{1}{4}x - \frac{5}{8}x = 20 - 47$

$$\frac{2}{8}x - \frac{5}{8}x = -27$$

$$-\frac{3}{8}x = -27$$

$$-\frac{8}{3} \cdot -\frac{3}{8}x = -\frac{8}{3} \cdot -27$$

$$x = 72$$

49. $\dfrac{x - 3}{2} = \dfrac{5 - 3}{2} = \dfrac{2}{2} = 1$

53. Addition should be used to solve the equation $12 = x - 5$. Specifically, 5 should be added to both sides of the equation.

57. answers may vary

61. Use $d = r \cdot t$, where $d = 390$ and $r = 60$.

$$d = r \cdot t$$

$$390 = 60 \cdot t$$

$$\frac{390}{60} = \frac{60t}{60}$$

$$\frac{13}{2} = t$$

It will take $\dfrac{13}{2} = 6.5$ hours to make the drive.

Exercise Set 11.4

1. $2x - 6 = 0$

$$2x - 6 + 6 = 0 + 6$$

$$2x = 6$$

$$\frac{2x}{2} = \frac{6}{2}$$

$$x = 3$$

5. $6 - n = 10$

$$6 - 6 - n = 10 - 6$$

$$-n = 4$$

$$\frac{-n}{-1} = \frac{4}{-1}$$

$$n = -4$$

9. $1.7 = 2y + 9.5$

$$1.7 - 9.5 = 2y + 9.5 - 9.5$$

$$-7.8 = 2y$$

$$\frac{-7.8}{2} = \frac{2y}{2}$$

$$-3.9 = y$$

13. $3x - 7 = 4x + 5$

$$3x - 7 - 5 = 4x + 5 - 5$$

$$3x - 12 = 4x$$

$$3x - 3x - 12 = 4x - 3x$$

$$-12 = x$$

17. $9 - 3x = 14 + 2x$

$$9 - 14 - 3x = 14 - 14 + 2x$$

$$-5 - 3x = 2x$$

$$-5 - 3x + 3x = 2x + 3x$$

$$-5 = 5x$$

$$\frac{-5}{5} = \frac{5x}{5}$$

$$-1 = x$$

21. $3(x - 1) = 12$

$$3x - 3 = 12$$

$$3x - 3 + 3 = 12 + 3$$

$$3x = 15$$

$$\frac{3x}{3} = \frac{15}{3}$$

$$x = 5$$

25. $35 - 17 = 3(x - 2)$

$$18 = 3x - 6$$

$$18 + 6 = 3x - 6 + 6$$

$$24 = 3x$$

$$\frac{24}{3} = \frac{3x}{3}$$

$$8 = x$$

29. $2t - 1 = 3(t + 7)$

$$2t - 1 = 3t + 21$$

$$2t - 1 - 21 = 3t + 21 - 21$$

$$2t - 22 = 3t$$

$$2t - 2t - 22 = 3t - 2t$$

$$-22 = t$$

33.
$$3r + 4 = 19$$
$$3r + 4 - 4 = 19 - 4$$
$$3r = 15$$
$$\frac{3r}{3} = \frac{15}{3}$$
$$r = 5$$

37.
$$8 - t = 3$$
$$8 - 8 - t = 3 - 8$$
$$-t = -5$$
$$\frac{-t}{-1} = \frac{-5}{-1}$$
$$t = 5$$

41.
$$9a + 29 = -7$$
$$9a + 29 - 29 = -7 - 29$$
$$9a = -36$$
$$\frac{9a}{9} = \frac{-36}{9}$$
$$a = -4$$

45.
$$11(x - 2) = 22$$
$$11x - 22 = 22$$
$$11x - 22 + 22 = 22 + 22$$
$$11x = 44$$
$$\frac{11x}{11} = \frac{44}{11}$$
$$x = 4$$

49.
$$-3c + 1 - 4c = -20$$
$$-3c - 4c + 1 = -20$$
$$-7c + 1 = -20$$
$$-7c + 1 - 1 = -20 - 1$$
$$-7c = -21$$
$$\frac{-7c}{-7} = \frac{-21}{-7}$$
$$c = 3$$

53.
$$-5 + 7k = -13 + 8k$$
$$-5 + 13 + 7k = -13 + 13 + 8k$$
$$8 + 7k = 8k$$
$$8 + 7k - 7k = 8k - 7k$$
$$8 = k$$

57.
$$-8(n + 2) + 17 = -6n - 5$$
$$-8n - 16 + 17 = -6n - 5$$
$$-8n + 1 = -6n - 5$$
$$-8n + 1 + 5 = -6n - 5 + 5$$
$$-8n + 6 = -6n$$
$$-8n + 8n + 6 = -6n + 8n$$
$$6 = 2n$$
$$\frac{6}{2} = \frac{2n}{2}$$
$$3 = n$$

61.
$$10 + 5(z - 2) = -4z + 1$$
$$10 + 5z - 10 = -4z + 1$$
$$5z = -4z + 1$$
$$5z + 4z = -4z + 4z + 1$$
$$9z = 1$$
$$\frac{9z}{9} = \frac{1}{9}$$
$$z = \frac{1}{9}$$

65.
$$7(6 + w) = 6(w - 2)$$
$$42 + 7w = 6w - 12$$
$$42 - 42 + 7w = 6w - 12 - 42$$
$$7w = 6w - 54$$
$$7w - 6w = 6w - 6w - 54$$
$$w = -54$$

69.
$$2(3z - 2) - 2(5 - 2z) = 4$$
$$6z - 4 - 10 + 4z = 4$$
$$10z - 14 = 4$$
$$10z - 14 + 14 = 4 + 14$$
$$10z = 18$$
$$\frac{10z}{10} = \frac{18}{10}$$
$$z = \frac{9}{5}$$

73. "The product of" indicates multiplication.
$$-5(-29) = 145$$

77. "The quotient of" indicates division.
$$\frac{100}{2(50)} = 1$$

81. The number of electronically filed returns is expected to be 70 million in 2006 and 90 million in 2009. The increase is expected to be 90 million − 70 million = 20 million returns.

85. The next step in solving $-3x = -1.2$ is to divide both sides of the equation by −3; a.

89. Use $C = \frac{5}{9}(F - 32)$ with $C = 57.8$.
$$C = \frac{5}{9}(F - 32)$$
$$57.8 = \frac{5}{9}(F - 32)$$
$$\frac{9}{5}(57.8) = \frac{9}{5} \cdot \frac{5}{9}(F - 32)$$
$$104.04 = F - 32$$
$$104.04 + 32 = F - 32 + 32$$
$$136.04 = F$$
The temperature was 136.04°F.

Exercise Set 11.5

1. "The sum of a number and five" is $x + 5$.

5. "Twenty decreased by a number" is $20 - x$.

9. "A number divided by 2" is $\frac{x}{2}$.

13. "A number added to −5 is −7" is
$$-5 + x = -7.$$

17. "A number subtracted from −20 amounts to 104" is
$$-20 - x = 104.$$

21. "A number subtracted from 11" is $11 - x$.

25. "Fifty decreased by eight times a number" is
$$50 - 8x.$$

29. "Three times a number, added to 9 is 33" is
$$9 + 3x = 33.$$
$$9 + 3x = 33$$
$$9 + 3x - 9 = 33 - 9$$
$$3x = 24$$
$$\frac{3x}{3} = \frac{24}{3}$$
$$x = 8$$

33. "The difference of a number and 3 is equal to the quotient of 10 and 5" is $x - 3 = \frac{10}{5}$.
$$x - 3 = \frac{10}{5}$$
$$x - 3 = 2$$
$$x - 3 + 3 = 2 + 3$$
$$x = 5$$

37. "40 subtracted from five times a number is 8 more than the number" is $5x - 40 = x + 8$.

$$5x - 40 = x + 8$$
$$5x - 40 + 40 = x + 8 + 40$$
$$5x = x + 48$$
$$5x - x = x - x + 48$$
$$4x = 48$$
$$\frac{4x}{4} = \frac{48}{4}$$
$$x = 12$$

41. "The product of 4 and a number is the same as 30 less twice that same number" is $4x = 30 - 2x$.

$$4x = 30 - 2x$$
$$4x + 2x = 30 - 2x + 2x$$
$$6x = 30$$
$$\frac{6x}{6} = \frac{30}{6}$$
$$x = 5$$

45. Let x be the number of inches that kelp can grow in one day. Since bamboo grows twice as fast, bamboo can grow $2x$ inches in one day. Since both can grow a total of 54 inches in one day, the sum of x and $2x$ is 54.

$$x + 2x = 54$$
$$3x = 54$$
$$\frac{3x}{3} = \frac{54}{3}$$
$$x = 18$$

Thus, kelp can grow 18 inches in one day and bamboo can grow $2 \cdot 18 = 36$ inches in one day.

49. Let x be the cost of the Gamecube. Since the cost of the games is 3 times the cost of the Gamecube alone, the cost of the games is $3x$. Since the total is \$600, the sum of x and $3x$ is 600.

$$x + 3x = 600$$
$$4x = 600$$
$$\frac{4x}{4} = \frac{600}{4}$$
$$x = 150$$

The cost of the Gamecube alone is \$150 and the cost of the games is $3 \cdot \$150 = \$450$.

53. Let x be the native American population of Washington state, in thousands. Since the population in California is three times the population in Washington state, the population in California is $3x$. Since the total of the two populations is 412 thousand, the sum of x and $3x$ is 412.

$$x + 3x = 412$$
$$4x = 412$$
$$\frac{4x}{4} = \frac{412}{4}$$
$$x = 103$$

The native American population of Washington state is 103 thousand, the native American population of California is $3 \cdot 103 = 309$ thousand.

57. Let x be the projected shortage of nurses in 2010. Then the projected shortage of nurses in 2020 is $x + 533,201$, and the sum of these two quantities is 1,083,631.

$$x + x + 533,201 = 1,083,631$$
$$2x + 533,201 = 1,083,631$$
$$2x + 533,201 - 533,201 = 1,083,631 - 533,201$$
$$2x = 550,430$$
$$\frac{2x}{2} = \frac{550,430}{2}$$
$$x = 275,215$$

The shortage of nurses is projected to be 275,215 in 2010 and $275,215 + 533,207 = 808,416$ in 2020.

61. Let x be the number of points scored by the Connecticut Huskies. Then the Tennessee Lady Volunteers scored 9 fewer points or $x - 9$ points, and the sum of these two quantities is 131 points.

$$x + x - 9 = 131$$
$$2x - 9 = 131$$
$$2x - 9 + 9 = 131 + 9$$
$$2x = 140$$
$$\frac{2x}{2} = \frac{140}{2}$$
$$x = 70$$

The Connecticut Huskies scored 70 points.

65. 1026 rounded to the nearest hundred is 1000.

69. answers may vary

73. Use $P = C + M$, where $P = 12$ and $C = 7$.

$$P = C + M$$
$$12 = 7 + M$$
$$12 - 7 = 7 - 7 + M$$
$$5 = M$$

The markup is \$5.

Chapter 11 Test

1. $\dfrac{3x - 5}{2y} = \dfrac{3 \cdot 7 - 5}{2(-8)}$

$$= \frac{21 - 5}{-16}$$
$$= \frac{16}{-16}$$
$$= -1$$

5. Area $=$ length $\cdot$ width

$$A = 4 \cdot (3x - 1)$$
$$= 4 \cdot 3x - 4 \cdot 1$$
$$= 12x - 4$$

The area is $(12x - 4)$ square meters.

9. $-\dfrac{5}{8}x = -25$

$$-\frac{8}{5} \cdot \frac{5}{8} x = -\frac{8}{5} \cdot -25$$
$$x = 40$$

13. $-4x + 7 = 15$

$$-4x + 7 - 7 = 15 - 7$$
$$-4x = 8$$
$$\frac{-4x}{-4} = \frac{8}{-4}$$
$$x = -2$$

17. $10y - 1 = 7y + 21$

$$10y - 1 + 1 = 7y + 21 + 1$$
$$10y = 7y + 22$$
$$10y - 7y = 7y - 7y + 22$$
$$3y = 22$$
$$\frac{3y}{3} = \frac{22}{3}$$
$$y = \frac{22}{3}$$

21. Use $A = \dfrac{1}{2} \cdot b \cdot h$, where $b = 5$ and $h = 12$.

$$A = \frac{1}{2} \cdot b \cdot h = \frac{1}{2} \cdot 5 \cdot 12 = 30$$

The area is 30 square feet.

25. Let x be the number of women runners entered. Then the number of men runners entered is $x + 112$, and the sum of these two quantities is 600.

$$x + x + 112 = 600$$
$$2x + 112 = 600$$
$$2x + 112 - 112 = 600 - 112$$
$$2x = 488$$
$$\frac{2x}{2} = \frac{488}{2}$$
$$x = 244$$

There were 244 women runners entered.

APPENDIX A

Exercise Set A.1

1.
$$\begin{array}{r} 1 \\ +4 \\ \hline 5 \end{array}$$

5.
$$\begin{array}{r} 3 \\ +9 \\ \hline 12 \end{array}$$

9.
$$\begin{array}{r} 9 \\ +5 \\ \hline 14 \end{array}$$

13.
$$\begin{array}{r} 5 \\ +5 \\ \hline 10 \end{array}$$

17.
$$\begin{array}{r} 2 \\ +9 \\ \hline 11 \end{array}$$

21.
$$\begin{array}{r} 6 \\ +4 \\ \hline 10 \end{array}$$

25.
$$\begin{array}{r} 9 \\ +8 \\ \hline 17 \end{array}$$

29.
$$\begin{array}{r} 7 \\ +5 \\ \hline 12 \end{array}$$

33.
$$\begin{array}{r} 4 \\ +3 \\ \hline 7 \end{array}$$

37.
$$\begin{array}{r} 7 \\ +1 \\ \hline 8 \end{array}$$

41.
$$\begin{array}{r} 2 \\ +4 \\ \hline 6 \end{array}$$

45.
$$\begin{array}{r} 3 \\ +6 \\ \hline 9 \end{array}$$

49.
$$\begin{array}{r} 2 \\ +5 \\ \hline 7 \end{array}$$

53.
$$\begin{array}{r} 8 \\ +3 \\ \hline 11 \end{array}$$

57.
$$\begin{array}{r} 0 \\ +5 \\ \hline 5 \end{array}$$

61.
$$\begin{array}{r} 6 \\ +7 \\ \hline 13 \end{array}$$

65.
$$\begin{array}{r} 0 \\ +7 \\ \hline 7 \end{array}$$

69.
$$\begin{array}{r} 4 \\ +1 \\ \hline 5 \end{array}$$

73.
$$\begin{array}{r} 7 \\ +9 \\ \hline 16 \end{array}$$

77.
$$\begin{array}{r} 1 \\ +0 \\ \hline 1 \end{array}$$

81.
$$\begin{array}{r} 2 \\ +8 \\ \hline 10 \end{array}$$

85.
$$\begin{array}{r} 5 \\ +0 \\ \hline 5 \end{array}$$

89.
$$\begin{array}{r} 9 \\ +2 \\ \hline 11 \end{array}$$

93.
$$\begin{array}{r} 2 \\ +7 \\ \hline 9 \end{array}$$

97.
$$\begin{array}{r} 6 \\ +8 \\ \hline 14 \end{array}$$

Exercise Set A.2

1.
$$\begin{array}{r} 1 \\ \times 1 \\ \hline 1 \end{array}$$

5.
$$\begin{array}{r} 8 \\ \times 4 \\ \hline 32 \end{array}$$

9.
$$\begin{array}{r} 2 \\ \times 2 \\ \hline 4 \end{array}$$

13.
$$\begin{array}{r} 3 \\ \times 2 \\ \hline 6 \end{array}$$

17.
$$\begin{array}{r} 4 \\ \times 6 \\ \hline 24 \end{array}$$

21.
$$\begin{array}{r} 5 \\ \times 8 \\ \hline 40 \end{array}$$

25.
$$\begin{array}{r} 9 \\ \times 6 \\ \hline 54 \end{array}$$

29.
$$\begin{array}{r} 6 \\ \times 9 \\ \hline 54 \end{array}$$

33.
$$\begin{array}{r} 4 \\ \times 9 \\ \hline 36 \end{array}$$

37.
$$\begin{array}{r} 9 \\ \times 4 \\ \hline 36 \end{array}$$

41.
$$\begin{array}{r} 8 \\ \times 6 \\ \hline 48 \end{array}$$

45.
$$\begin{array}{r} 9 \\ \times 0 \\ \hline 0 \end{array}$$

49.
$$\begin{array}{r} 3 \\ \times 5 \\ \hline 15 \end{array}$$

53.
$$\begin{array}{r} 1 \\ \times 0 \\ \hline 0 \end{array}$$

57.
$$\begin{array}{r} 0 \\ \times 6 \\ \hline 0 \end{array}$$

61.
$$\begin{array}{r} 9 \\ \times 2 \\ \hline 18 \end{array}$$

65.
$$\begin{array}{r} 6 \\ \times 6 \\ \hline 36 \end{array}$$

69.
$$\begin{array}{r} 7 \\ \times 5 \\ \hline 35 \end{array}$$

73.
$$\begin{array}{r} 8 \\ \times 5 \\ \hline 40 \end{array}$$

77.
$$\begin{array}{r} 9 \\ \times 1 \\ \hline 9 \end{array}$$

81.
$$\begin{array}{r} 1 \\ \times 5 \\ \hline 5 \end{array}$$

85.
$$\begin{array}{r} 3 \\ \times 7 \\ \hline 21 \end{array}$$

89.
$$\begin{array}{r} 8 \\ \times 2 \\ \hline 16 \end{array}$$

93.
$$\begin{array}{r} 4 \\ \times 1 \\ \hline 4 \end{array}$$

97.
$$\begin{array}{r} 3 \\ \times 6 \\ \hline 18 \end{array}$$

APPENDIX C

Exercise Set C.1

1. a. $\dfrac{\$16}{1\text{ hr}} \cdot \dfrac{40\text{ hr}}{1} = \dfrac{\$16 \cdot 40}{1 \cdot 1} = \$640$

Before deductions, your earnings for 40 hours are $640.

b. $\dfrac{\$240}{1} \cdot \dfrac{1\text{ hr}}{\$16} = \dfrac{240 \cdot 1\text{ hr}}{1 \cdot 16} = 15\text{ hr}$

It takes you 15 hours to earn $240 before deductions.

5. a. $\dfrac{1\text{ bed}}{155\text{ people}} \cdot \dfrac{31{,}000\text{ people}}{1} = \dfrac{1\text{ bed} \cdot 31{,}000}{155 \cdot 1}$
$$= 200\text{ beds}$$

There would be 200 hospital beds in the city.

b. $\dfrac{155\text{ people}}{1\text{ bed}} \cdot \dfrac{73\text{ beds}}{1} = \dfrac{155\text{ people} \cdot 73}{1 \cdot 1}$
$$= 11{,}315\text{ people}$$

The population is about 11,315 people.

9. $\dfrac{\$0.75}{1\text{ component}} \cdot \dfrac{26\text{ components}}{1\text{ hr}} \cdot \dfrac{33\text{ hr}}{1}$
$$= \dfrac{\$0.75 \cdot 26 \cdot 33}{1 \cdot 1 \cdot 1}$$
$$= \$643.50$$

Her pay before deductions was $643.50.

13. a. $\dfrac{16\text{ tortillas}}{1\text{ min}} \cdot \dfrac{60\text{ min}}{1\text{ hr}} \cdot \dfrac{7.5\text{ hr}}{1}$
$$= \dfrac{16\text{ tortillas} \cdot 60 \cdot 7.5}{1 \cdot 1 \cdot 1}$$
$$= 7200\text{ tortillas}$$

The machine would make 7200 tortillas in 7.5 hours.

b. $\dfrac{200\text{ tortillas}}{1} \cdot \dfrac{1\text{ min}}{16\text{ tortillas}} = \dfrac{200 \cdot 1\text{ min}}{1 \cdot 16}$
$$= 12\dfrac{1}{2}\text{ min}$$

It takes the machine $12\dfrac{1}{2}$ minutes to make 200 tortillas.

17. a. $\dfrac{45\text{ miles}}{1\text{ hr}} \cdot \dfrac{\frac{1}{4}\text{ hr}}{1} = \dfrac{45\text{ miles} \cdot \frac{1}{4}}{1 \cdot 1} = 11\dfrac{1}{4}\text{ miles}$

The cheetah has traveled $11\dfrac{1}{4}$ miles in $\dfrac{1}{4}$ hour.

b. $\dfrac{5\text{ miles}}{1} \cdot \dfrac{1\text{ hr}}{45\text{ miles}} = \dfrac{5 \cdot 1\text{ hr}}{1 \cdot 45} = \dfrac{1}{9}\text{ hr}$

$\dfrac{\frac{1}{9}\text{ hr}}{1} \cdot \dfrac{60\text{ min}}{1\text{ hr}} = \dfrac{\frac{1}{9} \cdot 60\text{ min}}{1 \cdot 1} = \dfrac{60}{9}\text{ min} = 6\dfrac{2}{3}\text{ min}$

It takes the cheetah $\dfrac{1}{9}$ hour or $6\dfrac{2}{3}$ minutes to run 5 miles.

INDEX

Photo Credits

ELAYN MARTIN-GAY: BASIC COLLEGE MATHEMATICS 3E, CHAPTER TEST PREP VIDEO CD

0-13-186832-2
© 2006 Pearson Education, Inc.
Pearson Prentice Hall
Pearson Education, Inc.
Upper Saddle River, NJ 07458
Pearson Prentice Hall™ is a trademark of Pearson Education, Inc.

YOU SHOULD CAREFULLY READ THE TERMS AND CONDITIONS BEFORE USING THE CD-ROM PACKAGE. USING THIS CD-ROM PACKAGE INDICATES YOUR ACCEPTANCE OF THESE TERMS AND CONDITIONS.

Pearson Education, Inc. provides this program and licenses its use. You assume responsibility for the selection of the program to achieve your intended results, and for the installation, use, and results obtained from the program. This license extends only to use of the program in the United States or countries in which the program is marketed by authorized distributors.

LICENSE GRANT
You hereby accept a nonexclusive, nontransferable, permanent license to install and use the program ON A SINGLE COMPUTER at any given time. You may copy the program solely for backup or archival purposes in support of your use of the program on the single computer. You may not modify, translate, disassemble, decompile, or reverse engineer the program, in whole or in part.

TERM
The License is effective until terminated. Pearson Education, Inc. reserves the right to terminate this License automatically if any provision of the License is violated. You may terminate the License at any time. To terminate this License, you must return the program, including documentation, along with a written warranty stating that all copies in your possession have been returned or destroyed.

LIMITED WARRANTY
THE PROGRAM IS PROVIDED "AS IS" WITHOUT WARRANTY OF ANY KIND, EITHER EXPRESSED OR IMPLIED, INCLUDING, BUT NOT LIMITED TO, THE IMPLIED WARRANTIES OF MERCHANTABILITY AND FITNESS FOR A PARTICULAR PURPOSE. THE ENTIRE RISK AS TO THE QUALITY AND PERFORMANCE OF THE PROGRAM IS WITH YOU. SHOULD THE PROGRAM PROVE DEFECTIVE, YOU (AND NOT PEARSON EDUCATION, INC. OR ANY AUTHORIZED DEALER) ASSUME THE ENTIRE COST OF ALL NECESSARY SERVICING, REPAIR, OR CORRECTION. NO ORAL OR WRITTEN INFORMATION OR ADVICE GIVEN BY PEARSON EDUCATION, INC., ITS DEALERS, DISTRIBUTORS, OR AGENTS SHALL CREATE A WARRANTY OR INCREASE THE SCOPE OF THIS WARRANTY.

SOME STATES DO NOT ALLOW THE EXCLUSION OF IMPLIED WARRANTIES, SO THE ABOVE EXCLUSION MAY NOT APPLY TO YOU. THIS WARRANTY GIVES YOU SPECIFIC LEGAL RIGHTS AND YOU MAY ALSO HAVE OTHER LEGAL RIGHTS THAT VARY FROM STATE TO STATE.

Pearson Education, Inc. does not warrant that the functions contained in the program will meet your requirements or that the operation of the program will be uninterrupted or error-free. However, Pearson Education, Inc. warrants the CD-ROM(s) on which the program is furnished to be free from defects in material and workmanship under normal use for a period of ninety (90) days from the date of delivery to you as evidenced by a copy of your receipt. The program should not be relied on as the sole basis to solve a problem whose incorrect solution could result in injury to person or property. If the program is employed in such a manner, it is at the user's own risk and Pearson Education, Inc. explicitly disclaims all liability for such misuse.

LIMITATION OF REMEDIES
Pearson Education, Inc.'s entire liability and your exclusive remedy shall be:
1. the replacement of any CD-ROM not meeting Pearson Education, Inc.'s "LIMITED WARRANTY" and that is returned to Pearson Education, or
2. if Pearson Education is unable to deliver a replacement CD-ROM that is free of defects in materials or workmanship, you may terminate this agreement by returning the program.

IN NO EVENT WILL PEARSON EDUCATION, INC. BE LIABLE TO YOU FOR ANY DAMAGES, INCLUDING ANY LOST PROFITS, LOST SAVINGS, OR OTHER INCIDENTAL OR CONSEQUENTIAL DAMAGES ARISING OUT OF THE USE OR INABILITY TO USE SUCH PROGRAM EVEN IF PEARSON EDUCATION, INC. OR AN AUTHORIZED DISTRIBUTOR HAS BEEN ADVISED OF THE POSSIBILITY OF SUCH DAMAGES, OR FOR ANY CLAIM BY ANY OTHER PARTY.

SOME STATES DO NOT ALLOW FOR THE LIMITATION OR EXCLUSION OF LIABILITY FOR INCIDENTAL OR CONSEQUENTIAL DAMAGES, SO THE ABOVE LIMITATION OR EXCLUSION MAY NOT APPLY TO YOU.

GENERAL
You may not sublicense, assign, or transfer the license of the program. Any attempt to sublicense, assign or transfer any of the rights, duties, or obligation hereunder is void.

This Agreement will be governed by the laws of the State of New York.

Should you have any questions concerning this Agreement, you may contact Pearson Education, Inc. by writing to:
ESM Media Development
Higher Education Division
Pearson Education, Inc.
1 Lake Street
Upper Saddle River, NJ 07458

Should you have any questions concerning technical support, you may write to:
New Media Production
Higher Education Division
Pearson Education, Inc.
1 Lake Street
Upper Saddle River, NJ 07458

YOU ACKNOWLEDGE THAT YOU HAVE READ THIS AGREEMENT UNDERSTAND IT, AND AGREE TO BE BOUND BY ITS TERMS AND CONDITIONS. YOU FURTHER AGREE THAT IT IS THE COMPLETE AND EXCLUSIVE STATEMENT OF THE AGREEMENT BETWEEN U THAT SUPERSEDES ANY PROPOSAL OR PRIOR AGREEMENT, OR OR WRITTEN, AND ANY OTHER COMMUNICATIONS BETWEEN U RELATING TO THE SUBJECT MATTER OF THIS AGREEMENT.

System Requirements
Windows
Pentium II 300 MHz processor
Windows 98, NT, 2000, ME, or XP
64 MB RAM (128 MB RAM required for Windows XP)
4.3 MB available hard drive space (optional-for minimum QuickTime installa
800 x 600 resolution
8x or faster CD-ROM drive
QuickTime 6.x
Sound card

Macintosh
PowerPC G3 233 MHz or better
Mac OS 9.x or 10.x
64 MB RAM
10 MB available hard drive space for Mac OS 9, 19 MB on OS X (optional—if QuickTime installation is needed)
800 x 600 resolution
8x or faster CD-ROM drive
QuickTime 6.x

Support Information
If you are having problems with this software, call (800) 677-6337 between 8:00 a.m. and 8:00 p.m. EST, Monday through Friday, and 5:00 p.m. through Midnight EST on Sundays. You can also get support by filling out the web for located at: http://247.prenhall.com/mediaform

Our technical staff will need to know certain things about your system in orde to help us solve your problems more quickly and efficiently. If possible, please be at your computer when you call for support. You should have the following information ready:
- Textbook ISBN
- CD-ROM ISBN
- corresponding product and title
- computer make and model
- Operating System (Windows or Macintosh) and Version
- RAM available
- hard disk space available
- Sound card? Yes or No
- printer make and model
- network connection
- detailed description of the problem, including the exact wording of any err messages.

NOTE: Pearson does not support and/or assist with the following:
- third-party software (i.e. Microsoft including Microsoft Office suite, Apple, Borland, etc.)
- homework assistance
- Textbooks and CD-ROMs purchased used are not supported and are non-replaceable. To purchase a new CD-ROM, contact Pearson Individual Orde Copies at 1-800-282-0693.